THE WILEY BICENTENNIAL—KNOWLEDGE FOR GENERATIONS

*E*ach generation has its unique needs and aspirations. When Charles Wiley first opened his small printing shop in lower Manhattan in 1807, it was a generation of boundless potential searching for an identity. And we were there, helping to define a new American literary tradition. Over half a century later, in the midst of the Second Industrial Revolution, it was a generation focused on building the future. Once again, we were there, supplying the critical scientific, technical, and engineering knowledge that helped frame the world. Throughout the 20th Century, and into the new millennium, nations began to reach out beyond their own borders and a new international community was born. Wiley was there, expanding its operations around the world to enable a global exchange of ideas, opinions, and know-how.

For 200 years, Wiley has been an integral part of each generation's journey, enabling the flow of information and understanding necessary to meet their needs and fulfill their aspirations. Today, bold new technologies are changing the way we live and learn. Wiley will be there, providing you the must-have knowledge you need to imagine new worlds, new possibilities, and new opportunities.

Generations come and go, but you can always count on Wiley to provide you the knowledge you need, when and where you need it!

WILLIAM J. PESCE
PRESIDENT AND CHIEF EXECUTIVE OFFICER

PETER BOOTH WILEY
CHAIRMAN OF THE BOARD

www.wiley.com/college/microsoft *or* call the MOAC Toll-Free Number: 1+(888) 764-7001 (North America Only)

www.wiley.com/college/microsoft *or* call the MOAC Toll-Free Number: 1+(888) 764-7001 (North America Only)

Microsoft® Official Academic Course

Microsoft® Office System 2007

www.wiley.com/college/microsoft *or* call the MOAC Toll-Free Number: 1+(888) 764-7001
(North America Only)

Microsoft Certified Application Specialist (MCAS)

Approved Courseware

What does this logo mean?

It means this courseware has been approved by the Microsoft® Certified Application Specialist program to be among the finest available for learning Microsoft® Office Word 2007, Microsoft® Office Excel 2007, Microsoft® Office PowerPoint 2007, Microsoft® Office Access 2007, or Microsoft® Office Outlook 2007. It also means that upon completion of this courseware, you may be prepared to take an exam for Microsoft Certified Application Specialist qualification.

What is a Microsoft Certified Application Specialist?

A Microsoft Certified Application Specialist is an individual who has passed exams for certifying his or her skills in one or more of the Microsoft Office desktop applications such as Microsoft Word, Microsoft Excel, Microsoft PowerPoint, Microsoft Outlook, or Microsoft Access. The Microsoft Certified Application Specialist program is the only program approved by Microsoft for testing proficiency in Microsoft Office desktop applications. This testing program can be a valuable asset in any job search or career development.

More Information

To learn more about becoming a Microsoft Certified Application Specialist and exam availability, visit www.microsoft.com/learning/msbc.

Microsoft, the Microsoft Office Logo, PowerPoint, and Outlook are trademarks or registered trademarks of Microsoft Corporation in the United States and/or other countries, and the Microsoft Certified Application Specialist logo is used under license from the owner.

www.wiley.com/college/microsoft *or* call the MOAC Toll-Free Number: 1+(888) 764-7001 (North America Only)

www.wiley.com/college/microsoft *or* call the MOAC Toll-Free Number: 1+(888) 764-7001
(North America Only)

Microsoft® Official Academic Course

Microsoft® Office System 2007

Credits

EXECUTIVE EDITOR	John Kane
SENIOR EDITOR	Gary Schwartz
DIRECTOR OF MARKETING AND SALES	Mitchell Beaton
MICROSOFT STRATEGIC RELATIONSHIPS MANAGER	Merrick Van Dongen of Microsoft Learning
GLOBAL MOAC MANAGER	Laura McKenna
DEVELOPMENT AND PRODUCTION	Custom Editorial Productions, Inc
EDITORIAL ASSISTANT	Jennifer Lartz
PRODUCTION MANAGER	Kelly Tavares
CREATIVE DIRECTOR/COVER DESIGNER	Harry Nolan
TECHNOLOGY AND MEDIA	Phyllis Bregman/Elena Santa Maria
COVER PHOTO	Corbis

Wiley 200th Anniversary logo designed by: Richard J. Pacifico

This book was set in Garamond by Aptara, Inc. and printed and bound by Courier Kendallville. The covers were printed by Phoenix Color.

Copyright © 2009, 2008 by John Wiley & Sons, Inc. All rights reserved.

No part of this publication may be reproduced, stored in a retrieval system or transmitted in any form or by any means, electronic, mechanical, photocopying, recording, scanning or otherwise, except as permitted under Sections 107 or 108 of the 1976 United States Copyright Act, without either the prior written permission of the Publisher, or authorization through payment of the appropriate per-copy fee to the Copyright Clearance Center, Inc. 222 Rosewood Drive, Danvers, MA 01923, (978) 750-8400, fax (978) 646-8600. Requests to the Publisher for permission should be addressed to the Permissions Department, John Wiley & Sons, Inc., 111 River Street, Hoboken, NJ 07030-5774, (201) 748-6011, fax (201) 748-6008. To order books or for customer service, please call 1-800-CALL WILEY (225-5945).

Microsoft, ActiveX, Excel, InfoPath, Microsoft Press, MSDN, OneNote, Outlook, PivotChart, PivotTable, PowerPoint, SharePoint, Visio, Windows, Windows Mobile, and Windows Vista are either registered trademarks or trademarks of Microsoft Corporation in the United States and/or other countries. Other product and company names mentioned herein may be the trademarks of their respective owners.

The example companies, organizations, products, domain names, e-mail addresses, logos, people, places, and events depicted herein are fictitious. No association with any real company, organization, product, domain name, e-mail address, logo, person, place, or event is intended or should be inferred.

The book expresses the author's views and opinions. The information contained in this book is provided without any express, statutory, or implied warranties. Neither the authors, John Wiley & Sons, Inc., Microsoft Corporation, nor their resellers or distributors will be held liable for any damages caused or alleged to be caused either directly or indirectly by this book.

ISBN 978-0-47044226-5

Printed in the United States of America

10 9 8 7 6 5 4 3

Foreword from the Publisher

Wiley's publishing vision for the Microsoft Official Academic Course series is to provide students and instructors with the skills and knowledge they need to use Microsoft technology effectively in all aspects of their personal and professional lives. Quality instruction is required to help both educators and students get the most from Microsoft's software tools and to become more productive. Thus our mission is to make our instructional programs trusted educational companions for life.

To accomplish this mission, Wiley and Microsoft have partnered to develop the highest quality educational programs for Information Workers, IT Professionals, and Developers. Materials created by this partnership carry the brand name "Microsoft Official Academic Course," assuring instructors and students alike that the content of these textbooks is fully endorsed by Microsoft, and that they provide the highest quality information and instruction on Microsoft products. The Microsoft Official Academic Course textbooks are "Official" in still one more way—they are the officially sanctioned courseware for Microsoft IT Academy members.

The Microsoft Official Academic Course series focuses on *workforce development*. These programs are aimed at those students seeking to enter the workforce, change jobs, or embark on new careers as information workers, IT professionals, and developers. Microsoft Official Academic Course programs address their needs by emphasizing authentic workplace scenarios with an abundance of projects, exercises, cases, and assessments.

The Microsoft Official Academic Courses are mapped to Microsoft's extensive research and job-task analysis, the same research and analysis used to create the Microsoft Certified Application Specialist (MCAS) and Microsoft Certified Application Professional (MCAP) exams. The textbooks focus on real skills for real jobs. As students work through the projects and exercises in the textbooks they enhance their level of knowledge and their ability to apply the latest Microsoft technology to everyday tasks. These students also gain resume-building credentials that can assist them in finding a job, keeping their current job, or in furthering their education.

The concept of life-long learning is today an utmost necessity. Job roles, and even whole job categories, are changing so quickly that none of us can stay competitive and productive without continuously updating our skills and capabilities. The Microsoft Official Academic Course offerings, and their focus on Microsoft certification exam preparation, provide a means for people to acquire and effectively update their skills and knowledge. Wiley supports students in this endeavor through the development and distribution of these courses as Microsoft's official academic publisher.

Today educational publishing requires attention to providing quality print and robust electronic content. By integrating Microsoft Official Academic Course products, *WileyPLUS*, and Microsoft certifications, we are better able to deliver efficient learning solutions for students and teachers alike.

Bonnie Lieberman
General Manager and Senior Vice President

www.wiley.com/college/microsoft *or* call the MOAC Toll-Free Number: 1+(888) 764-7001
(North America Only)

Preface

Welcome to the Microsoft Official Academic Course (MOAC) program for the 2007 Microsoft Office system. MOAC represents the collaboration between Microsoft Learning and John Wiley & Sons, Inc. publishing company. Microsoft and Wiley teamed up to produce a series of textbooks that deliver compelling and innovative teaching solutions to instructors and superior learning experiences for students. Infused and informed by in-depth knowledge from the creators of Microsoft Office and Windows Vista™, and crafted by a publisher known worldwide for the pedagogical quality of its products, these textbooks maximize skills transfer in minimum time. With MOAC, students are hands on right away—there are no superfluous text passages to get in the way of learning and using the software. Students are challenged to reach their potential by using their new technical skills as highly productive members of the workforce.

Because this knowledge base comes directly from Microsoft, architect of the 2007 Office system and creator of the Microsoft Certified Application Specialist (MCAS) exams, you are sure to receive the topical coverage that is most relevant to students' personal and professional success. Microsoft's direct participation not only assures you that MOAC textbook content is accurate and current; it also means that students will receive the best instruction possible to enable their success on certification exams and in the workplace.

■ The Microsoft Official Academic Course Program

The *Microsoft Official Academic Course* series is a complete program for instructors and institutions to prepare and deliver great courses on Microsoft software technologies. With MOAC, we recognize that, because of the rapid pace of change in the technology and curriculum developed by Microsoft, there is an ongoing set of needs beyond classroom instruction tools for an instructor to be ready to teach the course. The MOAC program endeavors to provide solutions for all these needs in a systematic manner in order to ensure a successful and rewarding course experience for both instructor and student—technical and curriculum training for instructor readiness with new software releases; the software itself for student use at home for building hands-on skills, assessment, and validation of skill development; and a great set of tools for delivering instruction in the classroom and lab. All are important to the smooth delivery of an interesting course on Microsoft software, and all are provided with the MOAC program. We think about the model below as a gauge for ensuring that we completely support you in your goal of teaching a great course. As you evaluate your instructional materials options, you may wish to use the model for comparison purposes with available products.

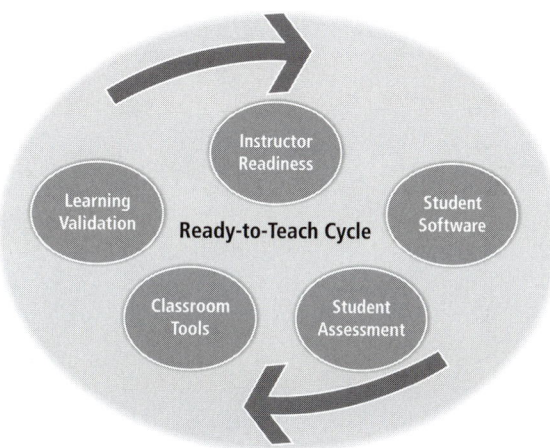

www.wiley.com/college/microsoft *or* call the MOAC Toll-Free Number: 1+(888) 764-7001 (North America Only)

www.wiley.com/college/microsoft *or* call the MOAC Toll-Free Number: 1+(888) 764-7001
(North America Only)

Illustrated Book Tour

▪ Pedagogical Features

MOAC for *2007 Microsoft Office System* is designed to cover all the learning objectives in the MCAS exams, referred to as "objective domains." The Microsoft Certified Application Specialist (MCAS) exam objectives are highlighted throughout the textbooks. Many pedagogical features have been developed specifically for *Microsoft Official Academic Course* programs. Unique features of our task-based approach include a Lesson Skills Matrix that correlates skills taught in each lesson to the MCAS objectives; Certification, Workplace, and Internet Ready exercises; and three levels of increasingly rigorous lesson-ending activities: Competency, Proficiency, and Mastery Assessment.

Presenting the extensive procedural information and technical concepts woven throughout the textbook raises challenges for the student and instructor alike. The Illustrated Book Tour that follows provides a guide to the rich features contributing to *Microsoft Official Academic Course* program's pedagogical plan. Following is a list of key features in each lesson designed to prepare students for success on the certification exams and in the workplace:

- Each lesson begins with a **Lesson Skill Matrix.** More than a standard list of learning objectives, the Skill Matrix correlates each software skill covered in the lesson to the specific MCAS "objective domain."
- Every lesson features a real-world **Business Case** scenario that places the software skills and knowledge to be acquired in a real-world setting.
- Every lesson opens with a **Software Orientation.** This feature provides an overview of the software features students will be working with in the lesson. The orientation will detail the general properties of the software or specific features, such as a ribbon or dialog box; and it includes a large, labeled screen image.
- Concise and frequent **Step-by-Step** instructions teach students new features and provide an opportunity for hands-on practice. Numbered steps give detailed, step-by-step instructions to help students learn software skills. The steps also show results and screen images to match what students should see on their computer screens.
- **Illustrations:** Screen images provide visual feedback as students work through the exercises. The images reinforce key concepts, provide visual clues about the steps, and allow students to check their progress.
- **Button images:** When the text instructs a student to click a particular toolbar button, an image of the button is shown in the margin.
- **Key Terms:** Important technical vocabulary is listed at the beginning of the lesson. When these terms are used later in the lesson, they appear in bold italic type and are defined. The Glossary contains all of the key terms and their definitions.
- Engaging point-of-use **Reader aids**, located throughout the lessons, tell students why this topic is relevant (*The Bottom Line*), provide students with helpful hints (*Take Note*), show alternate ways to accomplish tasks (*Another Way*), or point out things to watch out for or avoid (*Troubleshooting*). Reader aids also provide additional relevant or background information that adds value to the lesson.

- **Certification Ready?** features throughout the text signal students where a specific certification objective is covered. They provides students with a chance to check their understanding of that particular MCAS objective and, if necessary, review the section of the lesson where it is covered. MOAC offers complete preparation for MCAS certification.
- **New Feature:** The New Feature icon appears near any software feature that is new to Office 2007.
- **Competency, Proficiency, and Mastery Assessments** provide three progressively more challenging lesson-ending activities.
- **Internet Ready** projects combine the knowledge students acquire in a lesson with a Web-based research task.
- **Circling Back.** These integrated projects provide students with an opportunity to review and practice skills learned in previous lessons.
- **Workplace Ready.** These features preview how the 2007 Microsoft Office system applications are used in real-world situations.
- **Student CD:** The companion CD contains the data files needed for each lesson. These files are indicated by the CD icon in the margin of the textbook.

www.wiley.com/college/microsoft *or* **call the MOAC Toll-Free Number: 1+(888) 764-7001
(North America Only)**

Illustrated Book Tour | xv

Lesson Features

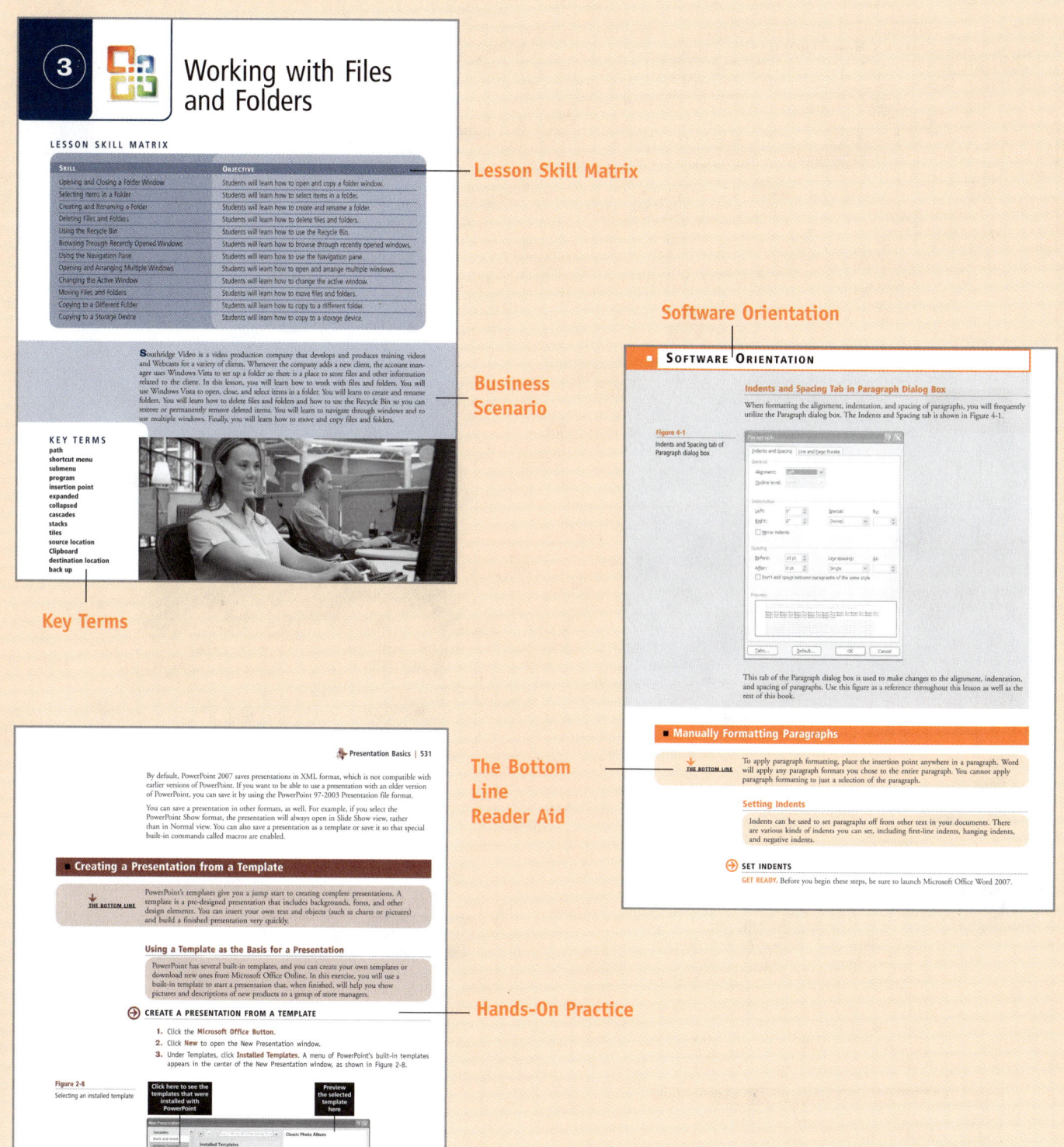

www.wiley.com/college/microsoft *or* call the MOAC Toll-Free Number: 1+(888) 764-7001 (North America Only)

xvi | Illustrated Book Tour

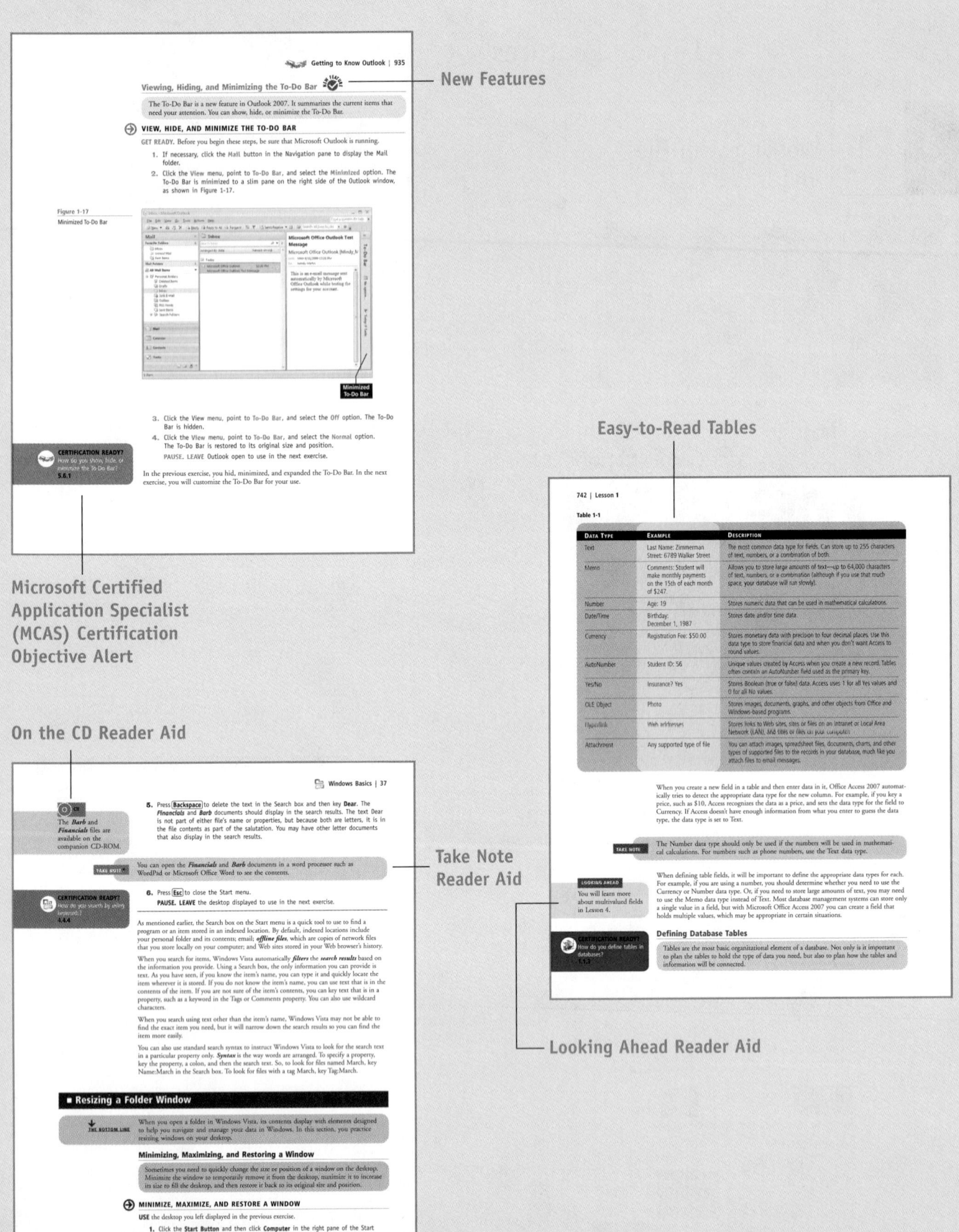

Illustrated Book Tour | xvii

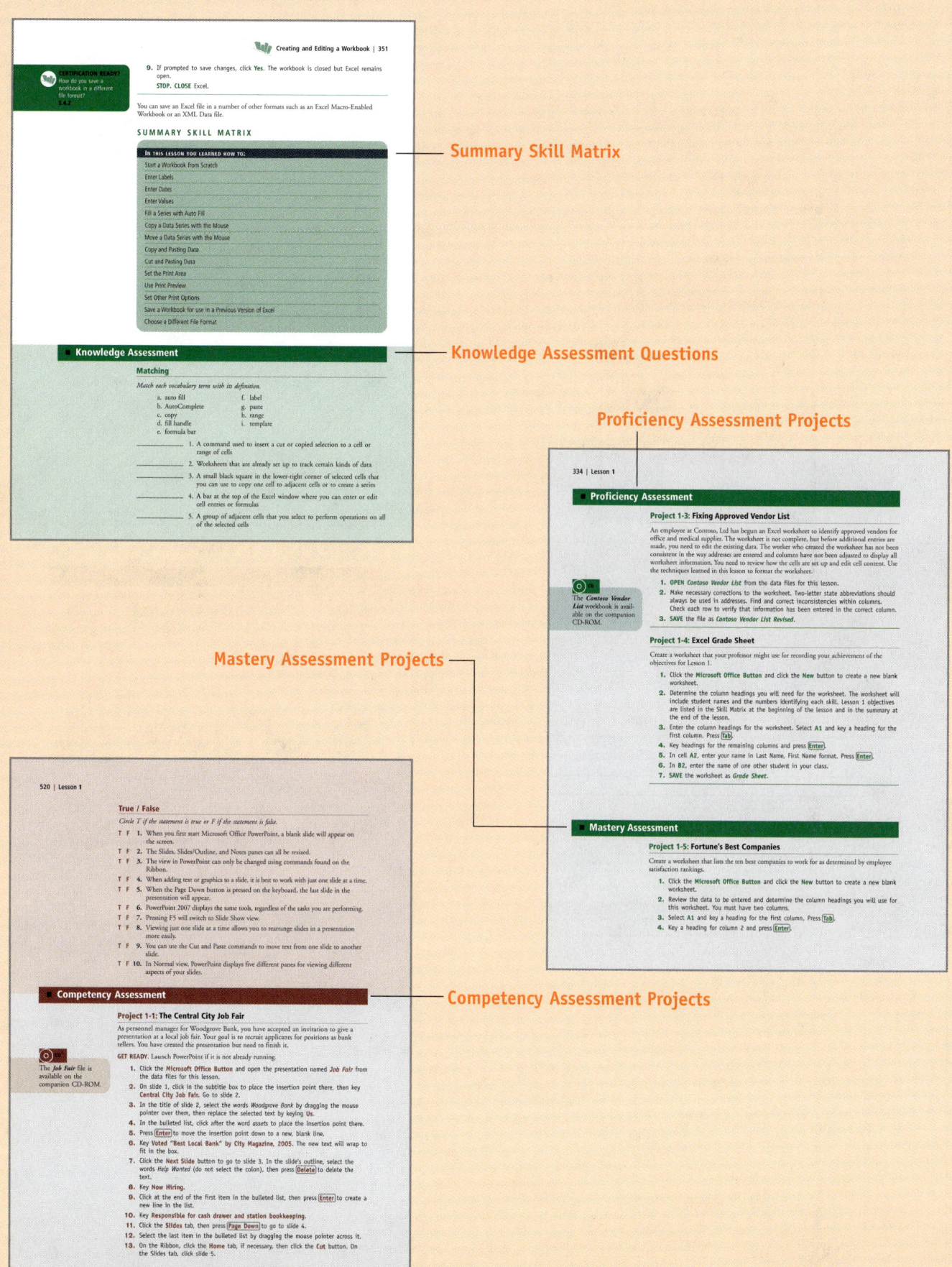

Summary Skill Matrix

Knowledge Assessment Questions

Proficiency Assessment Projects

Mastery Assessment Projects

Competency Assessment Projects

www.wiley.com/college/microsoft *or* call the MOAC Toll-Free Number: 1+(888) 764-7001 (North America Only)

xviii | Illustrated Book Tour

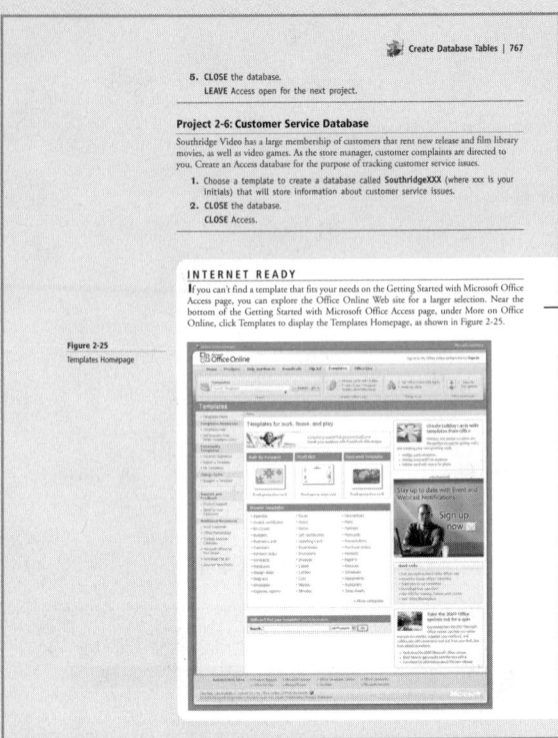

Internet Ready Project

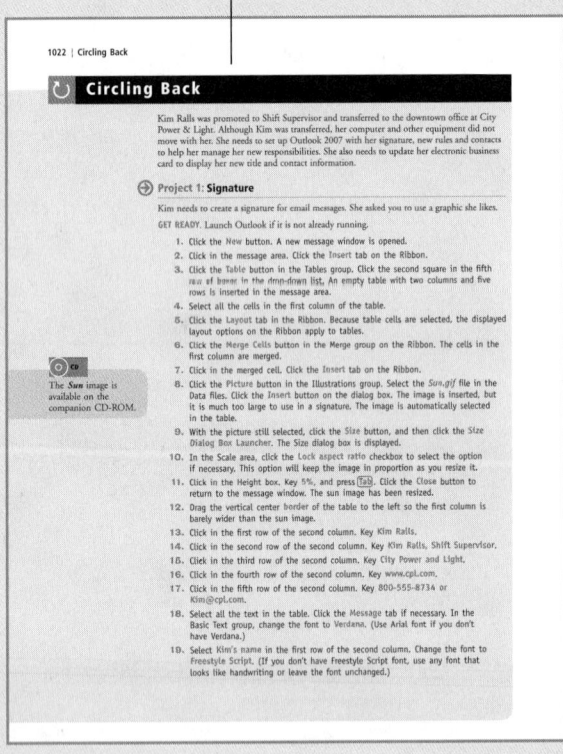

Circling Back Projects

Workplace Ready Scenario

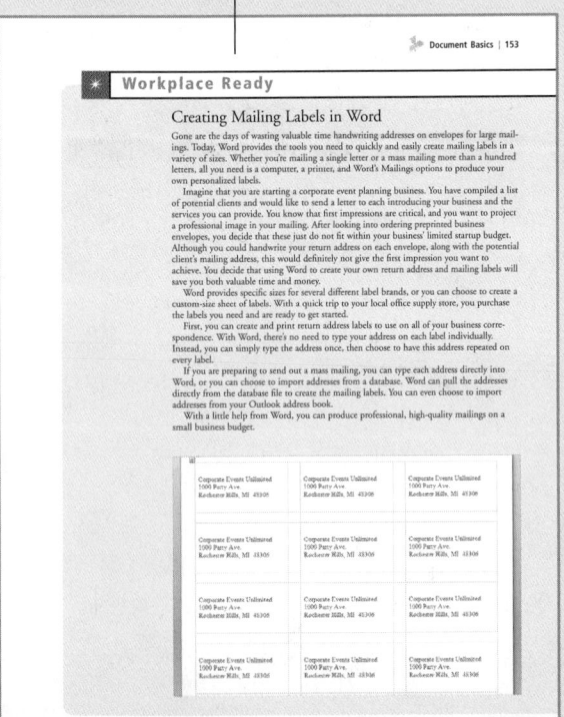

www.wiley.com/college/microsoft *or* **call the MOAC Toll-Free Number: 1+(888) 764-7001 (North America Only)**

Conventions and Features Used in This Book

This book uses particular fonts, symbols, and heading conventions to highlight important information or to call your attention to special steps. For more information about the features in each lesson, refer to the Illustrated Book Tour section.

Convention	Meaning
NEW FEATURE	This icon indicates a new or greatly improved Office 2007 feature in this version of the software.
THE BOTTOM LINE	This feature provides a brief summary of the material to be covered in the section that follows.
CLOSE	Words in all capital letters and in a different font color than the rest of the text indicate instructions for opening, saving, or closing files or programs. They also point out items you should check or actions you should take.
CERTIFICATION READY?	This feature signals the point in the text where a specific certification objective is covered. It provides you with a chance to check your understanding of that particular MCAS objective and, if necessary, review the section of the lesson where it is covered.
CD	This indicates a file that is available on the student CD.
TAKE NOTE*	Reader aids appear in shaded boxes found in your text. *Take Note* provides helpful hints related to particular tasks or topics.
ANOTHER WAY	*Another Way* provides an alternative procedure for accomplishing a particular task.
TROUBLESHOOTING	*Troubleshooting* covers common problems and pitfalls.
X REF	These notes provide pointers to information discussed elsewhere in the textbook or describe interesting features of Office 2007 that are not directly addressed in the current topic or exercise.
SAVE	When a toolbar button is referenced in an exercise, the button's picture is shown in the margin.
Alt + **Tab**	A plus sign (+) between two key names means that you must press both keys at the same time. Keys that you are instructed to press in an exercise will appear in the font shown here.
A *cell* is the area where data is entered.	Key terms appear in bold italic.
Key **My Name is.**	Any text you are asked to key appears in color.
Click **OK**.	Any button on the screen you are supposed to click on or select will also appear in color.
OPEN *FitnessClasses.*	The names of data files will appear in bold, italic, and color for easy identification.

www.wiley.com/college/microsoft *or* call the MOAC Toll-Free Number: 1+(888) 764-7001 (North America Only)

www.wiley.com/college/microsoft *or* call the MOAC Toll-Free Number: 1+(888) 764-7001 (North America Only)

Instructor Support Program

The *Microsoft Official Academic Course* programs are accompanied by a rich array of resources that incorporate the extensive textbook visuals to form a pedagogically cohesive package. These resources provide all the materials instructors need to deploy and deliver their courses. Resources available online for download include:

- **6-Month Office 2007 Trial Edition (available in North America only).** Students receive 6-months' access to Microsoft Office Professional 2007 when you adopt a MOAC 2007 Microsoft Office system textbook. The textbook includes the trial CD and a product key that allows students to activate the CD for a 6-month period.

- The **Instructor's Guide** contains Solutions to all the textbook exercises, Syllabi for various term lengths, and Data Files for all the documents students need to work the exercises. The Instructor's Guide also includes chapter summaries and lecture notes. The Instructor's Guide is available from the Book Companion site (www.wiley.com/college/microsoft) and from *WileyPLUS*.

- The **Test Bank** contains hundreds of multiple-choice, true-false, and short answer questions and is available to download from the Instructor's Book Companion site (www.wiley.com/college/microsoft) and from *WileyPLUS*. A complete answer key is provided. It is available as a computerized test bank and in Microsoft Word format.

- **PowerPoint Presentations and Images.** A complete set of PowerPoint presentations is available on the Instructor's Book Companion site (www.wiley.com/college/microsoft) and in *WileyPLUS* to enhance classroom presentations. Approximately 50 PowerPoint slides are provided for each lesson. Tailored to the text's topical coverage and Skills Matrix, these presentations are designed to convey key Office 2007 concepts addressed in the text.

  All figures from the text are on the Instructor's Book Companion site (www.wiley.com/college/microsoft) and in *WileyPLUS*. You can incorporate them into your PowerPoint presentations, or create your own overhead transparencies and handouts.

  By using these visuals in class discussions, you can help focus students' attention on key elements of Office 2007 and help them understand how to use it effectively in the workplace.

- **Microsoft Business Certification Pre-Test and Exams**. With each MOAC textbook, students receive information allowing them to access a Pre-Test, Score Report, and Learning Plan, either directly from Certiport, one of Microsoft's exam delivery partners, or through links from *WileyPLUS* Premium. They also receive a code and information for taking the certification exams.

- The **MSDN Academic Alliance** is designed to provide the easiest and most inexpensive developer tools, products, and technologies available to faculty and students in labs, classrooms, and on student PCs. A free 1-year membership is available to qualified MOAC adopters.

- **The Wiley Faculty Network** lets you tap into a large community of your peers effortlessly. Wiley Faculty Network mentors are faculty like you, from educational institutions around the country, who are passionate about enhancing instructional efficiency and effectiveness through best practices. Faculty Network activities include technology training and tutorials, virtual seminars, peer-to-peer exchanges of experience and ideas, personal consulting, and sharing of resources. To register for a seminar, go to www.wherefacultyconnect.com or phone 1-866-4FACULTY.

WileyPLUS

Broad developments in education over the past decade have influenced the instructional approach taken in the Microsoft Official Academic Course programs. The way that students learn, especially about new technologies, has changed dramatically in the Internet era. Electronic learning materials and Internet-based instruction is now as much a part of classroom instruction as printed textbooks. *WileyPLUS* provides the technology to create an environment where students reach their full potential and experience academic success that will last them a lifetime!

WileyPLUS is a powerful and highly-integrated suite of teaching and learning resources designed to bridge the gap between what happens in the classroom and what happens at home and on the job. *WileyPLUS* provides instructors with the resources to teach their students new technologies and guide them to reach their goals of getting ahead in the job market by having the skills to become certified and advance in the workforce. For students, *WileyPLUS* provides the tools for study and practice that are available to them 24/7, wherever and whenever they want to study. *WileyPLUS* includes a complete online version of the student textbook; PowerPoint presentations; homework and practice assignments and quizzes; links to Microsoft's Pre-Test, Learning Plan, and a code for taking the certification exam (in *WileyPLUS* Premium); image galleries; test-bank questions; gradebook; and all the instructor resources in one easy-to-use website.

Organized around the everyday activities you and your students perform in the class, *WileyPLUS* helps you:

- **Prepare & Present** outstanding class presentations using relevant PowerPoint slides and other *WileyPLUS* materials—and you can easily upload and add your own.
- **Create Assignments** by choosing from questions organized by lesson, level of difficulty, and source—and add your own questions. Students' homework and quizzes are automatically graded, and the results are recorded in your gradebook.
- **Offer context-sensitive help to students, 24/7.** When you assign homework or quizzes, you decide if and when students get access to hints, solutions, or answers where appropriate—or they can be linked to relevant sections of their complete, online text for additional help whenever—and wherever they need it most.
- **Track Student Progress:** Analyze students' results and assess their level of understanding on an individual and class level using the *WileyPLUS* gradebook, or export data to your own personal gradebook.
- **Administer Your Course:** *WileyPLUS* can easily be integrated with another course management system, gradebook, or other resources you are using in your class, providing you with the flexibility to build your course, your way.
- **Seamlessly integrate all of the rich *WileyPLUS* content and resources with WebCT and Blackboard**—with a single sign-on.

Please view our online demo at **www.wiley.com/college/wileyplus.** Here you will find additional information about the features and benefits of *WileyPLUS*, how to request a "test drive" of *WileyPLUS* for this title, and how to adopt it for class use.

MICROSOFT BUSINESS CERTIFICATION PRE-TEST AND EXAMS AVAILABLE THROUGH *WILEYPLUS* PREMIUM

Enhance your students' knowledge and skills and increase their performance on Microsoft Business Certification exams with adoption of the Microsoft Official Academic Course program for Office 2007.

With the majority of the workforce classified as *information workers*, certification on the 2007 Microsoft Office system is a critical tool in terms of validating the desktop computing knowledge and skills required to be more productive in the workplace. Certification is the primary tool companies use to validate the proficiency of desktop computing skills among employees. It gives organizations the ability to help assess employees' actual computer skills and select job candidates based on verifiable skills applying the latest productivity tools and technology.

Microsoft Pre-tests, delivered by Certiport, provide a simple, low-cost way for individuals to identify their desktop computing skill level. Pre-Tests are taken online, making the first step towards certification easy and convenient. Through the Pre-Tests, individuals can receive a custom learning path with recommended training.

To help students to study for and pass the Microsoft Certified Application Specialist, or MCAS exam, each MOAC textbook includes information allowing students to access a Pre-Test, Score Report, and Learning Plan, either directly from Certiport or through links from the *WileyPLUS* Premium course. Students also receive a code and information for taking the certification exams. Students who do not have access to *WileyPLUS* Premium can find information on how to purchase access to the Pre-Test and a code for taking the certification exams by clicking on their textbook at:

www.wiley.com/college/microsoft.

The Pre-Test can only be taken once. It provides a simple, low-cost way for students to evaluate and identify their skill level. Through the Pre-Test, students receive a recommended study plan that they can print out to help them prepare for the live certification exams. The Pre-Test is comprised of a variety of selected response questions, including matching, sequencing exercises, "hot spots" where students must identify an item or function, and traditional multiple-choice questions. After students have mastered all the certification objectives, they can use their code to take the actual Microsoft Certified Application Specialist (MCAS) exams for Office 2007.

WileyPLUS Premium includes a complete online version of the student textbook, PowerPoint® presentations, homework and practice assignments and quizzes, links to Microsoft's Pre-Test, Learning Plan and a certification voucher, image galleries, test bank questions, gradebook, and all the instructor resources in one, easy-to-use website. Together, with *WileyPLUS* and the MCAS Pre-Test and exams delivered by Certiport, we are creating the best of both worlds in academic learning and performance based validation in preparation for a great career and a globally recognized Microsoft certification—the higher education learning management system that accesses the industry-leading certification pre-test.

Contact your Wiley rep today about this special offer.

www.wiley.com/college/microsoft *or* call the MOAC Toll-Free Number: 1+(888) 764-7001 (North America Only)

> **MSDN ACADEMIC ALLIANCE—FREE 1-YEAR MEMBERSHIP**
> **AVAILABLE TO QUALIFIED ADOPTERS!**
>
> MSDN Academic Alliance (MSDN AA) is designed to provide the easiest and most inexpensive way for universities to make the latest Microsoft developer tools, products, and technologies available in labs, classrooms, and on student PCs. MSDN AA is an annual membership program for departments teaching Science, Technology, Engineering, and Mathematics (STEM) courses. The membership provides a complete solution to keep academic labs, faculty, and students on the leading edge of technology.
>
> Software available in the MSDN AA program is provided at no charge to adopting departments through the Wiley and Microsoft publishing partnership.
>
> **As a bonus to this free offer, faculty will be introduced to Microsoft's Faculty Connection and Academic Resource Center. It takes time and preparation to keep students engaged while giving them a fundamental understanding of theory, and the Microsoft Faculty Connection is designed to help STEM professors with this preparation by providing articles, curriculum, and tools that professors can use to engage and inspire today's technology students.**
>
> * Contact your Wiley rep for details.
>
> For more information about the MSDN Academic Alliance program, go to:
>
> http://msdn.microsoft.com/academic/

Adoption Options

To provide you and your students with the right choices for learning, studying, and passing the MCAS certification exams, we have put together various options for your adoption requirements.

All selections include the student CD. Please contact your Wiley rep for more information:

- Textbook with 6-month Microsoft Office Trial
- Textbook, 6-month Microsoft Office Trial, *WileyPLUS*
- Textbook, 6-month Microsoft Office Trial, *WileyPLUS* Premium (includes access to Certiport)
- *WileyPLUS* (includes full e-book)
- *WileyPLUS* Premium (includes full e-book and access to Certiport)

Important Web Addresses and Phone Numbers

To locate the Wiley Higher Education Rep in your area, go to the following Web address and click on the "*Who's My Rep?*" link at the top of the page.

www.wiley.com/college

Or Call the MOAC Toll Free Number: 1 + (888) 764-7001

To learn more about becoming a Microsoft Certified Application Specialist and exam availability, visit www.microsoft.com/learning/msbc.

www.wiley.com/college/microsoft *or* call the MOAC Toll-Free Number: 1+(888) 764-7001

www.wiley.com/college/microsoft *or* call the MOAC Toll-Free Number: 1+(888) 764-7001
(North America Only)

Student Support Program

Book Companion Website (www.wiley.com/college/microsoft)

The book companion site for the MOAC series includes the Instructor Resources the student CD files, and Web links to important information for students and instructors.

WileyPLUS

WileyPLUS is a powerful and highly-integrated suite of teaching and learning resources designed to bridge the gap between what happens in the classroom and what happens at home and on the job. For students, *WileyPLUS* provides the tools for study and practice that are available 24/7, wherever and whenever they want to study. *WileyPLUS* includes a complete online version of the student textbook; PowerPoint presentations; homework and practice assignments and quizzes; links to Microsoft's Pre-Test, Learning Plan, and a code for taking the certification exam (in *WileyPLUS* Premium); image galleries; test bank questions; gradebook; and all the instructor resources in one easy-to-use website.

WileyPLUS provides immediate feedback on student assignments and a wealth of support materials. This powerful study tool will help your students develop their conceptual understanding of the class material and increase their ability to answer questions.

- A **Study and Practice** area links directly to text content, allowing students to review the text while they study and answer. Access to Microsoft's Pre-Test, Learning Plan, and a code for taking the MCAS certification exam is available in Study and Practice. Additional Practice Questions tied to the MCAS certification that can be re-taken as many times as necessary, are also available.

- An **Assignment** area keeps all the work you want your students to complete in one location, making it easy for them to stay on task. Students have access to a variety of interactive self-assessment tools, as well as other resources for building their confidence and understanding. In addition, all of the assignments and quizzes contain a link to the relevant section of the multimedia book, providing students with context-sensitive help that allows them to conquer obstacles as they arise.

- A **Personal Gradebook** for each student allows students to view their results from past assignments at any time.

Please view our online demo at www.wiley.com/college/wileyplus. Here you will find additional information about the features and benefits of *WileyPLUS*, how to request a "test drive" of *WileyPLUS* for this title, and how to adopt it for class use.

6-Month Microsoft Office 2007 Trial Edition

MOAC textbooks provide an unparalleled value to students in today's performance-based courses. All MOAC 2007 Microsoft Office system textbooks sold in North America are packaged with a 6-month trial CD of Microsoft Office Professional 2007. The textbook includes the CD and a product key that allows students to activate Microsoft Office Professional 2007 for the 6-month trial period. After purchasing the textbook containing the Microsoft Office Professional 2007 Trial CD, students must install the CD onto their computer and, when prompted, enter the Office Trial product key that allows them to activate the software.

Installing the Microsoft Office Professional 2007 Trial CD provides students with the state-of-the-art 2007 Microsoft Office system software, allowing them to use the practice files on the Student CD and in *WileyPLUS* to learn and study by doing, which is the best and most effective way to acquire and remember new computing skills.

TAKE NOTE*

For the best performance, the default selection during Setup is to uninstall previous versions of Office. There is also an option to remove previous versions of Office. With all trial software, Microsoft recommends that you have your original CDs available to reinstall if necessary. If you want to return to your previous version of Office, you need to uninstall the trial software. This should be done through the Add or Remove Programs icon in Microsoft Windows Control Panel (or Uninstall a program in the Control Panel of Windows Vista).

Installation of Microsoft Office Professional 2007 6-Month Trial software will remove your existing version of Microsoft Outlook. However, your contacts, calendar, and other personal information will not be deleted. At the end of the trial, if you choose to upgrade or to reinstall your previous version of Outlook, your personal settings and information will be retained.

Installing the 2007 Microsoft Office System 6-Month Trial

1. Insert the trial software CD-ROM into the CD drive on your computer. The CD will be detected, and the Setup.exe file should automatically begin to run on your computer.
2. When prompted for the Office Product Key, enter the Product Key provided with the software, and then click **Next**.
3. Enter your name and organization user name, and then click **Next**.
4. Read the End-User License Agreement, select the *I Accept the Terms in the License Agreement* check box, and then click **Next**.
5. Select the install option, verify the installation location or click **Browse** to change the installation location, and then click **Next**.
6. Verify the program installation preferences, and then click **Next**.
7. Click **Finish** to complete the setup.

Upgrading Microsoft Office Professional 2007 6-Month Trial Software to the Full Product

You can convert the software into full use without removing or reinstalling software on your computer. When you complete your trial, you can purchase a product license from any Microsoft reseller and enter a valid Product Key when prompted during Setup.

Uninstalling the Trial Software and Returning to Your Previous Office Version

If you want to return to your previous version of Office, you need to uninstall the trial software. This should be done through the Add or Remove Programs icon in Control Panel (or Uninstall a program in the Control Panel of Windows Vista).

www.wiley.com/college/microsoft *or* call the MOAC Toll-Free Number: 1+(888) 764-7001 (North America Only)

Uninstall Trial Software

1. Quit any programs that are running.
2. In Control Panel, click **Add or Remove Programs** (or **Uninstall a program** in Windows Vista).
3. Click **Microsoft Office Professional 2007,** and then click **Remove** (or **Uninstall** in Windows Vista).

> **TAKE NOTE***
>
> If you selected the option to remove a previous version of Office during installation of the trial software, you need to reinstall your previous version of Office. If you did not remove your previous version of Office, you can start each of your Office programs either through the Start menu or by opening files for each program. In some cases, you may have to recreate some of your shortcuts and default settings.

Student CD

The CD-ROM included with this book contains the practice files that you will use as you perform the exercises in the book. By using the practice files, you will not waste time creating the samples used in the lessons, and you can concentrate on learning how to use Microsoft Office 2007. With the files and the step-by-step instructions in the lessons, you will learn by doing, which is an easy and effective way to acquire and remember new skills.

> **IMPORTANT**
>
> This course assumes that the 2007 Microsoft Office system has already been installed on the PC you are using. Note that Microsoft Product Support does not support this trial version.

Copying the Practice Files

Your instructor might already have copied the practice files before you arrive in class. However, your instructor might ask you to copy the practice files on your own at the start of class. Also, if you want to work through any of the exercises in this book on your own at home or at your place of business, you may want to copy the practice files. Note that you can also open the files directly from the CD-ROM, but you should be cautious about carrying the CD-ROM around with you as it could become damaged.

If you only want to copy the files for one lesson, you can open the Data folder and right-click the desired Lesson folder within the Data folder.

1. Insert the CD-ROM in the CD-ROM drive of your computer.
2. Start Windows Explorer.
3. In the left pane of Explorer, locate the icon for your CD-ROM and click on this icon. The folders and files contained on the CD will appear listed on the right.
4. Locate and select the **Data** folder. This is the folder that contains all of the practice files, separated by Lesson folders.
5. Right-click on the **Data** folder and choose **Copy** from the menu.
6. In the left pane of Windows Explorer, choose the location to which you would like to copy the practice files. This can be a drive on your local PC or an external drive.
7. Right-click on the drive/location to which you want to copy the practice files and choose **Paste.** This will copy the entire Data folder to your chosen location.
8. Close Windows Explorer.

Deleting the Practice Files

Use the following steps when you want to delete the practice files from your hard disk or other drive. Your instructor might ask you to perform these steps at the end of class. Also, you should perform these steps if you have worked through the exercises at home or at your place of business and want to work through the exercises again. Deleting the practice files and then

www.wiley.com/college/microsoft *or* **call the MOAC Toll-Free Number: 1+(888) 764-7001 (North America Only)**

reinstalling them ensures that all files and folders are in their original condition if you decide to work through the exercises again.

1. Start Windows Explorer.
2. Browse through the drives and folders to locate the practice files.
3. Select the **Data** folder.
4. Right-click on the **Data** folder and choose **Delete** from the menu.
5. Close Windows Explorer.

Locating and Opening Practice Files

If you only want to delete only the files for one lesson, you can open the Data folder and right-click the desired Lesson folder within the Data folder.

After you (or your instructor) have copied the practice files, all the files you need for this course will be stored in a folder named Data located on the disk you choose.

1. Click the **Office Button** in the top left corner of your application.
2. Choose **Open** from the menu.
3. In the Open dialog box, browse through the Folders panel to locate the drive and folder where you copied the files.
4. Double-click on the **Data** folder.
5. Double-click on the **Lesson** folder for the lesson on which you are working.
6. Select the file that you want and click **Open** or double-click on the file that you want.

Wiley Desktop Editions

You can use the Search function in the Open dialog box to quickly find the specific file for which you are looking.

Wiley MOAC Desktop Editions are innovative, electronic versions of printed textbooks. Students buy the desktop version for 50% off the price of the printed text, and get the added value of permanence and portability. Wiley Desktop Editions provide students with numerous additional benefits that are not available with other e-text solutions.

Wiley Desktop Editions are NOT subscriptions; students download the Wiley Desktop Edition to their computer desktops. Students own the content they buy to keep for as long as they want. Once a Wiley Desktop Edition is downloaded to the computer desktop, students have instant access to all of the content without being online. Students can also print out the sections they prefer to read in hard copy. Students also have access to fully integrated resources within their Wiley Desktop Edition. From highlighting their e-text to taking and sharing notes, students can easily personalize their Wiley Desktop Edition as they are reading or following along in class.

Please visit Microsoft Office Online for help using Office 2007, Clip Art, Templates, and other valuable information:
http://office.microsoft.com/

Preparing to Take the Microsoft Certified Application Specialist (MCAS) Exam

The Microsoft Certified Application Specialist program is part of the new and enhanced Microsoft Business Certifications. It is easily attainable through a series of verifications that provide a simple and convenient framework for skills assessment and validation.

For organizations, the new certification program provides better skills verification tools that help with assessing not only in-demand skills on the 2007 Microsoft Office system, but also the ability to quickly complete on-the-job tasks. Individuals will find it easier to identify and work towards the certification credential that meets their personal and professional goals.

www.wiley.com/college/microsoft *or* **call the MOAC Toll-Free Number: 1+(888) 764-7001 (North America Only)**

To learn more about becoming a Microsoft Certified Application Specialist and exam availability, visit www.microsoft.com/learning/msbc.

Microsoft Certified Application Specialist (MCAS) Program

The core Microsoft Office Specialist credential has been upgraded to validate skills with the 2007 Microsoft Office system as well as the new Windows Vista operating system. The Application Specialist certifications target information workers and cover the most popular business applications such as Word 2007, PowerPoint 2007, Excel 2007, Access 2007, and Outlook 2007.

By becoming certified, you demonstrate to employers that you have achieved a predictable level of skill in the use of a particular Office application. Employers often require certification either as a condition of employment or as a condition of advancement within the company or other organization. The certification examinations are sponsored by Microsoft but administered through exam delivery partners like Certiport.

Preparing to Take an Exam

Unless you are a very experienced user, you will need to use a test preparation course to prepare to complete the test correctly and within the time allowed. The *Microsoft Official Academic Course* series is designed to prepare you with a strong knowledge of all exam topics, and with some additional review and practice on your own. You should feel confident in your ability to pass the appropriate exam.

After you decide which exam to take, review the list of objectives for the exam. This list can be found in the MCAS Objectives Appendix at the back of this book. You can also easily identify tasks that are included in the objective list by locating the Lesson Skill Matrix at the start of each lesson and the Certification Ready sidebars in the margin of the lessons in this book.

To take the MCAS test, visit *www.microsoft.com/learning/msbc* to locate your nearest testing center. Then call the testing center directly to schedule your test. The amount of advance notice you should provide will vary for different testing centers, and it typically depends on the number of computers available at the testing center, the number of other testers who have already been scheduled for the day on which you want to take the test, and the number of times per week that the testing center offers MCAS testing. In general, you should call to schedule your test at least two weeks prior to the date on which you want to take the test.

When you arrive at the testing center, you might be asked for proof of identity. A driver's license or passport is an acceptable form of identification. If you do not have either of these items of documentation, call your testing center and ask what alternative forms of identification will be accepted. If you are retaking a test, bring your MCAS identification number, which will have been given to you when you previously took the test. If you have not prepaid or if your organization has not already arranged to make payment for you, you will need to pay the test-taking fee when you arrive.

Test Format

All MCAS certification tests are live, performance-based tests. There are no true/false or short-answer questions. Instructions are general: you are told the basic tasks to perform on the computer, but you aren't given any help in figuring out how to perform them. You are not permitted to use reference material.

As you complete the tasks stated in a particular test question, the testing software monitors your actions. An example question might be:

Open the file named *Wiley Guests* and select the word *Welcome* in the first paragraph. Change the font to 12 point, and apply bold formatting. Select the words *at your convenience* in the second paragraph, move them to the end of the first paragraph using drag and drop, and then center the first paragraph.

When the test administrator seats you at a computer, you will see an online form that you use to enter information about yourself (name, address, and other information required to process your exam results). While you complete the form, the software will generate the test from a master test bank and then prompt you to continue. The first test question will appear in a window. Read the question carefully, and then perform all the tasks stated in the test question. When you have finished completing all tasks for a question, click the Next Question button.

You have 45 to 50 minutes to complete all questions, depending on the test that you are taking. The testing software assesses your results as soon as you complete the test, and the test administrator can print the results of the test so that you will have a record of any tasks that you performed incorrectly. If you pass, you will receive a certificate in the mail within two to four weeks. If you do not pass, you can study and practice the skills that you missed and then schedule to retake the test at a later date.

Tips for Successfully Completing the Test

The following tips and suggestions are the result of feedback received from many individuals who have taken one or more MCAS tests:

- Make sure that you are thoroughly prepared. If you have extensively used the application for which you are being tested, you might feel confident that you are prepared for the test. However, the test might include questions that involve tasks that you rarely or never perform when you use the application at your place of business, at school, or at home. You must be knowledgeable in all the MCAS objectives for the test that you will take.
- Read each exam question carefully. An exam question might include several tasks that you are to perform. A partially correct response to a test question is counted as an incorrect response. In the example question on the previous page, you might apply bold formatting and move the words *at your convenience* to the correct location, but forget to center the first paragraph. This would count as an incorrect response and would result in a lower test score.
- You are not allowed to use the application's Help system. The Help function is always disabled for all exams.
- The test does display the amount of time that you have left. The test program also displays the number of items that you have completed along with the total number of test items (for example, "35 of 40 items have been completed"). Use this information to gauge your pace.
- If you skip a question, you can return to it later.

If You Do Not Pass the Test

If you do not pass, you can use the assessment printout as a guide to practice the items that you missed. There is no limit to the number of times that you can retake a test; however, you must pay the fee each time that you take the test. When you retake the test, expect to see some of the same test items on the subsequent test; the test software randomly generates the test items from a master test bank before you begin the test. Also expect to see several questions that did not appear on the previous test.

www.wiley.com/college/microsoft *or* call the MOAC Toll-Free Number: 1+(888) 764-7001 (North America Only)

Acknowledgments

MOAC Instructor Advisory Board

We would like to thank our Instructor Advisory Board, an elite group of educators who has assisted us every step of the way in building these products. Advisory Board members have acted as our sounding board on key pedagogical and design decisions leading to the development of these compelling and innovative textbooks for future Information Workers. Their dedication to technology education is truly appreciated.

Catherine Binder, Strayer University & Katharine Gibbs School–Philadelphia

Catherine currently works at both Katharine Gibbs School in Norristown, PA and Strayer University in King of Prussia, PA. Catherine has been at Katharine Gibbs School for 4 years. Catherine is currently the Department Chair/Lead instructor for PC Networking at Gibbs and the founder/advisor of the TEK Masters Society. Since joining Strayer University a year and a half ago she has risen in the ranks from adjunct to DIT/Assistant Campus Dean.

Catherine has brought her 10+ year's industry experience as Network Administrator, Network Supervisor, Professor, Bench Tech, Manager and CTO from such places as Foster Wheeler Corp, KidsPeace Inc., Victoria Vogue, TESST College, AMC Theatres, Blue Mountain Publishing and many more to her teaching venue.

Catherine began as an adjunct in the PC Networking department and quickly became a full-time instructor. At both schools she is in charge of scheduling, curricula and departmental duties. She happily advises about 80+ students and is committed to Gibbs/Strayer life, her students, and continuing technology education every day.

Penny Gudgeon, CDI College

Penny is the Program Manager for IT curriculum at Corinthian Colleges, Inc. Until January 2006, Penny was responsible for all Canadian programming and web curriculum for five years. During that time, Corinthian Colleges, Inc. acquired CDI College of Business and Technology in 2004. Before 2000 she spent four years as IT instructor at one of the campuses. Penny joined CDI College in 1997 after her working for 10 years first in programming and later in software productivity education. Penny previously has worked in the fields of advertising, sales, engineering technology and programming. When not working from her home office or indulging her passion for life long learning, and the possibilities of what might be, Penny likes to read mysteries, garden and relax at home in Hamilton, Ontario, with her Shih-Tzu, Gracie, and husband, Al.

Jana Hambruch, School District of Lee County

Ms. Hambruch currently serves as Director for the Information Technology Magnet Programs at The School District of Lee County in Ft Myers, Florida. She is responsible for the implementation and direction of three schools that fall under this grant program. This program has been recognized as one of the top 15 most innovative technology programs in the nation. She is also co-author of the grant proposal for the IT Magnet Grant prior to taking on the role of Director.

Ms. Hambruch has over ten years experience directing the technical certification training programs at many Colleges and Universities, including Barry University, the University of

South Florida, Broward Community College, and at Florida Gulf Coast University, where she served as the Director for the Center for Technology Education. She excels at developing alternative training models that focus on the tie between the education provider and the community in which it serves.

Ms. Hambruch is a past board member and treasurer of the Human Resources Management Association of SW Florida, graduate of Leadership Lee County Class of 2002, Steering Committee Member for Leadership Lee County Class of 2004 and a former board member of the Career Coalition of Southwest Florida. She has frequently lectured for organizations such as Microsoft, American Society of Training and Development, Florida Gulf Coast University, Florida State University, University of Nevada at Las Vegas, University of Wisconsin at Milwaukee, Canada's McGill University, and Florida's State Workforce Summit.

Dee Hobson, Richland College

Dee Hobson is currently a faculty member of the Business Office Systems and Support Division at Richland College. Richland is one of seven colleges in the Dallas County Community College District and has the distinction of being the first community college to receive the Malcolm Baldrige National Quality Award in 2005. Richland also received the Texas Award for Performance Excellence in 2005.

The Business Office Systems and Support Division at Richland is also a Certiport Authorized Microsoft Office testing center. All students enrolling in one of Microsoft's application software courses (Word, Excel, PowerPoint, and Access) are required to take the respective Microsoft certification exam at the end of the semester.

Dee has taught computer and business courses in K-12 public schools and at a proprietary career college in Dallas. She has also been involved with several corporate training companies and with adult education programs in the Dallas area. She began her computer career as an employee of IBM Corporation in St. Louis, Missouri. During her ten-year IBM employment, she moved to Memphis, Tennessee, to accept a managerial position and to Dallas, Texas, to work in a national sales and marketing technical support center.

Keith Hoell, Katharine Gibbs School–New York

Keith has worked in both non-profit and proprietary education for over 10 years, initially at St. John's University in New York, and then as full-time faculty, Chairperson and currently Dean of Information Systems at the Katharine Gibbs School in New York City. He also worked for General Electric in the late 80's and early 90's as the Sysop of a popular bulletin board dedicated to ASCII-Art on GE's pioneering GEnie on-line service before the advent of the World Wide Web. He has taught courses and workshops dealing with many mainstream IT issues and varied technology, especially those related to computer hardware and operating system software, networking, software applications, IT project management and ethics, and relational database technology. An avid runner and a member of The New York Road Runners, he won the Footlocker Five Borough Challenge representing Queens at the 2005 ING New York City Marathon while competing against the 4 other borough reps. He currently resides in Queens, New York.

Michael Taylor, Seattle Central Community College

Michael worked in education and training for the last 20 years in both the public and private sector. He currently teaches and coordinates the applications support program at Seattle Central Community College and also administers the Microsoft IT Academy. His experience outside the educational world is in Travel and Tourism with wholesale tour operations and cruise lines.

Interests outside of work include greyhound rescue. (He adopted 3 x-racers who bring him great joy.) He also enjoys the arts and is fortunate to live in downtown Seattle where there is much to see and do.

www.wiley.com/college/microsoft *or* call the MOAC Toll-Free Number: 1+(888) 764-7001 (North America Only)

MOAC Office 2007 Reviewers

We also thank the many reviewers who pored over the manuscript, providing invaluable feedback in the service of quality instructional materials.

Access
Susan Fry, Boise State University
Leslie Jernberg, Eastern Idaho Technical College
Dr. Deborah Jones, South Georgia Technical College
Suzanne Marks, Bellevue Community College
Kim Styles, Tri-County Technical College & Anderson School District 5
Fred Usmani, Conestoga College

Excel
Bob Gunderson, TriOS College
Christie Hovey, Lincoln Land Community College
Barbara Lave, Portland Community College
Trevor McIvor, Bow Valley College
Donna Madsen, Kirkwood Community College
James M. Veneziano, Davenport University—Caro
Dorothy Weiner, Manchester Community College

PowerPoint
Barbara Gillespie, Cuyamaca College
Caroline de Gruchy, Conestoga College
Tatyana Pashnyak, Bainbridge College
Michelle Poertner, Northwestern Michigan College
Janet Sebesy, Cuyahoga Community College

Outlook
Julie Boyles, Portland Community College
Joe LaMontagne, Davenport University—Grand Rapids
Randy Nordell, American River College
Echo Rantanen, Spokane Community College
Lyndsey Webster, TriOS College

Project
Janis DeHaven, Central Community College
Dr. Susan Jennings, Stephen F. Austin State University
Jack Maronowski, Curriculum Director, CDI College
Diane D. Mickey, Northern Virginia Community College
Linda Nutter, Peninsula College
Marika Reinke, Bellevue Community College

Word
Diana Anderson, Big Sandy Community & Technical College
Donna Hendricks, South Arkansas Community College
Dr. Donna McGill-Cameron, Yuba Community College—Woodland Campus
Patricia McMahon, South Suburban College
Jack Maronowski, Curriculum Director, CDI College
Nancy Noe, Linn-Benton Community College
Teresa Roberts, Wilson Technical Community College

www.wiley.com/college/microsoft *or* call the MOAC Toll-Free Number: 1+(888) 764-7001 (North America Only)

Focus Group and Survey Participants

Finally, we thank the hundreds of instructors who participated in our focus groups and surveys to ensure that the Microsoft Official Academic Courses best met the needs of our customers.

Jean Aguilar, Mt. Hood Community College
Konrad Akens, Zane State College
Michael Albers, University of Memphis
Diana Anderson, Big Sandy Community & Technical College
Phyllis Anderson, Delaware County Community College
Judith Andrews, Feather River College
Damon Antos, American River College
Bridget Archer, Oakton Community College
Linda Arnold, Harrisburg Area Community College– Lebanon Campus
Neha Arya, Fullerton College
Mohammad Bajwa, Katharine Gibbs School–New York
Virginia Baker, University of Alaska Fairbanks
Carla Bannick, Pima Community College
Rita Barkley, Northeast Alabama Community College
Elsa Barr, Central Community College – Hastings
Ronald W. Barry, Ventura County Community College District
Elizabeth Bastedo, Central Carolina Technical College
Karen Baston, Waubonsee Community College
Karen Bean, Blinn College
Scott Beckstrand, Community College of Southern Nevada
Paulette Bell, Santa Rosa Junior College
Liz Bennett, Southeast Technical Institute
Nancy Bermea, Olympic College
Lucy Betz, Milwaukee Area Technical College
Meral Binbasioglu, Hofstra University
Catherine Binder, Strayer University & Katharine Gibbs School–Philadelphia
Terrel Blair, El Centro College
Ruth Blalock, Alamance Community College
Beverly Bohner, Reading Area Community College
Henry Bojack, Farmingdale State University
Matthew Bowie, Luna Community College
Julie Boyles, Portland Community College
Karen Brandt, College of the Albemarle
Stephen Brown, College of San Mateo
Jared Bruckner, Southern Adventist University
Pam Brune, Chattanooga State Technical Community College
Sue Buchholz, Georgia Perimeter College
Roberta Buczyna, Edison College
Angela Butler, Mississippi Gulf Coast Community College
Rebecca Byrd, Augusta Technical College
Kristen Callahan, Mercer County Community College
Judy Cameron, Spokane Community College
Dianne Campbell, Athens Technical College
Gena Casas, Florida Community College at Jacksonville
Jesus Castrejon, Latin Technologies
Gail Chambers, Southwest Tennessee Community College
Jacques Chansavang, Indiana University–Purdue University Fort Wayne
Nancy Chapko, Milwaukee Area Technical College
Rebecca Chavez, Yavapai College
Sanjiv Chopra, Thomas Nelson Community College

www.wiley.com/college/microsoft *or* call the MOAC Toll-Free Number: 1+(888) 764-7001 (North America Only)

Greg Clements, Midland Lutheran College
Dayna Coker, Southwestern Oklahoma State University– Sayre Campus
Tamra Collins, Otero Junior College
Janet Conrey, Gavilan Community College
Carol Cornforth, West Virginia Northern Community College
Gary Cotton, American River College
Edie Cox, Chattahoochee Technical College
Rollie Cox, Madison Area Technical College
David Crawford, Northwestern Michigan College
J.K. Crowley, Victor Valley College
Rosalyn Culver, Washtenaw Community College
Sharon Custer, Huntington University
Sandra Daniels, New River Community College
Anila Das, Cedar Valley College
Brad Davis, Santa Rosa Junior College
Susan Davis, Green River Community College
Mark Dawdy, Lincoln Land Community College
Jennifer Day, Sinclair Community College
Carol Deane, Eastern Idaho Technical College
Julie DeBuhr, Lewis-Clark State College
Janis DeHaven, Central Community College
Drew Dekreon, University of Alaska–Anchorage
Joy DePover, Central Lakes College
Salli DiBartolo, Brevard Community College
Melissa Diegnau, Riverland Community College
Al Dillard, Lansdale School of Business
Marjorie Duffy, Cosumnes River College
Sarah Dunn, Southwest Tennessee Community College
Shahla Durany, Tarrant County College–South Campus
Kay Durden, University of Tennessee at Martin
Dineen Ebert, St. Louis Community College–Meramec
Donna Ehrhart, State University of New York–Brockport
Larry Elias, Montgomery County Community College
Glenda Elser, New Mexico State University at Alamogordo
Angela Evangelinos, Monroe County Community College
Angie Evans, Ivy Tech Community College of Indiana
Linda Farrington, Indian Hills Community College
Dana Fladhammer, Phoenix College
Richard Flores, Citrus College
Connie Fox, Community and Technical College at Institute of Technology
   West Virginia University
Wanda Freeman, Okefenokee Technical College
Brenda Freeman, Augusta Technical College
Susan Fry, Boise State University
Roger Fulk, Wright State University–Lake Campus
Sue Furnas, Collin County Community College District
Sandy Gabel, Vernon College
Laura Galvan, Fayetteville Technical Community College
Candace Garrod, Red Rocks Community College
Sherrie Geitgey, Northwest State Community College
Chris Gerig, Chattahoochee Technical College
Barb Gillespie, Cuyamaca College
Jessica Gilmore, Highline Community College
Pamela Gilmore, Reedley College
Debbie Glinert, Queensborough Community College

www.wiley.com/college/microsoft *or* **call the MOAC Toll-Free Number: 1+(888) 764-7001 (North America Only)**

Steven Goldman, Polk Community College
Bettie Goodman, C.S. Mott Community College
Mike Grabill, Katharine Gibbs School–Philadelphia
Francis Green, Penn State University
Walter Griffin, Blinn College
Fillmore Guinn, Odessa College
Helen Haasch, Milwaukee Area Technical College
John Habal, Ventura College
Joy Haerens, Chaffey College
Norman Hahn, Thomas Nelson Community College
Kathy Hall, Alamance Community College
Teri Harbacheck, Boise State University
Linda Harper, Richland Community College
Maureen Harper, Indian Hills Community College
Steve Harris, Katharine Gibbs School–New York
Robyn Hart, Fresno City College
Darien Hartman, Boise State University
Gina Hatcher, Tacoma Community College
Winona T. Hatcher, Aiken Technical College
BJ Hathaway, Northeast Wisconsin Tech College
Cynthia Hauki, West Hills College – Coalinga
Mary L. Haynes, Wayne County Community College
Marcie Hawkins, Zane State College
Steve Hebrock, Ohio State University Agricultural Technical Institute
Sue Heistand, Iowa Central Community College
Heith Hennel, Valencia Community College
Donna Hendricks, South Arkansas Community College
Judy Hendrix, Dyersburg State Community College
Gloria Hensel, Matanuska-Susitna College University of Alaska Anchorage
Gwendolyn Hester, Richland College
Tammarra Holmes, Laramie County Community College
Dee Hobson, Richland College
Keith Hoell, Katharine Gibbs School–New York
Pashia Hogan, Northeast State Technical Community College
Susan Hoggard, Tulsa Community College
Kathleen Holliman, Wallace Community College Selma
Chastity Honchul, Brown Mackie College/Wright State University
Christie Hovey, Lincoln Land Community College
Peggy Hughes, Allegany College of Maryland
Sandra Hume, Chippewa Valley Technical College
John Hutson, Aims Community College
Celia Ing, Sacramento City College
Joan Ivey, Lanier Technical College
Barbara Jaffari, College of the Redwoods
Penny Jakes, University of Montana College of Technology
Eduardo Jaramillo, Peninsula College
Barbara Jauken, Southeast Community College
Susan Jennings, Stephen F. Austin State University
Leslie Jernberg, Eastern Idaho Technical College
Linda Johns, Georgia Perimeter College
Brent Johnson, Okefenokee Technical College
Mary Johnson, Mt. San Antonio College
Shirley Johnson, Trinidad State Junior College– Valley Campus
Sandra M. Jolley, Tarrant County College

Teresa Jolly, South Georgia Technical College
Dr. Deborah Jones, South Georgia Technical College
Margie Jones, Central Virginia Community College
Randall Jones, Marshall Community and Technical College
Diane Karlsbraaten, Lake Region State College
Teresa Keller, Ivy Tech Community College of Indiana
Charles Kemnitz, Pennsylvania College of Technology
Sandra Kinghorn, Ventura College
Bill Klein, Katharine Gibbs School–Philadelphia
Bea Knaapen, Fresno City College
Kit Kofoed, Western Wyoming Community College
Maria Kolatis, County College of Morris
Barry Kolb, Ocean County College
Karen Kuralt, University of Arkansas at Little Rock
Belva-Carole Lamb, Rogue Community College
Betty Lambert, Des Moines Area Community College
Anita Lande, Cabrillo College
Junnae Landry, Pratt Community College
Karen Lankisch, UC Clermont
David Lanzilla, Central Florida Community College
Nora Laredo, Cerritos Community College
Jennifer Larrabee, Chippewa Valley Technical College
Debra Larson, Idaho State University
Barb Lave, Portland Community College
Audrey Lawrence, Tidewater Community College
Deborah Layton, Eastern Oklahoma State College
Larry LeBlanc, Owen Graduate School–Vanderbilt University
Philip Lee, Nashville State Community College
Michael Lehrfeld, Brevard Community College
Vasant Limaye, Southwest Collegiate Institute for the Deaf – Howard College
Anne C. Lewis, Edgecombe Community College
Stephen Linkin, Houston Community College
Peggy Linston, Athens Technical College
Hugh Lofton, Moultrie Technical College
Donna Lohn, Lakeland Community College
Jackie Lou, Lake Tahoe Community College
Donna Love, Gaston College
Curt Lynch, Ozarks Technical Community College
Sheilah Lynn, Florida Community College–Jacksonville
Pat R. Lyon, Tomball College
Bill Madden, Bergen Community College
Heather Madden, Delaware Technical & Community College
Donna Madsen, Kirkwood Community College
Jane Maringer-Cantu, Gavilan College
Suzanne Marks, Bellevue Community College
Carol Martin, Louisiana State University–Alexandria
Cheryl Martucci, Diablo Valley College
Roberta Marvel, Eastern Wyoming College
Tom Mason, Brookdale Community College
Mindy Mass, Santa Barbara City College
Dixie Massaro, Irvine Valley College
Rebekah May, Ashland Community & Technical College
Emma Mays-Reynolds, Dyersburg State Community College
Timothy Mayes, Metropolitan State College of Denver
Reggie McCarthy, Central Lakes College

Matt McCaskill, Brevard Community College
Kevin McFarlane, Front Range Community College
Donna McGill, Yuba Community College
Terri McKeever, Ozarks Technical Community College
Patricia McMahon, South Suburban College
Sally McMillin, Katharine Gibbs School–Philadelphia
Charles McNerney, Bergen Community College
Lisa Mears, Palm Beach Community College
Imran Mehmood, ITT Technical Institute–King of Prussia Campus
Virginia Melvin, Southwest Tennessee Community College
Jeanne Mercer, Texas State Technical College
Denise Merrell, Jefferson Community & Technical College
Catherine Merrikin, Pearl River Community College
Diane D. Mickey, Northern Virginia Community College
Darrelyn Miller, Grays Harbor College
Sue Mitchell, Calhoun Community College
Jacquie Moldenhauer, Front Range Community College
Linda Motonaga, Los Angeles City College
Sam Mryyan, Allen County Community College
Cindy Murphy, Southeastern Community College
Ryan Murphy, Sinclair Community College
Sharon E. Nastav, Johnson County Community College
Christine Naylor, Kent State University Ashtabula
Haji Nazarian, Seattle Central Community College
Nancy Noe, Linn-Benton Community College
Jennie Noriega, San Joaquin Delta College
Linda Nutter, Peninsula College
Thomas Omerza, Middle Bucks Institute of Technology
Edith Orozco, St. Philip's College
Dona Orr, Boise State University
Joanne Osgood, Chaffey College
Janice Owens, Kishwaukee College
Tatyana Pashnyak, Bainbridge College
John Partacz, College of DuPage
Tim Paul, Montana State University–Great Falls
Joseph Perez, South Texas College
Mike Peterson, Chemeketa Community College
Dr. Karen R. Petitto, West Virginia Wesleyan College
Terry Pierce, Onandaga Community College
Ashlee Pieris, Raritan Valley Community College
Jamie Pinchot, Thiel College
Michelle Poertner, Northwestern Michigan College
Betty Posta, University of Toledo
Deborah Powell, West Central Technical College
Mark Pranger, Rogers State University
Carolyn Rainey, Southeast Missouri State University
Linda Raskovich, Hibbing Community College
Leslie Ratliff, Griffin Technical College
Mar-Sue Ratzke, Rio Hondo Community College
Roxy Reissen, Southeastern Community College
Silvio Reyes, Technical Career Institutes
Patricia Rishavy, Anoka Technical College
Jean Robbins, Southeast Technical Institute
Carol Roberts, Eastern Maine Community College and University of Maine

Teresa Roberts, Wilson Technical Community College
Vicki Robertson, Southwest Tennessee Community College
Betty Rogge, Ohio State Agricultural Technical Institute
Lynne Rusley, Missouri Southern State University
Claude Russo, Brevard Community College
Ginger Sabine, Northwestern Technical College
Steven Sachs, Los Angeles Valley College
Joanne Salas, Olympic College
Lloyd Sandmann, Pima Community College–Desert Vista Campus
Beverly Santillo, Georgia Perimeter College
Theresa Savarese, San Diego City College
Sharolyn Sayers, Milwaukee Area Technical College
Judith Scheeren, Westmoreland County Community College
Adolph Scheiwe, Joliet Junior College
Marilyn Schmid, Asheville-Buncombe Technical Community College
Janet Sebesy, Cuyahoga Community College
Phyllis T. Shafer, Brookdale Community College
Ralph Shafer, Truckee Meadows Community College
Anne Marie Shanley, County College of Morris
Shelia Shelton, Surry Community College
Merilyn Shepherd, Danville Area Community College
Susan Sinele, Aims Community College
Beth Sindt, Hawkeye Community College
Andrew Smith, Marian College
Brenda Smith, Southwest Tennessee Community College
Lynne Smith, State University of New York–Delhi
Rob Smith, Katharine Gibbs School–Philadelphia
Tonya Smith, Arkansas State University–Mountain Home
Del Spencer – Trinity Valley Community College
Jeri Spinner, Idaho State University
Eric Stadnik, Santa Rosa Junior College
Karen Stanton, Los Medanos College
Meg Stoner, Santa Rosa Junior College
Beverly Stowers, Ivy Tech Community College of Indiana
Marcia Stranix, Yuba College
Kim Styles, Tri-County Technical College
Sylvia Summers, Tacoma Community College
Beverly Swann, Delaware Technical & Community College
Ann Taff, Tulsa Community College
Mike Theiss, University of Wisconsin–Marathon Campus
Romy Thiele, Cañada College
Sharron Thompson, Portland Community College
Ingrid Thompson-Sellers, Georgia Perimeter College
Barbara Tietsort, University of Cincinnati–Raymond Walters College
Janine Tiffany, Reading Area Community College
Denise Tillery, University of Nevada Las Vegas
Susan Trebelhorn, Normandale Community College
Noel Trout, Santiago Canyon College
Cheryl Turgeon, Asnuntuck Community College
Steve Turner, Ventura College
Sylvia Unwin, Bellevue Community College
Lilly Vigil, Colorado Mountain College
Sabrina Vincent, College of the Mainland
Mary Vitrano, Palm Beach Community College

www.wiley.com/college/microsoft *or* **call the MOAC Toll-Free Number: 1+(888) 764-7001 (North America Only)**

Brad Vogt, Northeast Community College
Cozell Wagner, Southeastern Community College
Carolyn Walker, Tri-County Technical College
Sherry Walker, Tulsa Community College
Qi Wang, Tacoma Community College
Betty Wanielista, Valencia Community College
Marge Warber, Lanier Technical College–Forsyth Campus
Marjorie Webster, Bergen Community College
Linda Wenn, Central Community College
Mark Westlund, Olympic College
Carolyn Whited, Roane State Community College
Winona Whited, Richland College
Jerry Wilkerson, Scott Community College
Joel Willenbring, Fullerton College
Barbara Williams, WITC Superior
Charlotte Williams, Jones County Junior College
Bonnie Willy, Ivy Tech Community College of Indiana
Diane Wilson, J. Sargeant Reynolds Community College
James Wolfe, Metropolitan Community College
Marjory Wooten, Lanier Technical College
Mark Yanko, Hocking College
Alexis Yusov, Pace University
Naeem Zaman, San Joaquin Delta College
Kathleen Zimmerman, Des Moines Area Community College

We would also like to thank Lutz Ziob, Sanjay Advani, Jim DiIanni, Merrick Van Dongen, Jim LeValley, Bruce Curling, Joe Wilson, and Naman Kahn at Microsoft for their encouragement and support in making the Microsoft Official Academic Course programs the finest instructional materials for mastering the newest Microsoft technologies for both students and instructors.

Brief Contents

Introduction Unit 1

Lesson 1: Introduction to Office 2007 3
Lesson 2: Windows Basics 23
Lesson 3: Working with Files and Folders 48
Lesson 4: Windows Vista Speech Recognition 75

↻ **Circling Back** 106

Word Unit 111

Lesson 1: Word Essentials 113
Lesson 2: Document Basics 132
Lesson 3: Character Formatting 154
Lesson 4: Paragraph Formatting 171
Lesson 5: Document Formatting 195

↻ **Circling Back** 209

Lesson 6: Managing Text Flow 213
Lesson 7: Editing Basics 228
Lesson 8: Creating Tables and Lists 247
Lesson 9: Adding Pictures and Shapes to a Document 270
Lesson 10: Customizing Word 296

↻ **Circling Back** 316

Excel Unit 319

Lesson 1: Excel Essentials 321
Lesson 2: Creating and Editing a Workbook 336
Lesson 3: Formatting Cells and Ranges 355
Lesson 4: Worksheet Formatting 381

↻ **Circling Back** 406

Lesson 5: Managing Worksheets 409
Lesson 6: Working with Data 430
Lesson 7: Using Basic Formulas and Functions 453
Lesson 8: Creating Charts from Your Data 481

⟳ Circling Back 500

PowerPoint Unit 504

Lesson 1: PowerPoint Essentials 505
Lesson 2: Presentation Basics 524
Lesson 3: Working with Text 555
Lesson 4: Designing a Presentation 593

⟳ Circling Back 628

Lesson 5: Adding Tables, Charts, and SmartArt Graphics to Slides 631
Lesson 6: Adding Graphics and Media Clips to a Presentation 660
Lesson 7: Delivering a Presentation 699

⟳ Circling Back 725

Access Unit 728

Lesson 1: Database Essentials 729
Lesson 2: Create Database Tables 748
Lesson 3: Work with Tables/Database Records 768
Lesson 4: Modifying Tables and Fields 794

⟳ Circling Back 826

Lesson 5: Create Forms 831
Lesson 6: Create Reports 853
Lesson 7: Create and Modify Queries 871
Lesson 8: Database Tools 899

⟳ Circling Back 917

Outlook Unit 923

Lesson 1: Getting to Know Outlook 925
Lesson 2: Email Basics 940
Lesson 3: Managing Mail with Folders 965
Lesson 4: Processing Messages with Rules 979
Lesson 5: Contact Basics 1002

www.wiley.com/college/microsoft *or* call the MOAC Toll-Free Number: 1+(888) 764-7001 (North America Only)

↻ **Circling Back 1022**

Lesson 6: Advanced Contact Management   1026

Lesson 7: Calendar Basics   1049

Lesson 8: Managing Meetings   1062

Lesson 9: Managing Tasks   1086

Lesson 10: Categories and Outlook Data Files   1108

↻ **Circling Back 1122**

Appendix A   1125

Appendix B   1137

Appendix C   1138

Glossary   1141

Index   1147

www.wiley.com/college/microsoft *or* call the MOAC Toll-Free Number: 1+(888) 764-7001
(North America Only)

www.wiley.com/college/microsoft *or* call the MOAC Toll-Free Number: 1+(888) 764-7001 (North America Only)

Contents

Introduction Unit 1

Lesson 1: Introduction to Office 2007 3

Lesson Skill Matrix 3
Key Terms 3
Software Orientation 4
Opening and Closing Office Applications 4
    Starting an Office Application 5
    Closing a Document 5
    Closing an Office Application 6
Working in the Office Window 6
    Using the Onscreen Tools 6
        Use the Ribbon 6
        Use the Mini Toolbar 8
        Use the Quick Access Toolbar 8
        Use KeyTips 9
Working with the Microsoft Office Button 10
    Using the Microsoft Office Button 10
    Opening an Existing Document 11
    Saving a Document 13
    Choosing a Printer 14
    Setting Standard Properties 14
    Assigning Keywords to a Document 15
Working with Microsoft Office Help 16
    Using the Microsoft Office Help button 16
Summary Skill Matrix 19
Assessment 19
    Knowledge Assessment 19
    Competency Assessment 20
    Proficiency Assessment 21
    Mastery Assessment 21
Internet Ready 22

Lesson 2: Windows Basics 23

Lesson Skill Matrix 23
Key Terms 23
Getting Started with Windows Vista 24
    Logging On to Windows Vista 24
Using the Mouse to Identify Desktop Items 27
Use the Start Menu 28
    Opening and Closing the Start Menu 28
    Identifying Items on the Start Menu 29
    Selecting Start Menu Settings 32
    Searching from the Start Menu 35
Resizing a Folder Window 37
    Minimizing, Maximizing, and Restoring a Window 37
Accessing Help and Support 40
    Accessing Help and Support 40
Shutting Down Windows Vista 42
    Shutting Down Windows Vista 42
Summary Skill Matrix 42
Assessment 43
    Knowledge Assessment 43
    Competency Assessment 45
    Proficiency Assessment 45
    Mastery Assessment 46
Internet Ready 47

Lesson 3: Working with Files and Folders 48

Lesson Skill Matrix 48
Key Terms 48
Using a Folder Window 49
    Opening and Closing a Folder Window 49
    Selecting Items in a Folder 52
Creating and Renaming a Folder 53
    Creating and Renaming a Folder 53
Deleting Files and Folders 55
Using the Recycling Bin 56
Navigating Through Windows 58
    Browsing Through Recently Opened Windows 58
    Using the Navigation Pane 59
Using Multiple Windows 62
    Opening and Arranging Multiple Windows 62
Changing the Active Window 65
Moving Files and Folders 66
    Moving Files and Folders 66
Managing Files and Folders 67
    Copying to a Different Folder 67
    Copying to a Storage Device 69
Summary Skill Matrix 70

www.wiley.com/college/microsoft *or* call the MOAC Toll-Free Number: 1+(888) 764-7001 (North America Only)

Assessment 70
  Knowledge Assessment 70
  Competency Assessment 71
  Proficiency Assessment 72
  Mastery Assessment 73
Internet Ready 74

Lesson 4: Windows Vista Speech Recognition 75

Lesson Skill Matrix 75
Key Terms 75
Setting Up Speech Recognition 76
  Setting Up the Microphone 76
  Learning How to Talk to Your Computer 79
  Training your Computer to Understand Your Speech 85
Speech Recognition Basics 86
  Turning Speech Recognition On and Off 87
  Using Voice Commands 89
  Navigating Speech Recognition 90
Working with Text in Speech Recognition 95
  Dictating Text 95
  Editing Text 96
  Formatting Text 100
Summary Skill Matrix 102
Assessment 102
  Knowledge Assessment 102
  Competency Assessment 103
  Proficiency Assessment 104
  Mastery Assessment 104
Internet Ready 105

Circling Back 106

Word Unit 111

Lesson 1: Word Essentials 113

Lesson Skill Matrix 113
Key Terms 113
Software Orientation 114
Working in Word 114
  Changing Word's View 115
    Change Document Views 115
    Use Show/Hide Commands 117
    Use Zoom 118
    Change Window Views 119
  Navigate a Document 122
    Scroll Through a Document Using the Mouse 122
    Use Keystrokes to Navigate a Document 123

Entering Text in a Document 124
Selecting, Replacing, and Deleting Text 125
Summary Skill Matrix 127
Assessment 127
  Knowledge Assessment 127
  Competency Assessment 128
  Proficiency Assessment 130
  Mastery Assessment 130
Internet Ready 131

Lesson 2: Document Basics 132

Lesson Skill Matrix 132
Key Terms 132
Creating a Document 133
  Starting a Business Letter 133
  Choosing a Different File Format 134
Changing a Document's Appearance 135
  Formatting a Document with Quick Styles 135
  Formatting a Document with a Theme 137
Printing a Document 140
  Using Print Preview 140
  Setting Other Print Options 141
Creating Envelopes and Labels 143
  Creating and Printing an Envelope 143
  Creating and Printing a Label 146
Summary Skill Matrix 148
Assessment 148
  Knowledge Assessment 148
  Competency Assessment 150
  Proficiency Assessment 151
  Mastery Assessment 152
Internet Ready 152
Workplace Ready 153

Lesson 3: Character Formatting 154

Lesson Skill Matrix 154
Key Terms 154
Software Orientation 155
Manually Formatting Characters 155
  Choosing Fonts and Font Sizes 155
  Applying Special Character Attributes 158
  Changing Case 159
  Highlighting Text 160
Copying and Removing Formatting 161
  Using the Format Painter 161
  Removing Formatting 162
Formatting Text with Styles 162
  Applying Styles 162

Modifying Styles 164
Summary Skill Matrix 165
Assessment 166
  Knowledge Assessment 166
  Competency Assessment 167
  Proficiency Assessment 168
  Mastery Assessment 169
Internet Ready 170

Lesson 4: Paragraph Formatting   171

Lesson Skill Matrix 171
Key Terms 171
Software Orientation 172
Manually Formatting Paragraphs 172
  Setting Indents 172
  Changing Alignment 174
  Setting the Line Spacing Within a Paragraph 176
  Setting the Spacing Around a Paragraph 177
  Creating a Numbered List 178
  Creating a Bulleted List 179
  Shading a Paragraph 180
  Placing a Border Around a Paragraph 182
Software Orientation 184
Setting Tabs 184
  Setting Tabs on the Ruler 184
  Using the Tabs Dialog Box 186
  Displaying Non-Printing Characters 187
  Clearing Tabs 188
Clearing the Formats from a Paragraph 188
Summary Skill Matrix 189
Assessment 190
  Knowledge Assessment 190
  Competency Assessment 192
  Proficiency Assessment 193
  Mastery Assessment 194
Internet Ready 194

Lesson 5: Document Formatting   195

Lesson Skill Matrix 195
Key Terms 195
Formatting a Document's Background 196
  Setting a Colored Background 196
  Adding a Watermark 196
  Placing a Border Around a Document's Pages 198
Inserting Headers and Footers 198
  Adding Page Numbers to a Document 199
  Inserting a Built-In Header or Footer 199
  Adding Content to a Header or Footer 201

Page Layout 202
  Setting Margins 202
  Selecting a Page Orientation 203
  Choosing a Paper Size 204
Summary Skill Matrix 205
Assessment 205
  Knowledge Assessment 205
  Competency Assessment 206
  Proficiency Assessment 207
  Mastery Assessment 207
Internet Ready 208

Circling Back 209

Lesson 6: Managing Text Flow   213

Lesson Skill Matrix 213
Key Terms 213
Controlling Paragraph Behavior 214
  Controlling Widows and Orphans 214
  Keeping a Paragraph's Lines on the Same Page 215
  Keeping Two Paragraphs on the Same Page 216
  Forcing a Paragraph to the Top of a Page 216
Working with Breaks 216
  Forcing a Page Break 217
  Inserting Section Breaks 218
Setting Up Columns 220
  Creating Columns 220
    Formatting Columns 221
  Changing Column Widths 221
Inserting a Blank Page Into a Document 222
Summary Skill Matrix 223
Assessment 223
  Knowledge Assessment 223
  Competency Assessment 224
  Proficiency Assessment 225
  Mastery Assessment 226
Internet Ready 227

Lesson 7: Editing Basics   228

Lesson Skill Matrix 228
Key Terms 228
Using Quick Parts to Add Content to a Document 229
  Using Built-In Building Blocks 229
  Inserting a Field from Quick Parts 230
  Creating Your Own Building Blocks 231
Copying and Moving Text 233
  Using the Clipboard to Copy and Move Text 233
  Using the Mouse to Copy or Move Text 234

www.wiley.com/college/microsoft *or* call the MOAC Toll-Free Number: 1+(888) 764-7001
(North America Only)

Finding and Replacing Text 235
- Finding Text in a Document 235
- Replacing Text in a Document 237

Navigating a Long Document 238
- Using the Go To Command 238
- Using the Document Map 239

Summary Skill Matrix 241

Assessment 242
- Knowledge Assessment 242
- Competency Assessment 244
- Proficiency Assessment 245
- Mastery Assessment 245

Internet Ready 246

Lesson 8: Creating Tables and Lists 247

Lesson Skill Matrix 247

Key Terms 247

Creating Tables 248
- Inserting a Table by Dragging 248
- Using the Insert Table Dialog Box 249
- Drawing a Table 249
- Inserting a Quick Table 251

Software Orientation 252

Formatting a Table 252
- Applying a Quick Style to a Table 252
- Turning Table Style Options On or Off 253

Software Orientation 254

Managing Tables 254
- Resizing a Row or Column 254
- Moving a Row or Column 256
- Setting a Table's Horizontal Alignment 257
- Creating a Header Row 257
- Sorting a Table's Contents 258
- Performing Calculations in Table Cells 259
- Merging and Splitting Table Cells 260
- Changing the Position of Text in a Cell 261
- Changing the Direction of Text in a Cell 261

Working with Lists 261
- Creating an Outline-Style List 262
- Sorting a List's Contents 263
- Changing a List's Formatting 263

Summary Skill Matrix 264

Assessment 265
- Knowledge Assessment 265
- Competency Assessment 266
- Proficiency Assessment 267
- Mastery Assessment 268

Internet Ready 268

Workplace Ready 269

Lesson 9: Adding Pictures and Shapes to a Document 270

Lesson Skill Matrix 270

Key Terms 270

Software Orientation 271

Inserting a Picture 271
- Using SmartArt Graphics 271
- Inserting and Resizing a Clip Art Picture 274
- Inserting a Picture from a File 275

Software Orientation 277

Adding Shapes 278
- Inserting Shapes 278
- Creating a Flowchart 280
- Adding Text to a Shape 281

Software Orientation 282

Formatting Pictures 282
- Cropping, Resizing, Scaling, and Rotating a Picture 282
- Applying a Quick Style to a Picture 284
- Adjusting a Picture's Brightness, Contrast, and Color 286
- Arranging Text Around a Picture 287
- Compressing a Picture 288
- Resetting a Picture 289

Summary Skill Matrix 290

Assessment 291
- Knowledge Assessment 291
- Competency Assessment 292
- Proficiency Assessment 293
- Mastery Assessment 294

Internet Ready 295

Lesson 10: Customizing Word 296

Lesson Skill Matrix 296

Key Terms 296

Software Orientation 297

Customizing Word 297
- Personalizing Word 297
- Changing Display Options 298
- Configuring Proofing Options 299
- Setting Save Options 301
- Using Advanced Options 302
- Customizing the Quick Access Toolbar 304
- Viewing and Managing Add-Ins 306
- Protecting Your Computer 307

Software Orientation 308

Changing Research Options 308

Summary Skill Matrix 310

www.wiley.com/college/microsoft or call the MOAC Toll-Free Number: 1+(888) 764-7001 (North America Only)

Assessment 310
   Knowledge Assessment 310
   Competency Assessment 312
   Proficiency Assessment 313
   Mastery Assessment 314
Internet Ready 315

   Circling Back 316

Excel Unit 319

Lesson 1: Excel Essentials 321

Lesson Skill Matrix 321
Key Terms 321
Software Orientation 322
Working in the Excel Window 322
   Changing Excel's View 322
   Splitting a Window 324
   Opening a New Window 325
Workplace Ready 326
Working with an Existing Workbook 326
   Navigating a Worksheet 326
   Entering Data in a Worksheet 328
   Selecting, Editing, and Deleting a Cell's Contents 329
Summary Skill Matrix 331
Assessment 332
   Knowledge Assessment 332
   Competency Assessment 332
   Proficiency Assessment 334
   Mastery Assessment 334
Internet Ready 335

Lesson 2: Creating and Editing a Workbook 336

Lesson Skill Matrix 336
Key Terms 336
Software Orientation 337
Creating a Workbook 337
   Starting a Workbook from Scratch 337
Populating a Worksheet with Data 338
   Entering Labels 338
   Entering Dates 339
   Entering Values 340
   Filling a Series with Auto Fill 342
Cutting, Copying, and Pasting Data 344
   Copying with the Mouse 344
   Moving a Data Series with the Mouse 344
   Copying and Pasting Data 345
   Cutting and Pasting Data 347
Printing a Worksheet 348
   Setting the Print Area 348
   Using Print Preview 349
   Setting Other Print Options 349
Saving a Workbook 350
   Saving a Workbook for Use in a Previous Version of Excel 350
   Choosing a Different File Format 350
Summary Skill Matrix 351
Assessment 351
   Knowledge Assessment 351
   Competency Assessment 352
   Proficiency Assessment 353
   Mastery Assessment 354
Internet Ready 354

Lesson 3: Formatting Cells and Ranges 355

Lesson Skill Matrix 355
Key Terms 356
Software Orientation 356
Inserting and Deleting Cells 357
   Adding a New Cell to a Worksheet 357
   Deleting a Cell from a Worksheet 358
Manually Formatting Cell Contents 359
   Selecting Cells and Ranges 359
   Aligning Cell Contents 360
   Choosing Fonts and Font Sizes 361
   Applying Special Character Attributes 362
   Changing Font Color 362
   Filling Cells with Color 363
   Applying Number Formats 364
   Wrapping Text in a Cell 365
   Merging and Splitting Merged Cells 366
   Placing Borders Around Cells 367
Copying Cell Formatting with the Format Painter 368
Formatting Cells with Styles 369
   Applying a Cell Style 369
   Modifying a Cell Style 370
Working with Hyperlinked Data 371
   Placing a Hyperlink in a Cell 371
   Removing a Hyperlink 372
Applying Conditional Formatting to Cells 372
   Using the Rule Manager to Apply Conditional Formats 373

www.wiley.com/college/microsoft *or* call the MOAC Toll-Free Number: 1+(888) 764-7001
(North America Only)

Contents

  Allowing Multiple Conditional Formatting Rules
   to Be True 374
  Applying Specific Conditional Formats 374
 Clearing a Cell's Formatting 375
 Summary Skill Matrix 376
 Assessment 376
  Knowledge Assessment 376
  Competency Assessment 377
  Proficiency Assessment 378
  Mastery Assessment 379
 Internet Ready 380

Lesson 4: Worksheet Formatting 381

 Lesson Skill Matrix 381
 Key Terms 381
 Software Orientation 382
 Working with Rows and Columns 382
  Inserting or Deleting a Row or Column 382
  Modifying Row Height and Column Width 383
  Formatting an Entire Row or Column 385
  Hiding and Unhiding a Row or Colum 386
 Using Themes 387
  Choosing a Theme for a Worksheet 388
  Customizing a Theme 389
  Customizing a Theme by Selecting Colors 389
  Customizing a Theme by Selecting a Font and Effects 390
 Modifying a Worksheet's On-Screen and Printed Appearance 391
  Formatting a Sheet Background 391
  Changing the Color of a Worksheet Tabs 392
  Viewing and Printing a Worksheet's Gridlines 393
  Viewing and Printing Column and Row Headings 393
 Inserting Headers and Footers 393
  Adding Page Numbers to a Worksheet 394
  Inserting a Predefined Header or Footer 395
  Adding Content to a Header or Footer 395
 Preparing a Document for Printing 396
  Adding and Moving a Page Break 396
  Setting Margins 397
  Setting a Worksheet's Orientation on the Page 398
  Scaling a Worksheet to Fit on a Printed Page 399
 Summary Skill Matrix 400
 Assessment 401
  Knowledge Assessment 401
  Competency Assessment 401
  Proficiency Assessment 403
  Mastery Assessment 404
 Internet Ready 405
  ↻ **Circling Back** 406

Lesson 5: Managing Worksheets 409

 Lesson Skill Matrix 409
 Key Terms 409
 Software Orientation 410
 Organizing Worksheets 410
  Copying a Worksheet 411
  Renaming a Worksheet 412
  Reposition the Worksheets in a Workbook 413
  Hiding and Unhiding a Worksheet 414
  Inserting a New Worksheet into a Workbook 415
  Deleting a Worksheet from a Workbook 416
  Working with Multiple Worksheets 416
  Hiding and Unhiding Worksheets in a Workbook 418
  Using Zoom and Scroll to Change Onscreen View 419
 Finding and Replacing Data 420
  Locating Data with the Find Command 420
  Replacing Data with the Replace Command 422
  Navigating a Worksheet with the Go To Command 423
 Summary Skill Matrix 424
 Assessment 425
  Knowledge Assessment 425
  Competency Assessment 426
  Proficiency Assessment 427
  Mastery Assessment 429
 Internet Ready 429

Lesson 6: Working with Data 430

 Lesson Skill Matrix 430
 Key Terms 430
 Software Orientation 431
 Ensuring Your Data's Integrity 431
  Restricting Cell Entries to Certain Data Types 431
  Allowing Only Specific Values to Be Entered in Cells 433
  Removing Duplicate Cells, Rows, or Columns
   from a Worksheet 434
 Sorting Data 435
  Sorting Data on a Single Criterion 435
  Sorting Data on Multiple Criteria 436
  Sorting Data by Using Conditional Formatting 437
  Sorting Data by Using Cell Attributes 438
 Filtering Data 439
  Using AutoFilter 439
  Creating a Custom AutoFilter 440
  Filtering Data by Using Conditional Formatting 441
  Filtering Data by Using Cell Attributes 442
 Subtotaling Data 442
  Grouping and Ungrouping Data for Subtotaling 442
  Subtotaling Data in a List 443

www.wiley.com/college/microsoft *or* call the MOAC Toll-Free Number: 1+(888) 764-7001 (North America Only)

Setting Up Data in a Table Format 444
   Formatting a Table with Quick Style 444
   Inserting a Total Row in a Table 445
   Adding and Removing Rows or Columns in a Table 445
Summary Skill Matrix 446
Workplace Ready 447
Assessment 448
   Knowledge Assessment 448
   Competency Assessment 449
   Proficiency Assessment 450
   Mastery Assessment 451
Internet Ready 452

Lesson 7: Using Basic Formulas and Functions 453

Lesson Skill Matrix 453
Key Terms 454
Software Orientation 454
Building Basic Formulas 455
   Creating a Formula that Performs Addition 455
   Creating a Formula that Performs Subtraction 456
   Creating a Formula that Performs Multiplication 456
   Creating a Formula that Performs Division 457
Using Cell References in Formulas 458
   Using Relative Cell References in a Formula 458
   Using Absolute Cell References in a Formula 460
   Referring to Data in Another Worksheet 461
   Referring to Data in Another Workbook 462
Using Cell Ranges in Formulas 463
   Naming a Range 463
   Changing the Size of a Range 465
   Keeping Track of Ranges 465
   Creating a Formula that Operates on a Named Range 466
Summarizing Data with Functions 466
   Using SUM 466
   Using COUNT 468
   Using COUNTA 468
   Using AVERAGE 469
   Using MIN 470
   Using MAX 470
Using Formulas to Create Subtotals 471
   Selecting Ranges for Subtotaling 471
   Modifying a Range in a Subtotal 472
   Building Formulas to Subtotal and Total 472
Controlling the Appearance of Formulas 473
   Displaying Formulas on the Screen 473
   Printing Formulas 474
Summary Skill Matrix 475
Assessment 475
   Knowledge Assessment 475
   Competency Assessment 477
   Proficiency Assessment 478
   Mastery Assessment 479
Internet Ready 480

Lesson 8: Creating Charts from Your Data 481

Lesson Skill Matrix 481
Key Terms 481
Software Orientation 482
Building Charts 482
   Selecting Data to Include in a Chart 482
   Choosing the Right Chart for Your Data 484
   Creating a Bar Chart 486
Formatting a Chart with a Quick Style 487
Manually Formatting the Parts of a Chart 488
   Changing the Chart's Fill Color or Pattern 488
   Changing the Chart's Border Line 489
   Formatting the Data Series 490
   Modifying a Chart's Legend 490
Modifying a Chart 491
   Adding Elements to a Chart 491
   Deleting Elements from a Chart 492
   Moving a Chart 493
   Resizing a Chart 493
   Choosing a Different Chart Type 494
Summary Skill Matrix 495
Assessment 495
   Knowledge Assessment 495
   Competency Assessment 497
   Proficiency Assessment 498
   Mastery Assessment 499
Internet Ready 499
   Circling Back 500

PowerPoint Unit 504

Lesson 1: PowerPoint Essentials 505

Lesson Skill Matrix 505
Key Terms 505
Software Orientation 506
Working with an Existing Presentation 506
   Viewing a Presentation in Different Ways 506
      Change PowerPoint's View 506
      Use Zoom 510
   Navigating a Presentation 511
      Scroll with the Mouse 511
      Navigate a Presentation from the Keyboard 513

www.wiley.com/college/microsoft *or* call the MOAC Toll-Free Number: 1+(888) 764-7001 (North America Only)

Working with Text   513
  Add Text to a Text Placeholder   513
  Add Text on the Outline Tab   515
  Select, Replace, and Delete Text   516
  Copy and Move Text from One Slide to Another   517
Summary Skill Matrix   519
Assessment   519
  Knowledge Assessment   519
  Competency Assessment   520
  Proficiency Assessment   522
  Mastery Assessment   522
Internet Ready   523

Lesson 2: Presentation Basics   524

Lesson Skill Matrix   524
Key Terms   524
Software Orientation   525
Creating a Blank Presentation   526
  Opening a Blank Presentation   526
  Changing a Slide's Layout   527
  Adding Text to a Blank Slide   528
Saving a Presentation with a Different File Format   529
  Choosing a Different File Format   530
Creating a Presentation from a Template   531
  Using a Template as the Basis for a Presentation   531
  Adding a New Slide to a Presentation   533
  Reusing a Slide from Another Presentation   534
Creating a New Presentation from an Existing One   536
Starting a Presentation from a Microsoft Word Outline   537
  Change Indent Levels in a List   538
Organizing Your Slides   540
  Rearranging the Slides in a Presentation   540
  Deleting a Slide   541
Adding Notes to Your Slides   542
Workplace Ready   544
Printing a Presentation   544
  Using Print Preview   544
  Setting Print Options   547
  Printing a Presentation in Grayscale Mode   548
Previewing a Presentation on the Screen   549
Summary Skill Matrix   550
Assessment   550
  Knowledge Assessment   550
  Competency Assessment   551
  Proficiency Assessment   552
  Mastery Assessment   553
Internet Ready   554

Lesson 3: Working with Text   555

Lesson Skill Matrix   555
Key Terms   555
Software Orientation   556
Choosing Fonts and Font Sizes   556
Applying Font Sizes and Effects   558
Changing Font Color   560
Copying Character Formats with the Format Painter   561
Formatting Paragraphs   562
  Aligning Paragraphs   562
  Setting Paragraph Line Spacing   564
Working with Lists   565
  Creating Numbered Lists   565
  Working with Bulleted Lists   567
Inserting and Formatting WordArt   568
  Inserting a WordArt Graphic   568
  Formatting a WordArt Graphic   570
    Changing the WordArt Fill Color   570
    Changing the WordArt Outline Color   571
    Applying Special Effects to WordArt   572
  Formatting Text with WordArt Styles   573
Creating and Formatting Text Boxes   574
  Adding a Text Box to a Slide   574
  Resizing a Text Box   575
  Setting Formatting Options for a Text Box   577
    Applying a Quick Style to a Text Box   577
    Applying Fill and Border Formatting to a Text Box   578
  Working with Text in a Text Box   580
    Aligning Text in a Text Box   580
    Orienting Text in a Text Box   581
    Setting Margins in a Text Box   583
    Setting Up Columns in a Text Box   584
  Deleting a Text Box   586
Summary Skill Matrix   587
Assessment   587
  Knowledge Assessment   587
  Competency Assessment   589
  Proficiency Assessment   590
  Mastery Assessment   591
Internet Ready   592

Lesson 4: Designing a Presentation   593

Lesson Skill Matrix   593
Key Terms   593
Software Orientation   594
Formatting Presentations with Themes   595

www.wiley.com/college/microsoft *or* call the MOAC Toll-Free Number: 1+(888) 764-7001 (North America Only)

Applying a Theme to a Presentation 595
Changing Theme Colors 596
Changing Theme Fonts 598

Changing Slide Backgrounds 599
Selecting a Theme Background 599
Applying a Textured Background 599

Working with Different Layouts 601

Inserting Date, Footer, and Slide Numbers 603

Linking to Web Pages and Other Programs 605
Adding a Hyperlink to a Slide 605
Adding an Action to a Slide 606
Testing Links in a Slide Show 608

Setting Up Slide Transitions 609
Applying a Transition 609
Modifying a Transition 610
Determining How Slides Will Advance 611

Animating Your Slides 612
Using Built-In Animations 612
Modifying an Animation 613
Creating a Customized Animation 614

Software Orientation 617

Customizing Slide Masters 618
Applying a Theme to a Slide Master 618
Changing a Slide Master's Background 619
Adding New Elements to a Slide Master 620

Summary Skill Matrix 622

Assessment 622
Knowledge Assessment 622
Competency Assessment 624
Proficiency Assessment 625
Mastery Assessment 626

Internet Ready 627

Circling Back 628

Lesson 5: Adding Tables, Charts, and SmartArt Graphics to Slides 631

Lesson Skill Matrix 631
Key Terms 631
Software Orientation 632
Creating Tables 632
Inserting a Table 632
Inserting an Excel Worksheet 635

Formatting Tables 638
Applying a Quick Style to a Table 638

Software Orientation 639

Building Charts 639
Inserting a Chart from a Content Placeholder 639

Choosing a Different Chart Type 642
Applying a Different Chart Layout 643

Workplace Ready 645

Formatting Charts with Quick Styles 645
Applying a Quick Style to a Chart 645

Software Orientation 647

Adding SmartArt to a Slide 647
Insert a SmartArt Diagram 647
Insert an Organization Chart 647
Add Text to a SmartArt Diagram 649
Converting a Bulleted List to a Diagram 651

Modifying SmartArt Graphics 653
Applying a Quick Style to a SmartArt Diagram 653

Summary Skill Matrix 654

Assessment 655
Knowledge Assessment 655
Competency Assessment 656
Proficiency Assessment 657
Mastery Assessment 658

Internet Ready 659

Lesson 6: Adding Graphics and Media Clips to a Presentation 660

Lesson Skill Matrix 660
Key Terms 661
Software Orientation 661
Adding a Picture to a Slide 662
Inserting a Clip Art Picture 662
Inserting a Picture from a File 665

Formatting Pictures 667
Using the Ruler, Gridlines, and Guides 667
Rotating an Object 669
Resizing Objects 670
Crop an Object 670
Size or Scale an Object 671
Formatting a Picture with a Quick Style 674
Adjusting a Picture's Color, Brightness, and Contrast 675
Adding Special Effects to a Picture 676
Compressing the Images in a Presentation 677

Adding Shapes to Slides 678
Drawing Lines 678
Inserting Basic Shapes 680
Adding Text to Shapes 681
Formatting Shapes 682

Organizing Objects on a Slide 684
Setting the Order of Objects 684
Aligning Objects with Each Other 687
Grouping Objects Together 688

www.wiley.com/college/microsoft *or* call the MOAC Toll-Free Number: 1+(888) 764-7001
(North America Only)

Adding Media Clips to a Presentation 690
 Adding a Sound File to a Slide 690
 Adding a Movie to a Slide 692
Summary Skill Matrix 693
Assessment 694
 Knowledge Assessment 694
 Competency Assessment 695
 Proficiency Assessment 696
 Mastery Assessment 697
Internet Ready 698

Lesson 7: Delivering a Presentation 699

Lesson Skill Matrix 699
Key Terms 699
Adjusting Slide Orientation and Size 700
 Selecting Slide Orientation 700
 Setting Slide Size 701
Customizing Audience Handouts 703
Workplace Ready 706
Choosing Slides to Display 706
 Omitting Selected Slides from a Presentation 706
 Creating a Custom Show 708
Rehearsing Your Delivery 709
Software Orientation 711
Setting Up a Slide Show 712
Working with Presentation Tools 713
 Use Presentation Tools 714
 Annotate Slides with the Pen 716
Packaging a Presentation for Delivery 718
Summary Skill Matrix 720
Assessment 720
 Knowledge Assessment 720
 Competency Assessment 722
 Proficiency Assessment 723
 Mastery Assessment 724
Internet Ready 724
 ↻ Circling Back 725

Access Unit 728

Lesson 1: Database Essentials 729

Lesson Skill Matrix 729
Key Terms 729
Software Orientation 730

Working in the Access Window 730
 Navigating Access 730
  Database Basics 731
Software Orientation 732
 Using the Navigation Pane 732
 Using Object Tabs 735
 Changing Views 737
Defining Data Needs and Types 739
 Defining Table Fields 739
 Defining Data Types for Fields 740
 Defining Database Tables 742
Summary Skill Matrix 744
Assessment 744
 Knowledge Assessment 744
 Competency Assessment 745
 Proficiency Assessment 746
 Mastery Assessment 746
Internet Ready 747
Workplace Ready 747

Lesson 2: Create Database Tables 748

Lesson Skill Matrix 748
Software Orientation 749
Creating a Database 749
 Using a Template to Create a Database 749
 Creating a Blank Database 754
Software Orientation 756
Creating a Database Table 756
 Creating a Table from a Template 757
 Creating a Table from Another Table 759
Saving a Database Object 762
 Saving a Table 762
Summary Skill Matrix 763
Assessment 763
 Knowledge Assessment 763
 Competency Assessment 765
 Proficiency Assessment 766
 Mastery Assessment 766
Internet Ready 767

Lesson 3: Work with Tables/Database Records 768

Lesson Skill Matrix 768
Key Terms 768
Navigating Among Records 769
 Navigating Using the Keyboard 769
 Navigating Using Navigation Buttons 770

Contents | Lv

Entering, Editing, and Deleting Records   771
Creating and Modifying Primary Keys   773
   Defining and Modifying a Primary Key   773
   Defining and Modifying a Multi-field Primary Key   774
Finding and Replacing Data   775
Attaching and Detaching Documents   777
Sorting and Filtering Data Within a Table   779
Software Orientation   779
   Sorting Data Within a Table   779
   Filtering Data Within a Table   781
   Removing a Filter   783
Understanding Table Relationships   784
Software Orientation   784
   Defining Table Relationships   785
   Modifying Table Relationships   786
   Printing Table Relationships   787
Summary Skill Matrix   789
Assessment   789
   Knowledge Assessment   789
   Competency Assessment   790
   Proficiency Assessment   791
   Mastery Assessment   792
Internet Ready   793

Lesson 4: Modifying Tables and Fields   794

Lesson Skill Matrix   794
Key Terms   794
Modifying a Database Table   795
   Modifying Table Properties   795
   Renaming a Table   797
   Deleting a Table   798
Software Orientation   799
Creating Fields and Modifying Field Properties   800
   Modifying Field Properties   800
Software Orientation   807
   Creating and Deleting Fields   807
   Creating and Modifying Multi-valued Fields   811
   Creating and Modifying Attachment Fields   817
Summary Skill Matrix   819
Assessment   819
   Knowledge Assessment   819
   Competency Assessment   821
   Proficiency Assessment   822
   Mastery Assessment   823

Internet Ready   825
   Circling Back   826

Lesson 5: Create Forms   831

Lesson Skill Matrix   831
Key Terms   831
Software Orientation   832
Creating Forms   832
   Creating a Simple Form   832
   Creating a Form in Design View   834
   Creating a Form in Layout View   836
   Creating a Datasheet Form   837
   Applying AutoFormat   840
   Sorting Data Within a Form   842
   Filtering Data Within a Form   844
      Filter Data With Common Filters   844
      Filter By Form   846
Summary Skill Matrix   848
Assessment   848
   Knowledge Assessment   848
   Competency Assessment   849
   Proficiency Assessment   850
   Mastery Assessment   851
Internet Ready   852

Lesson 6: Create Reports   853

Lesson Skill Matrix   853
Key Terms   853
Software Orientation   854
Creating Reports   854
   Creating a Simple Report   854
   Using the Report Wizard   856
   Creating a Report in Design View   859
   Applying an AutoFormat   861
   Sorting Data Within a Report   862
   Filtering Data Within a Report   864
Summary Skill Matrix   866
Assessment   867
   Knowledge Assessment   867
   Competency Assessment   868
   Proficiency Assessment   869
   Mastery Assessment   869
Internet Ready   870

www.wiley.com/college/microsoft *or* call the MOAC Toll-Free Number: 1+(888) 764-7001
(North America Only)

Lesson 7: Create and Modify Queries 871

Lesson Skill Matrix 871
Key Terms 871
Software Orientation 872
Creating a Query 872
    Creating a Query from a Table 872
        Create a Simple Query 872
        Create a Find Duplicates Query 874
    Creating a Query from Multiple Tables 876
        Create a Query from Multiple Tables 877
        Find Unmatched Reports 879
Software Orientation 882
Modifying a Query 882
    Adding a Table to a Query 882
    Remove a Table from a Query 884
    Adding Criteria to a Query 884
Sorting and Filtering Data Within a Query 888
    Sorting Data Within a Query 888
    Filtering Data Within a Query 891
Summary Skill Matrix 893
Assessment 893
    Knowledge Assessment 893
    Competency Assessment 895
    Proficiency Assessment 896
    Mastery Assessment 897
Internet Ready 898

Lesson 8: Database Tools 899

Lesson Skill Matrix 899
Key Terms 899
Maintaining a Database 900
    Backing Up a Database 900
    Compacting and Repairing a Database 901
Configuring Database Options 902
Software Orientation 904
Using Database Tools 905
    Encrypting a Database 905
    Identifying Object Dependencies 907
    Using the Database Documenter 908
    Using the Linked Table Manager 910
    Splitting a Database 911
Summary Skill Matrix 913
Assessment 913
    Knowledge Assessment 913
    Competency Assessment 914
    Proficiency Assessment 915
    Mastery Assessment 915

Internet Ready 916
Circling Back 917

Outlook Unit 923

Lesson 1: Getting to Know Outlook 925

Lesson Skill Matrix 925
Key Terms 925
Software Orientation 926
Working in the Outlook Window 926
    Using the On-Screen Tools 927
    Changing Outlook's View 928
Personalizing Outlook 933
    Working with the Reading Pane 933
    Viewing, Hiding, and Minimizing the To-Do Bar 935
    Customizing the To-Do Bar 936
Summary Skill Matrix 937
Assessment 937
    Knowledge Assessment 937
    Competency Assessment 938
    Proficiency Assessment 938
    Mastery Assessment 939
Internet Ready 939

Lesson 2: Email Basics 940

Lesson Skill Matrix 940
Key Terms 940
Software Orientation 941
Creating and Sending Messages 941
    Composing a Message 941
    Sending a Message 943
    Resending a Message 944
    Saving a Copy of a Sent Message in a Different Location 946
Reading and Replying to Messages 947
    Automatically Previewing Messages 947
    Sending a Reply to a Message 948
Forwarding a Message 949
Working with Attachments 951
    Attaching a File to a Message 951
    Previewing an Attachment in Outlook 952
    Saving an Attachment to a Specific Location 953
    Opening an Attachment 954
Personalizing Messages 956
    Creating a Personal Signature 956

www.wiley.com/college/microsoft *or* call the MOAC Toll-Free Number: 1+(888) 764-7001 (North America Only)

Adding a Signature to a Single Message   958
Adding a Signature to All Outgoing Messages   959

Working with Automated Replies   959
Creating an Internal Out of Office Message   959
Creating an External Out of Office Message   960

Summary Skill Matrix   961

Assessment   961
Knowledge Assessment   961
Competency Assessment   962
Proficiency Assessment   963
Mastery Assessment   963

Internet Ready   964

Lesson 3: Managing Mail with Folders   965

Lesson Skill Matrix   965

Key Terms   965

Software Orientation   966

Working with Folders   966
Creating and Moving a Mail Folder   966
Deleting and Restoring a Folder   968

Moving Messages to a Different Folder   969

Deleting and Archiving Outlook Items   971
Emptying the Deleted Items Folder   971
Archiving Outlook Items   971

Summary Skill Matrix   974

Assessment   974
Knowledge Assessment   974
Competency Assessment   976
Proficiency Assessment   977
Mastery Assessment   977

Internet Ready   978

Lesson 4: Processing Messages with Rules   979

Lesson Skill Matrix   979

Key Terms   979

Software Orientation   980

Using Rule Templates   980
Creating a Rule to Move Messages from a Template   980
Running a Rule   986

Creating and Editing Rules   987
Creating a Rule to Categorize Messages from a Selected Message   987
Creating a Rule to Forward a Message by Copying an Existing Rule   990
Creating a Rule to Delete Messages from Scratch   992

Managing Rules   994
Sequencing Rules   994
Turning Off a Rule   995
Deleting a Rule   995

Summary Skill Matrix   996

Assessment   996
Knowledge Assessment   996
Competency Assessment   998
Proficiency Assessment   999
Mastery Assessment   1000

Internet Ready   1001

Lesson 5: Contact Basics   1002

Lesson Skill Matrix   1002

Key Terms   1002

Software Orientation   1003

Creating and Modifying Contacts   1003
Creating a Contact from a Blank Contact   1004
Creating a Contact from an Existing Contact   1006
Modifying Contact Information   1006

Sending and Receiving Contacts   1008
Sending a Contact as an Attachment   1008
Saving a Contact as a Contact Record   1009
Creating a Contact from a Message Header   1011

Viewing and Deleting Contacts   1012

Creating and Modifying a Distribution List   1013
Creating a Distribution List   1013
Modifying a Distribution List   1015

Summary Skill Matrix   1017

Assessment   1017
Knowledge Assessment   1017
Competency Assessment   1019
Proficiency Assessment   1020
Mastery Assessment   1020

Internet Ready   1021

Circling Back   1022

Lesson 6: Advanced Contact Management   1026

Lesson Skill Matrix   1026

Key Terms   1026

Software Orientation   1027

Using Electronic Business Cards   1027
Editing an Electronic Business Card   1027
Sending an Electronic Business Card   1030
Creating a Contact from an Electronic Business Card   1032
Using an Electronic Business Card in a Signature   1033

www.wiley.com/college/microsoft *or* call the MOAC Toll-Free Number: 1+(888) 764-7001 (North America Only)

Contents

Finding Contact Information 1035
- Searching for Contacts 1035
- Searching for Items Related to a Contact 1037
- Creating a Custom Search Folder 1038

Creating a Secondary Address Book 1040
- Creating a Secondary Address Book for Personal Contacts 1040
- Importing a Secondary Address Book from a File 1041

Summary Skill Matrix 1043

Assessment 1043
- Knowledge Assessment 1043
- Competency Assessment 1045
- Proficiency Assessment 1046
- Mastery Assessment 1047

Internet Ready 1047

Workplace Ready 1048

Lesson 7: Calendar Basics 1049

Lesson Skill Matrix 1049

Key Terms 1049

Software Orientation 1050

Managing Appointments 1050
- Creating a One-Time Appointment 1050
- Scheduling a Recurring Appointment 1051
- Creating an Appointment from a Message 1053
- Creating an Appointment from a Task 1055
- Marking an Appointment as Private 1056

Managing Events 1057

Summary Skill Matrix 1058

Assessment 1058
- Knowledge Assessment 1058
- Competency Assessment 1059
- Proficiency Assessment 1059
- Mastery Assessment 1060

Internet Ready 1061

Lesson 8: Managing Meetings 1062

Lesson Skill Matrix 1062

Key Terms 1062

Software Orientation 1063

Creating a Meeting 1063
- Creating a One-Time Meeting 1063
- Inviting Mandatory and Optional Attendees 1065
- Determining When Attendees Can Meet 1066
- Responding to a Meeting Request 1068
- Tracking Responses to a Meeting Request 1069

Modifying a Meeting 1071
- Changing a Meeting Time 1071
- Proposing a New Meeting Time 1072
- Accepting a Proposed New Meeting Time 1074
- Adding and Updating a New Attendee 1075

Managing a Recurring Meeting 1076
- Creating a Recurring Meeting 1076
- Changing One Occurrence of a Recurring Meeting 1077

Scheduling a Meeting Resource 1078

Cancelling a Meeting 1079

Summary Skill Matrix 1081

Assessment 1081
- Knowledge Assessment 1081
- Competency Assessment 1082
- Proficiency Assessment 1083
- Mastery Assessment 1084

Internet Ready 1085

Lesson 9: Managing Tasks 1086

Lesson Skill Matrix 1086

Key Terms 1086

Software Orientation 1087

Creating New Tasks 1087
- Creating a One-Time Task 1088
- Creating a Recurring Task 1089
- Creating a Task from a Message 1091

Modifying and Completing a Task 1092
- Modify a Task 1092
- Making a Task Private 1093
- Completing a Task 1094

Working with Assigned Tasks 1095
- Assigning a Task to Someone Else 1095
- Responding to an Assigned Task 1097
- Reporting the Status of an Assigned Task 1098

Searching for Tasks 1099

Summary Skill Matrix 1101

Assessment 1101
- Knowledge Assessment 1101
- Competency Assessment 1103
- Proficiency Assessment 1104
- Mastery Assessment 1105

Internet Ready 1106

Workplace Ready 1107

Lesson 10: Categories and Outlook Data Files 1108

Lesson Skill Matrix 1108
Key Terms 1108
Software Orientation 1109
Working with Categories 1109
    Assigning Outlook Items to Color Categories 1109
    Modifying and Creating Color Categories 1111
    Sorting Items by Color Category 1112
    Searching for Items by Category 1112
Working with Data Files 1114
    Creating a Data File 1114
    Selecting a Data File for a Mail Account 1115
    Changing Data File Settings 1116
Summary Skill Matrix 1118

Assessment 1118
    Knowledge Assessment 1118
    Competency Assessment 1119
    Proficiency Assessment 1120
    Mastery Assessment 1121
Internet Ready 1121

Circling Back 1122

Appendix A 1125

Appendix B 1137

Appendix C 1138

Glossary 1141

Index 1147

www.wiley.com/college/microsoft *or* **call the MOAC Toll-Free Number: 1+(888) 764-7001 (North America Only)**

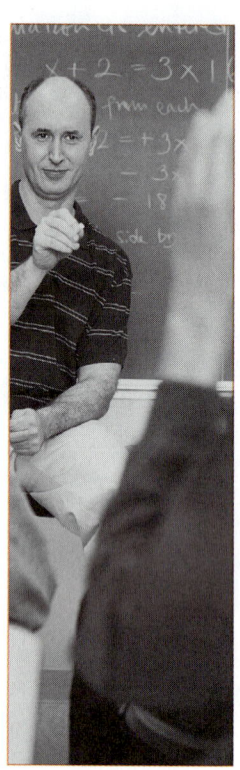

The first person to invent a car that runs on water...

...may be sitting right in your classroom! Every one of your students has the potential to make a difference. And realizing that potential starts right here, in your course.

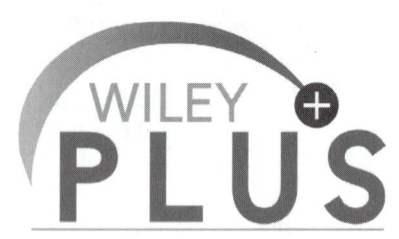

When students succeed in your course—when they stay on-task and make the breakthrough that turns confusion into confidence—they are empowered to realize the possibilities for greatness that lie within each of them. We know your goal is to create an environment where students reach their full potential and experience the exhilaration of academic success that will last them a lifetime. *WileyPLUS* can help you reach that goal.

*Wiley***PLUS** is an online suite of resources—including the complete text—that will help your students:

- come to class better prepared for your lectures
- get immediate feedback and context-sensitive help on assignments and quizzes
- track their progress throughout the course

And now, through *WileyPLUS*, Wiley is partnering with Certiport to create the best preparation possible for the Microsoft Certified Application Specialist (MCAS) examination. By combining the Microsoft Official Academic Course program for Office 2007 applications with Microsoft's Assessment, Learning Plan, and Certification Examination Vouchers delivered by Certiport and *WileyPLUS* Premium, we are creating the best environment in academic learning for future success in the workplace. Together, Wiley and Certiport are supplying online performance-based training to help students prepare for the globally recognized Microsoft certification exams so they get that job they want.

www.wiley.com/college/wileyplus

80% of students surveyed said it improved their understanding of the material.*

www.wiley.com/college/microsoft *or* call the MOAC Toll-Free Number: 1+(888) 764-7001 (North America Only)

FOR INSTRUCTORS

WileyPLUS is built around the activities you perform in your class each day. With **WileyPLUS** you can:

Prepare & Present
Create outstanding class presentations using a wealth of resources such as PowerPoint™ slides, image galleries, interactive simulations, and more. You can even add materials you have created yourself.

Create Assignments
Automate the assigning and grading of homework or quizzes by using the provided question banks, or by writing your own.

Track Student Progress
Keep track of your students' progress and analyze individual and overall class results.

Now Available with WebCT and Blackboard!

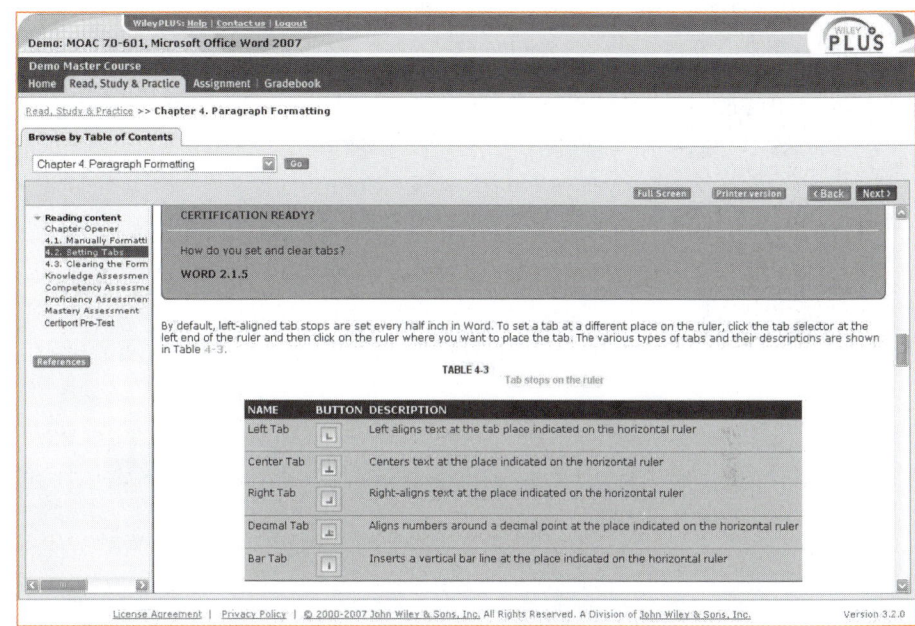

"It has been a great help, and I believe it has helped me to achieve a better grade."

Michael Morris,
Columbia Basin College

FOR STUDENTS

You have the potential to make a difference!

Wiley*PLUS* is a powerful online system packed with features to help you make the most of your potential and get the best grade you can!

With **WileyPLUS** you get:

A complete online version of your text and other study resources.

Problem-solving help, instant grading, and feedback on your homework and quizzes.

The ability to track your progress and grades throughout the term.

Access to Microsoft's Assessment, Learning Plan, and MCAS examination voucher.

For more information on what *WileyPLUS* can do to help you and your students reach their potential, please visit www.wiley.com/college/wileyplus.

76% of students surveyed said it made them better prepared for tests.*

*Based on a survey of 972 student users of *WileyPLUS*

www.wiley.com/college/microsoft *or* call the MOAC Toll-Free Number: 1+(888) 764-7001
(North America Only)

www.wiley.com/college/microsoft *or* call the MOAC Toll-Free Number: 1+(888) 764-7001
(North America Only)

Microsoft® Official Academic Course

Microsoft® Office System 2007

www.wiley.com/college/microsoft *or* call the MOAC Toll-Free Number: 1+(888) 764-7001 (North America Only)

Introduction to 2007
Microsoft® Office System

Introduction to 2007 Microsoft® Office System

LESSON SKILL MATRIX

Skill	Objective
Starting an Office Application	Students will learn how to start an Office application.
Closing a Document	Students will learn how to close an Office document.
Closing an Office Application	Students will learn how to close an Office application.
Using the Onscreen Tools	Students will learn how to use Office onscreen tools.
Using the Microsoft Office Button	Students will learn how to use the Microsoft Office Button.
Opening an Existing Document	Students will learn how to open an existing Office document.
Saving a Document	Students will learn how to save an Office document.
Choosing a Printer	Students will learn how to choose a printer in an Office application.
Setting Standard Properties	Students will learn how to set standard properties in an Office document.
Assigning Keywords to a Document	Students will learn how to assign keywords to an Office document.
Using the Microsoft Office Help button	Students will learn how to use the Microsoft Office Help button.

KEY TERMS
badges
command
Connection Status menu
desktop
dialog box
dialog box launcher
document properties
groups
KeyTips
keywords
menu
Mini toolbar
Microsoft Office Button
Quick Access toolbar
Redo
Ribbon
shortcut menu
tabs
Undo

Lesson 1

■ SOFTWARE ORIENTATION

Office's Opening Screen

Before you begin working in a Microsoft Office 2007 application, you should be familiar with the primary user interface. When you first launch an Office application, you will see a screen similar to that shown in Figure 1-1.

Figure 1-1
Office window

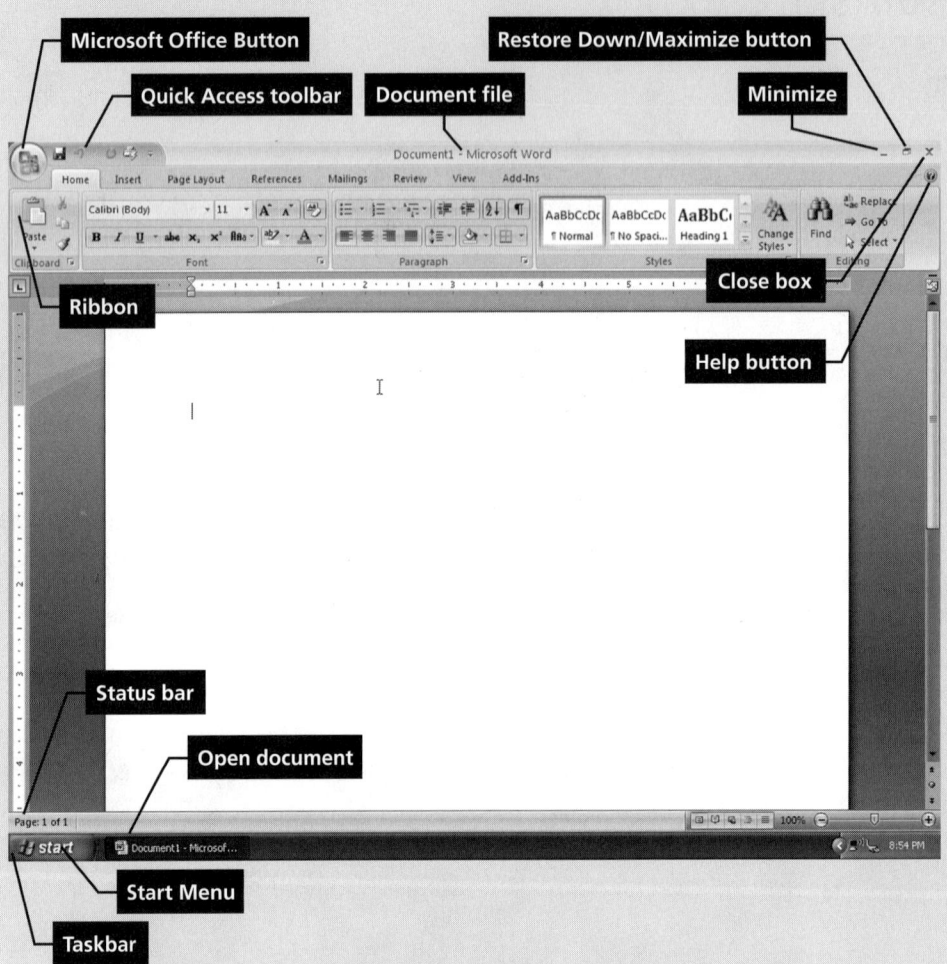

 Microsoft has designed the user interface to provide easier access to commands relevant to the document being created or edited. Your screen may vary if default settings have been changed or if other preferences have been set.

■ Opening and Closing Office Applications

THE BOTTOM LINE — Before you can begin working in an Office application, you must start the program. The opening screen of each Office program contains many common features.

Introduction to 2007 Microsoft® Office System | 5

Starting an Office Application

START AN OFFICE APPLICATION

GET READY. Before you begin these steps, be sure to turn on and/or log on to your computer.

1. On the Windows Taskbar, click the **Start** button and click **All Programs.** A menu of installed programs appears.
2. Click **Microsoft Office.** Another menu appears.
3. Click **Microsoft Office Word 2007** (see Figure 1-2). The program starts and a new, blank document appears.

 When Office was installed on your computer, shortcut icons may have been added to the Start menu or to your desktop. You can double-click a shortcut icon on your desktop to start an Office application without having to go through the Start menu.

Figure 1-2

Start an Office Application

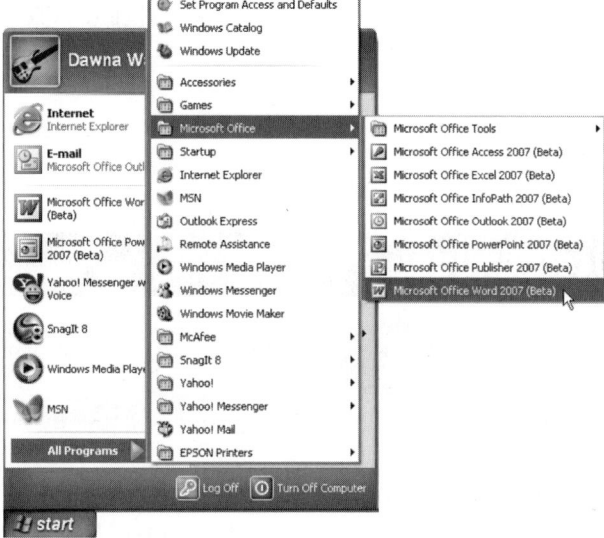

PAUSE. LEAVE the document open to use in the next exercise.

After you have started your computer, the screen you see is called the Windows *desktop*. Click the Start button in the lower-left corner of the Taskbar to open the Start menu and then click All Programs. A pop-up menu appears where you click Microsoft Office. Another pop-up menu appears where you can click the Office 2007 program you want to start.

Closing a Document

Closing a document removes it from the screen. It is a good idea to close a document before exiting a program.

CLOSE A DOCUMENT

USE the document that is open from the previous exercise.

1. Click the **Microsoft Office Button** and click **New.** A new blank document is opened.
2. Click the **Close** button. The document is removed from the screen.

PAUSE. LEAVE Word open to use in the next exercise.

When you are ready to close the document, click the Close button on the Microsoft Office window. You can also click the Microsoft Office Button and choose the Close command from the menu.

You should always save your file before closing it, so you do not lose any of the work you just finished. If you forget to save and click the Close button or Close command on the Microsoft Office Button when working in Word, Excel, or PowerPoint, a Microsoft Office window will appear, asking if you want to save your document. Choose Yes to save and close, No to close without saving, or Cancel to stop the Close command.

Closing an Office Application

Once you have closed all Office documents, you will need to close all Office applications. Be sure to exit all applications before turning off your computer.

→ CLOSE AN OFFICE APPLICATION

1. Click the **Close** button. The application is closed.
   STOP.

When you are ready to exit an Office application, click the Close button on the Microsoft Office window. Clicking the Close button on the last document open in an Office application also exits the application.

You can also click the Microsoft Office Button and choose the Exit command in the lower-right of the menu.

■ Working in the Office Window

THE BOTTOM LINE The Office 2007 window was designed to help you get your work done quickly. You will start exploring the Ribbon across the top right away. Also in this lesson, you will practice using other onscreen tools and features, such as the Microsoft Office Button and Office Help.

Using the Onscreen Tools

Office has many tools to help you create documents. In this section, you will explore the Ribbon, which displays common commands in groups arranged by tabs. You will also learn about other onscreen tools to help you get your work done faster, such as the Mini toolbar, the Quick Access toolbar, and KeyTips.

→ USE THE RIBBON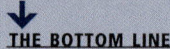

1. On the Windows Taskbar, click the **Start** button, click **All Programs**, click **Microsoft Office**, and then click **Microsoft Office Excel 2007**.
2. The Home tab is the active tab. As shown in Figure 1-3, the Ribbon is divided into groups of commands.

Figure 1-3

The Ribbon in Excel

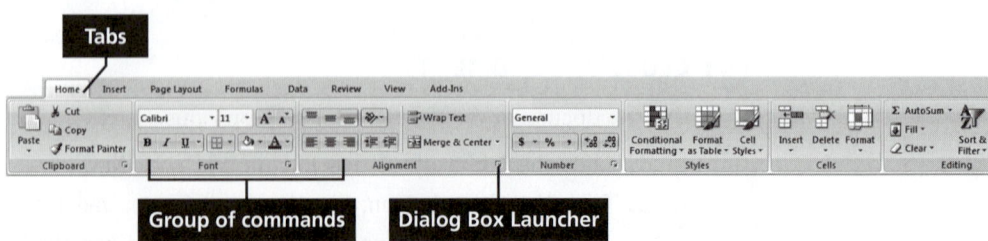

TAKE NOTE* The tabs on the Ribbon will vary, depending on which Office application you are working in.

3. Click **Page Layout** to make it the active tab. Notice that the groups of commands change.
4. Click the **Home** tab.
5. Click the dialog box launcher in the lower-right corner of the Font group, as shown in Figure 1-3. The Font Dialog Box, as shown in Figure 1-4, appears. Click **Cancel** to close the dialog box.

Figure 1-4

Format Cells dialog box

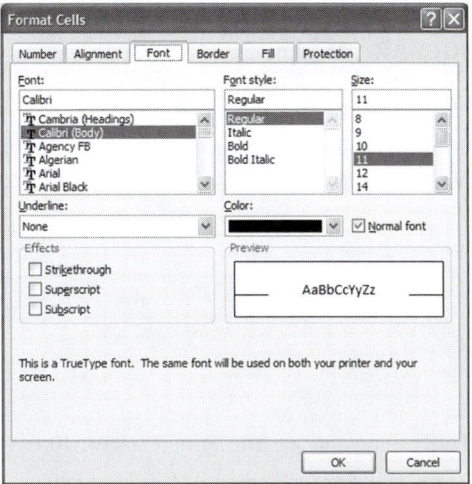

6. Click the arrow on the **Font** command in the Font group. In Figure 1-5, notice that the dropdown menu lists a variety of fonts.

Figure 1-5

Font menu

7. Click the arrow again to remove the menu.
8. Double-click the **Home** tab. Notice that the groups are hidden to give you more screen space to work on your document.
9. Double-click **Home** again to redisplay the groups.

   PAUSE. LEAVE the worksheet open to use in the next exercise.

You have just practiced using the **Ribbon**. It is divided into eight **tabs,** or areas of activity. Each tab contains **groups** of related commands. The Ribbon is contextual, which means it offers you commands related to the type of document or object you are working with.

8 | Lesson 1

Most groups have a *dialog box launcher*—a small arrow in the lower-right corner of the group—that you click to launch a dialog box. A *dialog box* displays additional options or information you can specify to execute a command. A *command* is a button you click or a box where you enter information that tells the application what you want it to do. Some commands on the Ribbon have small arrows pointing down. These arrows indicate that there is a *menu*, from which you can choose from a list of options. To choose an option from a menu, just drag the mouse pointer to the command you want and click.

→ **USE THE MINI TOOLBAR**

USE the worksheet that is open from the previous exercise.

1. Click in the first cell (A1) and key your name. Select your name and hover the cursor over the selection. A faint image of the Mini toolbar appears, as shown in Figure 1-6.

Figure 1-6

A faint version of the Mini toolbar appears when you point to selected text.

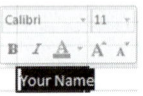

2. Point to the **Font** command on the Mini toolbar. Notice that the toolbar brightens.
3. Click the arrow on the **Font** command. A font menu appears.
4. Move the I-beam off the Mini toolbar to a blank cell and click the right mouse button. In addition to the Mini toolbar, a shortcut menu with commonly used commands appears (see Figure 1-7).

Figure 1-7

The shortcut menu and Mini toolbar

PAUSE. LEAVE the worksheet open to use in the next exercise.

The *Mini toolbar*—a small toolbar with popular commands—is available in Microsoft Office Word, Excel, and PowerPoint. The toolbar appears when you point to selected text. The image is very faint until you point to a command, then it brightens and becomes active. You can also display the Mini toolbar by clicking the right mouse button, whether text is selected or not. The *shortcut menu*, which displays a list of useful commands, also appears when you click the right mouse button.

→ **USE THE QUICK ACCESS TOOLBAR**

USE the worksheet that is open from the previous exercise.

1. Click the **Save** button on the Quick Access toolbar, shown in Figure 1-8.

Introduction to 2007 Microsoft® Office System | 9

Figure 1-8

The Quick Access toolbar

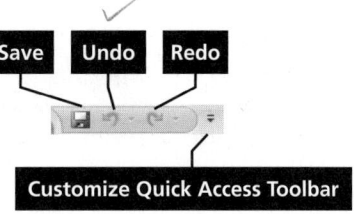

2. The Save As dialog box appears. Click **Cancel.**
3. Click the **Customize Quick Access toolbar** button. A menu appears, as shown in Figure 1-9.

Figure 1-9

Customize Quick Access toolbar menu

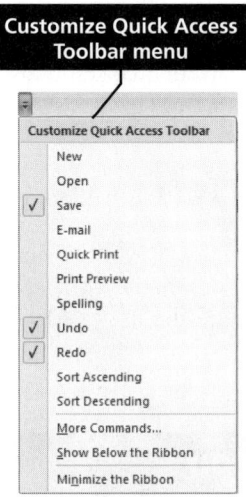

4. Click **Show Below the Ribbon**. The toolbar is moved.
5. Click the **Customize Quick Access toolbar** button again. Click **Show Above the Ribbon**.

PAUSE. LEAVE the worksheet open to use in the next exercise.

The *Quick Access toolbar* contains the commands that you use most often, such as Save, Undo, and Redo.

Click the Save button to quickly save an existing document as you are working on it or when you have finished. If you have not yet saved a document with a filename, the Save As dialog box will launch to prompt you to do so.

The *Undo* command lets you cancel or undo your last command. Click it as many times as necessary to undo previous commands. Click the arrow beside the Undo button, and a menu of actions you can undo appears. In much the same way, click the *Redo* command to repeat your last action. A command is not available if the button is dimmed.

Later in this book, you will learn to customize the toolbar, adding buttons so you can quickly find the commands you use most often. As you practiced in the preceding exercise, you can also place the toolbar below the Ribbon.

 USE KEYTIPS

USE the worksheet that is open from the previous exercise.

1. With the cursor in the first cell, press **Alt**. Letters and numbers appear on the Ribbon to let you know which key to use to access commands or tabs (see Figure 1-10).

Figure 1-10

KeyTips

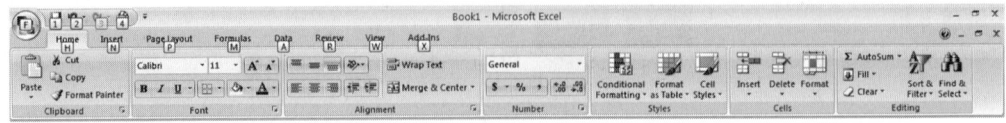

2. Press **H** to activate the Home tab.
3. Press **A** then **C** to center the cell contents.
4. Close the worksheet without saving changes.

   STOP. CLOSE Excel.

When you press the Alt key, small letters and numbers called **KeyTips** appear on the Ribbon in small square labels, called **badges**. To execute a command using KeyTips, press the Alt key then press the KeyTip or sequence of KeyTips that corresponds to the command you want to use. Every command on the Ribbon has a KeyTip.

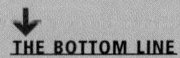

Shortcut keys are keys or combinations of keys pressed together to perform a command. Shortcut keys provide a quick way to give commands without having to move your hands off the keyboard and reach for a mouse. Keyboard shortcuts from previous versions of Office that began with Ctrl have remained the same. However, those that began with Alt are now different and require the use of KeyTips.

■ Working with the Microsoft Office Button

THE BOTTOM LINE

The Microsoft Office Button is a menu of commands that you will use for opening, saving, and printing documents. Standard document properties and keywords can be set using this button. As you will learn in later lessons, the Microsoft Office Button even contains some commands you will find important to know about when distributing and protecting your files.

Using the Microsoft Office Button

You will use the Microsoft Office Button when working in nearly every Office file you create, edit, or print.

➡ **USE THE MICROSOFT OFFICE BUTTON**

USE the document that is open from the previous exercise.

1. Start Microsoft Office PowerPoint 2007.
2. Click the **Microsoft Office Button**. A menu appears (see Figure 1-11).

Figure 1-11

Microsoft Office Button and menu

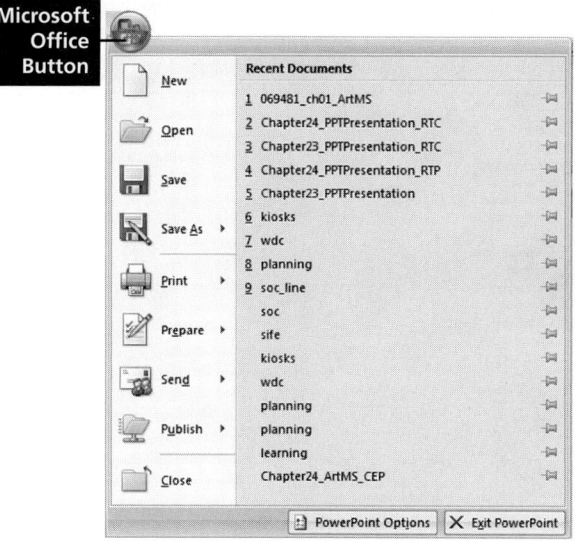

3. Point to the **Prepare** command to view the options available.
4. Point to other commands with the arrow to view more options.
5. Click the **Microsoft Office Button** again to remove the menu.

   PAUSE. LEAVE the presentation open to use in the next exercise.

The *Microsoft Office Button* is located in the upper-left corner of the screen. When clicked, it displays a menu of basic commands for opening, saving, and printing files, as well as more advanced options. Some commands have arrows indicating that another menu of options is available. When you click commands that do not have an arrow, a dialog box opens.

The Microsoft Office Button lists Recent Documents for easy access. It also displays an Options button at the bottom of the menu that allows you to customize the Office application. You can exit the Office application by clicking the Exit button.

Opening an Existing Document

Office provides three basic options for opening existing files. You can choose to open an original document, open a copy of a document, or open a document as a read-only file that cannot be changed.

 OPEN AN EXISTING DOCUMENT

1. Click the **Microsoft Office Button** to display the menu.
2. Click **Open.** The Open dialog box appears (see Figure 1-12).

Figure 1-12

The Open dialog box

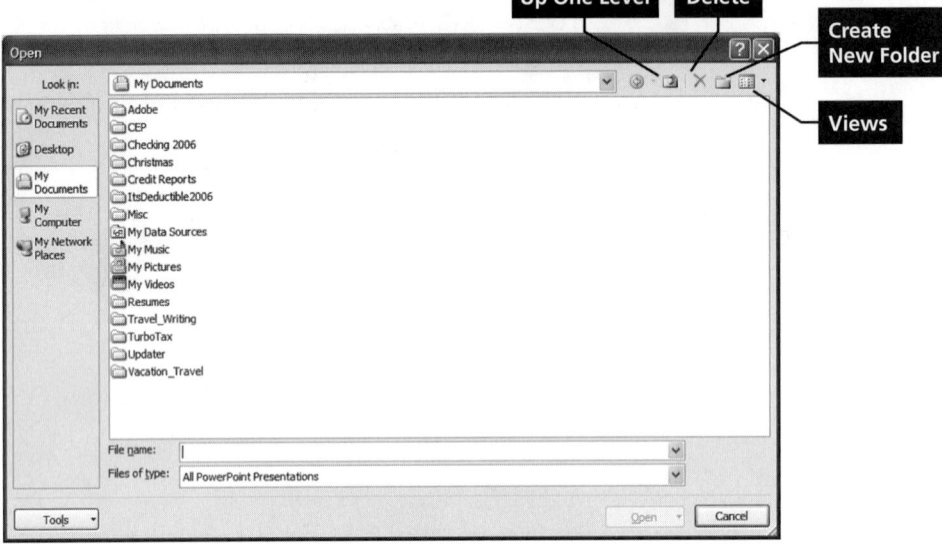

The *SalesMeeting* document is available on the companion CD-ROM.

3. In the Look In box, click the location of the data files for this lesson. Locate and click *SalesMeeting* one time to select it.
4. Click the **Open** button. The document appears, as shown in Figure 1-13.

Figure 1-13

SalesMeeting presentation

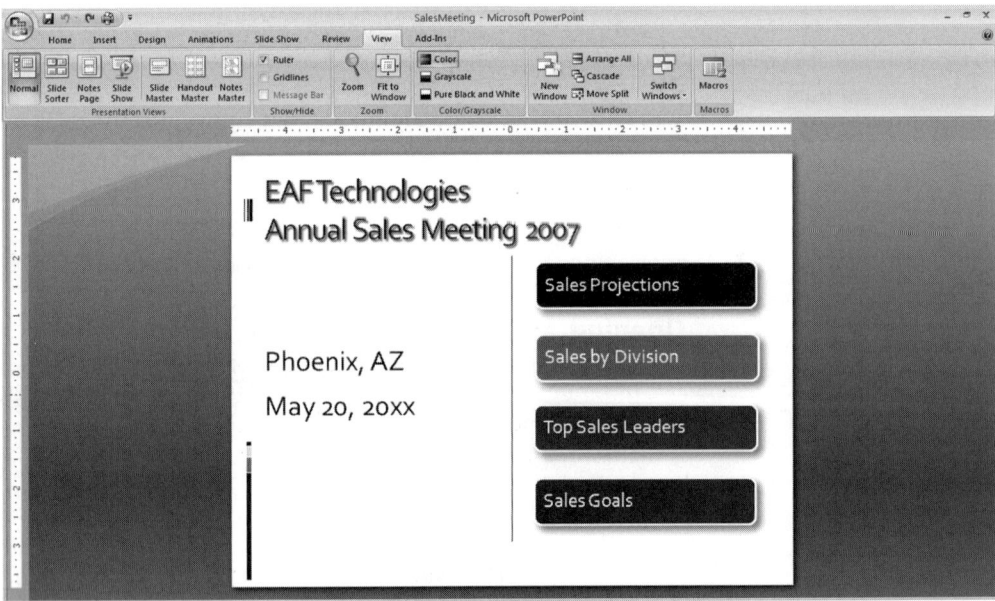

PAUSE. LEAVE the document open to use in the next exercise.

Use the Microsoft Office Button to open an existing document. The Open dialog box lets you find and open files wherever they may be located—on the desktop, in a folder on your computer, on a network drive, or on a CD or other removable media. The Look In box lists the available locations such as a folder, drive, or Internet location. Click the location, and the folders you can choose to open will be displayed in the folder list. When you find the file you want, double-click the filename to open it or click it once to select it and then click the Open button.

In the Open dialog box, the Files of Type menu lets you choose the type of file you want to open. The Tools button lets you delete, rename, print, map a network drive, or show a document's properties. The Up One Level button lets you go up a level in the folder organization to find a file. You can select a file in the Open dialog box and delete it with the

Delete button. The Create New Folder button helps you organize your files with new folders. The Views button lets you display contents of a folder by thumbnail, tiles, icons, lists, details, properties, preview, or Web view.

The Open dialog box also has options for choosing whether to open a document and edit it; open a copy of the document you can edit, leaving the original intact; or open the document as a read-only file that cannot be changed. Most likely, you will open an original document and edit it, so this is the default setting. To open a document another way, click the downward-pointing arrow beside the Open button and make your choice. This menu has a few more options that may not always be available—Open in Browser, Open with Transform, or Open and Repair.

Saving a Document

After creating or editing a document, it is important to save your work.

➔ SAVE A DOCUMENT

USE the presentation that is open from the previous exercise.

1. Click the **Microsoft Office Button**. The menu appears.
2. Click **Save As**. The Save As dialog box appears, as shown in Figure 1-14.

Figure 1-14

The Save As dialog box

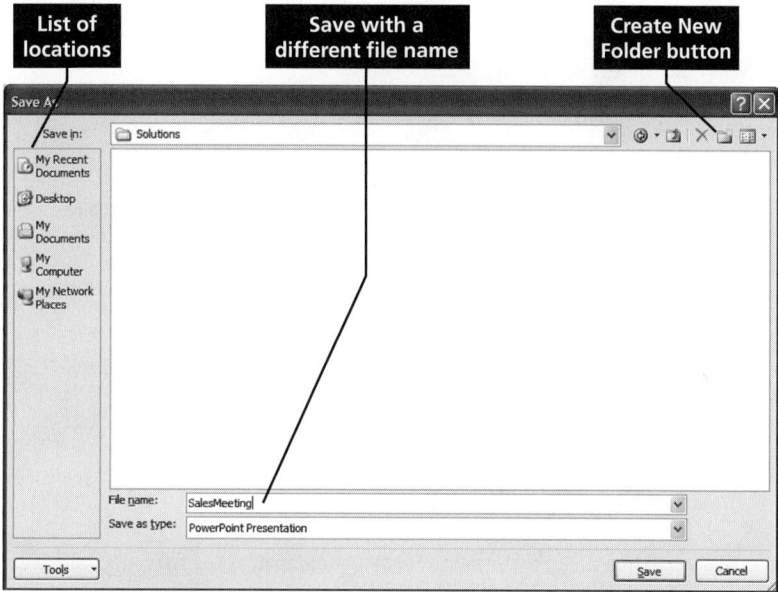

3. In the Save In box, click the location where you will save files.
4. If necessary, double-click a folder in the folder list where you will save your files.
5. Key **PhoenixSalesMeeting** in the File Name box.
6. Click **Save**.

   PAUSE. LEAVE the presentation open to use in the next exercise.

CERTIFICATION READY?
How do you save a document?
6.1.1

To save a document, use the Save command on the Microsoft Office Button. When saving a document for the first time or when specifying a new location or filename for a document, use the Save As command. The Save As dialog box will appear. You can specify in the Save In window the location where you want to store the document. In the main window, you can double-click to open a folder where you are storing documents. You will then key a filename for the document and click Save. After you have the document stored with a filename in the location where you want it, just click the Save button on the Quick Access toolbar each time you make changes.

Choosing a Printer

Before printing your document, you will need to make sure you have selected a printer. If your computer is already set up to print, you will not need to complete this exercise.

→ CHOOSE A PRINTER

USE the presentation that is open from the previous exercise.

> **ANOTHER WAY**
>
> You can also press **Ctrl + P** to display the Print dialog box.

1. Click the **Microsoft Office Button** and click **Print** to display the Print dialog box.
2. Click **Find Printer** to display the Find Printers dialog box.
3. In the Name list, choose the printer you want to use.
4. Click **OK** to close the Find Printers dialog box. The Print dialog box should still be open.

   PAUSE. LEAVE the document open to use in the next exercise.

Choosing a printer is a necessary step when printing for the first time. Now you are ready to set your print options and print your document.

> **TROUBLESHOOTING**
>
> You may need to set up a new printer before you can select it. To add a printer:
> In *Microsoft Windows Vista*
> 1. Click the Start button and then click Control Panel.
> 2. In the Control Panel, double-click Printers.
> 3. In the Printers dialog box, click Add Printer.
> 4. Follow the instructions in the Add Printer Wizard.
>
> In *Microsoft Windows XP*
> 1. Click the Start button and then click Printers and Faxes.
> 2. Under Printer Tasks, click Add a Printer.
> 3. Follow the instructions in the Add Printer Wizard.

> **TAKE NOTE***
>
> To set a printer as the default, right-click the printer icon and click **Set as Default Printer** on the shortcut menu. A checkmark will appear next to the default printer.

Setting Standard Properties

Standard properties are those such as author, title, and subject that are associated with a document by default.

→ SET STANDARD PROPERTIES

USE the document that is open from the previous exercise.

1. Click the **Microsoft Office Button**, point to **Prepare**, and then click **Properties**.
2. The standard properties views and options are displayed in the Document Information Panel, as shown in Figure 1-15.

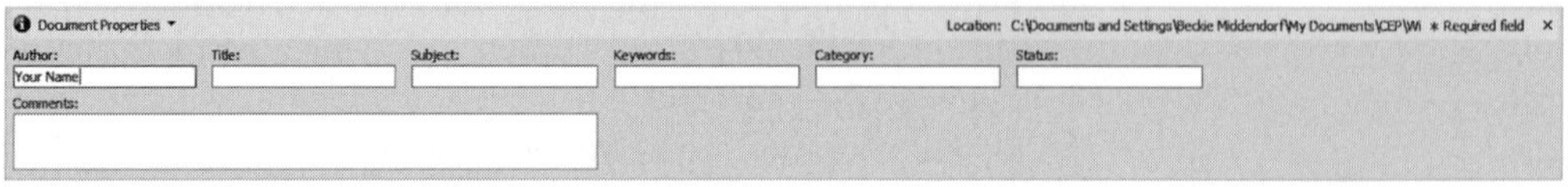

Figure 1-15

Document Information Panel

3. Key the following document properties:
   Author: **Your Name** (this may already be filled in—change if necessary)
   Title: **Phoenix 20XX**
   Subject: **Sales Meeting**

> **TAKE NOTE*** A document property field marked by a red asterisk indicates that the field is required. You will need to fill it in before you can save the document.

4. **SAVE** your presentation.
   PAUSE. LEAVE the presentation open to use in the next exercise.

> **ANOTHER WAY** When working in Microsoft Office Access 2007, you need to click the Microsoft Office Button, point to Manage, and then select Database Properties. The property fields appear in the Properties dialog box, rather than below the Ribbon.

You have just set some of the basic properties for a document that will help you identify and organize it later. ***Document properties*** are details that describe or identify a file. Table 1-1 describes each standard property. These properties can all be changed by the user; however, some properties, such as the file size, the number of words in a document, and the date the document was created or updated—are automatically updated and cannot be changed.

Document properties can be useful for locating a file later. For example, you could search for all the documents created before a certain date or for all the files that were last changed yesterday. The description of each document property is listed in Table 1-1.

Table 1-1

Standard Document Properties

PROPERTY NAME	DESCRIPTION
Author	The name of the individual who has authored the document
Title	Title of the document
Subject	Topic of the contents of the document
Keywords	A word or set of words that describes the document
Category	The category in which the document can be classified (e.g., "Documents from my manager")
Status	The status of the content (e.g., "Draft," "Reviewed," or "Final")
Comments	The summary or abstract of the contents of the document

Assigning Keywords to a Document

By assigning words that describe a document, you can later organize or locate the document more easily.

➔ ASSIGN KEYWORDS

USE the presentation that is open from the previous exercise.

1. The Document Information Panel should be open. If not, click the **Microsoft Office Button**, point to **Prepare**, and then click **Properties**.
2. In the Keywords box, key **EAF Technologies, Sales, Phoenix**.
3. In the Category box, key **sales meeting**.

16 | Lesson 1

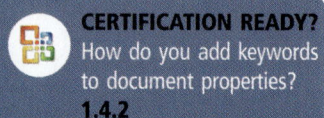

CERTIFICATION READY?
How do you add keywords to document properties?
1.4.2

4. Click the **Close** button in the upper-right corner of the Document Information Panel to close it.
5. **SAVE** the document and **CLOSE** the file.

STOP. CLOSE PowerPoint.

Keywords are words or sets of words that describe a document. When assigning keywords to a document, choose words that are descriptive and will help you identify it later when you are searching your files.

You can also view the keywords and other properties for any document when opening or saving a file. In the Open or Save As dialog box, clicking the downward-pointing arrow on the Views button and choosing Properties will display the document properties, as shown in Figure 1-16.

Figure 1-16

Document properties

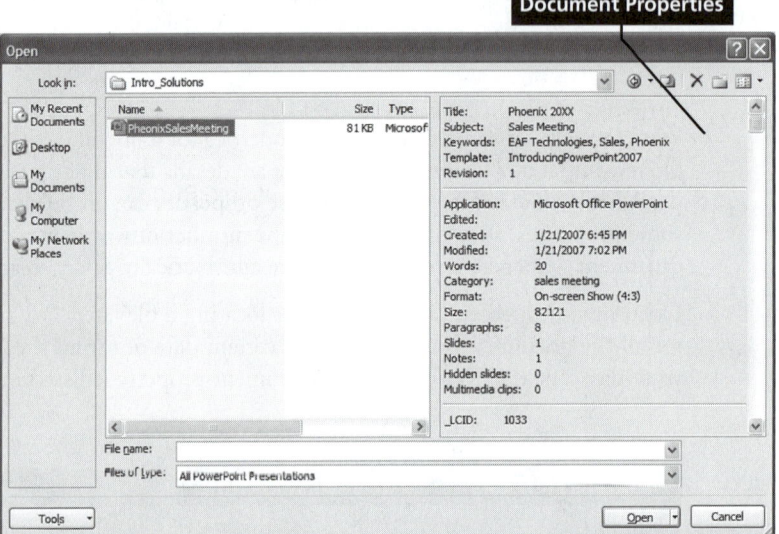

Working with Microsoft Office Help

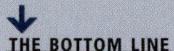

THE BOTTOM LINE

If you have questions, Microsoft Office Help has answers. You can key in search words, browse help topics, or choose a topic from the Table of Contents to get your answers.

Using the Microsoft Office Help Button

Many Microsoft Office Help topics are installed directly on your computer. Additional Help options are also available online.

TAKE NOTE*

When you rest the mouse pointer over a command on the Ribbon, a screen tip will appear displaying the name of the command. Office 2007 also has enhanced screen tips, which give more information about the command, as well as a Help button you can click to get more help.

→ **USE THE HELP BUTTON**

1. Start Microsoft Office Access 2007.
2. Click the **Microsoft Office Access Help** button in the upper-right corner of the screen. The Access Help dialog box appears, as shown in Figure 1-17. Notice the Connection Status command in the lower-right corner, indicating that Access is set

Figure 1-17

The Access Help dialog box when you're connected to Office online

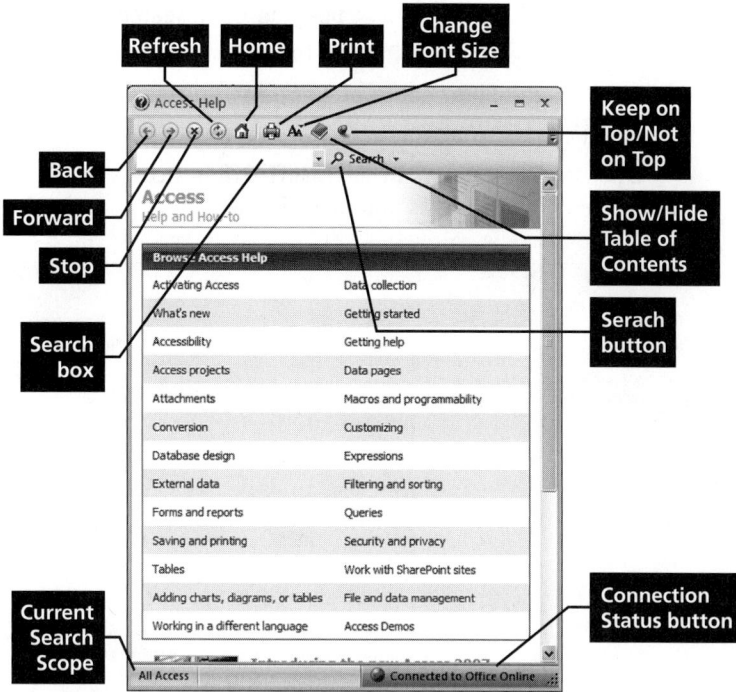

to Connected to Office Online to search online for help topics. If your Connection status is set to Offline, your screen will look different.

3. Click the **Connection Status** button. A menu appears, as shown in Figure 1-18.

Figure 1-18

Connection Status menu

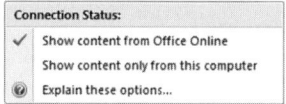

4. Click **Show content only from this computer.** Access Help appears, as shown in Figure 1-19.

Figure 1-19

Access Help dialog box when offline

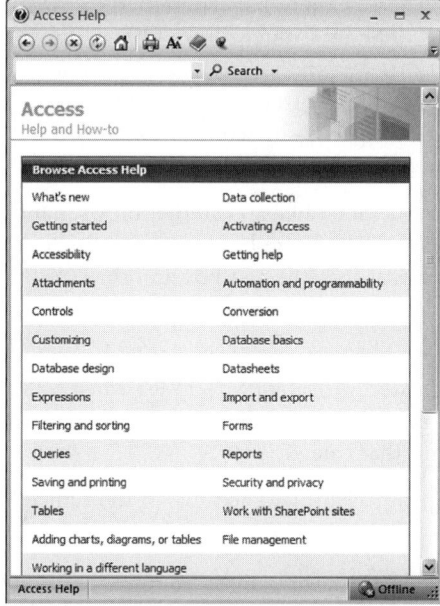

18 | Lesson 1

5. Key **ribbon** in the text box and click **Search**. A list of possible topics appears.
6. Click the **Use the Ribbon** link. The help topic appears.

7. Click the **Show Table of Contents** button.
8. Click the **What's new** link at the top.
9. Click **What's new in Microsoft Office Access 2007**. The text for the topic appears in the window, as shown in Figure 1-20.

Figure 1-20

Access Help with Table of Contents and topics displayed

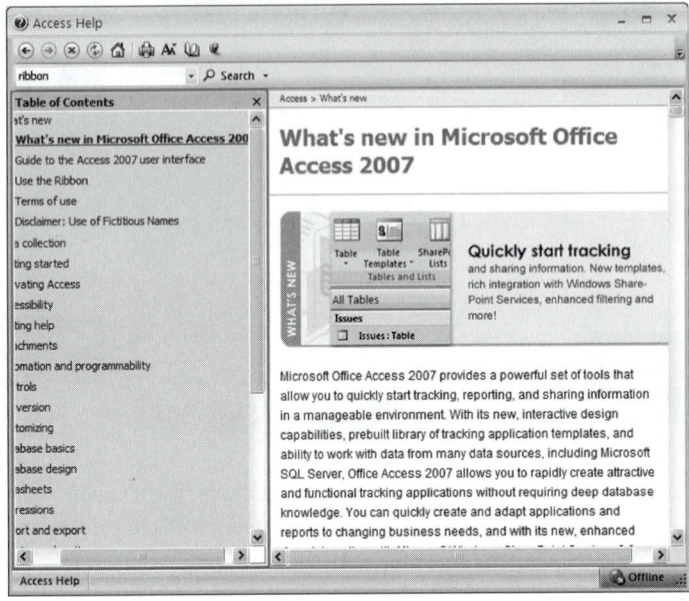

10. Click the **Home** button.
11. Click the **Close** button to close Microsoft Access Help.

PAUSE. LEAVE the document open to use in the next exercise.

The **Connection Status menu** in the lower-right corner of Office Help lets you choose between the help topics that are available online and the help topics installed on your computer for offline reference. If you are usually connected to the Internet, you might prefer to set the Connection Status to Show Content from Office Online to get the most up-to-date help available. But sometimes you cannot be, or do not want to be, online. In those instances, you can choose Show Content Only from this Computer to get offline help topics. You can also click the Search menu to specify the scope of topics you want to search, such as All Office, Office Help, Office Templates, Office Training, or Developer References.

Microsoft Office Help works much like an Internet browser and has many of the same buttons, such as Back, Forward, Stop, Refresh, Home, and Print. A quick way to find what you need is to key a word or words into the text box and then click the Search button. Office will display a list of related topics as links.

Another way to get help is to choose one of the available topics in the Browse Office Help list when online or the Browse Office 2007 Help list when offline. You can also click the Show Table of Contents button to list Office Help categories. Choose a category to see a list of related topics within that category.

If you need to print a topic, just display the topic in the Office Help main window and click the Print button.

For your convenience, the Office Help window can be resized and moved to another location on the screen. The On Top button toggles between Keep On Top, which ensures that the Help window is always on top of the document you are working on, and Not On Top, which keeps the document you are editing on top. You can also use the Change Font Size button to change the font size of the text in the window.

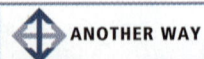

ANOTHER WAY

The Help button is positioned in some dialog boxes and screen tips for quick access to context-related help. Click it wherever you see it to launch Office Help.

SUMMARY SKILL MATRIX

IN THIS LESSON YOU LEARNED HOW TO:
Start an Office Application
Close a Document
Close an Office Application
Use the Onscreen Tools
Use the Microsoft Office Button
Open an Existing Document
Save a Document
Choose a Printer
Set Standard Properties
Assign Keywords to a Document
Use the Microsoft Office Help button

■ Knowledge Assessment

Matching

Match the term in Column 1 to its description in Column 2.

Column 1

1. Save
2. Desktop
3. Ribbon
4. Document Properties
5. Quick Print
6. Mini toolbar
7. Quick Access toolbar
8. KeyTips
9. Connection Status menu
10. Standard Properties

Column 2

a. command that saves changes to an existing file by overwriting the previous version
b. letters and numbers that appear on the Ribbon when you press the Alt key
c. lets you choose between the help topics available online and the help topics installed on your computer offline
d. details that describe or identify a file
e. contains commands you use most often, such as Save, Undo, and Redo.
f. used to print a document quickly using the default settings
g. organized by tabs and groups of commands
h. properties that are associated with a document by default
i. the first screen you see when you start Windows
j. appears when you point to selected text

True/False

Circle T if the statement is true or F if the statement is false.

T | F 1. When you start Word, Access, or PowerPoint, a new, blank document appears.
T | F 2. The Save As command can be used to save a copy of your document with a new filename or in a new location.
T | F 3. Comments are words or sets of words that describe a document.
T | F 4. The Undo button is on the Mini toolbar.
T | F 5. You can choose to save a document with a different theme from the Save As dialog box.
T | F 6. Quick printing a document sends the document straight to the printer.
T | F 7. You can use the Microsoft Office Button to save and print files.
T | F 8. The shortcut menu appears when you point to selected text.
T | F 9. File size, date created, and author are all standard file properties.
T | F 10. You can hide the Ribbon by double-clicking the active tab.

■ Competency Assessment

Project 1-1: Coho Database

You have compiled a database with contact information for Coho Winery's employees. You need to access the database to verify employee information.

GET READY. Before you begin these steps, start your computer and log on to your Windows Vista account. Close all open windows so you can see the desktop.

1. On the Windows Taskbar, click the **Start** button, click **All Programs**, click **Microsoft Office**, and click **Microsoft Office Access 2007**.
2. Click the **Microsoft Office Button** and choose **Open** from the menu.
3. In the Look In box, click the location of the data files for this lesson.
4. Locate and click **Coho_database** one time to select it.

   PAUSE. LEAVE the database open for the next project.

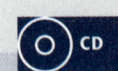

The *Coho_database* document is available on the companion CD-ROM.

Project 1-2: New Employee Information

One of Coho's employees recently retired. You need to update and save the database information.

USE the database that is open from the previous project.

1. Click once to the far left of Katherine Sue's database entry. The entire row should be selected.
2. Press the Delete key.
3. Click **Yes** to delete the record.
4. Click the **Microsoft Office Button**, click the arrow next to Save As, and select **Access 2007 Database**.
5. Click **Yes** to close the objects.
6. In the Save In box, click the location where you will save files.
7. Key **Coho_updated_database** in the File Name box.
8. Click **Save**.

   PAUSE. CLOSE Access.

■ Proficiency Assessment

Project 1-3: Reference Letter

A former employee at Tech Terrace Real Estate has asked for a reference letter. Open and add document properties so it will be easier to locate in the future.

GET READY. Launch Microsoft Office Word 2007.

The *reference_letter* document is available on the companion CD-ROM.

1. **OPEN** *reference_letter* from the data files for this lesson.
2. Click the **Microsoft Office Button**, point to **Prepare**, and then click **Properties**.
3. In the Document Information Panel, key the following:
   Author: **Your Name**
   Title: **Randall Jasmine letter**
   Subject: **reference**
   Keywords: **Jasmine, employee, reference**
   Category: **former employees**
4. **CLOSE** the Document Information Panel.
5. **SAVE** the document as *jasmine_reference*.

PAUSE. LEAVE Word open for the next project.

Project 1-4: Phone Interview Selection Letter

In your position at Tech Terrace Real Estate, you have already created a letter to decline pursing a candidate for employment any further after a phone interview. Open the document and save it with a different name.

GET READY. Launch Word if it is not already running.

The *selection_letter* document is available on the companion CD-ROM.

1. **OPEN** *selection_letter* from the data files for this lesson.
2. Click the **Microsoft Office Button** and then click **Save As** to open the Save As dialog box.
3. In the File Name box, key **decline_letter**.
4. Click **Save** to save the file with a different name.
5. **CLOSE** the document.

PAUSE. CLOSE Word.

■ Mastery Assessment

Project 1-5: Starting Presentation

As the Marketing Director for AEF Technologies, you often create new PowerPoint presentations. You need to start PowerPoint in order to create a new presentation.

GET READY. Launch Microsoft Office PowerPoint 2007.

1. Click the **Microsoft Office Button** and then click **New** to create a new presentation.

PAUSE. LEAVE the presentation open for the next project.

Project 1-6: Creating Marketing Presentation

You want to search for PowerPoint templates you can use when creating various presentations for AEF Technologies.

GET READY. Launch PowerPoint if it is not already running.

1. In the New Presentation dialog box, click **Presentations** under the Microsoft Office Online section at the far left.
2. Select **Business** from the Presentations section in the middle of the dialog box.
3. Click **Marketing plan presentation** once to select the template, and then click the **download** button.
4. Click **Continue** if you receive a Microsoft Office Genuine Advantage dialog box.
5. Save the presentation as *MarketingPlan*.
6. **CLOSE** the file.

   STOP. CLOSE PowerPoint.

INTERNET READY

Use Office Help to access online information about What's New in Office 2007. *Up to Speed with the 2007 Office system* provides an online short course or a demo explaining the new features. Browse these or other topics in Office Help online.

Windows Basics

LESSON SKILL MATRIX

Skill	Objective
Logging on to Windows Vista	Students will learn how to log on to Windows Vista.
Using the Mouse to Identify Desktop Items	Students will learn how to use the mouse to identify desktop items.
Opening and Closing the Start Menu	Students will learn how to open and close the Start menu.
Identifying Items on the Start Menu	Students will learn how to identify items on the Start menu.
Selecting Start Menu Settings	Students will learn how to select Start menu settings.
Searching from the Start Menu	Students will learn how to search from the Start menu.
Minimizing, Maximizing, and Restoring a Window	Students will learn how to minimize, maximize, and resize a window.
Accessing Help and Support	Students will learn how to access Help and Support.
Shutting Down Windows Vista	Students will learn how to shut down Windows Vista.

KEY TERMS
**background
button
context menu
files
filter
folders
gadgets
icon
index
indexed locations
maximize
menu
minimize
mouse
mouse pointer
offline files
panes
Recycle Bin
restore down
ScreenTip
search results
selects
shortcuts
sidebar
Start Button
Start menu
syntax
taskbar**

24 | Lesson 2

Northwind Traders is a small company that helps Inuit artists in Alaska market their work to customers around the globe. Originally, the owner was able to use a paper filing system for tasks such as invoicing and storing information about artists and buyers. Now that the business has grown, the owner has invested in a personal computer running the Windows Vista operating system. In this lesson, you will learn how to log on to Windows Vista and use your mouse to identify screen elements. You will open and close the Start menu, learning how to identify and select items on the menu. You will also learn how to search for items on your computer from the Start menu. Finally, you will learn how to minimize, maximize, and restore windows, get help while using Windows Vista, and shut down your computer.

■ Getting Started with Windows Vista

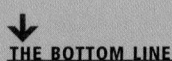
THE BOTTOM LINE

To use your computer, you must be able to use Windows Vista. Windows Vista is an operating system, which is the software that controls the way your computer communicates with you—the user—and with the other parts of the computer, such as the screen, the keyboard, and the printer. Once you log on to Vista, you can use it to access and manage information. In this section, you will log on to your computer and practice using the mouse.

Logging On to Windows Vista

To access the information on your computer, you must log on to your account.

➔ LOG ON TO WINDOWS VISTA

GET READY. Before you begin these steps, make sure your computer is turned on. The Welcome screen should be displayed, as shown in Figure 2-1.

Figure 2-1

Windows Vista Welcome screen

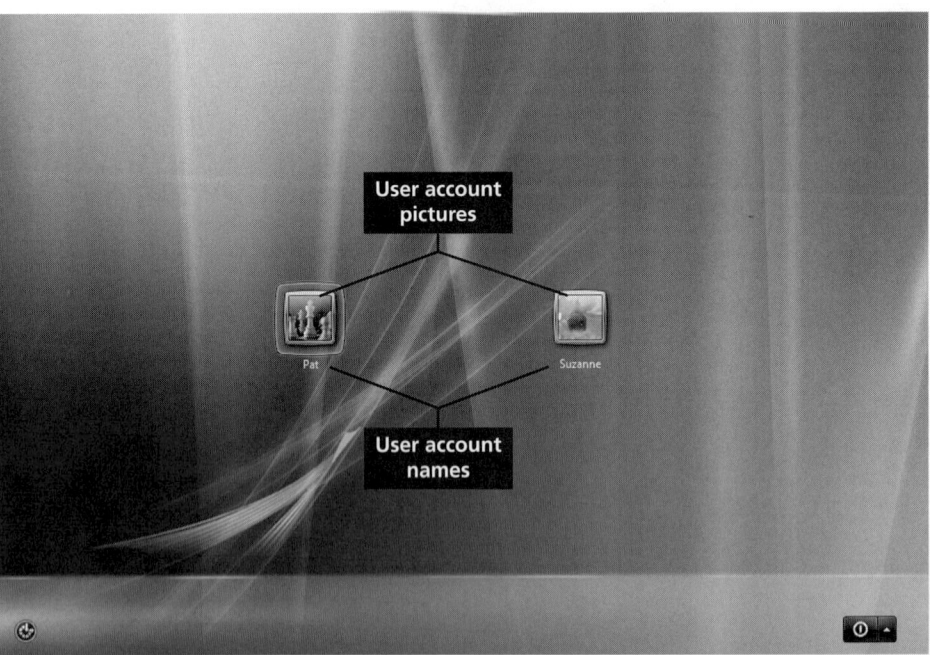

TROUBLESHOOTING

Your Welcome screen will not look exactly the same as the screen in Figure 2-1. The names on your Welcome screen will be the names of the users authorized to use your computer, and the pictures will be those assigned to each user account.

1. Move the mouse so that the mouse pointer touches your name on the Welcome screen.
2. Press and release the left mouse button one time. This is called a click. Either the Windows desktop or the Password screen displays.
3. If the Password screen displays, click in the password box, key your password, and then press **Enter**. A password is a string of characters, such as a word or phrase, that protects your account from unauthorized access. When you key the password, black dots display in the password box to hide the actual password from anyone who might be looking over your shoulder. The Windows Vista desktop displays. It should look similar to Figure 2-2.

> **TROUBLESHOOTING** If the Welcome Center window displays, click the Close button (the white X on the red background) in the upper-right corner of the window to close it so you can get a clear view of the desktop.

> **TROUBLESHOOTING** If you do not know your password, consult your instructor or your system administrator.

4. Take a moment to identify the elements of the desktop that are shown in Figure 2-2. Refer to Table 2-1 for a description of each element.

Table 2-1

Common Desktop Elements

ELEMENT	DESCRIPTION
Taskbar	The **taskbar** usually runs across the bottom of the desktop (although it can be moved to the top, left side, or right side). It displays buttons and icons to let you access the features that you use most frequently. A **button** is an element that you can click to select a command or action.
Start Button	The **Start Button** is a round button with the Microsoft Windows logo on it. You click the Start Button to open the **Start menu**, which provides access to everything stored on your computer. A **menu** is a list of choices.
Sidebar	The **sidebar** is a vertical bar usually located along the right side of the desktop. It displays **gadgets**, which are programs or tools designed to provide information at a glance. A clock, a slideshow, and an Internet news feed are the default gadgets.
Quick Launch toolbar	The Quick Launch toolbar is an area of the taskbar that displays **shortcuts** to frequently used programs. A shortcut is a link to a program, feature, or command.
Recycle Bin icon	The Recycle Bin icon represents the **Recycle Bin**, a folder where deleted items are stored until you remove them permanently or restore them to their original location.
Shortcut icons	Shortcut icons on the desktop let you quickly access programs, folders, and files that you use most often. The arrow in the lower-left corner indicates that the icon is a shortcut. The shortcut icons on your desktop depend on how your computer is set up. Many programs create icons on the desktop during installation, or you can create your own shortcut icons on the desktop, on the taskbar, and in folders.
Background	The **background** is the broad, empty area where windows open and display content. By default, the background displays a picture that you select when you first set up your user account, but you can change it at any time to a different picture, or to a solid color, like the one shown in Figure 2-2.
Notification area	At the right end of the taskbar is the notification area, where the time and information about the programs running on your computer displays.

Figure 2-2

Windows Vista desktop

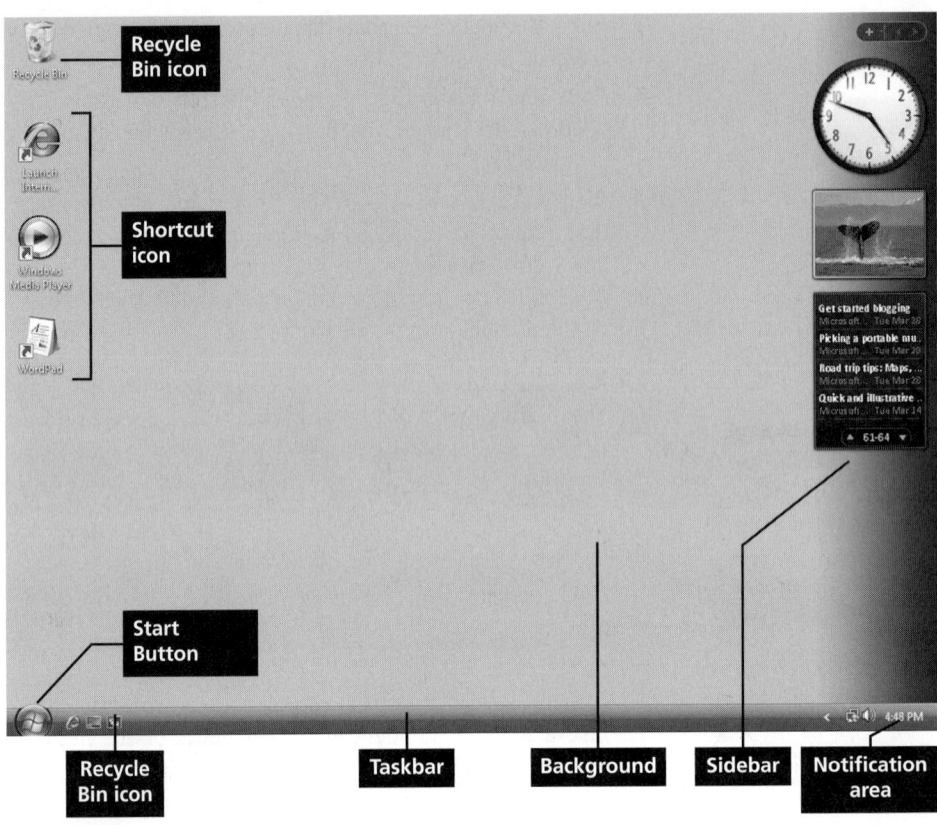

> As you will discover, Windows Vista can be easily customized and changed. Therefore, it is likely that the way your screen looks will often be different from the figures used throughout this book. For example, your Windows Vista desktop may not look the same as the desktop shown in Figure 2-2. It may display a different background, different colors, or different desktop icons.

PAUSE. LEAVE the desktop displayed to use in the next exercise.

As you have seen, in Windows Vista, the logon procedure always starts from the Welcome screen. However, the actual steps may vary, depending on how your system is set up.

- On some systems, you simply click your user name to log on.
- If your account has a password, you must key it when you reach the password screen to log on.

Also, because it is easy to customize Windows Vista, you will find that your screen may frequently look different from the screens used to illustrate this book.

The ***mouse*** is a device attached to your computer that lets you input commands. The ***mouse pointer*** is an icon that moves on the screen when you move the mouse on your desk. On the desktop, it usually looks like an arrow pointing up and to the left.

The ***desktop*** is the main work area that displays when Windows Vista is running.

In the next section, you will practice using the mouse while you familiarize yourself with the main components of the Windows Vista desktop.

 Windows Basics | 27

Using the Mouse to Identify Desktop Items

In Windows Vista, you use a mouse to point to and select items. The mouse pointer moves on the screen when you move the mouse on your desk.

USE THE MOUSE TO IDENTIFY DESKTOP ITEMS

USE the desktop you left displayed in the previous exercise.

1. Move the mouse on your desk or on a mouse pad on your desk so that the mouse pointer moves on the desktop. If you move the mouse to the left or right, the mouse pointer moves to the left or right. If you move the mouse away from yourself toward the back of your desk, the mouse pointer moves toward the top of the desktop. If you move the mouse toward yourself, the mouse pointer moves toward the bottom of the desktop.

TAKE NOTE* If the mouse reaches the edge of your desk or mouse pad before the mouse pointer is in the correct spot on the desktop, you can pick up the mouse and reposition it without moving the pointer on the screen.

2. Move the pointer so that it is touching the **Recycle Bin** icon. This is called "pointing to the Recycle Bin." Notice that the icon is highlighted and that a ScreenTip displays information about the Recycle Bin, as shown in Figure 2-3. An icon is a small picture that represents an item or command. A ScreenTip is a pop-up balloon that displays information about the item you are pointing at on the screen.

Figure 2-3

Point to the Recycle Bin icon

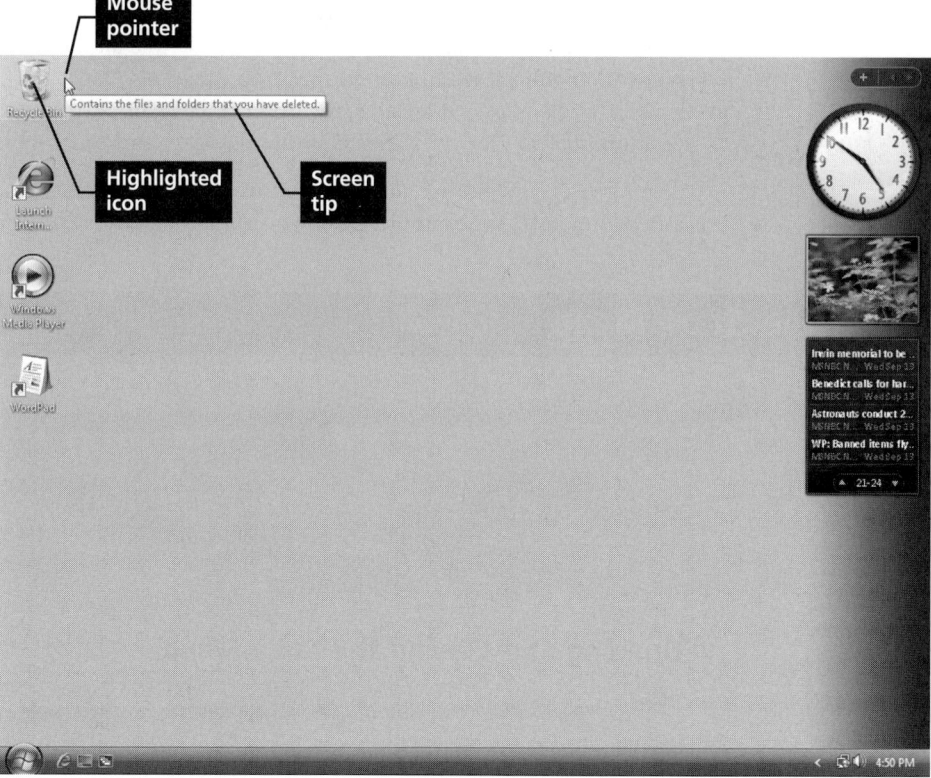

TROUBLESHOOTING If the mouse pointer changes to a hand with a pointing finger and the text label is underlined when you point to the Recycle Bin icon, it means your computer has been set to enable single-click launching of icons. If so, when you point at an icon, it becomes selected, and when you click it, it opens. If pointing selects the Recycle Bin icon, skip step 3. If you accidentally click the Recycle Bin icon, the folder window opens. Click the Close button in the upper-right corner to close it, and continue with step 4.

28 | Lesson 2

ANOTHER WAY

You can also cancel a selection by pressing Esc.

3. Click the **Recycle Bin** icon. This selects the Recycle Bin icon, which means it is marked as the item the next action or command will affect. Notice that the text label changes color, and that the highlight remains around the icon, even if you move the mouse.

4. Click a blank area of the desktop. This cancels the selection. The Recycle Bin icon is no longer highlighted.

5. Move the mouse on your desk so that the pointer is touching the **Start Button** at the left end of the taskbar at the bottom of the screen.

TROUBLESHOOTING

The taskbar is usually positioned across the bottom of the desktop, but you can move it to any side of the screen. If you do not see the taskbar at the bottom of the screen, look for it at the top, left, or right. If it does not display at all, it may be hidden. If so, move the mouse pointer to the side of the desktop where you think the taskbar is positioned (try the bottom first). It should display.

6. Use the mouse to point to the **current time** in the lower-right corner of the desktop, at the right end of the taskbar. The ScreenTip should display the current date.

PAUSE. LEAVE the desktop open to use in the next exercise.

In this exercise, you practiced using the mouse to point at and identify different items on the desktop and to *select* a desktop icon. Usually, when you point at an item on the desktop, a *ScreenTip* displays information about the item.

You can think of the Windows Vista desktop as similar to the top of your actual desk. On your desk, you might have an open folder or file and some papers such as a letter or report that you are reading or editing. You might also have pictures of your family or friends, a clock, a calendar, and a calculator. You can have all of these things on your Windows Vista desktop, too, so that you can access them quickly and easily while you work.

The *icons* on the taskbar and desktop provide access to frequently used programs, features, and commands. For example, when you click the Start Button, you open the Start menu.

■ Using the Start Menu

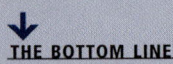

THE BOTTOM LINE

The Start menu is often the first element you use when you sit down at your computer because it provides access to all of your information. For example, from the Start menu you can start programs such as a word processor or database, locate files such as letters you have written, or access the Internet. In this section, you use your mouse to open and close the Start menu. You practice selecting and locating items on the Start menu and searching from the Start menu.

Opening and Closing the Start Menu

To open or close the Start menu, you point to the Start Button on the desktop and then click the left mouse button.

➔ **OPEN AND CLOSE THE START MENU**

USE the desktop you left displayed in the previous exercise.

1. Use your mouse to point to the **Start Button** in the lower-left corner of the desktop.

2. Click the **Start Button**. The Start menu opens, as shown in Figure 2-4. Take a moment to use the figure to locate the parts of the Start menu on your screen. (Of course, because Windows Vista is easily customized, your Start menu probably does not look exactly the same as the one in the figure.)

Figure 2-4

Windows Vista Start menu

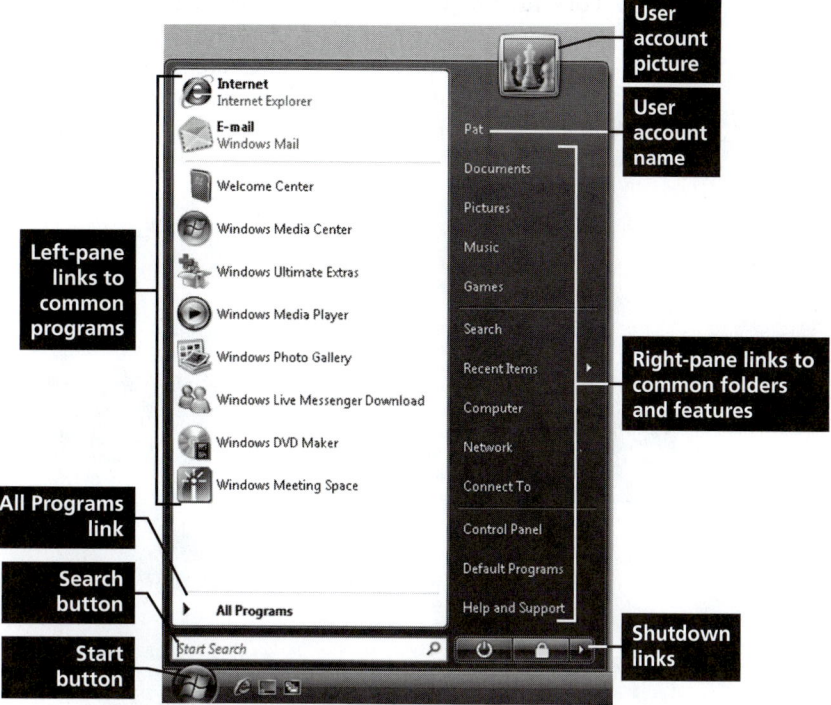

3. Click the **Start Button** again. The Start menu closes.

 **ANOTHER WAY** You can also open the Start menu by pressing the Windows logo key on your keyboard and close it by pressing Esc.

PAUSE. LEAVE the desktop open to use in the next exercise.

You may have noticed that the Start menu is divided into two main sections, which are called *panes*. The left pane is a menu of links to commonly used programs; the right pane is a menu of links to commonly used features and *folders*. Your user account name and picture display at the top of the right pane. A folder is a place where you can store items such as files and other folders. A *file* is a set of information stored with a single name. The tools you need to end your Windows session and shut off your computer are at the bottom of the right pane, and the tools you need to search your computer to find information are at the bottom of the left pane.

Identifying Items on the Start Menu

Most items on the Start menu are links to the programs, folders, and files that you use most often. Simply click a link to access the feature you need.

➔ **IDENTIFY ITEMS ON THE START MENU**

USE the desktop you left displayed in the previous exercise.

1. Click the **Start Button** to open the Start menu.
2. Point to the word **Documents** near the top of the right pane. It should highlight, and a ScreenTip should display. The highlighted item is often called the *current* or *active item,* which means that it is the item that the next command will affect.
3. Point to the word **Computer** in the right pane. You might notice that the picture at the top of the pane changes depending on the current item. When you point at Computer, the picture shows a computer system.

30 | Lesson 2

4. Click **All Programs** at the bottom of the left pane. A menu of all the programs installed on your computer displays in the left pane, as shown in Figure 2-5. (The programs on your computer are probably different from the ones shown in the figure.) Notice that each program on the menu has an icon next to it to represent the program type. If an item on the menu is a folder, it has a folder icon instead.

Figure 2-5

All Programs menu

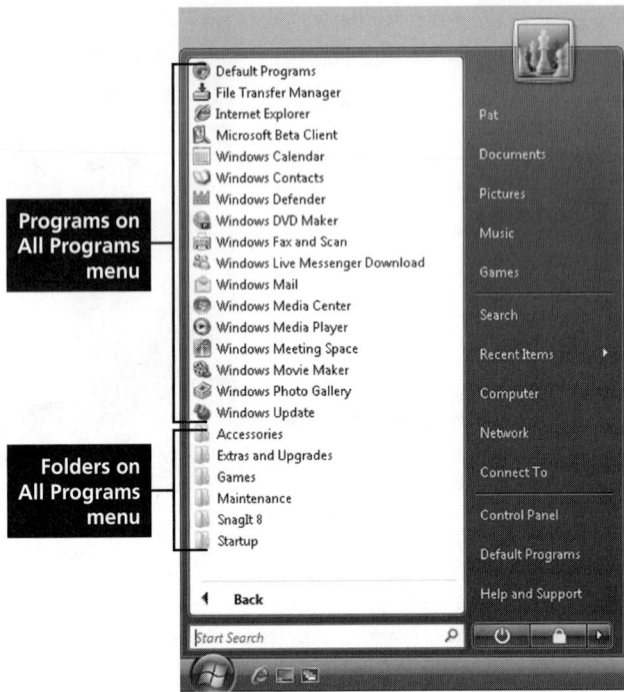

5. Click the **Accessories** folder on the All Programs menu. The folder opens—or expands—to display its contents, as shown in Figure 2-6.

Figure 2-6

Expand the Accessories folder

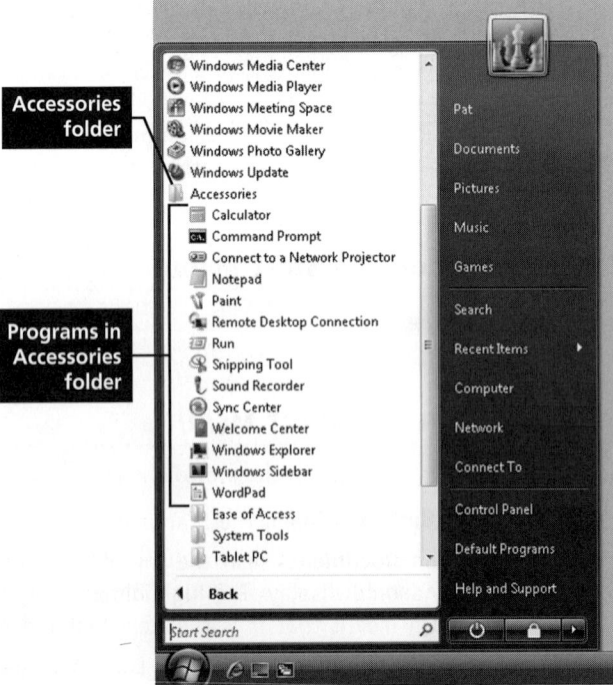

Windows Vista Windows Basics | 31

> **TROUBLESHOOTING** Sometimes there are too many items on the All Programs menu to display within the Start menu pane. In that case, a scrollbar displays along the right edge of the pane. You can drag the scrollbar up or down to see additional items on the menu.

6. Click **Calculator** on the Accessories menu. The Calculator displays on the desktop and the Start menu closes. (Notice that a button representing the window displays on the taskbar.) The Calculator is one of the accessory tools that come with Windows to help make your work easier. You can use the calculator to perform basic mathematical functions.

7. On the Calculator keypad, click **5**, click *****, click **3**, and then click **=5**. The result—15—shows in the Calculator display, as shown in Figure 2-7.

Figure 2-7

Calculator

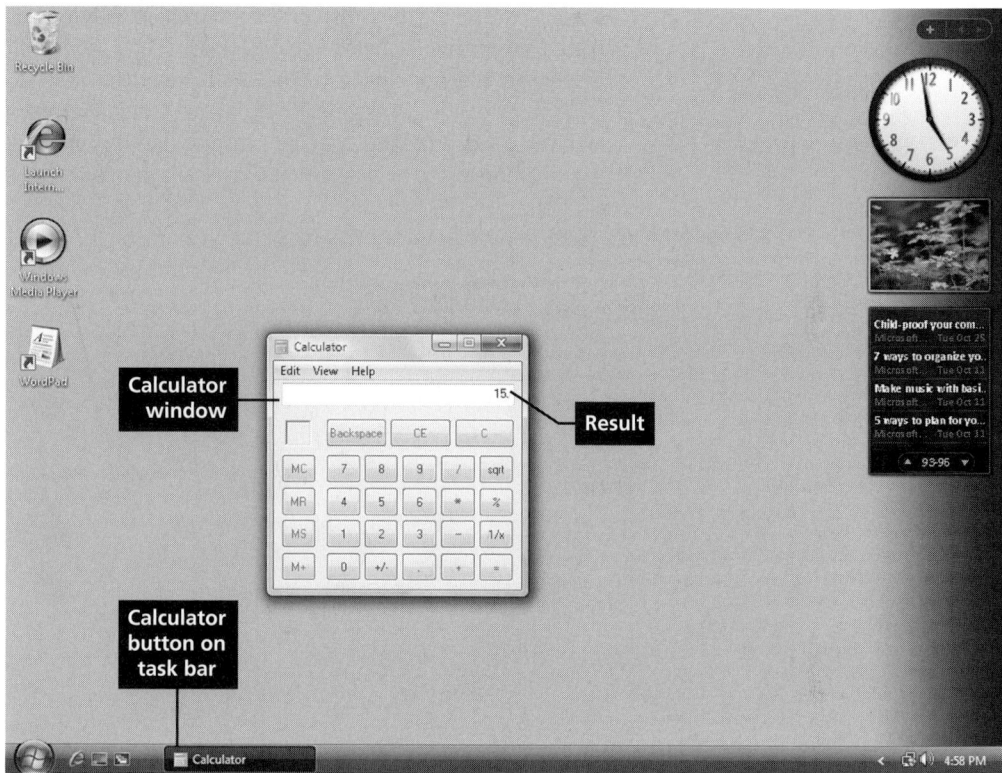

8. Click the **Close** button in the top right corner of the Calculator (the white X on a red background).

PAUSE. LEAVE the desktop open to use in the next exercise.

As you have seen, the Start menu displays links to the features and folders that you use most often. When you click a link on the Start menu, the feature starts or the folder opens. If there is a right-pointing arrow next to an item, it means that when you click the item a menu will display. For example, when you click All Programs, the All Programs menu displays. When you click a program icon, the program starts and displays in its program window and the Start menu closes. A button representing the open window displays on the taskbar.

Some of the items on the All Programs menu are organized into folders, such as Accessories and Maintenance. When you click a folder on All Programs, the folder expands on the menu so you can see its contents.

The Accessories folder stores useful tools and programs that come with Windows Vista. In addition to the Calculator, Windows Accessories usually include WordPad, a basic word processing program, and Paint, a graphics editing program. Other accessory programs may be available as well.

Selecting Start Menu Settings

The default Start menu settings make the most commonly used items available. In the Customize Start Menu dialog box, you can select the way links, icons, and menus display and behave. You can also set the number of recent programs you want on the menu and choose whether to display a link to your Internet browser and your email program.

→ SELECT START MENU SETTINGS

GET READY. Before you begin these steps, start your computer and log on to your Windows Vista account. Close all open windows so you can see the desktop.

1. Right-click a blank area of the Taskbar to display a shortcut menu and then click **Properties**. The Taskbar and Start Menu Properties dialog box displays.
2. Click the **Start Menu** tab and then click the **Customize . . .** button. The Customize Start Menu dialog box displays, as shown in Figure 2-8. The list at the top of the dialog box includes items such as links, icons, and programs that are available to display in the right pane of the Start menu, as well as options that control how each item opens. Other elements in the dialog box let you set the number of recently used programs that will display in the left pane and select the Internet and email programs to display. There is also a button that restores the default settings.

Figure 2-8

Customize Start Menu dialog box

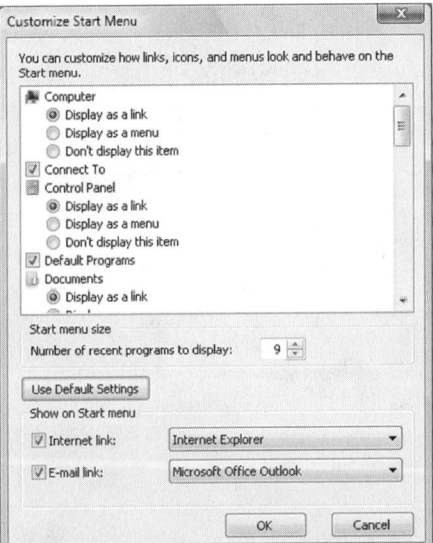

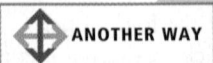

If the Customize Classic Start Menu dialog box displays, click Cancel to return to the Taskbar and Start Menu Properties dialog box, click the Start menu option button, and then click the Customize button.

ANOTHER WAY

To open the Taskbar and Start Menu dialog box with the Start Menu tab active, click the Start button, right-click a blank area of the Start menu, and click Properties.

3. Click the **Use Default Settings** button to restore the defaults. If necessary, click to select the **Internet link** and **E-mail link** checkboxes and then click **OK** to return to the Start Menu tab of the Taskbar and Start Menu Properties dialog box.
4. If necessary, click to select the **Store and display a list of recently opened files** checkbox and the **Store and display a list of recently opened programs** checkbox.
5. Click **OK** in the Taskbar and Start Menu Properties dialog box.

 **Windows Basics | 33**

6. Click the **Start** button to display the Start menu with the default settings. It should look similar to Figure 2-9, although the specific programs and item names on your computer may be different from the ones in the figure. Notice that nine recently used programs and an Internet and email program are listed in the left pane and links to standard folders are in the right pane. In the right pane, all but Recent Items are set to display as links, which means when you click the item the folder window opens. Recent Items is set to display as a menu, which means when you point to it or click it a menu of recently used items displays.

Figure 2-9

Default Start menu

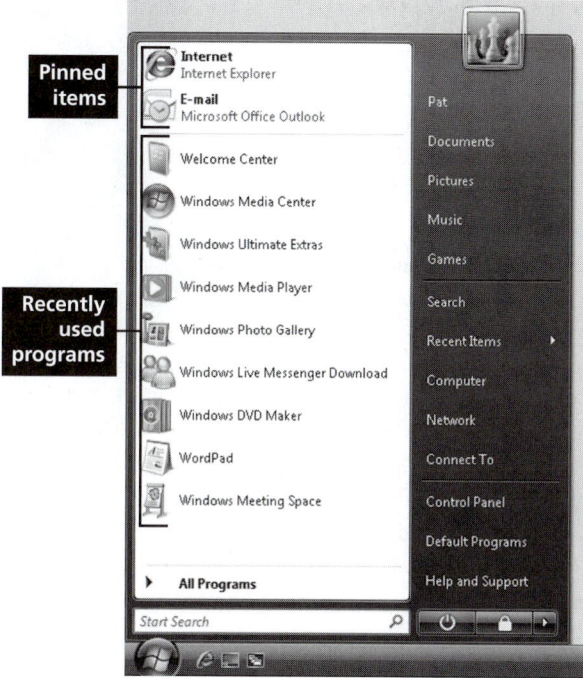

7. Right-click a blank area of the Taskbar and then click **Properties**. Click the **Start Menu** tab and then click the **Customize . . .** button to display the Customize Start Menu dialog box again. In the list at the top of the dialog box, you can select which items to display in the right pane and how you want the items to behave.
8. Under Computer, click the **Display as a menu** option button. This changes the way the item opens, from a link to a menu.
9. Click to clear the **Connect To** and **Default Programs** checkboxes. This removes the items from the right pane of the Start menu.
10. Scroll down the list, noting the available options. At the bottom of the list, click to clear the **Use Large Icons** checkbox.
11. Under Start menu size, click the down increment arrow to change the number of recent programs to display to four.
12. Under Show on Start menu, click to clear the **Internet link** and **E-mail link:** checkboxes.
13. Click **OK** and then click **Apply** in the Taskbar and Start Menu Properties dialog box.

Using smaller icons lets you fit more items on the Start menu.

TAKE NOTE* Clicking an Apply button in a dialog box applies the current options but leaves the dialog box open so that you can make additional changes.

14. Click the **Start Button**. The Start menu should look similar to Figure 2-10. In the left pane, notice that only four recently used programs are listed and that the icons are smaller. The Internet and email links do not display. In the right pane, notice that the Connect To and Default Programs items do not display and that Computer is now a menu. If you point to it, a menu of computer components, such as storage devices, displays.

Figure 2-10

Customized Start menu

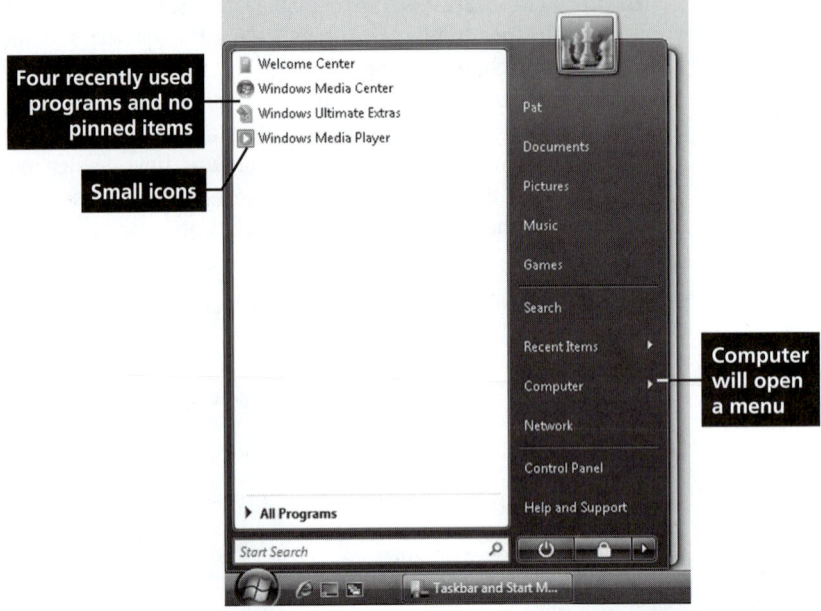

15. Press **Esc** to cancel the Start menu and click the **Customize** button on the Start Menu tab of the Taskbar and Start Menu Properties dialog box.
16. Click the **Use Default Settings** button to restore the default settings, click to select the **Internet link** and **E-mail link** checkboxes, and then click **OK**. Click **OK** in the Taskbar and Start Menu Properties dialog box to apply the changes and close the dialog box.

    PAUSE. LEAVE the desktop displayed to use in the next exercise.

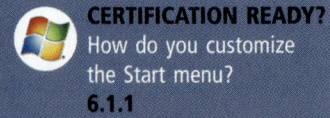

CERTIFICATION READY?
How do you customize the Start menu?
6.1.1

You can easily use the options in the Customize Start Menu dialog box to control the items that display in both the left and right panes of the Start menu. As you have seen, you can also select to display items in the right pane as menus instead of as links.

You might prefer using a menu if you want to go directly to an item stored in the main folder rather than having to navigate through folder windows. For example, if you frequently access a particular storage device, such as a flash drive, you can set Computer to display as a menu. Then, instead of opening the Computer folder and navigating to the flash drive, you can just select the flash drive from the Computer menu.

In addition to selecting items to display in the right pane, you may have noticed options for controlling general Start menu behavior, including the following:

- **Enable context menus and dragging and dropping.** *Context menu* is another term for shortcut menu. This option is selected by default. If you deselect this option, no shortcut menus display when you right-click a Start menu item, and you cannot drag an item to pin or unpin it to the Start menu.
- **Highlight newly installed programs.** This option is selected by default, so that when a new program is installed on your computer, the All Programs menu and the item on the All Programs menu are highlighted. If you deselect this option, newly installed programs are not highlighted.
- **Open submenus when I pause on them with the mouse pointer.** This option is selected by default. If you deselect this option, you must click an item to open a menu.
- **Sort All Programs menu by name.** This option is selected by default. Deselect this option if you want to arrange items on the All Programs menu in a different order, not alphabetically by name. You can drag the items to reposition them on the menu.

 **Windows Basics | 35**

Finally, in addition to selecting to display links to your Internet browser and email program, you can select the specific program to display. This is useful if you have more than one browser or email program installed. Simply click the dropdown arrow and click the program to use.

Searching from the Start Menu

> The Search box on the Start menu is a quick tool to use to find a program, file, or folder when you are not sure where the item is stored. From the Start menu, Windows Vista searches the indexed locations on your computer. An *indexed location* is one that is included in the Windows Vista *index*, which is a collection of information about the items stored on your computer. Windows Vista uses the index to increase the speed and accuracy of a search. In this exercise, you learn how to search from the Start menu using text and keywords.

➔ SEARCH FROM THE START MENU

GET READY. Before you begin these steps, start your computer and log on to your Windows Vista account. Close all open windows so you can see the desktop.

1. Click the **Start Button** and then navigate to the data files for this lesson.
2. Click the **Start Button** to display the Start menu. In the Search box at the bottom of the left pane, key **C**. As soon as you start keying characters into the Search box, Windows Vista starts looking for matching items. In this case, it starts searching for any item that is named with a word starting with the letter C. The text you type does not have to be the name of an item; it can be in the contents of the item or in a property. Windows Vista displays the search results in the left pane of the Start menu, organized by type. The search results are all of the items that match the criteria that you are looking for, which in this case is the text in the Search box. Your Start menu should look similar to Figure 2-11. However, the search results depend on the contents of your computer, so you may not have the exact items in the figure.

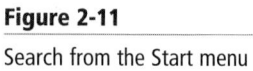

Figure 2-11

Search from the Start menu

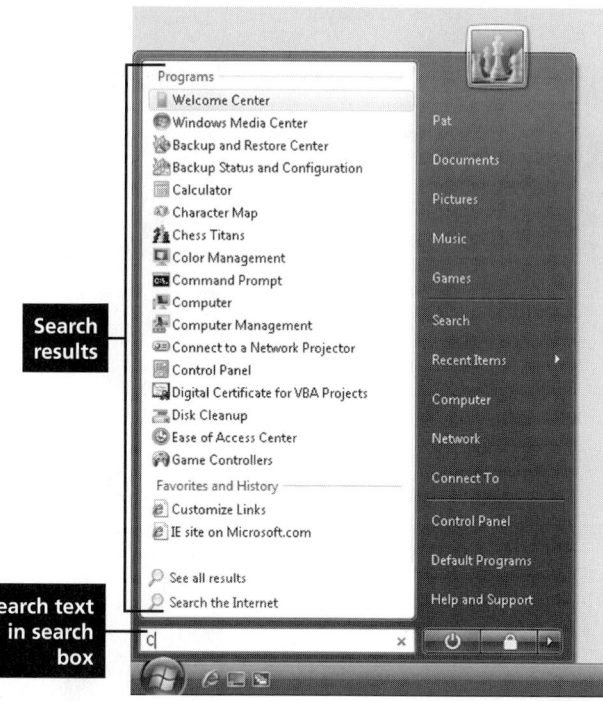

36 | Lesson 2

3. Key the letter **o**, so the text Co displays in the Search box. Windows Vista filters the search to find items with the text Co in the name, contents, or properties. To filter means to find items that meet certain criteria and exclude those that do not. In this case, the criteria are the text Co. Now, the search results listed should include the two folders Contoso and Company Info, as shown in Figure 2-12.

Figure 2-12

Filter the search to Co

4. Key **ntoso** to complete the word Contoso in the Search box. Now, the search results should look similar to Figure 2-13, with only the exact match Contoso and its contents displayed.

Figure 2-13

Filter the search to Contoso

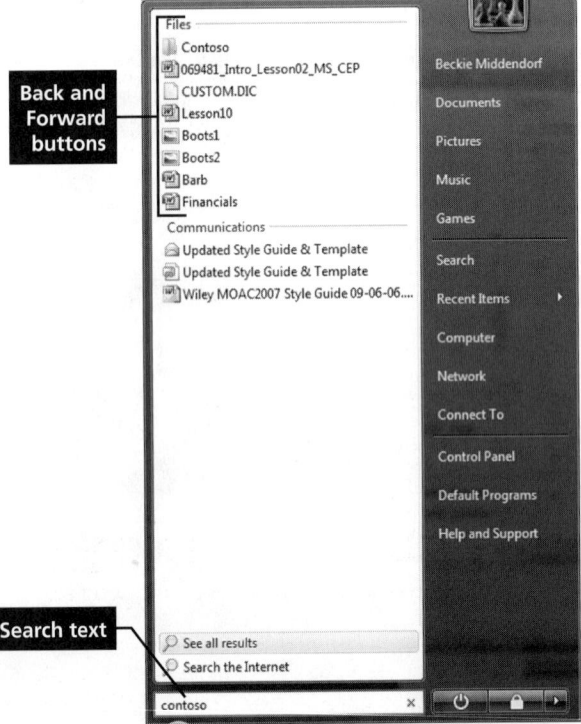

CD

The *Barb* and *Financials* files are available on the companion CD-ROM.

5. Press **Backspace** to delete the text in the Search box and then key **Dear**. The *Financials* and *Barb* documents should display in the search results. The text Dear is not part of either file's name or properties, but because both are letters, it is in the file contents as part of the salutation. You may have other letter documents that also display in the search results.

TAKE NOTE

You can open the *Financials* and *Barb* documents in a word processor such as WordPad or Microsoft Office Word to see the contents.

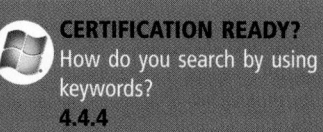

CERTIFICATION READY?
How do you search by using keywords?
4.4.4

6. Press **Esc** to close the Start menu.
   PAUSE. LEAVE the desktop displayed to use in the next exercise.

As mentioned earlier, the Search box on the Start menu is a quick tool to use to find a program or an item stored in an indexed location. By default, indexed locations include your personal folder and its contents; email; *offline files*, which are copies of network files that you store locally on your computer; and Web sites stored in your Web browser's history.

When you search for items, Windows Vista automatically *filters* the *search results* based on the information you provide. Using a Search box, the only information you can provide is text. As you have seen, if you know the item's name, you can type it and quickly locate the item wherever it is stored. If you do not know the item's name, you can use text that is in the contents of the item. If you are not sure of the item's contents, you can key text that is in a property, such as a keyword in the Tags or Comments property. You can also use wildcard characters.

When you search using text other than the item's name, Windows Vista may not be able to find the exact item you need, but it will narrow down the search results so you can find the item more easily.

You can also use standard search syntax to instruct Windows Vista to look for the search text in a particular property only. *Syntax* is the way words are arranged. To specify a property, key the property, a colon, and then the search text. So, to look for files named March, key Name:March in the Search box. To look for files with a tag March, key Tag:March.

■ Resizing a Folder Window

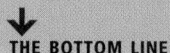

THE BOTTOM LINE

When you open a folder in Windows Vista, its contents display with elements designed to help you navigate and manage your data in Windows. In this section, you practice resizing windows on your desktop.

Minimizing, Maximizing, and Restoring a Window

Sometimes you need to quickly change the size or position of a window on the desktop. Minimize the window to temporarily remove it from the desktop, maximize it to increase its size to fill the desktop, and then restore it back to its original size and position.

➔ **MINIMIZE, MAXIMIZE, AND RESTORE A WINDOW**

USE the desktop you left displayed in the previous exercise.

1. Click the **Start Button** and then click **Computer** in the right pane of the Start menu. The Computer folder window opens. It displays the components of your computer system, including disk drives. Notice the common window elements.

2. Click the **Minimize** button in the upper-right corner of the window. The window is reduced to a button on the taskbar, as shown in Figure 2-14.

Figure 2-14

Minimize a window

3. Click the **Computer** taskbar button. The window opens.

4. Click the **Maximize** button in the upper-right corner of the window. The window expands to fill the desktop, as shown in Figure 2-15. Notice that some of the colors in the window change to indicate it is maximized and that the Maximize button is now replaced by the Restore Down button.

Figure 2-15

Maximize a window

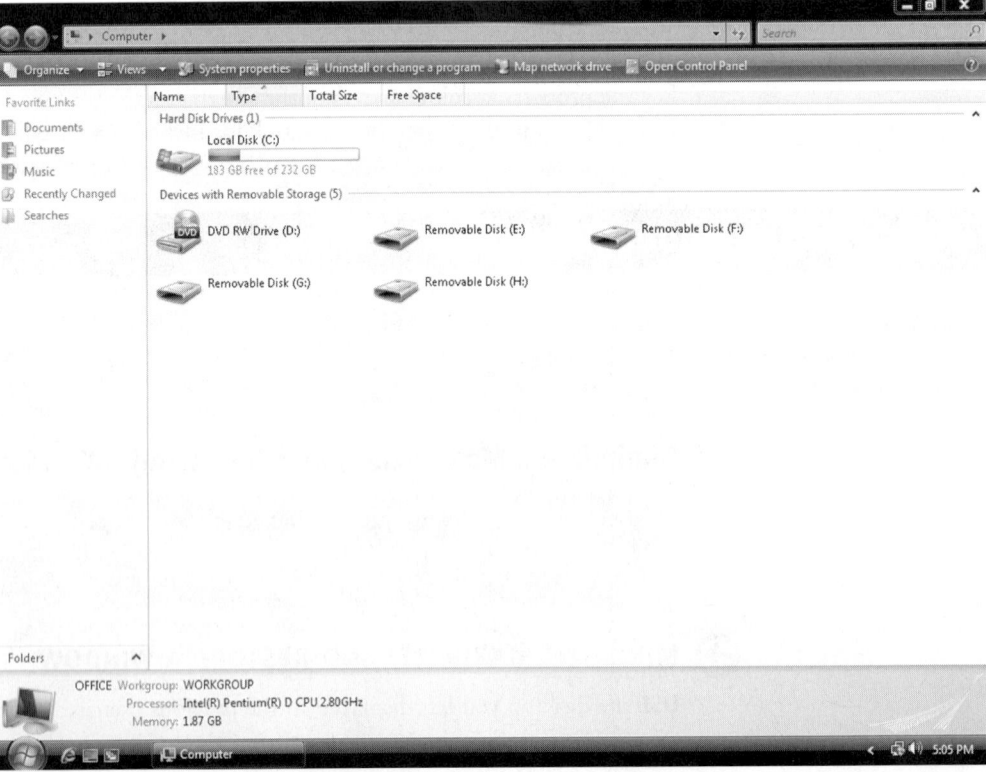

5. Click the **Minimize** button to once again reduce the window to a taskbar button.
6. Click the taskbar button to return the window to its previous size and position—in this case, maximized.

7. Click the **Restore Down** button in the upper-right corner of the window. The window returns to the size and position it had before you maximized it in step 4.
8. Click the **Close** button to close the Computer window.

PAUSE. LEAVE the desktop open to use in the next exercise.

When you *minimize* a window, you reduce it to a taskbar button. A minimized window is not closed. It remains running on your computer in a minimized state. When you *maximize* a window, you expand it to fill the desktop. You cannot see other items on the desktop behind it, but they are still there. When you *restore down* a window, it returns to its previous size and position. These commands become more and more useful as you start working with multiple windows at the same time, because they enable you to juggle many tasks at once. For example, you might be writing a letter with a word processing program in one window and need to look up a name and address in your contacts list at the same time. You can easily manipulate the windows so that you can access the information you need, when you need it.

You may have noticed that the Computer folder was divided into two sections.

- Hard Disk Drives, which lists the hard disks that are fixed inside your computer or attached externally.
- Devices with Removable Storage, which shows devices such as digital video disk (DVD) or compact disks (CD) drives, as well as universal serial bus (USB) devices such as flash drives, scanners, or cameras that are currently connected to your computer.

A drive is a device that reads and writes data on storage media, such as a CD or DVD. In Windows Vista, each drive is assigned a drive letter to help you identify it as part of your computer system. For example, the main hard disk drive is called drive C:, or Local Disk C:. See Table 2-2 for information about different types of storage devices.

Table 2-2

Disk drives and storage devices

Device name	Description
Hard disk	A hard disk is a device that contains one or more inflexible platters coated with material on which data can be recorded magnetically. Most personal computers have at least one primary hard disk fixed inside the computer. It is usually called drive C: or Local Disk C: and is the location where files and programs are typically stored. Some hard disks are attached externally to a computer. External drives can be removed and stored in a different location to safeguard data or attached to a different computer to transfer data.
Hard disk drive	A hard disk drive is the device that reads data from and writes data to a hard disk.
DVD drive	A DVD drive is a drive that reads data on DVDs or CDs. If the drive is a DVD burner, it can also write data on a DVD or CD. DVD burners may be labeled RW, which stands for "read and write." DVDs can store a large amount of data, making them suitable for storing videos, pictures, and music, as well as data.
CD drive	A CD drive reads data on a compact disk. If the drive is a CD burner, it can write data on a CD. A CD burner may be labeled RW, which stands for "read and write." Although they do not have as large a capacity as DVDs, CDs are suitable for storing music and pictures, as well as data.
Flash drive	A flash drive is a small storage device that plugs into a USB port on the computer. Flash drives can be moved from one computer to another, making it easy to share and transport information. Flash drives may also be called memory keys, key drives, pen drives, or thumb drives.
Network drive	A network drive is any type of drive that is connected to a network and that can be accessed by users on the network. A network drive makes it possible for people to share files and folders stored on that drive.
Other	Other types of storage devices include scanners, digital cameras, and digital video camcorders, which can be attached to a USB port. Data from the attached device can be transferred to the computer. A scanner is a device that converts a printed image to a digital file. A digital camera is a camera that records and stores pictures in digital format. A digital video camcorder records and stores video in digital format.

Accessing Help and Support

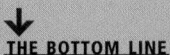

THE BOTTOM LINE When you have a question about a feature in Windows Vista, you can find useful information in the Help and Support Center. Access the Help and Support Center from the Start menu and use the home page to locate basic information about your computer or Windows Vista.

Accessing Help and Support

→ ACCESS HELP AND SUPPORT

USE the desktop you left open in the previous exercise.

1. Click the **Start Button** and then click **Help and Support** near the bottom of the right pane on the Start menu. The Windows Help and Support home page displays in a window, as shown in Figure 2-16. Notice that some elements in the window are the same as in a folder window, including the Back and Forward buttons, the Search box, and a toolbar.

Figure 2-16

Windows Help and Support home page

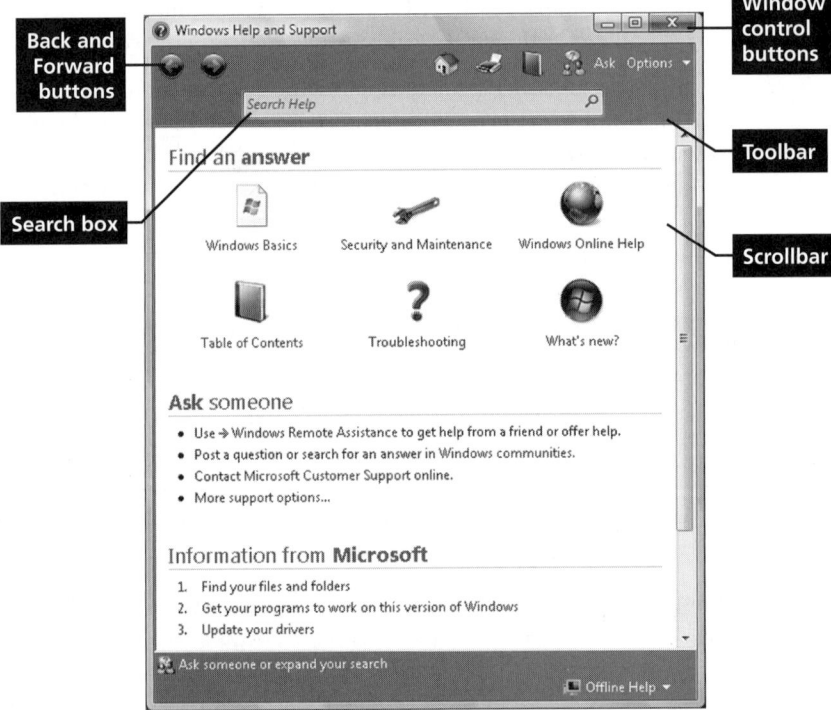

2. Click **Windows Basics** under the heading Find an answer. A page listing all of the Windows Basics topics displays. The topics are grouped under headings, and each topic is a link to a page of specific help information.

 **ANOTHER WAY** You can also open Help and Support from many locations in Windows Vista, simply by clicking the Help button. For example, in the Documents window, click Help to open the Working with the Documents folder Help and Support topic page.

3. Click **The Start menu (overview)** under the heading Desktop fundamentals. A page of information about the Start menu displays.

4. Drag the vertical scroll box down slowly so you can review the information about the Start menu.

Windows Vista Windows Basics | 41

5. Click the **Back** button to return to the previous page and then click **Working with windows**. A page of information about how to work with windows displays. You can also scroll down in this page.
6. Click the **Help and Support** home button on the toolbar. The home page displays. The Help and Support home button is available on all pages within Help and Support.
7. Click **Table of contents** to display the Contents page. Each item on the page is a link to a main topic.
8. Click **Getting Started** to display the Getting Started topic, as shown in Figure 2-17. Items that have a question mark icon are links to specific topics, and items that have books are links to subtopics.

Figure 2-17

Getting Started Help topic

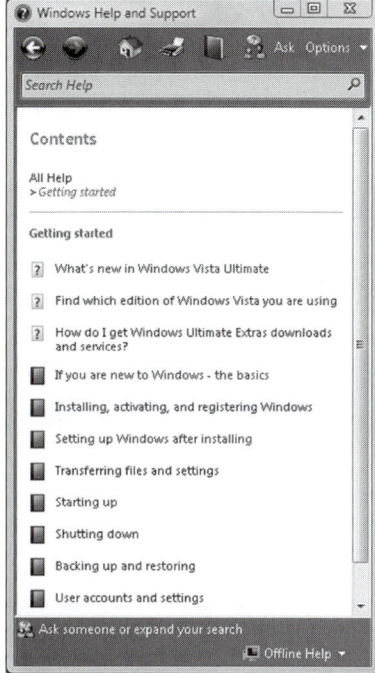

9. Click **Which edition of Windows Vista do I have**. The topic page displays. Some pages provide specific instructions for performing tasks. This page walks you through the steps for locating information about your version of Windows Vista.
10. On the help page, click **Click to open Welcome Center**. The Welcome Center window opens, and the Help and Support window stays open as well.
11. Next to the picture of the computer under your user name, locate the name of the Windows Vista edition you are using and then click the **Close** button to close the Welcome Center window.
12. Click the **Close** button in the Help and Support window.
    PAUSE. LEAVE your desktop open to use in the next exercise.

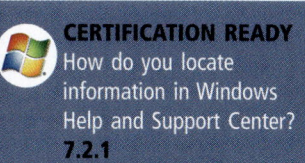

CERTIFICATION READY
How do you locate information in Windows Help and Support Center?
7.2.1

The Help and Support Center is chock full of information to help you accomplish any Windows task. It is organized as a series of linked pages that you can browse through in any order. Some pages provide information, and some walk you through specific steps. The color of text helps identify the type of link.

- Blue text links to another topic or to a specific task. The link may go to a location on a different page, on the same page, or in a different window. It may even go to a location on the Internet.
- Green text links to a definition. When you click the link, a definition displays in a ScreenTip.
- Violet text indicates a link that has already been used at least once. This can help you identify pages you have already accessed.

Shutting Down Windows Vista

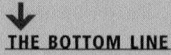

When you are finished using your computer, you should shut it down. Shutting down insures that your data is saved and your computer system is secure. It also saves energy. In this section, you learn how to shut down Windows Vista.

Shutting Down Windows Vista

When you want to shut down Windows and turn off all of your computer components, use the Shut Down command.

SHUTTING DOWN WINDOWS VISTA

1. Close all open windows.
2. Click the **Start Button** and then click the arrow to the right of the Lock button.
3. Click **Shut Down** on the menu. Your session ends, closing all open windows, and your computer turns off. If necessary, manually turn off your display.

Windows Vista provides other options when shutting down windows. In addition to those covered in this section, you may find other options on the Shut Down menu useful, such as Log Off, Lock, Restart, Sleep, and Hibernate.

You can use the Power button on the Welcome screen to shut down the computer. Click the button to shut off or click the arrow next to the button to display a menu of shutdown options.

SUMMARY SKILL MATRIX

IN THIS LESSON YOU LEARNED HOW TO:
Log on to Windows Vista
Use the Mouse to Identify Desktop Items
Open and Close the Start Menu
Identify Items on the Start Menu
Select Start Menu Settings
Search from the Start Menu
Minimize, Maximize, and Restore a Window
Access Help and Support
Shut Down Windows Vista

Knowledge Assessment

Multiple Choice

Select the best response for the following questions.

1. To access information on your computer, you must log on to which of the following?
   a. Internet Explorer
   b. User Account ✓
   c. Outlook
   d. Microsoft Office

2. An icon is a small picture that represents which of the following?
   a. item
   b. command
   c. both a and b ✓
   d. none of the above

3. How many items can be selected at one time in a file list?
   a. one
   b. two
   c. three or more ✓
   d. none

4. Which of the following is selected by default in Windows Vista?
   a. Sort All Programs menu
   b. Sort All Documents menu
   c. both a and b ✓
   d. none of the above

5. When does the Restore Down button display?
   a. always
   b. when a window is maximized ✓
   c. when a window is minimized
   d. both b and c

6. To select items that are not adjacent to one another, which of the following must be pressed and held?
   a. Shift key
   b. Ctrl key ✓
   c. Alt key
   d. all of the above

7. Which of the following refers to the way words are arranged?
   a. reference
   b. index
   c. list
   d. syntax ✓

8. The Customize Start Menu dialog box is used to control items displayed in which pane of the Start menu?
   a. left pane
   b. right pane
   c. both a and b
   d. none of the above ✓

9. The best way to get help and support for Windows Vista tasks is through which of the following methods?
   a. call Microsoft on the telephone
   b. send a letter to the Microsoft Help and Support center
   c. use the Help and Support option on the Start menu ✓
   d. send an email to the Microsoft Help and Support center

10. An area where you can key search text is known as which of the following?
    a. search results
    b. search pane
    c. search menu
    d. search box ✓

Fill in the Blank

Complete the following sentences by writing the correct word or words in the blanks provided.

1. The __Welcome__ screen lists the names of all of the people authorized to use the computer.
2. Another term for a shortcut menu is a(n) __Context__ menu.
3. The __desktop__ is the main work area that displays when Windows Vista is running.
4. A(n) __Index__ is a collection of information about items stored on a computer; used to increase the speed and accuracy of a search.
5. Items matching specified __Criteria__ are displayed in the search results.
6. __restore__ down a window to return it to its previous size and position.
7. __minimize__ a window to reduce it to a button on the taskbar.
8. __max__ a window to increase its size to fill the desktop.
9. Windows Vista looks for __Syntax__ text to locate programs, files, and folders stored on your computer.
10. The top of the Start menu's left pane displays __pin__ items.

Competency Assessment

Project 2-1: Identify Disk Drives

Use Windows Vista to learn about your computer system.

GET READY. Have a piece of paper and pen on hand to write down information about your computer.

1. Turn on your computer and monitor.
2. On the Welcome screen, click your **user name**.
3. If necessary, key your password in the Password box and then press **Enter** to display the desktop.
4. If necessary, click the **Close** button to close the Welcome Center.
5. Click the **Start Button** to open the Start menu.
6. Click **Computer** on the right pane of the Start menu to display the Computer folder window.
7. Click to select the icon representing your hard disk drive, which is usually named Local Disk(C:).
8. Count how many devices with removable storage you have and write the number on a piece of paper. If you can identify the type of drive, write that information down as well. For example, write down the letter of the CD drive, DVD drive, or network drive.
9. Click the **Close** button to close the Computer window.

    PAUSE. LEAVE the desktop displayed to use in the next project.

Project 2-2: Proper Shutdown

Use Help and Support to find out how to turn off your computer properly.

USE the desktop that is displayed from the previous project.

1. Click the **Start Button** to open the Start menu.
2. Click **Help and Support** to open the Help and Support home page.
3. Click **Windows Basics** to display the list of topics.
4. Click **Turning off your computer properly** to display the help topic.
5. Read the information on the help page.
6. At the end of the help topic, under the heading See also, click **Turning off a computer: frequently asked questions**.
7. Click **Is my data safe while my computer is asleep**. Read the answer and then write the explanation in your own words on the piece of paper.
8. Click the **Close** button to close the Help and Support window.

    PAUSE. LEAVE the desktop displayed to use in the next project.

Proficiency Assessment

Project 2-3: Find Program Files

While you were on vacation, a temporary worker deleted all of the program shortcuts from your Start menu. In this project, you will search from the Start menu for the Notepad, WordPad, and Paint programs.

USE the desktop that is displayed from the previous project.

1. Click **Start** to open the Start menu.

2. In the Search box at the bottom of the left pane of the Start menu, key **WordPad**. The program name should display in the search results in the left pane of the Start menu.
3. Delete the text **WordPad** from the Search box and key **Notepad**. View the search results.
4. Delete the text **Notepad** from the Search box and key **Paint**. View the search results.
5. Press Esc to close the Start menu.

   PAUSE. LEAVE the desktop displayed to use in the next project.

Project 2-4: Explore Sample Windows Vista Folders

Explore the picture and music samples that come with Windows Vista.

USE the desktop that is displayed from the previous project.

1. Use the Start menu to open the Pictures folder.
2. Select the Sample Pictures shortcut.
3. Double-click the **Sample Pictures** shortcut to open the Sample Pictures folder.
4. Maximize the window so you can see all of the picture files.
5. Click the Waterfall picture. If the Waterfall picture is not available, select a different picture.
6. Minimize the window.
7. Maximize the window and then restore it.
8. In the Navigation pane, click **Music** to open the Music folder.
9. Click the **Sample Music** shortcut icon to select it.
10. Double-click the **Sample Music** shortcut to open the Sample Music folder.
11. Click the **Back** button.
12. Close the folder window.

    PAUSE. LEAVE the desktop displayed to use in the next project.

■ Mastery Assessment

Project 2-5: Show Off Windows Vista

You recently hired an assistant who has never used a personal computer before. In this project, give him a tour of some of the basic features of Windows Vista.

USE the desktop that is displayed from the previous project.

1. Open your personal folder and select all items in the file list at the same time.
2. Maximize and then minimize the window.
3. Open the window and then restore it.
4. From the Start menu, key the word **games**. View the search results.
5. Press Esc to close the Start menu.
6. Open the Recycle Bin window and then close it.
7. Log off and then log back on.

   PAUSE. LEAVE the desktop displayed to use in the next project.

Project 2-6: New Computer

You just purchased a new computer and want to personalize it for your home. In this project, you will customize the Start menu by adding shortcuts, then restore the Start menu's default settings.

USE the desktop that is displayed from the previous project.

1. Click the Start button, right-click a blank area of the Taskbar, and then click **Properties**.
2. Customize the Start menu to display Computer, Control Panel, and Personal folder as menus.
3. Set the number of recent programs to display to 3.
4. Pin the Calculator, WordPad, and Paint programs to the Start menu.
5. Restore the Start menu's default settings.

    STOP. Log off your Windows Vista user account.

INTERNET READY

As mentioned at the beginning of this lesson, Northwind Traders is a small, growing company that helps Inuit artists in Alaska market their work to customers around the globe. To prepare for a press release announcing the company's expansion, use Internet search tools to locate information about the history of Inuit art. For example, you might find out the types of traditional Inuit art created over the years, as well as the type of art created by contemporary artists. Use the information you find to write a paragraph that you can include in the press release that summarizes the evolution of Inuit art from the past to the present.

3 Working with Files and Folders

LESSON SKILL MATRIX

Skill	Objective
Opening and Closing a Folder Window	Students will learn how to open and copy a folder window.
Selecting Items in a Folder	Students will learn how to select items in a folder.
Creating and Renaming a Folder	Students will learn how to create and rename a folder.
Deleting Files and Folders	Students will learn how to delete files and folders.
Using the Recycle Bin	Students will learn how to use the Recycle Bin.
Browsing Through Recently Opened Windows	Students will learn how to browse through recently opened windows.
Using the Navigation Pane	Students will learn how to use the Navigation pane.
Opening and Arranging Multiple Windows	Students will learn how to open and arrange multiple windows.
Changing the Active Window	Students will learn how to change the active window.
Moving Files and Folders	Students will learn how to move files and folders.
Copying to a Different Folder	Students will learn how to copy to a different folder.
Copying to a Storage Device	Students will learn how to copy to a storage device.

Southridge Video is a video production company that develops and produces training videos and Webcasts for a variety of clients. Whenever the company adds a new client, the account manager uses Windows Vista to set up a folder so there is a place to store files and other information related to the client. In this lesson, you will learn how to work with files and folders. You will use Windows Vista to open, close, and select items in a folder. You will learn to create and rename folders. You will learn how to delete files and folders and how to use the Recycle Bin so you can restore or permanently remove deleted items. You will learn to navigate through windows and to use multiple windows. Finally, you will learn how to move and copy files and folders.

KEY TERMS
path
shortcut menu
submenu
program
insertion point
expanded
collapsed
cascades
stacks
tiles
source location
Clipboard
destination location
back up

48

 **Working with Files and Folders | 49**

Using a Folder Window

↓ THE BOTTOM LINE

Imagine an office without file folders or desk drawers. Letters, reports, telephone lists, and other printed information might be strewn willy-nilly on the desk, chair, and even the floor! You would never be able to find anything when you needed it. With Windows Vista, you organize your electronic data in much the same way as you would organize an office. You create folders on your computer in which you can store information. When you open a folder, its contents display in a window that also has elements designed to help you manage your data and navigate in Windows. In this section, you will open and close folders that come with Windows Vista and practice selecting items in a folder.

Opening and Closing a Folder Window

You can easily open a folder that is listed on the Start menu by clicking it. If the icon is on the desktop, you double-click to open it. To close a window, click its Close button.

⊙ OPEN AND CLOSE A FOLDER WINDOW

USE the desktop you left displayed in the previous exercise.

1. Click the **Start Button** to open the Start menu.
2. Click your user account name at the top of the right pane of the Start menu. Your personal folder window opens. It should look similar to the one in Figure 3-1, although the name and the contents may be different, depending on your user name and the items stored in the folder. Notice that a button representing the window displays on the taskbar.
3. Take a moment to identify the elements of a folder window, as shown in Figure 3-1. Refer to Table 3-1 for descriptions of each element.

Figure 3-1

A personal folder window

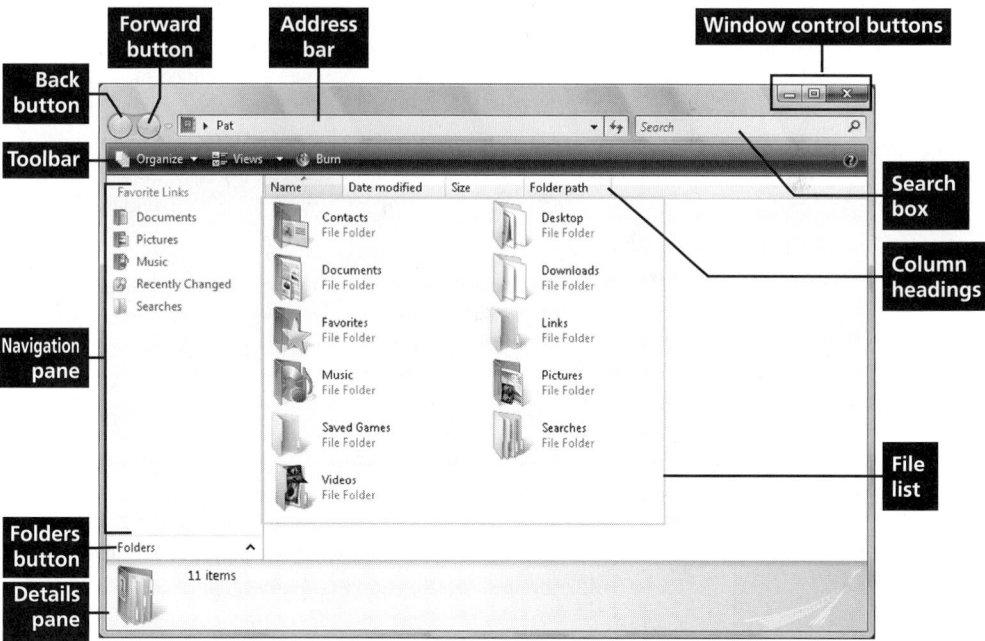

Table 3-1

Common window elements

Element	Description
File list	The file list displays the contents of the current folder, including programs, files, subfolders, and links to other locations. Double-click an item to open it.
Navigation pane	The Navigation pane displays links to other locations. Click a link to display that location.
Back and Forward buttons	Click the Back and Forward buttons to navigate to folders that you have been viewing.
Toolbar	The toolbar displays buttons for common tasks, such as organizing the contents of a folder or changing the way the file list displays.
Address bar	The Address bar displays the name of the current folder. It may also display the complete **path** to the location, with each part of the path separated by arrows. The path is the route Windows takes from a storage device through folders and subfolders to a specific destination. For example, the Address bar might display the name of your personal folder, an arrow, and then the name of the current folder. You can key a path in the Address bar to go to that location.
Headings	The column headings label the details displayed in the file list.
Search box	Key a word or phrase in the Search box to quickly locate a file in the current folder or its subfolders.
Details pane	The Details pane displays properties of the selected item, which are details or characteristics, such as name, size, and type.
Window control buttons	The three window control buttons let you control the size and position of the window on the desktop. Click the Minimize button to reduce the window to a button on the taskbar. Click the Maximize button to expand the window to fill the desktop. When the window is maximized, the Restore Down button displays. Click the Restore Down button to return the window to its previous size and location on the desktop. Click the Close button to close the window.
Folders button	Click the Folders button to display a hierarchical list of the contents of your computer system. Click it again to hide the list.

4. Click the **Close** button in the upper-right corner of the window. The window closes.
5. Point to the **Recycle Bin** icon on the desktop and then press and release the left mouse button twice in rapid succession. This is called a double-click. The Recycle Bin folder window opens. Notice that it has many of the same common elements as your personal folder window. The Recycle Bin folder contains items you have deleted but have not yet removed permanently.

TROUBLESHOOTING If your computer has been customized to enable single-click launching, you only have to click the Recycle Bin icon once to open the folder window.

6. In the Navigation pane, click **Documents**. The Documents folder opens, replacing the Recycle Bin folder in the window on your desktop.
7. Click the **Back** button. The previously opened folder—the Recycle Bin—displays in place of Documents.

Working with Files and Folders | 51

8. Click the **Forward** button. The Documents folder displays.

9. Click the **Close** button to close the window.

PAUSE. LEAVE the desktop open to use in the next exercise.

Recall that a folder is a storage location where you can keep files, subfolders—folders stored within other folders—and links. Most folder windows have the same common elements, so once you learn how to work in one folder you can work in any folder.

Windows Vista comes with a few special folders already set up to help you get started and to organize system information. Table 3-2 describes some of the special folders.

Table 3-2

Windows Vista folders

Folder name	Description
Personal	Each user account has a personal folder, named with the user name assigned to the account. It displays at the top of the right pane on the Start menu. The personal folder contains files that belong only to the assigned user and that are not shared with other people using the same computer. By default, it displays frequently used folders so that you can quickly access your stored data, including documents, pictures, and music.
Documents	The Documents folder is the default folder for storing document files, such as letters, presentations, reports, and spreadsheets. Many programs use Documents as the default storage location for new documents, which means they automatically store new files in Documents unless you specify a different location. The Documents folder is called My Documents in previous versions of Windows.
Computer	The Computer folder provides access to drives and other storage devices as well as to network locations connected to your computer. The Computer folder is called My Computer in previous versions of Windows.
Pictures	The Pictures folder is set up to store and display digital pictures. Many graphics and photo editing programs use Pictures as the default storage location for picture files. The Pictures folder is called My Pictures in previous versions of Windows.
Music	The Music folder is set up to store and organize digital music. Many digital music players use Music as the default storage location for music files. The Music folder is called My Music in previous versions of Windows.
Recycle Bin	The Recycle Bin folder stores items you have deleted but have not yet removed permanently from your computer. You can restore items from the Recycle Bin if you realize you deleted them in error or you can empty the Recycle Bin to remove the items permanently.

Selecting Items in a Folder

To perform any type of command or action on an item, you must first select it. For example, you must select a file to move it. You can select one or more items by using your mouse.

➔ SELECT ITEMS IN A FOLDER

USE the desktop you left displayed in the previous exercise.

1. Click the **Start Button** and then click your personal folder to open it.
2. In the file list, click the **Documents** folder to select it. To select means to mark an item to indicate that it will be affected by the next action or command. The selected item is highlighted and has a selection box around it, as shown in Figure 3-2. A description of the item displays in the Details pane.

Figure 3-2

Select an item

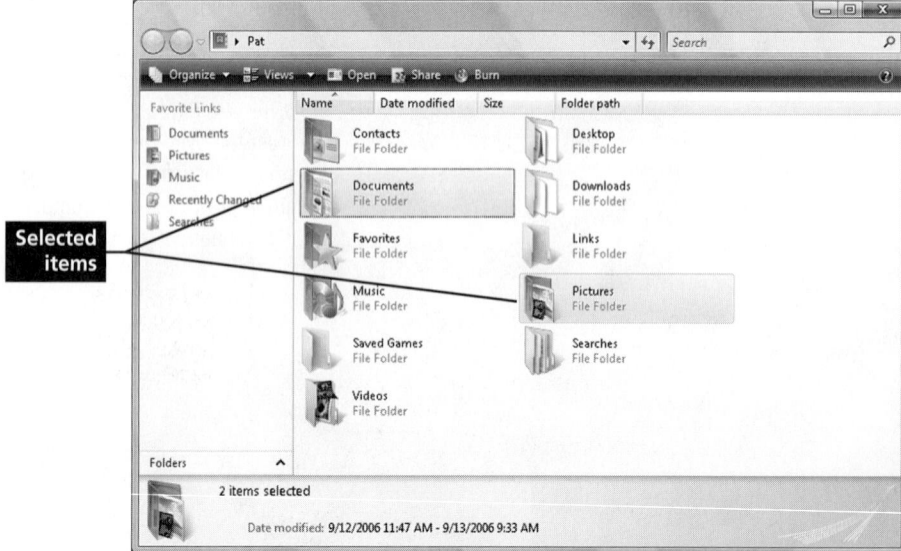

TROUBLESHOOTING

If your computer has been customized to enable single-click launching, you only have to point at an item to select it.

3. In the file list, click the **Pictures** file folder to select it. Notice that Documents is no longer selected.
4. Press and hold down **Ctrl** on your keyboard and then click the **Documents** file folder. Now both items are selected, as shown in Figure 3-3. You can select multiple items anywhere in the list by holding down **Ctrl** while you click.

Figure 3-3

Select multiple items

Working with Files and Folders | 53

> **ANOTHER WAY**
>
> You can also click and drag the mouse pointer around items to select them.

5. Click the first item in the file list—it may be the Contacts file folder—press and hold down Shift on your keyboard, and then click the last item in the file list—it may be Videos. All items in the list are selected. You can select multiple items that are adjacent in a list by holding down Shift while you click.
6. Click any blank area in the file list to deselect the items.
7. Double-click the **Documents** folder icon. The Documents folder opens, replacing your personal folder in the open window.
8. Click the **Back** button to return to your personal folder.
9. Click the **Close** button to close the window.

   PAUSE. LEAVE the desktop open to use in the next exercise.

When you select an item, you make it current, or active. Recall that the current item is the one on which the next action or command will occur. For example, you select a file before you move it or print it.

The easiest way to select an item is to click it. When you want to select more than one item, you combine the click with a key press.

- Press and hold Ctrl while you click to select items that are not adjacent to one another.
- Press and hold Shift while you click to select items that are adjacent to one another.

To cancel a selection, click a blank area in the window or press Esc.

■ Creating and Renaming a Folder

> **THE BOTTOM LINE**
>
> You use folders in Windows Vista to store your computer files just as you use folders to store printed files in a filing cabinet. Every file on your computer is stored in a folder, so it is important to know how to create and name folders. By giving each folder a unique and descriptive name, you can quickly recognize it and know what files it contains. In this exercise, you create a new folder on the desktop, name it, and then rename it.

➔ CREATE AND RENAME A FOLDER

GET READY. Before you begin these steps, start your computer and log on to your Windows Vista account. Close all open windows so you can see the desktop.

1. Point to any blank area of the desktop and then press and release the right mouse button. Recall that this is called right-clicking. A shortcut menu displays.
2. Point to **New** on the shortcut menu to display a submenu, as shown in Figure 3-4. The New submenu displays a list of the types of files, folders, and other items that you can create. The list depends on the programs you have installed on your computer, so the one you see on your desktop is probably not the same as the one in the figure.

Figure 3-4

Shortcut menu

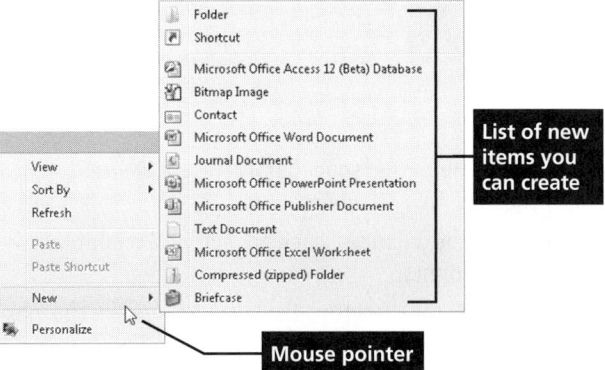

54 | Lesson 3

ANOTHER WAY

To display a shortcut menu by using the keyboard, select an item and then press Shift +F10.

3. Click **Folder** at the top of the New submenu. Windows Vista creates a new folder on the desktop, as shown in Figure 3-5. The default name—New Folder—is selected. In Windows Vista, and most programs that run on Windows Vista, selected text is replaced when you key new text.

Figure 3-5

New folder with default name

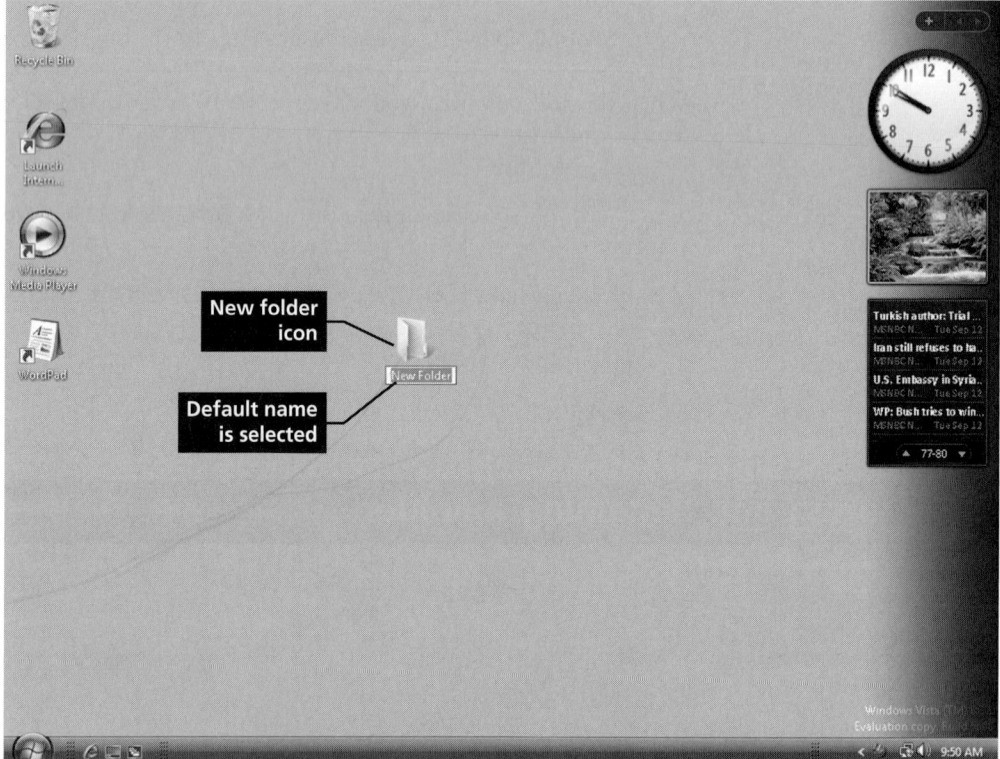

4. Key **Accounts** and then press **Enter**. The new folder is renamed Accounts.
5. Right-click the **Accounts folder icon** and then click **Rename** on the shortcut menu. The folder name—Accounts—is selected.
6. Move the mouse pointer to the left of the first character in the name—A—and click. The text is deselected, and an insertion point displays to the left of the folder name, as shown in Figure 3-6.

Figure 3-6

Renaming a folder

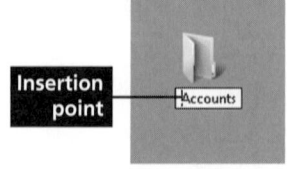

ANOTHER WAY

You can also select a folder name by selecting the folder icon and then clicking the folder name.

7. Key **Active**, press the **spacebar** to insert a space, and then press **Enter**. The folder name changes to Active Accounts.
8. The folder name changes back to Active Accounts. This name is more descriptive than just Accounts.

PAUSE. LEAVE the desktop displayed to use in the next exercise.

 Working with Files and Folders | 55

You can create folders in any storage location on your computer, including disk drives, removable devices, and in other folders. Where you create a folder is important, because it helps you stay organized. If you use a folder often, you may want it on the desktop so you can access it quickly at any time. Sometimes, you might create a *subfolder*, which is a folder within another folder. For example, if you work for a company that has many clients, you might have a folder for each client. In a client's folder, you might have a folder for storing correspondence and a folder for storing invoices.

Using a descriptive name for a folder helps you to identify the folder contents at a glance. For example, if you name a folder Information, you cannot tell what information it contains. If you name the folder Regional Sales Information, you know exactly what the folder contains.

A *shortcut* menu is a list of commands or options relevant to the current task that displays when you right-click an item. The list that appears depends on which *programs* are installed on your computer. Programs, sometimes called applications, are sets of instructions that a computer uses to perform tasks, such as word processing or photo editing.

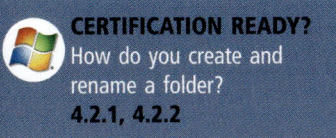
CERTIFICATION READY?
How do you create and rename a folder?
4.2.1, 4.2.2

A folder name can have up to 260 characters, but that includes the complete path to the folder. There are nine characters that you cannot use in a folder name: \ / ? : * " >< |. If you try to key these characters in a folder name, Windows Vista displays a ScreenTip to remind you that they are unavailable. You can begin keying a folder name at the *insertion point*. An insertion point is a blinking vertical bar that indicates the location where text will be inserted.

■ Deleting Files and Folders

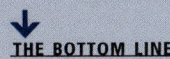
THE BOTTOM LINE

Over time, you will accumulate many files and folders on your computer. Some may continue to be useful, others you may not need any more. To keep your computer from getting cluttered with unnecessary information, you can delete the files and folders that you no longer need. Deleting sends items to the Recycle Bin. In this section, you delete files and folders.

The *Schedule* file is available on the companion CD-ROM.

→ DELETE FILES AND FOLDERS

USE the desktop you left displayed in the previous exercise.

1. Navigate to the data files for this lesson, right-click the *Schedule* file, and then click **Delete** on the shortcut menu. Windows Vista displays a confirmation dialog box, as shown in Figure 3-7, asking if you are sure you want to move the file to the Recycle Bin.

Figure 3-7
Delete confirmation dialog box

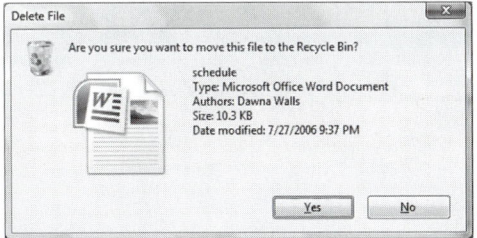

TROUBLESHOOTING

If the confirmation dialog box does not display, someone customized the Recycle Bin settings on your computer so that deleted items are automatically moved to the bin without confirmation. To change this setting, right-click the Recycle Bin icon on the desktop and click Properties. In the Recycle Bin Properties dialog box, click to select the Display delete conformation dialog check box and then click OK.

56 | Lesson 3

2. Click **Yes** to delete the file. Windows Vista deletes the Schedule file from the data folder.
3. Click the **Tailspin Toys Account** folder to select it.
4. Press  on your keyboard. This is an alternative method of deleting an item. Windows Vista displays the confirmation dialog box.
5. Click **Yes** to delete the folder.

> **TAKE NOTE**
>
> You can delete more than one item at a time. Simply select all the items to delete and then press Delete on your keyboard. Or, right-click the selection and click Delete. The confirmation dialog box lists the number of items you have selected.

PAUSE. LEAVE the desktop displayed use in the next exercise.

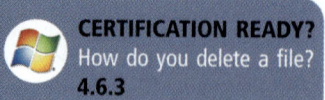

CERTIFICATION READY?
How do you delete a file?
4.6.3

When you delete a folder, note that all items in the folder are deleted as well. For that reason, it is a good idea to open and check the contents of a folder before you delete it.

■ Using the Recycle Bin

> **THE BOTTOM LINE**
>
> The Recycle Bin folder that comes with Windows Vista is the storage location for items that you delete. Items stay in the Recycle Bin until you remove them permanently or restore them to their original location. In this section, you open the Recycle Bin and restore a deleted folder. You then permanently remove a deleted file.

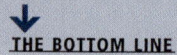 **Use the Recycle Bin**

USE the desktop you left displayed in the previous exercise.

1. On the desktop, double-click the **Recycle Bin** icon to open the Recycle Bin folder window. It should look similar to Figure 3-8. If you or someone else using your computer has deleted other items, they may be listed in the Recycle Bin as well.

Figure 3-8

Items in the Recycle Bin

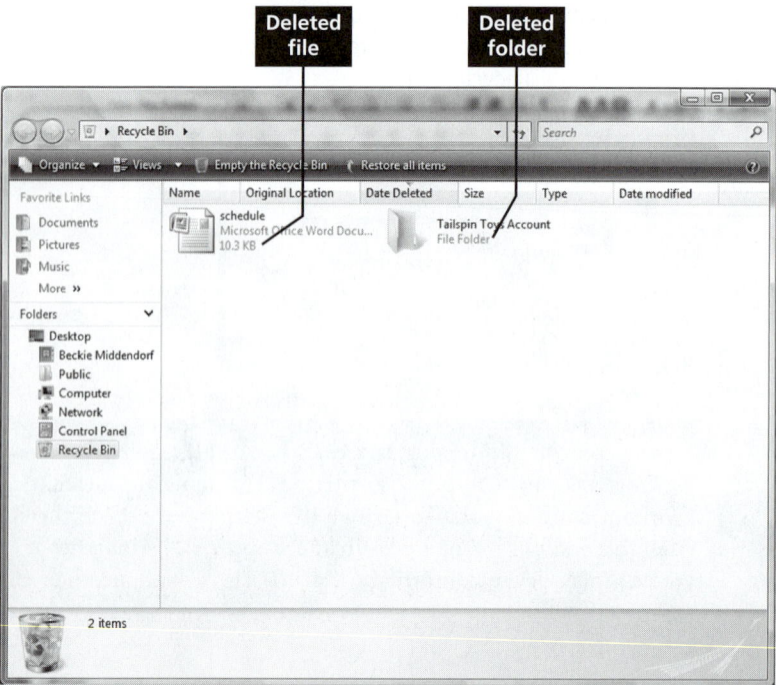

 **Working with Files and Folders | 57**

2. Click the **Tailspin Toys Account** folder to select it.
3. On the Recycle Bin window toolbar, click **Restore this item**. Windows Vista removes the folder from the Recycle Bin and restores it to its original storage location—in this case, the data folder.

> **TROUBLESHOOTING** If you see the button Restore all items instead of Restore this item, it means you did not select an item to restore.

4. Click the **Minimize** button in the Recycle Bin window. The Tailspin Toys Account folder should display in the data folder.

> **TROUBLESHOOTING** The restored folder icon may not display in the same place on the desktop where it displayed before it was deleted. If you don't see it right away, look for it in a line with other icons.

5. Delete the Tailspin Toys Account folder to send it back to the Recycle Bin.
6. Click the **Recycle Bin** window taskbar button to restore the window.
7. On the Recycle Bin window toolbar, click **Empty the Recycle Bin**. Windows Vista displays a confirmation dialog box, as shown in Figure 3-9, asking if you are sure you want to permanently delete the items.

Figure 3-9

Delete confirmation dialog box

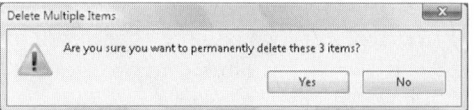

8. Click **Yes** to permanently delete the items. The Recycle Bin folder is now empty.
9. **CLOSE** the Recycle Bin folder window.

   PAUSE. LEAVE the desktop displayed use in the next exercise.

> **TAKE NOTE** To permanently delete an item without emptying the entire bin, right-click the item in the Recycle Bin and click Delete on the shortcut menu.

The Recycle Bin can save you from many an errant deletion, because you can always locate a file or folder and restore it. Note that when you restore a folder, all of the items in the folder that were deleted are restored as well.

You may be tempted to leave every deleted item in your Recycle Bin forever, just in case you need it in the future. However, items in the Recycle Bin take up storage space on your disk drive. If you never empty the Recycle Bin, some day space will run low. Once you are certain you no longer need the items in the bin, you should empty it to free up space.

You may have noticed that the Recycle Bin icon on the desktop changes depending on whether it contains items or is empty. If it is empty, the icon resembles an empty basket. If it contains items, paper is in the basket.

You can empty the Recycle Bin without opening the folder window by right-clicking the icon on the desktop and clicking Empty Recycle Bin, but you must open the window to restore items.

You can permanently delete or restore individual items using shortcut menus. Just right-click the item to affect and then select the desired command.

58 | Lesson **3**

■ Navigating through Windows

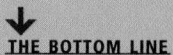
THE BOTTOM LINE

To locate and organize the data you have stored on your computer system, it is important to know how to navigate from one storage location to another. You can use the many navigational tools that Windows Vista provides to browse forward and back through folders or jump directly to a specific location.

Browsing through Recently Opened Windows

Use the Forward and Back buttons on a window's toolbar to browse through windows you have opened recently. Click the Back button to view the previous window. Click the Forward button to return to the window that was open before you clicked Back. Use the Recent Pages dropdown menu to select from a list of recently opened windows.

→ BROWSE THROUGH RECENTLY OPENED WINDOWS

USE the desktop you left displayed in the previous exercise.

1. Click **Start** and then click **Computer** to open the Computer folder window. Recall that the Computer window displays components of your computer system, such as disk drives and other devices.

2. In the file list, double-click the **Local Disk (C:)** icon to change to the folder that displays the contents of your hard disk drive.

TROUBLESHOOTING

By default, Windows Vista replaces the contents of the current window with the next folder that you open, but it can be customized to open each folder in a separate window. If the Local Disk (C:) folder opens in a new, separate window, your system has been customized. To restore the default settings, click Organize on the window's toolbar, click Folder and Search options, click the Restore Defaults button, and then click OK.

3. In the file list, double-click the **Program Files** folder to change to the Program Files folder. The Program Files folder is where Windows Vista stores the files for the programs installed on your computer. It should look similar to Figure 3-10, although the specific contents depend on the programs you have installed.

Figure 3-10

Program Files folder

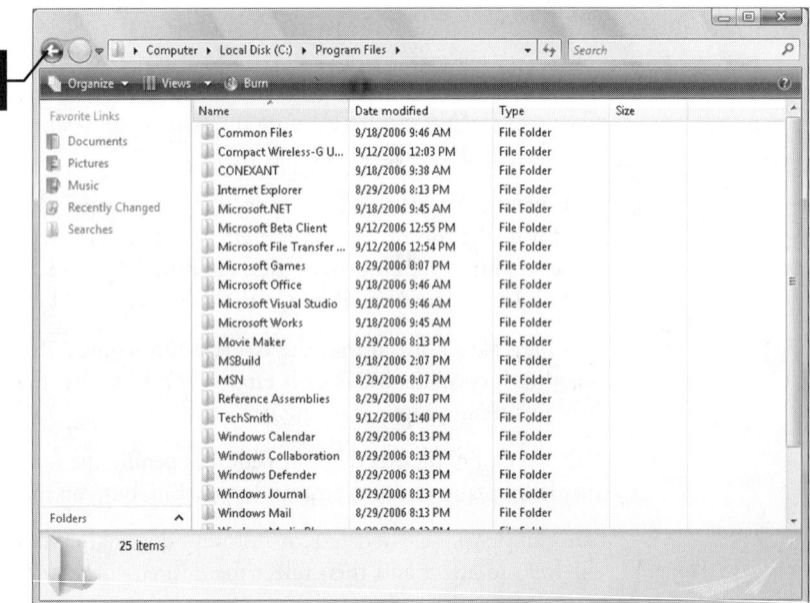

 Working with Files and Folders | 59

4. Click the **Back** button on the Program Files window toolbar. The previous folder displays—in this case, the Local Disk (C:) window. Notice that once you click Back, the Forward button becomes available as well.

5. Click the **Forward** button on the window toolbar. The folder that was open before you clicked Back displays again—in this case, Program Files. Now only the Back button is available, because there are no other folders to go forward to.

6. Double-click the **Windows Photo Gallery** folder icon to change to the folder where the files for the Windows Photo Gallery program are stored. (You may have to scroll down the file list to locate the folder.) Windows Photo Gallery comes with Windows Vista. It is a program for viewing and organizing pictures.

7. Click the **Back** button on the window toolbar to return to the previous folder (Program Files) and then click the **Back** button again to return to folder open prior to that—Local Disk (C:).

8. Click the **Forward** button to change to the Program Files folder and then click the **Forward** button again to change to the Windows Photo Gallery folder.

9. Click the **Recent Pages** dropdown arrow to the right of the Forward button. A menu of all the locations you have viewed during the current session displays, as shown in Figure 3-11. A checkmark indicates the current location.

Figure 3-11

Recent Pages menu

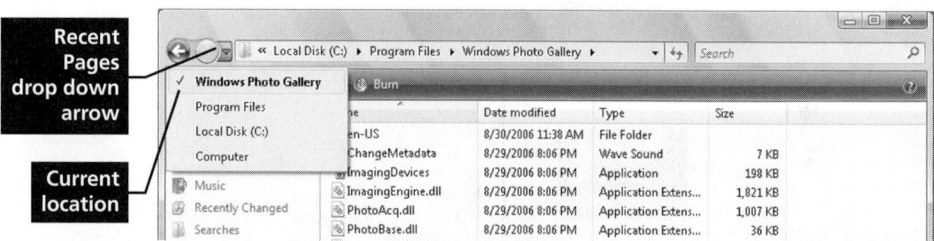

You can use ScreenTips to help identify buttons on the window toolbar, including the Recent Pages dropdown arrow. You'll notice that the ScreenTip for the Back and Forward buttons changes to indicate the window that will display when you click the button. For example, the ScreenTip for the Back button might say Back to Computer if the previous window was Computer.

10. Click **Computer** on the Recent Pages menu to change to the Computer folder. When you click a location on the Recent Pages menu, you go directly to that folder instead of browsing through all previously opened folders.

    PAUSE. LEAVE the Computer folder open to use in the next exercise.

Browsing lets you easily move back and forth among the folders you have been using. However, it may not be convenient when you need to access a completely different storage location. In the next section, you practice navigating using the options in the Navigation pane.

Using the Navigation Pane

The Favorite Links in the Navigation pane let you quickly open common folders, such as Documents or Pictures. You can expand the Folders list to access any location on your system.

USE THE NAVIGATION PANE

USE the Computer folder you left open in the previous exercise.

1. In the Favorite Links list in the Navigation pane, click **Pictures** to change to the Pictures folder.

2. Click **Music** to change to the Music folder.

60 | Lesson 3

3. Click **Documents** to change to the Documents folder.

4. To expand the Folders list, click **Folders**, or the up arrow icon to the right of the word Folders, at the bottom of the Navigation pane. The Folders list displays the contents of your computer as a hierarchical, or tree, diagram at the top is the root folder, which is the desktop. All folders and subfolders branch off the root.

> **TROUBLESHOOTING** To see more items in the Folders list, increase the height of the current window by dragging a top or bottom window border or by maximizing the window.

5. Move the mouse pointer over your personal folder near the top of the Folders list. Arrowheads display to the left of items that contain subfolders or files, as shown in Figure 3-12. A solid black arrowhead—the collapse arrow—indicates that the folder is *expanded*, which mean that the contents of the folder display in the list. A clear arrowhead—the expand arrow—indicates that the folder is *collapsed*, which means its contents are hidden.

Figure 3-12

Folders list

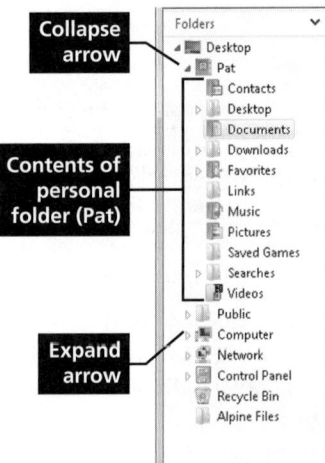

6. Click your personal folder in the Folders list. Clicking an item in the Folders list makes that item current. The contents display in the File list area of the window.

7. Click the collapse arrow to the left of your personal folder in the Folders list. The folder collapses in the Folders list to hide its subfolders, but it is still current, and its contents still display in the window's File list. Once the folder is collapsed, the arrow changes to an expand arrow.

8. Click the **expand arrow** to the left of Computer in the Folders list. The Folders list expands to display the contents of the Computer folder, and the arrow changes to a collapse arrow, as shown in Figure 3-13. Notice that clicking the arrowhead does not make the Computer folder current. The contents of your personal folder still display in the File list.

Working with Files and Folders | 61

Figure 3-13

Collapse and expand the Folders list

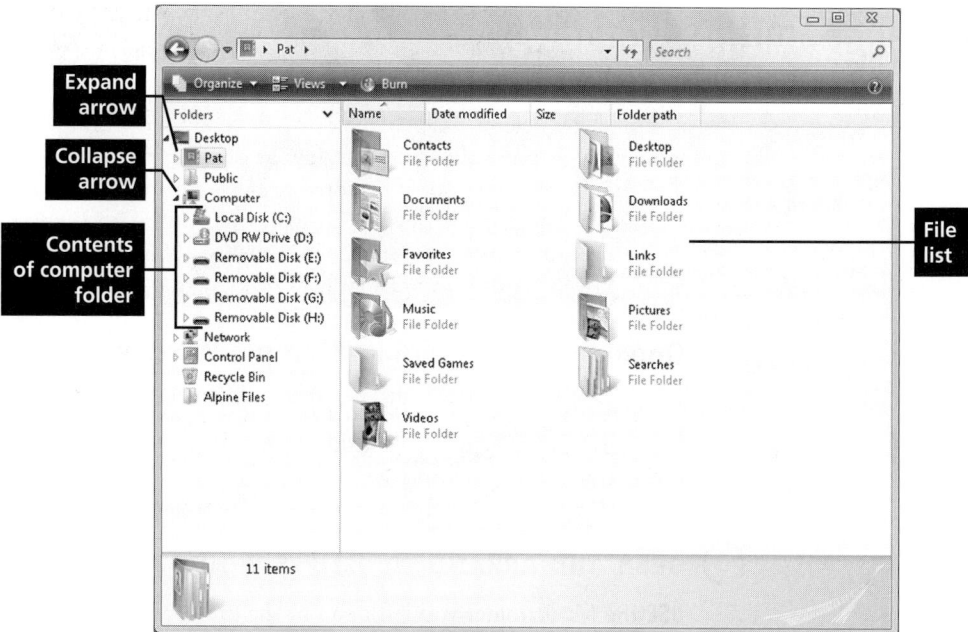

TAKE NOTE* You can change the width of the Navigation pane by dragging the border between the pane and the File list. For example, to make the pane wider, drag the border to the right. To make the pane narrower, drag the border to the left.

9. Click **Local Disk (C:)** in the Folders list to make it current.
10. Click the **expand arrow** to the left of your personal folder and then click the **expand arrow** to the left of Favorites. (You may have to scroll the Folders list to locate the items.) The Folders list expands, but the current folder is still Local Disk (C:).
11. Click the collapse arrow to the left of Favorites and then click **Music**. Music is now the current folder.
12. Click **Folders**, or the down arrow icon to the right of Folders, to collapse the entire Folders list.

    PAUSE. LEAVE the Music folder open to use in the next exercise.

The Folders list in the Navigation pane is useful because you can see the entire storage system of your computer while working with the contents of a specific folder. You can easily move among the many storage locations without browsing through multiple folders, simply by expanding the folder list and then clicking the location you want to make current. The contents of an *expanded* folder are displayed in a list. A clear arrowhead—the expand arrow—indicates that the folder is *collapsed*, which means its contents are hidden.

You can also work with folders in the Navigation pane in much the same way you work with them in their storage locations. For example, you can rename a folder or delete it. Simply right-click the folder in the Folders list to display a shortcut menu and then select the command you want to use.

Using Multiple Windows

THE BOTTOM LINE

Although by default each folder opens in the same window, sometimes you might want to work with more than one window at once. For example, you might want to compare the contents of two folders or copy or move an item from one folder to another or from a folder to a removable device. Or, you might want to use the Calculator while you view an invoice document. You can open a new window at any time. In this section, you open multiple windows, arrange windows on the desktop, and change the active window.

Opening and Arranging Multiple Windows

There is no limit to the number of windows you can have open at once. To open additional windows, simply click the Start Button and select the window you want to open. You can arrange multiple windows so that you can see each window in its entirety or so that they overlap evenly. In this section, you practice arranging multiple windows.

OPEN AND ARRANGE MULTIPLE WINDOWS

USE the Music folder you left open in the previous exercise.

1. Click the **Start Button** and then click your personal folder. It opens in a new window, overlapping the Music window, which was already open.
2. Click the **Start Button** again and then click **Computer** to open the Computer folder in a new window. Now three windows are open, as shown in Figure 3-14. (The size and position of the three windows on your screen may differ from the illustration.)

Figure 3-14

Three windows open at once

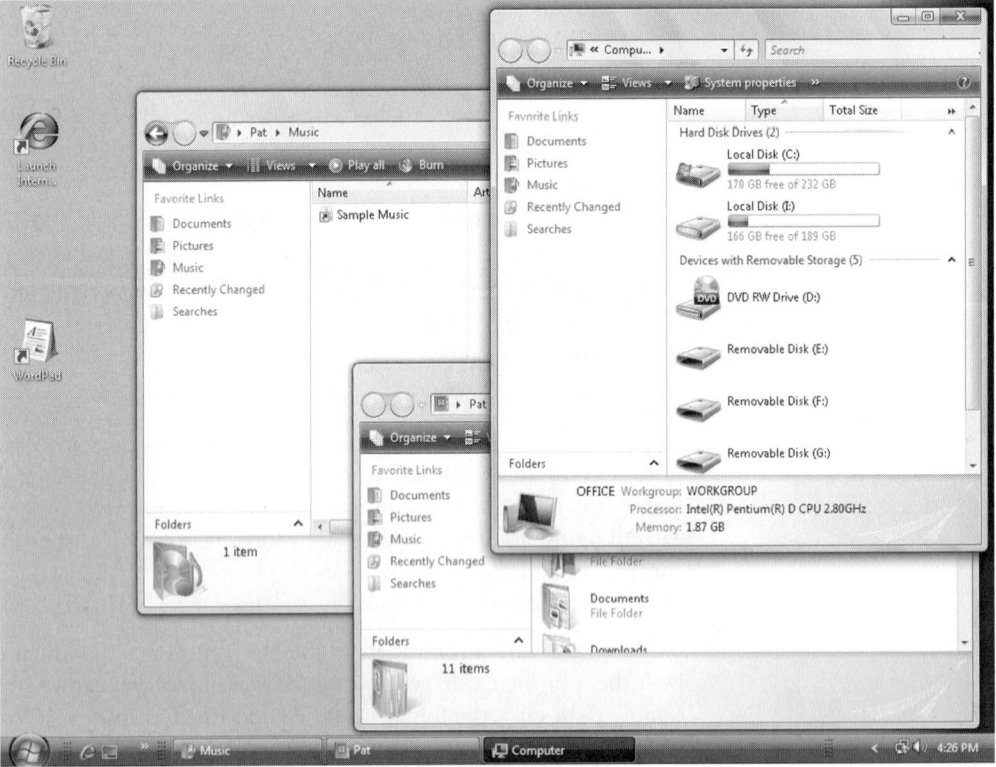

3. Right-click a blank area of the Windows taskbar. A shortcut menu displays.
4. Click **Cascade Windows** on the shortcut menu. Windows Vista cascades the open windows, which means that they overlap one another in an orderly fashion, starting in the upper-left corner of the desktop, as shown in Figure 3-15. The active window, which is on top, displays in its entirety, and only the top and left of the other windows are visible.

 **Working with Files and Folders | 63**

Figure 3-15

Cascading windows overlap

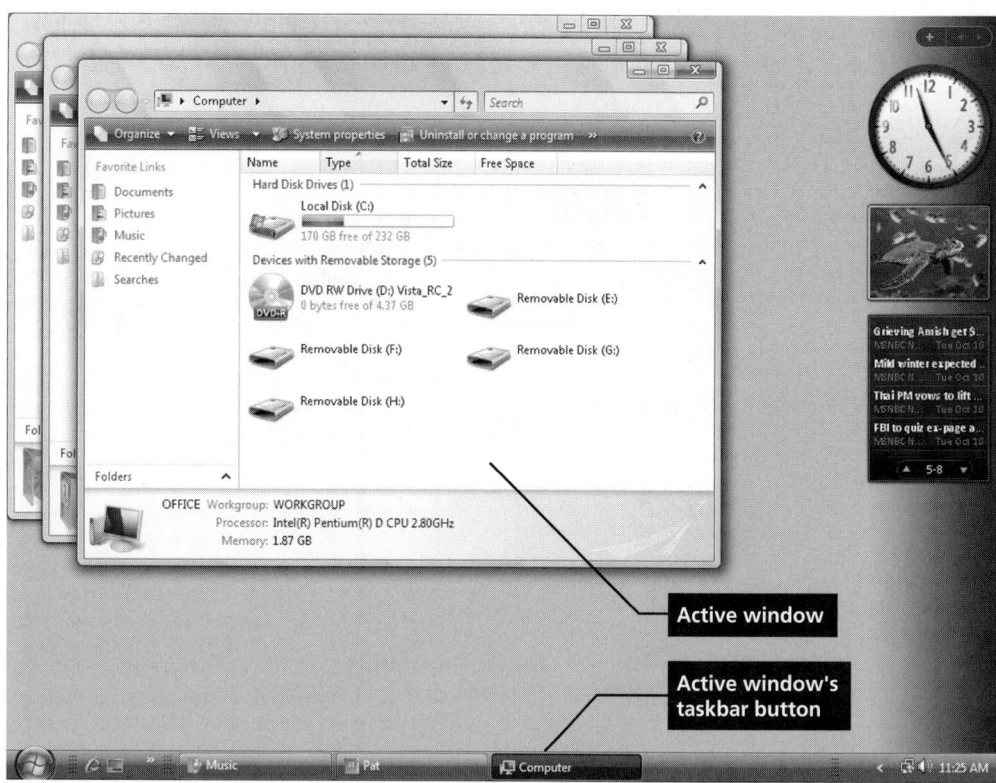

5. Right-click a blank area of the taskbar and click **Show Windows Stacked**. Windows Vista stacks the windows, or tiles them horizontally, which means they are sized to display one above the other without overlapping, as shown in Figure 3-16.

Figure 3-16

Stacked windows are tiled horizontally

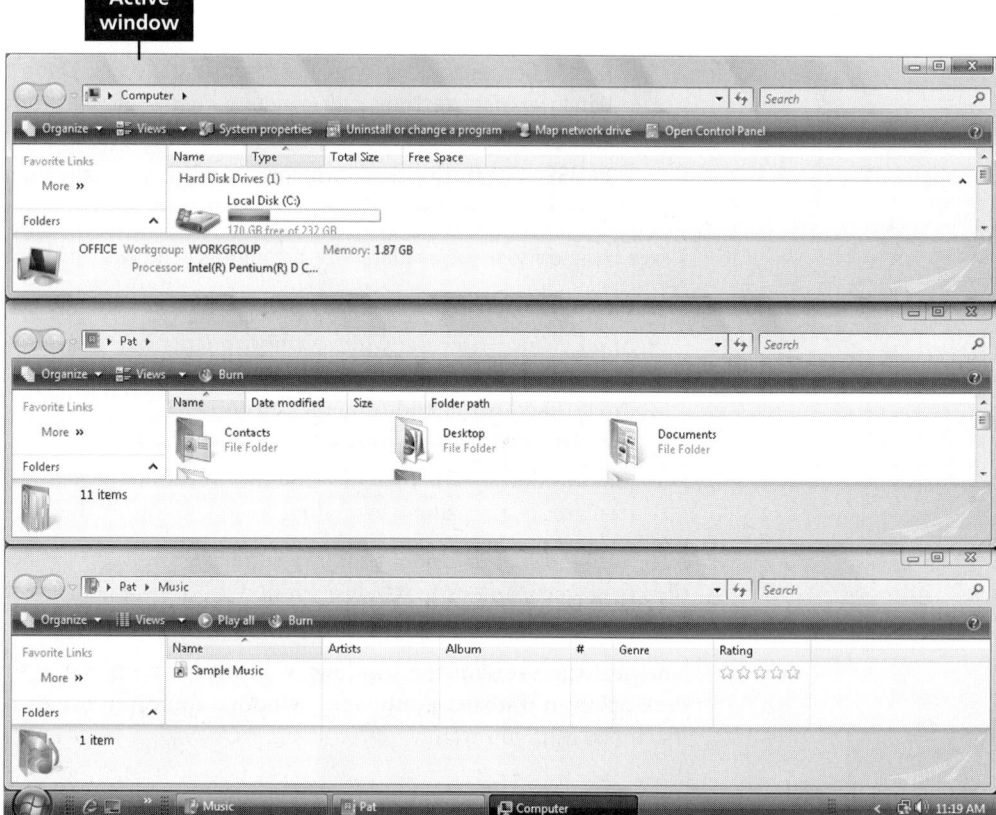

6. Right-click a blank area of the taskbar and click **Show Windows Side by Side**. Windows Vista tiles the window vertically, which means they are sized to display next to each other without overlapping, as shown in Figure 3-17.

Figure 3-17

Side by side windows are tiled vertically.

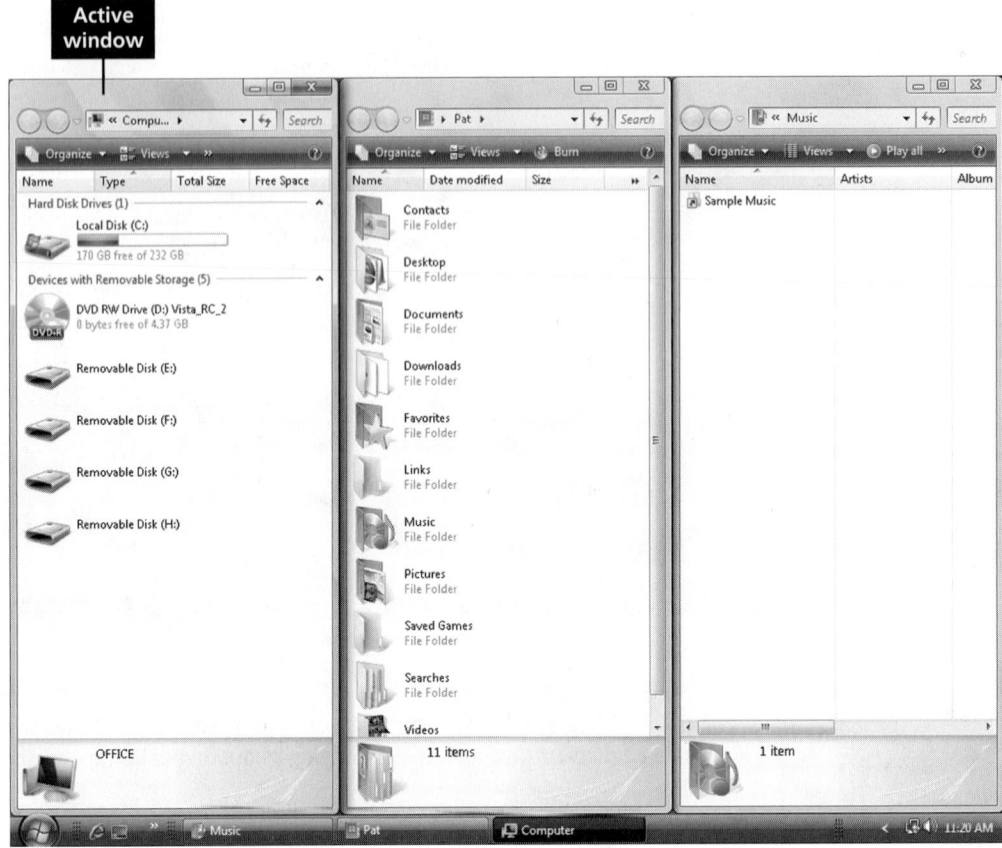

7. Right-click a blank area of the taskbar and click **Undo Show Side by Side**. Windows Vista restores the windows to the previous arrangement, in this case stacked vertically.

   PAUSE. LEAVE the three windows stacked vertically to use in the next exercise.

Three basic options are available for arranging windows on the desktop:

- *Cascade*, which overlaps the windows evenly, with the active window on top.
- *Stack*, which *tiles* the windows horizontally one above the other. Each window displays in its entirety. If there are only two or three windows, each window extends across the width of the screen. If there are more than three windows, they are sized to fit so that none of them overlap.
- Side by side, which tiles the windows vertically next to each other. Each window displays in its entirety, extending from the top of the screen to the bottom.

Keep in mind that the more windows you have open, the smaller each one displays when tiled or stacked. You can exclude a window from an arrangement by minimizing it before selecting the command to cascade, stack, or arrange side by side.

The next time you open a window, it displays in its previous size and position on the desktop, even if it is the only open window. You can move or resize the window, or maximize it, if you want.

 **Working with Files and Folders | 65**

Changing the Active Window

No matter how many windows are open, only one can be active, or current. You can easily change the active window.

→ CHANGE THE ACTIVE WINDOW

USE the stacked windows you left open in the previous exercise.

1. Click the **Music** window. Clicking a window makes it active. Notice that the Close button in the active window is red, and that the window's taskbar button appears pressed in. In addition, the window's border and background are brighter.
2. Right-click a blank area of the taskbar and click **Cascade Windows**. When the windows are cascaded, it may be difficult to click in the one you want to make active.
3. Click the taskbar button for your personal folder. Clicking a taskbar button makes the window active. Notice that the active window moves in front of the other open windows.
4. Press and hold **Alt** and then press **Tab**. A pane opens in the middle of the desktop, displaying previews of each open window, as shown in Figure 3-18. A selection rectangle displays around one preview, and the window name displays at the top of the pane.

Figure 3-18

Alt + Tab switching

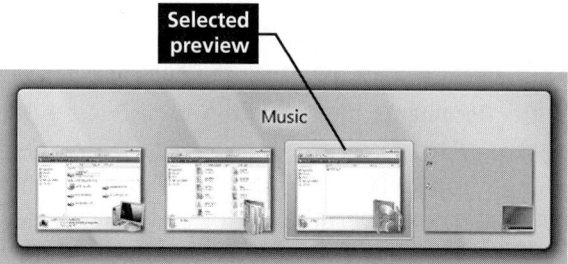

5. While continuing to hold down **Alt**, press **Tab** again, and the selection rectangle moves to the next preview. Press **Tab** until the selection rectangle is around Computer, then release **Tab** and **Alt**. Computer becomes active. This procedure is called Alt + Tab switching, and you can use it to cycle through all open windows.
6. Close the Computer window. Make your personal folder active and then close it. Make Music active and then close it.

   PAUSE. LEAVE the desktop displayed to use in the next exercise.

You can only work in the active window, no matter how many windows are open at the same time. Windows Vista provides many tools for changing the active window.

- The easiest way to make a window active is to click in it.
- You can click a taskbar button to make its window active.
- Use Alt + Tab switching to cycle through all open windows. Release both the Alt key and the Tab key when the window you want to make active is selected.

TAKE NOTE* On some systems, the Quick Launch toolbar on the taskbar displays a Switch Between Windows button. When you click the button, Windows Vista displays a 3-D view of all open windows. You can click a window to make it active.

Moving Files and Folders

THE BOTTOM LINE

You can move a file or folder from one storage location to another. This is useful for reorganizing your storage system. In addition, you can move a file or folder to a removable disk to give to someone else or to take to a different computer, or you can move a file or folder to a network drive so others can access it. You can move items by using the Cut and Paste commands or by dragging them to the new location.

Moving Files and Folders

➔ MOVE FILES AND FOLDERS

USE the desktop you left displayed in the previous exercise.

1. Click **Start** and then click **Documents** to open the Documents folder. Click the **Minimize b**utton to minimize the Documents window.
2. Right-click a blank area of the desktop, point to **New** on the shortcut menu, and then click **Folder**.
3. Key **Alpine Files** and then press [Enter] to rename the new folder.
4. Right-click the **Alpine Files** folder and click **Cut** on the shortcut menu. The Cut command moves an item from its source location and places it in the Clipboard. A source location is the location where the item was originally stored. The Clipboard is a temporary storage area that can hold one item at a time.
5. Click the **Documents** taskbar button to restore the window.
6. Right-click a blank area of the File list in the Documents window and click **Paste** on the shortcut menu. The Paste command copies the item from the Clipboard to its destination location, which is the new storage location. (The destination is sometimes called the target.) In this case, Windows Vista pastes the Alpine Files folder into the Documents window.
7. Right-click a blank area of the File list, point to **New**, and then click **Folder**. Key **Ad Text** and press [Enter] to rename the new folder.
8. Drag the **Ad Text** folder icon onto the Alpine Files folder icon, as shown in Figure 3-19. Notice that when you drag the item over a potential destination, it displays an arrow and the message Move to *destination name*.

TAKE NOTE*

Note that only one item can be stored on the Clipboard at a time. Each item that you cut—or copy—replaces the item currently on the Clipboard.

TAKE NOTE*

When you move a folder, any items stored in the folder also are moved.

Figure 3-19

Drag an item to move it

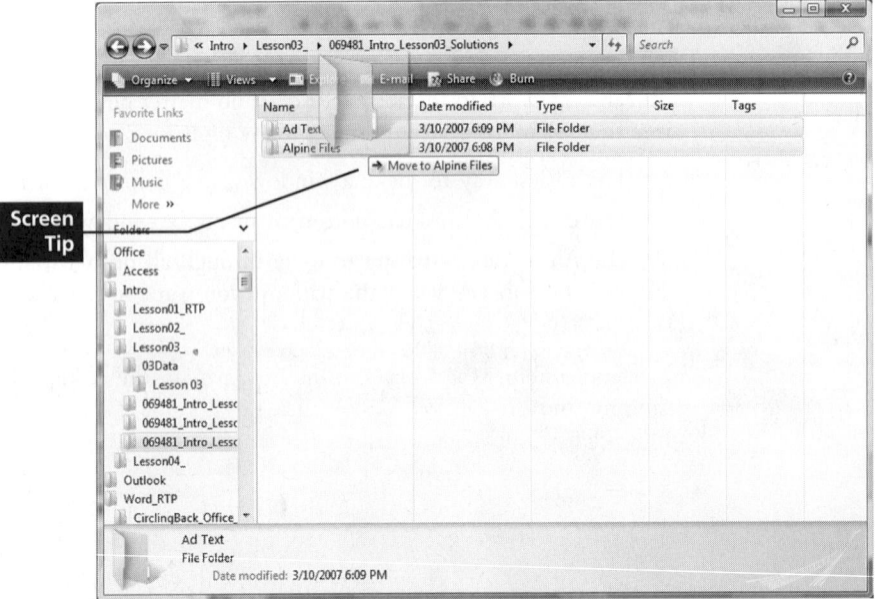

 **Working with Files and Folders | 67**

9. When the ScreenTip message is Move to Alpine Files, release the mouse button. Windows Vista moves the file. Notice that the Ad Text file icon no longer displays in the Documents file list.
10. Double-click the **Alpine Files** folder icon to open it. The Ad Text folder displays in the File list.

You can use the Folders list in the Navigation pane to move folders. Expand the Folders list so you can see both the original location and the destination, then drag the item from the original location to the destination. You can also drag items from the File list to a folder in the Folders list, and vice versa. Alternatively, right-click the item that you want to move and then click Cut. Then right-click the destination and click Paste.

PAUSE. LEAVE the Alpine Files folder open to use in the next exercise.

As you have just seen, moving an item deletes it from its original *source location* and places it in a new *destination location*. As with most tasks, Windows Vista provides multiple options for moving files and folders. Each has benefits for use in different situations. As you become more comfortable working with Windows Vista, you will be able to select the method that works best for you.

The Cut and Paste commands provide a versatile method for moving files and folders, because once an item is cut to the *Clipboard*, you can navigate away from the source to locate the destination. Each item stays on the Clipboard until you cut—or copy—another item. That means that you can paste an item from the Clipboard as many times as you want, into many different locations. In addition, Cut and Paste are available on shortcut menus, so they are easily accessible from any location.

The drag and drop method is useful when you can see both the source and the destination locations on the screen at the same time. For example, you can move an item to a subfolder in the same folder you used in the previous exercise. You can also stack or arrange windows side by side so you can drag items from one window to another or use the Folders list in the Navigation pane. Dragging is quick and easy and does not require any menus or commands.

You can move multiple items at the same time using either the Cut and Paste commands or the drag and drop methods. Simply select all of the items you want to move and then move the items.

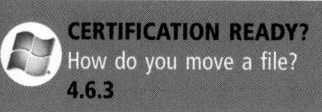

Both the Clipboard and drag and drop methods are also used in programs that run on Windows Vista to move selected data, such as text, graphics, and even formulas in a spreadsheet. So, once you learn to move files and folder in Windows Vista, you will be able to transfer that knowledge to your application programs.

■ Managing Files and Folders

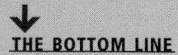

You copy files and folders from one location to another in order to have multiple versions of the same item available. Copying does not delete the original file—it simply creates an exact replica that can be stored for safekeeping, shared with someone else, or taken to a different computer. The methods for copying are similar to those for moving. You can use the Copy and Paste commands or you can press and hold Ctrl while dragging an item to the new location.

Copying to a Different Folder

You can easily copy a file or folder to a different folder on your computer. You—or others—can edit the copy while the original remains unchanged in its original location. In this exercise, you will copy a file—supplied with this book—from the data files storage location to the Alpine Files folder. You will then create a new folder and copy two files into it.

68 | Lesson 3

→ **COPY TO A DIFFERENT FOLDER**

The ***Alpine_Photo1*** file is available on the companion CD-ROM.

USE the Alpine Files folder you left open in the previous exercise.

1. Navigate to the *Alpine_Photo1* file in the data files for this lesson.
2. Right-click the *Alpine_Photo1* file icon and then click **Copy** on the shortcut menu. This copies the item to the Clipboard, leaving the original file in its source location.
3. Navigate to the Alpine Files folder.
4. Right-click a blank area of the File list and then click **Paste** on the shortcut menu. Windows Vista pastes a copy of the *Alpine_Photo1* file into the Alpine Files folder.
5. In the Alpine Files folder, create a new folder named **Files for Review**.
6. Right-click the *Ad Text* folder in the Alpine Files folder and then click **Copy** on the shortcut menu.
7. Right-click the **Files for Review** folder icon and then click **Paste** on the shortcut menu. Windows Vista pastes a copy of the Ad Text folder into the Files for Review folder.
8. Double-click the **Files for Review** folder to open it.
9. Click **Start**, click **Documents**, and then double-click the **Alpine Files** folder to open it.
10. Right-click a blank area of the taskbar and click **Show Windows Stacked** on the shortcut menu. With the windows stacked on the screen, you can see both copies of the Ad Text folder.
11. Press and hold **Ctrl** and drag the *Alpine_Photo1* file from the Alpine Files folder window to the Files for Review folder window. A plus sign displays with the icon as you drag, and the ScreenTip indicates that you are copying—not moving—the item. Also, a vertical bar indicates the location where the copied file will be inserted.
12. Release the mouse button to copy the file into the Files for Review folder. Now both the **Ad Text** folder and *Alpine_Photo1* files are stored in the **Alpine Files** folder and in the **Files for Review** folder.
13. Close the Files for Review window.

    PAUSE. LEAVE the Alpine Files folder open to use in the next exercise.

The same rules apply to the Clipboard when you copy as when you cut.

- Only one item can be stored on the Clipboard at a time. As long as the item is on the Clipboard, you can paste it into many different locations.
- You can copy multiple items at the same time by using either the Cut and Paste commands or the drag and drop method. Simply select all items you want to copy before performing the copy action.
- Both the Clipboard and drag and drop methods are used in programs that run on Windows Vista to copy selected data.

Be careful when you copy files and folders that you do not clutter your computer with too many copies of the same item, because you may have trouble keeping track of which item is which. It is a good idea to rename copied items so you can tell them apart.

Copying a file to a different folder on the same computer is not a good way to back up your data. To ***back up*** means to create a copy of data for safekeeping. A mechanical failure that causes the drive to stop working or a disaster, such as a fire or flood, would affect both files. To keep a copy safe, you must copy it to a remote location, such as a network, or to a removable device so you can physically take it to a different location, such as a safe.
In the next section, you copy items to a removable storage device.

 **Working with Files and Folders | 69**

Copying to a Storage Device

When you want to create a copy of a file or folder that you physically take away from your computer, you can copy it to a removable storage device. This is useful for keeping a copy safe in a different location, creating a copy you can use on your home computer, or giving a copy to someone else. Use the Send to command to quickly copy an item to a storage device.

➔ COPY TO A STORAGE DEVICE

GET READY. Before you begin these steps, insert a removable storage device into your computer. For example, insert a CD or DVD into a compatible drive, insert a floppy disk into a floppy disk drive, or plug a flash drive into a USB port. You may also use an external hard drive attached to a USB port or a network drive. If an AutoPlay window displays, click the Close button.

1. Right-click the **Files for Review** folder in the Alpine Files folder window.
2. Point to **Send To** on the shortcut menu. A menu of available locations displays, as shown in Figure 3-20. (The locations on your computer will be different from those in the illustration, depending on the number and type of devices you have available.)

Figure 3-20

Send To menu

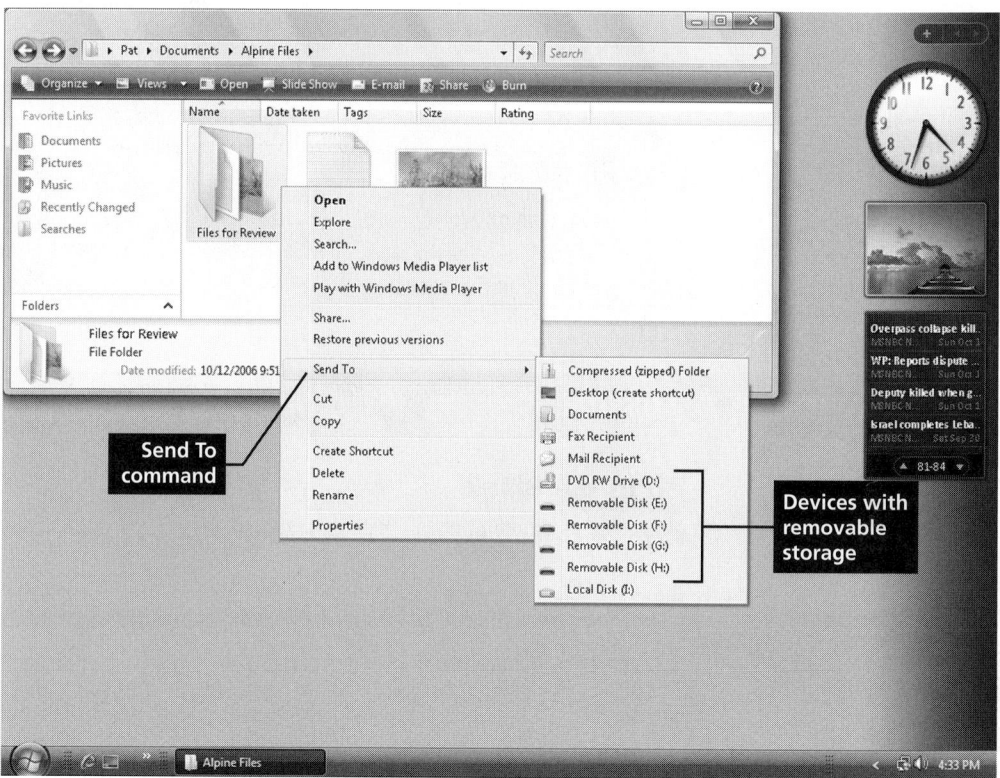

3. On the menu, click the device in which you have inserted the removable media. Windows Vista copies the folder and opens a window for the device.

TROUBLESHOOTING Some devices, such as CD and DVD drives, may prompt you to prepare or format the disk before copying the items. Click OK or Next, or press Enter to continue.

4. In the device window, double-click the **Files for Review** folder to open it. Notice that when you copy a folder, all items in the folder are copied as well.
5. Close the device window. Remove the media and label it **Files for Review**, with your name.

   STOP. Log off and shut down your computer.

70 | Lesson 3

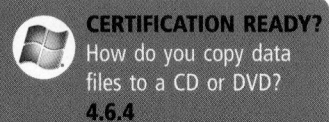

CERTIFICATION READY?
How do you copy data files to a CD or DVD?
4.6.4

You can also use the Copy and Paste commands and drag and drop method to copy or move items to a removable or network device. Also, most CD and DVD drives come with their own software programs that you can use to transfer data—including music, pictures, and videos—onto a disk.

SUMMARY SKILL MATRIX

IN THIS LESSON YOU LEARNED HOW TO:
Open and Close a Folder Window
Select Items in a Folder
Create and Rename a Folder
Delete Files and Folders
Use the Recycle Bin
Browse Through Recently Opened Windows
Use the Navigation Pane
Open and Arrange Multiple Windows
Change the Active Window
Move Files and Folders
Copy to a Different Folder
Copy to a Storage Device

■ Knowledge Assessment

Fill in the Blank

Complete the following sentences by writing the correct word or words in the blanks provided.

1. A(n) __shortcut__ menu is a list of commands or options relevant to the current task that displays when you right-click and item.
2. A menu that opens off of another menu is called a(n) __submenu__.
3. By __stacking__ windows, you tile them horizontally so that they display one above the other without overlapping.
4. The blinking vertical bar that indicates the location where text will be inserted is called the insertion __insertion__.
5. Arranging windows to overlap one another in an orderly fashion, starting in the upper-left corner of the desktop, is also known as __cascading__ the windows.
6. You must __sel__ an item to indicate that it will be affected by the next action or command.
7. You can have as many __win.__ as you want open at the same time.
8. You can __expand__, or display, the contents of a folder in a list or menu by clicking an arrow next to the folder name.
9. You can have __one__ active window(s) at a time.
10. Pressing the __back__ button displays the previously viewed folder.

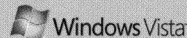 **Working with Files and Folders | 71**

True/False

Circle T if the statement is true or F if the statement is false.

T **(F)** 1. There is no limit to the length of a folder name. up to 260

T **(F)** 2. You can only delete one item at a time using Windows Vista.

(T) F 3. You cannot use a question mark in a folder name.

T **(F)** 4. You can only select one item at a time in a file list.

(T) F 5. You can hide the contents of a folder in a list or menu by clicking the collapse arrow next to the folder name.

T **(F)** 6. Stacking a window changes the active window.

(T) F 7. The Send to command can be used to quickly copy a file or folder to a storage device.

(T) F 8. The new storage location for a moved or copied file is the destination location.

T **(F)** 9. When you delete a file, it is permanently erased from your computer.

T **(F)** 10. Items in the Recycle Bin are stored in your computer's memory, so they do not take up any storage space on your disk drive.

■ Competency Assessment

Project 3-1: Prepare for Family Photos

A relative plans to send you family photos in digital format so you can select one to use for a New Year's Card. In this exercise, you will prepare a folder for storing the digital files. When the relative fails to send the photos, you delete the folder.

GET READY. Before you begin these steps, start your computer and log on to your Windows Vista account. Close all open windows so you can see the desktop.

1. Right-click a blank area of the desktop to display the shortcut menu.
2. Point to **New** on the shortcut menu to display a submenu.
3. Click **Folder** on the submenu to create a new folder.
4. Key **Card Photos** and then press **Enter** to rename the folder.
5. Right-click the **Card Photos** folder icon and then click **Rename**.
6. Key **NY Card Photos** and then press **Enter**.
7. Right-click a blank area of the desktop and then click **Undo Rename** to restore the name to Card Photos.
8. Double-click the **Card Photos** folder to open it.
9. Close the Card Photos folder and then press **Delete**. Click **Yes** in the confirmation dialog box.
10. Double-click the **Recycle Bin** icon on the desktop to open it.
11. Click **Empty the Recycle Bin** on the toolbar and then click **Yes** in the confirmation dialog box to permanently delete all items.
12. **CLOSE** the Recycle Bin folder window.

PAUSE. LEAVE the desktop displayed to use in the next project.

Project 3-2: Explore Sample Windows Vista Folders

Explore the music and picture samples that come with Windows Vista.

1. Use the Start menu to open the Music folder.
2. Double-click the **Sample Music** shortcut to open the Sample Music folder.

72 | Lesson 3

3. Click the **Amanda** music file. If the Amanda file is not available, select a different file. Write down the filename, date, author, and size.
4. In the Navigation pane, click **Pictures** to open the Pictures folder.
5. Double-click the **Sample Picture** shortcut to open the Sample Picture folder.
6. Click the first picture in the file list.
7. Click the **Back** button.
8. **CLOSE** the folder window.

   PAUSE. LEAVE the desktop displayed to use in the next project.

■ Proficiency Assessment

Project 3-3: Potential Clients

Your manager asks you to prepare folders for storing information about two potential clients. The clients never sign a contract, so you must then delete the folders.

1. Right-click a blank area of the desktop, point to **New** on the shortcut menu, and then click **Folder**.
2. Key **Potential Clients** and then press **Enter**.
3. Open the **Potential Clients** folder.
4. Right-click a blank area of the folder window, point to **New**, and then click **Folder**.
5. Key **Trey Research** and then press **Enter**.
6. Right-click a blank area of the folder window, point to **New**, and then click **Folder**.
7. Key **Contoso, Inc.** and then press **Enter**.
8. Right-click the **Contoso, Inc.** folder icon and then click **Rename**.
9. Key **Contoso, Ltd.** and then press **Enter**.
10. Right-click the **Trey Research** folder icon and then click **Delete**. Click **Yes** in the confirmation dialog box to send the folder to the Recycle Bin.
11. Right-click the **Contoso, Ltd.** folder icon and then click **Delete**. Click **Yes** in the confirmation dialog box to send the folder to the Recycle Bin.
12. Close the **Potential Clients** folder.
13. Right-click the **Potential Clients** folder icon on the desktop and then click **Delete**. Click **Yes** in the confirmation dialog box to send the folder to the Recycle Bin.
14. Double-click the **Recycle Bin** icon on the desktop to open it. Click **Empty the Recycle Bin** on the toolbar and then click **Yes** in the confirmation dialog box to permanently delete all items.
15. **CLOSE** the Recycle Bin folder window.

    PAUSE. LEAVE the desktop open to use in the next project.

Project 3-4: Catalog Photo

The *Catalog_Photo* file is available on the companion CD-ROM.

An equipment manufacturer has submitted a picture for use in an Alpine Ski House catalog. In this project, you must locate the picture in the data files and copy it to the Design Project folder.

1. Navigate to the *Catalog_Photo* file in the data files for this lesson, right-click it, and then click **Copy** on the shortcut menu.
2. In the Navigation pane of the folder window, click **Folders** to display the Folders list.

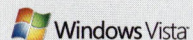

Working with Files and Folders | 73

3. Click the **expand arrow** next to your personal folder in the Folders list and then click **Documents** to display the contents of the Documents folder in the File list.
4. Right-click a blank area of the File list and then click **Paste** on the shortcut menu to paste the *Catalog_Photo* file into the Documents folder.
5. Click the **Close** button in the upper-right corner of the Documents window to close it.

   PAUSE. LEAVE the desktop open to use in the next project.

■ Mastery Assessment

Project 3-5: Telephone List

You are working on a design project with four coworkers, and you want to be able to contact them even when you are working at home. In this project, you copy a telephone list to a removable device so you can take it home.

GET READY. Before you begin these steps, start your computer and log on to your Windows Vista account. Insert a blank disk such as a CD, DVD, or floppy into the appropriate drive. Close all open windows so you can see the desktop.

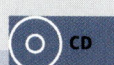

The *Phone List* file is available on the companion CD-ROM.

1. Click **Start** and then click **Documents** to open the Documents folder window.
2. Navigate to the location of the data files for this lesson and right-click the *Phone List* file.
3. Point to the **Send To** command, and then click the device in which you have inserted a disk.
4. When the drive is finished copying the file to the disk, remove the disk and label it with your name, the date, and the filename—Phone List.
5. **CLOSE** the Documents window.

   PAUSE. LEAVE the desktop displayed to use in the next project.

Project 3-6: Telephone List

To keep your design project organized, you must keep all files in the same storage location. In this project you create a folder for storing the files, you locate and copy the Phone List text file into the folder, and then move the entire folder to your Documents folder.

The *Phone_List* file is available on the companion CD-ROM.

1. Navigate to the *Phone_List* text file in the data files for this lesson, right-click the file, and click **Copy**. Then, to paste the file into the Documents folder, navigate to your Documents folder, right-click the Files list area, and click **Paste**. Close the Documents folder window.
2. Right-click a blank area of the desktop, point to **New** on the shortcut menu, and then click **Folder** on the submenu to create a new folder.
3. Key **Design Project** and then press [Enter] to rename the folder.
4. Right-click the **Design Project** icon on the desktop and then click **Cut** on the shortcut menu to move the folder to the Clipboard.
5. Click the **Start Button** and then click **Documents**.
6. Right-click a blank area of the File list in the Documents window and then click **Paste** on the shortcut menu to paste the Design Project folder from the Clipboard into the Documents folder.
7. Double-click the **Design Project** folder icon to open it.
8. Click the **Start** button and then click **Documents** to open the Documents folder window.

9. Right-click a blank area of the taskbar and click **Show Windows Stacked** to tile the Documents window and the Design Project window horizontally on the desktop.
10. Click the *Phone List* file icon in the Documents window, drag it to the **Design Project** window, and then drop it in the File list area.
11. **CLOSE** the Documents window.
12. **CLOSE** the Design Project window.
13. Navigate to the Documents folder, right-click on the **Design Project** folder, and click **Delete** on the shortcut menu.

    STOP. Log off and shut down your computer.

INTERNET READY

Southridge Video develops and produces digital videos. The technical director wants all employees to understand the different types of digital video file formats that might be used. In this exercise, use Web search tools to locate definitions for at least five digital video formats. Create a text file and use Notepad to record the file format names, extensions, and definitions. Save the file with a descriptive filename.

Windows Vista Speech Recognition

4

LESSON SKILL MATRIX

Skill	Objective
Setting Up a Microphone	Students will learn how to set up a microphone.
Talking to Your Computer	Students will learn how to talk to their computer.
Training Your Computer to Understand Your Speech	Students will learn how to train their computer to understand their speech.
Turning Speech Recognition On and Off	Students will learn how to turn speech recognition on and off.
Using Voice Commands	Students will learn how to use voice commands.
Navigating Speech Recognition	Students will learn how to navigate speech recognition.
Dictating Text	Students will learn how to dictate text.
Editing Text	Students will learn how to edit text.
Formatting Text	Students will learn how to format text.

As a Travel Agent with Global Destinations, you often find yourself juggling several tasks at once. Limiting the amount of time you spend keying information into your computer and increasing your productivity would be extremely beneficial in your position. Using Windows Speech Recognition, you discover that you can interact with your computer using only your voice. You can start and switch between applications, control computer settings, dictate text for documents and emails, fill out online forms, and even browse the Internet. In this lesson, you will learn how to work with Speech Recognition in Windows Vista. Specifically, you will learn how set up speech recognition on your computer, how to turn the option on and off, how to use voice commands, and how to navigate this tool. Finally, you will learn how to use speech recognition to dictate, edit, and format text.

KEY TERMS
speech recognition
speech recognition rate
speech user interface
microphone
warning icon

75

Setting Up Speech Recognition

THE BOTTOM LINE

Windows Speech Recognition allows you to use your voice to control your computer. Using speech recognition, you can dictate and edit text, issue verbal commands to your computer, and even browse the Internet. In this section, you will learn how to set up your computer for speech recognition, including setting up a microphone, learning how to talk to your computer, and training your computer to understand your speech.

Setting Up the Microphone

Before you can begin using Windows Speech Recognition, you must first set up a microphone to use on your computer. Windows Vista provides a wizard that will walk you through the necessary steps.

 **SET UP THE MICROPHONE**

GET READY. Before you begin these steps, start your computer and log on to your Windows Vista account. Ensure that you have a properly working microphone connected to your computer.

TAKE NOTE* Headset-style microphones are the best for speech recognition. When using other microphone types, such as desktop units, the computer is more likely to have trouble understanding your speech.

1. Click the **Start Button** and point to **All Programs**. Click **Accessories**, click **Ease of Use**, and select **Microsoft Speech Recognition**, as shown in Figure 4-1.

Figure 4-1

Starting Microsoft Speech Recognition

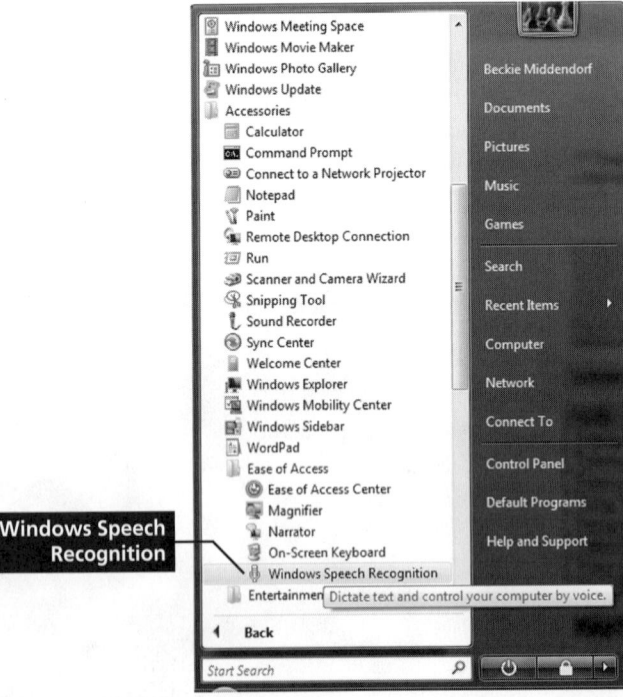

2. The Set up Speech Recognition dialog box will appear (see Figure 4-2). Click the **Next** button.

Windows Vista Speech Recognition | 77

Figure 4-2

Set up Speech Recognition dialog box

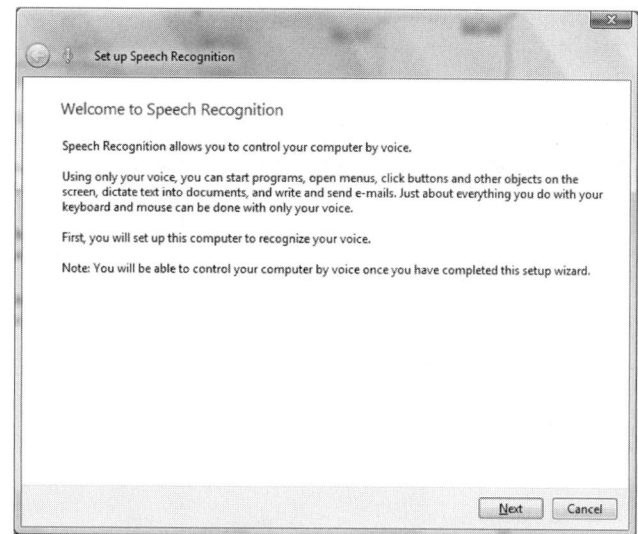

> **TROUBLESHOOTING**
>
> If you need to return to a previous screen while setting up Windows Speech Recognition, click the Back button in the upper-left corner of any dialog box.

3. Select the type of microphone you would like to use from the dialog box, as shown in Figure 4-3, then click the **Next** button.

Figure 4-3

Select microphone

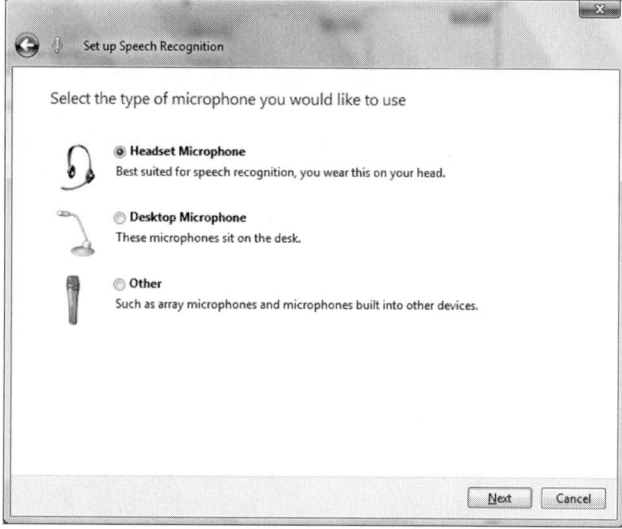

4. Read the information on proper microphone placement, as shown in Figure 4-4, then click the **Next** button.

Figure 4-4

Set up your microphone

5. In a natural speaking voice, read aloud the sentence provided on the dialog box (see Figure 4-5). Once you have finished reading the sentence, click the **Next** button.

Figure 4-5

Adjust the microphone volume

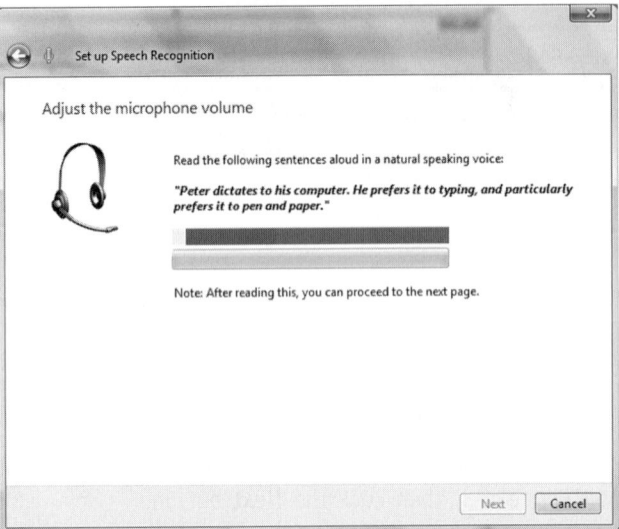

> If the computer is unable to hear your voice, you will receive the dialog box shown in Figure 4-6. Check to ensure that your microphone is properly connected to your computer or that it is not set to mute. Once the problem has been corrected, click the Next button to read the sentence again.

TROUBLESHOOTING

Figure 4-6

Microphone error

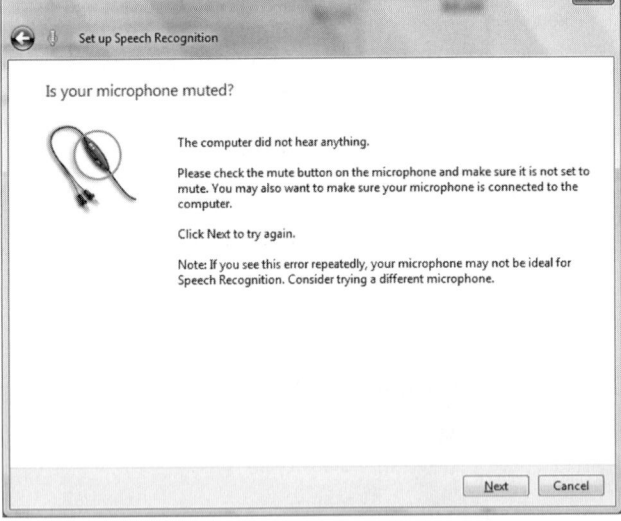

6. Once the computer is able to recognize your voice, the confirmation screen shown in Figure 4-7 appears. Click the **Next** button.

Figure 4-7

Your microphone is now set up

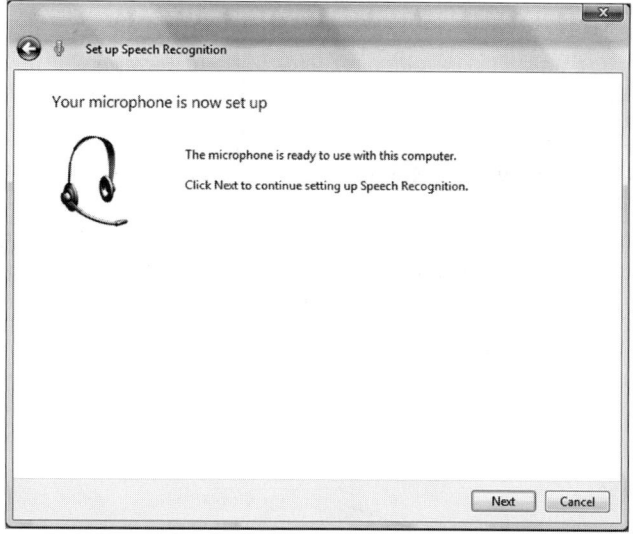

PAUSE. LEAVE the wizard open to use in the next exercise.

Speech recognition is the process of converting a speech signal to a sequence of words. Windows Speech Recognition, which comes with Windows Vista, is a useful tool for interacting with your computer using only your voice. Before using the tool for the first time, you must set up a *microphone* on your computer. The *speech recognition rate* is directly related to the quality of the microphone you use. The most common types of microphones used for speech recognition are headsets and desktops. Headset microphones are less likely to pick up extraneous sounds.

Learning How to Talk to Your Computer

Windows Vista provides a speech training tutorial that will help you learn how to talk to your computer and use some of the basic Windows Speech Recognition commands.

➔ LEARN HOW TO TALK TO YOUR COMPUTER

USE the wizard that is open from the previous exercise.

   1. Choose **Enable document review**, as shown in Figure 4-8, then click the **Next** button.

Figure 4-8

Enable document review

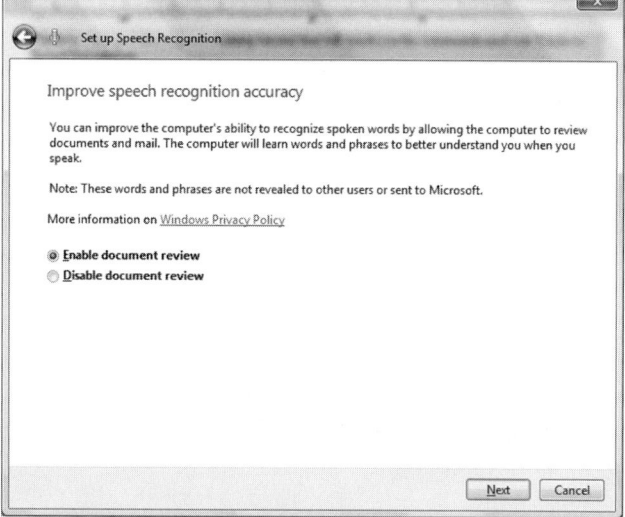

TAKE NOTE* Enabling document review allows Windows Speech Recognition to review emails and documents on your computer for commonly used words and phrases. This can help improve the accuracy of your speech recognition.

2. Click the **View Reference Sheet** button, as shown in Figure 4-9.

Figure 4-9

View Reference Sheet

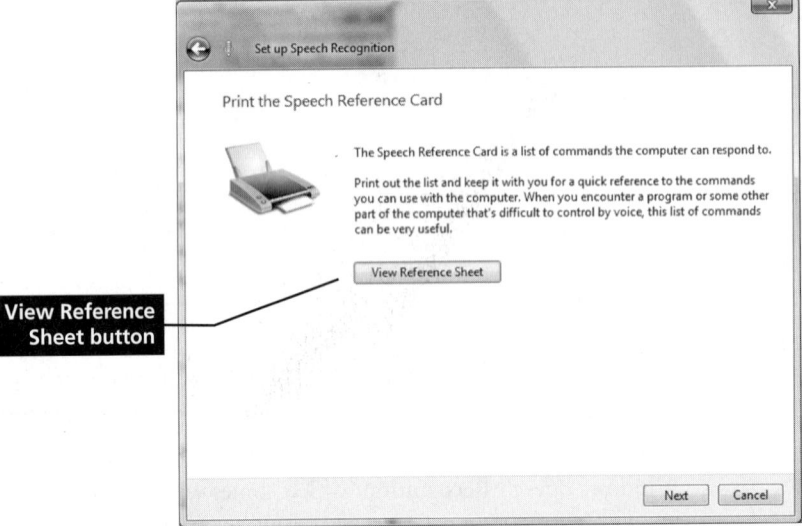

3. Windows Help and Support opens to the Common commands in Speech Recognition topic. Click the **Show all** button (see Figure 4-10).

Figure 4-10

Windows Help and Support

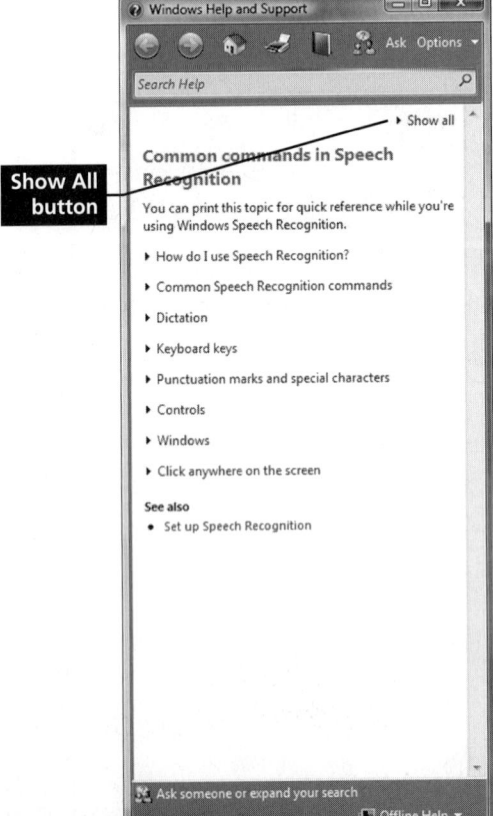

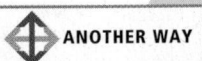 **ANOTHER WAY** Once Windows Speech Recognition is running, you can view the Common commands in Speech Recognition topic by saying "What can I say?"

 **Windows Vista Speech Recognition | 81**

4. Review the reference information, as shown in Figure 4-11, then click the **Close** button on the Windows Help and Support window. Table 4-1 lists many commonly used speech recognition commands.

Figure 4-11

Common commands in Speech Recognition

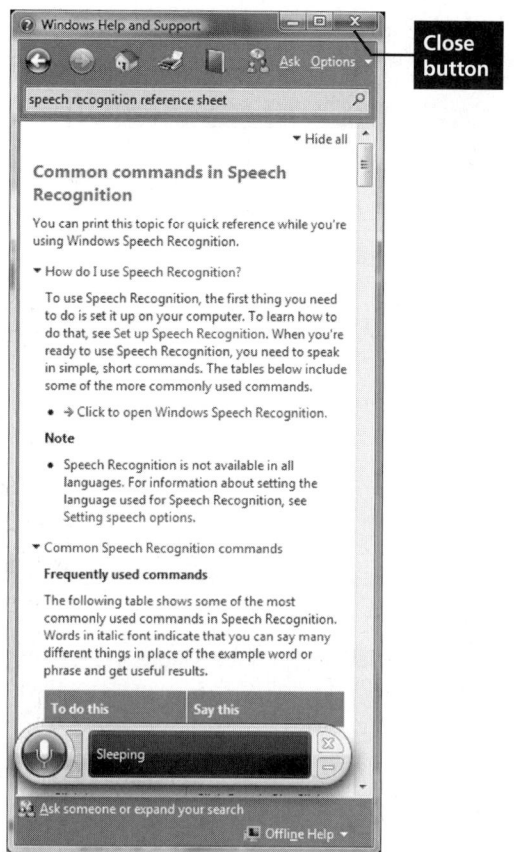

Table 4-1

Commonly Used Speech Recognition Commands

TO DO THIS...	SAY THIS...
Click any item by its name	File; Start; View
Click item	Click Recycle Bin; Click Computer; Click File
Double-click item	Double-click Recycle Bin; Double-click Computer; Double-click File
Switch to an open program	Switch to Paint; Switch to WordPad; Switch to program name; Switch application
Insert a new paragraph or new line in a document	New paragraph; New line
Select a word and start to correct it	Correct word
Select and delete specific words	Delete word
Show a list of applicable commands	What can I say?
Update the list of speech commands that are currently available	Refresh speech commands
Make the computer listen to you	Start listening
Make the computer stop listening	Stop listening
Move the microphone out of the way	Move speech recognition
Minimize the microphone bar	Minimize speech recognition

82 | Lesson 4

5. In the Set up Speech Recognition dialog box, click the **Next** button.
6. Leave the **Run Speech Recognition at startup** box checked, as shown in Figure 4-12, then click the **Next** button.

Figure 4-12

Run Speech Recognition at startup

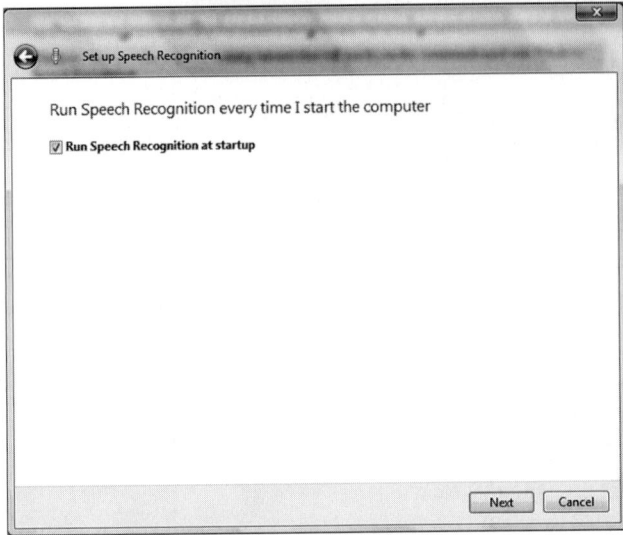

7. Click the **Start Tutorial** button (see Figure 4-13).

Figure 4-13

Start Tutorial

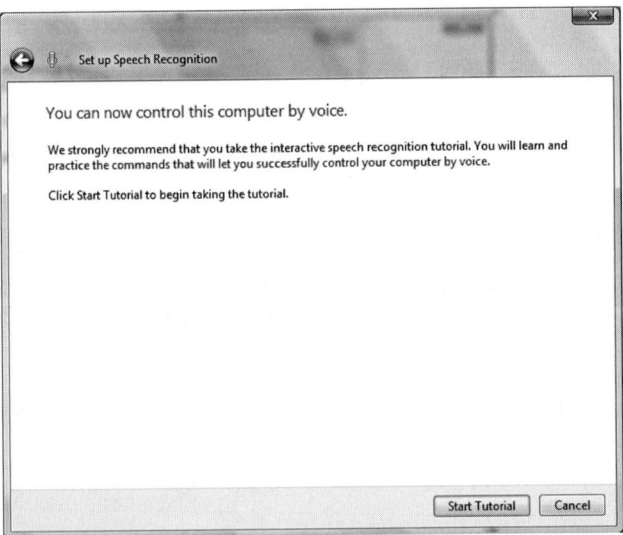

8. The Speech Recognition Tutorial begins, as shown in Figure 4-14. Navigate through the tutorial topics.

Figure 4-14

Speech Recognition Tutorial

> **TAKE NOTE*** Before you begin the Windows Vista speech recognition training, you should ensure that you have at least 30 minutes to dedicate to completing the tutorial.

> **ANOTHER WAY** If you do not have time to view the entire tutorial now, you can choose to start it at a later time from the Speech Options shortcut menu (see step 10).

9. Once you have completed the tutorial, the speech user interface appears on the screen, along with a confirmation message that Speech Recognition configuration has finished (see Figure 4-15).

Figure 4-15

Speech user interface

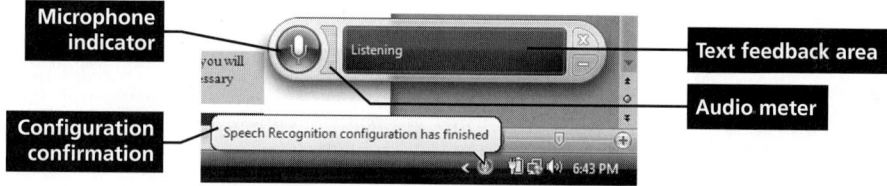

10. Say "**Show speech options.**" The Speech Options shortcut menu appears, as shown in Figure 4-16.

Figure 4-16

Speech Options shortcut menu

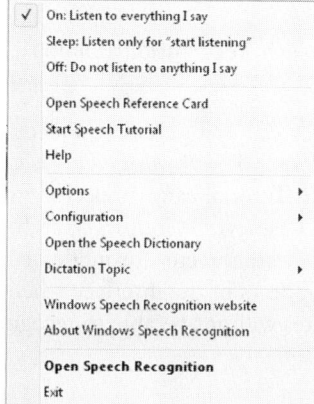

 **ANOTHER WAY** You can also right-click on the Microphone indicator to open the Speech Options shortcut menu.

   11. Say "**Sleep.**" The Text feedback area of the speech user interface reads Sleeping, as shown in Figure 4-17.

Figure 4-17

Speech user interface—Sleeping

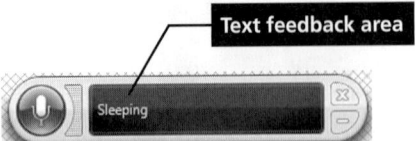

 **ANOTHER WAY** You can also say "Stop listening" to change the Microphone User Interface to sleep mode.

TAKE NOTE* When the speech user interface indicates Sleeping, Windows Speech Recognition will only listen for and recognize the audio command "Start listening."

   12. Say "**Start listening.**" The Text feedback area of the speech user interface changes back to Listening.
   13. Say "**I had a good weekend.**" The speech user interface did not recognize a command (see Figure 4-18).

Figure 4-18

Speech user interface—What was that?

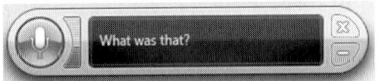

   14. After a few seconds, the speech user interface will again read Listening.

TROUBLESHOOTING If a warning icon appears in the speech user interface, as shown in Figure 4-19, commands will not be accepted in the active window. The icon should only stay visible for a few seconds. Once the icon has disappeared, Windows Speech Recognition will be ready to accept voice commands.

Figure 4-19

Warning icon

PAUSE. LEAVE Microsoft Speech Recognition running to use in the next exercise.

Windows Vista provides a Speech Tutorial that guides you through many of the commands and options available in Windows Speech Recognition. This is a great tool for learning how to talk to your computer. The Speech Tutorial can be selected from the ***speech user interface***. This interface appears on the screen whenever Windows Speech Recognition is running on your computer. The interface will indicate the current mode of speech recognition; Sleeping, Listening, or Off. A ***warning icon*** appears in the interface when the tool is busy. While the warning icon is visible, your computer will not be able to recognize verbal commands.

 Windows Vista Speech Recognition | 85

Training your Computer to Understand Your Speech

> Windows Speech Recognition provides a voice-training wizard that helps the computer learn to recognize your speech.

➔ TRAIN YOUR COMPUTER TO UNDERSTAND YOUR SPEECH

Speech Recognition should be running from the previous exercise.

1. Say "**Show speech options.**"
2. Say "**Configuration.**"
3. Say "**Improve voice recognition.**"
4. The Speech Recognition Voice Training wizard shown in Figure 4-20 opens.

Figure 4-20

Speech Recognition Voice Training Wizard

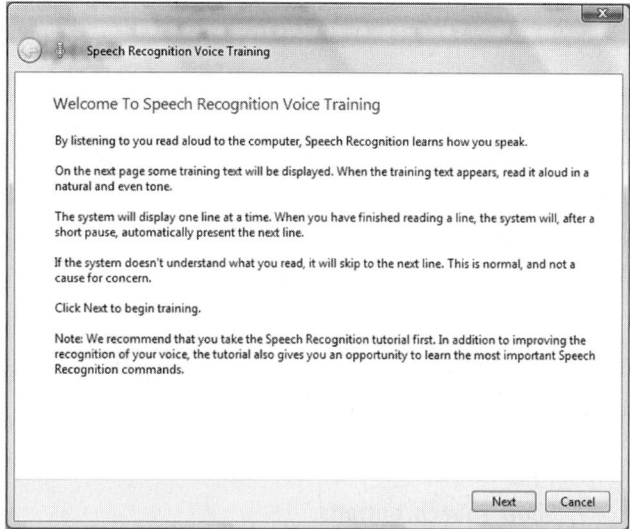

5. Say "**Next.**" Read aloud the text as it appears (see Figure 4-21).

Figure 4-21

Training text

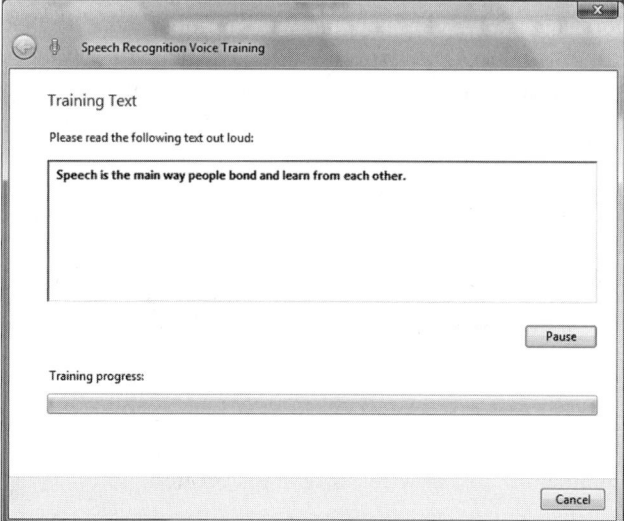

6. When training is complete, the screen shown in Figure 4-22 appears.

Figure 4-22

Speech Recognition Training is complete

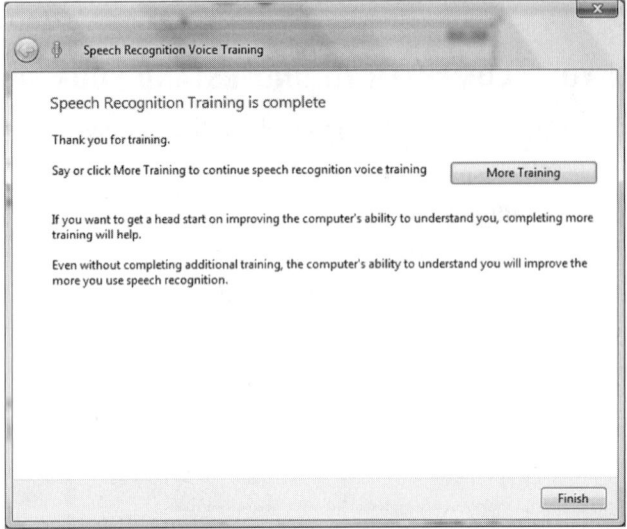

7. Say "**Finish**."

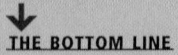

Speech recognition is not available in all languages. Windows Speech Recognition supports the English, German, French, Spanish, Japanese, Traditional Chinese, and Simplified Chinese languages.

8. Say "**Show speech options**."
9. Say "**Exit**."

   PAUSE. Microsoft Speech Recognition should remain closed before starting the next exercise.

The more you use Windows Speech Recognition, the better the computer will become at understanding your speech patterns and pronunciations. Windows Speech Recognition provides a Voice Training wizard that steps you through the dictation of numerous sentences to your computer. Each time you speak one of the sentences, the computer is remembering certain aspects of your speech for future reference.

■ Speech Recognition Basics

THE BOTTOM LINE

Once Windows Speech Recognition has been set up on your computer, you are ready to start exploring all that this tool has to offer. In this section, you will learn the basics of Windows Speech Recognition, including how to turn the tool on and off, how to use voice commands, and how to navigate speech recognition.

Windows Vista Speech Recognition | 87

Turning Speech Recognition On and Off

If you chose the Run Speech Recognition at startup option while configuring Windows Speech Recognition, this tool will start as soon as you log on to Windows Vista. If not, you will need to know how to turn this tool on manually.

➔ TURN SPEECH RECOGNITION ON AND OFF

1. Click **Start**, point to **All Programs**, click **Accessories**, click **Ease of Access**, and then click **Windows Speech Recognition**, as shown in Figure 4-23.

Figure 4-23

Starting Windows Speech Recognition

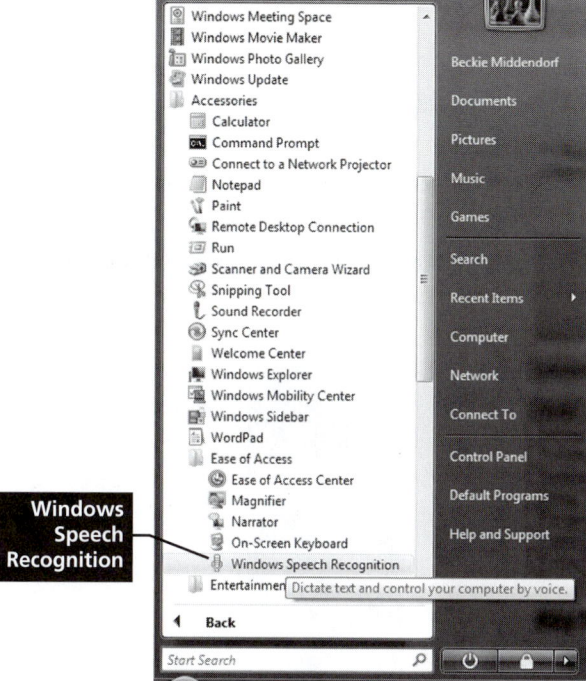

2. The speech user interface appears on the screen (see Figure 4-24) in sleep mode.

Figure 4-24

Speech user interface—Sleeping

3. Say "**Start listening.**"
4. Say "**Show speech options.**"
5. Say "**Off.**" The speech user interface reads Off, as shown in Figure 4-25.

Figure 4-25

Speech user interface—Off

88 | Lesson 4

6. Right-click the **Microphone indicator** on the speech user interface, then click **On: Listen to everything I say** (see Figure 4-26).

Figure 4-26

On: Listen to everything I say

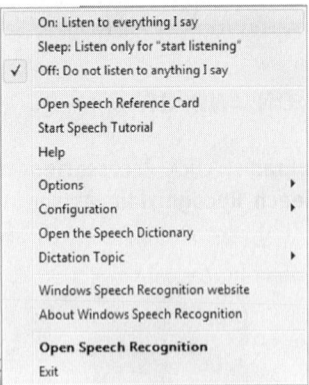

7. Say "**Show speech options.**"
8. Say "**Exit.**"
9. Click the Start menu, and then click **Windows Speech Recognition** in the list of recently accessed programs (see Figure 4-27).

Figure 4-27

Windows Speech Recognition in Start menu list

PAUSE. LEAVE Windows Speech Recognition open to use in the next exercise.

Windows Speech Recognition can be set up to start automatically when you log on to Windows Vista. You can also turn the tool on manually from the Start menu.

 **Windows Vista Speech Recognition | 89**

Using Voice Commands

With Windows Speech Recognition running, you can use your voice to send commands to your computer, rather than using your keyboard or mouse.

→ USE VOICE COMMANDS

Windows Speech Recognition should be running from the previous exercise.

1. Say "**Open WordPad.**" The WordPad application opens.
2. Say "**Open calculator.**" The calculator opens.
3. Say "**Switch to WordPad.**" WordPad becomes active again.
4. Say "**Switch to Desktop.**" The Windows Vista Desktop becomes active, and all other windows are minimized.
5. Say "**Switch to calculator.**" The calculator becomes active again.
6. Say "**Press 5.**"
7. Say "**Press times.**"
8. Say "**Press 8.**"
9. Say "**Press equals.**" The calculator shows a total of 40.
10. Say "**View.**" The View menu appears, as shown in Figure 4-28.

Figure 4-28

Calculator—View menu

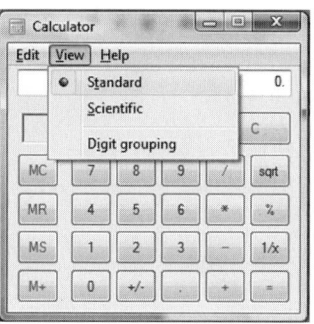

11. Say "**Scientific**" to switch to the scientific calculator.
12. Say "**View,**" then say "**Standard**" to switch back to the standard calculator.
13. Say "**Help**" to view the Help menu.
14. Say "**Cancel**" to close the Help menu.
15. Say "**Close calculator**" to close the calculator.
16. Say "**Switch to WordPad.**"
17. Say "**Insert**" to view the Insert menu, then say "**Date and Time**" to view the Date and Time dialog box (see Figure 4-29).

Figure 4-29

WordPad—Date and Time dialog box

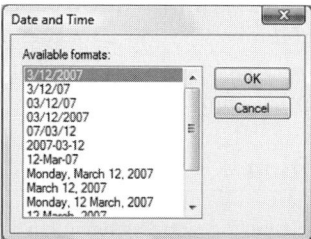

18. Say "**Cancel**" to close the dialog box.

19. Say "**Show Numbers.**" A number is displayed for each available option in WordPad, as shown in Figure 4-30.

Figure 4-30

WordPad—Show Numbers

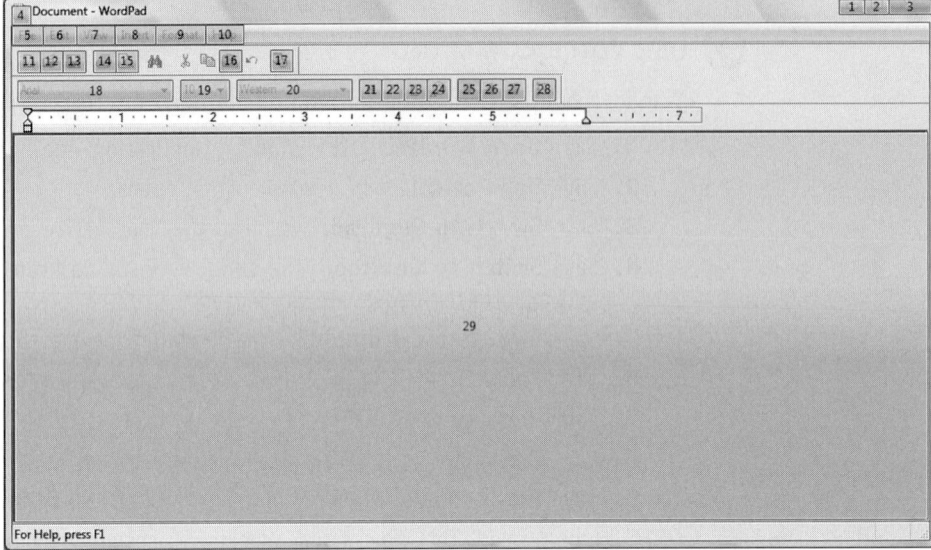

20. Say "**Five**," then say "**OK**" to display the File menu.

21. Say "**Show Numbers.**" A number is displayed for each available option in the File menu, as shown in Figure 4-31.

Figure 4-31

WordPad File menu—
Show Numbers

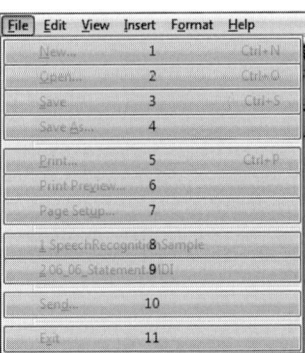

22. Say "**Eleven**" to choose the Exit option, then say "OK" to close WordPad.

PAUSE. LEAVE Windows Speech Recognition open to use in the next exercise.

You can open and close applications, switch between applications, navigate menu options, and much more using only voice commands with Windows Speech Recognition. If you are unsure of an item's name, the Show Numbers option associates a number with each available option on the active screen. A number appears over each option, allowing you to choose the desired option by voicing the appropriate number.

Navigating Speech Recognition

Many options are available in Windows Speech Recognition. You can view commonly used commands, change configuration settings, and even personalize the speech recognition dictionary.

 **Windows Vista Speech Recognition | 91**

NAVIGATE SPEECH RECOGNITION

Windows Speech Recognition should be running from the previous exercise.

1. Say "**Show speech options.**"
2. Say "**Help.**" Read about what you can do with speech recognition (see Figure 4-32).

Figure 4-32

What can I do with Speech Recognition?

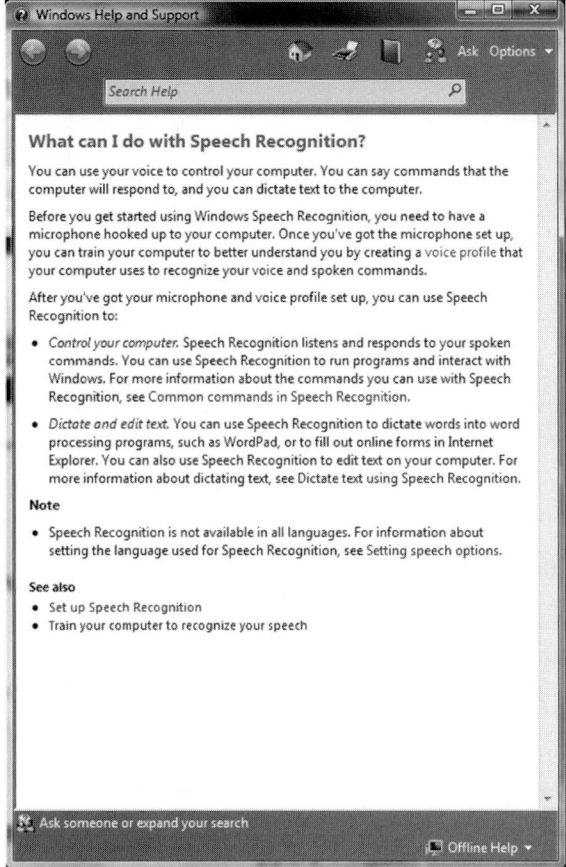

3. Say "**Close Help.**"
4. Say "**Show speech options.**"
5. Say "**Open the Speech Dictionary.**" The Speech Dictionary dialog box appears, as shown in Figure 4-33.

Figure 4-33

Speech Dictionary dialog box

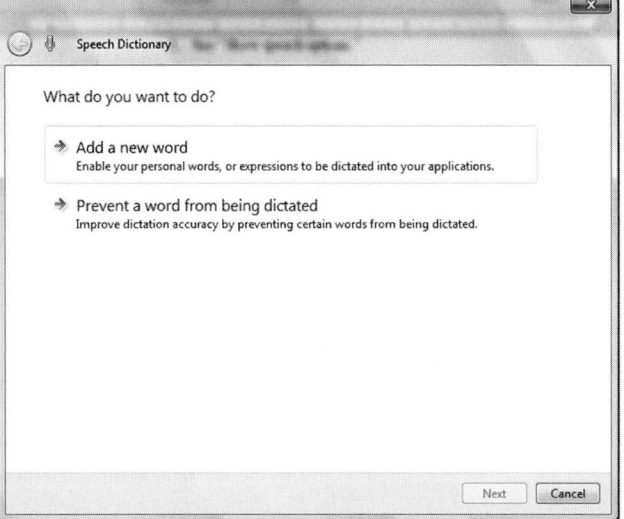

6. Say "**Add a new word.**"
7. Say your name (see Figure 4-34), then say "**Next.**"

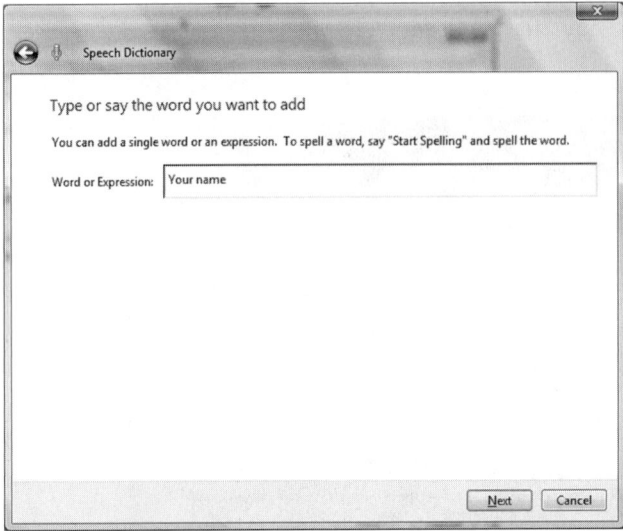

Figure 4-34

Type or say the word you want to add

8. On the next screen, shown in Figure 4-35, say "**Finish.**"

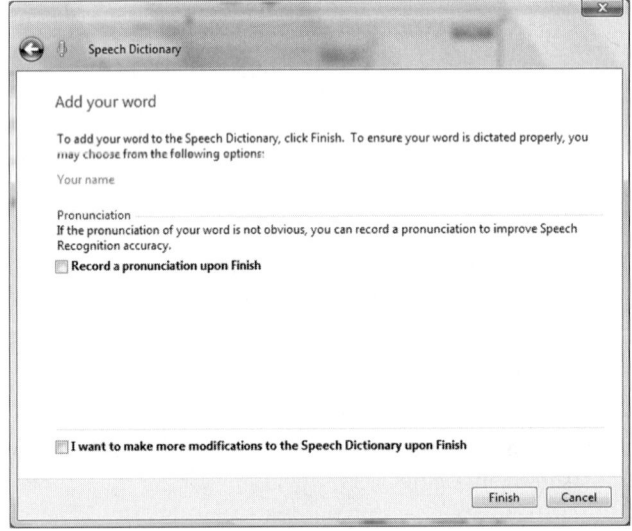

Figure 4-35

Add your word

9. On the next screen, shown in Figure 4-36, say "**Three.**"

Figure 4-36

Say "three"

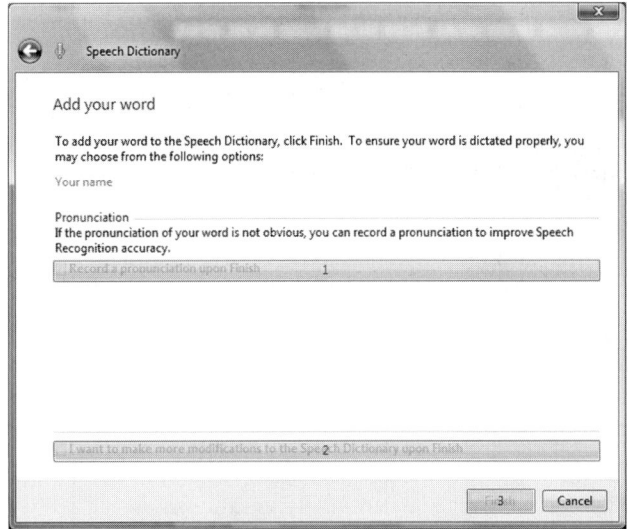

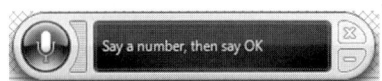

10. On the next screen, shown in Figure 4-37, say "**OK**."

Figure 4-37

Say "OK"

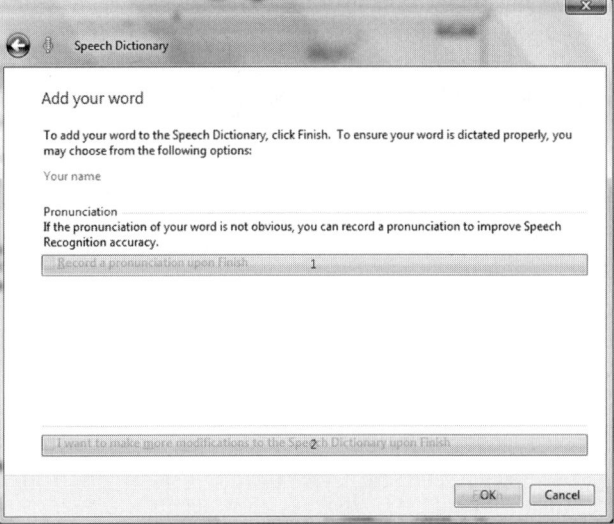

11. Say "**Show speech options.**"
12. Say "**Configuration.**"
13. Say "**Open Speech Recognition Control Panel.**"

14. The Speech Recognition Control Panel appears, as shown in Figure 4-38; say "**OK**."

Figure 4-38

Speech Recognition Control Panel

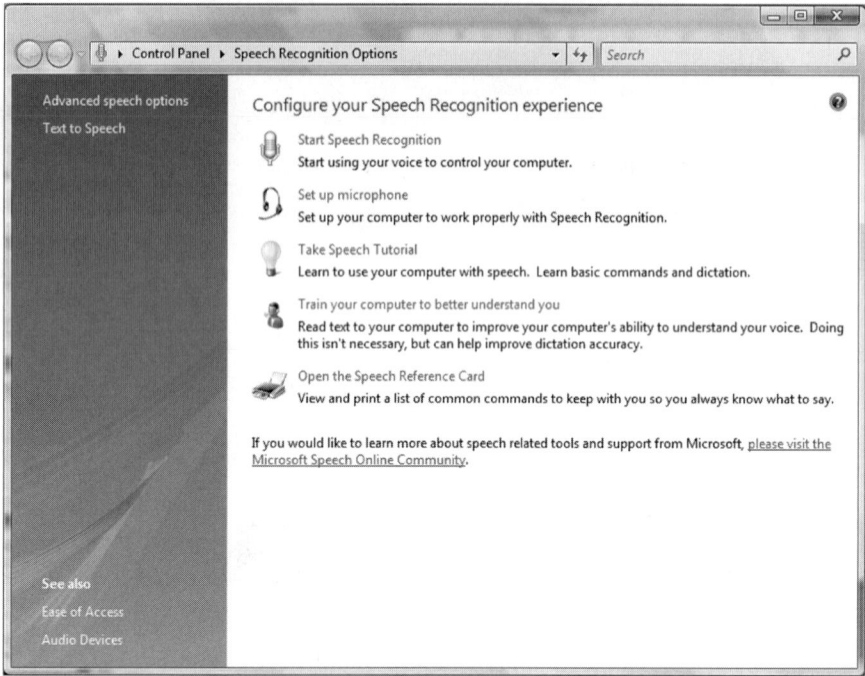

15. Say "**Advanced speech options**" to open the Speech Properties dialog box (see Figure 4-39).

Figure 4-39

Speech Properties dialog box

16. Say "**Close**."

PAUSE. LEAVE Windows Speech Recognition open to use in the next exercise.

The speech options shortcut menu provides you with several options, including the ability to change the microphone configuration, improve voice recognition, and open the Speech Recognition Control Panel. The Control Panel provides access to several speech recognition items, including Advanced speech options, such as Language, Voice Properties, and other options for text-to-speech translation.

 Windows Vista Speech Recognition | 95

Working with Text in Speech Recognition

THE BOTTOM LINE

Windows Speech Recognition can be used to manipulate text in documents, emails, and more. With practice, you can limit your use of the keyboard and mouse, while increasing your productivity. In this section, you will learn how to use speech recognition to dictate, edit, and format text.

Dictating Text

You can dictate text to your computer much more quickly than you can type on the keyboard. By using a clear, well-pronounced speaking voice, you will limit the computer's number of mistakes and improve your overall productivity.

→ DICTATE TEXT

Windows Speech Recognition should be running from the previous exercise.

1. Say "**Start WordPad.**"
2. In a clear and concise voice, read the following text:

   Potential Client List
   Enter
   Craig Johnson
   comma
   Karen West
   comma
   Jon and Mary Smith
   comma
   Ben Stuart

TAKE NOTE* Speech recognition will not add punctuation for you, so remember to say any punctuation marks aloud as you dictate to the computer.

3. Your screen should look similar to Figure 4-40.

Figure 4-40

WordPad—Potential client list

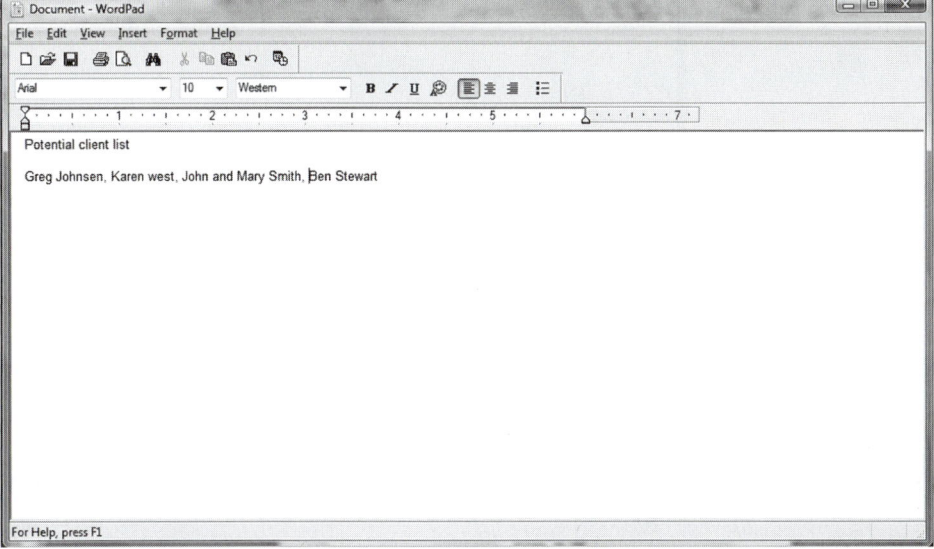

TROUBLESHOOTING Due to the differences in speech patterns and dialect, some of the words on your screen may have been entered differently than those shown in Figure 4-38. If so, don't worry. You will learn how to edit text later in this lesson.

PAUSE. LEAVE WordPad and Windows Speech Recognition open to use in the next exercise.

Be sure to speak clearly, pronouncing each word correctly as you dictate text to your computer. Because everyone's speech differs slightly, the computer may interpret some of your words incorrectly. The more you dictate to the computer, the better it will become at recognizing your particular speech style. This means that as you become more experienced with speech recognition, the number of dictation mistakes that your computer makes will decrease. Windows Speech Recognition will not automatically add punctuation marks or hard returns, so you will need to speak these commands aloud as you dictate text.

Editing Text

When you need to make changes to text, you can easily do so using only voice commands.

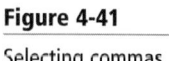 **EDIT TEXT**

WordPad and Windows Speech Recognition should be running from the previous exercise.

1. Say "**Select comma**," then say "**OK**" to select the third comma (see Figure 4-41).

Figure 4-41

Selecting commas

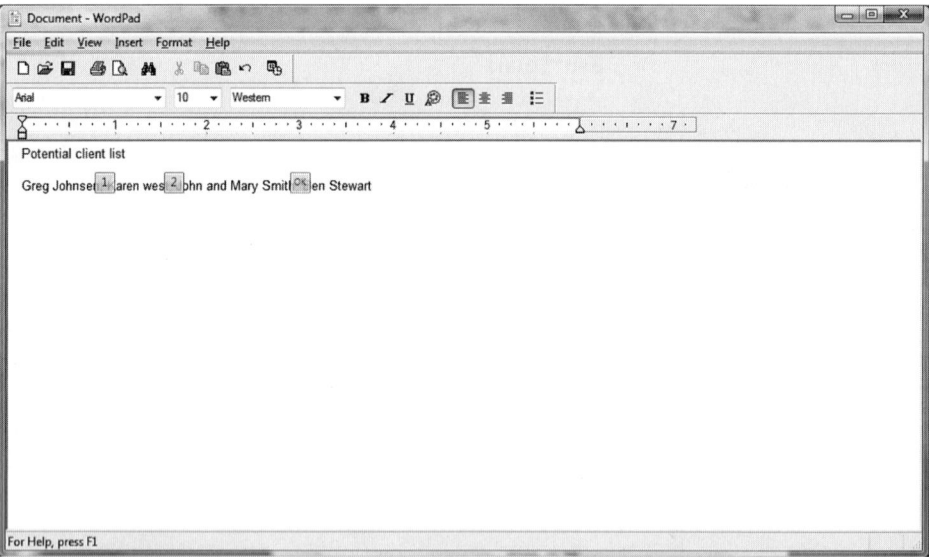

2. Say "**Delete**," say "**Enter**," then say "**Delete**." Your screen should look similar to Figure 4-42.

   **Windows Vista Speech Recognition | 97**

Figure 4-42

Third comma removed, line added

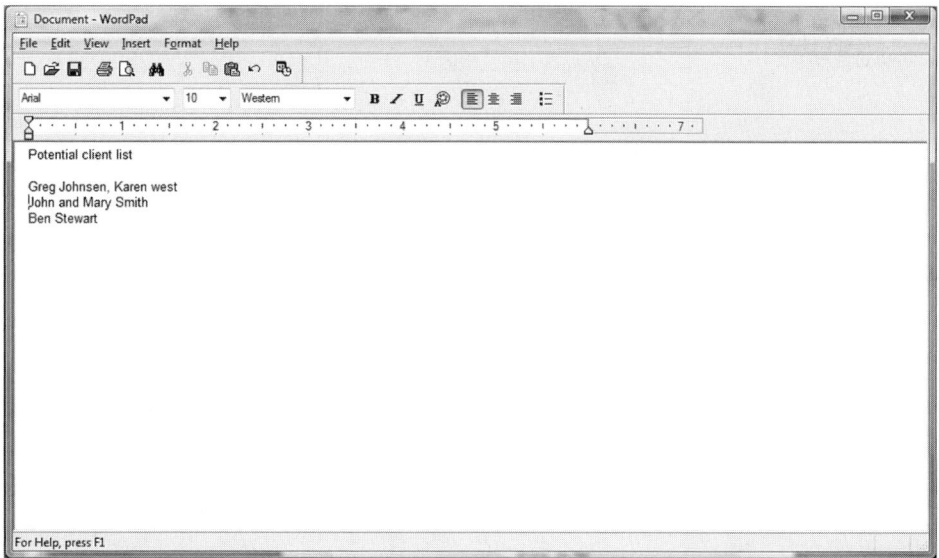

3. Say "**Select comma**," then say "**OK**" to select the second comma.
4. Say "**Delete**," say "**Delete**," say "**Enter**," then say "**Enter**."
5. Say "**Undo**" to remove the extra blank line. Your screen should look similar to Figure 4-43.

Figure 4-43

Second comma removed, line added

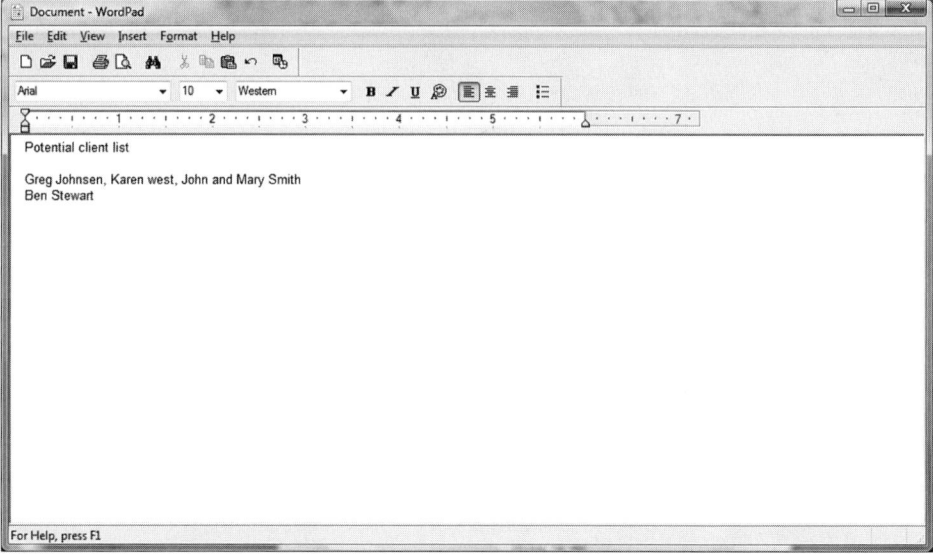

6. Say "**Select comma**," say "**Delete**," say "**Delete**," then say "**Enter**."
7. Say "**Go to west**." The cursor should move to the beginning of Karen West's last name.
8. Say "**Delete**" to remove the lowercase letter w.
9. Say "**Spell it**."
10. With the Spelling panel open, say "**Capital W as in win**" (see Figure 4-44). When the correct letter appears in the Spelling panel, say "**OK**."

Figure 4-44

Spelling panel

> **TROUBLESHOOTING** If the letter you intended to add does not appear in the Spelling panel, simply say the number directly above the incorrect letter, then say the correct letter again. Make sure you speak clearly and pronounce the letter correctly.

11. The Add word to dictionary dialog box appears (see Figure 4-45). Say **"Simply insert."**

Figure 4-45

Add word to dictionary dialog box

> **TAKE NOTE*** If you are spelling out a complete word, you may want to add it to the speech recognition dictionary for future reference. On the Add word to dictionary dialog box, select whether the word is always capitalized or sometimes capitalized, then click the Add word button.

12. Say **"Backspace"** to remove the extra space in the name West. Your screen should look similar to Figure 4-46.

Figure 4-46

West corrected

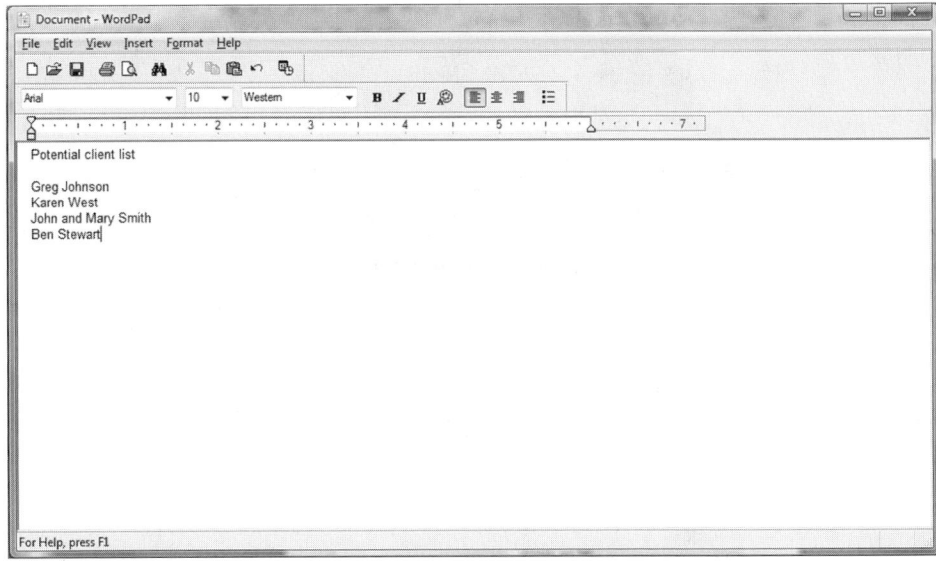

13. Say "**Go to client**." Say "**Delete**" to remove the lowercase letter c.
14. Say "**Press Shift c**." A capital letter C is entered.
15. Say "**Go to list**." Say "**Delete**," then say "**Press shift l**" to enter a capital letter L.

> **TROUBLESHOOTING** Your computer is learning as you correct errors. Once a particular error has been corrected in Windows Speech Recognition, the same error is unlikely to appear again.

PAUSE. LEAVE WordPad and Windows Speech Recognition open to use in the next exercise.

Windows Speech Recognition provides several options for editing text. Table 4-2 lists several common phrases used to edit text in speech recognition.

Table 4-2

Common phrases used in speech recognition editing

SAY THIS . . .	TO DO THIS . . .
Start New paragraph	Start a new paragraph.
Start New line	Start a new line.
Correct word	Correct a particular word.
Select word	Select a particular word.
Go to word	Move cursor to the beginning of a particular word.
Go after word	Move cursor to the end of a particular word.
Go to the end of the document	Move cursor to the end of the document.
Delete word	Delete a particular word.
Delete that	Delete the last item(s) spoken; delete item(s) selected.
Press key	Press any key; press any combination of keys.

As you become more familiar with Windows Speech Recognition, you will learn that several phrases often can be used to perform the same task.

Formatting Text

Once you have dictated and edited text, you can then format the text using only voice commands through Windows Speech Recognition.

➔ FORMAT TEXT

WordPad and Windows Speech Recognition should be running from the previous exercise.

1. Say "**Select Potential Client List**."
2. Say "**Press Control b**." The words become bold. Your screen should look similar to Figure 4-47.

Figure 4-47

Title bolded

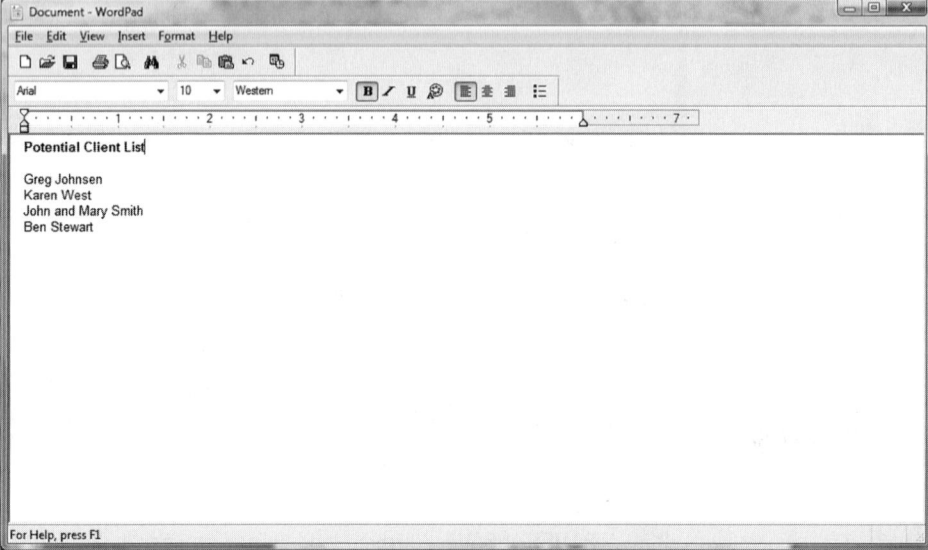

 ANOTHER WAY

To bold selected text, you can also say "Format" to select Format from the menu bar, and then say "Font" to open the Font dialog box. Next, say the attribute you would like to add to the text, such as "bold." If the correct attribute is selected in the Font dialog box, say "OK."

3. Say "**Select Greg to Stewart**." The entire list of names is selected.
4. Say "**Undo**." The list is unselected, and the words Potential Client List are selected again.
5. Say "**Press control u**." The selected words are now underlined.
6. Say "**Move to Greg**," then say "**tab**." A tab is added before Greg's name.
7. Say "**Move to Karen**," then say "**tab**" to add a tab before Karen's name. Continue adding tabs before each name in the list. Your screen should look similar to Figure 4-48.

 **Windows Vista Speech Recognition** | 101

Figure 4-48

Tabs added to list

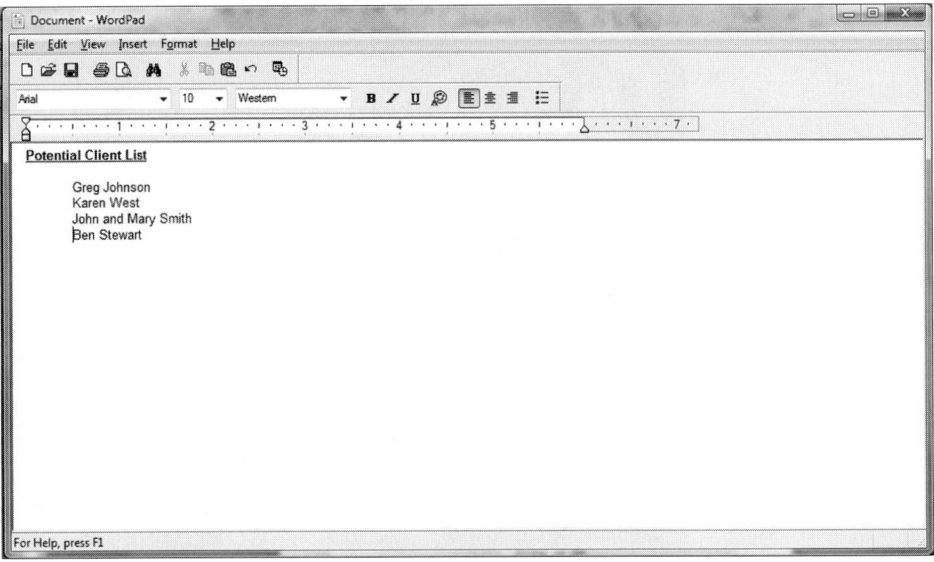

> **TROUBLESHOOTING** If you are having trouble remembering a particular command while using Windows Speech Recognition, simply say "What can I say" to open the Speech Reference Card.

8. Say "**Close WordPad.**"
9. The WordPad dialog box appears, as shown in Figure 4-49.

Figure 4-49

WordPad dialog box

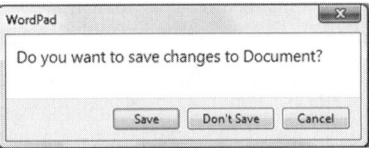

10. Say "**Don't save**" to close WordPad without saving the file.

   STOP. Exit Windows Speech Recognition.

You likely know that many common formatting commands, such as Ctrl + B to bold a selection, can be used throughout most Microsoft programs. You can also speak these key combinations to add the appropriate formatting to selected text using Windows Speech Recognition. Alternately, you can access formatting options from the menu bar of most programs using only your voice. As with all other aspects of speech recognition, the more you use this tool, the more comfortable you will become with the various voice commands for editing text.

SUMMARY SKILL MATRIX

IN THIS LESSON YOU LEARNED HOW TO:
Set Up the Microphone
Talk to Your Computer
Train Your Computer to Understand Your Speech
Turn Speech Recognition On and Off
Use Voice Commands
Navigate Speech Recognition
Dictate Text
Edit Text
Format Text

■ Knowledge Assessment

Fill in the Blank

Complete the following sentences by writing the correct word or words in the blanks provided.

1. Before you can use Windows Speech Recognition, you must first setup a _____ on your computer.

2. Speech recognition is the process of converting a speech _____ to a sequence of words.

3. The user _____ appears on the screen whenever Windows Speech Recognition is turned on.

4. Speech recognition _____ is directly related to the quality of the microphone you use.

5. The two most common types of microphones used for speech recognition are headset and _____.

6. You can choose to spell out a word by saying "Spell _____."

7. When the speech user interface is in Sleep mode, Windows Speech Recognition will only recognize the "Start _____" audio command.

8. A _____ icon appears in the speech user interface when the tool is busy.

9. The _____ Numbers option displays a number for each available item on your screen.

10. You can dictate, edit, and format _____ in documents and emails using Windows Speech Recognition.

True / False

Circle T if the statement is true or F if the statement is false.

T | F 1. Your computer is most likely to have trouble recognizing your voice commands when you use a headset microphone.

T | F 2. Enabling document review can help improve the accuracy of your speech recognition.

T | F 3. Windows Speech Recognition can be set to start automatically when you log on to Windows Vista.

T | F 4. To view the common commands in Windows Speech Recognition topics, say "View Topics."

T | F 5. Windows Speech Recognition automatically adds punctuation as you dictate text.

T | F 6. The more you use Windows Speech Recognition, the better able it becomes at recognizing your speech.

T | F 7. Windows Speech Recognition will not automatically add hard returns as you dictate text.

T | F 8. Windows Speech Recognition is available in all languages.

T | F 9. Windows allows you to personalize your speech recognition dictionary.

T | F 10. As you correct errors, Windows Speech Recognition is remembering your changes for future reference and is unlikely to make the same mistake again.

■ Competency Assessment

Project 4-1: Starting Speech Recognition

You have logged on to your Windows Vista account at Global Destinations and want to use Windows Speech Recognition to navigate your computer. First, you must start the tool.

GET READY. Before you begin these steps, start your computer and log on to your Windows Vista account.

1. From the Start menu, click **All Programs**, **Accessories**, **Ease of Access**, **Windows Speech Recognition**.
2. Say **"Start Listening."**

   PAUSE. LEAVE Windows Speech Recognition running to use in the next project.

Project 4-2: Use Speech Recognition to Open Programs

Now that Windows Speech Recognition is running, you are ready to begin navigating your computer. You want to open the calculator, as well as WordPad.

1. Say **"Open calculator."**
2. Say **"Open WordPad."**

   PAUSE. LEAVE Windows Vista Speech Recognition, WordPad, and the calculator running to use in the next project.

■ Proficiency Assessment

Project 4-3: Add New Project

As an Independent Realtor, you have several figures from recent home sales that you need to calculate. You decide to use Windows Speech Recognition to complete the calculations.

1. Say "**Switch to calculator.**"
2. Using Windows Speech Recognition, find the sum of your new home sales for the previous month. The sales amounts are listed below:
   $240,000
   $230,000
   $234,000
3. Switch to WordPad and enter the total amount.
4. Switch back to the calculator.
5. Find the average sale price for the previous month (divide the total from step 2 by 3).
6. Switch to WordPad and enter the average sales amount.
   PAUSE. LEAVE Windows Vista Speech Recognition, WordPad, and the calculator running to use in the next project.

Project 4-4: Close a Program

You have finished your calculations and need to close the calculator.

1. Switch back to the calculator.
2. Using Windows Speech Recognition, close the calculator.
   PAUSE. LEAVE Windows Vista Speech Recognition and WordPad running to use in the next project.

■ Mastery Assessment

Project 4-5: Add New Project

Now, add text to accompany the figures you entered into WordPad.

1. Make WordPad active.
2. Move to the beginning of the document.
3. Add the following title before the first figure:
   Total New Home Sales
4. Add a hard return between the text and the amount.
5. Move to just before the second figure.
6. Add the following title before the second figure:
   Average New Home Sale
7. Add a hard return between the text and the amount.
   PAUSE. LEAVE Windows Vista Speech Recognition and WordPad running to use in the next project.

Project 4-6: Add New Project

Finally, add formatting to the text and figures you entered into the WordPad document.

1. Use Windows Speech Recognition to select the first title, Total New Home Sales.
2. Bold the selection.
3. Underline the selection.
4. Use Windows Speech Recognition to select the first dollar amount.
5. Italicize the amount.
6. Add the same formatting to the second title and the second dollar amount.
7. Use Windows Speech Recognition to close WordPad without saving changes.

   STOP. Log off and shut down your computer.

INTERNET READY

The more you work with Windows Vista Speech Recognition, the more natural it will become. Your accuracy will improve with practice. Microsoft offers additional training and tutorials for speech recognition on its website. To access the site, make sure Windows Speech Recognition is running. Say "Show speech options," then say "Windows Speech Recognition website." The website will open, as shown in Figure 4-50. Navigate throughout the site to learn more about the benefits of speech recognition.

Figure 4-50

Windows Speech Recognition website

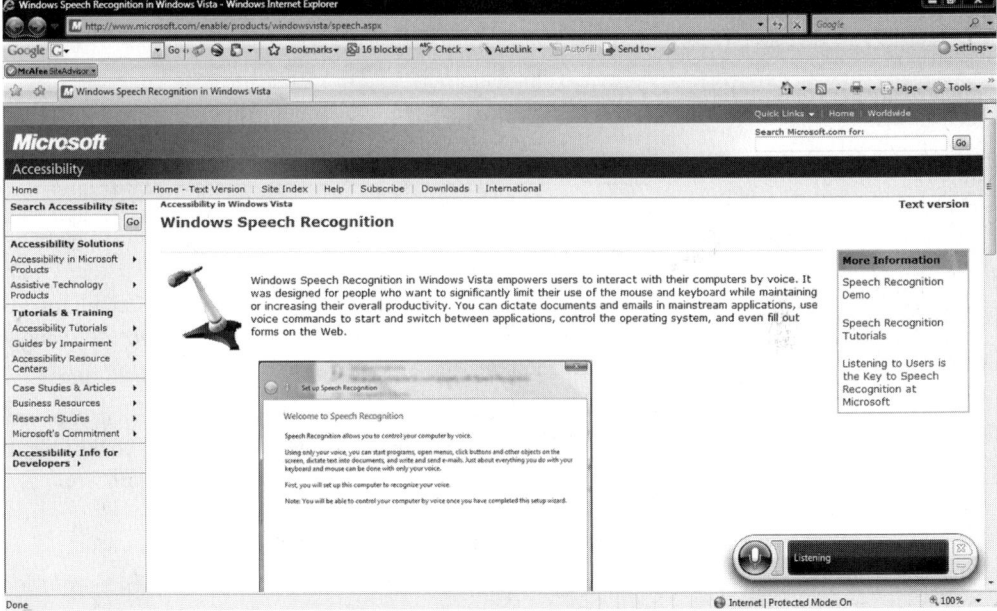

Circling Back

The Baldwin Museum of Science is sponsoring a series of four seminars for high school science teachers. The manager of special events has hired you as a temporary assistant to help with planning and organizing the seminars. In particular, you will be responsible for organizing information for seminar participants. Your manager has already given you a list of tasks that she needs completed quickly, including calculating the cost of lunch for the participants and organizing files for the seminar handbook.

Project 1: Folder Structure

Log on to your Windows Vista account and create folders, subfolders, and a text file for use in later projects.

GET READY. Before you begin these steps, make sure your computer is connected to a printer or to a network that has a printer. Verify that the printer has paper and that the printer is active, or turned on.

1. Start your computer and log on to your Windows Vista account.
2. Open the **Start** menu and then click **Documents**.
3. Create a new folder and rename it **Seminars**.
4. Open the **Seminars** folder and create a new text document named **Lunch**.
5. In the **Seminars** folder, create a folder named **Memos**.
6. Move the **Lunch** document into the **Memos** folder.
7. Open the **Lunch** document in Notepad.
8. Minimize the **Memos** folder window.

PAUSE. LEAVE the document open to use in the next project.

Project 2: Lunch Costs

Use Windows Vista Speech Recognition and the calculator to determine the total cost of lunch for 57 participants. Use Windows Vista Speech Recognition to insert the information into a text document, print the document, and then delete it.

GET READY. Before you begin these steps, ensure that your microphone is properly set up and working on your computer before beginning this project.

USE the file that is open from the previous project.

1. Start Windows Vista Speech Recognition.
2. If necessary, user Windows Vista Speech Recognition to switch to Notepad.
3. On the first line, use Windows Vista Speech Recognition commands to key **Memorandum** and then press the [Enter] key twice.
4. Use Windows Vista Speech Recognition commands to enter the following:
   Today's date [Enter]
   To: Manager of Special Projects [Enter]
   From: Your Name [Enter twice]
   Based on the estimated cost of $9.85 per person, [Enter]
   I have calculated that the total cost of lunch for the [Enter]
   57 teachers attending the first seminar is [Enter]
5. Save the changes to the file.

6. Using Windows Vista Speech Recognition, open the calculator.
7. On the calculator keypad, use Windows Vista Speech Recognition to click **5**, click **7**, and then click *****.
8. On the calculator keypad, use Windows Vista Speech Recognition to click **9**, click the decimal point, click **8**, click **5**, and then click **=**.
9. Arrange the open windows side by side and make the **Lunch** document active.
10. Using Windows Vista Speech Recognition, move the insertion point to the end of the file, press [spacebar], and key the result of the calculation as a dollar value followed by a period to end the sentence.
11. Using Windows Vista Speech Recognition, press [Enter] twice and key **Please let me know if you have any questions**. Your desktop should look similar to Figure 1.

Figure 1
Open windows side by side

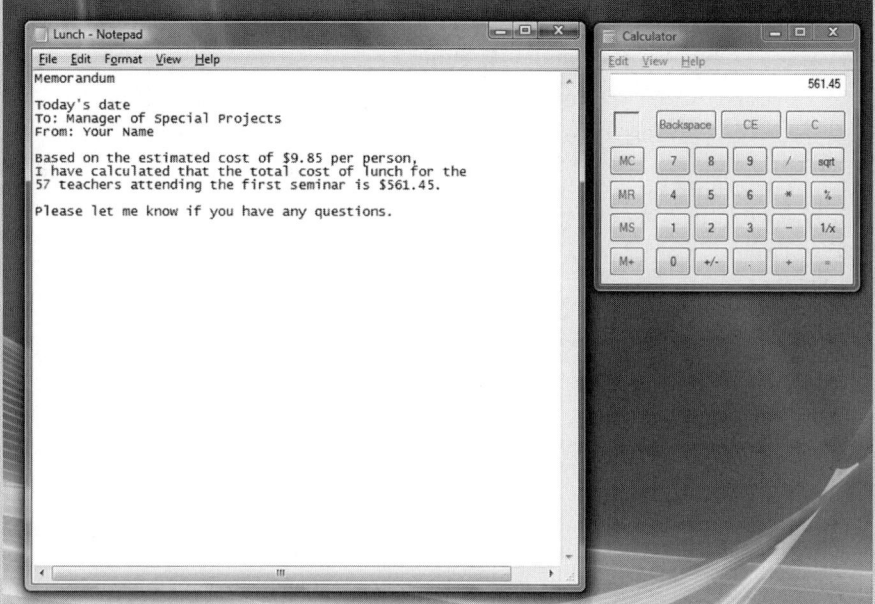

12. Save the changes to the **Lunch** document and then close it.
13. Close the Calculator window.
14. Maximize the **Memos** folder window.
15. Print the **Lunch** text document.
16. Delete the **Lunch** text document.
17. Restore the **Memos** folder window and then close it.
    PAUSE. LEAVE the desktop open to use in the next project.

Project 3: Handbook Files

Set up a folder for the seminar handbook files and then create a text file in the folder, listing the topics and dates of each seminar. You will locate two picture files that might be suitable for the handbook cover and then copy them into the folder.

1. Open the **Documents** folder and then open the **Seminars** folder.
2. Create a new folder named **Handbook**.
3. Open the **Handbook** folder, create a new text document file, and name it **Schedule**.
4. Open the **Schedule** text document in Notepad.
5. On the first line, key your name and then press [Enter].

6. Key today's date and then press **Enter** twice.
7. Key the following list, pressing **Enter** once to start a new line or twice to leave a blank line:

   Seminar 1, October 15

   Our Changing Climate

   [blank line]

   Seminar 2, January 10

   Exploring Space

   [blank line]

   Seminar 3, March 12

   Animal Habitats

   [blank line]

   Seminar 4, June 7

   Everyday Physics

8. Save the changes to the file. It should look similar to Figure 2.

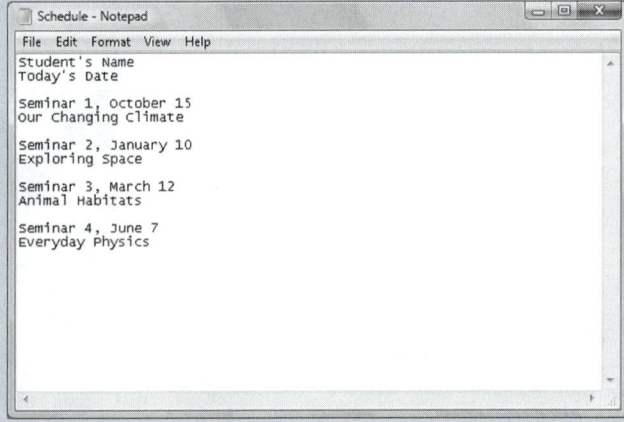

Figure 2

Schedule Notepad document

The *Handbook_Picture1* file is available on the companion CD-ROM.

9. Print the **Schedule** file and then close it.
10. Navigate to the data files for this lesson and locate **Handbook_Picture1**.
11. Right-click the **Handbook_Picture1** picture file and click **Copy**. Then navigate to your Handbook folder, right-click the Files list area, and click **Paste** to paste the file into the folder.

The *Handbook_Picture2* file is available on the companion CD-ROM.

12. Locate the **Handbook_Picture2** file in the data files and copy it to the Handbook folder.

    PAUSE. LEAVE the Handbook folder open to use in the next project.

Project 4: Removable Files

The manager of special events is leaving on a brief business trip and wants to review the handbook files you have been working on. In this project, you will copy the entire Handbook folder to a removable device.

GET READY. Before you begin these steps, insert a blank disk such as a CD, DVD, or floppy into the appropriate drive. If necessary, close the AutoPlay window.

The *Schedule*, *Handbook_Picture3*, and *Handbook_Picture4* files are available on the companion CD-ROM.

USE the Handbook folder containing the Schedule text document, the **Handbook_Picture1** file, and the **Handbook_Picture2** file that you created in Project 2, or create a new Handbook folder and use the **Handbook_Picture3** and **Handbook_Picture4** files from the data files for this Lesson.

1. Open the **Handbook** folder.
2. If necessary, navigate to the data files for this lesson and then copy the *Schedule* text file and the *Handbook_Picture3* and *Handbook_Picture4* picture files to the **Handbook** folder. Rename *Handbook_Picture3* to **Handbook_Picture1**. Rename *Handbook_Picture4* to **Handbook_Picture2**.
3. Right-click the **Handbook** folder icon on the desktop, point to the **Send To** command, and then click the device in which you have inserted a disk.
4. Navigate to the Documents folder.
5. Delete the Seminars folder and its contents.
6. Navigate to the Recycle Bin.
7. Empty the Recycle Bin.
8. Close all open windows.
9. Log off of your Windows Vista user account and shut down Windows Vista.
10. Shut off your computer.

Microsoft® Office
Word® 2007

Word Essentials

LESSON SKILL MATRIX

Changing Word's View	Students will learn how to change Word's view.
Navigating a Document	Students will learn how to navigate a Word document.
Entering Text in a Document	Students will learn how to enter text in a Word document.
Selecting, Replacing, and Deleting Text	Students will learn how to select, replace, and delete text in a Word document.

Star Bright Satellite Radio is the nation's leading satellite radio company. The company sells its subscription service to automobile owners, home listeners, and people on the go with portable satellite radios. The public relations department is responsible for promoting a favorable image of Star Bright Satellite Radio to the media, potential customers, and current customers. Microsoft Word 2007 is the perfect tool for creating and editing a wide variety of professional-looking documents that enhance Star Bright's image on a daily basis. In this lesson, you will learn to open, navigate, edit, save, print, and close a document.

KEY TERMS
gridlines
I-beam
insertion point
multi-selection
ruler
scroll box
scroll buttons
thumbnails

Software Orientation

Microsoft Word's Opening Screen

Before you begin working in Microsoft Word, you should be familiar with the primary user interface. When you first launch Microsoft Word, you will see a screen similar to that shown in Figure 1-1.

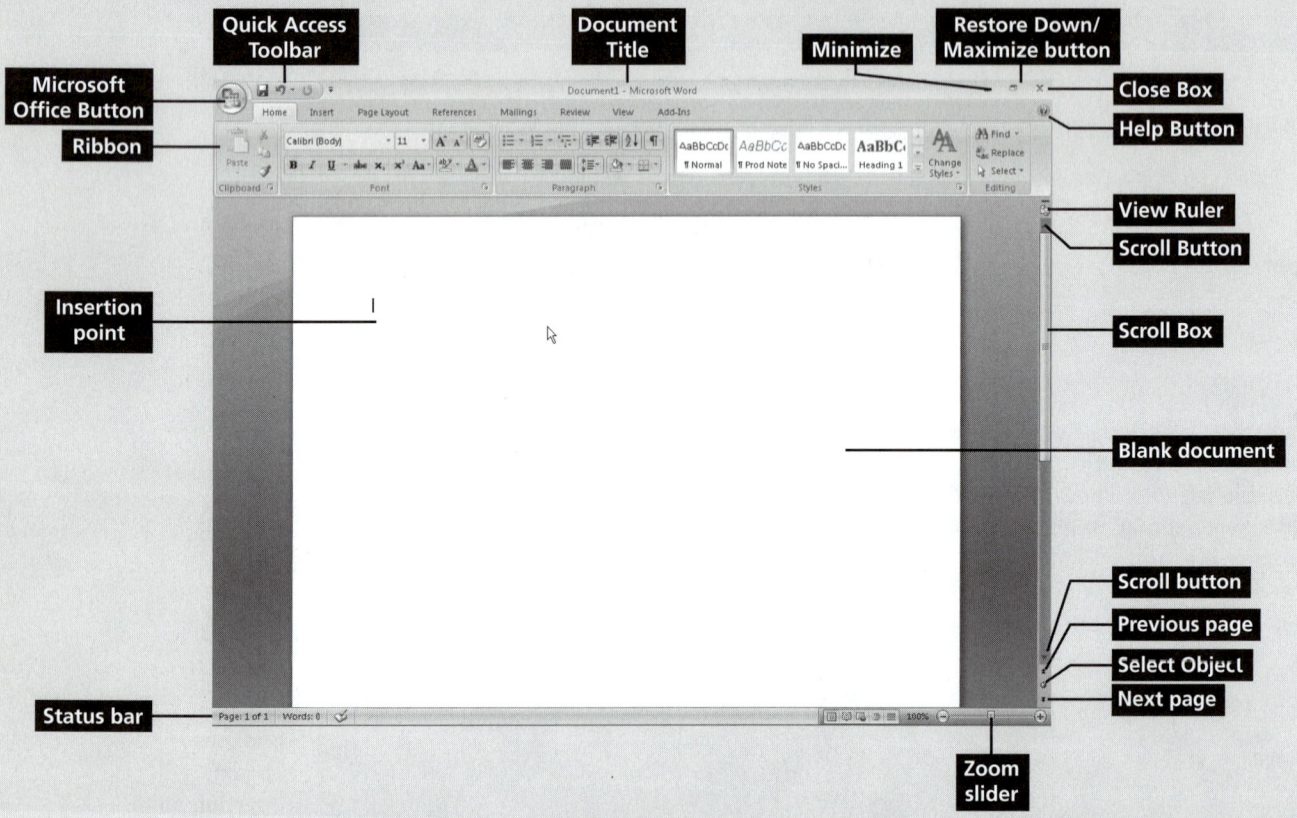

Figure 1-1
Word document window

Microsoft has designed the user interface to provide easier access to commands relevant to the document being created or edited. Your screen may vary if default settings have been changed or if other preferences have been set.

Working with an Existing Document

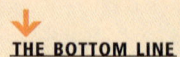

THE BOTTOM LINE

The great thing about creating and editing documents using Word is the convenience with which you can later reopen documents to make changes. In this lesson, you will open an existing document and learn to navigate it. You will also enter, select, replace, and delete text.

Word Essentials | 115

Changing Word's View

Word has different ways you can view a document. The View tab on the ribbon has groups of commands for Document Views, Show/Hide, Zoom, Window, and Macros. In this section, you will learn about various ways to view documents in Word.

➔ CHANGE DOCUMENT VIEWS

GET READY. Before you begin these steps, be sure to launch Microsoft Word 2007.

1. Browse to the location of the data files for this lesson and open the *SBpressrelease* file.
2. Click the **View** tab to activate it, as shown in Figure 1-2. Notice the command groups that are available.

The *SBpressrelease* document is available on the companion CD-ROM.

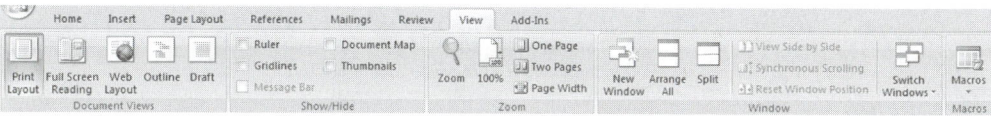

Figure 1-2

The View tab

3. In the Document Views group, click the **Full Screen Reading** view button to change to Full Screen Reading view, as shown in Figure 1-3.

Figure 1-3

Full Screen Reading view

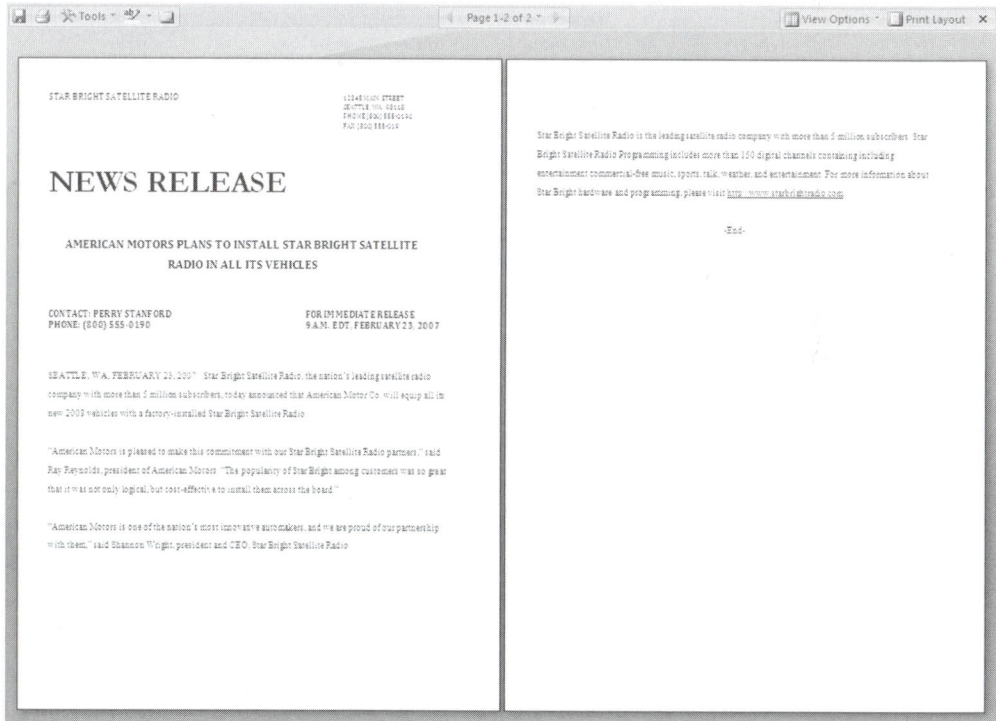

Figure 1-4

View Options menu

4. Click the **View Options** menu, shown in Figure 1-4.

5. Notice all the options for viewing the document. Choose **Increase Text Size**. The text size is temporarily increased for better reading on the screen.
6. Click **View Options** and **Show One Page**. The document is displayed on the page one screen at a time.
7. Press **Esc** to turn off Full Screen Reading view.
8. Click the **Web Layout** view button.
9. Click the **Outline** view button. Notice the Outline tab and the groups of commands that appear for editing outlines. Click **Close Outline View**.
10. Click the **View** tab and click the **Draft** view button.
11. Click the **Print Layout** view button.

   PAUSE. LEAVE the document open to use in the next exercise.

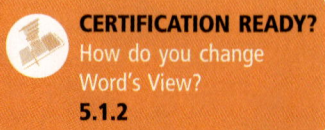

CERTIFICATION READY?
How do you change Word's View?
5.1.2

Word has five main views:

• Print Layout is the most common view. It displays the document as it will look when printed and enables you to use the ribbon to create and edit your document.
• Full Screen Reading view is made for reading documents on the screen. You have many options for customizing this view.
• Web Layout view shows how the document would look as a web page.

- Outline view displays the document as an outline and shows an outline tab with commands for creating and editing outlines.
- Draft view lets you view the document as a draft. Headers, footers, and other elements do not appear.

 **ANOTHER WAY** The view commands are also accessible in the View button portion of the status bar located at the bottom of the screen.

 USE SHOW/HIDE COMMANDS

USE the document that is open from the previous exercise.

1. In the Show/Hide group, click the **Ruler** box to insert a checkmark. Rulers appear, as shown in Figure 1-5.
2. Click the **Gridlines** box. A grid appears behind text on the page, as shown in Figure 1-5.
3. Click the **Thumbnails** box. Small pages appear in the left pane of the window, as shown in Figure 1-5.

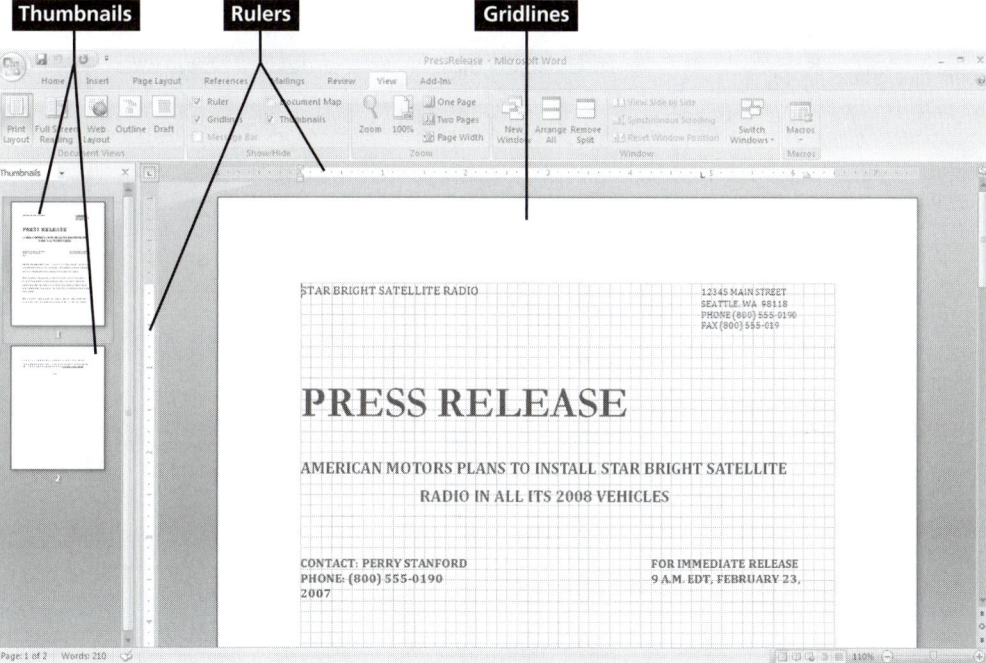

Figure 1-5

Rulers, gridlines, and thumbnails

4. Click the **Document Map** box to insert a checkmark. The document map appears in the left pane, replacing the thumbnails.
5. Click the **Document Map** box to remove the checkmark. The thumbnails and window pane disappear.
6. Click the **Gridlines** box to remove the gridlines.
7. Click the **Ruler** box to remove the rulers from view.

   PAUSE. LEAVE the document open to use in the next exercise.

118 | Lesson 1

ANOTHER WAY

You can also use the View Ruler button on the document window to display the ruler.

The Show/Hide command group lets you show or hide various features to help with the creation, editing, and navigation of your documents. In this exercise, you displayed the *rulers*, which are measuring tools to help you align text. Both the horizontal and vertical rulers display margins, while the horizontal ruler also displays indents and tabs.

Gridlines provide a grid of vertical and horizontal lines that help you align graphics and other objects in your documents. They can only be displayed in Print Layout view.

For long documents, it is helpful to use the document map, which appears in the left pane of the window and shows you the structure of a document. A *thumbnail* is a small picture of a page. Because the document map and thumbnails are both displayed in the left pane, they cannot be displayed at the same time. The message bar is a to-do list for the document, displaying tasks that need to be completed.

→ USE ZOOM

USE the document that is open from the previous exercise.

1. Click the **View** tab, if necessary.
2. Click the **One Page** button. The entire page is shown on the screen.
3. Click the **Two Pages** button. Two pages are shown on the screen.
4. Click the **Zoom** button. The Zoom dialog box appears, as shown in Figure 1-6.

Figure 1-6

Zoom dialog box

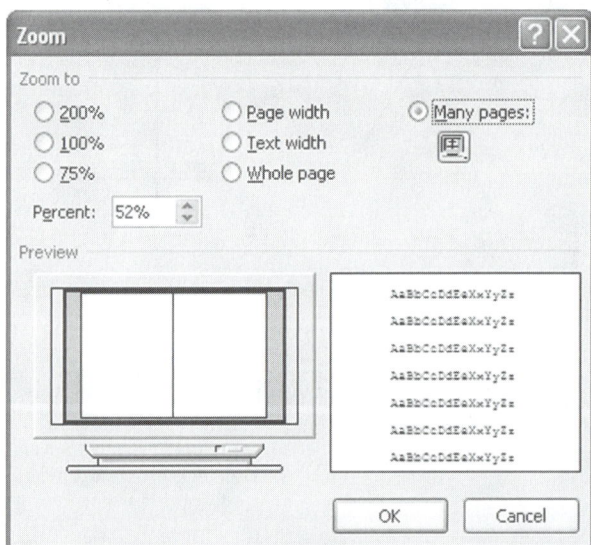

5. Click the button beside **200%** and click **OK**.
6. Click the **Zoom Out** button on the zoom slider at the bottom right of the screen, shown in Figure 1-7. Notice it decreases the zoom by 10 percent with each click.

Figure 1-7

Zoom slider

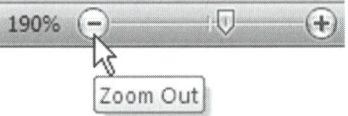

7. Drag the slider all the way to the left beside the **Zoom Out** button. Notice the document is reduced to thumbnail size.
8. In the Zoom group, click the **Page Width** button. The document expands to the width of the window.

   PAUSE. LEAVE the document open to use in the next exercise.

Word Essentials | 119

ANOTHER WAY

You can also click the percentage displayed in the zoom slider to display the Zoom dialog box.

The Zoom group of commands lets you zoom in to get a closer view of a page or zoom out to see more of the document at a smaller size. In the previous exercise, you used the Zoom commands to view one page at a time and two pages at a time.

The Page Width button expands the document to the width of the window. The Zoom button launches the Zoom dialog box, where you have more options for zooming in and out. You can even enter a specific number in the percent box. In the Zoom To section, click to choose a specific amount of zoom, such as 200%. The preview section shows how the document will look on the screen.

You can also use the zoom slider, located on the status bar, to zoom in and out.

CHANGE WINDOW VIEWS

USE the document that is open from the previous exercise.

1. In the Window group, click the **New Window** button. A new window with the same document, titled *SBpressrelease:2* appears, as shown in Figure 1-8. It is now the active document.

Figure 1-8

New window

2. Click the **View** tab. In the Window group, click the **Switch Windows** button. A menu of open windows appears, as shown in Figure 1-9.

Figure 1-9

Switch Windows button and menu

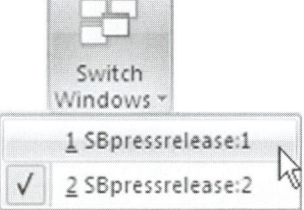

3. Click *SBpressrelease:1*. The original document is now the active document.
4. Click the **Arrange All** button. The two windows are placed on the top and bottom of your screen, as shown in Figure 1-10.

Figure 1-10

Arrange All

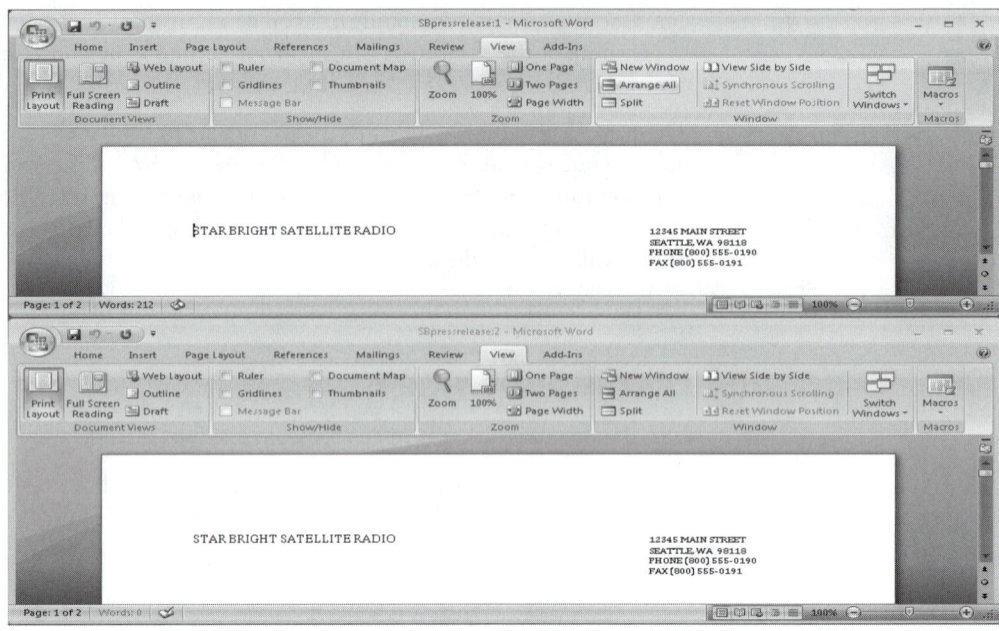

5. Click the **View Side by Side** button. The windows are arranged side by side.
6. Click in the window of *SBpressrelease:2* to make it the active document. Click the **Close** button to close it.
7. In the remaining document, click the **Maximize** button to make the document fill the screen again.
8. Click the **Split** button. Notice you have a vertical split bar and a double-sided arrow. Position the split bar below *News Release* and click the mouse button. The document window is now split in two (see Figure 1-11).

Figure 1-11

Split window

9. Click **Remove Split**.
10. Click the **Minimize** button, shown in Figure 1-12. The document is minimized to the Windows Taskbar at the bottom of the screen.

Figure 1-12

Minimize, Restore Down, and Close buttons

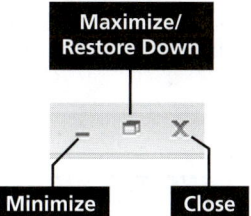

11. Click the *SBpressrelease* document in the Taskbar to maximize the document back on the screen.
12. Click the **Restore Down** button.
13. Position the mouse pointer on the lower right corner of the document window where you see the pattern of dots. Your mouse pointer becomes a double-sided arrow, as shown in Figure 1-13.

Figure 1-13

Size a window

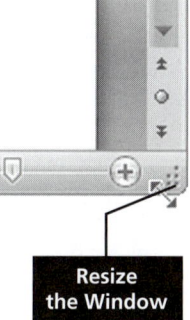

14. Click and drag toward the middle of the screen to decrease the size of the window.
15. Click the sizing corner again and drag the double-sided arrow to the lower right corner to increase the size of the window.

   PAUSE. LEAVE the document open to use in the next exercise.

You can view a document in a variety of ways using the Window group of commands. In the previous exercise, you created a new window with the New Window button. The Arrange All button places two or more windows on the screen at the same time. This is useful when comparing documents or using some information from one document in another document.

The Split command divides one document window into two windows that scroll independently. This enables you to view two parts of the document at the same time.

You can view two documents next to each other using the View Side by Side button. You can use the Synchronous Scrolling command to set the scrolling of two documents to work together. And the Reset Window Position repositions two side-by-side documents equally on the screen.

You can change which window is the current active document using the Switch Windows button. When you click the button, a menu of open documents appears. Click the document you want to make active. The active document is the document that is ready to accept commands.

You may have a need to move a window on your screen out of the way without exiting the application. The three buttons in the upper right corner of Windows documents let you minimize, restore down/maximize, or close a window. Click the Minimize button to minimize the document window, removing it from the screen and sending it to the Taskbar. The Restore

Down and Maximize button toggles back and forth. Click Restore Down and you are able to size a window. Click Maximize to return the window to its maximum size on the screen.

Navigating a Document

In this section, you will use scrollbars, scroll boxes, and scroll buttons to help you navigate a document. In addition, you can use certain keystrokes to make your way through a document.

⊙ **SCROLL THROUGH A DOCUMENT USING THE MOUSE**

USE the document that is open from the previous exercise.

1. Click the **Scroll Down button**, shown in Figure 1-14. The document scrolls down one line at a time.

Figure 1-14

Scrollbars, scroll box, and scroll buttons

Word Essentials | 123

2. Click and hold the **Scroll Down** button until you scroll all the way to the end of the document.
3. Position the mouse pointer on the **scroll box**. Click and hold to see a screen tip appear, letting you know your current location in the document (see Figure 1-15).

Figure 1-15

Screen tip on scroll box

4. Drag the **scroll box** all the way to the top of the scrollbar. The page quickly scrolls to the beginning of the document.
5. Click the **Next Page** button to move to the next page, which in this case is page 2.
6. Click the **Select Browse Object** button. A menu appears with various places you can choose to browse (see Figure 1-16).

Figure 1-16

Select Browse Object menu

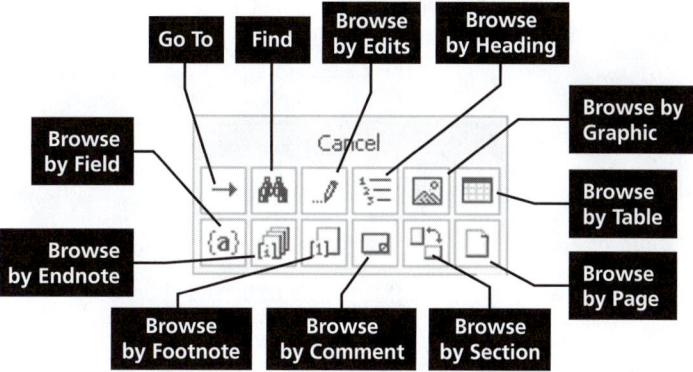

7. Move the mouse pointer over each button to see its name appear in the display box.
8. Click in a blank space in the document to remove the menu.
9. Click the **Previous Page** button to move back to page 1.

   PAUSE. LEAVE the document open to use in the next exercise.

Vertical *scrollbars* appear on the right and/or bottom of the document window, enabling you to move up and down through the document. Click the *scroll buttons* to move up or down one line at a time. Click and hold a scroll button to move more quickly. Click the scroll box to see a display of your position in the document. Click and drag the *scroll box* to move even more quickly horizontally or vertically through a document.

You can click the Previous Page button to move back to the previous page; click the Next Page button to move to the following page. The Select Browse Object button has a pop-up menu of ways to move quickly to and browse by field, endnote, footnote, comment, edits, section, page, graphic, or table. You will learn more about these items throughout the book.

➡ **USE KEYSTROKES TO NAVIGATE A DOCUMENT**

USE the document that is open from the previous exercise.

1. In the first line of the body of the document, position the insertion point before the *S* in *Seattle*.

2. On the keyboard, press the `Right arrow` key to move one character to the right.
3. Press the `Left arrow` key to move one character to the left.
4. Press the `Down arrow` key to move down one line.
5. Press the `End` key to move to the end of the line.
6. Press the `Page Down` key to move down one screen.
7. Press the `Home` key to move to the beginning of the page.

   PAUSE. LEAVE the document open to use in the next exercise.

You can press certain keys on the keyboard or use a combination of keys to navigate through a document. Table 1-1 displays common keyboard shortcuts for moving through a document.

Table 1-1

Keyboard shortcuts for navigating a document

Shortcut Key	To Move
Left Arrow	One character to the left
Right Arrow	One character to the right
Up Arrow	Up one line
Down Arrow	Down one line
End	End of a line
Home	Beginning of a line
Page Up	Up one screen
Page Down	Down one screen
Ctrl+Page Down	Down one page
Ctrl+Page Up	Up one page
Ctrl+Home	To beginning of the document
Ctrl+End	To end of the document

Entering Text in a Document

In this section, you will learn how to enter text where you want it in a document.

ENTER TEXT

USE the document that is open from the previous exercise.

1. Move the pointer over the title of the document. Notice the pointer changes to an I-beam.
2. Position the I-beam on the left side of the *V* in the word *VEHICLES* and click. The I-beam becomes the blinking insertion point.
3. Key **2008** and press the .
4. Position the insertion point in the middle of the second paragraph, to the left of the *T* in *The popularity*.
5. Key **Their excellent programming provides our customers with an endless variety of entertainment options**. Press the `spacebar`. Your screen should look similar to Figure 1-17.

Figure 1-17

Text entered in a document

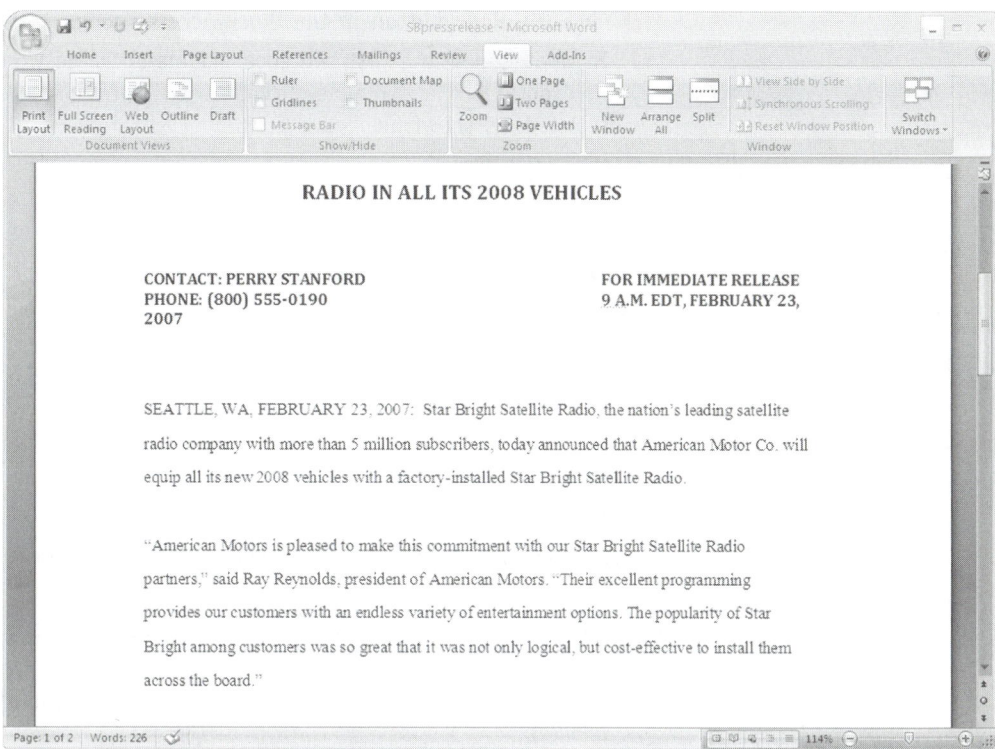

TAKE NOTE

As you key, Word automatically checks the spelling and grammar of the words you key. If it detects a mistake, it inserts a wavy red or green line underneath. Ignore these for now. You will learn more about checking spelling and grammar in later lessons.

PAUSE. LEAVE the document open to use in the next exercise.

When you move the mouse in the text area of a document, it is shaped like an *I-beam*. Position the I-beam where you want to key text and click. Now it becomes a blinking *insertion point*, ready for you to start keying. Text will be inserted to the left of the insertion point.

When you key text, Word automatically wraps text for you when you reach the end of a line. If you want to start a new paragraph, press Enter.

Selecting, Replacing, and Deleting Text

Before making any change to text, you have to select it. In this section, you will learn to use the mouse and keyboard to select text. Then you will learn to delete or replace it with new text.

➔ SELECT, REPLACE, AND DELETE TEXT

USE the document that is open from the previous exercise.

1. At the beginning of the document, position the insertion point to the left of the *N* in *News Release*. Click and drag across the word *News* to select it.
2. Key **PRESS**. The word *NEWS* is replaced with the word *PRESS*.
3. In the first paragraph of the body of the document, position the insertion point after the *5* in *5 million*.
4. Press **Backspace** to delete the number *5*. Key **8**.
5. Scroll to the bottom of the document. Position the insertion point in any word in the last paragraph. Triple-click the mouse. The entire paragraph is selected.
6. Click in a blank part of the page, such as the margin, to deselect the paragraph.
7. Press the **Ctrl** key and click *Star*, the first word of the first sentence of the last paragraph. The sentence is selected.
8. Press **Backspace** to delete the sentence.
9. Click the **Undo** button in the Quick Access Toolbar to undo the action.

10. Click the **Redo** button in the Quick Access Toolbar to redo the action.
11. In what is now the first sentence, double-click the word *containing* to select it. Hold down **Ctrl** and double-click the word *entertainment*. Both words are now selected, as shown in Figure 1-18.

Figure 1-18

Multi-selection

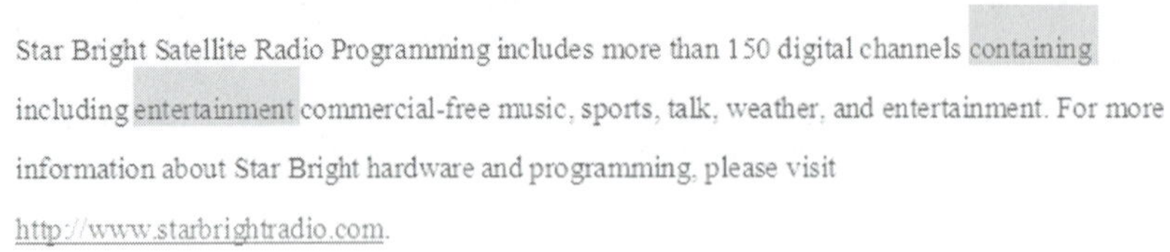

Star Bright Satellite Radio Programming includes more than 150 digital channels containing including entertainment commercial-free music, sports, talk, weather, and entertainment. For more information about Star Bright hardware and programming, please visit http://www.starbrightradio.com.

-End-

12. Press **Delete** to delete the words.
13. In the last paragraph, first sentence, position the insertion point to the left of the first *e* in *entertainment*.
14. Press and hold **Ctrl**, press and hold **Shift**, and press the **Right arrow** key. The word *entertainment* is selected.
15. Key **traffic updates**. The word *entertainment* is replaced with the words *traffic updates*.
16. Click the **Microsoft Office Button**, choose Save As, and key **PressRelease** as the new file name.
17. **CLOSE** the file.

    STOP. CLOSE Word.

When you select text, the text you key replaces the selected text. To cancel a selection, click on white space in the document.

When the mouse pointer is in the left margin, it changes to a selection arrow that enables you to drag to select a character, word, lines, or paragraphs of text. You can also click to position the insertion point and then drag to select text. Table 1-2 shows ways you can select text with the mouse.

Table 1-2

Selecting text with the mouse

To Select	Do This
Any amount of text	Click and drag across the text
Word	Double-click the word
Line	Click in the left margin with the mouse pointer
Multiple lines	Drag in the left margin
Sentence	Hold Ctrl and click anywhere in the sentence
Paragraph	Double-click in the left margin or triple-click in the paragraph
Entire Document	Triple-click in the left margin

ANOTHER WAY

The Select button in the Editing group of the Home tab lets you select all text in a document, select objects behind text, or select text with similar formatting.

In the previous exercise, you practiced ***multi-selection***, which is a feature of Word that enables you to select multiple pieces of text that are not next to each other. Just select the first piece of text, press the Ctrl key, and select additional items.

You can also use the keyboard to select text. Table 1-3 shows keys you can press to select text.

Word Essentials | 127

Table 1-3

Selecting text with the keyboard

To Select	Do This
One character to the right	Shift+Right Arrow
One character to the left	Shift+Left Arrow
To the end of a word	Ctrl+Shift+Right Arrow
To the beginning of a word	Ctrl+Shift+Left Arrow
To the end of a line	Shift+End
To the beginning of a line	Shift+Home
To the end of a document	Ctrl+Shift+End
To the beginning of a document	Ctrl+Shift+Home
The entire document	Ctrl+A
To the end of a paragraph	Ctrl+Shift+Down Arrow

You can delete text in a number of ways.

- Press the Backspace key to delete characters to the left of the insertion point.
- Press the Del key to delete characters to the right of the insertion point.
- Select text and press the Del or Backspace key.

To replace text, select the text and key new text.

SUMMARY SKILL MATRIX

In this lesson you learned How to:
Change Word's View
Navigate a Document
Enter Text in a Document
Select, Replace, and Delete Text

■ Knowledge Assessment

Matching

Match the term in Column 1 to its description in Column 2.

Column 1

Column 2

1. Arrange All *d*
2. desktop *i*
3. Scrollbars *g*

a. helps you align text and displays indents, tabs, and margins

b. divides one document window into two windows that scroll independently

c. Headers, Footers, and other elements do not appear in this view

4. multi-selection F
5. thumbnail h
6. insertion point j
7. Print Layout view e
8. Split command d
9. Draft view c
10. ruler g

d. places all open windows on the screen at the same time
e. most commonly used view
f. enables you to select multiple pieces of text that are not next to each other
g. appear on right and/or bottom of a document window
h. small picture of a page
i. the first screen you see when you start Windows
j. blinking I-beam appears at this place in a document

True/False

Circle T if the statement is true or F if the statement is false.

T F 1. When you start Word, a new, blank document appears.
T **F** 2. The New Window button splits the window in two.
T F 3. When you select text, the first text you key replaces text.
T **F** 4. The Undo button is on the Mini toolbar.
T **F** 5. Full Screen Reading view displays the document as it will look when printed.
T F 6. View commands are accessible on the status bar.
T F 7. Gridlines can be used to help align graphics and other objects in a document.
T **F** 8. The Microsoft Office Button is used to change a document's view.
T **F** 9. The zoom slider is located in the View menu.
T F 10. The zoom dialog box can be displayed by clicking the percentage displayed in the zoom slider.

■ Competency Assessment

Project 1-1: Coffee Shop Sign

GET READY. Launch Word if it is not already running.

The Grand Street Coffee Shop places a sign on the door and near the order counter listing the featured coffees of the day. Update today's sign.

1. Click the **Microsoft Office Button** and choose **Open** from the menu.
2. In the Look In box, click the location of the data files for this lesson.
3. Locate and click **sign** one time to select it.
4. Click **Open**.
5. Position the I-beam before the *M* in *Morning Blend*. Drag over the words to select *Morning Blend*.
6. Key **Grand Street Blend**.
7. Position the I-beam before the *K* in *Kona* and click to place the insertion point.
8. Press and hold **Shift** and press the **Right arrow** key four times to select the entire word.
9. Key **Hawaiian**.
10. Position the I-beam before the *T* in *Try Me* and click to place the insertion point.
11. Key **$1** and press the **spacebar**.

The *sign* document is available on the companion CD-ROM.

Word Essentials | 129

12. In the last line, double-click the word *Mocha* to select it.
13. Key **White Chocolate**.
14. Click the **View** tab. In the Zoom group, click **One Page**.
15. Click **Page Width**.
16. Click the **Microsoft Office Button** and choose **Save As** from the menu.
17. In the Save In window, click the location where you will save the file. If necessary, double-click the folder in the main window where you will save files.
18. Key **newsign** in the File Name box and click **Save**.
19. Click the **Microsoft Office Button**. Point to Print and then click Quick Print.
20. Click the **Microsoft Office Button** and choose **Close** from the menu.
    PAUSE. LEAVE Word open for the next project.

Project 1-2: Job Description

Star Bright Satellite Radio is hiring. Edit the job description so that it can be sent on to the human resources department for processing and posting.

The *jobdescription* document is available on the companion CD-ROM.

1. Click the **Microsoft Office Button** and choose **Open** from the menu.
2. In the Look In box, click the location of the data files for this lesson. Locate and click *jobdescription* one time to select it.
3. Click **Open**.
4. In the second line of the document, position the I-beam before the *D* in *Date* and click to place the insertion point.
5. Beginning at the *D*, click and drag down and to the right until *Date Posted* and the line below it, *5/15/07*, is selected.
6. Press **Backspace** to delete both lines.
7. In the *Duties & Responsibilities* heading, position the insertion point before the &. Press **Shift** and then press the **Right arrow** key to select &.
8. Key **and**. The & is replaced with the word *and*.
9. Position the mouse pointer in the left margin beside the line in the first bulleted list that reads *Define the web site's look and feel*. Click to select the line.
10. Press **Del** to delete it.
11. In the *Education and/or Experience* heading, position the I-beam to the right of the letter *r* in *or*.
12. Press **Backspace** three times to delete the *r*, *o*, and */*.
13. In the first line of the bulleted list that begins *College degree required...*, click to position the insertion point after the last *e* in *degree*.
14. Press the **spacebar** and key **preferred**.
15. Click the **Microsoft Office Button** and choose **Save As** from the menu.
16. In the Save In window, click the location where you will save the file. If necessary, double-click the folder in the main window where you will save files.
17. Key **updatedjobdescription** in the File Name box and click **Save**.
18. Click the **Microsoft Office Button** and choose **Close** from the menu.
    PAUSE: LEAVE Word open for the next project.

■ Proficiency Assessment

Project 1-3: Committee Meeting Schedule

You are chair of the New Neighbor Welcoming Committee in your neighborhood. The group meets monthly at a committee member's house. A different committee member is responsible for bringing refreshments to each meeting. Use Word to create a schedule to share with members.

The *schedule* document is available on the companion CD-ROM.

1. OPEN *schedule* from the data files for this lesson.
2. Complete the schedule. For the May 11 meeting details, key **D. Lorenzo, 7501 Oak, 8 p.m.** Beside *refreshments*, key **S. Wilson**.
3. The June 15 meeting details are **R. Mason, 7620 Oak, 8 p.m.** and **J. Estes** is bringing the refreshments.
4. SAVE the document as *updatedschedule* and then CLOSE the file.

   PAUSE: LEAVE Word open for the next project.

Project 1-4: Updating the Coffee Shop Sign

You already know the featured coffees for tomorrow, so go ahead and update the sign with the new coffees.

The *newsign* document is available on the companion CD-ROM.

1. OPEN *newsign* from the data files for this lesson.
2. Change the light coffee to **Colombian**.
3. Change the dark coffee to **French Roast**.
4. Change the $1 Try Me Special to **French Vanilla Latte**.
5. SAVE the document as *updatedsign* and then CLOSE the file.

   PAUSE: LEAVE Word open for the next project.

■ Mastery Assessment

Project 1-5: Fixing the Coffee Shop Menu

A co-worker for the Grand Coffee Shop has been working on a new menu for the coffee shop. She asks you to take a look at it before she sends it out to a graphic designer. You find the old menu file and decide to compare the two.

The *menu* document is available on the companion CD-ROM.

1. OPEN *menu* from the data files for this lesson.
2. OPEN *oldmenu* from the data files for this lesson.
3. View the two files side by side to compare.
4. Find and insert two items that are missing from the new menu.
5. Find and change five pricing errors on the new menu.
6. SAVE the corrected menu as *newmenu* and then CLOSE the file.
7. CLOSE the *oldmenu* file.

   PAUSE: LEAVE Word open for the next project.

The *oldmenu* document is available on the companion CD-ROM.

Project 1-6: Meeting Schedule Memo

Create a memo to committee members to include with the schedule you created.

The *schedulememo* document is available on the companion CD-ROM.

1. **OPEN** *schedulememo* from the data files for this lesson.

2. Leave two blank lines after the subject line and key the following:

   Thank you for volunteering to be on the New Neighbor Welcoming Committee. Enclosed please find the meeting and refreshment schedule for the next six months. See you in January!

   Committee Members:

3. **SAVE** the file as *decschedulememo*.

4. **OPEN** the *updatedschedule* document you saved in Project 1-3.

5. Display both documents on your screen using the Arrange All command. Scroll through the meeting schedule document to see the names of committee members. Key the names of the eight committee members below the *Committee Members* heading in the memo.

6. **SAVE** the *decschedulememo* document and then **CLOSE** the file.

7. **CLOSE** the *updatedschedule* document without saving.

   STOP: CLOSE Word.

INTERNET READY

Use Word Help to access online information about What's New in Word 2007. Up to Speed with Word 2007 provides an online short course or a demo explaining the new features. Browse these or other topics in Word Help online.

Document Basics

LESSON SKILL MATRIX

Creating a Document	Students will learn how to create a Word document.
Choosing a Different File Format	Students will learn how to choose a different file format.
Formatting a Document with Quick Styles	Students will learn how to format a Word document with Quick Styles.
Formatting a Document with a Theme	Students will learn how to format a Word document with a Theme.
Using Print Preview	Students will learn how to use print preview.
Setting Other Printing Options	Students will learn how to set other printing options.
Creating and Printing an Envelope	Students will learn how to create and print an envelope.
Creating and Printing a Label	Students will learn how to create and print a label.

Tech Terrace Real Estate is a real estate agency that works with clients to buy, sell, and rent homes in the neighborhood bordering a local university. Agents regularly create letters, sales data, and other real estate information to be mailed to current and prospective clients. Microsoft Word is the perfect tool for this task. In this lesson, you will learn how to create, save, format, and print a business letter. In addition, you will learn how to create and print the envelopes and labels you need to mail this material.

KEY TERMS
document theme
Print Preview
Quick Styles
Save
Save As

Creating a Document

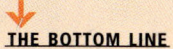
THE BOTTOM LINE

When you open Word, a blank document called *Document1* is automatically displayed, as shown in Figure 2-1. Each new document you create during a Word session will be numbered consecutively. Starting a new document is like having a blank piece of paper on which you can begin keying text or entering data.

Figure 2-1

Blank document titled *Document1*

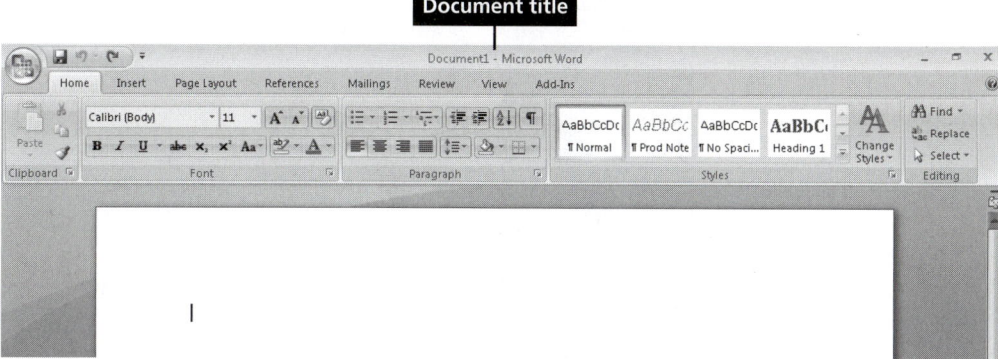

→ START A BUSINESS LETTER

GET READY. Before you begin these steps, be sure to launch Microsoft Office Word 2007 and open a new, blank document.

1. On the line where the blinking insertion point appears, key today's date.
2. Press **Enter** twice.
3. Key the delivery address as shown:

   Miriam Lockhart
   764 Crimson Avenue
   Boston, MA 02136

4. Press **Enter** twice.
5. Key **Dear Ms. Lockhart:**.
6. Press **Enter** twice.
7. Key the following text:

   We are pleased that you have chosen to list your home with Tech Terrace Real Estate. Our office has bought, sold, renovated, appraised, leased, and managed more homes in the Tech Terrace neighborhood than anyone—and now we will be putting that experience to work for you.

   Our goal is to sell your house quickly for the best possible price.

   The enclosed packet contains a competitive market analysis, complete listing data, a copy of the contracts, and a customized house brochure. Your home has been input into the MLS listing and an Internet ad has been posted on our website. We will be contacting you soon to determine the best time for an open house.

   We look forward to working with you to sell your home. Please don't hesitate to call if you have any questions.

8. Press **Enter** twice.
9. Key **Sincerely,**.
10. Press **Enter** twice.
11. Key **Steve Buckley**. Your document should appear as shown in Figure 2-2.

Figure 2-2

Business letter with text entered

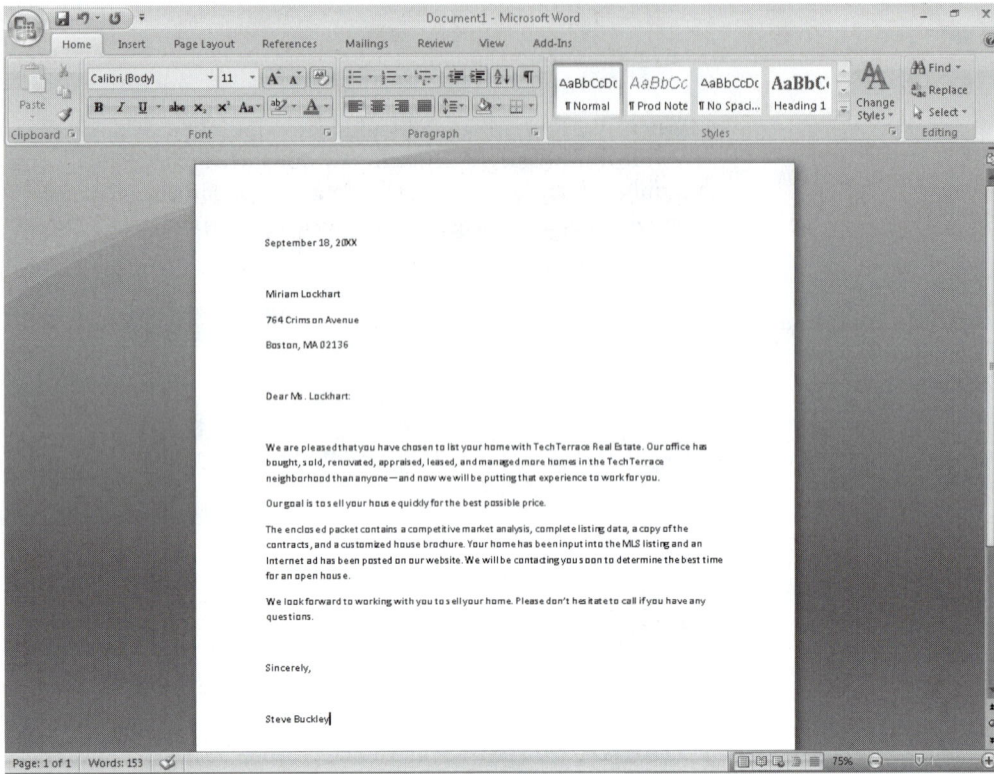

12. Save the file as *TechTerrace_letter*.

PAUSE. LEAVE the document open to use in the next exercise.

You have just created a business letter from scratch in a Word document. Later in this lesson, you will learn how to save, format, and print the document.

Choosing a Different File Format

If you need your document available in a different format, you can choose to save it as another type of file.

CHOOSE A DIFFERENT FILE FORMAT

USE the document that is open from the previous exercise.

1. Click the **Microsoft Office Button** and then click **Save As** to open the Save As dialog box.
2. In the Save As type box, click the downward-pointing arrow and choose **Word 97-2003 Document**, as shown in Figure 2-3.

Figure 2-3

Save As type menu

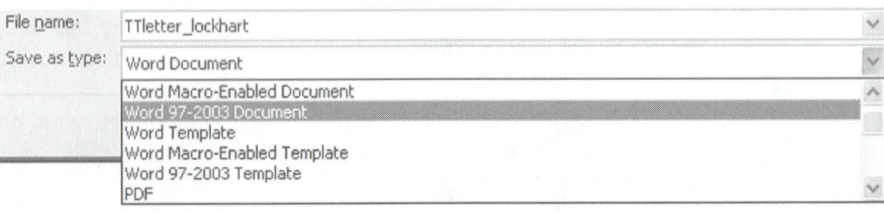

Document Basics | 135

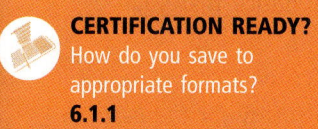

CERTIFICATION READY?
How do you save to appropriate formats?
6.1.1

3. **SAVE** the document and **CLOSE** the file.

PAUSE. LEAVE Word open for the next exercise.

You just saved a copy of your document in a different file format. The format you chose enables a user who has an earlier version of Word to open your document without any difficulty. You can choose from many different file formats, depending on your needs. For example, you may choose to save the document as a web page if it will be viewed with a browser. Or, you may want to save your document as plain text if you do not want it to include any formatting. Unless you have a specific reason for saving your document in a different file format, you will usually choose to accept the default Word format when saving.

> **TAKE NOTE***
>
> PDF files are a popular save-as format for documents. This preserves the formatting so that it can be viewed exactly as you intended, without allowing data to be changed or copied. In order to save in PDF format, you must download the appropriate add-in from *www.microsoft.com*.

■ Changing a Document's Appearance

THE BOTTOM LINE

Once you have created your document, it is time to think about how you might improve its appearance. In Word, it is easy to change a document using features such as Quick Styles and themes to make it look more professional and appealing.

Formatting a Document with Quick Styles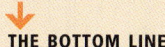

You can save time when formatting a document by choosing from a gallery of predefined Quick Styles available in Word.

→ FORMAT USING QUICK STYLES

OPEN the *TechTerrace_letter* file from the location where you saved it earlier.

1. Click anywhere in your document.
2. On the Home tab, in the Styles group, click the **Change Styles** button.
3. Click **Style Set** to display the menu of Quick Style options, as shown in Figure 2-4.

Figure 2-4

Style Set menu options

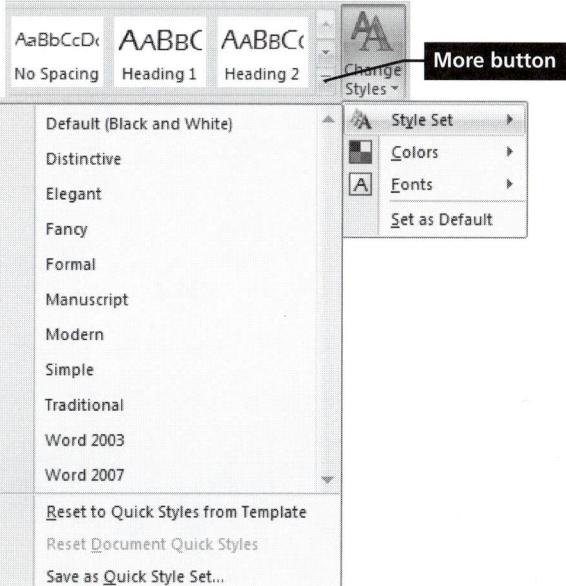

4. Place your pointer over any choice on the Style Set menu and notice that your document changes to show you a preview of that style.
5. Click **Distinctive**.
6. Select the paragraph that reads *Our goal is to sell your house quickly for the best possible price*.
7. On the Home tab, in the Styles group, click the **More** button. A Quick Style gallery appears, as shown in Figure 2-5.

Figure 2-5

Quick Style gallery

8. Place your pointer over any thumbnail in the gallery and notice that the paragraph changes to show you a preview of that style.
9. Click the **Intense Quote** thumbnail. Notice that style is applied to the paragraph you previously selected. Your document should look similar to Figure 2-6.

Figure 2-6

Document formatted with Quick Styles

If items are grey and can't access them:
— Click MS button
— Sel Convert

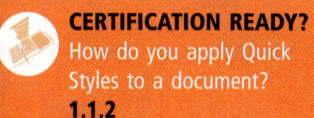

 CERTIFICATION READY?
How do you apply Quick Styles to a document?
1.1.2

10. **SAVE** your document.

    PAUSE. LEAVE the document open to use in the next exercise.

You have just formatted a business letter using Quick Styles. **Quick Styles** are predefined formats that you can apply to your document to instantly change its look and feel. Word eliminates the guesswork by allowing you to preview the formatting changes in your document before you commit to applying the style.

Formatting a Document with a Theme

Document themes are another way to quickly change the overall design of your document using formatting choices that are predefined by Word.

→ **FORMAT USING A DOCUMENT THEME**

USE the document that is open from the previous exercise.

1. On the Page Layout tab, in the Themes group, click **Themes**, as shown in Figure 2-7.

138 | Lesson 2

Figure 2-7

Document themes

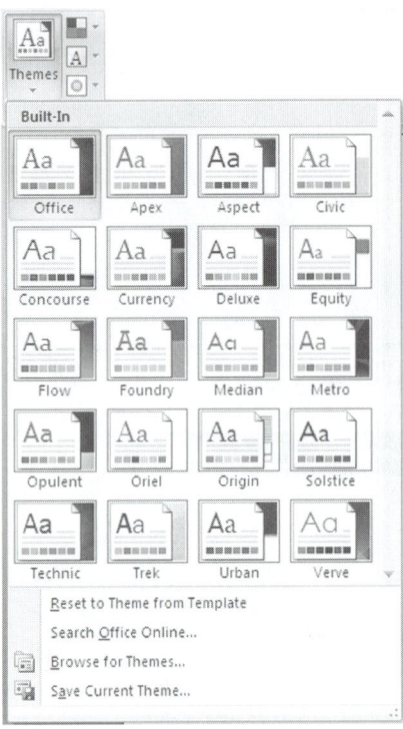

2. Place your pointer over any built-in theme and notice that the document changes to show you a preview of that theme.

> **TAKE NOTE**
>
> Although you used a theme to change the overall design of the entire document, you can also change individual elements by using the Theme Colors, Theme Fonts, and Theme Effects buttons.

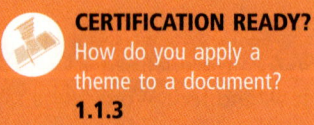

CERTIFICATION READY?
How do you apply a theme to a document?
1.1.3

3. Click **Concourse**. The colors, fonts, and effects for that theme are applied to your document.
4. **SAVE** your document.

   PAUSE. LEAVE the document open to use in the next exercise.

You have just used a document theme to format your letter. A ***document theme*** is a set of predefined formatting options that includes theme colors, fonts, and effects. You can use the choices Word provides or you can create your own document theme. Document themes contain the following elements:

- Theme colors contain four text and background colors, six accent colors, and two hyperlink colors. Click the Theme Colors button to change the colors for the current theme, as shown in Figure 2-8.

Document Basics | 139

Figure 2-8

Theme Colors menu

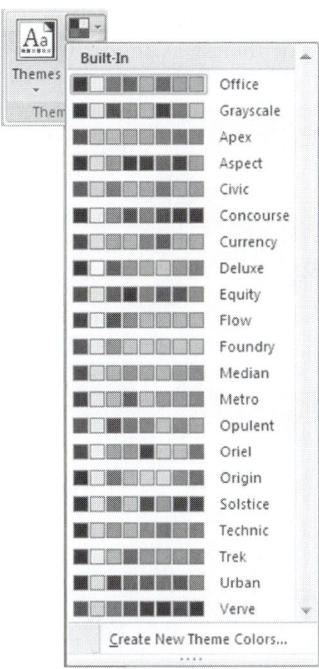

- Theme fonts contain a heading font and a body text font. Click the Theme Fonts button to change the fonts for the current theme, as shown in Figure 2-9.

Figure 2-9

Theme Fonts menu

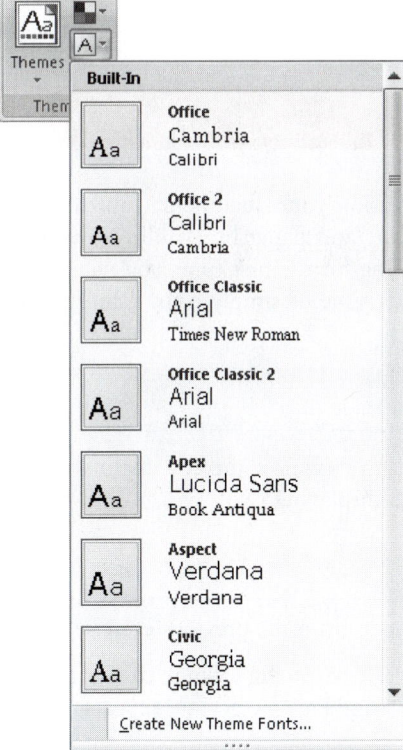

140 | Lesson 2

- Theme effects are sets of lines and fill effects. Click the Theme Effects button to change the effects for the current theme, as shown in Figure 2-10.

Figure 2-10

Theme Effects menu

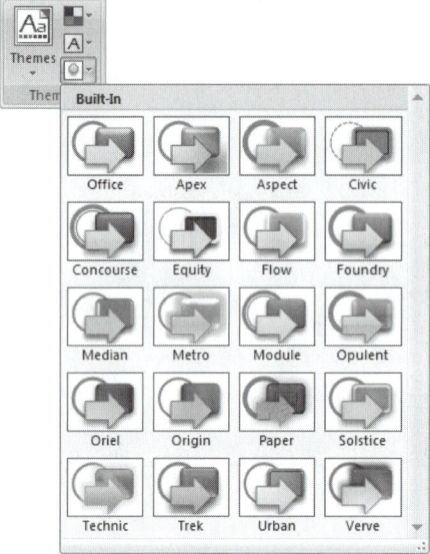

CERTIFICATION READY?
How do you add keywords to document properties?
1.3.3

If you make any changes to the colors, fonts, or effects of the current theme, you can save it as a custom document theme and then apply it to other documents.

■ Printing a Document

THE BOTTOM LINE

After you have finished creating your document, you can preview it to see how it will look in print. This saves time and paper by enabling you to make any necessary changes before printing. When printing for the first time, you will need to choose a printer. You can choose printing options each time or simply print using the default options.

Using Print Preview

Print Preview enables you to view how the document will appear when it is printed, with options such as zoom and displaying two pages.

USE PRINT PREVIEW

USE the document that is open from the previous exercise.

1. Click the **Microsoft Office Button**, point to the arrow next to **Print**, and then click **Print Preview**. The Print Preview screen appears, as shown in Figure 2-11.

Figure 2-11

Print Preview

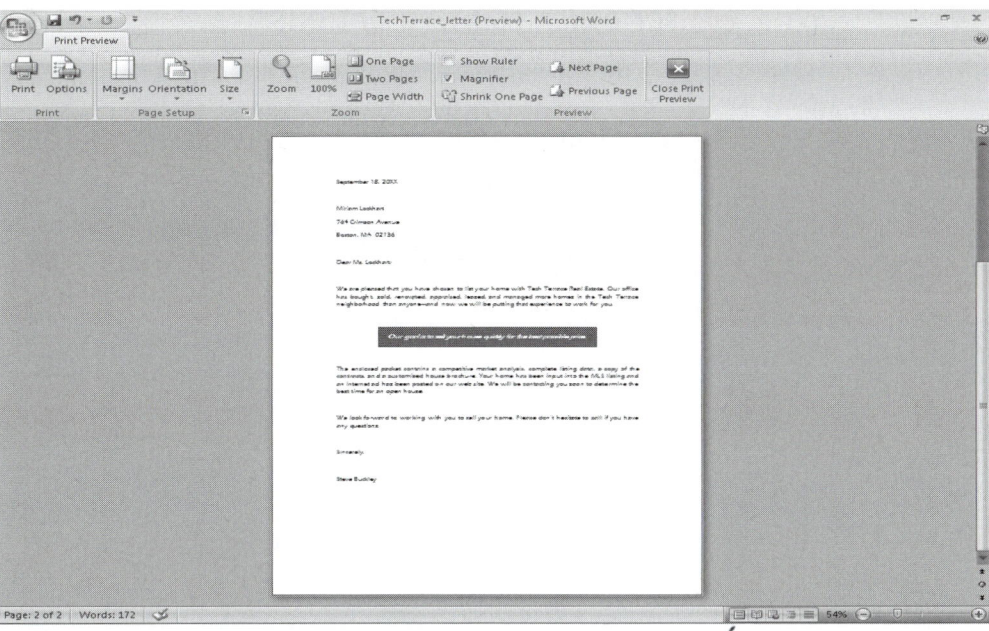

 **ANOTHER WAY** Move the pointer over the document and notice that it changes to a magnifying glass. Click the document to zoom in to 100% and again to zoom out to 50%.

2. Use the **Zoom** controls on the bottom right of the window to zoom in to 100%.
3. In the Zoom group, click the **One Page** button so that the entire page fits in the window.
4. In the Page Setup group, click the **Margins** button and then click **Normal**. Notice the document margins change in the preview window.
5. In the Zoom group, click the **Page Width** button so that the width of the page matches the width of the window.
6. In the Preview group, click **Previous Page** to display the top of the document.
7. Click the **Close Print Preview** button.
8. **SAVE** your document.

   PAUSE. LEAVE the document open to use in the next exercise.

Print Preview enables you to view your document as it will appear when it is printed and make any necessary changes before printing.

TAKE NOTE* Print Preview is an example of how the standard tabs on the ribbon are replaced with program tabs relevant to the task you are performing.

Setting Other Printing Options

You can choose various printing options before sending your document to the printer, such as the number of copies or the range of pages to print.

142 | Lesson 2

➔ **SET OTHER PRINTING OPTIONS**

USE the document that is open from the previous exercise.

1. The Print dialog box should still be open, as shown in Figure 2-12. If it is not, click the **Microsoft Office Button** and click **Print**.

Figure 2-12

Print dialog box

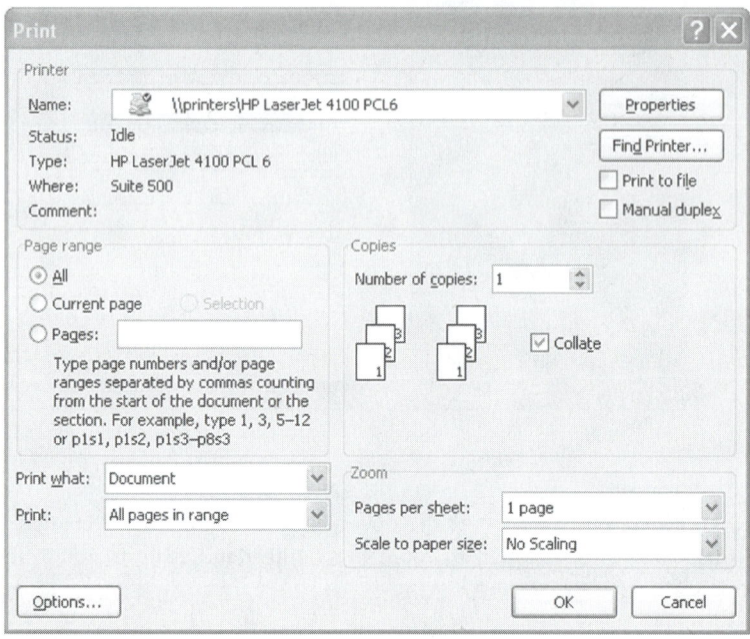

2. Click the **Options** button to display the Word Options dialog box, as shown in Figure 2-13.

Figure 2-13

Word Options dialog box

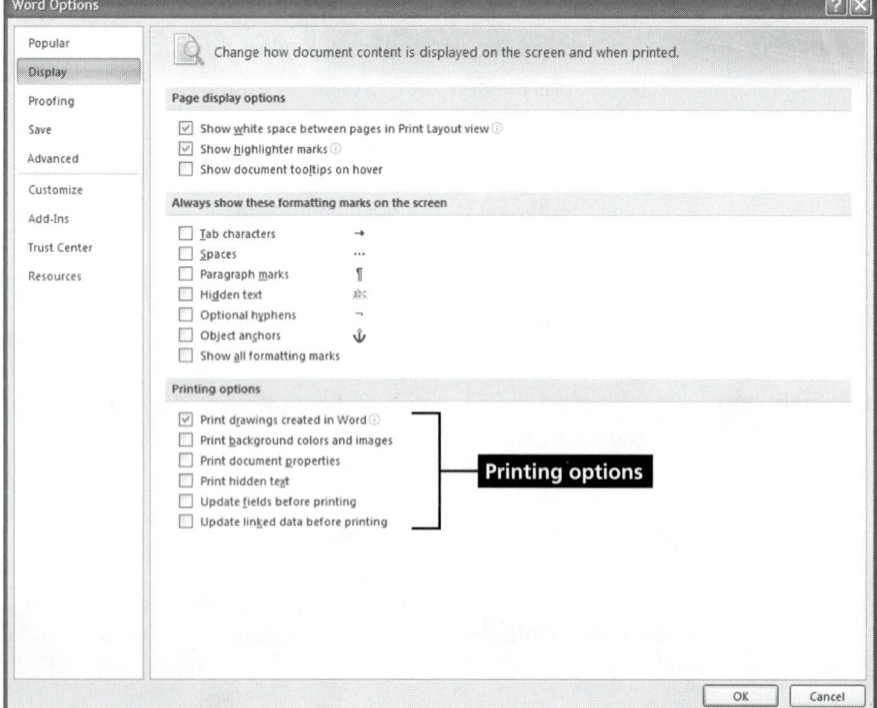

3. Notice the printing options at the bottom of the dialog box that can be selected to change the way you print your documents. Click **Cancel** to return to the Print dialog box.
4. In the Copies section, click the upward-pointing arrow next to the Number of Copies box to change it to **2**.
5. Click **OK** to print two copies of the letter.

 To print a document quickly, you can skip the Print dialog box and use the default settings by clicking **Quick Print** from the Print option on the Microsoft Office Button menu.

PAUSE. LEAVE the document open to use in the next exercise.

In this activity, you learned about some of the options available when printing a document. When you make changes in the Word Options dialog box, they will be applied to any Word document you print. Changes that you make in the Print dialog box will only be applied to that particular document.

You chose to print two copies of the letter in this activity. If the document were longer, you could have chosen other options, such as printing a range of pages, collating the pages, or printing multiple pages per sheet.

 You will learn more about printing documents with different layouts—including margins, orientations, and paper sizes—in Lesson 5.

■ Creating Envelopes and Labels

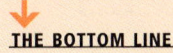 Creating and printing envelopes and labels in Word is a similar process that uses the same dialog box. If you have a return address stored, it can be used as the default address to save time.

Creating and Printing an Envelope

To send the letter you have been working on, you will now create and print an envelope that you can save with the document.

144 | Lesson 2

➲ CREATE AND PRINT AN ENVELOPE

USE the document that is open from the previous exercise.

1. On the Mailings tab, in the Create group, click **Envelopes**. The Envelopes and Labels dialog box appears, as shown in Figure 2-14.

Figure 2-14

Envelopes and Labels dialog box

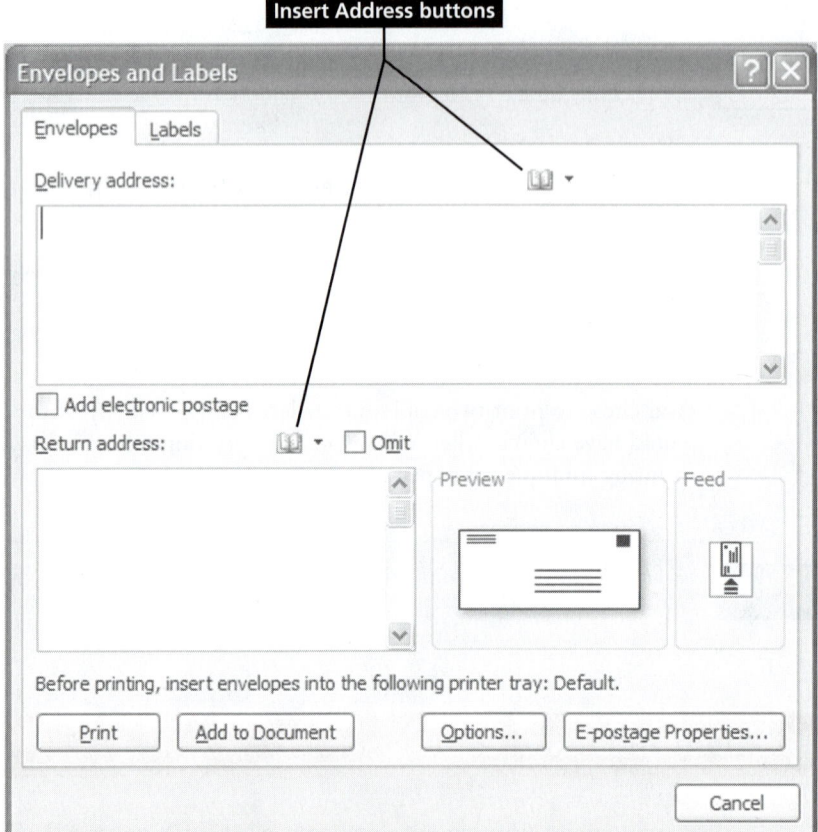

2. In the Delivery Address box, key:

   Miriam Lockhart
   764 Crimson Avenue
   Boston, MA 02136

   (Note: If the Delivery address is already pre-populated with the address above, go to the next step.)

> **TAKE NOTE***
>
> If you wanted to choose an address from the electronic address book on your computer, you could click the **Insert Address button.**

TAKE NOTE*

The current document theme determines what font is used on the envelope. To change the font, select the address, then right-click and choose **Font** from the shortcut menu.

3. In the Return Address box, key:

   Tech Terrace Real Estate
   1218 Hutchinson Road
   Boston, MA 02136

4. Click the **Add to Document button**. (When a dialog box appears asking if you want to save the new return address as the default, click **No**.) This saves the envelope with the document you have been working on as Page 0, as shown in Figure 2-15.

Figure 2-15

Envelope added to document

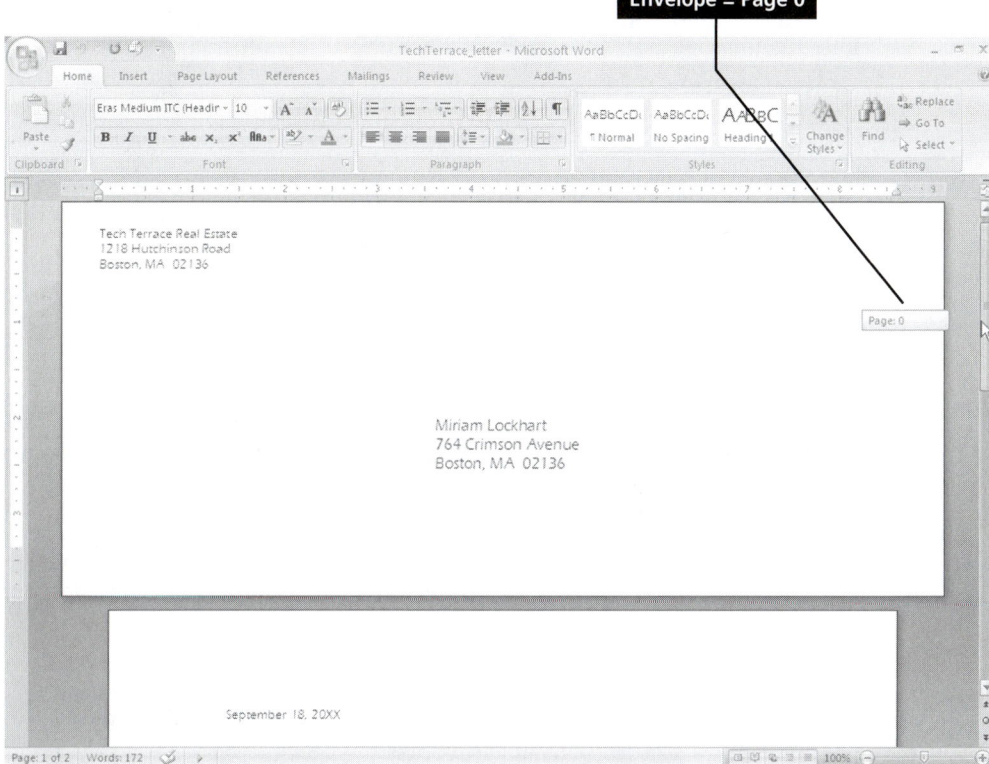

5. Click **Ctrl** + **P** to open the Print dialog box.
6. In the Print dialog box, in the Page Range section, click **Pages** and key **0**. This will print only the envelope and not the accompanying letter.
7. Insert the envelope in the printer's manual feeder and click **OK**.
8. **SAVE** the document and then **CLOSE** the file.

   PAUSE. LEAVE Word open for the next exercise.

CERTIFICATION READY?
How do you create an envelope?
4.5.3

In this activity, you printed a single envelope that will enable you to mail your letter. If the return address were one that you would be using regularly, you could have chosen to save it as the default. This would save you the time of keying it again later and the address would be available for printing envelopes, labels, or inserting into a document. The Omit checkbox in the Envelopes and Labels dialog box allows you to keep the return address for future use, but not include it on the current envelope.

If you add an envelope to a document, it is stored as page 0 and saved with the document. You can print only the envelope by choosing to print page 0 of the document. If you do not add the envelope to the document, it is not stored for future use. Simply click the Print button to send it directly to the printer.

If you have electronic postage software installed, you can add electronic postage to your envelope before printing. To set postage options, click the E-postage Properties button from the Envelopes and Labels dialog box.

146 | Lesson 2

TROUBLESHOOTING

Before sending an envelope through your printer, you should check to make sure it is set up correctly.

1. On the Mailings tab, in the Create group, click **Envelopes**.
2. Click **Options** and then click the **Envelope Options** tab.
3. In the Envelope Size box, click the choice that matches the size of your envelope.
4. Click the **Printing Options** tab. Information about which way the envelope should be loaded into the printer is displayed here.
5. Load the envelope as indicated in the dialog box.
6. Click **OK**.

Creating and Printing a Label

Word makes it easy to create and print labels. You can select from a number of popular paper label styles and shapes to print a single label or create a full sheet of identical labels to use as return address labels.

➔ CREATE AND PRINT A LABEL

1. **OPEN** a new, blank Word document.

TAKE NOTE* To create labels in Word, you must first open a blank document or the label commands will not be available.

2. On the Mailings tab, in the Create group, click **Labels**. The Envelopes and Labels dialog box appears with the Labels tab displayed, as shown in Figure 2-16.

Figure 2-16

Labels tab of Envelopes and Labels dialog box

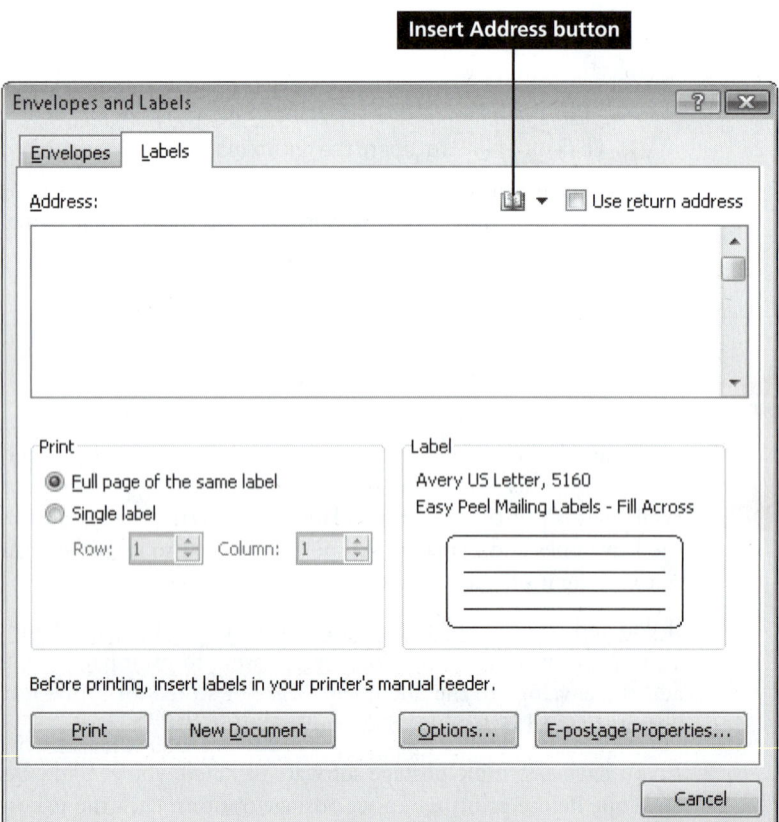

Document Basics | 147

3. In the Address box, key:

   Tech Terrace Real Estate
   1218 Hutchinson Road
   Boston, MA 02136

4. Click the **Options** button. The Label Options dialog box appears, as shown in Figure 2-17.

Figure 2-17

Labels Options dialog box

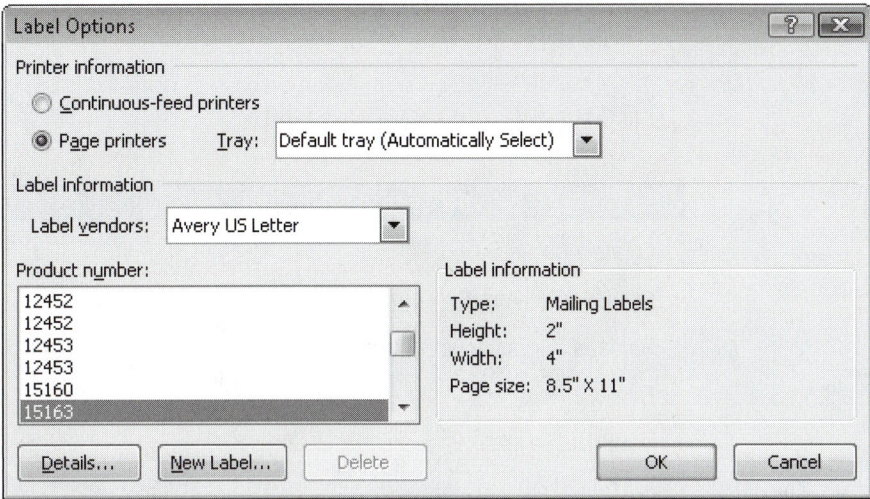

CERTIFICATION READY?
How do you create a label?
4.5.3

5. In the Label Information section, choose the type of label you are using.
6. Click **OK** to return to the Labels and Envelopes dialog box.
7. In the Print section, be sure **Full page of the same labels** is selected.

TAKE NOTE*

To print just one label, click the **Single Label** options and choose the numbers that correspond with the label row and column on the sheet you are using to print.

8. Click the **New Document** button. This creates a separate document with a full sheet of labels.
9. Save the document as *TT_return_labels*.
10. Insert the labels into your printer's manual feeder.
11. Print the labels.
12. **SAVE** the document and then **CLOSE** the file.

   STOP. CLOSE Word.

TAKE NOTE*

When you create a full sheet of labels in a separate document, you can make formatting changes to the text on each individual label just as you would in any Word document.

In this activity, you printed a full sheet to use as return address labels. If you need only one label, it is easy to print a single label by specifying the row and column number of the label on the sheet.

Several of the options in the Label tab of the Envelopes and Labels dialog box are similar to the Envelope tab. You can use an address from the electronic address book by clicking the Insert Address button, or click the E-postage Properties button to use the electronic postage feature. To send labels directly to the printer without previewing them, click the Print button.

To change formatting, select the text, right-click and then click Font or Paragraph on the shortcut menu. To use the return address that is stored, click the Use Return Address box.

TROUBLESHOOTING

If none of the choices in the Label Options dialog box match your labels, you will need to create a custom setting.

1. Click the **New Label** button to open the Label Details dialog box.
2. Key the label name.
3. Enter the dimensions and other options for your label.
4. Click **OK**.
5. To use your custom label setting, choose **Other/Custom** in the Label products list.

SUMMARY SKILL MATRIX

In this lesson you learned How to:
Create a Document
Choose a Different File Format
Format a Document with Quick Styles
Format a Document with a Theme
Use Print Preview
Set Other Printing Options
Create and Print an Envelope
Create and Print a Label

■ Knowledge Assessment

Fill in the Blank

Complete the following sentences by writing the correct word or words in the blanks provided.

1. When you open Word, a _____ document called *Document1* is automatically displayed.

2. When you open Word, a _____ document called Document1 is automatically displayed.

3. If you need your document in a different _____ you can choose to save it as another type of file.

4. The Word _____ Document file format allows users with a(n) earlier version of Word to open the document without any difficulty.

5. When choosing the _____ _____ option, you must choose the numbers that correspond with the label row and column on the sheet you are using to print.

6. Quick _____ are predefined formats that can be used to instantly change the look and feel of a document.

7. If you make any changes to the colors, fonts, or effects of the current _____ you can save it as a custom version that can be applied to other documents.

8. Document themes are the same throughout all _____ programs.

9. Print _____ allows you to view how a document will appear when it is printed.

10. If you have a _____ address stored, it can be used as the default address to save time when creating envelopes or labels.

Multiple Choice

Select the best response for the following statements and questions.

1. How many times should you press Enter between each section of information in a business letter?
   a. once
   b. twice
   c. three times
   d. four times

2. Predefined formats that you can apply to your document to instantly change its look and feel are called
   a. Theme Colors
   b. Standard Properties
   c. Pre-Formats
   d. Quick Styles

3. A document theme includes sets of
   a. colors
   b. fonts
   c. effects
   d. all of the above
   e. none of the above

4. Which of the following is popular Save As file format that is used to preserve formatting and prevent data from being changed or copied?
   a. PDF
   b. Word 97-2003 Document
   c. Word Template
   d. Word Macro-Enabled Document

5. When previewing a document, which command enables you to see your document close-up or see the page at a reduced size?
   a. Magnify
   b. Zoom
   c. Percentage
   d. Quick View

6. Choosing the number of copies or range of pages are options that are available when performing what process on a document?
   a. Previewing
   b. Assigning keywords
   c. Printing
   d. Saving in a different format

7. An envelope that is saved with a document is added as which page?
   a. 0
   b. 1
   c. 2
   d. the last one

8. When the pointer is placed over a any choice on the Style Set menu, which of the following occurs?
   a. the style is applied to the selected text
   b. the style is previewed in the document
   c. the Style Set dialog box appears
   d. none of the above

9. To preview a style or a theme,
   a. place your pointer over the choice
   b. print the document
   c. set up the document properties
   d. it is not possible to preview a style or theme

10. Which of the following options are not available in Print Preview?
    a. zoom
    b. show ruler
    c. page size
    d. all of the above
    e. none of the above

■ Competency Assessment

Project 2-1: Phone Interview Selection Letter

In your position at Tech Terrace Real Estate, you previously created a letter to declining a candidate for employment following a phone interview. Open the document and save it in a different format.

GET READY. Launch Word if it is not already running.

The **selection_letter** document is available on the companion CD-ROM.

1. **OPEN** *selection_letter* from the data files for this lesson.
2. Click the **Microsoft Office Button** and then click **Save As** to open the Save As dialog box.
3. In the File Name box, key **decline_letter**.
4. Click **Save** to save the file with a different name.
5. Press **F12** to open the Save As dialog box again.
6. In the Save As type box, click the downward-pointing arrow and choose **Word 97-2003 Document**.
7. Click **Save** to save the document in a different format.
8. **CLOSE** the file.
   LEAVE Word open for the next project.

Project 2-2: Reference Letter

You previously created a reference letter for a former employee at Tech Terrace Real Estate. Open and format the document.

1. **OPEN** *reference_letter* from the data files for this lesson.
2. On the Home tab, in the Styles group, click the **Change Styles** button.
3. On the Set Styles menu, click **Formal**.
4. On the Page Layout tab, in the Themes group, click **Themes**.
5. Click **Origin** on the gallery menu.
6. **SAVE** the document as *jasmine_reference* and then **CLOSE** the file.

   LEAVE Word open for the next project.

The *reference_letter* document is available on the companion CD-ROM.

■ Proficiency Assessment

Project 2-3: Creating Return Address Labels

You are paying bills at home and decide to save time writing your return address on every envelope by creating a sheet of return address labels to use.

1. **OPEN** a new, blank Word document.
2. Create a full sheet of return address labels with your name and address. Use **Avery US Letter 5160** as the label type.
3. **SAVE** the new document as *personal_labels*.
4. Change the style on the labels to **Traditional**.
5. Use Print Preview and to see what the labels will look like when printed.
6. **PRINT** the labels.
7. **SAVE** the document and **CLOSE** the file.

   LEAVE Word open for the next project.

Project 2-4: Welcome Back to School Letter

As a second grade teacher at the local elementary school, you have to send out letters to all your students letting them know you will be their teacher and welcoming them back to school.

1. **OPEN** *school_letter* from the data files for this lesson.
2. Set document properties, including keywords, for the letter. Use words that apply to the document.
3. Format the document using a style that you think looks good from the Style Set menu.
4. Select the last paragraph that begins *I hope to see you...*
5. Choose an option from the Quick Style gallery to emphasize the paragraph.
6. **SAVE** the document as *welcome_letter*.
7. Preview and then print the document.
8. **CLOSE** the file.

   LEAVE Word open for the next project.

The *school_letter* document is available on the companion CD-ROM.

Mastery Assessment

Project 2-5: Create a Custom Theme

Tech Terrace Real Estate has decided to give all their documents a branded look by creating a custom theme to be used for all client-facing business documents.

CERTIFICATION READY?
How do you customize a theme?
WORD 1.1.4

1. **OPEN** a new, blank Word document.
2. Use the **Word Help** button to get more information about creating a custom theme.
3. Choose a custom set of colors, fonts, and/or effects that you feel would be a good choice for Tech Terrace Real Estate.
4. **SAVE** the theme as *custom_xxx* (where xxx are your initials).
5. Key a short paragraph explaining what colors, fonts, or effects you chose. Format the paragraph with your custom theme.
6. **SAVE** the document as *custom_theme* and **CLOSE** the file.

   LEAVE Word open for the next project.

Project 2-6: Customizing an Envelope

Your sister needs to print an envelope for an invitation she will create and mail, but she is not as familiar with the process as you are. She has a particular size envelope and wants a certain font. She asks you to help set up the envelope, add it to a document, and be sure it prints correctly.

1. **OPEN** a new, blank Word document.
2. Create an envelope with the following information:

   Delivery address:

   Beth Patterson
   211 Spring Road
   Kearney, NE 68845

   Return address:

   Carole Bass
   14451 Cypress Lane
   Garden City, KS 67846

3. Change the format of the delivery address to **Comic Sans MS, bold, size 12**.
4. Change the format of the return address to **Comic Sans MS, regular, size 10**.
5. Set the envelope size to **Size 6 3/4 (3 5/8 X 6 1/2)**.
6. Add the envelope to the document so that your sister can create the invitation later. Do not save the return address as the default.
7. Print just the envelope.
8. **SAVE** the document as *invitation_envelope* and then **CLOSE** the file.

   STOP. CLOSE Word.

INTERNET READY

You began this lesson by creating a business letter from scratch. Now you will use those skills to write a cover letter for your resume in which you request an interview for the office manager position at Tech Terrace Real Estate. Use web search tools to find out what information should be contained in a cover letter and how to format it. The OWL at Purdue is a good online source for writing help. Print the letter and an envelope or label to go with it.

Workplace Ready

Creating Mailing Labels in Word

Gone are the days of wasting valuable time handwriting addresses on envelopes for large mailings. Today, Word provides the tools you need to quickly and easily create mailing labels in a variety of sizes. Whether you're mailing a single letter or a mass mailing more than a hundred letters, all you need is a computer, a printer, and Word's Mailings options to produce your own personalized labels.

Imagine that you are starting a corporate event planning business. You have compiled a list of potential clients and would like to send a letter to each introducing your business and the services you can provide. You know that first impressions are critical, and you want to project a professional image in your mailing. After looking into ordering preprinted business envelopes, you decide that these just do not fit within your business' limited startup budget. Although you could handwrite your return address on each envelope, along with the potential client's mailing address, this would definitely not give the first impression you want to achieve. You decide that using Word to create your own return address and mailing labels will save you both valuable time and money.

Word provides specific sizes for several different label brands, or you can choose to create a custom-size sheet of labels. With a quick trip to your local office supply store, you purchase the labels you need and are ready to get started.

First, you can create and print return address labels to use on all of your business correspondence. With Word, there's no need to type your address on each label individually. Instead, you can simply type the address once, then choose to have this address repeated on every label.

If you are preparing to send out a mass mailing, you can type each address directly into Word, or you can choose to import addresses from a database. Word can pull the addresses directly from the database file to create the mailing labels. You can even choose to import addresses from your Outlook address book.

With a little help from Word, you can produce professional, high-quality mailings on a small business budget.

Corporate Events Unlimited 1000 Party Ave. Rochester Hills, MI 48306	Corporate Events Unlimited 1000 Party Ave. Rochester Hills, MI 48306	Corporate Events Unlimited 1000 Party Ave. Rochester Hills, MI 48306
Corporate Events Unlimited 1000 Party Ave. Rochester Hills, MI 48306	Corporate Events Unlimited 1000 Party Ave. Rochester Hills, MI 48306	Corporate Events Unlimited 1000 Party Ave. Rochester Hills, MI 48306
Corporate Events Unlimited 1000 Party Ave. Rochester Hills, MI 48306	Corporate Events Unlimited 1000 Party Ave. Rochester Hills, MI 48306	Corporate Events Unlimited 1000 Party Ave. Rochester Hills, MI 48306
Corporate Events Unlimited 1000 Party Ave. Rochester Hills, MI 48306	Corporate Events Unlimited 1000 Party Ave. Rochester Hills, MI 48306	Corporate Events Unlimited 1000 Party Ave. Rochester Hills, MI 48306

Character Formatting 3

LESSON SKILL MATRIX

Choosing Fonts and Font Sizes	Students will learn how to choose fonts and font sizes.
Applying Special Character Attributes	Students will learn how to apply special character attributes.
Changing Case	Students will learn how to change case.
Highlighting Text	Students will learn how to highlight text.
Using the Format Painter	Students will learn how to use the format painter.
Removing Formatting	Students will learn how to remove formatting.
Applying Styles	Students will learn how to apply styles.
Modifying Styles	Students will learn how to modify styles.

With more than 20 million members and 2,600 facilities, the YMCA (Y) is the nation's largest community service organization. The health and fitness programs offered at the Y include group exercise for adults and youth as well as personal fitness programs. The staff and volunteers at the Y need to create various types of documents for announcing and advertising programs throughout the year as well as organizing and registering members for participation in the programs. Microsoft Word is a great tool for creating all sorts of documents easily and quickly. In this lesson, you will learn how to format text manually and with Quick Styles to create a document that describes the group exercise classes offered at the YMCA.

KEY TERMS
character
character styles
font
paragraph styles
point size

154

Character Formatting | 155

■ SOFTWARE ORIENTATION

The Font Group

As you learn to format text, it is important to become familiar with the group of commands you will use. The Font group, shown in Figure 3-1, is displayed in the Home tab of the ribbon. It contains most of the commands you will need to format characters in this lesson.

Figure 3-1
The Font group

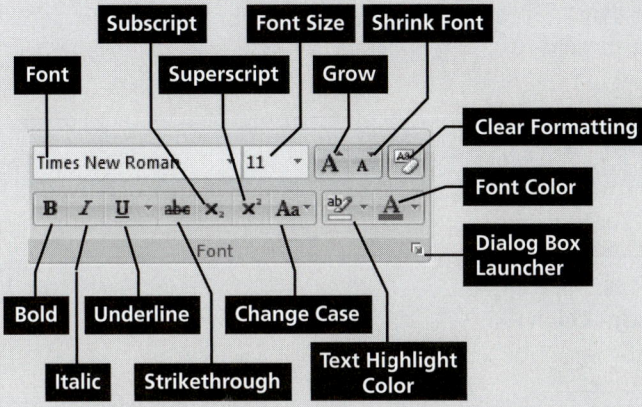

The Font group contains commands for changing the appearance of text.

■ Manually Formatting Characters

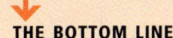 **THE BOTTOM LINE**   Formatting characters makes your text more appealing and more readable.

Choosing Fonts and Font Sizes

Microsoft Word has a variety of fonts and font sizes to help you communicate your intended message in a document, whether it is casual for your personal life or formal for the workplace.

➔ CHANGE FONTS AND FONT SIZES

GET READY. Before you begin these steps, be sure to launch Microsoft Office Word 2007 and **OPEN** the *class_descriptions* document from the data files for this lesson.

 The *class_descriptions* document is available on the companion CD-ROM.

1. Select *Preston Creek Family YMCA*.
2. In the **Font** group of the **Home** tab, click the downward-pointing arrow on the **Font** menu. The menu appears as shown in Figure 3-2.

Figure 3-2

The Font menu

3. Scroll down the list and position the mouse pointer on **Arial**. Notice that as you point to each font in the list, the selected text changes with a live preview of what your text would look like with each different font.
4. Click **Arial**.
5. With the text still selected, click the arrow on the **Font Size** menu. The menu appears, as shown in Figure 3-3.

Figure 3-3

The Font Size menu

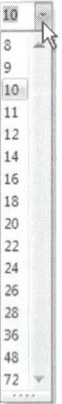

6. Click **18**.
7. Select *Group Exercise Class Descriptions*.
8. Click the **Font** menu and click **Arial**.
9. With the text still selected, click the **Font Size** menu and click **14**.
10. Select the remainder of text in the document. Point to selected text to display the Mini toolbar. Click the **Font** menu on the Mini toolbar and choose **Calibri** (see Figure 3-4).

Figure 3-4

The Font menu on the Mini toolbar

11. With text still selected, click the **Font Size** menu on the Mini toolbar and choose **12**.
12. Click in a blank area of the document to remove the selection.
13. Select *Preston Creek Family YMCA*. In the Font group, click the **Grow Font** button to increase the size of the text. Notice that each time you click it, the number in the Font Size menu changes.
14. Click **Grow Font** two more times until the point size is 24.
15. Save the document as *classes*.

    PAUSE. LEAVE the document open to use in the next exercise.

A ***character*** is any single letter, number, symbol, or punctuation mark. Select a character to change its format.

A ***font*** is a set of characters that have the same design. Each font has a unique name.

Font sizes are measured in points. **Point size** refers to the height of characters, with one point equaling approximately 1/72 of an inch. Point sizes range from the very small 8-point size to 72 points or higher. Select text to change its font or size. Here are a few examples of fonts and sizes.

This is an example of Garamond 10 point.

This is an example of Arial 14 point.

This is an example of Juice ITC 18 point.

The Font group in the Home tab contains the Font menu for changing the Font, and the Font Size menu for changing its size. You can also access these commands on the Mini toolbar. The shortcut menu also has the Font command, which opens the Font dialog box.

Another way to change the size of text is to select it and click the Grow Font button to increase the size of a font, or click the Shrink Font button to decrease the size.

> **TAKE NOTE**
>
> Some fonts, such as Times, have tiny lines at the ends of characters, called *serifs*. Sans serif fonts, like Calibri, don't have the lines. Serif fonts are usually more suitable for large amounts of text.

Applying Special Character Attributes

In addition to changing the font and font size, you can also change the appearance of characters to give them special emphasis.

→ APPLY SPECIAL CHARACTER ATTRIBUTES

USE the document that is open from the previous exercise.

1. Select the title of the document, *Preston Creek Family YMCA*. In the Font group, click the **Bold** button.

 **ANOTHER WAY** You can also use the keyboard to apply bold. Select text and press **Ctrl+B**.

2. Select the subtitle, *Group Exercise Class Descriptions*, and click the **Italic** button.

 **ANOTHER WAY** You can also use the keyboard to apply italics. Select text and press **Ctrl+I**.

3. Select *Active Older Adults* and click the **Bold** button.
4. With the text still selected, click the **Underline** button.

 **ANOTHER WAY** You can also use the keyboard to apply underline. Select text and press **Ctrl+U**.

5. With text still selected, click the arrow beside the **Underline** button. A menu of underlining choices appears, as shown in Figure 3-5.

Figure 3-5
The Underline menu

6. Click **Thick Underline**, the third line down in the menu.
7. Select the title, *Preston Creek Family YMCA*. In the Font group, click the **Dialog Box Launcher**. The Font dialog box appears, as shown in Figure 3-6.

Figure 3-6

The Font dialog box

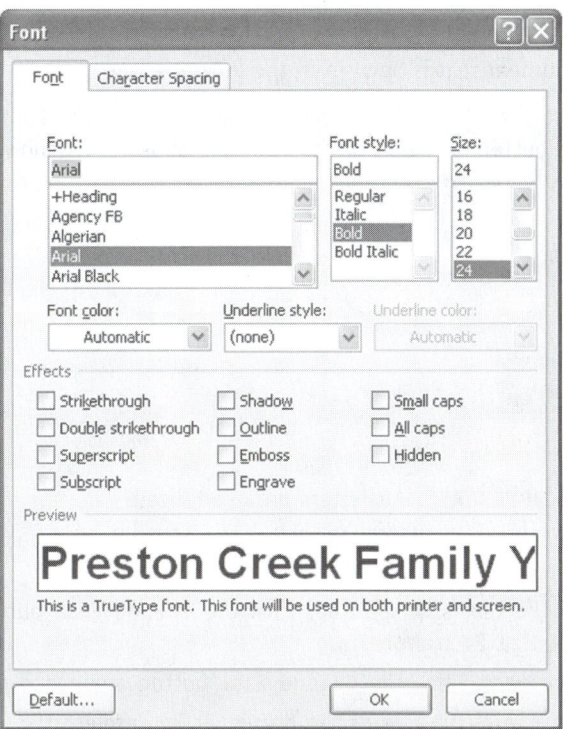

8. In the Effects section, click the **Outline** box to insert a checkmark.
9. Click the arrow on the **Font Color** menu. A menu of colors appears. Click **Red** from the Standard Colors section at the bottom.

 **ANOTHER WAY** You can also click the Font Color button on the ribbon to launch a menu of colors you can use to change the color of text.

10. Click **OK**.
11. In the Font group, click the **Dialog Box Launcher** again. In the Font dialog box, click the **Outline** box to remove the checkmark. Click **OK**.
12. **SAVE** the document.

    PAUSE. LEAVE the document open to use in the next exercise.

The Font group in the Home tab includes the commands for changing the style of text—bold, italic, and underline. You learned that applying any of these commands gives text special emphasis. You can use one at a time, such as **Bold**, or use two, such as **Bold Underline**. Just select the text you want to change and click the command in the Font group. You can also use the Bold and Italic commands on the Mini toolbar.

The Font dialog box has more options for formatting characters. You can change the Font, Font style, and Font size. In addition, you can specify a Font color, underline style, and a variety of effects, such as small caps, strikethrough, superscript, and shadow. Click the Dialog Box Launcher in the Font Group to display the Font dialog box.

Changing Case

When you need to change the case of text, Word provides several case options and an easy way to choose the one you want.

CHANGE CASE

USE the document that is open from the previous exercise.

1. Select the title, *Preston Creek Family YMCA*. In the Font group, click the **Change Case** button. A menu of case options appears, as shown in Figure 3-7.

Figure 3-7

The Change Case menu

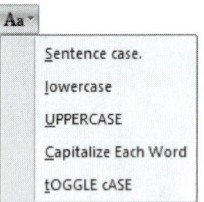

2. Click **UPPERCASE**. All letters are capitalized.
3. With the text still selected, click the **Change Case** button again and click **lowercase**.
4. With the text still selected, click the **Change Case** button again and click **Capitalize Each Word**.
5. Select *Ymca*. Click the **Change Case** button again and choose **UPPERCASE**.
6. Click in a blank area of the document to deselect the text.
7. **SAVE** the document.

   PAUSE. LEAVE the document open to use in the next exercise.

The Change Case menu in the Font group has five options for changing the capitalization of text:

- Sentence case: capitalizes the first word in each sentence
- Lowercase: changes all characters to lowercase
- UPPERCASE: changes all characters to caps
- Capitalize Each Word: Capitalizes the first character of Each Word
- tOGGLE cASE: changes each character to its opposite case

In the Effects section of the Font dialog box, you can change selected text to all caps or small caps.

Highlighting Text

Sometimes you might really want text to be noticed quickly. The Highlighting tool in the Font group lets you do just that.

HIGHLIGHT TEXT

USE the document that is open from the previous exercise.

1. In the Font group, click the **Text Highlight Color** button. Highlighting is turned on and the pointer changes to a highlighter pen icon.
2. Under *Core Express*, select the last sentence, *This new class is open to all fitness levels!* When you release the mouse button, the text is highlighted.
3. Click the **Text Highlight Color** button again to turn off Highlighting.
4. Select the text again. Click the arrow beside the **Text Highlight Color** button. A menu of colors appears, as shown in Figure 3-8. Click **Turquoise**. Notice the highlight color in the text and the **Text Highlight Color** button in the ribbon have changed to turquoise.

Figure 3-8

The Text Highlight Color menu

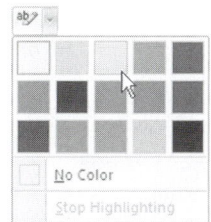

5. Select the text again. Click the **Text Highlight Color** button again to remove the highlight color.
6. **SAVE** the document.

   PAUSE. LEAVE the document open to use in the next exercise.

You have just learned to use the Text Highlight Color button in the Font group to highlight text, making it look like it was marked with a highlighting pen. Click the Text Highlight Color button to turn on highlighting. Click and drag across the text you want to highlight. When you're finished, click the Text Highlight Color button again to turn off highlighting.

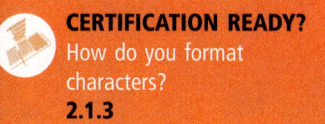

CERTIFICATION READY?
How do you format characters?
2.1.3

You can also select text first and click the Text Highlight Color button to apply yellow highlighting. If you'd like a different highlight color, click the arrow to display a menu of colors.

To remove highlighting, select the highlighted text and choose No Color from the Text Highlight Color menu.

■ Copying and Removing Formatting

THE BOTTOM LINE

Formatting text often requires copying formats or removing formats in the process of getting the look and feel you want. The Format Painter will help you copy formats to use in other areas of the document. And if you ever need to remove formatting, the Clear Formatting button will do it for you.

Using the Format Painter

When you find a tool that saves time and makes your work easier, it becomes invaluable. The Format Painter is such a tool. You can use it to copy formatting and apply it in other places, making document formatting easier and faster.

⊕ **USE THE FORMAT PAINTER**

USE the document that is open from the previous exercise.

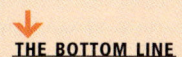

1. Select the *Active Older Adults* heading.
2. On the Home tab, in the Clipboard group, click the **Format Painter** button. The pointer changes to a paintbrush icon.
3. Select the next heading, *Boot Camp*. The copied format is applied and the Format Painter is turned off.
4. With **Boot Camp** still selected, double-click the **Format Painter** button. The mouse pointer becomes a paintbrush icon.
5. Select the next heading, *Cardio Combo*. The copied format is applied.
6. Select the next heading, *Cardio Kickboxing*. The copied format is applied.

7. Select the remaining headings to apply the copied format. When you are finished with the last heading, click the **Format Painter** button to turn it off.
8. **SAVE** the document.

   PAUSE. LEAVE the document open to use in the next exercise.

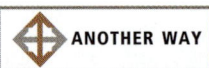

ANOTHER WAY

The Format Painter button is also available on the Mini toolbar.

The Format Painter command in the Clipboard group lets you copy the attributes, or format, of text and apply those attributes to different text. Select the formatted text you want to copy and click the Format Painter button. The mouse pointer becomes a paintbrush icon. Now select the text where you want to apply the format and click.

You can double-click the Format Painter button to copy the format to multiple places.

Removing Formatting

When you are formatting documents, sometimes you need to try a few different options before you get the appearance you want.

USE THE CLEAR FORMATTING BUTTON

USE the document that is open from the previous exercise.

1. Select *Active Older Adults*. In the Font group, click the **Clear Formatting** button. Formatting is removed and the plain text remains.
2. Press and hold **Ctrl** and select *Boot Camp*. Still holding the **Ctrl** key, select the remaining headings using multi-selection and click the **Clear Formatting** button. Formatting is removed on all the remaining headings at once.
3. **SAVE** the document

   PAUSE. LEAVE the document open to use in the next exercise.

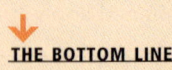

X REF

Refer to Lesson 2 for more information regarding multi-selection.

The Clear Formatting button in the Font group lets you clear formatting from selected text. Select the text with the formatting you want to clear and click the Clear Formatting button.

■ Formatting Text with Styles

THE BOTTOM LINE

Word has included predefined Quick Styles you can use to format text. When your own formatting is not producing the results you want, you might try a Quick Style. You can also modify Quick Styles to suit your needs. As you get more familiar with using the styles and exploring what is available, you'll be able to use the styles to produce results more quickly.

Applying Styles

Word's Quick Styles has two kinds of styles—paragraph styles and character styles.

APPLY A STYLE

USE the document that is open from the previous exercise.

1. Select the *Active Older Adults* heading. In the Styles group, click **Heading 1**. The style is applied to the heading.
2. Use multi-selection to select all the headings and then click **Heading 1**. The Heading 1 style is applied to all the headings.

Character Formatting | 163

3. In the second sentence of the *Active Older Adults* description, select *low-impact*. In the Styles group, click the **Dialog Box Launcher**. The Styles window appears, as shown in Figure 3-9.

Figure 3-9

Styles window

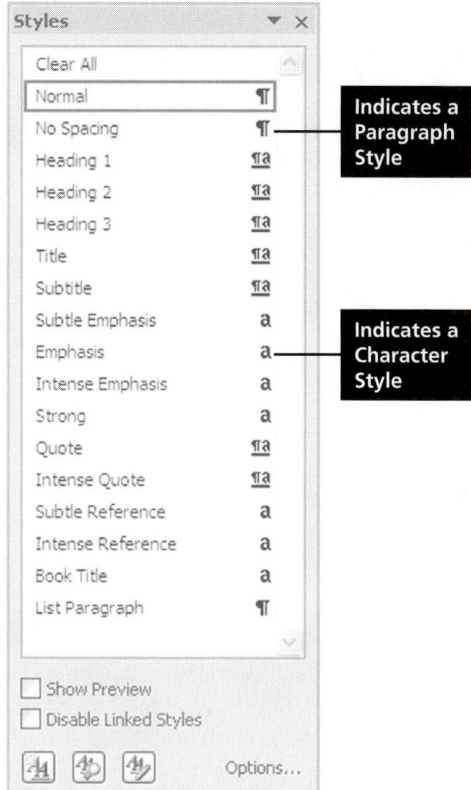

4. Point to **Subtle Emphasis**. Notice a screen tip appears and the lowercase *a* to the right of the style name becomes an arrow. Click **Subtle Emphasis**. The style is applied.
5. In the *Boot Camp* description, select *challenging* and click **Subtle Emphasis** in the Styles window.
6. In the *Core Express* description, select *strengthen* and click **Subtle Emphasis** in the Styles window.
7. In the *Indoor Cycling* description, select *high-energy* and click **Subtle Emphasis** in the Styles window.
8. In the *Yoga* description, select *breathing* and *relaxation* and click **Subtle Emphasis** in the Styles window.
9. **SAVE** the document.

   PAUSE. LEAVE the document open to use in the next exercise.

The Styles window lists the same Quick Styles as are displayed in the Styles Gallery. A paragraph mark to the right of the style name denotes a style created for paragraphs. When you choose ***paragraph styles***, the formats are applied to all the text in the paragraph where your insertion point is located, whether or not you have it all selected.

Character styles have a lowercase letter *a* beside them. ***Character styles*** are applied to individual characters or words that you have selected within a paragraph rather than affecting the entire paragraph.

Sometimes, a style can be used for either a paragraph or characters. These linked styles have a paragraph symbol as well as a lowercase *a* beside them. Select the text to which you want to apply a linked style.

When you point to a style in the list, a screen tip displays the style's properties.

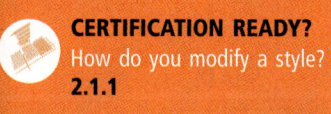

CERTIFICATION READY?
How do you modify a style?
2.1.1

Modifying Styles

When the style you have selected needs a little tweaking, Word lets you modify it.

➔ MODIFY A STYLE

USE the document that is open from the previous exercise.

1. In the Styles Window, click the arrow to the right of **Subtle Emphasis** to display the Subtle Emphasis menu, shown in Figure 3-10.

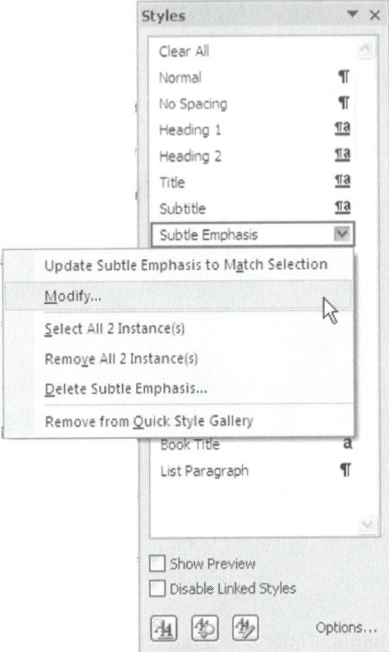

Figure 3-10

Subtle Emphasis dropdown menu

2. Click **Modify**. The Modify Styles dialog box appears, as shown in Figure 3-11.

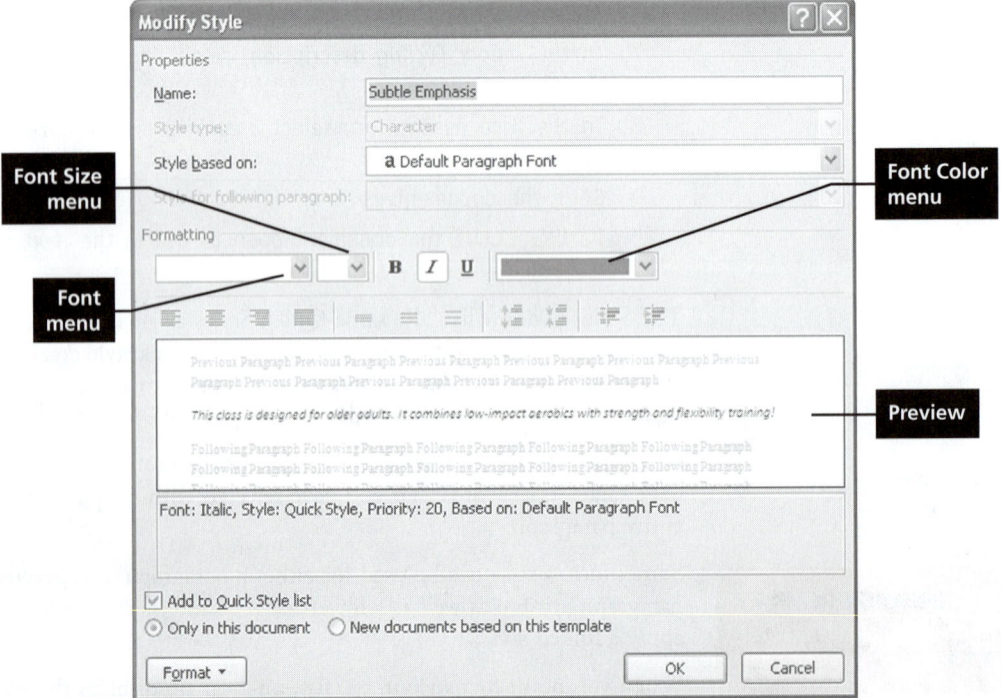

Figure 3-11

Modify Styles dialog box

3. Click the **Bold** button.
4. Click the **Font Color** menu and click **Red** in the Standard Colors section. Notice the preview in the dialog box changes.
5. Click **OK**.
6. Click the arrow beside **Heading 1** and click **Modify**.
7. Click the **Font Color** menu and choose **Red**.
8. Click the **Font Size** menu and click **12**.
9. Click **OK**. All the headings with the Heading 1 style are updated to the new color and size.
10. **SAVE** the document and **CLOSE** the file.

    STOP. CLOSE Word.

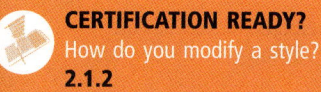

CERTIFICATION READY?
How do you modify a style?
2.1.2

You just learned that the Modify dialog box has basic formatting commands like the Font menu; Font size menu; bold, italic, and underline buttons; and Font color menu. When you modify paragraph fonts, you can also change alignment, indents, and spacing.

When you make a change, Word automatically renames the style, or you can give it a name yourself.

You can also click the box to Add to Quick Style list or Automatically Update. Click the button to Only use in this document or New documents based on this template.

SUMMARY SKILL MATRIX

IN THIS LESSON YOU LEARNED HOW TO:
Choose Fonts and Font Sizes
Apply Special Character Attributes
Change Case
Highlight Text
Use the Format Painter
Remove Formatting
Apply Styles
Modify Styles

Knowledge Assessment

Matching

Match the term in Column 1 to its description in Column 2.

Column 1

1. point size
2. character
3. font
4. change case
5. highlighting text
6. Format Painter
7. clear formatting
8. serifs
9. Grow Font button
10. character style

Column 2

a. a set of characters that have the same design
b. makes text look like it was marked with a highlighting pen
c. lets you copy the format of text and apply those attributes to different text
d. tiny lines at the ends of characters
e. removes formatting from selected text, leaving plain text
f. increases the size of text
g. refers to the height of characters, with one point equaling approximately 1/72 of an inch.
h. formats are applied to individual characters or words that you have selected within a paragraph rather than affecting the entire paragraph
i. any single letter, number, symbol, or punctuation mark
j. refers to changing the capitalization of text

True/False

Circle T if the statement is true or F if the statement is false.

T F 1. Toggle Case changes each character to its opposite case.
T F 2. Applying bold to text gives it special emphasis.
T F 3. The Format Painter is on the Mini toolbar.
T F 4. The Font dialog box has commands for highlighting text.
T F 5. The Shrink Font button increases point size.
T F 6. The Clear Formatting button clears text from one location and lets you apply it in another location.
T F 7. You can only highlight text with the colors yellow or turquoise.
T F 8. To apply a Quick Style, select the text and click the style you want.
T F 9. You cannot modify Quick Styles.
T F 10. The Font dialog box has options for adding effects such as strikethrough, superscript, and shadow.

■ Competency Assessment

Project 3-1: Sales Letter

Star Bright Satellite Radio will be sending sales letters to people who have just purchased new vehicles equipped with their radios. Add some finishing formatting touches to this letter.

GET READY. Launch Word if it is not already running.

1. **OPEN** *letter* from the data files for this lesson.

 The *letter* document is available on the companion CD-ROM.

2. In the second paragraph, select the first sentence, *Star Bright Satellite*....
3. Click **Bold**.
4. In the second paragraph, select the fifth sentence, *Star Bright also broadcasts*....
5. Click the **Italic** button.
6. In the fourth paragraph, select the first sentence, *Star Bright is only $10.95 a month*.
7. Click **Bold**.
8. In the second sentence of the fourth paragraph, select *Subscribe*.
9. Click the **Change Case** button and click **UPPERCASE**.
10. With the word still selected, click **Bold**.
11. **SAVE** the document as *sales_letter* and **CLOSE** the file.

   LEAVE Word open for the next project.

Project 3-2: YMCA Flyer

The YMCA's sports program needs volunteer coaches for youth sports. They ask for your help in creating a flyer.

1. **OPEN** *volunteercoaches* from the data files for this lesson.

 The *volunteercoaches* document is available on the companion CD-ROM.

2. Select *We Need You!* Click the **Font** menu and click **Arial Black**.
3. Click the **Font Size** menu and click **48**.
4. Select *Volunteer Coaches Needed For Youth Sports*. Click the **Font** menu and click **Arial Black**.
5. Click the **Font Size** menu and click **18**.
6. Select *Sports include* and the four lines below it. Click the **Font** menu and click **Calibri**. Click the **Font Size** menu and click **18**.
7. Select the four sports listed and click **Italic**.
8. Select the three lines of contact information, beginning with *Contact Patrick Edelstein*... Click the **Font** menu and click **Arial Black**. Click the **Font Size** menu and click **11**.
9. Select *YMCA*. Click the **Font Color** button and click **Red** from the Standard Colors section.

10. With the text still selected, click **Bold**. Click the **Font** menu and click **Arial Black**. Click the **Font Size** menu and choose **36**.
11. **SAVE** the document as *volunteers* and **CLOSE** the file.

    LEAVE Word open for the next project.

■ Proficiency Assessment

Project 3-3: Coffee Shop Flyer

The Grand Street Coffee Shop has decided to install a wireless Internet service for customers. To announce the news, create a flyer for distribution in the coffee shop.

1. **OPEN** *wireless* from the data files for this lesson.

    The *wireless* document is available on the companion CD-ROM.

2. Follow the directions in Figure 3-12 to format the document.

Figure 3-12

Formatting instructions for WiFi document

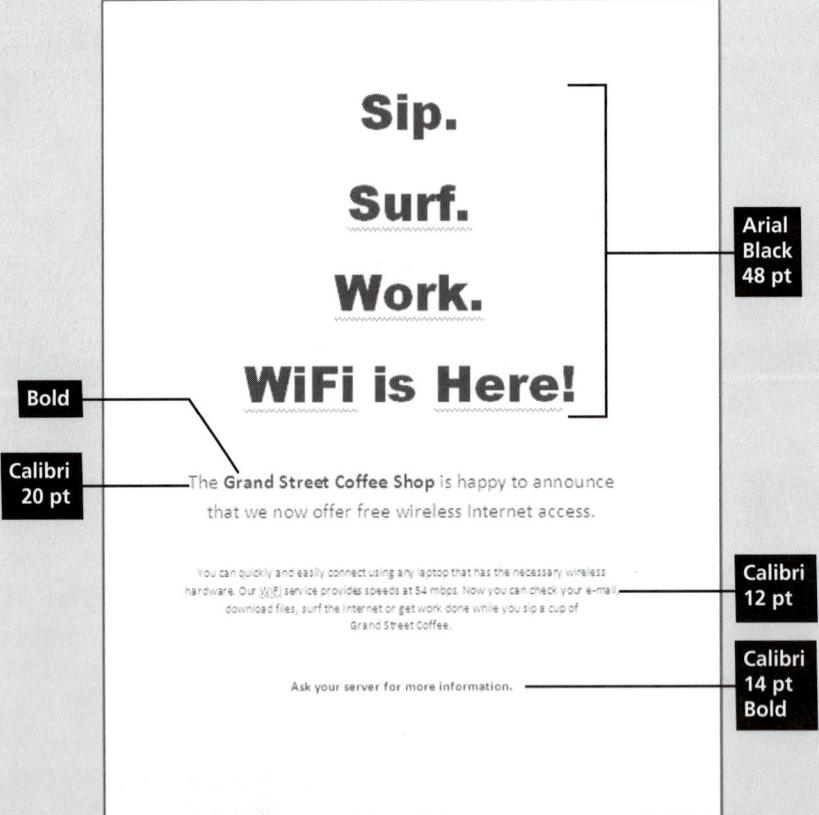

3. **SAVE** the document as *WiFi* and **CLOSE** the file.

    LEAVE Word open for the next project.

Project 3-4: Nutritional Information

Customers of the Grand Street Coffee Shop have asked about the nutritional makeup of some of the blended coffee items on the menu. Format a document you can post or make available for customers to take with them.

1. **OPEN** *nutritioninfo* from the data files for this lesson.

The *nutritioninfo* document is available on the companion CD-ROM.

2. Select *Grand Street Coffee Shop*. On the **Font** menu, click **Juice ITC**.
3. With the text still selected, change the font size to **28**.
4. Click the **Font Color** menu and click **Dark Blue** from the Standard Colors section.
5. Select *Nutritional Information*.
6. In the Font group, click the **Dialog Box Launcher**. Click the **Small Caps** box and change the font size to **12** and the font color to **Dark Blue**. Click **OK**.
7. Select *Brewed Coffee* and click **Title** from the Quick Styles Gallery. In the Styles group, click the **Dialog Box Launcher**.
8. In the Styles window, click the downward-pointing arrow on the **Title** style. Choose **Modify**.
9. In the Modify Style dialog box, change the font color to **Dark Blue** and the font size to **14**. Click **OK**.
10. Select the three lines of text under the *Brewed Coffee* heading. Click **Intense Emphasis** on the Styles Gallery.
11. Apply the **Title** style to the remaining headings, and apply the **Intense Emphasis** style to the remaining text.
12. **SAVE** the document as *nutrition* and **CLOSE** the file.

    LEAVE Word open for the next project.

■ Mastery Assessment

Project 3-5: Resume

Your friend Mike asks you to help him with his resume. Format the resume so that it looks professional.

1. **OPEN** *resume* from the data files for this lesson.

The *resume* document is available on the companion CD-ROM.

2. Format the resume to the following specifications:
   - Format Mike's name with Cambria, 24 pt., bold.
   - Change his address, phone, and email information to Times New Roman 9 pt.
   - For the main headings, use the Emphasis style with Cambria font size 16 bold and italic.
   - For job titles, use Times New Roman 12 pt. small caps, bold.
   - Italicize the sentence or sentences before the bulleted lists.
   - For places and years of employment, as well as the college name, use Times New Roman 12 pt. small caps.

3. **SAVE** the document as *mzresume* and **CLOSE** the file.
   LEAVE Word open for the next project.

Project 3-6: References

Your friend Mike liked your work on his resume so much that he asks you to format his reference list with the same design as his resume.

1. **OPEN** *references* from the data files for this lesson.

 The *references* document is available on the companion CD-ROM.

2. Refer to the resume you formatted in Project 3-5. Format the list of references using the same fonts, styles, sizes, and attributes as in his resume, so that they look consistent when compared side by side.
3. **SAVE** the document as *mzreferences* and **CLOSE** the file.
   CLOSE Word.

INTERNET READY

Search the Internet for information on the national YMCA or your local YMCA. Create a document that lists some of the programs available. The list will be mailed with a letter soliciting donations and volunteers for the Y, so make sure to choose fonts, sizes, and effects that have an appropriate look and feel. Create a heading for each program in the list with a description underneath.

Paragraph Formatting

LESSON SKILL MATRIX

Setting Indents 172	Students will learn how to set indents.
Changing Alignment 174	Students will learn how to change alignment.
Setting the Line Spacing within a Paragraph 176	Students will learn how to set the line spacing within a paragraph.
Setting the Spacing Around a Paragraph 177	Students will learn how to set the spacing around a paragraph.
Creating a Numbered List 178	Students will learn how to create a numbered list.
Creating a Bulleted List 179	Students will learn how to create a bulleted list.
Shading a Paragraph 180	Students will learn how to shade a paragraph.
Placing a Border Around a Paragraph 182	Students will learn how to place a border around a paragraph.
Setting Tabs on the Ruler 184	Students will learn how to set tabs on the ruler.
Using the Tabs Dialog Box 186	Students will learn how to use the tabs dialog box.
Displaying Non-Printing Characters 187	Students will learn how to display non-printing characters.
Clearing Tabs 188	Students will learn how to clear tabs.
Clearing Formats from a Paragraph 188	Students will learn how to clear formats from a paragraph.

You are employed at Books and Beyond, an independent used book store. Your responsibilities include receiving and assessing used books, issuing trade credit, stocking the bookshelves, and placing special orders. Because you are computer literate, your job also involves creating and modifying documents needed at the store. Currently, you are working on the employee handbook. In this lesson, you will learn how to use Word's formatting features to change the appearance of paragraphs. You will learn how to set indents, change alignment and line spacing, create numbered and bulleted lists, and use shading and borders. You will also learn how to use tabs and clear the formatting from paragraphs.

KEY TERMS
first-line indent
hanging indent
horizontal alignment
indent
leaders
line spacing
negative indent
non-printing characters
paragraph spacing
vertical alignment

Software Orientation

Indents and Spacing Tab in Paragraph Dialog Box

When formatting the alignment, indentation, and spacing of paragraphs, you will frequently utilize the Paragraph dialog box. The Indents and Spacing tab is shown in Figure 4-1.

Figure 4-1

Indents and Spacing tab of Paragraph dialog box

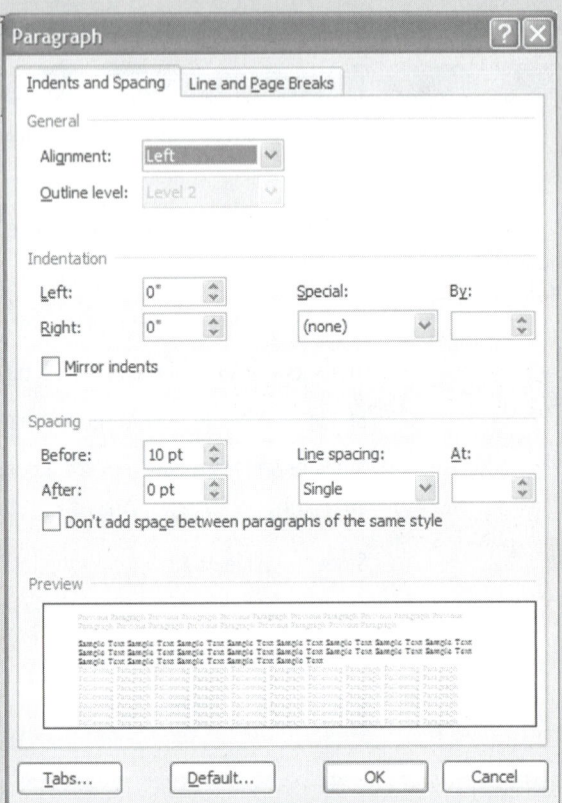

This tab of the Paragraph dialog box is used to make changes to the alignment, indentation, and spacing of paragraphs. Use this figure as a reference throughout this lesson as well as the rest of this book.

■ Manually Formatting Paragraphs

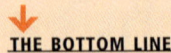

THE BOTTOM LINE

To apply paragraph formatting, place the insertion point anywhere in a paragraph. Word will apply any paragraph formats you chose to the entire paragraph. You cannot apply paragraph formatting to just a selection of the paragraph.

Setting Indents

Indents can be used to set paragraphs off from other text in your documents. There are various kinds of indents you can set, including first-line indents, hanging indents, and negative indents.

➔ SET INDENTS

GET READY. Before you begin these steps, be sure to launch Microsoft Office Word 2007.

Paragraph Formatting | 173

The *acknowledgement* document is available on the companion CD-ROM.

1. **OPEN** *acknowledgement* from the data files for this lesson.
2. Click to place the insertion point in the first paragraph.
3. On the Home tab, in the Paragraph group, click the **Dialog Box Launcher** to display the Paragraph dialog box. The **Indents and Spacing** tab should be selected.
4. In the Special list under Indentation, click **First line**. In the By box, the amount of space that you want the first line to be indented should be set to 0.5 inches.
5. Click **OK**.

 **ANOTHER WAY**
Click to place the insertion point before the first line in the paragraph and drag the First Line Indent marker on the ruler (see Figure 4-2) to the place where you want the text to be indented.

6. Place the insertion point in the second paragraph.
7. On the horizontal ruler, drag the **Hanging Indent** marker to 0.5 inches, as shown in Figure 4-2.

Figure 4-2

Ruler with hanging indent marker

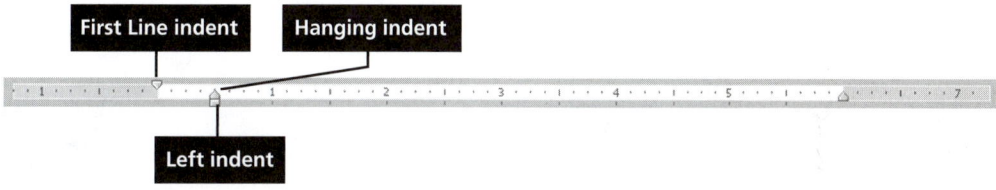

TROUBLESHOOTING
If the horizontal ruler is not visible along the top of the document, click the View Ruler button at the top of the vertical scrollbar to display it.

8. Place the insertion point in the third paragraph.
9. On the Page Layout tab, in the Paragraph group, click the upward-pointing arrow next to Indent Left five times to indent the left side of the paragraph by **0.5 inches**.
10. Click the **upward-pointing arrow** next to Indent Right five times to indent the right side of the paragraph by **0.5 inches**.

 **ANOTHER WAY**
To indent the first line of a paragraph, click in front of the line and press **Tab**. To indent an entire paragraph, click in front of any line but the first line and click **Tab**.

11. Place the insertion point in the last paragraph.
12. On the ruler, drag the **Left Indent** marker into the left margin at −0.5 inches, as shown in Figure 4-3.

Figure 4-3

Ruler with negative indent

Figure 4-4

Document with indents

13. Your document should look similar to Figure 4-4.

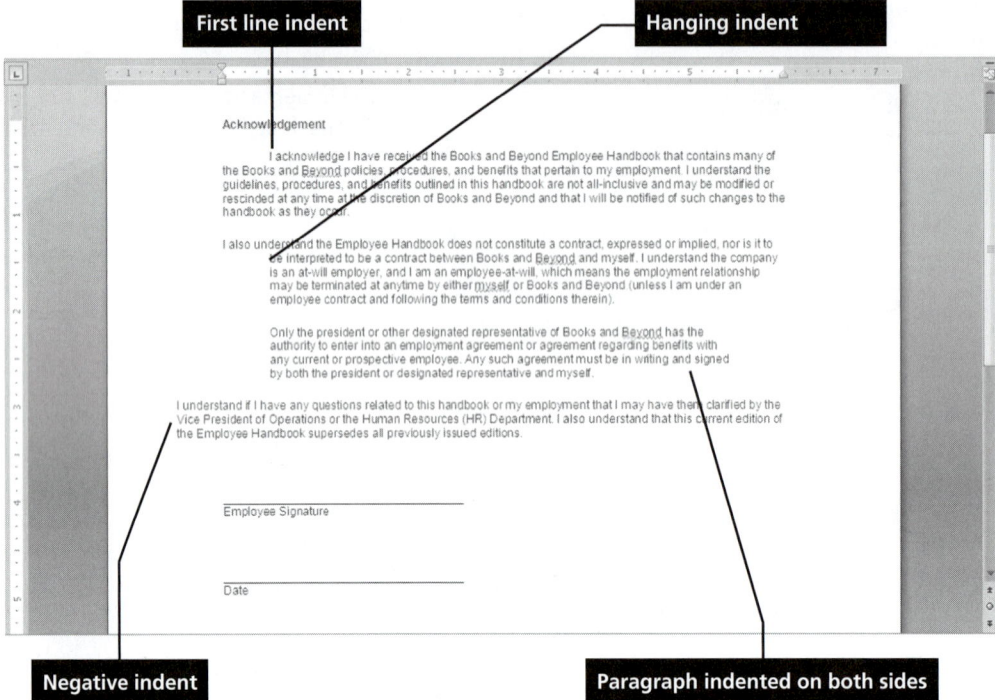

CERTIFICATION READY?
How do you format paragraphs?
2.1.4

14. **SAVE** the document as *handbook_acknowledgement* and close the file.

    PAUSE. LEAVE Word open for the next exercise.

An *indent* is the space between a paragraph and the document's left and/or right margin. In this activity, you learned about various types of indents. A *first-line indent* is where the first line of a paragraph indents more than the following lines. A *hanging indent* is created when the first full line of text in a paragraph is not indented, but the following lines are. Hanging indents are common in legal documents or reference lists. A *negative indent* is when the paragraph extends into the left margin. You can also increase or decrease the indentation of a whole paragraph from the left or right margin, or both. This is often done to set off a long quotation.

Changing Alignment

Depending on the document you are creating, you may need to change the horizontal or vertical alignment of text. Alignment refers to how text is positioned between the margins.

➔ CHANGE ALIGNMENT

1. **OPEN** *introduction* from the data files for this lesson.
2. Click to place the insertion point in the first paragraph.
3. On the Home tab, in the Paragraph group, click the **Justify** button (shown in Table 4-1).
4. Place the insertion point in the second paragraph.
5. On the Home tab, in the Paragraph group, click the **Dialog Box Launcher** to display the Paragraph dialog box. The **Indents and Spacing** tab should be selected.
6. In the Alignment list under General, click **Centered** and then click **OK**.

 **CD**

The *introduction* document is available on the companion CD-ROM.

Paragraph Formatting | 175

7. Place the insertion point in the third paragraph.
8. Press Ctrl+R to align the text on the right. Your document should appear similar to Figure 4-5.

Figure 4-5

Document with various horizontal alignments

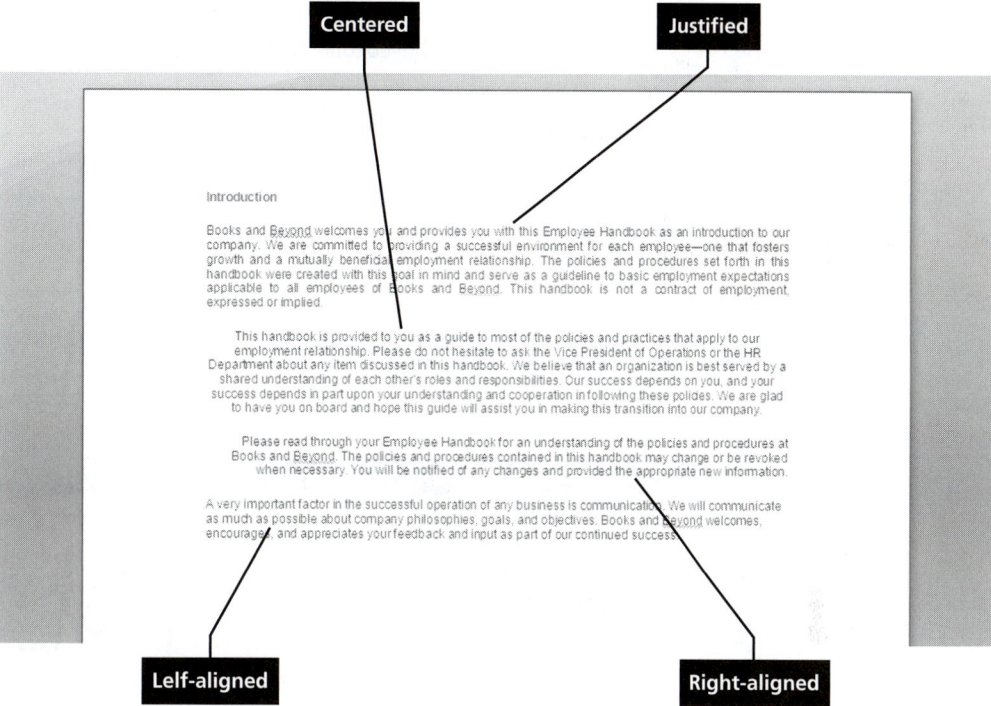

9. On the Page Layout tab, in the Page Setup group, click the **Dialog Box Launcher** and then click the Layout tab, shown in Figure 4-6.

Figure 4-6

Layout tab of Page Setup dialog box

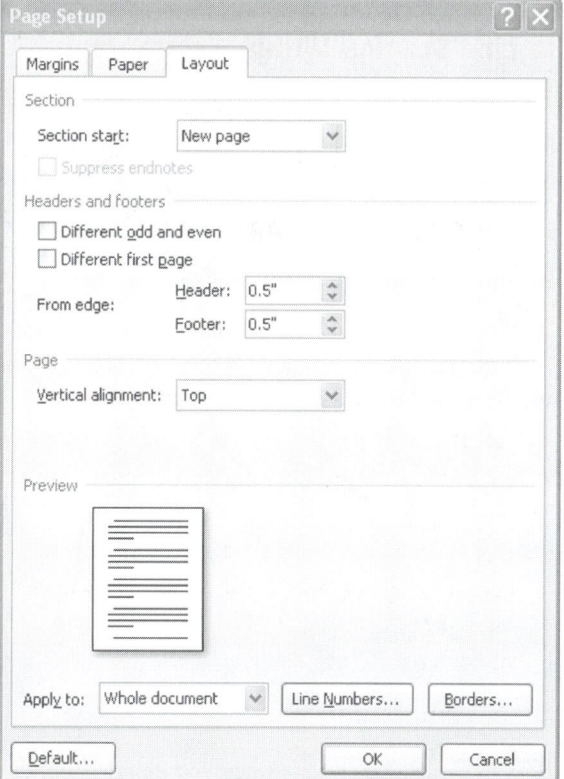

10. In the Vertical alignment list under Page, click **Center**.
11. In the Apply To list under Preview, **Whole document** should be selected. You could also choose to apply the vertical alignment option from that point forward.
12. Click **OK**. All the text is centered on the page.
13. **SAVE** the document as *handbook_introduction*.

    PAUSE. LEAVE the document open to use in the next exercise.

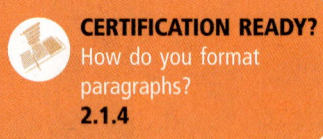

CERTIFICATION READY?
How do you format paragraphs?
2.1.4

Horizontal alignment refers to how text is positioned between the left and right margins. You can left-align, center, right-align, or justify text using the alignment commands. *Vertical alignment* refers to how text is positioned between the top and bottom margins of the page. You can align text vertically at the top, at the bottom, centered on the page, or justified.

By default, text is left-aligned at the top of the page. You can change vertical alignment in the Layout tab of the Page Setup dialog box. You can change horizontal alignment in the Indents and Spacing tab of the Paragraph dialog box or using the buttons and shortcut keys shown in Table 4-1.

Table 4-1

Horizontal alignment options

Option	Button	Shortcut Keys	Description
Align Left		Ctrl+L	Lines up text flush with the left margin, leaving a ragged right edge
Align Right		Ctrl+R	Lines up text flush with the right margin, leaving a ragged left edge
Center		Ctrl+E	Centers text between the left and right margins, leaving ragged edges on both sides
Justify		Ctrl+J	Lines up text flush on both the left and right margins, adding extra space between words as necessary, for a clean look

Setting the Line Spacing Within a Paragraph

By default, paragraphs in Word are single-spaced. You can change the amount of space between lines in a paragraph by setting the line spacing.

➔ SET LINE SPACING WITHIN A PARAGRAPH

USE the document that is open from the previous exercise.

1. Click to place the insertion point in the first paragraph.
2. On the Home tab, in the Paragraph group, click the **Line Spacing** button to display the Line Spacing menu, as shown in Figure 4-7.
3. Click 2.0 to double-space the selected text.

Figure 4-7

Line Spacing menu

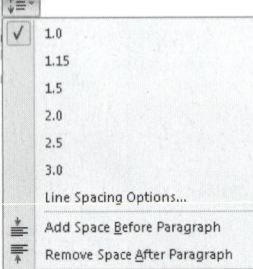

Paragraph Formatting | 177

4. Place the insertion point in the second paragraph.
5. On the Home tab, in the Paragraph group, click the **Line Spacing** button to display the menu.
6. To set more precise spacing measurements, click **Line Spacing Options** to display the Indents and Spacing tab of the Paragraph dialog box.
7. In the Line Spacing list under Spacing, click **Exactly**. In the At list, click the **upward-pointing arrow** until it reads 14 pt.
8. Click **OK**.
9. **SAVE** the document.

   PAUSE. LEAVE the document open to use in the next exercise.

> **CERTIFICATION READY?**
> How do you format paragraphs?
> 2.1.4

Line spacing is the amount of space between lines of text in a paragraph. The lines in a paragraph are single-spaced by default. Line spacing options available in the Indents and Spacing tab of the Paragraph dialog box are explained in Table 4-2.

Table 4-2

Line spacing options

OPTION	DESCRIPTION
Single	Default option that accommodates the largest font in that line, plus a small amount of extra space
1.5	One-and-one-half times the amount of space as single
Double	Twice as much space as single
At least	Sets the spacing at the minimum amount needed to fit the largest font on the line
Exactly	Sets the spacing at a fixed amount that Word does not adjust
Multiple	Sets the spacing at an amount that is increased or decreased from single spacing by a percentage that you specify e.g., Setting the line spacing to 1.3 will increase the space by 30%

Setting the Spacing Around a Paragraph

By default, the space after a paragraph is slightly more than single-spaced lines. You can change the amount of space before or after a paragraph by setting the paragraph spacing.

➔ SET SPACING AROUND A PARAGRAPH

USE the document that is open from the previous exercise.

1. Click to place the insertion point in the third paragraph.
2. On the Home tab, in the Paragraph group, click the **Dialog Box Launcher** to display the Paragraph dialog box. The **Indents and Spacing** tab should be selected.
3. In the Spacing section, click the **upward-pointing arrow** next to Before until it reads **24 pt**.
4. Click the **upward-pointing arrow** next to After until it reads **24 pt**.
5. Click **OK**.
6. With the insertion point still in the third paragraph, click the **Line Spacing** button in the Paragraph group to display the Line Spacing menu.
7. Click **Remove Space Before Paragraph**.
8. **SAVE** the document and **CLOSE** the file.

   PAUSE. LEAVE Word open for the next exercise.

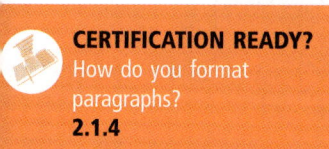

> **CERTIFICATION READY?**
> How do you format paragraphs?
> 2.1.4

Paragraph spacing is the amount of space above or below a paragraph. To increase or decrease paragraph spacing, click the Before and After upward-pointing or downward-pointing arrows in the Indents and Spacing tab of the Paragraph dialog box. You can also click the Line Spacing button in the Paragraph group and use the Remove Space Before Paragraph and Remove Space After Paragraph commands. If no space is currently before or after the selected paragraph, the commands will be Add Space Before Paragraph and Add Space After Paragraph.

Creating a Numbered List

You can quickly add numbers to existing lines of text to create a list, or Word can automatically create a numbered list as you key.

➔ CREATE A NUMBERED LIST

1. **OPEN** *alarm* from the data files for this lesson.
2. Select the four sentences under the *Set Alarm* heading.
3. On the Home tab, in the Paragraph group, click the **Numbering** button (see Figure 4-8).
4. Click to place the insertion point at the end of the fourth numbered sentence.
5. Press [Enter]. Notice that Word automatically numbers the next line sequentially.
6. Key **Leave the premises immediately**.
7. Select the four sentences under the *Deactivate Alarm* heading.
8. On the Home tab, in the Paragraph group, click the **Numbering** button.
9. Select the numbered list under the *Set Alarm* heading.
10. To change the format of the numbered list, click the **downward-pointing arrow** next to the Numbering button to display the menu shown in Figure 4-8.

CD

The *alarm* document is available on the companion CD-ROM.

Figure 4-8

Number formatting options

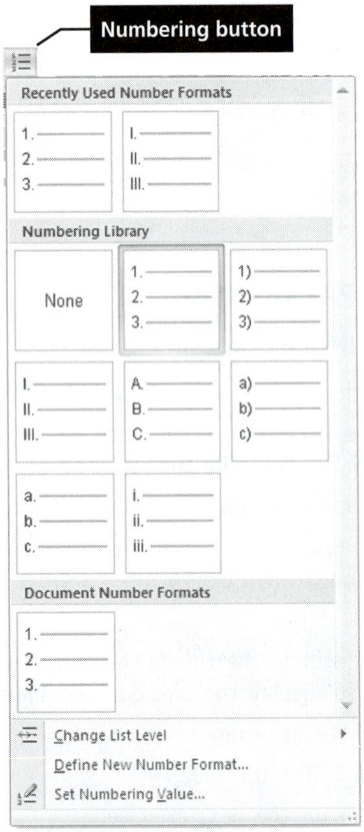

Paragraph Formatting | 179

11. Notice that when you point your mouse to an option on the menu, the changes are previewed in your document. Click the last option on the first row in the Numbering Library.

> **TAKE NOTE*** To change the formatting of the numbers, click any number to select the entire list. If you select the text, the formatting of both the text and the numbering changes.

> **CERTIFICATION READY?**
> How do you format paragraphs?
> **2.1.4**
> How do you create tables and lists?
> **4.2.1**

12. Select the numbered list under the *Deactivate Alarm* heading.
13. Click the **downward-pointing arrow** next to the Numbering button.
14. On the menu under Recently Used Number Formats, choose the same number format that you just applied.
15. **SAVE** the document as *handbook_alarm*.

    PAUSE. LEAVE the document open to use in the next exercise.

Numbers can be added to an already existing list or you can create a numbered list from scratch. To remove the numbers, select the list and then click the Numbers button. To change the format of a numbered list, select it and click the downward-pointing arrow next to the Numbering button.

> **TROUBLESHOOTING** If you key an asterisk (*) or a number one (1.), Word recognizes that you are trying to start a bulleted or numbered list and will automatically continue it. If you occasionally don't want the text you are keying to be turned into a list, you can undo a list by clicking the AutoCorrect Options button ⌧ that appears.
>
> To turn the feature off completely, click the Microsoft Office button, then choose Word Options, Proofing, AutoCorrect Options, and then the AutoFormat As You Type tab. Under Apply as You Type, select or clear the Automatic Bulleted Lists checkbox or the Automatic Numbered Lists checkbox.

Creating a Bulleted List

> Bulleted lists are very similar to numbered lists. You can change existing lines of text to a bulleted list or Word can automatically create one as you key.

➔ CREATE A BULLETED LIST

USE the document that is open from the previous exercise.

1. Select the two sentences below the phrase *Please keep in mind:*.
2. On the Home tab, in the Paragraph group, click the **Bullets** button.
3. Click to place the insertion point at the end of the second bulleted sentence.
4. Press [Enter]. Notice that Word automatically continues the bulleted list.
5. Key **If you do not know your four-digit code and password, please get it from the HR department**.
6. Select the entire bulleted list.
7. To change the format of the bulleted list, click the **downward-pointing arrow** next to the Bullets button to display the menu shown in Figure 4-9.

Figure 4-9

Bullet formatting options

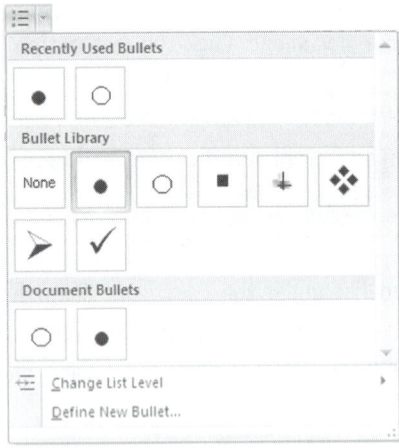

> **TAKE NOTE** To change a bulleted list to a numbered list (or vice versa), select the list and then click either the Numbering or Bullets button.

   8. Click the last option on the first row of the Bullets Library.
   9. Your document should look similar to the one shown in Figure 4-10.

Figure 4-10

Document with bulleted and numbered lists

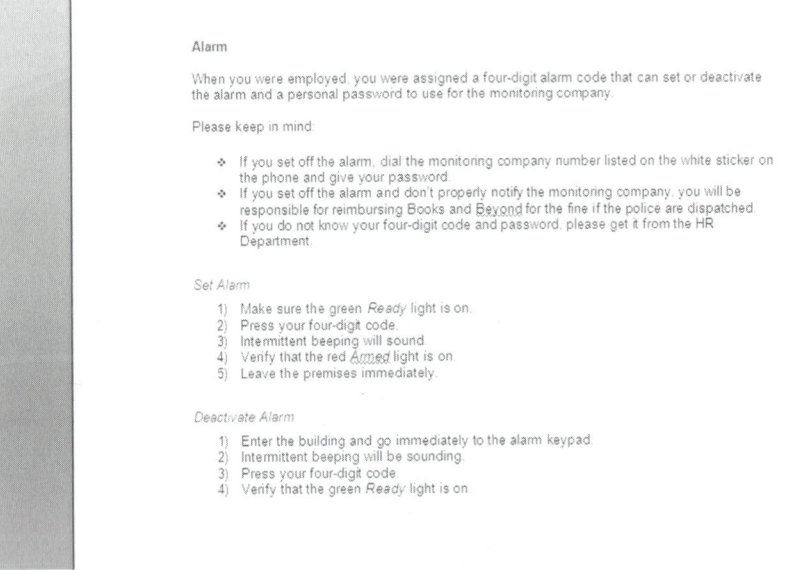

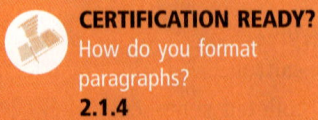

CERTIFICATION READY?
How do you format paragraphs?
2.1.4
How do you create tables and lists?
4.2.1

   10. **SAVE** the document and **CLOSE** the file.
       PAUSE. LEAVE Word open for the next exercise.

Bullets can be added to an already existing list or you can create a bulleted list from scratch. To remove the bullets, select the list and then click the Bullets button. To change the format of a bulleted list, select it and click the downward-pointing arrow next to the Bullets button.

You will learn more about working with lists and multilevel lists in Lesson 8.

Shading a Paragraph

> You can use the Shading feature to color the background behind the selected text or paragraph.

Paragraph Formatting | 181

→ **SHADE A PARAGRAPH**

The *diversity* document is available on the companion CD-ROM.

1. **OPEN** *diversity* from the data files for this lesson.
2. Click to place the insertion point in the first paragraph.
3. On the Home tab, in the Paragraph group, click the **downward-pointing arrow** next to the **Shading** button to display the menu shown in Figure 4-11.

Figure 4-11

Shading menu

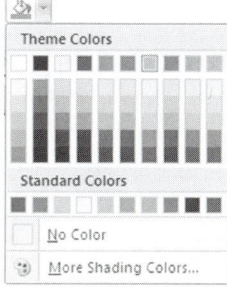

CERTIFICATION READY?
How do you format paragraphs?
2.1.4

4. In the Theme Colors palette, click the color on the third row down on the last column (Orange, Accent 6, Lighter 40%).
5. **SAVE** the document as *handbook_diversity*.

   PAUSE. LEAVE the document open to use in the next exercise.

If you want to apply the previously chosen shading to a paragraph, click the Shading button. To choose another color, click the downward-pointing arrow next to the Shading button, and you will be able to choose a color in the current theme or a standard color from the Shading menu. To remove shading, click No Color.

If you want more color choices, click More Colors to open the Colors dialog box, where you can choose standard colors in the Standard tab, shown in Figure 4-12. In the Custom tab, shown in Figure 4-13, you can create a custom color and even enter the exact RGB numbers if you know them.

Figure 4-12

Standard tab of Colors dialog box

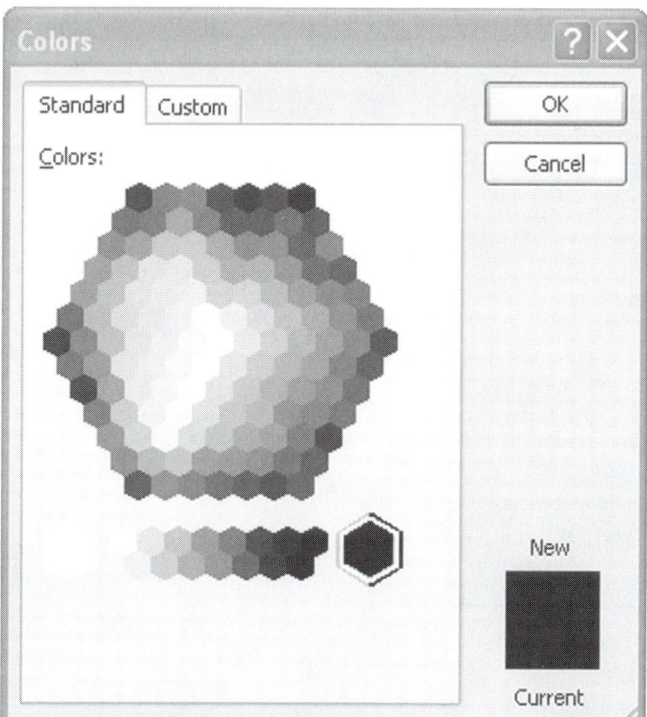

Figure 4-13

Custom tab of Colors dialog box

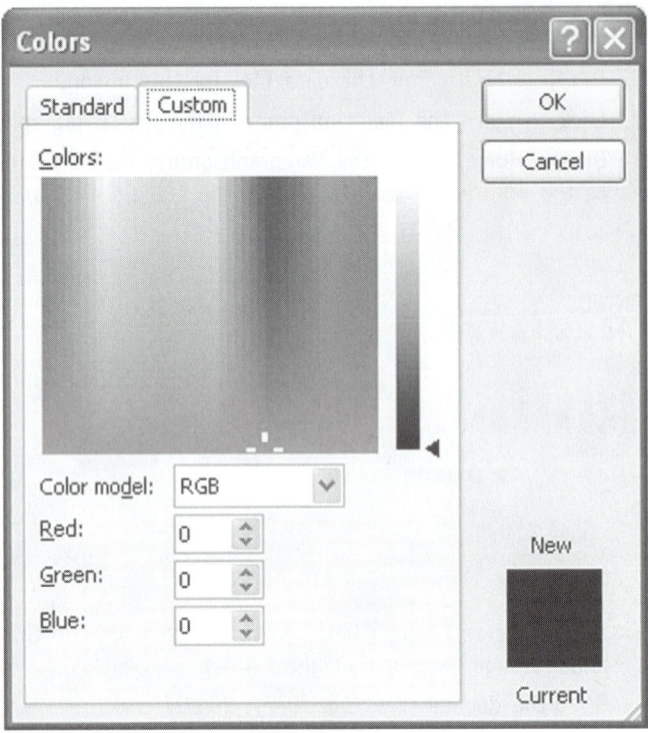

Placing a Border Around a Paragraph

Like shading, borders can add interest and emphasis to paragraphs. Borders can be formatted with a variety of styles, colors, and widths.

→ **PLACE A BORDER AROUND A PARAGRAPH**

USE the document that is open from the previous exercise.

1. Click to place the insertion point in the second paragraph.
2. On the Home tab, in the Paragraph group, click the **downward-pointing arrow** next to the **Border** button to display the menu shown in Figure 4-14.

Figure 4-14

Border menu

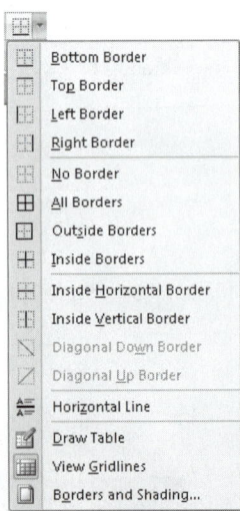

Paragraph Formatting | 183

3. Click **Outside Borders** on the menu.
4. Your document should look similar to Figure 4-15.

Figure 4-15

Document with shading and border

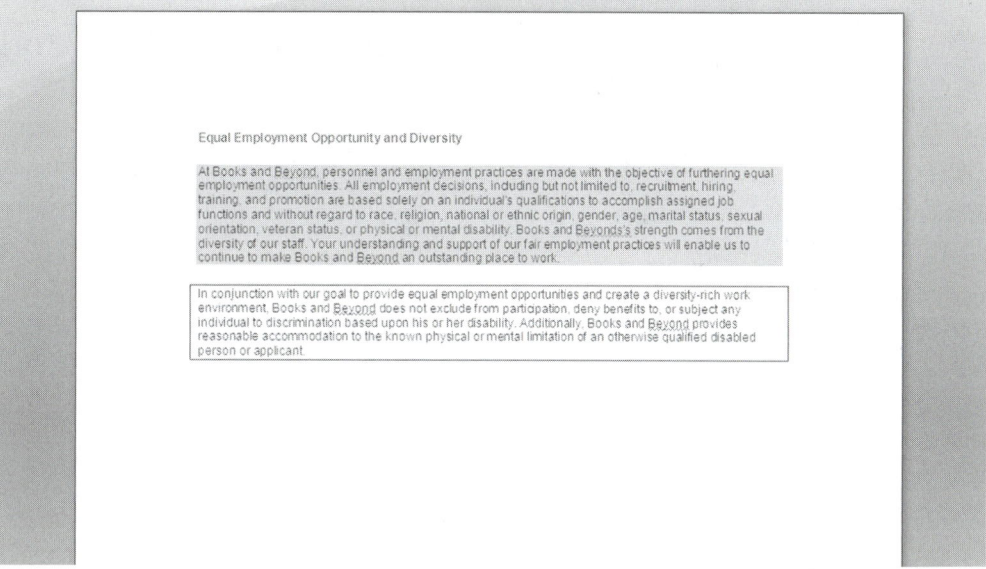

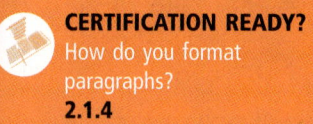

CERTIFICATION READY?
How do you format paragraphs?
2.1.4

5. **SAVE** the document and **CLOSE** the file.

   PAUSE. LEAVE Word open for the next exercise.

If you want to apply the previously chosen border to a paragraph, click the Border button. To place a different border around selected text, click the downward-pointing arrow next to the Border button.

For more options, click the Borders and Shading option on the Border menu to display the Borders tab of the Borders and Shading dialog box, shown in Figure 4-16. Here you can change the style, color, and width of the borders and preview the changes. To remove a border, click None in the Setting section. This dialog box also contains tabs for page border options and shading.

Figure 4-16

Borders tab of the Borders and Shading dialog box

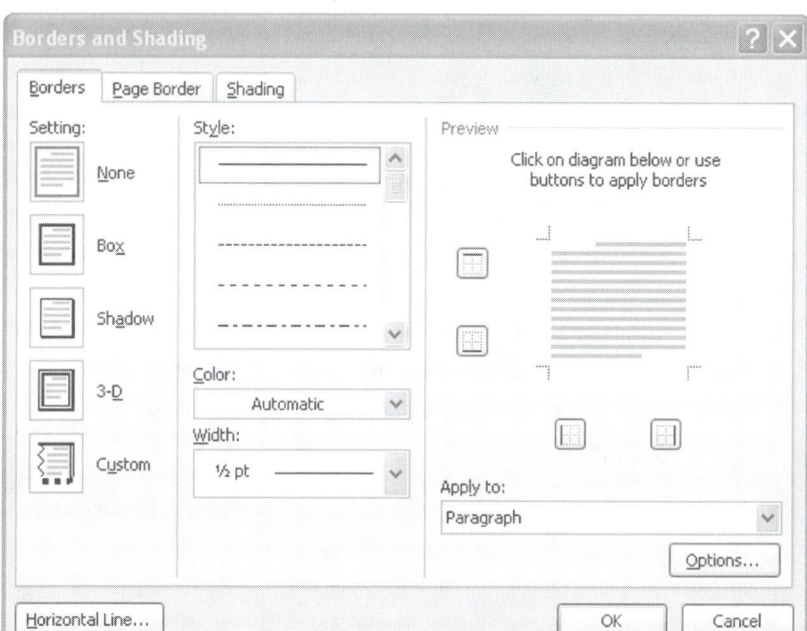

TAKE NOTE*

Borders can also be added to pages, sections, tables, cells, graphic objects, and pictures.

Software Orientation

Tab Dialog Box

When setting and clearing tabs, you will frequently use the Tabs dialog box, shown in Figure 4-17.

Figure 4-17

Tabs dialog box

Use this figure as a reference throughout the activities on setting tabs as well as the rest of the book.

Setting Tabs

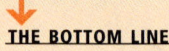
THE BOTTOM LINE
You can set tabs quickly on the ruler. Or you can open the Tabs dialog box to set more precise tabs and have more options.

Setting Tabs on the Ruler

To set tabs quickly, you can click the tab selector at the left end of the ruler until it displays the type of tab that you want and then click the ruler at the place where you want to set it.

 **SET TABS ON THE RULER**

1. **OPEN** *perdiem* from the data files for this lesson.
2. Place the insertion point on the line below the *Meals & Incidentals Breakdown* heading.

The *perdiem* document is available on the companion CD-ROM.

Paragraph Formatting | 185

3. Click the tab selector at the left of the ruler until the Center tab appears. The tab selector and horizontal ruler are shown in Figure 4-18.

Figure 4-18

Tab selector and horizontal ruler with tabs set

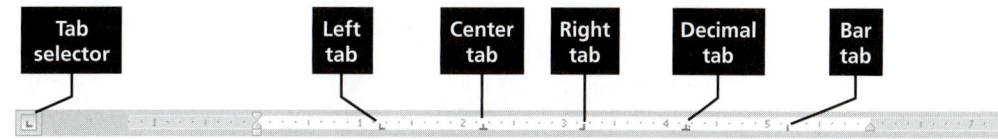

TROUBLESHOOTING If the horizontal ruler is not visible along the top of the document, click the View Ruler button at the top of the vertical scrollbar to display it.

4. Click the ruler at the 2.5-inch mark to set a center tab.
5. Click the ruler at the 4-inch mark to set a center tab.
6. Press Tab and key *Chicago*.
7. Press Tab and key *New York*.
8. Select the list of words at the end of the document, starting with *Breakfast*.
9. Click the tab selector until the right tab appears.
10. Click the ruler at the 1-inch mark to set a right tab.
11. Place the insertion point in front of each word and press Tab to align it at the right tab. Your document should look similar to Figure 4-19.

Figure 4-19

Document formatted with tabs

CERTIFICATION READY?
How do you set and clear tabs?
2.1.5

12. **SAVE** the document as *handbook_perdiem*.

PAUSE. LEAVE the document open to use in the next exercise.

By default, left-aligned tab stops are set every half inch in Word. To set a tab at a different place on the ruler, click the tab selector at the left end of the ruler and then click on the ruler where you want to place the tab. The various types of tabs and their descriptions are shown in Table 4-3.

Table 4-3

Tab stops on the ruler

Name	Button	Description
Left Tab		Left aligns text at the tab place indicated on the horizontal ruler
Center Tab		Centers text at the place indicated on the horizontal ruler
Right Tab		Right-aligns text at the place indicated on the horizontal ruler
Decimal Tab		Aligns numbers around a decimal point at the place indicated on the horizontal ruler
Bar Tab		Inserts a vertical bar line at the place indicated on the horizontal ruler

After tabs are set, when you press the Tab key, the insertion point will stop at the place you specified with a tab stop. To move a tab stop to a different position on the ruler, click and drag it left or right to a new position.

Using the Tabs Dialog Box

The Tabs dialog box is useful for setting tabs at precise locations on the ruler, clearing all tabs, and setting tab leaders.

 USE THE TABS DIALOG BOX

USE the document that is open from the previous exercise.

1. Select the list of words at the end of the document, starting with *Breakfast*.
2. On the Home tab, in the Paragraph group, click the **Dialog Box Launcher**.
3. Click the **Tabs** button on the bottom left to display the Tabs dialog box.
4. In the Tab stop box, key **2.6**. In the Alignment section, select **Right**. In the Leader section, select **2**. Then click **Set**.
5. In the Tab stop box, key **4.1**. In the Alignment section, select **Right**. In the Leader section, select **2**. Then click **Set**.
6. Click **OK**.
7. Place the insertion point after the word *Breakfast* and press Tab.
8. Key **$10** and press Tab.
9. Key **$12**. Repeat this process for each line, keying the numbers shown in Figure 4-20.

ANOTHER WAY

To open the Tabs dialog box, double-click any tab stop on the ruler.

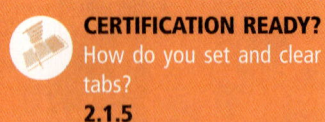

CERTIFICATION READY?
How do you set and clear tabs?
2.1.5

Figure 4-20

Document formatted with tabs

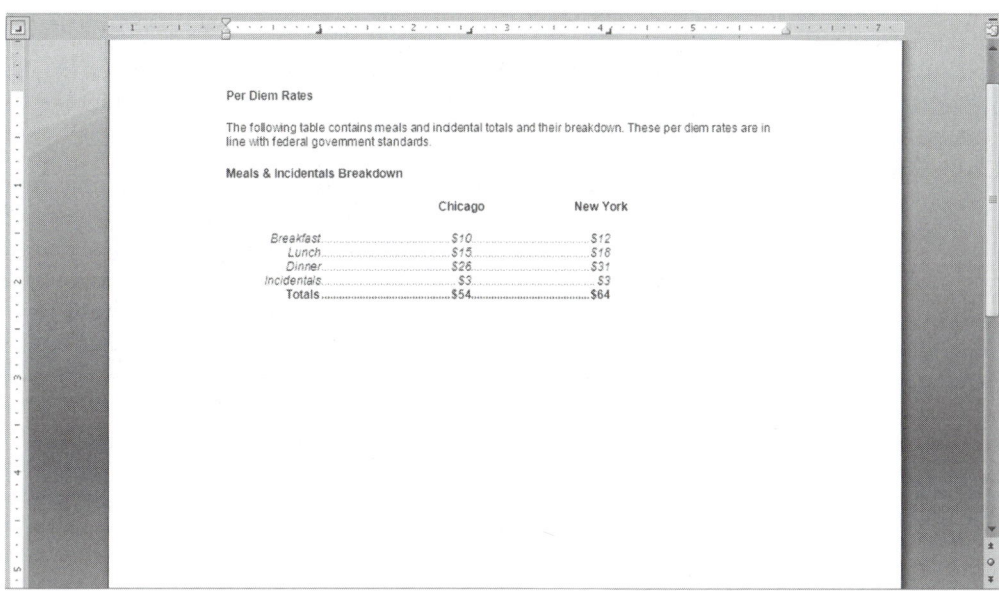

10. **SAVE** the document.

   PAUSE. LEAVE the document open to use in the next exercise.

In this activity, you learned how to use the Tabs dialog box to set tabs and specify leaders. Tab *leaders* are dotted, dashed, or solid lines that fill the space before a tab.

Displaying Non-Printing Characters

When you format documents, Word inserts symbols in the document that are usually hidden from view. However, these non-printing characters—such as paragraph marks or tab indents—can be displayed.

➔ DISPLAY NON-PRINTING CHARACTERS

USE the document that is open from the previous exercise.

1. On the Home tab, in the Paragraph group, click the **Show/Hide Paragraph** button to display the non-printing characters in the document. Your screen should look similar to Figure 4-21.

Figure 4-21

Document with non-printing characters displayed

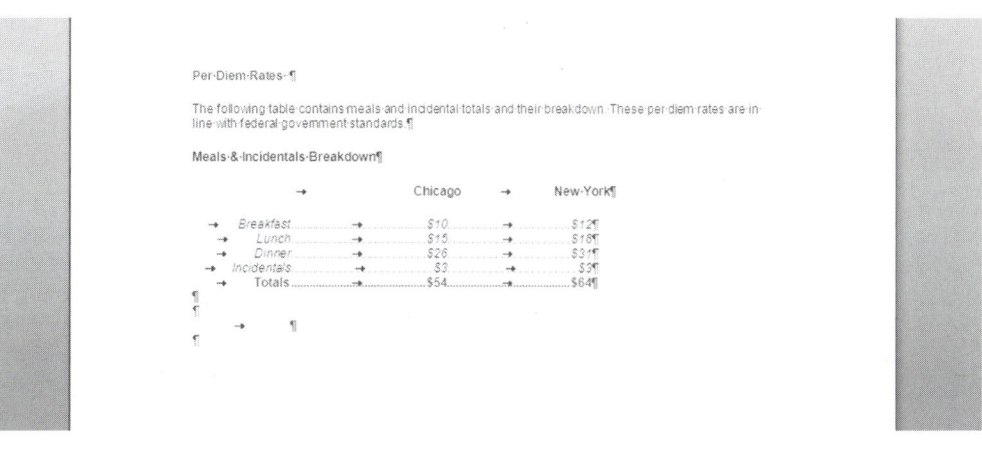

188 | Lesson 4

To display non-printing characters, press **Ctrl+Shift+***.

2. Click the Show/Hide Paragraph button again to hide the non-printing characters.
3. SAVE the document.

PAUSE. LEAVE the document open to use in the next exercise.

Non-printing characters are symbols that Word inserts into a document when you use certain formatting commands, such as paragraphs and indents. These symbols are usually hidden from view, but you can display them by clicking the Show/Hide Paragraph button in the Paragraph group of the Home tab. Seeing the exact locations of these symbols can help you edit text. When you are done, click the Show/Hide Paragraph button again to hide the symbols.

Clearing Tabs

You can quickly remove a single tab by dragging it off the ruler, or you can use the Tabs dialog box to clear one or all tabs.

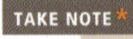 **CLEAR TABS**

USE the document that is open from the previous exercise.

1. Click to place the insertion point on the last line (*Total*).
2. Click the tabs stop at **4.1"**.
3. Drag it down off the ruler and release the mouse button to remove it.
4. On the Home tab, in the Paragraph group, click the **Dialog Box Launcher**.
5. Click the Tabs button on the bottom left to display the Tabs dialog box.
6. In the Tab stop position list, click **2.6"** and then click Clear to clear that tab.
7. Click the Clear All button to clear all tabs on that line.
8. Click OK.
9. Select all the text on the *Totals* line and click the **Delete** button to delete it.
10. SAVE the document and CLOSE the file.

PAUSE. LEAVE Word open for the next exercise.

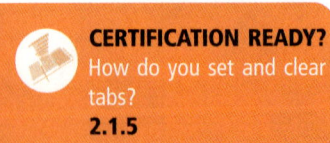

CERTIFICATION READY?
How do you set and clear tabs?
2.1.5

To remove a tab stop from the ruler, click and drag it off the ruler. When you release the mouse button, the tab stop disappears. Or open the Tabs dialog box, where you can choose to clear one tab or all of them.

TAKE NOTE* Many of the predesigned document layout options in Word 2007 make it possible to create documents such as an index or table of contents without having to set any tabs manually.

■ Clearing the Formats from a Paragraph

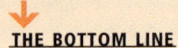 **THE BOTTOM LINE** Just as you learned how to clear the formatting from characters in the previous lesson, you can similarly clear the formatting from an entire paragraph.

Clearing Formats from a Paragraph

You may decide after making changes that you no longer want any formatting in a paragraph or that you want to start over. The Clear Formatting command makes it easy change a paragraph back to plain text, no matter how many formats you have applied to it.

Paragraph Formatting | 189

 **CLEAR PARAGRAPH FORMATS**

Clear Formatting was also discussed in Lesson 3.

1. **OPEN** the *handbook_diversity* document that you saved earlier in this lesson.
2. Select the two paragraphs.
3. On the Home tab, in the Styles group, click the **More** button to display the gallery of styles.
4. Click the **Clear Formatting** option.

ANOTHER WAY
You can also return the paragraph to plain text by clicking the Clear Formatting button on the Home tab in the Font group.

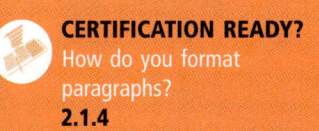
CERTIFICATION READY?
How do you format paragraphs?
2.1.4

5. Change the font of the two paragraphs to **Arial** and the size to **9**.
6. Insert a blank line after the document title and between the paragraphs.
7. **SAVE** the document as *handbook_eeo* and **CLOSE** the file.
   STOP. **CLOSE** Word.

The Clear Formatting command provides an easy way to change a paragraph back to plain text. Not only is all the formatting removed, but the font and font size also revert to the default.

SUMMARY SKILL MATRIX

IN THIS LESSON YOU LEARNED HOW TO:
Set Indents
Change Alignment
Set the Line Spacing within a Paragraph
Set the Spacing Around a Paragraph
Create a Numbered List
Create a Bulleted List
Shade a Paragraph
Place a Border Around a Paragraph
Setting Tabs on the Ruler
Using the Tabs Dialog Box
Displaying Non-Printing Characters
Clearing Tabs
Clearing Formats from a Paragraph

Knowledge Assessment

Fill in the Blank

Complete the following sentences by writing the correct word or words in the blanks provided.

1. To indent the first line of a paragraph, click in front of the line and press ___tab___.
2. A(n) ___horizontal Alignment___ is the space between a paragraph and the document's left and/or right margin. *(indent)*
3. If you key a(n) ___(*) or a # one (1) p.179___, Word recognizes that you are trying to start a bulleted list and will automatically continue it.
4. When setting tabs, you can do so quickly by setting them on the ___ruler (184)___.
5. By default, left-aligned tabs stops are set every ___½ inch (185)___ in Word.
6. A bar tab inserts a(n) ___Vertical (186)___ bar line at the place indicated on the horizontal ruler.
7. Tab ___leaders (187)___ are dotted, dashed, or solid lines that fill the space before a tab.
8. Non-printing characters are ___Symbols___ that Word inserts into a document when you use certain formatting commands.
9. The ___Clear Formating___ command makes it easy to change a paragraph back to plain text, no matter how many formats you have applied to it.
10. ___Single (177)___ line spacing is the default option that accommodates the largest font in that line, plus a small amount of extra space.

Multiple Choice

Select the best response for the following statements.

1. Which of the following is not a type of indent?
   a. hanging
   b. negative
   c. positive — 172
   d. first-line

2. Which word(s) refers to how text is positioned between the top and bottom margins of the page?
   a. horizontal alignment
   b. vertical alignment — 176
   c. justified
   d. line spacing

3. Which line spacing command sets the spacing at a fixed amount that Word does not adjust?
   a. Exactly — 177
   b. Double
   c. Multiple
   d. At Least

4. Which command do you use to remove shading from a paragraph?
   a. Remove Shading
   b. Delete Color
   c. Undo Shading
   d. No Color

5. Which property of borders can be changed in the Borders tab of the Borders and Shading dialog box?
   a. color
   b. width
   c. style
   d. all of the above
   e. none of the above

6. Where is the View Ruler button located?
   a. in the Tabs dialog box
   b. at the top of the vertical scrollbar
   c. in the Paragraph group
   d. all of the above
   e. none of the above

7. What does dragging a tab off the ruler do?
   a. moves it to another position
   b. turns it into a left-aligned tab
   c. clears it
   d. hides it from view

8. When applying shading to text or a paragraph, you can choose which of the following?
   a. a color in the current theme
   b. a standard color
   c. a custom color
   d. all of the above

9. Which Word feature would you use to extend a paragraph into the left margin?
   a. indent
   b. line spacing
   c. horizontal alignment
   d. shading

10. Which button do you click to display non-printing characters?
    a. Display Non-Printing Characters
    b. Show/Hide Paragraph
    c. View Formatting Commands
    d. none of the above

Competency Assessment

Project 4-1: Lost Art Photos

You are employed in the marketing department at Lost Art Photos and have been asked to format a promotional document.

GET READY. Launch Word if it is not already running.

The *photos* document is available on the companion CD-ROM.

1. **OPEN** *photos* from the data files for this lesson.
2. Select the title.
3. On the Home tab, in the Paragraph group, click the **Border** button.
4. Click **Borders and Shading** . . . on the menu to open the Borders and Shading dialog box.
5. In the Setting list, click **Shadow**. On the Width list, click **3 pt**.
6. Click **OK**.
7. On the Home tab, in the Paragraph group, click the **downward-pointing arrow** next to the Shading button.
8. Under Theme Colors, click the color that is labeled **Olive Green, Accent 3, 60%**.
9. Select the first paragraph.
10. On the Home tab, in the Paragraph group, click the **Line Spacing** button.
11. Click **1.0** on the menu.
12. Select *Affordable Prints*.
13. Click the **downward-pointing arrow** next to the **Borders and Shading** button.
14. Click **Outside Borders** on the menu.
15. Click the **downward-pointing arrow** next to the Shading button.
16. Click the color that is labeled **Olive Green, Accent 3, 40%**.
17. Copy the formatting of *Affordable Prints* to each of the other headings—*Quality Product, Options, Options, Options,* and *Satisfaction Guaranteed*.
18. **SAVE** the document as *lost_art_photos* and **CLOSE** the file.

   LEAVE Word open for the next project.

Project 4-2: General Performance Expectation Guidelines

In your job at Books and Beyond, you continue to work on documents that will be part of the employee handbook.

The *guidelines* document is available on the companion CD-ROM.

1. **OPEN** *guidelines* from the data files for this lesson.
2. Select the two lines that begin *Verbal discussion* . . . and *Written warning* . . . .
3. On the Home tab, in the Paragraph group, click the **Numbering** button to change the lines into a numbered list.
4. Place the insertion point after the second sentence in the list and press **Enter**.
5. Key **Termination** as the third numbered item.
6. Select the double-spaced lines beginning with *abuse, misuse* . . . and ending with *engaging in conduct* . . . .
7. On the Home tab, in the Paragraph group, click the **Bullets** button to change the lines into a bulleted list.
8. Select the first paragraph.
9. On the Home tab, in the Paragraph group, click the **Justify** button.
10. Place your insertion point at the beginning of the first line of the first paragraph and click **Tab** to create a first-line indent.

Paragraph Formatting | 193

11. Select each of the remaining paragraphs in the document and repeat steps 9 and 10 to justify them and create first line indents.
12. **SAVE** the document as *handbook_guidelines* and **CLOSE** the file.
    LEAVE Word open for the next project.

■ Proficiency Assessment

Project 4-3: PTA Officers

The *pta* document is available on the companion CD-ROM.

You are a volunteer at the local elementary school and have been asked to format a PTA document that lists the officers for the upcoming school year.

1. **OPEN** *pta* from the data files for this lesson.
2. Format the document as shown in Figure 4-22.

Figure 4-22
Formatted PTA document

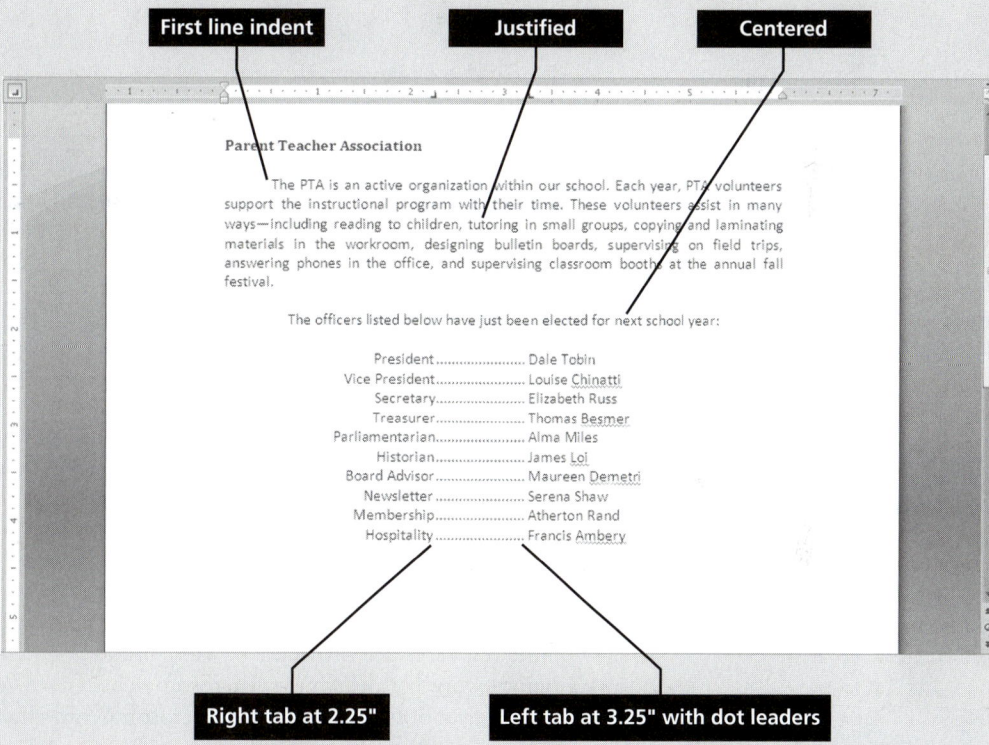

3. **SAVE** the document as *pta_officers* and **CLOSE** the file.
   LEAVE Word open for the next project.

Project 4-4: Phone List

You want to create a list of numbers that you call frequently to keep beside your phone.

1. **CREATE** a new Word document.
2. Create a numbered list with the names of at least ten family members, friends, or businesses that you call frequently.
3. Create a tab with dot leaders and then key the phone number beside each name. For example:

   1) Gary Evans......................555-1212

4. Format every other line with shading so it is easier to read.
5. **SAVE** the document as *phone_list* and **CLOSE** the file.
   LEAVE Word open for the next project.

■ Mastery Assessment

Project 4-5: Developer Job Description

You are a content specialist at a software development company. Your supervisor asks you to format the job description for the developer position.

The *developer* document is available on the companion CD-ROM.

1. **OPEN** *developer* from the data files for this lesson.
2. Use the skills you have learned in this lesson—such as alignment, line spacing, shading, borders, tabs, and bulleted lists—to format the document attractively.
3. **SAVE** the document as *developer_description* and **CLOSE** the file.
   LEAVE Word open for the next project.

Project 4-6: Rabbit Show

You are a volunteer at the annual Falls Village Fair and have been given a document about one of the exhibits. You will need to correctly format the document. The person who created the document was not as familiar with line spacing, tabs, and lists as you are.

The *rabbit* document is available on the companion CD-ROM.

1. **OPEN** *rabbit* from the data files for this lesson.
2. Make any adjustments necessary to correctly format the tabs, line spacing, and lists.
3. Adjust the text so that it all fits on one page.
4. **SAVE** the document as *rabbit_show* and **CLOSE** the file.
   CLOSE Word.

INTERNET READY

Many online resources can provide you with solutions to challenges that you might face during a typical workday. Search the Microsoft website for Work Essentials—a place where you can find information on how to use Microsoft Word efficiently to perform typical business tasks and activities. Explore the resources and content that Work Essentials offers and write a short paragraph about one particular tool or solution that could be useful on the job and how you could use it to be more productive.

Document Formatting

5

LESSON SKILL MATRIX

Setting a Colored Background — 196	Students will learn how to set a colored background
Adding a Watermark — 196	Students will learn how to add a watermark
Placing a Border Around a Document's Pages — 198	Students will learn how to place a border around a document's pages
Adding Page Numbers to a Document — 199	Students will learn how to add page numbers to a document.
Inserting a Built-In Header or Footer — 199	Students will learn how to insert a built-in header or footer.
Adding Content to a Header or Footer — 201	Students will learn how to add contents to a header or footer.
Setting Margins — 202	Students will learn how to set margins.
Selecting a Page Orientation — 203	Students will learn how to select a page orientation.
Choosing a Paper Size — 204	Students will learn how to choose a paper size.

You are employed at Montgomery, Slade & Parker, a global strategic management consulting firm offering consulting services to senior management in a wide variety of industries. A large healthcare corporation that owns hospitals in many major cities in the United States has hired your company to research and recommend the best place to relocate their corporate headquarters. As part of the strategy and operations team, you will be involved in this process. In this lesson, you will format the first draft of a short proposal to submit to the client.

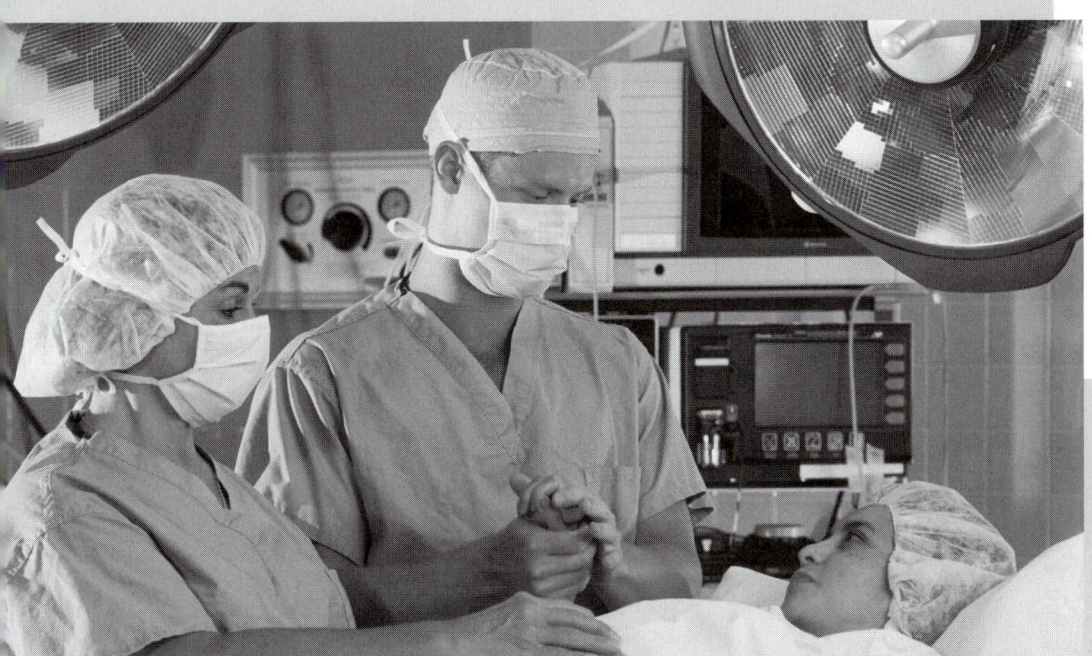

KEY TERMS
content controls
footer
header
landscape orientation
margins
portrait orientation
watermark

Formatting a Document's Background

THE BOTTOM LINE

Word has three commands for formatting a document's background. You can insert a watermark, change the page color, or add a border. Adding these elements to a page can give a document visual importance and help set it apart from other printed materials.

Setting a Colored Background

You are probably familiar with the use of colored backgrounds for text on Web pages. Colored backgrounds can also be used when creating print documents. Adding a colored background to the title page of a report, for example, can help to establish a certain feel for the content of the report and make it easily recognizable. However, it is important to use colored backgrounds in moderation and to use light colors that will not interfere with the text on a page.

→ INSERT A PAGE COLOR

GET READY. Before you begin these steps, be sure to launch Microsoft Office Word 2007.

The *proposal* document is available on the companion CD-ROM.

1. **OPEN** *proposal* from the data files for this lesson.
2. Click the **Page Layout** tab.
3. In the Page Background group, click the **Page Color** menu and click **Aqua, Accent 5, Lighter 80%**, as shown in Figure 5-1. The page color is applied.

Figure 5-1

The Page Color menu

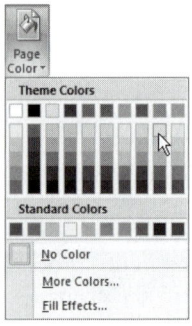

4. Save the document as *USA_proposal*.

   PAUSE. LEAVE the document open to use in the next exercise.

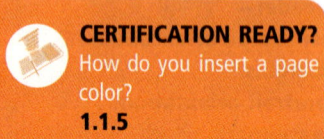

CERTIFICATION READY?
How do you insert a page color?
1.1.5

You can change a page's background color using the Page Color menu from the Page Background group. The Page Color menu lists Theme colors and Standard colors as well as a No Color option. The More Colors command lets you choose a custom color and the Fill Effects command displays the Fill Effects dialog box, where you can insert a page background with a gradient, texture, pattern, or picture.

Adding a Watermark

Words such as *confidential*, *draft*, or *urgent* are often used as watermarks to identify a document as needing special treatment. Graphic images are sometimes used as watermarks for added interest.

Document Formatting | 197

 ADD A WATERMARK

USE the document that is open from the previous exercise.

1. In the Page Background group of the Page Layout tab, click the **Watermark** menu and scroll down to select **DRAFT 1: "DRAFT" Watermark Gray Diagonal Text**, as shown in Figure 5-2. The watermark is inserted on all pages (see Figure 5-3).

Figure 5-2

The Watermark menu

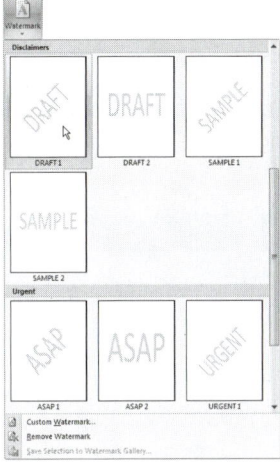

Figure 5-3

Watermark

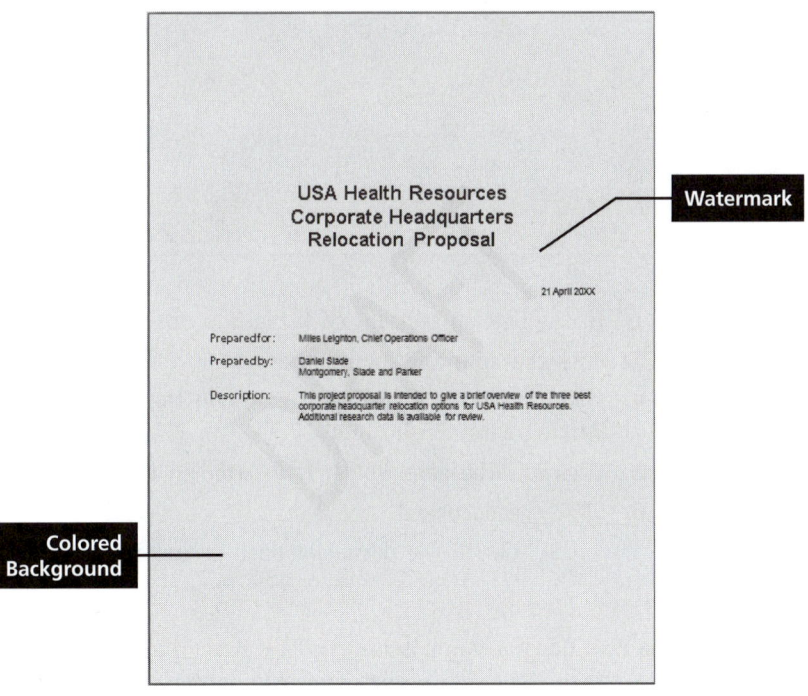

2. **SAVE** the document.

   PAUSE. LEAVE the document open to use in the next exercise.

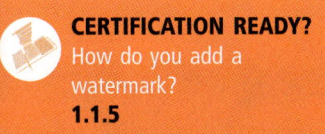

CERTIFICATION READY?
How do you add a watermark?
1.1.5

A ***watermark*** is text or a graphic that is printed lightly behind the text of a document. To insert a watermark, click the Watermark menu in the Page Background group. The menu displays a list of watermark choices as well as the Custom Watermark and Remove Watermark commands.

Choose the Custom Watermark command to create a custom watermark with a picture or custom text in the Printed Watermark dialog box. When you want to delete a watermark from the page, click the Remove Watermark command.

Placing a Border around a Document's Pages

Adding a line or border around a document's pages can help add a graphic element to the page or frame a page. Because you can change the color, width, and style of the border to zigzag, dotted, thick, thin, or double lines, page borders can also serve the purpose of surrounding text that you want to emphasize.

➔ INSERT A PAGE BORDER

USE the document that is open from the previous exercise.

1. In the Page Background group of the Page Layout tab, click the **Page Borders** button. The Borders and Shading dialog box appears, as shown in Figure 5-4.

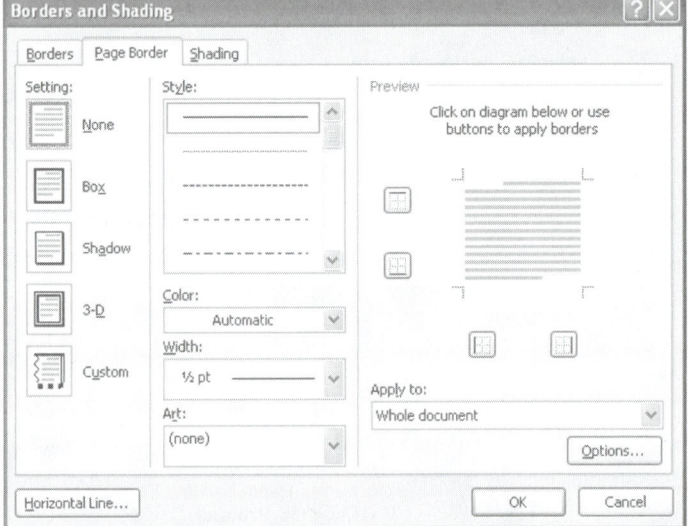

Figure 5-4

The Borders and Shading dialog box

2. In the Setting section, click the **Box** option.
3. Click the downward-pointing arrow on the **Width** menu and choose **1/4 pt**.
4. Click the downward-pointing arrow on the **Apply To** menu and click **This Section—First Page Only**.
5. Click **OK**. The page border is inserted in the first page only.
6. **SAVE** the document.

   PAUSE. LEAVE the document open to use in the next exercise.

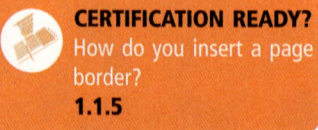

CERTIFICATION READY?
How do you insert a page border?
1.1.5

The Page Borders command in the Page Background group lets you insert a border around a page. When you click the command, the Borders And Shading dialog box appears. The Page Border tab has options for the setting, style, color, width, and art, if any, you want to use in the border you are inserting.

■ Inserting Headers and Footers

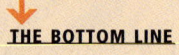

THE BOTTOM LINE

When you need to repeat information in the same place on every page of a document, use headers and footers to arrange and display that information.

Adding Page Numbers to a Document

It is often necessary to number the pages of documents that contain multiple pages, especially if the document will be printed. Not only does this help the reader keep loose pages in order, but it also enables the recipient to refer to information on a specific page when discussing a document.

ADD PAGE NUMBERS

USE the document that is open from the previous exercise.

1. Make sure the insertion point is located at the top of the first page.
2. Click the **Insert** tab.
3. In the Header and Footer group, click the **Page Number** menu, click **Bottom of Page**, and scroll down to select **Plain Number 2**, as shown in Figure 5-5. Page numbers are inserted on all pages.

Figure 5-5

Page Number menu and submenus

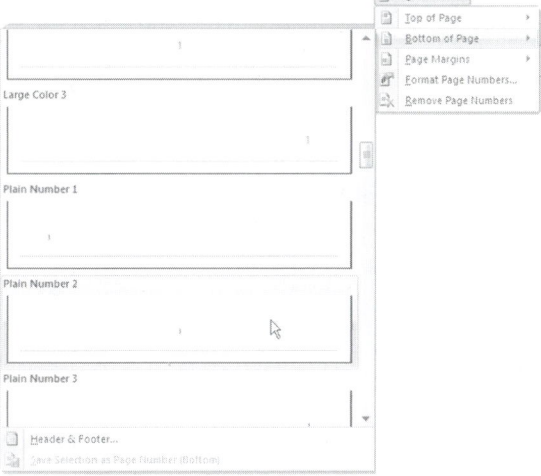

4. SAVE the document.

    PAUSE. LEAVE the document open to use in the next exercise.

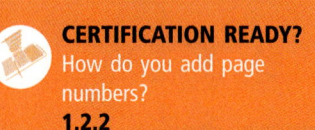

CERTIFICATION READY?
How do you add page numbers?
1.2.2

The Page Number menu in the Header and Footer group has commands for inserting page numbers at the top, bottom, or in the margin of a page. You can also use the Format Page Numbers command to choose the type of numbering you want, such as 1, 2, 3. . . or i, ii, iii. . . and the number you want to start with. To delete page numbers, click the Remove Page Numbers command.

Inserting a Built-In Header or Footer

Word's built-in headers and footers offer you instant design for page numbers and other text that you want to appear on each page of a document.

INSERT A HEADER OR FOOTER

USE the document that is open from the previous exercise.

1. In the Header and Footer group of the Insert tab, click the **Header** menu and scroll down to select **Pinstripes**, as shown in Figure 5-6. The header is inserted.

Figure 5-6

Header menu

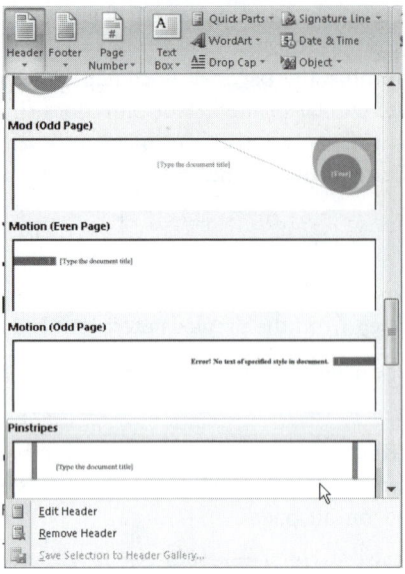

2. Notice the Header & Footer Tools that are displayed in the Design tab's ribbon (see Figure 5-7).

Figure 5-7

Header & Footer Tools

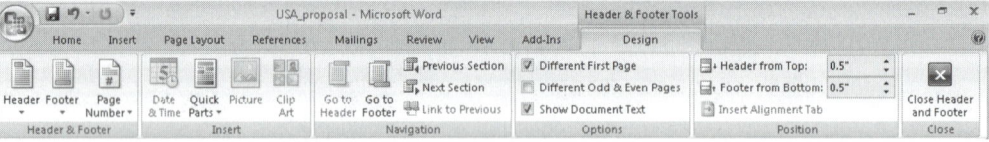

3. In the Options group of the Design tab, click the **Different First Page** box. The header and the page number are removed from the first page.

4. Click in the header area of page 2. In the Header and Footer group, click the **Footer** button and scroll down to click **Pinstripes**. Notice the new footer replaces the page number you inserted in the previous exercise (see Figure 5-8).

Figure 5-8

Header and Footer

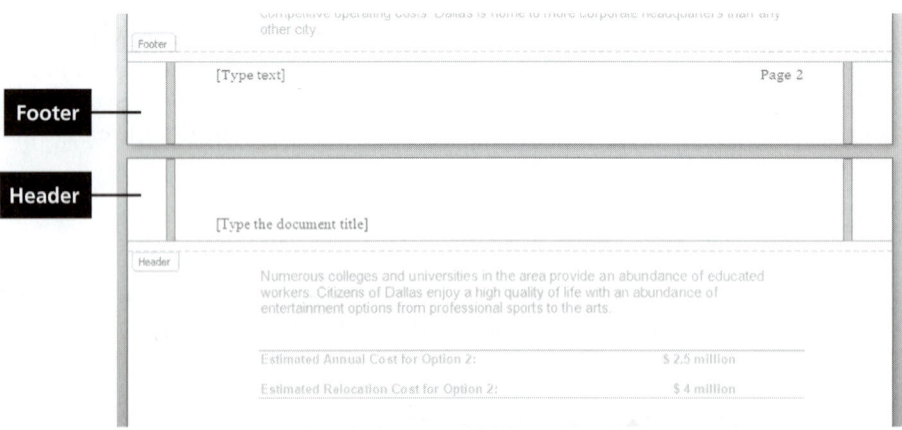

5. **SAVE** the document.

   PAUSE. LEAVE the document open to use in the next exercise.

Document Formatting | 201

CERTIFICATION READY?
How do you insert a built-in header or footer?
1.2.2

CERTIFICATION READY?
How do you insert a formatted header or footer from Quick Parts?
4.1.3

You will learn more about Quick Parts in Lesson 7.

A ***header*** is text such as the title of a document that is located at the top of the page. A ***footer*** includes the text, such as a page number, at the bottom of the page. Headers and footers are usually printed on all or most of the pages of a document. To insert a header or footer, click the Insert tab. The Header and Footer group has commands for inserting headers, footers, and page numbers. Word provides a variety of built-in header and footer designs. Just click the one you want.

When you insert a header, Word displays Header & Footer Tools in the ribbon. The Header and Footer group displays the Header, Footer, and Page Number commands. The Insert group lets you insert the Date & Time, Quick Parts (reusable pieces of content), Picture, or Clip Art you want in a header or footer. In the Navigation group, you can switch between Go To Header and Go To Footer. You can also navigate the document by Previous Section, Next Section, or Link To Previous. In the Options group, click Different First Page to remove the header or footer from the first page. Click Different Odd & Even pages if you want one header or footer on the odd pages and a different one on the even pages. The Show Document Text command toggles to show the text of the document or hide it when you are working with a header or footer.

The Position group lets you specify the location of the header from the top of the document or the location of the footer from the bottom of the document. You can also click the Insert Alignment tab to align text within a header.

Adding Content to a Header or Footer

Headers and footers can provide a convenient and functional place to insert a company logo, the title of a document, or other content that you want to display on each page of a document.

ADD CONTENT TO A HEADER OR FOOTER

USE the document that is open from the previous exercise.

1. Move the mouse pointer to the header on the second page of the document and double-click to activate the header.
2. Click **[Type the Document Title]** to select it.
3. Key **Relocation Proposal** (see Figure 5-9).

Figure 5-9
Title in header

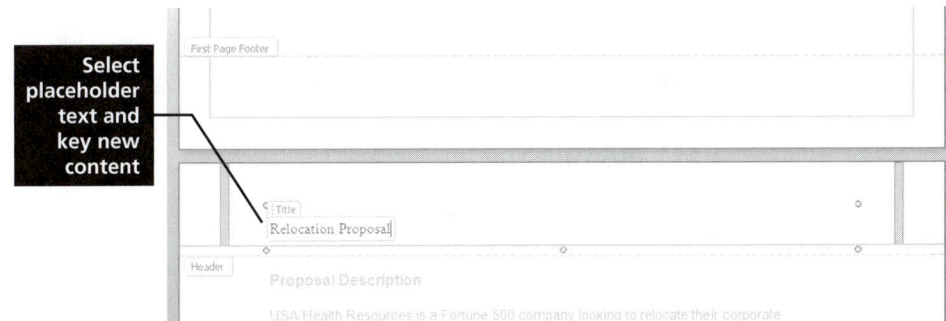

4. Scroll down to the footer of page 2. Click **[Type Text]** to select it. Key **Montgomery, Slade & Parker**.
5. Select all the text in the footer. Point to selected text to display the Mini toolbar. Click the **Font** menu and select **Arial**.
6. Click the **Font Size** menu and select **11**.
7. Click the **Italic** button.
8. Click outside the footer to deselect it.
9. Select the text in the header and display the Mini toolbar.

10. Click the Font menu and select Arial.
11. Click the Font Size menu and select 12.
12. Click the Italic button and then click the Bold button.
13. SAVE the document

   PAUSE. LEAVE the document open to use in the next exercise.

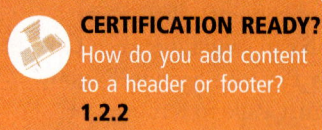

CERTIFICATION READY?
How do you add content to a header or footer?
1.2.2

After you insert a header or footer, you will want to add your own content. Just double-click the header or footer, which is grayed out, to make it active. When you activate a header or footer, the Header & Footer Tools appear with options for inserting content, such as Date & Time, Quick Parts, a Picture, or Clip Art.

Some built-in headers and footers contain **content controls**, which are tiny programs that include a label for instructing you on the type of text to include and a placeholder that reserves a place for your new text. Click the placeholder text in the header or footer to select it, and then key your content. After you key your own content, the content control will disappear. You can remove a content control by right-clicking it and choosing Remove Content Control from the shortcut menu.

After inserting your content, you can format it with the Mini toolbar or commands in the ribbon.

■ Page Layout

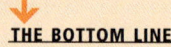
THE BOTTOM LINE

The layout of a page helps to communicate your message. Obviously, the content of your document is very important, but having appropriate margins, page orientation, and paper size all contribute to the success of your document.

Setting Margins

Changing the size of the margins in a document can change not only the look of the document, but also the number of pages it includes. Sometimes you might want to adjust margin sizes slightly to decrease or increase the number of pages in a document. When choosing margin sizes, it is important to keep in mind how the document will be used. For example, a document that will be inserted in a three-ring binder should have plenty of space in the left margin to accommodate the binder.

➔ SET MARGINS

USE the document that is open from the previous exercise.

1. Click the Page Layout tab.
2. In the Page Setup group, click the Margins menu and choose Moderate, as shown in Figure 5-10.

Document Formatting | 203

Figure 5-10

Margins menu

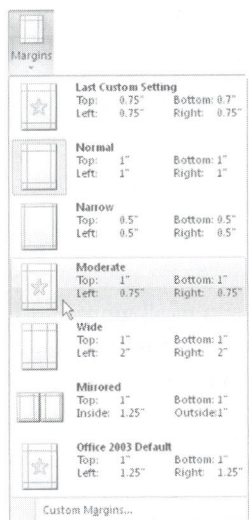

3. **SAVE** the document.

PAUSE. LEAVE the document open to use in the next exercise.

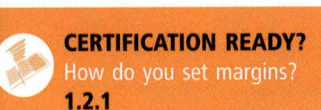

CERTIFICATION READY?
How do you set margins?
1.2.1

Margins are the blank spaces at the top, bottom, and sides of the page. To change the margins of a document, click the Page Layout tab. In the Page Setup group, click the Margins menu. Predefined margin settings are available for you to choose from. A good margin size to use for most documents is the default margin size of 1 inch for the top, bottom, left, and right margins. Click the setting of your choice and all the pages in the document will change to the setting. Click the Custom Margins command to display the Page Setup dialog box, where you can specify custom margin sizes.

Selecting a Page Orientation

As you plan and format your document, you also need to decide on the page orientation that best displays the content of your document. Word lets you change the orientation easily from portrait to landscape and back again if you need to, so you can choose the layout that is best for your document.

→ SELECT A PAGE ORIENTATION

USE the document that is open from the previous exercise.

1. In the Page Setup group of the Page Layout tab, click the **Orientation** menu and select **Landscape**, as shown in Figure 5-11. The page orientation changes to Landscape.

Figure 5-11

Orientation menu

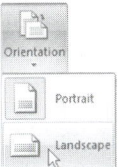

2. Click the Orientation menu and select **Portrait**. The orientation is changed back to portrait.
3. **SAVE** the document.

PAUSE. LEAVE the document open to use in the next exercise.

204 | Lesson 5

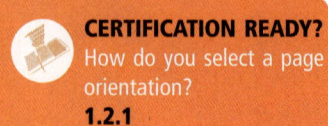

CERTIFICATION READY?
How do you select a page orientation?
1.2.1

Orientation refers to the layout of a document. A document in *portrait orientation* is taller than it is wide. A document in *landscape orientation* is wider than it is tall.

Change the orientation for a page or entire document using the Orientation command in the Page Setup group. Click the Orientation command to display a menu with the choices of Portrait or Landscape orientation.

Choosing a Paper Size

Microsoft Word helps you create documents of all kinds and sizes. When you need to print an invitation, postcard, legal document, or report, you can choose the paper size you need so that your document will print correctly on the paper.

CHOOSE A PAPER SIZE

USE the document that is open from the previous exercise.

1. From the Page Setup group of the Page Layout tab, click the **Size** menu and select **Legal (8 1/2 x 14 in)**, as shown in Figure 5-12.

Figure 5-12

Size menu

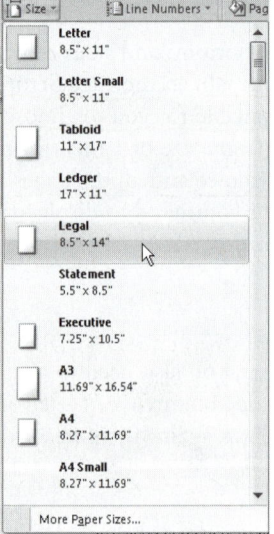

2. Click the **Size** menu and click **Letter (8 1/2 x 11 in)**.
3. **SAVE** and **CLOSE** the document.
   STOP. CLOSE Word.

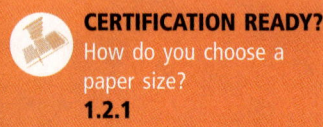

CERTIFICATION READY?
How do you choose a paper size?
1.2.1

Many printers provide options for printing on various sizes of paper. In the Page Setup group, click the Size menu to choose a paper size. A menu appears with common paper sizes. If you need a custom paper size, click More Paper Sizes to display the Page Setup dialog box. In the Paper tab, you can enter a custom paper size and select the paper source. A preview shows what your printed page will look like. Click the Print Options button for more printing specifications.

SUMMARY SKILL MATRIX

In this lesson you learned how to:
Set a Colored Background
Add a Watermark
Place a Border Around a Document's Pages
Add Page Numbers to a Document
Insert a Built-In Header or Footer
Add Content to a Header or Footer
Set Margins
Select a Page Orientation
Choose a Paper Size

Knowledge Assessment

Matching

Match the term in Column 1 to its description in Column 2.

Column 1

1. watermark — g
2. Header & Footer Tools — f
3. content controls — e
4. page border — a
5. page color — h
6. footer — i
7. portrait orientation — c
8. landscape orientation — j
9. margins — d
10. header — b

Column 2

a. a line inserted around the page
b. text or graphics located at the top of the document
c. a page that is taller than it is wide
d. the blank spaces at the sides, top, and bottom of a document
e. tiny programs that include a label for instructing you on the type of text to include and a placeholder that reserves a place for your new text
f. are displayed in the ribbon after you insert a header or footer
g. text or a graphic that is printed lightly behind the text of a document
h. refers to the background color of a page
i. text or graphics located at the bottom of a document
j. a page that is wider than it is tall

True/False

Circle T if the statement is true or F if the statement is false.

T **F** 1. You can only insert page numbers at the top or bottom of a document.
T F 2. Watermarks can be text or graphics.
T **F** 3. Triple-click to activate a header or footer.
T **F** 4. The default margin size is 1.5 inches for the top, bottom, left, and right margins.
T F 5. Built-in headers and footers provide instant design.
T F 6. In the Borders And Shading dialog box, you can specify to insert a page border on only the first page of a document.
T **F** 7. Paper size refers to landscape or portrait orientation.
T F 8. You can insert a picture as a page background.
T **F** 9. You cannot use a header in a document without also inserting a footer.
T F 10. You can specify a different header for odd and even pages.

■ Competency Assessment

Project 5-1: Certificate of Appreciation

Create a Certificate of Appreciation for a volunteer who has helped with the health and fitness programs at the YMCA this year.

GET READY. Launch Word if it is not already running.

The *Certificate of Appreciation* document is available on the companion CD-ROM.

1. **OPEN** *Certificate of Appreciation* from the data files for this lesson.
2. In the Page Layout tab, click the **Orientation** menu and select **Landscape**.
3. Click the **Margins** menu and select **Narrow**.
4. Click the **Page Borders** button and choose a box border with a rope style.
5. **SAVE** the document as *certificate* and **CLOSE** the file.

   LEAVE Word open for the next project.

Project 5-2: Elevator Communications

Montgomery, Slade & Parker uses elevator communications for in-house announcements, invitations, and other employee relations documents. In each elevator, a durable 8 1/2 × 14-inch clear plastic frame has been installed in which announcements can be inserted and changed on a regular basis. Create a document that recognizes employee award winners and also invites employees to a reception to honor these the award winners.

The *congratulations* document is available on the companion CD-ROM.

1. **OPEN** *congratulations* from the data files for this lesson.
2. Click the **Page Layout** tab. In the **Page Background** group, click the **Page Color** menu. In the Theme Colors section, choose a green for the background color. Choose **Olive Green, Accent 3, Lighter 60%**.
3. Click the **Page Borders** button. In the Borders and Shading dialog box, click **Shadow** in the Setting section. Click the **Width** menu and choose 3/4 pt.
4. In the Page Setup group, click the **Orientation** menu and select **Portrait**.
5. Click the **Size** menu and click **Legal (8 1/2 × 14 in)**.
6. **SAVE** the document as *elevatorcom* and **CLOSE** the file.

   LEAVE Word open for the next project.

Proficiency Assessment

Project 5-3: Two-Page Resume

Your friend Mike has revised and added some information to his resume, and it is now two pages. Update the formatting to include a header.

CD

The *mzresume2* document is available on the companion CD-ROM.

1. **OPEN** *mzresume2* from the data files for this lesson.
2. Click the **Page Layout** tab. Click the **Margins** menu and select **Custom Margins**. In the Page Setup dialog box, key **1.25** in the Top box. Press the **Tab** key and key **1.25** in the Bottom box.
3. Press **Tab** and key **1.25** in the Left box. Press **Tab** and key **1.25** in the Right box.
4. Click **OK**.
5. Click the **Insert** tab. In the Header and Footer group, click the **Header** menu and select **Stacks**.
6. In the header, click **[Type the document title]** and key **Resume of Michael J. Zuberi**.
7. In the Options group, click the **Different First Page** box.
8. Click on page 2 to insert the insertion point anywhere on the page.
9. Click the **Footer** button and click **Stacks**.
10. Right-click **[Type the Company Name]**. In the shortcut menu, click **Remove Content Control**.
11. **SAVE** the document as *mzresume2updated* and **CLOSE** it.

    LEAVE Word open for the next project.

Project 5-4: Letterhead

The Grand Street Coffee Shop needs new letterhead. Create one using Word.

1. **OPEN** a new blank document.
2. Insert the **Tiles** built-in header and key the document title as **Grand Street Coffee Shop**. Change the text to bold, size 18 point.
3. Click the **Year** content control and then click the downward-pointing arrow. In the calendar that appears, click **Today**.
4. Insert the Tiles built-in footer and key the company address as **1234 Grand Street, Forest Grove, OR 97116**.
5. **SAVE** the document as *gsletterhead* and **CLOSE** the file.

    LEAVE Word open for the next project.

Mastery Assessment

Project 5-5: Postcard

It's soccer season again, and the YMCA is sending out postcards to all participants who played last season. Use Word to create the postcard.

CD

The *soccer* document is available on the companion CD-ROM.

1. **OPEN** *soccer* from the data files for this lesson.
2. In the Page Setup group, change the Page Size to **4 X 6 in**, the page orientation to **Landscape**, and the margins to **Narrow**.
3. In the Page Background group, click the **Page Borders** button and insert a red double-line page border (Box setting) that is 3/4 pt. wide.

4. Click the **Page Color** menu and click **Fill Effects**. In the Fill Effects dialog box in the Colors section, click **One Color**. In the Shading styles section, click Horizontal. Click the sample *horizontal* pattern in the lower right corner.
5. Click the **Watermark** menu and click **Custom Watermark**. In the Printed Watermark dialog box, click **Text Watermark** and select **ASAP**. Key **YMCA SOCCER**. Click the **Horizontal** button and click **OK**.
6. **SAVE** the document as *postcard* and **CLOSE** the file.
   LEAVE Word open for the next project.

Project 5-6: Thank You Notes

Create thank you notes that match the style of Mike's new two-page resume.

1. Create a new blank document.
2. Choose the Statement (5.5 x 8.5) paper size, portrait orientation, and narrow margins. Keep in mind that the note will be folded in the middle and the words *Thank You* will be on the front of the note.
3. Referring to the *mzresume2updated* document, insert the same footer. Key **Thank You** where the company name would go. Be sure to use the same font, size, and style as Mike's name on the resume.
4. **SAVE** the document as *thankyou* and **CLOSE** the file.
   CLOSE Word.

INTERNET READY

Research the cities that have been rated the "Best Places to Live." Choose one of the top ten and find out why it ranked so high. Create a promotional document touting the positive ranking and listing reasons for the ranking. The document could be a flyer, postcard, or letter that city officials could mail to prospective businesses and families who request information about the city.

Circling Back

The National Association of Professional Consultants is a professional organization that serves a varied membership of consultants. Each year, the association has a three-day professional development conference. The association is now planning the upcoming conference. As the association's membership manager, your job includes a wide variety of tasks related to organizing and communicating information related to membership. In addition, you are working with the conference planning committee to help secure speakers for the conference and market the conference to members.

Project 1: LETTER

Create a letter using a template from Microsoft Office Online requesting a speaker for the conference's banquet. Modify and customize the letter.

GET READY. Launch Word if it is not already running.

1. Click the **Microsoft Office Button** and click **New**.
2. Choose and download the Request for Paid Speaker at Banquet template. You should find it under Letters, Business, Meeting and Seminar Planning.
3. Replace the fields in the document by keying the following information:
   [Your Name]: **Susan Pasha**
   [Street Address]: **5678 Circle St.**
   [City, ST ZIP Code]: **Kansas City, MO 64163**
   [Recipient Name]: **Daniel Slade**
   [Title]: **President, Strategies and Operations**
   [Company Name]: **Montgomery, Slade and Parker**
   [Street Address]: **3333 Lakeside Way**
   [City, ST ZIP Code]: **Chicago, IL 60611**
   [Recipient Name]: **Mr. Slade**
   [Your Name]: **Susan Pasha**
   [Title]: **President**
4. Save the document as *conf_speaker*.
5. If a message box opens telling you that the document will be converted to the Word 2007 file format, click **OK**.
6. Change the date of the letter to **June 15, 20XX**.
7. In the first sentence of the body of the letter, select *travel agents'* and key **consultants'**.
8. In the second sentence, select *Alpine Ski House in Breckenridge, Colorado* and key **Lakeview Towers in South Lake Tahoe, California**.
9. Select the text you just keyed and apply the **Emphasis** style.
10. Change the date of the evening to **September 16** and apply the **Emphasis** style.
11. In the last sentence of the letter, select *convention* and key **conference**.
12. **SAVE** the document.
13. On the Insert tab, in the Header & Footer group, insert the **Transcend (Even)** header.

14. Select the **Title** placeholder text and key **National Association of Professional Consultants**.
15. Change the font to **Arial Unicode MS 12 pt. bold**.
16. Click the **arrow** on the Pick the Date content control and click **Today**.
17. Click the **Date** content control to select it. In the Header and Footer Tools tab, Insert group, click **Date & Time**. Change the format to **00-Month-00**.
18. Change the font to **Arial Unicode MS 10 pt**.
19. Insert the **Transcend (Odd Page)** footer.
20. At the blinking insertion point, key **5678 Circle Street, Kansas City, MO 64163**. (The address should be right aligned.)
21. Change the font to **Arial Unicode MS 12 pt**.
22. Select the page number and change its font to **Arial Unicode MS 12 pt**.
23. Change the margins of the page to **Moderate**.
24. Double-click in the body of the document to de-activate the headers.
25. On the View tab, in the Zoom group, click the **One Page** button to view the document on the screen.
26. Click **Page Width**.
27. Insert three blank lines before the return address to center the letter on the page.
28. On the Page Layout tab, in the Themes group, click the **Theme Colors** menu and choose **Opulent**.
29. **SAVE** the changes.

    PAUSE. LEAVE Word and the document open for the next project.

Project 2: Envelope

Create an envelope in which you can mail the letter.

USE the document that is open from the previous project.

1. Select the recipient's name, title, company name, and address.
2. On the Mailings tab, in the Create group, click **Envelopes**. The selected address should appear in the Delivery Address box.
3. In the Return Address box, key:

   Susan Pasha

   5678 Circle St.

   Kansas City, MO 64163
4. Click the **Add to Document** button. (When a dialog box appears asking if you want to save the new return address as the default, click **No**.)
5. Click **Ctrl** + **P** to open the Print dialog box.
6. In the Print dialog box, in the Page Range section, click **Pages** and key **0**. This will print only the envelope and not the accompanying letter.
7. Insert the envelope in the printer's manual feeder and click **OK**.
8. **SAVE** the changes and **CLOSE** the file.

   PAUSE. LEAVE Word open for the next project.

Project 3: Postcard

Create a postcard to announce the date of the conference to members and to solicit early registrations.

1. Create a new blank document.
2. On the Page Layout tab, in the Page Setup group, use the **Size** command to create a custom paper size of **4.25"** wide and **5.5"** high.
3. Change the document to landscape orientation with narrow margins.
4. On the Insert tab, in the Header & Footer group, insert the **Transcend (Even)** header.
5. Select the **Date** placeholder text and key **20XX**. Change the font to **Calibri 18 pt. bold**.
6. Select the **Title** placeholder and key **NAPC PROFESSIONAL CONFERENCE**. Change the font to 18 pt. bold.
7. Double-click in the body of the postcard and key the following text:

    September 14–16

    Lakeview Towers in South Lake Tahoe, California

    Early Bird Registration $329; Regular Rate $389

    Admission to all keynotes, seminars, and breakout sessions

    Ticket to Saturday night banquet

    All meals included

    Early Bird Deadline is August 1, 20XX

    Register online at www.napc20XX.com or call 800-555-5678

8. Make sure you do not press `Enter` after the last line of keyed text.
9. Select *September 14–16*, change the font to Calibri 20 pt. Bold, and center it.
10. Select the *Lakeview Towers* . . . line of text, change it to 14 pt., and center it.
11. Click the **View Ruler** button to display the ruler if it isn't displayed already.
12. Place the insertion point before the *E* in *Early Bird Registration*. . . . Click on the .5" position to insert a left tab.
13. Press the `Tab` key to indent the paragraph.
14. Select the three lines of text under the registration costs information and format them as a bulleted list.
15. Select *$329*. Change the font color to **Purple, Accent 4, Lighter 40%** and bold it.
16. On the Home tab, in the Clipboard group, use the Format Painter to copy the format of $329 and apply it to **$389**, **August 1, 20XX**, **www.napc20XX.com**, and **800-555-5678**.
17. Beginning with *Lakeview Towers*, select all the remaining text. On the Page Layout tab, in the Paragraph group, adjust the spacing after the paragraph to **6 pt**.
18. Select the last two lines of text and center them.
19. In the Page Background group, use the Page Borders command to insert a ½ **pt**. wide box page border, using the color **Purple, Accent 4, Lighter 60%**.
20. Use the **Watermark** command to create a custom horizontal watermark with the text **SAVE THE DATE** using **Calibri font**.
21. Select the last paragraph, which begins *Register online* . . . .
22. On the Home tab, in the Paragraph group, use the Shading command to insert shading using the color **Purple, Accent 4, Lighter 40%**.

23. In the Page Layout tab, in the Themes group, use the Theme Colors menu to change the color to **Opulent**.
24. Your document should look similar to Figure 1. Make any necessary adjustments.

Figure 1

NAPC Postcard

25. **SAVE** the document as *napc_postcard* and **CLOSE** the file.
    STOP. CLOSE Word.

Managing Text Flow

LESSON SKILL MATRIX

Controlling Widows and Orphans – 214	Students will learn how to control widows and orphans.
Keeping a Paragraph's Lines on the Same Page – 215	Students will learn how to keep a paragraph's lines on the same page.
Keeping Two Paragraphs on the Same Page – 216	Students will learn how to keep two paragraphs on the same page.
Forcing a Paragraph to the Top of a Page – 216	Students will learn how to force a paragraph to the top of a page.
Forcing a Page Break – 217	Students will learn how to force a page break.
Inserting Section Breaks – 218	Students will learn how to insert section breaks.
Creating Columns – 220	Students will learn how to create columns.
Formatting Columns – 221	Students will learn how to format columns.
Changing Column Widths – 221	Students will learn how to change column widths.
Inserting a Blank Page – 222	Students will learn how to insert a blank page.

As a marketing associate for First Bank, you are involved in a wide variety of marketing and communications projects. You are responsible for creating and maintaining marketing collateral—brochures, posters, and other printed product information—that supports the sale of a product. It is time to update the Personal Checking Choices document that your bank provides to people interested in opening new accounts. Microsoft Word is a great tool for producing documents such as this that can be easily updated. In this lesson, you will learn to control paragraph behavior, work with section and page breaks, create and format columns, and insert a blank page.

KEY TERMS
columns
orphan
page break
section break
widow

■ Controlling Paragraph Behavior

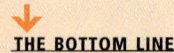

THE BOTTOM LINE Word works behind the scenes to control how text flows in your document. Automatic page breaks are inserted within multi-page documents, helping you create professional-looking documents. However, you may need to adjust or override automatic page breaks from time to time so that you can control where a paragraph ends or begins.

Controlling Widows and Orphans

For professional-looking documents, it is best to avoid leaving a single line of text at the bottom or top of a page. Word can help you avoid this situation by keeping at least two lines together at the bottom of the page or at the top of a new page.

→ **TURN ON WIDOW/ORPHAN CONTROL**

GET READY. Before you begin these steps, be sure to launch Microsoft Office Word 2007 and **OPEN** the *checking* document from the data files for this lesson.

1. Scroll to the top of page 2 and notice the widow *experience...* at the top of the page.
2. Select the four-line paragraph under *Preferred Checking,* including the widow.
3. On the **Home** tab, in the **Paragraph** group, click the **dialog box launcher.** The Paragraph dialog box appears.
4. Click the **Line and Page Breaks** tab, as shown in Figure 6-1.

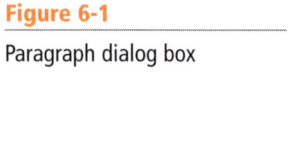

The *checking* document is available on the companion CD-ROM.

Figure 6-1

Paragraph dialog box

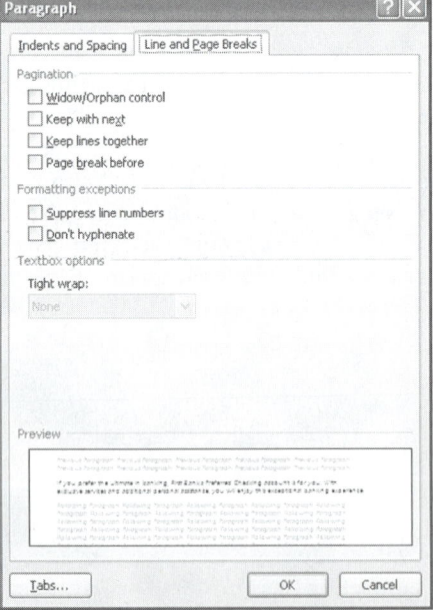

5. Click to select the **Widow/Orphan Control** box and then click **OK**. Notice that another line of the paragraph is moved to the second page.
6. Save the document as *checkingchoices*.

   PAUSE. LEAVE the document open to use in the next exercise.

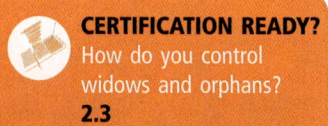

CERTIFICATION READY?
How do you control widows and orphans?
2.3

A ***widow*** is the last line of a paragraph that is left alone at the top of a page. See Figure 6-2.

Figure 6-2
Widow

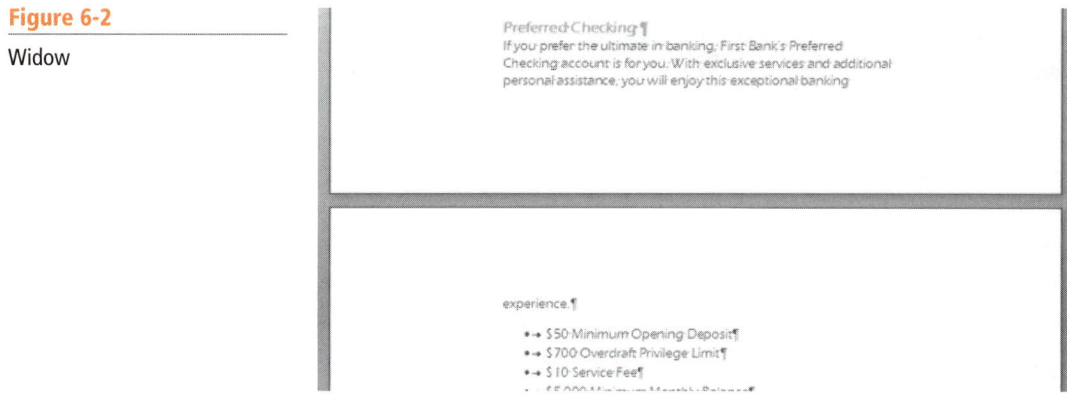

An ***orphan*** is the first line of a paragraph that is left alone at the bottom of a page. See Figure 6-3.

Figure 6-3
Orphan

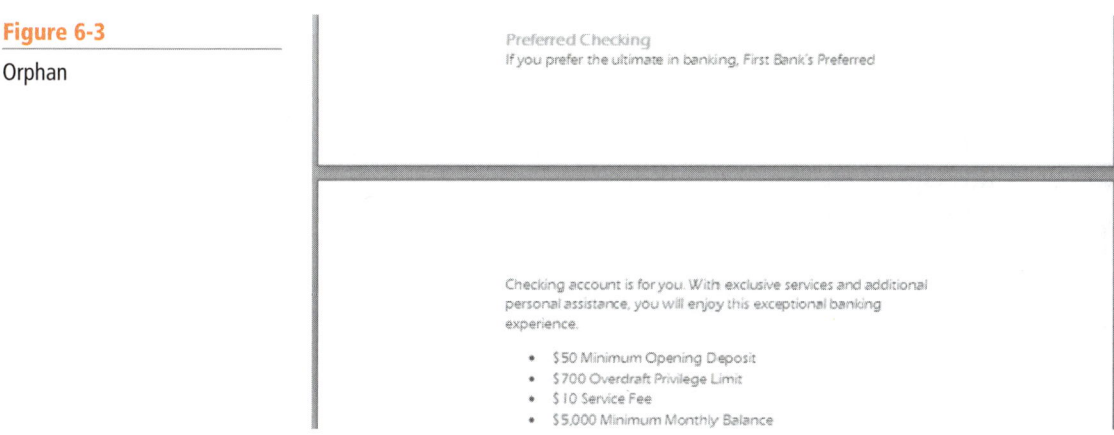

You can avoid having widows and orphans in your document by turning on Widow/Orphan Control in the Paragraph dialog box. When creating a new document, this option is turned on by default. Click to select or deselect the Widow/Orphan Control box to turn the option on or off.

Keeping a Paragraph's Lines on the Same Page

Sometimes you may not want a paragraph to split across two pages. Word's Keep Lines Together command can solve this problem.

→ KEEP LINES TOGETHER

USE the document that is open from the previous exercise.

1. Select the four-line paragraph under *Preferred Checking*, if necessary.
2. On the **Home** tab, in the **Paragraph** group, click the **dialog box launcher**. The Paragraph dialog box appears.
3. On the **Line and Page Breaks** tab, click to select the **Keep Lines Together** box and then click **OK**. Notice that the two lines that were at the bottom of page 1 moved to page 2.
4. **SAVE** the document.

   PAUSE. LEAVE the document open to use in the next exercise.

CERTIFICATION READY?
How do you keep a paragraph's lines on the same page?
2.3

When you need to keep all the lines of a paragraph together on the same page, select the entire paragraph and click to select the Keep Lines Together box in the Paragraph dialog box.

Keeping Two Paragraphs on the Same Page

Word considers any line of text that is followed by a return to be a paragraph. So, a heading, even if it is only one or two words, is considered a paragraph. When you need to keep two paragraphs together on the same page, such as a heading and the text below it, use Word's Keep with Next command.

→ **KEEP TWO PARAGRAPHS ON THE SAME PAGE**

USE the document that is open from the previous exercise.

1. Select the *Preferred Checking* heading and the four-line paragraph below it.
2. On the **Home** tab, in the **Paragraph** group, click the **dialog box launcher**. The Paragraph dialog box appears.
3. On the **Line and Page Breaks** tab, click to select the **Keep with Next** box and then click **OK**. Notice that the two paragraphs (the heading and paragraph that follows) stayed together and moved to page 2.
4. **SAVE** the document.

   PAUSE. LEAVE the document open to use in the next exercise.

Keeping two paragraphs together on the same page is easy in Word. To do so, select both paragraphs and click to select the Keep with Next box in the Paragraph dialog box.

CERTIFICATION READY?
How do you keep two paragraphs on the same page?
2.3

Forcing a Paragraph to the Top of a Page

Although automatic page breaks usually occur at acceptable places in a Word document, there may be times when you need to force a paragraph to the top of a page.

→ **FORCE A PARAGRAPH TO THE TOP OF A PAGE**

USE the document that is open from the previous exercise.

1. Position the insertion point before the *S* in the *Senior Preferred Checking* heading.
2. On the **Home** tab, in the **Paragraph** group, click the **dialog box launcher**. The Paragraph dialog box appears.
3. On the **Line and Page Breaks** tab, click to select the **Page Break Before** box and then click **OK**. Notice that the paragraph is forced to the top of a new page.
4. **SAVE** the document.

   PAUSE. LEAVE the document open to use in the next exercise.

CERTIFICATION READY?
How do you force a paragraph to the top of a page?
2.3

You just read about how you can force a paragraph to begin at the top of a page by clicking to select the Page Break Before box in the Paragraph dialog box.

■ Working with Breaks

THE BOTTOM LINE

There may be times when you will be working with documents that contain various objects or special layouts that require you to step in and control where a page or section breaks. When you need to be in control, you can do so with Word's page breaks and section breaks commands.

Forcing a Page Break

You just learned about how Word not only inserts automatic page breaks into a document, but also about how you can set specific options for those page breaks. There may also be times when you need to insert a manual page break.

➡ INSERT AND DELETE A MANUAL PAGE BREAK

USE the document that is open from the previous exercise.

1. Position the insertion point before the *V* in the *Value Checking* heading.
2. On the **Insert** tab, in the **Pages** group, click the **Page Break** button. A manual page break is inserted and the *Value Checking* paragraphs start a new page, as shown in Figure 6-4.

Figure 6-4

Page Break in Print Layout view

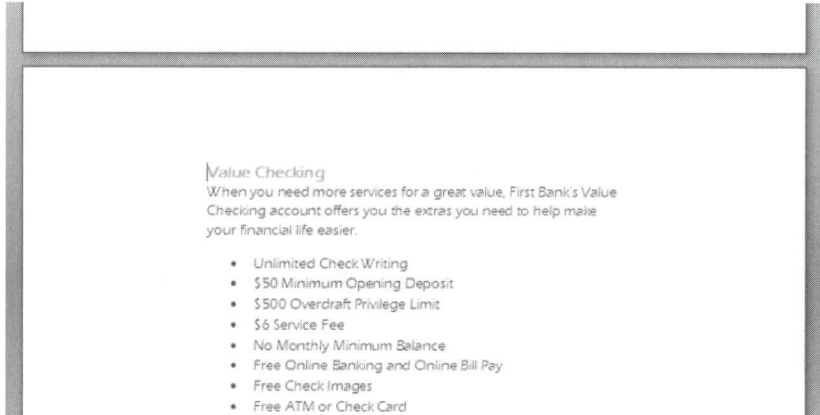

3. Position the insertion point before the *P* in the *Preferred Checking* heading.
4. On the **Page Layout** tab, in the **Page Setup** group, click the **Breaks** menu. The Breaks menu appears, as shown in Figure 6-5.

Figure 6-5

Breaks menu

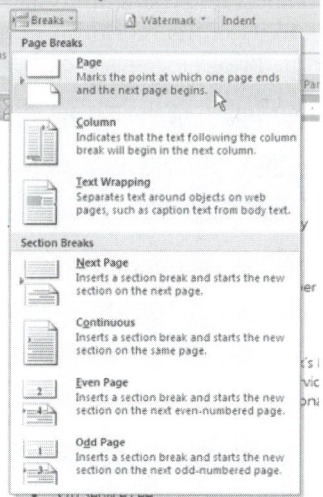

5. Select **Page** from the menu. A manual page break is inserted.
6. On the Home tab, in the Paragraph group, click the **Show/Hide ¶** button. The hidden paragraph marks, page break markers, and other formatting marks are displayed.

7. Scroll to the first page and notice the manual page break marker, shown in Figure 6-6.

Figure 6-6

Manual page break with hidden formatting marks displayed

8. Select the Page Break marker and press the Backspace key. The page break is deleted.
9. Select the Page Break marker below the Value Checking information and press the Backspace key.
10. SAVE the document.

    PAUSE. LEAVE the document open to use in the next exercise.

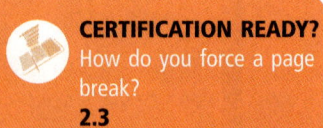

CERTIFICATION READY?
How do you force a page break?
2.3

A *page break* is the location in a document where one page ends and a new page begins. Pages are easy to distinguish in Word. In Print Layout view, Word displays a document page by page, one after the other, on a blue background (as was shown earlier in Figure 6-4).

In this exercise, you inserted page breaks using two different methods. To insert a manual page break, position the insertion point where you want to start a new page. Then, on the Insert tab, in the Pages group, click to select the Page Break button. Or, on the Page Layout tab, in the Page Setup group, click the Breaks menu and choose Page.

The Breaks menu contains options for inserting three types of breaks:

- Page: inserts a manual page break where one page ends and a new page begins
- Column: inserts a manual column break where text will begin in the next column after the column break
- Text Wrapping: separates the text around objects on a Web page, such as caption text from body text

TAKE NOTE

Click the **Show/Hide ¶** button to view page breaks and section breaks for editing purposes.

ANOTHER WAY

You can also insert a manual page break by pressing **Ctrl+Enter**.

Inserting Section Breaks

You can use section breaks to create a section, or separate portion, of a document. For example, you can create a section in your document that contains a page that has different margins than the rest of the document.

INSERT A SECTION BREAK

USE the document that is open from the previous exercise.

1. Position the Insertion point before the *F* in the *Free Checking* heading. Press Enter to insert a blank line.

2. On the **Page Layout** tab, in the **Page Setup** group, click the Breaks menu.
3. Under Section Breaks, select Continuous. A section break is inserted, as shown in Figure 6-7.

Figure 6-7

Section Break

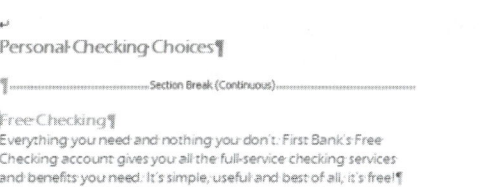

4. On the **Page Layout** tab, in the **Page Setup** group, click Margins and select Narrow. The margins of the section are changed while the margins of the other part of the document remain the same.
5. **SAVE** the document.

   PAUSE. LEAVE the document open to use in the next exercise.

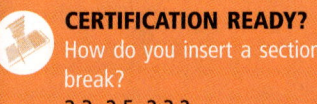

CERTIFICATION READY?
How do you insert a section break?
2.3, 2.5, 2.3.2

A *section break* is used to create layout or formatting changes in a portion of a document. In this exercise, you inserted a Continuous section break and then changed the margins of that section.

It is useful to insert a section break when you want to change the following types of formatting for a portion of your document:

- Columns
- Footnotes and endnotes
- Headers and footers
- Line numbering
- Margins
- Page borders
- Page numbering
- Paper size or orientation
- Paper source for a printer
- Vertical alignment of text on a page

To insert a section break, position the insertion point where you want the section to begin. On the Page Layout tab, in the Page Setup group, click the Breaks menu and then select one of the four available options for creating section breaks:

- Next Page: inserts a section break and starts the new section on the next page
- Continuous: inserts a section break and starts the new section on the same page
- Even Page: inserts a section break and starts the new section on the next even-numbered page
- Odd Page: inserts a section break and starts the new section on the next odd-numbered page

You can select and delete section breaks just as you can remove page breaks. Just remember that when you delete a section break, you remove the section formatting as well.

■ Setting Up Columns

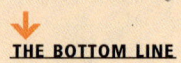

THE BOTTOM LINE

Columns are often used in newspapers, magazines, and newsletters that contain large amounts of text. When text is formatted into columns, the lines are shorter, white space is added, and a document generally becomes more reader friendly. When setting up columns in a document, you can specify the number of columns, formatting options, and column widths.

Creating Columns

You can create columns for all the text within a document or for only a portion of the text.

→ **CREATE COLUMNS**

USE the document that is open from the previous exercise.

1. On the Page Layout tab, in the Page Setup group, click **Columns**. The Columns menu appears, as shown in Figure 6-8.

Figure 6-8

Columns menu

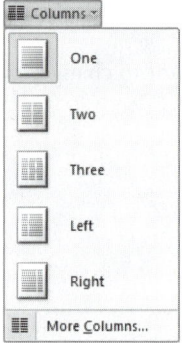

2. Select **Two**. The text in the document following the *Personal Checking Choices* heading is formatted into two columns.
3. **SAVE** the document.

PAUSE. LEAVE the document open to use in the next exercise.

Columns are vertical blocks of text in which text flows from the bottom of one to the top of the next. As you learned in this exercise, you can easily create columns in your document. On the Page Layout tab, in the Page Setup group, the Columns menu, shown in Figure 6-8, lists options for creating common column formats:

- One: formats the text into a single column
- Two: formats the text into two even columns
- Three: formats the text into three even columns
- Left: formats the text into two unequal columns—a narrow one on the left and a wide one on the right
- Right: formats the text into two uneven columns—a narrow one on the right and a wide one on the left
- More Columns: contains options for customizing columns

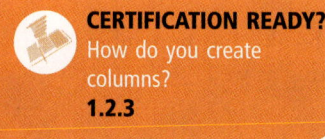

CERTIFICATION READY?
How do you create columns?
1.2.3

Managing Text Flow | 221

Formatting Columns — Customize

In addition to Word's common column formats, you can customize column formats to fit the text and the purpose of your document.

→ FORMAT COLUMNS

USE the document that is open from the previous exercise.

1. On the Page Layout tab, in the Page Setup group, click the **Columns** menu.
2. Select **More Columns**. The Columns dialog box appears, as shown in Figure 6-9.

Figure 6-9

Columns Dialog box

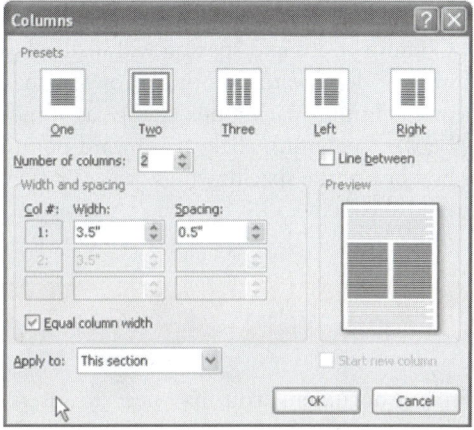

3. Select **2**, if necessary, in the Number of Columns box and key 3.
4. Click the **Line Between** box.
5. Click **OK**.
6. Position the insertion point before the *S* in the *Senior Preferred* heading.
7. On the **Home** tab, **Paragraph** group, click the **dialog box launcher**. In the Line and Page Breaks tab, click to deselect the **Page Break Before** box and click **OK**.
8. **SAVE** the document.

   PAUSE. LEAVE the document open to use in the next exercise.

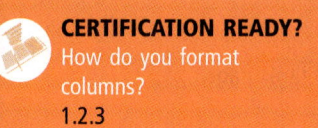

CERTIFICATION READY?
How do you format columns?
1.2.3

You have many options for formatting columns. The More Columns command at the bottom of the Columns menu displays the Columns dialog box. From here, you can choose one of the preset column formats or create a format of your own containing up to 15 columns.

Click the Line Between box to insert a vertical line between columns.

 ### Changing Column Widths

Documents that contain columns with even widths are formal and conservative. If you want to make a document more casual, or if the information you are displaying calls for columns of different widths, you can specify varying column widths easily in Word.

→ CHANGE COLUMN WIDTHS

USE the document that is open from the previous exercise.

1. On the Page Layout tab, in the Page Setup group, click the **Columns** menu.
2. Select **More Columns**. The Columns Dialog Box appears.
3. Key **2** in the Number of columns box.

4. Select the text in the Width box and key 3.25. Press the Tab key to move to the Spacing box. Notice that the spacing adjusted automatically to 1. Click **OK**.

5. On the Page Layout tab, in the Page Setup group, click the **Columns** menu and select **More Columns**.

6. Click the **Three** columns button. Select the text in the **Width** box and key 2.3. Press the Tab key to move to the Spacing box. Notice that the spacing adjusted automatically to .3. Click **OK**.

7. **SAVE** the document.

PAUSE. LEAVE the document open to use in the next exercise.

> **CERTIFICATION READY?**
> How do you change column widths?
> **1.2.3**

Columns can be formatted with even or uneven widths in the Columns dialog box. If you want all the columns in a document to have the same widths, make sure the Even column width box is checked. Column width and spacing will be displayed for the first column only. Click the upward-pointing or downward-pointing arrows in the Width box or key in a specific width. The measurements in the Spacing box change as you change the width. If you want to change the spacing between columns, click the upward-pointing or downward-pointing arrows in the Spacing box or key the spacing you want. The preview adjusts to show your changes. When you are finished, click OK.

■ Inserting a Blank Page Into a Document

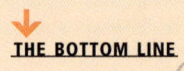

THE BOTTOM LINE

When creating or editing a document, you may need to insert a blank page on which to add more text, graphics, or a table. Rather than pressing the Enter key enough times to insert a blank page, Word provides a Blank Page command.

Inserting a Blank Page

You can insert a blank page at any point within a document—the beginning, middle, or end.

 INSERT A BLANK PAGE

USE the document that is open from the previous exercise.

1. Position the insertion point after the *k* in *First Bank*.
2. On the Insert tab, in the Pages group, click **Blank Page**. A blank page is inserted.
3. Click the **Undo** button on the Quick Access Toolbar.
4. Click the **Show/Hide ¶** button.
5. **SAVE** and then **CLOSE** the file.

STOP. CLOSE Word.

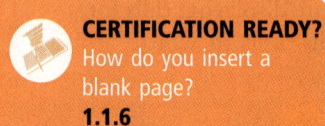

> **CERTIFICATION READY?**
> How do you insert a blank page?
> **1.1.6**

In this exercise, you inserted a blank page in the middle of the document. To insert a blank page wherever you need it, position the insertion point and click the Blank Page command in the Pages group on the Insert tab. To delete a blank page, use the Show/Hide ¶ button to display hidden characters, then select and delete the page break.

SUMMARY SKILL MATRIX

IN THIS LESSON YOU LEARNED HOW TO:
Control Widows and Orphans
Keep a Paragraph's Lines on the Same Page
Keep Two Paragraphs on the Same Page
Force a Paragraph to the Top of a Page
Force a Page Break
Insert Section Breaks
Create Columns
Format Columns
Change Column Widths
Insert a Blank Page

■ Knowledge Assessment

Matching

Match the term in Column 1 to its description in Column 2.

Column 1

1. widow (f)
2. orphan (i)
3. page break (h)
4. section break (b)
5. columns (a)
6. Blank Page command (j)
7. More Columns command (c)
8. Keep with Next (d)
9. Keep Lines Together (e)
10. Widow/Orphan Control (g)

Column 2

a. vertical blocks of text in which text flows from the bottom of one column to the top of the next
b. used to create layout or formatting changes in a portion of a document
c. displays the Columns dialog box
d. keeps two paragraphs together on the same page
e. keeps all lines of a paragraph together on the same page
f. the last line of a paragraph that is left alone at the top of a page
g. keeps at least two lines together at the bottom of the page or at the top of a new page
h. the location in a document where one page ends and a new page begins
i. the first line of a paragraph that is left alone at the bottom of a page
j. inserts a blank page at the insertion point

True/False

Circle T if the statement is true or F if the statement is false.

T F 1. Widow/Orphan Control is turned on by default.

T **F** 2. Use Widow/Orphan Control to keep all the lines of a paragraph together on the same page.

T F 3. Word considers a heading a paragraph.

T F 4. Columns can be formatted with even or uneven widths.

T **F** 5. You can see page break and section break markers in Print Layout view.

T **F** 6. A Continuous section break starts the new section on the next page.

T F 7. A page break is the location in a document where one page ends and a new page begins.

T F 8. The Even column width box should be checked only when you want all columns to have the same width.

T **F** 9. You can only insert a blank page at the beginning or at the end of a document.

T F 10. Section breaks are useful when you want to change the margin setting for a portion of the document.

■ Competency Assessment

Project 6-1: YMCA Newsletter

Format some data for the YMCA into a two-column newsletter.

GET READY. Launch Word if it is not already running.

The *ynews* document is available on the companion CD-ROM.

1. **OPEN** *ynews* from the data files for this lesson.
2. Click the **Show/Hide ¶** button.
3. Position the insertion point before the *M* in *Mother's Day Out . . . .*
4. On the Page Layout tab, in the Page Setup group, click the **Breaks** menu and select **Continuous**.
5. On the Page Layout tab, in the Page Setup group, click the **Columns** menu and select **Two**.
6. Position the insertion point before the *F* in the *Fall Soccer . . .* heading.
7. On the Page Layout tab, in the Page Setup group, click the **Breaks** menu and select **Column**.
8. On the Page Layout tab, in the Page Setup group, click the **Columns** menu and click **More Columns**.
9. In the Columns dialog box, click the **up arrow** on the Width box until it reads **2.8**. The number in the Spacing box should adjust to **.9"**.
10. Click the **Line Between** box and click **OK**.
11. Click the **Show/Hide ¶** button.
12. **SAVE AS** *ymcanewsletter* and then **CLOSE** the file.

    PAUSE. LEAVE Word open for the next project.

Managing Text Flow | 225

Project 6-2: Computer Use Policy

You are updating First Bank's computer use policy and you need to adjust the flow of text on the page.

The *computerusepolicy* document is available on the companion CD-ROM.

1. **OPEN** *computerusepolicy* from the data files for this lesson.
2. Scroll to the top of page 3. Position the insertion point before the *e* in *engaging in illegal activity*.
3. On the Home tab, in the Paragraph group, click the **dialog box launcher**. On the Line and Page Breaks tab, click to select the **Widow/Orphan Control** box and click **OK**.
4. Position the insertion point in the last line of page 3 that begins *D. Anyone obtaining....*
5. On the Home tab, in the Paragraph group, click the **dialog box launcher**. On the Line and Page Breaks tab, click the **Keep Lines Together** box and click **OK**.
6. Position the insertion point before the *S* in the *Section Ten* heading.
7. On the Home tab, in the Paragraph group, click the **dialog box launcher**. On the Line and Page Breaks tab, click the **Page Break Before** box and click **OK**.
8. **SAVE** the document as *newcupolicy* and **CLOSE** the file.

   PAUSE. LEAVE Word open for the next project.

■ Proficiency Assessment

Project 6-3: Coffee Shop Brochure

Your supervisor at the Grand Street Coffee Shop asks you to format the information within their coffee menu as a brochure.

The *coffeemenu* document is available on the companion CD-ROM.

1. **OPEN** *coffeemenu* from the data files for this lesson.
2. Change the page orientation to **Landscape**.
3. Position the insertion point before the *M* in the *Menu* heading and insert a **Continuous** section break.
4. Create an uneven, two-column format using the **Left** column setting.
5. Position the insertion point before the *N* in the *Nutritional* heading and insert a **Column** break.
6. Increase the amount of space between columns to **.7"**.
7. **SAVE** the document as *coffeeshopbrochure* and **CLOSE** the file.

   PAUSE. LEAVE Word open for the next project.

Project 6-4: Mom's Favorite Recipes

Your mom asks you to help her create a small cookbook filled with her favorite recipes that she can share with family and friends. She has emailed you a Word document containing a few recipes to help you get started with creating a format.

The *recipes* document is available on the companion CD-ROM.

1. **OPEN** *recipes* from the data files for this lesson.
2. Click the **Show/Hide ¶** button to display hidden formatting marks.
3. Position the insertion point before the *C* in the *Chicken Pot Pie* heading and insert a **Continuous** section break.
4. Position the insertion point before the *B* in the *Breads* heading and insert a **Next Page** section break.
5. Position the insertion point before the *B* in the *Banana Nut Bread/Chocolate Chip Muffins* headings and insert a **Continuous** section break.

6. Position the insertion point anywhere within the Chicken Pot Pie recipe.
7. Format the recipes in this section into two even columns with .7" spacing between columns and a line between.
8. Position the insertion point anywhere within the Banana Nut Bread recipe.
9. Format the recipes in this section into two even columns with .7" spacing between columns and a line between.
10. Position the insertion point before the *R* in the *Ranch Chicken* heading and insert a column break.
11. Position the insertion point before the *E* in the *Easy Pumpkin Bread/Muffins* heading and insert a column break.
12. Position the insertion point before the *C* in the *Chocolate Zucchini Bread* heading and insert a column break.
13. Position the insertion point in the *Main Dishes* heading and insert the Alphabet header style. Select the *Title* placeholder and key **Mom's Favorite Recipes**.
14. Click the **Show/Hide ¶** button to hide formatting marks.
15. SAVE the document as *favorite recipes* and CLOSE the file.

    PAUSE. LEAVE Word open for the next project.

■ Mastery Assessment

 CD

The *checkingacctchoices* document is available on the companion CD-ROM.

Project 6-5: Three-fold Bank Brochure

Reformat the Checking Choices document to create a three-fold brochure.

1. OPEN *checkingacctchoices* from the data files for this lesson.
2. Reformat the document using a page size of 8 1/2 X 14 with landscape orientation. Create the brochure to look like the one shown in Figure 6-10.

Figure 6-10

Checking brochure

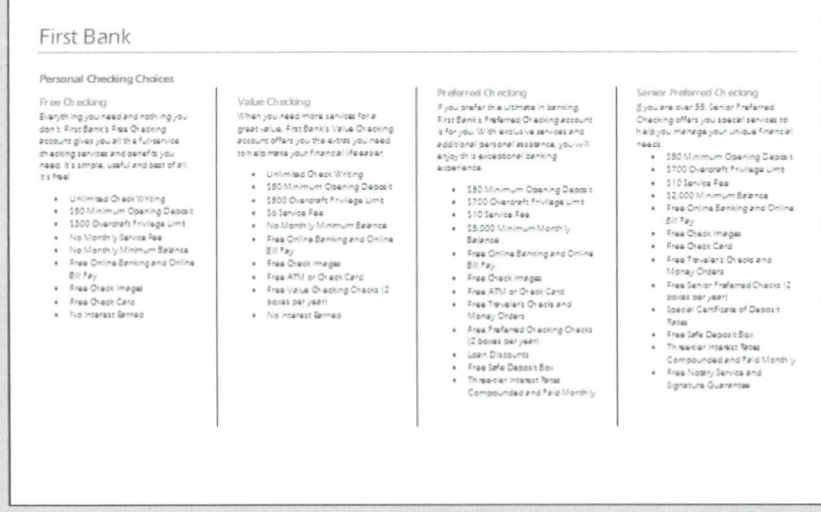

3. Make any adjustments necessary to format the document professionally.
4. SAVE the document as *checkingbrochure* and CLOSE the file.

   PAUSE. LEAVE Word open for the next project.

Project 6-6: Reformat the YMCA Newsletter

As an alternative to the layout you created earlier, reformat the YMCA newsletter with two uneven columns.

1. Open *ynewsletter* from the data files for this lesson.
2. Reformat the newsletter with two uneven columns using the **Right** column setting.
3. Make any adjustments necessary to format the document professionally on one page.
4. **SAVE** the document as *rightymcanewsletter* and **CLOSE** the file.

   STOP. CLOSE Word.

The *ynewsletter* document is available on the companion CD-ROM.

INTERNET READY

Have you considered starting your own business someday? Use the Internet to research small business checking accounts for three different banks. What are the fees? What services are offered? What are the restrictions? Create a three-column document comparing the account features of each bank side by side.

7 Editing Basics

LESSON SKILL MATRIX

Using Built-In Building Blocks — 229	Students will learn how to use built-in building blocks.
Inserting a Field from Quick Parts — 230	Students will learn how to insert a field from Quick Parts.
Creating Your Own Building Blocks — 231	Students will learn how to create your own building blocks.
Using the Clipboard to Copy and Move Text — 233	Students will learn how to use the clipboard to copy and move text.
Using the Mouse to Copy or Move Text — 234	Students will learn how to use the mouse to copy or move text.
Finding Text in a Document — 235	Students will learn how to find text in a document.
Replacing Text in a Document — 237	Students will learn how to replace text in a document.
Using the Go To Command — 238	Students will learn how to use the Go To command.
Using the Document Map — 239	Students will learn how to use the Document Map.

You are a content manager for Flatland Hosting Company, a position in which you are responsible for writing and editing all client-facing material, such as hosting guidelines and agreements. When creating and revising documents, several Word commands can help you work more efficiently. In this lesson, you will learn how to add content to a document using Quick Parts, copy and move text using the Clipboard and the mouse, find and replace text, and navigate a long document.

KEY TERMS
building blocks
copy
cut
field
paste
wildcards

Editing Basics | 229

Using Quick Parts to Add Content to a Document

THE BOTTOM LINE

Word has many features that can help simplify the process of creating documents. The Quick Parts feature enables you to easily insert reusable pieces of content within your document. In these activities, you will learn how to use built-in building blocks and how to create your own. You will also learn how to insert Quick Parts such as fields into a document.

Using Built-In Building Blocks

To save time when creating a document, you can use built-in building blocks already stored in galleries. Just choose the one you want and insert it.

The *hosting* document is available on the companion CD-ROM.

USE BUILT-IN BUILDING BLOCKS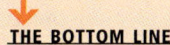

GET READY. Before you begin these steps, be sure to launch Microsoft Office Word 2007.

1. **OPEN** *hosting* from the data files for this lesson.
2. On the Insert tab, in the Text group, click the **Quick Parts** button to display the menu shown in Figure 7-1.

Figure 7-1

Quick Parts menu

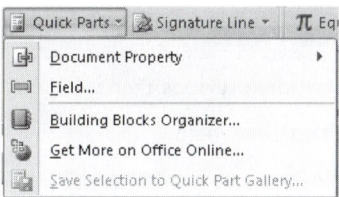

3. Click **Building Blocks Organizer** to display the dialog box shown in Figure 7-2.

Figure 7-2

Building Blocks Organizer

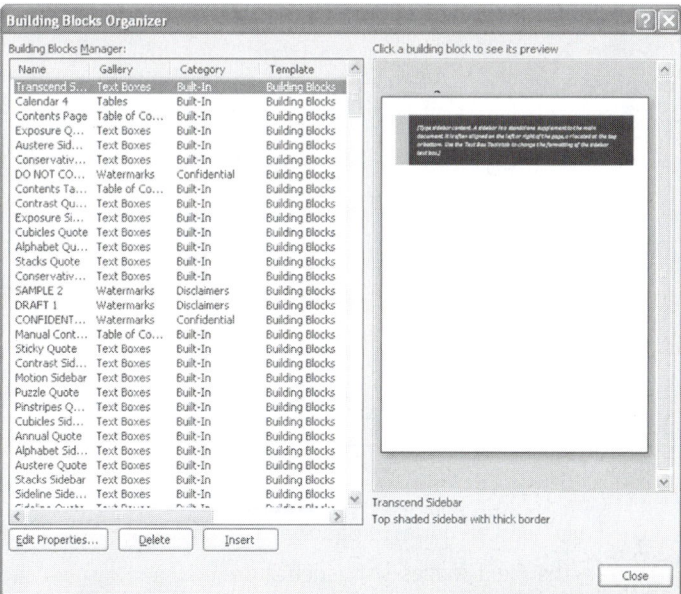

4. Click the **Name** heading to sort the building blocks by name.
5. Scroll down and select the **Confidential 1** building block.

> **TROUBLESHOOTING** If the names are not entirely visible, you can change the width of the Name column by pointing to the right edge of the heading and dragging the resize bar to the right.

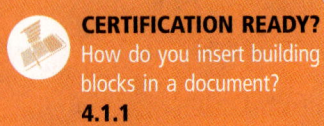

CERTIFICATION READY?
How do you insert building blocks in a document?
4.1.1

6. Click the **Insert** button. The Confidential watermark appears behind the text on each page of your document.
7. **SAVE** the document as *hosting_terms*.

   PAUSE. LEAVE the document open to use in the next exercise.

X REF

Headers and footers are another type of building block. You already learned how to insert headers and footers from Quick Parts in Lesson 5.

Building blocks are reusable pieces of content or other document parts that are stored in galleries and can be inserted into a document whenever needed. The Building Blocks Organizer enables you to manage building blocks by editing, deleting, and/or inserting them. You can sort the building blocks by name, gallery, category, or template, and you can also preview any of the building blocks that are stored in the galleries. A description of a selected building block appears below the preview pane.

Inserting a Field from Quick Parts

When you add fields from Quick Parts into a document, Word automatically inserts specific information in place of each field when you open the document.

➔ INSERT A FIELD FROM QUICK PARTS

USE the document that is open from the previous exercise.

1. Place the insertion point two lines below the last line in the document.
2. Key **Last Updated:** in bold.
3. On the Insert tab, in the Text group, click the **Quick Parts** button.
4. Click **Field** on the menu. The dialog box shown in Figure 7-3 will be displayed.

Figure 7-3

Field dialog box

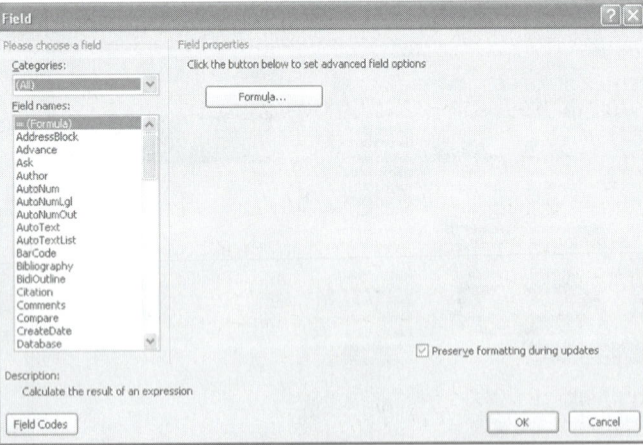

5. From the Categories dropdown list, click **Date and Time**.
6. In the Field Names list, click **Date**.
7. In the Date Formats list, select the ninth option with the **d MMMM yyyy** format and click **OK**. The end of your document should look similar to Figure 7-4.

Figure 7-4
Document with Date and Time field inserted

CERTIFICATION READY?
How do you insert fields from Quick Parts?
4.1.4

8. **SAVE** the document.

   PAUSE. LEAVE the document open to use in the next exercise.

A ***field*** is a placeholder that tells Word to insert changeable data into a document. Word automatically uses fields when you use certain commands, such as inserting a page number or creating a table of contents. You can also manually insert fields into your document. Word automatically updates fields when a document is opened, so the information stays up to date.

Fields—also called field codes—appear between curly brackets ({ }) when displayed. To display field codes in your document instead of the resulting information, press **Alt+F9**. To edit a field, right-click the field and then click Edit Field.

Creating Your Own Building Blocks

If you have customized text that you frequently insert into documents, you can store it as a building block and then reuse it again whenever you need it.

CREATE YOUR OWN BUILDING BLOCKS

USE the document that is open from the previous exercise.

1. Select the four paragraphs of text under the *2. Account Information* heading.
2. On the Insert tab, in the Text group, click the **Quick Parts** button.
3. Click **Save Selection to Quick Part Gallery** on the menu. The Create New Building Block dialog box appears, as shown in Figure 7-5.

Figure 7-5
Create New Building Block dialog box

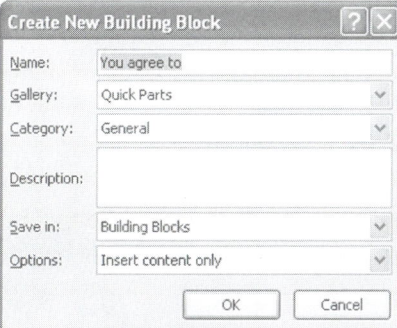

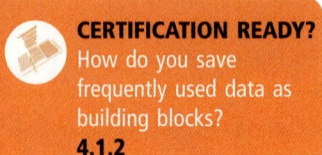

CERTIFICATION READY?
How do you save frequently used data as building blocks?
4.1.2

4. In the Name: box, key **Account Information XXX** (where XXX = your initials).
5. In the Description: box, key **text from hosting terms document**.
6. Click **OK**.

PAUSE. LEAVE the document open to use in the next exercise.

Building blocks enable you to store frequently needed information so that it can be easily accessed and used again. In this activity, you stored the account information text so that you can easily insert it into other documents in the future.

Table 7-1 describes the information you fill out in the Create New Building Block dialog box. This same information is available if you need to modify a building block.

Table 7-1

Create New Building Block information

Name	Description
Name	Unique and descriptive name for the building block.
Gallery	Gallery where the building block will appear.
Category	Category in which the building block will be located. User may choose an existing category from the dropdown list or create a new category.
Description	General description of the building block.
Save In	Name of the template where the building block will be saved, selected from the dropdown list.
Options	The **Insert Content in Its Own Page** option ensures the building block is placed on a separate page.
	The **Insert Content in Its Own Paragraph** option is used for content that should not become part of another paragraph.
	The **Insert Content Only** option is used for all other content.

TROUBLESHOOTING To store paragraph formatting such as indentation, alignment, line spacing, and pagination in a building block, you must include the paragraph mark (¶) in the selection. To view paragraph marks, from the Home tab, in the Paragraph group, click Show/Hide.

When you close Word, a message will appear asking if you want to save the changes you have made to building blocks, as shown in Figure 7-6. To keep the changes, click Yes.

Figure 7-6

"Save changes to building blocks" message

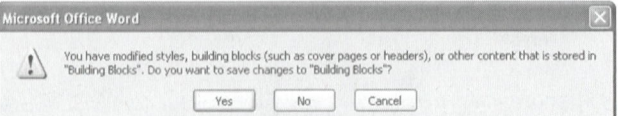

Editing Basics | 233

■ Copying and Moving Text

THE BOTTOM LINE

It is often necessary to copy or remove text from one location in a document and place it in another. In the following activities, you will learn two different ways to copy and move text—using the Clipboard and using the mouse.

Using the Clipboard to Copy and Move Text

The Clipboard enables you to cut or copy multiple items and paste them into any Office document.

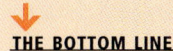

USE THE CLIPBOARD TO COPY AND MOVE TEXT

USE the document that is open from the previous exercise.

1. In the first section of the document, select the entire second paragraph, which begins *Questions or comments regarding* . . ..
2. On the Home tab, in the Clipboard group, click the **Cut** button shown in Figure 7-7.

Figure 7-7

Clipboard group on the Home tab

To copy items to the Clipboard using the keyboard, press **Ctrl+C**. To cut an item using the keyboard, press **Ctrl+X**.

3. Place the insertion point on the line below the document title.
4. On the Home tab, click the **Clipboard dialog box launcher** to display the Clipboard task pane.
5. Move your mouse pointer to the text you just collected on the Clipboard and click the downward-pointing arrow, as shown in Figure 7-8.

Figure 7-8

Clipboard task pane

TAKE NOTE*

Your Clipboard task pane may look different depending on how many items have been collected there.

6. Click **Paste** to insert the text into the document in the new location.

234 | Lesson 7

To paste the item most recently collected on the Clipboard, press **Ctrl+V** on the keyboard.

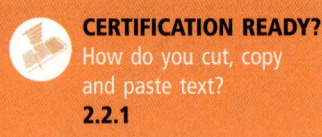

CERTIFICATION READY?
How do you cut, copy and paste text?
2.2.1

7. Click the **Close** button on the Clipboard task pane.
8. **SAVE** the document.
   PAUSE. LEAVE the document open to use in the next exercise.

When you *cut* text, you remove it. When you *copy* text, you make a duplicate. When you *paste* text, you place the cut or copied text in a different location. In this activity, you moved text to a new location in a document. The process for copying an item is the same.

When you cut or copy an item, it is added to the Clipboard collection. Collected items stay on the Clipboard until you exit all Office programs or click the Clear All button. To turn off the Clipboard, click the Close button on the Clipboard task pane.

The Clipboard holds up to 24 items. If you add a 25th item, the first item is deleted from the Clipboard. The newest entry is always added to the top. Each entry includes an icon representing the source Office program and a portion of copied text or a thumbnail of a copied graphic. By default, a message appears in the lower corner of your screen when you collect an item on the Clipboard, as shown in Figure 7-9.

Figure 7-9

Clipboard icon and status message

To control how the Clipboard is displayed, click the Options button on the Clipboard task pane. Table 7-2 describes the various options available.

Table 7-2

Options for displaying the Clipboard

OPTION	DESCRIPTION
Show Office Clipboard Automatically	Automatically displays the Clipboard when copying items.
Show Office Clipboard When Ctrl+C Pressed Twice	Automatically displays the Clipboard when you press **Ctrl**+**C** twice.
Collect Without Showing Office Clipboard	Automatically copies items to the Clipboard without displaying the Clipboard task pane.
Show Office Clipboard Icon on Taskbar	Displays the Clipboard icon in the status area of the system Taskbar when the Clipboard is active. Turned on by default.
Show Status Near Taskbar When Copying	Displays the "collected item" message when copying items to the Clipboard. Turned on by default.

Using the Mouse to Copy or Move Text

When you want to move a selection of text, you can use your mouse to drag and drop the selection.

USE THE MOUSE TO COPY OR MOVE TEXT

USE the document that is open from the previous exercise.

1. Select the phrase *Flatland Hosting* in the second paragraph of *6. Security/Software*.
2. Press the **Ctrl** key as you click, drag, and drop the phrase in the first paragraph before the words *login ID and password*. As you can see in Figure 7-10, the pointer shows a plus sign (+) as you drag, indicating that you are copying the selected text.

Figure 7-10

Copying text using the drag-and-drop feature

6. Security/Software

You agree to take all steps reasonable, necessary, and prudent to protect your login ID and password.

You agree not to attempt to undermine or cause harm to any server, software, system or customer of Flatland Hosting.

You agree to maintain your computing equipment responsibly, including running virus software.

Uploading a virus to a Flatland Hosting server will result in account termination, service charges and/or prosecution.

CERTIFICATION READY?
How do you cut, copy and paste text?
2.2.1

3. **SAVE** the document.

   PAUSE. LEAVE the document open to use in the next exercise.

To move or copy text by using the mouse, first select the text and then click the selection. Drag the text to a new position, or hold the Ctrl key while you drag to copy the text. As you drag, the pointer shows a box when you are moving text or a box with a plus sign (+) when you are copying it. When you copy or move text using the mouse, the item is not stored on the Clipboard.

TROUBLESHOOTING By default, drag-and-drop editing is turned on so that you can drag the pointer to move and copy text. This option can be turned on or off by clicking the Microsoft Office Button and then clicking Word Options.

Click Advanced and, under Editing options, select or clear the Allow Text to Be Dragged and Dropped checkbox.

■ Finding and Replacing Text

THE BOTTOM LINE A big advantage of online documents over hard copy is the ability to quickly search for and/or replace text. These features may be accessed from the Find and Replace dialog box.

Finding Text in a Document

You can use the Find command to search for specific text in a document, or you can use it to move quickly to a particular word or place in the document.

➡ FIND TEXT IN A DOCUMENT

USE the document that is open from the previous exercise.

1. Place the insertion point at the beginning of the document.
2. On the Home tab, in the Editing group, click the **Find** button, shown in Figure 7-11.

Figure 7-11

Editing group on Home tab

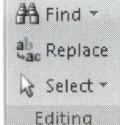

ANOTHER WAY

To open the Find tab in the Find and Replace dialog box using the keyboard, press **Ctrl+F**.

3. The Find tab of the Find and Replace dialog box should be displayed. In the Find What box, key **Products**.
4. Click the **Find Next** button to find each occurrence.
5. When a message appears saying "Word is finished searching the document," click **OK**.
6. Click the **More >>** button, if necessary, to display more search options (see Figure 7-12).

Figure 7-12

Find tab of the Find and Replace dialog box

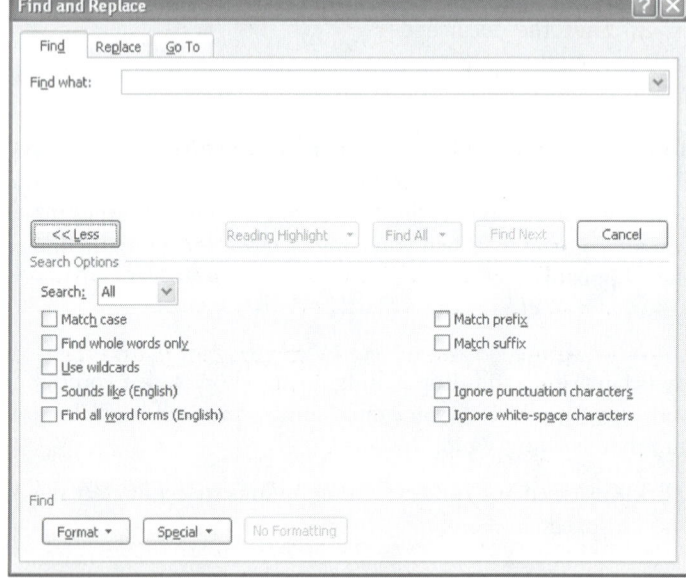

TAKE NOTE

To cancel a search in progress, press **Esc**.

CERTIFICATION READY?

How do you find and replace text? How do you move around in a document quickly by using the Find and Go To commands?

2.2.2, 5.1.1

7. In the Search dropdown list, click **All** if it is not already selected.
8. Click to select the **Match Case** checkbox.
9. Click **Find Next**. Notice that this time Word only finds one occurrence because all the others are lowercase.
10. **SAVE** the document.

   PAUSE. LEAVE the document open to use in the next exercise.

In the Find dialog box, key the text that you want to search for and click Find Next to locate the next instance of the word or phrase. To find all instances of a specific word or phrase in the document, click Find All and then click Main Document.

 TAKE NOTE Do not select text before starting the search. Otherwise, Word will only search through the selected text, rather than the entire document.

To highlight every occurrence of a word or phrase on the screen, click Reading Highlight and then click Highlight All. The highlighting will not be visible when the document is printed. To clear the highlighting, click Reading Highlight and click Clear Highlighting. Figure 7-13 shows part of a document with reading highlight applied to the word *information*.

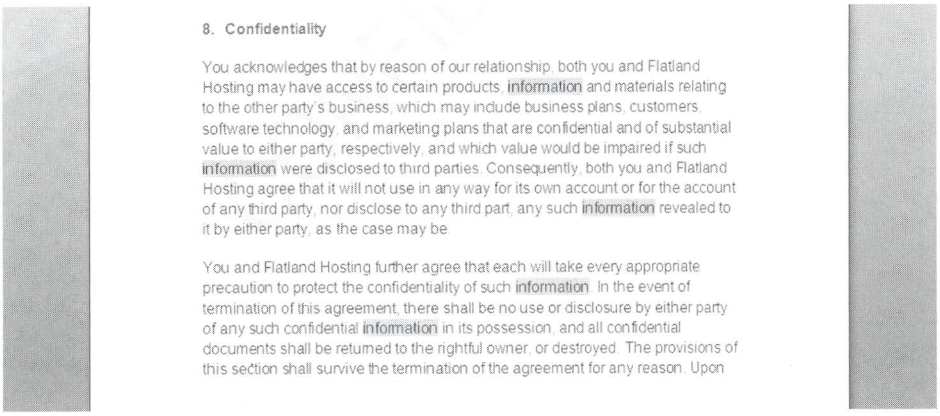

8. Confidentiality

You acknowledges that by reason of our relationship, both you and Flatland Hosting may have access to certain products, information and materials relating to the other party's business, which may include business plans, customers, software technology, and marketing plans that are confidential and of substantial value to either party, respectively, and which value would be impaired if such information were disclosed to third parties. Consequently, both you and Flatland Hosting agree that it will not use in any way for its own account or for the account of any third party, nor disclose to any third part, any such information revealed to it by either party, as the case may be.

You and Flatland Hosting further agree that each will take every appropriate precaution to protect the confidentiality of such information. In the event of termination of this agreement, there shall be no use or disclosure by either party of any such confidential information in its possession, and all confidential documents shall be returned to the rightful owner, or destroyed. The provisions of this section shall survive the termination of the agreement for any reason. Upon

Figure 7-13

Text with reading highlight

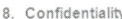

For more options, click the More>> button and choose additional criteria to refine the search process, such as matching the case or finding whole words only. You can use ***wildcard*** characters to find words or phrases that contain specific letters or combinations of letters. Key a question mark (?) to represent a single character—for example, keying b?t will find *bat*, *bet*, *bit*, and *but*. Key an asterisk (*) to represent a string of characters—for example, m*t will find *mat*, *moment*, or even *medium format*.

Click the Format button to find specific formatting such as a font, paragraph, or style. Click the Special button to find special elements in a document such as a field, footnote mark, or section break.

Replacing Text in a Document

The Replace command can be used to automatically replace a word or phrase with another. The Replace tab of the Find and Replace dialog box is similar to the Find tab, except that it enables you to replace text instead of just searching for it.

REPLACE TEXT IN A DOCUMENT

USE the document that is open from the previous exercise.

1. Place the insertion point at the beginning of the document.
2. On the Home tab, in the Editing group, click the **Replace** button.
3. Click to deselect the Match Case check box. Click the **<< Less** button to hide the options. The Replace tab of the Find and Replace dialog box should now look similar Figure 7-14.

Figure 7-14

Replace tab of Find and Replace dialog box

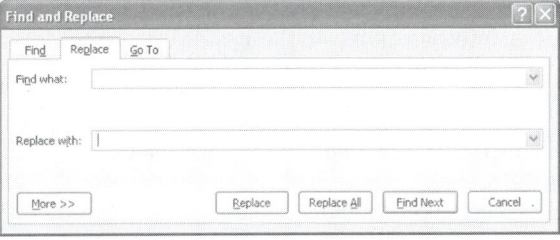

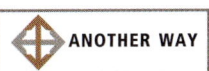

ANOTHER WAY

To open the Replace tab in the Find and Replace dialog box using the keyboard, press **Ctrl+H**.

4. In the Find What box, key **clients**.
5. In the Replace with box, key **customers**.
6. Click **Find Next**. Word searches for the first occurrence of the word *clients* and highlights it.
7. Click **Replace**.

238 | Lesson 7

TAKE NOTE When replacing text, it is usually a good practice to click Replace instead of Replace All so that you can confirm each replacement to make sure it's correct.

8. Click **Replace All**. Word searches for all occurrences of the word *clients*, replaces them all with the word *customers*, and then displays a message telling you how many replacements were made (see Figure 7-15).

Figure 7-15

Find and replace message

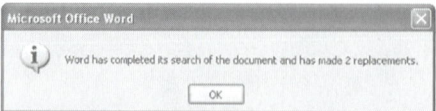

9. Click **OK**.
10. Click the **Close** button to close the Find and Replace dialog box.
11. **SAVE** the document.

    PAUSE. LEAVE the document open to use in the next exercise.

CERTIFICATION READY?
How do you find and replace text? How do you move around in a document quickly by using the Find and Go To commands?
2.2.2, 5.1.1

The Replace command is versatile. Besides text, you can also search for and replace formatting. For example, you can find a specific word or phrase and change the font color, or find specific formatting such as italics and remove or change it. It is also possible to search for and replace special characters and document elements such as page breaks and tabs.

■ Navigating a Long Document

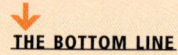 **THE BOTTOM LINE** In a longer document, you might want to go directly to a specific place without having to scroll or quickly locate a particular heading. The Go To and Document Map commands provide ways to navigate through longer documents easily.

Using the Go To Command

You can navigate to a specific page, line number, footnote, comment, or other object using the Go To command.

USE THE GO TO COMMAND

USE the document that is open from the previous exercise.

1. Place the insertion point at the beginning of the document.
2. On the Home tab, in the Editing group, click the downward-pointing arrow next to the Find button and then click **Go To**.
3. The Go To tab of the Find and Replace dialog box is displayed, as shown in Figure 7-16.

Figure 7-16

Go To tab in Find and Replace dialog box

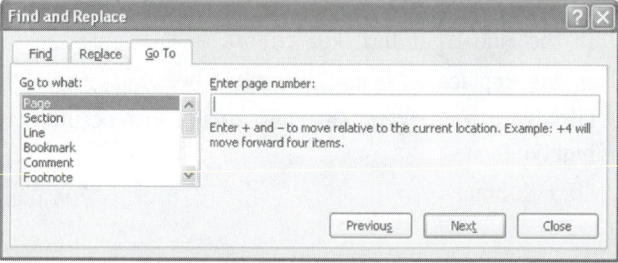

Editing Basics | 239

 **ANOTHER WAY** To open the Go To tab in the Find and Replace dialog box using the keyboard, press **Ctrl+G**.

 **CERTIFICATION READY?**
How do you find and replace text? How do you move around in a document quickly by using the Find and Go To commands?
2.2.2, 5.1.1

4. In the Go To What box, **Page** should be selected. In the Enter Page Number Box, key **6** and then click Go To. The insertion point moves to page 6 of the document.
5. In the Go To What box, select **Line**. In the Enter Line Number box, key **23** and then click Go To. The insertion point moves to line 23 in the document.
6. In the Go To What box, select **Field**. In the Enter Field Number box, **Any Field** should be selected. Click Next. The insertion point moves to the field you inserted into the document earlier in this lesson.
7. Click the **Close** button to close the Find and Replace dialog box.
   PAUSE. LEAVE the document open to use in the next exercise.

You can use the Go To command to jump to a specific page, table, graphic, equation, or other item in your document. To go to the next or previous item of the same type, leave the Enter box empty and then click Previous or Next.

 TAKE NOTE Word keeps track of the last three locations where you typed or edited text. To go to a previous editing location in your document, press **Shift+F5**.

Using the Document Map

Use the Document Map to quickly navigate through a document and keep track of your location within it.

➔ **USE THE DOCUMENT MAP**

USE the document that is open from the previous exercise.

1. Place the insertion point at the beginning of the document.
2. On the View tab, in the Show/Hide group, click to select the **Document Map** checkbox.
3. The Document Map pane appears, as shown in Figure 7-17.

Figure 7-17

Document Map pane

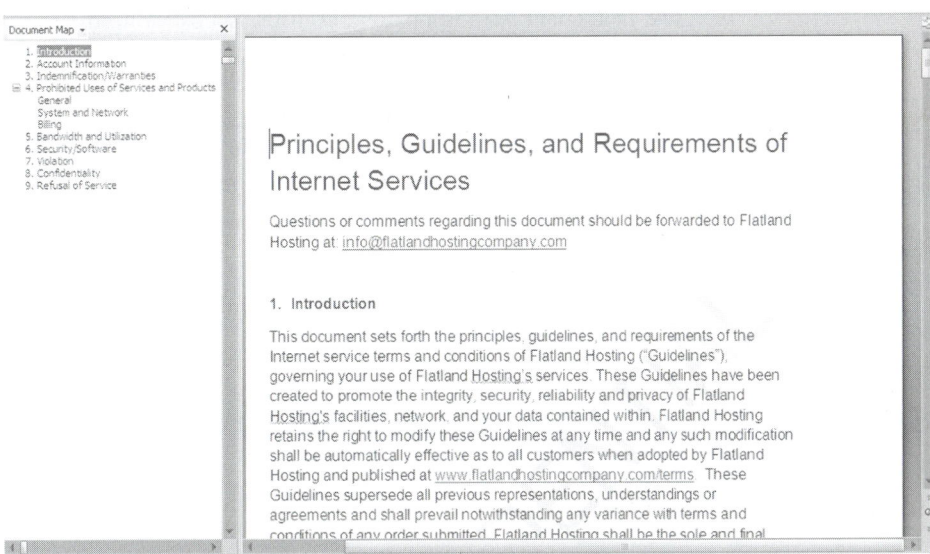

240 | Lesson 7

> **TROUBLESHOOTING** If the headings are too long, you can change the width of the Document Map by pointing to the right edge of the pane and dragging the resize bar to the right. Or you can hover the pointer over an individual heading to view it.

4. In the Document Map pane, click the *5. Bandwidth and Utilization* heading. The insertion point moves to that location in the document.
5. Click the minus sign (-) next to the *4. Prohibited Uses of Products and Services* heading to collapse the subheadings.
6. Click the downward-pointing arrow next in the Document Map dropdown list and click **Thumbnails**. The pane shows a thumbnail of each page, as shown in Figure 7-18.

Figure 7-18

Document Map thumbnails

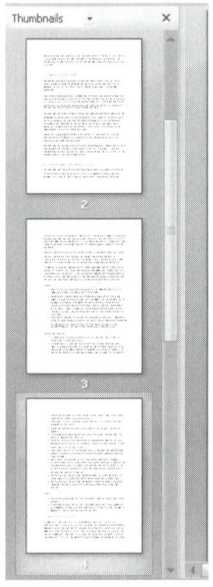

7. Click the **Close** button to close the Document Map pane.
8. **SAVE** and **CLOSE** the document.
   STOP. CLOSE Word.

> **CERTIFICATION READY?**
> How do you find and replace text? How do you move through a document quickly by using the Find and Go To commands? How do you change window views?
> **2.2.2, 5.1.1, 5.1.2**

The Document Map is a pane that displays a list of headings so that you can navigate through a structural view of the document. When you click a heading in the pane, Word jumps to the corresponding heading in the document and highlights it in the Document Map. You can display small versions of each page by clicking the downward-pointing arrow in the Document Map pane and then clicking Thumbnails.

> **TROUBLESHOOTING** Document headings must be formatted with built-in heading styles to display in the Document Map.

Editing Basics | 241

You can choose the level of detail to display in the Document Map by right-clicking a heading and clicking a number on the shortcut menu, as shown in Figure 7-19. To display the subheadings under a heading, click the plus sign (+) next to it. To collapse the subheadings under a heading, click the minus sign (-). To close the Document Map, click the Close button.

Figure 7-19

Document Map shortcut menu

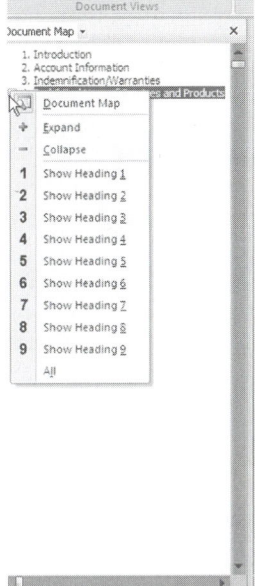

SUMMARY SKILL MATRIX

IN THIS LESSON YOU LEARNED HOW TO:
Use Built-In Building Blocks
Insert a Field from Quick Parts
Create Your Own Building Blocks
Use the Clipboard to Copy and Move Text
Use the Mouse to Copy or Move Text
Find Text in a Document
Replace Text in a Document
Use the Go To Command
Use the Document Map

Knowledge Assessment

Fill in the Blank

Complete the following sentences by writing the correct word or words in the blanks provided.

p.230 1. The Building Blocks _Organizer_ gives you a way to manage building blocks by editing, deleting, and/or inserting them.

p.231 2. A _field_ is a placeholder that tells Word to insert changeable data into a document.

p.235 3. When you copy or move text using the _Mouth_, the item is not stored on the Clipboard.

p.237 4. You can use _wildcard_ characters to find words or phrases that contain specific letters or combinations of letters.

p.238 5. You can navigate to a particular page, line number, footnote, comment, or other object using the _GO TO_ command.

p.240 6. The _Document_ Map is a pane that displays a list of headings so that you can navigate through a structural view of the document.

p.234 7. When you _Paste_ text, you place it in another location.

p.234 8. If you add more items to the Clipboard than it can hold, the first item is _Deleted_.

p.234 9. When you want to move a selection of text, you can use the _drag & drop_ feature with your mouse.

p.237 10. The Replace command is very similar to the _Find_ command, except that you can replace text instead of just searching for it.

Multiple Choice

Select the best response for the following statements.

1. You can sort the building blocks by all EXCEPT which of the following?
    a. name
    b. creator
    c. gallery
    d. category

2. The Clipboard holds up to how many items?
    a. 10
    b. 14
    c. 20
    d. 24

3. To control how the Clipboard is displayed, click which button in the Clipboard task pane?
    a. Options
    b. Display
    c. Settings
    d. View

4. To copy text using the mouse, which key do you hold while you drag?
   a. Tab
   b. Shift
   c. Alt
   d. Ctrl

5. To highlight every occurrence of a word or phrase on the screen, click
   a. Reading Highlight.
   p. 226 **b. Highlight All.**
   c. View All.
   d. Highlight Next.

6. You can display small versions of each page by clicking the downward-pointing arrow in the Document Map pane and clicking
   a. Display Small.
   b. Thumbnails.
   c. View Page.
   d. Miniature.

7. When displayed in the document, field codes appear between what?
   a. parentheses
   b. quotations
   p.231 **c. curly brackets**
   d. dashes

8. If you have customized text that you frequently insert into documents, you can reuse it by storing it as
   a. a wildcard.
   b. Clipboard content.
   c. a Document Map.
   d. a building block.

9. The Replace command can be used to search for
   a. text.
   b. formatting.
   c. special characters.
   d. all of the above.
   e. none of the above.

10. Which command could NOT be used to navigate a longer document?
    a. Find
    b. Go To
    c. Clipboard
    d. Document Map

■ Competency Assessment

Project 7-1: Compiling Books and Beyond Handbook

In your job at Books and Beyond, you have started compiling the documents you have been working on into an employee handbook.

GET READY. Launch Word if it is not already running.

1. **OPEN** *perdiemrates* from the data files for this lesson.
2. Press **Ctrl**+**A** to select all the text in the *perdiemrates* document.
3. On the Home tab, in the Clipboard group, click the **Copy** button to copy the text to the Clipboard.
4. Click the **Microsoft Office Button** and click **Close** to close the *perdiemrates* document.
5. **OPEN** *booksbeyond* from the data files for this lesson.
6. On the Home tab, in the Editing group, click the Find arrow and then click **Go To**.
7. In the Go To What box, select **Page** if necessary. In the Enter Page Number box, key **6**.
8. Click the **Go To** button to go to page 6, which is blank.
9. Click the **Close** button to close the Find and Replace dialog box.
10. On the Home tab, click the **Clipboard task pane launcher**.
11. In the Clipboard task pane, click the per diem text you just copied to the Clipboard to insert it on page 6.
12. Click the **Close** button to close the Clipboard task pane.
13. **SAVE** the document as *booksbeyond_handbook*.

    PAUSE. LEAVE the document open to use in the next project.

The *perdiemrates* document is available on the companion CD-ROM.

The *booksbeyond* document is available on the companion CD-ROM.

Project 7-2: Editing Books and Beyond Handbook

Now that you have compiled all the individual documents into one employee handbook for Books and Beyond, you need to make some changes.

1. Place the insertion point at the beginning of the document.
2. On the Home tab, in the Editing group, click the Find arrow and then click **Go To**.
3. In the Go To What box, select **Line**. In the Enter Line Number box, key **1**.
4. Click the **Go To** button to go to the first line of the document.
5. Click the **Replace** tab in the Find and Replace dialog box.
6. In the Find What box, key **HR**.
7. In the Replace With box, key **Human Resources**.
8. Click the **More >>** button, if necessary, to display more options.
9. Select the **Match Case** box.
10. Click **Find Next** and then **Replace**.
11. Click **Replace All** and then **OK** to close the message box when all replacements have been made.
12. Click **Close** to close the Find and Replace dialog box.
13. On the Insert tab, in the Text group, click the **Quick Parts** button.
14. Select **Building Blocks Organizer** on the menu.
15. Sort by name and then scroll down and click the **Draft 1** building block.
16. Click the **Insert** button to insert the watermark into the document.

17. **SAVE** the document then **CLOSE** the file.

PAUSE. LEAVE Word open for the next project.

■ Proficiency Assessment

Project 7-3: Inserting Your Custom Building Block

You are creating a new hosting agreement document for Flatland Hosting and to save time, you want to use the building block that you saved earlier.

1. **OPEN** *agreement* from the data files for this lesson.
2. Place the insertion point at the end of the document.
3. On the Insert tab, in the Text group, click the **Quick Parts** button.
4. Select **Building Blocks Organizer** from the menu.
5. Insert the **Account Information XXX** building block that you saved earlier in the document.
6. **SAVE** the document as *flatland_agreement* and then **CLOSE** the file.

PAUSE. LEAVE Word open for the next project.

> **CD**
> The *agreement* document is available on the companion CD-ROM.

Project 7-4: Editing a Document

As an employee of Cornwall Village Bank and Trust, you frequently work with bank documents. The bank has just started a new service for customers called the Discretionary Overdraft Service, and you need to make some changes to the document describing it.

1. **OPEN** *overdraft* from the data files for this lesson.
2. Select the first paragraph under the Introduction title.
3. Create a reusable building block named **Cornwall Intro XXX** (where XXX = your initials).
4. Search for every occurrence of the & symbol in the document and replace it with the word *and*.
5. Use the Document Map to navigate to the *If You Need Help* heading.
6. Copy the phone number from the end of that paragraph.
7. Use the Go To command to go to the first page.
8. Paste the phone number on first line below the title of the document.
9. **SAVE** the document as *overdraft_service* and then **CLOSE** the file.

PAUSE. LEAVE Word open for the next project.

> **CD**
> The *overdraft* document is available on the companion CD-ROM.

■ Mastery Assessment

Project 7-5: Store a Personal Quick Part

It would be helpful to be able to insert your name, class name, and the date on documents that you create in class without keying the items each time. You decide to create a personal building block for this purpose.

1. **OPEN** a new blank document.
2. Create a building block that includes your name, the class, and the current date. Use a field to insert the date.

3. Format the text however you want. You could even put the information in a header or footer.
4. Save the building block as your full name.
5. Open a document you have previously created in class and insert the building block you just created.
6. **SAVE** the document as *personal_block* and then **CLOSE** the file.
7. Without saving, close the document you used to create the building block.
8. **SAVE** the changes to building blocks when prompted.

   PAUSE. LEAVE Word open for the next project.

Project 7-6: Building Blocks Help

You want to be able to create a report template that provides your template users with two cover letter types to choose from when they create their own report based on your template. You have heard that it is possible to do this by saving and distributing building blocks with a template, and you decide to use Word Help to find out more.

1. **OPEN** a new blank document.
2. Use Word Help to look up information on building blocks.
3. Find the information that deals specifically with saving and distributing building blocks with a template.
4. Read the Word Help information and then copy and paste the information into the blank document.
5. **SAVE** the document as *buildingblocks_help* and **CLOSE** the file.

   STOP. CLOSE Word.

INTERNET READY

One benefit to being connected to the Internet while you are working in Word is that you have access to additional resources. As you saw in Figure 7-1 at the beginning of this lesson, the Quick Parts menu has a **More on Office Online** choice. Select this option to go directly to the Word building blocks page in the online Templates site. This resource improves as more people contribute. Consider submitting a building block others might find useful to the Community Templates section. Or, download an existing building block and then participate by rating or commenting on it.

Creating Tables and Lists

8

LESSON SKILL MATRIX

Inserting a Table by Dragging — 248	Students will learn how to insert a table by dragging.
Using the Insert Table Dialog Box — 249	Students will learn how to use the insert table dialog box.
Drawing a Table — 249	Students will learn how to draw a table.
Inserting a Quick Table — 251	Students will learn how to insert a Quick Table.
Applying a Quick Style to a Table — 252	Students will learn how to apply a Quick Style to a table.
Turning Table Style Options On or Off — 253	Students will learn how to turn table style options on or off.
Resizing a Row or Column — 254	Students will learn how to resize a row or column.
Moving a Row or Column — 256	Students will learn how to move a row or column.
Setting a Table's Horizontal Alignment — 257	Students will learn how to set a table's horizontal alignment.
Creating a Header Row — 257	Students will learn how to create a header row.
Sorting a Table's Contents — 258	Students will learn how to sort a table's contents.
Performing Calculations in Table Cells — 259	Students will learn how to perform calculations in table cells.
Merging and Splitting Table Cells — 260	Students will learn how to merge and split table cells.
Changing the Position of Text in a Cell — 261	Students will learn how to change the position of text in a cell.
Changing the Direction of Text in a Cell — 261	Students will learn how to change the direction of text in a cell.
Creating an Outline-Style List — 262	Students will learn how to create an outline-style list.
Sorting a List's Contents — 263	Students will learn how to sort a list's contents.
Changing a List's Formatting — 263	Students will learn how to change a list's formatting.

Karen Archer is an executive recruiter. Many large companies hire her to find professional talent to fill communications and marketing executive positions within their firms. You have just been hired as her assistant. Although the business is small, you are still expected to display a high degree of professionalism, confidentiality, and integrity. Because it is a small business, you will be asked to perform many different duties. One of your main duties is to assist Ms. Archer with the constant updating of tables that contain data related to current clients, potential clients, and potential candidates for placement. Microsoft Word's table tools can help you successfully manage this information. In this lesson, you will learn to format lists as well as create, format, and manage tables.

KEY TERMS
ascending
cells
descending
formula
header row
merge cells
Quick Tables
sort
split cells
table

Creating Tables

THE BOTTOM LINE

Tables are ideal for organizing information in an orderly manner. Calendars, invoices, and contact lists are all examples of tables that you see and use every day. Word gives you several options for creating tables. You can create a table using the dragging method, the Insert Table dialog box, by drawing a table, or inserting a Quick Table.

Inserting a Table by Dragging

When you know exactly how many rows and columns you need for a new table, the quickest way to create a table is by dragging over the Table grid in the Tables menu to select the desired number of rows and columns.

➔ INSERT A TABLE BY DRAGGING

GET READY. Before you begin these steps, be sure to launch Microsoft Office Word 2007 and **OPEN** a new blank Word document.

1. On the **Insert** tab, in the **Tables** group, click the **Table** button. The Insert Table menu appears.
2. Point to the cell in the **fifth column, second row**. The menu title should read *5X2 Table*, as shown in Figure 8-1. Click the mouse button to create the table.

Figure 8-1

Insert Table menu

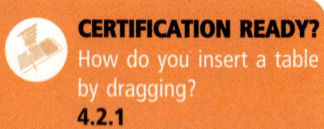

CERTIFICATION READY?
How do you insert a table by dragging?
4.2.1

3. Click below the table and press **Enter** to insert a blank line.
4. **SAVE** the document as *tables*.

PAUSE. LEAVE the document open to use in the next exercise.

A *table* is an arrangement of data made up of horizontal rows and vertical columns. *Cells* are the rectangles that are formed when rows and columns intersect. See Figure 8-2.

Figure 8-2

Table

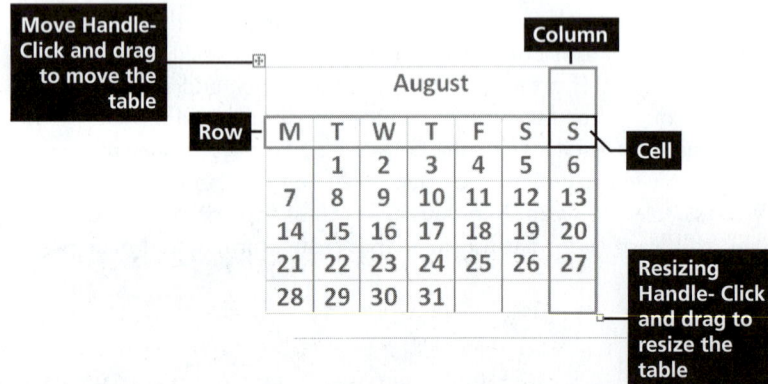

Creating Tables and Lists | 249

As you just learned in the previous exercise, you can quickly create a table from the Table menu by dragging the mouse pointer to specify the number of rows and columns that you want. In this way, you can create a new empty table with up to 8 rows and 10 columns.

Using the Insert Table Dialog Box

The Insert Table dialog box lets you create large tables by specifying up to 63 columns and thousands of rows. You probably will not be working with tables that large very often, but the Insert Table dialog box gives you the option of creating a table with exactly the number of columns and rows you need.

USE THE INSERT TABLE DIALOG BOX

USE the document that is open from the previous exercise.

1. On the **Insert** tab, in the **Tables** group, click the **Table** button. Select **Insert Table** from the menu. The Insert Table dialog box appears.
2. In the **Number of Columns** box, click the upward-pointing arrow until **9** is displayed.
3. In the Number of rows box, click the upward-pointing arrow until **3** is displayed, as shown in Figure 8-3.

Figure 8-3

Insert Table dialog box

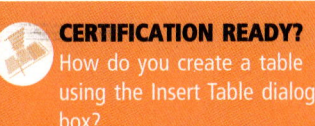

CERTIFICATION READY?
How do you create a table using the Insert Table dialog box?
4.2.1

4. Click **OK** to insert the table.
5. Click below the table and press [Enter] to insert a blank line.
6. **SAVE** the document.

   PAUSE. LEAVE the document open to use in the next exercise.

You just used the Insert Table dialog box to insert a table with nine columns and three rows. From the Insert Table dialog box, you can click the upward- and downward-pointing arrows or key in the number of columns and rows you want in a table.

Drawing a Table

When you need to draw a complex table, you can use the Draw Table command, which lets you draw a table as you would with a pencil and piece of paper. The Draw Table command enables you to draw an outline of a table and then draw the rows and columns exactly where you want them.

DRAW A TABLE

USE the document that is open from the previous exercise.

1. Click the **View Ruler** button to display the rulers, if necessary.
2. On the **Insert** tab, in the **Tables** group, click the **Table** button. Select **Draw Table** from the menu. The pointer becomes a pencil tool.

250 | Lesson 8

3. To begin drawing the table shown in Figure 8-4, click at the blinking insertion point and drag down and to the right until you draw a rectangle that is approximately 3 inches high and 6 inches wide.

Figure 8-4

Draw a Table

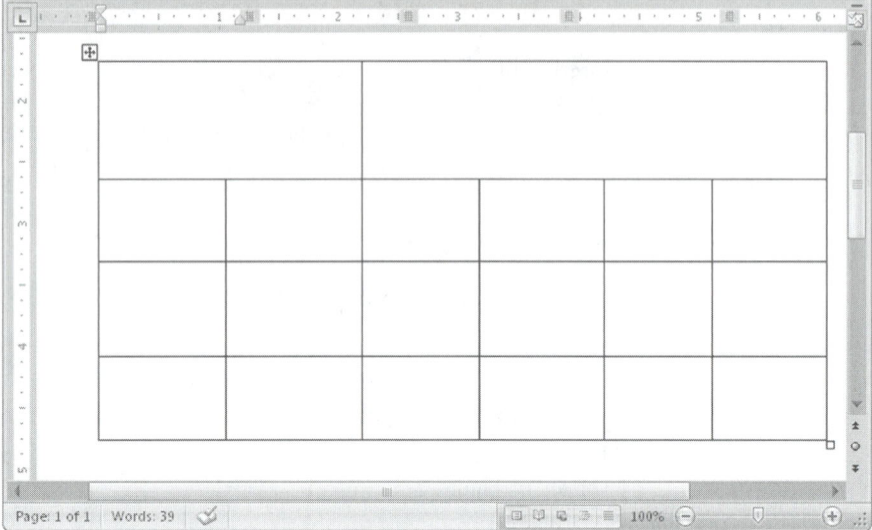

4. Starting at about 0.5 inch down from the top, click and drag the pencil from the left border to the right border to draw a horizontal line.
5. Draw two more horizontal lines about 0.5 apart.
6. Starting at about 1 inch from the left side, click and drag the pencil from the first line you drew to the bottom to create a column (see Figure 9-4).
7. Move over about 1 inch and draw a line from the top of the table to the bottom.
8. Draw three more vertical lines about 1 inch apart from the first horizontal line to the bottom of the table to create a total of six columns. Your table should look similar to Figure 9-4.
9. Click below the table and press Enter to create a blank line.
10. SAVE the document.

    PAUSE. LEAVE the document open to use in the next exercise.

When you choose the Draw Table command from the Table menu, the mouse pointer becomes a pencil tool you can use to draw a table.

TAKE NOTE*

You have learned four ways to insert a blank table. If you have data that is separated by commas, tabs, paragraphs, or another character, you can easily convert it to a table with the Convert Text to Table command on the Table menu.

TROUBLESHOOTING

When you are drawing tables with the pencil tool, remember that it will draw squares and rectangles as well as lines. If you are trying to draw a straight line and you move the pencil off your straight path, Word may think you are trying to draw a rectangle and insert one for you. If this happens, just click the Undo button on the Quick Access toolbar and try again. It might take a little bit of practice to learn the difference between drawing straight lines and rectangles.

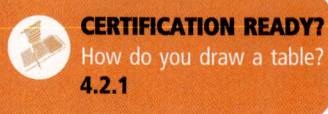

CERTIFICATION READY?
How do you draw a table?
4.2.1

Creating Tables and Lists | 251

Inserting a Quick Table

As you have learned in previous lessons, Word provides many predefined building blocks, such as headers and footers, that can help you create professional-looking documents. In the same way, Word provides a variety of Quick Tables you can insert into your documents.

→ **INSERT A QUICK TABLE**

USE the document that is open from the previous exercise.

1. On the Insert tab, in the Tables group, click the **Table** button. Select **Quick Tables** from the menu. A gallery of built-in Quick Tables appears, as shown in Figure 8-5.

Figure 8-5

Built-in Quick Table gallery

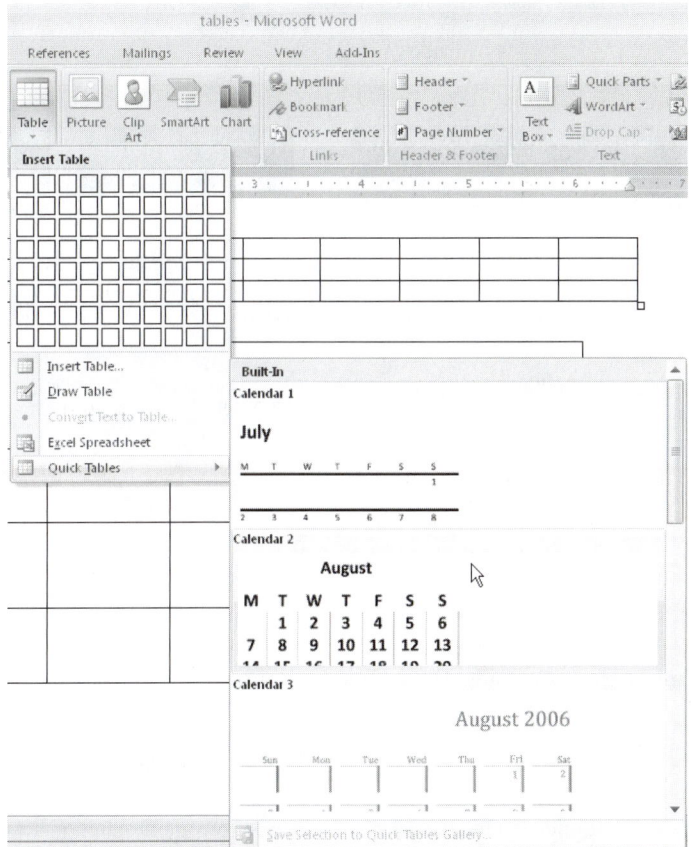

2. Select **Calendar 2**.
3. **SAVE** the document and **CLOSE** the file.
   PAUSE. LEAVE Word open to use in the next exercise.

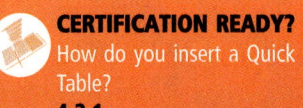

CERTIFICATION READY?
How do you insert a Quick Table?
4.2.1

Quick Tables are built-in preformatted tables, such as calendars and tabular lists, you can insert and use in your documents.

You just inserted a Quick Table calendar into a document. You can edit a calendar, if necessary, to reflect the current month and year.

> **TAKE NOTE**
>
> You can move a table to a new page or a new document by clicking the Move handle to select the table and then using the Cut and Paste commands. Use the Copy command to leave a copy of the table in the original location.

SOFTWARE ORIENTATION

Design Tab on the Table Tools Ribbon

After you insert a table, Word displays Table Tools in the ribbon as shown in Figure 8-6. You can use these tools to work with your table. Because this is a new set of tools you have not seen before, it is important to become familiar with the commands that are available.

Figure 8-6

Design Tab on the Table Tools Ribbon

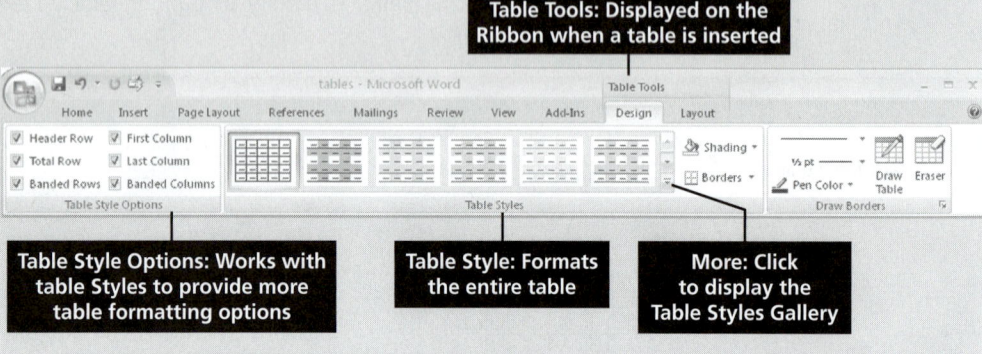

Use this figure as a reference throughout this lesson as well as the rest of this book.

Formatting a Table

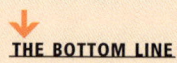

THE BOTTOM LINE

You can format rows and columns individually and experiment with different combinations of formats, which would take some time. However, if you are interested in creating a professional-looking table quickly, apply a Quick Style. Then, if you need to, you can adjust the style using Table Style Options.

Applying a Quick Style to a Table

With Quick Styles, Word makes it easy to quickly change a table's formatting. You can apply styles to tables in much the same way you learned to apply styles to text in previous lessons.

APPLY A QUICK STYLE TO A TABLE

OPEN *clients* from the data files for this lesson.

1. Click anywhere in the table to position the insertion point.
2. On the Design tab, in the Table Styles group, click the **More** button 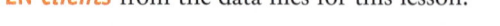 to view a gallery of Quick Styles.
3. Scroll through the available styles. Notice that as you point to a style, Word displays a live preview, showing you what your table will look like if you choose that style.
4. Scroll down to the fourth row under the Built-in section and select the fourth style over in the row, the green **Medium Shading 1 - Accent 3** style, shown in Figure 8-7.

CD

The *clients* document is available on the companion CD-ROM.

Figure 8-7

Quick Style gallery

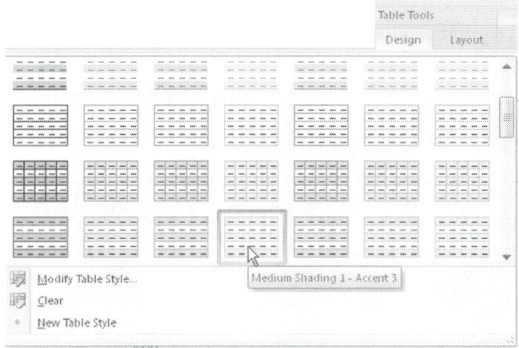

CERTIFICATION READY?
How do you apply a Quick Style to a table?
4.3.1

5. **SAVE** the document as *client_table*.

   PAUSE. LEAVE the document open to use in the next exercise.

In the previous exercise, you applied a Quick Style to a table. Remember to position the insertion point in the table before selecting a style from the Quick Styles gallery. If you decide later that you do not like the current style, you can always go back and use the same procedure to choose a different style.

Turning Table Style Options On or Off

✓ Table Style Options work with Quick Styles to give you even more formatting options.

→ **TURN TABLE STYLE OPTIONS ON OR OFF**

USE the document that is open from the previous exercise.

1. Position the insertion point anywhere in the table.
2. On the Design tab, in the Table Style Options group, click the **First Column** checkbox. Notice that the format of the first column of the table changes, as do the Table Styles in the Quick Style gallery.
3. Click the **Banded Rows** checkbox to turn the option off. Color is removed from the rows.
4. Click the **Banded Rows** checkbox to turn it on again. Color is reapplied to every other row.
5. **SAVE** the document.

   PAUSE. LEAVE the document open to use in the next exercise.

CERTIFICATION READY?
How do you turn Table Style Options on or off?
4.3.2

In the previous exercise, you learned to turn Table Style Options on or off by clicking each option's checkbox. Table Style Options are used globally throughout the table. For example, if you turn on Banded Columns, all even columns in the table will be formatted differently than the odd columns. Table Style Options relate back to the Table Styles. So, if you turn on an option, such as Banded Columns, the Table Style gallery will include various designs with banded columns.

The following are Table Style Options you can turn on or off:
- Header Row: Formats the top row of the table specially
- Total Row: Formats the last row, which usually contains column totals, specially
- Banded Rows: Formats even rows differently than odd rows
- First Column: Formats the first column of the table specially
- Last Column: Formats the last column of the table specially
- Banded Columns: Formats even columns differently than odd columns

■ Software Orientation

Layout Tab on the Table Tools Ribbon

As you have already learned, when you are working with tables, Word displays Table Tools in the ribbon. You can switch between the Design tab and the Layout tab to edit tables. The Layout tab, as shown in Figure 8-8, includes commands for changing the format of an entire table as well as commands for changing the appearance of individual table components, such as cells, columns, and rows.

Figure 8-8

Layout Tab on the Table Tools Ribbon

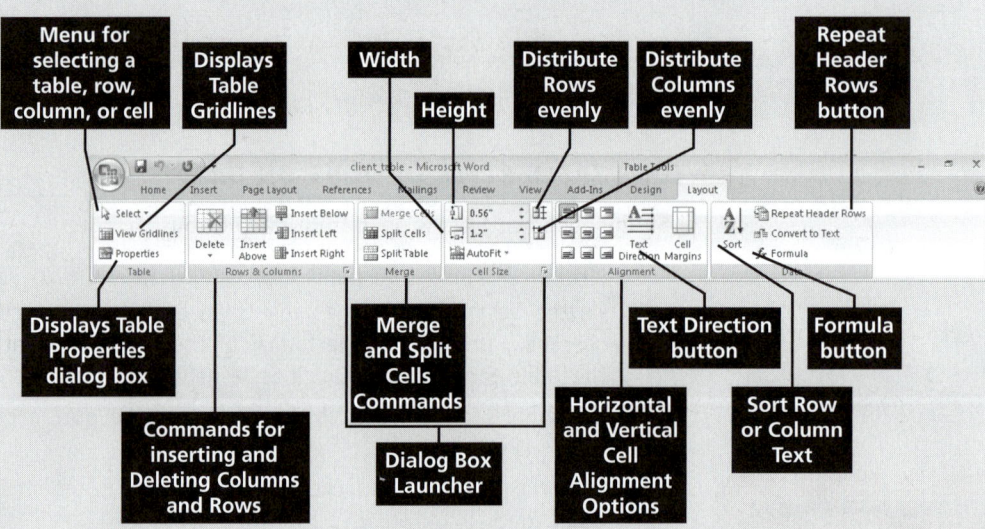

Use this figure as a reference throughout this lesson as well as the rest of this book.

■ Managing Tables

After you create a table, you can resize rows or columns, move rows or columns, set a table's horizontal alignment, create a header row, sort a table's contents, perform calculations, merge and split cells, change the position of text in a cell, and change the direction of text in a cell.

Resizing a Row or Column

As with any document that you edit, some adjustments are always necessary when you work with tables. You may need to resize columns or rows to better fit your data.

Creating Tables and Lists | 255

RESIZE A ROW OR COLUMN

USE the document that is open from the previous exercise.

1. On the Layout tab, in the Table group, click the **View Gridlines** button.
2. Position the mouse pointer over the right border of the table, in the first row. The pointer changes to a double-headed arrow, shown in Figure 8-9.

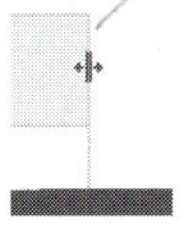

Figure 8-9

Double-headed arrow

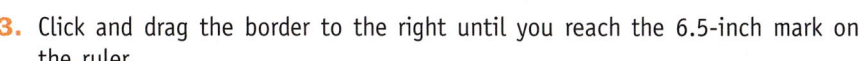

3. Click and drag the border to the right until you reach the 6.5-inch mark on the ruler.
4. On the Layout tab, in the Cell Size group, click the **AutoFit** button. On the dropdown menu, click **AutoFit Contents**, as shown in Figure 8-10. Each column width changes to fit the data in the column.

Figure 8-10

AutoFit button and menu

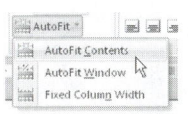

5. Position the pointer outside the table, above the column with the phone numbers. The pointer changes to a downward-pointing selection arrow. Click to select the column.
6. On the Layout tab, in the Cell Size group, click the upward-pointing arrow in the **Width** box until it reads **1.1**. The column width changes.
7. Select the first row. On the Layout tab, in the Cell Size group, click the **Dialog Box Launcher**. The Table Properties dialog box appears.
8. Click the **Row** tab. Click the **Specify Height** checkbox. In the Height box, click the upward-pointing arrow until the box reads **0.5"**, as shown in Figure 8-11.

Figure 8-11

Table Properties dialog box

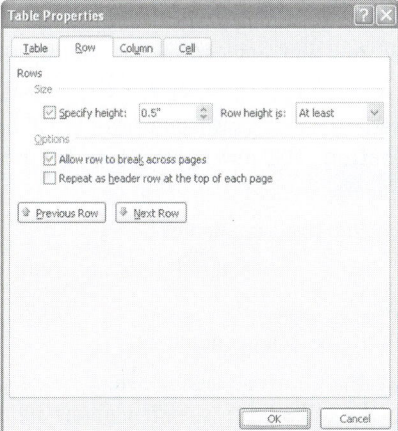

9. Click the Next Row button. Notice the selection moves down one row. Click **OK**.
10. Click in any cell to remove the selection.
11. **SAVE** the document.

PAUSE. LEAVE the document open to use in the next exercise.

As you just saw, Word makes it easy to resize a column or row instantly. When you position the pointer over a row or column boundary, it becomes a double-headed arrow pointer. Now you can click and drag the boundary to resize the row or column.

Displaying a table's gridlines can make editing easier. The View Gridlines button is located on the Layout tab in the Table group.

You can also resize a column or row using the commands in the Cell Size group on the Layout tab. Select cells or an entire row and click the arrows in the Height box to adjust the height. Select cells or a column and click the arrows or key in a measurement to adjust the width. The AutoFit command provides three options for automatically adjusting column width:

- AutoFit Contents: Adjusts column width to fit the size of its contents
- AutoFit Window: Adjusts column width to fit the size of the window
- Fixed Column Width: Forces column to a remain at a fixed width

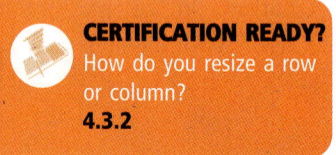

CERTIFICATION READY?
How do you resize a row or column?
4.3.2

If you need to be more precise or change the size of several rows or columns at one time, select the rows or columns you want to resize and use the Table Properties dialog box to specify the height of a row or the width of a column. You can also specify whether you want the row height or column width to be exactly that measurement or at least that measurement.

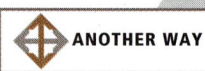

ANOTHER WAY You can access the Table Properties dialog box from the shortcut menu by right-clicking anywhere in the table and selecting Table Properties.

Moving a Row or Column

When you are working with tables, it is important to know how to rearrange columns and rows to better display your data.

→ **MOVE A ROW OR COLUMN**

USE the document that is open from the previous exercise.

1. Select the fourth row of data, which contains the information for Proseware, Inc.
2. Click on the selected row and hold down the mouse button. Notice the mouse pointer changes to a move pointer with a dotted insertion point.
3. Drag the dotted insertion point down and position it before the *W* in *Wingtip Toys*. Release the mouse button. The row is moved to the position above the Wingtip Toys row.
4. Select the column listing the first names.
5. Position the pointer inside the selected cells and right-click to display the shortcut menu. Select **Cut**.
6. Select the column with the phone numbers.
7. Right-click to display the shortcut menu. Select **Paste Columns**. The first name column is moved to the left of the selected phone number column.
8. **SAVE** the document.

   PAUSE. LEAVE the document open to use in the next exercise.

You can use drag-and-drop editing to move rows or columns. Select the entire column or row that you want to move and then click within the selection and hold the mouse button. The mouse pointer changes to a move pointer, which looks like a pointer with an empty rectangle underneath it. The insertion point becomes a dotted line. Drag the dotted insertion point to the location where you want to move the row or column and release the mouse button.

Creating Tables and Lists | 257

Another way to move rows and columns is to cut and paste. You have already learned to cut and paste text. The concept is the same for rows and columns. Select the entire row or column. Right-click to display the shortcut menu and then select the Cut command. Select the column to the right or the row below where you want the copied data to appear and select either Paste Columns or Paste Rows from the shortcut menu.

TAKE NOTE When moving a row, you can click the Home tab and use the Cut and Paste commands in the Clipboard group. However, using the commands on the shortcut menu saves you time by keeping the Table Tools displayed in the Ribbon.

Setting a Table's Horizontal Alignment

A table can be aligned on a page at the left margin, right margin, or in the center. When you insert a table within a report, such as a sales projections table, you can adjust its horizontal alignment on the page to maintain the flow of the report.

SET A TABLE'S HORIZONTAL ALIGNMENT

USE the document that is open from the previous exercise.

1. Position the insertion point anywhere inside the table. On the Layout tab, in the Table group, click the **Select** button. Then click **Select Table** from the menu.
2. On the Layout tab, in the Table group, click **Properties**. The Table Properties dialog box appears.
3. Click the **Table** tab. In the Alignment section, click **Center**, as shown in Figure 8-12.

Figure 8-12

Table Properties dialog box

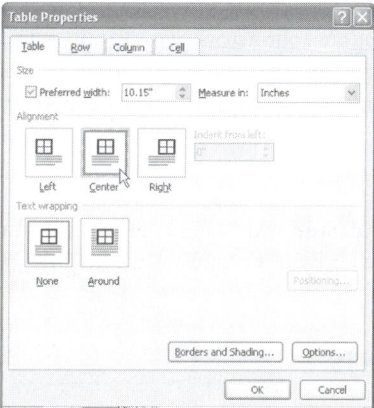

4. Click **OK**. The table is centered horizontally on the page.
5. **SAVE** the document.

   PAUSE. LEAVE the document open to use in the next exercise.

CERTIFICATION READY?
How do you set a table's horizontal alignment?
4.3.2

To set a table's horizontal alignment, click in any table cell to position the insertion point somewhere within the table you want to align. Alternatively, you can select the table. On the Layout tab, in the Table group, click Properties to display the Table Properties dialog box. In the Alignment section, click Left, Center, or Right. If you want to indent the table from the left margin, first choose Left in the Alignment section, then use the upward- and downward-pointing arrow or key in the amount of space you want to indent from the left margin.

Creating a Header Row

When you specify a header row in the Table Style Options group, the row is formatted specially and provides a great place for column headings.

258 | Lesson 8

CREATE A HEADER ROW

USE the document that is open from the previous exercise.

1. Select the first row of the table.
2. On the Layout tab, in the Rows & Columns group, click **Insert Above**. A new blank row is inserted.
3. On the Design tab, in the Table Style Options group, click the **Header Row** checkbox. The header row is formatted differently.
4. Key headings in each cell within the first row of the table, as shown in Figure 8-13.

Figure 8-13

Header row

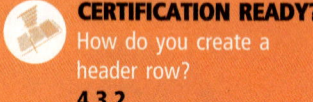

Company Name	Contact Person	Phone Number	Number of Current Open Positions	Position Title	Date Posted	Notes
Contoso Pharmaceuticals	Caron	Rob	469-555-0109	0		
Litware, Inc.	Bankert	Julie	469-555-0167	0		

5. Select the first row of the table.
6. On the Layout tab, in the Data group, click the **Repeat Heading Rows** button. Scroll down and see that the headings have been repeated on the second page.
7. **SAVE** the document.

   PAUSE. LEAVE the document open to use in the next exercise.

TAKE NOTE*

Repeating rows are only visible in Print Layout view or on a printed document.

A **header row** is the first row of the table that is formatted differently, and it usually contains headings for the entire table. When you click the Header Row checkbox in the Header Style Options group, you specify special formatting for the header row.

When you have long tables that are split across two or more pages, you may need to repeat the header row or rows on each page. Similar to the way you practiced in the previous exercise, select the row or rows that you want to repeat and click the Repeat Heading Rows button.

CERTIFICATION READY?
How do you create a header row?
4.3.2

Sorting a Table's Contents

It is often helpful to display data in order. For example, an office contact list that displays employees in alphabetical order by last name would help the reader find information for a particular employee quickly.

SORT A TABLE'S CONTENTS

USE the document that is open from the previous exercise.

1. Select the **Company Name** column.
2. On the Layout tab, in the Data group, click the **Sort** button. The Sort dialog box appears, as shown in Figure 8-14.

Figure 8-14

Sort dialog box

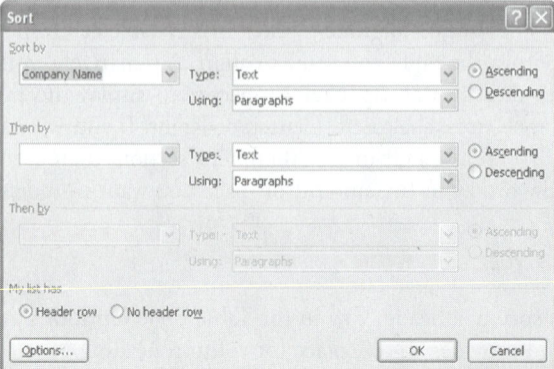

Creating Tables and Lists | 259

3. Click **OK**. Note that the table now appears sorted in ascending alphabetical order by company name.
4. **SAVE** the document.

    PAUSE. LEAVE the document open to use in the next exercise.

To *sort* data means to arrange it alphabetically, numerically, or chronologically. Word can sort text, numbers, or dates in ascending or descending order. ***Ascending*** order sorts text from beginning to end, such as from A to Z, 1 to 10, and January to December. ***Descending*** order sorts text from the end to the beginning, such as from Z to A, 10 to 1, and December to January.

To sort text, numbers, or dates in a column, you first need to select the column. Then click the Sort command on the Layout tab in the Data group to display the Sort dialog box. The column you have selected will be displayed in the Sort By box. Select the type of data you are sorting, then choose ascending or descending order.

The Sort dialog box lets you sort up to three columns of data in a table. For example, you could sort text in one column by last name, and then sort text in another column by first name.

> **CERTIFICATION READY?**
> How do you sort a table's contents?
> 4.2.2

Performing Calculations in Table Cells

Tables provide a professional format for displaying numbers, such as sales figures. In a Word table, you can easily perform basic calculations, such as adding all of the sales figures in a column.

PERFORM CALCULATIONS IN TABLE CELLS

USE the document that is open from the previous exercise.

1. Select the *Woodgrove Bank* row.
2. On the Layout tab, in the Rows & Columns group, click the **Insert Below** button . A new blank row is inserted at the bottom of the table.
3. On the Design tab, in the Table Styles Options group, click the **Total Row** checkbox.
4. Click in the last cell of the *Number of Current Open Positions* column, which should be an empty cell.
5. On the Layout tab, in the Data group, click the **Formula** button. The Formula dialog box appears, as shown in Figure 8-15.

Figure 8-15

Formula dialog box

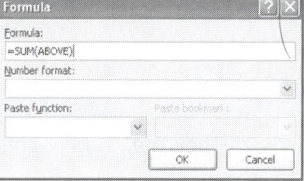

6. Click **OK** to accept the default settings. The sum is displayed in the formula cell.
7. Key **TOTAL** in the first cell of the Total row.
8. **SAVE** the document.

    PAUSE. LEAVE the document open to use in the next exercise.

A *formula* is a set of mathematical instructions used to perform calculations in a table cell. Word provides basic formulas that can be used in tables to perform calculations like totaling sales figures in a column.

To insert a formula, click the cell that will contain the formula and click the Formula button on the Data group. The Formula dialog box appears from which you can key in a formula or insert one from the Paste Functions menu.

A formula must begin with an equal sign (=) for Word to consider any text that follows to be a formula. Next, key a function in all caps or choose one of the 18 functions available from the Paste Functions menu. Functions include SUM, AVERAGE, and COUNT. In parentheses after the function, key the addresses of the cells you want Word to consider in the calculation. You can key ABOVE to tell Word to consider all the cells above the formula cell. You can also specify cell references such as LEFT, RIGHT, or BELOW.

TAKE NOTE

If you want to specify individual cells, combine the column letter with the row number. For example, the cell in the first column in the first row would be A1. This is known as the cell address.

CERTIFICATION READY?
How do you perform calculations in table cells?
4.3.4

Merging and Splitting Table Cells

The ability to merge and split table cells gives you flexibility to create tables that fit your data.

MERGE AND SPLIT TABLE CELLS

USE the document that is open from the previous exercise.

1. Scroll to the header row located at the top of page 1. Select the cell that contains the *Contact Person* heading and the empty cell to the right of it.
2. On the Layout tab, in the Merge group, click the **Merge Cells** button.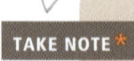
3. In the *Position Title* column, on the *Lucerne Publishing* row, select the cell that contains *Director Marketing VP Public Relations*.
4. On the Layout tab, in the Merge group, click the **Split Cells** button 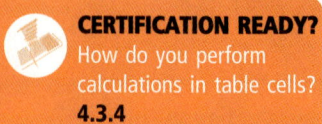. The Split Cells dialog box appears, as shown in Figure 8-16.

Figure 8-16

Split Cells dialog box

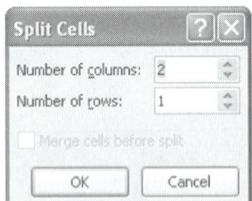

5. Click **OK** to accept the settings as they are. A new column is inserted within the cell.
6. Select *VP Public Relations* and press the Backspace key to delete it.
7. Position the insertion point in the new cell and key **VP Public Relations**.
8. **SAVE** the document.

   PAUSE. LEAVE the document open to use in the next exercise.

ANOTHER WAY

You can access the Merge Cells command on the shortcut menu.

To *merge cells* means to combine two or more cells into one. Merging cells is useful when you want to create a heading that spans several columns. Merging cells is simple. Select the cells you want to merge and click the Merge Cells command, located in the Merge group of the Layout tab.

Creating Tables and Lists | 261

| **CERTIFICATION READY?** How do you merge and split table cells? 4.3.3 |

To ***split cells*** means to divide one cell into two or more cells. You may want to split cells when you have more than one type of data that needs to fit in one cell. To split a cell, select it and click the Split Cells command. The Split Cells dialog box enables you to split a cell vertically into columns or horizontally into rows. Use the upward- and downward-pointing arrows or key in the number you want and click OK.

Changing the Position of Text in a Cell

Word provides you with nine options for aligning text in a cell. These options enable you to control the horizontal and vertical alignment of cells, such as Top Left, Top Center, and Top Right.

➔ CHANGE THE POSITION OF TEXT IN A CELL

USE the document that is open from the previous exercise.

1. Select the first row, with the headings.
2. On the Layout tab, in the Alignment group, click the **Align Bottom Center** button.
3. Select the *Number of Current Open Positions* column and click the **Align Center** button.
4. **SAVE** the document.

   PAUSE. LEAVE the document open to use in the next exercise.

| **CERTIFICATION READY?** How do you change the position of text in a cell? 4.3.5 |

As you just practiced, you can easily align text in a cell. Select the cell or cells you want to align and click one of the nine alignment buttons in the Alignment group on the Layout tab (see Figure 8-8). These alignment buttons let you align the text horizontally and vertically within the cell.

Changing the Direction of Text in a Cell

Rotating text in a cell provides you with additional options for creating interesting and effective tables. Changing the direction of text in a heading can be especially helpful.

➔ CHANGE THE DIRECTION OF TEXT IN A CELL

USE the document that is open from the previous exercise.

1. Select the cell that contains the *Company Name* heading.
2. On the Layout tab, in the Alignment group, click the **Text Direction** button three times to see the rotating text option.
3. **SAVE** the document and **CLOSE** the file.

   PAUSE. LEAVE Word open to use in the next exercise.

| **CERTIFICATION READY?** How do you change the direction of text in a cell? 4.3.5 |

As you just saw, you can change the direction of text in a cell. Clicking the button three times will cycle you through the three available directions.

■ Working with Lists

THE BOTTOM LINE

From lists of supplies needed for a project to To Do lists, everyone uses lists. Bulleted lists, numbered lists, and multilevel lists are used in documents to provide small, quick, user-friendly pieces of information. Word can help you create and format lists to fit your documents.

Creating an Outline-style List

Outline-style lists, also called multilevel lists, are often used to create outlines for long documents. Outline-style lists are also used to create documents such as meeting agendas and legal documents.

CREATE AN OUTLINE-STYLE LIST

The *outline* document is available on the companion CD-ROM.

OPEN *outline* from the data files for this lesson.

1. Position the insertion point on the blank line after the *Discussion Outline* heading.
2. On the Home tab, in the Paragraph group, click the **Multilevel** List button. A menu of list formats appears. Notice that when you position the mouse pointer over the formats, they enlarge and expand.
3. Click the format style in the *Current List* section, as shown in Figure 9-8. The number *1.* is inserted for you.

Figure 9-8

Multilevel List menu

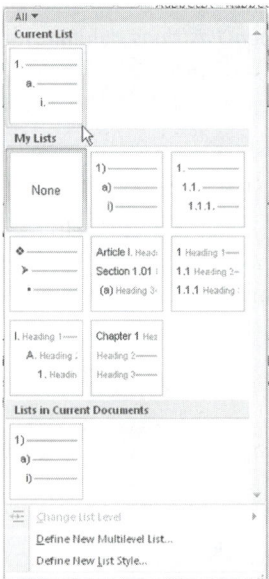

4. Key **Experience** and press the `Enter` key.
5. Key **Communication with Client** and press the `Enter` key.
6. Press the `Tab` key and key **Initial Meeting**. Press the `Enter` key.
7. Press the `Tab` key and key **Identify Position**. Press the `Enter` key.
8. Press the `Tab` key and key **Qualifications**. Press the `Enter` key.
9. Key **Compensation Package** and press the `Enter` key.
10. Key **Time Frame** and press the `Enter` key.
11. Press `Shift` + `Tab` twice to move back two levels. Key **Progress Reporting** and press the `Enter` key.
12. Press `Shift` + `Tab` to move back one level. Key **Methods for Finding Candidates** and press the `Enter` key.
13. Press the `Tab` key. Key **Database** and press the `Enter` key.
14. Key **Contacts** and press the `Enter` key.
15. Key **Networking**.
16. **SAVE** the document as *discussion_outline*.

PAUSE. LEAVE the document open for use in the next exercise.

Creating Tables and Lists | 263

CERTIFICATION READY?
How do you create an outline-style list?
4.2.1

To create a multilevel list, position the insertion point at the location where you want the list to begin. Click the Multilevel List button in the Paragraph group of the Home tab. Select a multilevel list style from the gallery. Key the list, using the Tab key or Shift+Tab to move to different levels.

Sorting a List's Contents

You can sort a single-level list in much the same way as you sort a column in a table.

SORT A LIST'S CONTENTS

USE the document that is open from the previous exercise.

1. Select the bulleted list under the *Philosophy* section.
2. On the Home tab, in the Paragraph group, click the **Sort** button . The Sort Text dialog box appears. Click **OK**.
3. **SAVE** the document.

   PAUSE. LEAVE the document open to use in the next exercise.

You just sorted a bulleted list. The Sort Text dialog box probably looked familiar because it is the same as the one you used for sorting text in a table. Like sorting column content, you can specify to sort lists with text, numbers, or dates in ascending or descending order.

CERTIFICATION READY?
How do you sort a list's contents?
4.2.2

You can sort single-level lists, such as bulleted lists or numbered lists, but if you sort a multi-level list, Word will alphabetize each line and your outline will become jumbled and out of correct order.

Changing a List's Formatting

Word provides several options for changing the look of a list. You can change a list's formatting by changing the type of bullet or numbering that is displayed. Some formats, such as round bullets, work well for most documents. Sometimes, however, you may prefer to use different shaped bullets.

CHANGE A LIST'S FORMATTING

USE the document that is open from the previous exercise.

1. Select the bulleted list.
2. On the Home tab, in the Paragraph group, click the downward-pointing arrow on the **Bullets** button. A menu appears.
3. Click the square bullet format in the Bullet Library, as shown in Figure 8-18.

Figure 8-18

Bullets menu

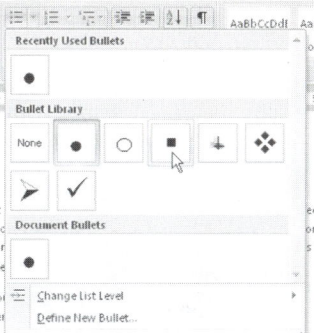

4. Select the multilevel list you keyed earlier.
5. On the Home tab, in the Paragraph group, click the downward-pointing arrow on the **Multilevel List** button. A menu appears.
6. Under List Library, click the second format on the top row.
7. **SAVE** the document and **CLOSE** the file.

   STOP and **CLOSE** Word.

> **CERTIFICATION READY?**
> How do you change a list's formatting?
> 4.2.3

As you just learned, you can change the formatting of lists easily by highlighting the list and choosing a new format from the library of formats on the Bullets, Numbering, or Multilevel List menus. You can also customize bullets, numbering, or multilevel lists with the Define New commands on the menus.

SUMMARY SKILL MATRIX

IN THIS LESSON YOU LEARNED HOW TO:
Insert a Table by Dragging
Use the Insert Table Dialog Box
Draw a Table
Insert a Quick Table
Apply a Quick Style to a Table
Turn Table Style Options On or Off
Resize a Row or Column
Move a Row or Column
Set a Table's Horizontal Alignment
Create a Header Row
Sort a Table's Contents
Perform Calculations in Table Cells
Merge and Split Table Cells
Change the Position of Text in a Cell
Change the Direction of Text in a Cell
Create an Outline-Style List
Sort a List's Contents
Change a List's Formatting

Knowledge Assessment

Matching

Match the term in Column 1 to its description in Column 2.

Column 1

1. sort (h)
2. ascending (g)
3. descending (e)
4. merge cells (a)
5. split cells (i)
6. table (b)
7. header row (j)
8. formulas (f)
9. Quick Tables (c)
10. cells (d)

Column 2

a. to combine two or more cells into one
b. an arrangement of data made up of horizontal rows and vertical columns
c. built-in preformatted tables you can insert and use in your documents
d. the rectangles that are formed when rows and columns intersect
e. sorts text from the end to the beginning (Z-A)
f. a set of mathematical instructions used to perform calculations in a table cell
g. sorts text from the beginning to the end (A-Z)
h. to arrange data alphabetically, numerically, or chronologically
i. to divide one cell into two or more cells
j. the first row of a table that is formatted differently from the rest of the table and usually contains headings for the entire table

True/False

Circle T if the statement is true or F if the statement is false.

T F 1. When you know how many rows and columns you need in a table, the quickest way to create one is by dragging over a grid in the Table menu.

T F 2. Turning Table Style Options on or off has no effect on the Quick Styles in the Table Styles gallery.

T **F** 3. The Total Row is the first row of the table.

T F 4. You can move a column or row using Cut and Paste.

T **F** 5. You can only sort one column of data at a time.

p.260 **T** F 6. A formula must begin with an equal sign (=).

T F 7. You can align text horizontally and vertically in a cell.

T **F** 8. Word gives you four options for changing the direction of text in a cell.

T F 9. You can sort single-level lists, such as bulleted lists or numbered lists, but you should not sort multilevel lists.

T F 10. In a multilevel list, press Shift+Alt to move the insertion point back one level.

Competency Assessment

Project 8-1: Placements Table

Ms. Archer, the executive recruiter, asks you to start working on a placements table that will list the candidates that have been placed, the companies that hired them, and the date of hire.

GET READY. Launch Word if it is not already running.

1. **OPEN** *placements* from the data files for this lesson.
2. Select the last column.
3. On the Layout tab, in the Cell Size group, click the downward-pointing arrow in the **Width** box until it reads .9".
4. Select the first column.
5. On the Layout tab, in the Cell Size group, click the downward-pointing arrow in the **Width** box until it reads .9".
6. Select the *Company* column and change the width to 1.5".
7. Select the *Date of Placement* column and change the width to 1.3".
8. On the Design tab, in the Table Style Options group, click the **Header Row** checkbox and **Banded Rows** checkbox to turn them on.
9. On the Design tab, in the Table Styles group, select the **Medium Shading 1 - Accent 1** style in the fourth row.
10. Select the last column.
11. On the Layout tab, in the Data group, click the **Sort** button. In the Sort dialog box, click **OK**.
12. On the Layout tab, in the Table group, click the **Select** menu and choose **Select Table**.
13. On the Layout tab, in the Table group, click the **Properties** button.
14. In the Table Properties dialog box, click **Center** alignment and click **OK**.
15. Select the first row, the header row.
16. On the Layout tab, in the Alignment group, click **Align Center**.
17. **SAVE** the document as *placements_table* and **CLOSE** the file.

    PAUSE. LEAVE Word open for the next project.

The *placements* document is available on the companion CD-ROM.

Project 8-2: Quarterly Sales Data

Create a table showing the quarterly sales for Coho Vineyard.

1. Create a new blank document.
2. On the Insert tab, in the Tables group, click the **Table** button. Drag to create a table that has 5 columns and 7 rows.
3. Enter the following data in the table:

20XX Sales

	First Quarter	Second Quarter	Third Quarter	Fourth Quarter
Mark Hanson	19,098	25,890	39,088	28,789
Terry Adams	21,890	19,567	32,811	31,562
Max Benson	39,400	35,021	19,789	21,349
Cathan Cook	34,319	27,437	28,936	19,034
Totals				

Creating Tables and Lists | 267

4. Select the first row. On the Layout tab, in the Merge group, click the **Merge Cells** button.
5. With the row still selected, center the title. On the Layout tab, in the Alignment group, click the **Align Center** button.
6. Position the insertion point in the second column, bottom row.
7. On the Layout tab, in the Data group, click the **Formula** button to insert a SUM formula in the *Totals* row. In the Formula dialog box, click **OK**.
8. Insert SUM formulas in the *Totals* row for the *Second Quarter*, *Third Quarter* and *Fourth Quarter* columns.
9. On the Design tab, in the Table Styles Options group, click the **Total Row** checkbox to turn it on. The Header Row, First Column, and Banded Rows options should be turned on already.
10. On the Design tab, in the Table Styles gallery, click the **More** button to display the gallery. On the eleventh row, seventh column, choose the orange **Dark List - Accent 6**.
11. **SAVE** the document as *quarterly_sales* and **CLOSE** the file.
    PAUSE. LEAVE Word open for the next project.

■ Proficiency Assessment

Project 8-3: Sales Table

Ms. Archer asks you to create a sales table including data from the past two years. She can use this table to set goals and project future income.

The ***sales*** document is available on the companion CD-ROM.

1. **OPEN** *sales* from the data files for this lesson.
2. Select the columns with the months and change the text direction for all the months so that they begin at the bottom of the column and extend to the top.
3. Increase the row height of the row with the months to 0.9 inches so that the text all fits on one line.
4. Select all the columns with the months and select AutoFit Contents.
5. Insert SUM formulas in the bottom row for each month.
6. Make sure the **Header Row**, **Total Row**, **Banded Columns**, and **First Column** Table Style Options are the only ones turned on.
7. Merge all the cells in the first row.
8. Merge all the cells in the second row.
9. Choose the **Medium Shading 2 - Accent 2** Table Style format.
10. **SAVE** the document as *sales_table* and **CLOSE** the file.
    PAUSE. LEAVE Word open for the next project.

Project 8-4: Client Contact Table

Ms. Archer needs you to create a quick contact list.

The ***client_table_2*** document is available on the companion CD-ROM.

1. **OPEN** *client_table_2* from the data files for this lesson.
2. Delete the four last columns: *Number of Current Open Positions*, *Position Title*, *Date Posted*, and *Notes*.
3. Change the page orientation to **Portrait**.
4. Change the width of the *Company Name* column to 1.9 inches.

5. Select the *Contoso Pharmaceuticals* row and change its height to 0.2 inches.
6. Delete the *Total* row and turn off the Total Row option in Table Styles Options.
7. Change the style to the blue **Light Grid–Accent 1** style.
8. Center the table horizontally on the page.
9. Select the header row and change its height to 0.4 inches.
10. **SAVE** the document as *new_client_table* and **CLOSE** the file.
    PAUSE. LEAVE Word open for the next project.

■ Mastery Assessment

Project 8-5: Correct the Quarterly Sales Table

The Coho Winery's Quarterly Sales Table includes some formatting mistakes. Find and correct the five problems within this document.

1. **OPEN** *problem* from the data files for this lesson.
2. Find and correct five errors in the table.
3. **SAVE** the document as *fixed_quarterly_sales* and **CLOSE** the file.
   PAUSE. LEAVE Word open for the next project.

*The **problem** document is available on the companion CD-ROM.*

Project 8-6: Soccer Team Roster

As coach of your child's soccer team, you need to distribute a roster to all of your players with contact information, uniform numbers, and assigned snack responsibilities. You received a rough list from the league and you would like to convert it to table form. You haven't converted text to a table before, but you're confident you can do it.

1. **OPEN** *soccer_team* from the data files for this lesson.
2. Select all the text.
3. On the Insert tab, in the Tables group, click the **Table** button. Select **Convert Text to Table** from the menu.
4. In the Convert Text to Table dialog box, key **4** in the Number of Columns box. Click the **Commas** button under the Separate Text At section and click **OK**.
5. Use what you learned in this lesson to format the table. Start by removing extra spaces or words, adjusting column widths, and aligning text. Sort the table by snack date, insert a header row with headings for each column, and choose a Table Style format.
6. **SAVE** the document as *soccer_roster* and **CLOSE** the file.
   STOP and **CLOSE** Word.

*The **soccer_team** document is available on the companion CD-ROM.*

INTERNET READY

Search the Internet for job openings that interest you. Create a table to record data about at least five positions. Include columns for the job title, salary, location, contact person, and any other information that would help you in a job search. Use what you have learned in this chapter to format the table in an attractive way that you could easily maintain.

Workplace Ready

Creating Tables and Performing Calculations in Word

Most everyone working in business is familiar with the many advantages of using Excel for creating tables and performing calculations. What some people may not realize is that Word provides many of these same capabilities. By creating a table and performing basic calculations directly within a Word document, you can turn an ordinary word processing document into a comprehensive business illustration.

Having just completed your college education, you are excited to begin your new career with Woodgrove Bank. As a Banking Associate in the Mortgage Department, one of your main responsibilities will be to produce a monthly Mortgage status memo. This memo will include monthly information on the number of new mortgage applications, the dollar amount of each, and their current status.

Presenting this information in a table format will provide for the most appealing design. However, you also need to include a brief introductory paragraph recapping the monthly information, as well as calculations for the total dollar amount of new mortgage applications. This report should be sent out in a memo format. By using Word, you can easily meet all of your objectives in just one program.

A co-worker reminds you that Word provides several memo templates, and you decide to choose one when initially creating your document. Memo templates provide replaceable text for To, From, Subject, Date and CC information. Below this, you can enter your monthly recap paragraph. Finally, you can use Word's Table options to create and format a table with the desired number of columns and rows.

Once the table has been created and the information has been entered into the appropriate cells, you can use Word's Table Layout and Design tools to enhance your table's appearance. Word provides many of the same capabilities you would find in Excel, such as merging cells, splitting cells, aligning text, auto-fitting text, sorting and much more. You can also insert formulas to perform basic calculations.

With so many possibilities, Word is a true all-in-one business tool.

INTEROFFICE MEMORANDUM

TO:	WOODGROVE BANK MORTGAGE DEPARTMENT
FROM:	SHAUN BEASLEY
SUBJECT:	OCTOBER MORTGAGE STATUS MEMO
DATE:	2/4/20XX
CC:	FILE

OCTOBER MORTGAGE STATUS MEMO

Although we saw a slight decrease in the number of new mortgage applications in October, the total dollar amount of new mortgage applications actually increased over the previous month. This is likely due to the increase in new and existing home sale prices throughout the tri-state region.

Woodgrove Bank October 20XX Mortgage Statistics		
New Mortgages	Mortgage $ Amount	Current Status
Alexander, Michelle	$149,000	Approved
Bischoff, Jim & Denise	$234,900	Pending
Harrington, Mark	$210,500	Denied
MacDonald, Scott	$180,000	Approved
Steele, Bill & Laura	$205,500	Approved
Wood, John & Karen	$199,900	Pending
TOTAL $ AMOUNT	**$1,179,800**	

9 Adding Pictures and Shapes to a Document

LESSON SKILL MATRIX

Using SmartArt Graphics — 271	Students will learn how to use SmartArt graphics.
Inserting and Resizing a Clip Art Picture — 274	Students will learn how to insert and resize a clip art picture.
Inserting a Picture from a File — 275	Students will learn how to insert a picture from a file.
Inserting Shapes — 278	Students will learn how to insert shapes.
Creating a Flow Chart — 280	Students will learn how to create a flow chart.
Adding Text to a Shape — 281	Students will learn how to add text to a shape.
Cropping, Resizing, Scaling, and Rotating a Picture — 280	Students will learn how to crop, resize, scale, and rotate a picture.
Applying a Quick Style to a Picture — 284	Students will learn how to apply a Quick Style to a picture.
Adjusting a Picture's Brightness, Contrast, and Color — 286	Students will learn how to adjust a picture's brightness, contrast, and color.
Arranging Text Around a Picture — 287	Students will learn how to arrange text around a picture.
Compressing a Picture — 288	Students will learn how to compress a picture.
Resetting a Picture — 281	Students will learn how to reset a picture.

You work as a travel agent at Margie's Travel, a full-service travel agency that specializes in providing services to senior citizens. Margie's Travel offers tours, cruises, adventure activities, group travel, and vacation packages all geared toward seniors. On the job, you frequently need to enhance a document with graphics, pictures, or drawings. Word makes it easy to provide eye-catching travel information, signs, brochures, and flyers using SmartArt, clip art, and shapes. In this lesson, you will learn how to insert SmartArt graphics, clip art, pictures, and shapes containing text in a document. You will work with pictures to resize; scale; crop; rotate; apply a Quick Style; adjust color, brightness, and contrast; and compress.

KEY TERMS
clip art
compress
crop
embedded object
floating object
inline object
linked object
reset
SmartArt graphics

Adding Pictures and Shapes to a Document | 271

Software Orientation

Illustrations Group on Insert Tab

The Insert tab, shown in Figure 9-1, contains a group of features that you can use to add graphics to your document. The Illustrations group has options for several types of graphics you can use to enhance your Word documents—Shapes, SmartArt, charts, pictures, and clip art.

Figure 9-1

Illustrations group on the Insert tab

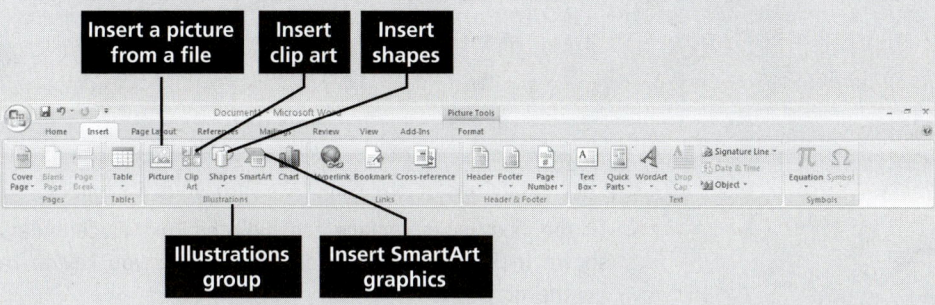

Use this figure as a reference throughout this lesson, as well as the rest of the book.

Inserting a Picture

THE BOTTOM LINE SmartArt, pictures, and clip art are graphics that can be inserted into a document and then formatted using a variety of options.

Using SmartArt Graphics

SmartArt graphics, designer-quality illustrations, can be quickly and easily created by choosing from among many different available layouts, depending on what information you want to convey. SmartArt graphics can be used to illustrate a process, hierarchy, cycle, or relationship.

USE SMARTART GRAPHICS

GET READY. Before you begin these steps, be sure to launch Microsoft Office Word 2007 and **OPEN** a new, blank document.

1. On the Insert tab, in the Illustrations group, click **SmartArt**. The Choose a SmartArt Graphic dialog box appears.

2. Click the **Relationship** category and then click **Equation** as shown in Figure 9-2.

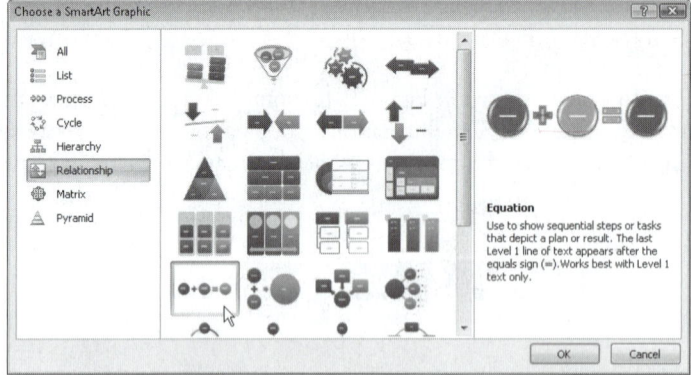

Figure 9-2

Choose a SmartArt graphic dialog box

3. Click **OK** to insert the SmartArt into your document.
4. In the Text pane, replace the bulleted text placeholders with the information shown in Figure 9-3. Notice how the text you key in the placeholder also appears on the graphic.

Figure 9-3

Replace SmartArt graphic text with your own

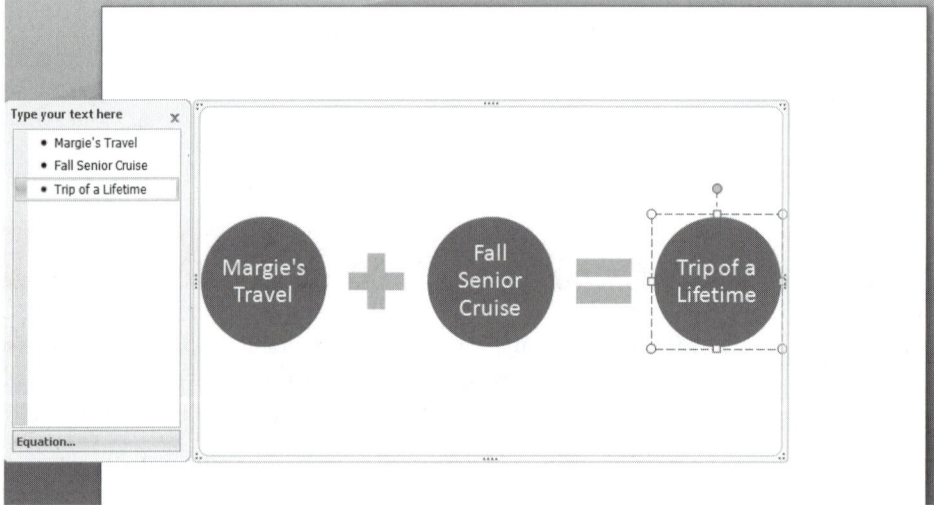

5. SmartArt Tools are available to make changes to SmartArt graphics. On the Design tab, in the Layouts group, click **Vertical Equation**.
6. Click the **Change Colors** button and then click **Colorful-Accent Colors**, shown in Figure 9-4. Your document should also look similar to the figure.

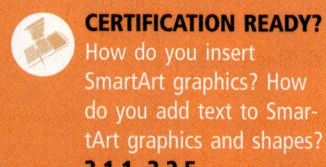

CERTIFICATION READY?
How do you insert SmartArt graphics? How do you add text to SmartArt graphics and shapes?
3.1.1, 3.2.5

Adding Pictures and Shapes to a Document | 273

Figure 9-4

SmartArt Tools and document

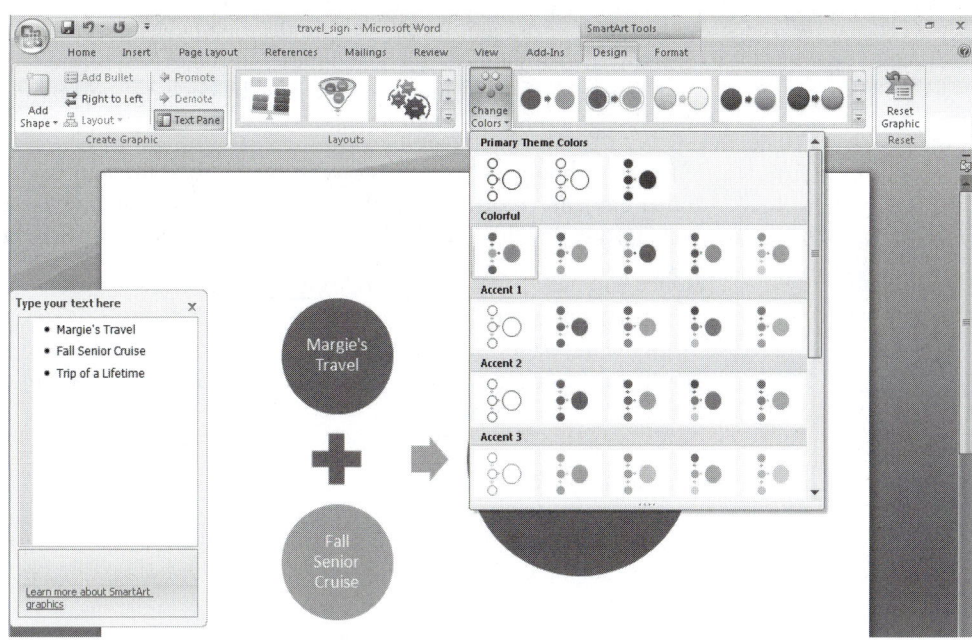

7. **SAVE** the document as *travel_sign* and **CLOSE** the file.
   PAUSE. LEAVE Word open to use in the next exercise.

 SmartArt graphics are visual representations of information that can help communicate your message or ideas more effectively. Table 9-1 gives some examples of the type of information you can display with each category of SmartArt graphics.

Table 9-1

SmartArt graphic categories

Type	Purpose
List	Show nonsequential or grouped blocks of information
Process	Show a progression of steps in a process, timeline, task, or workflow
Cycle	Show a continuing sequence of stages, tasks, or events in a circular flow
Hierarchy	Show a decision tree or create an organization chart
Relationship	Illustrate connections or interlocking ideas; show related or contrasting concepts
Matrix	Show how parts relate to a whole
Pyramid	Show proportional, foundation-based, containment, overlapping, or interconnected relationships

When a SmartArt graphic is selected, the Text pane appears to the left. As you key text to replace the placeholders, the text appears in the corresponding location on the Text pane. You can choose to show or hide the Text pane by clicking the Text Pane button in the Create Graphic group on the Design tab.

After you choose a layout, it is easy to switch to a different layout. Most of your text and other content, colors, styles, effects, and text formatting are automatically carried over to the new layout. Try different layouts until you find one that works best with your message.

Once you have inserted a SmartArt graphic, you can alter it using the SmartArt Tools. There are many options for changing the graphic. For example, you can add shapes to the graphic, alter the direction, change the layout, and change the colors. At any time if you want to revert to the original graphic, click the Reset Graphic button to discard the formatting changes you have made.

Inserting and Resizing a Clip Art Picture

To illustrate a specific concept in your document, you can insert clip art pictures—including drawings, movies, sounds, or stock photography.

INSERT AND RESIZE A CLIP ART PICTURE

OPEN a new, blank Word document.

1. Centered on the page, key **Explore the Globe** in Cambria, 48 pt. font.
2. Press **Enter**.
3. On the Insert tab, in the Illustrations group, click **Clip Art**. The Clip Art pane appears to the right of your document.
4. In the Search For box, key **travel**.
5. In the Search In box, click the downward-pointing arrow and click **Everywhere**.
6. In the Results Should Be box, click the downward-pointing arrow and select only the **Clip Art** checkbox.
7. Click **Go**.
8. In the Results pane, click the clip art with **baggage and Earth**, as shown in Figure 9-5.

Figure 9-5

Clip art pane

Adding Pictures and Shapes to a Document | 275

9. Hold the [Shift] key (to maintain the proportions of the clip art picture) as you click and drag the **bottom right sizing handle** of the clip art to make it larger, as shown in Figure 9-6.

Figure 9-6

Resizing clip art

X REF

Besides resizing, there are many other ways to format clip art. You will learn to use the various Picture Tools options later in this lesson.

10. **SAVE** the document as *travel_flyer*.

PAUSE. LEAVE the document open to use in the next exercise.

Clip art refers to picture files that can be inserted into a document. In the Clip Art task pane, you can also search for photographs, movies, and sounds. To include any of those media types, select the checkbox next to each in the *Results Should Be* box.

In the Clip Art pane, you can click Organize Clips... to open the Microsoft Clip Organizer, shown in Figure 9-7. From here, clips can be arranged and categorized into collections for easy access. You can also add, delete, copy, and move clips, as well as change keywords and captions.

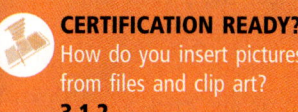

CERTIFICATION READY?
How do you insert pictures from files and clip art?
3.1.2

Figure 9-7

Microsoft Clip Organizer

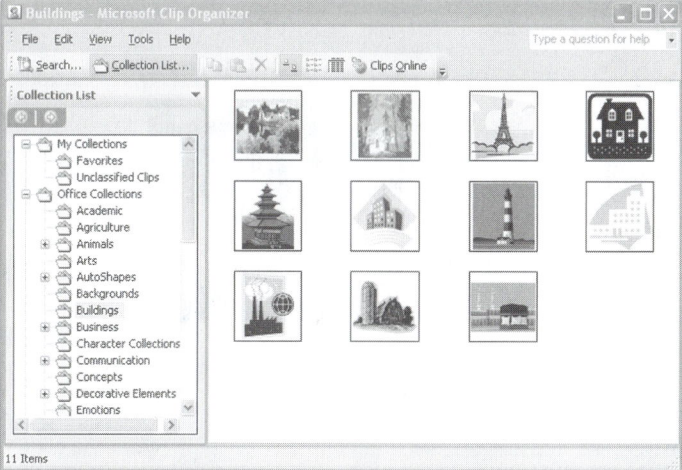

Inserting a Picture from a File

Additional sources of graphics include photographs or pictures that you might have stored on your computer. If you have your own picture that you would like to add to a document, you can insert it from a file.

INSERT A PICTURE FROM A FILE

USE the document that is open from the previous exercise.

1. On the line below the clip art, centered on the page, key **Picture Yourself Here** in Cambria, 28 pt. font.
2. Press **Enter**.
3. On the Insert tab, in the Illustrations group, click **Picture**. The Insert Picture dialog box appears, similar to Figure 9-8. (Your screen will look different, depending on the pictures that you have in the My Pictures folder on your computer.)

Figure 9-8

Insert Picture dialog box

 **CD**

The **beach** picture file is available on the companion CD-ROM.

4. Navigate to where the data files for this lesson are located. Select the picture file named *beach*.
5. Click **Insert**.
6. Hold the **Shift** key (to maintain the proportions of the picture) as you click and drag the **bottom right sizing handle** of the picture to make it smaller. Reduce the size of the picture until the entire document fits on one page. The bottom half of the document should look similar to Figure 9-9.

Figure 9-9

Picture inserted into a document

 REF

You will learn more about how to format a picture using Picture Tools later in this lesson.

Adding Pictures and Shapes to a Document | 277

CERTIFICATION READY?
How do you insert pictures from files and clip art?
3.1.2

7. **SAVE** the document.

   PAUSE. LEAVE the document open to use in the next exercise.

When you insert a picture into a document, Word makes it an ***embedded object*** by default, which means that it becomes part of the document. Another option is to insert the pictures as a ***linked object***, which creates a connection between the document and picture. This can reduce the file size of the document. In the Insert Picture dialog box, click the arrow next to Insert and then click Link to File.

You can copy or move a picture just as you would any other object or text. Select the picture and then choose the Copy, Cut, or Paste command.

■ SOFTWARE ORIENTATION

Shapes Menu and Drawing Tools Format

When you click the Shapes button in the Illustrations group, the Shapes menu is displayed, as shown in Figure 9-10. This menu contains options for a variety of ready-made shapes, including lines, arrows, stars, and banners. After inserting a shape, you can use the Drawing Tools, shown in Figure 9-11, to format a shape's style, fill, color, outline, and many other attributes.

Figure 9-10

Shapes menu

Figure 9-11

Drawing Tools

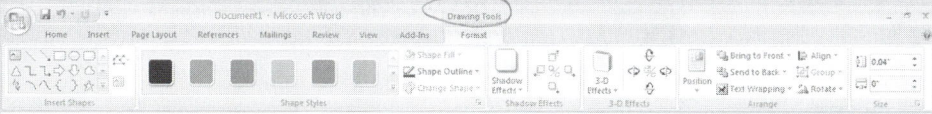

Use these figures as a reference throughout this lesson, as well as the rest of the book.

Adding Shapes

THE BOTTOM LINE

A drawing refers to a single drawing object or multiple drawing objects that are grouped together. A drawing object can include lines, arrows, callouts, stars, banners, or any other shape.

When inserting a drawing object in Word, you can place it in a drawing canvas—a frame-like boundary between the drawing and the rest of the document. Because a drawing canvas can help keep multiple drawing objects together, it is best to use one when adding more than one shape to your illustration—for example, if you are creating a flowchart.

Inserting Shapes

With a few simple clicks, you can insert a variety of different shapes into your Word document. There are many ready-made shapes to choose from—lines, basic shapes, block arrows, flowchart symbols, callouts, stars, and banners.

⊙ INSERT SHAPES

USE the document that is open from the previous exercise.

1. Select the *Picture Yourself Here* text and the picture below it.
2. On the Home tab, in the Paragraph group, click the **Align Text Right** button.
3. On the Insert tab, in the Illustrations group, click the **Shapes** button to display the Shapes menu.
4. In the Block Arrows section, click the **Curved Right Arrow** shape. The insertion point turns into a crosshair (+).
5. Place the crosshair in front of the word *Picture*. Click and drag downward and toward the chairs on the left of the photograph to create the arrow shown in Figure 9-12.

Figure 9-12

Block arrow shape

TROUBLESHOOTING If the shape you are drawing does not turn out the right size the first time, you can adjust the shape by selecting it and then dragging one of the sizing handles.

6. On the Insert tab, in the Illustrations group, click the **Shapes** button to display the Shapes menu.
7. In the Basic Shapes section, click the **Smiley Face** shape.

Adding Pictures and Shapes to a Document | 279

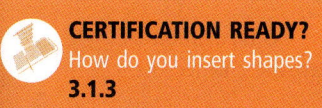

CERTIFICATION READY?
How do you insert shapes?
3.1.3

8. Place the crosshair (+) inside the curve of the arrow. Click and drag to create a small smiley face that fits in the space available there.
9. **SAVE** the document and **CLOSE** the file.

   PAUSE. LEAVE Word open to use in the next exercise.

The shapes on the Shapes menu are all inserted the same way. Click to select the one you want to insert. Then click in the document where you want to begin drawing and drag until the shape is the size and shape you want.

Drawing Tools provides many options for formatting shapes. Click the More button in the Shape Styles group to see the Quick Style options for changing the overall visual style of the shape, as shown in Figure 9-13.

Figure 9-13

Shape Styles gallery

You can change the look of your shape by changing its fill or by adding effects, such as shadows, glows, reflections, soft edges, bevels, and 3-D rotations. For example, click the Shadow Effects button to see all the options for applying a shadow to your shape. Or, click the 3-D Effects button to enhance your shape with a 3-D effect, as shown in Figure 9-14. There are so many ways to format a shape that it is not possible to cover them all here—but, do not be afraid to experiment.

Figure 9-14

3-D Effects button and menu

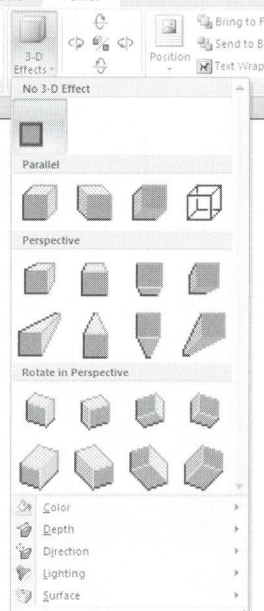

Creating a Flowchart

Q.5

A flowchart can be created using the flowchart symbols available on the Shapes menu. You can then connect the symbols using a variety of line options—arrows, connectors, curves, freeform, and even scribbles.

  CREATE A FLOWCHART

OPEN a new, blank Word document.

1. At the top of the document, centered on the page, key **Margie's Travel** in Cambria, 24 pt. font. Press Enter.
2. Centered on the page, key **Organization Chart** in Cambria, 20 pt. font. Press Enter.
3. On the Insert tab, in the Illustrations group, click the **Shapes** button.
4. At the bottom of the Shapes menu, click **New Drawing Canvas**. The frame of a drawing canvas appears on the document.
5. On the Insert tab, in the Illustrations group, click the **Shapes** button.
6. In the Flowchart section, click the **Flowchart: Alternate Process** symbol.
7. At the top center of the drawing canvas, click and drag the crosshair (+) to create a shape that is approximately 2 inches wide by 1 inch high.
8. Repeat steps 5–7 to draw the same shape in the bottom left of the drawing canvas.
9. On the Insert tab, in the Illustrations group, click the **Shapes** button.
10. In the Lines section, click the **Elbow Arrow Connector** symbol.
11. Click the crosshair (+) on the bottom center of the top shape and drag to the top center of the bottom shape, as shown in Figure 9-15.

Figure 9-15

Flowchart shapes and connector

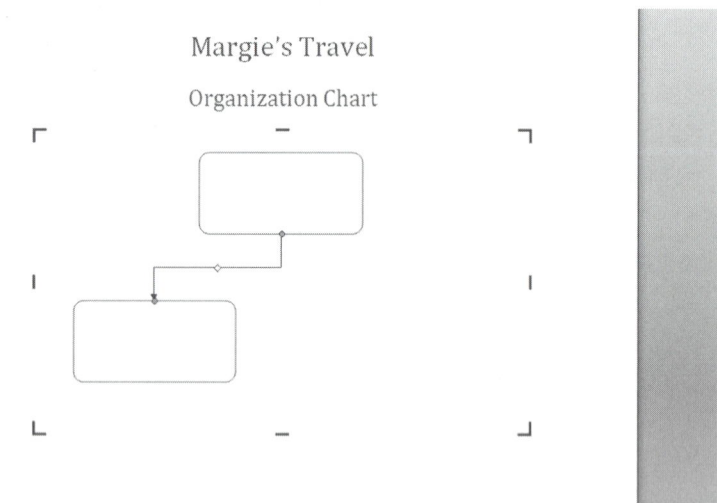

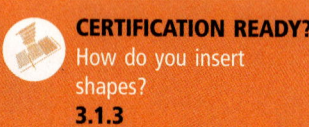

CERTIFICATION READY?
How do you insert shapes?
3.1.3

12. **SAVE** the document as *travel_flowchart*.

   PAUSE. LEAVE the document open to use in the next exercise.

Adding Pictures and Shapes to a Document | 281

Flowcharts are useful for creating process documents, decision trees, or small organization charts. Because a flowchart is comprised of multiple drawing objects, it is easier to arrange them by first clicking New Drawing Canvas on the Shapes menu to insert a document canvas.

Insert flowchart symbols and size them just as you would any other shape. To connect them, use the connector options in the Lines section of the Shapes menu.

 To create organization charts that are already formatted and arranged, choose a SmartArt graphic from the Hierarchy category.

Adding Text to a Shape

You can add text to shapes and then format or edit the text just as you would text in a document. You can also use the Text Box Tools to format the text box just as you would a shape.

 ADD TEXT TO A SHAPE

USE the document that is open from the previous exercise.

1. Select the top box.
2. On the Format tab, in the Insert Shapes group, click the **Edit Text** button. An insertion point appears within the shape.
3. Key **Josh Barnhill**, press **Enter**, and key **President**.
4. Select the text and use the Mini toolbar that appears to center the text and change it to **14 pt**.
5. Select the bottom box.
6. On the Format tab, in the Insert Shapes group, click the **Edit Text** button. An insertion point appears within the shape.
7. Key **Jeanne Bourne**, press **Enter**, and key **Vice President**.
8. Select the text and use the Mini toolbar that appears to **center** the text and change it to **12 pt**.
9. Click outside the drawing canvas. Your document should look similar to Figure 9-16.

Figure 9-16

Shapes with text inserted

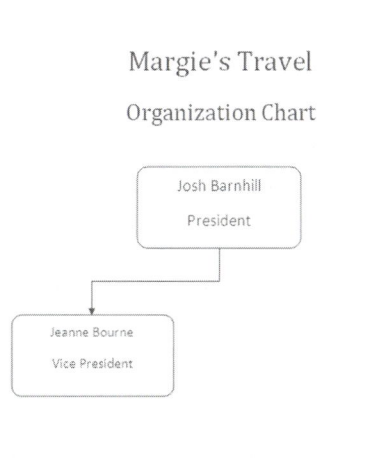

282 | Lesson 9

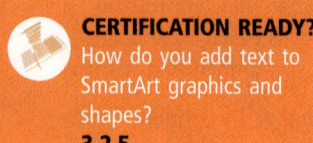

CERTIFICATION READY?
How do you add text to SmartArt graphics and shapes?
3.2.5

10. **SAVE** the document and **CLOSE** the file.

PAUSE. LEAVE Word open to use in the next exercise.

To add text to a flowchart symbol, or any shape, select the symbol or shape and then click the Edit Text button in the Insert Shapes group on the Format tab. An insertion point appears within the shape. After keying text, you can format or edit it just as you would regular text. The Text Box Tools, shown in Figure 9-17, are available at the top of the screen for formatting the text box.

Figure 9-17

Text Box Tools

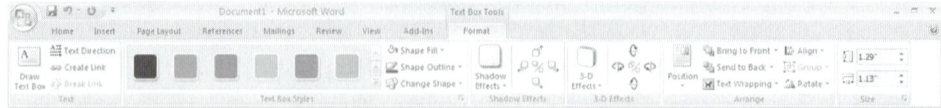

TAKE NOTE *

If the shape does not allow for text, such as a line, then the Edit Text button will be unavailable.

Software Orientation

Picture Tools

The Picture Tools tab, shown in Figure 9-18, is a contextual command tab that appears only when a picture is selected. Many formatting options are available for you to make changes, including borders, effects, cropping, and resizing.

Q.4

Figure 9-18

Picture Tools

Use this figure as a reference throughout this lesson, as well as the rest of the book.

Formatting Pictures

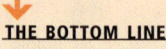

THE BOTTOM LINE

To format a picture, first select the picture. Then you can choose from the many Picture Tools options, such as adjusting the contrast, rotating the picture, or compressing the picture to reduce the size.

Q.6 (P.292)

Cropping, Resizing, Scaling, and Rotating a Picture

Q.5

Cropping a picture enables you to remove unwanted parts. You can resize a picture by changing the height and width measurements or scale the picture by changing the height and width percentages. You can rotate a picture to change its position.

Adding Pictures and Shapes to a Document | 283

CROP, RESIZE, SCALE, AND ROTATE A PICTURE

OPEN a new, blank Word document.

1. Key **Visit the Palm Trees of California** centered on the first line of the document.
2. On the Home tab, in the Styles group, click the **More** button.
3. Click the **Title** option in the Quick Style gallery to apply the style and then press Enter.
4. On the Insert tab, in the Illustrations group, click the **Picture** button.
5. Navigate to the data files for this lesson, select the *palms* picture, and click **Insert**. The picture should be selected and the Picture Tools displayed.
6. On the Format tab, in the Size group, click the **Crop** button. The insertion point becomes a cropping tool and cropping handles appear on the edges of the picture.
7. Position the cropping tool over the **top right cropping handle**. Then click and drag down and left until it is past the street signs in the picture, as shown in Figure 9-19.

The *palms* picture file is available on the companion CD-ROM.

Figure 9-19

Cropping a picture

8. Release the mouse button to crop the picture. Click the **Crop** button again to remove the cropping handles.
9. On the Format tab, click the **Size Dialog Box Launcher** to display the Size dialog box, similar to Figure 9-20.

Figure 9-20

Size dialog box

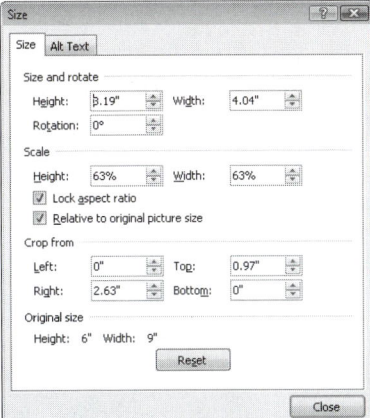

284 | Lesson 9

10. In the Size and Rotate section, click the **Height downward-pointing arrow** until = **3"** appears. Click the **Rotation downward-pointing arrow** until **350°** appears.

 **ANOTHER WAY** You can also rotate a picture by selecting it and dragging the rotation handle—the round arrow that appears at the top of a selected picture or shape—in the direction you want to rotate the picture.

11. In the Scale section, both checkboxes should be selected. Click the **Height upward-pointing arrow** until **65%** appears.
12. Click the **Close** button.
13. **SAVE** the document as *travel_palms*.

    PAUSE. LEAVE the document open to use in the next exercise.

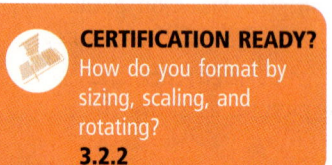 **CERTIFICATION READY?**
How do you format by sizing, scaling, and rotating?
3.2.2

When you *crop* a picture, you trim the horizontal or vertical edges to get rid of unwanted areas. To crop a picture, select the picture and click the Crop button. The insertion point becomes a cropping tool and cropping handles appear on the edges of the picture. Drag the cropping handles until only the portion of the picture you want to remain is outlined. Release the mouse button and then click the Crop button again to remove the cropping handles. You can also crop by precise measurements using the Size box.

To resize, scale, rotate, or crop a picture, click the Size Dialog Box Launcher. In the Size dialog box, you can either resize the picture by changing the exact measurements of the height and width or rescale it by changing the height and width percentages. If the Lock Aspect Ratio box is selected, the width will change proportionally when you change the height or vice versa. If the Relative to Original Picture Size box is selected, the size and scale numbers are displayed with respect to the original size of the picture, which is shown at the bottom. To reset a picture to its original size, click the Reset button.

You can also rotate a picture right 90° or left 90°, flip it horizontally, or flip it vertically by clicking the Rotate button in the Arrange group, as shown in Figure 9-21.

Figure 9-21

Rotate button and menu

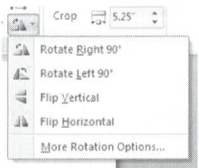

Applying a Quick Style to a Picture

Applying a Quick Style to a picture is similar to applying a Quick Style to text. You can choose from the preformatted options available in the gallery.

APPLY A QUICK STYLE TO A PICTURE

USE the document that is open from the previous exercise.

1. To display the Picture Tools, select the picture if it is not already selected,.
2. On the Format tab, in the Picture Styles group, click the **More** button to display the Quick Style gallery, shown in Figure 9-22.

Adding Pictures and Shapes to a Document | 285

Figure 9-22

Picture Quick Style gallery

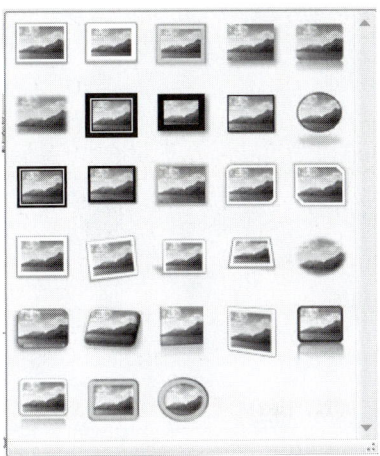

3. Click **Bevel Rectangle**. Your document should look similar to Figure 9-23.

Figure 9-23

Picture with Quick Style applied

4. **SAVE** the document.

   PAUSE. LEAVE the document open to use in the next exercise.

CERTIFICATION READY?
How do you apply QuickStyles?
3.2.3

You can use a Quick Style to add interest to your picture. Some styles are shown in the Picture Styles group. Click the More button to see the other options. In the Picture Styles group, you can also add a border using the Picture Border menu, shown in Figure 9-24, to specify the color, width, and line style for the outline of the picture. Or you can add an effect using the Picture Effects menu, shown in Figure 9-25. To see an effect without actually applying it, just hover the mouse cursor over the option for a live preview.

Figure 9-24

Picture Border menu

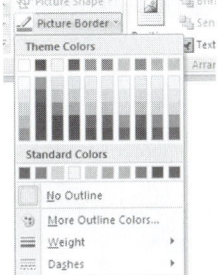

Figure 9-25

Picture Effects menu

Adjusting a Picture's Brightness, Contrast, and Color

Although Word does not have all the advanced features of a stand-alone photo editing program, it does offer many ways for you to make adjustments to a picture—including changing a picture's brightness, contrast, and color.

ADJUST A PICTURE'S BRIGHTNESS, CONTRAST, AND COLOR

USE the document that is open from the previous exercise.

1. To display the Adjust Tools, select the picture if it is not already selected.
2. On the Format tab, in the Adjust group, click the **Brightness** button to display the menu shown in Figure 9-26.

Figure 9-26

Brightness menu

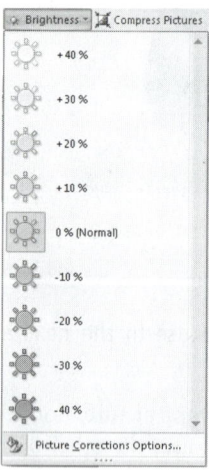

3. Click **+10%** to increase the brightness of the picture.
4. On the Format tab, in the Adjust group, click the **Contrast** button to display the menu.
5. Click **−20%** to decrease the contrast of the picture.
6. On the Format tab, in the Adjust group, click the **Recolor** button to display the menu shown in Figure 9-27.

Adding Pictures and Shapes to a Document | 287

Figure 9-27

Recolor menu

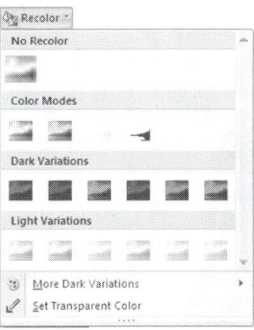

7. In the Dark Variations section, click the **Accent color 3 Dark** option.
8. **SAVE** the document.

   PAUSE. LEAVE the document open to use in the next exercise.

CERTIFICATION READY?
How do you set contrast, brightness, and coloration?
3.2.4

You can quickly make adjustments to a picture that has been inserted into a document by using the Brightness, Contrast, and Recolor menus. On the Brightness and Contrast menus, choose the percentage that you want the picture to vary from normal. On the Recolor menu, turn the picture into a grayscale, sepia-toned, washed-out, or black-and-white version or apply a light or dark color variation.

Arranging Text Around a Picture

The Text Wrapping command changes the way text wraps around the picture or other drawing object.

ARRANGE TEXT AROUND A PICTURE

USE the document that is open from the previous exercise.

1. Place the insertion point on the line below the picture and key the following text:

   Our charming desert cities, warm sun, and hot mineral springs make California the perfect vacation destination. So come visit the palm trees and experience this magical place.

2. To display the Adjust Tools, select the picture if it is not already selected.
3. On the Format tab, in the Arrange group, click the **Text Wrapping** button to display the menu shown in Figure 9-28.

Figure 9-28

Text Wrapping options

4. Click **Square**. All the text moves to the right, including the title.
5. Select the picture and drag it downward slightly until the title returns to the top and all the text is positioned on the right of the picture, as shown in Figure 9-29.

Figure 9-29

Text wrapped around a picture

6. **SAVE** the document.

PAUSE. LEAVE the document open to use in the next exercise.

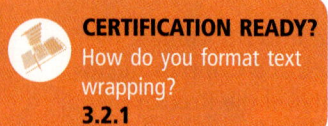

To configure the picture as an ***inline object*** that moves along with the text around it, select the In Line with Text option. Or, you can choose a text wrapping style that changes a picture to a ***floating object*** that can be positioned precisely on the page, including behind or in front of text.

Click More Layout Options on the Text Wrapping menu to open the Advanced Layout dialog box, shown in Figure 9-30.

Figure 9-30

Advanced Layout dialog box

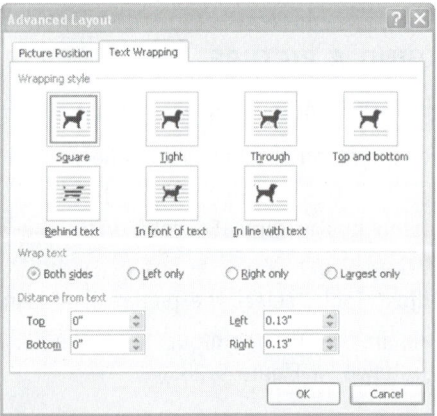

In this dialog box, you can choose precisely how to wrap the text and determine the distance between the text and the picture. You can also click the Picture Position tab to choose options for exactly how you want to position the picture on the page vertically or horizontally.

Compressing a Picture

When you compress a picture, it reduces the file size and makes documents easier to manage.

COMPRESS A PICTURE

USE the document that is open from the previous exercise.

1. To display the Adjust Tools, select the picture if it is not already selected.
2. On the Format tab, in the Adjust group, click the **Compress Pictures** button to display the Compress Pictures dialog box, shown in Figure 9-31.

Adding Pictures and Shapes to a Document | 289

Figure 9-31

Compress Pictures dialog box

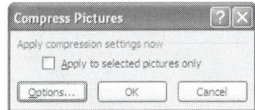

3. Click the **Options** button to display the Compression Settings dialog box, shown in Figure 9-32.

Figure 9-32

Compression Settings dialog box

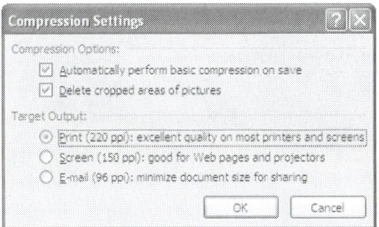

4. In the Target Output section, select **E-mail (96 ppi)**.
5. Click **OK**.
6. In the Compress Pictures dialog box, select the **Apply to Selected Pictures Only** checkbox.
7. Click **OK**.

> **TROUBLESHOOTING**
> You will not see the compression take place. To verify that the file is smaller after compressing pictures, you can compare the document's properties before and after performing the command. Keep in mind that if your picture is already smaller than the compression option chosen, no compression will occur.

8. **SAVE** the document.

   PAUSE. LEAVE the document open to use in the next exercise.

CERTIFICATION READY?
How do you compress pictures?
3.2.6

When you *compress* a picture, you decrease the size of the file by reducing the resolution. Inserting large picture files can make a document difficult to manage. You can work more efficiently by compressing the pictures to reduce the file size of the document. This helps save room on your hard disk, enables documents to open and save more quickly, and reduces download time for files you plan to share.

In the Compression Settings dialog box, you can choose to reduce the resolution to print, screen, or email quality, depending on what you plan to do with the pictures. You can also choose to delete cropped areas of pictures, which discards the extra information for the hidden parts of the picture that are still stored in the file after the picture is cropped.

Resetting a Picture

> Resetting a picture will discard all formatting changes you made to the picture, including changes to contrast, color, brightness, and style.

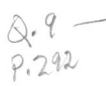 **RESET A PICTURE**

USE the document that is open from the previous exercise.

1. To display the Picture Tools, select the picture if it is not already selected.
2. On the Format tab, in the Adjust group, click **Reset Picture**. Formatting changes you made to the picture are discarded.

3. **SAVE** the document as *travel_reset* and **CLOSE** the file.
   STOP and **CLOSE** Word.

Q.10 P.292

Reset a picture when you want to discard all the formatting changes that you made. You can undo changes that you made to a picture's contrast, color, or brightness using the Reset Picture command. Or, you can choose to discard only certain formatting changes. In the Picture Styles group, click the dialog box launcher to open the Format Picture dialog box. To reset just the brightness and contrast, click Picture and then click the Reset Picture button. Or, to remove a style that you applied, click 3-D Format to display the options shown in Figure 9-33. Then click the Reset button.

Figure 9-33

Format Shape dialog box

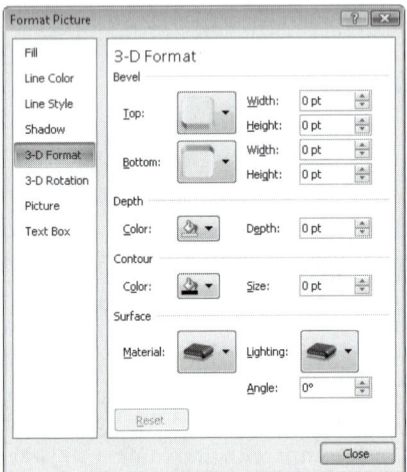

SUMMARY SKILL MATRIX

IN THIS LESSON YOU LEARNED HOW TO:
Use SmartArt Graphics
Insert and Resizing a Clip Art Picture
Insert a Picture from a File
Insert Shapes
Create a Flow Chart
Add Text to a Shape
Crop, Resize, Scale, and Rotate a Picture
Apply a Quick Style to a Picture
Adjust a Picture's Brightness, Contrast, and Color
Arrange Text Around a Picture
Compress a Picture
Reset a Picture

Adding Pictures and Shapes to a Document | 291

Knowledge Assessment

Fill in the Blank

Complete the following sentences by writing the correct word or words in the blanks provided.

1. <u>SmartArt</u> graphics can be used to illustrate a process, hierarchy, cycle, or relationship. P. 271
2. To illustrate a specific concept in your document, you can insert a <u>ClipArt</u> picture—including drawings, movies, sounds, or stock photography. P. 274
3. It is easier to arrange multiple drawing objects by first creating a document <u>Canvas</u>.
4. Picture Tools is a contextual command tab that appears only when a picture is <u>Selected</u>.
5. You can <u>resize</u> a picture by changing the height and width measurements.
6. The <u>Text Wrapping</u> command changes the way text wraps around the picture or other drawing object.
7. A <u>floating</u> object is a picture or drawing object that can be positioned precisely on the page, including behind or in front of text.
8. When you insert a picture into a document, Word makes it an <u>embedded object</u> by default, which means that it becomes part of the document.
9. <u>Flowcharts</u> are useful for creating process documents, decision trees, or small organization charts.
10. When you scale a picture, you change the height and width <u>Percentage</u>.

Multiple Choice

Select the best response for the following statements.

1. In the Clip Art pane, you can click Organize Clips … to open the
   a. ClipArt Organizer.
   b. Result task pane.
   c. Microsoft Clip Organizer.
   d. Manage Pictures dialog box.

2. What is it called when you decrease the size of a picture file by reducing the resolution?
   a. compress - P. 289
   b. rotate
   c. crop
   d. resize

3. Lines, block arrows, stars, and banners are examples of what?
   a. diagrams
   b. shapes - P. 278
   c. flowcharts
   d. Quick Styles

4. Which tools provide options for formatting shapes?
   a. Drawing P. 277
   b. Picture
   c. Text
   d. Effects

5. Which is *not* a type of line option?
   a. connectors
   b. callouts — P. 280
   c. freeform
   d. scribbles

6. Which command enables you to remove unwanted parts from a picture?
   a. SmartArt
   b. Contrast
   c. Rotate
   d. Crop

7. Which option is *not* available on the Recolor menu?
   a. Grayscale
   b. Position — P. 287
   c. Sepia
   d. Washout

8. Which type of picture is configured to move along with the text around it?
   a. inline — P. 288
   b. wrap
   c. square
   d. flipped

9. Which is *not* an option in the Compression Settings dialog box?
   a. print
   b. optimal — P. 289
   c. screen
   d. e-mail

10. Which command do you use to discard all the formatting changes you made to a picture?
    a. Original
    b. Undo
    c. Reset — P. 290
    d. Discard

■ Competency Assessment

Project 9-1: House for Sale

In your position at Tech Terrace Real Estate, you are asked to add a photo to a flyer advertising a house for sale and format it attractively.

GET READY. Launch Word if it is not already running.

1. **OPEN** *tech_house* from the data files for this lesson.
2. Place the insertion point on the first line of the document.
3. On the Insert tab, in the Illustrations group, click **Picture**.
4. Navigate to the data files for this lesson and select the *housephoto* file.
5. On the Format tab, in the Size group, click the **Crop** button.
6. Click the **bottom right cropping handle** and drag up until the sidewalk is outside the selection area and release the mouse button to crop out the sidewalk.

The *tech_house* document is available on the companion CD-ROM.

Adding Pictures and Shapes to a Document | 293

The *housephoto* picture file is available on the companion CD-ROM.

7. On the Format tab, in the Picture Styles group, click the **More** button.
8. Click **Reflected Bevel, Black** in the gallery.
9. On the Format menu, in the Adjust group, click the **Recolor** button.
10. In the Color Modes section, click **Grayscale**.
11. **SAVE** the document as *house_flyer* and **CLOSE** the file.

   PAUSE. LEAVE Word open for the next project.

Project 9-2: Server Model

In your position at Flatland Hosting Company, you are asked to create a process diagram to present to clients. Your development process operates on a three-server model, so you want to find a SmarArt graphic that fits the information you are trying to illustrate.

1. **OPEN** a new, blank Word document.
2. On the first line, key **Flatland Hosting Company Development Process**.
3. On the Home tab, in the Styles group, click the **More** button.
4. Click the **Heading 1** option in the gallery.
5. On the Home tab, in the Paragraph group, click **Center** to center the text.
6. Press **Enter**.
7. On the Insert tab, in the Illustrations group, click the **SmartArt** button.
8. Click **Process** in the list on the left.
9. Click the **Alternating Flow** option.
10. In the Text pane, enter the text shown below:
    - Dev Server
      - internal
      - developer access
    - Stage Server
      - intermediate
      - client access
    - Live Server
      - launched
      - public access
11. **SAVE** the document as *server_model* and **CLOSE** the file.

    PAUSE. LEAVE Word open for the next project.

■ Proficiency Assessment

Project 9-3: Adding to the Organization Chart

You need to make some additions and changes to the organization chart your created for Margie's Travel.

1. **OPEN** *travel_flowchart* from the location where you saved it earlier in this lesson.
2. Use the knowledge you have gained about shapes in this lesson to add to the organization chart and format it, as shown in Figure 10-34.

Figure 9-34

Formatted organization chart

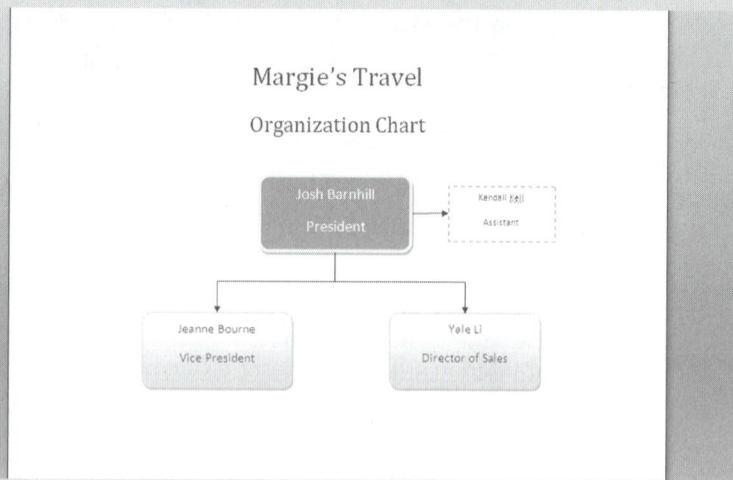

3. **SAVE** the document as *travel_orgchart* and **CLOSE** the file.

   PAUSE. LEAVE Word open for the next project.

Project 9-4: Creating a Room Layout

Your teacher needs your help creating a drawing of your classroom's layout, including various shapes to indicate the location of desks, computers, printers, and any other significant items.

1. **OPEN** a new, blank Word document.
2. On the Insert menu, in the Illustrations group, click the Shapes button and choose **New Drawing Canvas** to insert a document canvas.
3. Use the available shapes to draw a layout map of the classroom.
4. Label each shape and format the shapes attractively.
5. **SAVE** the document as *room_layout* and **CLOSE** the file.

   PAUSE. LEAVE Word open for the next project.

■ Mastery Assessment

Project 9-5: Party Invitation

You are having a party and want to create your own invitation using Word and clip art.

1. **OPEN** a new, blank Word document.
2. Use the knowledge you have gained in this lesson to create a party invitation using at least two pieces of clip art that reflect the type of party you are having.
3. Include the time, date, and location of the party. Use the Text Wrapping command to position the clip art around your text. Be creative!
4. **SAVE** the document as *party_invitation* and **CLOSE** the file.

   PAUSE. LEAVE Word open for the next project.

Project 9-6: Formatting a Flyer

The *rose_bushes* document is available on the companion CD-ROM.

A coworker at Keyser Garden & Nursery tried to create a sales flyer about roses, but was not familiar with formatting tools and ran into trouble. She asks if you can open the file and try to correct the problems and help format it.

1. **OPEN** *rose_bushes* from the data files for this lesson.

Adding Pictures and Shapes to a Document | 295

2. Use the skills learned in this lesson to correct the problems and format the document to look like Figure 9-35.

Figure 9-35

Formatted flyer

3. **SAVE** the document as *rose_sale* and **CLOSE** the file.
   STOP. CLOSE Word.

INTERNET READY

When creating a document, you are not limited to inserting only the clip art and other media that comes installed with Word. A single click can open up a whole new world of options. At the bottom of the Clip Art pane, notice the Clip Art on Office Online link. Click the link to connect to the Clip Art and Media home page, as shown in Figure 9-36. You can browse dozens of categories, download the clip of the day, view featured collections, and get clip tips. Next time you need to enhance your document with clip art or other media, expand your options by going online.

Figure 9-36

Clip Art and Media page

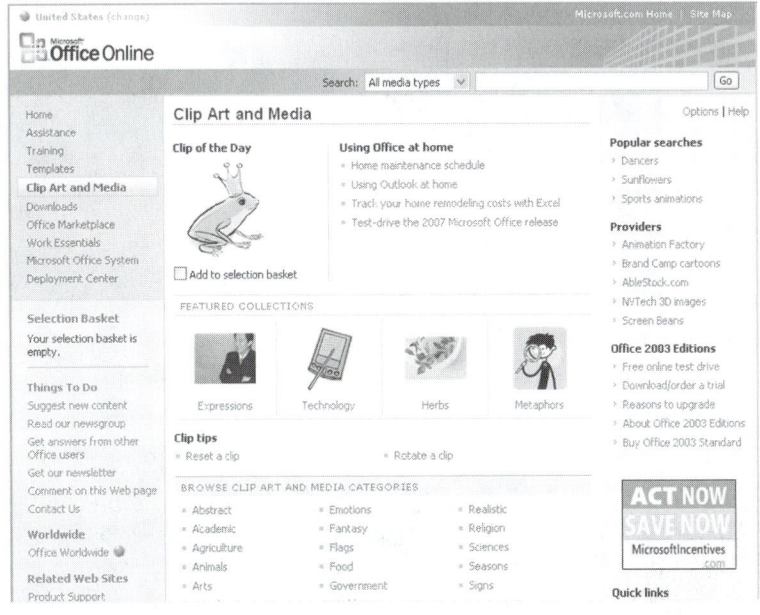

10 Customizing Word

LESSON SKILL MATRIX

Personalizing Word — 297	Students will learn how to personalize Word.
Changing Display Options — 298	Students will learn how to change display options.
Configuring Proofing Options — 299	Students will learn how to configure proofing options.
Setting Save Options — 301	Students will learn how to set save options.
Using Advanced Options — 302	Students will learn how to use advanced options.
Customizing the Quick Access Toolbar — 234	Students will learn how to customize the Quick Access toolbar.
Viewing and Managing Add-Ins — 306	Students will learn how to view and manage Add-Ins.
Protecting Your Computer — 307	Students will learn how to protect their computer.
Changing Research Options — 308	Students will learn how to change research options.

You are employed as a researcher at A. Datum Corporation, a company that provides custom consulting services to information technology companies. Many of the default options for Word are suitable, but there are times you need to make changes to settings for features such as compatibility, editing, printing, and saving. In this lesson, you will learn how to access options that enable you to customize Word to best fit the tasks that you perform. You will learn how to personalize Word, change display options, configure proofing options, set save options, use advanced options, customize the Quick Access toolbar, view and manage add-ins, protect your computer, and change research options.

KEY TERMS
add-in

Customizing Word | 297

■ SOFTWARE ORIENTATION

Word Options

The Word Options dialog box provides a wide variety of methods to customize how Word is used. Nine different option groups are provided. To access these options, click the Microsoft Office Button and then click the Word Options button on the menu, as shown in Figure 10-1.

Figure 10-1

Word Options button

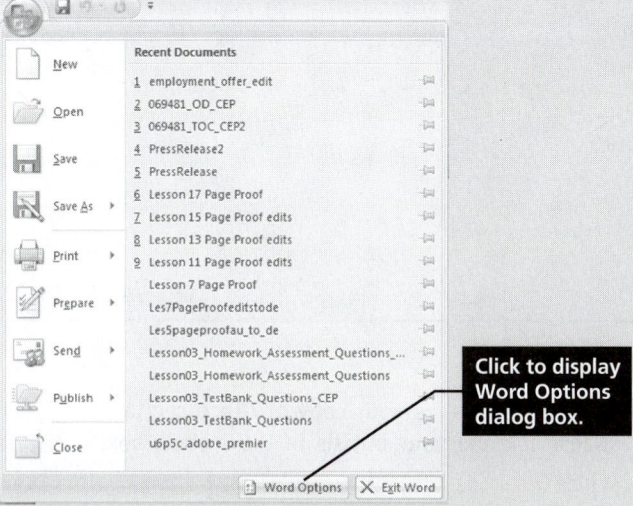

Use this figure as a reference throughout this lesson as well as the rest of this book.

■ Customizing Word

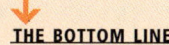

THE BOTTOM LINE Word can be customized through the different options available in the Word Options dialog box.

Personalizing Word

The Popular screen of the Word Options dialog box contains some of the most popular options that can be customized in Word, including changing your name and initials.

⮕ PERSONALIZE WORD

GET READY. Before you begin these steps, be sure to launch Microsoft Office Word 2007.

1. **OPEN** *a_datum* from the data files for this lesson.
2. Click the **Microsoft Office Button** and then click the **Word Options** button to display the Word Options dialog box.
3. Click **Popular** on the left to display the personalize options, shown in Figure 10-2.

The *a_datum* file is available on the companion CD-ROM.

Figure 10-2

Popular options screen

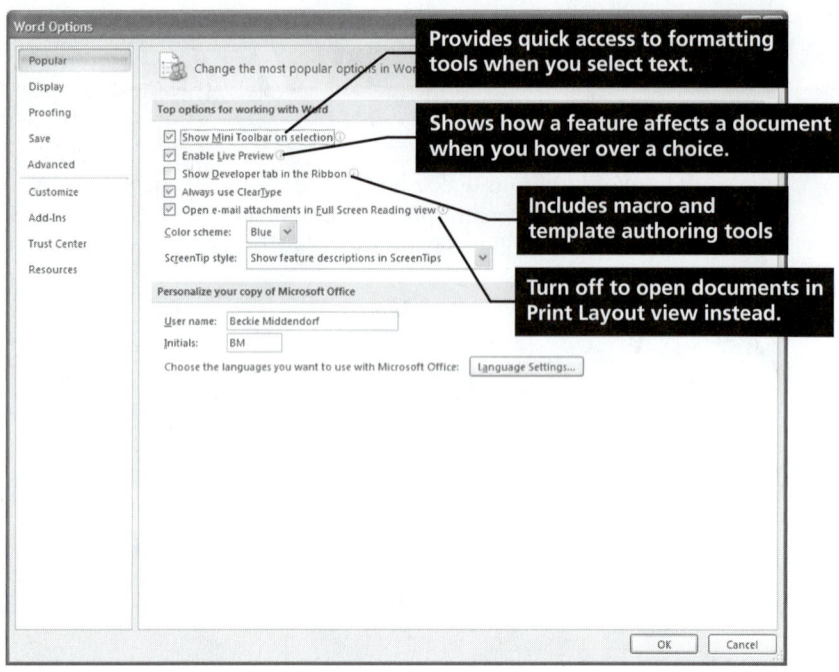

4. In the Personalize your copy of Office section, key your name in the User Name box and your initials in the Initials box, if they are not there already.
5. Click **OK**.
6. Click the **Microsoft Office Button**, click **Prepare**, and then click **Properties**. Notice the Author box in the Document Information Panel has your name.
7. Click the **Close** button to close the Document Information Panel.

   PAUSE. LEAVE the document open to use in the next exercise.

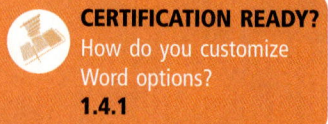

CERTIFICATION READY?
How do you customize Word options?
1.4.1

The popular options are some of the most frequently used when customizing Word. When creating a new document, Word sets the Author property based on the user name setting. The user name and initials specified here are also displayed in comments and tracked changes.

Take time to explore the contents of each screen of the Word Options dialog box, because there are too many choices to cover in this lesson, The more familiar you become with the options available, the better able you will be to customize Word to suit your needs.

Changing Display Options

The Display screen of the Word Options dialog box contains options for changing how document content is displayed both on the screen and when printed.

 CHANGE DISPLAY OPTIONS

USE the document that is open from the previous exercise.

1. Click the **Microsoft Office Button** and then click the **Word Options** button to display the Word Options dialog box.
2. Click **Display** on the left to view the display options, shown in Figure 10-3.

Figure 10-3

Display options screen

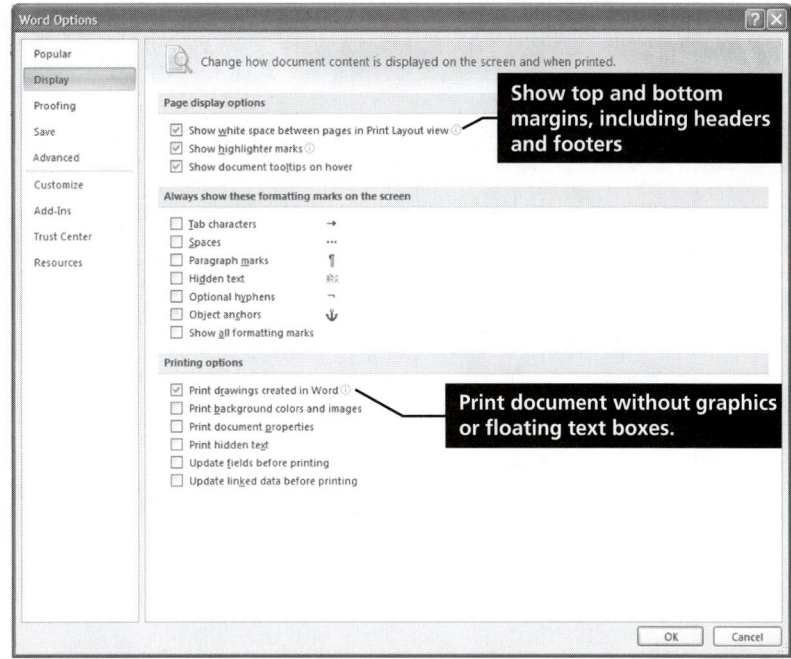

3. In the Always show these formatting marks on the screen section, select the **Paragraph Marks** checkbox.
4. Click **OK**. Notice the paragraph marks are displayed in the document.
5. Open the Word Options dialog box and deselect the Paragraph Marks checkbox on the Display screen.
6. Click **OK**.
7. **CLOSE** the document without saving the changes.

   PAUSE. LEAVE Word open to use in the next exercise.

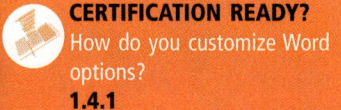

CERTIFICATION READY?
How do you customize Word options?
1.4.1

Changing options on the Display screen of the Word Options dialog box affects how content is displayed both on your computer screen and when printed for all documents, not just the document that is currently open. Select or deselect the checkbox for any option you want to turn on or off.

Configuring Proofing Options

The Proofing screen of the Word Options dialog box contains options for changing how Word corrects and formats your text.

➔ CONFIGURE PROOFING OPTIONS

OPEN a new, blank Word document.

1. Click the **Microsoft Office Button** and then click the **Word Options** button to display the Word Options dialog box.
2. Click **Proofing** on the left to display the Proofing options screen, shown in Figure 10-4.

Figure 10-4

Proofing options screen

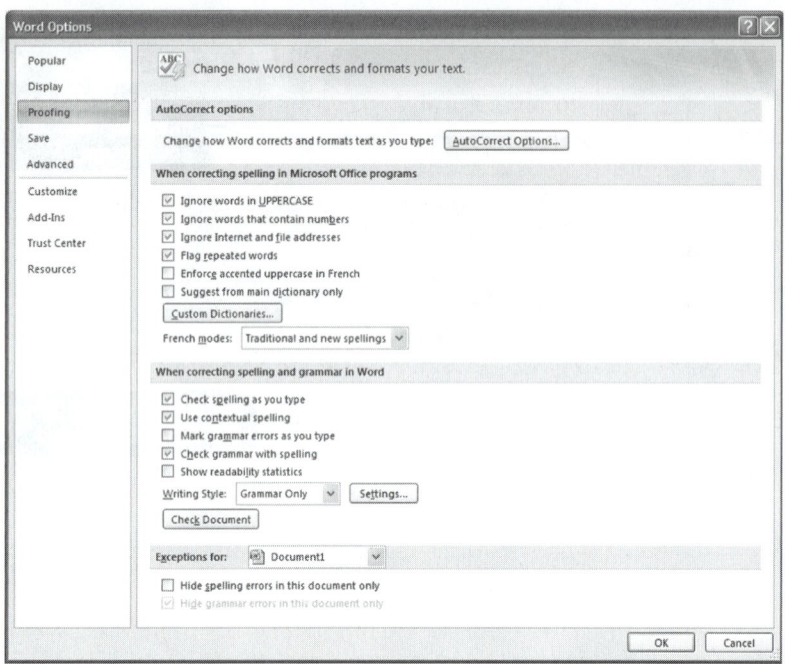

3. Click the **AutoCorrect Options** button to display the AutoCorrect: English (U.S.) dialog box, shown in Figure 10-5.

Figure 10-5

AutoCorrect: English (U.S.) dialog box

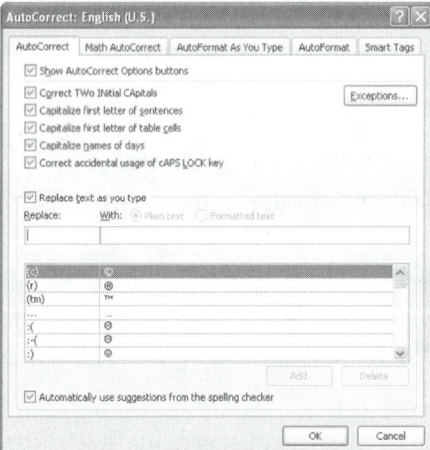

4. Click each of the tabs at the top to view the various options in the AutoCorrect dialog box.
5. Click **OK**.
6. In the When correcting spelling and grammar in Word section, click the **Settings** button to open the Grammar Settings dialog box, shown in Figure 10-6.

Figure 10-6

Grammar Settings dialog box

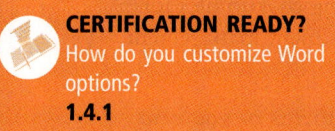

CERTIFICATION READY?
How do you customize Word options?
1.4.1

7. Scroll down to see all the grammar and style options.
8. Click **OK**.
9. Leave the Word Options dialog box open for the next exercise.

   PAUSE. LEAVE Word open to use in the next exercise.

Use the proofing options to specify how Word corrects spelling and grammar. The default options usually work well for most people, but you can customize options to suit your needs.

Click the AutoCorrect Options button to open the AutoCorrect dialog box and make choices about how Word corrects and formats text as you type—for example, having Word automatically correct capitalization errors or replace certain text as you type. Click the Settings button to open the Grammar Settings dialog box and choose which grammar and style options you want Word to check.

Setting Save Options

The Save screen of the Word Options dialog box contains options for customizing how documents are saved.

SET SAVE OPTIONS

1. From the Word Options dialog box, click **Save** on the left to display the save options, shown in Figure 10-7.

Figure 10-7

Save options screen

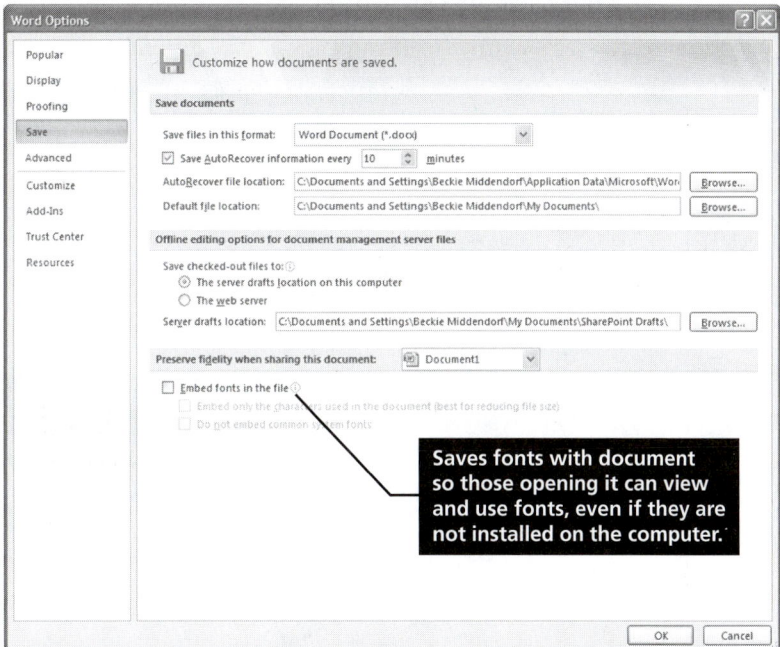

2. In the Save documents section, click the **downward-pointing arrow** in the Save files in this format box. The menu displays the options available for changing the default file format used when saving backup files.
3. In the Save AutoRecover information every box, click the **downward-pointing** arrow to change the number of minutes to **9**.
4. Leave the Word Options dialog box open for the next exercise.

   PAUSE. LEAVE Word open to use in the next exercise.

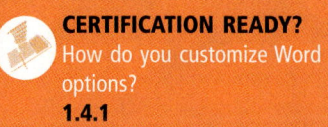

CERTIFICATION READY?
How do you customize Word options?
1.4.1

Use the save options to determine how documents are saved, including backup files for preserving information for your documents, sharing files using a document management server, and embedding fonts in a file.

For example, you can change the default format used to save documents or you can change how often your documents are backed up by using the AutoRecover feature. The My Documents folder, located on drive C, is the default working folder for all the documents created in Microsoft Office programs. On the Save screen, you can choose a different default working folder.

TAKE NOTE Any change made to the default working folder applies only to the program that you are currently using. For example, if a different default working folder is selected for Word, the default working folder for Excel will remain My Documents.

Using Advanced Options

The Advanced screen of the Word Options dialog box contains advanced options for working with Word.

 USE ADVANCED OPTIONS

1. From the Word Options dialog box, click **Advanced** on the left to display the advanced options. There are several advanced options, many of which are shown in Figures 10-8 thru 10-11.

Figure 10-8

Advanced options screen; Editing and Cut, copy, and paste options

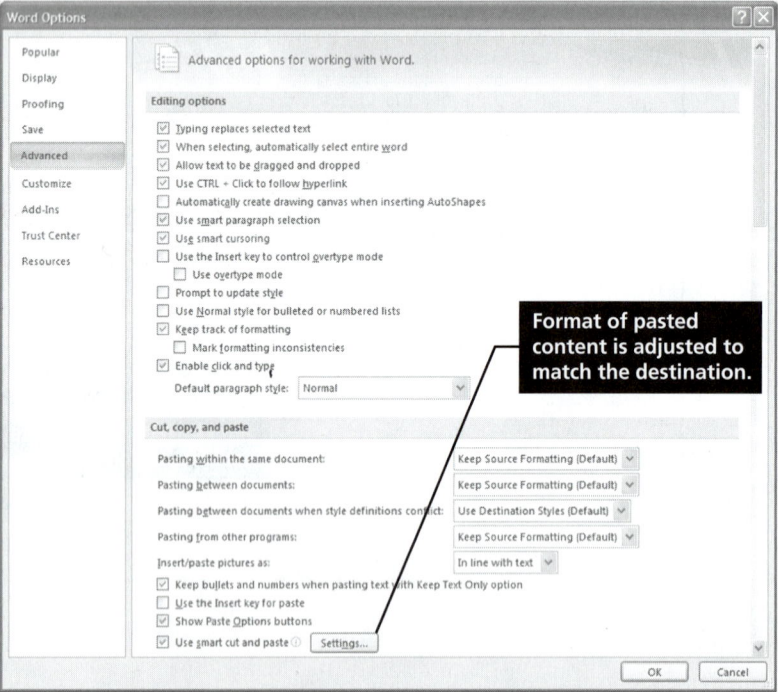

2. Scroll down and in the Display section (shown in Figure 10-9), click the upward-pointing arrow in the Number of documents in the Recent Document list box to change it to **10**.

Figure 10-9

Advanced options screen; Show document content and Display options

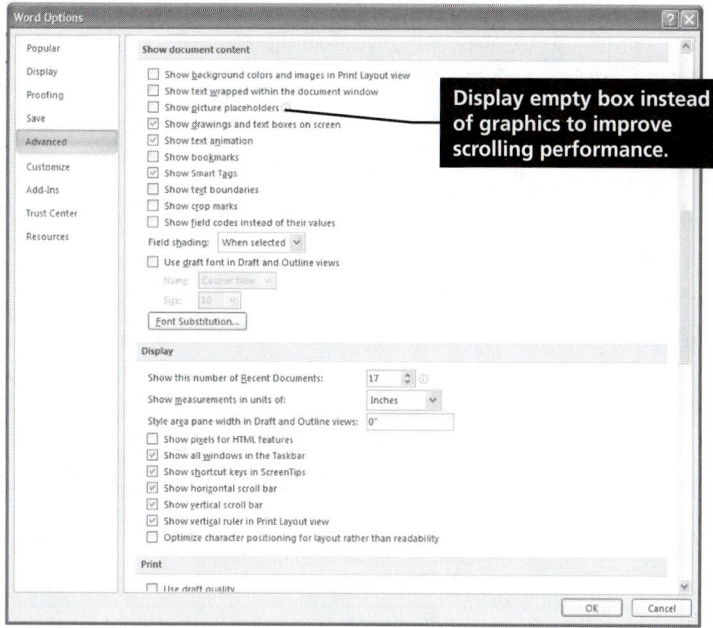

3. Click **OK**.
4. Click the **Microsoft Office Button** and notice that the Recent Document list now displays ten documents, but only the first nine are numbered.
5. Click the **Word Options** button to display the Word Options dialog box.
6. On the Advanced screen, scroll down to the Save section (shown in Figure 10-10) and click to select the **Prompt before saving Normal template** checkbox. Now if you change the default template, Word will ask if you want to save the changes.

Figure 10-10

Advanced options screen; Print and Save options

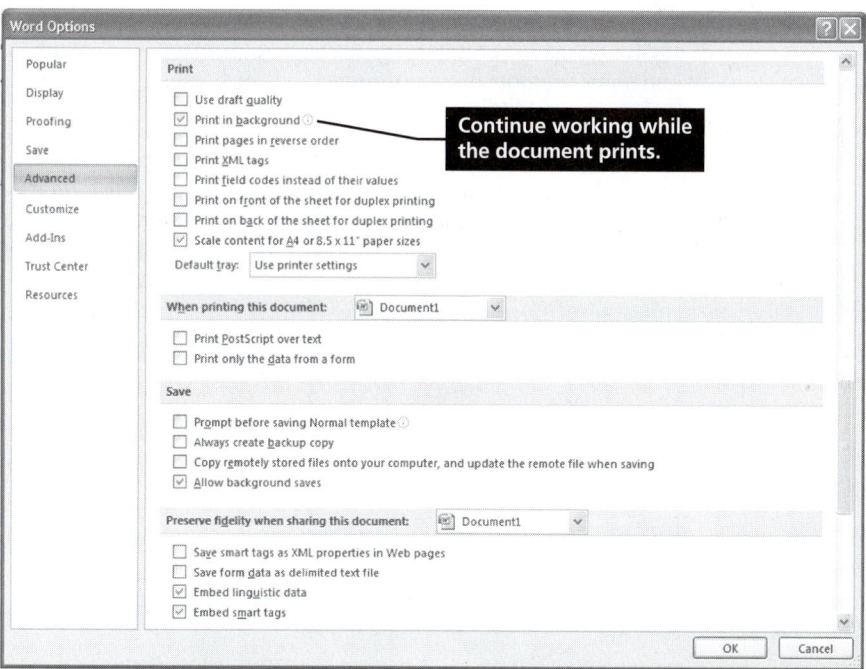

7. In the General section (shown in Figure 10-11), key your name and address in the Mailing address box.

Figure 10-11

Advanced options screen; General and Compatibility options

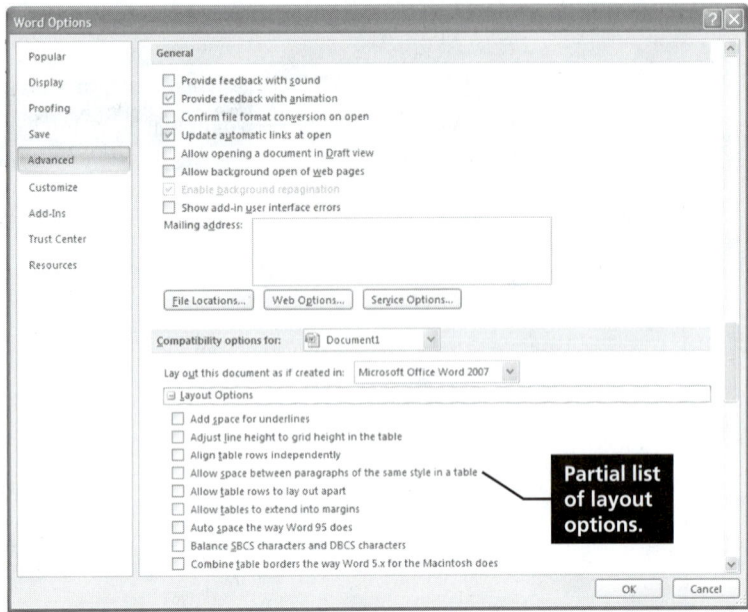

8. Click **OK**.
9. **OPEN** a new, blank Word document.
10. On the Mailings tab, in the Create group, click the **Labels** button.
11. In the Envelopes and Labels dialog box, click to select the **Use return address** checkbox. Notice that your name and address is displayed in the Address box.
12. Click **Cancel**.

   PAUSE. LEAVE Word open to use in the next exercise.

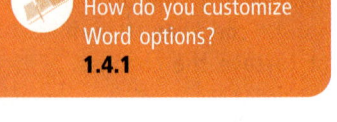

CERTIFICATION READY?
How do you customize Word options?
1.4.1

The Advanced screen contains many advanced choices for working with Word documents, including options for editing, displaying, printing, and saving. Some are selected by default and some are not. Browse through and see how you might use some of the options to work more efficiently in Word.

In addition to the multitude of options found on this screen, several dialog boxes can be accessed for additional customization. For example, clicking the Settings button will open the Settings dialog box, shown in Figure 10-12. From here, you can set formatting options to be used when cutting, copying, and pasting.

Figure 10-12

Settings dialog box

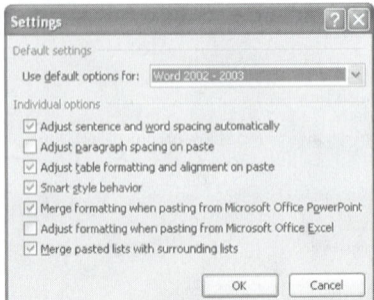

Customizing the Quick Access Toolbar

The Customize screen of the Word Options dialog box enables you to customize the Quick Access Toolbar and keyboard shortcuts.

Customizing Word | 305

CUSTOMIZE THE QUICK ACCESS TOOLBAR

1. From the Word Options dialog box, click **Customize** on the left to display the customization options, shown in Figure 10-13.

Figure 10-13

Customize options screen

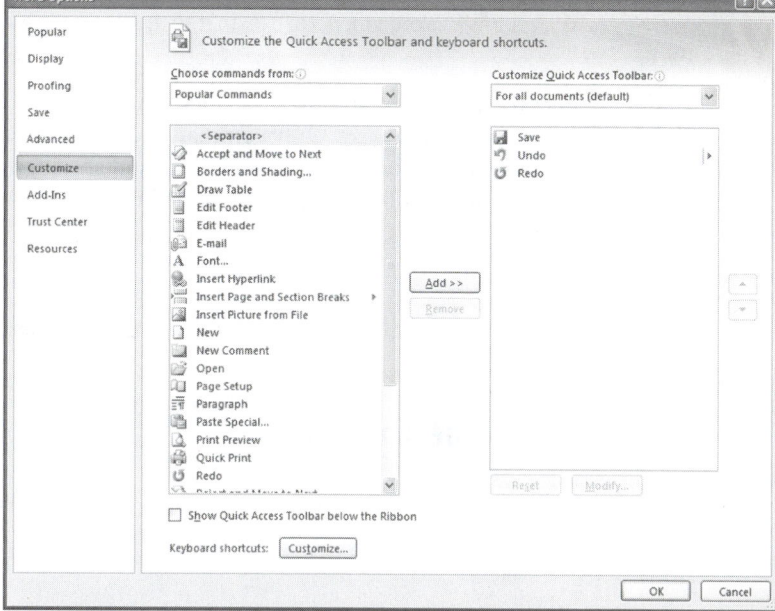

X REF

You first learned about the Quick Access Toolbar in Lesson 1.

2. In the Choose commands from list, choose **Office Menu**.
3. In the list of commands, click **New**.
4. Click **Add**.
5. Click **OK**. Notice the New command button is now on the Quick Access Toolbar.
6. Open the Word Options dialog box, click Customize on the left, and from the customization screen, click the **Customize** button. The Customize Keyboard dialog box appears, as shown in Figure 10-14.

Figure 10-14

Customize Keyboard dialog box

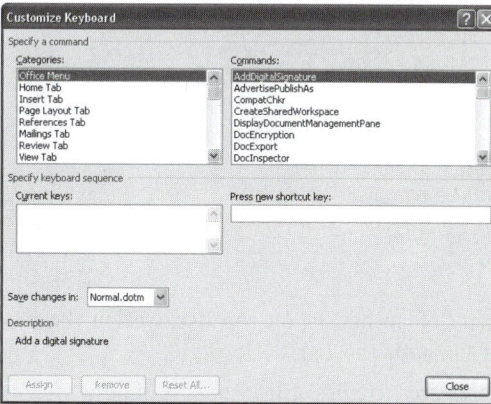

7. In the Categories box, click **Home tab**.
8. In the Commands box, click **Bold**.
9. In the Current keys box, select **Ctrl** + **Shift** + **B**.
10. Click the **Remove** button.
11. Click **Close**.

12. Leave the Word Options dialog box open for the next exercise.

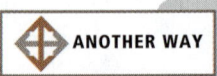 **ANOTHER WAY**: You can also add an item to the Quick Access Toolbar in the Ribbon by clicking the Customize Quick Access Toolbar button, or by right-clicking anywhere on the bar.

PAUSE. LEAVE Word open to use in the next exercise.

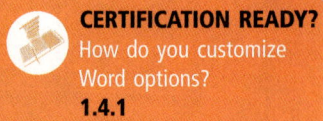
CERTIFICATION READY?
How do you customize Word options?
1.4.1

Adding frequently used commands to the Quick Access Toolbar ensures that those commands are always just a single click away. Only commands can be added to the Quick Access Toolbar. The contents of most lists, such as indent and spacing values and individual styles, which also appear on the Ribbon, cannot be added to the Quick Access Toolbar.

Viewing and Managing Add-Ins

The Add-Ins screen of the Word Options dialog box provides a way to view and manage Office add-ins.

VIEW AND MANAGE ADD-INS

1. From the Word Options dialog box, click **Add-Ins** on the left to display the add-ins options, shown in Figure 10-15.

Figure 10-15

Add-Ins options screen

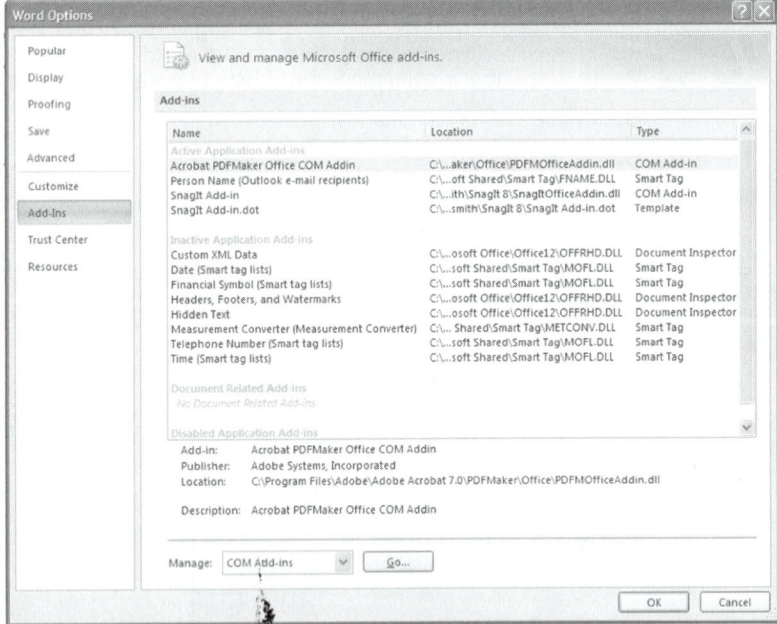

2. Click the name of an add-in on the list. Notice the description of the program is displayed beneath the list.

3. In the Manage box, choose **COM Add-ins** if it is not already selected.

4. Click the **Go** button. The COM Add-ins dialog box is displayed, as shown in Figure 10-16. Use this dialog box to add or remove add-ins.

Figure 10-16

COM Add-ins dialog box

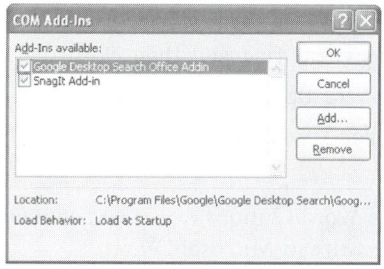

CERTIFICATION READY?
How do you customize Word options?
1.4.1

5. Click **Cancel**.

   PAUSE. LEAVE Word open to use in the next exercise.

TAKE NOTE

Once you've added an add-in program, it can be accessed from the Add-Ins tab on the Ribbon.

An ***add-in*** is a supplemental program that can be installed to extend the capabilities of Word by adding custom commands and specialized features. An example of an add-in program would be the Google Desktop Search Office Add-in.

For an add-in to be available whenever Word is started, the add-in must be stored in the Startup folder. To conserve memory and increase the speed of Word, it is a good idea to unload add-in programs that are not often used. When an add-in that is located in your Startup folder is unloaded, it is made unavailable for the current Word session but is automatically reloaded the next time Word is started. To delete an add-in from Word, remove it from the COM Add-ins dialog box.

Protecting Your Computer

The Trust Center screen of the Word Options dialog box provides ways to keep your documents safe, your computer secure, and your privacy protected.

→ PROTECT YOUR COMPUTER

1. Click the **Microsoft Office Button** and then click the **Word Options** button to display the Word Options dialog box.
2. Click **Trust Center** on the left to display the Trust Center options, shown in Figure 10-17.

Figure 10-17

Trust Center options screen

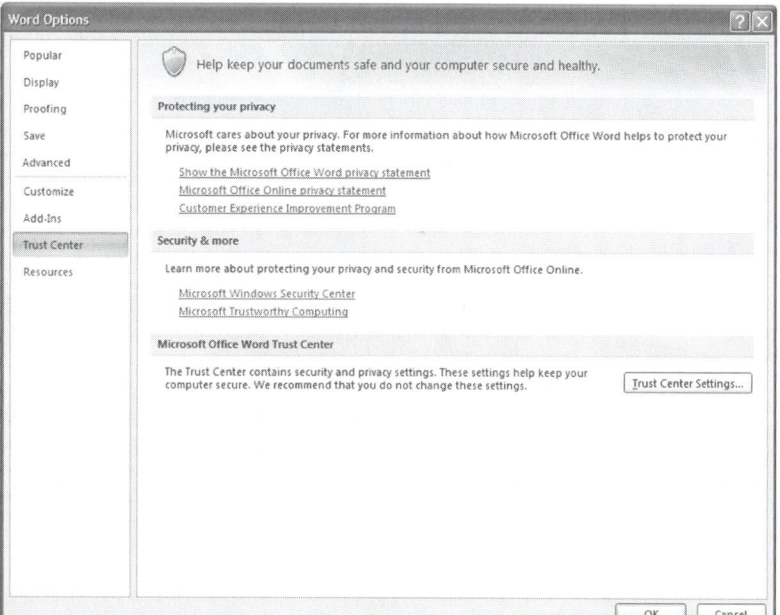

308 | Lesson 10

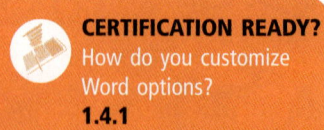

CERTIFICATION READY?
How do you customize Word options?
1.4.1

3. In the Security & more section, click the **Microsoft Trustworthy Computing** link.
4. Read about trustworthy computing and then close the browser window.
5. Click **OK** to close the Word Options dialog box.

   PAUSE. LEAVE Word open to use in the next exercise.

The Trust Center screen of the Word Options dialog box contains links to information about protecting your privacy and security in Microsoft Word.

Clicking the Trust Center Settings button opens the Trust Center dialog box, which contains security and privacy settings to help keep your computer secure. It is recommended that these settings *not* be changed.

■ SOFTWARE ORIENTATION

Research Task Pane

The Research Task Pane, shown in Figure 10-18, enables you to search various research and reference services for information related to keyed-in text.

Figure 10-18

Research Task Pane

Use this figure as a reference throughout this lesson as well as the rest of this book.

■ Changing Research Options

THE BOTTOM LINE

The Research command is used to search through available reference materials. The Research Options dialog box enables you to activate a service for searching.

Changing Research Options

Manage the available research options by adding, removing, and updating services, or setting parental controls.

Customizing Word | 309

CHANGE RESEARCH OPTIONS

1. On the Review tab, in the Proofing group, click the **Research** button. The Research Task Pane is displayed.

 **ANOTHER WAY** Another way to open the Research Task Pane is by clicking the Alt key, then clicking on a word in your Word document. Note that the word you click on will automatically be entered into the Search for box of the task pane.

2. Click **Research Options** to display the Research Options dialog box, shown in Figure 10-19.

Figure 10-19

Research Options dialog box

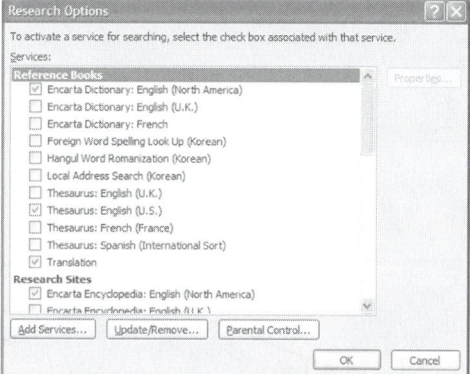

3. Scroll down to the Research Sites section, select **Factiva iWorks™**, and click **Properties** to display the Service **Properties** dialog box, shown in Figure 10-20.

Figure 10-20

Service Properties dialog box

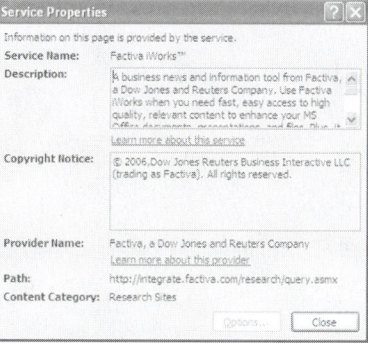

4. Click **Close**.
5. Click **Cancel**.
6. In the Search for box in the Research Task Pane, key **immigration**.
7. Click the **Start searching** green arrow beside the box.
8. Scroll down to see the search results.
9. Just below the Search for box, click the **downward-pointing** arrow and select **All Research Sites**.
10. Scroll down to see the search results.
11. Just below the Search for box, click the **downward-pointing** arrow and select **All Business and Financial Sites**.
12. Click the **plus sign (+)** next to Thomson Gale Company Profiles to display the available information.

310 | Lesson 10

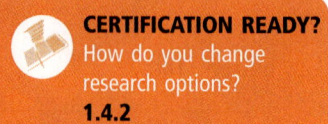

CERTIFICATION READY?
How do you change research options?
1.4.2

13. Click the **Close** button to close the Research Task Pane.
   STOP. **CLOSE** Word.

Open the Research Task Pane to search reference materials such as dictionaries, encyclopedias, and translation services. Click the Research Options link to open the Research Options dialog box, where you can manage the available search services. To see details about a service, select it and click the Properties button.

Clicking the Parental Controls button opens the Parental Controls dialog box, shown in Figure 10-21, where you can choose to filter content to ensure that services block offensive material. You can also ensure that only search services that have the ability to block offensive material are used. By specifying a password on this dialog box, you prevent unauthorized users from changing the Parental Control settings.

Figure 10-21

Parental Controls dialog box

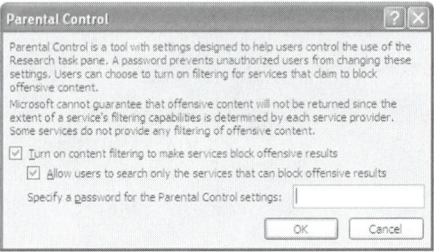

SUMMARY SKILL MATRIX

IN THIS LESSON YOU LEARNED HOW TO:
Personalize Word
Change Display Options
Configure Proofing Options
Set Save Options
Use Advanced Options
Customize the Quick Access Toolbar
View and Manage Add-Ins
Protect Your Computer
Change Research Options

■ Knowledge Assessment

Fill in the Blank

Complete the following sentences by writing the correct word or words in the blanks provided.

1. You can change your name and initials on the _____ screen of the Word Options dialog box.

2. The Display screen of the Word Options dialog box contains options to change how document content is displayed on the _____ and when _____.

3. The _____ screen contains options to change how Word corrects and formats your text.

4. The option for choosing a different default file format is found on the _____ screen.

5. The _____ folder is the default working folder for all the documents created in Microsoft Office programs.

6. The _____ screen contains the largest number of options available in the Word Options dialog box.

7. The Customization screen of the Word Options dialog box enables you to customize the Quick Access Toolbar and _____.

8. An _____ is a supplemental program that can be installed to extend the capabilities of Word by adding custom commands and specialized features.

9. The _____ screen of the Word Options dialog box provides ways to keep your documents safe, your computer secure, and your privacy protected.

10. The _____ command is used to search through available reference materials and services.

Multiple Choice

Select the best response for the following statements.

1. How many option groups are listed in the Word Options dialog box?
    a. three
    b. five
    c. seven
    d. nine

2. What button do you click to display the menu with the Word Options button?
    a. Insert
    b. Advanced
    c. Microsoft Office Button
    d. Display

3. Which Word Office dialog box screen contains the most popular options?
    a. Popular
    b. Save
    c. Resources
    d. Tools

4. Changes made to options on the Display screen will affect
    a. all Word documents.
    b. the document currently in use.
    c. all Office documents.
    d. any document in the My Documents folder.

5. Correct TWo INitial CAps is a proofing option found in which dialog box?
    a. CorrectCaps
    b. AutoCorrect
    c. Grammar Settings
    d. Exceptions

6. The Quick Access Toolbar is for
   a. frequently used commands.
   b. commands from the File menu.
   c. contents of lists on the Ribbon.
   d. recently used documents.
7. Which dialog box is used to add or remove add-ins?
   a. Add/Remove Add-Ins
   b. Manage Add-ins
   c. Add-in Wizard
   d. COM Add-ins
8. It is recommended that the settings in the Trust Center
   a. be updated regularly.
   b. not be changed.
   c. be accessed using keyboard shortcuts.
   d. all of the above.
9. Which reference materials or services are available using the Research Task Pane?
   a. dictionaries
   b. encyclopedias
   c. translation services
   d. all of the above
10. You can choose to filter content to block offensive material in which dialog box?
    a. Filter Content
    b. Parental Control
    c. Block Material
    d. User Controls

■ Competency Assessment

Project 10-1: Lost Art Photos Return Address

In your position as a marketing assistant at Lost Art Photos, you frequently mail promotional letters. You prepare envelopes for these mailings in Word, and making the company's return address your default option would save time. Change your Word options to set this up.

GET READY. Launch Word if it is not already running.

1. **OPEN** a new, blank Word document.
2. Click the **Microsoft Office Button** and then click the **Word Options** button to display the Word Options dialog box.
3. Click **Advanced** on the left to display the advanced options.
4. Scroll down to the General section and in the Mailing address box, key:
   LostArtPhotos
   5500 Bissell Street
   Grand Junction, CO 98445
5. Click **OK**.
6. On the Mailings tab, in the Create group, click **Envelopes**.

7. In the Envelopes and Labels dialog box, key your name and address in the Delivery address box. Notice that the company's return address is already in the Return address box.
8. Click the Add to Document button.
9. **SAVE** the document as *lostart_envelope* and **CLOSE** the file.
   PAUSE. LEAVE Word open for the next project.

Project 10-2: Set Research Options

A. Datum Corporation has an overseas branch in the United Kingdom. In your position as a researcher, you sometimes need to take this into account when using Word to look up information. Set the research options accordingly.

1. On the Review tab, in the Proofing group, click the **Research** button to display the Research Task Pane.
2. Click **Research Options** to display the Research Options dialog box.
3. In the Reference Books section, click the checkboxes to select **Encarta Dictionary: English (U.K.)** and **Thesaurus: English (U.K.)**.
4. In the Research Sites section, click the checkboxes to select **Encarta Encyclopedia: English (U.K.)** and **MSN Search U.K.**
5. In the Business and Financial Sites section, click the checkbox to select **MSN Money Stock Quotes U.K.**
6. Click **OK**. Your research options are now set to include those specific to the United Kingdom.
   PAUSE. LEAVE Word open for the next project.

■ Proficiency Assessment

Project 10-3: Customizing the Quick Access Toolbar

As a paralegal in a busy legal practice, you are always looking for ways to streamline your work. As you learn more about Word, you want to use the available options to help customize the program for your daily tasks.

1. **OPEN** the Word Options dialog box.
2. Display the Customization screen.
3. Choose five commands that you use frequently, but that are not currently located on the Quick Access Toolbar. Add the commands to the Quick Access Toolbar.
4. **CLOSE** the Word Options dialog box.
   PAUSE. LEAVE Word open for the next project.

Project 10-4: Finding Readability Statistics

You are a fourth grade teacher, and a research paper that you are presenting at a national conference will be distributed to members of a discussion panel. You are interested in finding out the readability statistics of your paper, an option that you know is available in Word.

The *research_readability* document is available on the companion CD-ROM.

1. **OPEN** *research_readability* from the data files for this lesson.
2. Open the Word Options dialog box and display the Proofing screen.
3. In the When correcting spelling and grammar in Word section, select the **Show readability statistics** checkbox if it is not already selected.
4. Click **OK**.

5. On the Review tab, in the Proofing group, click the **Spelling & Grammar** button.
6. Click **Ignore All** each time Word displays a possible spelling mistake.
7. When a message appears that the spelling and grammar check is complete, click **OK**. The Readability Statistics dialog box is displayed.
8. On a piece of paper, jot down the numbers displayed for the Flesch Reading Ease and the Flesch-Kincaid Grade Level tests.
9. Click **OK** to close the dialog box.

   PAUSE. LEAVE the document open for the next project.

■ Mastery Assessment

Project 10-5: Understanding Readability Statistics

Now that you have found the readability statistics for your research paper, you need to understand what they mean. Use Word help to locate this information.

1. **OPEN** Word help and search for *readability*.
2. Read the information about testing a document's readability.
3. In a new Word document, briefly explain the Flesch Reading Ease test and the Flesch-Kincaid Grade Level test.
4. List the readability scores that you wrote down for the *research_readability* document and explain whether they are considered good scores.
5. **SAVE** the document as *test_scores* and **CLOSE** the file.
6. **CLOSE** the *research_readability* document without saving.

   PAUSE. LEAVE Word open for the next project.

Project 10-6: Word Options

You are a volunteer in the business office of the ANHH (Association of National Historic Homes) and have been assigned a variety of tasks that require an advanced knowledge of Word options.

1. **OPEN** a new, blank Word document.
2. Using what you have learned in this chapter, explore the Word Options dialog box as needed to find the answers to the following questions:
   a. You want to use XML-related features. How would you display the necessary commands in the Ribbon?
   b. You want blank boxes to be printed in place of graphics. What option would you disable?
   c. You do not want Word to replace fractions (1/2) with fraction characters (½). What option in what dialog box would you access to change this?
   d. You want Word to always check and require a comma before the last item in a list. What setting would you change?
   e. You want to use draft quality to print the rough draft of a long document. Where would you access this option?
   f. You want to diagnose and repair a problem with your Office applications. How would you do this from the Word Options dialog box?
3. Key your answers into the Word document.
4. **SAVE** the document as *word_options* and **CLOSE** the file.

   STOP. CLOSE Word.

Customizing Word | 315

INTERNET READY

From the Resources screen of the Word Options dialog box, shown in Figure 10-22, you can contact Microsoft, find online resources, and maintain the health and reliability of your Office applications.

Figure 10-22

Resources screen of Word Options dialog box

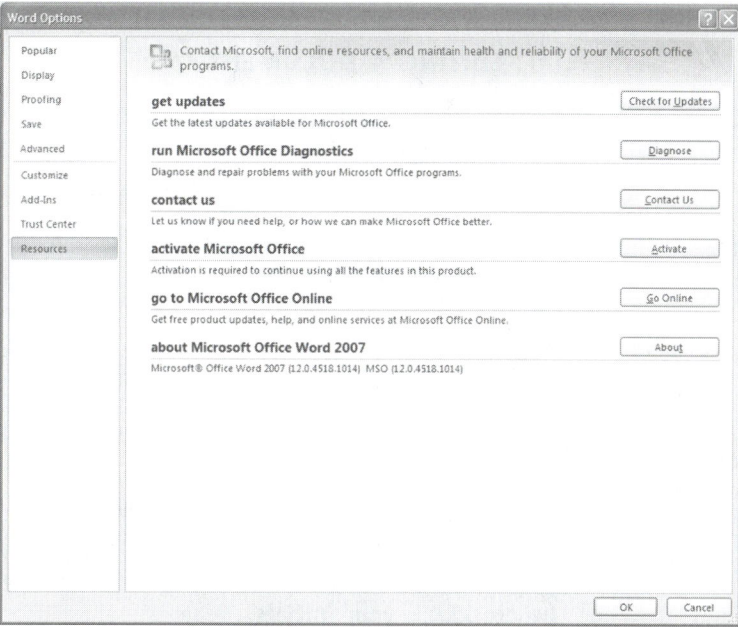

To ensure that your computer is up-to-date, click the Check for Updates button to open the Microsoft update site, shown in Figure 10-23. From here, you can check to see if you need updates for your programs, hardware, or devices.

Figure 10-23

Microsoft update site

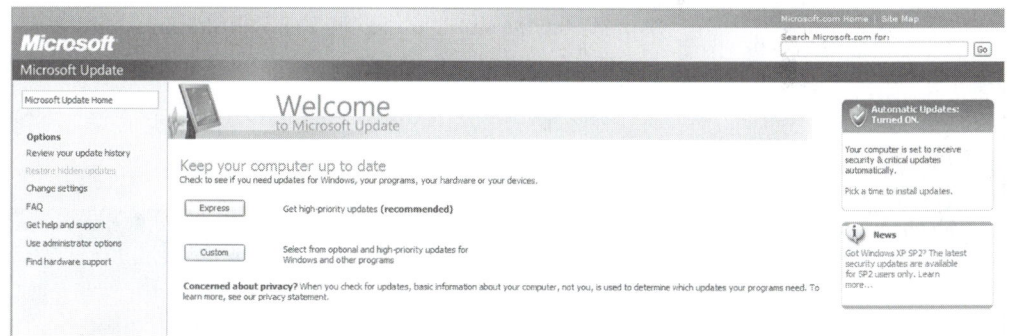

Circling Back

As the scheduling manager for Consolidated Messenger, a full-service conference and retreat center, you use Word to create and revise all documents and forms used in coordinating the facility's events.

Project 1: EDITING A DOCUMENT

You are working on a promotional piece for the conference center, but need to make some changes and add a logo. Open and revise the document.

GET READY. Launch Word if it is not already running.

The *consolidated_logo* file is available on the companion CD-ROM.

The *consolidated_intro* file is available on the companion CD-ROM.

1. Open *consolidated_logo* from the data files for this lesson. Select the logo and copy it to the Clipboard.
2. OPEN *consolidated_intro* from the data files for this lesson.
3. Place the insertion point on the first line of the document and paste the logo.
4. On the **Home** tab, in the **Editing** group, click the **Find** button.
5. In the **Replace** tab, search for all occurrences of the word *Gallery* and replace them with the word *Theatre*.
6. Select the first two paragraphs of the document.
7. On the **Insert** tab, in the **Text** group, click the **Quick Parts** button.
8. Click Save Selection to Quick Parts Gallery with the name *consolidatedXXX* **(where XXX = your initials)**.
9. Place the insertion point at the beginning of the first sentence of the document.
10. On the **Insert** tab, in the **Illustrations** group, click the **Picture** button.
11. Locate *conference_photo* in the data files for this lesson and click **Insert**.
12. On the **Format** tab, in the **Arrange** group, click the **Text Wrapping** button.
13. Click **Square**.
14. On the **Format** tab, in the **Size** group, click the **Crop** button.
15. Crop the picture and position it in the document so that it looks similar to Figure 1.

The *conference_photo* picture file is available on the companion CD-ROM.

Figure 1

Promotional document with photo

16. On the **Format** tab, in the **Picture Styles** group, click the **More** button.
17. Click the **Rotated, White** option.
18. Make any adjustments necessary to fit the entire document on one page.

19. **SAVE** the document as *consolidated_promo*.

PAUSE. LEAVE the document open to use in the next project.

Project 2: AUDIO VISUAL EQUIPMENT TABLE

Create a table that contains a list of the audio and visual equipment available for rent at the conference center.

USE the document that is open from the previous project.

1. Place the insertion point below the logo.
2. In Cambria, 24 pt. font, key the title *Audio Visual Equipment Rental*.
3. Create a table that has three columns and eight rows.
4. Change column widths as necessary and key the information shown in Figure 2 into the table.

Figure 2
Audio visual equipment table

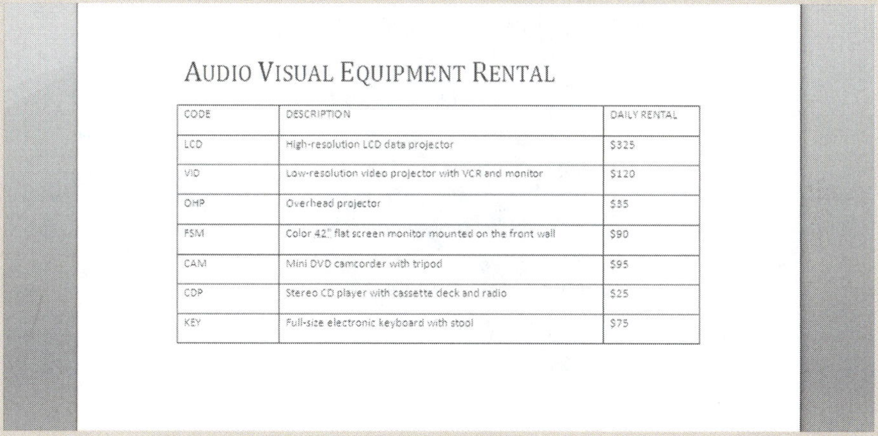

CODE	DESCRIPTION	DAILY RENTAL
LCD	High-resolution LCD data projector	$325
VID	Low-resolution video projector with VCR and monitor	$120
OHP	Overhead projector	$55
FSM	Color 42" flat screen monitor mounted on the front wall	$90
CAM	Mini DVD camcorder with tripod	$95
CDP	Stereo CD player with cassette deck and radio	$25
KEY	Full-size electronic keyboard with stool	$75

5. Place the insertion point anywhere in the table.
6. On the **Design** tab, in the **Table Styles** group, click the **More** button to view a gallery of Quick Styles.
7. Scroll down and click the **Medium Shading 1 - Accent 1** option.
8. On the **Layout** tab, in the **Data** group, click the **Sort** button. Sort by the *Daily Rental* column in descending order.
9. Select the first row.
10. On the **Layout** tab, in the **Alignment** group, click **Align Top Center**.
11. Select all the numbers in the *Daily Rental* column.
12. On the **Layout** tab, in the **Alignment** group, click **Align Center Right**.
13. **SAVE** the document as *consolidated_equipment* and **CLOSE** the file.

PAUSE. LEAVE Word open for the next project.

Project 3: FORMATTING A DOCUMENT

You began creating a document to serve as a guide for introducing guests to the conference center. Open and format the document.

The *consolidated_guests* file is available on the companion CD-ROM.

1. **OPEN** *consolidated_guests* from the data files for this lesson.
2. Use what you have learned in this unit to complete the following tasks. You do not have to complete them in this order, but your goal is to make the document look similar to Figure 3.

Figure 3

Finished document

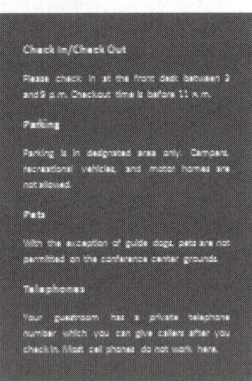

a. Use section breaks to create a section for the text and then put the text into two columns.
b. Create a drop cap for the first sentence.
c. Apply Snip Diagonal Corner, White to the photograph.
d. Create a pull quote using the Tiles Quotes style in the **Accent 2** theme color using this text: *We are rated the most unique conference center in the country.*
e. Arrange elements on the page and make any other necessary adjustments to make your document look like Figure 3.

3. **SAVE** the document as *consolidated_guide* and **CLOSE** the file.
   STOP. CLOSE Word.

Microsoft® Office
Excel® 2007

Excel Essentials

LESSON SKILL MATRIX

Changing Excel's Views — 322	Students will learn how to change Excel's views.
Splitting a Window — 324	Students will learn how to split a window.
Opening a New Window — 325	Students will learn how to open a new window.
Navigating a Worksheet — 326	Students will learn how to navigate a worksheet.
Entering Data in a Worksheet — 328	Students will learn how to enter data in a worksheet.
Selecting, Editing, and Deleting a Cell's Contents — 329	Students will learn how to select, edit, and delete a cell's contents.

Contoso, Ltd provides specialty healthcare for the entire family—prenatal through geriatric care. The practice, owned by Dr. Stephanie Bourne, has an expanding patient list. It currently employs a staff of 36, which includes three additional family practice physicians. Each physician has unique patient-contact hours; the office is open from 7 a.m. to 7 p.m. on Mondays and from 8 a.m. to 4 p.m. other weekdays. The office manager must track revenue and expenses for the practice and maintain a large volume of employee data. Microsoft Excel is an ideal tool for organizing and analyzing such data. In this lesson, you will learn how to enter text and numbers into an Excel worksheet to keep up-to-date employee records.

KEY TERMS
active cell
cell
column
row
workbook
worksheet

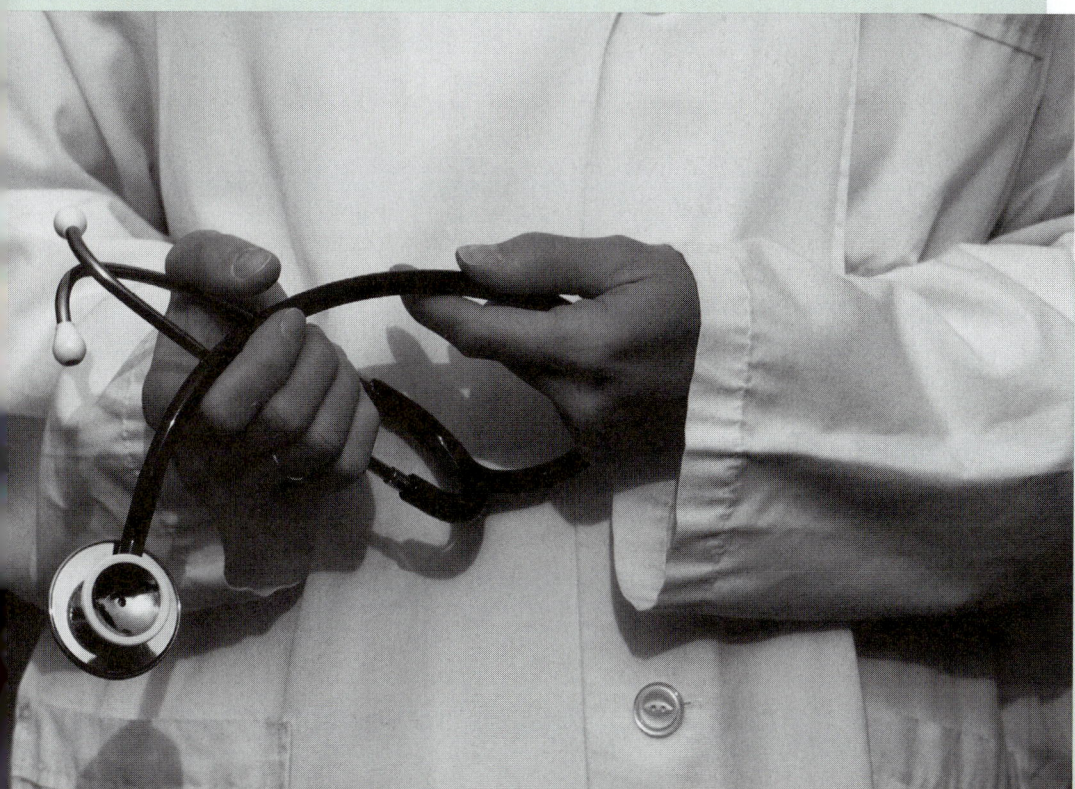

Software Orientation

Microsoft Excel's Opening Screen

Microsoft Office Excel 2007 provides new and improved powerful tools that enable users to organize, analyze, manage, and share information easily.

When you first launch Excel, you will see a screen similar to the one shown in Figure 1-1. The Developer and Add-Ins tabs may not appear on your screen if default settings have been changed or other preferences have been set. Use Figure 1-1 as a reference throughout this lesson and the rest of this book.

Figure 1-1

Excel's opening screen

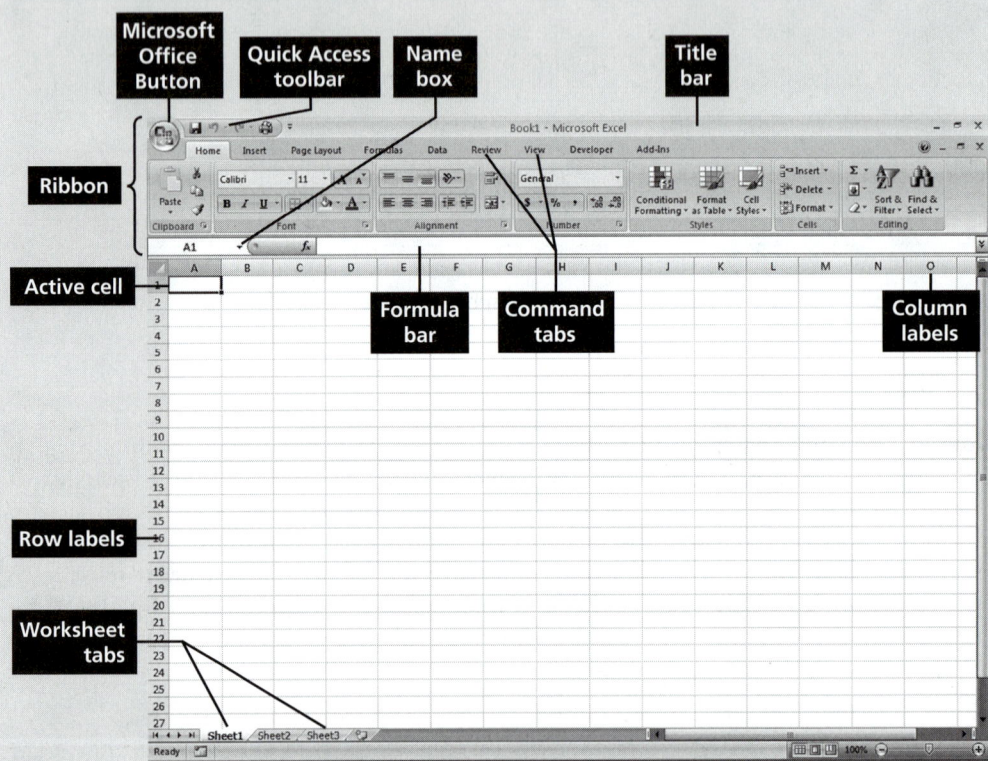

Changing Excel's View

When you open Excel, a blank workbook is displayed. The filename (Book1) and the program name (Microsoft Excel) appear in the title bar at the top of the screen. A new *workbook* contains three worksheets—similar to pages in a document or a book. The sheet tabs are located just above the Status bar and are identified as Sheet1, Sheet2, and Sheet3. Worksheets can be renamed to identify their content and additional worksheets can be added as needed.

A *worksheet* (sometimes called a spreadsheet) is a grid comprised of rows, columns, and cells. Worksheet *columns* go from top to bottom and are identified by letters; *rows* go from left to right and are identified by numbers. Information is entered into a cell. Each box on the grid is a *cell* and is identified by the intersection of a column and a row. Thus, the first cell in an open worksheet is A1. The *active* cell is outlined by a bold black line. When you key information, it will be entered in the outlined cell.

While you are working, you can see your worksheet as it will appear when printed. To preview your printed worksheet, click the Ribbon's View tab, then click Page Layout in the Workbook View group (first section).

Excel Essentials | 323

CHANGE EXCEL'S VIEW

GET READY. Before beginning these steps, be sure to launch Microsoft Office Excel 2007.

1. The Home tab should be active. If it is not, click **Home**.
2. Select the **A1** cell to make it active. Key **456** and press Tab.
3. Click the arrow in the lower-right corner of the Font group of commands. The Format Cells dialog box, shown in Figure 1-2, opens.

Figure 1-2

Format Cells dialog box

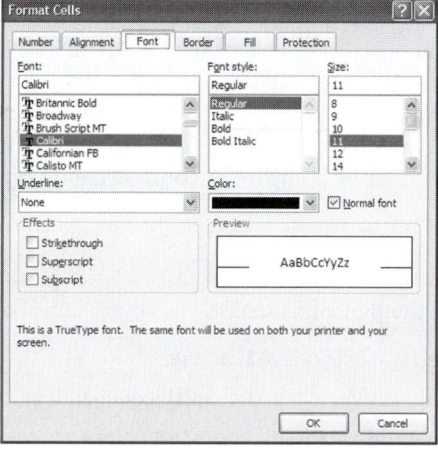

4. Notice that the Font tab of the box is active. Change the font to **Arial** and click **OK**.
5. Cell B1 should be the active cell. Key **456** and press Tab. Notice the difference in size and appearance between this number and the one you keyed in cell A1.
6. Click the **View** tab.
7. Click **Page Layout View**. Your workbook should look like Figure 1-3. From this view, you can see the margins, and you can add a header or footer in this view.

Figure 1-3

Worksheet in Page Layout View

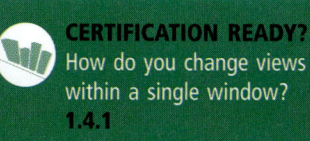

CERTIFICATION READY?
How do you change views within a single window?
1.4.1

324 | Lesson 1

 **ANOTHER WAY**

You can also access the Format Cells dialog box by right-clicking in a cell or on a column or row label.

PAUSE. LEAVE the worksheet open to use in the next exercise.

Page Layout view is useful when preparing your data for printing. This view enables you to fine-tune pages before printing. You can change the data's layout and format in this view as well as the Normal view. You can also use the rulers to measure the width and height of the data and determine whether you need to change the margins or print orientation. These commands will be presented in later lessons.

Splitting a Window

When a worksheet contains a great deal of data, Normal and Page Layout views allow you to see only a small portion of the worksheet at a time. The Split command allows you to view the worksheet in four quadrants. The scroll bars on the right and at the bottom of the window allow you to display different sections of the worksheet at the same time. You can more easily compare or contrast data.

➔ SPLIT A WINDOW

USE the worksheet from the previous exercise.

1. Press **Ctrl+Home** to make cell **A1** active.
2. With the View tab active, click the **Split** command in the Window group.
3. Choose the lower-right quadrant and scroll down to row 30.
4. Key **235** in cell **H30** and press **Enter**. The data you entered in cells A1 and B1 should be visible as well as what you just entered in cell H30. See Figure 1-4.

Figure 1-4

Split window

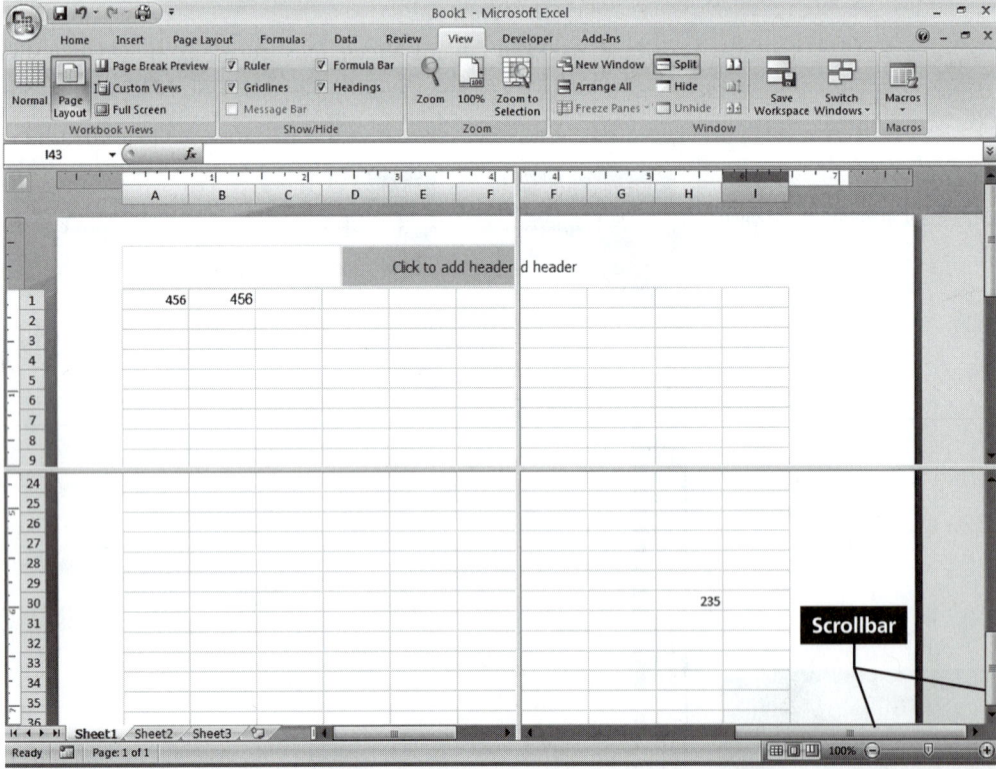

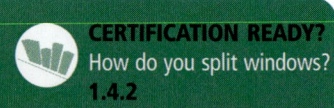

CERTIFICATION READY?
How do you split windows?
1.4.2

5. Click **Split** to remove the split. The data in cell H30 is no longer visible. If you click the **Split** command, you will again see all the data in this worksheet.

PAUSE. LEAVE the worksheet open to use in the next exercise.

Excel Essentials | 325

TAKE NOTE The Split command is especially useful when you need to compare various portions of a long worksheet.

When you use a worksheet that contains a small amount of data, it is easy to scroll through the worksheet and focus on specific cells. Worksheets that you create and work with in the future, however, could be much larger. The ability to view more than one section of a worksheet at the same time is especially useful when you need to compare various sections of data.

Opening a New Window

Splitting a window allows you to look at two sections of a worksheet side by side. You can also view two sections of a worksheet by using the New Window command.

→ **OPEN A NEW WINDOW**

USE the worksheet from the previous exercise.

1. Make **A1** the active cell.
2. With the View tab active, click **New Window** in the Window group. A new window titled Book1:2 opens.
3. Scroll down the window until cell H30 is visible. As illustrated in Figure 1-5, you can see the data in H30. Although cell A1 is not visible, it is still the active cell. It is important to note that you have opened a new view of the active worksheet—not a new worksheet.

Figure 1-5

New window

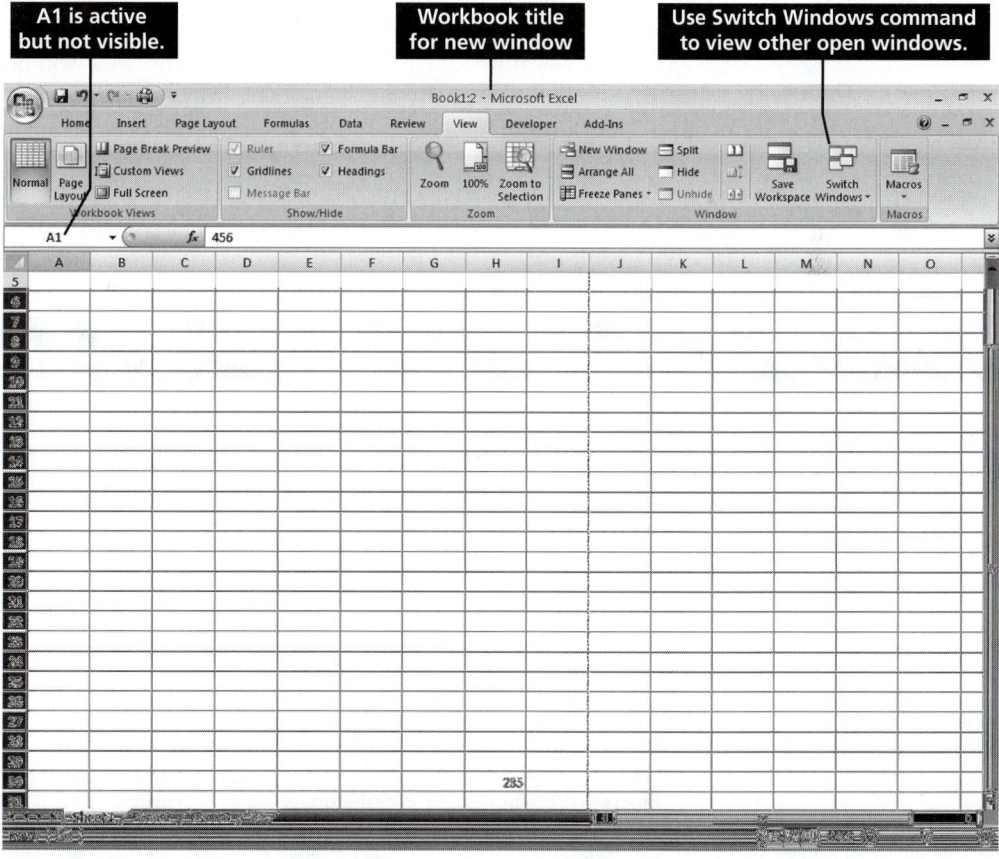

326 | Lesson 1

4. Click **Switch Windows**. Book1:2 is checked, which indicates that it is the active window.
5. Click **Book1:1.** You see the original view of the worksheet with cell A1 active.
6. Click **Switch Windows** and make Book1:2 active.
7. Click the **Close** button to close Book1:2. The window closes and the title Book1 tells you that this is the only open view of this workbook.

> **TAKE NOTE**
> If you use the Microsoft Office Button, you will close the workbook. The Close window option will close only the new window opened at the beginning of this exercise.

CERTIFICATION READY?
How do you open and arrange new windows?
1.4.3

8. Click the **Microsoft Office Button** and then click **Close**.
9. When asked if you want to save the changes to Book1, click **No**.
   PAUSE. LEAVE Excel open to use in the next exercise.

When you open a new window, you can move between the windows as you did in this exercise. You can also use the Arrange All command on the View tab to display the windows side by side to compare or contrast various parts of a worksheet. This function is especially useful when you work with workbooks that contain more than one worksheet.

✱ Workplace Ready

Contoso, Ltd provides health insurance and other benefits to its employees who work 30 or more hours each week. The office manager has created a workbook for employee information so that he can more easily track which employees are eligible for benefits. In the following exercises, you will update existing data and add additional employees to an Excel worksheet.

■ Working with an Existing Workbook

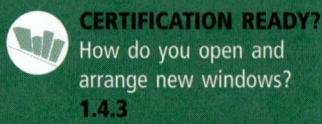

When an Excel 2007 file is saved, the extension *xlsx* is automatically added to the name assigned to the file. When you want to open a file, the filename extension identifies the program in which the file can be opened. To open a file, you must identify the drive and folder that contains the file. In the following exercise, you will open a file created by Contoso's office manager.

Rows   Columns
Million + 16,000+

Navigating a Worksheet

The *Contoso Employee Info* workbook is available on the companion CD-ROM.

An Excel worksheet can contain more than a million rows and more than sixteen thousand columns. There are several ways to move through worksheets that contain numerous rows and columns. You can use the arrow keys, the scrollbars, or the mouse to navigate through a worksheet. In the following exercises, you will explore several ways to move through a worksheet.

NAVIGATE A WORKSHEET

BEFORE you begin this exercise, put the companion CD in the computer.

1. Browse to the location of the data files for this lesson and open the *Contoso Employee Info* file (see Figure 1-6).

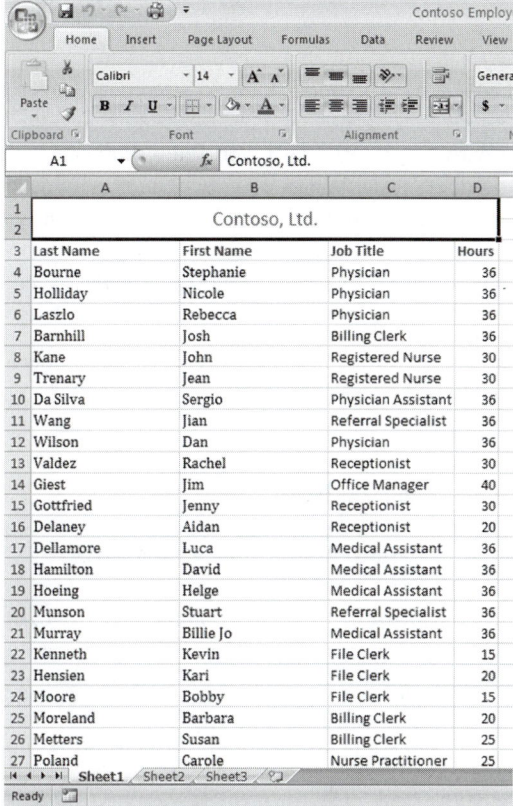

Figure 1-6

Existing worksheet

2. Press **Ctrl+Home** to move to the beginning of the document (cell A1).
3. Press **Ctrl+End** to move to the end of the document (cell D27).
4. Make cell **A27** the active cell and press **Page Up**. The cursor moves to cell A1.
5. Click the **A3** cell to make it active, and press **Ctrl+Down Arrow** to go to the last row of data (cell A27).
6. Press **Ctrl+Right Arrow**. The cursor moves to D27, the last column in the range of data.
7. Press **Ctrl+Down Arrow**. The cursor moves to the last possible row in the worksheet. The unused cells below the data are considered a range.
8. Press **Ctrl+Home**.
9. Press **Scroll Lock** while you press the **Right Arrow** key. This moves the sheet one column to the right.

TAKE NOTE

Ctrl+Arrow allows you to move to the start and end of ranges of data. The title, which spans all the columns, is not considered part of the worksheet's data range.

TAKE NOTE

When you use the scroll options, the view of the worksheet changes, but the active cell does not change.

10. Use the vertical scrollbar to move from the beginning to the end of the data.
11. If your mouse has a wheel button, roll the wheel button on the mouse forward and back to scroll quickly through the worksheet.

ANOTHER WAY

The name box is located below the Ribbon at the left end of the formula bar. You can key a cell location in this box and press Enter. The cursor moves to that cell.

TAKE NOTE

When Scroll Lock is on, *scroll lock* is displayed on the left side of the Status bar. If you want to use the arrow keys to move between cells, you must turn off Scroll Lock.

PAUSE. LEAVE the workbook open to use in the next exercise.

If you are familiar with Microsoft Word, you know that the beginning of the document is displayed when you open a file. When you open an Excel workbook, the active cell and view were determined when the file was saved. For example, when you opened the Contoso Employee Info workbook, A22 was the active cell displayed in Normal view because A22 was the active cell displayed in Normal view when the file was saved. This feature enables you to continue working in the same location when you return to the workbook.

In the preceding exercise, you learned a variety of ways to view and navigate through data. As you continue to create and edit worksheets, you will select the navigation methods that work best for you.

Entering Data in a Worksheet

You can key data directly into a worksheet cell or cells. You can also copy and paste information from another worksheet or from other programs. To enter data in a cell within a worksheet, you must make the desired cell active and then key the data. To move to the next column after text has been entered, press Tab. When you have finished keying the entries in a row, press Enter to move to the beginning of the next row. You can also use the arrow keys to move to an adjacent cell. If the first few characters you key in a cell match an existing entry in that column, Excel enters the remaining characters automatically. Press Enter to accept the proposed entry or continue keying. In the following exercise, you will add a new employee's information to the worksheet.

XREF

Other methods of entering worksheet data will be addressed in Lesson 2.

➔ **ENTER DATA IN A WORKSHEET**

USE the worksheet from the previous exercise.

1. Move to cell **A28**.
2. Key **Simon** and press Tab.
3. Key **Britta** and press Tab.
4. Key **Administrative Assistant** and press Tab.
5. Key **36** and press Enter.
6. Double-click the marker between columns C and D to so that the entire text is visible in column C.

PAUSE. LEAVE the workbook open to use in the next exercise.

TAKE NOTE

When you key text that is longer that the cell, the text extends into the next cell. However, when you press Tab and move to the next cell, the overflow text is not displayed. The text is still there. You will learn more about adjusting the column width in Lesson 2.

You added data to an exisiting worksheet in this exercise. However, column width has been established based on the existing data. When you added an entry in column C that was longer than other entries in the column, it was necessary to adjust the column width to accommodate the entry.

Selecting, Editing, and Deleting a Cell's Contents

One advantage of electronic records versus manual ones is that changes can be made quickly and easily. To edit information in a worksheet, you can make changes directly in the cell or edit the contents of a cell in the formula bar. Before changes can be made, however, you must select the information that is to be changed. Selecting text means that you highlight the text that is to be changed. You can select a single cell, a row, a column, a range of cells, or an entire workbook. You can select a single cell, a row, a column, a range of cells, or an entire workbook.

➔ SELECT, EDIT, AND DELETE A CELL'S CONTENTS

USE the workbook from the previous exercise.

1. Select cell **A22** as shown in Figure 1-7.

Figure 1-7

Edit in the cell or in the formula bar

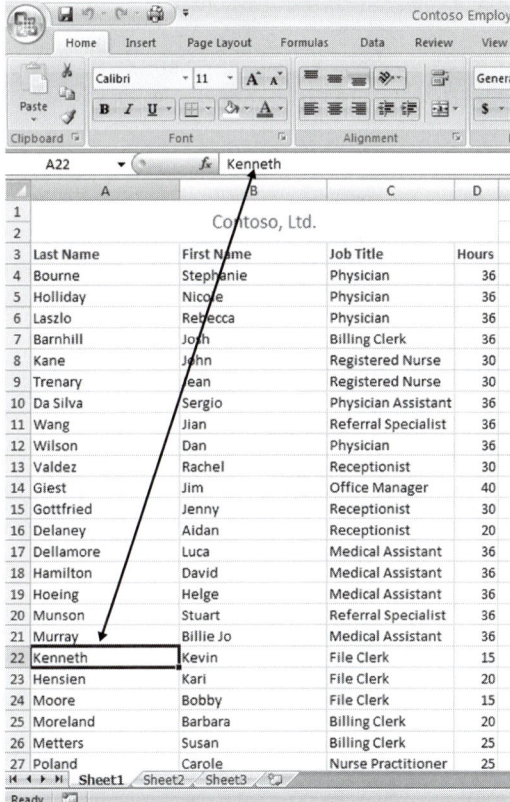

2. Select the existing text. Key **Kennedy** and press **Enter**.
3. Click cell **A15**. Hold down the left mouse button and drag to cell **D15**. You have selected the entire record for Jenny Gottfried.
4. Press **Delete**. The information is deleted and row 15 is now blank.
5. With cells A15 to D15 still selected, right-click to display the shortcut menu.
6. Press **Delete**. The Delete dialog box will be displayed.

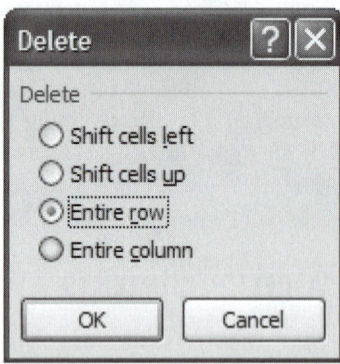

7. Click **Entire row** as shown in Figure 1-8, and then click **OK**.

Figure 1-8

Delete a row from a worksheet

8. Click the **Select All** button. As you can see in Figure 1-9, all cells on the worksheet are selected.

Figure 1-9

Select all cells

	A	B	C	D
1		Contoso, Ltd.		
2				
3	Last Name	First Name	Job Title	Hours
4	Bourne	Stephanie	Physician	36
5	Holliday	Nicole	Physician	36
6	Laszlo	Rebecca	Physician	36
7	Barnhill	Josh	Billing Clerk	36
8	Kane	John	Registered Nurse	30
9	Trenary	Jean	Registered Nurse	30
10	Da Silva	Sergio	Physician Assistant	36
11	Wang	Jian	Referral Specialist	36
12	Wilson	Dan	Physician	36
13	Valdez	Rachel	Receptionist	30
14	Giest	Jim	Office Manager	40
15	Delaney	Aidan	Receptionist	20
16	Dellamore	Luca	Medical Assistant	36
17	Hamilton	David	Medical Assistant	36
18	Hoeing	Helge	Medical Assistant	36
19	Munson	Stuart	Referral Specialist	36
20	Murray	Billie Jo	Medical Assistant	36
21	Kenneth	Kevin	File Clerk	15
22	Hensien	Kari	File Clerk	20
23	Moore	Bobby	File Clerk	15
24	Moreland	Barbara	Billing Clerk	20
25	Metters	Susan	Billing Clerk	25

TAKE NOTE*

If you edit a cell's contents and change your mind before you press Enter, press Esc and the original text will be restored. If you change the content of a cell and then do not want the change, click Undo on the Quick Access Toolbar. The deleted text will be restored.

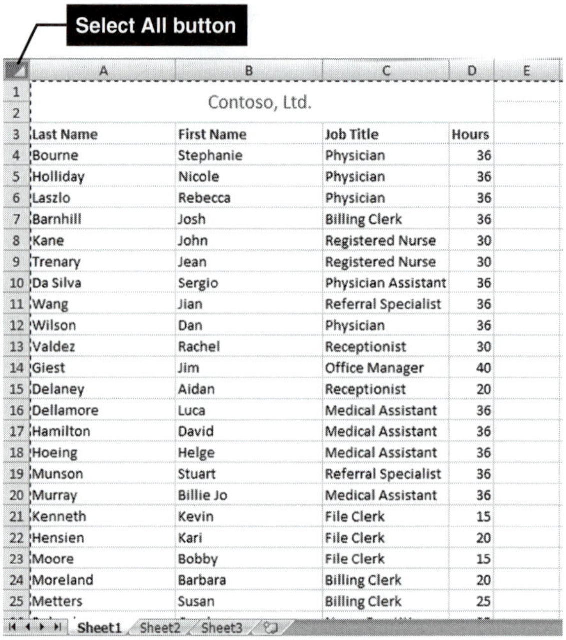

9. Click any worksheet cell to deselect the worksheet.
10. To select all cells containing data, select **A1** and press Ctrl+A. Click any worksheet cell to deselect the cells.
11. **SAVE** the worksheet as ***Contoso Employee Info Revised*** and **CLOSE** the file.

STOP. CLOSE Excel.

As you have seen in the preceding exercises, there are several ways to modify the values or text you have entered into a cell:

- Erase the cell's contents.
- Replace the cell's contents with something else.
- Edit the cell's contents.

To erase the contents of a cell, simply double-click the cell and press Delete. To erase more than one cell, select all of the cells that you want to erase and then press Delete. Pressing Delete removes the cell's contents, but does not remove any formatting (such as bold, italic, or a different number format) that you may have applied to the cell.

 **ANOTHER WAY**

You can right-click a cell or a selected range of cells and choose Delete from the menu that appears.

 **ANOTHER WAY**

Place the cursor in the cell you want to edit, press F2, and edit directly in the cell.

To replace the contents of a cell with something else, simply click the cell and key the new entry. This replaces the cell's previous contents. Any formatting that you previously applied to the cell remains in place and is applied to the new content.

If the cell contains only a few characters, replacing the contents by keying new data usually is easiest. But if the cell contains lengthy text or a complex formula and you need to make only a slight modification, it is probably easier to edit the cell rather than re-enter information.

When you begin editing a cell, the insertion point appears as a vertical bar, and you can move the insertion point by using the direction keys. Use Home to move the insertion point to the beginning of the cell, and use End to move it to the end of the cell. You can add new characters at the location of the insertion point. To select multiple characters, press Shift while you use the arrow keys. You also can use the mouse to select characters while you are editing a cell. Just click and drag the mouse pointer over the characters that you want to select.

SUMMARY SKILL MATRIX

IN THIS LESSON YOU LEARNED HOW TO:
Change Excel's Views
Split a Window
Open a New Window
Navigate a Worksheet
Enter Data in a Worksheet
Select, Edit, and Delete a Cell's Contents

Knowledge Assessment

Fill in the Blank

Complete the following sentences by writing the correct word or words in the blanks provided.

1. A worksheet's margins are displayed in __page__ Layout view.
2. A selected cell is called the __active__.
3. In order to use arrow keys to move between cells in a worksheet, __scroll__ Lock must be turned off.
4. After a file has been saved, the filename appears in the __workbook (Title)__.
5. When you split a window, the window is divided into __4__ panes.
6. When you are changing the contents of a cell, you are in the __edit__ mode.
7. A cell is formed by the intersection of __Column & Row__.
8. You can select a single __cell__, a row, a column, a range of cells, or an entire workbook.
9. A new Excel workbook opens with __blank__ worksheets.
10. The active cell is identified in the __Name box__ that appears on the left side of the formula bar.

True/False

Circle T if the statement is true or F if the statement is false.

T **F** 1. Three worksheets is the maximum number that can be included in one workbook.
T F 2. The Split command is useful for viewing different sections within a large worksheet.
T **F** 3. When data is too wide for a cell, the part of the data that will not fit is automatically deleted.
T F 4. After a file has been saved, the file name appears in the title bar.
T F 5. Excel opens with a new blank workbook displayed.
T **F** 6. The columns in a worksheet are indentified by numbers.
T F 7. The active cell is outlined by a bold black line.
T F 8. Excel provides a Select All button that can be used to select all cells in a worksheet.
T **F** 9. Using the **Delete** key will remove both text and formats from a cell.
T F 10. Edits can be made in the formula bar.

Competency Assessment

Project 1-1: Scenic Drives in the United States

Create a worksheet listing the top scenic drives in the United States (according to Orbitz.com). Identify the state and the scenic route.

GET READY. Launch Excel if it is not already running.

1. Click the **Microsoft Office Button**, click **New**, click **Blank Workbook**, and click **Create**.
2. Select **A1**, key **State**, and press **Tab**.
3. In **B1**, key **Scenic Route**.

4. Beginning in cell **A2**, key the following data.

State	Scenic Route
AK	Seward Highway
CA	California 1
WY and MT	Beartooth Highway
UT	Zion National Park Scenic Byway
SD	Custer Scenic Byway
MN	North Shore Drive
LA	Old Spanish Trail
VT	Vermont 100
VA and NC	Blue Ridge Parkway
GA	Sea Islands

5. Double-click the boundary between columns B and C to adjust the width of column B to display all of the text.
6. Click the **Quick Print** icon on the Quick Access Toolbar.
7. **SAVE** the worksheet as *Road Trip* and then **CLOSE** the file.

    LEAVE Excel open for the next project.

Project 1-2: Pro Football Hall of Fame

Eleven colleges have five or more of their football alumni who have been inducted into the Pro Football Hall of Fame.

College	Number of Inductees
Notre Dame	10
Southern California	10
Michigan	7
Alabama	6
Illinois	6
Ohio State	6
Minnesota	5
Oregon	5
Penn State	5
Southern Methodist	5
Syracuse	5

1. Press **Ctrl+N** to open a new blank worksheet to enter the data.
2. Create columns for **College** and **Number of Inductees**. Enter the data.
3. Adjust column widths to fit the text contained in each column.
4. **SAVE** the worksheet as *Hall of Fame* and then **CLOSE** the file.

    LEAVE Excel open for the next project.

Proficiency Assessment

Project 1-3: Fixing Approved Vendor List

An employee at Contoso, Ltd has begun an Excel worksheet to identify approved vendors for office and medical supplies. The worksheet is not complete, but before additional entries are made, you need to edit the existing data. The worker who created the worksheet has not been consistent in the way addresses are entered and columns have not been adjusted to display all worksheet information. You need to review how the cells are set up and edit cell content. Use the techniques learned in this lesson to format the worksheet.

1. **OPEN** *Contoso Vendor List* from the data files for this lesson.
2. Make necessary corrections to the worksheet. Two-letter state abbreviations should always be used in addresses. Find and correct inconsistencies within columns. Check each row to verify that information has been entered in the correct column.
3. **SAVE** the file as *Contoso Vendor List Revised* and **CLOSE** the file.

    LEAVE Excel open for the next exercise.

The *Contoso Vendor List* workbook is available on the companion CD-ROM.

Project 1-4: Excel Grade Sheet

Create a worksheet that your professor might use for recording your achievement of the objectives for Lesson 1.

1. Click the **Microsoft Office Button**, click **New**, click **Blank Workbook**, and click **Create**.
2. Determine the column headings you will need for the worksheet. The worksheet will include student names and the numbers identifying each skill. Lesson 1 objectives are listed in the Skill Matrix at the beginning of the lesson and in the summary at the end of the lesson.
3. Enter the column headings for the worksheet. Select **A1** and key a heading for the first column. Press `Tab`.
4. Key headings for the remaining columns and press `Enter`.
5. In cell **A2**, enter your name in Last Name, First Name format. Press `Enter`.
6. In **B2**, enter the name of one other student in your class.
7. **SAVE** the workbook as *Grade Sheet* and **CLOSE** the file.

    LEAVE Excel open for the next exercise.

Mastery Assessment

Project 1-5: Fortune's Best Companies

Create a worksheet that lists the ten best companies to work for as determined by employee satisfaction rankings.

1. Create a new blank Workbook.
2. Review the data to be entered and determine the column headings you will use for this worksheet. You must have two columns.
3. Select **A1** and key a heading for the first column. Press `Tab`.
4. Key a heading for column 2 and press `Enter`.

5. Enter the following data, starting in cell **A2**.

Companies in Rank Order
Genentech
Wegmans
Valero Energy
Griffin Hospital
W. L. Gore
Container Store
Vision Service Plan
J. M. Smucker
REI
S. C. Johnson and Son

Source: Fortune.com

6. **SAVE** the worksheet as *Best Companies* when all data has been entered and **CLOSE** the file.

   LEAVE Excel open for the next project.

Project 1-6: Updating an Existing Worksheet

The *Contoso Employees* workbook is available on the companion CD-ROM.

1. **OPEN** *Contoso Employees* from the data files for this lesson.
2. Add your name as a new employee. You have been hired as a file clerk. You will work 15 hours each week.
3. With the Home tab active, select the entire worksheet.
4. Click the arrow in the Dialog Box Launcher in the Font command group. The Format Cells dialog box will open.
5. Change the font to **Times New Roman** and press Enter.
6. **SAVE** the worksheet as *Contoso Employees 1-6* and **CLOSE** the file.

   STOP. CLOSE Excel.

INTERNET READY

In this lesson you learned how to select a cell, a row, and an entire worksheet. Use Excel's Help to gain further knowledge of selecting data.

1. Click the **question mark** on the right side of the ribbon.
2. On the Excel Help dialog box, key **Select text** in the Search box at the top of the Help window.
3. Click **Search**. From the search result, open a topic that will provide information about selecting cells.
4. Print the topic. **CLOSE** Excel.

2 Creating and Editing a Workbook

LESSON SKILL MATRIX

Starting a Workbook from Scratch — 337	Students will learn how to start a workbook from scratch.
Entering Labels — 338	Students will learn how to enter labels.
Entering Dates — 339	Students will learn how to enter dates.
Entering Values — 340	Students will learn how to enter values.
Filling a Series with Auto Fill — 342	Students will learn how to fill a series with AutoFill.
Copying a Data Series with the Mouse — 344	Students will learn how to copy a data series with the mouse.
Moving a Data Series with the Mouse — 344	Students will learn how to move a data series with the mouse.
Copying and Pasting Data — 345	Students will learn how to copy and paste data.
Cutting and Pasting Data — 347	Students will learn how to cut and paste data.
Setting the Print Area — 348	Students will learn how to set the print area.
Using Print Preview — 349	Students will learn how to use print preview.
Setting Other Print Options — 349	Students will learn how to set other print options.
Saving a Workbook for use in a Previous Version of Excel — 350	Students will learn how to save a workbook for use in a previous version of Excel.
Choosing a Different File Format — 350	Students will learn how to choose a different file format.

Purchasing a home is usually the biggest financial investment most people make in a lifetime. Real estate agents advise and assist those who want to buy a new home or sell their present home. Agents must be licensed by the state. Many licensed agents also become Realtors®. This is a trademarked name that an agent can use only when he or she joins the local, state, and national associations of Realtors®. Fabrikam, Inc., located in Columbus, Ohio, is owned by Richard Carey and David Ortiz. Fabrikam has five full-time sales agents. Fabrikam uses an Excel workbook to track each agent's sales data with the date of the agent's last sale.

KEY TERMS
auto fill
AutoComplete
copy
copy pointer
cut
fill handle
formula bar
label
move pointer
Office Clipboard
paste
range
template

Creating and Editing a Workbook | 337

■ SOFTWARE ORIENTATION

Excel's Home Tab

In Excel, when the Home tab is displayed, you see the Clipboard group. This group contains the command buttons to cut, copy, and paste data. These commands allow you to revise, move, and repeat data within a worksheet. Commands related to editing worksheet data are grouped together in the Editing group. Use commands in this group to fill adjacent cells, to sort and filter data, and to find specific data within a worksheet.

Figure 2-1

Home tab groups and commands

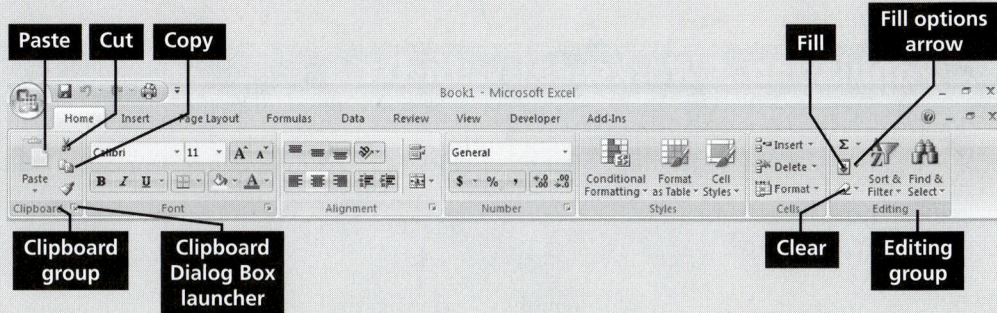

■ Creating a Workbook

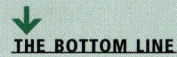
THE BOTTOM LINE

There are three ways to create a new Microsoft Excel workbook. You can open a new, blank workbook using the Microsoft Office Button. You can open an existing Excel workbook, enter new or additional data, and save the file with a new name, thus creating a new workbook. You can also use a *template* to create a new workbook. A template is a model that has already been set up to track certain kinds of data, such as sales reports, invoices, etc.

Starting a Workbook from Scratch

When you want to create a new workbook, launch Excel and a blank workbook is ready for you to begin working. If you have already been working in Excel and want to begin a new workbook, click the Microsoft Office Button, click New, and then click Create to create a blank workbook.

Worksheets usually begin with a title. The primary title is often followed by a secondary title. A title sets the stage for the reader's interpretation of the data contained in a worksheet. You will create a sales report for Fabrikam in the following exercises.

START A WORKBOOK FROM SCRATCH

GET READY. Before beginning these steps, be sure to launch Microsoft Office Excel 2007.

1. A blank workbook opens with A1 as the active cell.
2. Key **Fabrikam, Inc.** This is the primary title for the worksheet. Note that as you key, the text appears in the cell and in the Formula bar.
3. Press Enter. The text is entered into cell A1, but looks like it flows over into B1.
4. In cell A2, key **Monthly Sales Report**. Press Enter.
5. Click the **Microsoft Office Button**, and then click **New** in the Options pane. The New Workbook dialog box will open. Sometimes you need to open a new workbook when you are already working in Excel.

When you are working in Excel, you can open a blank workbook with the shortcut combination Ctrl+N.

338 | Lesson 2

6. In the right pane, click **Blank Workbook** if necessary.
7. Click the **Create** button. A second Excel workbook is opened.
8. Click the **Microsoft Office Button**, and then click **Close**. Book2 is closed. Book1 remains open.

   PAUSE. LEAVE the workbook open to use in the next exercise.

TAKE NOTE

Text is stored in only one cell even when it appears to extend into adjacent cells. If an entry is longer that the cell width and the next cell contains data, the entry appears in truncated form.

Populating a Worksheet with Data

THE BOTTOM LINE

You can enter three types of data into Excel: text, numbers, and formulas. In the following exercises, you will enter text (labels) and numbers (values). You will learn to enter formulas in Lesson 7. Text entries contain alphabetic characters and any other character that does not have a purely numeric value.

The real strength of Excel is its ability to calculate and to analyze numbers based on the numeric values you enter. For that reason, accurate data entry is crucial.

Entering Labels

Labels are used to identify the numeric data and are the most common type of text entered in a worksheet. Labels are also used to sort and group data. If the first few characters that you type in a column match an existing entry in that column, Excel automatically enters the remaining characters. This *AutoComplete* feature works only for entries that contain text or a combination of text and numbers.

ENTER LABELS

USE the workbook from the previous exercise.

TROUBLESHOOTING

To verify that AutoComplete is enabled, click the Microsoft Office Button, and then click Excel Options. Click Advanced. In the Editing options section, click the Enable AutoComplete for cell values check box if it is not already checked. Click OK.

1. Select **A4** to enter the first column label. Key **Agent** and press Tab.
2. Key **Last Closing** and press Tab.
3. In cell C4, key **January** and press Enter.

TAKE NOTE

When you press Tab to enter data in several cells in a row and then press Enter at the end of the row, the selection moves to the beginning of the next row.

Creating and Editing a Workbook | 339

4. Select **A5** to enter the first row label and key **Richard Carey**.
5. Select **A6** and key **David Ortiz**.
6. Select **A7** and key **Kim Akers**.
7. Select **A8** and key **Nicole Caron**.
8. Select **A9** and key **R**. As shown in Figure 2-2, AutoComplete is activated when you key the *R* because it matches the beginning of a previous entry in this column. AutoComplete displays the entry for Richard Carey.

Figure 2-2

Excel's AutoComplete

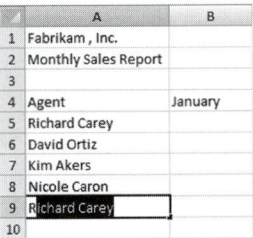

9. Key a **y**. The AutoComplete entry disappears. Finish keying an entry for **Ryan Calafato**.
10. Double-click the marker between columns A and B.
11. Double-click the marker between columns B and C. All worksheet data should be visible.

TAKE NOTE Excel bases the list of potential AutoComplete entries on the active cell column. Entries that are repeated within a row are not automatically completed.

PAUSE. LEAVE the workbook open to use in the next exercise.

As you experienced in the preceding exercise, when the beginning of a new column entry matches an existing entry and AutoComplete is activated, the remaining text is selected, and you can accept or reject it. To accept an AutoComplete entry, press Enter or Tab. When you accept AutoComplete, the completed entry will exactly match the pattern of uppercase and lowercase letters of the existing entry. To replace the automatically entered characters, continue keying. To delete the automatically entered characters, press Backspace. Entries that contain only numbers, dates, or times are not automatically completed. If you do not want to see the AutoComplete option, the feature can be turned off.

The *formula bar* is located between the Ribbon and the worksheet. As you can see in Figure 2-3, when you enter data in a cell, the text or numbers appear in the cell and in the formula bar. You can also enter or edit data directly in the formula bar.

Entering Dates

Dates are often used in worksheets to track data over a specified period of time. Dates can also be used in formulas and in developing graphs and charts. In Excel 2007, the default date format uses four digits for the year. Also by default, dates are right-justified in the cells.

ENTER DATES

USE the workbook from the previous exercise.

1. Click cell **B5**, key **1/4/XX** (with XX representing the current year), and press [Enter]. The number is entered in B5 and B6 becomes the active cell.
2. Key **1/25/XX** and press [Enter]. The number is entered in B6 and B7 becomes the active cell.
3. Key **1/17** and press [Enter]. 17-Jan is entered in the cell, and 1/17/current year appears in the formula bar.
4. Key **1/28** and press [Enter].
5. Key **January 21, 2008** and press [Enter]. 21-Jan-08 will appear in the cell. The date formats in column B are not consistent. You will apply a consistent date format in the next lesson.

PAUSE. LEAVE the workbook open to use in the next exercise.

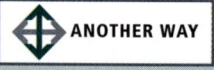 **ANOTHER WAY**

Ctrl+; (semicolon) will enter the current date into a worksheet cell; Ctrl+: (colon) will enter the current time.

Like text, dates can be used as row and column headings. However, dates are considered serial numbers, which means that they are sequential and can be added, subtracted, and used in calculations. The way a date is initially displayed in a worksheet cell depends upon the format in which you enter it.

Excel interprets two-digit years from 00 to 29 as the years 2000 to 2029; two-digit years from 30 to 99 are interpreted as 1930 to 1999. If you enter 1/28/08, the date will be displayed as 1/28/2008 in the cell. If you enter 1/28/37, the cell will display 1/28/1937.

If you key January 28, 2008, the date will display as 28-Jan-08, as shown in Figure 2-3. If you key 1/28 without a year, Excel interprets the date to be the current year. 28-Jan will display in the cell, and the formula bar will display 1/28/ followed by the current year. In the next lesson, you will learn to apply a consistent format to series of dates.

Figure 2-3

Date formats

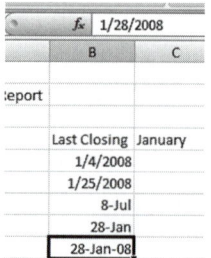

When you enter a date into a cell in a particular format, the cell is automatically formatted. Subsequent numbers entered in that cell will be converted to the date format of the original entry. In the preceding exercise, if you enter a date in a different format than what is specified and then key the format specified, your worksheet may not reflect the results described.

 **TAKE NOTE**

Regardless of the date format displayed in the cell, the formula bar displays the date in month/day/four-digit-year format because that is the format required for calculations and analyses.

Entering Values

Numeric values are the foundation for Excel's calculations, analyses, charts, and graphs. Numbers can be formatted as currency, percentages, decimals, and fractions. By default, numeric entries are right-justified in a cell.

Applying formatting to numbers changes their appearance but does not affect the cell value that Excel uses to perform calculations. The value is not affected by formatting or special characters that are entered with a number. The true value is always displayed in the formula bar.

 ENTER VALUES

USE the workbook from the previous exercise.

1. Click cell **C5**, key **$275,000**, and press **Enter**. Be sure to include the $ and the comma in your entry. The number is entered in C5 and C6 becomes the active cell. The number is displayed in the cell with a dollar sign and comma; however, the formula bar displays the true value and disregards the special characters.
2. Key **125000** and press **Enter**.
3. Key **209,000** and press **Enter**. The number is entered in the cell with a comma separating the digits; the comma does not appear in the formula bar.
4. Key **258,000** and press **Enter**.
5. Key **145700** and press **Enter**. See Figure 2-4.

Figure 2-4

Value unaffected by formatting

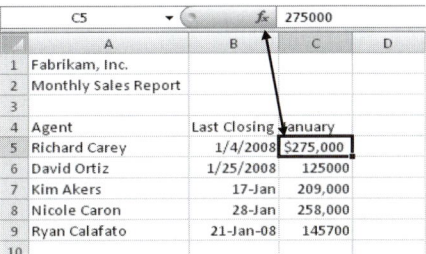

PAUSE. LEAVE the worksheet open to use in the next exercise.

A numeric entry contains a combination of the digits 0 through 9. Special characters that indicate the type of value can also be included in the entry. The following chart illustrates special characters that can be entered with numbers.

Character	Used to
+	Indicate a positive value
- or ( )	Indicate a negative value
$	Indicate a currency value
%	Indicate a percentage
/	Indicate a fraction
.	Indicate a decimal
,	Separate the digits of an entry

A number entered in Excel is considered positive unless it is combined with a special character to indicate otherwise. If you enter a plus sign with a number, Excel ignores it. Negative numbers can be entered with a minus sign or with parentheses. By default, Excel shows negative numbers with a minus sign. When you enter a dollar sign or another of the characters shown, Excel automatically assigns a number format to the entry.

Filling a Series with Auto Fill

Excel provides *auto fill* options that will automatically fill cells with data and/or formatting. To populate a new cell with data that exists in an adjacent cell, use the Fill command. You can choose the direction from which you want the data to be copied.

The *fill handle* is a small black square in the lower-right corner of the selected cell. When you point to the fill handle, the pointer changes to a black cross. You can drag the fill handle from a cell containing data to fill adjacent cells with existing data or have Excel automatically continue a series of numbers, numbers and text combinations, dates, or time periods, based on an established pattern.

→ FILL A SERIES WITH AUTO FILL

USE the workbook from the previous exercise.

1. Select **D4** and click **Fill**. See Figure 2-5.

Figure 2-5

Fill command

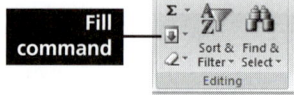

ANOTHER WAY

To quickly fill a cell with the contents of the cell above, press Ctrl+D; press Ctrl+R to fill the cell to the right.

2. From the Options box, click **Right**. The contents of C4 (January) is filled into cell D4.
3. Select **C10** and click the **Fill** button. Choose **Down**. The content of C9 is copied into C10.
4. Click the fill handle in C5, as shown in Figure 2-6, and drag to F5. The Auto Fill Options button appears in G6.

Figure 2-6

Fill handle

TAKE NOTE

A *range* is a group of adjacent cells that you select to perform operations on all of the selected cells. When you refer to a range of cells, the first cell and last cell are written with a colon, for example, D5:F5.

5. Point to the Auto Fill Options button, click the arrow, and choose **Fill Formatting Only**.
6. Click the fill handle in C4 and drag to H4. Excel recognizes January as the beginning of a natural series and completes the series as far as you take the fill handle.
7. Select **C13**, key **2007**, and press **Enter**.
8. Click the fill handle in C13 and drag to D13. The contents of C13 are copied.
9. In D13, key **2008** and press **Enter**. You have created a series of years.
10. Select **C13** and **D13**. Click the fill handle and drag to G13. The cells are filled with consecutive years. When you enter sufficient data for Excel to recognize a series, you can drag the fill handle to complete the series as far as you want.

Creating and Editing a Workbook | 343

TAKE NOTE: When Excel recognizes a series, the default fill option is to complete the series. When you use the fill handle and a series is not present, the default is to copy the cell contents. The Fill Options button also allows you to fill formatting only or to fill without formatting.

11. Select cells **F4:H4**. With the range selected, press **Delete**.
12. Select **C10:G13**. Press **Delete**. You have cleared your Sales Report worksheet of unneeded data. Your worksheet should look like Figure 2-7.

Figure 2-7

Sales Report worksheet

	A	B	C	D	E
1	Fabrikam , Inc.				
2	Monthly Sales Report				
3					
4	Agent	Last Closing	January	February	March
5	Richard Carey	1/4/2008	$275,000		
6	David Ortiz	1/25/2008	125000		
7	Kim Akers	8-Jul	209,000		
8	Nicole Caron	28-Jan	258,000		
9	Ryan Calafato	28-Jan-08	145700		
10					

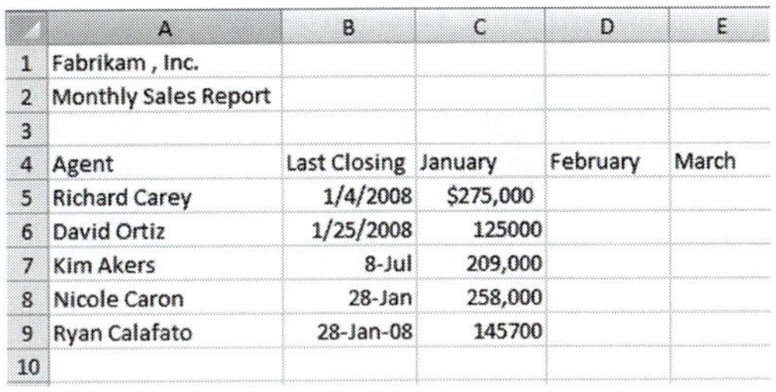

PAUSE. LEAVE the workbook open to use in the next exercise.

CERTIFICATION READY?
How do you fill a series using Auto Fill?
1.1.1

To display the fill handle, hover the cursor over the lower-right corner of the cell until it turns into a +. Click and drag the handle from cells that contain data to the cells you want to fill with that data.

After you fill cells using the fill handle, the Auto Fill Options button appears so that you can choose how the selection is filled. As shown in Figure 2-8, the default is to copy the original content and formatting. In the illustrated example, the content of the original cell appears in each cell in the filled range. When you point to the Auto Fill Options button and click the arrow that appears, you can choose other fill options.

Figure 2-8

Auto Fill Options button

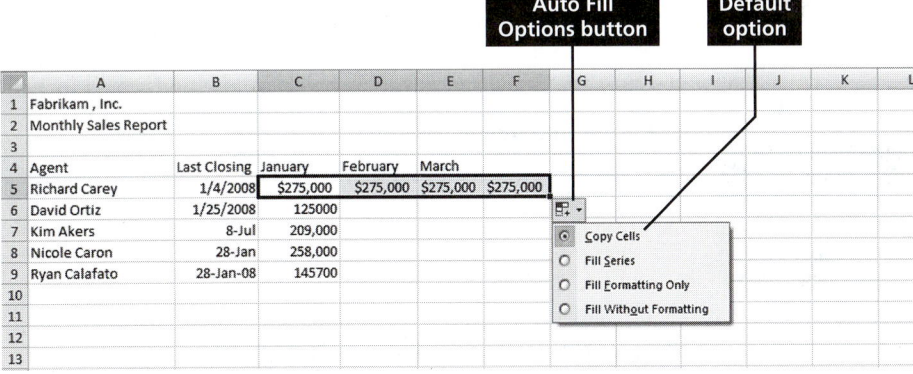

If you choose to fill formatting only, the contents are not copied, but any number that you key into a cell in the selected range will be formatted like the original cell, such as Currency. If you click Fill Series, the copied cells will read $275,001, $275,002, etc. The Auto Fill Options button remains until you perform another function.

The fill handle can be used to complete a natural series or any series that you create. For example, to record daily sales, you might want to have consecutive columns labeled with the days of the week. If you key Monday in the first cell, you can fill in the rest of the days by dragging the fill handle from the Monday cell to complete the series. When you key sufficient data for Excel to recognize a series, the fill handle will do the rest.

Cutting, Copying, and Pasting Data

THE BOTTOM LINE

You can use Excel's Cut, Copy, and Paste commands to copy or move entire cells with their contents, formats, and formulas. You can also copy specific contents or attributes from the cells. For example, you can copy the format only without copying the cell value or copy the resulting value of a formula without copying the formula itself. You can also copy the value from the original cell but retain the formatting of the destination cell.

Copying a Data Series with the Mouse

By default, drag-and-drop editing is turned on so that you can use the mouse to *copy* (duplicate) or move cells. Just select the cells or range of cells you want to copy and hold down Ctrl while you point to the border of the selection. When the pointer becomes a *copy pointer*, 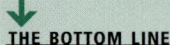 you can drag the cell or range of cells to the new location. As you drag, a scrolling ScreenTip identifies where the selection will be copied if you released the mouse button.

COPY A DATA SERIES WITH THE MOUSE

USE the workbook from the previous exercise.

1. Select the range **A4:A9**.
2. Press Ctrl and point the cursor at the bottom border of the selected range. The copy pointer is displayed. Be sure to hold down the Ctrl key the entire time, or you will move the value instead of copying it.
3. With the copy pointer displayed, hold down the left mouse button and drag the selection down until A12:A17 is displayed in the scrolling ScreenTip below the copy box.
4. Release the mouse button. The data in A4:A9 appears in A12:A17.

   PAUSE. LEAVE the workbook open to use in the next exercise.

After you have entered data into a worksheet, you frequently need to rearrange or reorganize some of it to make the worksheet easier to understand and analyze. As you practiced in this exercise, cut, copy, and paste functions can be performed in a variety of ways:

- using the mouse
- using Ribbon commands
- using shortcut commands
- using the Office Clipboard task pane

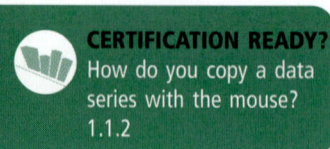

CERTIFICATION READY?
How do you copy a data series with the mouse?
1.1.2

Moving a Data Series with the Mouse

Data can be moved from one location to another within a workbook in much the same way as copying. To move a data series, select the cell or range of cells and point to the border of the selection. When the pointer becomes a *move pointer*, you can drag the cell or range of cells to a new location. When data is moved, it replaces any existing data in the destination cells.

➔ MOVE A DATA SERIES WITH THE MOUSE

USE the workbook from the previous exercise.

1. Select **B4:B9**.
2. Point the cursor at the bottom border of the selected range. The move pointer is displayed.
3. With the move pointer displayed, hold down the left mouse button and drag the selection down until B12:B17 is displayed in the scrolling ScreenTip below the box.
4. Release the mouse button. In your worksheet, the destination cells are empty; therefore, you are not concerned with replacing existing data. The data previously in B4:B9 is now in B12:B17.
5. Select the range of cells from **C4:E9**.
6. Point the cursor at the left border of the selection to display the move arrows.
7. Drag left and drop the range of cells in the same rows in column B.

   PAUSE. LEAVE the workbook open to use in the next exercise.

When you attempt to move a selection to a location that contains data, a caution dialog box, shown in Figure 2-9, opens. "Do you want to replace the contents of the destination cells?" is a reminder that moving data to a new location replaces the existing data.

Figure 2-9

Dialog box to move cells

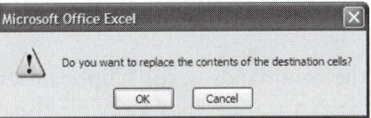

Copying and Pasting Data

The ***Office Clipboard*** collects and stores up to 24 copied or cut items. You can then ***paste*** (insert) selected items from the Clipboard to a new location in the worksheet. ***Cut*** data is removed from the worksheet but is still available for you to use in multiple locations. Items on the Office Clipboard are available to be used in the active workbook, in other workbooks, and in other Microsoft Office programs. To use more than the last item cut or copied, however, the Clipboard task pane must be open. If Collect Without Showing Office Clipboard is selected in Clipboard Options, cut or copied items will be stored on the clipboard, but you must display the task pane to paste any item except the last one.

➔ COPY AND PASTE DATA

USE the workbook from the previous exercise.

1. Click the **Clipboard Dialog Box Launcher** to open the Office Clipboard task pane. The Clipboard task pane opens on the left side of the worksheet. (Task panes opened on the right in Excel 2003.)
2. Select **C5** and key **305000**. Press `Enter`.
3. Select **C5** and click **Copy** in the Clipboard group. The border around C5 becomes a flashing marquee.

 **ANOTHER WAY**

To copy, you can use Ctrl+C or right-click and then click Copy on the shortcut menu. You can use Ctrl+V to paste the last cut or copied data.

4. Select **C8**; the flashing marquee identifies the item that will be copied. Click **Paste** in the Clipboard group.
5. Select **D5**. Right-click and then click **Paste** on the shortcut menu. The flashing border remains.
6. With D5 selected, press **Delete** to remove the data from D5. When you perform any function other than paste, the flashing border is removed from C5. You can no longer paste the item unless you use the Clipboard pane.
7. Select **C6**, key **185000**, and press **Enter**.
8. You can copy data from one worksheet or workbook and paste it to another worksheet or workbook. Select **A1:A9** and click **Copy**.
9. Click the **Sheet2** tab to open the worksheet.
10. Select **A1** and click **Paste**. Point to Paste Options and click the arrow. Click **Keep Source Column Widths**.

> **TAKE NOTE**
> To paste a range of cells, select the first cell in the range to copy or select a range the same size as the one copied.

11. Click **Sheet1**. With C9 active, click the **$305,000** item in the task pane. The item is pasted. Click **Undo** to clear C9.

   PAUSE. LEAVE the workbook open to use in the next exercise.

You have just practiced using the commands in the Clipboard group. You can select a range of data, click copy, move the cursor to a new location, and click Paste. If you copy additional items and then click Paste, only the last item copied will be pasted. To access multiple items, open the Clipboard task pane.

> **TAKE NOTE**
> When you cut or copy data and then paste the data using the Office Clipboard, the Paste command on the Ribbon, or press Ctrl+V, the default is to paste the original cell contents and formatting. Additional options are available when you click the arrow below the Paste command. You can copy a range of data in a column and click Transpose to paste the data into columns. Other options allow you to copy formulas, to copy values instead of formulas, and to copy cells containing borders and paste the data without the border.

When you paste data, the Paste Options button appears below the pasted data. Click the button to choose how the destination cell or range will be formatted. Paste options are illustrated in Figure 2-10.

Figure 2-10

Paste options

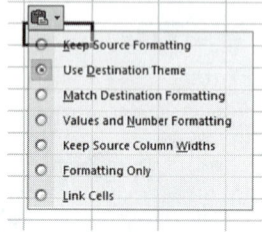

To display the Office Clipboard task pane, click the Clipboard Dialog Box Launcher. The most recently copied item is always added at the top and it is the item that will be copied when you click Paste or use a shortcut command. As illustrated in Figure 2-11, the Clipboard stores items copied from other programs as well as those from Excel. The program icon and the beginning of the copied text are displayed.

Creating and Editing a Workbook | 347

Figure 2-11

Office Clipboard task pane

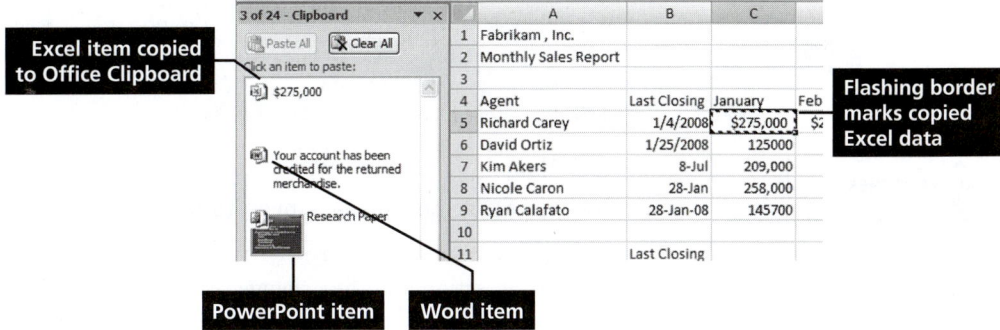

When you copy or cut data from a worksheet, a flashing border appears around the item and remains visible after you paste the data to one or more new locations. It will continue to flash until you perform another action or press Esc. As long as the marquee flashes, you can paste that item to multiple locations without the Clipboard being open.

When you move the cursor over a Clipboard item, an arrow appears on the right side that allows you to paste the item or delete it. You can delete individual items, or click Clear All to delete all Clipboard items. When the task pane is open, you can still use the command buttons or shortcuts to paste the last copied item.

Clipboard Options allow you to display the Clipboard automatically. If you do not have the Clipboard automatically displayed, it is a good idea to check Collect Without Showing Office Clipboard so that you can access items you cut or copied when you open the Clipboard.

To close the Clipboard task pane, click the Dialog Box Launcher or the Close button at the top of the pane. Clipboard items remain, however, until you exit all Microsoft Office programs. If you want the Clipboard task pane to be displayed when Excel opens, click the Options button at the bottom of the Clipboard task pane and check the Show Office Clipboard Automatically option.

Press Ctrl+C twice to display the Office Clipboard task pane. If this shortcut does not open the Clipboard, open the Clipboard with the Dialog Box Launcher, click Clipboard Options, and enable this shortcut.

Cutting and Pasting Data

CERTIFICATION READY?
How do you copy and paste a data series?
1.3.1

Most of the options for copying and pasting data also apply to cutting and pasting. The major difference is that data copied and pasted remains in the original location as well as in the destination cell or range. Cut and pasted data appears only in the destination cell or range.

CUT AND PASTE DATA

USE the workbook from the previous exercise.

1. Click **Sheet2** if necessary.
2. Select **A8** and click **Cut** in the Clipboard group.
3. Select **A9** and click **Paste**.

348 | Lesson 2

TAKE NOTE When you delete text, it is not stored on the clipboard. If you want to remove data but think that you might use the text later, use Cut rather than Delete. Deleted text can be restored only with Undo.

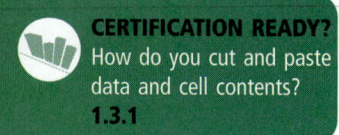

ANOTHER WAY

You can press Ctrl+Z to undo and Ctrl+Y to redo.

   4. Click **Undo**. The data is restored to A8.

   PAUSE. LEAVE the workbook open to use in the next exercise.

If you complete an action and then change your mind, Excel's Undo is extremely useful. If you mistakenly paste into a cell or range that already contains data, that data will not be available on the Clipboard. You must undo the paste to recover the data.

You can undo and repeat up to 100 actions in Excel. You can undo one or more actions by clicking Undo on the Quick Access Toolbar. To undo several actions at once, click the arrow next to Undo and select the actions that you want to reverse. Click the list and Excel will reverse the selected actions.

To redo an action that you undid, click Redo on the Quick Access Toolbar. When all actions have been undone, the Redo command changes to Repeat.

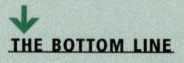

CERTIFICATION READY?
How do you cut and paste data and cell contents?
1.3.1

In the preceding exercises you learned that Excel provides a number of options for populating a worksheet with data. There are also several ways you can accomplish each of the tasks. To cut, copy, and paste, you can use Ribbon commands, shortcut key combinations, or right-click and use a shortcut menu. As you become more proficient in working with Excel, you will decide which method is most efficient for you.

Printing a Worksheet

THE BOTTOM LINE

When you click Quick Print, the entire open worksheet is printed. That option does not allow you to customize the printed report. The Page Layout tab commands allow you to tailor how a worksheet looks when it is printed. The commands on this tab let you set a print area, determine the page orientation, adjust page breaks, and decide whether you want the grid lines to print.

Setting the Print Area

Defining a print area gives you more control over what shows up on the printed page. If a worksheet has a defined print area, Excel will print only the specified print area. The print options in the Print dialog box will not override a defined area. You can set print areas to print a completed portion of a worksheet or to restrict publication of some data.

SET THE PRINT AREA

USE the workbook from the previous exercise.

   1. With Sheet1 active, select **C1:C9**.
   2. Click the **Microsoft Office Button** and select **Print**. The Print dialog box will open. The default printer will appear in the Name box.
   3. In the Print what section, click **Selection**.
   4. Click **OK**. Only the portion of the worksheet that you selected is printed. If you want to print a second copy of this portion of the worksheet, you have to repeat Steps 1–3.
   5. Select A1:B9. On the Page Layout tab, click **Print Area** in the Page Setup command group as shown in Figure 2-12.

Figure 2-12

Use Page Layout commands to prepare for printing

> **TROUBLESHOOTING**: If you click the Print Area without selecting the range of data you want to print, you will print only the active cell.

6. Click **Set Print Area** on the dropdown list. When you print from this worksheet, only the area A1:B9 will be printed.

   PAUSE. LEAVE the workbook open to use in the next exercise.

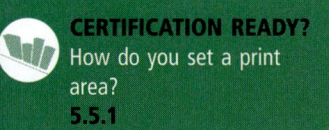

CERTIFICATION READY?
How do you set a print area?
5.5.1

With this print area setting, regardless of the method you use to print, only the January sales information will appear in the printed document. When a print area has been set, it will remain outlined on the worksheet as you continue to work. If you later want to print the entire worksheet, you must clear the print area or check Ignore print areas on the Print dialog box.

Using Print Preview

You have two options for seeing how your page will look when printed.

- Click the Microsoft Office Button, point to the Print arrow, and then click Print Preview.
- Click the Microsoft Office Button, click Print, and click Preview on the Print dialog box.

➔ USE PRINT PREVIEW

USE the workbook from the previous exercise.

1. Click the **Microsoft Office Button** and point to the arrow next to Print.
2. Click **Print Preview** from the options panel. The worksheet is displayed as it will be printed. Only the cell contents will be printed; the gridlines will not be printed.
3. Click **Close Print Preview**.
4. Click the **Page Layout** tab if necessary. Check the Print box in the Gridlines section of the Sheet Options command group. Although gridlines are visible on the work surface, the lines will not print unless the Print box is checked.
5. Click the **Microsoft Office Button**, point to Print, and choose **Print Preview**. The gridlines are shown in the preview window.
6. **CLOSE** the Print Preview window.

   PAUSE. LEAVE the workbook open to use in the next exercise.

Setting Other Printer Options

The Print dialog box options allow you to print multiple copies, print selected pages of a multi-page document, print an entire workbook, and ignore a set print area. You can also view document properties and preview the printed document.

SET OTHER PRINTER OPTIONS

USE the workbook from the previous exercise.

1. Click the **Microsoft Office Button**.
2. Click **Print**. The Print dialog box is displayed.
3. Click **Ignore print areas**. The print area will be ignored for this printing only. It will remain set and be visible in your worksheet.
4. Click **OK**. The active worksheet will be printed.

   PAUSE. LEAVE the workbook open to use in the next exercise.

Saving a Workbook

Saving a Workbook for Use in a Previous Version of Excel

Files created in earlier versions can be opened and revised in Excel 2007. You can save a copy of an Excel 2007 workbook (xlsx) that is fully compatible with Excel 97 through Excel 2003 (xls) versions. The program symbol displayed with the filenames will be different, but it is a good idea to give the earlier edition file a different name.

SAVE A WORKBOOK FOR USE IN A PREVIOUS VERSION OF EXCEL

USE the workbook from the previous exercise.

1. Click the **Microsoft Office Button** and point to **Save As**.
2. In the Save a copy of the document pane, click **Excel 97-2003 Workbook**.
3. In the Save As dialog box, key **Fabrikam First Qtr Sales 97-03**. Click **Save**. Close the workbook.
4. Press **Ctrl**+**O** to display the Open dialog box. Select **Fabrikam First Qtr. Sales 97-03**. Scroll right to view the file type and see that it is saved to be compatible with earlier Excel editions.
5. Click **Open**.

   PAUSE. LEAVE the workbook open to use in the next exercise.

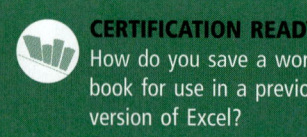

CERTIFICATION READY?
How do you save a workbook for use in a previous version of Excel?
5.4.1

Choosing a Different File Format

You can save an Excel 2007 file in a format other than xlsx or xlx. The file formats that are available in the Save As dialog box depend upon what type of sheet is active. When you save a file in another file format, some of the formatting, data, and/or features may be lost.

CHOOSE A DIFFERENT FILE FORMAT

USE the workbook from the previous exercise.

1. Click the **Microsoft Office Button** and point to Save As. Click **Other Formats**.
2. Choose **Single File Web Page** in the Save as type box.
3. Click **Change Title**. Key **January Sales**. Click **OK**.
4. Click **Selection:Sheet** and click **Publish**.
5. In the Publish as Web Page dialog box, select **Print Area**.
6. Click **Publish**. A browser window opens with January Sales displayed.
7. Close the browser window.
8. Click the **Microsoft Office Button** and click **Close**.

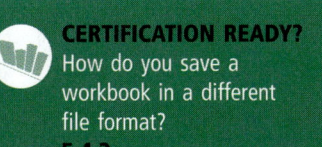

CERTIFICATION READY?
How do you save a workbook in a different file format?
5.4.2

9. If prompted to save changes, click **Yes**. The workbook is closed but Excel remains open.
   STOP. CLOSE Excel.

You can save an Excel file in a number of other formats such as an Excel Macro-Enabled Workbook or an XML Data file.

SUMMARY SKILL MATRIX

In this lesson you learned how to:
Start a Workbook from Scratch
Enter Labels
Enter Dates
Enter Values
Fill a Series with Auto Fill
Copy a Data Series with the Mouse
Move a Data Series with the Mouse
Copy and Pasting Data
Cut and Pasting Data
Set the Print Area
Use Print Preview
Set Other Print Options
Save a Workbook for use in a Previous Version of Excel
Choose a Different File Format

■ Knowledge Assessment

Matching

Match each vocabulary term with its definition.

a. auto fill
b. AutoComplete
c. copy
d. fill handle
e. formula bar
f. label
g. paste
h. range
i. template

_____g_____ 1. A command used to insert a cut or copied selection to a cell or range of cells

_____i_____ 2. Worksheets that are already set up to track certain kinds of data

_____d_____ 3. A small black square in the lower-right corner of selected cells that you can use to copy one cell to adjacent cells or to create a series

_____e_____ 4. A bar at the top of the Excel window where you can enter or edit cell entries or formulas

_____h_____ 5. A group of adjacent cells that you select to perform operations on all of the selected cells _____c_____ 6. To place a duplicate of a selection on the Office Clipboard

_____b_____ 7. An Excel feature that helps you quickly enter data into cells

_____a_____ 8. An Excel feature that automatically fills cells with data from another cell or range or completes a data series

_____f_____ 9. Entries that identify the numeric data in a worksheet

True / False

Circle T if the statement is true or F if the statement is false.

(T) F 1. You can accept an AutoComplete entry by pressing Tab or Enter.

T **F** 2. If you key **June 5** in a cell, the formula bar will display June 5 as well.

(p 340) T **(F)** 3. Use Ctrl+: to enter the current date in a worksheet cell. Ctrl+ ;(semicolon)

T **(F)** 4. When you paste data into a cell or range of cells that contain data, the data that is replaced is copied to the Office Clipboard.

T **(F)** 5. When you set a print area, the setting lasts for one printing only. If you want to print that range again, you will need to reset the print area.

(T) F 6. Use the fill handle to create a natural series such as the months of the year.

T **(F)** 7. You can use Quick Print to print selected pages of a long document.

T **(F)** 8. The Office Clipboard collects items cut or copied from Excel worksheets only.

(T) F 9. You cannot make changes to a worksheet in the Print Preview window.

T **(F)** 10. By default, gridlines will print in an Excel worksheet.

■ Competency Assessment

Project 2-1: Advertising Budget

Create a new worksheet for Fabrikam, Inc., that can be used to compare actual expenses with budgeted amounts.

GET READY. Launch Excel if it is not already running.

1. Click the **Microsoft Office Button** and click **New**.
2. Click **Blank Workbook** and then click **Create**.
3. Select **A1** and key **Fabrikam, Inc.**
4. Select **A2** and key **Advertising Budget**.
5. Beginning in A4, key the following labels and values.

Media	*Vendor*	*Monthly Budget*
Print	**Lucerne Publishing**	2000
Radio	**Northwind Traders**	$1,500
Door-to-Door	**Consolidated Messenger**	1200
Print	**Graphic Design Institute**	500
Television	**Southridge Video**	3000

6. If necessary, double-click the marker between columns to adjust the column width to display all of the text.
7. **SAVE** the workbook in the Lesson 2 folder you created in an exercise. Save the workbook as *Advertising Budget 2-1*.
8. **CLOSE** the file.

   LEAVE Excel open for the next project.

Creating and Editing a Workbook | 353

Project 2-2: Advertising Budget for Use in Previous Versions of Excel

The *Advertising Budget* document is avilable on the companion CD-ROM.

Fabrikam, Inc. needs their advertising budget worksheet saved for use in a previous version of Excel.

1. **OPEN** *Advertising Budget* from the CD data files.
2. Click the **Microsoft Office Button**.
3. Click **Save As**.
4. Change the Save As type to Excel 97-2003 Workbook.
5. Change the File name to *Advertising Budget 2-2*.
6. Click the **Save** button and **CLOSE** the file.

   LEAVE Excel open for the next project.

■ Proficiency Assessment

Project 2-3: Monthly Advertising Expense

The *Advertising Expense* document is available on the companion CD-ROM.

Use an existing workbook to create a new workbook that will track monthly advertising costs.

1. **OPEN** *Advertising Expense* from the CD data files.
2. Select **D4** and key **January**.
3. Select **D4**. Use the fill handle to enter the months of the year.
4. Select **A10**. Click **Fill** in the Editing group on the Home tab.
5. Choose **Down** and press `Enter`.
6. Select **B10**, key **Trey Research**, and press `Enter`.
7. Select **C10**, key **2500**, and press `Enter`.
8. **SAVE** the workbook in your Lesson 2 folder as *Advertising Expense 2-3* and **CLOSE** the file.

   LEAVE Excel open for the next project.

Project 2-4: Advertising Expenditures

Fourth Coffee specializes in unique coffee and tea blends. Create a workbook to track and classify expenditures for January.

1. Click the **Microsoft Office Button**. Open a new blank workbook.
2. In A1 key **Fourth Coffee**.
3. In A2 key **January Expenditures**.
4. Enter the following column headings in row 4.

Date	Check No.	Paid to	Category	Amount

5. Enter the following expenditures:

   - **January 3**, paid **$3000** to **Wide World Importers** for **coffee**, Check No. **4076**.
   - **January 20**, paid **$600** to **Northwind Traders** for **tea**, Check **4077**.
   - **January 22**, paid **$300** to **City Power and Light** for **utilities**.
   - **January 28**, paid **$200** to **A. Datum Corporation** for **advertising**.

6. Checks are written sequentially. Use the fill handle to enter the missing check numbers.

7. Adjust column headings as needed.
8. **SAVE** the workbook as *Expenses 2-4* and **CLOSE** the file.
   LEAVE Excel open for the next project.

■ Mastery Assessment

Project 2-5: Home Sales Data

Fabrikam receives sales research data from the local association of Realtors, which it uses as a benchmark for evaluating its sales performance.

OPEN *Sales Research* from the CD data files.

The *Sales Research* document is available on the companion CD-ROM.

1. **OPEN** the **Office Clipboard**. If it contains items, click **Clear All** so that only data for this project will be on the Clipboard.
2. Use AutoFill to add the remaining months in column A.
3. The data for March and April are reversed. Use the Copy command to place the data for March (B6:G6) on the Clipboard. Copy the data as one item.
4. Use the mouse to move B7:G7 to B6:G6. Paste the April data from the Clipboard to B7:G7.
5. Beginning with A1, set the Print Area to include all data for January through June. Print the selected area.
6. Click the **Select All** button in the upper-left corner of the worksheet. Copy the entire worksheet to the Clipboard.
7. Paste the data to Sheet2. Adjust column widths if necessary.
8. **SAVE** the workbook as *Sales Research 2-5*. **CLOSE** the workbook.
   LEAVE Excel open for the next project.

Project 2-6: Fourth Coffee

An employee has begun an inventory worksheet for Fourth Coffee. You want to use the company name and logo from the inventory sheet to create a banner for a website.

OPEN *FC Inventory* from the CD data files.

The *FC Inventory* document is available on the companion CD-ROM.

1. **SAVE** the workbook as a Single File Web Page.
2. **PUBLISH** Selection A1:E1.
3. Click **Publish**. You have just created the banner for the company's new Web page.
   STOP. CLOSE Excel.

INTERNET READY

More than fifteen shortcut combinations were given in the first two lessons. Create a worksheet to list at least fifteen shortcut combinations. Decide how many columns you will need. Each column must have a label that identifies its contents.

Use the Excel Help on your computer and Microsoft Help online. Save your file as *Excel Shortcuts*.

Formatting Cells and Ranges

3

LESSON SKILL MATRIX

Adding a New Cell to a Worksheet — 357	Students will learn how to add a new cell to a worksheet.
Deleting a Cell from a Worksheet — 358	Students will learn how to delete a cell from a worksheet.
Selecting Cells and Ranges — 359	Students will learn how to select cells and ranges.
Aligning Cell Contents — 360	Students will learn how to align cell contents.
Choosing Fonts and Font Sizes — 361	Students will learn how to choose fonts and font sizes.
Applying Special Character Attributes — 362	Students will learn how to apply special character attributes.
Changing Font Color — 362	Students will learn how to change font color.
Filling Cells with Color — 363	Students will learn how to fill cells with color.
Applying Number Formats — 364	Students will learn how to apply number formats.
Wrapping Text in a Cell — 365	Students will learn how to wrap text in a cell.
Merging and Splitting Merged Cells — 366	Students will learn how to merge and split merged cells.
Placing Borders Around Cells — 367	Students will learn how to place borders around cells.
Copying Cell Formatting with the Format Painter — 368	Students will learn how to copy cell formatting with the format painter.
Applying a Cell Style — 369	Students will learn how to apply a cell style.
Modifying a Cell Style — 370	Students will learn how to modify a cell style.
Placing a Hyperlink in a Cell — 371	Students will learn how to place a hyperlink in a cell.
Removing a Hyperlink — 372	Students will learn how to remove a hyperlink.
Using the Rule Manager to Apply Conditional Formats — 373	Students will learn how to use the rule manager to apply conditional formats.
Allowing Multiple Conditional Formatting Rules to Be True — 374	Students will learn how to allow multiple conditional formatting rules to be true.
Allowing Specific Conditional Formats — 374	Students will learn how to allow specific conditional formats.
Clearing a Cell's Formatting — 375	Students will learn how to clear a cell's formatting.

KEY TERMS
attribute
character
conditional formatting
default
font
Format Painter
hyperlink
merged cells
Mini toolbar
point
select
style

Contoso, Ltd's income is generated by the four physicians and the physician assistant (PA). Ideally, physicians are scheduled to see no more than 35 patients per day, but every effort is made to accommodate patients who need immediate medical attention. Working in collaboration with the physicians, the PA sees patients who need an appointment when all the physicians' schedules are full. Many chronically ill patients whose conditions require frequent monitoring are scheduled with the PA. By law, a PA can treat no more than 25 patients a day. The firm is considering adding a nurse practitioner (NP) to balance the patient load. An NP is a registered nurse who provides some of the same care as physicians. In most states, an NP can prescribe medications.

■ SOFTWARE ORIENTATION

Formatting Excel Worksheets

The Home tab displayed in Figure 3-1 contains the formatting commands that you will use to enhance the appearance of the worksheets you create. You will use commands from every group as you learn to insert and delete cells, apply basic formatting to text, copy formatting, and apply styles and conditional formatting.

Figure 3-1

Apply formatting using the Home tab

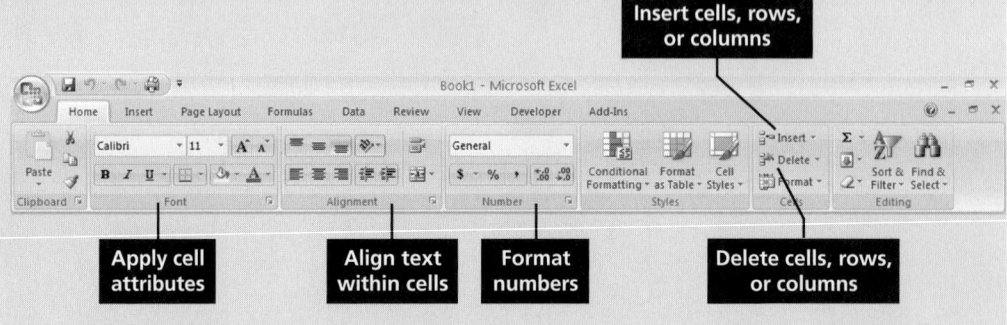

Formatting Cells and Ranges | 357

■ Inserting and Deleting Cells

THE BOTTOM LINE

As shown in Figure 3-2, when you click the arrow next to Insert, you can insert cells, worksheet rows, worksheet columns, or a new worksheet into a workbook.

Similar options apply to deleting cells. You can delete a cell, a worksheet row, a worksheet column, or a worksheet from a workbook. In the exercises that follow, you will add and delete cells.

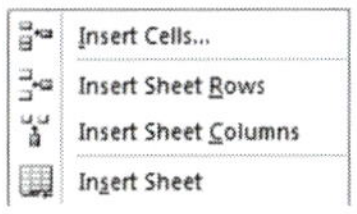

Figure 3-2

Insert options

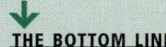

Looking Ahead

In Lesson 4, you will insert and delete worksheet rows and columns. In Lesson 5 you will add a worksheet to an existing workbook and delete a worksheet from a workbook.

Adding a New Cell to a Worksheet

After creating a worksheet, you may decide that you need to add additional data or delete unnecessary data. To enter additional text or values within the existing data, you need to insert cells. You can insert a cell or cells and shift down other cells in the same column, or you can shift other cells in the same row to the right.

CD

The *Contoso Patient Visits* workbook is available on the companion CD-ROM.

→ ADD A NEW CELL TO A WORKSHEET

GET READY. Before you begin these steps, be sure to launch Microsoft Office Excel 2007.

1. The Home tab should be active.
2. **OPEN** *Contoso Patient Visits* from the data files for this lesson.
3. Click **F5** and click **Insert** in the Cells group. F5 is now blank and the cells in the range F5:F8 have shifted down one row.
4. Key **604** and press **Enter**.
5. Select **J4**.
6. Click the **Insert** arrow, and click **Insert Cells**. The Insert dialog box opens.
7. Click **Shift cells right** and click **OK**. A blank cell is inserted and the data is shifted to the right.

ANOTHER WAY

You can select a cell or range, right-click, and click Insert to open the Insert dialog box. In the dialog box, click the direction in which you want to shift the cells.

ANOTHER WAY

You can repeat the action of inserting a cell by clicking Redo on the Quick Access Toolbar.

8. Key **580** and press **Enter**.
9. Select **K7:L7** and click the **Insert** arrow.
10. Click **Insert Cells**.
11. Click **Shift cells right** and click **OK**. The data has shifted two cells to the right.
12. Select **K7**, key **475**, and press **Tab**.
13. Key **611** and press **Enter**.

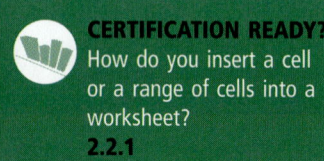

CERTIFICATION READY?
How do you insert a cell or a range of cells into a worksheet?
2.2.1

14. Select **N3:N9**. Click the **Insert** arrow and click **Insert Cells**.
15. Click **Shift cells right** and click **OK**. Cells are inserted so that November's data can be entered later.

    PAUSE. LEAVE the workbook open to use in the next exercise.

Additions and changes are common activities in Microsoft Office Excel 2007 workbooks. In the previous exercise, Contoso created an Excel workbook to track the number of patients treated during a month to determine whether to hire a nurse practitioner. After creating and saving the workbook, the administrative assistant discovered that corrections are needed and additional data must be added to the workbook.

If you click Insert in the Cells group, a blank cell is inserted and, by default, existing cells move down in the column. When you click the arrow next to Insert and click Insert Cells, the Insert dialog box shown in Figure 3-3 opens, and you can choose to shift cells to the right. The dialog box also allows you to insert a row or a column in a worksheet.

Figure 3-3
Insert dialog box

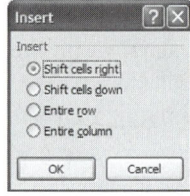

To insert blank cells in a worksheet, select the cell or the range of cells where you want to insert the new blank cells. Select the number of cells that you want to insert. As Figure 3-4 illustrates, if you want to insert two cells, you must select two cells.

Figure 3-4
Selection must match cells to be inserted

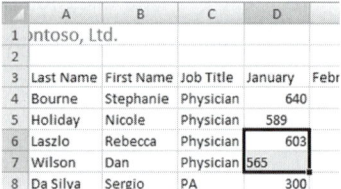

With the cells selected, click the arrow next to Insert, and then click Insert Cells. When the Insert dialog box opens, click the direction you want to shift the cells.

Deleting a Cell from a Worksheet

You can use Delete in the Cells group to delete cells, ranges, rows, or columns. The principles are the same as those you used to insert cells except that the direction the cells shift is reversed.

➔ DELETE A CELL FROM A WORKSHEET

USE the workbook from the previous exercise.

1. Select **C3:C9**. Click **Delete** in the Cells group. The Job Title data is removed from the worksheet and the remaining columns are shifted left.
2. Select **A9:N9** and click **Delete**. The duplicate row of data is removed.
3. Select **K13:K18** and click **Cut** in the Clipboard group.
4. Select **M3** and click **Paste**.

   PAUSE. LEAVE the workbook open to use in the next exercise.

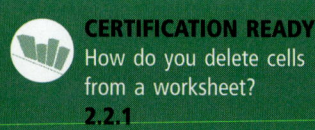

CERTIFICATION READY?
How do you delete cells from a worksheet?
2.2.1

Formatting Cells and Ranges | 359

Click Delete in the Cells group to eliminate cells from a worksheet. Any data to the right of the deleted cell or cells will automatically shift left. If you want to shift cells up rather than left, click the arrow next to Delete and click Delete Cells to open the Delete dialog box.

You can right-click and click Delete on the shortcut menu to open the Delete dialog box and delete cells. Remember that when you use the Delete command, the cells are deleted. When you use the Cut command or press Delete on the keyboard, only the cell contents are deleted. The cells and any formatting remain.

■ Manually Formatting Cell Contents

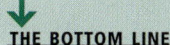
THE BOTTOM LINE

The commands in the Font, Alignment, and Number groups (Figure 3-5) contain the basic formatting commands. Using only those groups, you can significantly change the appearance of a worksheet. Use Font commands to change the font and font size; to bold, italicize, and underline data; and to add color, fill, and borders. Use Alignment commands to choose how data is aligned within cells. Use Number commands to apply a format to values and to increase or decrease the number of digits after a decimal.

Figure 3-5

Basic formatting command groups

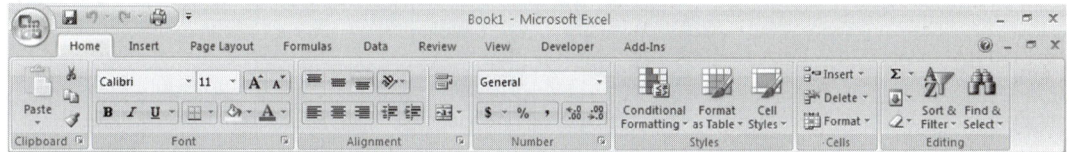

Selecting Cells and Ranges

To apply formatting to text and values in an existing worksheet, you must first *select* the data. When you select data, you identify the cell or range of cells in which you want to enter data or apply formatting. You can select cells, ranges, rows, columns, or the complete worksheet. The cells in a range can be adjacent or nonadjacent. You can also place a cell in editing mode and select all or part of its contents.

➔ SELECT CELLS AND RANGES

USE the workbook from the previous exercise.

1. Select **A3**. Hold down the left mouse button and drag to **B8** to select the range.
2. Click the row heading to select the entire row.
3. Click the column **C** header, press and hold **Ctrl**, and click **E**, **G**, and **I** to select nonadjacent columns.

TAKE NOTE If a worksheet has been protected, you may not be able to select cells on the worksheet.

4. Click the **Microsoft Office Button** and then click **Save As**.
5. When the Save As dialog box opens, create a Lesson 3 folder.
6. **SAVE** your workbook in the folder and name it *Patient Visits*.

   PAUSE. LEAVE the workbook open to use in the next exercise.

Table 3-1 illustrates a variety of ways to select portions or all of a worksheet.

Table 3-1

Options for selecting cells and ranges

To Select	Do This
A single cell	Click the cell or press the arrow keys to move to the cell.
A range of cells	Click the first cell in the range and drag to the last cell, or hold down Shift while you press the arrow keys to extend the selection.
A large range of cells	Click the first cell in the range and hold down Shift while you click the last cell.
All cells on a worksheet	Click the Select All button (intersection of the column and row headings), or press Ctrl+A.
Nonadjacent cells or cell ranges	Select the first cell or range and hold down Ctrl while you select the other cells or ranges.
An entire row or column	Click the row or column heading.
Adjacent rows or columns	Drag across the row or column headings.
Nonadjacent rows or columns	Click the column or row heading of the first row or column of the selection. Hold down Ctrl while you click the column or row headings of other rows or columns you want to add to the selection.
The contents of a cell	Double-click the cell and then drag across the contents that you want to select.

When you make a selection, the cell or range is highlighted on the screen. These highlights do not appear in a printout, however. If you want cells to be highlighted when you print a worksheet, you must use formatting features to apply shading.

Excel provides many ways to format labels and values in a worksheet. In the business world, worksheets are usually printed or shared with others electronically. Therefore, you want your worksheet or workbook to be as eye-catching and understandable as possible. You can improve the design of a worksheet in several ways.

- Change the alignment.
- Change the font style and enlarge the text for titles.
- Format titles and labels in bold and/or italics.
- Apply special formatting attributes.

Aligning Cell Contents

Text and numbers in a worksheet can be aligned to the left, to the right, or at the center. By default, when you enter alphabetic characters or alphabetic characters combined with numbers or symbols, the cell content is left-aligned. When you enter numbers, the content is right-aligned. You can use Alignment commands to change default alignment or to override previous alignment formatting.

Formatting Cells and Ranges | 361

ANOTHER WAY

Press Ctrl+L to left align or Ctrl+R to right align text.

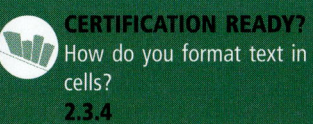
CERTIFICATION READY?
How do you format text in cells?
2.3.4

ALIGN CELL CONTENTS

USE the workbook from the previous exercise.

1. Select **A3:N3**.
2. In the Alignment group, click **Center**. The column labels are horizontally centered.
3. Click **C4**, press **Shift**, and click **N8**. The cell range containing the values is selected. Click **Align Text Right**. All cells containing values are now right-aligned.

   PAUSE. LEAVE the workbook open to use in the next exercise.

As illustrated in Figure 3-6, the alignment that has been applied to the active cell is shown by the highlighted commands in the Alignment group. Proper alignment and spacing greatly improve the readability of worksheet data.

Figure 3-6

Active cell alignment is highlighted

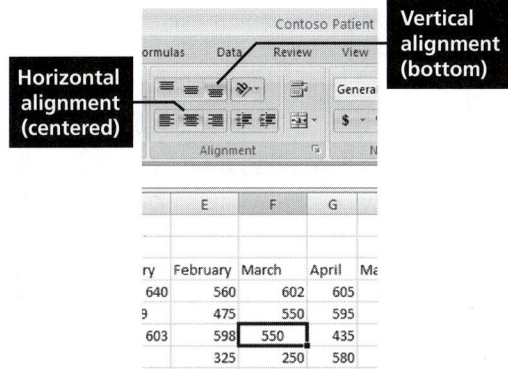

Choosing Fonts and Font Sizes

A ***font*** is a set of text characteristics designed to appear a certain way. The font determines the appearance of the cell contents. The ***default***, or predefined, font for Excel 2007 is 11-point Calibri. This is an easy-to-read font that takes up less space than Arial, which was the default in earlier Excel versions.

CHOOSE FONTS AND FONT SIZES

USE the workbook from the previous exercise.

1. Select the column labels in row 3.
2. Click the **Font** arrow. Scroll down the list of font names and click **Arial**. Notice that the font size is unchanged (still 11 point), but Arial is larger than the default Calibri font.
3. With row 3 still selected, click **Decrease Font Size**. The number 10 appears in the Font Size box and the labels now fit within the column width.

   PAUSE. LEAVE the workbook open to use in the next exercise.

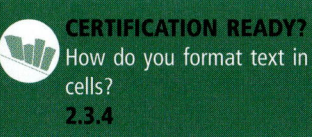
CERTIFICATION READY?
How do you format text in cells?
2.3.4

You can change the default font in Excel Options. If you chose a different default font and/or font size, that font is used only in new workbooks that you create after you change the default and restart Excel. Existing workbooks are not affected.

You can change the font for a selected cell, a range of cells, or for characters within text. To change the font, select the font that you want in the Font box Calibri. You can change the size in the Font Size box 11 or click Increase Font Size or Decrease Font Size until the size you want is displayed in the Font Size box. To improve the overall design of a worksheet, the font size is usually enlarged for titles and labels.

Font size is measured in ***points***. Each time you click Decrease Font Size or Increase Font Size, the size changes by a set amount that matches the size options on the Font Size list. Points refer to the measurement of height of characters in a cell. A point is equal to 1/72 inch.

Applying Special Character Attributes

In addition to changing the font and font size, you can apply special *attributes* to the font that add visual appeal. An attribute is a formatting characteristic, such as bold, italic, or underlined text. Applying special characteristics to specific text or values adds interest to a worksheet and calls attention to specific data.

→ APPLY SPECIAL CHARACTER ATTRIBUTES

USE the workbook from the previous exercise.

1. Select **A4**. Hold down the left mouse button and drag to B8. Click **Bold** **B** in the Font group.
2. Click **A3**. Press Shift and click **N3** to select the column labels. Click **Italic** *I* in the Font group, then click **Bold**.

   PAUSE. LEAVE the workbook open to use in the next exercise.

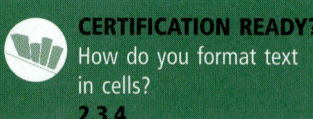

CERTIFICATION READY?
How do you format text in cells?
2.3.4

Although you are adding multiple special formatting to the worksheet in these exercises to improve your skills, it is wise to have a clear, logical design plan that presents the data in an easy-to-understand format. It is best not to overuse special character attributes. Keep in mind that the focus is on the data and the information that it conveys.

When you select text for formatting, you can use the **Mini toolbar**, shown in Figure 3-7, to apply selected formatting features. This unique formatting tool is new in Excel 2007. When you right-click, the Mini toolbar displays above the shortcut menu. Just click any of the available features to apply them to selected text. Unlike the Quick Access Toolbar, which can be customized, you cannot customize the Mini toolbar. You can turn off the Mini toolbar in Excel Options.

Figure 3-7

Mini toolbar

Changing Font Color

Color enhances the visual appeal of a worksheet. You can change the color of the text in cells. To add color, select the cell, range of cells, text, or *characters* that you want to format with a different color. A character can be a letter, number, punctuation mark, or symbol.

→ CHANGE FONT COLOR

USE the workbook from the previous exercise.

1. Select the column labels. Click the **Font Color** arrow.
2. Click **Blue** in the standard colors.
3. Select **A4:B8**. Click the **Font Color** arrow. Click **Red** in the standard colors.

   PAUSE. LEAVE the workbook open to use in the next exercise.

TAKE NOTE*

If you choose a color and change your mind, click Undo on the Quick Access Toolbar or press Ctrl+Z.

Black is the default, or automatic, font color, but you can easily change the color. The most recently applied color appears on the Font Color button . To apply that color, make a selection and click Font Color. To apply a different text color, click the arrow next to Font Color. You can choose a theme color or a standard color. You can also click More Colors to open the Colors dialog box where you can choose from additional standard colors or create colors to your specifications.

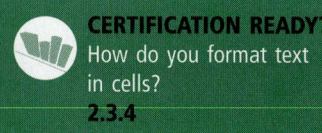

CERTIFICATION READY?
How do you format text in cells?
2.3.4

Looking Ahead — You will learn about Document Themes in Lesson 4. The default Office theme is the basis for the colors that appear under Theme Colors and Standard Colors on the Font Color menu.

Filling Cells with Color

You can call attention to cells by adding a background color and pattern. You can use a solid color or apply special effects, such as gradients, textures, and pictures. Use the Fill Color command in the Font group to change the background color. The most recently used fill color appears on the Fill Color button.

→ FILL CELLS WITH COLOR

USE the workbook from the previous exercise.

1. Select **A3:N3**.
2. Click the **Font** Dialog Box Launcher.
3. Click the **Fill** tab.
4. In the Background Color section, click the light blue color (second box) in column 5.
5. Add a second color in the Pattern Color box. Click the arrow and click the third box in column 5.
6. Click the **Pattern Style** arrow and click the pattern at the end of the first row. At the bottom of the dialog box, you can see a sample of how the pattern and color will look in the selected cells.
7. Click **OK** to apply the color and the fill pattern.
8. **SAVE** and **CLOSE** the *Patient Visits* workbook.

   PAUSE. LEAVE Excel open to use in the next exercise.

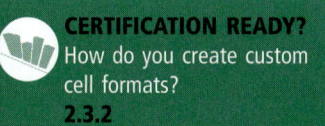

CERTIFICATION READY?
How do you create custom cell formats?
2.3.2

No color (clear) is the default background. To add color and shading, select cells to which you want to add special effects. The color palate you used to apply font color is also used for background color. To apply the color shown on the Fill Color button, make a selection and click the button. To apply a different fill color, click the arrow next to Fill Color and apply a theme color or a standard color. You can also click More Colors to open the Colors dialog box and custom blend colors.

You can apply a background color and add a pattern effect. Select the range of cells to which you want to apply a background color with fill effects. Click the Font group's Dialog Box Launcher. The Format Cells dialog box opens. Click the Fill tab. As shown in Figure 3-8, make a selection in the Pattern Style box to add a pattern to the background color.

Figure 3-8

Add a pattern to cell background color

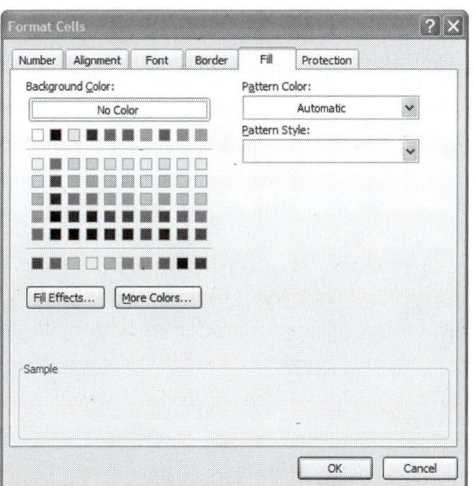

Applying Number Formats

Most of the data that you use in Excel is numeric. Applying accurate formatting to numeric data makes it easier to interpret and, therefore, more useful. Number formatting can be applied to cells before data is entered, or data can be selected and formatted after it has been entered. Formatting changes the appearance of numbers; it does not change their value. The actual value is always displayed in the formula bar.

→ APPLY NUMBER FORMATS

GET READY. Before you begin these steps, be sure that Microsoft Excel is running.

1. **OPEN** *Contoso Revenue*. Click the **Sheet1** tab if necessary to make it the active worksheet.
2. Select **B4:D10** and click **Accounting Number Format ($)** in the Number group. The data is reformatted to monetary values, the decimal points are aligned, and column width is increased to accommodate the selected number format.
3. With the text still selected, click **Decrease Decimal** in the Number group twice. The data is rounded to whole dollars.
4. Select **B10:D10**. Click **Comma Style (,)**. Click **Decrease Decimal** twice to show whole numbers. Row 10 data relates to the number of patients, not monetary values. Accounting style was inappropriately applied to this data.
5. Click the **Sheet2** tab.
6. Select **B7:B11**. Click the **Number** Dialog Box Launcher.
7. Click **Number** in the Category area. Key **0** in the Decimal places box and check the **Use 1000 Separator** box. Click **OK**.
8. Format B6 with **Accounting** and zero decimals.
9. Select **C7:C11**. Click the **Number** Dialog Box Launcher.
10. On the Number tab, click **Date** in the Category area. Click the **03/14/01** date style. Click **OK**.
11. **SAVE** the workbook as *Revenue*.

    PAUSE. LEAVE the workbook open to use in the next exercise.

The *Contoso Revenue* worksheet is available on the companion CD-ROM.

CERTIFICATION READY?
How do you apply number formats?
2.3.1

- General
- Special

In this exercise you applied formatting to Contoso's first-quarter revenue data. When you enter a number in Excel, the default format is General, which displays the data exactly as you enter it. If you include a special character such as $ or % when you enter a number, the special character will appear in the cell. The format does not affect the actual cell value.

To change how numeric data appears, you can select one of the formatting options in the Number group on the Home tab, or you can launch the Format Cells dialog box and click the Number tab. The most commonly applied number formats are summarized in Table 3-2.

Formatting Cells and Ranges | 365

Table 3-2

Number-formatting categories

Format Category	Description
General	This is the default number format that Excel applies when you key a number. Numbers are displayed just the way you key them. If a cell is not wide enough to show the entire number, a number with decimals will be rounded.
Number	This format is used for the general display of numbers. You can specify the number of decimal places that you want to use, whether you want to use a thousands separator, and how you want to display negative numbers.
Currency	This format is used for general monetary values and displays the default currency symbol with numbers. You can specify the number of decimal places that you want to use, whether you want to use a thousands separator, and how you want to display negative numbers.
Accounting 	This format is also used for monetary values. Currency symbols and decimal points are aligned.
Date	Displays days, month, and years in various formats such as January 7, 2008, 7-Jan, and 1/7/2008.

If number symbols (###) appear in a cell, it means that the number entered is wider than the cell. If you plan to apply a number format to the data, it is not necessary to adjust column width because the column width is adjusted automatically when you apply a number format.

After you choose a number format, you will need to further specify how you want the numbers to appear. You can use the commands in the Number group to apply formats and to increase or decrease the number of decimal places displayed in worksheet data. When you decrease the decimal, data becomes less precise because numbers following the decimal are rounded. The lack of preciseness is insignificant, however, when you deal with large numbers.

Wrapping Text in a Cell

When a cell is formatted to wrap text, data in the cell wraps to fit the column width. If you change the column width, text wrapping adjusts automatically. When text is wrapped, row height is adjusted to accommodate the wrap.

➔ WRAP TEXT IN A CELL

USE the workbook from the previous exercise.

1. Select **Sheet1**. Select **A7** and click **Wrap Text** in the Alignment group. The row height is adjusted and the cell's full text is displayed on two lines.

TAKE NOTE* If you format a cell for text wrapping and all wrapped text is not visible, it may be because the row is set to a specific height. You will learn to modify row height in Lesson 4.

2. Double-click **A4**. *Edit* is displayed on the Status bar, indicating that the cell is in edit mode.

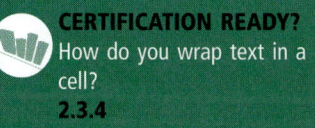

CERTIFICATION READY?
How do you wrap text in a cell?
2.3.4

3. Place the cursor just to the left of the word *Coverage* and press **Alt** + **Enter**. A manual line break is inserted. Press **Enter**.

   PAUSE. LEAVE the workbook open to use in the next exercise.

TAKE NOTE

Remember that you can edit a cell in the formula bar as well as in the cell.

Alt+Enter

If you want the text in a cell to appear on multiple lines, you can format the cell so that the text wraps automatically, or you can enter a manual line break. To wrap text automatically, select the text you want to format and click Wrap Text in the Alignment group. To start a new line of text at a specific point in a cell, double-click the cell to place it in edit mode. Click the location where you want to break the line and press Alt+Enter.

Merging and Splitting Merged Cells

You can use the Merge and Center command in the Alignment group to merge cells. A *merged cell* is created by combining two or more adjacent horizontal or vertical cells. When you merge cells, the selected cells become one large cell that spans multiple columns or rows. You can split cells that have been merged into separate cells again, but you cannot split a single worksheet cell that has not been merged.

 **MERGE AND SPLIT MERGED CELLS**

USE the workbook from the previous exercise.

1. Select **A1:D1**. Click **Merge and Center** in the Alignment group. The content previously in A1 is now centered across columns A, B, C, and D.
2. Select **A2:D2**. Click **Merge and Center**.
3. Select **A4:A5** and click **Merge and Center**. A dialog box opens to remind you that the data in A5 will be deleted in the merge.
4. Click **OK**. A4 and A5 are merged and the data originally in A4 is centered in the merged cell.
5. Click the arrow next to Merge and Center and click **Unmerge Cells**. The cells are unmerged, but the data from A5 has been deleted.
6. Select **A5**, key **Medicare/Medicaid**, and press **Enter**.
7. Select **A4:A5** and click **Align Text Left** in the Alignment group.

PAUSE. LEAVE the workbook open to use in the next exercise.

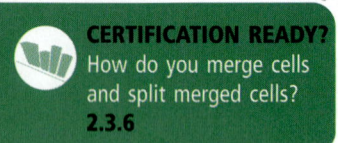

ANOTHER WAY

With a merged cell active, you can click Merge and Center to unmerge the cells.

CERTIFICATION READY?
How do you merge cells and split merged cells?
2.3.6

When you merge cells, the data that you want to appear in the merged cells must be in the upper-left cell of the selected range. Only the data in the upper-left cell will remain in the merged cell. Data in the other cells to be merged will be deleted. Cells can be merged in a row or column, and the content of the upper-left cell will be centered in the merged cell. If the cells to be merged contain information that will be deleted in the merge, the Excel dialog box shown in Figure 3-9 opens to caution you that if you merge the cells, only the content of the upper-left cell will remain after the merge.

Figure 3-9

Merge cells warning

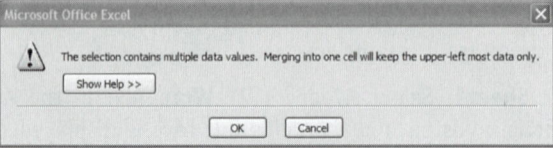

To merge cells without centering the contents of the upper-left cell, click the arrow next to Merge and Center, and click Merge Cells. Text you enter in such a merged cell will be left aligned.

With a merged cell active, click Merge and Center to split the merged cell. You can also use the arrow next to Merge and Center and choose Unmerge Cells.

TROUBLESHOOTING

If the Merge and Center button is unavailable, the selected cells may be in editing mode. To cancel editing mode, press Enter or Escape (Esc).

Formatting Cells and Ranges | 367

A merged cell takes the name of the original upper-left cell. As shown in Figure 3-10, when you merged A1:D1 in the previous exercise, the merged cell is named A1.

Figure 3-10

Merged cells have one name

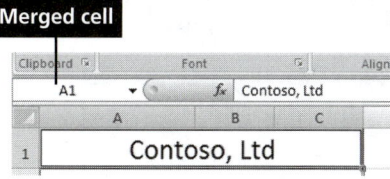

Placing Borders around Cells

You can use borders to enhance a worksheet's visual interest and to make it easier to read. You can apply Excel's predefined border styles, or you can customize borders by specifying a line style and a color of your choice. Borders are often used to set off headings, labels, or totals.

→ **PLACE BORDERS AROUND CELLS**

USE the workbook from the previous exercise.

1. Select **A1** and click the arrow next to Bottom Border.
2. Click **More Borders**. The Format Cells dialog box opens with the Borders tab displayed.
3. Under Line, click the Style displayed in the lower-right corner.
4. Click the **Color** arrow and then click **Red**.
5. Under Presets, click **Outline**. The red border is previewed in the Border box.
6. Click **OK**. The dialog box closes and the border is applied to A1.
7. With A1 selected, click **Increase Font Size** until the value in the Font Size box is 20 points.

   PAUSE. LEAVE the workbook open to use in the next exercise.

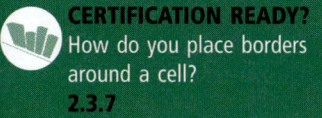

CERTIFICATION READY?
How do you place borders around a cell?
2.3.7

To add a border, select the cell or range of cells to which you want to call attention. For example, you may want to place a border around the titles, around the cells displaying the total revenue for the first quarter, or around the labels that identify the months.

In the Font group, the Border button displays the most recently used border style, and the button's name changes to that style name. Click the Border button (not the arrow) to apply that style, or you can click the arrow and choose a different border style. Click More Borders to apply a custom or diagonal border. On the Borders tab of the Format Cells dialog box, click a Line Style and a color. Select a border style from the Presets or create a style with line-placement options in the Border area. Notice that Figure 3-11 displays the two diagonal borders.

Figure 3-11

Borders options

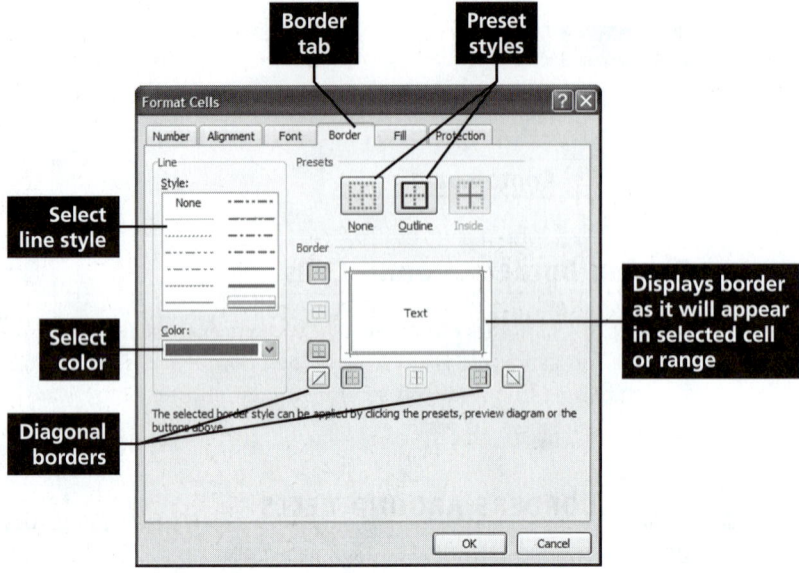

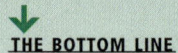 **TAKE NOTE** If you apply two different types of borders to a shared cell boundary, the most recently applied border is displayed.

■ Copying Cell Formatting with the Format Painter

THE BOTTOM LINE The *Format Painter* is an Excel feature that allows you to copy formatting from a cell or range of cells to another cell or range of cells. Located in the Clipboard group on the Home tab, it is one of Excel's most useful tools. It allows you to quickly copy attributes that you have already applied and "paint" those attributes to other data.

➔ COPY CELL FORMATTING WITH THE FORMAT PAINTER

USE the workbook from the previous exercise.

1. With A1 active, click **Format Painter**. A flashing border appears around A1, the formatting to be copied.
2. Click A2.
3. Select **A2** and right-click to display the Mini toolbar. Click the **Font Size** arrow and click **14**. The font size of the subtitle is reduced.
4. Select **A1:A2** and click **Format Painter**.
5. Click the **Sheet2** tab and select **A1:A2**. The formatting from the Sheet1 titles have been applied to the Sheet2 titles.
6. Click the **Sheet1** tab.

   PAUSE. LEAVE the workbook open to use in the next exercise.

ANOTHER WAY

The Format Painter is available on the Mini toolbar as well as in the Clipboard group.

You can use the Format Painter to copy formats, including font, font size, font style, font color, alignment, indentation, number formats, and borders and shading. To copy formatting from one location to another, select the cell or range that has the formatting you want to copy. Click Format Painter in the Clipboard group. The mouse pointer turns into a white plus sign with the paint brush beside it. Drag the mouse pointer across the cell or range of cells that you want to format.

To copy the formatting to several cells or ranges of cells, double-click Format Painter, and then drag the mouse pointer across each cell or range of cells that you want to format. When you're done, click Format Painter again or press Esc to turn off the Format Painter.

■ Formatting Cells with Styles

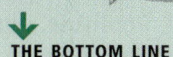

THE BOTTOM LINE

A *style* is a set of formatting attributes that you can apply to a cell or range of cells more easily than setting each attribute individually. Style attributes include fonts and font sizes, number formats, and borders and shading. Excel has several predefined styles that you can apply or modify; you can also modify or duplicate a cell style to create a custom cell style.

Applying a Cell Style

To apply a cell style to an active cell or range, click Cell Styles in the Styles group on the Home tab. Click the cell style that you want to apply. You can apply more than one style to a cell or range.

→ **APPLY A CELL STYLE**

USE the workbook from the previous exercise.

1. Select **A1:A2** and click **Cell Styles** in the Styles group. The Cell Styles gallery opens.
2. Click **20% - Accent4** under Themed Cell Styles. The themed shading is applied to A1 and A2. The style changes the font size as well as adding the shading.
3. Select **A1** and click **Cell Styles**.
4. Click **Heading 1** under Titles and Headings.
5. Select **A2** and click **Cell Styles**.
6. Click **Heading 2** under Titles and Headings.
7. Select **A8:D8** and click **Cell Styles**.
8. Click **Total** under Titles and Headings.

   PAUSE. LEAVE the workbook open to use in the next exercise.

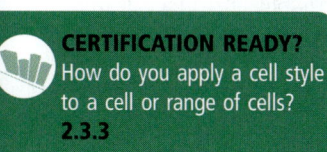

CERTIFICATION READY?
How do you apply a cell style to a cell or range of cells?
2.3.3

When you view defined styles in the Cell Styles gallery, you can see the formatting that will be used when you apply each style. This feature allows you to assess the formatting without actually applying it.

Experiment with combining styles to achieve the desired effect. For example, you can click a themed cell style, which will apply shading to the cell. Then, you can click Cell Styles again and click Heading 1, which applies font face, font size, and special formatting effects such as bold or italics.

TAKE NOTE

You cannot delete the Normal cell style.

If you are not pleased with a style you apply, you can Undo the style or apply another style to the cell or range. To remove a cell style from selected cells without deleting the cell style, select the cells that are formatted with that cell style. Click Cell Styles and click Normal. To delete the cell style and remove it from all cells formatted with that style, right-click the cell with the cell style, and then click Delete.

Modifying a Cell Style

You can modify or duplicate a cell style to create your own custom cell style. You can add additional attributes to the style and delete attributes.

→ MODIFY A CELL STYLE

USE the worksheet from the previous exercise.

1. With A12 active, click **Cell Styles** in the Styles group. The Cell Styles gallery opens.
2. Right-click **20% - Accent6** under Themed Cell Styles. Click **Duplicate**. The Style dialog box opens.
3. Key **Accent Revised** in the Style name box.
4. Click **Format**. Click the **Font** tab.
5. Click **Italic** in the Font style box.
6. Click **12** in the Size box.
7. Click the **Border** tab and click your choice of a broken line in the Line Style box.
8. Click the two diagonal borders below the Border box. Click **OK**. Your formatting modifications will be shown in the Style dialog box.
9. Click **OK** to close the dialog box.
10. Click **Cell Styles** in the Styles group. Your Accent Revised cell style should be the first style in the Custom section. Click **Accent Revised** to apply the style to A12.
11. Use the Format Painter to apply your style to **B12:D12**.

    PAUSE. LEAVE the workbook open to use in the next exercise.

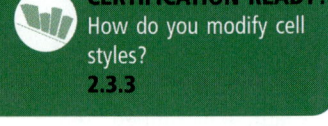

CERTIFICATION READY?
How do you modify cell styles?
2.3.3

In this exercise, you duplicated a cell style and then modified the style to create your own custom style. Your custom style was added to the styles gallery. If you had used the Modify command, the existing style would have reflected the formatting changes you made. Duplicating an existing style, and then modifying it is preferable. To modify an existing style, click Cell Styles in the Styles group. When the styles gallery is displayed, right-click the cell style that you want to change, and then click Modify. The Style dialog box shown in Figure 3-12 opens with the current style name displayed but not accessible. This tells you that any changes you make to the style will be made to the existing style rather than a customized style.

Figure 3-12

Style dialog box

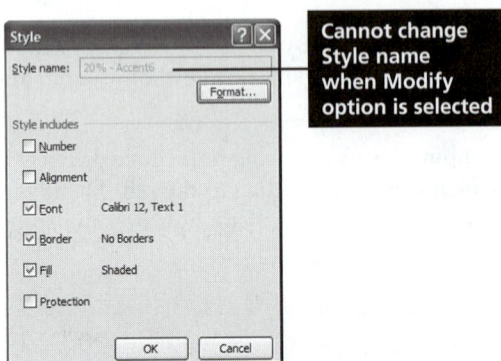

Key an appropriate name for the new cell style you want to create. To change the cell style, click Format. The Format Cells dialog box opens. On the various tabs in the dialog box, select the formatting that you want for the new style. Click OK when you have completed your changes. The changes will be reflected on the Style dialog box. When you are satisfied with the style attributes, click OK. The new cell style is added to the styles gallery and identified as a custom style.

■ Working with Hyperlinked Data

THE BOTTOM LINE

For quick access to related information in another file or on a Web page, you can insert a hyperlink in a worksheet cell. Hyperlinks enable you to supplement worksheet data with additional information and resources.

A *hyperlink* is an image or a sequence of characters that opens another file or Web page when you click it. The target file or Web page can be on the World Wide Web, on an intranet, or on your personal computer. In a workbook containing your personal banking records, for example, you might insert a hyperlink to jump to your bank's online bill-paying service.

Placing a Hyperlink in a Cell

It is easy to embed a hyperlink in a workbook cell. Just click the cell where you want to create a hyperlink and identify the source to which you want to connect. Each hyperlink appears in the cell as blue underlined text. When you point to a hyperlink, a ScreenTip describing the link or giving the location of the file appears.

→ PLACE A HYPERLINK IN A CELL

USE the workbook from the previous exercise. Verify that you can access the Internet.

1. Click **A15**.
2. Click the Ribbon's **Insert** tab.
3. Click **Insert Hyperlink** in the Links group. The Insert Hyperlink dialog box opens.
4. In the Text to display box, key **Microsoft**. This is the blue, underlined text that will appear in A15.
5. Click **ScreenTip**. The Set Hyperlink ScreenTip dialog box opens.
6. Key **Go to Microsoft's Help and Support Center**. Click **OK**. The text you keyed will replace the default ScreenTip.
7. In the Address box, key **www.support.microsoft.com** and click **OK**. The hyperlink appears in A15.

ANOTHER WAY

Ctrl+K will insert a hyperlink in a cell, or you can right-click and then click Hyperlink on the shortcut menu.

TAKE NOTE*

When you key www, Excel recognizes it as the beginning of a Web address and *http://* is supplied automatically.

8. Point to the cell containing the hyperlink.
9. Click the left mouse button to open the hyperlink. The Web browser opens and connects to Microsoft's Help and Support.
10. Click the **Excel** button on the taskbar to return to your workbook.
11. Key your email address in D17. If you do not have an email address, key **someone@example.com**.

    PAUSE. LEAVE the workbook open to use in the next exercise.

CERTIFICATION READY?
How do you create a hyperlink in a worksheet cell?
2.3.8

In this exercise, you created a hyperlink using the Hyperlink command on the Insert tab. You can also create a hyperlink to an email address or an Internet address by typing the address directly in the cell. For example, if you key someone@example.com or www.microsoft.com in a worksheet cell, an automatic hyperlink is created.

The default ScreenTip identifies the full address of the hyperlink and provides instructions for following the link. You can specify the information you want in the tip when you create the link or you can edit it later.

To edit a hyperlink, click and hold to select the cell containing the hyperlink. Right-click and then click Edit Hyperlink to open the Edit Hyperlink dialog box. You can edit the text that displays in the link, the ScreenTip text, or the address where the link will take you. You can cut or copy a hyperlink and paste it into another cell in the worksheet or paste it into another worksheet.

Removing a Hyperlink

You can delete a hyperlink and the text that represents it, turn off a single hyperlink, or turn off several hyperlinks at once.

REMOVE A HYPERLINK

USE the workbook from the previous exercise.

1. Right-click the link in D17.
2. Click **Clear Contents** on the shortcut menu. The hyperlink and text are removed.
3. Right-click **B17** and click **Remove Hyperlink**. The hyperlink is removed and the text remains in the cell.
4. **SAVE** and **CLOSE** the *Revenue* workbook.

   PAUSE. LEAVE Excel open to use in the next exercise.

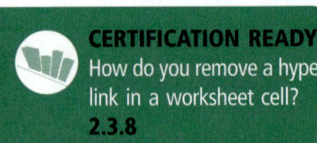

CERTIFICATION READY?
How do you remove a hyperlink in a worksheet cell?
2.3.8

As demonstrated in this exercise, you can remove a hyperlink and the associated text, or you can remove the link and retain the text. To remove multiple links, press Shift and select the hyperlinks to be removed or deleted. Right-click and click the appropriate action.

■ Applying Conditional Formatting to Cells

THE BOTTOM LINE

There are times when you want to format cells in a particular way only if they meet a specific condition. Conditional formatting allows you to specify how cells that meet a given condition should be displayed. Thus, *conditional formatting* means that Excel applies formatting automatically, based on established criteria.

When you analyze data, you often ask questions, such as:

- Who are the highest performing sales representatives?
- In what months were revenues highest or lowest?
- What are the trends in profits over a specified time period?

Conditional formatting helps to answer such questions by highlighting interesting cells or ranges of cells. With conditional formatting, fonts become visual guides that help the reader understand data distribution and variation.

Using the Rule Manager to Apply Conditional Formats

On what conditions or criteria do you want to analyze the data contained in a worksheet? That is the basis for establishing conditional formats. Once data is selected, you can choose one of five preset specific conditional formats that provide a visual analysis of a worksheet or selected range of data.

For example, you can specify that when the value in a cell is greater than a given number, the value will be displayed with a particular font or background color. You can establish multiple conditional format rules for a data range.

➔ USE THE RULE MANAGER TO APPLY CONDITIONAL FORMATS

GET READY. Open the *Patient Visit Data* file.

1. Select **A1:N1**. Merge and center the range and apply the Heading 1 style.
2. Select **A2:N2**. Merge and center the range and apply the Heading 2 style.
3. Select **C4:N7** and click **Conditional Formatting** in the Styles group.
4. Click **Highlight Cell Rules** and click **Greater Than**.
5. In the Greater Than dialog box, key **600** and click **OK**. The highlighted data represents the months in which the doctors were seeing more than the ideal number of patients.
6. With the range still selected, click **Conditional Formatting**.
7. Click **Highlight Cell Rules** and click **Less Than**.
8. In the Less Than dialog box, key **560**. In the *with* box, select **Green Fill with Dark Green Text** and click **OK**. The highlight now contrasts the months in which the patient load was less than expected.
9. Click **Conditional Formatting** and click **Top/Bottom Rules**.
10. Click **Top 10%**. In the dialog box, accept 10% and click **Yellow Fill with Dark Yellow Text**. Click **OK**.
11. Click **Conditional Formatting** and click **Manage Rules** at the bottom of the list.
12. In the *Show Formatting Rules for* box, click **This Worksheet**. The three conditional formatting rules you have applied are displayed. Position the Conditional Formatting Rules Manager dialog box below the worksheet data so you can view the data and the conditional formatting rules. Notice that the first and third rules apply to overlapping data. Therefore, if a cell value exceeds 600 and that value also falls within the top 10%, the 10% formatting will be applied.
13. Click the **Cell Value>600** rule and click the **up arrow** to move the rule to the top of the list. Click **Apply**. All values greater than 600 are formatted with the dark red font.
14. Click the **Close** button to close the dialog box.

    PAUSE. LEAVE the workbook open to use in the next exercise.

The *Patient Visit Data* worksheet is available on the companion CD-ROM.

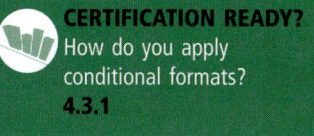

CERTIFICATION READY?
How do you apply conditional formats?
4.3.1

In this lesson's exercises, you have worked with data related to the number of patients treated each month at Contoso, Ltd. You can use Excel's Rule Manager to apply conditional formatting to provide visual analyses of the data in the *Patient Visits* Data workbook.

You can display the Conditional Rules Manager to see what rules are in effect for the worksheet and to apply those rules at an appropriate time. From the Conditional Formatting Rules Manager, you can add new rules, edit the existing rules, or delete one or all of the rules. The rules are applied in the order in which they are listed in the Conditional Formatting Rules Manager. You can apply all the rules or you can apply specific rules to analyze the data. As you can see in Figure 3-13, formatting is visible while the Conditional Formatting Rules Manager is open. Thus, you can experiment with the formats you want to apply and the order in which they are applied.

Figure 3-13

Conditional Formatting Rules Manager

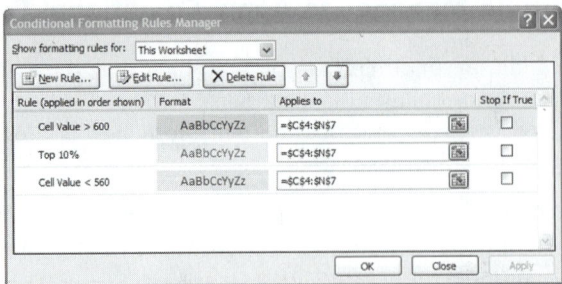

Conditional formatting is applied in the order it appears in the Rule Manager. The top rule is the latest condition created and it takes precedence. However, you can use the arrow keys to adjust rule precedence. If two rules conflict, the rule that is higher on the list is applied.

Allowing Multiple Conditional Formatting Rules to Be True

Multiple conditional formatting rules can be true. By default, new rules are always added to the top of the list and therefore have a higher precedence. Conditional formatting takes precedence over manual formatting that has been applied.

➔ ALLOW MULTIPLE CONDITIONAL FORMATTING RULES TO BE TRUE

USE the workbook from the previous exercise.

1. Select **C8:N8**. Click **Conditional Formatting** and click **Highlight Cells Rules**.
2. Click **Less Than**. Key **300** in the value box and click **Red Text**. Click **OK**.
3. Click **Conditional Formatting** and click **Manage Rules**. In the Show Formatting Rules for box, click **This Worksheet**. Although the last rule has the highest precedence, it applies only to the PA's schedule and therefore does not conflict with any of the rules that apply to the physicians' schedules.
4. Click the **Close** button to close the dialog box.

   PAUSE. LEAVE the workbook open to use in the next exercise.

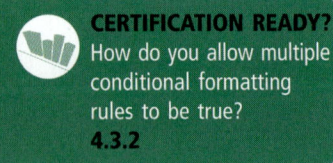

CERTIFICATION READY?
How do you allow multiple conditional formatting rules to be true?
4.3.2

Applying Specific Conditional Formats

Excel has three preset conditional formats that use color and symbols to provide visual guides to help you understand data distribution and variation: color scales, icon sets, and data bars.

➔ APPLY SPECIFIC CONDITIONAL FORMATS

USE the workbook from the previous exercise.

1. Click **Conditional Formatting**.
2. Click **Clear Rules** and then click **Clear Rules from Entire Sheet**. All conditional formatting is cleared from the data.
3. Select **C4:N8**. Click **Conditional Formatting**.

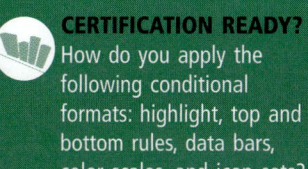

CERTIFICATION READY?
How do you apply the following conditional formats: highlight, top and bottom rules, data bars, color scales, and icon sets?
4.3.3

4. Click **Data Bars** and click **Blue Data Bar**. The longer the dark blue portion of the bar is, the higher the value is in relation to other cells in the data range.
5. Clear the data bars. Select the data range and click **Conditional Formatting**.
6. Click **Color Scales** and click the **Yellow–Red Color Scale** (first option in the second row). The darker colors indicate the lower values.
7. Clear the formatting rules. Click **Conditional Formatting**. Click **Icon Sets**. Click the **3 Flags** set.
8. **SAVE** the workbook as *Patient Visits with Icons*.

   PAUSE. LEAVE the workbook open to use in the next exercise.

A two-color scale helps you compare a range of cells by using a gradation of two colors. The shade of the color represents higher or lower values. The shade of the color in a three-color scale represents higher, middle, and lower values.

You can use an icon set to interpret and classify data into three to five categories. Each icon represents a range of values. For example, in the three-flag icon set, the green flag represents higher values, the yellow represents middle values, and the red represents lower values.

A data bar helps you see the value of a cell relative to other cells in the data range. The length of the data bar represents the value in the cell. A longer bar represents a higher value and a shorter bar represents a lower value. Data bars are useful in spotting higher and lower numbers, especially with large amounts such as a retailer's after-Thanksgiving sales report.

■ Clearing a Cell's Formatting

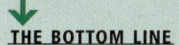

THE BOTTOM LINE

The Clear command in the Editing group on the Home tab lets you clear contents and formatting or allows you to selectively remove the contents or the formatting. When you want to redesign the appearance of an existing worksheet, click Clear and then click Clear Formats. The content will remain and you can choose to apply manual formatting, styles, or conditional formatting. Clearing all formatting ensures that you are starting with a clean formatting slate.

➔ CLEAR A CELL'S FORMATTING

USE the worksheet from previous exercise.

1. Click **Select All** to select the entire worksheet.
2. Click **Clear** in the Editing group.
3. Click **Clear Formats**. All formatting is cleared from the data. If you selected **Clear All**, the data would be removed as well as the formatting.
4. **CLOSE** the file without saving.

   STOP. CLOSE Excel.

If you select Clear All, contents and formatting are removed. Selecting Clear Contents will remove the data within the selected range, but the formatting will remain.

SUMMARY SKILL MATRIX

In This Lesson You Learned how to:
Add a New Cell to a Worksheet
Delete a Cell from a Worksheet
Select Cells and Ranges
Align Cell Contents
Choose Fonts and Font Sizes
Apply Special Character Attributes
Change Font Color
Fill Cells with Color
Apply Number Formats
Wrap Text in a Cell
Merge and Splitting Merged Cells
Place Borders Around Cells
Copy Cell Formatting with the Format Painter
Apply a Cell Style
Modify a Cell Style
Place a Hyperlink in a Cell
Remove a Hyperlink
Use the Rule Manager to Apply Conditional Formats
Allow Multiple Conditional Formatting Rules to Be True
Allow Specific Conditional Formats
Clear a Cell's Formatting

Knowledge Assessment

True / False

Circle T if the statement is true or F if the statement is false.

357 — T **(F)** 1. When you insert a cell into a row, all data in that row is shifted down. to the right

T **(F)** 2. When you shift cells down and data in another cell is replaced, that data is copied to the Office Clipboard.

(T) F 3. You can select a large range of cells by selecting the first cell in the range, pressing Shift, and selecting the last cell in the range.

T **(F)** 4. You can merge cells horizontally, but not vertically.

p.365 **(T)** F 5. If you want the dollar sign and decimals to align in a column, apply Accounting format.

365 **(T)** F 6. When you wrap text in a cell, the row height is automatically adjusted to accommodate the multiple-line text.

Formatting Cells and Ranges | 377

T (F) 7. Any cell in a worksheet can be split. — 366, no, if not merged

(T) F 8. When you apply a style to text, any conflicting formatting in the cell or range is replaced by the style format.

T (F) 9. When you remove a hyperlink, the link and the text are removed.

(T) F 10. When you select the entire worksheet and click Clear and Clear All, the worksheet will be blank.

Fill in the Blank

Complete the following sentences by writing the correct word or words in the blanks provided.

1. When a single cell is created by combining two or more selected cells, the new cell is referred to as a(n) **Merged cell**.

2. A(n) **Style** is a set of formatting attributes that you can apply as a group to a selected cell or range of cells.

3. A shortcut or jump that opens a stored document or connects with the Internet is called a(n) **hyperlink**.

4. When formatting is applied to data based on established criteria, it is said to be **Conditional** formatting. — p.372

5. Bold, italic, or underlining are examples of formatting **attributes** — 362.

6. You can apply formatting to multiple cells with the **Format painter**.

7. By default, a new Excel 2007 feature call the **minipoints** displays above the right-click shortcut menu.

8. Font sizes are measured in **points**.

9. A letter, number, punctuation mark, or symbol is considered a(n) **characters**.

10. Small windows that display descriptive text when you rest the pointer on a command are called **screen tips**.

■ Competency Assessment

Project 3-1: Apply Basic Formatting

Apply formatting attributes to a workbook used to track annual utilities expenses.

GET READY. Launch Excel if it is not already running.

The *Utilities* workbook is available on the companion CD-ROM.

1. Click the **Microsoft Office Button** and click **Open**.
2. Open the *Utilities* file from the data files for this lesson.
3. Select **A8:G8**. Click the **Insert** arrow in the Cells group and click **Insert Cells**.
4. Click **OK** on the Insert dialog box to shift the cells down.
5. Select **A27:G27** and click **Cut** in the Clipboard group.
6. Select **A8** and click **Paste** in the Clipboard group.
7. Select **A2:G2**. Click **Bold** in the Font group.
8. Select the column labels and click **Center** in the Alignment group.
9. With the column labels still selected, click the **Font Color** arrow and click **Red**.
10. Select **A3:A15** and click **Align Left**.
11. Click **Quick Print** on the Quick Access Toolbar.

12. Click the **Microsoft Office Button**. Click **Save As**.
13. **SAVE** the workbook as *Utilities 3-1* in your Lesson 3 folder.
    LEAVE the workbook open for the next project.

Project 3-2: Enhance Worksheet Appearance

Apply additional formatting attributes to an existing workbook.

USE the workbook from Project 3-1.

1. Select **A1**. Click the arrow in the Font box and click **Cambria**.
2. With A1 still selected, click **Increase Font Size** until the Font Size box shows 16 point.
3. Apply the **Green** font color to the title.
4. Select **A1:G1** and click **Merge & Center** in the Alignment group.
5. With only the merged A1 cell still selected, click **Middle Align** in the Alignment group.
6. Select **F2** and click **Wrap Text** in the Alignment group.
7. With F2 selected, click the **Format Painter** in the Clipboard group. Drag the Format Painter across all column labels.
8. Adjust column width if necessary so that column labels are completely visible.
9. Select the labels and click **Middle Align**.
10. Click **B3**, press [Shift], and click **G15** to select the range that contains values. Apply the Number format to the range.
11. Print the worksheet.
12. **SAVE** the workbook as *Utilities 3-2* in the Lesson 3 folder and **CLOSE** the file.
    LEAVE Excel open for the next project.

■ Proficiency Assessment

Project 3-3: Format Training Budget

Graphic Design Institute's Training Department provides in-house technical and soft-skills training for the firm's 1,200 employees. Apply the formatting skills you learned in Lesson 3 to give the Training Budget worksheet a professional finish.

The *Training Budget* workbook is available on the companion CD-ROM.

1. **OPEN** *Training Budget* from the data files for this lesson.
2. Merge and center cells A1:E1.
3. Key **Graphic Design Institute** as the worksheet title.
4. Click **Cell Styles** in the Styles group and apply the 40% - Accent 1 style to the title.
5. Click Cell Styles and apply the Heading 1 style.
6. Merge and center cells A2:E2. Key the subtitle **Training Department Budget**.
7. Apply the 20% - Accent 1 fill to the subtitle. Apply the Heading 2 style.
8. Merge and center the blank row above the column labels.
9. Select the column labels and apply the Note style. Click **Center** in the Alignment group.
10. Key **TOTAL** in A18 and apply the Total style to row 18.
11. Select **D6:E17**. Click the **Number** group Dialog Box Launcher. Click the **Number** category, set decimal places to 0, and check **Use 1000 separator**.
12. In the Cell Name box, key **D5:E5, E18** to select the nonadjacent cells. Apply the Currency format and reduce decimals to 0.

13. Print the worksheet.
14. **SAVE** the workbook as *Training Budget 3-3*.
    LEAVE the workbook open for the next project.

Project 3-4: Hyperlinks

Create and edit hyperlinks that connect a worksheet with selected web pages. Insert links to send e-mail messages to selected recipients.

USE the *Training Budget 3-3* worksheet that is open from Project 3-3.

1. Label column B **Contact**.
2. Click the **Insert** tab.
3. Select **B5** and click **Hyperlink**.
4. Key **A. Datum Corporation** as the text to display.
5. Key **www.adatum.com** in the address box. Click **OK**.
6. In B11, create a hyperlink that displays as Lucerne Publishing at www.lucernepublishing.com.
7. In B16 create a hyperlink for Margie's Travel. The address is www.margiestravel.com.
8. Select **B16** and click **Hyperlink** to open the Edit Hyperlink dialog box. Edit the ScreenTip to read **Corporate contract for all travel**.
9. Select **B13** and create an email link for the consultant: someone@example.com.
10. **PRINT** the worksheet. **SAVE** the workbook as *Training Budget 3-4* and then **CLOSE** the file.
    LEAVE Excel open for the next project.

■ Mastery Assessment

Project 3-5: Format Sales Report

The *Litware Sales* workbook is available on the companion CD-ROM.

Litware, Inc. wants to apply Font and Alignment group formatting to enhance its sales report's appearance and readability.

1. **OPEN** *Litware Sales* from the data files for this lesson.
2. Merge and center the title and apply the Heading 1 style.
3. Merge and center the subtitle and apply the Heading 2 style.
4. Select A1:G2. Click the **Border** arrow to open the Format Cells dialog box.
5. Under Line Styles, select the last line style in column 2.
6. Click the **Color** arrow and click **Red**.
7. Click **Outline** and **Inside** in Presets. Click **OK**.
8. Select **B4** and use the fill handle to extend the months across the remaining columns of data.
9. Select the labels in row 4. Center the labels and apply the Red font color. Add a Thick Box border.
10. Apply the Accounting format to the values in row 5. Reduce decimals to 0.
11. Select **B6:G12** and apply the Number format with comma separator and 0 decimals.
12. Apply the Total style to row 13.
13. **PRINT** the workbook. **SAVE** the workbook as *Litware Sales 3-5*.
    LEAVE the workbook open for the next project.

Project 3-6: Apply Conditional Formatting to Sales Report

Apply conditional formatting to the Litware, Inc. sales report to highlight the top performing sales representatives.

USE the workbook that is open from Project 3-5.

1. Select **B13:G13**.
2. Click **Conditional Formatting** and click **Highlight Cells Rules**.
3. Click **Greater Than**. In the Greater Than dialog box, key **140,000** and click **OK**. Total sales exceed $140,000 for February and May.
4. Select **B5:G12**. Click **Conditional Formatting**, click **Top/Bottom Rules**, and then click **Top 10%**. When the dialog box opens, four cells are highlighted.
5. Drag the dialog box below the data range. Change the Top percentage number to 1. Format cells that rank in the Top 1% with a red border. Deborah Poe was the top sales performer with $25,874 for the month of May.
6. Click **Conditional Formatting** and click **Icon Sets**. Click **3 Flags**. Colored flags are applied to the sales data. Green flags mark the top 10%; red flags mark the bottom 10%; and yellow flags mark the middle range.
7. Print the worksheet.
8. Click **Conditional Formatting** and click **Manage Rules**.
9. On the dialog box, show the formatting for This Worksheet. The formatting rules are listed in the order you created them.
10. Delete the **Icon Sets** rule.
11. **PRINT** the worksheet. **SAVE** the workbook as *Litware Sales 3-6* and then **CLOSE** the file.

    STOP. CLOSE Excel.

INTERNET READY

OPEN a new, blank worksheet.

In this lesson you applied formatting styles that are preset in Excel. You also created a custom style. Open Excel Help and key **create style** in the Excel Help Search box. Open the *Apply, create, or remove a cell style* link. Click **Create a custom cell style**.

Merge four cells in an open worksheet and key **your name** in the cell. Follow the steps provided and create a custom style. Use your first name as the style name. Include the following formats in the style:

• Alignment	Horizontal Center
	Vertical Center
• Font	CG Omega, 16 point, Italic
• Border	Broken line (your choice)
	Green line color
	Outline Preset
• Fill	Yellow Pattern Color
	Thin Vertical Stripe Pattern Style

Key your name in cell A1 of a new blank workbook. Apply the style to your name. Save the workbook as *My Style*.

Worksheet Formatting

LESSON SKILL MATRIX

Inserting or Deleting a Row or Column — 382	Students will learn how to insert and delete rows and columns.
Modifying Row Height and Column Width — 383	Students will learn how to modify row height and column width.
Formatting an Entire Row or Column — 385	Students will learn how to format a row or column.
Hiding and Unhiding a Row or Column — 386	Students will learn how to hide and unhide a row or column.
Choosing a Theme for a Worksheet — 388	Students will learn how to choose a theme for a worksheet.
Customizing a Theme by Selecting Colors — 389	Students will learn how to customize a theme by selecting colors.
Customizing a Theme by Selecting a Font and Effects — 390	Students will learn how to customize a theme by selecting a font and effects.
Formatting a Sheet Background — 391	Students will learn how to format a sheet background.
Changing the Color of a Worksheet Tab — 392	Students will learn how to change the color of a worksheet tab.
Viewing and Printing a Worksheet's Gridlines — 393	Students will learn how to view and print a worksheet's gridlines.
Viewing and Printing Column and Row Headings — 393	Students will learn how to view and print column and row headings.
Adding Page Numbers to a Worksheet — 394	Students will learn how to add page numbers to a worksheet.
Inserting Predefined Header or Footer — 395	Students will learn how to insert a predefined header or footer.
Adding Content to a Header or Footer — 395	Students will learn how to add content to a header or footer.
Adding and Moving a Page Break — 396	Students will learn how to add and move a page break.
Setting Margins — 397	Students will learn how to set margins.
Setting a Worksheet's Orientation on the Page — 398	Students will learn how to set a worksheet's orientation.
Scaling a Worksheet to Fit on a Printed Page — 399	Students will learn how to scale a worksheet to fit on a printed page.

KEY TERMS
**boundary
column heading
column width
document theme
footer
gridlines
header
orientation
page break
Page Break Preview
Print Preview
row heading
row height
scaling**

A travel agency sells travel-related products and services to clients on behalf of third parties such as airlines, hotels, and cruise lines. Margie's Travel custom designs corporate and leisure travel packages for its clients. The owner, Margie Shoop, specializes in creative, detailed, and personalized service to assure clients they will have an enjoyable and trouble-free travel experience. She employs experienced and knowledgeable travel consultants whose goal is to save the client time, effort, and money. The company maintains a 24/7 emergency service hotline and nationwide toll-free accessibility for business travelers and tourists.

■ SOFTWARE ORIENTATION

Page Layout Commands

One of the easiest ways to share information in a worksheet or workbook is to print copies for others to review. You will continue to use some of the Home tab command groups as you format worksheets, but you will primarily use the Page Layout command groups shown in Figure 4-1 to prepare worksheets for printing and distribution. Applying formatting techniques from these command groups will ensure that your printed worksheets are more useful, more readable, and more attractive.

Figure 4-1

Use Page Layout command groups to prepare worksheets for printing

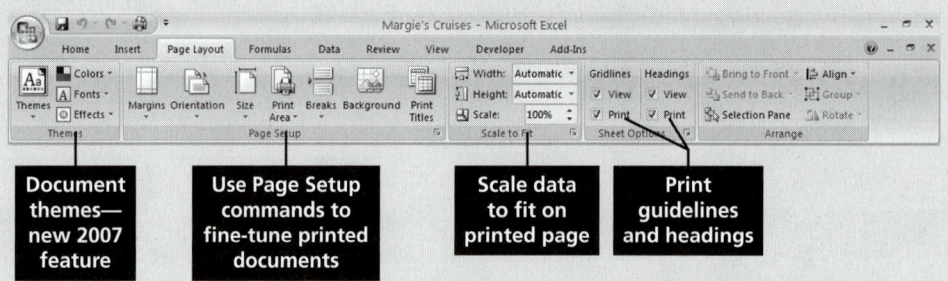

■ Working with Rows and Columns

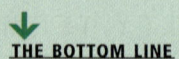

THE BOTTOM LINE

When you open a new worksheet, columns and rows are uniform. However, uniformity rarely fits the data you want to include in a worksheet or workbook. For some columns, you need only two or three characters; for others, you need to increase the *column width* to accommodate more data than will fit in the default column width of 8.43 characters.

Inserting or Deleting a Row or Column

After some data has been entered, you often need to insert additional rows or columns. To insert a row, select the row or a cell in the row below which you want the new row to appear. The new row is inserted above the selected cell or row. For example, to insert a row above row 10, click any cell in row 10. To insert multiple rows, select the same number of rows as you want to insert.

Inserting columns works the same way. If you want to insert a column to the left of column D, click any cell in column D. Columns are inserted to the left of the selected cell, and by default, the inserted column is formatted the same as the column to the left.

The same principles apply when you need to delete a row or column. In the following exercise, you will delete an entire row from a worksheet.

Worksheet Formatting | 383

TAKE NOTE: It does not matter which column you use to select cells when you want to insert rows or which row you select when you want to insert columns.

➔ INSERT OR DELETE A ROW OR COLUMN

GET READY. Before beginning these steps, be sure to launch Microsoft Office Excel 2007 and place the CD that accompanies this text in your computer.

1. **OPEN** *Margie's Cruises* from the data files for this lesson. The Home tab should be active.
2. Select any cell in row 12; press `Ctrl` and select a cell in row 17. Click the arrow next to **Insert** in the Cells group and click **Insert Sheet Rows**.
3. Select any cell in column A. Click the arrow next to Insert and then click **Insert Sheet Columns**.
4. In A5, key **Destination**.
5. Select **A6:A11**. Click **Merge and Center** in the Alignment group.
6. Select **A13:17**. Click **Merge and Center**.
7. Select **A19:23**. Click **Merge and Center**.
8. Label the merged cells **Mexico**, **Hawaii**, and **Alaska**.
9. Select **A6:A23**. Click **Center** and **Middle Align** in the Alignment group and **Bold** in the Font group.
10. Select any cell in row 2. Click the arrow next to Delete and click **Delete Sheet Rows**. Repeat this process to delete the new row 2.

   PAUSE. LEAVE the workbook open to use in the next exercise.

CD: The *Margie's Cruises* workbook is available on the companion CD-ROM.

ANOTHER WAY: After you insert a row or column, you can select the location where you want to insert another row or column and press Ctrl+Y.

CERTIFICATION READY? How do you insert rows or columns into a worksheet? 2.2.1

An associate at Margie's Travel prepared the workbook you opened in the previous exercise for a corporate client that rewards its top sales representatives with a cruise. The workbook contains cruise data for dates and locations specified by the client. In the following exercises, you will continue to apply formatting tools to make the workbook easier to understand and improve the presentation of the data to the client.

Modifying Row Height and Column Width

By default, all columns in a new worksheet are the same width and all rows are the same height. In most worksheets, you will want to change some column or row defaults to accommodate more or less data. Changes can be made using the Format commands in the Cells group on the Home tab.

Modifying row height and column width can make a worksheet's contents easier to read and increase its visual appeal. You can set a row or column to a specific height or width, change the height or width to fit the contents, or change the height or width by dragging the *boundary*, the line between rows or columns.

➔ MODIFY ROW HEIGHT AND COLUMN WIDTH

USE the workbook from the previous exercise.

1. Click the column **D** heading. Press and hold the mouse button and drag to select column **E**.
2. Click **Format** in the Cells group.
3. Under Cell Size, click **Column Width** on the options list shown in Figure 4-2.

Figure 4-2

Cell Size options

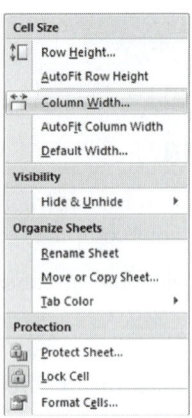

4. In the Column Width dialog box shown in Figure 4-3, key **15**. Click **OK**.

Figure 4-3

Key a column width number in the box

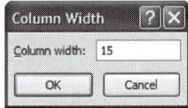

X REF

In previous lessons, when you double-clicked the right column boundary, you utilized the AutoFit Column Width option.

5. Select column **C**. Click **Format** and click **AutoFit Column Width**. This command adjusts the column width to fit the longest entry in the column.
6. Click the column **G** right boundary and drag to the right until the ScreenTip says *Width: 17.00*.
7. Click any cell in column A. Click **Format** in the Cells group.
8. Under Cell Size, click **Column Width**.
9. In the Column Width dialog box, key **16**. Click **OK**.
10. Set the width for column B to 30 characters.
11. Select row **3** and click **Format**. Click **Row Height** and key **25** in the Row Height dialog box. Click **OK**.

    PAUSE. LEAVE the workbook open to use in the next exercise.

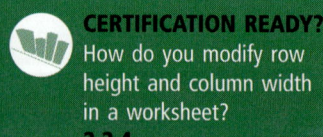

CERTIFICATION READY?
How do you modify row height and column width in a worksheet?
2.2.4

Row height, the top-to-bottom height, is measured in points; one point is equal to 1/72 inch. The default row height is 15 points, but you can specify a row height of 0 to 409 points. Although you can specify a column width of 0 to 255 characters, the default column width is 8.43 characters (based on the default font and font size). If the column width or row height is set to 0, the column or row is hidden.

As you learned in Lesson 2, when the text you enter exceeds the column width, the text overflows to the next column or it is truncated when the next cell contains data. If the value entered in a column exceeds the column width, a series of #### symbols, shown in Figure 4-4, indicate the number is larger than the cell width.

Looking Ahead

You will hide rows and columns later in this lesson.

Figure 4-4

Number is larger than column width

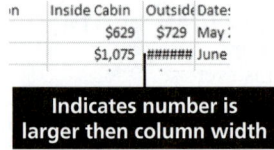

Indicates number is larger then column width

ANOTHER WAY

To quickly autofit the entries in all rows on the worksheet, click Select All and then double-click one of the column boundaries.

Worksheet Formatting | 385

Depending upon the alignment of data within columns, worksheet data may appear crowded when you use the AutoFit Column Width option because it adjusts column width to the exact width of the longest entry in the column. After you use the option, you may want to use the mouse to drag the right column boundary when a column with right-aligned data is adjacent to one with left-aligned data, as shown in Figure 4-5.

Figure 4-5

Drag column boundary to separate right-aligned and left-aligned columns

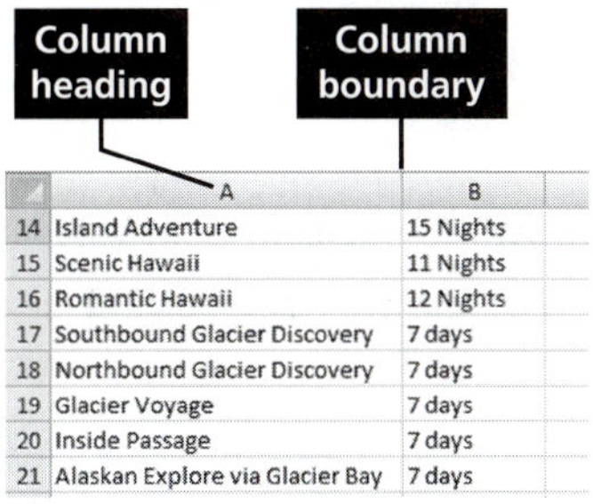

When you drag the boundary, the width of the column in characters and pixels appears in a ScreenTip above the column headings. See Figure 4-6.

Figure 4-6

Column width shown as you drag boundary

ANOTHER WAY

You can also use the Format Painter to copy the width of one column to other columns. Select the heading of the first column, click Format Painter, and then click the heading of the column or columns to which you want to apply the column width.

TAKE NOTE

When you are more familiar with the ways to modify rows and columns, you will likely use one method consistently.

You can change the default width for all columns on a worksheet or a workbook. Click Format and under Cell Size, click Default Width. In the Standard Width dialog box, key a new default column measurement. If you change the default column width for a worksheet that contains data, only empty columns will be changed. Columns that contain data or that have been previously formatted retain their formatting.

Formatting an Entire Row or Column

To save time, to achieve a consistent appearance, and to align cell contents in a consistent manner, you often want to apply the same format to an entire row or column. To apply formatting to a row or column, click the ***row heading*** or ***column heading*** (its identifying letter or number) to select it. Then apply the appropriate format or format style.

➔ FORMAT AN ENTIRE ROW OR COLUMN

USE the workbook from the previous exercise.

1. Select **A1:G1**, and then click **Merge & Center**. With A1 selected, click **Cell Styles** in the Styles group and click **Heading 1** under Titles and Headings.
2. Key **Margie's Travel** and press Enter.
3. With A1 selected, click **Increase Font Size** until the font size is **20** points. Notice that the height of row 1 increased to accommodate the larger font size.

TROUBLESHOOTING If you select row 1 rather than the data range and apply the style, the bottom border style effect will extend to the end of the row (cell XFD1).

4. Merge and center A2:G2. Apply the Heading 2 style.
5. Key **Cruise Options, Prepared for Fabrikam, Inc.** Increase the font size to 16 points.
6. Select **A3:G3** and apply Heading 3 style to the column labels. Increase font size to 12 points.
7. Select row 3. Click **Middle Align** and **Center** in the Alignment group.
8. Select columns **D** and **E**. Click the **Number Format** box and click **Accounting**.

TAKE NOTE Accounting format will be applied to any number you enter in column C or D, even if, for example, you enter the number as currency.

9. Select rows **4-9** and click the **Font Color** arrow in the Font group.
10. Click **Green** under Standard Colors.
11. Select rows **11-15**. Click the **Font Color** arrow and click **Purple** under Standard Colors.
12. Select rows **17-21**. Click the **Font Color** arrow and click **Red** under Standard Colors.

PAUSE. LEAVE the workbook open to use in the next exercise.

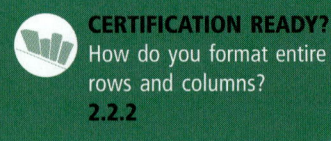

CERTIFICATION READY?
How do you format entire rows and columns?
2.2.2

Formatting rows and columns rather than applying formatting to the range of cells containing data has an advantage. When you insert rows or columns or add additional data to a worksheet, it will be formatted correctly.

Hiding and Unhiding a Row or Column

You may not want or need all rows and columns to be visible all the time, particularly if a worksheet contains a large number of rows or columns. You can hide a row or a column by using the Hide command or by setting the row height or column width to zero. When rows are hidden, they do not appear on the screen or in printouts.

→ HIDE AND UNHIDE A ROW OR COLUMN

USE the workbook from the previous exercise.

1. Click the column D heading to select the entire column. Click **Format** in the Cells group.
2. Point to Hide & Unhide and click **Hide Columns**.
3. Click the row 11 heading, press [Shift], and click the row 15 heading. Click **Format** in the Cells group.
4. Point to Hide & Unhide and click **Hide Rows**.
5. Click **Quick Print** on the Quick Access Toolbar. The boundary line in the row or column heading displays as a thicker line than normal when rows or columns are hidden. As you can see in Figure 4-7, you also recognize when rows or columns are hidden because numbers are skipped in the row headings or letters are skipped in the column headings.

Figure 4-7

Hidden rows marked by thicker boundary and missing headings

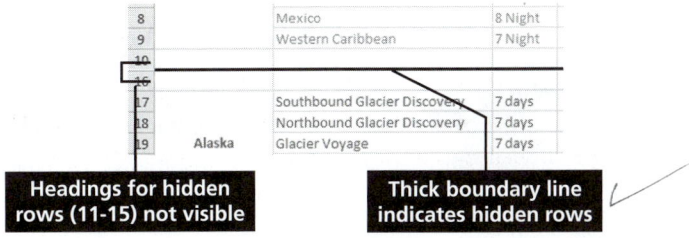

6. Select columns **C** and **E** (columns on each side of hidden column).
7. Click **Format**, point to Hide & Unhide, and click **Unhide Columns**. Column D is again visible.

TAKE NOTE

You must click the row or column heading to select the entire row or column when you want to display a hidden row or column. Selecting the data in the rows will not release the hidden rows or columns.

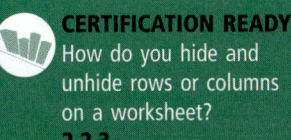

CERTIFICATION READY?
How do you hide and unhide rows or columns on a worksheet?
2.2.3

8. Select row **10**, press Shift, and select row **16**. Click **Format**. Point to Hide & Unhide and click **Unhide Rows**.

   PAUSE. LEAVE the workbook open to use in the next exercise.

A worksheet may contain rows or columns of sensitive data that you are not using or do not want to be visible while you are working in other areas of the worksheet. For example, if the person working with the Margie's Cruises worksheet wants to focus on or print the cruises to only one of the destinations, the rows containing the data for the other destinations can be hidden.

To make hidden rows visible, select the row above and the row below the hidden row or rows and use the Format commands to Unhide Rows. If the first row is hidden, use the Go To feature to make the row visible. To display hidden columns, select the adjacent columns and follow the same steps used for displaying hidden rows.

When you select rows 10 and 16 to unhide the rows, you must select them in a way that includes the hidden rows. Press Shift when you select row 16 or select row 10 and drag to include row 16. If you select row 10, press Ctrl, and click row 16, the rows will not unhide.

Looking Ahead

You will learn to use the Go To feature in Lesson 5.

■ Using Themes NEW FEATURE

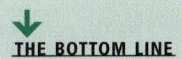

THE BOTTOM LINE

A *document theme* is a predefined set of colors, fonts, lines, and fill effects that can be applied to an entire workbook or to specific items within a workbook, such as charts or tables. In Excel 2007, you can use document themes to quickly and easily format an entire document, giving it a fresh, professional look.

Themes can be shared across other Office 2007 applications such as Microsoft Office Word and Microsoft Office PowerPoint. Because document themes can be shared, this feature enables you to give all your Office documents a uniform look in terms of colors, fonts, and effects. Effects, such as shadows or bevels, modify the appearance of an object.

Choosing a Theme for a Worksheet

Excel has several predefined document themes. When you apply a theme to a worksheet or workbook, the colors, fonts, and effects contained within that theme replace any styles that were applied to cells or ranges.

TROUBLESHOOTING: If you or another user has customized one or more document themes, those themes will appear at the top of the list and you may have to scroll down to see all built-in themes.

➔ CHOOSE A THEME FOR A WORKSHEET

USE the workbook from the previous exercise.

1. Click the **Page Layout** tab to make it active.
2. Click **Themes**. The 20 built-in themes are displayed in a preview window (see Figure 4-8). Point to each theme and observe the changes in the title lines of your worksheet.

Figure 4-8

Excel's built-in document themes

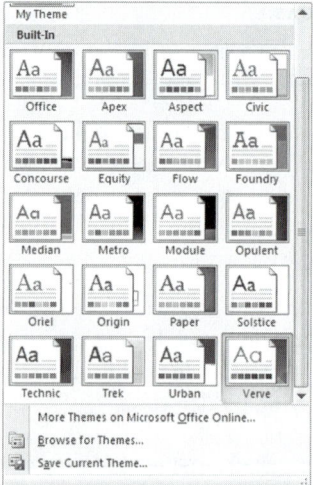

3. Click **Verve** (last theme listed) to apply it to your worksheet.
4. Click **Save As** and create a Lesson 4 folder. Name your workbook **Verve Theme** and save it in the Lesson 4 folder. You changed the default document theme by selecting another predefined document theme. As you can see, document themes that you apply immediately affect the styles that have been applied in your document.

TAKE NOTE: Because you increased the font size after you applied Heading 1 to the title, the font size remains at 20 points. If you had changed the font size before applying the heading style, the title would be displayed in points, because that is the default font size for themes.

5. Click **Themes** and click **Opulent**. The appearance of your document is significantly changed.
6. Click **Save As** and save the workbook in the Lesson 4 folder. Name your workbook **Opulent Theme**.

   PAUSE. LEAVE the workbook open to use in the next exercise.

Figure 4-8 shows the 20 built-in themes for Excel 2007. The styles that you applied in the previous exercises were the styles associated with the default Office theme. When you opened the styles gallery, the colors, fonts, and effects that were displayed were those that make up the Office theme.

Remember that styles are used to format specific cells or ranges within a worksheet; document themes are used to apply sets of styles (colors, fonts, lines, and fill effects) to an entire document. All of the default Office theme styles you applied to the titles in a previous exercise were changed when you applied a different theme.

In this exercise, you applied two document themes so that the owner of Margie's Travel can select the one that will be used on all company documents. Because themes are consistent in Microsoft Office 2007 programs, all of Margie's Travel company documents can have a uniform appearance.

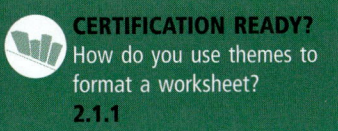

CERTIFICATION READY?
How do you use themes to format a worksheet?
2.1.1

Many companies create a customized document theme and use it consistently. You can experiment by applying various predefined themes until you decide on the "look" that appeals to you, or you can design a customized theme, as you will do in the next exercise.

Customizing a Theme

You can create a customized theme by making changes to one or more of the theme components—theme colors, fonts, or line and fill effects that are used. You can customize one of the existing themes to create your own theme. Changes you make to one or more of the theme components immediately affect the styles that you have applied in the active document.

Customizing a Theme by Selecting Colors

When you change any of the colors to create a customized theme, the colors that are shown in the Theme Colors button and next to the Theme Colors name change accordingly.

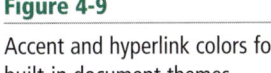 **CUSTOMIZE A THEME BY SELECTING COLORS**

USE the workbook from the previous exercise.

1. On the Page Layout tab, in the Themes group, click **Theme Colors**. Figure 4-9 illustrates the color array for each of the built-in themes.

Figure 4-9

Accent and hyperlink colors for built-in document themes

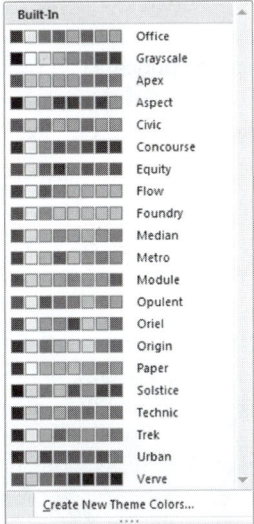

2. Click **Create New Theme Colors**. The Create New Theme Colors dialog box opens (see Figure 4-10), showing the colors used in the Opulent theme that is currently applied to the worksheet. Move the dialog box so that you can see the worksheet titles and column labels.

Figure 4-10

Create New Theme Colors dialog box

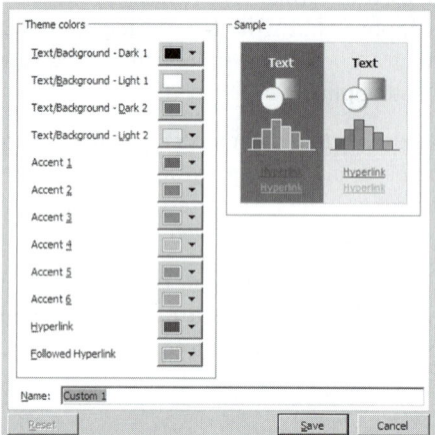

3. Click the **Text/Background – Dark 2** arrow. The current color is highlighted under Theme Colors. Click **Accent 6** to change the color to orange.
4. Click the arrow next to **Accent 1** in the dialog box and click **Accent 6** under Theme Colors. In the Name box, key **My Colors**. Click **Save**. The font and line color in the worksheet titles reflect the customized theme colors.

   PAUSE. LEAVE the workbook open to use in the next exercise.

TAKE NOTE

To return all theme color elements to their original theme colors, you can click Reset before you click Save.

In the Create New Theme Colors dialog box, click the button next to the theme color element that you want to change. The theme colors are presented in every color gallery with a set of lines and shades based on those colors. By selecting colors from this expanded matched set, you can make formatting choices for individual pieces of content that will still follow the themes. When the theme colors change, the gallery of colors changes and so does all document content using them.

It is easy to create your own theme that can be applied to all of your Excel workbooks and other Office 2007 documents. You can choose any of the color combinations you see in Figure 4-9, which represent the built-in themes, or you can create your own combination of colors.

When you clicked Create New Theme Colors, the dialog box shown in Figure 4-10 opened. Theme colors contain four text and background colors, six accent colors, and two hyperlink colors. You can change any or all of these when you customize a theme.

Customizing a Theme by Selecting a Font and Effects

Now that you have customized the color of your themes, you are ready to choose the font for your theme. Use fonts and effects that create a unique image for your documents. Themes contain a heading font and a body font. When you click the Theme Fonts button, you see the name of the heading font and body text font that is used for each theme font below the Theme Fonts name.

Worksheet Formatting | 391

➔ CUSTOMIZE A THEME BY SELECTING A FONT AND EFFECTS

USE the workbook from the previous exercise.

1. On the Page Layout tab, click **Fonts** in the Themes group.
2. Click **Create New Theme Fonts**. In the Heading font box, click **Lucida Calligraphy**.
3. In the Body font box, click **Lucida Handwriting**. The sample is updated with the fonts that you selected.

> **TROUBLESHOOTING** If your customized theme font is not automatically applied, click Cell Styles and click the customized heading font to apply it.

4. In the Name box, key **My Fonts** as the name for the new theme fonts. Click **Save**. Your customized theme fonts will be available for you to use to customize any of the built-in themes or to use the next time you click Cell Styles on the Home tab.
5. Click your theme to apply it to the open worksheet.
6. On the Page Layout tab, in the Themes group, click **Effects**.
7. Click the **Aspect** effect.
8. In the Themes group, click **Themes**. Click **Save Current Theme**.
9. In the File name box, key **My Theme**. Click **Save**. Your customized document theme is saved in the Document Themes folder, and it is automatically added to the list of custom themes that now appears at the top of the themes preview window.

PAUSE. LEAVE the workbook open to use in the next exercise.

> **CERTIFICATION READY?**
> How do you use themes to format worksheets?
> 2.1.1

You can customize the built-in themes by the manner in which you apply the attributes of the theme. For example, you like the colors in the Verve theme, but you want to use a different font. Apply the Verve theme, and then click Theme Fonts and apply the font of your choice. You can then save that theme and apply it to other documents. You cannot customize theme effects, but you can apply a different built-in effect to modify appearance by changing the shading, beveling, or other effects.

■ Modifying a Worksheet's On-Screen and Printed Appearance

> **THE BOTTOM LINE**
> You can add interest to a worksheet's on-screen appearance by displaying a background picture. You can also add color to worksheet tabs. Gridlines, row headings, and column headings are displayed by default, but they are not printed automatically. **Gridlines** are the lines that display around the worksheet cells.

Formatting a Sheet Background

> You can use a picture as a sheet background for display purposes only. A sheet background is saved with your worksheet, but it is not printed and it is not retained in a worksheet or as an item that you save as a web page. Because a sheet background is not printed, it cannot be used as a watermark.

➔ FORMAT A SHEET BACKGROUND

The *Sunset* image and the *Open Sea* image are available on the companion CD-ROM.

USE the workbook from the previous exercise.

1. On the Page Layout tab, in the Page Setup group, click **Background**.
2. Click the *Sunset* image on the companion CD, and then click **Insert**. The selected picture is displayed behind the text and fills the sheet.
3. In the Sheet Options group, click **View** to remove the gridlines.

4. Select **A1:G21**, click the **Home** tab, and click the **Fill Color** arrow. To improve readability, click **Lavender Background 2** to add solid color shading to cells that contain data.
5. Click in the worksheet. Click the **Page Layout** tab. In the Page Setup group, click **Delete Background**. The background is removed; the shading applied to the data range remains.
6. On the Page Layout tab, in the Page Setup group, click **Background** and click the *Open Sea* image on the companion CD. Click **Insert**.
7. **SAVE** the file in the Lesson 4 folder as *Background*. The background will be saved with the worksheet.
8. Click **Delete Background** in preparation for the next exercise.
9. Select **A1:G21**. Click the **Home** tab, click the **Fill Color** arrow, and click **No Fill**.
   PAUSE. LEAVE the workbook open to use in the next exercise.

> **CERTIFICATION READY?**
> How do you insert and format a picture as a worksheet background?
> 2.1.4

The owner of Margie's Travel often uses worksheets in presentations to clients as well as providing the client with printed copies. You can increase the effectiveness of the worksheet presentation by adding an appropriate background picture and adding color to worksheet tabs. It is best to remove gridlines when a sheet background is used, but printing gridlines makes printed worksheets easier to read. Printing column and row headings can help to identify the location of data during discussions.

Changing the Color of a Worksheet Tab

> By default, a new workbook contains three blank worksheets identified as Sheet1, Sheet2, and Sheet3. You often use more than one worksheet to enter related data because it is easier to move between sheets than to scroll up and down through large amounts of data. Adding color to the worksheet tabs makes it easy to locate needed information.

➔ CHANGE THE COLOR OF A WORKSHEET TAB

USE the workbook from the previous exercise.

1. Right-click the **Sheet1** tab and click **Tab Color**. Under Standard Colors, click **Green**.
2. Right-click the **Sheet2** tab and click **Tab Color**. Click **Purple**.
3. Right-click the **Sheet3** tab and click **Tab Color**. Click **Red**.
4. Click the **Sheet1** tab. Click the **Home** tab in the Ribbon. Select **A1:A3**. Click **Copy**.
5. Click **Sheet2**. Select **A1** and click **Paste**.
6. Click the **Paste Options** button and click **Keep Source Column Widths**.
7. Click **Sheet3**. Select **A1** and click **Paste**.
8. Click the **Paste Options** button and click **Keep Source Column Widths**.
9. On the Sheet1 worksheet, select **A11:G15** and click **Cut**.
10. On the Sheet2 worksheet, select **A4** and click **Paste**.
11. Cut the Alaska data from Sheet1 and paste it to A4 on Sheet3.
    PAUSE. LEAVE the workbook open to use in the next exercise.

> **Looking Ahead**
> You will rename worksheets in Lesson 5.

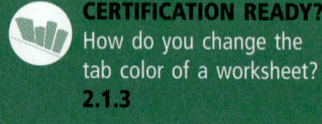

> **CERTIFICATION READY?**
> How do you change the tab color of a worksheet?
> 2.1.3

The workbook contained data about cruises to three destinations in one worksheet. In this exercise, you separated the data so that data related to each destination is on a separate worksheet in the workbook.

Worksheet Formatting | 393

Viewing and Printing a Worksheet's Gridlines

TAKE NOTE
Worksheets print faster if you print without gridlines.

You can have gridlines visible on your work surface or work without them. By default, gridlines are present when you open a worksheet. You can also choose whether gridlines are printed. A printed worksheet is easier to read when gridlines are included.

→ VIEW AND PRINT A WORKSHEET'S GRIDLINES

USE the workbook from the previous exercise.

1. Click the **Sheet1** tab. On the Page Layout tab, in the Sheet Options group, remove the checkmark from the View option in the Gridlines section if necessary.
2. In the Page Setup group, click **Orientation** and click **Landscape**. In the Scale to Fit group, click **1 page** in the Width box.
3. Click **Quick Print** on the Quick Access Toolbar. Gridlines are not present on the work surface or in the printout.
4. Click the **Sheet2** tab to make it the active worksheet. Click the **Print** checkbox under Gridlines. Click **Orientation** and click **Landscape**.
5. In the Scale to Fit group, click **1 page** in the Width box. Click **Quick Print**. Although gridlines are not present on the work surface, they are included on the printout.
6. With Sheet3 as the active worksheet, check **View** and **Print** under Gridlines. Click **Orientation** and **Landscape**.
7. Click **Quick Print**. Gridlines are present on the work surface and in the printout.

PAUSE. LEAVE the workbook open to use in the next exercise.

CERTIFICATION READY?
How do you show and hide gridlines?
2.1.2

Viewing and Printing Column and Row Headings

Column and row headings are displayed by default, but they are not printed automatically. Displaying row and column headings makes it easier to identify data in a printout.

→ VIEW AND PRINT COLUMN AND ROW HEADINGS

USE the workbook from the previous exercise.

1. Click **Sheet1.** On the Page Layout tab, in the Sheet Options group under Headings, click **View** to remove the check. Column and row headings are removed from the display.
2. Check the **View** box again. Headings are restored. Click the **Print** check box under Headings.
3. Click the **View** tab and click **Page Layout** in the Workbook Views group. Column and row headings appear in the worksheet as it will be printed. Page Layout View allows you to see the worksheet exactly as it will appear on a printed page. You can use this view to see where pages begin and end.

PAUSE. LEAVE the workbook open to use in the next exercise.

CERTIFICATION READY?
How do you show and print column and row headings?
2.1.2

■ Inserting Headers and Footers

THE BOTTOM LINE

You can add headers or footers to your worksheets to provide useful information about the worksheet, such as who prepared it, the date it was created or last modified, the page number, and so on. Headers and footers are visible in Page Layout View and they are printed on printouts.

394 | Lesson 4

A ***header*** is a line of text that appears at the top of each page of a printed worksheet. ***Footers*** appear at the bottom of each page. You can add predefined header or footer information; insert elements such as page numbers, the date and time, and the file name; or add your own content to a header or footer.

Adding Page Numbers to a Worksheet

To add or to change a header or footer, click the Insert tab and click Header & Footer in the Text group. The worksheet displays in Page Layout View, a Design tab as shown in Figure 4-11 is added to the Ribbon, and the Header & Footer Tools command groups are displayed.

Figure 4-11

Design tab added to Ribbon

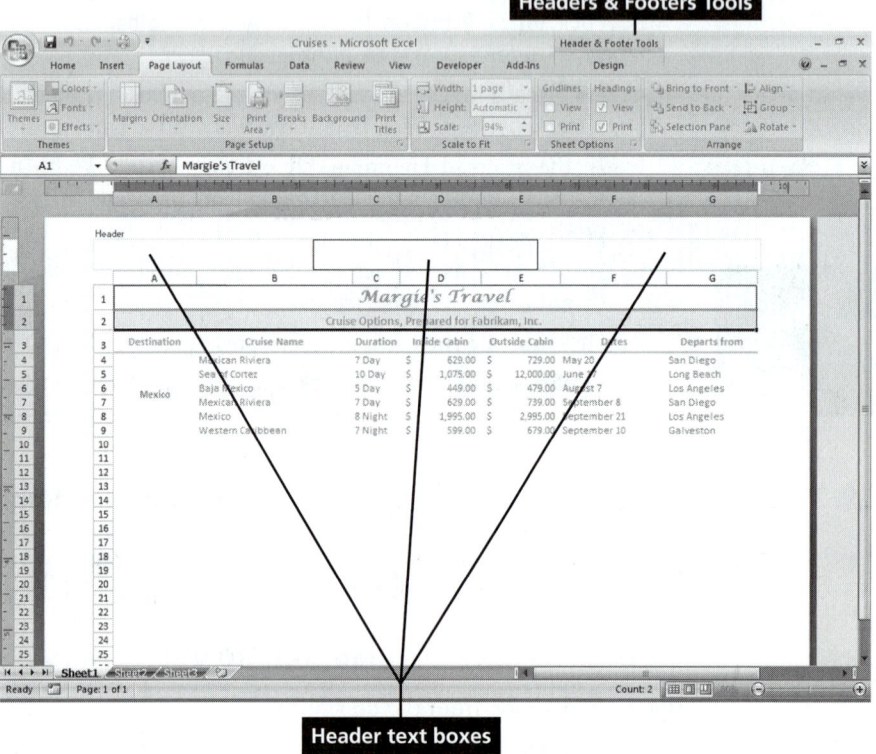

The addition of the Design tab illustrates an advantage of Excel's Ribbon interface. Instead of every command being available all the time, some commands appear only in response to an action you take.

➔ ADD PAGE NUMBERS TO A WORKSHEET

USE the workbook from the previous exercise.

1. Click the **Sheet1** tab if necessary. Click the **Insert** tab, and click **Header & Footer**. The worksheet is displayed in Page Layout View. The Center Header text box is active. The Design tab is added to the Ribbon. Header & Footer Tools command groups are available for you to use in the worksheet.
2. Press Tab to move to the right text box in the Header section of the worksheet.
3. Click **Page Number** in the Header & Footer Elements group. The code &[Page] appears in the text box. This symbol indicates that the appropriate page number will be added to each page of the printed worksheet.
4. Click **Go To Footer** in the Navigation group.

5. Click the left text box in the footer and click **Sheet Name** in the Header & Footer Elements group. Press **Tab** twice.
6. Click **Current Date** in the Header & Footer Elements group. Click anywhere in the worksheet outside the header and footer to close the Design tab.
7. **SAVE** the workbook in the Lesson 4 folder as *Cruises*.

   PAUSE. LEAVE the workbook open to use in the next exercise.

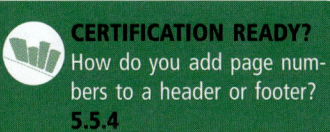

CERTIFICATION READY?
How do you add page numbers to a header or footer?
5.5.4

You can create headers and footers by keying the text that you want to appear or, as you practiced in this exercise, you can click one of the predefined elements to insert codes for headers or footers that Excel provides. When the workbook is printed, Excel replaces the codes with the current date, current time, and so on.

Inserting a Predefined Header or Footer

> On the Design tab, the Header & Footer group contains predefined headers and footers that allow you to automatically add text to the header or footer such as the date, page number, number of pages, the name of the sheet, and so on.

→ **INSERT A PREDEFINED HEADER OR FOOTER**

USE the workbook from the previous exercise.

1. Click the **Sheet3** worksheet. Click the **View** tab if necessary.
2. Client **Page Layout View** in the Workbook Views group.
3. Click the center **Header** text box. Click **Sheet Name** in the Header and Footer Elements group.
4. Click **Go To Footer** in the Navigation group. Click the left **Footer** box.
5. Click **Footer** in the Header and Footer group and click the last option in the list, which combines Prepared by, Current Date, and Page Number. Because the footer is wider than the left footnote pane, the majority of the footnote is moved to the center pane and the page number appears in the right footer pane.

   PAUSE. LEAVE the workbook open to use in the next exercise.

CERTIFICATION READY?
How do you insert a predefined header or footer?
5.5.4

ANOTHER WAY

You can access the Header and Footer text boxes by clicking Page Layout View on the right side of the status bar.

Many of the predefined headers and footers combine one or more of the elements. In the previous exercise, you inserted a combined entry by clicking it. In Page Layout view, you can create text for a header or footer.

Adding Content to a Header or Footer

> The content of the header and footer elements or the predefined headers and footers will not always meet your needs. In that case, simply key any text into one of the header or footer text boxes.
>
> You may be familiar with the watermark functionality that is available in Microsoft Word. You cannot insert a watermark in Excel, but you can mimic one by displaying a graphic in a header or footer. The graphic will appear behind the text and it will display and print like a watermark.

→ **ADD CONTENT TO A HEADER OR FOOTER**

USE the workbook from the previous exercise.

1. Click **Sheet3**. Click the center **Header** text box and delete the existing header.
2. Key **For Presentation to Client**. Press **Tab** to move to the right Header text box.

396 | Lesson 4

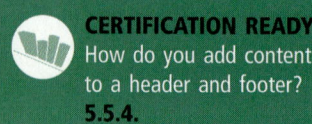

The *Sailing* image is available on the companion CD-ROM.

CERTIFICATION READY?
How do you add content to a header and footer?
5.5.4.

3. Click **Picture** in the Header and Footer Elements group. Click the *Sailing* image from the companion CD and click **Insert**.
4. Click **Format Picture**.
5. On the Format Picture dialog box, under Size & Rotate, set height to **8.5"** and accept the default width. Click **OK**. The image appears behind the text. You can resize or scale the graphic to fill the page, to appear below the text, or to appear as a graphic image in one of the header or footer boxes.
6. Click the center header text box.

PAUSE. SAVE and **CLOSE** the workbook.

You can create header or footer content by entering text that is not available in the predefined headers and footers. To enter text, click the header or footer text box where you want the text to appear and key the text that you want.

TAKE NOTE

If you want to create a multi-line header or footer, press Enter and key text or add a predefined element.

■ Preparing a Document for Printing

THE BOTTOM LINE

When worksheet data prints on more than one page, you can use the Page Break Preview command on the View tab to control where the page breaks occur. This allows you to break data where it is most logical, so that printed documents are well-organized and easy to read.

The Page Layout view is new in Excel 2007. Figure 4-12 illustrates that when you click Page Layout View on the View tab, you can view headers and footers, view (but not change) page breaks, and change page margins at the top, sides, and bottom of the worksheet.

Figure 4-12
Page Layout View

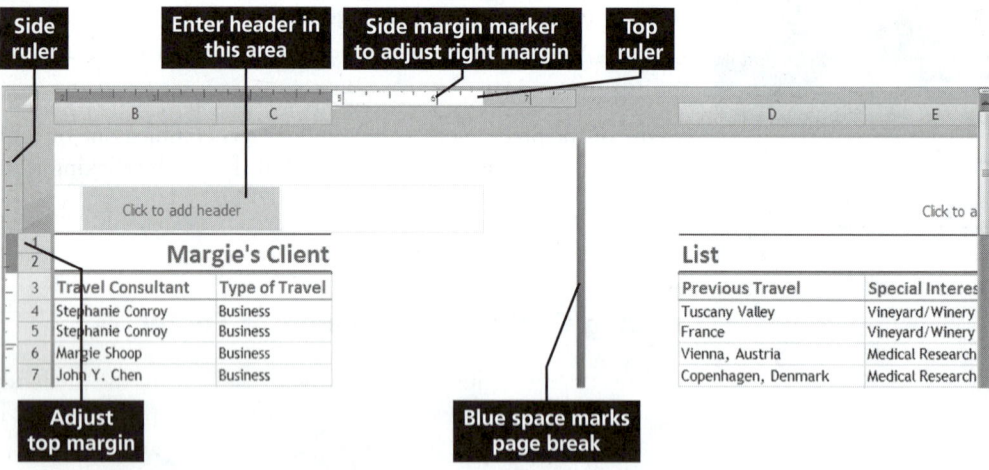

Adding and Moving a Page Break

The **Print Preview** window displays a full-page view of the worksheet just as it will be printed. You can check the format and overall layout before actually printing. You cannot make changes to the document in print preview. A **page break** is a divider that breaks a worksheet into separate pages for printing. Excel inserts automatic vertical page breaks (broken line) based on the paper size, margin settings, scaling options, and the positions of any manual page breaks (solid line) that you insert. In the *Page Break Preview* window, shown in Figure 4-13, you can quickly adjust automatic page breaks to achieve a more desirable printed document.

Figure 4-13

Page Break Preview window

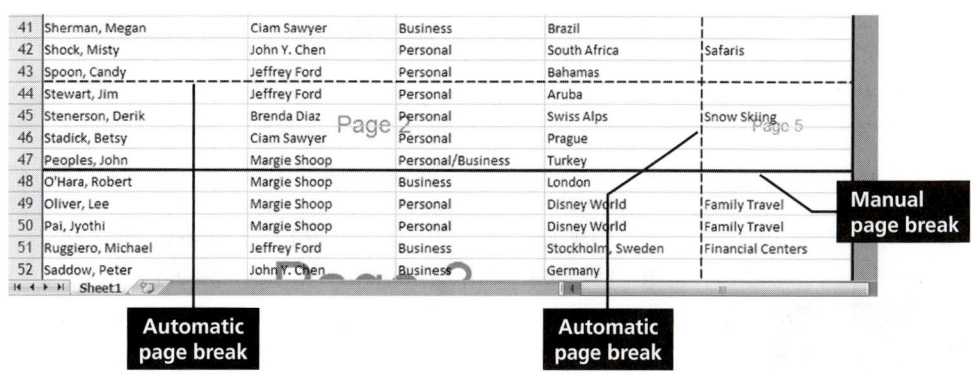

The *Margie's Client List* workbook is available on the companion CD-ROM.

TAKE NOTE

When you move an automatic page break, it becomes a manual page break.

CERTIFICATION READY?
How do you insert or move a page break?
5.5.2

➡ ADD AND MOVE A PAGE BREAK

OPEN *Margie's Client List* from the companion CD.

1. Click the View tab. In the Workbook Views group, click Page Break Preview. If a dialog box welcoming you to the view is displayed, click OK. The worksheet will print on four pages. An automatic page break occurs after row 45 and another automatic page break occurs between columns D and E.

2. Click the horizontal page break and drag it below row 40. The automatic page break is now a manual page break represented by a solid blue line.

3. Click row A22. Click the Page Layout tab. In the Page Setup group, click Breaks and click Insert Page Break. A horizontal page break is added above row 22. Press Ctrl + Home to move to cell A1.

   PAUSE. LEAVE the workbook open to use in the next exercise.

Use manual page breaks to control the page break locations. Drag the automatic page break to a new location to convert an automatic page break to a manual page break.

Setting Margins

Margins are an effective way to manage and optimize the white space on a printed worksheet. Achieving balance between data and white space adds significantly to the readability and appearance of a worksheet. You can choose one of three built-in margin sets shown in Figure 4-14 or create customized margins using the Page Setup dialog box.

Figure 4-14

Built-in margin sets

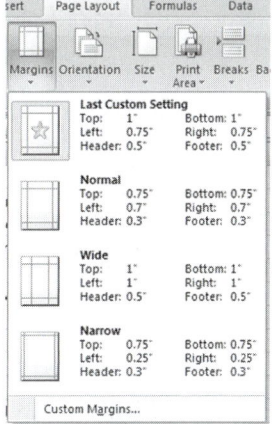

➡ SET MARGINS

USE the workbook from the previous exercise.

1. Click the **View** tab. In the Workbook Views group, click **Page Layout View**.
2. Click the **Page Layout** tab. In the Page Setup group, click **Margins** and click **Narrow**.
3. Click **Zoom In** on the status bar and increase the zoom to **100%** if necessary.

4. Click **Page Break Preview** on the Status bar. The margin adjustment has moved the vertical page break to between columns E and F.
5. Click **Margins** and click **Custom Margins**. On the Page Setup dialog box, change the left and right margins to 0.5. Click **OK**.
6. Click cell A22, click Breaks in the Page Setup group, and click **Remove Page Break**.
7. Click the vertical page break line and drag it to the right of column E.
8. Click the **Microsoft Office Button.** Point to **Print** and click **Print Preview**. The worksheet will now print on two pages, with all columns fitting to one page wide.
9. Print the worksheet or **CLOSE** the Print Preview window without printing.

PAUSE. CLOSE the workbook without saving any changes.

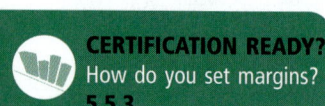

CERTIFICATION READY?
How do you set margins?
5.5.3

The Normal margin setting is the default for a new workbook. The custom margins shown in Figure 4-14 were set in the workbook you used in the exercise. Narrower margins allow more area for data when you print the workbook. You can change the margin settings to fit the needs of each workbook. When you click Custom Margins at the bottom of the Margins list, the Page Setup dialog box will open with the settings that have been applied to the open worksheet. You can change any of the settings to create a custom margin setting. Header and footer margins automatically adjust when you change the page margins.

Worksheets that do not fill the entire page can be centered vertically and horizontally, thereby evenly distributing the page's white space. Use the Margins tab of the Page Setup dialog box for this function.

You can also alter the margins in Page Layout View by clicking the top or bottom border on the margin area in the ruler. When a vertical two-headed arrow appears, drag the margin to the size you want.

Setting a Worksheet's Orientation on the Page

Printed worksheets are easiest to read and analyze when all of the data appears on one piece of paper. Excel's orientation and scaling features give you control over the number of printed pages of worksheet data. You can change the *orientation* of a worksheet so that it prints either vertically or horizontally on a page. A worksheet printed vertically uses the Portrait orientation and looks like the document shown in Figure 4-15. Portrait orientation is the default setting. A worksheet printed horizontally uses the Landscape orientation, also shown in Figure 4-15.

Figure 4-15

Portrait and landscape orientation

Worksheet Formatting | 399

 SET A WORKSHEET'S ORIENTATION ON THE PAGE

OPEN Margie's Client List again from the companion CD.

1. On the **Page Layout** tab, click Orientation and click Portrait. Notice that column E no longer fits on the same page with columns A–D.
2. Click **Orientation** in the Page Setup group and click **Landscape**. Scroll through the document to see that it will now print on two pages with each page containing all columns.
3. In the Page Setup group, click **Print Titles**. The Page Setup dialog box opens. Click the Collapse dialog box next to *Rows to repeat at top*.
4. Click row **3** (the column labels). Row 3 data is identified in the dialog box. Press Enter. Click **OK** to close the dialog box.
5. Click the **Microsoft Office Button**, point to Print, and click **Print Preview**. Press Page Down. Notice that the column labels appear on page 2 of the document.
6. **CLOSE** the Print Preview.

   PAUSE. LEAVE the workbook open to use in the next exercise.

> **CERTIFICATION READY?**
> How do you change the orientation of a worksheet?
> 5.5.5

Use the Landscape orientation when the width of the area you want to print is greater than the height. Data is easier to read when all the columns fit on one page. This can be accomplished by changing the orientation to landscape. When you can't fit all of the data on one printed page by changing the orientation, you can shrink or reduce it by using Excel's scaling options described in the next exercise.

Scaling a Worksheet to Fit on a Printed Page

 ***Scaling*** refers to shrinking or stretching the printed output to a percentage of its actual size. Before attempting to change the scaling for a worksheet's output, the maximum width and height must be set to "Automatic" to use the scaling feature. See Figure 4-16.

Figure 4-16

Scaling a worksheet to fit

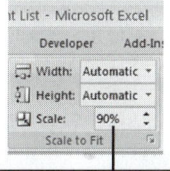

 SCALE A WORKSHEET TO FIT ON A PRINTED PAGE

USE the workbook from the previous exercise.

1. On the page layout tab, click **Orientation** and click **Portrait**. Notice that column E no longer fits on the same page with columns A–D.
2. In the Scale to Fit group, click the **Width** arrow and click **1 page**. Click the Height arrow and click 1 page. The scale is reduced to fit all columns and rows on the same page.
3. Click the **Microsoft Office Button**. Point to the arrow next to Print and click **Print Preview**. All columns appear on the page, and the height is one page as well. When output is reduced, it shrinks the height and width proportionally.
4. Close Print Preview. Save the workbook as ***Client List*** and **CLOSE** the file.

   STOP. CLOSE Excel.

>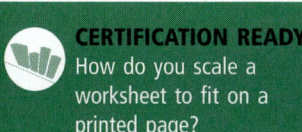
> **CERTIFICATION READY?**
> How do you scale a worksheet to fit on a printed page?
> 5.5.6

The most common reason for scaling a worksheet is to shrink it so that you can print it on one page. You can also enlarge the sheet so that data appears bigger and fills up more of the printed page. When the Width and Height boxes are set to automatic, you can click the arrows in the Scale box to increase or decrease scaling of the printout. Each time you click the arrow, the scaling changes by 5%.

> **TAKE NOTE**
>
> Remember that width and height must be set to automatic if you want to specify a scale, such as 75%.

SUMMARY SKILL MATRIX

IN THIS LESSON YOU LEARNED HOW TO:
Insert or Delete a Row or Column
Modify Row Height and Column Width
Format an Entire Row or Column
Hide and Unhide a Row or Column
Choose a Theme for a Worksheet
Customize a Theme by Selecting Colors
Customize a Theme by Selecting a Font and Effects
Format a Sheet Background
Change the Color of a Worksheet Tab
View and Print a Worksheet's Gridlines
View and Print Column and Row Headings
Add Page Numbers to a Worksheet
Insert Predefined Header or Footer
Add Content to a Header or Footer
Add and Move a Page Break
Set Margins
Set a Worksheet's Orientation on the Page
Scale a Worksheet to Fit on a Printed Page

Worksheet Formatting | 401

Knowledge Assessment

True / False

Circle T if the statement is true or F if the statement is false.

T F 1. You can insert a graphic in the header or footer of a worksheet.
T F 2. Column width and row height can be changed.
T **F** 3. After you enter a manual page break, you cannot remove it.
398— T **F** 4. You can center a worksheet's data horizontally, but not vertically.
386— **T** F 5. You can hide a column by setting the column width to zero.
386— T **F** 6. Hidden rows are not displayed on the screen but they will appear when the page is printed.
T F 7. You can change page endings in the Page Break Preview.
T F 8. You can use one of Excel's predefined Header & Footer elements to enter the worksheet author's name.
396— **T** F 9. You cannot make changes to a worksheet in the Print Preview window.
T F 10. By default, gridlines will print in an Excel worksheet.

Fill in the Blank

Complete the following sentences by writing the correct word or words in the blanks provided.

1. The _Scaling_ option allows you to enlarge or shrink worksheet data to achieve a more logical fit on the printed page.
2. There are _3_ header and footer text boxes on a workbook page where you can enter information.
3. You can manually adjust page breaks in the _page break_ view.
4. You can mimic a watermark on printouts by adding a(n) _picture - graphic_ as a header or footer.
5. Applying a(n) _Theme_ will override any formatting styles that have been applied to a data range.
6. To format an entire row or column, you must select its _headings_.
7. A(n) _header_ is a line of text that appears at the top of each printed page.
8. The row _height_ will automatically expand to accommodate increased font size.
9. Document themes are used to apply sets of styles including colors, fonts, and _effects_.
10. _Orientation_ is a setting that specifies the direction a worksheet appears on the printed page.

Competency Assessment

Project 4-1: Work with Rows and Columns

The School of Fine Art has developed a workbook to track enrollment for the academic year. Enrollments for courses in two departments have been entered. You will apply formatting techniques learned in Lesson 4 to enhance the appearance of the two worksheets in the workbook.

The *SFA Enrollment* workbook is available on the companion CD-ROM.

GET READY. Launch Excel if it is not already running.

1. **OPEN** *SFA Enrollment* from the data files for this lesson. Sheet1 should be active and the Home tab should be displayed.
2. Select **A1,** click the **Insert** arrow in the Cells group, and click **Insert Sheet Rows**.
3. Select **A1:C1** and click **Merge & Center** in the Alignment group.
4. Select **A1** and key **School of Fine Art**.
5. Select **A2:C2** and click **Merge & Center**. Key **Fine Arts Department**, replacing the existing text.
6. Merge and center A3:C3 and key **Enrollment**, replacing the existing text.
7. Click the row 4 heading, click the **Insert** arrow, and click **Insert Sheet Rows**.
8. In A5, key **Call No**.
9. In B5, key **Course**.
10. In C5, key **Fall**, replacing the existing text.
11. Select row **5**. Click **Bold** and **Italic** in the Font group. Click **Center** in the Alignment group.
12. Select row **1**. Click **Format** in the Cells group and click **Row Height** under Cell Size.
13. Key **20** in the Row Height dialog box and click **OK**.
14. Click the bottom boundary for row 2 and drag down until the ScreenTip says the height is 18 points.
15. Click the **Sheet2** tab and repeat steps 2-14. If necessary, double-click the boundary between columns to adjust the column width to display all of the text.
16. In A2, key **Media Studies Department**.
17. **SAVE** the workbook in your Lesson 4 folder. Name the workbook *SFA Enrollment 4-1* and **CLOSE** the file.

    LEAVE Excel open for the next project.

Project 4-2: Work with Rows and Columns

Insert columns and rows to add additional data to the client list for Margie's Travel. Apply styles and a document theme to add visual appeal.

1. **Open** *Client Update* from the CD data files for this lesson.
2. Select column **E**. Click the **Insert** arrow in the Cells group and click **Insert Sheet Columns**.
3. In E3, key **Anticipated Travel**.
4. Insert a row above row 3.
5. Select columns **C** and **D**. Click **Format** in the Cells group. Under Visibility, point to Hide & Unhide and click **Hide Columns**.
6. Open the **Page Layout** tab and click **Themes** in the Themes group. Click **Metro**.
7. Select **A1**. Open the **Home** tab and click **Cell Styles**. Apply Heading 1. Click **Middle Align** in the Alignment group.
8. Select row **A4:F4**. Click **Cell Styles**. Apply Heading 3 to the column labels.
9. Enter the following anticipated travel for the listed clients:

    Kiel, Kendall   Romantic Hawaii Cruise
    Nash, Mike   Aruba
    Li, Yale   Paris

10. **SAVE** the workbook as *Client Update 4-2*.

    LEAVE the workbook open for the next project.

The *Client Update* workbook is available on the companion CD-ROM.

Proficiency Assessment

Project 4-3: Modify a Worksheet's On-Screen Appearance

Create a customized theme for Margie's Travel. Prepare the document for printing on two pages.

USE the workbook that is open from Project 4-2.

1. Click the **Home** tab.
2. Select **A1**. Increase the font size to 20.
3. Select row **4**. Increase the font size to 14.
4. Click the **Page Layout** tab.
5. Click **Theme Colors** and click **Create New Theme Colors**.
6. Change the third Text/Background to Purple.
7. Key your name in the Name box. Click **Save**.
8. Set gridlines to print.
9. Insert a footer that prints the File Name in the Left Footer text box.
10. Insert a footer that prints the Page Number in the Right Footer text box.
11. Click **Print** under headings on the Page Layout tab. Set the column headings to print on the second page. Click **Page Break Preview**. Move the horizontal automatic page break to the bottom of row 40 and move the vertical page break to the right of column F.
12. **PRINT** the worksheet.
13. **SAVE** the workbook in your Lesson 4 folder as *Client Update 4-3* and then **CLOSE** the file.

    LEAVE Excel open for the next project.

Project 4-4: Prepare a Worksheet for Printing

Apply styles and a theme to a School of Fine Art worksheet. Create and apply a custom margin setting, and print the worksheet with gridlines and headings.

The *SFA Enrollment Update* workbook is available on the companion CD-ROM.

1. **OPEN** *SFA Enrollment Update* from the CD data files for this lesson.
2. **OPEN** Sheet1. Apply Heading 1 to A1.
3. Apply Heading 2 to A2.
4. Apply Heading 3 to A3.
5. Apply the Oriel theme to the worksheets.
6. Click **Margins** and **Custom Margins** to open the Page Setup dialog box.
7. For Sheet1, set top, bottom, left, and right margins to 1.5.
8. Center the data horizontally and vertically.
9. Print Sheet2 with gridlines.
10. Print Sheet1 with headings.
11. Add Blue color to the Sheet1 tab and Green to the Sheet2 tab.
12. **SAVE** the workbook as *SFA Enrollment 4-4*.

    LEAVE the workbook open for the next project.

Mastery Assessment

Project 4-5: Updating and Printing a Workbook

Add additional data to an existing workbook and prepare the workbook for printing.
USE the workbook that is open from Project 4-4.

1. On Sheet1, select **A1:C5**. Copy the heading to Sheet3.
2. Click the **Paste Options** button. Click **Keep Source Column Widths**.
3. Enter the data for the Biomedical Art Department enrollments.

MED114	Principles of Biology	463
MED115	Human Forms	236
MED116	Biomedical Art Methods	365
MED351	Traditional and Digital Color	446
MED352	3D Modeling	234
MED353	Advanced Problem in Biomedical Art	778
MED354	3D Texture	567
ILL302	Digital Imaging and Illustration	643
ILL303	Storyboarding	234
ILL304	Drawing Beyond Observation	123
DRG333	Visual Editor	434

4. Color the Sheet3 tab Orange.
5. Insert a footer in the center text box that reads **Academic Year 20XX** (with XX being the current year).
6. In the Left Footer text box, key **Current as of** and click **Current Date**.
7. Center Sheet3 vertically and horizontally.
8. Print the sheet with gridlines.
9. **SAVE** the workbook as **SFA Enrollment 4-5** and **CLOSE** the file.
   LEAVE Excel open for the next project.

Project 4-6: Page Layout—Challenge

The owner of Margie's Travel plans to meet with each travel consultant to discuss his or her client list. Insert manual page breaks in a worksheet so that each consultant's data prints on a separate page.

1. **OPEN** *Anticipated Travel* from the CD data files for this lesson.
2. Remove all existing headers and footers.
3. In the right Header box, insert the *Lighthouse* image from the CD data files for this lesson. Click **Format Picture**. Set the scale to 10% of its original size, so that it appears only in the header.
4. In the center Footer box, click **Footer** and click the last option in the predefined footers.
5. Unhide columns C and D.
6. Set the orientation to landscape.
7. Open the Page Break Preview and move and add page breaks so that each consultant's client list appears on a different page.
8. Titles and column labels should print on each page.
9. Scale the data so that it is only one page wide.
10. Print the complete worksheet with gridlines. You should have a page for each consultant.

The *Anticipated Travel* workbook and the *Lighthouse* image are available on the companion CD-ROM.

11. **SAVE** the workbook as *Anticipated Travel 4-6*. **CLOSE** the workbook.

    LEAVE Excel open for the next project.

INTERNET READY

You and two friends from your class have an appointment with Stephanie Conroy, a travel consultant with Margie's Travel, to plan your next vacation.

Using the *Anticipated Travel 4-6* file from the previous project, add your name and your friends' names to the client list. Identify Stephanie as your consultant. List at least one special interest for each of you.

Go online and find an ideal vacation spot that will fulfill the special interests for all of you. For example, if the three interests were golfing, theater, and swimming, where could you vacation that would satisfy the three interests?

SAVE the revised workbook as *My Vacation*.

Circling Back

Cross Cultural Solutions is a nonprofit organization that is recognized by the United Nations as an expert in the field of international volunteering. Whereas well-known programs such as the Peace Corps and Volunteer Service Overseas (VSO) require a two-year commitment, Cross Cultural Solutions provides volunteer opportunities ranging from 1 to 12 weeks. The organization offers a choice of three programs with year-round start dates. The goal is to provide a balance of volunteer work, cultural activities, and learning activities with time to explore the host country.

As an employee in the organization's home office, you create, edit, and format worksheets related to the programs and the individuals who volunteer.

Project 1: Create and Format a Worksheet

The 2- to 12-week **Volunteer Abroad** program is Cross Cultural Solutions' most popular program because it offers the greatest flexibility of locations and start dates. Volunteer work is personalized to the volunteer's skills and interests. Create a worksheet that contains details about this program.

GET READY. Launch Excel if it is not already running.

1. Click the **Microsoft Office Button** and click **New** if necessary. Click the **Create** button. The Home tab should be active.
2. Select A2 and key **Volunteer Abroad**.
3. In row 4, key the column labels:

    Country

    Location

    Language
4. SAVE the document as *Volunteer Abroad*.
5. Select columns **A** and **C**. Click **Format**, click **Column Width**, and change the column width to 20 characters.
6. Change the width of column B to 25 characters.
7. Enter data for the countries and locations where the Volunteer Abroad program is available.

    Ghana, Volta Region

    Tanzania, Arusha

    Tanzania, Kilimanjaro

    China, Xi'an

    Thailand, Bangkok

    Thailand, Trang

    India, New Delhi

    India, Dharamsala (Himalayas)

    Brazil, Salvador

    Costa Rica, San Carlos

    Costa Rica, Cartago

    Guatemala, Guatemala City

    Peru, Lima

    Peru, Ayacucho

    Russia, Yaroslavl

8. Click any cell in column A. Click the **Insert** arrow and click **Insert Sheet Columns**.
9. Select **A4** and key **Continent**.
10. Select **A5:A7**. Click **Merge & Center** and key **Africa**.
11. Select **A8:A12**. Click **Merge & Center** and key **Asia**.
12. Select **A13:A18**. Click **Merge & Center**. Key **Latin America**. Click **Wrap Text**.
13. Select **A19** and key **Europe**. Click **Center** in the Alignment group.
14. Format column A as follows:

    Click **Middle Align**.

    Increase the font size to 14.

    Set the Font Color to Blue.

    Double-click the column A boundary to autofit the contents.
15. Select a continent and the three columns associated with that continent. Click **Format** and click **Format Cells**. Click the **Border** tab. Place an outline around each continent's data.
16. Merge and center A2:D2. Click **Cell Styles** and apply Heading 2 style.
17. With A1 active, click **Insert** and click **Sheet Rows**.
18. In A1, key **Cross Cultural Solutions**. Merge and center the title above the columns and apply Heading 1 style.
19. Merge and center A2:D2; then merge and center A4:D4.
20. Apply Heading 3 style to the column labels and a light blue fill color.
21. Click the **Microsoft Office Button**, point to Print, and click **Print Preview**.
22. Click **Page Setup** and make the following selections.

    Portrait Orientation

    Center Vertically and Horizontally
23. **PRINT** the worksheet.
24. **SAVE** the changes. **CLOSE** the file.

    LEAVE Excel open for the next project.

Project 2: Format Cells and Ranges

In addition to the Volunteer Abroad program, the organization offers a 2- to 12-week **Intern Abroad** program for students interested in an international internship or academic credit and a 1-week **Insight Abroad** program. You have prepared a workbook with data related to volunteers who will depart for their assignments within the next two months. After preparing the workbook, you learned that assignments are made by the on-site coordinators. You need to edit and format the worksheet.

The *Cross Cultural Volunteers* file is available on the companion CD-ROM.

1. **OPEN** *Cross Cultural Volunteers* from the data files.
2. With Sheet1 active and the Home tab displayed, delete column E.
3. Click the row **18** heading to select the entire row. Press Ctrl and select row **23**. Continue to scroll through the worksheet, selecting the blank rows.

TROUBLESHOOTING If you hold down Ctrl before you select the first row to delete, you will receive an error message when you attempt to delete the rows. Select the first row and then press Ctrl.

4. Click **Delete** and click **Delete Sheet Rows**.

5. On the Insert tab, click **Header & Footer**. Key **July and August Departures** in the center Header pane.
6. Click **Go To Footer** and key **Prepared by (your name)** in the left Footer pane.
7. Move to the center Footer pane and click the **Current Date** button.
8. Move to the right Footer pane and click the **Page Number** button.
9. Right-click the **Sheet1** tab and change the tab color to purple.
10. Right-click **Sheet2** and change the tab color to green.
11. With Sheet1 active, select column **E**, click the **Home** tab, and display the Number dialog box. Format dates to display as day-month (i.e., 20-Jul).
12. Click the **Sheet2** tab to make it the active worksheet. Format columns B and C as Currency and decrease the decimals to zero.
13. **SAVE** the workbook as *Volunteers Project 2*.

   LEAVE the workbook open for the next project.

Project 3: Prepare Worksheets for Printing and Display

USE the *Volunteers Project 2* workbook from the previous project.

1. With Sheet1 active, set a Wide Margin.
2. Click **Page Break Preview** and move the page breaks so that page 1 ends with row 30 and page 2 ends with row 60.
3. Prepare the workbook for printing.
   Use Landscape Orientation.
   Print the gridlines.
   Print the titles (row 4) at the top of all pages.
4. Examine the Print Preview to verify that the printout will be in landscape orientation, that column labels print on pages 2 and 3, and that only cells that contain data are included in the printout.
5. Print the entire workbook.
6. Prepare Sheet1 for display at a meeting. On the Page Layout tab, click **Background**. Select the *Blue Hills* image from the data files and click **Insert**.
   Remove gridlines and headings from the viewed worksheet.
   Double-click the **Ribbon** tab to minimize the Ribbon.
   Zoom in until the worksheet data fills the screen.
7. **SAVE** the workbook as *Volunteers Project 3* and then **CLOSE** the file.
   STOP. CLOSE Excel.

The *Blue Hills* image file is available on the companion CD-ROM.

Managing Worksheets

5

LESSON SKILL MATRIX

Copying a Worksheet	Students will learn how to copy a worksheet.
Renaming a Worksheet	Students will learn how to rename a worksheet.
Repositioning the Worksheets in a Workbook	Students will learn how to reposition the worksheets in a workbook.
Hiding and Unhiding a Worksheet	Students will learn how to hide and unhide a worksheet.
Inserting a New Worksheet into a Workbook	Students will learn how to insert a new worksheet into a workbook.
Deleting a Worksheet from a Workbook	Students will learn how to delete a worksheet from a workbook.
Working with Multiple Worksheets	Students will learn how to work with multiple worksheets.
Working with Multiple Worksheets in a Workbook	Students will learn how to work with multiple worksheets in a workbook.
Hiding and Unhiding Worksheets in a Workbook	Students will learn how to hide and unhide worksheets in a workbook.
Use Zoom and Scroll to Change Onscreen View	Students will learn how to use zoom and scroll to change onscreen view.
Locating Data with the Find Command	Students will learn how to locate data with the Find command.
Replacing Data with the Replace Command	Students will learn how to replace data with the Replace command.
Navigating a Worksheet with the Go To Command	Students will learn how to navigate a worksheet with the Go To command.

The School of Fine Art (SFA) is a private college that is recognized as a leader in art education. More than 2,500 students are enrolled in its four-year programs of study. Admission requires an audition and/or portfolio presentation. Students pursue a BA degree in one of six majors: Fine Arts, Media Studies, Biomedical Art, Dramatic Arts, Interior Design, and Advertising and Graphic Arts. The school also offers a degree program for students who wish to combine major areas of concentration. In addition to its degree programs, SFA offers continuing education courses and Saturday and summer courses for children, teens, and adults who hope to pursue a career in the creative arts or who have exceptional artistic talent.

KEY TERMS
freeze
group worksheets
hide
string
unhide
zoom

409

■ Software Orientation

Worksheet Management

An Excel workbook should contain information about a unique subject. For example, SFA might have a workbook for enrollment data, one for faculty course assignments, and one for summer workshop course offerings. Each worksheet within a workbook contains a subset of information about that subject. The number of worksheets that a workbook can contain is limited only by the available memory of your computer. In this lesson, you will learn to move between worksheets, manage and reorganize sheets, and use Excel's search tools to find and replace information in a worksheet or workbook. To accomplish these tasks, you will use commands in the Home tab's Cells and Editing groups.

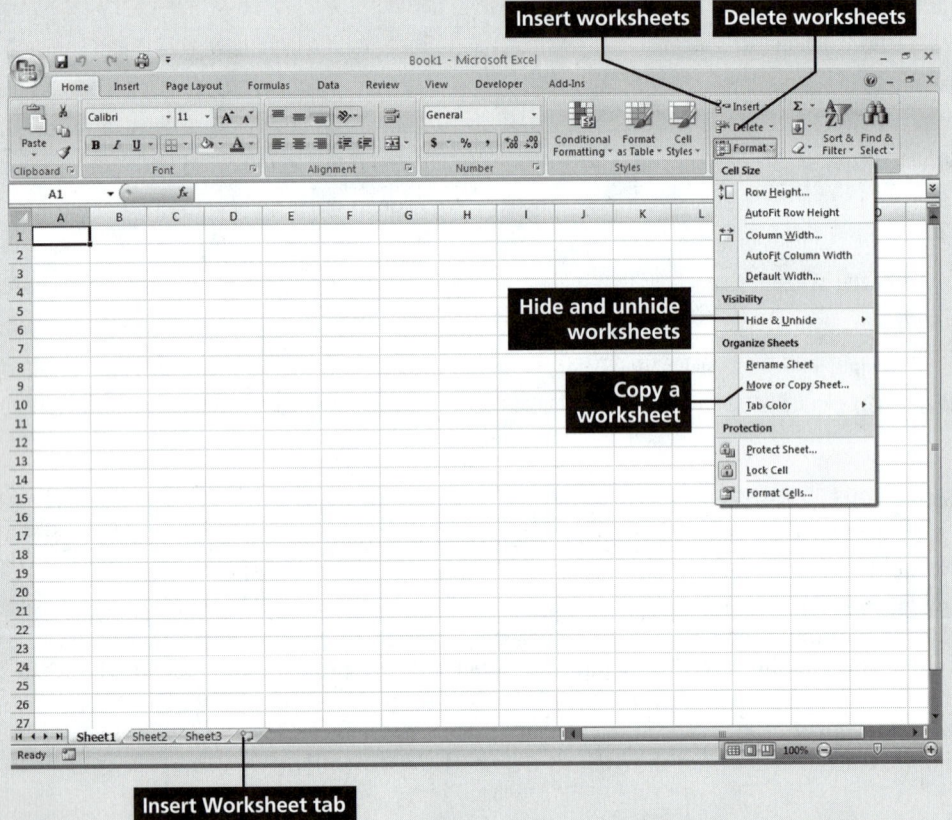

Figure 5-1

Commands to organize worksheets

■ Organizing Worksheets

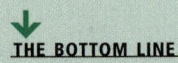

THE BOTTOM LINE

A new, blank Excel workbook has three worksheets. You can add to, delete from, and move and copy worksheets as desired. You can also rename worksheets and hide and unhide worksheets when you need to do so. The flexibility to organize worksheets with similar subject matter together in one file enables you to effectively and efficiently manage related data.

Managing Worksheets | 411

Copying a Worksheet

Just as you can copy data from one cell or range in a worksheet to another cell or range, you can copy data from one worksheet to another within a workbook. For example, when a new worksheet will contain similar information to that contained in an existing worksheet, you can copy the worksheet and delete cell contents or overwrite existing data with new data. When you copy a worksheet, you retain the structure and formatting of the original worksheet so that you don't need to rebuild it from scratch. You can copy a worksheet using the Home tab's Format commands, the mouse, or the shortcut menu.

→ COPY A WORKSHEET

GET READY. Before you begin these steps, be sure to launch Microsoft Office Excel 2007.

1. **OPEN** *School of Fine Art* from the data files for this lesson.
2. Click the **Sheet1** tab and click **Format** in the Cells group on the Home tab.
3. Click **Move or Copy Sheet**. The dialog box shown in Figure 5-2 opens.

The *School of Fine Art* worksheet is available on the companion CD-ROM.

Figure 5-2

Move or Copy dialog box

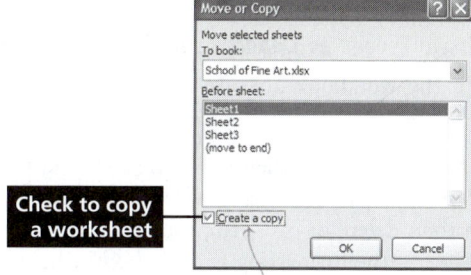

You can right-click a sheet tab to display the shortcut menu. Click Move or Copy to display the dialog box.

4. Sheet1 is selected by default. Select the **Create a copy** box as shown in Figure 5-2 and click **OK**. A copy of Sheet1 is inserted to the left of Sheet1.
5. Click the **Sheet3** tab and hold down the left mouse button. A down arrow appears at the boundary between Sheet2 and Sheet3 and the cursor becomes an arrow pointing to a blank document symbol.
6. Press and hold **Ctrl**. A plus sign appears in the cursor document. Move the cursor to the right until the down arrow appears on the right side of Sheet3. Release the cursor. The new sheet is named Sheet3 (2).
7. With Sheet3 (2) active, select **A2** and key **Dramatic Arts Department**.
8. Select **A6:C18** and press **Delete**.

Rather than delete the existing data, you can overwrite it. Select A6 and begin keying new data. Press Tab and key the data for B6. Press Tab and key the data for C6 and press Enter, etc. As you move to the next cell, the existing text is selected and it will be deleted when you enter new text.

9. Enter the data for the Dramatic Arts Department, beginning in A6.

DRAM321	Acting Studio I: Discover the Actor	106
DRAM322	Naturalism and Realism Techniques	95
DRAM326	Acting Studio: Improvisation	87
DRAM302	Acting Studio: Comedy	69
DRAM301	Fundamentals of Dance	110
DRAM312	Acting Studio: Shakespeare	95
DRAM315	Acting Studio: Iconoclastic Voices	95
DRAM400	Dialects and Accents	95
DRAM401	Advanced Voice and Diction	75
DRAM420	Theatre History	125
DRAM435	Acting for Film and TV	76
DRAM460	Auditioning Techniques	95

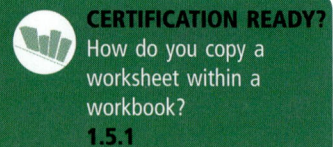

CERTIFICATION READY?
How do you copy a worksheet within a workbook?
1.5.1

10. If necessary, adjust column widths to display all data.
11. Click the **Microsoft Office Button** and click **Save As**. Create a Lesson 5 folder and **SAVE** the worksheet as *Department Enrollments*.

    PAUSE. LEAVE the workbook open to use in the next exercise.

When an existing worksheet contains the formatting that you want to use in a new worksheet, it is more efficient to copy the existing worksheet rather than start the new worksheet from scratch. You can then delete or overwrite the data with new data. You will not need to format the new worksheet—the formatting is copied with the data. You can be assured that formatting is consistent among the worksheets within the workbook.

In the preceding exercise, you used two methods to copy a worksheet, and the workbook now has five worksheets. When you copy a worksheet, the new sheet is identified as a copy by a number in parentheses following the worksheet name. When you click and hold the left mouse button on the worksheet tab, the cursor becomes a new workbook icon and an arrow appears next to the active worksheet tab as shown in Figure 5-3.

Figure 5-3

Copy a worksheet using the mouse

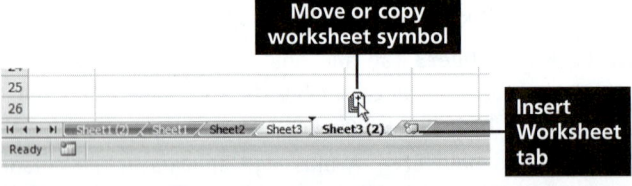

TAKE NOTE Notice that when a worksheet is copied, the tab color is copied as well as the worksheet contents and formatting.

When you use the Format command or the shortcut menu to copy a worksheet, the Move or Copy dialog box shown in Figure 5-2 lets you identify the worksheet you want to copy. The copied worksheet is inserted before the sheet you select in the dialog box.

Renaming a Worksheet

When a workbook contains multiple worksheets with data, it is helpful to replace the generic Sheet1, Sheet2, etc. names with names that identify the data contained in the sheet. Each of the worksheets contains information about one department within the School of Fine Art. Renaming the tabs with department names will allow you to quickly locate needed enrollment data.

Managing Worksheets | 413

 RENAME A WORKSHEET

USE the workbook you saved in the previous exercise.

1. Double-click the **Sheet1 (2)** tab to select the tab name.
2. Key **Interior Design** and press [Enter]. The new name appears on the worksheet tab.
3. Key **Interior Design Department** in A2 of the sheet. Select **A6:C19** and press [Delete]. You will enter data for this department in a later exercise.
4. Click the **Sheet1** tab. Click **Format** and click **Rename Sheet**. Key **Fine Arts** and press [Enter].
5. Click the **Sheet2** tab. Rename the sheet **Media Studies** and press [Enter].
6. Click the **Sheet3** tab. Rename the sheet **Biomedical Arts** and press [Enter].
7. Click **Sheet3 (2)**. Rename the sheet **Dramatic Arts** and press [Enter].
8. Check each worksheet to ensure that the shortened name on the sheet tab matches the department name in A2.

   PAUSE. LEAVE the workbook open to use in the next exercise.

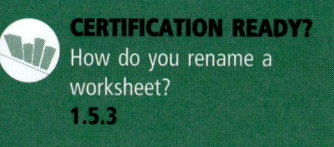

CERTIFICATION READY?
How do you rename a worksheet?
1.5.3

By naming the worksheets, it will be much easier to locate enrollment data for any course within a department. Each worksheet name indicates the type of data contained in the sheet.

Repositioning the Worksheets in a Workbook

Now that the worksheets in the Department Enrollments workbook are appropriately named, you can rearrange them in any way you wish. An alphabetical arrangement is a logical way to organize the worksheets in this workbook. In the following exercise, click the tab for the sheet you want to move.

 REPOSITION THE WORKSHEETS IN A WORKBOOK

USE the workbook from the previous exercise.

1. Click the **Biomedical Arts** tab. Click **Format** in the Cells group.
2. Click **Move or Copy Sheet**. The Move or Copy dialog box opens. You want this sheet to be the first sheet. *Interior Design* is selected. Click **OK** to move Biomedical Arts **before** Interior Design.
3. Click the **Dramatic Arts** tab. Hold down the mouse button and move the worksheet to the left. Release the mouse when the down arrow is on the right side of the Biomedical Arts tab.
4. Click the **Fine Arts** tab. Click **Format** and click **Move or Copy Sheet**.
5. Click **Interior Design** in the dialog box. Click **OK** to move Fine Arts before Interior Design. The Fine Arts sheet is moved to the third position and the sheets are now in alphabetic order.
6. Click the **Dramatic Arts** tab. Click **Format** and click **Tab Color**. Click **Red** under Standard Colors. As noted previously, when you copied worksheets, the tab color was copied as well as the contents and formatting. Changing the tab color for the copied worksheets ensures that each tab has a different color.
7. Right-click the **Interior Design** tab, click **Tab Color**, and click **Purple** under Standard Colors.
8. **SAVE** the workbook with the same name.

   PAUSE. LEAVE the workbook open to use in the next exercise.

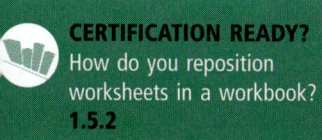

CERTIFICATION READY?
How do you reposition worksheets in a workbook?
1.5.2

Hiding and Unhiding a Worksheet

In Lesson 4, you hid columns and rows when you wanted to exclude particular columns or rows from a printout or when you wanted to hide sensitive or confidential information while you worked with other data in the worksheet. You can apply the same procedure to *hide* (make a worksheet invisible) and *unhide* (make visible again) worksheets. For example, because the Interior Design worksheet does not contain data at this time, you would hide that sheet if you wanted to print the entire workbook.

HIDE AND UNHIDE A WORKSHEET

USE the workbook from the previous exercise.

1. Select the **Interior Design** worksheet. Click **Format** in the Cells group.
2. Click **Hide & Unhide** and click **Hide Sheet**. The Interior Design worksheet is no longer visible. Click the **Fine Arts** tab.

TAKE NOTE: Right-click any worksheet tab. If worksheets are hidden, the Unhide option will be active on the shortcut menu.

3. Click **Format**, click **Hide & Unhide**, and click **Unhide Sheet**. The Unhide dialog box shown in Figure 5-4 opens.

Figure 5-4

Unhide dialog box

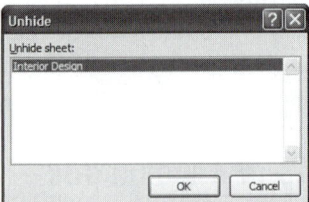

4. Click **OK** to unhide the Interior Design worksheet. Enter the following enrollment information.

ID201	Elements of Design I	103
ID205	Interior Design I	106
ID207	History of Interiors	110
ID232	Drawing and Composition	121
ID320	Interior Design II	86
ID322	Architectural Drafting	98
ID325	Elements of Design II	95
ID330	Color Theory	89
ID335	Textiles	121
ID405	CAD I	82
ID432	CAD II	75
ID430	Perspectives in Design	63
ID461	Furniture Design	59
ID465	Lighting Design	49

5. **SAVE** your workbook.

PAUSE. LEAVE the workbook open to use in the next exercise.

CERTIFICATION READY?
How do you hide and unhide a worksheet in a workbook?
1.5.4

Managing Worksheets | 415

You can hide several worksheets at the same time. Hold down Ctrl and click the tab of the sheets you want to hide. You cannot, however, select multiple worksheets in the Unhide dialog box; you must unhide worksheets individually.

Inserting a New Worksheet into a Workbook

You can insert one or multiple worksheets into an existing workbook. The Insert Worksheet tab (Figure 5-5) at the bottom of a worksheet is a new Excel 2007 feature that allows you to quickly insert a new worksheet at the end of the existing worksheets. To insert a new worksheet before an existing worksheet, select the worksheet tab before which you want the new sheet and use the Cells group Insert command.

Figure 5-5

Insert Worksheet tab

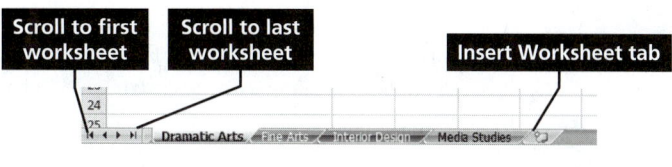

(Shift + F11)

 INSERT A NEW WORKSHEET INTO A WORKBOOK

USE the workbook from the previous exercise.

1. Click the **Insert Worksheet** tab next to the Media Studies tab. A new worksheet is inserted.
2. Click the **Biomedical Arts** tab and click the **Insert** arrow in the Cells group to display the options shown in Figure 5-6. Click **Insert Sheet**. A blank sheet is inserted before the Biomedical Arts worksheet.

Figure 5-6

Insert options

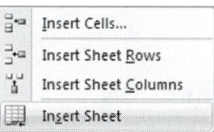

TROUBLESHOOTING: If the Biomedical Arts tab is not visible, use the scroll arrow to move to the first worksheet.

3. Double-click the **Sheet7** tab, key **Advertising**, and press **Enter**.
4. Click the **Dramatic Arts** tab and click the **Insert** arrow in the Cells group. Click **Insert Sheet**.
5. Click Advertising, press and hold **Shift**, and click **Biomedical Arts**.
6. Click **Insert** and **Insert Sheet**. Two worksheets are inserted after the **Biomedical Arts** worksheet.

PAUSE. LEAVE the workbook open to use in the next exercise.

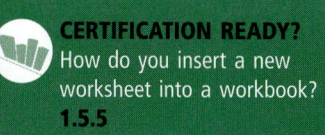

CERTIFICATION READY?
How do you insert a new worksheet into a workbook?
1.5.5

As more worksheets are added to a workbook, you may not be able to see all worksheet tabs. Use the scroll arrows, shown in Figure 5-6, to move through all worksheets.

When you copied a worksheet in a previous exercise, the tab name and tab color were copied with the worksheet's contents and formatting. When you insert a new worksheet, it is blank and has the generic Sheet1 title. When you inserted a worksheet before the existing sheets were named, the new sheet was given the next consecutive number, such as Sheet6.

You can right-click a worksheet tab and click Insert on the shortcut menu to insert a worksheet. The Insert dialog box shown in Figure 5-7 opens and you can insert a blank worksheet from the General tab, insert a worksheet based on a template from the Spreadsheet Solutions tab, or insert an online template if you are connected to the Internet.

Figure 5-7

Insert dialog box

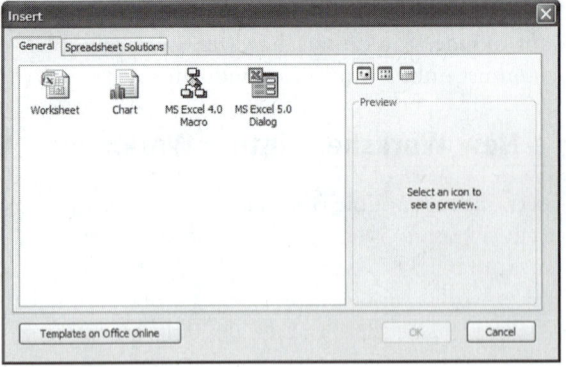

TROUBLESHOOTING When you open the Insert dialog box, multiple Excel files may be shown on the General tab. The listed files represent templates that have been downloaded, created by you, or created by another user.

To insert multiple worksheets at the same time, press and hold Shift, and then select the same number of worksheet tabs that you want to insert in the open workbook. In the exercise, when you selected the tabs of two existing worksheets, clicked Insert, and clicked Insert Sheet, two new worksheets were inserted.

Deleting a Worksheet from a Workbook

If a workbook contains blank worksheets or worksheets that contain data that is no longer needed, you can delete the unnecessary sheets.

→ **DELETE A WORKSHEET FROM A WORKBOOK**

USE the workbook from the previous exercise.

1. Click **Sheet6** and click the **Delete** arrow in the Cells group.
2. Click **Delete Sheet**.
3. Click the Sheet8 tab, press and hold [Shift], and click the **Sheet9** tab. The selection should include Sheet10 as well as Sheet8 and Sheet9.
4. Click the **Delete** arrow and click **Delete Sheet**.
5. **SAVE** the workbook.

   PAUSE. LEAVE the workbook open to use in the next exercise.

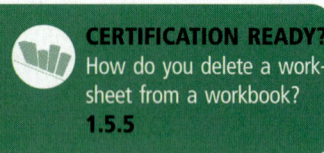

CERTIFICATION READY?
How do you delete a worksheet from a workbook?
1.5.5

You can right-click the tab of a worksheet you do not need and click Delete. The worksheet will be deleted.

Working with Multiple Worksheets

You can *group worksheets*, a feature that allows you to enter and edit data on several worksheets at the same time or apply formatting to multiple worksheets. When sheets are grouped, you can enter data in one worksheet and have it appear in multiple worksheets in a workbook. When multiple worksheets are selected, [*Group*] appears in the title bar at the top of the worksheet. Be cautious. When you change data in grouped sheets, you may accidentally replace data on other sheets.

Managing Worksheets | 417

Working with Multiple Worksheets in a Workbook

Working with a group of worksheets is a time-saving technique. You can view several worksheets within a workbook at the same time. This feature allows you to make quick visual comparisons and ensures that changes made to grouped sheets will not overwrite existing data. You can group worksheets and enter data on all worksheets within the group at the same time.

→ WORK WITH MULTIPLE WORKSHEETS IN A WORKBOOK

USE the workbook from the previous exercise.

1. Right-click a worksheet tab and click **Select All Sheets**. The title bar reads *Departmental Enrollments [Group]*.

ANOTHER WAY
If you want to group some but not all worksheets within a workbook, press Ctrl and click the tab of each worksheet you want to include in the group.

2. In B20, key **Total Enrollment**.

TAKE NOTE
If you copy a data range from a worksheet to grouped worksheets, the Paste Options button does not appear. Some formatting, such as column width, is not copied.

3. Right-click a worksheet tab and click **Ungroup Sheets**.
4. Click the **View** tab if necessary. With Biomedical Arts data displayed, click **New Window** in the Windows group.
5. Click the **Dramatic Arts** tab and click **New Window**.
6. Click the **Fine Arts** tab to make the sheet active and click **Arrange All** in the Windows group. The Arrange Windows dialog box opens. Click **Vertical** as shown in Figure 5-8. Click **Windows of active workbook**.

Figure 5-8

Arrange Windows dialog box

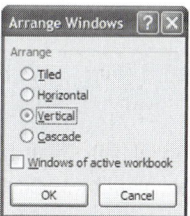

TAKE NOTE
Data that you copy or cut in grouped sheets cannot be pasted on another sheet because the size of the copy area includes all layers of the selected sheets and is therefore different from the paste area in a single sheet. Make sure that only one sheet is selected before you attempt to copy or move data to another worksheet.

7. Click **OK**. Your screen should look like Figure 5-9 with the three worksheets displayed side by side.

Figure 5-9

Vertically tiled worksheets

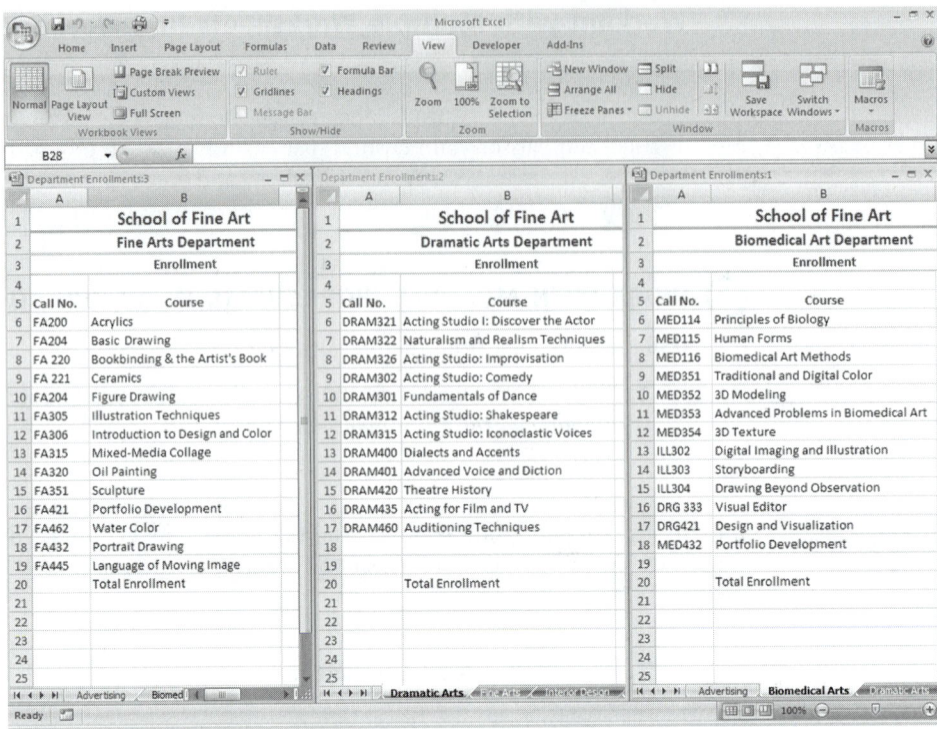

PAUSE. LEAVE the workbook open to use in the next exercise.

The New Window and Arrange All options enable you to display worksheets side by side for a quick visual comparison. You can enter and edit data, scroll, and move around in the individual windows just as you would in a normal-view window. You can click a cell in any of the displayed worksheets to make changes or to select cells or ranges.

Hiding and Unhiding Worksheets in a Workbook

You can replace any worksheet in the view by clicking the tab of another worksheet. You can also hide and unhide worksheets or an entire workbook in this view.

➔ HIDE AND UNHIDE WORKSHEETS IN A WORKBOOK

USE the workbook from the previous exercise.

1. Click any cell in the Fine Arts window.
2. Click **Hide Window** in the Window group of the View tab. The Fine Arts window is closed; the Dramatic Arts and Biomedical windows remain visible.
3. Click **Unhide Window**. Select the sheet you want to unhide and click **OK**.
4. Click the **Close** button in the upper-right corner of the Fine Arts and Dramatic Arts windows. Restore the Biomedical Arts window to full-screen view.
5. **SAVE** and **CLOSE** the file.

PAUSE. LEAVE Excel open to use in the next exercise

If you click Hide in the Window group with one worksheet window open, the entire workbook is hidden. Excel remains open, but the Taskbar no long displays the worksheet name. This feature allows you to quickly mask confidential data from view. In a later exercise, you will group worksheets and enter data on all of them at one time.

TROUBLESHOOTING Do not confuse the Hide and Unhide commands you used in this lesson with those you used in Lesson 4. The View tab commands in this lesson are used to hide and unhide what is in the active window—in most cases a complete worksheet. The Hide and Unhide commands in the Format options on the Home tab are used to hide and unhide rows, columns, and worksheets. You can hide a worksheet with either Hide command. When you hide a sheet with the Format command, other worksheets in the workbook remain visible and accessible. When you use the Hide Window command, all worksheets are hidden. You must use the Unhide command to access any worksheet in the workbook.

Using Zoom and Scroll to Change Onscreen View

Excel's *Zoom* feature allows you to make a worksheet appear bigger (zoom in) or smaller (zoom out) on your screen. You can use this feature to zoom in on a portion of a worksheet so that it appears larger and the data is easier to read. Or you can zoom out to get a better perspective of the entire worksheet, making it easier to identify formatting inconsistencies or problematic spacing or alignment.

The Freeze Panes feature lets you *freeze* a pane, which means that you keep rows or columns visible while the rest of the worksheet scrolls. You often want to freeze the row that contains column labels and the column that contains row headings so that it is always clear what the data you see represents.

➔ USE ZOOM AND SCROLL TO CHANGE ONSCREEN VIEW

OPEN *SFA Staff Directory* from the data files for this lesson.

1. Select a data cell in the **SFA Staff Directory** worksheet. Click **Zoom to Selection** on the View tab. Zoom is increased to 400%.
2. Click **Undo** on the Quick Access Toolbar to return to 100% zoom.
3. Click **Zoom** on the View tab. In the Zoom dialog box, under Magnification, click **200%**. Click **OK**.
4. Click **Zoom** and under Magnification, click **Custom**. Key **150** in the percentage box and click **OK**.
5. Click **100%** in the Zoom group.
6. Select **A5**. Click **Freeze Panes** in the Window group on the View tab. Click **Freeze Panes** in the dropdown list.
7. Press **Ctrl** + **End**. Row 4 with the column labels appears at the top of the screen to let you know what each column represents, even when the active cell is the last cell in the data range.

   PAUSE. LEAVE the workbook open to use in the next exercise.

The *SFA Staff Directory* worksheet is available on the companion CD-ROM.

You can use the Zoom scale on the Status bar to customize magnification. To zoom in (magnify), select a size greater than 100%; to zoom out (shrink), select a size less than 100%.

Some mouse devices have built-in zooming capabilities. If your mouse has a wheel, hold down Ctrl while you rotate the wheel forward or back to increase and decrease zoom.

If the SFA Staff Directory worksheet contained more columns than you could view at one time, you can freeze column A and the row containing the column labels. The Freeze First Column and Freeze First Row commands shown in Figure 5-10 are quick and easy to use if your worksheet begins with column headings, but when the data is preceded by a title and subtitle, you must tell Excel where you want the "freeze" to be located. That is why you need to select the cell below the line that you want to be visible as you move through the worksheet.

Figure 5-10

Freeze Panes options

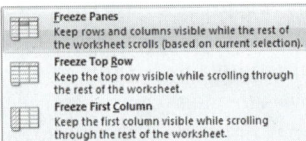

The column labels will be visible as you make changes to the worksheet in the next exercises.

> **TAKE NOTE**
> The Freeze First Row and Freeze First Column commands do not work together. When you want to freeze the first row and first column at the same time, locate the "freeze point" and use the Freeze Panes command.

■ Finding and Replacing Data

> 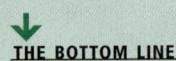 **THE BOTTOM LINE**
> The Find and Replace options let you locate specific data quickly and, if necessary, replace it with new data. These features are most effective in large worksheets in which all of the data is not visible on the screen, thus saving you the time of scanning through vast amounts of data to find the information you need.

Locating Data with the Find Command

Excel's Find feature lets you look for specific data. If you want to locate a particular item of data that isn't immediately visible, you can scan the worksheet visually to look for the needed data. A much easier and quicker way is to use the Find & Select commands shown in Figure 5-11

Figure 5-11

Find & Select commands

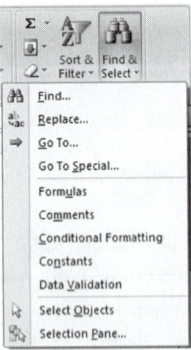

⊙ **LOCATE DATA WITH THE FIND COMMAND**

USE the workbook from the previous exercise.

1. Select **Find & Select** in the Editing group on the Home tab.
2. Click **Find**. The Find and Replace dialog box opens with the Find tab displayed.
3. Key **tutor** in the *Find what* box. It does not matter whether you key the text in uppercase or lowercase—Excel will find it.

>  **ANOTHER WAY**
> You can open the Find and Replace dialog box with the keyboard shortcut Ctrl+F.

> **TAKE NOTE**
> It does not matter which cell is currently the active cell when you enter a search string. If you do not select a range of cells, Excel will search the entire worksheet.

4. Click **Find All**. The box is expanded to list the occurrences of *tutor* in the worksheet and you see that the search results lists both academic and writing tutors, so you need to refine the search criteria.
5. Key **writing tutor** in the Find what box and click **Find All**. The worksheet contains data for two individuals whose title is Writing Tutor.
6. Click **Options** on the dialog box to view the default settings for the **Find** feature.
7. **CLOSE** the dialog box.

   PAUSE. LEAVE the workbook open to use in the next exercise.

When you enter the text or number that you want to find and click Find All, Excel locates all occurrences of the search string and lists them at the bottom of the dialog box, as shown in Figure 5-12. A *string* is any sequence of letters or numbers in a field.

Figure 5-12

Results of Find All search

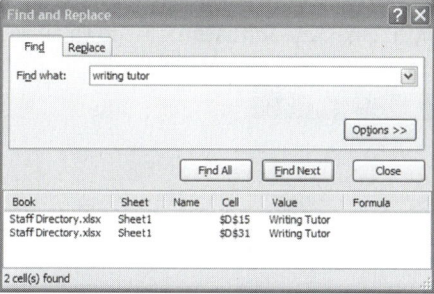

If you click Find Next after you key the search string, Excel selects the cell in which the first occurrence of the string is found. You can edit the cell or click Find Next and continue to browse through the worksheet. The cursor will stop at each cell where the search string is located.

The Options button on the Find tab allows you to set additional parameters for the search. As shown in Figure 5-13, the default is to search the active worksheet, but you can also search an entire workbook. You can locate instances in which only the case (capitals or lower case) matches the search string you key or the entire cell contents match the search string—more precise search strings create more concise search results.

Figure 5-13

Set search parameters

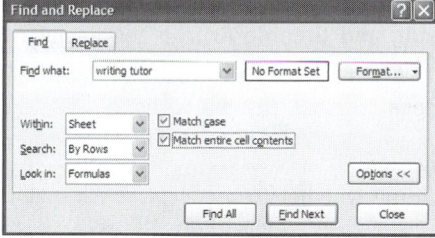

TROUBLESHOOTING: If you had selected the Match case checkbox when you searched for *tutor*, the search would not have found any data because the word *tutor* is capitalized each time it occurs in the worksheet. Therefore, a data match would not be found if you searched for a lowercase word. When the search was completed, a dialog box would have informed you that Excel could not find the data you requested.

Looking Ahead: The Look in box on the Find and Replace dialog box lets you look for data in formulas, values, or comments. You will work with formulas in Lesson 7.

Replacing Data with the Replace Command

To look for specific data and replace it with other data, you will use the Replace tab on the Find and Replace dialog box. You can quickly find and replace all or some occurrences of a character string in a worksheet. Replacing data with the click of a button can save you the time of finding occurrences of the data and repeatedly keying replacement data.

→ REPLACE DATA WITH THE REPLACE COMMAND

USE the worksheet from the previous exercise.

1. Click **Find & Select** in the Editing group.
2. Click **Replace**. The Find and Replace dialog box opens with the Replace tab displayed.
3. In the Find what box, key **Johnson**.
4. In the Replace with box, key **Johnston** as shown in Figure 5-14.

Figure 5-14

Replace tab of Find and Replace dialog box

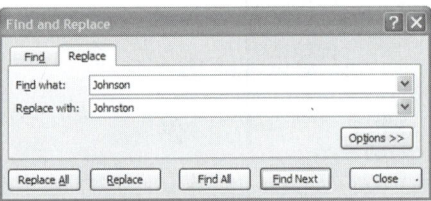

5. Click **Options** to expand the dialog box. In the Search box, click **By Columns** and click **Find Next**. The first occurrence of Johnson is not the one you are looking for, so click **Find Next** until you locate the entry for Tamara Johnson.

TROUBLESHOOTING: If the Find and Replace dialog box obstructs your view of column A where the search data will be located, click the title bar and drag the box to the right so that you have a clear view of columns A and B.

6. Click **Replace** and click **Close**.
7. Click **Find & Select** and then click **Replace**. Key **Advertising** in the Find what field and key **Advertising and Graphic Arts** in the Replace with field.
8. Click **Replace All**. A dialog box tells you that Excel made 9 replacements. Click **OK** and then click **Close** to close the dialog box.

TROUBLESHOOTING: Use discretion when deciding whether to use Replace All or Find Next when looking for specific data. When you needed to correct the spelling of a last name, you did not know whether there were other entries with the last name Johnson. Therefore, as a precaution, you needed to find the entry and decide whether to replace it with the corrected spelling. If you had chosen Replace All, you would have incorrectly changed two other last names in the directory.

9. **SAVE** your worksheet in the Lesson 5 folder. Name the file **Staff Directory**.

PAUSE. LEAVE the worksheet open to use in the next exercise.

As you have seen in this exercise, the Replace All command allows you to quickly change the contents of multiple cells. When the staff directory was created, it was easier to key *Advertising* rather than the complete name, *Advertising and Graphic Arts*. You corrected all nine occurrences of the department name, however, by clicking Replace All.

Navigating a Worksheet with the Go To Command

As you learned in an earlier lesson, you can key a cell location in the Name box, press Enter, and Excel makes the designated cell active. Another method of moving to a specific cell is to use the Go To feature. In the following exercise, you will use the Go To feature to navigate the worksheet and enter new data and to unhide the first worksheet row.

➔ NAVIGATE A WORKSHEET WITH THE GO TO COMMAND

USE the worksheet you saved in the previous exercise.

1. On the View tab, click **Freeze Panes** and click **Unfreeze Panes**. This removes the freeze so you can display the hidden row 1.
2. Click the **Home** tab. Click **Find & Select** and then click **Go To**. The Go To dialog box is displayed.
3. Key **A1** in the Reference box and click **OK**. A2 becomes the active cell, but A1 is still hidden.
4. In the Cells group, click **Format**, click **Hide & Unhide**, and click **Unhide Rows**. Row 1 is displayed.
5. Click **Find & Select** and click **Go To**. Key **E67** in the Reference box and click **OK**.
6. Key **5/15/06** in **B46** as the date on which Professor Young was hired. Press Enter.
7. Click **Find & Select** and click **Go To Special.**
8. On the Go To Special dialog box, click **Blanks** and click **OK**. The blank cells within the data range are highlighted.
9. Press Tab three times until E13, the first blank cell in the Date Hired column, is the active cell. Enter **6/8/87** and press Tab to move to the next blank cell. Enter the following dates. Press Tab after each entry.

Gronchi	12/8/05
Hasselberg	10/20/00
Kahn	11/2/03
Liu	6/5/07
Male	7/10/00
Vande Velde	3/01/01
Wadia	6/1/02
Yang	6/1/02

10. **SAVE** the *Staff Directory* worksheet and **CLOSE** the file.
    STOP. CLOSE Excel.

ANOTHER WAY

Ctrl+G is the keyboard command to display the Go To dialog box.

TROUBLESHOOTING

The reason you needed to tab three times to reach E13 is the blank cells in the heading rows. Remember that when cells are merged, entries in the merged cells are considered to be in the upper-left cell. Therefore, Excel considers the remaining cells in the merge to be blank.

As you experienced in the preceding exercises, the Find & Select features allow you to find and, if necessary, quickly replace existing data. The Go To feature is a fast way to move to specific cell references, especially in a large worksheet.

When you opened the worksheet, row 1 was hidden. By using the Go To feature, you were able to make row 1 visible. In Lesson 4 you learned to select the row before and after the hidden row to unhide a row. However, to unhide the first row or column, you need to use the Go To feature before you click Format, click Hide & Unhide, and click Unhide Rows to unhide the first row or first column.

You used one of several Go To Special commands, shown in Figure 5-15, when you located and filled blank cells in the worksheet. You will use the Special commands to go to conditional formatting in Lesson 6 and to go to formulas in Lesson 7.

Figure 5-15

Go to Special dialog box

In the exercises you completed as you learned new Excel features, you worked with relatively small amounts of data. In the business world, you often work with worksheets that contain massive amounts of data. The Find & Select and Go To features are most effective in large worksheets where it can take a significant amount of time to scan numerous rows and/or columns to find the data you need.

SUMMARY SKILL MATRIX

IN THIS LESSON YOU LEARNED HOW TO:
Copy a Worksheet
Rename a Worksheet
Reposition the Worksheets in a Workbook
Hide and Unhide a Worksheet
Insert a New Worksheet into a Workbook
Delete a Worksheet from a Workbook
Work with Multiple Worksheets
Work with Multiple Worksheets in a Workbook
Hide and Unhide Worksheets in a Workbook
Use Zoom and Scroll to Change Onscreen View
Locate Data with the Find Command
Replace Data with the Replace Command
Navigate a Worksheet with the Go To Command

Knowledge Assessment

Matching

Match each vocabulary term with its definition.

a. Hide command
b. freeze
c. group worksheets
d. string
e. search and replace
f. Unhide command
g. zoom in
h. zoom out
i. Go To Special
j. Arrange All command

___f___ 1. To make a hidden workbook or worksheet visible.
___b___ 2. To make certain rows or columns remain visible on your screen even when you scroll your worksheet.
___g___ 3. To make a worksheet appear larger on the screen.
___a___ 4. To make a workbook or worksheet invisible.
___d___ 5. Any sequence of letters or numbers that you type.
___h___ 6. To make a worksheet appear smaller on the screen.
___c___ 7. Selecting multiple worksheets to enter and edit data on them.
___i___ 8. A command you can use to locate blank cells in a worksheet.
___e___ 9. A feature you can use to locate and replace specific data in a worksheet.
___j___ 10. A feature that allows you to visually compare worksheets. *(p. 326)*

Multiple Choice

Circle the choice that best completes or responds to the following statements.

1. To find data using the Find and Replace dialog box, you must enter a sequence of characters called a
   a. range.
   b. string.
   c. cell address.
   d. menu.

2. You can tell that worksheets are grouped by
   a. a bracket around the grouped sheets.
   b. the word *group* on the sheet tabs.
   c. the word *group* in the title bar.
   d. the words *grouped sheets* on the Status bar.

3. When Sheet1 has been copied, the new worksheet title says
   a. copy of Sheet1.
   b. Sheet1 (2).
   c. Sheet1 Copy.
   d. Sheet2.

4. Which of the following is **not** a way to insert a new worksheet into a workbook?
   a. On the Home tab, click Insert and click Insert Sheet.
   b. Right-click a sheet tab, click Insert, and click Insert Worksheet.

c. On the Insert tab, click New Sheet.

d. On the Home tab, click Format, click Move or Copy Sheet, and click Create a Copy.

5. To insert multiple worksheets at one time, what action is needed in addition to selecting the same number of tabs as the number of sheets to insert?
   a. Press and hold Shift as you select the tabs.
   b. Press and hold Ctrl as you select the tabs.
   c. Press Shift after you select the tabs.
   d. Press Ctrl after you select the tabs.

6. To enter data in multiple worksheets at one time, you must
   a. use the Arrange command in the Window group on the View tab.
   b. use the Freeze command in the Window group on the View tab.
   c. use the Format command in the Cells group on the Home tab.
   d. group all worksheets and enter data in the open worksheet.

7. If you want to magnify data on the screen,
   a. decrease zoom to less than 100%.
   b. increase zoom to 100%.
   c. increase zoom to more than 100%.
   d. increase the font size in the data range.

8. When a worksheet is hidden,
   a. Unhide is active on the shortcut menu.
   b. a bold line appears where the sheet is hidden.
   c. the word Hidden appears on the Status bar.
   d. the word Hidden appears in the title bar.

9. To hide a workbook that has multiple worksheets,
   a. click Format and click Hide in the Cells group on the Home tab.
   b. click Hide in the Window group on the View tab.
   c. right-click a sheet tab and click Hide.
   d. group all worksheets and click Format, click Hide & Unhide, and click Hide Sheet.

10. When you use the Freeze command,
    a. data cannot be entered in the worksheet.
    b. you cannot scroll through the worksheet.
    c. you cannot change the worksheet view.
    d. the column and/or row headings remain visible as you scroll through the worksheet.

■ Competency Assessment

Project 5-1: School of Fine Art

You will move and copy worksheets, rename worksheets, change the tab color, and rearrange worksheets within a workbook.

The *SFA Enrollments* workbook is available on the companion CD-ROM.

GET READY. Launch Excel if it is not already running.

1. OPEN *SFA Enrollments* from the data files for this lesson.
2. Click Advertising to make it the active worksheet. If the tab is not visible, click the scroll arrow to take you to the first worksheet.

Managing Worksheets | 427

3. Click **Format** in the Cells group on the Home tab. Click **Move or Copy Sheet**.
4. In the Move or Copy dialog box, click the **Create a copy** box and click **OK**.
5. On the Advertising (2) worksheet, select **A2** and key **Foundational Studies**. Press [Enter].
6. Select **A6:C20** and press [Delete].
7. Click **Format**, click **Rename Sheet**, and key **Foundations**. Press [Enter].
8. Click **Format**, click **Tab Color**, and click **Dark Red**.
9. Click **Format** and click **Move or Copy Sheet**. In the Before sheet box, click **(move to end)** and click **OK**.
10. **SAVE** the worksheet as *SFA Enrollments 5-1* and then **CLOSE** the file.
    LEAVE Excel open for the next project.

Project 5-2: Graphic Design Institute

You will rename worksheets, hide and unhide worksheets, and insert and delete worksheets from a workbook.

The *Training Expenditures* workbook is available on the companion CD-ROM.

1. **OPEN** *Training Expenditures* from the data files for this lesson.
2. Right-click **Sheet1**. Click **Rename** and key **Budget**. Press [Enter].
3. Double-click the **Sheet2** tab. Key **January.** Press [Enter].
4. Rename Sheet3 **March** and press [Enter].
5. Rename Sheet4 **Previous Qtr** and press [Enter].
6. Click the **Insert Worksheet** tab. Rename the new sheet **Summary**.
7. Click the **March** tab and click the **Insert** arrow in the Cells group on the Home tab. Click **Insert Sheet**.
8. Name the new worksheet **February**.
9. Click the **Previous Qtr** tab. Click **Format**, click **Hide & Unhide**, and click **Hide Sheet**.
10. Click **Format**, click **Hide & Unhide**, and click **Unhide Sheet**. In the Unhide dialog box, click **OK**.
11. Click the **Previous Qtr** tab. Click the arrow next to **Delete** and click **Delete Sheet**. Click **Delete** on the dialog box to confirm that you want to delete the Previous Qtr sheet.
12. **SAVE** the worksheet as *Training Expenditures 5-2*.
    LEAVE the workbook open for the next project.

■ Proficiency Assessment

Project 5-3: Graphic Design Institute

You will move between worksheets, change the workbook view, and group worksheets to enter data on multiple sheets.

USE the workbook from the previous project.

1. Click the **View** tab to make it active.
2. On the Budget worksheet, select **E18** and click **Zoom to Selection** in the Zoom group.
3. Click **100%** in the Zoom group.
4. Click **Zoom In** on the Status bar and increase magnification to 150%.
5. Click the **January** tab and click **Select All**. Click **Copy**.
6. Click the **Summary** sheet tab, select **A1**, and click **Paste**.

7. On the February worksheet, select **A1**, right-click, and click **Paste**. Click the **Paste Options** button and click **Keep Source Formatting**.

> **TROUBLESHOOTING** If the formatting is not copied, make the January worksheet active and select the text containing the formatting. Double-click the Format Painter and apply the formatting to the necessary cells.

8. Double-click **A2** to put it in Edit mode (noted on Status bar). Select **January**, key **February**, and press `Enter`.
9. Select **C4** and key **February**.
10. Delete the January expenditures from C5:C17. Then enter the February expenditures for the items listed below. (Not all items have February expenditures; leave those cells blank.)

Courseware development	$2,500
Courseware purchase	400
Certification	250
Train-the-trainer	1,200
Hardware purchases	10,500
Consulting fees	150
Instructor fees	4,000
Travel	600
Per diem	400

11. Select **A2** on the **Summary** worksheet and key **Quarterly Expenditures**.
12. Copy **C4:C18** from the **February** worksheet to the **Summary** sheet. Paste the data next to the January data.
13. Copy **C4:C18** from the March worksheet to the Summary sheet. Paste the data next to the February data.
14. Select **A1:E1** and click **Merge & Center** two times.
15. Click **Merge & Center** two times for cells **A2:E2**.
16. **SAVE** the workbook as *Training Expenditures 5-3*. **CLOSE** the workbook.
    LEAVE Excel open for the next project.

Project 5-4: School of Fine Art

Update the school's staff directory.

OPEN *Updated Directory* from the data files for this lesson.

The *Updated Directory* workbook is available on the companion CD-ROM.

1. At the bottom of the worksheet, add information for three new staff members.

DeGrasse, Kirk	Media Studies	Associate Professor	2/15/07
Sheperdigian, Janet	Student Services	Academic Advisor	3/1/07
Playstead, Craig	Administration	Associate Dean	4/1/07

2. Gail Erickson has been promoted to Professor. Click **Find & Select**. Change her title.
3. Use the Find & Select feature to replace BioMedical with **Biomedical Art**.
4. Use Find & Select to go to **A33**. Sidney Higa's title should be **Vice President**.
5. Click **Format** and change the name of Sheet1 to **Directory**.
6. Click **Sheet2**. Press `Ctrl` and click **Sheet3**. Click **Format** and hide the blank worksheets.
7. Name the workbook *Staff Directory 5-4*.
8. **SAVE** and **CLOSE** the workbook.
    LEAVE Excel open for the next project.

Managing Worksheets | 429

Mastery Assessment

Project 5-5: School of Fine Art

Debra Core, an academic advisor, has asked you to search the enrollment data and highlight courses for some of the continuing education students with whom she is working.

The *Advisor Recommendations* workbook is available on the companion CD-ROM.

1. **OPEN** *Advisor Recommendations* from the data files for this lesson.
2. Identify the courses that investigate various aspects of color.
    a. Use the **Find & Select** options to search the entire workbook.
    b. Use **color** as the search string.
    c. In the Within field, click **Workbook**.
    d. Find all courses that have color as part of the course name.
3. Your search should return a list of six courses. Add Yellow fill color to highlight each course.
    a. Click the first course (Biomedical Arts). Click **Fill Color**.
    b. Click the second course and click **Fill Color** in the Fonts group.
    c. Continue until the six courses have been highlighted.
4. Identify the available painting courses.
    a. Use **painting** as the search string.
    b. Search the workbook and mark painting courses with a Light Blue fill.
5. Mark photography courses with a Light Green fill.
6. **SAVE** the worksheet as *Advisor Recommendations 5-5*. **CLOSE** the file.
    LEAVE Excel open for the next project.

Project 5-6: Contoso, Ltd

Use the Find & Select command to locate specific information and fill blank spaces in a worksheet. Freeze the column headings so they remain visible as you scroll through the list of Contoso employees.

The *Contoso Employees* worksheet is available on the companion CD-ROM.

1. **OPEN** *Contoso Employees* from the data files for this lesson.
2. Use the Freeze Panes command so that the column headings in row 4 remain visible as you scroll to the end the data range.
3. Find and Replace all occurrences of Billing Clerk with **Accounts Receivable Clerk**.
4. Use Find and Replace options to find all blank cells on the worksheet. Key **Records Management** in each blank in column C.
5. **SAVE** the worksheet as *Contoso Employees 5-6* and **CLOSE** the file.
    STOP. CLOSE Excel.

INTERNET READY

OPEN *College Comparisons* in the data files for this lesson.

In this lesson you worked with data files for the School of Fine Art. Go online and investigate colleges that offer degrees in your career interest. Use the College Comparisons worksheet to record information about three colleges that offer a degree program in your area of interest.

Fill in as much information as you can locate about each college. Based on your limited research, indicate which college would be your choice to pursue the degree you investigated.

The *College Comparisons* workbook is available on the companion CD-ROM.

6 Working with Data

LESSON SKILL MATRIX

Restricting Cell Entries to Certain Data Types - 431	Students will learn how to restrict cell entries to certain data types.
Allowing Only Specific Values to Be Entered in Cells - 433	Students will learn how to allow only specific values to be entered in cells.
Removing Duplicate Cells, Rows, or Columns from a Worksheet - 434	Students will learn how to remove duplicate cells, rows, or columns from a worksheet.
Sorting Data on a Single Criterion - 435	Students will learn how to sort data on a single criterion.
Sorting Data on Multiple Criteria - 436	Students will learn how to sort data on multiple criteria.
Sorting Data by Using Conditional Formatting - 437	Students will learn how to sort data by using conditional formatting.
Sorting Data by Using Cell Attributes - 438	Students will learn how to sort data by using cell attributes.
Using AutoFilter - 439	Students will learn how to use AutoFilter.
Creating a Custom AutoFilter - 440	Students will learn how to create a custom AutoFilter.
Filtering Data by Using Conditional Formatting - 441	Students will learn how to filter data by using conditional formatting.
Filtering Data by Using Cell Attributes - 442	Students will learn how to filter data by using cell attributes.
Grouping and Ungrouping Data for Subtotaling - 442	Students will learn how to group and ungroup data for subtotaling.
Subtotaling Data in a List - 443	Students will learn how to subtotal data in a list.
Formatting a Table with a Quick Style - 444	Students will learn how to format a table with a Quick Style.
Inserting a Total Row in a Table - 445	Students will learn how to insert a total row in a table.
Adding and Removing Rows or Columns in a Table - 445	Students will learn how to add and remove rows or columns in a table.

KEY TERMS

ascending order
AutoFilter
comparison operator
criteria
descending order
duplicate value
filter
grouping
outline symbols

Working with Data | 431

An employee's name is added to the list of Contoso, Ltd.'s employees when he or she joins the company. However, viewing the employee list according to the employees' positions would be more useful to the office manager when he develops the work schedule. Reorganizing the data enables the office manager to ensure that the office is fully staffed when it is open. The office manager also needs to update employee data files with additional data. Because other employees often need to access the files, he plans to restrict the data that can be entered in some files to ensure that valid results are obtained when data entry is complete and the data is analyzed for decision making.

SOFTWARE ORIENTATION

Excel's Data Tab

Excel is primarily a tool for organizing, analyzing, and presenting numerical information. Sorting data from highest to lowest or smallest to largest, for example, lets you quickly and easily identify trends and generate forecasts or probabilities. In this lesson you will learn to use commands on Excel's Data tab, shown in Figure 6-1, to sort, filter, and display data needed for specific purposes.

Figure 6-1
Data tab

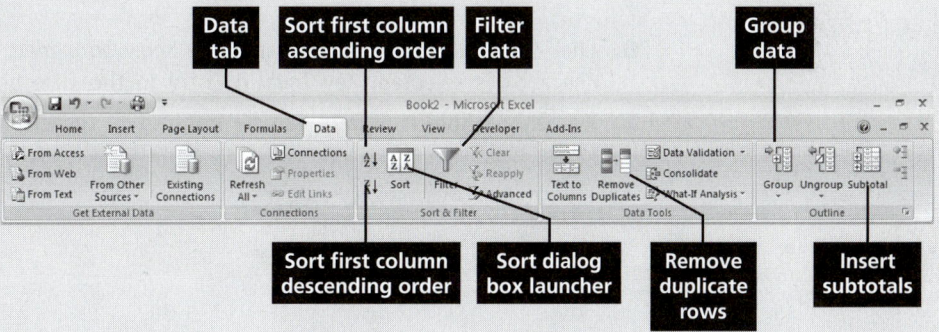

The commands on this tab enable you to sort and filter data, convert text to columns, ensure valid data entry, conduct what-if analysis, and outline data. You can also get external data into Excel by using Data commands. Use Figure 6-1 throughout this lesson as a guide to various commands.

■ Ensuring Your Data's Integrity

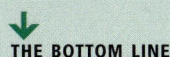
THE BOTTOM LINE

In many worksheets that you create, other users may enter data to get desired calculations and results. Ensuring valid data entry is an important task. Restricting the type of data that can be entered in a cell is one way to ensure data integrity. You may want to restrict data entry to a certain range of dates, limit choices by using a dropdown list, or make sure that only positive whole numbers are entered.

Restricting Cell Entries to Certain Data Types

Once you decide what validation you want to use on a worksheet, you are ready to set up the validation *criteria*, which is the test that Excel uses to filter data that is to be entered or displayed. When data entry is restricted, it is necessary for you to provide immediate feedback to instruct users about the data that is permitted in a cell. You can provide an input message when a restricted cell is selected or provide an instructive message when an invalid entry is made. Clear feedback to users assures a smooth, trouble-free data entry experience.

432 | Lesson 6

→ **RESTRICT CELL ENTRIES TO CERTAIN DATA TYPES**

GET READY. Before you begin these steps, be sure to launch Microsoft Office Excel 2007.

The *Employee Data* workbook is available on the companion CD-ROM.

1. **OPEN** *Employee Data* from the data files for this lesson.
2. Select **D3:D50**.
3. On the Data tab, in the Data Tools group, click **Data Validation**.
4. On the Settings tab of the Data Validation dialog box, select **Whole number** in the Allow box.
5. Key **15** in the Minimum box and **40** in the Maximum box. The Data Validation dialog box should look like Figure 6-2.

Figure 6-2

Restrict data entry using the Data Validation dialog box

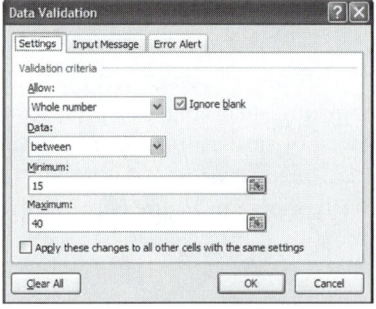

6. Click the **Error Alert** tab. Be sure the *Show error alert after invalid data is entered* checkbox is selected. Key **Invalid Entry** in the Title box.
7. Key **Only whole numbers can be entered** in the error message box as shown in Figure 6-3.

Figure 6-3

Error Alert message

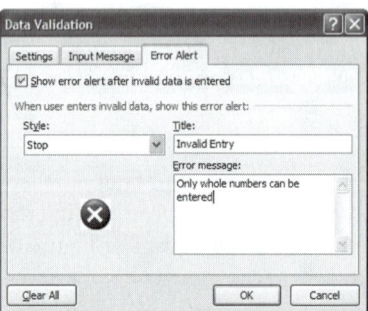

8. Click the **Input Message** tab and key **Enter a whole number between 15 and 40**. Click **OK**.
9. Select cell **D6**, key **35.5**, and press [Enter]. The Invalid Entry dialog box (Figure 6-4) opens, displaying the error message you created.

Figure 6-4

Invalid Entry message

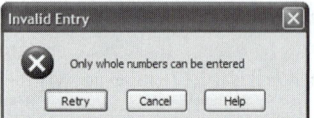

10. Click **Retry**; key **36**, and press [Enter].
11. Use the following employee information to key values in row 29.
    Patricia Doyle was hired today as a receptionist. She will work 20 hours each week.
12. Create a Lesson 6 folder and **SAVE** the file as *Contoso Data*.
    PAUSE. LEAVE the workbook open to use in the next exercise.

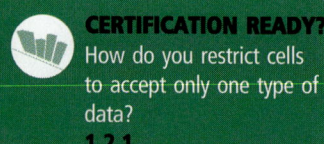

CERTIFICATION READY?
How do you restrict cells to accept only one type of data?
1.2.1

You have just taken the first step toward ensuring the integrity of data entered in the Contoso Data workbook. An employee cannot inadvertently enter text or values that are outside the parameters you set in the validation criteria. By extending the range beyond the current data, when new employee data is entered, the validation criteria will be applied.

You can specify how you want Excel to respond when invalid data is entered. In the preceding exercise, you accepted the default value, Stop, in the Style box on the Error Alert tab (Figure 6-3). If you select Warning in the Style box, you will be warned that you have made an entry that is not in the defined range, but you can choose to ignore the warning and enter the invalid data.

> **TAKE NOTE**
> If you do not enter an Error Alert title or text, the Excel default message will be displayed: *The value you entered is not valid. A user has restricted values that can be entered in this cell.*

Allowing Only Specific Values to Be Entered in Cells

To make data entry easier, or to limit entries to predefined items, you can create a dropdown list of valid entries. The entries on the list can be forced-choice (i.e., yes, no) or can be compiled from cells elsewhere in the workbook. A dropdown list displays as an arrow in the cell. To enter information in the restricted cell, click the arrow and then click the entry you want.

→ ALLOW ONLY SPECIFIC VALUES TO BE ENTERED IN CELLS

USE the workbook from the previous exercise.

1. Select **E3:E29**. Click **Data Validation**.
2. On the Settings tab, in the Allow box, select **List**. The *In-cell dropdown* checkbox is selected by default.
3. In the Source box, key **Yes, No**. Click **OK**.
4. Select **E3**. Click the arrow to the right of the cell.
5. If the value in column D is 30 or more hours, choose **Yes**. If it is less than 30 hours, select **No**.
6. Continue to select from the list for each cell in **E4:E29**. **SAVE** the workbook.

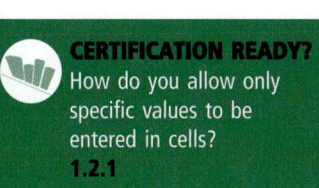

CERTIFICATION READY?
How do you allow only specific values to be entered in cells?
1.2.1

> **Looking Ahead**
> When you learn to create formulas in Lesson 7, you will be able to create a formula that will analyze the number of hours worked and enter Yes or No based on the analysis.

PAUSE. LEAVE the workbook open to use in the next exercise.

In the previous exercise, Contoso, Ltd. provided health insurance benefits to those employees who work 30 or more hours each week. By applying a Yes, No list validation, the office manager can quickly identify employees who are entitled to insurance benefits. You restricted the input for column E to two choices, but a list can include multiple choices. As you did in the exercise, the choices can be defined in the Source box on the Settings tab.

Use a comma to separate choices. For example, if you wanted to rate a vendor's performance, you might have three choices: Low, Average, and High.

There are a variety of other ways to limit data that can be entered into a cell range. You can base a list on criteria contained in the active worksheet, within the active workbook, or in another workbook. Enter the range of cells in the Source box on the Settings tab or key the cell range for the criteria. You can calculate what will be allowed based on the content of another cell. For example, you can create a data validation formula that enters yes or no in column E based on the value in column D. You will learn to create formulas in the next lesson.

Data validation can be based on a decimal with limits, a date within a timeframe, or a time within a timeframe. You can also specify the length of the text that can be entered within a cell.

434 | Lesson 6

TROUBLESHOOTING Always test the data validation to make sure that it works correctly. Try entering both valid and invalid data in the cells to make sure that your settings work as you intend and that the expected message appears when invalid data is entered.

Removing Duplicate Cells, Rows, or Columns from a Worksheet

A *duplicate value* occurs when all values in the row are an exact match of all the values in another row. In a very large worksheet, data may be inadvertently entered more than once. This is even more likely to happen when more than one individual enters data into a worksheet. Duplicate rows or duplicate columns need to be removed before data is analyzed. When you remove duplicate values, only the values in the selection are affected. Values outside the range of cells are not altered or removed.

→ **REMOVE DUPLICATE CELLS, ROWS, OR COLUMNS FROM A WORKSHEET**

USE the workbook from the previous exercise.

1. Select **A3:E29**. In the Data Tools group, click **Remove Duplicates**. The Remove Duplicates dialog box shown in Figure 6-5 opens.

Figure 6-5

Identify duplicate values to be removed

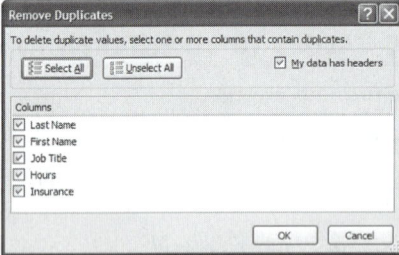

2. Remove the check from Hours and Insurance. You want to identify duplicate employee data based on last name, first name, and job title.
3. *My data has headers* is selected by default. Click **OK**. Duplicate rows are removed and the confirmation box shown in Figure 6-6 appears informing you that two duplicate values were found and removed.

Figure 6-6

Duplicate values removed

TROUBLESHOOTING Because you are permanently deleting data, it is a good idea to copy the original range of cells to another worksheet or workbook before removing duplicate values. You saved the file at the end of the previous exercise; therefore, you have a backup if you inadvertently remove data that you do not intend to remove.

Later in this lesson you will to learn to filter data. You can filter for unique values first to confirm that the results of removing duplicate values will return the result you want.

PAUSE. LEAVE the workbook open to use in the next exercise.

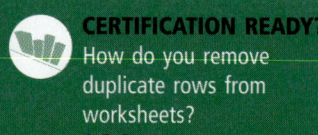

CERTIFICATION READY?
How do you remove duplicate rows from worksheets?
1.2.2

TAKE NOTE

You are working with a relatively small amount of data in the practice exercises, and it would not take a great deal of time to review the data and identify duplicate entries. However, if a company has hundreds of employees, you can see the benefit of this Excel feature.

You can specify which columns should be checked for duplicates. When the Remove Duplicates dialog box (Figure 6-5) opens, all columns are selected by default. If the range of cells contains many columns and you want to select only a few columns, you can quickly clear all columns by clicking Unselect All and then selecting the columns you want to check for duplicates. In the data used for this exercise, it is possible that an employee had been entered twice, but the number of hours was different. If you accepted the default and left all columns selected, that employee would not have been removed.

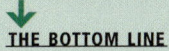**SHOOTING**

Regardless of the format applied to and displayed in a cell, the cell's true value is displayed in the Formula bar. Duplicate values are determined by the value displayed in the cell and not necessarily the true value stored in the cell. This is an important distinction when dates are entered in different formats. For example, if Aug 5, 2008 is entered in one row and 08/05/2008 is entered in another row, the values are considered unique—not duplicate. It is a good idea to check formatting before removing duplicate values.

Sorting Data

THE BOTTOM LINE

Excel's most important function is its ability to perform calculations. However, it also includes database functions that allow you to sort by text, numbers, dates, and times in one or more columns, that is, on a single criterion or on multiple criteria. Sorting data enables you to quickly visualize and understand the data better. You can rearrange and locate the data that you need to make more effective decisions.

Sorting Data on a Single Criterion

Data can be sorted on a single criterion (one column) in ascending or descending order. In *ascending order*, alphabetic data appears A to Z, numeric data appears from lowest to highest or smallest to largest, and dates appear from oldest to most recent. In *descending order*, the opposite is true—alphabetic data appears Z to A, numeric data appears from highest to lowest or largest to smallest, and dates appear from most recent to oldest.

➔ SORT DATA ON A SINGLE CRITERION

USE the workbook from the previous exercise.

1. Select **D2:D27** (column heading and data in column D).
2. On the Data tab, Click **Sort Smallest to Largest**.
3. A Sort Warning message prompts you to expand the data selection. With only one column selected, the data will not be sorted properly. With the *Expand the selection* option selected, click **Sort**. The data is sorted by Hours.
4. Select any cell in column A and click **Sort A to Z**. Data is sorted by last name.
5. Select **A2:E27** and click **Sort** to launch the Sort dialog box shown in Figure 6-7.

Figure 6-7

Specify sort criterion in the Sort dialog box

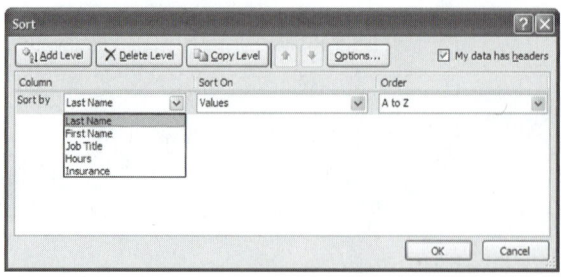

6. The first column is the default in the *Sort by* box. Click the arrow and select **Job Title**. Click **OK**.
7. Click **Sort**. The data range is automatically selected and the Sort dialog box opens. Select **Hours** in the *Sort by* box. In the Order box, select **Largest to Smallest**. Click **OK**.

   PAUSE. LEAVE the workbook open to use in the next exercise.

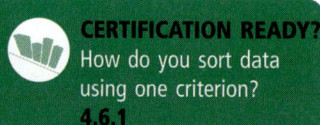

CERTIFICATION READY?
How do you sort data using one criterion?
4.6.1

TAKE NOTE
Sort and Filter commands are in the Editing group on the Home tab as well as the Sort & Filter group on the Data tab.

In this exercise, you sorted data on one criterion. Unless the worksheet contains multiple merged cells, you do not need to select data to use the Sort commands. The Sort A to Z and Sort Z to A commands automatically sort the data range on the column that contains the active cell.

It is best to have column headings that have a different format than the data when you sort a data range. By default, the heading is not included in the sort operation. In your worksheet, a heading style was applied to the column headings. Therefore, Excel recognized the header row and *My data has headers* was selected by default on the Sort dialog box.

Sorting Data on Multiple Criteria

You can sort data by more than one column. For example, in the following exercise, you will sort the Contoso employee data by job title and then sort the names alphabetically within each job category. In the Sort dialog box, identify each criterion by which you want to sort.

 **SORT DATA ON MULTIPLE CRITERIA**

USE the workbook from the previous exercise.

1. Select the range **A2:E27**, if necessary.
2. Click **Sort** to open the dialog box.
3. Select **Job Title** in the *Sort by* box and **A to Z** in the Order box.
4. Click **Add Level** to identify the second sort criteria. A new criterion line is added to the dialog box.
5. Select **Last Name** as the second criterion. A to Z should be the default in the Order box as shown in Figure 6-8. Click **OK**.

Figure 6-8

Create a multiple-criteria sort

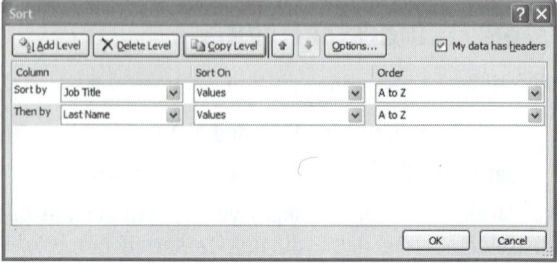

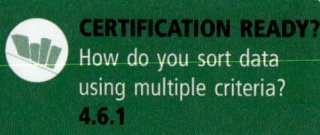

CERTIFICATION READY?
How do you sort data using multiple criteria?
4.6.1

6. **SAVE** the workbook.

Working with Data | 437

 **TAKE NOTE** You can sort by up to 64 columns. For best results, the range of cells that you sort should have column headings.

PAUSE. LEAVE the workbook open to use in the next exercise.

When working with large files, you often need to perform a multiple-criteria sort. Figure 6-8 illustrates a two-criteria sort. You can continue to add levels as well as delete or copy a criterion level. To change the sort order, select the criterion and click the up or down arrow. Entries higher in the list are sorted before entries lower in the list. To sort by case sensitivity, click the Options button to open the Sort Options dialog box shown in Figure 6-9. If Case sensitive is activated, lowercase entries will be sorted before uppercase entries.

Figure 6-9

Use case-sensitive criteria to sort data

Sorting Data by Using Conditional Formatting

If you have conditionally formatted a range of cells with an icon set, you can sort by the icon. As you learned in Lesson 3, an icon set can be used to annotate and classify data into categories. Each icon represents a range of values. For example, in a three-color arrow set, the green up arrow represents the highest values, the yellow sideways arrow represents the middle values, and the red down arrow represents the lower values.

SORT DATA BY USING CONDITIONAL FORMATTING

USE the workbook from the previous exercise.

1. On the Home tab, click **Find & Select** and click **Conditional Formatting**. A message is returned that no cells in the worksheet contain conditional formatting. Click **OK** to close the dialog box.
2. Select **D3:D27**. Click **Conditional Formatting** and then click **Icon Sets**.
3. Click **3 Arrows (Colored)**. Each value in the column now has an arrow that represents whether the value falls within the high, middle, or low range.
4. Select **A3:E27**. On the Home tab, click **Sort & Filter** and then click **Custom Sort**.
5. Select **Hours** in the *Sort by* box. Select **Cell Icon** under Sort On. Click the green arrow under Order.

TROUBLESHOOTING The sort resulted in the green arrows (highest values) on top. However, the medium and low range values are not sorted. You need to implement a multiple-criteria sort.

6. Select **Hours** in the *Then by* box. Select **Cell Icon** under Sort On and accept the yellow arrow and **On top** in the Order field. Click **OK**. Data is sorted by icon set.
7. **SAVE** your worksheet as *Contoso Icons*. **CLOSE** the workbook.

PAUSE. LEAVE Excel open to use in the next exercise.

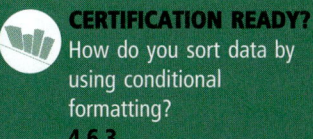

CERTIFICATION READY?
How do you sort data by using conditional formatting?
4.6.3

The first time you perform a sort, you must select the entire range of cells, including the column header row. When you want to sort the data using different criteria, select any cell within the data range and the entire range will be selected for the sort. You need to select the data only if you want to use a different range for a sort.

438 | Lesson 6

Sorting Data by Using Cell Attributes

If you have formatted a range of cells by cell color or by font color, you can create a custom sort to sort by colors. To sort by cell attribute, use the Sort & Filter command on the Home tab. When you select Custom Sort, the Sort dialog box opens and you can select the order in which you want the colors sorted.

→ SORT DATA BY USING CELL ATTRIBUTES

1. **OPEN** *MA Assignments* from the data files for this lesson.
2. Select the data range (including the column headings). On the Data tab, click **Sort**.
3. On the Sort dialog box, accept **Last name** in the *Sort by* box. Under Sort On, select **Cell Color**.
4. Under Order, select **Pink** and **On Top**.
5. Click **Add Level** and select **Last Name** in the *Sort by* box. Under Sort On, select **Cell Color**. Select **Yellow** and **On Top**.
6. Add a level for Green and then add a level for Blue. You should have a criterion for each color as illustrated in Figure 6-10. Click **OK**.

The *MA Assignments* workbook is available on the companion CD-ROM.

Figure 6-10

Multiple cell attribute sort

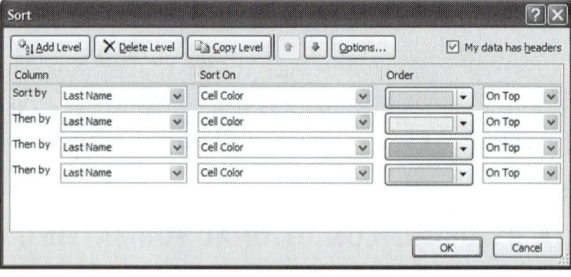

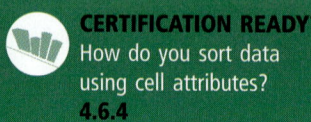

CERTIFICATION READY?
How do you sort data using cell attributes?
4.6.4

7. **SAVE** the worksheet in your Lesson 6 folder as *MA Assignments*.

PAUSE. LEAVE the workbook open to use in the next exercise.

TROUBLESHOOTING

When a worksheet contains unevenly sized merged cells, if you do not select data before you open the Sort dialog box, you will receive an error message that tells you a sort requires merged cells to be identically sized. The *MA Assignments* worksheet contained two rows with merged cells. Therefore, you had to select the data range (including column labels) the first time you sorted the worksheet. If you performed additional sorts, Excel would remember the data range and you would not need to select it again.

At Contoso, Ltd., each medical assistant is assigned to work with a specific physician. To assist with scheduling, the office manager created the *MA Assignments* worksheet with the physician/medical assistant assignments color coded. The color coding is a reminder that the two must be scheduled for the same days and hours when the weekly schedule is created. The color coding enabled you to sort the data so that the physician and his or her medical assistant were grouped.

Most sort operations are by columns, but you can custom sort by rows. Create a custom sort by clicking Options on the Sort dialog box. You can then choose *Sort left to right* under Orientation (see Figure 6-9).

Sort criteria are saved with the workbook so that you can reapply the sort each time the workbook is opened. Table 6-1 summarizes Excel's default ascending sort orders. The order is reversed for a descending sort.

Table 6-1

Default ascending sort order

VALUE	ASCENDING SORT ORDER
Numbers	Smallest negative number to largest positive number
Dates	Earliest date to most recent date
Text	Alphanumeric data is sorted left to right, character by character. For example, A5, A501, A51 are correctly sorted. Numbers and symbols are sorted before text. If the Case sensitive option is active, lowercase text is sorted before uppercase text.
Logical values	False is placed before true.
Blank cells	In both ascending and descending sorts, blank cells are placed last.

Filtering Data

THE BOTTOM LINE

Worksheets can hold as much data as you need, but you may not want to work with all of the data at the same time. You can temporarily isolate specific data in a worksheet by placing a restriction, called a *filter*, on the worksheet. Filtering data enables you to focus on the data pertinent to a particular analysis by displaying only the rows that meet specified criteria and hiding rows you do not want to see.

Using AutoFilter

X REF

See *Setting Up Data in a Table Format* later in this lesson.

AutoFilter is a built-in set of filtering capabilities. Using AutoFilter to isolate data is a quick and easy way to find and work with a subset of data in a specified range of cells or table columns. You can use AutoFilter to create three types of filters: list value, format, or criteria. Each is mutually exclusive. For example, you can filter by list value or format, but not both.

➔ USE AUTOFILTER

USE the workbook from the previous exercise.

1. Select **A3:E28**. Click **Filter** on the Data tab in the Sort & Filter group. A down arrow is added to each column heading.
2. Click the arrow in the Job Title column. The AutoFilter menu shown in Figure 6-11 is displayed.

Figure 6-11

Select text values to filter

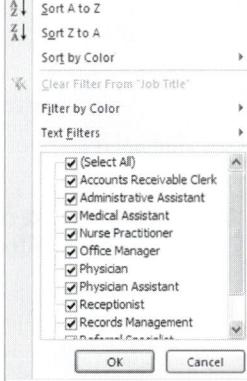

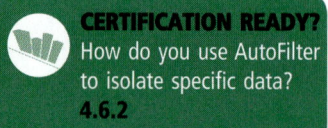

TAKE NOTE* To make the AutoFilter menu wider or longer, click and drag the grip handle at the bottom.

3. Currently the data is not filtered, so all job titles are selected. Click **Select All** to deselect all titles.
4. Click **Accounts Receivable Clerk** and **Receptionist**. Click **OK**. Data for six employees is displayed. All other employees are filtered out.

   PAUSE. LEAVE the workbook open with the filtered data displayed to use in the next exercise.

CERTIFICATION READY?
How do you use AutoFilter to isolate specific data?
4.6.2

In this exercise, you used two text filters to display only the receptionists and accounts receivables clerks. This information is especially useful when the office manager is creating a work schedule. This feature allows him to isolate relevant data quickly.

Creating a Custom AutoFilter

You can create a custom AutoFilter to further filter data by two comparison operators. A *comparison operator* is a sign that is used in criteria to compare two values. For example, you might create a filter to identify values *greater than* 50 but *less than* 100. Greater than and less than are comparison operators. Such a filter would display values from 51 to 99.

→ **CREATE A CUSTOM AUTOFILTER**

USE the workbook from the previous exercise.

1. With the filtered list displayed, click the arrow in column D. Point to Number Filters. As shown in Figure 6-12, the menu expands to allow you to customize the filter.

Figure 6-12

Numeric comparison criteria

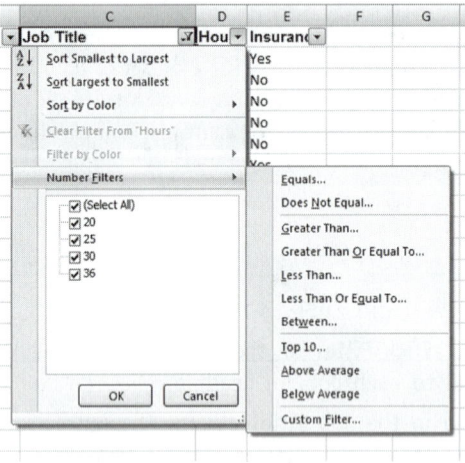

2. Select **Less Than** on the expanded menu and key **30** in the amount box. Click **OK**. The filtered list is reduced to four employees.
3. Click **Filter** to display all data. Select the data range and click **Filter**.
4. Click the arrow in column D. Point to Number Filters and select **Greater Than**. Key **15** and press **Tab** twice.
5. Click the arrow and select **is less than** as the second comparison operator and press **Tab**. Key **30** and click **OK**. The list should be filtered to six employees.
6. Click **Filter** to display all data.
7. **SAVE** and **CLOSE** the workbook.

   PAUSE. LEAVE Excel open to use in the next exercise.

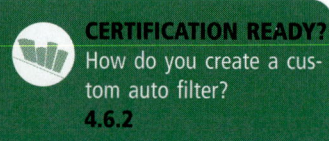

CERTIFICATION READY?
How do you create a custom auto filter?
4.6.2

Comparison operators are used to create a formula that Excel uses to filter numeric data. The operators are identified in Table 6-2.

Table 6-2

Comparison operators

Operator	Meaning
=	Equal to
>	Greater than
<	Less than
>=	Greater than or equal to
<=	Less than or equal to
<>	Not equal to

Equal to and *Less than* are options for creating custom text filters. Text Filter options also allow you to filter text that begins with a specific letter (Begins With option) or text that has a specific letter anywhere in the text (Contains option).

As illustrated in Figure 6-13, you can design a two-criterion custom filter that selects data that contains both criteria (*And* option) or selects data that contains one or the other of the criteria (*Or* option). If you select *Or*, less data will be filtered out.

Figure 6-13

Two-criterion custom filter

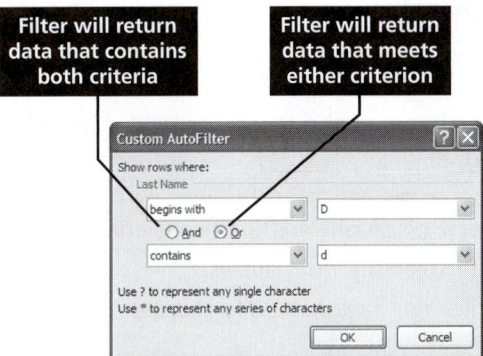

Filtering Data by Using Conditional Formatting

If you have conditionally formatted a range of cells, you can filter the data by that format. In the following exercise, icon sets are used to identify the number of hours employees work each week, and font color has been used to identify the medical assistant assigned to each physician.

➔ FILTER DATA BY USING CONDITIONAL FORMATTING

OPEN *Conditional Format* from the data files for this lesson.

1. Select **A3:E32**. On the Data tab, click **Filter**.
2. Click the arrow in column D. Point to Filter by Color. Click the green flag under *Filter by Cell Icon*. Data formatted with a green flag (highest number of work hours) is displayed.
3. Click the filter arrow in column D. Point to Filter by Color. Click the red flag under *Filter by Cell Icon*. The data formatted by a green flag is replaced by data formatted with a red flag (lowest number of work hours).
4. Click **Filter** to remove the filter arrows.

    PAUSE. LEAVE the workbook open to use in the next exercise.

The *Conditional Format* worksheet is available on the companion CD-ROM.

442 | Lesson 6

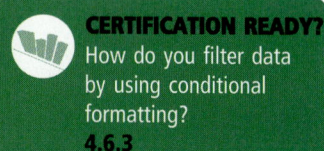

CERTIFICATION READY?
How do you filter data by using conditional formatting?
4.6.3

As you learned in Lesson 3, a conditional format is a visual guide that helps you quickly understand variation in a worksheet's data. By using conditional formatting as a filter, you can easily highlight interesting cells or ranges in order to emphasize the values based on one or more criteria.

Filtering Data by Using Cell Attributes

If you have formatted a range of cells with fill color or font color, you can filter on those attributes. It is not necessary to select the data range to filter using cell attributes. Excel will search for any cell that contains either background or font color.

➔ **FILTER DATA BY USING CELL ATTRIBUTES**

USE the workbook from the previous exercise.

1. Select any cell in the data range and click **Filter**.
2. Click the arrow next to the title and point to Filter by Color. Click **More Font Colors**. A dialog box opens that displays the font colors used in the worksheet.
3. As in Figure 6-14, the first color appears in the *Selected* field. Click **OK**. The heading rows are displayed. These are the colors in the Oriel theme that was applied to this worksheet.

Figure 6-14

Colors used in worksheet displayed in dialog box

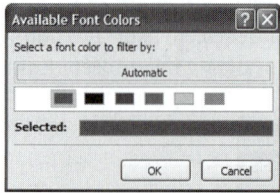

4. Click the filter arrow at the top of the worksheet and click **Clear Filter From "(Column A)"**.
5. Click the filter arrow and point to Filter by Color. Select **Purple**. Data for Dr. Blythe (new physician) and his two medical assistants is displayed.
6. Click **Filter** to clear the filter arrows.
7. **CLOSE** the file. You have not made changes to the data, so it is not necessary to save the file.

   PAUSE. LEAVE Excel open to use in the next exercise.

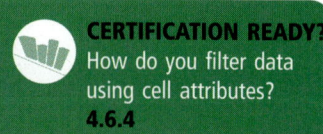

CERTIFICATION READY?
How do you filter data using cell attributes?
4.6.4

In the preceding exercises, you used Excel's Sort and Filter features to group data using a variety of criteria. Both Sort and Filter allow you to select and analyze specific data. The two functions have a great deal in common. In both instances, you can focus on data that meets specific criteria. Unrelated data is displayed when you sort; it is hidden when you use the filter command.

■ Subtotaling Data

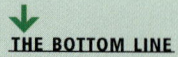

THE BOTTOM LINE

Excel provides a number of features that enable you to organize large groups of data into more manageable groups. Data in a list can be summarized by inserting a subtotal. Before you can subtotal, however, you must first sort the list by the field on which you want the list subtotaled.

Grouping and Ungrouping Data for Subtotaling

If you have a list of data that you want to group and summarize, you can create an outline. *Grouping* refers to organizing data so that it can be viewed as a collapsible and expandable outline. To group data, each column must have a label in the first row and the column must contain similar facts. The data must be sorted by the column or columns for that group.

Working with Data | 443

GROUP AND UNGROUP DATA FOR SUBTOTALING

The *Salary* worksheet is available on the companion CD-ROM.

OPEN *Salary* from the data files for this lesson.

1. Select any cell in the data. Click **Sort** on the Data tab.
2. On the Sort dialog box, sort first by Job Category in ascending order.
3. Add a sort level, sort by Job Title in ascending order, and click **OK**.
4. Select row **14**, press Ctrl, and select row **27**. On the Home tab, click the **Insert** arrow and click **Insert Sheet Rows**. This step inserts rows to separate the job categories.
5. In C14, key **Subtotal**. Select **F14** and click **AutoSum**. The values above F14 are selected. Press Enter and the category is subtotaled.
6. In C28, key **Subtotal**. Select **F28** and click **AutoSum**. Press Enter.
7. In C36, key **Subtotal**. Select **F36** and click **AutoSum**. Press Enter.
8. In C37, key **Grand Total**. Select **F37** and click **AutoSum**. The three subtotals are selected. Press Enter.
9. Select a cell in the data range. On the Data tab, click the arrow below **Group**, and then click **Auto Outline**. A three-level outline is created.

PAUSE. LEAVE the workbook open to use in the next exercise.

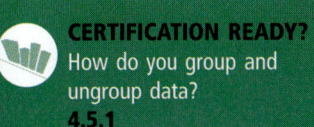

CERTIFICATION READY?
How do you group and ungroup data?
4.5.1

In the preceding exercises, you manually grouped and subtotaled salary data for Contoso, Ltd. You will use Excel's automatic subtotal feature in the next exercise.

To outline data by rows, you must have summary rows that contain formulas that reference cells in each of the detail rows for that group. In the preceding exercise, your outline contained three levels: the grand total level, the subtotals level, and the detail rows level. You can create an outline of up to eight levels.

Each inner level displays detail data for the preceding outer level. Inner levels are represented by a higher number in the ***outline symbols***, which are symbols that you use to change the view of an outlined worksheet. You can show or hide detailed data by pressing the plus sign, minus sign, and the numbers 1, 2, or 3 that indicate the outline level.

Subtotaling Data in a List

You can automatically calculate subtotals and grand totals for a column by using the Subtotal command in the Outline group on the Data tab. You can display more than one type of summary function for each column. The Subtotal command outlines the list so that you can display and hide the detail rows for each subtotal.

SUBTOTAL DATA IN A LIST

USE the worksheet from the previous exercise.

1. In the Outline group on the Data tab, click the **Ungroup** arrow and then click **Clear the Outline.**
2. Select rows 14, 28, 36, and 37 and then delete all selected rows.
3. Select the data range. Include the column labels in the selection.
4. Click **Subtotal** in the Outline group on the Data tab. The Subtotal dialog box is displayed.
5. Select **Job Category** in the *At each change in* box.
6. Under *Add subtotal to*, click **Salary**. Click **OK** to accept the remaining defaults. Figure 6-15 illustrates the appropriate selections. Subtotals are inserted for each of the three job categories and a grand total is calculated at the bottom of the list.

Figure 6-15

Subtotal a data range.

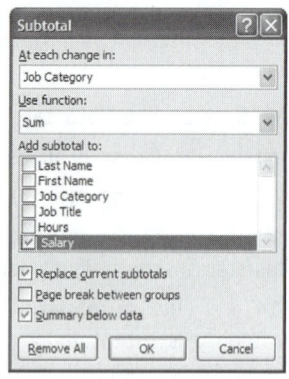

CERTIFICATION READY?
How do you insert subtotals in a list?
4.5.2

7. **SAVE** the workbook as *Salaries* and **CLOSE** the file.

   LEAVE Excel open for the next exercise.

TAKE NOTE

If the workbook is set to automatically calculate formulas, the Subtotal command recalculates subtotal values automatically as you edit the detail data.

When the data you want to subtotal can be grouped according to a category, such as Job Category in this exercise, the Subtotal command is the best choice. However, when data is not categorized, you can manually insert subtotals as you did in the previous exercise.

You can subtotal groups within categories. For example, you could subtotal the salaries for the accounts receivable clerks or the records management employees as well as find a total for the entire office staff.

Setting Up Data in a Table Format

THE BOTTOM LINE

When you create a table in Excel, you can manage and analyze data in the table independently of data outside the table. For example, you can filter table columns, add a row for totals, apply table formatting, and publish a table to a server that is running Microsoft SharePoint Services 3.0.

Formatting a Table with a Quick Style

When you create a table, Table Tools become available, and a Design tab appears on the Ribbon. You can use the tools on the Design tab to customize or edit the table. Four table styles are displayed in the Table Styles group. Click the arrows to the right of the styles to display additional styles.

FORMAT A TABLE WITH A QUICK STYLE

1. **OPEN** *Salary* from the data files for this lesson.
2. Select any cell in the data. Click **Sort** on the Data tab.
3. On the Sort dialog box, sort first by Job Category in ascending order.
4. Add a sort level and sort by Job Title in ascending order. Click **OK**.
5. On the Home tab, click **Format as Table** in the Styles Group.
6. Click **Table Style Medium 5** from the format gallery. The Format as Table dialog box opens.
7. Click the arrow in *Where is the data for your table?* The dialog box collapses.
8. Select **A27:F32** as shown in Figure 6-16 and press **Enter**. Your table does not have headers, so click **OK**. The banded rows style format is applied and filtering column headers are inserted.

CD

The *Salary* worksheet is available on the companion CD-ROM.

CERTIFICATION READY?
How do you apply Quick Styles to tables?
2.4.1

Figure 6-16

Identify data to include in table

PAUSE. LEAVE the workbook open to use in the next exercise.

You can turn a range of cells into an Excel table and manage and analyze a group of related data independently. By default, when you insert a table, the table has filtering enabled in the header row so that you can filter or sort your table quickly. As you will see in the next exercise, you can add a Totals row that provides a dropdown list of functions for each cell in the total row. You can insert more than one table in the same worksheet.

Inserting a Total Row in a Table

You could insert a new row at the end of the table, but it is faster to total the data in an Excel table by using the Total Row command in the Table Styles Options group on the Design tab.

TAKE NOTE

Because the data selected for the table did not have headers, default names (i.e., Column1) are displayed above the table.

ANOTHER WAY

You can also right-click on a table row or column to open the shortcut menu. Point to Insert and options to insert rows or columns appear.

 INSERT A TOTAL ROW IN A TABLE

USE the worksheet from the previous exercise.

1. Select a cell in the table and click **Total Row** in the Table Style Options on the Design tab. A row is inserted below the table and the salaries in column F of the table are totaled.
2. Click a blank cell to deselect the table. Adjust the column width to display the total amount if necessary.

   PAUSE. LEAVE the workbook open to use in the next exercise.

If you press Tab in the last cell of the last row of the table, a blank row will be added at the end of the table, which would allow you to add new data to the table. Once a Totals row has been added to the table, however, pressing Tab will not add a new row.

Adding and Removing Rows or Columns in a Table

After you create a table in your worksheet, you can easily add rows or columns. You can add adjacent rows to the table by using the mouse to drag the resize handle down to select rows or drag to the right to select columns. You can enter text or values in an adjacent row or column that you want to include in the table. You can add a blank row at the end of the table, or insert table rows or columns anywhere in the table.

CERTIFICATION READY?
How do you create a total row in a table?
2.4.2

 ADD AND REMOVE ROWS OR COLUMNS IN A TABLE

USE the worksheet from the previous exercise.

1. On the Design tab, in the Properties group, click **Resize Table**.
2. Collapse the Resize Table dialog box, and select **A27:F35**. Press **Enter**. Click **OK**. The physician assistant data is moved above the total line and the total is recalculated.
3. Select **C28**. On the Home tab, click the **Delete** arrow and click **Delete Table columns**. Column C is deleted.
4. Click the **Column1** heading and key **Last Name**. Press **Tab**. Key **First Name** and press **Tab**. Key **Job Title** and press **Tab**.

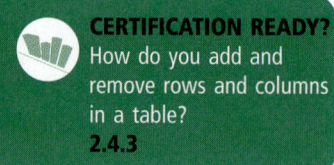

CERTIFICATION READY?
How do you add and remove rows and columns in a table?
2.4.3

5. Key **Hours** in column 5. Press Tab. Click **Yes** to continue when the Invalid Entry dialog box opens. Key **Salary** in the column 6 heading.
6. Adjust the column E width to display the total salary amount.
7. In the Properties group on the Design tab, select the text in the Table Name box and key **Schedule**. This table represents the individuals with whom patients schedule appointments.
8. **SAVE** the file as *Table* and then **CLOSE** the file.
   EXIT Excel.

When you resize a table, the table headers must remain in the same row, and the revised table range must overlap the original table range. In the exercise, you added a row from below to the table, but you would not be able to add a row from above the table. You can click the resizing handle in the lower-right corner of the table and drag it to the right to add a column.

When you finish working with table, you can click Convert to Range in the Tools group and convert the table to a data range. The formatting, column headers, and table total remain.

In a previous exercise, you restricted column E to whole numbers. When you keyed the column heading, the Invalid Entry dialog box opened, allowing you to override the data restriction. The text was accepted when you clicked Yes to continue.

SUMMARY SKILL MATRIX

In This Lesson You Learned how to:
Restrict Cell Entries to Certain Data Types
Allow Only Specific Values to Be Entered in Cells
Remove Duplicate Cells, Rows, or Columns from a Worksheet
Sort Data on a Single Criterion
Sort Data on Multiple Criteria
Sort Data by Using Conditional Formatting
Sort Data by Using Cell Attributes
Use AutoFilter
Create a Custom AutoFilter
Filter Data by Using Conditional Formatting
Filter Data by Using Cell Attributes
Group and Ungroup Data for Subtotaling
Subtotal Data in a List
Format a Table with a Quick Style
Insert a Total Row in a Table
Add and Remove Rows or Columns in a Table

Workplace Ready

Using a Template with Built-in Formulas

Microsoft Excel provides numerous templates that can be downloaded and used to start new worksheets. Templates are time-saving tools that eliminate the need for you to spend time setting up the structure of a worksheet and applying complex formatting and formulas. All you need to do is enter the raw data, because the template has built-in formatting and formulas.

When you click the Microsoft Office Button and click New, the New Workbook window opens, as shown in the following figure. Recently used templates are shown in the window's middle pane. The Templates pane lists categories of templates that can be downloaded from Microsoft Office Online. Although some are personal-use templates, the majority are business templates. You can browse templates by category and select and download a template of your choice. You can then use it as the basis for a new workbook

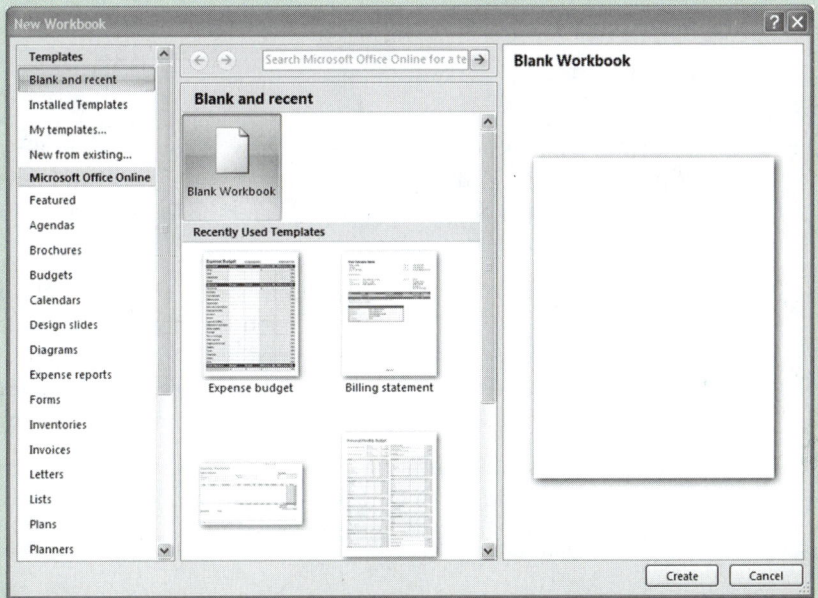

The Expense Budget template can be downloaded from Microsoft Office Online. Download the *Expense Budget* file and explore this template that could be used in a business setting. This template, shown in the following figure, makes it easy for you to perform calculations because formulas and other worksheet features are already set up for you.

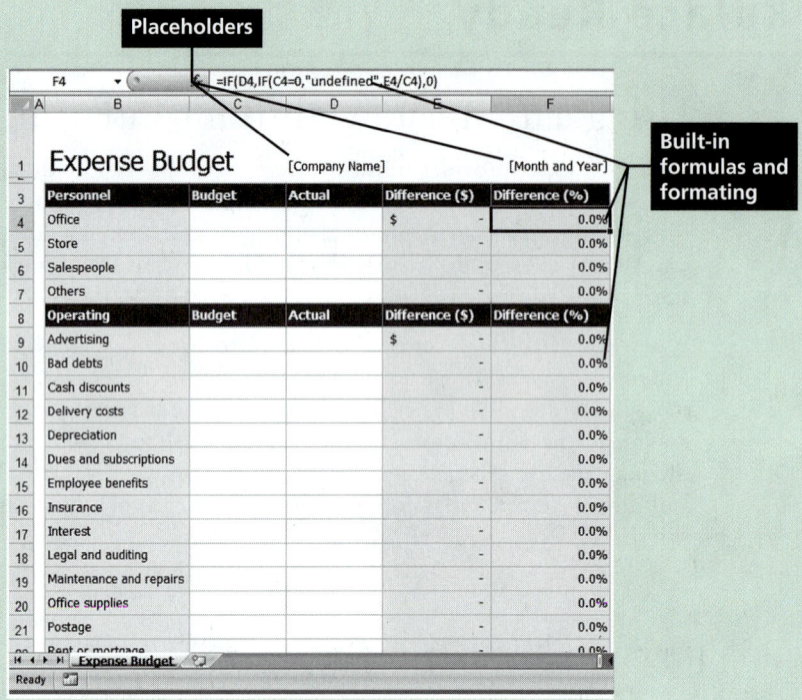

Placeholders mark cells in which to enter your company's name and the date. Categories of expenses are identified in column A. You can insert cells and rows if necessary. The existing cells and rows can be deleted or moved and the labels can be edited to reflect the line items in your company's budget.

You can key the data for your company's budget amounts and actual expenditures in columns B and C. The data cells in columns D and E contain formulas to calculate the difference between budget and actual expenditures as values and percentages. When you enter data, both calculations are completed automatically. When you scroll to the bottom of the worksheet, you see that formulas have been created to total each column.

You can easily see that using this template to create a company expense budget would take far less time than creating the worksheet from scratch. With a template you just enter the data—Excel provides the formulas and performs all the calculations.

■ Knowledge Assessment

Fill in the Blank

Complete the following sentences by writing the correct word or words in the blanks provided.

1. The process of organizing data so that it can be viewed as a collapsible and expandable outline is __Grouping__.
2. Values in the row that are an exact match of all the values in another row are referred to as __duplicate__.
3. Excel uses __filter__ rules to determine which worksheet rows to display.
4. In __descending__, sorted values appear Z to A or highest to lowest.

Working with Data | 449

5. The <u>Criteria</u> are conditions specified to limit which records to include in the result of a sort or filter.

6. A sign used in criteria to compare two values is a(n) <u>Comparison Operator</u>.

7. Using a(n) <u>Autofilter</u> allows you to apply a built-in set of filtering capabilities.

8. In <u>Ascending</u> sort order, values appear A to Z or smallest to largest.

9. You can use outline <u>Symbols</u> to change the view of an outlined worksheet.

10. You can quickly rearrange the data sequence when you use Excel's <u>Sorting</u> feature.

True/False

Circle T if the statement is true or F if the statement is false.

P.437 **(T)** F 1. You can sort a data range using conditional formatting.

T **(F)** 2. When numbers are sorted in ascending order, the largest number is on top.

P.440 **(T)** F 3. You can create a custom AutoFilter that will isolate data that falls between a high and low number.

(T) F 4. You can filter data to display all cells with a specific background color and cells that contain specific text.

(T) F 5. In a case-sensitive sort, lowercase letters will be sorted before uppercase letters.

T **(F)** 6. To temporarily isolate a specific list of rows in a worksheet containing data, use the Sort feature.

T **(F)** 7. The Data Validation command enables you to locate and remove duplicate values in a worksheet.

(T) F 8. To outline data, the data must have a blank line that includes a formula that references all the cells in the detail rows for that group.

444 - **(T)** F 9. When a table is inserted in a worksheet, the Design tab is added to the Ribbon and Table tools are available.

(T) F 10. Data validation enables you to allow only specific values to be entered in cells.

■ Competency Assessment

Project 6-1: Analyze Semiannual Sales Data

Litware, Inc. has divided its sales representatives into two teams that are in competition for sales rewards. The sales report worksheet has been color coded to identify team members.

GET READY. Launch Excel if it is not already running.

The *Semiannual Sales* worksheet is available on the companion CD-ROM.

1. **OPEN** *Semiannual Sales* from the data files for Lesson 6.
2. Click the **Data** tab to make it active.
3. Select **A4:H12**. The data range should include the column headings but not the monthly totals.
4. Click **Sort** in the Sort & Filter group. *My data has headers* should be selected by default. If not, select it.
5. On the Sort dialog box, select **Total** (or Column H) in the *Sort by* field. In the Sort On field, select **Values**. Select **Largest to Smallest** (descending) in the Order field. Click **OK**. The sales representative with the highest total sales is listed first. The rest are listed in descending order.

6. With the data still selected, click **Sort**. Sort by Sales Representative. Sort on Font Color. In the Order fields, select **Red** and **On Top**. Click **OK**. The red team is listed first. Within the red team, representatives are listed in descending order in terms of sales.
7. **SAVE** the workbook as *Semiannual Sales 6-1*. **CLOSE** the file.

   LEAVE Excel open for the next project.

Project 6-2: Ensuring Data Integrity

Create a worksheet that you will use to collect survey responses from a random sample of students at your college. Your survey will consist of ten questions, and you will survey ten students.

1. Click the **Microsoft Office Button** and open a new blank worksheet.
2. Select **A2**, key **Survey Questions**, and press Tab.
3. Key **Student 1** and press Tab. Key **Student 2** and press Tab.
4. Select **B2:C2**. Use the fill handle to complete the series to Student 10 (Cell K2).
5. Select **A3** and key **In what year did you begin college?** Press Enter.
6. Key **Have you met with an advisor this year?** Press Enter.
7. Key **How many hours per week do you study?** Press Enter.
8. Select **B3:K3**. On the Data tab, click **Data Validation**.
9. On the Settings tab, in the Allow box, select **Whole number**. In the Data box, select **less than or equal to**. In the Maximum field, enter the current year in 20XX format.
10. Click the **Input Message** tab. In the *Input message* box, key **Enter year in 20XX format**. Click **OK**. The input message should be displayed when you close the dialog box.
11. Select **B4:K4**. Click **Data Validation**.
12. Click the **Settings** tab if necessary. In the Allow box, select **List**. In the Source box, key **Yes, No**. Click **OK**. A dropdown arrow should be displayed next to the active cell.
13. Resize the columns if necessary.
14. **SAVE** the workbook as *Survey 6-2* and then **CLOSE** the file.

    LEAVE Excel open for the next project.

Proficiency Assessment

Project 6-3: Filter Data on Multiple Criteria

The Litware sales manager needs to filter the sales report data in a variety of ways that he can use in team meetings to acknowledge those who have achieved sales objectives and to motivate the teams. Create the filters for the sales manager.

The *Sales Teams* workbook is available on the companion CD-ROM.

GET READY. Launch Excel if it is not already running.

1. **OPEN** *Sales Teams* from the data files for this lesson.
2. Select **A4:H12**. Click **Filter**. Click the arrow in the Total column.
3. Click **Number Filter** and then click **Greater Than**. Key **100,000** on the dialog box. Click **OK**. Four sales representatives are displayed.

Working with Data | 451

4. Click **Filter** to display all data. Select any cell that contains data and create a filter to display the Red Team's statistics. (Hint: Because entire rows are color coded, you do not have to select the data. Data does not have to be sorted when you filter for color.)
5. **SAVE** the workbook as *Red Team*.
6. Click **Filter** to display all data. Click **Filter** again to display the filter arrows.
7. Click a filter arrow and display the Blue Team's statistics.
8. **SAVE** the workbook as *Blue Team*. **CLOSE** the file.
   LEAVE Excel open for the next project.

Project 6-4: Sort and Filter Using Conditional Formatting

Each year *Fortune Magazine* surveys employees and publishes a list of the ten best employers based on employee ranking. The Top Ten worksheet contains additional information about the top ten companies in terms of their size (number of employees), percentage of minorities, and percentage of women.

The *Top Ten* workbook is available on the companion CD-ROM.

1. **OPEN** *Top Ten* from the data files for this lesson.
2. Select the data range, including the column headings. Click **Sort** on the Data tab.
3. Sort the data by % Minorities. Click **Cell Icon** in the Sort On field.
4. Under Order, place the green flagged data (highest) on top. Click **OK**. Because you sorted by one criterion, the highest is on top, but the Red and Yellow are intermixed.
5. Click **Sort** to add a second criterion to sort on yellow flags, which represent the middle range.
6. With the data range selected, click **Filter**. Arrows are added to the column headings.
7. Click the filter arrow in the % Women column. Choose to filter by color.
8. Select the green arrow. Women comprise more than 60 percent of the workforce in two of the top ten companies.
9. **SAVE** the workbook as *Top Ten 6-4*. **CLOSE** the file.
   LEAVE Excel open for the next project.

■ Mastery Assessment

Project 6-5: Subtotal Data

As a motivational tool, Litware's sales manager wants to group the teams and enter a subtotal as well as the grand total.

The *Semiannual Sales* workbook is available on the companion CD-ROM.

1. **OPEN** *Semiannual Sales* from the data files for this lesson.
2. Select the data range only and sort by font color with the Blue Team on top.
3. Clear contents and formatting from the Totals row.
4. Select the Blue Team and group the rows. Group the Red Team.
5. Insert a column to the left of column A. Merge and center the title and subtitle to include the new column.
6. Key **Team** in A4. Select **B4:B14**.
7. Click the **Format Painter** and format column A. In column A, key **Red** or **Blue** to identify the salesperson's team.
8. Create team subtotals in the Total column.

9. Collapse the outline to Level 2 so that only the team totals and grand total are displayed.
10. **SAVE** the workbook as *Teams 6-5*, and then **CLOSE** the file.
    LEAVE Excel open for the next project.

Project 6-6: Create a Table in a Worksheet

The Records Management Director at Contoso has asked you to create a table within the Salary workbook.

The *Salary* worksheet is available on the companion CD-ROM.

1. **OPEN** *Salary* from the data files for this lesson.
2. Sort the data by Job Category and then by Job Title.
3. Click **Format as Table** on the Home tab. Select **Table Style Light 10** on the Quick Styles list.
4. In the Format As Table dialog box, select the records management personnel data as the data for the table.
5. Apply Table Style 10.
6. Add a Total Row to the table.
7. Rename the table column labels to match those in the worksheet (Last Name, First Name, Job Category, Job Title, Hours, and Salary).
8. **SAVE** the workbook as *Records Management Table*. **CLOSE** the file.
   STOP. CLOSE Excel.

INTERNET READY

In this lesson, you worked with salary data for a medical facility. The salary figures were based on average earnings for employees in medical care facilities in the Midwest. Go online and research salary data for your chosen profession. Identify three positions in which you might like to work. Conduct research into the average salary in those professions in three different cities in different parts of the country. For example, you might find earnings information for accountants in New York City; St. Louis, Missouri; and Seattle, Washington.

Create a worksheet to report your research findings. Format all data appropriately. **SAVE** your worksheet as *Salary Research*. **CLOSE** Excel.

Using Basic Formulas and Functions

LESSON SKILL MATRIX

Creating a Formula that Performs Addition – 455	Students will learn how to create a formula that performs addition.
Creating a Formula that Performs Subtraction – 456	Students will learn how to create a formula that performs subtraction.
Creating a Formula that Performs Multiplication – 456	Students will learn how to create a formula that performs multiplication.
Creating a Formula that Performs Division – 457	Students will learn how to create a formula that performs division.
Using Relative Cell References in a Formula – 458	Students will learn how to use relative cell references in a formula.
Using Absolute Cell References in a Formula – 460	Students will learn how to use absolute cell references in a formula.
Referring to Data in Another Worksheet – 461	Students will learn how to refer to data in another worksheet.
Referring to Data in Another Workbook – 462	Students will learn how to refer to data in another workbook.
Naming a Range – 463	Students will learn how to name a range.
Changing the Size of a Range – 465	Students will learn how to change the size of a range.
Keeping Track of Ranges – 465	Students will learn how to keep track of ranges.
Creating a Formula that Operates on a Named Range – 466	Students will learn how to create a formula that operates on a named range.
Using SUM – 467	Students will learn how to use SUM.
Using COUNT – 468	Students will learn how to use COUNT.
Using COUNTA – 469	Students will learn how to use COUNTA.
Using AVERAGE – 469	Students will learn how to use AVERAGE.
Using MIN – 470	Students will learn how to use MIN.
Using MAX – 470	Students will learn how to use MAX.
Selecting Ranges for Subtotaling – 471	Students will learn how to select ranges for subtotaling.
Modifying a Range in a Subtotal – 472	Students will learn how to modify a range in a subtotal.
Building Formulas to Subtotal and Total – 473	Students will learn how to build formulas to subtotal and total.
Displaying Formulas on the Screen – 473	Students will learn how to display formulas on the screen.
Printing Formulas – 474	Students will learn how to print formulas.

Most people agree that it is vitally important for a business to have a realistic budget. It is equally important for an individual to have a personal budget—a plan for managing income and expenses.

Katie Jordan has been managing, or more accurately, spending her money without a formal budget. In fact, the only budget she prepared was one she scribbled on the back of her résumé immediately after being offered what she considered to be her dream job. Since that time, Katie has changed jobs several times. Now, she wants to purchase a condominium, and she realizes that she needs to create a comprehensive personal budget that will enable her to realize her goal of home ownership.

Katie uses Excel in her job as a marketing analyst at Tailspin Toys. She plans to use Excel to track her expenditures and to develop a realistic budget. She has conducted online research and developed a preliminary budget. This is her first step toward financial independence.

KEY TERMS
absolute cell reference
constant
external reference
formula
function
mathematical operator
mixed reference
name
operand
reference
relative cell reference
scope

SOFTWARE ORIENTATION

The Formulas Tab

Formulas make Excel a powerful tool. In this lesson, you will learn to write simple formulas and use many of Excel's functions that have built-in formulas that enable you to perform many types of calculations by clicking a command on the Formulas tab illustrated in Figure 7-1.

Figure 7-1
Formulas tab

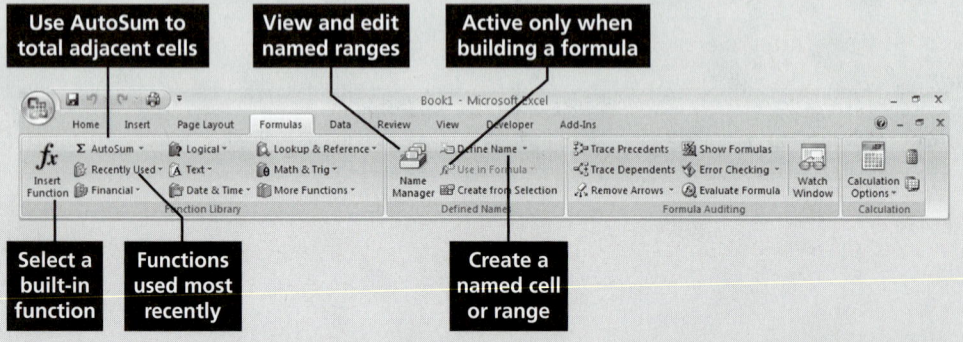

Use this illustration as a reference throughout this lesson as you become familiar with the command groups on the Formulas tab and use them to create formulas.

Building Basic Formulas

THE BOTTOM LINE

The real strength of Excel is its ability to perform common and complex calculations. In the following exercises, you will learn how to perform basic Excel calculations with formulas. A *formula* is an equation that performs calculations on values in a worksheet. When you enter a formula in a cell, the formula is stored internally and the results are displayed in the cell. Formulas give results and solutions that help you assess and analyze data.

Creating a Formula that Performs Addition

A formula consists of two elements: operands and mathematical operators. *Operands* identify the values to be used in the calculation. An operand can be a constant value, a cell reference, a range of cells, or another formula. A *constant* is a number or text value that is entered directly into a formula. *Mathematical operators* specify the calculations to be performed. In the following exercises, you will create basic formulas using different methods to enter the formulas.

→ CREATE A FORMULA THAT PERFORMS ADDITION

GET READY. Before you begin these steps, be sure launch to Microsoft Office Excel 2007 and open a blank workbook.

1. Select **A1** and key **=25+15**. Press Tab. The value in A1 is 40.
2. In B1, key **+18+35**. Press Tab. The sum of the two numbers is 53.

TAKE NOTE

Formulas should be keyed without spaces, but if you key spaces, Excel eliminates them when you press Enter.

3. Select **B1**. As illustrated in Figure 7-2, although you entered + to begin the formula, when you pressed Enter, Excel replaced the + with = as the beginning mathematical operator.

Figure 7-2

Equal sign marks the beginning of a formula

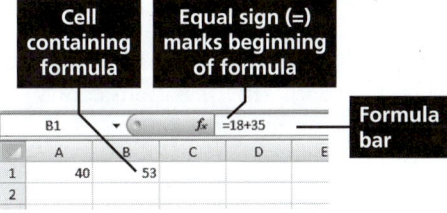

TAKE NOTE

When you click the Formula bar, you are automatically in Edit mode.

4. Select **A3**. Click the **Formula bar** and key **=94+89+35**. Press Enter. The sum of the three numbers is 218.
5. Select **A3** and click the **Formula bar**. Select **89** and key **98**. Press Enter.

   PAUSE. LEAVE the workbook open to use in the next exercise.

CERTIFICATION READY?
How do you create a formula that performs addition?
3.1.1

To begin creating a formula, select the cell in which you want the formula to appear. To allow Excel to distinguish formulas from data, all formulas begin with an equal sign (=).

TAKE NOTE

You can begin a formula with a + or − as the beginning mathematical operator, but Excel changes it to = when you press Enter.

When you build a formula, it appears in the Formula bar and in the cell itself. As illustrated in Figure 7-2, when you complete the formula and press Enter, the value displays in the cell and the formula displays in the Formula bar. As you practiced in this exercise, you can edit a formula in the cell or in the Formula bar the same as you can edit a data entry.

Creating a Formula that Performs Subtraction

The same methods you used to create a formula to perform addition can be used to create a formula to perform subtraction. When you create a subtraction formula, enter = followed by the positive number and then enter a minus sign to indicate subtraction.

CREATE A FORMULA THAT PERFORMS SUBTRACTION

USE the workbook from the previous exercise.

1. Select **A5**. Key **=456–98**. Press Enter. The value in A5 should be 358.
2. Select **A6** and key **=45–13–8**. Press Enter. The value in A6 should be 24.
3. In A8, create a formula to subtract 125 from 189. The value in A8 should be 64.

TROUBLESHOOTING If your formula returned a negative value (i.e., –64), you reversed the order in which the numbers should have been entered.

PAUSE. LEAVE the worksheet open to use in the next exercise.

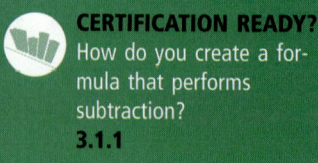

CERTIFICATION READY?
How do you create a formula that performs subtraction?
3.1.1

When you create a subtraction formula, the minus sign must precede the number to be subtracted. When you entered a formula to subtract 125 from 189, you could have entered =189–125 or = –125+189. Either formula would yield a positive 64. If the positive number is entered first, it not necessary to enter a plus sign.

Creating a Formula that Performs Multiplication

The formula to multiply 33 times 6 is =33*6. If a formula contains two or more operators, operations are not necessarily performed in the order in which you read the formula. The order is determined by the rules of mathematics, but you can override standard operator priorities by using parentheses. Operations contained in parentheses are completed before those outside parentheses.

CREATE A FORMULA THAT PERFORMS MULTIPLICATION

USE the worksheet from the previous exercise.

1. Select **D1**. Key **=125*4** and press Enter. The value should be 500.
2. Select **D3** and key **=2*7.50*2**. Press Enter. The value should be 30.
3. Select **D5** and key **=5*3**. Press Enter. The value should be 15.
4. Select **D7** and key **=5+2*8**. The value should be 21.
5. Select **D9** and key **=(5+2)*8**. The value should be 56.

PAUSE. LEAVE the workbook open to use in the next exercise.

CERTIFICATION READY?
How do you create a formula that performs multiplication?
3.1.1

When you added parentheses to the last formula you entered in this exercise, you changed the order of the calculations. When you entered the formula without parentheses, Excel multiplied 2 times 8 and added 5 for a value of 21. When you entered (5+2)*8, Excel performed the addition first and returned a value of 56. The order of calculations will be further illustrated in the next exercise.

Using Basic Formulas and Functions | 457

Creating a Formula that Performs Division

> The forward slash is the mathematical operator for division. When a calculation includes multiple values, use parentheses to indicate the part of the calculation that should be performed first.

CREATE A FORMULA THAT PERFORMS DIVISION

USE the workbook from the previous exercise.

1. Select **D7** and create the formula **=795/45**. Press Enter. The value in D7 is 17.66667.
2. Select **D7**. The Number format has been applied to D7. Click the **Accounting Number Format ($)** button. Accounting format is applied and the number is rounded to $17.67 because two decimal places is the default format for the Accounting format.
3. Select **D9** and create the formula **=65−29*8+97/5**. Press Enter. The value in D9 is −147.6.
4. Select **D9**. Click in the Formula bar and place parentheses around 65−29. Press Enter. The value in D9 is 307.4.
5. **CLOSE** but do not save the workbook.

   PAUSE. LEAVE Excel open to use in the next exercise.

CERTIFICATION READY?
How do you create a formula that performs division?
3.1.1

Because the cells in this worksheet were not formatted before you entered data, the default General format was applied to the numbers you entered. When you created the formula =795/45, Excel returned a value of 17.66667 and the Number format was applied to cell D7. The results of the formula calculation rounded the value after the seventh digit (eighth character) because the standard column width is 8.43. In other words, the value was rounded at that number of places only because of the column width.

When you inserted parentheses into the formula, the results were different than when there were no parentheses. Excel does not necessarily perform the operations in the same order that you enter or read them in a formula, which is left to right. Excel uses the rules of mathematics to determine which operations to perform first when a formula contains multiple operators. The order is:

- negative number (−)
- percents (%)
- exponentiation (^)
- multiplication (*) and division (/)
- addition (+) and subtraction (−)

BEDMAS

For example, consider the following equation.

$$5 + 6 * 15 / 3 - 1 = 34$$

Following mathematical operator priorities, the first operation would be 6 multiplied by 15 and that result would be divided by 3. Then 5 would be added and finally, 1 would be subtracted. Figure 7-3 illustrates the formula entered into Excel.

Figure 7-3

Structure of a formula

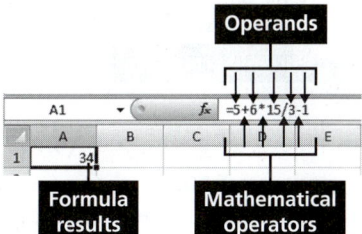

458 | Lesson 7

When you use parentheses in a formula, you indicate which calculation to perform first, which overrides the standard operator priorities. Therefore, the result of the following equation would be significantly different from the previous one. Figure 7-4 illustrates the Excel formula. Here is the mathematical formula.

$$(5 + 6) * 15 / (3 - 1) = 83$$

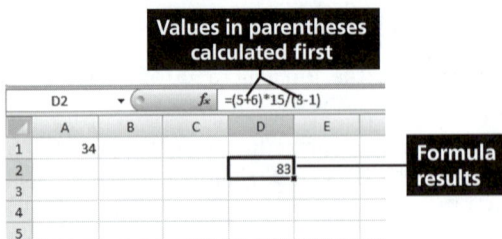

Figure 7-4

Use parentheses to control the order of operations

Using Cell References in Formulas

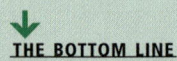

THE BOTTOM LINE

A *reference* identifies a cell or a range of cells on a worksheet and tells Excel where to look for the values you want to use in a formula. With references, you can use values contained in different parts of a worksheet in one formula or use the value from one cell in several formulas. You can also refer to cells on another worksheet in the same workbook and to other workbooks.

Using Relative Cell References in a Formula

Using cell references in formulas rather than constant amounts enables you to copy formulas without having to manually change cell references. When you include a cell reference in a formula and copy that formula, Excel changes the reference to match the column or row to which the formula is copied. A *relative cell reference* is, therefore, one whose references change "relative" to the location where it is copied or moved.

➔ USE RELATIVE CELL REFERENCES IN A FORMULA

GET READY. Launch Microsoft Excel if it is not already open.

1. **OPEN** *Personal Budget* from the data files for this lesson.
2. Select **B7** and key **=sum(B4:** (colon). As shown in Figure 7-5, cell B4 is outlined in blue, and the reference to B4 in the formula is also blue. The ScreenTip below the formula identifies B4 as the first number in the formula.

The *Personal Budget* worksheet is available on the companion CD-ROM.

Figure 7-5

Color-coordinated cell references

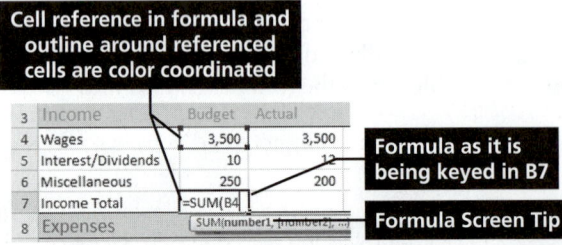

3. Key **B6** and press **Enter**. The total of the cells (3,760) appears in B7.
4. Select **B15**. Key **=sum(** and click **B10**. As shown in Figure 7-6, B10 appears in the Formula bar and a flashing marquee appears around B10.

Figure 7-6

Selecting a cell to include in a formula

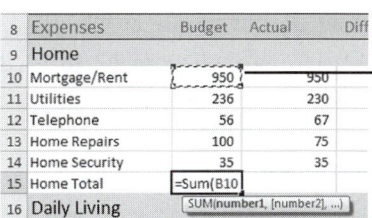

TAKE NOTE: You can use either uppercase or lowercase when you key a cell reference in a formula. For example, it would not matter whether you keyed B4 or b4 in the formula you entered.

5. Drag the flashing marquee to B14. As shown in Figure 7-7, the Formula bar reveals that values within the B10:B14 range will be summed (added).

Figure 7-7

Extend the cell range for a formula

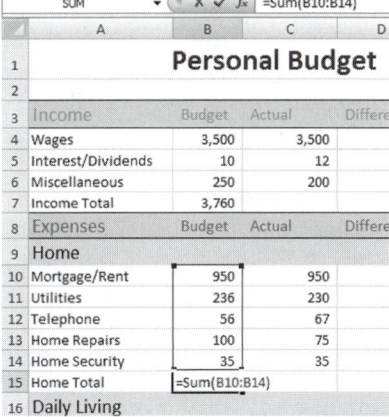

6. Press **Enter** to accept the formula. Select **B15**. As illustrated in Figure 7-8, the value is displayed in B15 and the formula is displayed in the Formula bar.

Figure 7-8

Formula always displayed in the Formula bar

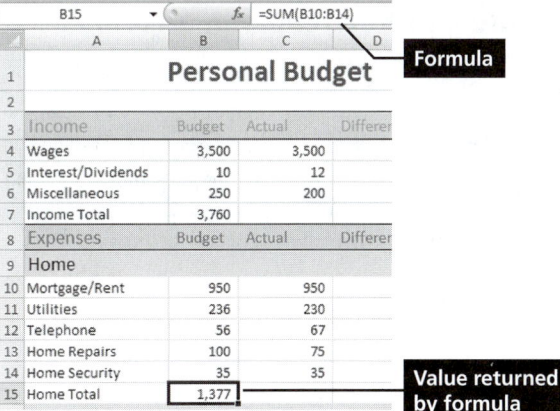

7. Select **D4** and key **=**. Click **B4** and key **–**. Click **C4** and press **Enter**. By default, when a subtraction formula yields no difference, Excel enters a hyphen.

TAKE NOTE: Open the Format Cells dialog box to change the way Excel displays "no difference" results. On the Numbers tab, you can choose to display 0, for example.

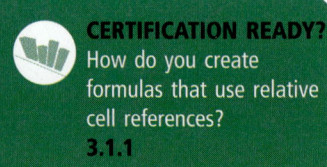

CERTIFICATION READY?
How do you create formulas that use relative cell references?
3.1.1

You can select a cell and click the Formula bar to key a formula.

8. Select **D4**. Click and drag the fill handle to D7.
9. Use the fill handle to copy the formula in B7 to C7. Notice that the amount in D7 changes when the formula is copied.
10. Select **D7** and click **Copy**. Select **D10:D15** and click **Paste**.
11. Select **D17:D21** and click **Paste**.
12. Create a Lesson 7 folder and **SAVE** your worksheet as **Budget**.

    PAUSE. LEAVE the workbook open to use in the next exercise.

In this exercise, you copied formulas rather than entering a formula repeatedly. You saved a considerable amount of time by copying a cell with a completed formula and pasting it in a destination cell.

To understand a relative cell reference, let's examine the formula in B7, which is =sum(B4:B6). The reference to B4 is based on its relative position to B7, the cell that contains the formula. When you copied the formula to C7, the position of the cell containing the formula changed, so the reference changed to C7. You use relative cell references when you want the reference to automatically adjust when you copy or fill the formula across rows or down columns. By default, new formulas use relative references.

In this exercise, you used two methods to create formulas using relative references:

- Key an equal sign to mark the entry as a formula. Then, key the formula, including cell references, constant values, and mathematical operators directly into the cell.
- Key an equal sign and click a cell or the range of cells included in the formula instead of keying cell references.

The second method is usually quicker and eliminates the possibility of typing an incorrect cell or range reference. Cell references and the borders around the corresponding cells are color coded to make it easier to verify that you selected the desired cell.

As you saw in Figure 7-8, when you build a formula, it appears in the Formula bar and in the cell. When you complete the formula and press Enter, the value displays in the cell and the formula displays in the Formula bar.

Using Absolute Cell References in a Formula

Sometimes you do not want a cell reference to change when you move or copy it. For example, when you review your personal budget, you might want to know what percentage of your income is budgeted for each category of expenses. Each formula you create to calculate those percentages will refer to the cell that contains the total income amount. The reference to the total income cell is an *absolute cell reference*—a reference that does not change when the formula is copied or moved.

USE ABSOLUTE CELL REFERENCES IN A FORMULA

USE the worksheet from the previous exercise.

1. Select **B15**. Use the fill handle to copy the formula to C15.
2. Select **B21**. Key **=sum(** and select **B17:B20**. Press **Enter**.

It is not necessary to key the closing parenthesis when you complete the selection for a formula. Excel supplies it when you press Enter.

3. Select **B21** and drag the fill handle to C21.
4. Select **E10**. Key **=** and click **B10**. Key **/** and click **B7**. Press [Enter].
5. Select **E10**. Click the **Formula bar** and edit the formula to make B7 an absolute reference. The edited formula should read =B10/$B$7. Press [Enter].

> **TROUBLESHOOTING**
> When you enter a formula that will yield a result less than a whole number, be sure the cell is formatted for decimals. If the cell is formatted for whole numbers, the cell will display 0 or 1 rather than the expected value.

> **CERTIFICATION READY?**
> How do you create a formula that contains an absolute cell reference?
> 3.1.1

6. Select **E10** and drag the fill handle to E15.
7. With E10:E15 selected, click the **Percent Style** button (**%**) in the Numbers group. Click **Increase Decimal**. The values should display with one decimal place and a %.
8. **SAVE** your worksheet.

   PAUSE. LEAVE the workbook open to use in the next exercise.

You can recognize an absolute cell reference by the inclusion of one or more dollar signs in the formula. The absolute cell reference $B$7 in the preceding exercise will always refer to cell B7 because both column B ($B) and row 7 ($7) have been made absolute. When you copy or fill the formula across rows or down columns, the absolute reference will not adjust to the destination cells. By default, new formulas use relative references, and you must edit them if you want them to be absolute references.

You can also create a mixed reference in which either a column or a row is absolute and the other is relative. For example, if the cell reference in the formula were $B7 or B$7, you would have a ***mixed reference*** in which one component is absolute and one is relative. The column is absolute and the row is relative if the reference is $B7.

If you copy or fill a formula across rows or down columns, the relative reference automatically adjusts, and the absolute reference does not adjust. For example, if you copied or filled a formula containing the mixed reference $B7 to a cell in column C, the formula in the destination cell would be =$B8. The column reference would be the same because that portion of the formula is absolute. The row reference would adjust because it is relative.

Referring to Data in Another Worksheet

> You can refer to the contents of cells in another worksheet within the same workbook. This strategy is often used to create a summary of data contained in several worksheets. The formula-building principles operate the same as for building formulas from data within a worksheet.

➔ REFER TO DATA IN ANOTHER WORKSHEET

USE the workbook you saved in the previous exercise.

1. Click **Sheet2** to make it the active sheet.
2. Select **B4**. Key **=** to indicate the beginning of a formula. Click **Sheet1** and select **B7**. Press [Enter]. The value of cell B7 on Sheet1 is displayed in cell B4 of Sheet2. The Formula bar displays =Sheet1!B7.
3. Select **B4** and drag the fill handle to D4. The values from Sheet1 row 4 are copied to Sheet2 row 4.
4. On the Home tab, click **Format** and click **Rename Sheet**.
5. Key **Summary** and press [Enter].
6. Make Sheet1 active. Click **Format** and click **Rename Sheet**.

CERTIFICATION READY?
How do you create a formula that refers to data in another worksheet?
3.1.2

7. Key **Expenses** and press Enter.
8. Make Summary active and select **B4**. The Formula bar now shows the formula as =Expenses!B7.
9. **SAVE** your worksheet.

    PAUSE. LEAVE the worksheet open to use in the next exercise.

In this exercise, you referenced data in another worksheet within the Budget workbook. In the next exercise, you will reference data in another workbook. By renaming the worksheets within this workbook, you have prepared it for the next exercise.

Referring to Data in Another Workbook

An *external reference* refers to a cell or range on a worksheet in another Excel workbook, or to a defined name in another workbook. External references are useful when it is not practical to keep large worksheets together in the same workbook.

 REFER TO DATA IN ANOTHER WORKBOOK

USE the worksheet you saved in the previous exercise.

1. Click the **Microsoft Office Button** and click **Excel Options**.
2. On the Excel Options window, click **Advanced**.
3. Click **Show all windows in the Taskbar** if necessary, and click **OK**.

Looking Ahead
You will name a range of cells later in this lesson.

TROUBLESHOOTING
If your system administrator has disabled the *Show all windows in the Taskbar* option, you will need to use the Switch Windows command in the Windows group on the View tab to move between the two workbooks.

The *Financial Obligations* worksheet is available on the companion CD-ROM.

4. Make the Summary worksheet active. In A10, key **Other Expenses** and press Tab.
5. **OPEN** *Financial Obligations* from the data files for this lesson. This is the source workbook. The **Budget** workbook is the destination workbook.
6. Switch to the destination workbook, and select **B10** on the Summary worksheet.
7. Key **=** to indicate the beginning of a formula. Select **B8** in the source workbook. A flashing marquee identifies the cell reference.
8. Press Enter to complete the external reference formula. The Formula bar displays square brackets around the name of the source workbook, indicating that the workbook is open.
9. **CLOSE** the source workbook. The Formula bar now displays the entire path for the source workbook.
10. **SAVE** the destination workbook.

    PAUSE. LEAVE the workbook open to use in the next exercise.

CERTIFICATION READY?
How do you create a formula that refers to data in another workbook?
3.1.2

Although external references are similar to cell references, there are important differences. You normally use external references when working with large amounts of data and complex formulas that encompass several workbooks.

When you create external references, the workbook or workbooks must be open. In a previous exercise, you created a reference to another worksheet within the same workbook. An exclamation point in the formula for that reference indicated that the source was in the same workbook.

Using Basic Formulas and Functions | 463

Formulas with external references are displayed in two ways, depending upon whether the workbook that contains the referenced data is open or closed. When the source is open, the external reference encloses the workbook name in square brackets, followed by the worksheet name, an exclamation point (!), and the cell range on which the formula depends. When the source workbook is closed, the brackets are removed and the entire file path is shown in the formula.

Using Cell Ranges in Formulas

THE BOTTOM LINE

You can simplify formula building by naming ranges of data so that you can easily identify their content and specify the name when making selections or building formulas rather than keying or selecting the cell range each time you use it in a formula. By default, a named range becomes an absolute reference in a formula.

Naming a Range

A *name* is a meaningful shorthand that makes it easier to understand the purpose of a cell reference, constant, formula, or table. You can create your own names to represent cells, ranges of cells, formulas, constant values, or Excel tables. Naming a range clarifies the purpose of the data within the range of cells. A named range in a formula is easily understood, whereas a reference to a cell range is difficult to comprehend at first glance, especially when the referenced range is not visible.

➔ NAME A RANGE

USE the workbook you saved in the previous exercise.

1. Select **B7** on the Expenses worksheet and click **Define Name** in the Defined Names group on the Formulas tab. The New Name dialog box shown in Figure 7-9 opens with Excel's suggested name for the range.

Figure 7-9

Accept default name or create a name

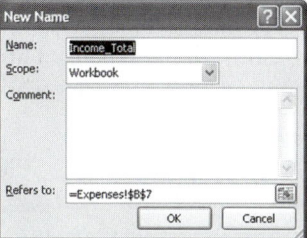

2. Click **OK** to accept Income_Total as the name for B7.

TAKE NOTE

There are several syntax rules for creating names. For example, the first character must be a letter, an underscore character (_), or a backslash (\). You cannot use a C, c, R, or r as a defined name, and you must use the underscore or period as word separators rather than spaces.

3. Select **B36**. Click **Define Name.** Click the **Name** box and key **Expenses**. Accept the default in the Scope box.
4. Click **Collapse Dialog** to select the range that makes up total expenses.

TAKE NOTE

You can name a range using the shortcut menu. Select the range and right-click. Click Name a Range to open the New Name dialog box.

5. Select and delete the text in the *Refers to* box. Press **Ctrl** and click **B15**, **B21**, **B28**, and **B33**, and then click **Expand Dialog**. Click **OK** to close the New Name dialog box. Some of the selected cells are blank. In the following exercises, you will use the names you create to fill them.

> **TROUBLESHOOTING**
>
> If, in the process of naming a range, you receive a message that the name already exists, display the Name Manager (discussed later in this lesson) and edit the existing name or delete it and begin again.

6. Select **B23:B27** and select the text in the **Name box** to the left of the Formula bar. Key **Transportation** and press **Enter**.
7. Select **B30:B32** and click **Define Name**. Key **Entertainment** in the Name box on the dialog box. Click **OK**.
8. Select **A15:B15**. Click **Create from Selection**. Click **Left column**, if necessary, on the dialog box that opens (shown in Figure 7-10). Click **OK**. The dialog box closes and it appears that nothing has happened, but a range has been named, as you will see in a later exercise.

Figure 7-10

Create a name from a row or column label

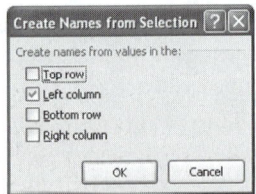

PAUSE. LEAVE the workbook open to use in the next exercise.

> **CERTIFICATION READY?**
> How do you manage named cells?
> 3.1.3

All names have a scope, either to a specific worksheet or to the entire workbook. The *scope* of a name is the location within which the name is recognized without qualification. For example, when you created the name Income_Total for cell B7, the New Name box, shown in Figure 7-9, identified the scope as part of the workbook. This means the named cell can be used in formulas on the Expenses and the Summary worksheets in this workbook.

In this exercise, you used three methods to name cells and ranges of cells. You created names by

- clicking Define Name on the Formulas tab and selecting the cell or range to be included in the name.
- selecting a cell or range and entering a name in the Name box next to the Formula bar.
- selecting a cell or range that included a label and clicking the Create from Selection button on the Formulas tab.

> **TROUBLESHOOTING**
>
> You must select the range of cells you want to name before you use the Name box to create a named range. When you create a name using the Define Name command, you have the opportunity to select the range after you enter the name. This option is not available when you use the Name box.

Naming ranges or an individual cell according to the data they contain is a time-saving technique, even though it may not seem so when you work with limited data files in practice exercises. In the business environment, you will often use a worksheet that contains data in hundreds of rows and columns. After you name a range, you can select it from the Name box and then perform a variety of functions, such as cutting and pasting it to a different workbook as well as using it in a formula.

Changing the Size of a Range

If you need to change the parameters of a named range, you can easily redefine the range by using the Name Manager on the Formulas tab. In the following exercise you will edit the range for Home_Total.

→ CHANGE THE SIZE OF A RANGE

USE the worksheet from the previous exercise.

1. Click **Name Manager** on the Formulas tab. Select **Home_Total** and click **Edit**. The Edit Name dialog box opens. You want to change the range rather than the name.

TAKE NOTE: This is the range you named in an earlier exercise using the Create from Selection command. Although it appeared that nothing happened when you created the named range, it was created, and now you can edit it.

2. The Home_Total range is identified in the *Refers to* box at the bottom of the dialog box. Click **Collapse Dialog** and select **B10:B14**.
3. Click **Expand Dialog** to view the dialog box as shown in Figure 7-11. Click **OK** to close the dialog box.

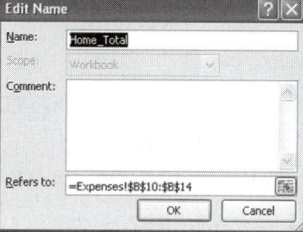

Figure 7-11

Edit the size of a range

4. Click **Close** to close the Name Manager dialog box.

PAUSE. LEAVE the workbook open to use in the next exercise.

In the previous exercise, you used the Name Manager dialog box to extend the reference for a named range. You can also rename a range, or use the Filter function to display names that meet a specific criterion, such as names scoped to the worksheet or names scoped to the workbook.

Keeping Track of Ranges

Use the Name Manager dialog box to work with all of the defined names in the workbook. From this dialog box you can also add, change, or delete names. You can use the Name Manager as a convenient way to confirm the value and reference of a named reference or to determine its scope.

→ KEEP TRACK OF RANGES

USE the workbook from the previous exercise.

1. Click **Name Manager** on the Defined Names group on the Formulas tab.
2. Select **Income_Total** and click **Edit**.
3. Select **_Total** in the Name field and press **Delete**. Click **OK** to close the dialog box.
4. Click **New**. Key **Short\Over** in the Name box. Be sure to use the backslash.

TROUBLESHOOTING

You will receive an error message if you use the forward slash in a name. Although the forward slash is used in the Short/Over label on the worksheets, you can use only the underscore or the backslash as a word divider in a named range.

5. In the *Refers to* box, key **=Income-Expenses**. Click **OK**.
6. Click **Close** to close the Name Manager dialog box.

   PAUSE. LEAVE Excel open to use in the next exercise.

If you defined a named reference after you entered a cell reference in a formula, you may want to update the existing cell reference to the defined name. Select an empty cell, click the arrow next to Define Name, and click Apply Names. On the Apply Names dialog box, click one or more names, and click OK.

You can create a list of defined names in a workbook. Select an area of a worksheet with two empty columns, one for the name and one for a description. Select the upper-left cell of the list. Click Use in Formula and click Paste Names. Click Paste List.

Creating a Formula that Operates on a Named Range

You can use a named range in a formula. You have created several named ranges, which you can now use to fill cells on the worksheets in your Budget workbook.

➔ **CREATE A FORMULA THAT OPERATES ON A NAMED RANGE**

USE the worksheet from the previous exercise.

1. On the Expenses worksheet, select **B28**. Key **=sum(**. Click **Use in Formula** in the Defined Names group on the Formulas tab.
2. Click **Transportation** on the dropdown list. Key the closing parenthesis and press **Enter**.
3. Select **B33**. Click **Use in Formula**. Select **Entertainment**. Click the **Formula bar**. Enter the rest of the formula, **=sum(Entertainment)**, and press **Enter**.
4. Select **B36**. Key the formula **=sum(** and click **Use in Formula**. Select **Expenses** from the list of named cells and ranges. Press **Enter**.

   PAUSE. LEAVE the worksheet open to use in the next exercise.

CERTIFICATION READY?
How do you create a formula that operates on a named range?
3.1.4

Use the Name Manager dialog box to work with all of the defined names in the workbook. You can view or edit the scope or sort and filter the list of names.

Summarizing Data with Functions

THE BOTTOM LINE

A *function* is a predefined formula that performs a calculation. Excel's built-in functions are designed to perform all sorts of calculations—from simple to complex. When you apply a function to specific data, you eliminate the time involved in manually constructing a formula. Using functions ensures the accuracy of the formula's results.

Using SUM

Adding a range of cells is one of the most common calculations performed on worksheet data. You can use the SUM function to easily and accurately select the cells to be included in a calculation. The AutoSum function makes that even easier.

Using Basic Formulas and Functions | 467

 **USE SUM**

USE the workbook from the previous exercise.

1. On the Expenses worksheet, select **C28**. Click **Insert Function** in the Function Library group on the Formulas tab. The Insert Function dialog box shown in Figure 7-12 opens.

Figure 7-12

Accept default name or create a name

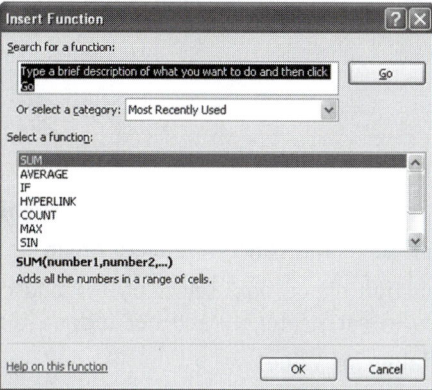

2. Select **SUM** if necessary. Click **OK**.
3. On the Function Arguments box, illustrated in Figure 7-13, the default range is C26:C27. Click **Collapse Dialog** in the Number1 field and select **C23:C27**.

Figure 7-13

Accept default range or select a new range

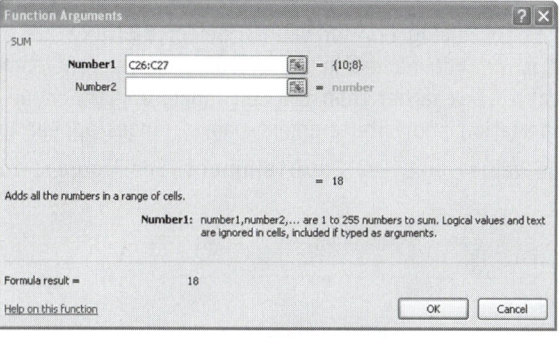

TROUBLESHOOTING

AutoSum, by default, calculates the total only from the active cell to the first nonnumeric cell. Because C25 is blank, you need to edit the range to be calculated.

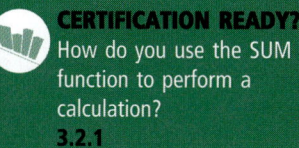

CERTIFICATION READY?
How do you use the SUM function to perform a calculation?
3.2.1

4. Click **Expand Dialog** and click **OK**.
5. Select **C33** and click **AutoSum** in the Function Library group.
6. Press **Enter** to accept **C30:C32** as the range to sum.

PAUSE. LEAVE the workbook open to use in the next exercise.

In previous exercises, you created a formula to perform addition by keying or selecting the cells to include and connected them with the plus sign. Using SUM or AutoSum function is a much easier way to achieve the same result.

A function consists of a function name and function arguments. The arguments are enclosed in parentheses in the formula. Depending upon the function, an argument can be a constant value, a single-cell reference, a range of cells, or even another function. If a function contains multiple arguments, the arguments are separated by commas.

TAKE NOTE: Because it is used so frequently, AutoSum is available on the Formulas tab in the Function Library group and on the Home tab in the Editing group.

Using COUNT

Statistical functions, such as SUM and COUNT, are used to compile and classify data to present significant information. Use the COUNT function to count the number of numeric entries in a range.

→ **USE COUNT**

USE the workbook from the previous exercise.

1. On the Expenses worksheet, select **A39** and key **Expense Categories**. Press Tab.
2. Click **Insert Function** in the Function Library group on the Formulas tab.
3. On the Insert Function dialog box, select **COUNT** and click **OK**. You want to count only the expenses in each category and not include the category totals.
4. Click **Collapse Dialog** for Value1.
5. Select **B10:B14** and press Enter.
6. Click **Collapse Dialog** for Value2 and select **B17:20**. Press Enter.

TAKE NOTE: As you add arguments, the Value fields on the Function Arguments dialog box expand to allow you to enter multiple arguments.

7. Collapse the dialog box for Value3. Select **B23:B27** and press Enter. The identified range is one you named in a previous exercise. That name (Transportation) appears in the Value3 box rather than the cell range, and the values of the cells in the Transportation and Entertainment named ranges appear to the right of the value boxes.
8. In the Value4 box, key **Entertainment**. See Figure 7-14.

Figure 7-14

Include named ranges in function

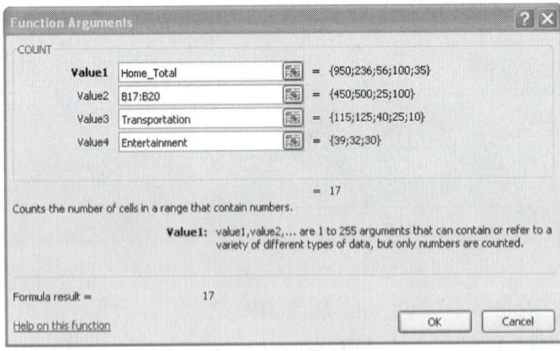

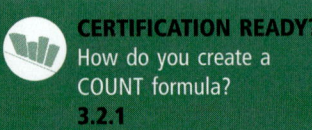

CERTIFICATION READY?
How do you create a COUNT formula?
3.2.1

9. Click **OK** to accept the function arguments.

PAUSE. LEAVE the workbook open to use in the next exercise.

Text or blank cells are ignored in a COUNT formula. If a cell contains a value of 0 (zero), the COUNT function will count it as a cell with a number.

Using CountA

Use the COUNTA function to count the number of cells in a range that are not empty. COUNTA counts both text and values in a selected data range.

Using Basic Formulas and Functions | 469

→ **USE COUNTA**

USE the workbook from the previous exercise.

1. On the Expenses worksheet, select **A40** and key **Cells Containing Data**. Press Tab.
2. Click **Insert Function** in the Function Library group on the Formulas tab.
3. On the Insert Function dialog box, select **COUNTA**. If COUNTA does not appear in your list, key **COUNTA** in the *Search for a function* box and click **Go**. The function will appear at the top of the function list and be selected by default. Click **OK**.

By default the most recently used functions are displayed when the Insert Function dialog box opens. You can click the arrow in the category field and select All to display a list of all functions.

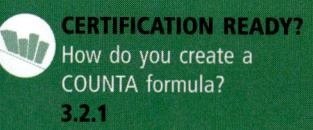

CERTIFICATION READY?
How do you create a COUNTA formula?
3.2.1

4. Select **B4:B33** in the Value1 box. Click **OK**. The formula returns a value of 26.

PAUSE. LEAVE the worksheet open to use in the next exercise.

COUNTA returns a value that indicates the number of cells that contain data. Empty cells within the data ranges are ignored.

Using AVERAGE

The AVERAGE function adds a range of cells and then divides by the number of cell entries. It might be interesting to know the average difference between what you budgeted for expenses and the amount you actually spent during the month. Before you can calculate the average, however, you will need to finish calculating the differences.

→ **USE AVERAGE**

USE the worksheet from the previous exercise.

1. Select **D21** and right-click. Click **Copy**.
2. Select **D23**, right-click, and click **Paste**.
3. Use the fill handle to copy the formula to D24:D28.
4. Copy the formula in D28 and paste it to D30.
5. Use the fill handle to copy the formula to D31:D33.
6. In A41, key **Average Difference** and press Tab.
7. Click **Recently Used** in the Function Library group and click **AVERAGE**.
8. Click **Collapse Dialog** in Value1. Press Ctrl and select the category totals (**D15**, **D21**, **D28**, and **D33**). Notice that the arguments are separated by a comma.
9. Click **Expand Dialog**. Click **OK**. There is a $38 average difference between the amount budgeted and the amount you spent in each category.
10. **SAVE** and **CLOSE** the *Budgets* workbook.

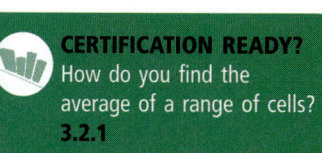

CERTIFICATION READY?
How do you find the average of a range of cells?
3.2.1

PAUSE. LEAVE Excel open to use in the next exercise.

Although you entered the numbers (cell references) as one number, if you open the Function Arguments dialog box after the formula has been entered, each cell reference is in a separate Number box.

The exact value returned for the AVERAGE formula was 38.25. Because column B is formatted for zero decimals, the value returned by the formula is 38.

Using MIN

The MIN formula returns the smallest number in a set of values. For example, a professor would use the MIN function to determine the lowest test score; a sales organization would determine which sales representative earned the lowest commission or which employee earns the lowest salary. Maximum values are usually calculated for the same set of data.

 USE MIN

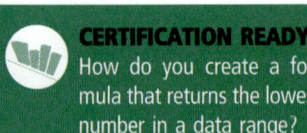

The *Personnel* worksheet is available on the companion CD-ROM.

OPEN *Personnel* from the data files for Lesson 7.

1. Select **A22** and key **Minimum Salary**. Press Tab.
2. Click **Recently Used** in the Function Library group on the Formulas tab. The MIN function is not available. Key **=min** in **B22** and click **MIN** when it appears on the popup list. Press Tab. An opening parenthesis is added to your formula.

 You can display the Insert Function dialog box by clicking the Insert Function button on the Formula bar.

3. Select **E6:E19** and press Enter.
4. **SAVE** the workbook as *Analysis*.

   PAUSE. LEAVE the workbook open to use in the next exercise.

CERTIFICATION READY?
How do you create a formula that returns the lowest number in a data range?
3.2.1

In this exercise, you calculated the lowest (minimum) value in a data range. The arguments typed into the Function Arguments dialog box can be cell references, a named range, or a number. If the arguments contain no number, MIN returns 0.

Using MAX

The MAX function returns the largest value in a set of values. Minimum values are usually calculated for the same set of data.

 USE MAX

USE the worksheet from the previous exercise.

1. In A23, key **Maximum Salary** and press Tab.
2. Click **Insert Function** in the Function Library group and click **MAX**. Click **OK**.
3. Click **Collapse Dialog** in Value1 and select **E6:E19**.
4. Click **Expand Dialog**. Click **OK**. The maximum salary is $89,000.
5. **SAVE** and **CLOSE** the workbook.

   PAUSE. LEAVE Excel open to use in the next exercise.

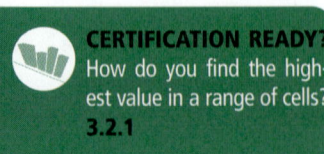

CERTIFICATION READY?
How do you find the highest value in a range of cells?
3.2.1

The arguments for the MAX function can be numbers, names, or references that contain numbers. Empty cells within the range are ignored.

Using Basic Formulas and Functions | 471

Using Formulas to Create Subtotals

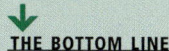
THE BOTTOM LINE

You can calculate subtotals using the SUBTOTAL function, but it is generally easier to create a list by using the Subtotal command in the Outline group on the Data tab. After the subtotal list has been created, you can edit it in the SUBTOTAL function.

Selecting Ranges for Subtotaling

Groups are created for subtotaling by sorting the data. Data must be sorted by groups to insert a subtotal function. Subtotals are calculated with a summary function, and you can use the SUBTOTAL function to display more than one type of summary function for each column.

→ SELECT RANGES FOR SUBTOTALING

The *Personnel* worksheet is available on the companion CD-ROM.

1. **OPEN** *Personnel* from the data files for this lesson.
2. Select **A5:F19** (the data range and the column labels). Click **Sort** in the Sort & Filter group on the Data tab.

TROUBLESHOOTING If you do not include the labels in the data selection, Excel will prompt you to include the labels so that you can sort by label rather than the column heading.

3. On the Sort dialog box, select **Department** as the sort by criterion. Select the *My data has headers* checkbox if it is not selected. Click **OK**. The list is sorted by department.
4. Select the data range (**A5:F19**) and click **Subtotal** in the Outline group on the Data tab. The Subtotal dialog box opens.
5. Select **Department** in the *At each change in* box. Sum is the default in the Use function box.
6. Select **Salary** in the *Add subtotal to* box. Deselect any other column labels. Select **Summary below data** if it is not selected. Click **OK**. Subtotals are inserted below each department with a grand total at the bottom.
7. With the data selected, click **Subtotal**. On the dialog box, click **Average** in the *Use function* box.
8. Click **Replace current subtotals** to deactivate it. Click **OK**.
9. **SAVE** the workbook as *Dept Subtotals*.

   PAUSE. LEAVE Excel open to use in the next exercise.

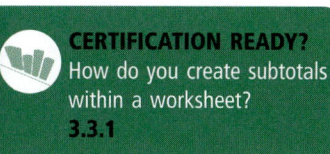
CERTIFICATION READY?
How do you create subtotals within a worksheet?
3.3.1

Subtotals are calculated with a summary function, such as Sum, Count, or Average. You can display more than one type of summary function for each column. Grand totals, on the other hand, are derived from the detail data, not from the values in the subtotals. Therefore, when you used the Average summary function, the grand total row displays an average of all detail rows in the list, not an average of the values in the subtotal rows.

SUBTOTAL function numbers specify which subtotal function to use in calculating subtotals within your list. When you use the Subtotal command on the Data tab, you choose the summary function from a dropdown list and the function number is automatically included in the subtotal formula. When you use the SUBTOTAL function, you will need to enter the function number. Table 7-1 lists the function numbers.

Table 7-1

SUBTOTAL function numbers

Function_num (includes hidden values)	Function_num (ignores hidden values)	Function
1	101	AVERAGE
2	102	COUNT
3	103	COUNTA
4	104	MAX
5	105	MIN
6	106	PRODUCT
7	107	STDEV
8	108	STDEVP
9	109	SUM
10	110	VAR
11	111	VARP

Modifying a Range in a Subtotal

You can change the way data is grouped and subtotaled by modifying the subtotal range using the SUBTOTAL function. This option is not available when you create subtotals from the Data tab commands.

→ MODIFY A RANGE IN A SUBTOTAL

USE the worksheet you saved in the previous exercise.

1. Insert a row above the Grand Total row.
2. Key **Sales/Marketing Total** in B29.
3. Copy the subtotal formula from E27 to E29.
4. In the Formula bar, change the function to 109 to exclude subtotals within the data range.
5. Replace the range in the Formula bar with E15:E25 and press **Enter**. The salaries for the sales and marketing departments combined are $310,000.
6. **SAVE** the workbook as *Dept Subtotals Revised*. **CLOSE** the workbook.

   PAUSE. LEAVE Excel open to use in the next exercise.

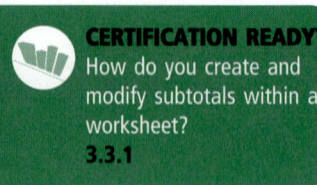

CERTIFICATION READY?
How do you create and modify subtotals within a worksheet?
3.3.1

When you modified the function number (changed 9 to 109) in the exercise, you excluded the sum and average subtotals for the individual departments. If you had not changed the function number to 109, the formula result would have included the average salary and the total salaries as well as the salaries for the individual employees.

Building Formulas to Subtotal and Total

In the previous exercise, you copied and modified a formula to create a subtotal for a combined group. You can accomplish the same result by using the SUBTOTAL function to build a formula and add subtotals to data that you cannot or do not want to sort into one category in order to use the built-in function in the Data tab's subtotal function.

Using Basic Formulas and Functions | 473

→ **BUILD FORMULAS TO SUBTOTAL AND TOTAL**

The *Personnel* worksheet is available on the companion CD-ROM.

1. **OPEN** *Personnel* from the data files for this lesson.
2. Insert a row above row 11.
3. Select **E11** and click **Recently Used** in the Formula Library group on the Formulas tab. Click **SUBTOTAL**.
4. Key **9** in the Function_num box on the Function Arguments dialog box.
5. Click **Collapse Dialog** in Ref1 and select **E6:E10**.
6. Click **Expand Dialog** and click **OK** to close the dialog box.
7. Select **B11** and key **Support Staff Total**.
8. Select **B21** and key **Sales and Marketing Total**.
9. Select **E21** and click **Recently Used**. Click **SUBTOTAL**. Create a subtotal for the values in E12:E20. Format the subtotal for currency.
10. Press `Ctrl` and select row **11** and row **21**. Click **Bold** on the Home tab to emphasize the subtotals.
11. **SAVE** the workbook as *Combined Depts*.

    PAUSE. LEAVE the workbook open to use in the next exercise.

When you use the Subtotal command on the Data tab, subtotal entries have a predefined format, and you can create multiple subtotals, as you did in a previous exercise. When you use the SUBTOTAL function, you must build the formula and label and format the subtotal entries manually.

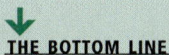 If the workbook is set to automatically calculate formulas, the Subtotal command recalculates subtotal and grand total values automatically when you edit the detail data.

Controlling the Appearance of Formulas

THE BOTTOM LINE

When you work with extremely large worksheets that contain numerous formulas, you sometimes need to see all formulas to audit the calculations in the worksheet. You can display and print the worksheet with all formulas visible.

Displaying Formulas on the Screen

When you create a formula, the result of the calculation is displayed in the cell and the formula is displayed in the Formula bar. You may need to see all formulas on the screen in order to audit them. You can click the Show Formulas command to display the formula in each cell instead of the resulting value.

→ **DISPLAY FORMULAS ON THE SCREEN**

USE the workbook from the previous exercise.

1. Click **Show Formulas** in the Formula Auditing group on the Formulas tab. All worksheet formulas are displayed.
2. Click **Show Formulas**. Values are displayed.
3. **SAVE** and **CLOSE** the workbook. When you open the workbook again, it will open with values displayed.

474 | Lesson 7

 **ANOTHER WAY** You can also press Ctrl+` (grave accent) to switch between formulas and their values. The accent is located to the left of the number 1 key on most keyboards.

TAKE NOTE For security reasons, you may want to hide formulas from other workbook users.

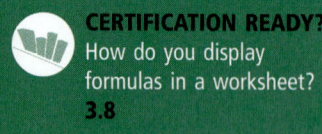

CERTIFICATION READY?
How do you display formulas in a worksheet?
3.8

PAUSE. LEAVE Excel open to use in the next exercise.

If you work with dates and times, you will find it useful to understand Excel's date and time system. Although you normally do not have to be concerned with serial numbers, when you displayed the worksheet formulas in the preceding exercise, you probably wondered what happened to the numbers in your worksheet. Excel stores dates as sequential serial numbers. By default, January 1, 1900, is serial number 1, and January 2, 1900, is serial number 2, and so on. This serial number date system allows you to use dates in formulas. For example, you can enter a formula to calculate the number of days you have lived by creating a formula to subtract your birth date from today's date.

Printing Formulas

When you audit the formulas in a large worksheet, you may find it useful to print the worksheet with the formulas displayed. To gain maximum benefit from the printed copy, print gridlines and row and column headers.

→ PRINT FORMULAS

1. **OPEN** *Budget* from your Lesson 7 folder. This is the exercise you saved earlier.
2. Click **Show Formulas** in the Formula Auditing group on the Formulas tab.
3. Click the **Page Layout** tab and click **Print Gridlines** and **Print Headings** in the Sheet Options group.
4. Click **Orientation** in the Page Setup group and click **Landscape**.
5. Click the **Microsoft Office Button**. Point to **Print** and click **Print Preview**.
6. On the Print Preview tab, click **Page Setup**.
7. On the Page tab, click **Fit to 1 page wide**.
8. Click the **Header/Footer** tab. Click **Custom Header** and key your name in the left section. Click **OK**. Close the Page Setup dialog box.
9. Click **Print** on the Print Preview tab. Click **OK** to print the document.
10. **SAVE** the workbook with the same name. **CLOSE** the file.

STOP. CLOSE Excel.

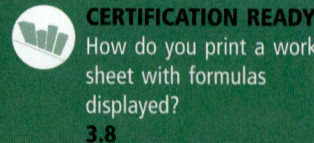

CERTIFICATION READY?
How do you print a worksheet with formulas displayed?
3.8

Using Basic Formulas and Functions | 475

SUMMARY SKILL MATRIX

In This Lesson You Learned how to:
Create a Formula that Performs Addition
Create a Formula that Performs Subtraction
Create a Formula that Performs Multiplication
Create a Formula that Performs Division
Use Relative Cell References in a Formula
Use Absolute Cell References in a Formula
Refer to Data in Another Worksheet
Refer to Data in Another Workbook
Name a Range
Change the Size of a Range
Keep Track of Ranges
Create a Formula that Operates on a Named Range
Use SUM
Use COUNT
Use COUNTA
Use AVERAGE
Use MIN
Use MAX
Select Ranges for Subtotaling
Modify a Range in a Subtotal
Build Formulas to Subtotal and Total
Display Formulas on the Screen
Print Formulas

■ Knowledge Assessment

Matching

a. absolute cell reference
b. constant
c. external reference
d. formula
e. function
f. operand
g. mathematical operator
h. relative cell reference
i. mixed reference
j. scope

_____h_____ 1. In formulas, cell references that change in relation to the location where they are moved or copied.

_____e_____ 2. A predefined formula that performs calculations on values in a worksheet.

_____f_____ 3. The components of a formula that identify the values to be used in the calculation.

_____b_____ 4. Numbers or text values entered directly into a formula. These values are not calculated.

____a____ 5. In a formula, a reference to a specific cell that does not change when the formula is copied or moved.

____c____ 6. A reference to a cell or range on a worksheet in another Excel workbook.

____d____ 7. An equation that performs calculations on values in a worksheet.

_____ 8. The formula component that specifies what calculations are to be performed.

____i____ 9. A cell reference in which the column is absolute and the row is relative or vice versa.

____j____ 10. The location within which a name is recognized without qualification.

Multiple Choice

Circle the choice that best completes the following statements.

1. Which of the following is not a mathematical operator?
   a. ×
   b. +
   c. −
   d. *

2. Which function automatically totals cells directly above or to the left of the cell containing the formula?
   a. COUNT
   b. AutoFill
   c. AutoSum
   d. SUM

3. Which of the following shows a formula for an external reference?
   a. =Sum(Expenses)
   b. =Sum(B6:b10)
   c. =Expenses!B7
   d. ='[Financial Obligations.xlsx]Sheet1'!$B$2

4. Which of the following shows a formula for a reference to another worksheet in the same workbook?
   a. =Sum(Expenses)
   b. =Sum(B6:b10)
   c. =Expenses!B7
   d. ='[Financial Obligations.xlsx]Sheet1'!$B$2

5. Which of the following shows a formula that references a named range?
   a. =Sum(Expenses)
   b. =Sum(B6:b10)
   c. =Expenses!B7
   d. ='[Financial Obligations.xlsx]Sheet1'!$B$2

6. Which character designates a cell reference as absolute?
   a. ^
   b. @
   c. $
   d. #

Using Basic Formulas and Functions | 477

7. The COUNTA function
   a. counts the number of cells in a range that contain values.
   b. counts all cells in the range.
   c. counts the number of cells that are not empty.
   d. counts the text entries in the range.

8. The COUNT function is an example of a ___c___ function.
   a. logical
   b. financial
   c. statistical
   d. text

9. Which of the following is an acceptable name for a named range?
   a. C
   b. C_Contracts
   c. C/Contracts
   d. C Contracts

10. Which of the following statements accurately describes the default selection for AutoSum?
    a. By default, AutoSum totals all entries above the cell in which the formula is located.
    b. By default, AutoSum calculates the total from the active cell to the first nonnumeric cell.
    c. AutoSum does not have a default selection.
    d. You must make the selection before clicking AutoSum.

■ Competency Assessment

Project 7-1: Create Formulas to Calculate Income and Expenses

An employee at Tailspin Toys has entered second quarter income and expense data into a worksheet. You will enter formulas to calculate monthly and quarterly totals.

GET READY. Launch Excel and open a new blank worksheet.

The *Tailspin Toys* worksheet is available on the companion CD-ROM.

1. **OPEN** *Tailspin Toys* from the data files for this lesson.
2. Select **E4** and key **=B4+C4+D4** and press **Enter**.
3. Select **B6**. On the Formulas tab, in the Function Library group, click **Insert Function**.
4. On the Insert Function dialog box, select **SUM** and click **OK**.
5. On the Function Arguments dialog box, click **Collapse Dialog** and click **B4**. Key **-** and click **B5**.
6. Expand Dialog and click **OK** to close the dialog box.
7. Select **B6** and use the fill handle to copy the formula to C6:D6.
8. Click **B11** and click **AutoSum** in the Function Library group. Press **Enter** to accept B8:B10 as the cells to total.
9. Select **B11** and use the fill handle to copy the formula to C11:D11.
10. Select **B13** and click **Insert Function** in the Function Library group. On the Insert Function dialog box, select **SUM** and click **OK**.
11. Click **Collapse Dialog** for Number1 and click **B6**, key **-** and click **B11**. Press **Enter** and click **OK** to close the dialog box.
12. Select **B13** and use the fill handle to copy the formula to C13:D13.

13. Select **E4**. Click **AutoSum** in the Function Library group. Press Enter to accept the range as B4:D4. Copy the formula to E5:E14. Then delete the data in cells E7 and E12.
14. Select **B15**, key =B13−B14, and press Enter. Copy the formula to C15:E15.
15. **SAVE** the worksheet as *Tailspin Toys 7-1* and then **CLOSE** the file.

    LEAVE Excel open to use in the next project.

Project 7-2: Use AutoSum to Total Sales; Calculate Percentage of Increase

Blue Yonder Airlines has created a worksheet to analyze sales for its first four years of operation. Enter formulas to determine the total sales for each division and the percentage increase/decrease each year.

The *Blue Yonder* workbook is available on the companion CD-ROM.

1. **OPEN** *Blue Yonder* from the data files for this lesson.
2. Select **F4** and click **AutoSum** in the Function Library group on the Formulas tab.
3. Press Enter to accept B4:E4 as the range to add.
4. Use the fill handle to copy the formula in F4 to F5:F8.
5. Select **B12** and key =(C4−B4)/C4. Press Enter. This formula calculates the percentage increase in sales from 2005 to 2006. The numbers in parentheses yield the amount of the increase. The increase is then divided by the 2006 sales.
6. Select **B12**. Use the fill handle to copy the formula to B13:B15.
7. Select **B12:B15**. Use the fill handle to copy the formulas in the selected range to C12:D15.
8. Select **F12**. Key =(E4−B4)/E4 and press Enter. This enters a formula to calculate the percentage increase from the first year (2005) to the most recent (2008).
9. Copy the formula in F12 to F13:F15.
10. **SAVE** the worksheet as *Blue Yonder 7-2* and then **CLOSE** the file.

    LEAVE Excel open for the next project.

■ Proficiency Assessment

Project 7-3: Calculate Totals and Percentages

In the previous project, you calculated total sales for Blue Yonder's first four years of operation. You also calculated the percentage of increase or decrease in sales for each year. In this project, you will calculate expense totals and percentage increase or decrease.

The *Blue Yonder Expenses* workbook is available on the companion CD-ROM.

1. **OPEN** *Blue Yonder Expenses* from the data files for this lesson. Expense History should be the active worksheet.
2. Select **B8** and click **AutoSum** to total the 2005 expenses.
3. Copy the formula in B8 to C8:F8.
4. Select **F4** and click **AutoSum** to total Corporate Contract expenses for the four-year period.
5. Copy the formula in F4 to F5:F7.
6. In B12, create a formula to calculate the percentage increase in Corporate Contracts expenses from 2005 to 2006. Begin with 2006 expenses minus 2005 expenses, divided by 2006. Use parentheses to instruct Excel which function to perform first.
7. Copy the formula from B12 to B13:B15 and to C12:D15.
8. In F12, create a formula to calculate the percentage increase in expenses from 2005 to 2008. Remember to construct the formula to subtract and then divide.
9. Click **Percentage Style** (%) in the Number group. If necessary, click **Increase Decimal** to display one position after the decimal point.

Using Basic Formulas and Functions | 479

10. Copy the formula in F12 to F13:F15.
11. **SAVE** the workbook as *Blue Yonder Expenses 7-3* and then **CLOSE** the file.
    LEAVE Excel open for the next project.

Project 7-4: Create Formulas in a Template Worksheet

Tailspin Toys wants to project income and expenses for the third quarter based on its performance in the second quarter. A template has been created for the projections. In this project, you will create formulas for the calculations that affect only this worksheet. In the next exercise, you will create formulas that refer to data in another worksheet in this workbook. You are creating a template, so the values returned by your formulas will be $0 until you use the template in the next exercise.

The *Tailspin Projections* workbook is available on the companion CD-ROM.

1. **OPEN** *Tailspin Projections* from the data files for this lesson.
2. In the Third Qtr worksheet, key **0** (zero) as a placeholder in B4 and in B5.
3. Select **B6** and enter a formula to subtract the cost of goods sold from sales. The value returned will be $0.
4. Key **0** as a placeholder in B8:B10.
5. Select **B11** and click **AutoSum** to calculate total expenses.
6. Select **B13** and enter a formula to subtract total expenses from the gross margin.
7. Federal taxes are estimated to be 34% net income. Select **B14** and enter a formula to multiply net income before taxes by 34%.
8. In B15, enter a formula to calculate net income after taxes.
9. **SAVE** the worksheet as *Tailspin Projections 7-4*.
    LEAVE the workbook open for the next project.

■ Mastery Assessment

Project 7-5: Refer to Data in Another Worksheet

Tailspin Toys wants to set goals for the third quarter based on its performance in the second quarter. Its goal is to increase sales by 10% while keeping costs and expenses to 5%. You will create formulas to calculate the projections.

USE the workbook you saved in Project 7-4.

1. Make Third Qtr the active sheet and display the Formulas tab. The formula to establish the sales goal for third quarter will be second quarter total sales + (second quarter total sales *10%).
2. Select **B4**, click **Recently Used** in the Function Library group, and click **Sum**. Select **Second Qtr E4** as the Number1 function argument. Click **Expand Dialog**.
3. In the Number2 argument box, key **+(** and click **Second Qtr**. Select **E4**.
4. In the Number2 arguments box, key ***10%)** and press [Enter]. Your completed formula should read =Sum('SecondQtr'!E4, + ('SecondQtr'!E4*10%)).
5. On the Third Quarter worksheet, select **B5**. Click **Recently Used** in the Function Library group and click **Sum**. Select **Second Qtr E5** as the Number1 function argument.
6. In the Number2 argument box, key **+(** and click **Second Qtr**. Select **E5**.
7. In the Number2 arguments box, key ***5%)** and press [Enter].
8. Copy the formula in B5 to B8:B10.
9. **SAVE** the workbook as *Tailspin Projections 7-5* and then **CLOSE** the file.
    LEAVE Excel open for the next project.

Project 7-6: Name a Range and Use the Range in a Formula

Blue Yonder Airlines wants to analyze the sales and expense data from its four-year history.

The *Income Analysis* workbook is available on the companion CD-ROM.

1. **OPEN** *Income Analysis* from the data files for this lesson.
2. Select **B4:E4** and click **Define Name** on the Formulas tab. Accept the defaults on the dialog box and click **OK**.
3. Repeat Step 2 and name the other three income sources.
4. On the Analysis worksheet, select **B5** and create a formula to calculate the four-year average for corporate contract sales. Use the Corporate Contracts named range in the formula.
5. Create a formula using the appropriately named range in B6, B7, and B8.
6. In column C, create a formula to calculate the maximum sales for each division.
7. Show the formulas on the screen. Adjust column width, if necessary, to display the entire formulas.
8. Print the Analysis worksheet in landscape orientation with gridlines and column headings included.
9. **SAVE** the workbook as *Income Analysis 7-6* and then **CLOSE** the file.
   STOP. CLOSE Excel.

INTERNET READY

As mentioned at the beginning of this lesson, a personal budget helps you make sound financial decisions and enables you to reach financial goals. Various governmental organizations and private financial counselors recommend percentages of your income to allocate for housing, transportation, etc. Use Web search tools to find recommended guidelines for the percentage of income you should allocate in various spending categories. Be sure to use "personal budget guidelines" to avoid business and government budget sites.

From your research, create a worksheet that lists the categories and percentages that you think are reasonable for your personal or family budget. **SAVE** the workbook as *My Budget*.

Creating Charts from Your Data

LESSON SKILL MATRIX

Selecting Data to Include in a Chart	Students will learn how to select data to include in a chart.
Choosing the Right Chart for Your Data	Students will learn how to choose the right chart for their data.
Creating a Bar Chart	Students will learn how to create a bar chart.
Formatting a Chart with a Quick Style	Students will learn how to format a chart with a Quick Style.
Changing the Chart's Fill Color or Pattern	Students will learn how to change the chart's fill color or pattern.
Changing the Chart's Border Line	Students will learn how to change the chart's border line.
Formatting the Data Series	Students will learn how to format the data series.
Modifying a Chart's Legend	Students will learn how to modify a chart's legend.
Adding Elements to a Chart	Students will learn how to add elements to a chart.
Deleting Elements from a Chart	Students will learn how to delete elements from a chart.
Moving a Chart	Students will learn how to move a chart.
Resizing a Chart	Students will learn how to resize a chart.
Choosing a Different Chart Type	Students will learn how to choose a different chart type.

Fourth Coffee owns espresso cafes in 15 major markets. Its primary income is generated from the sale of trademarked, freshly-brewed coffee and espresso drinks. The cafes also sell a variety of pastries, packaged coffees and teas, deli-style sandwiches, and coffee-related accessories and gift items. In preparation for an upcoming budget meeting, the corporate manager wants to create charts to show trends in each of the five revenue categories for a five-year period and to project those trends to future sales.

KEY TERMS
axis
chart
chart area
chart sheet
data labels
data marker
data series
embedded chart
legend
legend keys
plot area
title

Software Orientation

The Insert Tab

Excel 2007 makes it easy to create professional-looking charts. A ***chart*** is a graphical representation of numeric data in a worksheet. To create a basic chart in Excel that you can modify and format later, start by entering the data for the chart on a worksheet. Then, you can select that data and choose a chart type to graphically display the data. Simply by choosing a chart type, a chart layout, and a chart style—all of which are within easy reach on the Ribbon—you will have instant professional results every time you create a chart.

Use Figure 8-1 as a reference throughout this lesson as you become familiar with and use Excel's charting capabilities to create attention-getting illustrations that communicate an analysis of your data.

Figure 8-1

Insert tab

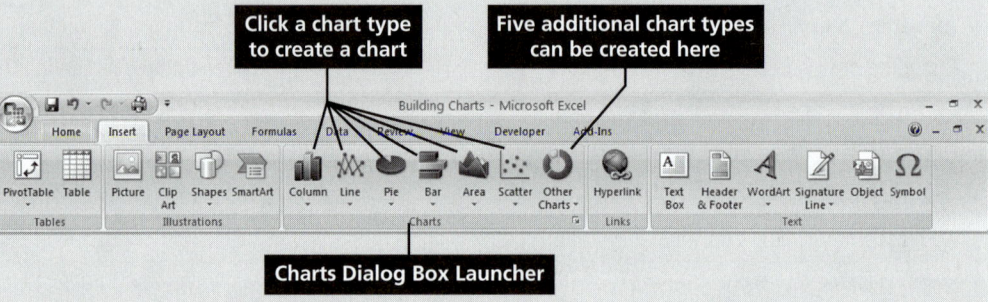

Building Charts

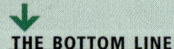

THE BOTTOM LINE

Because Excel allows you to track and work with substantial amounts of data, it is sometimes difficult to see the big picture by looking at the details in a worksheet. With Excel's charting capabilities, you can summarize and highlight data, reveal trends, and make comparisons that might not be obvious when looking at the raw data. Creating a chart is quick and easy, and Excel provides a variety of chart types from which to choose. In the following exercises, you will learn the types of charts available in Excel 2007 and how to create them. You will also learn how to modify, format, and move charts and chart elements.

Selecting Data to Include in a Chart

Excel's Ribbon interface makes it incredibly simple to create a chart. As you will see in the following exercise, you can create one of the common chart types by clicking its image on the Insert tab. More important than the chart type, however, is the selection of the data you want to display graphically. What aspects of the data do you want viewers to notice? The answer to that question is a major factor in selecting an appropriate chart type.

→ **SELECT DATA TO INCLUDE IN A CHART**

GET READY. Before you begin these steps, be sure to launch Microsoft Office Excel 2007.

The *Financial History* workbook is available on the companion CD-ROM.

1. **OPEN** *Financial History* from the data files for this lesson.
2. Select **B4:B10** (the 2004 data) on the Sales History worksheet.
3. Click **Pie** in the Charts group on the Insert tab. Click the first **2-D Pie** chart. A pie chart is displayed.

Creating Charts from Your Data | 483

TROUBLESHOOTING Notice that the chart is color-coded and the sections are identified by number. However, the pie has seven sections, and Fourth Coffee has only five sales categories that should be contrasted in the graphic. The pie chart includes the column label (2004) as the largest portion. The total sales amount is the second largest portion. These amounts should not be included in an analysis of sales for 2004.

4. Click in the chart's white space and press Delete.
5. Select **B5:B9**, click **Pie** in the Charts group, and click the first **2-D Pie** chart. The correct data is displayed, but the chart is difficult to interpret with only numbers to identify the parts of the pie.

TAKE NOTE* Use the Insert tab to create a chart. When a chart is inserted, the Ribbon displays the Format tab. You must select the Insert tab each time you want to insert a chart.

6. Click in the chart's white space and press Delete.
7. Select **A4:B9** and click **Pie** in the Charts group. Click the first **2-D Pie**. As illustrated in Figure 8-2, the data is clearly identified with a title and a label for each pie section.

Figure 8-2

Accurate data selection is essential in building a chart

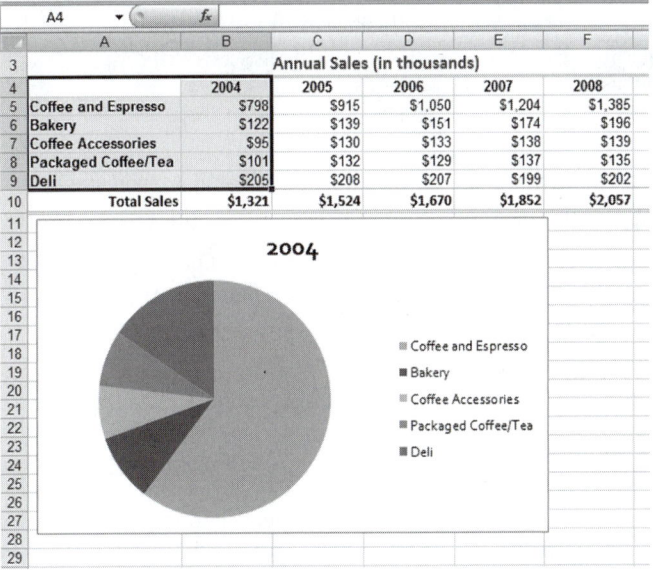

CERTIFICATION READY?
How do you select appropriate data sources for charts?
4.1.1

8. Create a Lesson 8 folder and **SAVE** the workbook as **Building Charts**.

   PAUSE. LEAVE the workbook open to use in the next exercise.

Excel did not distinguish between the column B label and its data when you selected only the data in column B. Although the label is formatted as text, because the column label was numeric, it was interpreted as data to be included in the graph. When you expanded the selection to include the row labels, 2004 was correctly recognized as a label and displayed as the title for the pie chart. This exercise illustrates that the chart's data selection must contain sufficient information to interpret the data at a glance. You will improve the display in subsequent exercises when you apply predefined layouts and styles.

When you selected data and created a pie chart, the chart was placed on the worksheet. This is referred to as an *embedded chart*, meaning it is placed on the worksheet rather than on a separate *chart sheet*, a sheet that contains only a chart.

Choosing the Right Chart for Your Data

Excel supports numerous types of charts to help you display data in ways that are meaningful to your audience. You can create most charts, such as column and bar charts, from data that you have arranged in rows or columns in a worksheet. Some charts, such as pie and bubble charts, require a specific data arrangement.

→ CHOOSE THE RIGHT CHART FOR YOUR DATA

USE the workbook from the previous exercise.

1. Delete the pie chart on the Sales History worksheet.

TAKE NOTE: To delete a chart, click in the white space. If you click on the graphic or another chart element and press Delete, only the selected element will be deleted.

2. Select **A4:F9** and click **Column** in the Charts group on the Insert tab. Click **3-D Clustered Column** on the dropdown list (first subtype under 3-D Column). The column chart illustrates the sales for each of the revenue categories for the five-year period.

TAKE NOTE: The pie chart was useful for displaying data in a single column, which illustrated the portion of total income generated by each revenue source. The pie chart cannot be used for comparisons across periods of time or for analyzing trends. The column chart works well for comparisons; in this case, it illustrates the significant increase in coffee and espresso sales during the five-year period.

3. Drag the chart below the worksheet data and position it at the far left.
4. Click outside the column chart to deselect it.
5. Select **A4:F9** and click **Line** in the Charts group. Click **2-D Line with Markers** (first chart in the second row). Position the line chart next to the column chart.
6. **SAVE** the workbook with the same name.

PAUSE. LEAVE the workbook open to use in the next exercise.

CERTIFICATION READY?
How do you select appropriate chart types to represent data sources?
4.1.2

The column and line charts provide two views of the same data, illustrating that the chart type you choose depends upon the analysis you want the chart to portray. The pie chart, which shows values as part of the whole, accurately displayed the distribution of sales for one year. Column and line charts allow you to make comparisons over a period of time as well as comparisons among items.

The line chart shown in Figure 8-3 includes data markers to indicate each year's sales. A ***data marker*** is a bar, area, dot, slice, or other symbol in a chart that represents a single data point or value that originates from a worksheet cell. Related data markers in a chart constitute a ***data series***.

Figure 8-3

Line chart with data markers

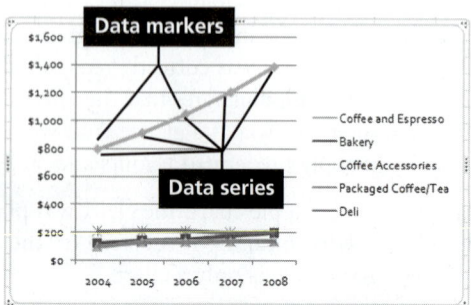

Creating Charts from Your Data | 485

In a 2-D or 3-D column chart, each data marker is represented by a column. In a stacked column, data markers are stacked so that a column represents a data series.

The line chart is a good analysis tool. The chart you created illustrates not only the growth in coffee and espresso sales, but reveals a modest increase in bakery sales and static activity in the sale of packaged products.

When you want to create a chart or change an existing chart, you can choose from 11 chart types and subtypes within each chart type. Table 9-1 gives a brief description of each Excel chart type.

Table 8-1
Chart types

Icon	Chart Name	Function	Data Arrangement
	Column	Useful for showing data changes over a period of time or illustrating comparisons among data. Values are represented with vertical bars.	Columns or rows
	Line	Useful for showing trends in data at equal intervals. Displays continuous data over time set against a common scale. Values are represented as points along a line.	Columns or rows
	Pie	Useful for showing the size of items in one data series, proportional to the sum of the items. Data points are displayed as a percentage of a circular pie.	One column or row
	Bar	Useful for illustrating comparisons among individual items. Useful when axis labels are long or values are durations. Values are represented as horizontal rectangles.	Columns or rows
	Area	Useful for emphasizing magnitude of change over time; can be used to draw attention to the total value across a trend. Shows relationship of parts to the whole. Values represented as shaded areas.	Columns or rows
	XY (Scatter)	Useful for showing relationships among the numeric values in several data series or plotting two groups of numbers as one series of xy coordinates.	Columns or rows
	Stock	Useful for illustrating the fluctuation of stock prices or scientific data.	Columns or rows in a specific order
	Surface	Useful for finding optimum combinations between two sets of data. Use this chart when categories and data series are numeric values.	Columns or rows
	Donut	Useful for displaying relationship of parts to a whole; can contain more than one data series. Values represented as sections of a circular band.	Columns or rows
	Bubble	Useful for comparing three sets of values. The third value determines the size of the bubble marker.	Columns with x values in first column and y values in adjacent columns
	Radar	Useful for showing the trends of values relative to a center point; represent values as points that radiate from the center. Lines connect values in the series.	Columns or rows

Creating a Bar Chart

Bar charts are similar to column charts and can be used to illustrate comparisons among individual items. Data that is arranged in columns or rows on a worksheet can be plotted in a bar chart. Clustered bar charts compare values across categories. Stacked bar charts show the relationship of individual items to the whole of that item.

USE the workbook from the previous exercise.

1. Click the **Expense History** tab.
2. Select **A4:F9**. Click **Bar** in the Charts Group on the Insert tab.
3. Click the **Clustered Bar in 3-D** subtype.

TAKE NOTE: A ScreenTip displays the chart type name when you rest the mouse pointer over a chart type or chart subtype.

4. Position the clustered bar chart on the left below the worksheet data.
5. Deselect the chart and select **A4:F9**. Click **Bar** in the Charts group.
6. Click **Stacked Bar in 3-D**.
7. Position the stacked bar graph next to the 3-D bar graph.
8. **SAVE** and **CLOSE** the file.

   PAUSE. LEAVE Excel open to use in the next exercise.

TAKE NOTE: The 3-D Bar graph displays the rectangles in 3-D but not the data.

CERTIFICATION READY?
How do you select appropriate chart types to represent data sources?
4.1.2

The side-by-side bar charts you created in this exercise illustrate two views of the same data. You can experiment with chart types and select the one that best portrays the message you want to convey to your target audience.

The Charts group on the Insert tab contains six of the eleven chart types. To create one of these charts, select the worksheet data and click the icon. You can insert one of the other five chart types by clicking the Charts dialog box launcher to open the Insert Chart dialog box shown in Figure 8-4.

Figure 8-4

Insert Chart dialog box

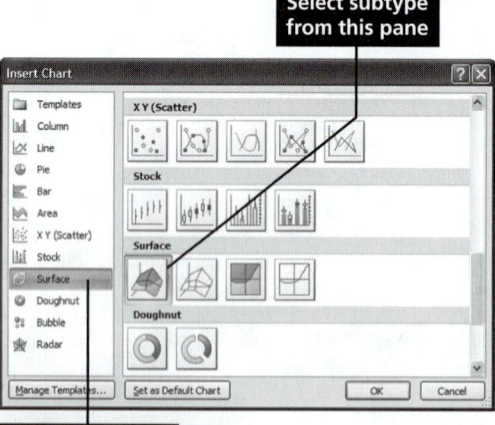

 **ANOTHER WAY**

You can open the Insert Chart dialog box by clicking Other Charts and then clicking All Chart Types at the bottom of the dropdown list.

When you click a chart type in the left pane of the dialog box, the first chart of that type is selected in the right pane. You can also scroll through the right pane and select any chart subtype.

When you apply a predefined chart style, the chart is formatted based on the document theme that you have applied. The Metro theme was applied to the Financial History workbook. The Metro theme colors were therefore applied to the charts you created in the preceding exercises.

Creating Charts from Your Data | 487

■ Formatting a Chart with a Quick Style

THE BOTTOM LINE

After you create a chart, you can instantly change its appearance by applying a predefined layout or style. Excel provides a variety of useful quick layouts and quick styles from which you can choose. As shown in Figure 8-5, when you create a chart, the chart tools become available and the Design, Layout, and Format tabs are added to the Ribbon.

Figure 8-5

Ribbon tabs added when chart is inserted

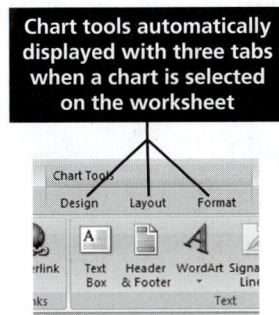

FORMAT A CHART WITH A QUICK STYLE

GET READY. Launch Microsoft Excel if it is not already open.

1. **OPEN** *Financial History* from the data files for this lesson.
2. On the Expense History worksheet, select **A4:A9**. Press Ctrl and select **F4:F9**.
3. Click **Pie** in the Charts group and click **Pie** under 2-D. The 2008 data is displayed and the Design tab is active.
4. In the Chart Layouts group on the Design tab, click **Layout 1**. The pie chart now displays the percentage that each sales category contributes to total sales.
5. In the Chart Styles group, click **Style 4**. The chart's color scheme is changed. Position the chart below the data.
6. On the Sales History worksheet, select **A4:A9**. Press Ctrl and select **F4:F9**.
7. Click **Bar** in the Charts group and click **Clustered Horizontal Cylinder** (third row).
8. Drag the chart below the worksheet data.
9. Click **Layout 2** in the Chart Layouts group on the Design tab. Click **Style 4** in the Chart Styles group.
10. **SAVE** the workbook as *Chart Styles*.

PAUSE. LEAVE the workbook open to use in the next exercise.

CD

The *Financial History* workbook is available on the companion CD-ROM.

TAKE NOTE*

To see all predefined styles, click More next to the last displayed style.

CERTIFICATION READY?
How do you format charts using Quick Styles?
4.1.3

When you applied Layout 1 and Style 4 to the expense chart, additional information was added to the chart and the appearance changed. Predefined layouts and styles are timesaving features that you can use to enhance the appearance of your charts.

Manually Formatting the Parts of a Chart

THE BOTTOM LINE

You can format individual chart elements. The following list defines some of the chart elements, which are illustrated in Figure 8-6. To format a chart element, click the chart element that you want to change

- *chart area*—the entire chart and all its elements.
- *plot area*—the area bounded by the axes.
- *axis*—a line bordering the chart plot area used as a frame of reference for measurement.
- *title*—descriptive text that is automatically aligned to an axis or centered at the top of a chart.
- *data labels*—text that provides additional information about a data marker, which represents a single data point or value that originates from a worksheet cell.
- *legend*—a box that identifies the patterns or colors that are assigned to the data series or categories in a chart.

Figure 8-6

Chart elements

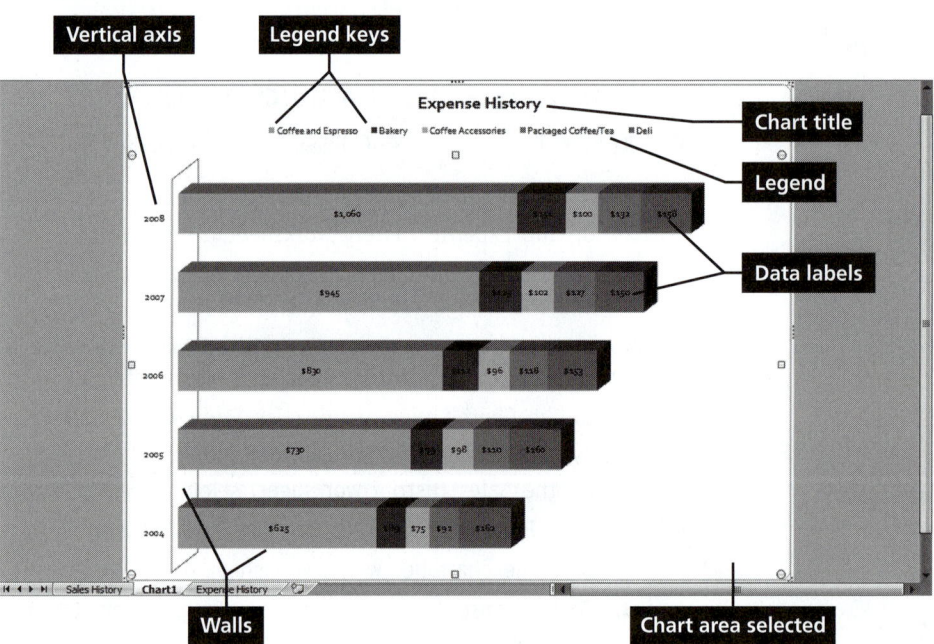

Changing the Chart's Fill Color or Pattern

Use commands on the Format tab to add or change fill colors or patterns applied to chart elements. When you select any chart element and click Format Selection, an element-specific dialog box opens. For example, if you click the data series, the Format Data Series dialog box opens. You also can use the Shape Fill command to fill any shape with color, gradient, or texture.

➔ CHANGE THE CHART'S FILL COLOR OR PATTERN

USE the workbook from the previous exercise.

1. Click in the chart area of the **Clustered Horizontal Cylinder** chart on the Sales History worksheet to display the Chart Tools.
2. Click the **Format** tab and click **Format Selection**. The Format Chart Area dialog box opens.

3. Click **Solid fill**. Click the **Color** arrow and click **Green, Accent 1, Lighter 80%**. A light green fill has been added to the entire chart area.
4. Click **Picture or texture fill**. Click the **Texture** arrow and click **Newsprint** (center of selection options). The textured format replaced the color fill in the chart area.
5. Click **Close** to close the dialog box.
6. Select **Plot Area** in the Current Selection group.
7. Click **More** next to the colored outlines in the Shape Styles group.
8. Click **Subtle Effect – Accent 1**.
9. Select **Legend** in the Current Selection group. Press Delete.

> **TAKE NOTE**
> *Legend keys* appear to the left of legend entries and identify the color-coded data series. Because this chart contains only one data series, the legend is unnecessary.

10. **SAVE** your workbook.

    PAUSE. LEAVE the workbook open to use in the next exercise.

You can use the mouse to select a chart element to format. When you use the mouse to point to an element in the chart, the element name appears in a ScreenTip. You can also select the element you want to format by clicking the arrow next to the Chart Elements box in the Current Selection group on the Format tab. Figure 8-7 shows the list of chart elements in the bar chart on the Sales History worksheet. This list is chart specific. Legend is not listed because you deleted that element from the chart. When you click the arrow, the list will include all elements that you have included in the displayed chart.

Figure 8-7

Chart elements

The Format tab provides a variety of ways to format chart elements. Select the element to format and launch the Format dialog box or use the commands in the Shape Styles group on the Format tab, shown in Figure 8-8, to add fill color or a pattern to the selected chart element. The Shape Fill color choices are those associated with the theme applied to the worksheet.

Figure 8-8

Format tab with Chart Tools

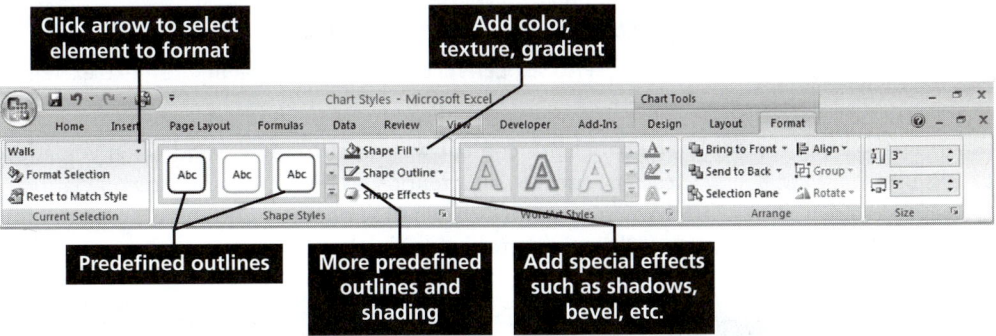

Changing the Chart's Border Line

You can apply a border around any chart element as well as around the entire chart. Select an element or the chart and use the colored outlines in the Shape Styles group or click Shape Outlines and choose a Theme or Standard color for the border.

TAKE NOTE

To display the Chart Tools, you must select the chart. If a worksheet cell is active, the Design, Layout, and Format tabs are not available.

➔ CHANGE THE CHART'S BORDER LINE

USE the worksheet you saved in the previous exercise.

1. Click the arrow in the **Current Selection** group and click **Chart Area**.
2. Click **Colored Outline – Accent 1** in the Shape Styles group. The chart is outlined with a green border.
3. Click **Plot Area** in the Current Selection group and click **Colored Outline – Accent 2**. A red border is placed around the plot area.
4. Click **Walls** in the Current Selection group and click **Colored Outline – Dark 1**.
5. **SAVE** your workbook.

PAUSE. LEAVE the workbook open to use in the next exercise.

You can outline any or all chart elements. Just select the element and apply one of the predefined outlines or click Shape Outline to format the shape of a selected chart element.

Formatting the Data Series

You can apply fill color to the data series, outline the series with a border, change the shape, or add special effects to the columns, bars, etc., that represent the data series.

➔ FORMAT THE DATA SERIES

USE the workbook you saved in the previous exercise.

1. Select the chart on the Sales History worksheet, then select **Series "2008"** in the Current Selection group on the Format tab.
2. Click **Shape Fill**.
3. Point to **Texture**. Click **Denim**.
4. Select **Series "2008" Data Labels** in the Current Selection.
5. Click **Shape Outline** in the Shape Styles group.
6. Click **Blue** under Standard Colors.
7. Select the data series for coffee and espresso. Drag the box above the bar so that the label is completely visible.
8. Click in the chart area to select it. Click **Print** in the Quick Access Toolbar. The Print dialog box opens with Selected Chart as the default print area. Click **Print**.
9. Click the **Expense History** worksheet tab. Select the **chart title**. Key **Expenses** at the end of the existing text. The title should read *2008 Expenses*.
10. **SAVE** the workbook. **CLOSE** the file.

PAUSE. LEAVE Excel open to use in the next exercise.

The bar chart's content was easier to understand when you added the data series and formatted the series to call attention to the figures. When you clarified the chart title in the pie chart, you clarified the chart's contents. The chart is a communication tool. Use formatting to call attention to significant data.

TAKE NOTE

The data series is the most important element of the chart. Use formatting tools to call attention to the graphic and the label.

Modifying a Chart's Legend

You can modify the content of the legend, expand or collapse the legend box, edit the text that is displayed, and change character attributes. A finished chart should stand alone—that is, the chart should contain sufficient data to convey the intended data analysis.

Creating Charts from Your Data | 491

MODIFY A CHART'S LEGEND

The *Financial History* workbook is available on the companion CD-ROM.

1. **OPEN** Financial History from the data files for this lesson.
2. On the Sales History worksheet, select **A4:F9**. Click **Column** on the Insert tab.
3. Select **Stacked Column in 3D** from the Column chart listing.
4. Click the down arrow next to the Chart Layouts group on the Design tab and click **Layout 4**. The legend appears below the plot area.
5. Select the legend and click **Colored Outline – Accent 1** in the Shape Styles on the Format tab to enclose the legend in a green border.
6. Select the **legend** and right-click to display the shortcut menu. Click **Font**.
7. On the Font dialog box, click **Small Caps** and click **OK**.
8. Select **Coffee and Espresso** in the legend, right-click to display the shortcut menu, and click **Font**.
9. Click **Font color** and click **Green**. Click **OK**.
10. Repeat step 9 for each legend item and apply the following font colors.
    Bakery – Red
    Coffee Accessories – Orange
    Packaged Coffee/Tea – Light Blue
    Deli - Blue
11. **SAVE** the file as *Chart 1*.
    PAUSE. LEAVE the workbook open to use in the next exercise.

Changing the font colors in the legend to match the blocks in the columns provides an additional visual aid that enables the viewer to quickly see the income contribution for each category. When you applied Layout 4 to the column chart, the legend was placed at the bottom of the chart. You can click the legend border and move it to any location on the chart. All other elements of the quick layout will remain the same.

■ Modifying a Chart

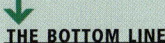

THE BOTTOM LINE

You can modify a chart by adding or deleting elements or by moving or resizing the chart. You can also change the chart type without having to delete the existing chart and create a new one.

Adding elements to a chart can provide additional information that was not available in the data you selected to create the chart. For example, the stacked column chart in the previous exercise does not have a title and it does not indicate that the sales amounts are in thousands.

Adding Elements to a Chart

Labels make it easy to understand chart data. You can display series names, category names, and percentages in data labels. To prevent data labels from overlapping and to make them easier to read, you can adjust their positions on the chart. Use the Layout tab commands to add chart labels.

ADD ELEMENTS TO A CHART

USE the workbook from the previous exercise.

1. Display the Layout tab.
2. Click **Axis Titles** and click **Primary Vertical Axis Title**.

3. Click **Vertical Title**. Key **(in Thousands)** in the title textbox.
4. Click **Chart Title** in the Labels group. Click **Above Chart**. A text box displaying *Chart Title* is inserted above the columns.
5. Select the text and key **Sales History**.
6. Click **Data Labels** in the Labels group. Click **Show**. Labels are added to each column showing the dollar amount of sales in each category.

Looking Ahead Because of the chart size, the data labels are difficult to read. You will correct this in a subsequent exercise.

7. Click **Gridlines** in the Axes group. Click **Primary Vertical Gridlines** and click **Major Gridlines**.
8. Click **Axis Titles** and click **Primary Horizontal Axis Title**.
9. Click **Title Below Axis**.
10. Key **Annual Sales** in the Axis Title textbox.

 **ANOTHER WAY** Rather than select and replace the text in the textboxes, you can key the new text in the formula bar. When you press Enter, the new text replaces the generic text in the title boxes.

11. **SAVE** the workbook with the same name.

    PAUSE. LEAVE the workbook open to use in the next exercise.

Chart axes are used to measure and categorize data. A column or bar chart typically has two axes. The vertical axis (y axis) usually contains the data. In your chart, the y axis contains the amount of sales. It is important for the viewer to understand that sales amounts in this chart are expressed in thousands. Therefore, it was necessary to add a label to the y axis.

The horizontal axis (x axis) contains the categories. In your chart, the categories are self-explanatory. Thus, the x axis label is less critical.

Deleting Elements from a Chart

When a chart becomes too cluttered, you may need to delete nonessential elements. You can use the Layout tab commands to delete chart elements, or you can select an element on the chart and press the Delete key. You can also select an element in the Current Selection group and press Delete.

➔ DELETE ELEMENTS FROM A CHART

USE the workbook from the previous exercise.

1. Display the Layout tab.
2. Click **Axis Titles** and click **Primary Horizontal Axis Title**. Click **None**.
3. Click **Gridlines in the Axes** group, click **Primary Vertical Gridlines**, and click **None**.
4. Click the **Design** tab and click **Switch Row/Column**. The data display is changed to have all sales for one category stacked.
5. Click **Undo**.
6. **SAVE** the workbook.

   PAUSE. LEAVE the workbook open to use in the next exercise.

Creating Charts from Your Data | 493

You can delete any element from a chart. Use the commands in the Labels group to add or remove a category of labels or select an element on the chart and press Delete. You can also right-click on a chart element and press Delete.

Moving a Chart

When you insert a chart, by default, it is embedded in the worksheet. You can click a corner of a chart or the midpoint of any side to display move handles (four-sided arrow). You can use the move handles to drag the chart to any location on the worksheet. Sometimes you want a chart to be on a chart sheet so that it can be reviewed without the worksheet data.

➔ MOVE A CHART

USE the workbook from the previous exercise.

1. Click a blank area in the Sales History chart.
2. Drag the chart so that it is centered in columns B to G.
3. With the chart selected, click the **Design** tab.
4. Click **Move Chart Location**. The Move Chart dialog box shown in Figure 8-9 opens, with the default setting—placing the chart as an object in the worksheet.

Figure 8-9

Choose where a chart is placed

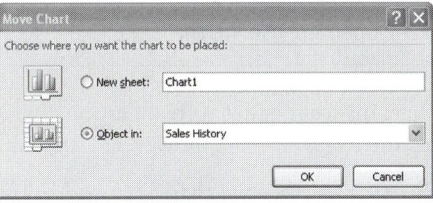

5. Click **New Sheet** and key **Sales History Chart** in the text box. Click **OK**. A chart worksheet is inserted before the Sales History sheet.
6. Click **Legend** in Labels group on the Layout tab. Click **Show Legend at Right**.

TAKE NOTE

The Chart Tools that you used on the Design, Layout, and Format tabs can be applied to the Chart Sheet. The data series amounts were difficult to read when you applied them to the embedded chart. They are easy to read and can be used for analysis when the chart is moved to a chart sheet.

7. **SAVE** and **CLOSE** the workbook.

PAUSE. LEAVE Excel open to use in the next exercise.

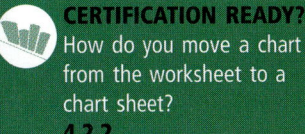

CERTIFICATION READY?
How do you move a chart from the worksheet to a chart sheet?
4.2.2

You can move chart elements or move the entire chart. In previous exercises, you moved an embedded chart by dragging it to a new location. When you move the chart to a new sheet, it becomes even more important for the chart to be self-explanatory. Moving the legend to the right makes it easier to identify the building blocks in the stacked columns.

Resizing a Chart

You can click a corner of a chart or the midpoint of any side to display sizing handles (two-sided arrow). Use the side handles to change chart height or width. Use the corner sizing handles to change both height and width.

RESIZE A CHART

GET READY. Launch Microsoft Excel if it is not already open.

1. OPEN *Financial History 2* from the data files for this lesson.
2. Click a blank area in the chart on the Expense History worksheet.
3. Click the **top-left sizing handle** and drag the left edge of the chart to the bottom of row 9 at the left edge of the worksheet.
4. Click the **top-right sizing handle** and align the right edge of the chart with the column G right boundary.
5. Click the **bottom-center sizing handle** and drag the chart boundary to the bottom of row 35.
6. Open the Sales History worksheet. Click a blank area in the chart. Click the **Format** tab.
7. In the Size group, click the **Shape Height** up arrow until the height is 3.5.
8. In the Size group, click the **Shape Width** down arrow until the width is 4.0.

You can click the Dialog Box Launcher in the Size group and enter the desired chart height and width.

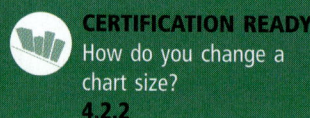

CERTIFICATION READY?
How do you change a chart size?
4.2.2

9. SAVE the workbook as *Chart 2*. CLOSE the workbook.

   PAUSE. LEAVE Excel open to use in the next exercise.

Increasing the size of a chart makes it easier to read, especially an embedded chart. Be cautious when you reduce the size of a chart, however. Titles and legends must be readable.

It is important to remember that whether the chart is embedded in the worksheet or located on a chart sheet, the chart is linked to the worksheet data. Any changes in the worksheet data will be reflected in the chart. Likewise, if the worksheet data is deleted, the chart will be deleted as well.

Choosing a Different Chart Type

For most 2-D charts, you can change the type of the entire chart and give it a completely different look. If a chart contains multiple data series, you can also select a different chart type for any single data series, creating a combined chart. You cannot combine a 2-D and a 3-D chart, however.

CHOOSE A DIFFERENT CHART TYPE

GET READY. Launch Microsoft Excel if it is not already open.

1. OPEN *Financial History* from the data files for this lesson.
2. On the Expense History worksheet, select **A4:F9**.
3. On the Insert tab, click **Bar** and click **Stacked Bar in 3-D**.
4. Click **Layout 2** on the Design tab.
5. Select the chart title text box and key **Expense History** in the formula bar. Press **Enter**.
6. On the Design tab, click **Change Chart Type**.
7. Click **Stacked Horizontal Cylinder** and click **OK**.
8. On the Sales History worksheet, select **A4:B9**. On the Insert tab, click **Pie**. Click **Pie**.
9. Click **Layout 1** on the Design tab.
10. Click **Change Chart Type** and click **Exploded pie in 3-D**. Click **OK**.
11. SAVE the workbook as *Chart 3*. CLOSE the workbook.

    END. CLOSE Excel.

The *Financial History* workbook is available on the companion CD-ROM.

SUMMARY SKILL MATRIX

IN THIS LESSON YOU LEARNED HOW TO:
Select Data to Include in a Chart
Choose the Right Chart for Your Data
Create a Bar Chart
Format a Chart with a Quick Style
Change the Chart's Fill Color or Pattern
Change the Chart's Border Line
Format the Data Series
Modify a Chart's Legend
Add Elements to a Chart
Delete Elements from a Chart
Move a Chart
Resize a Chart
Choose a Different Chart Type

■ Knowledge Assessment

Matching

a. axis
b. chart
c. chart area
d. chart sheet
e. data labels
f. data marker
g. data series
h. embedded chart
i. legend
j. title

____i____ 1. A box that identifies the patterns or colors that are assigned to a data series or categories in a chart.

____b____ 2. A graphical representation of numeric data in a worksheet.

____f____ 3. A bar, area, dot, slice, or other symbol in a chart that represents a single data point or value that originates from a worksheet cell.

____h____ 4. A chart that is placed on a worksheet rather than on a separate sheet.

____d____ 5. A sheet in a workbook that contains only a chart.

____c____ 6. The entire chart and all its elements.

____g____ 7. Related data points that are plotted in a chart.

____a____ 8. A line bordering the chart plot area used as a frame of reference for measurement.

_____j_____ 9. Descriptive text that is automatically aligned to an axis or centered at the top of a chart.

_____e_____ 10. A label that provides additional information about a data marker, which represents a single data point or value that originates from a worksheet cell.

Multiple Choice

Circle the choice that best completes the following statements.

1. Which chart type shows values as parts of a whole?
   a. column
   b. bar
   c. area
   d. pie

2. A(n) _____ chart appears on a worksheet with other data.
   a. chart sheet
   b. embedded
   c. Pivot chart
   d. mixed

3. What part of a chart do you click when you want to select the entire chart?
   a. chart area
   b. plot area
   c. chart title
   d. legend

4. What happens to a chart if the source data is deleted?
   a. Nothing.
   b. The chart will move to the area where the data was located.
   c. The data in the chart is deleted.
   d. You will be asked if you want the chart deleted.

5. What is the first step that should be taken when creating a chart?
   a. providing a name for the chart
   b. selecting the chart type
   c. selecting the range of cells that contain the data the chart will use
   d. choosing the data labels that will be used in the chart

6. If you want to print only the chart in a worksheet, what should you do before printing?
   a. click the chart to select it and then print
   b. select the *Print chart only* option in the Page Setup dialog box
   c. move the chart to a new sheet by itself and then print that sheet
   d. cannot print only the chart if it is part of a larger worksheet

7. To change the location of a legend on a chart, use the Legend command on this Ribbon tab.
   a. Insert
   b. Format
   c. Layout
   d. Design

Creating Charts from Your Data | 497

8. A column chart represents values as
   a. horizontal bars.
   b. vertical bars.
   c. horizontal lines.
   d. vertical lines.

9. To move a chart from a worksheet to a chart sheet,
   a. use the move handles and drag it to the new location.
   b. use the Move Chart Location command on the Design tab.
   c. cut the chart from the worksheet and paste it to a new workbook sheet.
   d. You cannot move the chart after it has been created.

10. Which of the following statements is **not** true?
    a. You can change both the height and width of a chart with commands on the Format tab.
    b. You can use the sizing handles to change the height and width of a chart.
    c. You must delete an existing chart in order to have the data displayed in a different chart type.
    d. When a chart sheet is created it no longer appears on the worksheet containing the data series.

■ Competency Assessment

Project 8-1: Create a Pie Chart

Blue Yonder Airlines has created a worksheet to analyze sales for its first four years of operation. The manager wants to create charts that reflect an analysis of the data.

GET READY. Launch Excel.

The *BY Financials* worksheet is available on the companion CD-ROM.

1. **OPEN** *BY Financials* from the data files for this lesson.
2. On the Income worksheet, select **A3:A7**. Press **Ctrl** and select **E3:E7**.
3. Click the **Insert** tab. Click **Pie** and click **Pie in 3-D**.
4. Click **Layout 1** in the Chart Layouts group on the Design tab.
5. Click **Move Chart Location**.
6. Select **New Sheet** and click **OK**.
7. Right-click the **Chart1** tab and click **Rename**.
8. Key **2008 Income Chart** and press **Enter**.
9. **SAVE** the worksheet as *BY Financials 8-1*.
10. **CLOSE** the file.
    PAUSE. LEAVE open for the next project.

Project 8-2: Create a Bar Chart

Create a bar chart to analyze trends in Fourth Coffee's income before taxes.

The *Financial History* workbook is available on the companion CD-ROM.

1. **OPEN** *Financial History* from the data files for this lesson.
2. Make the Income worksheet active. Select **A4:F9** and click the **Insert** tab.
3. Click **Bar** in the Charts group and click **100% Stacked Horizontal Cylinder**.
4. Click in the **Chart Area** and click the **Layout** tab.

5. Click **Legend** and click **Show Legend at Bottom**.
6. Click the **Chart Area** to display the move handles. Move the chart so that the top-left corner is aligned with B12.
7. Click the bottom-right sizing handle and increase the size of the chart so that it fills B12:G29.
8. **SAVE** the worksheet as *Financial History 8-2*.

   LEAVE the workbook open to use in the next project.

■ Proficiency Assessment

Project 8-3: Modify a Bar Chart

In the previous project, you created a bar chart to analyze trends in Fourth Coffee's income before taxes. Modify the chart by adding additional chart elements.

USE the workbook from the previous project.

1. Select the chart area and click **Chart Title** in the Labels group on the Layout tab.
2. Click **More Title Options** and click **Gradient fill**.
3. In the Preset colors box, click **Moss** and click **Close**. The Chart Title text box is selected.
4. In the formula bar, key **Income Before Taxes** and press [Enter].
5. Click **Axis Titles** and click **Primary Vertical Axis Title**.
6. Click **Rotated Title**. The Axis Title text box is selected.
7. In the formula bar, key **in thousands** and press [Enter].
8. Right-click the **axis title** text box and click **Font**.
9. Click **Font color** and click **Green**. Click **OK**.
10. **SAVE** the workbook as *Financial History 8-3* and then **CLOSE** the file.

    LEAVE Excel open for the next project.

Project 8-4: Create a Line Chart

The *BY Financials* workbook is available on the companion CD-ROM.

1. **OPEN** *BY Financials* from the data files for this lesson.
2. On the Annual Sales worksheet, select **A3:E7**. Click **Line**.
3. Click **Stacked line with Markers**.
4. Apply **Layout 3**.
5. Click **Chart Title** and key **Blue Yonder Airlines** in the formula bar.
6. Click **Plot Area** and click **Format Selection**.
7. Click **Border Color** and click **Gradient line**.
8. Click **Preset colors** and click **Day Break**.
9. Click **Direction** and click **Linear Diagonal**. Click **Close**.
10. Click **Chart Area**, click **Format Selection**, and click **Solid fill**.
11. Click **Color** and click **Blue, Accent1, Lighter 80%**.
12. Click **Close**.
13. **SAVE** the worksheet as *BY Financials 8-4*.

    LEAVE the workbook open for the next project.

Mastery Assessment

Project 8-5: Create a Doughnut Chart

USE the workbook from the previous project.

1. Click the **Annual Expenses** tab. Select **A3:E7** and click **Other Charts** on the Insert tab.
2. Click **Doughnut**.
3. Click **Layout 2**.
4. Click the **Size Dialog Box Launcher**. Set both height and width to 5 inches.
5. Key **Annual Expenses** as the chart title.
6. Print the chart only.
7. SAVE the workbook as *BY Financials 8-5*. CLOSE the file.

   LEAVE Excel open for the next project.

Project 8-6: Format Chart Elements

Fourth Coffee's corporate manager wants to change the chart type and some of the formatting in the chart prepared in a previous exercise.

The *Income Chart* workbook is available on the companion CD-ROM.

1. OPEN *Income Chart* from the data files for this lesson.
2. Select the chart. Click the **Design** tab.
3. Click **Layout 3**.
4. On the Layout tab, click **Axis Title** and key **Percentage of Income** below the axis.
5. Click **Data Labels** and add data labels to the bars.
6. Click **Chart Title**. Right-click and click **Font**. Click **Font color** and click **Pink – Accent 2** under Theme Colors.
7. Click **Small Caps** and click **OK**.
8. On the Layout tab, click **Legend** in the Current Selection group.
9. Click **Colored Outline – Accent 2** on the Format tab.
10. On the Design tab, click **Move Chart Location**. Click **New Sheet**.
11. SAVE the workbook as *Income Chart 8-6* and then CLOSE the file.

    STOP. CLOSE Excel.

INTERNET READY

Customized chart styles cannot be saved and applied to other charts. However, you can save a customized chart as a template. Use Excel Help to learn how to save a chart as a template that can be used later. Open your Income Chart 9-6 workbook and save it as a template file. SAVE the workbook as *Chart Template*.

Circling Back

Cross-Cultural Solutions, a nonprofit organization, offers three short-term international volunteer programs. Volunteers can choose from ten countries, with year-round start dates and programs that are 1–12 weeks long.

As international volunteers with Cross-Cultural Solutions, individuals work side-by-side with local people on locally designed and locally driven projects, allowing them to see and learn about a country through the eyes of its people. The organization sends more than 1000 volunteers abroad each year. Excel is a valuable tool for organizing data related to volunteers, the programs they choose, and the start date and duration of their volunteer activity.

Project 1: Sort and Filter Data

Sort and filter the list of volunteers who are scheduled to begin their volunteer experience in July and August.

GET READY. Launch Excel if it is not already running.

The *Volunteers* file is available on the companion CD-ROM.

1. **OPEN** *Volunteers* from the data files.
2. With the Data tab active, select any cell in column D. Click **Sort** in the Sort & Filter group.
3. The Sort dialog box opens. In the *Sort by* field, select **Program**.
4. Click **Add Level**. In the *Then by* box, select **Location**.
5. Click **Add Level**. In the *Then by* box, select **Start Date**. Click **OK**.
6. **SAVE** the document as *Volunteers Project 1*.
7. Click **Filter** in the Sort & Filter group.
8. Click the arrow in the Duration column. On the dropdown list, click the **(Select All)** checkbox to deselect all filters. Click the **6 weeks** checkbox and click **OK**.
9. Click the arrow in the Start Date column and deselect **August**. Click **OK**.
10. Click **Quick Print** to print the list of volunteers who will depart in July and remain on location for six weeks.
11. Select any cell in the data range. Click **Remove Duplicates** in the Data Tools group.
12. On the Remove Duplicates dialog box, click **Select All** and click **OK**. A dialog box indicates that one duplicate entry was removed.
13. Click **Filter** to display all data.
14. **SAVE** the workbook.

    LEAVE the workbook open for the next project.

Project 2: Manage Worksheets in a Workbook

Data can be accessed easily if you organize the data and create a worksheet for each program.

GET READY. Use the workbook from the previous project.

1. Select **A1:F19** and click **Copy** in the Clipboard group on the Home tab.
2. Select **Sheet2**, click **A1**, and click **Paste** in the Clipboard group.
3. Click the **Paste Options** button and click **Keep Source Column Widths**.
4. With Sheet2 active, click **Format** on the Home tab and click **Move or Copy Sheet**. On the Move or Copy dialog box, in the Before Sheet list, select **Sheet3**. Click **Create a Copy** and click **OK**.

5. Click the **Insert Worksheet** icon. This creates Sheet5.
6. With Sheet1 active, click **Format** and click **Rename Sheet**. Key **Summary** and press Enter. Click the **Sheet2** tab and rename it **Insight Abroad**.
7. Click the **Sheet2(2)** tab and rename the worksheet **Intern Abroad**. Click the **Sheet3** tab and rename the worksheet **Volunteer Abroad**.
8. On the Summary worksheet, select **A20:F45** (Intern Abroad volunteers) and click **Copy**. Click the **Intern Abroad** tab and select **A5**. Click **Paste**. This replaces data on the worksheet.
9. On the Summary worksheet, select **A1:F4** and click **Copy**. Click the **Volunteer Abroad** tab, select **A1**, and click **Paste**.
10. Click the **Paste Options** button and click **Keep Source Column Widths**.
11. Select **A46:F87** on the Summary worksheet and click **Copy**. Select **A5** on the Volunteer Abroad worksheet and click **Paste**.
12. With the Summary worksheet active, press Ctrl and click the **Sheet5** tab to group the two worksheets.
13. Click **Format**, point to **Hide & Unhide**, and click **Hide Sheet**. Three worksheets remain visible.
14. Click the **Microsoft Office Button** and click **Print**. On the Print dialog box, click **Entire workbook**.
15. Click **Format**. Point to **Hide & Unhide** and click **Unhide Sheet**. Select **Summary** and click **OK**. Select **Format** and unhide Sheet5.
16. With Sheet5 active, click the **Delete** arrow, and click **Delete Sheet**.
17. Click the **Summary** tab and click **Format**. Click **Move or Copy Sheet**. On the Move or Copy dialog box, click **(move to end)**. Click **OK**.
18. **SAVE** the workbook as *Volunteers Project 2* and **CLOSE** the file.

   LEAVE Excel open for the next project.

Project 3: Sort and Subtotal Data

Cross-Cultural Solutions is supported in part by individual and corporate tax-deductible contributions. Contributors are asked to select a fund to which their contribution will apply.

The *Contributions* file is available on the companion CD-ROM.

1. **OPEN** *Contributions* from the data files.
2. Click the **Data** tab.
3. Select any data cell. Click **Sort** in the Sort & Filter group on the Data tab.
4. On the Sort dialog box, select **Fund** and click **OK**.
5. Click **Subtotal** in the Outline group on the Data tab. The Subtotal dialog box opens.
6. In the *At each change in* box, select **Fund**. Select or accept **Sum** in the *Use function* box and **Amount** in the *Add subtotal to* box. Click **OK**.
7. Adjust column widths if necessary to display all data.
8. **SAVE** the workbook as *Contributions Project 3* and **CLOSE** the file.

   LEAVE Excel open for the next project.

Project 4: Use Formulas and Functions

In Project 3, you determined the amount contributed to each fund. Use formulas and functions to perform additional analyses in preparation for Cross-Cultural Solutions' annual fundraising drive.

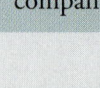

The *Contributions* file is available on the companion CD-ROM.

1. OPEN *Contributions* from the data files.
2. Click the Formulas tab. Select A36. Key Total Contributions.
3. Select C36 and click AutoSum in the Function Library group. C5:C35 should be selected by default. Press Enter.
4. Select A36:C36. Click Cell Styles on the Home tab. Click Total under Titles and Headings.
5. Select A38 and key Count. Press Tab.
6. On the Formulas tab, click Insert Function. Select Count and click OK.
7. Select C5:C35 in the Value1 box. Click OK.
8. In A39, key Contributions <$1,000 and press Tab.
9. Click Insert Function and select SUMIF. Click OK. Select C5:C35 in the Range box.

TROUBLESHOOTING If the function you want to use is not visible in the *Select a function* box on the Insert Function dialog box, key the function in the *Search for a function* box and click Go.

10. In the Criteria box, key <1000. Click OK.
11. Select A40 and key Average Individual. Press Tab.
12. Click Insert Function and click AVERAGE. Click OK. Select C25:C35 in the Number1 box. Click OK. A triangle appears in the upper-left corner of B40 and an error message button is displayed. Click the arrow and click ignore error.
13. Select A41, key Contributions >=5000, and press Tab.
14. Click Recently Used in the Function Library group and click SUMIF.
15. In the Range box, select C5:C35 and press Tab.
16. In the Criteria box, key >=5000. Click OK.
17. Select B39:B41 and click Accounting Number Format in the Number group on the Home tab.
18. Click Decrease Decimal twice.
19. SAVE the workbook as *Contributions Project 4* and CLOSE the file.

    LEAVE Excel open for the next project.

Project 5: Create a Column Chart

Create a chart that compares budgeted amounts with contributions received to date. This comparison will be used to establish the fundraising goal.

The *Contributions 5* workbook is available on the companion CD-ROM.

1. OPEN *Contributions 5* from the data files.
2. Click the Insert tab. On the Budget worksheet, select A4:C8 and click Column.
3. Click 3-D Clustered Column.
4. SAVE the document as *Contributions Project 5*.
5. Select Layout 2.
6. Select Chart Title in the Current Selection group on the Layout tab and key Budgeted vs. Received. Press Enter.
7. Delete the legend.

8. Select **Budgeted** in the chart title, click **Text Fill** on the Format tab, and click **Pink Accent 1** under Theme Colors.
9. Select **Received** in the chart title, click **Text Fill**, and click **Purple**.
10. Select **Series "Budgeted Amount" Data Labels** in the Current Selection group on the Layout tab and apply **Pink Accent 1** text fill.
11. Select **Series "Received to Date" Data Labels** and apply **Purple** text fill.
12. Move the chart to a new sheet.
13. Name the chart sheet **Budgeted vs. Received**.
14. Select the **Horizontal (Category) Axis** and select **Text Fill**. Click **Purple**.
15. If necessary, select and move the series amounts so that they are completely visible.
16. **SAVE** and **CLOSE** the file.

    STOP. CLOSE Excel.

Microsoft® Office
PowerPoint® 2007

PowerPoint Essentials

1

LESSON SKILL MATRIX

Viewing a Presentation in Different Ways 506	Students will learn how to view PowerPoint presentations in different ways.
Using Zoom 510	Students will learn how to use the Zoom option.
Scrolling with a Mouse 511	Students will learn how to scroll through a presentation using a mouse.
Navigating a Presentation from the Keyboard 513	Students will learn how to navigate a presentation from the keyboard.
Adding Text to a Text Placeholder 513	Students will learn how to add text to a text placeholder.
Adding Text on the Outline Tab 515	Students will learn how to add text on the Outline tab.
Selecting, Replacing, and Deleting Text 516	Students will learn how to select, replace, and delete text.
Copying and Moving Text from One Slide to Another 517	Students will learn how to copy and move text from one slide to another.

Blue Yonder Airlines is a small but rapidly growing company that offers charter flights to adventurous or exotic locations. The service is designed for small groups, such as corporate management teams or directors, who want to mix business and pleasure in a packaged getaway. As an enterprise account manager, your job is to introduce Blue Yonder to executives in mid-size and large companies. Your goal is to convince these managers to use your charter service when arranging off-site gatherings that require group travel. Microsoft PowerPoint 2007 provides the perfect set of tools for presenting this information to your potential customers. In this lesson, you will start PowerPoint and open an introductory presentation about Blue Yonder Airlines. You will learn to navigate, edit, save, print, and close a presentation.

KEY TERMS
current slide
Normal view
Notes Page view
placeholder
Slide Show view
Slide Sorter view

505

Software Orientation

Microsoft PowerPoint's Opening Screen

Before you begin working in Microsoft PowerPoint, you should be familiar with the primary user interface. When you first start Microsoft PowerPoint, you will see a screen similar to the one shown in Figure 1-1.

Figure 1-1

The PowerPoint window

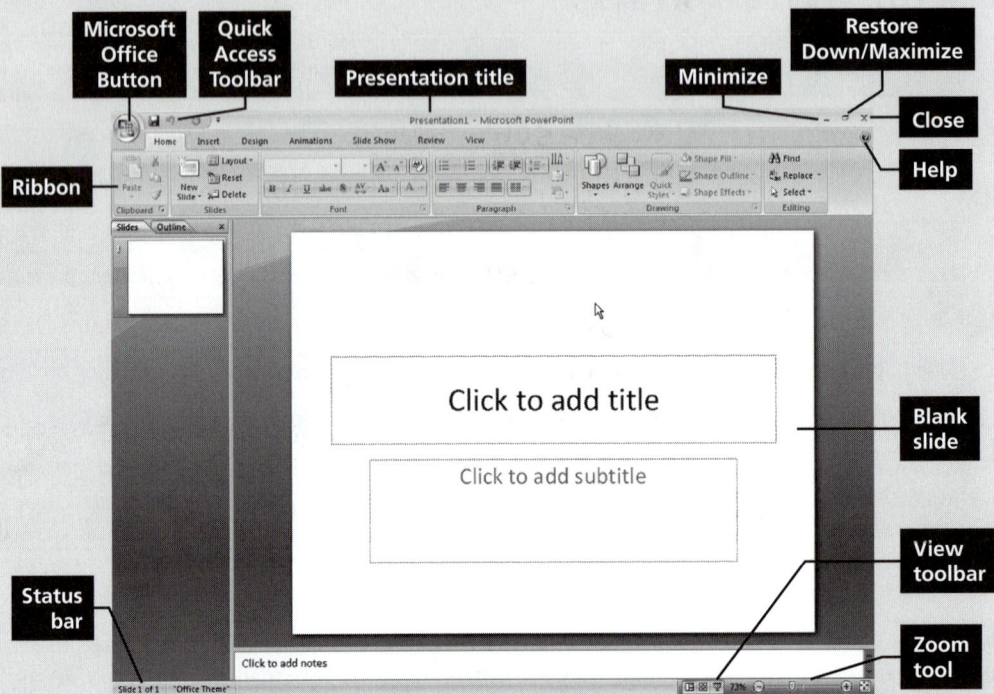

In PowerPoint 2007, it is easier to access commands and features than in previous versions of the application. PowerPoint 2007 displays the tools that are most relevant to the tasks you are performing at the moment. (Note that if default settings or other preferences have been changed on your system, your screen may look somewhat different from Figure 1-1.)

Viewing a Presentation in Different Ways

PowerPoint lets you see your presentation in a variety of ways. For example, you can work with just one slide at a time, which is helpful when you are adding text or graphics to a slide. Or, you can view all the slides in a presentation at the same time, which makes it easy to rearrange the slides. The following exercises show you how to change PowerPoint's views and how to change the magnification level of your slides for easier viewing.

➔ CHANGE POWERPOINT'S VIEWS

GET READY. Before you begin these steps, be sure to launch Microsoft Office PowerPoint 2007.

1. In the data files for this lesson, locate and open *Blue Yonder Overview*. The presentation appears on your screen, as shown in Figure 1-2.

> The *Blue Yonder Overview* file is available on the companion CD-ROM.

PowerPoint Essentials | 507

Figure 1-2

The Blue Yonder Overview presentation

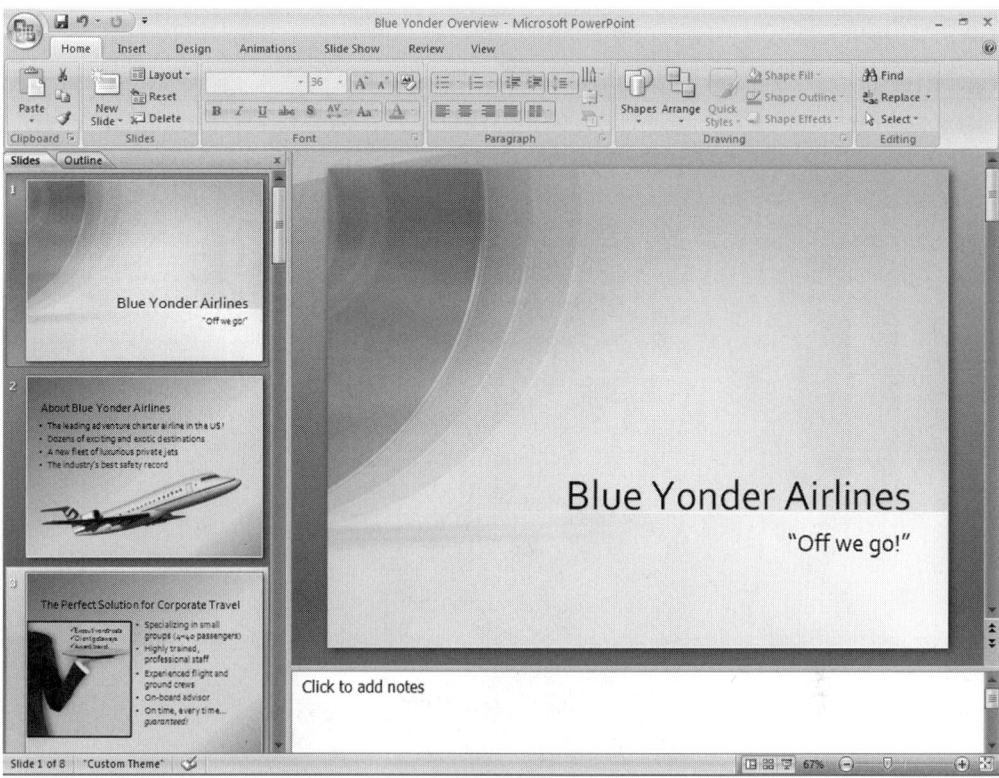

2. Click the **View** tab, as shown in Figure 1-3. Notice that the Normal button is highlighted; this is the default view.

Figure 1-3

Normal view, with the View tab selected

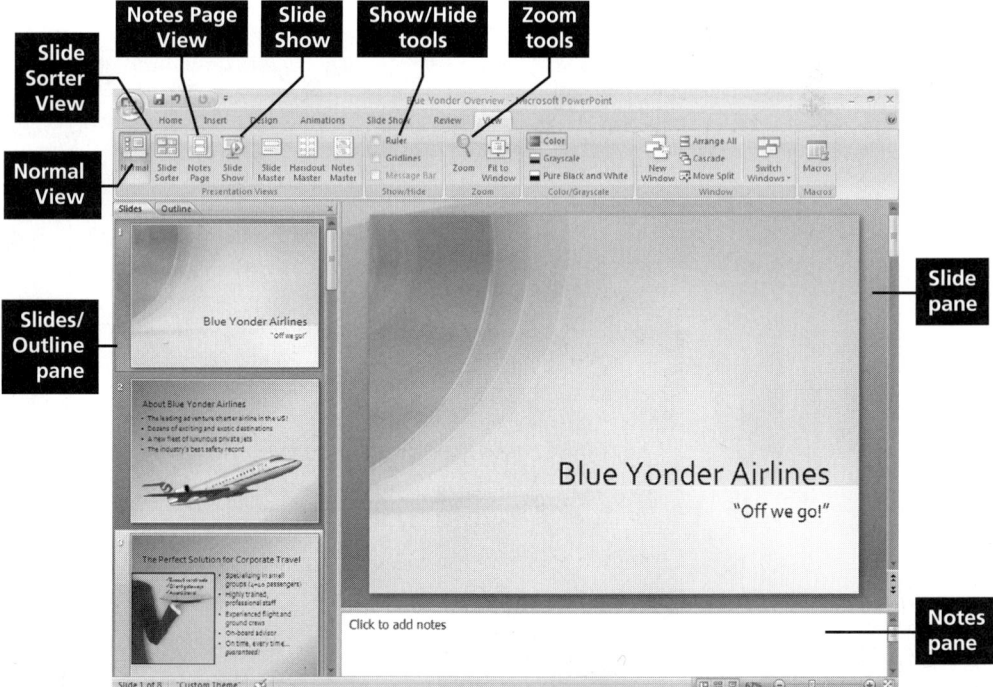

TAKE NOTE If formatted slides are hard to read in Slide Sorter view, press **Alt** and click a slide to see its heading clearly.

3. In the Presentation Views group, click the **Slide Sorter View** button to change to Slide Sorter view, as shown in Figure 1-4.

Figure 1-4

Slide Sorter view

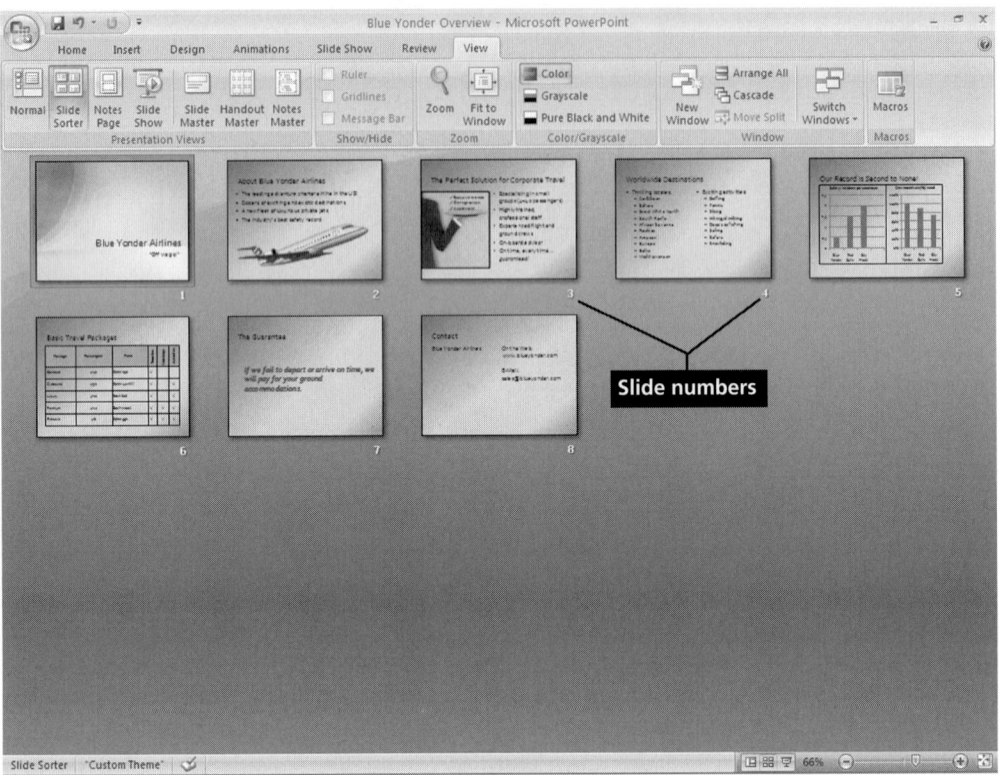

4. Click slide 2, then click the **Notes Page View** button in the Presentation Views group. PowerPoint switches to Notes Page view, as shown in Figure 1-5.

Figure 1-5

Notes Page view

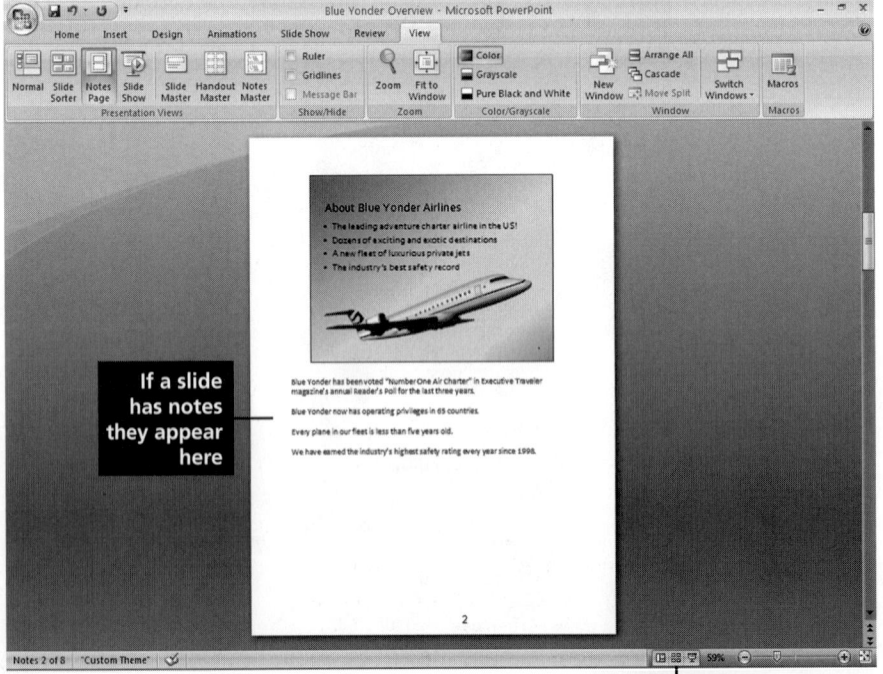

 **ANOTHER WAY**
Instead of using the Ribbon to change views, you can use the View toolbar in the lower-right corner of the PowerPoint window.

5. In the Presentation Views group, click **Slide Show**. The first slide of the presentation fills the screen, as shown in Figure 1-6.

Figure 1-6
Slide Show view

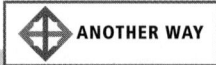 **ANOTHER WAY**
You can switch to Slide Show view by pressing **F5**.

6. Press Esc to exit Slide Show view and return to Notes Page view.
7. Click the **Normal View** button in the Presentation Views group. PowerPoint switches back to Normal view.
    PAUSE. LEAVE the presentation open to use in the next exercise.

PowerPoint has four main views:

- *Normal view* is the default view that lets you focus on an individual slide. The slide you are currently editing is called the *current slide*. The current slide appears in the Slide pane, which is the largest of the view's three panes. Below the Slide pane is the Notes pane, where you can add and edit notes you want to associate with the current slide. In the left pane—called the Slides/Outline pane—you can use the Slides tab to jump from one slide to another, as you will see later in this lesson. On the Outline tab, you can add text to a slide or copy or move text from one slide to another.
- *Slide Sorter view* displays all the slides in a presentation on a single screen. (If there are more slides than can fit in one screen, you can use scroll bars to move slides in and out of view.) In Slide Show view, you can reorganize a slide show by dragging slides to different positions. You can also duplicate and delete slides in this view.
- *Notes Page view* shows one slide at a time, along with any notes that are associated with the slide. This view lets you create and edit notes. You may find it easier to work with notes in this view than in Normal view. You can also print out notes pages for your presentation; they are printed as they appear in Notes Page view.
- *Slide Show view* lets you preview your presentation on the screen, so you can see it the way your audience will see it.

ANOTHER WAY

You can drag the Zoom control's slider bar to the right or left to change the zoom level.

→ **USE ZOOM**

USE the presentation that is open from the previous exercise.

1. Make sure that the View tab is active on the Ribbon.
2. On the View tab, click the **Zoom** button. The Zoom dialog box appears, as shown in Figure 1-7.

Figure 1-7

The Zoom dialog box

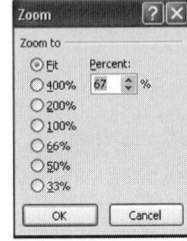

ANOTHER WAY

You can click the Zoom level indicator at the far left of the Zoom control to display the Zoom dialog box.

3. Click the **200%** option button, then click **OK**. In the Slide pane, the slide is magnified by 200%. Notice that you can no longer see the entire slide.
4. Click the **Zoom Out** button at the left end of the Zoom control, at the lower-right of the screen, as shown in Figure 1-8. Continue clicking the button until the zoom level drops to 100%. Notice that, even at 100% magnification, the slide is too large for the Slide pane.

Figure 1-8

Using the Zoom control

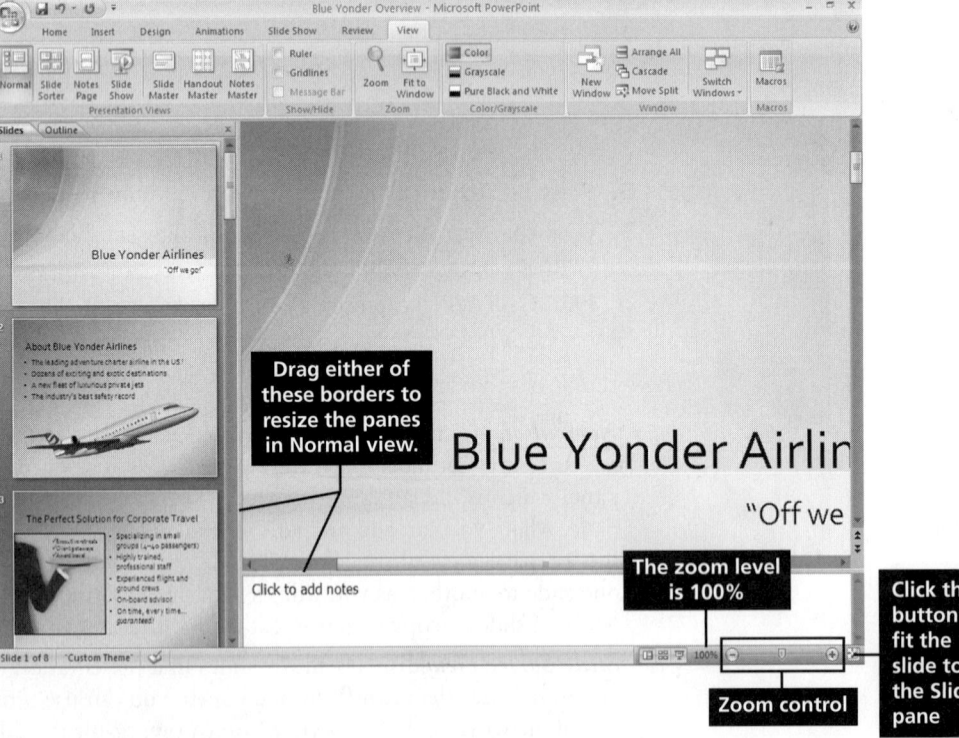

TAKE NOTE

You can resize the Slide pane by dragging its bottom border up or down, or by dragging its left-hand border to the right or left. The Slides/Outline pane and Notes pane also change size when you drag the borders.

5. Click the **Fit slide to current window** button at the far right end of the Zoom control. PowerPoint zooms out to fit the entire slide in the Slide pane.

PAUSE. LEAVE the presentation open to use in the next exercise.

PowerPoint's zoom tools let you change the magnification of slides on the screen. By zooming out, you can see an entire slide; by zooming in, you can inspect one area of the slide. Both views have advantages: Higher magnifications make it easier to position objects on the slide, and lower magnifications enable you to see how all the parts of a slide look as a whole.

You can use either the Zoom dialog box or the Zoom control to change magnification levels. In the Zoom dialog box, you can zoom in or out by choosing one of seven pre-set magnification levels, or you can use the Percent spin control to set the zoom level precisely. If you click the *Fit slide to current window* button on the Zoom control (there is also one on the View tab), PowerPoint changes the magnification level so the entire slide fits in the Slide pane.

All zoom options are available in Normal view. In Slide Sorter view, some zoom options are available, but the *Fit slide to current window* tool is not.

Navigating a Presentation

PowerPoint provides a number of tools that let you move around in—or navigate—a presentation. You can use onscreen tools such as scroll bars to view your slides in order, moving either forward or backward. There are also ways to jump from one slide to another in any order. Like all the Microsoft Office applications, PowerPoint also lets you use the keyboard to navigate a presentation. In the following exercise, you will practice using all these navigation tools.

➔ SCROLL WITH THE MOUSE

USE the presentation that is open from the previous exercise.

1. Click the **scroll down** button on the right side of the Slide pane, as shown in Figure 1-9. Because the zoom level is set at *Fit slide to current window,* slide 2 appears on the screen.

Figure 1-9

Scroll tools

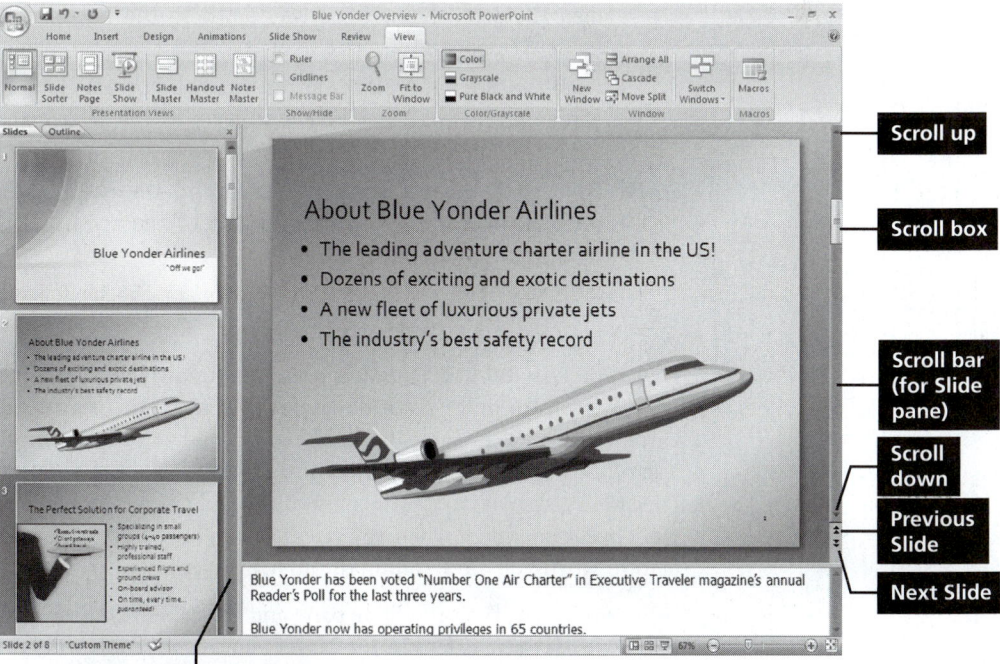

512 | Lesson 1

TAKE NOTE

The current slide's number always appears in the lower-left corner of the status bar.

2. Change the zoom level to 100%, then click the **scroll down** button twice. Because the slide is now larger than the Slide pane, the scroll button scrolls the slide down in small increments instead of jumping to the next slide.
3. Click the **Fit to Window** button on the Ribbon.
4. At the bottom of the scroll bar, click the **Next Slide** button twice. Slide 3 appears, then slide 4 appears.
5. In the Slides tab of the Slides/Outline pane, click slide 5. The selected slide appears in the Slide pane, as shown in Figure 1-10.

Figure 1-10

You can click a slide's picture on the Slides tab to jump to that slide

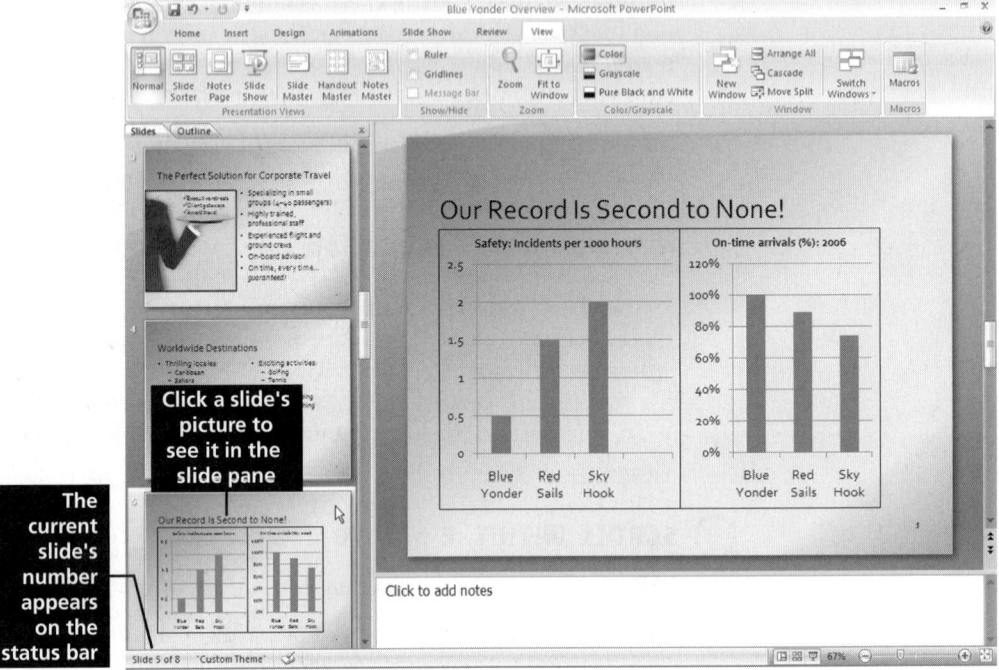

6. Point to the **scroll box** that appears to the right of the Slides/Outline pane, then drag the scroll box all the way down to the bottom of the scroll bar. The last slide (slide 8) appears on the Slides tab, but slide 5 remains visible in the Slide pane.
7. Click the **Previous Slide** button (at the bottom right of the Slide pane, as shown earlier in Figure 1-9). Slide 4 appears in the Slide pane; notice that the slide also appears highlighted on the Slides tab.
8. Point to the **scroll box** that appears to the right of the Slide pane, then drag the scroll box all the way up to the top of the scroll bar. You return to the beginning of the presentation.

   PAUSE. LEAVE the presentation open for the next exercise.

PowerPoint's scroll bars let you move up and down through your presentation. Click the scroll buttons to move up or down one line at a time or one slide at a time, depending on the current zoom level. Click and hold a scroll button to move more quickly. You can also drag a scroll box to move even more quickly. When you drag the scroll box in the Slide pane, PowerPoint displays a ScreenTip with the slide number and slide title to show you which slide will appear on screen when you release the mouse button. The scroll box's ScreenTip is helpful when you are scrolling through a presentation with a lot of slides.

In Normal view, both the Slide pane and the Slides/Outline pane have scroll bars, buttons, and boxes. If there is text in the Notes pane, scroll tools will appear there to let you move up and down through the text, if necessary. In Slide Sorter view and Notes Page view, scroll tools will appear on the right side of the window if they are needed.

In Normal view, you can click the Previous Slide button to move up to the previous slide and click the Next Slide button to move to the following slide.

NAVIGATE A PRESENTATION FROM THE KEYBOARD

USE the presentation that is open from the previous exercise.

1. With slide 1 visible in the Slide pane, press ↓ on your keyboard. Slide 2 appears.
2. Press **Page Down** to jump to slide 3.
3. Press → to jump to slide 4.
4. Press **Page Up** to go back to slide 3.
5. Press ← to move up to slide 2.
6. Press ↑ to view slide 1.
7. Press **End** to jump to slide 8, the last slide in the presentation.
8. Press **Home** to return to slide 1.

   PAUSE. LEAVE the presentation open to use in the next exercise.

Your keyboard's cursor control keys let you jump from one slide to another, as long as no text or object is selected on a slide. If text is selected, the arrow keys move the insertion point within the text; however, the Page Up, Page Down, Home, and End keys will still let you move from slide to slide.

Working with Text

> It is easy to add text to a slide. In most slides, text is contained in boxes called placeholders. You can work with text directly in a placeholder, or you can use the Outline tab. PowerPoint offers many of the same editing and formatting tools found in Microsoft Word. In the following exercises, you will practice adding text to a placeholder; adding text to the Outline tab; selecting, replacing, and deleting text on a slide; and copying and moving text from one slide to another.

ADD TEXT TO A TEXT PLACEHOLDER

USE the presentation that is open from the previous exercise.

1. Click the **Home** tab. On slide 1, click at the beginning of the slide's title (*Blue Yonder Airlines*). The borders of the title's placeholder appear, as shown in Figure 1-11, and a blinking insertion point appears before the word *Blue*.

Figure 1-11

The title placeholder and insertion point

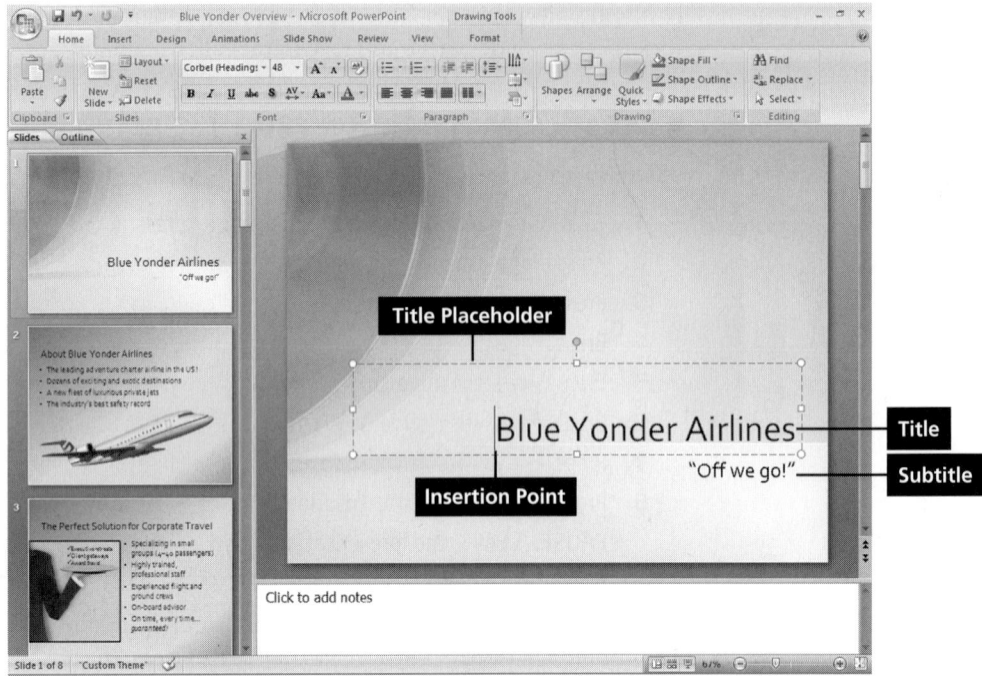

2. Click the slide's subtitle, which is the second line of text. The subtitle's placeholder appears, as does the insertion point.
3. Go to slide 4.
4. Click after the word *Snorkeling* in the second column. The insertion point appears.
5. Press [Enter] to start a new line, and key **Scuba**.
6. Press [Enter], then key **Sightseeing**. Your slide should look like the one shown in Figure 1-12.

Figure 1-12

Slide 4 with added text

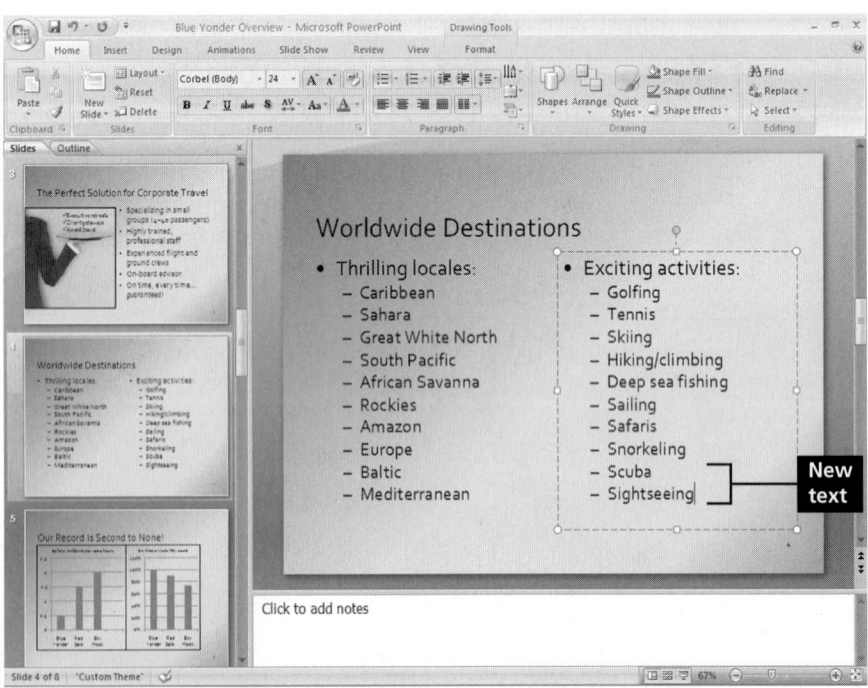

PAUSE. LEAVE the presentation open for the next exercise.

In this exercise, you practiced entering text in a ***placeholder***, which is a special box that holds text on a slide. (As you will see in upcoming lessons, placeholders can also hold objects such as pictures, tables, or charts.) Several types of slides, such as title slides, have text placeholders built into them. In the Blue Yonder presentation, slide 1 is an example of a title slide. A title slide almost always includes a title and a subtitle. Placeholders make it easy to add text—just click in the placeholder, then key the text.

➔ ADD TEXT ON THE OUTLINE TAB

USE the presentation that is open from the previous exercise.

1. Go to slide 8. This slide is supposed to contain contact information, but the mailing address and telephone number are missing.
2. In the Slides/Outline pane, click the **Outline** tab. Because slide 8 is the current slide, its text is highlighted on the tab.
3. On the Outline tab, click after the word *Airlines* to place the insertion point there.
4. Press **Enter** to start a new line.
5. On the new line, key **12 Ferris St.**, then press **Enter**. As you key the new text on the Outline tab, notice that it appears on the slide.
6. Key **Diehard, TN 34567**, then press **Enter**.
7. Key **(707) 555-AWAY**. Your slide should look like the one shown in Figure 1-13.

Figure 1-13

Text added to the Outline tab appears on the slide

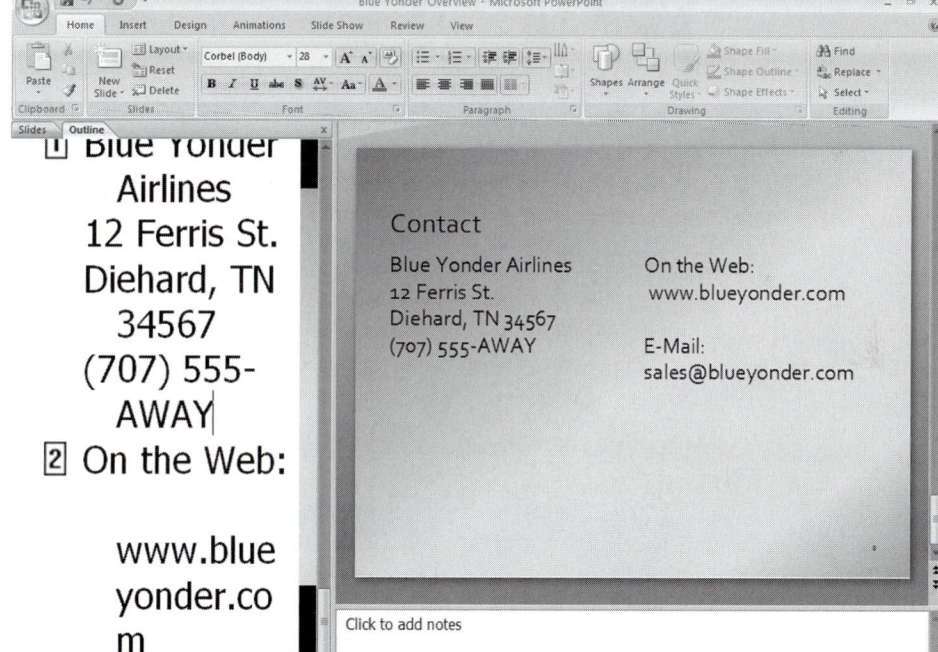

8. In the Slides/Outline pane, click the **Slides** tab.

PAUSE. LEAVE the presentation open for the next exercise.

Working on the Outline tab is like working in a word processor. PowerPoint displays the text from each slide on the Outline tab, without any backgrounds, placeholders, or anything else that might distract you from your writing. You can navigate a presentation on the Outline tab the same way you use the Slides tab—scroll to the desired slide's outline, then click it.

➔ SELECT, REPLACE, AND DELETE TEXT

USE the presentation that is open from the previous exercise.

1. Go to slide 3 and look at the right-hand column of text.
2. In the fourth item of the bulleted list, double-click the word *advisor* to select it, as shown in Figure 1-14.

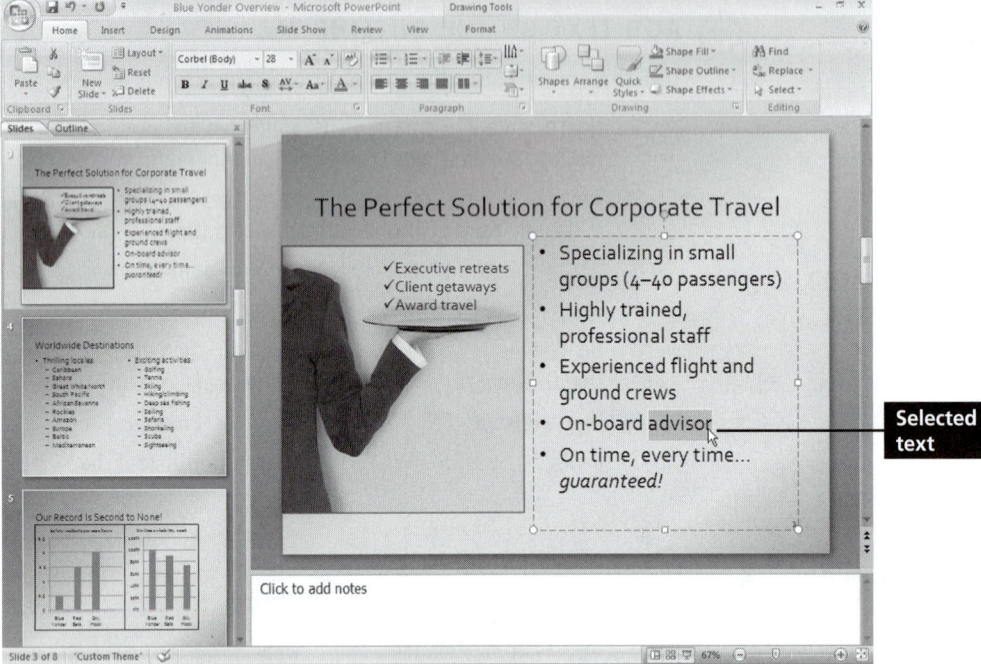

Figure 1-14

Selected text

3. While the text is selected, key **concierge**. The new text replaces the selected text.
4. Go to slide 7. This slide contains an unneeded word.
5. Select the word *ground* by dragging the mouse pointer over it. (The mouse pointer changes from an arrow to an I-beam whenever it is in a text placeholder, as shown in Figure 1-15.)

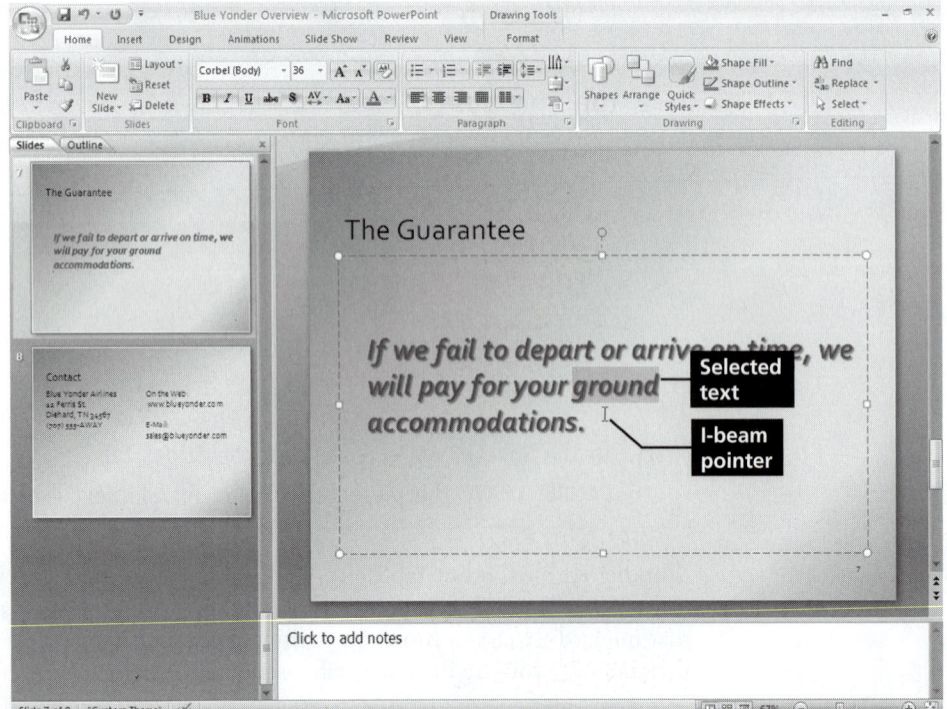

Figure 1-15

Selecting text and the I-beam pointer

PowerPoint Essentials | 517

   6. Press **Delete** to delete the word from the slide.

   PAUSE. LEAVE the presentation open for the next exercise.

As mentioned previously, working with text in PowerPoint is a lot like using a word processor. You can edit, replace, and delete text directly on a slide. First, you must select the text, to let PowerPoint know you want to edit it. You can select any amount of text by dragging the mouse pointer across it. When you move the mouse pointer over text, it changes to an *I-beam pointer*, a vertically oriented pointer that resembles the letter *I*. This pointer makes it easy to select text precisely. Whenever you select text in PowerPoint—whether it is a single character or all the text on a slide—it is highlighted with a colored background. Once the text is selected, you can type new text in its place or delete it.

COPY AND MOVE TEXT FROM ONE SLIDE TO ANOTHER

USE the presentation that is open from the previous exercise.

   1. Go to slide 2.
   2. In the slide's title placeholder, select B*lue Yonder Airline*s by dragging the mouse pointer across the text. You will make a copy of the selected text, then paste the copy into another slide.
   3. On the Home tab, click the **Copy** button, as shown in Figure 1-16.

You can issue the Copy command by pressing **Ctrl+C**.

Figure 1-16
The Clipboard tools

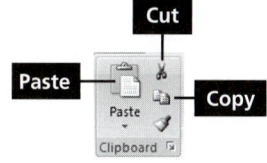

   4. Go to slide 7.
   5. Click between the two words of the title to place the insertion point before the word *Guarantee*.
   6. On the Home tab, click the **Paste** button. PowerPoint inserts the copied text at the insertion point's position, as shown in Figure 1-17. Press **Spacebar** if necessary to insert a space before the word *Guarantee*.

You can issue the Paste command by pressing **Ctrl+V**.

Figure 1-17
The selected text has been copied to slide 7

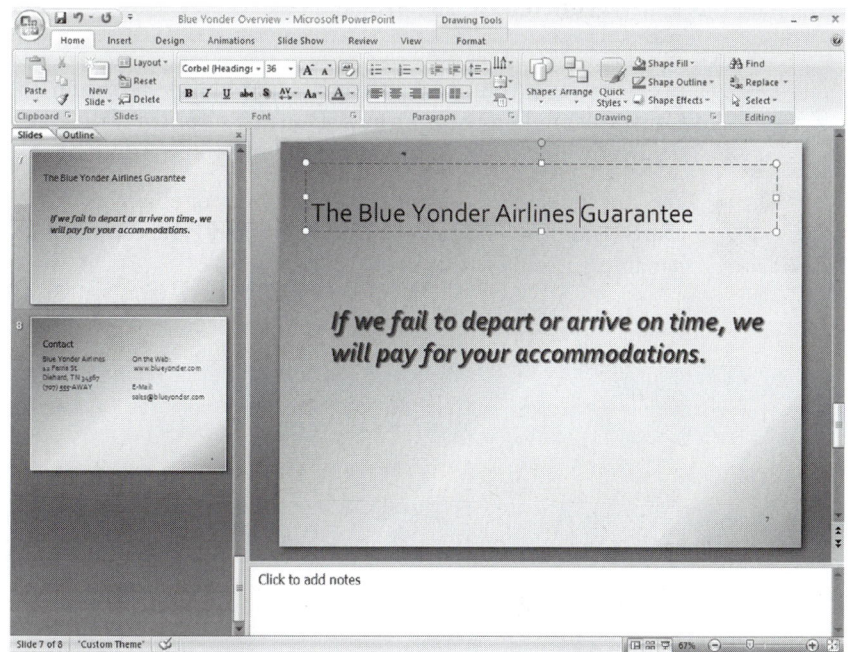

518 | Lesson 1

7. Go to slide 3.
8. Select the last item of the bulleted list, on the right side of the slide.
9. On the Home tab, click the **Cut** button. The selected item is removed from the list.
10. Go to slide 2.
11. Click below the last item of the bulleted list, just above the airplane's tail.
12. On the Home tab, click the **Paste** button. The item appears at the bottom of the list.
13. Click anywhere in the blank area around the slide to clear the placeholder's border from the screen. Your slide should look like the one shown in Figure 1-18.

You can issue the Cut command by pressing **Ctrl+X**.

Figure 1-18

The selected text has been moved to slide 2

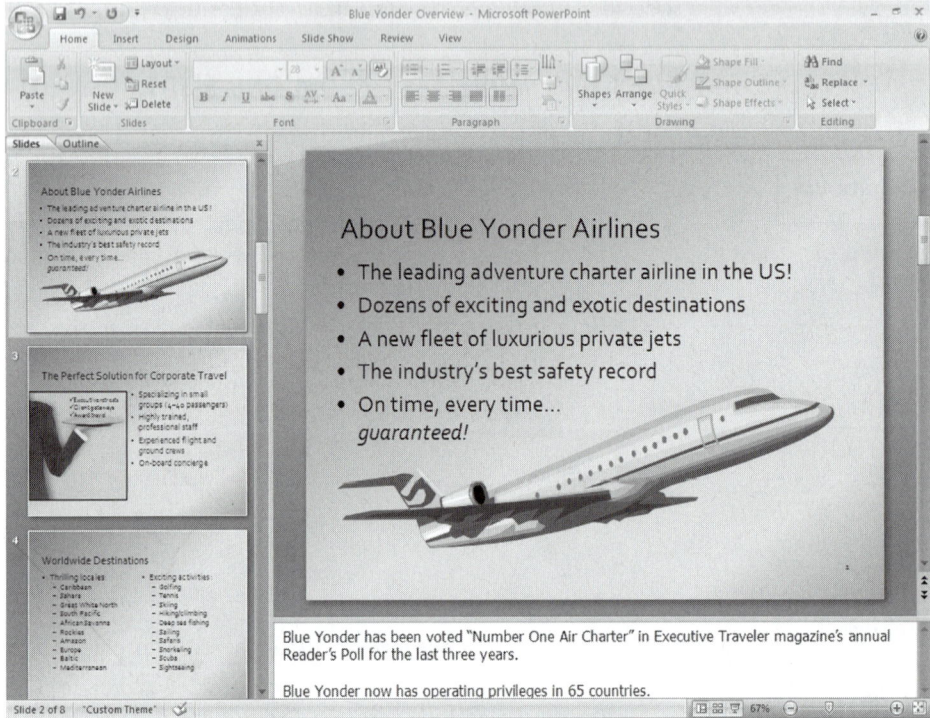

14. Save the presentation as **Blue Yonder Itroduction** and then **CLOSE** the file.
    STOP. CLOSE PowerPoint.

In this exercise, you practiced copying and moving text from one slide to another, using the Copy, Cut, and Paste commands. Don't be surprised if these commands become your most frequently used tools, because they can save you a great deal of typing.

You can use these commands on many kinds of objects in PowerPoint, including pictures, charts, and placeholders. The Cut, Copy, and Paste commands are used throughout the remaining lessons of this book.

CERTIFICATION READY?
How do you copy and move text from one slide to another slide?
2.3.2

SUMMARY SKILL MATRIX

IN THIS LESSON YOU LEARNED HOW TO:

View a Presentation in Different Ways

Use Zoom

Scroll with a Mouse

Navigate a Presentation from the Keyboard

Add Text to a Text Placeholder

Add Text on the Outline Tab

Select, Replace, and Delete Text

Copy and Move Text from One Slide to Another

Knowledge Assessment

Matching

Match the term in Column 1 to its description in Column 2.

Column 1		Column 2	
1. Ctrl + X	(c)	a.	includes the Slide, Notes, and Slide/Outline panes
2. Page Up key	(e)	b.	As you move it over text, the mouse pointer changes to this.
3. Normal view	(a)	c.	Cuts selected text
4. current slide	(g)	d.	to highlight text for editing
5. Slide Show view	(f)	e.	Moves to the previous slide in a presentation.
6. ScreenTip	(h)	f.	Allows you to preview a presentation on the screen.
7. placeholder	(j)	g.	the slide you are editing
8. Ctrl + V	(i)	h.	Displayed as you drag the scroll box in the Slide pane.
9. I-beam	(b)	i.	Pastes selected text.
10. select	(d)	j.	a box, built into many slides, that holds text or an object

True / False

Circle T if the statement is true or F if the statement is false.

T F 1. When you first start Microsoft Office PowerPoint, a blank slide will appear on the screen.

T F 2. The Slides, Slides/Outline, and Notes panes can all be resized.

T **F** 3. The view in PowerPoint can only be changed using commands found on the Ribbon.

T F 4. When adding text or graphics to a slide, it is best to work with just one slide at a time.

T **F** 5. When the Page Down button is pressed on the keyboard, the last slide in the presentation will appear.

T **F** 6. PowerPoint 2007 displays the same tools, regardless of the tasks you are performing.

T F 7. Pressing F5 will switch to Slide Show view.

T **F** 8. Viewing just one slide at a time allows you to rearrange slides in a presentation more easily.

T F 9. You can use the Cut and Paste commands to move text from one slide to another slide.

T **F** 10. In Normal view, PowerPoint displays five different panes for viewing different aspects of your slides.

■ Competency Assessment

Project 1-1: The Central City Job Fair

As personnel manager for Woodgrove Bank, you have accepted an invitation to give a presentation at a local job fair. Your goal is to recruit applicants for positions as bank tellers. You have created the presentation but need to finish it.

The *Job Fair* file is available on the companion CD-ROM.

GET READY. Launch PowerPoint if it is not already running.

1. Click the **Microsoft Office Button** and open the presentation named *Job Fair* from the data files for this lesson.
2. On slide 1, click in the subtitle box to place the insertion point there, then key **Central City Job Fair.** Go to slide 2.
3. In the title of slide 2, select the words *Woodgrove Bank* by dragging the mouse pointer over them, then replace the selected text by keying **Us**.
4. In the bulleted list, click after the word *assets* to place the insertion point there.
5. Press [Enter] to move the insertion point down to a new, blank line.
6. Key **Voted "Best Local Bank" by City Magazine, 2005.** The new text will wrap to fit in the box.
7. Click the **Next Slide** button to go to slide 3. In the slide's outline, select the words *Help Wanted* (do not select the colon), then press [Delete] to delete the text.
8. Key **Now Hiring**.
9. Click at the end of the first item in the bulleted list, then press [Enter] to create a new line in the list.
10. Key **Responsible for cash drawer and station bookkeeping**.
11. Click the **Slides** tab, then press [Page Down] to go to slide 4.
12. Select the last item in the bulleted list by dragging the mouse pointer across it.
13. On the Ribbon, click the **Home** tab, if necessary, then click the **Cut** button. On the Slides tab, click slide 5.

14. Click at the end of the last item in the bulleted list to place the insertion point there, then press **Enter**.
15. On the Ribbon, click the **Paste** button. The item you cut from slide 4 is pasted into slide 5.
16. **SAVE** the presentation as *Central City Job Fair* and then **CLOSE** the file.
    LEAVE PowerPoint open for the next project.

Project 1-2: Messenger Service

Consolidated Messenger is a new company offering in-town courier service to corporate and private customers. As the company's owner, you want to tell as many people as possible about your new service, and a presentation can help you do it. You need to review your presentation, make some minor changes, and print it.

The *Pitch* file is available on the companion CD-ROM.

1. Click the **Microsoft Office Button** and open the presentation named *Pitch* from the data files for this lesson.
2. Read slide 1. On the Slides tab, click slide 2 and read it.
3. Click the **scroll down** box to go to slide 3, then read it.
4. Click the **Next Slide** button to go to slide 4, then read it.
5. Press **Page Down** to go to slide 5, then read it.
6. Press ↓ to go to slide 6, then read it.
7. Press **Home** to return to the beginning of the presentation.
8. On slide 1, select the words *and Delivery* by dragging the mouse pointer over them.
9. Press **Delete** to delete the selected text from the subtitle. Go to slide 2.
10. On slide 2, select the word *delayed* and key **scheduled** in its place.
11. Select the third item in the bulleted list (*24-hour emergency service*) by dragging the mouse pointer over it.
12. On the Home tab of the Ribbon, click the **Copy** button. Go to slide 5.
13. On slide 5, click at the end of the last item in the bulleted list to place the insertion point there.
14. Press **Enter** to move the insertion point down to a new, blank line. On the Ribbon, click the **Paste** button.
15. Click at the end of the newly pasted line to move the insertion point there, then key **: $250**. Go to slide 6.
16. On slide 6, click at the end of the last line of text in the left-hand column, then press **Enter**.
17. Key **555-1087 (daytime)**, then press **Enter**.
18. Key **555-1088 (emergency)**, then press **Enter**.
19. Key **555-1089 (fax)**.
20. Go to slide 1. Click the **Microsoft Office Button**.
21. When the menu opens, point to **Print**, then click **Quick Print** to print the presentation.
22. **SAVE** the presentation as *Messenger Pitch* and then **CLOSE** the file.
    LEAVE PowerPoint open for the next project.

522 | Lesson 1

■ Proficiency Assessment

Project 1-3: The Big Meeting

You are the director of documentation at Litware, Inc., which develops software for use in elementary schools. You have scheduled a conference with the writing staff and are working on an agenda for the meeting. Because the agenda is a single PowerPoint slide, you can display it on a projection screen for reference during the meeting.

The *Agenda* file is available on the companion CD-ROM.

1. **OPEN** the *Agenda* file from the data files for this lesson.
2. Copy the second line of the bulleted list. Paste the copied item below the currently selected item.
3. In the newly pasted line, replace the word *Upcoming* with **Revised**.
4. On the Outline tab, add a new line to the end of the agenda. On the new line, key **Adjourn**.
5. Quick-print the presentation.
6. **SAVE** the presentation as *Final Agenda* and then **CLOSE** the file.

   LEAVE PowerPoint open for the next project.

Project 1-4: Job Fair, Part 2

You have decided to make some last-minute changes to your presentation before going to the job fair.

The *Central City Job Fair* file is available on the companion CD-ROM.

1. **OPEN** *Central City Job Fair* from the data files for this lesson.
2. Copy the word *Woodgrove* on slide 1. In the title of slide 2, delete the word *Us* and paste the copied word in its place.
3. On slide 2, change the word *owned* to **managed**.
4. On slide 4, add the line **References a must** to the bottom of the bulleted list.
5. Quick-print the presentation.
6. **SAVE** the presentation as *Final Job Fair* and then **CLOSE** the file.

   LEAVE PowerPoint open for the next project.

■ Mastery Assessment

Project 1-5: Price-Fixing

You are the general manager of the restaurant at Coho Winery. It's time to update the staff on the restaurant's new wine selections and prices, and a slide show is a good way to give everyone the details. An easy way to handle this job is to open last season's presentation and update it with new wines and prices.

The *Wine List* file is available on the companion CD-ROM.

1. **OPEN** *Wine List* from the data files for this lesson.
2. Move *Coho Premium Chardonnay - $29.99* from slide 2 to the bottom of slide 4.
3. On slide 3, increase the price of every wine by one dollar.
4. Quick-print the presentation.
5. **SAVE** the presentation as *New Wine List* and then **CLOSE** the file.

   LEAVE PowerPoint open for the next project.

Project 1-6: A Trip to Toyland

As a product manager for Tailspin Toys, you introduce new products to many other people in the company, such as the marketing and sales staff. You need to finalize a presentation about several new toys.

The *Toys* file is available on the companion CD-ROM.

1. **OPEN** *Toys* from the data files for this lesson.
2. Copy *List Price: $14.99* on slide 2 and paste it at the bottom of the bulleted lists on slides 3 and 4.
3. Change the teddy bear's name from *Rory* to **George**.
4. Change the top's speed from *800* to **1,200**.
5. Quick-print the presentation.
6. **SAVE** the presentation as *New Toys* and then **CLOSE** the file.
   STOP. CLOSE PowerPoint.

INTERNET READY

Use PowerPoint Help to access online information about *What's New in PowerPoint 2007. Up to Speed with PowerPoint 2007* provides a short online course or demo explaining the new features. Browse these or other topics in PowerPoint's Help online.

2 Presentation Basics

LESSON SKILL MATRIX

Opening a Blank Presentation — 526	Students will learn how to open a blank presentation.
Changing a Slide's Layout — 527	Students will learn how to change a slide's layout.
Adding Text to a Blank Slide — 529	Students will learn how to add text to a blank slide.
Choosing a Different File Format — 530	Students will learn how to choose a different file format.
Using a Template as the Basis for a Presentation — 531	Students will learn how to use a template as the basis for a presentation.
Adding a New Slide to a Presentation — 533	Students will learn how to add a new slide to a presentation.
Reusing a Slide from Another Presentation — 534	Students will learn how to reuse a slide from another presentation.
Creating a New Presentation from an Existing One — 536	Students will learn how to create a new presentation from an existing one.
Starting a Presentation from a Microsoft Office Word Outline — 537	Students will learn how to start a presentation from a Microsoft Office Word Outline.
Rearranging the Slides in a Presentation — 540	Students will learn how to rearrange the slides in a presentation.
Deleting a Slide — 540	Students will learn how to delete a slide.
Adding Notes to Your Slides — 542	Students will learn how to add notes to your slides.
Using Print Preview	Students will learn how to use Print Preview.
Setting Print Options	Students will learn how to set print options.
Printing a Presentation in Grayscale Mode	Students will learn how to print a presentation in grayscale mode.
Previewing a Presentation on the Screen — 549	Students will learn how to preview a presentation on the screen.

KEY TERMS
handout
indent level
layout
note
Presenter view
template
theme
thumbnails

Northwind Traders is a retailer of high-quality outdoor apparel and accessories for men, women, and children. The company has six stores in the Minneapolis–St. Paul area and a thriving online presence. As an assistant general manager, you help oversee the company's daily operations, hire and train new employees, and develop strategic plans. You also perform day-to-day functions assigned by the general manager. Your job frequently requires you to present information to an audience—for example, when training new workers on company policies or when providing executives with information about revenue or expenses. These duties often require you to create presentations from scratch, and PowerPoint 2007 lets you do that in several ways. In this lesson, you will learn different methods for creating presentations. You will also learn how to organize the slides in a presentation, add notes to your slides, select printing options, preview a slide show, and save a presentation for the first time.

■ Software Orientation

Microsoft PowerPoint's New Presentation Dialog Box

PowerPoint's New Presentation window gives you many choices for creating a new presentation. Figure 2-1 shows the New Presentation window.

Figure 2-1

The New Presentation window

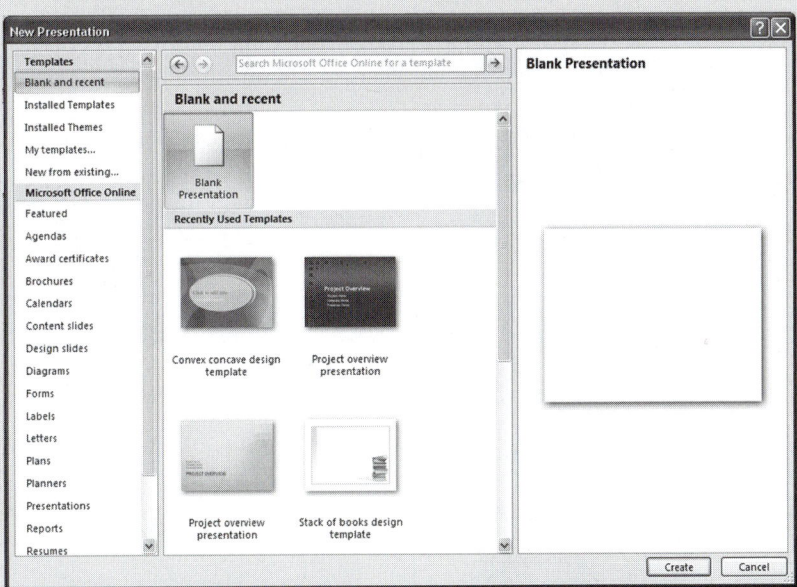

This window enables you to create a new, blank presentation; work from a template or theme stored on your computer; search for templates online; or create a new presentation from an existing one. (Note that if your copy of PowerPoint already has been used to create presentations, your screen may look somewhat different from Figure 2-1.)

Creating A New Blank Presentation

THE BOTTOM LINE The fastest and simplest way to create a new presentation is to start with a blank presentation. You can add text to the presentation, then format the slides later.

Opening a Blank Presentation

In the following exercises, you will create a short slide show from a blank presentation.

OPEN A BLANK PRESENTATION

GET READY. Before you begin these steps, be sure to launch Microsoft Office PowerPoint 2007.

1. Click the **Microsoft Office Button**.
2. Click **New**. The New Presentation window opens, as shown previously in Figure 2-1.

TAKE NOTE When you start PowerPoint, a new, blank slide appears. You can use that slide to create a new presentation. You need to use the New Presentation window only when another presentation is open or when no presentation is open.

3. Click the **Blank Presentation** icon, then click **Create**. A new, blank presentation appears in Normal view, as shown in Figure 2-2.

Figure 2-2

A blank presentation begins with a title slide

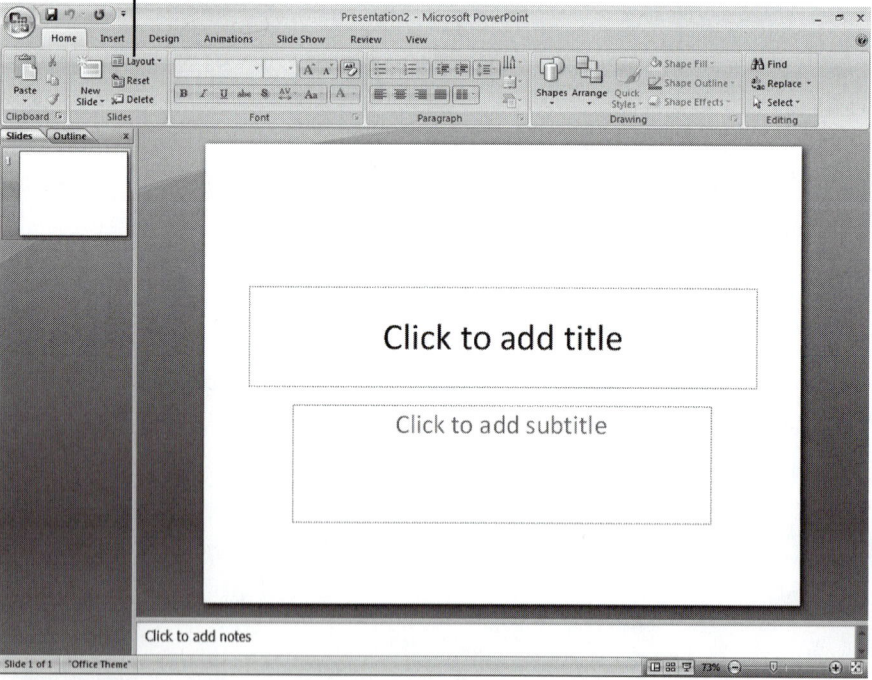

ANOTHER WAY Press **Ctrl+N** to open a new, blank presentation without using the New Presentation window. If another presentation is on the screen, the blank presentation opens on top of it.

PAUSE. LEAVE the blank presentation open to use in the next exercise.

There are two advantages to using a blank presentation to start a slide show. First, PowerPoint displays a blank presentation every time the program starts, so you always have immediate access to the first slide of a new presentation. Second, because the presentation is not formatted (meaning there are no backgrounds, colors, or pictures), you can focus on writing your text. Many experienced PowerPoint users prefer to start with a blank presentation because they know they can format their slides after the text is finished.

Changing a Slide's Layout

You can change a slide's layout at any time to arrange text or objects on the slide exactly the way you want. The following exercise shows you how to apply a different layout to the current slide.

CHOOSE A DIFFERENT LAYOUT

USE the new, blank presentation that is still open from the previous exercise.

1. Click the **Home** tab to make it active, if necessary, then click **Layout**. A drop-down menu (called a *gallery*) appears, displaying PowerPoint's default layouts, as shown in Figure 2-3.

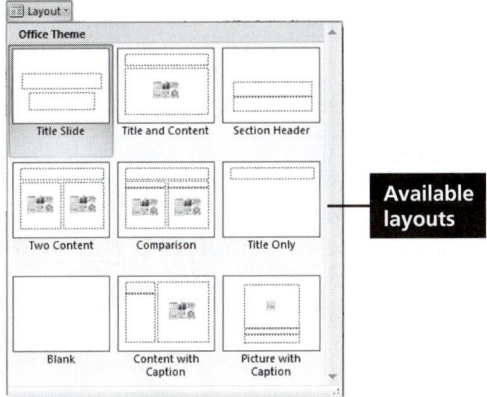

Figure 2-3

Choosing a new layout

 **ANOTHER WAY**

To change a slide's layout, right-click a blank area of the slide outside a placeholder. When the shortcut menu opens, click Layout, then click a layout.

2. Click **Title and Content**. The gallery closes and PowerPoint applies the chosen layout to the current slide, as shown in Figure 2-4.

Figure 2-4

The new layout applied to the current slide

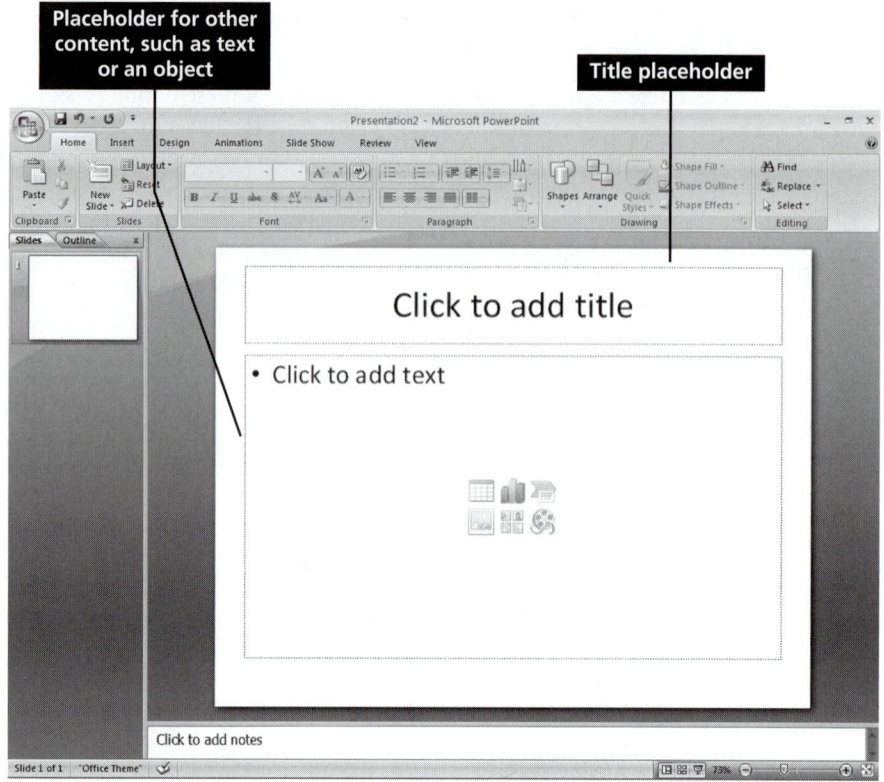

PAUSE. LEAVE the presentation open to use in the next exercise.

Most slides have a *layout*—a predefined arrangement of placeholders for text or objects (such as charts or pictures). PowerPoint has a variety of built-in layouts that you can use any time. Layouts are shown in the Layout gallery as *thumbnails*—small pictures showing each available layout. Choose the layout that is best suited to display the text or objects you want to place on the slide. In this exercise, you chose the Title and Content layout, which contains a placeholder for the slide's title and a second placeholder that can display text, a picture, a table, or some other kind of object.

You can change a slide's layout whether the slide is blank or contains text. If the slide already has text, PowerPoint will fit the text into the new layout's placeholders.

Adding Text to a Blank Slide

If a blank slide has one or more text placeholders, you can easily add text to the slide. In the following exercise, you will enter text into a blank slide's placeholders to create a set of discussion points for a meeting of store managers.

X REF

You will work with other slide layouts in Lesson 4.

ADD TEXT TO A BLANK SLIDE

USE the slide that is still on the screen from the preceding exercise.

1. Click the title placeholder at the top of the slide. The text *Click to add title* disappears and a blinking insertion point appears in the placeholder.
2. Key **Discussion Points**.
3. Click the text at the top of the lower placeholder. The words *Click to add text* disappear and the insertion point appears.

Presentation Basics | 529

TAKE NOTE

If you click any of the icons in the lower placeholder, PowerPoint will display tools for adding non-text content, such as a table or chart. These types of content are covered in later lessons.

4. Key **Customer surveys**, then press Enter to move the insertion point down to a new line.
5. Key **Inventory tracking** and press Enter.
6. Key **Absenteeism policy** and press Enter.
7. Key **Break** and press Enter.
8. Key **Store security** and press Enter.
9. Key **Store closing procedures** and press Enter.
10. Key **Cash drawer management**, then click anywhere in the blank area outside the placeholder to clear its borders from the screen. Your slide should look like the one shown in Figure 2-5.

Figure 2-5

The completed slide

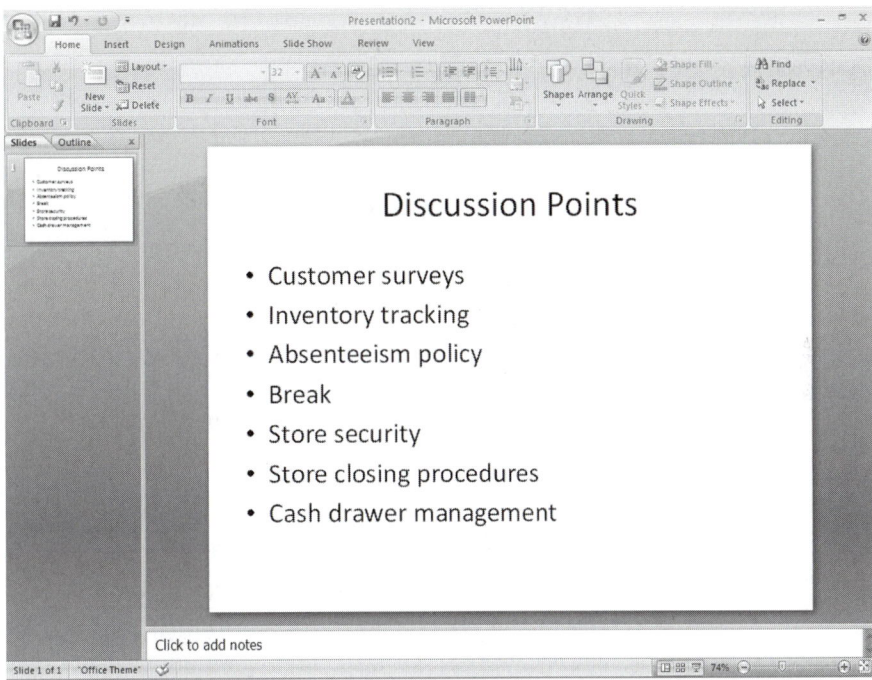

PAUSE. LEAVE the presentation open to use in the next exercise.

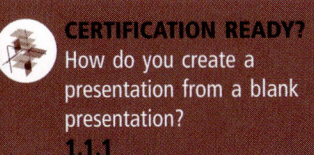

CERTIFICATION READY?
How do you create a presentation from a blank presentation?
1.1.1

In this exercise, you practiced adding text to a blank slide, creating a one-slide presentation that can be left on the screen for reference during a meeting. Even when a multiple-slide presentation is not needed at a meeting, displaying an agenda, a list of discussion points, or a list of breakout rooms can be helpful for the group.

PowerPoint makes it easy to add text to a slide with built-in text placeholders. In this exercise, the slide has a title placeholder and a content placeholder that can hold text and other types of content. To enter text, just click the sample text in the placeholder, then type your text.

■ Saving a Presentation with a Different File Format

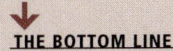

THE BOTTOM LINE

If you want to keep a presentation, you must save it on a disk. The following exercises show you how to save a new presentation to a disk in a different file format.

Choosing a Different File Format

PowerPoint can save presentations in several different file formats. In this exercise, you will save your presentation in a format that is compatible with earlier versions of PowerPoint.

⊖ **CHOOSE A DIFFERENT FILE FORMAT**

USE the presentation that is still open from the previous exercise.

1. Click the **Microsoft Office Button**, then point to the **Save As** command. A submenu of options appears.
2. On the submenu, click **PowerPoint 97-2003 Presentation**, as shown in Figure 2-6. The Save As box opens.

Figure 2-6

PowerPoint's Save As options

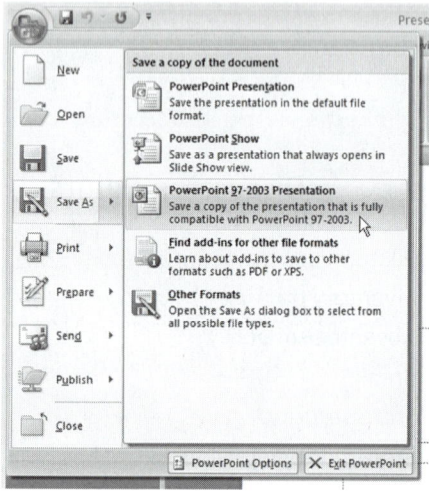

3. Navigate to the folder where you want to save your files.
4. In the File name box, key **Old Format Discussion Points**.
5. Look at the Save as type box. Notice that the PowerPoint 97-2003 file format is already selected. Click the drop-down arrow at the right end of the box to view other available file formats, as shown in Figure 2-7.

Figure 2-7

Viewing formats for saving presentations

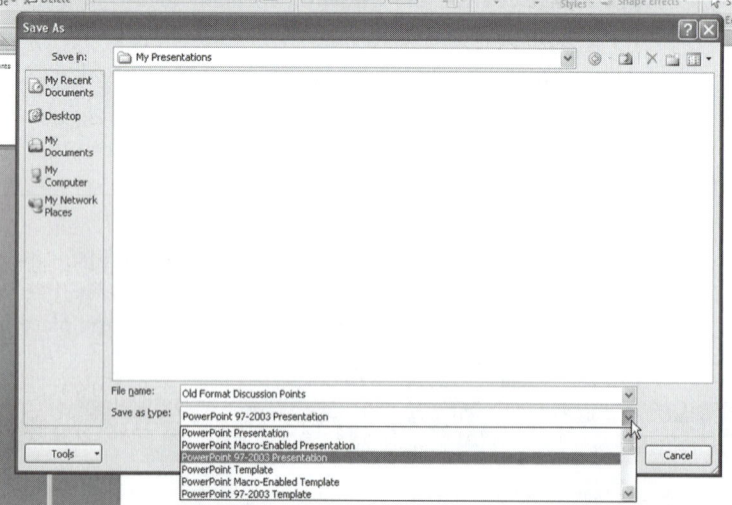

6. Because the desired format is already selected, click in the blank area to the right of the Save as type box to close the drop-down list.
7. Click **Save**, then **CLOSE** the file.

PAUSE. LEAVE PowerPoint open to use in the next exercise.

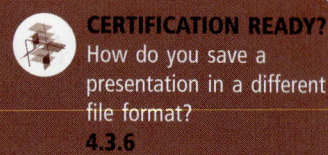

CERTIFICATION READY?
How do you save a presentation in a different file format?
4.3.6

Presentation Basics | 531

By default, PowerPoint 2007 saves presentations in XML format, which is not compatible with earlier versions of PowerPoint. If you want to be able to use a presentation with an older version of PowerPoint, you can save it by using the PowerPoint 97-2003 Presentation file format.

You can save a presentation in other formats, as well. For example, if you select the PowerPoint Show format, the presentation will always open in Slide Show view, rather than in Normal view. You can also save a presentation as a template or save it so that special built-in commands called macros are enabled.

■ Creating a Presentation from a Template

THE BOTTOM LINE

PowerPoint's templates give you a jump start to creating complete presentations. A template is a pre-designed presentation that includes backgrounds, fonts, and other design elements. You can insert your own text and objects (such as charts or pictures) and build a finished presentation very quickly.

Using a Template as the Basis for a Presentation

PowerPoint has several built-in templates, and you can create your own templates or download new ones from Microsoft Office Online. In this exercise, you will use a built-in template to start a presentation that, when finished, will help you show pictures and descriptions of new products to a group of store managers.

➔ CREATE A PRESENTATION FROM A TEMPLATE

1. Click the **Microsoft Office Button**.
2. Click **New** to open the New Presentation window.
3. Under Templates, click **Installed Templates**. A menu of PowerPoint's built-in templates appears in the center of the New Presentation window, as shown in Figure 2-8.

Figure 2-8

Selecting an installed template

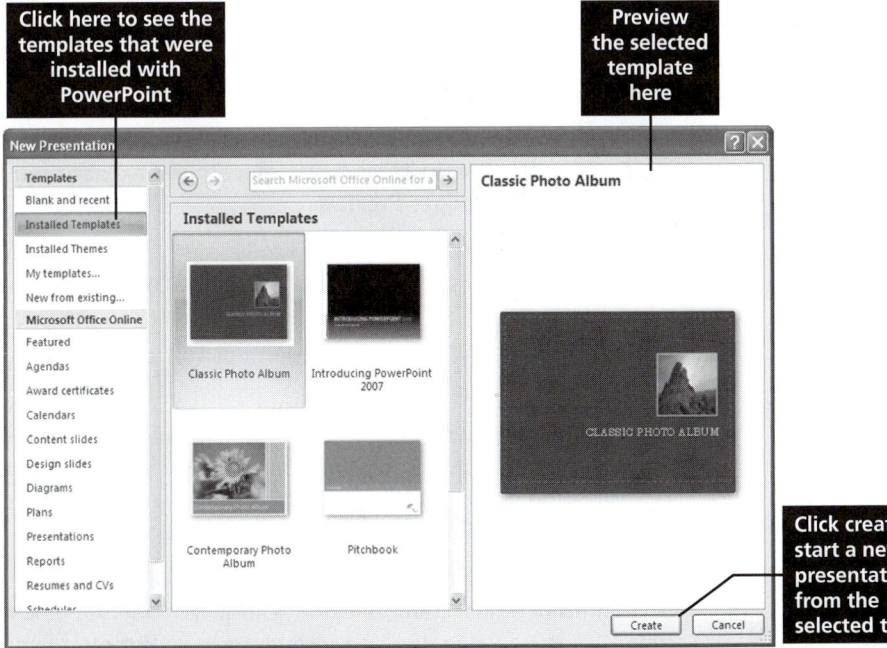

4. Click **Classic Photo Album**, then click **Create**. PowerPoint opens a new presentation based on the selected template.

> **TAKE NOTE**
>
> If none of the installed templates suits your needs, download one from Office Online. In the New Presentation window, click one of the categories under Microsoft Office Online. Select a template in the center of the window to preview it. If you like it, click Download. The template appears in the PowerPoint window, ready to edit.

5. On the Zoom control, click the **Fit slide to current window** button. Your screen should look like the one shown in Figure 2-9.

Figure 2-9

A new presentation based on the Classic Photo Album template

6. On slide 1, select the type CLASSIC PHOTO ALBUM and replace it with **NORTHWIND TRADERS**.
7. Click the text in the subtitle placeholder to place the insertion point there, then key **New Product Preview**.
8. On the Quick Access Toolbar, click **Save**. The Save As dialog box appears.
9. Navigate to the folder where you want to save your files, then save the presentation with the file name *New Product Preview*.

PAUSE. LEAVE the presentation open to use in the next exercise.

A ***template*** is a predesigned presentation that includes a background, layouts, coordinating fonts, and other elements that work together to create an attractive finished slide show. Most templates also have a ***theme***, which is a color scheme with complementing colors for the backgrounds, bullets, text, borders, and other parts of the presentation.

PowerPoint's templates, however, are more than just formatting. They can help you decide what kinds of information to add to your presentations. Some templates contain just one slide—for example, to display a meeting agenda. But most templates include multiple slides that are set up to hold specific combinations of content. For example, one slide may be ready to display pictures and descriptions, another might hold a chart and a bulleted list, and another might contain a table. Such templates often display instructions that tell you what kind of information to place in each slide.

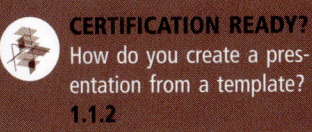

CERTIFICATION READY?
How do you create a presentation from a template?
1.1.2

You can choose from many different templates. A few templates are included with PowerPoint, but you can find many more on Office Online.

It is important to choose a template that is appropriate for your audience and your message. If you need to deliver business information to a group of managers, for example, choose a template that looks professional and does not have elements that will distract the audience from getting your message. Conversely, a whimsical template might work better for a group of young people.

Adding a New Slide to a Presentation

You can add as many new slides as you want to a presentation. The following exercise shows you how to insert a new slide into the current presentation.

➔ ADD A NEW SLIDE

USE the presentation that is still open from the previous exercise.

1. With slide 1 still selected, make sure that the Home tab is active.
2. Click the drop-down arrow under the **New Slide** button. A gallery opens, showing thumbnail images of the slide layouts that are available for this template, as shown in Figure 2-10.

Figure 2-10
The New Slide gallery

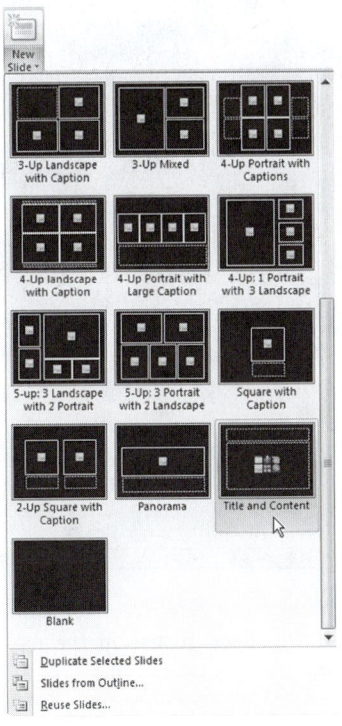

3. Scroll down to the bottom of the gallery, then click **Title and Content**.

TAKE NOTE
To view the New Slide gallery, you must click the New Slide button's drop-down arrow. If you click the New Slide button, PowerPoint will insert the default new slide for the current template.

4. On the new slide, click the title placeholder and key **THIS YEAR'S NEW PRODUCTS**.
5. Click the sample text at the top of the second placeholder, then key the following items, placing each item on its own line:

   Women's jackets
   Men's jackets
   Boots
   Backpacks
   Flannel shirts
   Fleece
   Turtlenecks
   Underwear
   Socks

6. Click in the area surrounding the slide to clear the placeholder's border. When you are done, your slide should look like the one shown in Figure 2-11.

Figure 2-11

The inserted slide

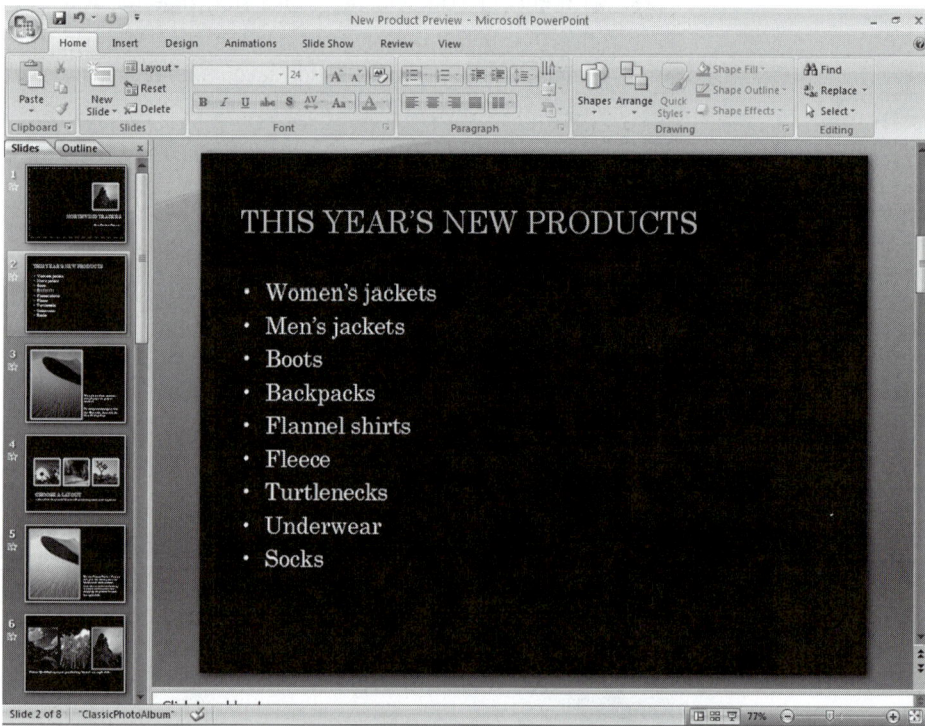

PAUSE. LEAVE the presentation open to use in the next exercise.

Reusing a Slide from Another Presentation

It is easy to reuse a slide from one presentation in another. This technique frees you from creating the same slide from scratch more than once. The following exercise shows you how to locate a slide from a different presentation and insert it into the current presentation.

➔ REUSE A SLIDE FROM A DIFFERENT PRESENTATION

USE the presentation that is still open from the previous exercise.

1. Click the drop-down arrow under the **New Slide** button. At the bottom of the gallery, click **Reuse Slides**. The Reuse Slides task pane opens on the right side of the PowerPoint window, as shown in Figure 2-12.

Figure 2-12

The Reuse Slides task pane

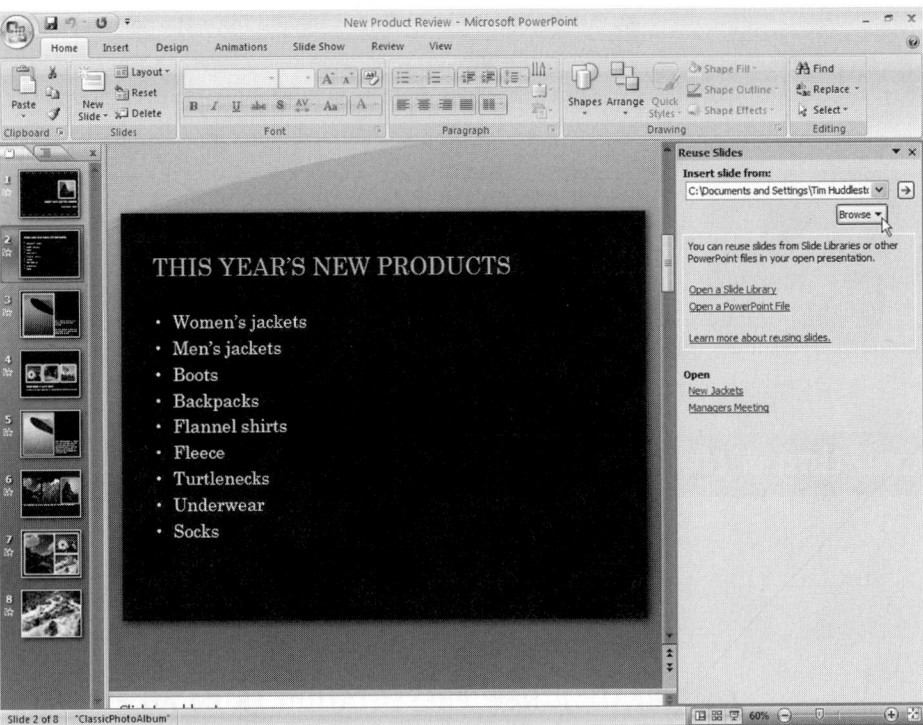

The *New Jackets* file is available on the companion CD-ROM.

2. In the task pane, click the **Browse** button. A drop-down list opens. Click **Browse File**. The Browse dialog box opens.

3. Locate and open *New Jackets*. The presentation's slides appear in the task pane, as shown in Figure 2-13.

Figure 2-13

Selecting a slide to reuse in the New Product Preview presentation

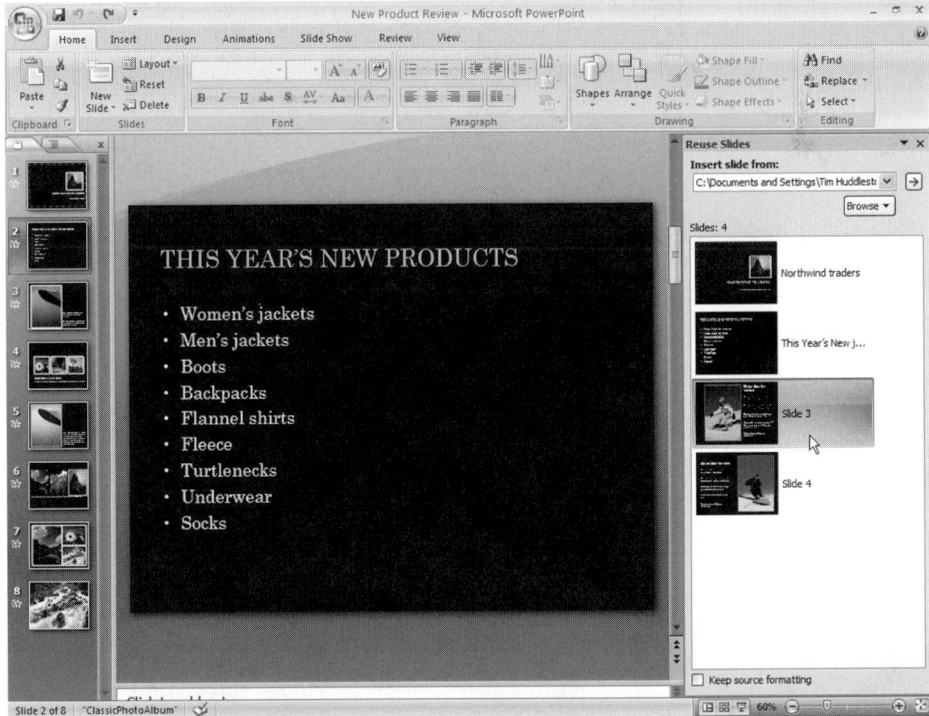

4. In the task pane, click slide 3. The slide is inserted into the *New Product Preview* presentation.
5. Click the **Close** button in the upper-right corner of the task pane.
6. **SAVE** and **CLOSE** the *New Product Preview* presentation.

    PAUSE. LEAVE PowerPoint open to use in the next exercise.

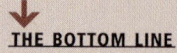

CERTIFICATION READY?
How do you reuse a slide from one presentation in another presentation?
2.3.1

Over time, you will probably create many presentations, and some of them may share common information. The Reuse Slide command lets you copy slides from one presentation to another. By copying finished slides in this manner, you can avoid re-creating similar slides over and over again.

■ Creating a New Presentation from an Existing One

THE BOTTOM LINE

You don't need to start a new presentation from scratch if you have already created another one that is similar. Instead, you can use the existing presentation as the basis for the new one.

→ CREATE A NEW PRESENTATION FROM AN EXISTING ONE

1. Click the **Office Button**.
2. Click **New** to open the New Presentation window.
3. Under Templates, click **New from existing**. The New from Existing Presentation dialog box opens, as shown in Figure 2-14.

Figure 2-14

The New from Existing Presentation dialog box

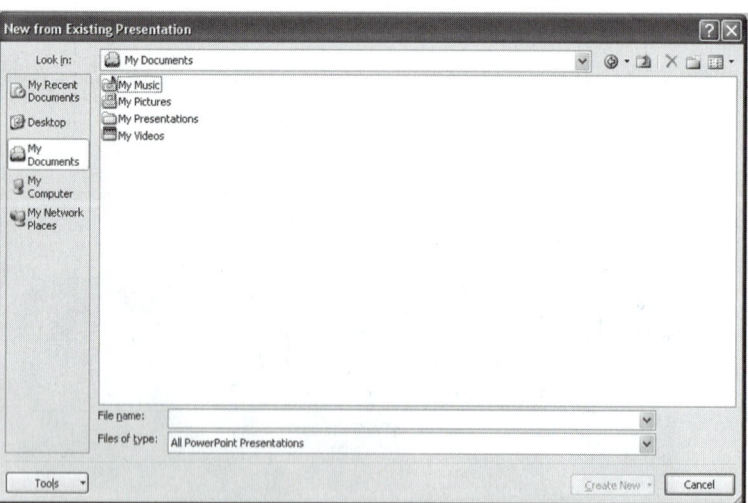

CD

The *Cashier Training* file is available on the companion CD-ROM.

4. Locate and open *Cashier Training*.
5. Look at PowerPoint's title bar, at the top of the screen. Notice that the presentation's name does not appear there. You can now save this presentation as though you just created it from scratch.
6. On the Quick Access Toolbar, click **Save**. The Save As dialog box appears.
7. **SAVE** the presentation as *Phone Sales Training*. You can now edit the slides as needed to suit a different audience or message.
8. **CLOSE** the file without making any changes to it.

    PAUSE. LEAVE PowerPoint open to use in the next exercise.

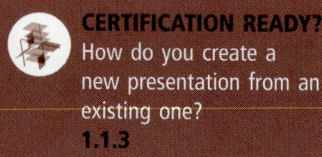

CERTIFICATION READY?
How do you create a new presentation from an existing one?
1.1.3

Starting a Presentation from a Microsoft Word Outline

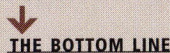
THE BOTTOM LINE

You can use text created in another application (such as Microsoft Word) as the basis for a new presentation. In the following exercises, you create a new presentation, then add content from a Microsoft Word outline. You also learn how to change the indent levels of items in a list.

➔ START A PRESENTATION FROM A WORD OUTLINE

1. Click the **Microsoft Office Button**.
2. Click **New** to open the New Presentation window.
3. Click **Create**. A new, blank title slide appears in the PowerPoint window.
4. Click in the slide's title placeholder, then key **Computer Use Policy**.
5. Click in the subtitle placeholder, then key **Northwind Traders**.

TAKE NOTE

Don't worry if a wavy red line appears under some words, such as *Northwind*. This is PowerPoint's spelling checker telling you that the word may be misspelled. To clear the underlining, right-click the word, then click Ignore All. PowerPoint will ignore the word from now on.

6. Click outside the text placeholder to clear its border.
7. On the Ribbon's Home tab, click the **New Slide** drop-down arrow. At the bottom of the gallery of slide layouts, click **Slides from Outline**. The Insert Outline dialog box appears, as shown in Figure 2-15.

Figure 2-15

The Insert Outline dialog box

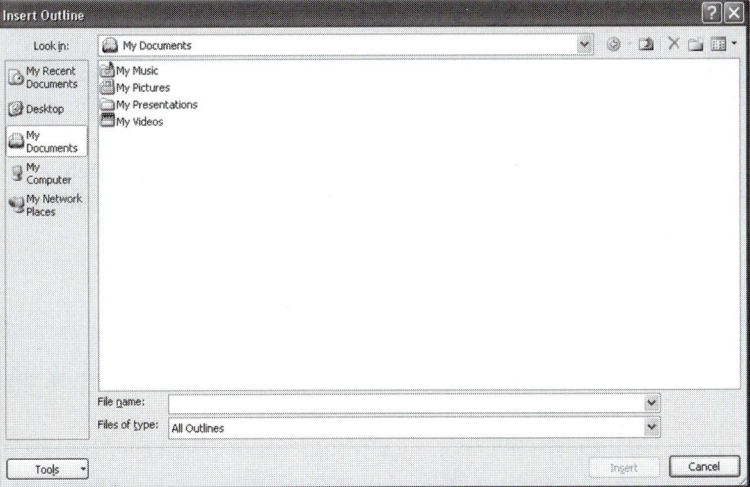

CD

The *Computer Use Policy* file is available on the companion CD-ROM.

8. Locate and select the Microsoft Word document named **Computer Use Policy**. Click **Insert**. PowerPoint imports the text from the outline and uses it to create five new slides, as shown in Figure 2-16.

Figure 2-16

New slides created from a Word outline

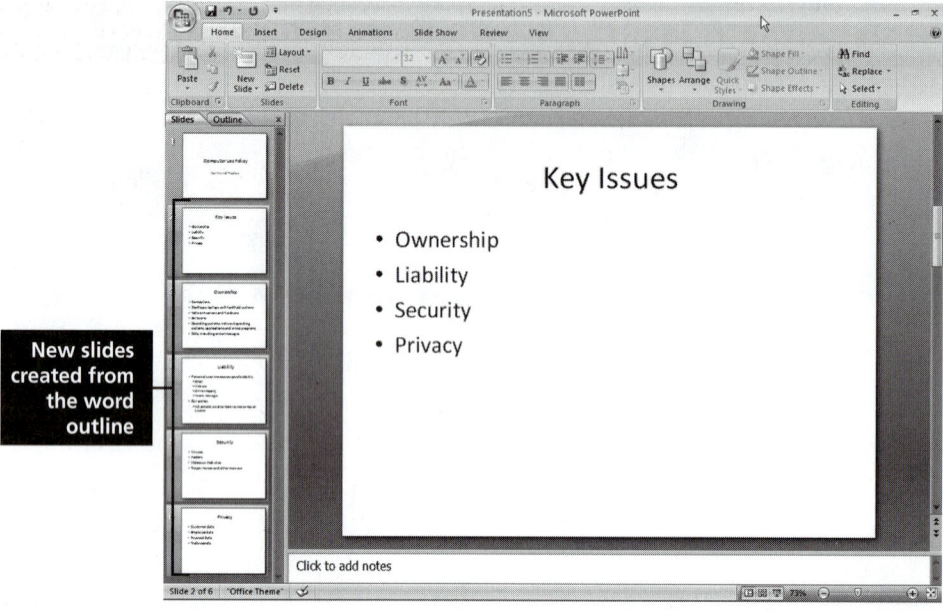

ANOTHER WAY

You can also create a presentation from an outline by opening a properly formatted Word outline in PowerPoint. Click the Microsoft Office Button, then click Open. In the Open dialog box, click the Files of type drop-down arrow, then click All Files. Select the outline, then click Open.

9. Press **Home** to return to slide 1, then navigate through the slides to see them all. When you have seen all the slides, go to slide 3.

   PAUSE. LEAVE the presentation open to use in the next exercise.

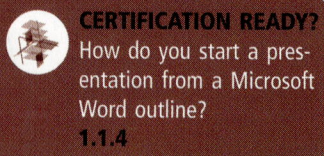

CERTIFICATION READY?
How do you start a presentation from a Microsoft Word outline?
1.1.4

If you create an outline in Microsoft Word, you can import it into PowerPoint and generate slides from it. Before you can create slides from a Word outline, the outline must be formatted correctly. Paragraphs formatted with Word's Heading 1 style become slide titles. Paragraphs formatted with subheading styles (such as Heading 2 or Heading 3) are converted into bulleted lists in the slides' subtitle placeholders.

CHANGE INDENT LEVELS IN A LIST

USE the presentation that is still open from the previous exercise.

1. With slide 3 still selected, click the second line of the bulleted list (*Desktops, laptops and handheld systems*).
2. On the Ribbon, click the **Increase List Level** button. In the list, the line's indent increases, making it subordinate to the preceding line (*Computers:*), as shown in Figure 2-17.

Figure 2-17

Increasing the indent of an item in a list

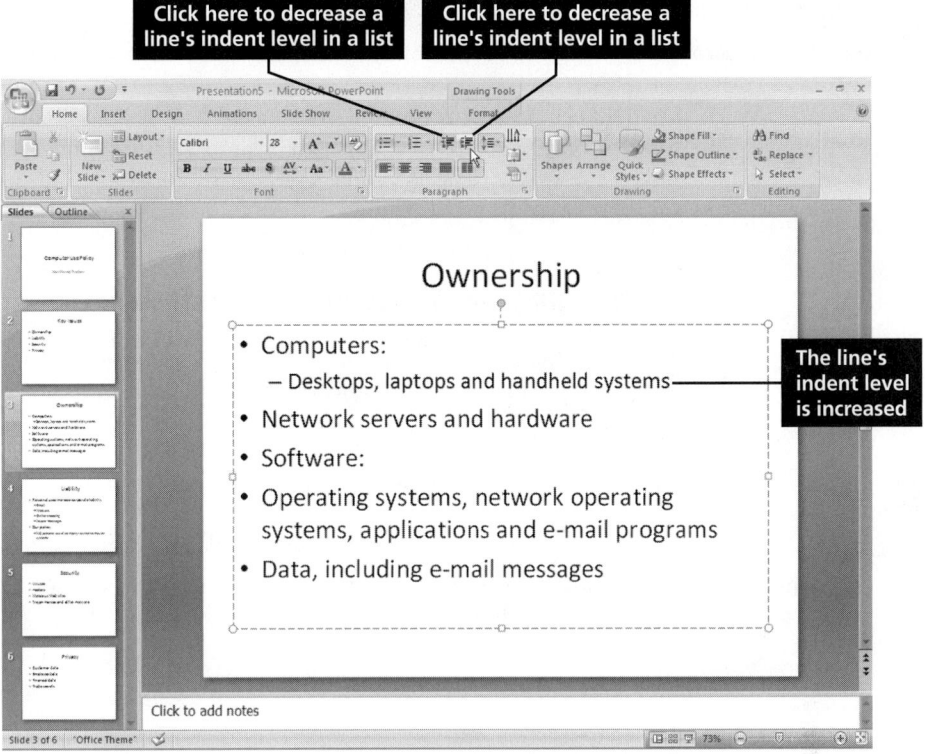

3. Click the next line in the list (*Network servers and hardware*), then click the **Increase List Level** button.

 **ANOTHER WAY** You can click the Repeat button on the Quick Access Toolbar to repeat the last action you took.

4. In the Slides/Outline pane, click the **Outline** tab. On the Outline tab, notice that all the text from slide 3 is highlighted.
5. Click just outside the highlighting to clear it from the text, then select the last two bulleted items by dragging the mouse pointer across them.
6. Click the **Increase List Level** button to increase the indent level of the two selected items.
7. In the Slides/Outline pane, click the **Slides** tab.
8. On the Quick Access Toolbar, click **Save**. The Save As dialog box appears.
9. **SAVE** the presentation as *Computer Use Policy*, then **CLOSE** the file.
   PAUSE. LEAVE PowerPoint open to use in the next exercise.

Just like the headings in a book's outline, some of the items in a list are superior while others are subordinate. In a PowerPoint slide, the relationship between items in a list is shown by indent level. An item's ***indent level*** is the distance it is indented from the placeholder's left border. Superior items are indented less than subordinate ones. You can change the indent level of an item in a list by using the Decrease List Level and Increase List Level buttons on the Home tab of the Ribbon.

Another way to increase a paragraph's indent level is to press Tab at the beginning of a line. To reduce a paragraph's indent level (called *outdenting*), press Shift+Tab. This method is especially helpful when you are keying text, because you don't have to remove your fingers from the keyboard to click a button to change indent levels.

■ Organizing Your Slides

THE BOTTOM LINE

As you work on a presentation, you may decide that some of the slides need to be in different places. PowerPoint makes it easy to view multiple slides and move them to different positions. The following exercises show you how to rearrange the slides in a presentation and how to remove a slide from a presentation.

Rearranging the Slides in a Presentation

You can reorganize your slides in either Normal view or Slide Sorter view. Moving a slide is a simple procedure, as you will learn in the following exercise.

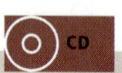

→ REARRANGE THE SLIDES IN A PRESENTATION

1. Locate and open the *Management Values* presentation.
2. Switch to Slide Sorter view. The presentation's slides appear together in a single window, as shown in Figure 2-18.

The *Management Values* file is available on the companion CD-ROM.

Figure 2-18

Viewing the presentation in Slide Sorter view

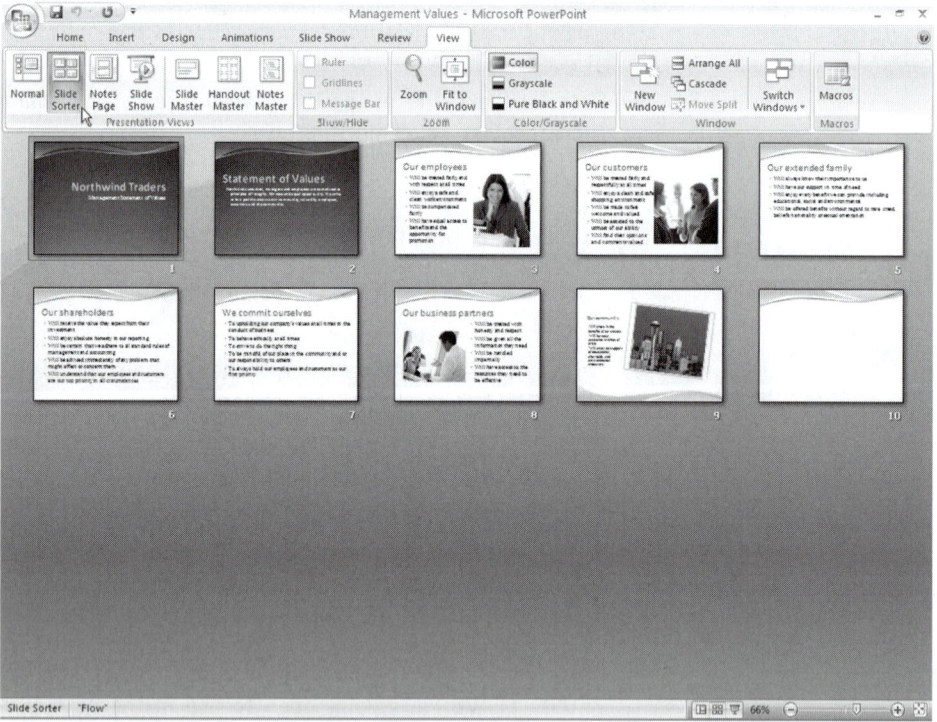

3. Click slide 5 and drag it to the left. When a vertical line appears between slides 3 and 4 (as shown in Figure 2-19), release the mouse button. The moved slide is now slide 4.

Figure 2-19

Moving a slide in Slide Sorter view

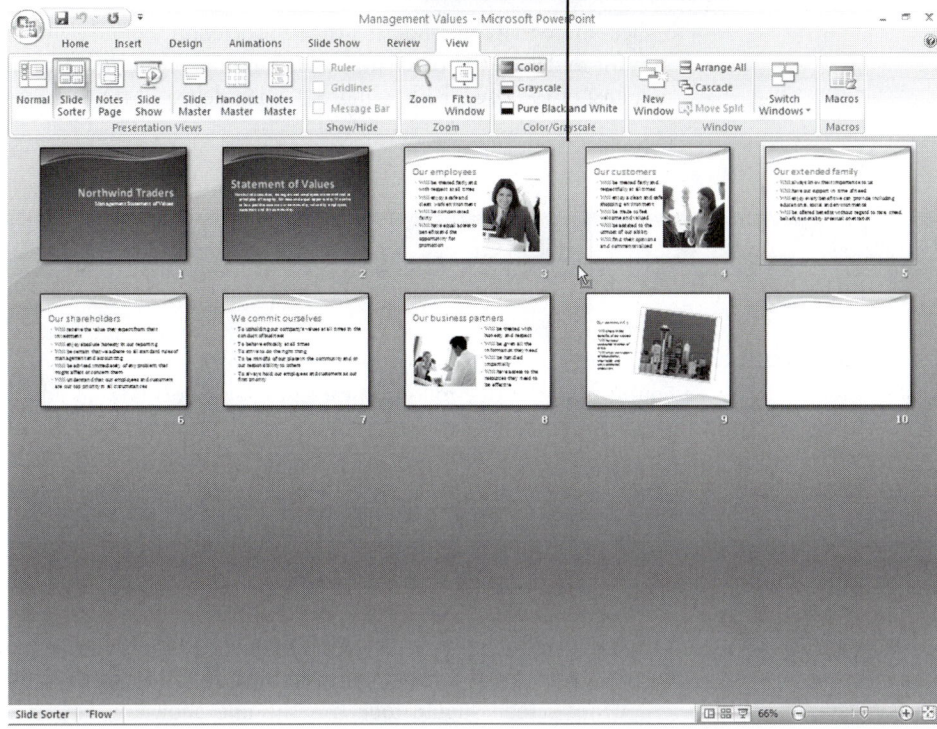

4. Click slide 7 and drag it to the right. When a vertical line appears between slides 9 and 10, release the mouse button. The moved slide is now slide 9.

 You can also drag slides to new positions in the Slides tab (Normal view). Click a slide and drag it up or down in the tab, then drop it where you want it.

PAUSE. LEAVE the presentation open to use in the next exercise.

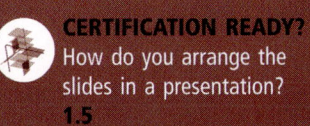

CERTIFICATION READY?
How do you arrange the slides in a presentation?
1.5

It is important to organize your slides so they best support your message. In PowerPoint, reorganizing slides is a simple drag-and-drop procedure. In Slide Sorter view (or on the Slides tab in Normal view), you can click a slide and drag it to a new location in the presentation. A line shows you where the slide will be placed when you drop it.

Deleting a Slide

When you don't want to keep a slide in a presentation, you can delete it. The following exercise shows you how.

➔ DELETE A SLIDE

USE the presentation that is still open from the previous exercise.

1. In Slide Sorter view, click slide 10.
2. On the Ribbon, click the **Home** tab to activate it, if necessary.
3. In the Slides group, click the **Delete** button. The selected slide is removed from the presentation.
4. **SAVE** the presentation as *New Management Values*.

   PAUSE. LEAVE the presentation open to use in the next exercise.

You can also delete a selected slide by pressing **Delete**.

PowerPoint does not ask whether you are sure if you want to delete a slide, so it's important to be careful before deleting. If you accidentally delete a slide, click the Undo button right away to bring the slide back.

To select more than one slide at a time for deletion, hold down the Ctrl key and click each slide you want to delete. (If you change your mind, you can deselect the selected slides by clicking in a blank area of the PowerPoint window.) Then delete all the selected slides at the same time.

■ Adding Notes to Your Slides

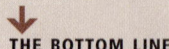
THE BOTTOM LINE

A note is a piece of additional information you associate with a slide. Notes do not appear on the screen when you show your presentation to an audience, but you can view notes in a couple of ways. The following exercises show you how to add notes to your slides.

 ADD NOTES IN THE NOTES PANE

USE the presentation that is still open from the previous exercise.

1. Switch to Normal view, then go to slide 2.
2. Click in the Notes pane (below the Slide pane) to place the insertion point there.
3. In the Notes pane, key **All Northwind employees are required to sign a statement of values, which binds them to ethical behavior on the job.** Your screen should look like the one shown in Figure 2-20.

> **ANOTHER WAY**
>
> You can move from one pane to another in Normal view by pressing **F6**.

Figure 2-20

Adding a note in the Notes pane

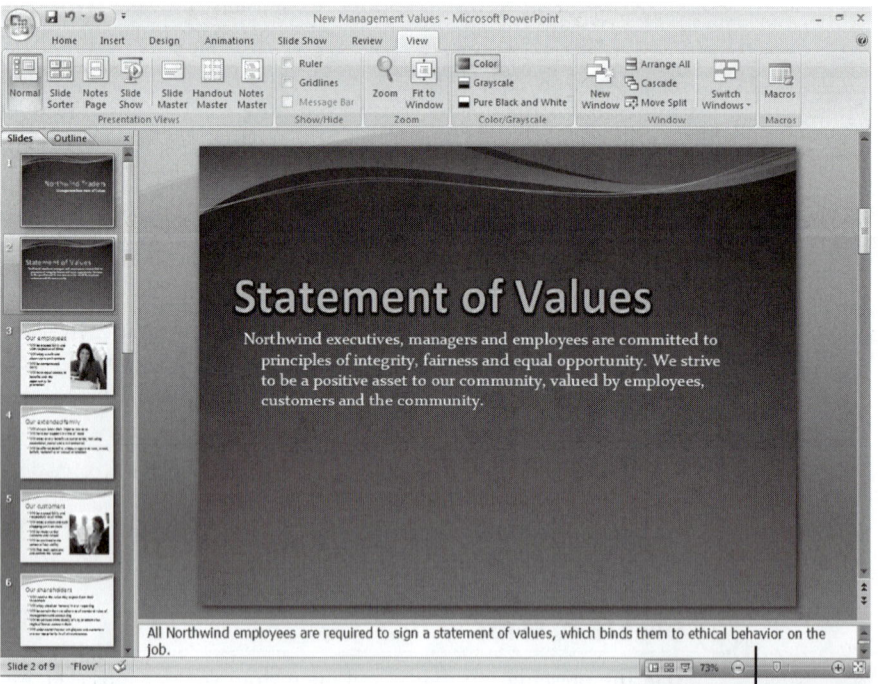

> **TAKE NOTE**
>
> You can edit and delete text in the Notes pane just as you can in the Slide pane or on the Outline tab. Select text with the mouse pointer; use the **Delete** and **Backspace** keys to delete text.

4. **SAVE** the presentation.

   PAUSE. LEAVE the presentation open to use in the next exercise.

Notes are extra information that might not fit on a slide, but which the presenter wants to tell the audience as they view the slide. Suppose, for example, you are using a chart to show financial data to the audience but do not have room on the slide for a lot of details. You can add those details as notes, and they will remind you to share the details with your audience during your presentation.

Notes do not appear on the screen in Slide Show view, so the audience does not see them. You can see your notes by printing them or by using PowerPoint's **Presenter view**. Presenter view lets you use two monitors when delivering your presentation to an audience. One monitor displays your slides in Slide Show view. You can use the second monitor to view your notes, among other things.

➜ ADD NOTES IN NOTES PAGE VIEW

USE the presentation that is still open from the previous exercise.

1. Switch to Notes Page view. On the scroll bar, click **Next Slide** to go to slide 3. Your screen should look like the one shown in Figure 2-21.

Figure 2-21

Viewing a slide and its notes in Notes Page view

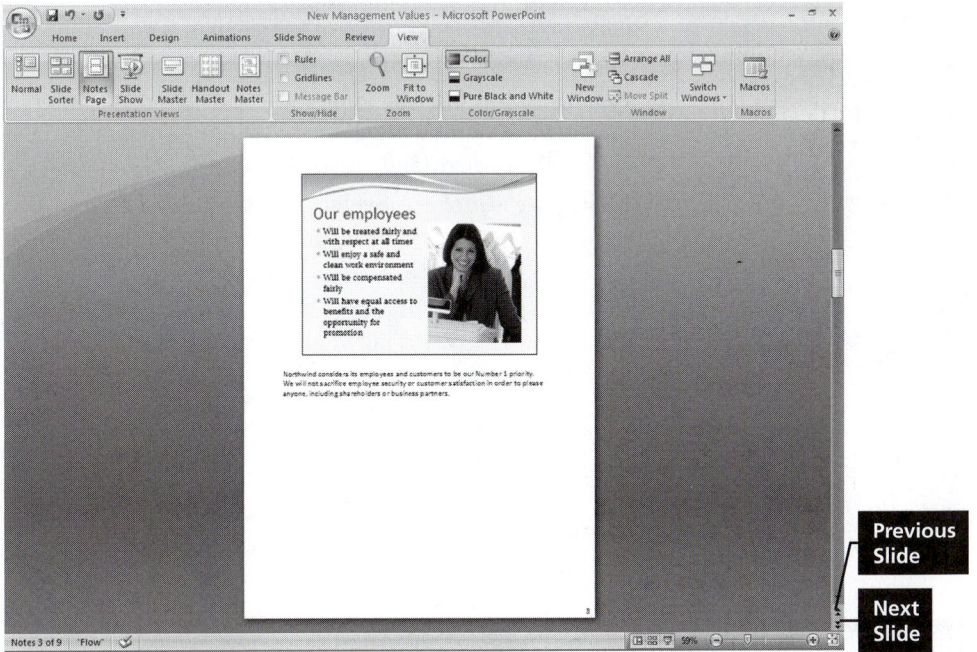

2. Go to slide 5. Click in the notes placeholder (below the slide) to place the insertion point there.
3. In the notes placeholder, key **All Northwind employees receive special training in customer relations.**
4. **SAVE** the presentation.

   PAUSE. LEAVE the presentation open to use in the next exercise.

> **TAKE NOTE**
>
> If your slides' content is too small to read in Notes Page view, use the Zoom control to enlarge the view.

Notes Page view is a special view that displays each slide along with its associated notes. Each slide and its notes appear on a white background; the content is sized as it would appear when printed on a standard sheet of paper. You can view and edit notes directly in the note placeholder, which is located below the slide.

Workplace Ready

Presenting with a Purpose

Many professionals have experienced "death by PowerPoint." They can tell you what it's like to sit through a presentation that is boring or too long and will usually tell you that the presenter did not understand how to use slides effectively. But an ineffective presentation can be worse than dull; it can actually prevent your audience from getting your message.

The following guidelines will help you (and your audience) get the most from a slide show:

- **Be brief:** Make only one major point per slide, using only a few bullets to support that point. A presentation should include only enough slides to support its major points.
- **Write concisely:** Keep your text short; sentence fragments work well on slides.
- **Focus on content:** Formatting is nice, but too much formatting can overwhelm the text and obscure your message.
- **Keep graphics relevant:** A nice picture can enhance a slide's meaning; a chart or table may support your point better than words alone. But use graphics only where they are needed.
- **Be consistent:** Use the same fonts, background, and colors throughout the presentation. If you use different design elements on each slide, your audience will become distracted (and maybe irritated).
- **Make sure slides are readable:** Ask someone else to review your slides before you show them to your audience. Make sure the reviewer can read all the text and see the graphics clearly.
- **Practice, practice, practice:** Never deliver a presentation "cold." Practice running the slide show and delivering your comments along with it. Practice your spoken parts out loud. Be sure to work on your timing, so you know just how long to keep each slide on the screen before going to the next one. Ask someone to watch you practice and offer feedback.

Printing a Presentation

THE BOTTOM LINE

PowerPoint gives you many options for printing your slides. In the following exercises, you learn how to preview a presentation before printing it, how to choose a printer, how to set print options, and how to print a presentation in both color and grayscale mode.

Using Print Preview

PowerPoint's Print Preview feature shows you how your slides will look on paper before you print them. This exercise shows you how to use Print Preview.

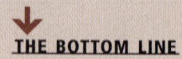
USE PRINT PREVIEW

USE the presentation that is still open from the previous exercise.

1. Go to slide 1. Click the **Microsoft Office Button**. When the menu appears, point to **Print**, then click **Print Preview**. The presentation's first slide appears in the Print Preview window, as shown in Figure 2-22.

Figure 2-22

Viewing a presentation in Print Preview

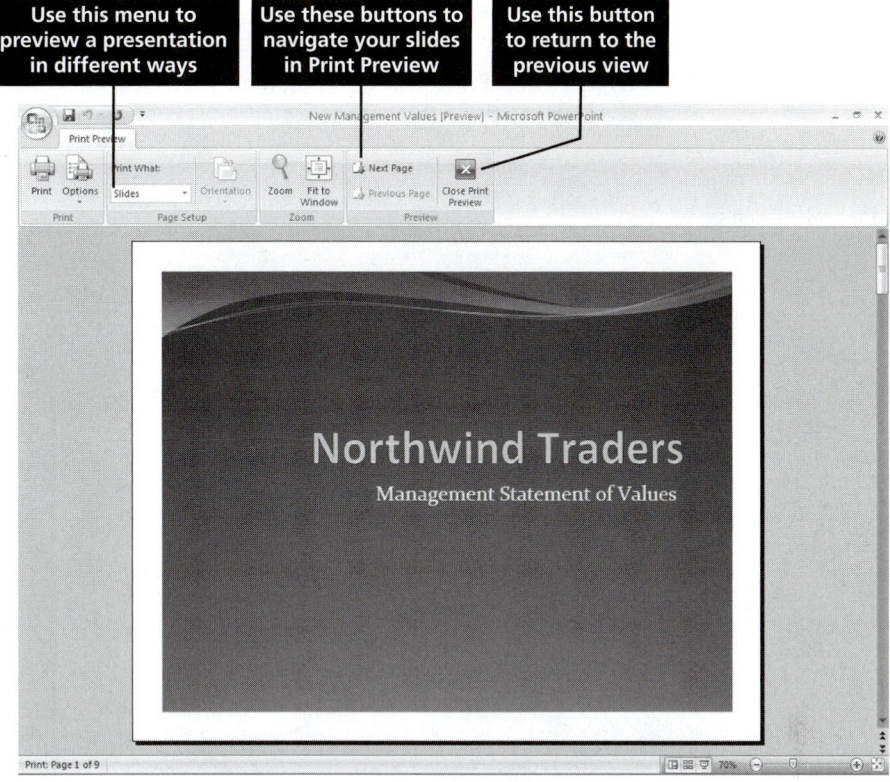

> **TAKE NOTE**
>
> If you are using a black-and-white printer, Print Preview will display your slides in grayscale.

2. On the Print Preview tab, click the **Next Page** button eight times to view each slide in the presentation. Then press the **Home** key to return to slide 1.
3. Click the **Print What** drop-down arrow, then click **Handouts (2 Slides Per Page)**. PowerPoint shows you how a printed handout would appear with two slides printed on each page, as shown in Figure 2-23.

Figure 2-23

Previewing a handout with two slides per page

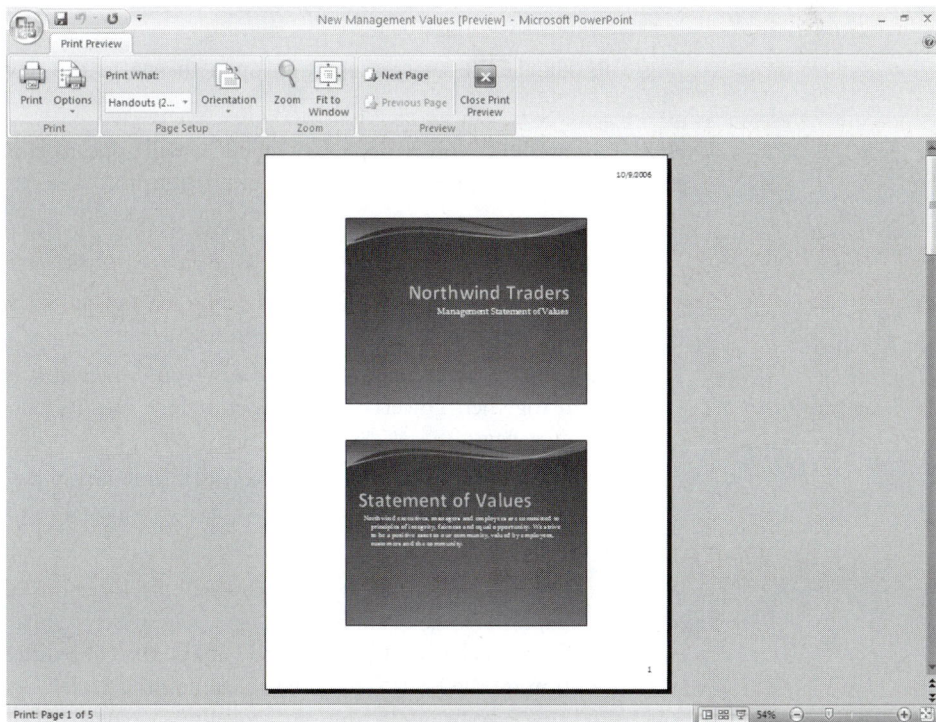

4. Click the **Print What** drop-down arrow, then click **Notes Pages**. PowerPoint shows you how your notes pages will appear when printed.
5. Click the **Print What** drop-down arrow, then click **Outline View**. PowerPoint displays the outline as it would appear when printed, as shown in Figure 2-24.

Figure 2-24

Previewing the presentation's outline

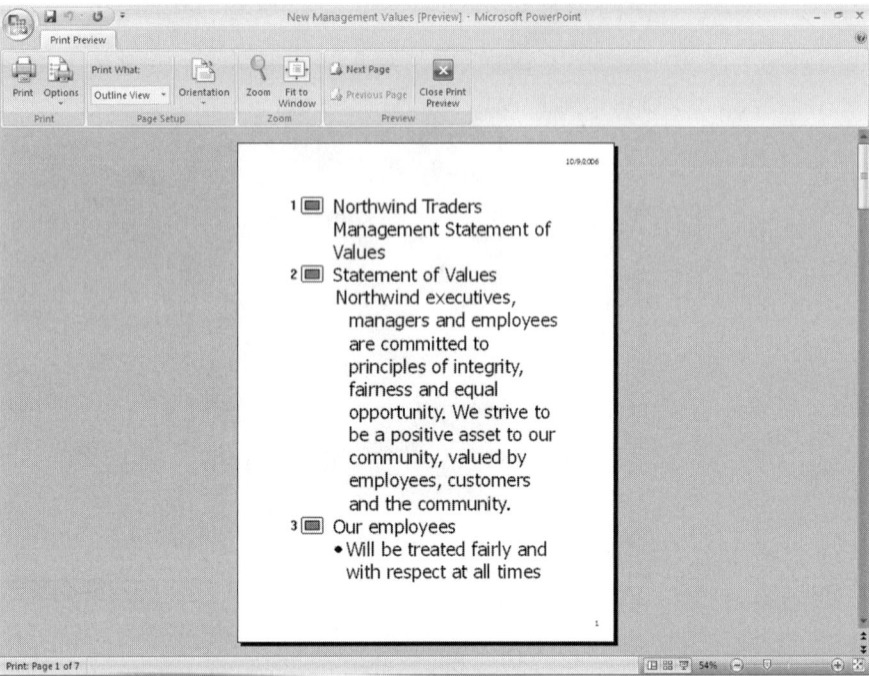

TAKE NOTE

If the preview does not fit in the window, use the Zoom button or the Fit slide to current window button on the Print Preview tab to change the magnification. These tools function in Print Preview just as they do in Normal view.

6. Click the **Close Print Preview** button to return to Notes Page view.
7. Switch to Normal view.

   PAUSE. LEAVE the presentation open to use in the next exercise.

Print Preview allows you to see how your slides will appear before you print them. You can preview and print a presentation in several different formats:

- **Slides:** When you select this option, PowerPoint shows you how the slides will look when printed one per page, using your current print settings.
- **Handouts:** A *handout* is a printed copy of your slides, which you can give to the audience. You can print handouts with up to nine slides on each sheet.
- **Notes Pages:** This view shows you how your slides and notes will appear when printed together. PowerPoint prints each slide and its associated notes on an individual page.
- **Outline View:** PowerPoint allows you to print only the text (the outline) of your presentation, without any graphics. This view shows you how the outline will appear when printed.

If you are using a color printer, Print Preview will display your slides in color mode, showing all colors and graphics. To save ink, however, you may want to print your slides in grayscale or black and white. To check the presentation's appearance in a different color mode, click the Options button on the Print Preview tab, then point to Color/Grayscale; a submenu of options appears. Click the color mode you want, and Print Preview will display the slides in that mode.

Presentation Basics | 547

Setting Print Options

PowerPoint lets you set a number of attributes before printing a presentation. The following exercise shows you how to set some of these printing options.

→ SET PRINT OPTIONS

USE the presentation that is still open from the previous exercise.

1. Click the **Microsoft Office Button**. When the menu appears, point to Print, then click Print. The Print dialog box appears, as shown in Figure 2-25.

Figure 2-25

The Print dialog box

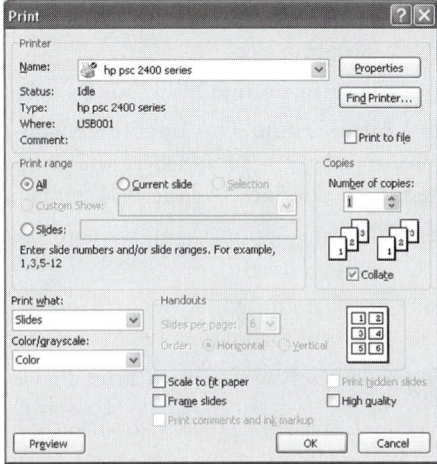

Press **Ctrl+P** to open the Print dialog box.

2. To select a different printer, click the **Name** drop-down arrow, then click the name of the printer you want to use.
3. In the Print range group, click the **All** option button if it is not already selected.
4. Click the **Print what** drop-down arrow, then click **Handouts**. Notice that the Handouts group becomes available.
5. In the Handouts group, click the **Slides per page** drop-down arrow, then click **2**.
6. Click the **Color/grayscale** drop-down arrow and click **Color**, if it is not already selected.
7. If the **Frame slides** check box is selected, click it to deselect it.
8. Click **OK**. PowerPoint prints your presentation, using the options you just selected.

PAUSE. LEAVE the presentation open to use in the next exercise.

The Print dialog box provides an array of options that help you print your presentations exactly the way you want. You can select a printer by choosing one from the Name drop-down list or choose properties that are specific to your chosen printer by clicking the Properties button. The Find Printer button helps you locate a printer that is attached to your computer or network but which does not appear in the Name list.

The Print range group lets you determine how many of the slides to print:

- **All:** Prints all the slides in the presentation.
- **Current slide:** Prints only the slide that is currently active on the screen.
- **Slides:** Prints only the slides you specify. For example, if you want to print only the first four slides of your presentation, click the Slides option button, then key 1-4 in the text box. If you want to print only the first and third slides, key 1,3 in the box.

TAKE NOTE

When you set printing options and then save your presentation, the options are saved as well.

The Copies group lets you determine how many copies of the presentation (or selected slides) to print. Click the Number of copies spinner control to set the number of copies. By default, PowerPoint collates multiple copies when printing. If you do not want the copies to be collated, clear the Collate check box.

Use the Print what drop-down list to determine how to print your presentation. You can print a presentation as slides only, handouts with multiple slides per page, notes pages, or outline.

The Color/grayscale drop-down list lets you set the color mode for printing. The following exercise shows you how to use this tool.

The Print dialog box offers the following options as well:

- **Scale to fit paper:** If your printer uses odd size sheets, this option tells PowerPoint to scale the slides to fit on the paper.
- **Frame slides:** This option prints a fine black border around each slide.
- **Print comments and ink markup:** This option lets you print out any comments and handwritten notes that have been added to the presentation. The option is not available if the presentation does not include comments or markups.
- **Print hidden slides:** Click this option if you want to include hidden slides in the printout.
- **High quality:** If your slides are formatted with shadows under text or graphics, choose this option to print the shadows.
- **Preview:** This button switches PowerPoint to Print Preview mode.

X REF

Comments are covered in Lesson 9.

Printing a Presentation in Grayscale Mode

Grayscale mode lets you print a presentation without color. This setting can save time and reduce your use of colored ink or toner.

➔ **PRINT A PRESENTATION IN GRAYSCALE MODE**

USE the presentation that is still open from the previous exercise.

1. Click the **Microsoft Office Button**. When the menu appears, point to **Print**, then click **Print**. The Print dialog box appears.
2. Click the **Color/grayscale** drop-down arrow, then click **Grayscale**.
3. Click **OK**. PowerPoint prints your presentation in grayscale mode.
4. **SAVE** the presentation.

   PAUSE. LEAVE the presentation open to use in the next exercise.

Even if you have a color printer and your presentation uses a colored background or fonts, you can still print the slides in grayscale mode. In this mode, PowerPoint converts the colors to shades of gray for printing. (The colors in the presentation itself are not changed.) Grayscale mode offers a couple of advantages over color printing. First, it saves time because color printers generally print faster in grayscale or black-and-white mode. Second, by omitting the colors from your printout, you reduce your use of colored ink or toner.

CERTIFICATION READY?
How do you print a presentation in grayscale mode?
4.4.2

PowerPoint can also print slides in pure black and white. To choose this option, click the Color/grayscale drop-down arrow, then click Pure Black and White. In this mode, slides are printed in black and white only, without any gray. This is the fastest way to print, but only the darkest parts of your presentation will print recognizably. Use black-and-white mode only for presentations that have no color or shading in them.

Previewing a Presentation on the Screen

THE BOTTOM LINE Before you show your presentation to an audience, you should preview it in Slide Show view. This exercise shows you how to use PowerPoint's tools for running a slide show on your own computer's screen.

PREVIEW A PRESENTATION

USE the presentation that is still open from the previous exercise.

1. Go to slide 1, if necessary.
2. On the Ribbon, click the **View** tab, if necessary.
3. Click **Slide Show**. PowerPoint changes to Slide Show view and the first slide appears in full-screen mode, as shown in Figure 2-26.

TAKE NOTE
You can also switch to Slide Show view by pressing **F5**.

Figure 2-26
Previewing a presentation in Slide Show view

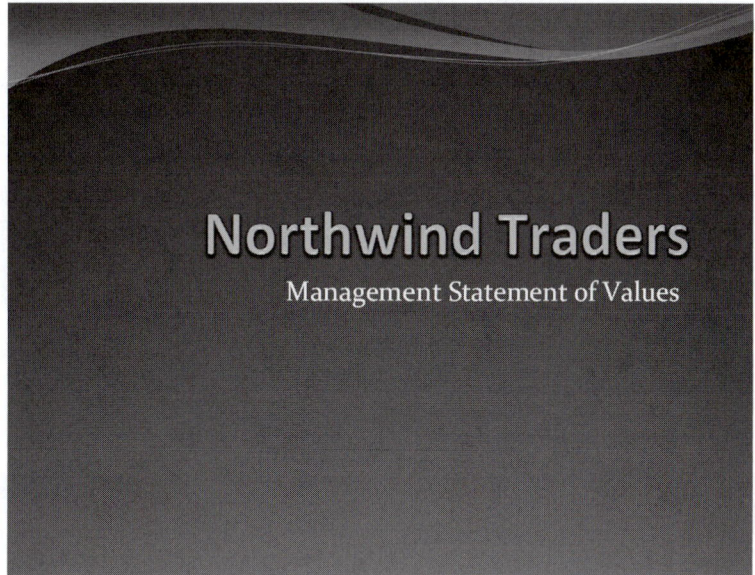

4. Click the left mouse button nine times to view the slides in order. When you click the mouse on the last slide, PowerPoint displays a black screen.
5. Click the left mouse button once more to return to Normal view.
6. **SAVE** and **CLOSE** the file.

   CLOSE PowerPoint.

TAKE NOTE
You can exit from Slide Show view at any time by pressing **Esc**.

In Slide Show view, PowerPoint displays every slide in the presentation, in order from beginning to end. To advance to the next slide, you can click the left mouse button.

SUMMARY SKILL MATRIX

IN THIS LESSON YOU LEARNED HOW TO:
Open a Blank Presentation
Change a Slide's Layout
Add Text to a Blank Slide
Choose a Different File Format
Use a Template as the Basis for a Presentation
Add a New Slide to a Presentation
Reuse a Slide from Another Presentation
Create a New Presentation from an Existing One
Start a Presentation from a Microsoft Office Word Outline
Rearrange the Slides in a Presentation
Delete a Slide
Add Notes to Your Slides
Use Print Preview
Set Print Options
Print a Presentation in Grayscale Mode
Preview a Presentation on the Screen

Knowledge Assessment

Matching

Match the term in Column 1 to its description in Column 2.

Column 1

1. note (c)
2. template (h)
3. handout (i)
4. Print Preview (a)
5. Presenter view (j)
6. theme (e)
7. layout (d)
8. thumbnail (f)
9. grayscale (b)
10. indent level (g)

Column 2

a. shows how a presentation will appear on paper
b. a printing mode that saves colored ink or toner
c. additional information associated with a slide
d. a predefined arrangement of placeholders
e. a scheme of complementing colors
f. a small picture of a slide
g. the distance from a placeholder's left border
h. a predesigned presentation
i. a printed copy of a presentation
j. lets you see notes on one screen while the audience sees slides on another

Presentation Basics | 551

True / False

Circle T if the statement is true or F if the statement is false.

T F 1. You can search Microsoft Office Online for templates and themes from the New Presentation window.

T **F** 2. Once a layout has been applied to a slide, it cannot be changed.

T F 3. When you save a presentation for the first time, the Save As dialog box appears.

T F 4. If you want to be able to use a presentation with an older version of PowerPoint, you can save it by using the PowerPoint 97-2003 Presentation file format.

T **F** 5. Many PowerPoint templates feature a set of complementing colors, called a layout. *(theme)*

T F 6. If you click the New Slide button, PowerPoint displays the New Slide gallery.

T F 7. To copy a slide, right-click its thumbnail, then click Copy.

T **F** 8. Notes appear on the screen with the slides in Slide Show view.

T F 9. PowerPoint can print just the text of your slide, without printing any graphics.

T F 10. If you use a black-and-white printer, your slides will appear in grayscale when viewed in Print Preview.

■ Competency Assessment

Project 2-1: Tonight's Guest Speaker

As director of the Citywide Business Alliance, one of your jobs is to introduce the guest speaker at the organization's monthly meeting. To do this, you will create a new presentation from a template, then reuse a slide with information about the speaker-from a different presentation.

GET READY. Launch PowerPoint if it is not already running.

1. Click the **Microsoft Office Button**, then click **New** to open the New Presentation window.
2. Click **Installed Templates**. Click **Introducing PowerPoint 2007** then click **Create**.
3. Switch to Slide Sorter view, then delete slides 2 through 18.
4. Switch to Normal view.
5. On slide 1, select the title by dragging the mouse pointer over it. Press **Delete**, then key **Citywide Business Alliance**.
6. Select the subtitle by dragging the mouse pointer over it. Press **Delete**, then key **Tonight's Guest Speaker**. Click outside the subtitle's placeholder to deselect it.
7. On the Ribbon, click the **New Slide** button. At the bottom of the gallery, click **Reuse Slides**.
8. In the Reuse Slides task pane, click the **Browse** button, then click **Browse File**.
9. When the Browse dialog box appears, locate and open the presentation named **Bourne**.
10. In the Reuse Slides task pane, click slide 1. The slide is added to your new presentation. Close the task pane.
11. Click the **Microsoft Office Button**, point to **Print**, then click **Print**. The Print dialog box opens.
12. In the Print dialog box, click the **Color/grayscale** drop-down arrow, then click **Grayscale**. Click **OK** to print the presentation in grayscale mode.
13. Click the **Microsoft Office Button**, point to **Save As**, then click **PowerPoint 97-2003 Presentation**. The Save As dialog box opens.

The *Bourne* file is available on the companion CD-ROM.

14. Navigate to the folder where you want to save the presentation.
15. Select the text in the File name box, press **Delete**, then key **Speaker**.
16. Click **Save**. If the Compatibility Checker task pane appears, click **Continue**. **CLOSE** the file.

    LEAVE PowerPoint open for the next project.

Project 2-2: Advertise with Us

As an account manager for The Phone Company, you are always trying to convince potential customers of the benefits of advertising in the local phone directory. A PowerPoint presentation can help you make your case. You need to create a presentation from a Word document that lists some reasons why businesses should purchase ad space in your directory.

1. **OPEN** the New Presentation window and click **Create**. A new, blank title slide appears in the PowerPoint window.
2. Click in the slide's title placeholder, then key **Why Advertise with Us?**
3. Click in the subtitle placeholder, then key **The Phone Company**.
4. Click outside the text placeholder to clear its border.
5. On the Ribbon's Home tab, click the **New Slide** drop-down arrow. At the bottom of the gallery of slide layouts, click **Slides from Outline**.
6. In the Insert Outline dialog box, locate and select the Microsoft Word document named *Ad Benefits*. Click **Insert**. PowerPoint inserts five new slides using content from the outline.
7. Switch to Slide Sorter view. Click slide 5 and drag it to the left, then drop it after slide 1.
8. Click slide 6, then press **Delete** to remove the slide from the presentation.
9. Switch to Notes Page view, then go to slide 1.
10. Click in the text box below the slide, then key **Give the client a copy of the directory**.
11. Switch to Normal view.
12. On the Quick Access Toolbar, click **Save**. The Save As dialog box opens.
13. Navigate to the folder where you want to save the presentation.
14. Select the text in the File name box, then key **Benefits**.
15. Click **Save**. **CLOSE** the file.

    LEAVE PowerPoint open for the next project.

The *Ad Benefits* file is available on the companion CD-ROM.

■ Proficiency Assessment

Project 2-3: Send People to Their Room

You are an assistant marketing manager at Contoso, Ltd., which develops process control software for use in manufacturing. You are coordinating a set of panel discussions at the company's annual sales and marketing meeting. At the start of the afternoon session, you must tell the groups which conference rooms to use for their discussions. To help deliver your message, you need to create a single-slide presentation that lists the panels' room assignments. You can display the slide on a projection screen for reference while you announce the room assignments.

1. **CREATE** a new, blank presentation.
2. Change the blank slide's layout to Title and Content. In the slide's title placeholder, key **Panel Discussions**.

3. In the second placeholder, key the following items, placing each item on its own line:

   Aligning with Partners, Room 104
   Building Incentives, Room 101
   Creating New Value, Room 102
   Managing Expenses, Room 108
   Opening New Markets, Room 112
   Recapturing Lost Accounts, Room 107
   Strengthening Client Relationships, Room 110

4. In the Notes pane, key **Refreshments will be delivered to each room during the 3:00 PM break**.
5. Print the presentation in grayscale mode.
6. **SAVE** the presentation as *Room Assignments*, then **CLOSE** the file.
   LEAVE PowerPoint open for the next project.

Project 2-4: Editorial Services

You are the editorial director for Lucerne Publishing, a small publishing house that provides editorial services to other businesses. Your sales manager has asked you to prepare a simple presentation that lists the services offered by your editorial staff. You can create this presentation from an outline that was created earlier.

The *Editorial Services* file is available on the companion CD-ROM.

The *About Lucerne* file is available on the companion CD-ROM.

1. **CREATE** a new, blank presentation.
2. Key **Lucerne Publishing** in the title placeholder.
3. Key **Editorial Services** in the subtitle placeholder, then click outside the placeholder.
4. Use the **Slides from Outline** command to locate the Microsoft Word document named *Editorial Services*, then click **Insert**.
5. In the Slides/Outline pane, click slide 6.
6. Use the Reuse Slides command to locate and open the *About Lucerne* presentation, then add slide 3 from that presentation to the end of your new presentation.
7. Print the presentation in grayscale mode.
8. **SAVE** the presentation as *Lucerne Editorial Services*, then **CLOSE** the file.
   LEAVE PowerPoint open for the next project.

■ Mastery Assessment

Project 2-5: The Final Gallery Crawl

As director of the Graphic Design Institute, you have volunteered to coordinate your city's last-ever gallery crawl—an annual charity event that enables the public to visit several art galleries for one price. Fortunately, this year's event is almost identical to last year's crawl, so when you create a presentation for the local arts council, you can use last year's presentation as the basis for a new one.

The *Gallery Crawl* file is available on the companion CD-ROM.

1. **OPEN** the New Presentation window, then click **New from existing**. Locate and open *Gallery Crawl*.
2. In Slide Sorter view, switch slides 6 and 7.
3. In Normal view, reword the subtitle of slide 1 to read **Our last ever!**
4. View the presentation in Print Preview.
5. Print the presentation in grayscale mode.

6. Preview the presentation from beginning to end in Slide Show view.
7. **SAVE** the presentation as *Final Gallery Crawl*, then **CLOSE** the file.
   LEAVE PowerPoint open for the next project.

Project 2-6: The Final, Final Gallery Crawl

Having just finished your presentation for the last-ever gallery crawl, you realize that one of the museum curators uses an older version of PowerPoint. You need to save a copy of the presentation so he can use it on his computer.

1. **OPEN** *Final Gallery Crawl* from the data files for this lesson.
2. **SAVE** the presentation with the file name *Compatible Gallery Crawl* in PowerPoint 97-2003 format. **CLOSE** the file without making any other changes.
   CLOSE PowerPoint.

The *Final Gallery Crawl* file is available on the companion CD-ROM.

INTERNET READY

Use PowerPoint Help to access online information about presentation templates. Learn how to download new templates from Office Online, then download at least one new template to your computer.

Working with Text

3

LESSON SKILL MATRIX

Choosing Fonts and Font Sizes (Table) – 556	Students will learn how to choose fonts and font sizes.
Applying Font Styles and Effects – 558	Students will learn how to apply font styles and effects.
Changing Font Color – 560	Students will learn how to change font color.
Copying Character Formats with the Format Painter – 561	Students will learn how to copy character formats with the format painter.
Aligning Paragraphs – 563	Students will learn how to align paragraphs.
Setting Paragraph Line Spacing – 564	Students will learn how to set paragraph line spacing.
Creating Numbered Lists – 565	Students will learn how to create numbered lists.
Working with Bulleted Lists (Color--) 1. Bullets & #ing 2. " – P.567	Students will learn how to work with bulleted lists.
Inserting a WordArt Graphic – 568	Students will learn how to insert a WordArt graphic.
Formatting a WordArt Graphic – 570	Students will learn how to format a WordArt graphic.
Formatting Text with WordArt Styles – 573	Students will learn how to format text with WordArt styles.
Adding a Text Box to a Slide – 574	Students will learn how to add a text box to a slide.
Resizing a Text Box – 575	Students will learn how to resize a text box.
Setting Formatting Options for a Text Box – 577	Students will learn how to set formatting options for a text box.
Working with Text in a Text Box – 580	Students will learn how to work with text in a text box.
Deleting a Text Box – 58	Students will learn how to delete a text box.

Fourth Coffee is a "boutique" company devoted to producing and distributing fine coffees and teas. As the sales manager for Fourth Coffee, you often produce and deliver presentations to your staff and managers on topics such as realizing the full profit potential of your delivery systems. Whenever you create a presentation, consider how the information appears to your viewers. If the text in your slides is difficult to read or haphazardly formatted, or if

KEY TERMS
bulleted list
fonts
Format Painter
formatting
line spacing
numbered list
Quick Style
text box
WordArt

555

you cram too much text into your slides, then your presentations will not be professional-looking. In this lesson, you learn some basics of text formatting, including formatting characters and paragraphs, creating and formatting lists, using WordArt to "jazz up" your text, and creating and modifying text boxes.

■ Software Orientation

Microsoft PowerPoint's Basic Text Formatting Tools

Most of PowerPoint's basic text formatting tools are found on the Home tab of the Ribbon, as shown in Figure 3-1. These are the tools you will use most often when working with text.

Figure 3-1

Basic text formatting tools

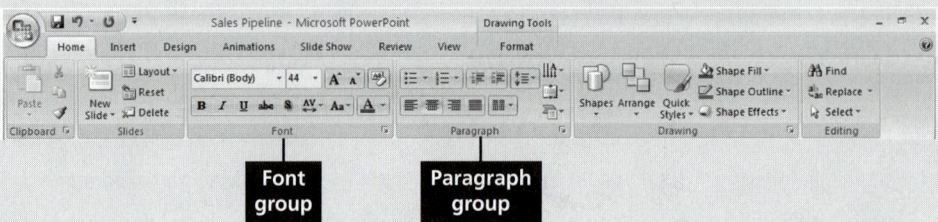

There are two groups of text formatting tools on the Ribbon: the Font group and the Paragraph group. They allow you to fine-tune the text on your slides, right down to an individual character. These groups also provide access to the Font and Paragraph dialog boxes, which give you even more control over your text's appearance.

■ Formatting Characters

> **THE BOTTOM LINE**
>
> All PowerPoint presentations are formatted with specific fonts, font sizes, and font attributes such as style and color. You can change the way characters look on a slide by using commands in the Font group on the Home tab or the Mini toolbar. The Format Painter can save you time by allowing you to copy formats from selected text to other text items.

Choosing Fonts and Font Sizes

> You can change the font and font size at any time on your slides. The following exercise shows you how.

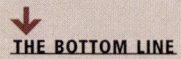

The *Sales Pipeline* file is available on the companion CD-ROM.

→ **CHOOSE FONTS AND FONT SIZES**

GET READY. Before you begin these steps, be sure to launch Microsoft Office PowerPoint 2007.

1. Locate and open *Sales Pipeline*.
2. Go to slide 2. In the first row of the table, double-click **Timing**. The Mini toolbar appears above the selected text.
3. Move the mouse pointer up to the Mini toolbar so you can see it better.
4. Click the **Font** drop-down arrow. A list of fonts appears, as shown in Figure 3-2.

TAKE NOTE

When you select text to change its font or font size, the Mini toolbar that appears is at first transparent.

Figure 3-2

Choosing a new font

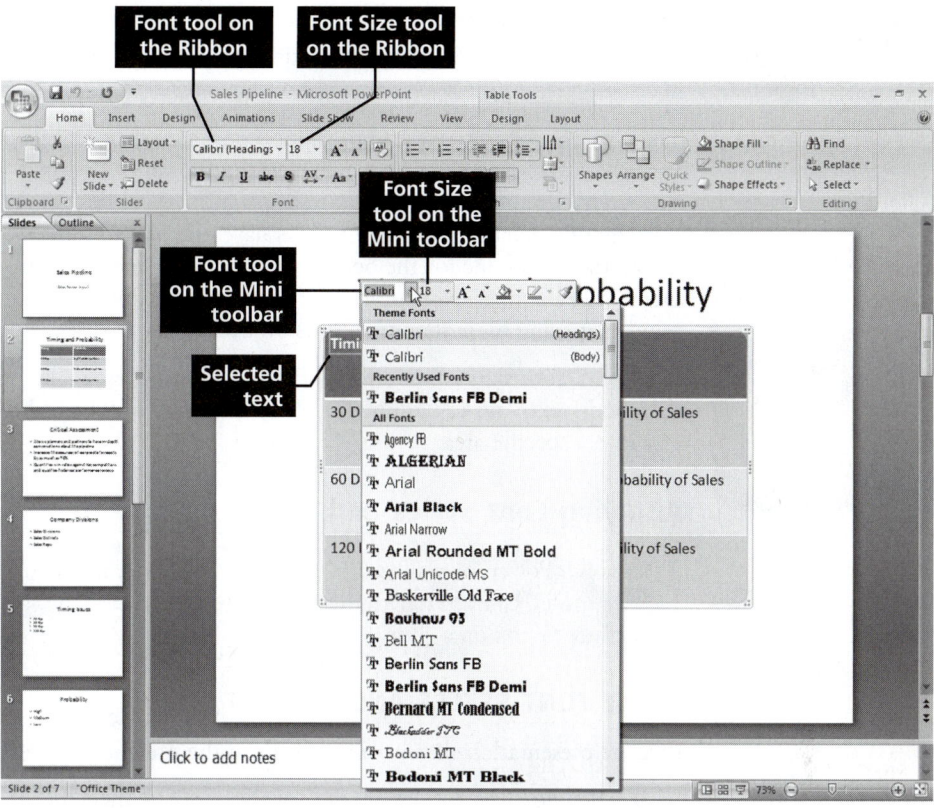

ANOTHER WAY

You can also select a font and font size from the Font group on the Ribbon's Home tab.

5. Click **Berlin Sans FB Demi**. PowerPoint applies the chosen font to the selected text.
6. Click the **Font Size** drop-down arrow. A list of font sizes appears.
7. Click **32**. PowerPoint applies the chosen font size to the selected text.
8. Double-click **Probability** in the top right cell of the table.
9. Select the **Berlin Sans FB Demi** font and size **32** from the Mini toolbar.
10. Click anywhere in the blank area outside the table to clear the Mini toolbar from your screen. Your slide should look like the one shown in Figure 3-3.

Figure 3-3

The new font and font size applied to the current slide

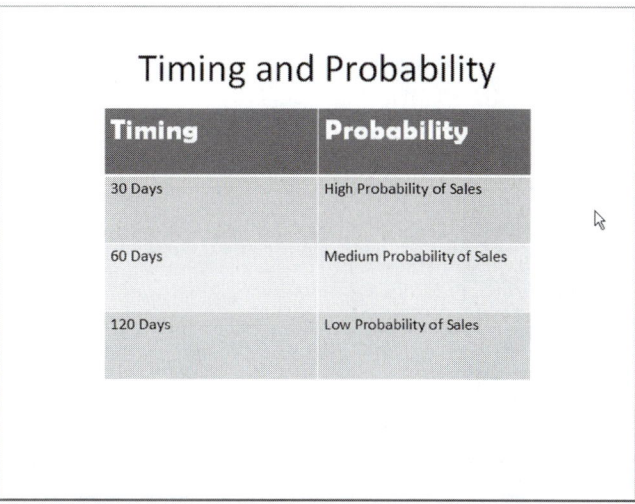

558 | Lesson 3

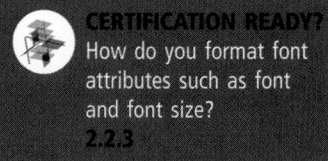

TAKE NOTE

All PowerPoint presentations have themes applied. Even a new, blank presentation uses a theme, the Office theme.

CERTIFICATION READY?
How do you format font attributes such as font and font size?
2.2.3

11. **SAVE** the presentation as *Sales Pipeline Formats*.
    PAUSE. LEAVE the presentation open to use in the next exercise.

The term *formatting* refers to the appearance of text or objects on a slide. Most of PowerPoint's tools are devoted to formatting the various parts of your slides. *Fonts* are sets of characters, numbers, and symbols in a specific style or design. (Fonts are sometimes also called *typefaces*.) By default, PowerPoint slides have one or two fonts per presentation: one font for the headings and one for the body text, such as bulleted or numbered items. Each PowerPoint theme supplies its own set of fonts. You can change these default fonts as you like, but keep in mind that using more than two fonts on a slide can be distracting to the viewer.

Like fonts, font sizes are controlled by the current theme. Slide titles have a larger font size than body text. You can adjust the font size of any text on a slide to emphasize it or fit the text into a specific area.

Applying Font Styles and Effects

Text on a PowerPoint slide can be boldfaced, underlined, italicized, or formatted with other special character attributes. In the following exercise, you will apply a font style and an effect to text on a slide.

APPLY FONT STYLES AND EFFECTS

USE the presentation that is still open from the previous exercise.

1. Double-click **Timing** in the top left cell of the table. The Mini toolbar appears above the selected text.
2. Point to the Mini toolbar so you can see it better.
3. Click the **Italic** button on the Mini toolbar. PowerPoint formats the selected text in italic, as shown in Figure 3-4.

Figure 3-4

Text formatted in italics

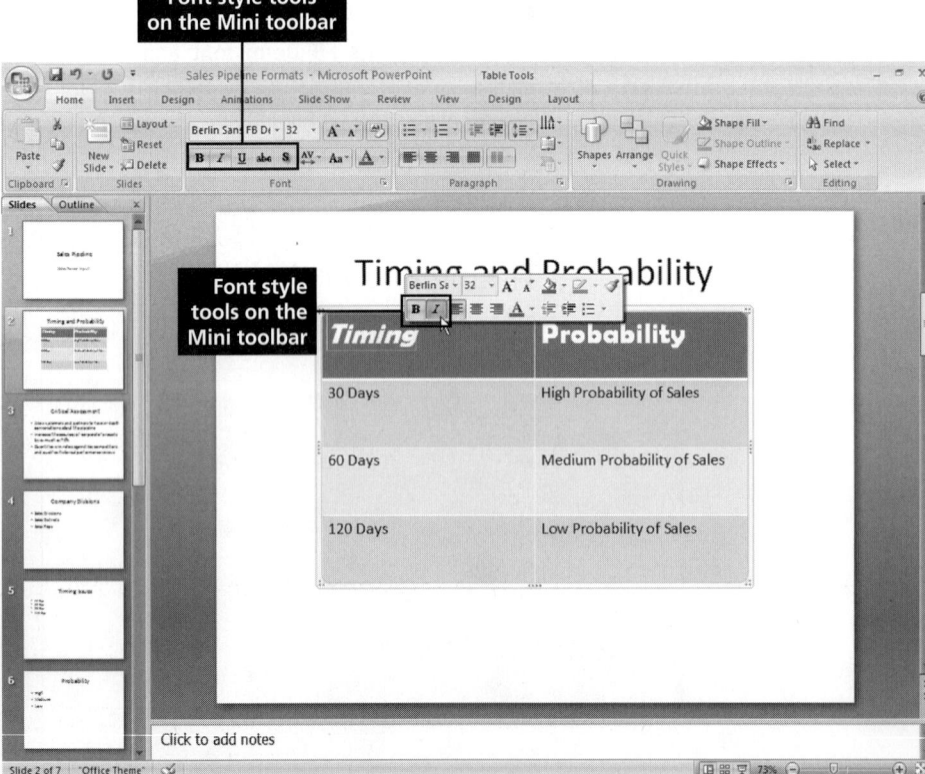

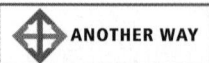 **ANOTHER WAY**

To apply italic formatting to a selection, press **Ctrl+I**. You can also click the Italic button in the Font group of the Ribbon.

4. Double-click **Probability** in the top right cell of the table.
5. Click the **Italic** button on the Mini toolbar. PowerPoint formats the selected text in italic.
6. Double-click **Timing** in the top left cell of the table, then click the Font dialog box launcher.
7. In the Font dialog box, click the **Character Spacing** tab, as shown in Figure 3-5.

Figure 3-5

Setting the character spacing for the selected text

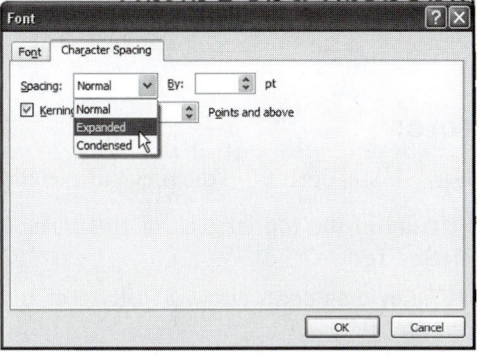

To repeat the last command you issued, press **Ctrl+Y**.

8. Click the **Spacing** drop-down arrow, click **Expanded**, then click **OK**. PowerPoint places 1 point of spacing between the letters.
9. Double-click **Probability** in the top right cell of the table, then click the **Repeat** button on the Quick Access Toolbar. PowerPoint repeats the last command you issued, applying the new character spacing to the selected text. Your slide should look like the one shown in Figure 3-6.

Figure 3-6

The slide with new character spacing in the table's column headings

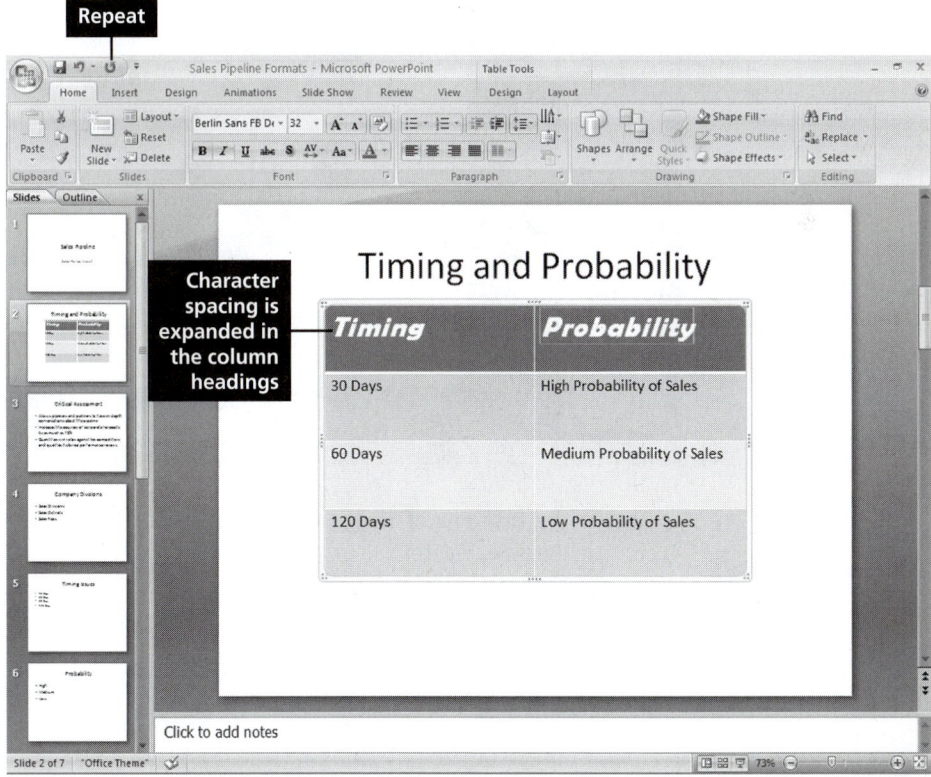

PAUSE. LEAVE the presentation open to use in the next exercise.

560 | Lesson 3

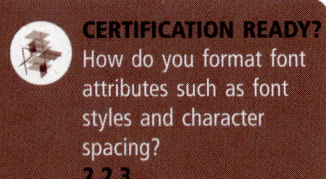

CERTIFICATION READY?
How do you format font attributes such as font styles and character spacing?
2.2.3

Use font styles and effects to emphasize text on a slide. Besides the standard font styles—bold, italic, and underline—PowerPoint provides strikethrough and shadow styles. You can also adjust character spacing and case to give your text a special look. To access more font effects, click the Font group's dialog box launcher to open the Font dialog box. The Font dialog box allows you to apply effects such as superscripts and subscripts, all caps, and small caps.

Changing Font Color

An easy way to change text appearance is to modify its color. Use the Font Color button in the Font group to access a palette of colors you can apply to selected text.

➔ CHANGE FONT COLOR

USE the presentation that is still open from the previous exercise.

1. Double-click **Timing** in the top left cell of the table. The Mini toolbar appears above the selected text.
2. Click the **Font Color** drop-down arrow. A palette of colors appears, as shown in Figure 3-7.

Figure 3-7

Changing a font's color

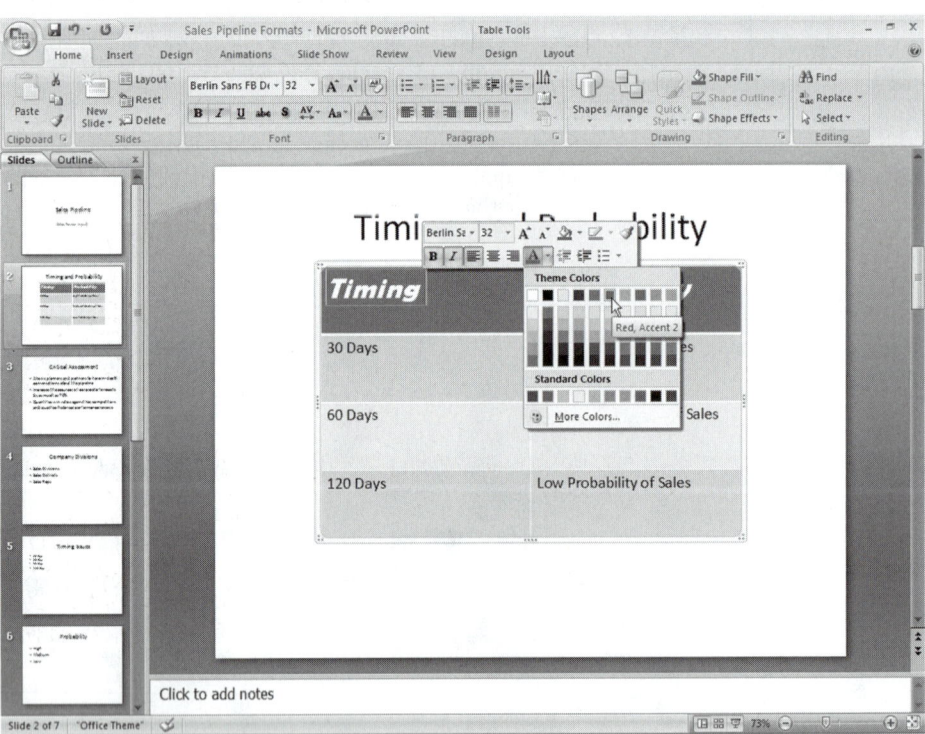

TAKE NOTE

When you hold the mouse pointer over a color box, the color's name appears in a ScreenTip.

3. In the first row of theme colors, click **Red, Accent 2**. PowerPoint applies the color to the selected text.
4. Double-click **Probability** in the top right cell of the table, then apply the color **Red, Accent 2** to it. Your slide should resemble the one shown in Figure 3-8.

Figure 3-8

The slide with the new color applied

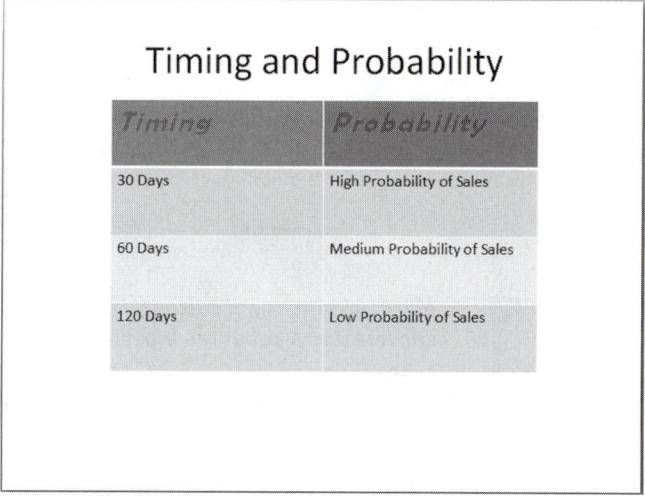

PAUSE. LEAVE the presentation open to use in the next exercise.

PowerPoint provides an almost limitless selection of colors that can be applied to fonts. You can select any color for your text, but it is usually best to use one of the colors provided by the presentation's theme. Each PowerPoint theme includes a set of coordinating colors, which appear in the color palette when you click the Font Color button. By selecting one of the theme's colors, you can be sure that all the font colors in your slides will look good together on the screen, making them easier to read.

If you want to use a color that is not included in the theme, select one of the Standard Colors at the bottom of the color palette or click More Colors to open the Colors dialog box. In the Colors dialog box, you can choose from dozens of standard colors or create a custom color.

Copying Character Formats with the Format Painter

As you format text in your presentations, you will want to keep similar types of text formatted the same way. Use the Format Painter to copy formatting from one character, word, phrase, or paragraph to another character, word, phrase, or paragraph.

➔ COPY CHARACTER FORMATS WITH THE FORMAT PAINTER

USE the presentation that is still open from the previous exercise.

1. Go to slide 2, if necessary.
2. Select the text in the title placeholder.
3. Change the font color to **Blue, Accent 1, Darker 25%**.
4. Click the **Bold** button in the Ribbon's Font group to apply the bold font style.
5. Click the **Shadow** button in the Font group to apply the shadow font style.
6. With the text still selected, click the **Format Painter** button in the Clipboard group.
7. Go to slide 3. Click just to the left of the first word in the title so that the placeholder border displays, hold down the mouse button, and then drag the Format Painter pointer over the title text. The title displays the same character formats you applied on slide 2, as shown in Figure 3-9.

Figure 3-9

Formatting copied to the title of slide 3

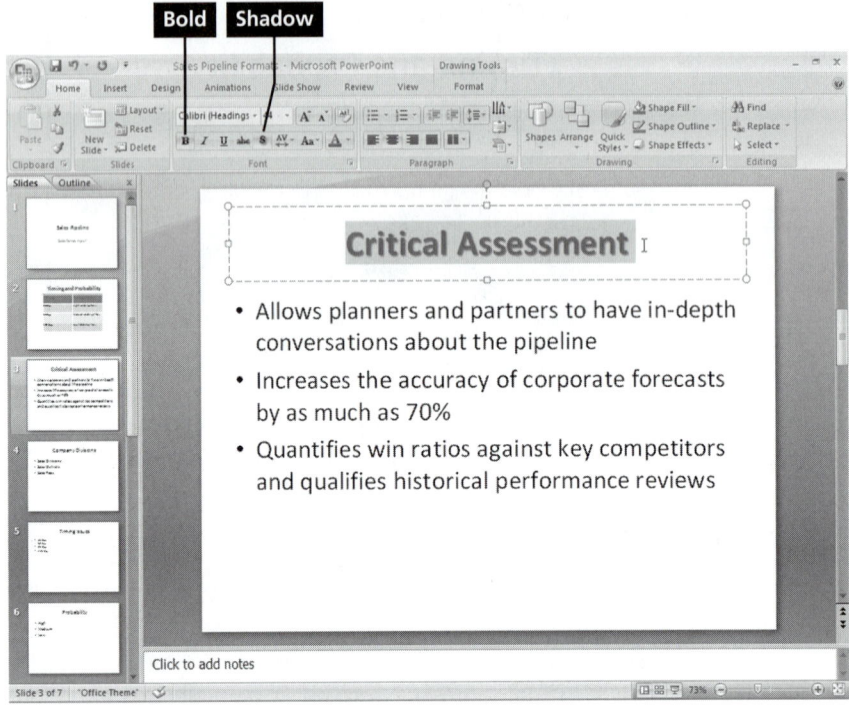

8. With the title text on slide 3 still selected, double-click the **Format Painter** button in the Clipboard group.
9. Go to each remaining slide and drag the Format Painter pointer over the title text.
10. Click the **Format Painter** in the Clipboard group to deselect it.

   PAUSE. LEAVE the presentation open to use in the next exercise.

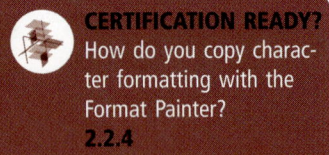

CERTIFICATION READY?
How do you copy character formatting with the Format Painter?
2.2.4

Consistency is the name of the game in a presentation. PowerPoint provides a number of tools to help you format text consistently on every slide. The ***Format Painter*** is one of those tools. Use it to copy formats from one text item to another on the same slide or on another slide. If you want to copy a format only once, simply click the button. To copy a format multiple times, double-click the button. Not only does this tool reduce your workload, it also ensures consistency throughout a presentation.

The Format Painter copies not only character formats but paragraph formats such as alignments and line spacing. You learn about paragraph formats in the next section.

■ Formatting Paragraphs

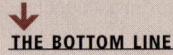 **THE BOTTOM LINE** You can change the look of paragraph text by modifying alignment or line spacing. When you apply formatting to a paragraph, all the text within that paragraph receives the same formatting.

Aligning Paragraphs

In this exercise, you change the default alignment of items in a bulleted list to customize a slide's appearance.

 **ALIGN PARAGRAPHS**

USE the presentation that is still open from the previous exercise.

1. Go to slide 4.
2. Click in the second bulleted item (*Sales Districts*).
3. Click the **Center** button in the Ribbon's Paragraph group. PowerPoint aligns the paragraph in the center of the text box.
4. Click in the third bulleted item (*Sales Reps*).
5. Click the **Align Text Right** button in the Paragraph group. PowerPoint aligns the paragraph to the right side of the text placeholder. Your slide should look like the one shown in Figure 3-10.

Figure 3-10

Aligning paragraphs to the left, center, and right

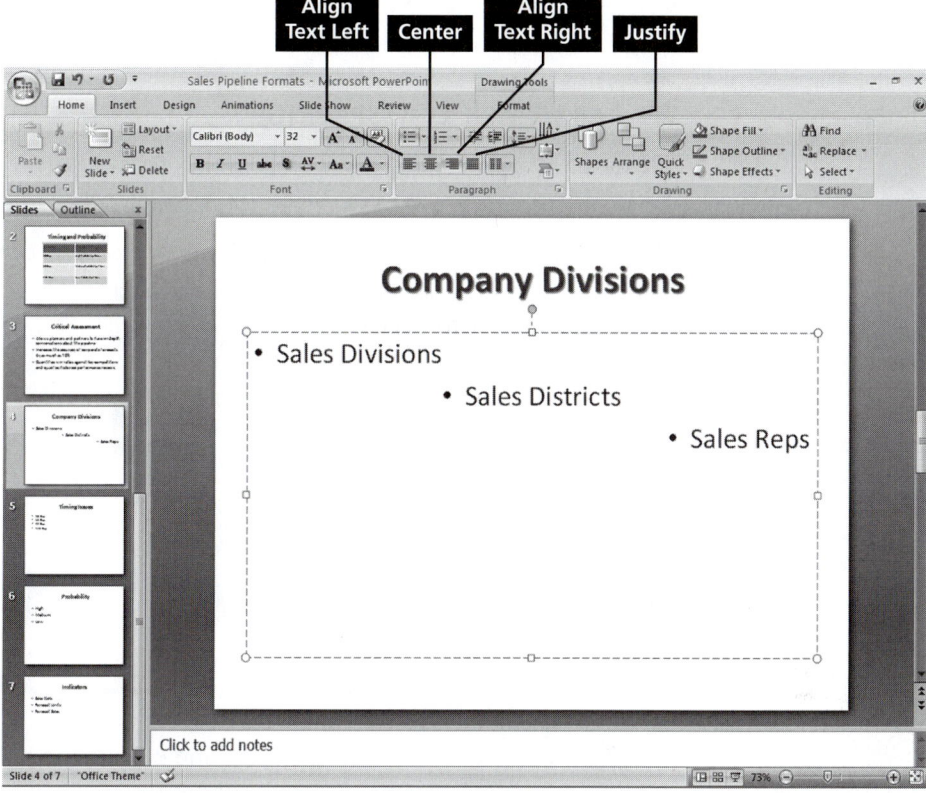

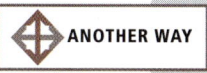 **ANOTHER WAY** The paragraph alignment tools also appear on the Mini toolbar when you right-click within a paragraph of text.

PAUSE. LEAVE the presentation open to use in the next exercise.

When you apply paragraph formats such as alignment, you do not have to select the entire paragraph of text. Just click anywhere in the paragraph and apply the format. The formatting applies to the entire paragraph, even if the paragraph is several lines or sentences long.

When you begin a new paragraph by pressing Enter after an existing paragraph, the new paragraph keeps the same alignment and formatting as the paragraph above it. For example, if you start a new paragraph after a paragraph aligned to the right, the new paragraph aligns to the right as well.

564 | Lesson 3

ANOTHER WAY

To left-align text, press **Ctrl+L**. To center text, press **Ctrl+E**. To right-align text, press **Ctrl+R**.

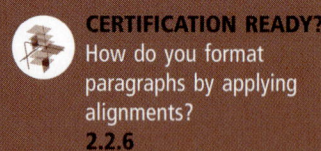

CERTIFICATION READY?
How do you format paragraphs by applying alignments?
2.2.6

PowerPoint provides four paragraph-alignment options:

- **Align Text Left** aligns the paragraph at the left edge of the object in which the text resides, whether the object containing the text is a placeholder, a table cell, or a text box.
- **Center** aligns the paragraph in the center of the object.
- **Align Text Right** aligns the paragraph at the right edge of the object.
- **Justify** distributes the paragraph of text evenly across the width of the object, if possible. PowerPoint justifies text by adding spaces between words and characters.

Setting Paragraph Line Spacing

Adjust paragraph *line spacing* to allow more or less room between lines of a paragraph. Line spacing changes can help you display text more attractively or fit more text on a slide.

 **SET PARAGRAPH LINE SPACING**

USE the presentation that is still open from the previous exercise.

1. Go to slide 3.
2. Click in the first bulleted item (*Allows planners and partners . . .*).
3. Click the **Line Spacing** drop-down arrow in the Paragraph group. A list of line spacing options appears, as shown in Figure 3-11.

Figure 3-11

PowerPoint's Line Spacing options

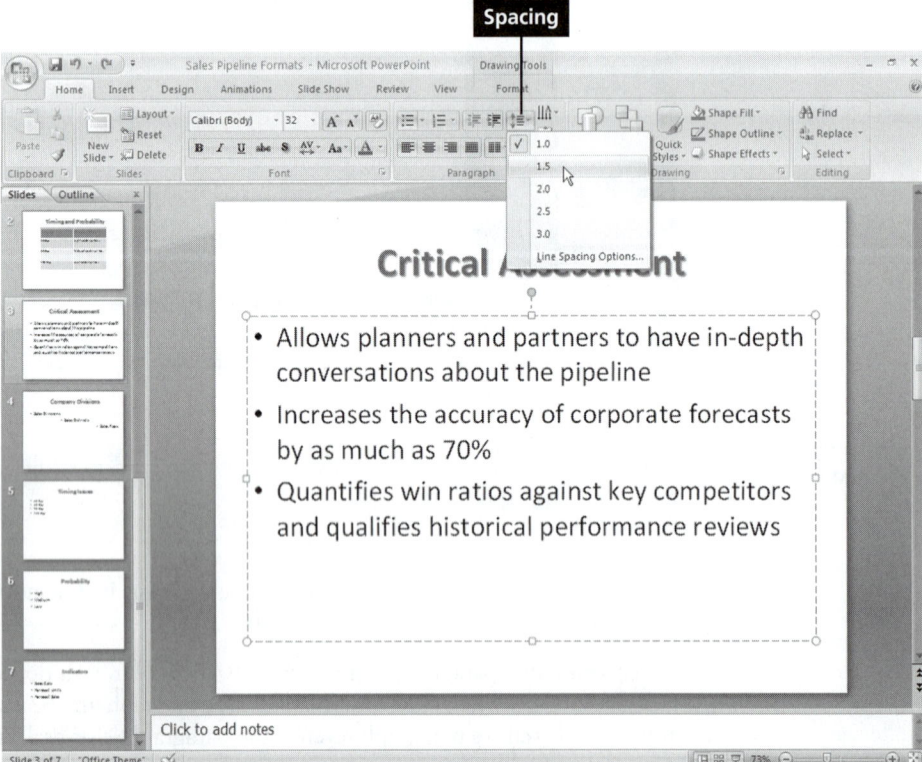

4. Select **1.5**. PowerPoint formats the paragraph's lines so they are separated by 1.5 lines of blank space.
5. Drag the mouse pointer over the first bulleted item to select the text.

TAKE NOTE

PowerPoint enables you to specify spacing before and after paragraphs. Click the Line Spacing button's drop-down arrow and click Line Spacing Options. Set the Before and After options to the settings you desire.

6. Click the **Format Painter** button once to copy the paragraph format.
7. Drag the Format Painter pointer over the remaining two bulleted items to apply the 1.5 line spacing. Your slide should look like the one shown in Figure 3-12.

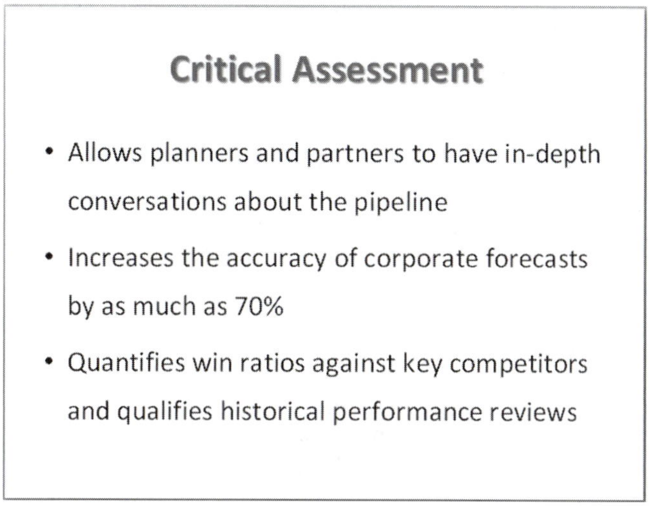

Figure 3-12

The text with different line spacing

Critical Assessment

- Allows planners and partners to have in-depth conversations about the pipeline
- Increases the accuracy of corporate forecasts by as much as 70%
- Quantifies win ratios against key competitors and qualifies historical performance reviews

8. **SAVE** the presentation and **CLOSE** the file.
   PAUSE. LEAVE PowerPoint open to use in the next exercise.

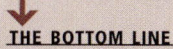

CERTIFICATION READY?
How do you format paragraphs by adjusting line spacing?
2.2.6

By default, PowerPoint formats your paragraphs so that one line of blank space lies between each paragraph and between the lines within a paragraph. Use the Line Spacing button to adjust the spacing to 1.0, 1.5, 2.0, 2.5, or 3.0. You also can use the Line Spacing Options command to display the Paragraph dialog box. With this dialog box, you can finely tune the spacing between each paragraph.

■ Working with Lists

THE BOTTOM LINE

Lists make the information on slides easy to read and remember. PowerPoint provides for several levels of bulleted lists that you can modify for a special effect. You can also create numbered lists when your slide text implies a specific order.

 **CD**

The *Leveraging Corporate Cash* file is available on the companion CD-ROM.

Creating Numbered Lists

PowerPoint enables you to create numbered lists to place your information in numeric order. Numbered lists are used for procedural steps, action items, and other information where order is required. In the following exercise, you create a numbered list from a list of items on a slide.

➔ CREATE NUMBERED LISTS

1. **OPEN** the *Leveraging Corporate Cash* presentation.

2. Go to slide 2.
3. Click in the first line of the text in the text placeholder (*Determine inventory turnover*).
4. Click the **Numbering** button in the Paragraph group. PowerPoint formats the sentence with a number 1.
5. Select the last three lines in the text placeholder.
6. Click the **Numbering** button. PowerPoint applies numbers 2 through 4.

 **ANOTHER WAY** To number a paragraph, right-click the paragraph, then click Numbering on the shortcut menu.

7. Click outside the text placeholder to clear its border. Your slide should look like the one shown in Figure 3-13.

Figure 3-13

A numbered list

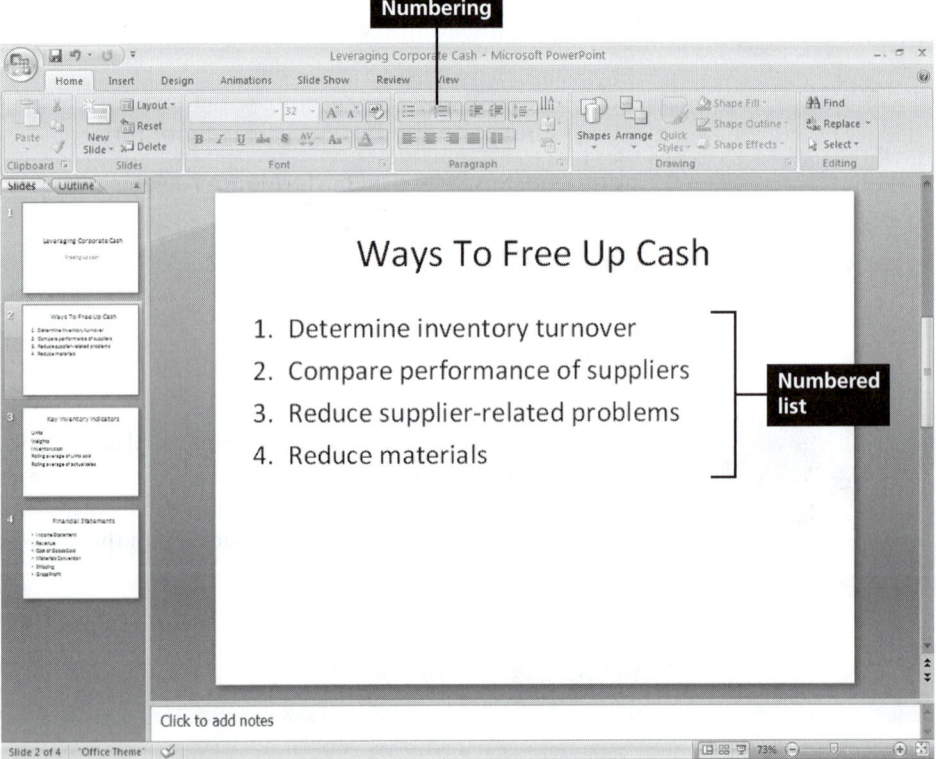

8. **SAVE** the presentation as *Leveraging Corporate Cash Lists*.

PAUSE. LEAVE the presentation open to use in the next exercise.

When you create a *numbered list* on a slide, you can continue it automatically after the last item by pressing Enter. PowerPoint automatically numbers the new paragraph with the next number in the sequence of numbers so you can continue the list uninterrupted.

By default, PowerPoint numbers items using numerals followed by periods. You can, however, change the numbering format to numerals followed by parentheses, upper- or lowercase Roman numerals, or upper- or lowercase letters. To change the numbering format, click the Numbering button's drop-down arrow and select a new format from the gallery. For more control over the numbering format, click Bullets and Numbering on the gallery to display the Bullets and Numbering dialog box. You can use this dialog box to choose what number to start the list with, change the size of the numbers, or change their color.

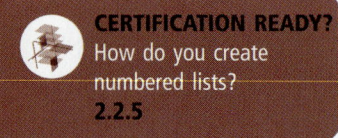

CERTIFICATION READY?
How do you create numbered lists?
2.2.5

Working with Bulleted Lists

Bulleted lists are the most popular way to present items on PowerPoint presentations. In fact, most of PowerPoint's text placeholders automatically format text as a bulleted list. In the following exercise, you will change the formats of a bulleted list.

➔ WORK WITH BULLETED LISTS

USE the presentation that is still open from the previous exercise.

1. Go to slide 3. In this slide, the text is already set up as a bulleted list.
2. Select all of the text in the text placeholder by dragging the mouse pointer over it.
3. Click the **Bullets** drop-down arrow in the Paragraph group. PowerPoint displays a gallery of bullet styles, as shown in Figure 3-14.

Figure 3-14

Gallery of bullet styles

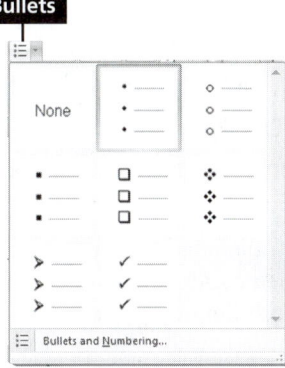

TAKE NOTE If a series of paragraphs does not have bullets, you can add them by selecting the paragraphs, then clicking the Bullets button in the Paragraph group.

4. Click **Hollow Square Bullets**. PowerPoint applies the bullet style to the selected paragraphs.
5. With the text still selected, click the **Bullets** drop-down arrow again, then click **Bullets and Numbering**. The Bullets and Numbering dialog box appears, as shown in Figure 3-15.

Figure 3-15

The Bullets and Numbering dialog box

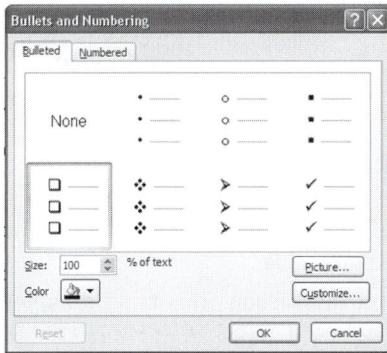

6. Select the value in the Size spin control by dragging the mouse pointer over it, then key **80**. This reduces the bullets' size to 80% of the text's size.
7. Click the **Color** drop-down arrow, then click **Blue, Accent 1**. This changes the color of the bullets.

8. Click **OK**. Your slide should look like the one shown in Figure 3-16.

Figure 3-16

The bullets with different formatting

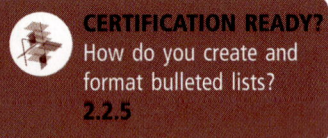

9. **SAVE** the presentation and **CLOSE** the file.

PAUSE. LEAVE PowerPoint open to use in the next exercise.

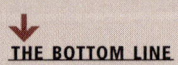

CERTIFICATION READY?
How do you create and format bulleted lists?
2.2.5

Bullets are small dots, arrows, circles, diamonds, or other graphics that appear before a short phrase or word. Each PowerPoint theme supplies bullet characters for up to nine levels of bullets, and these characters differ according to theme. When you create a *bulleted list* on your slide, you can continue it automatically after the last item by pressing Enter. PowerPoint automatically adds the new paragraph with a bullet.

■ Inserting and Formatting WordArt

THE BOTTOM LINE

PowerPoint's WordArt feature can change standard text into flashy, eye-catching graphics. Use WordArt's formatting options to change the WordArt fill or outline color or apply special effects. You can also apply WordArt styles to any slide text to give it special emphasis.

Inserting a WordArt Graphic

In this exercise, you choose a WordArt style and then key your own text to create the graphic.

→ **INSERT A WORDART GRAPHIC**

The *Full Profit Potential* file is available on the companion CD-ROM.

1. **OPEN** the *Full Profit Potential* presentation. Notice that the first slide has a subtitle, but no title placeholder.
2. Click the **Insert** tab on the Ribbon. This tab allows you to insert a number of different objects.
3. Click the **WordArt** button to display a gallery of WordArt styles, as shown in Figure 3-17.

Figure 3-17

Gallery of WordArt styles

4. Click the **Gradient Fill – Accent 1** WordArt style. PowerPoint displays the WordArt graphic with the sample text *Your Text Here*.
5. Key **Full Profit** to replace the sample text. Your slide should resemble Figure 3-18.

Figure 3-18

A new WordArt graphic on a slide

6. **SAVE** the presentation as *Full Profit*.

   PAUSE. LEAVE the presentation open to use in the next exercise.

The ***WordArt*** feature allows you to use text to create a graphic object. WordArt graphics can add special "pizzazz" on a slide. For the best appearance, limit the number of words in the graphic.

> **TAKE NOTE**
>
> When you create WordArt, the information appears as text, but PowerPoint treats the object as a graphics object—a picture. However, you can search for text formatted as WordArt when using the Find tool.

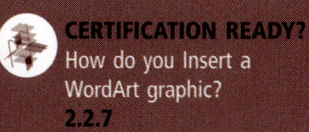

CERTIFICATION READY?
How do you Insert a WordArt graphic?
2.2.7

After you have inserted the WordArt graphic, you can format it in a number of ways. You can change the style from the WordArt gallery, you can modify the fill or the outline, or you can apply any of a number of interesting special effects. You can also modify the text of the graphic at any time. Click the graphic to open the placeholder, just as when editing a slide's title or body text, and then edit the text as desired.

Formatting a WordArt Graphic

To format a WordArt graphic, you use the tools on one of PowerPoint's contextual tabs, the Drawing Tools Format tab. In the next several exercises, you will use these tools to modify the WordArt's fill and outline and apply an effect.

CHANGING THE WORDART FILL COLOR

The WordArt fill color is the color you see inside the WordArt characters. You can change the fill color by using the color palette for the current theme or any other available color.

CHANGE THE WORDART FILL COLOR

USE the presentation that is still open from the previous exercise.

1. Select the WordArt graphic on slide 1. Note that the Drawing Tools Format tab becomes active on the Ribbon.
2. Click the **Drawing Tools Format** tab and locate the WordArt Styles group.
3. Click the **Text Fill** drop-down arrow. PowerPoint displays the Theme Colors palette as shown in Figure 3-19.

Figure 3-19
Selecting a new WordArt fill color

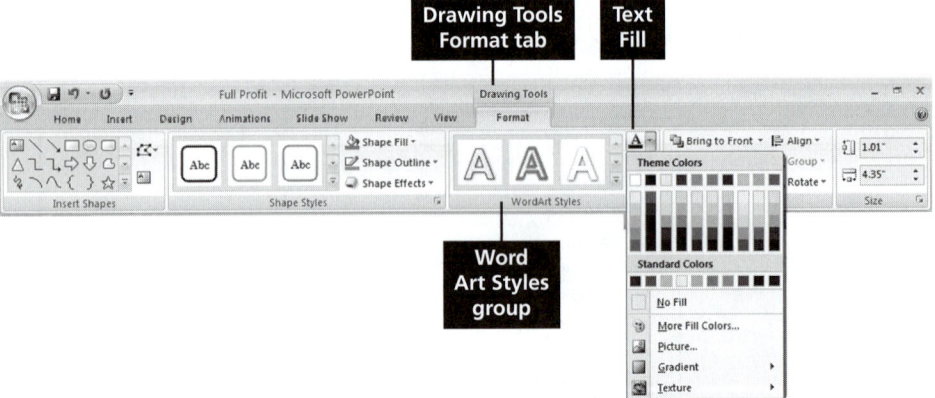

4. Click the **Blue, Accent 2, Darker 25%** theme color as the fill color. PowerPoint changes the fill of the graphic.

You can right-click a WordArt object, select Format Text Effects, and then click Text Fill in the Format Text Effects dialog box. Click the Color button's drop-down arrow and select a fill color.

5. Click outside the graphic to clear its border. Your slide should look like the one in Figure 3-20.

Figure 3-20

The WordArt object with a new fill color

PAUSE. LEAVE the presentation open to use in the next exercise.

One way to fine-tune the graphic you have inserted is to change the fill color of the WordArt object. You can use any of the colors on the Theme Colors palette to make sure the object coordinates with other items in the presentation.

You can also choose from the Standard Colors palette or select another color from the Colors dialog box. To access these colors, click More Fill Colors on the Theme Colors palette to open the Colors dialog box. You can "mix" your own colors on the Custom tab or click the Standard tab to choose from a palette of premixed colors.

The Theme Colors palette gives you additional fill options. You can search for a picture that will fill the graphic characters, apply a gradient (a gradient is a gradation of several colors), or apply one of PowerPoint's default textures.

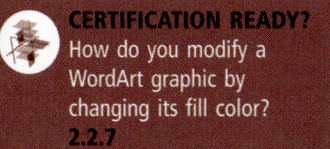

CERTIFICATION READY?
How do you modify a WordArt graphic by changing its fill color?
2.2.7

CHANGING THE WORDART OUTLINE COLOR

Most WordArt styles include a colored outline around the edges of the WordArt characters. You can change the outline color to fine-tune the graphic.

CHANGE THE WORDART OUTLINE COLOR

USE the presentation that is still open from the previous exercise.

1. Select the WordArt graphic on slide 1 if necessary.
2. Click the **Text Outline** drop-down arrow. PowerPoint displays the Theme Colors palette.
3. Click **Blue, Accent 2, Darker 50%**.

 ANOTHER WAY
You can right-click a WordArt object, select Format Text Effects, and then click Text Outline in the Format Text Effects dialog box. Click the Color button's drop-down arrow and select an outline color.

4. Click outside the graphic to clear its border. Your slide should look like the one in Figure 3-21.

Figure 3-21

The WordArt object with a new outline color

PAUSE. LEAVE the presentation open to use in the next exercise.

Just as with a WordArt object's fill color, you can fine-tune the outline color of the object. You have the same color options as for changing a fill color. The Text Outline Theme Colors palette also allows you to remove the outline, change its weight, or apply a dash style to the outline.

APPLYING SPECIAL EFFECTS TO WORDART

You can apply special effects to your WordArt objects, such as shadows, reflections, glows, transformations, and more.

APPLY SPECIAL EFFECTS TO WORDART

USE the presentation that is still open from the previous exercise.

1. Select the WordArt graphic on slide 1, if necessary.
2. Click the **Text Effects** drop-down arrow. PowerPoint displays the Text Effects menu.
3. Click **Reflection**. PowerPoint displays the reflection special effects, as shown in Figure 3-22.

Figure 3-22

WordArt special effects

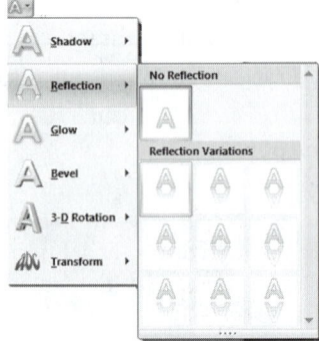

4. Click **Tight Reflection, touching**. PowerPoint adds the reflection special effect to the WordArt object.
5. Click outside the graphic to clear its border.
6. Move the WordArt graphic close to the subtitle, approximately where the slide title would be, as shown in Figure 3-23.

Figure 3-23

A reflection special effect added to the WordArt object

PAUSE. LEAVE the presentation open to use in the next exercise.

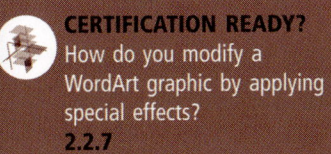

CERTIFICATION READY?
How do you modify a WordArt graphic by applying special effects?
2.2.7

WordArt special effects provide a way to spice up an ordinary slide. Although you should not use WordArt special effects on all your slides, you may want to look for spots in your presentations where a little artistic punch will liven up your slide show. Always consider your audience and your topic when adding special effects. For example, a presentation discussing plant closings and layoffs would not be an appropriate place for a cheerful-looking WordArt graphic.

Formatting Text with WordArt Styles

You do not have to insert a WordArt graphic to use the WordArt styles. You can apply WordArt styles to any text in a slide.

➔ **FORMAT TEXT WITH WORDART STYLES**

USE the presentation that is still open from the previous exercise.

1. Go to slide 2.
2. Select the slide title, *On-Time Delivery*.
3. Click the **Drawing Tools Format** tab.
4. Click the **More** button for the WordArt styles gallery to display all available styles.
5. Click the **Fill – Accent 2, Warm Matte Bevel** WordArt style.
6. Click outside the text placeholder to clear its border. Your slide should look like the one shown in Figure 3-24.

Figure 3-24

Formatting text with a WordArt style

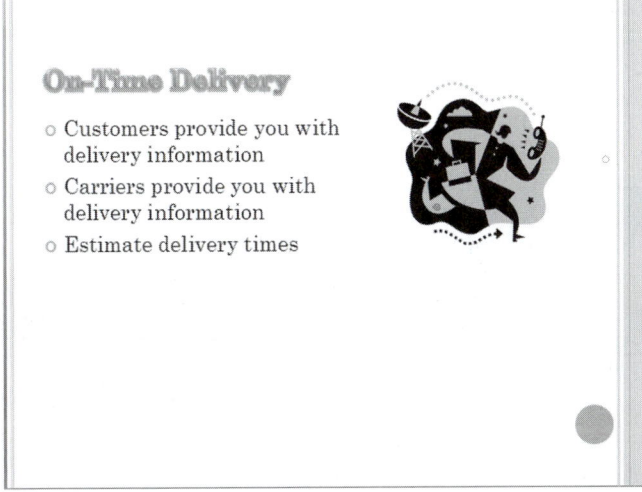

7. **SAVE** and **CLOSE** the file.

PAUSE. LEAVE PowerPoint open to use in the next exercise.

Applying WordArt styles to regular text in a presentation is an additional way to format the text to customize the presentation. You can use the same features you used to format the WordArt graphic to format a title or bulleted text: Text Fill, Text Outline, and Text Effects.

■ Creating and Formatting Text Boxes

THE BOTTOM LINE You can use text boxes as containers for text or graphics. Text boxes make it easy to position content anywhere on a slide.

Adding a Text Box to a Slide

Text boxes can be used to place text on a slide anyplace you want it. In this exercise, you add a text box to a slide and then insert text into the text box.

 ADD A TEXT BOX TO A SLIDE

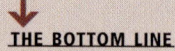

The *Profit Analysis* file is available on the companion CD-ROM.

1. **OPEN** the *Profit Analysis* presentation.
2. Go to slide 1, if necessary.
3. Click the **Insert** tab on the Ribbon.
4. Click **Text Box** in the Text group. The cursor changes to a text insertion pointer.
5. Move the pointer to the right side of the slide about two-thirds of the way up.
6. Click and hold down the mouse button. Drag the mouse down and to the right to create a rectangle.
7. Release the mouse button. The rectangle changes to a text box, as shown in Figure 3-25.

Figure 3-25

Inserting a text box

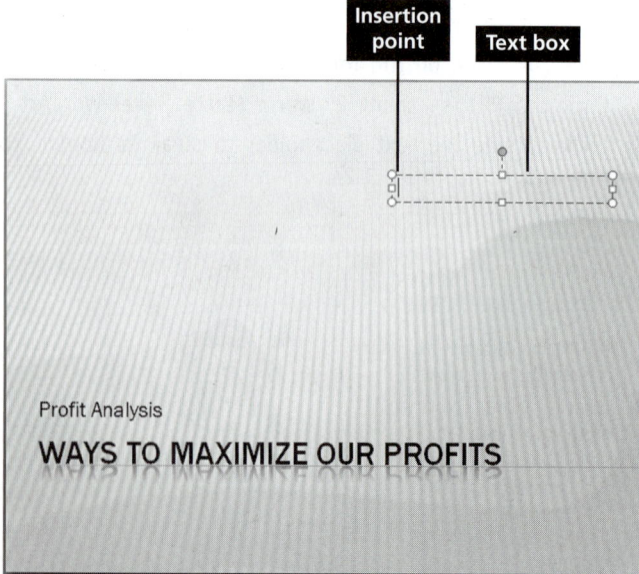

TAKE NOTE

When you release the mouse button after creating a text box, the Ribbon automatically displays the Home tab once more.

8. Key **Fourth Coffee** in the text box.
9. Click outside the text box to clear its border. Your slide should look like the one shown in Figure 3-26.

Figure 3-26

A text box with text inserted

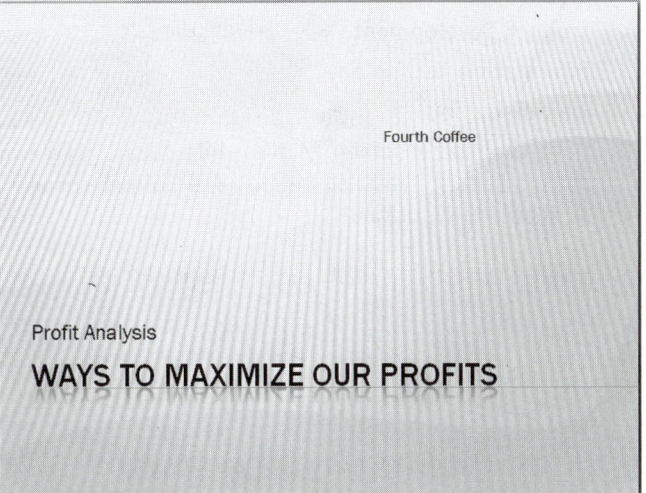

10. **SAVE** the presentation as *Profit Analysis Boxes*.

PAUSE. LEAVE the presentation open to use in the next exercise.

Although PowerPoint layouts are very flexible and provide a number of ways to insert text, you may occasionally need to insert text in a location for which there is no default placeholder. ***Text boxes*** are the answer in this circumstance. You can use a text box to hold a few words, an entire paragraph of text, or even several paragraphs of text.

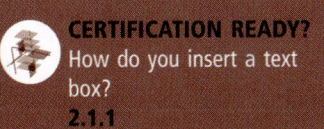

CERTIFICATION READY?
How do you insert a text box?
2.1.1

You have two options when creating a text box. If you simply click the slide with the text box pointer, you create a text box in which text will not wrap. As you enter text, the text box expands horizontally to accommodate the text. If you want to create a text box that will contain the text in a specific area, with text wrapping from line to line, you draw a desired width with the text box pointer. When text reaches that border, it wraps to the next line.

Resizing a Text Box

Text boxes can be resized so other text boxes or objects can be added to a slide without interfering with the text box or to rearrange a text box's contents.

➔ RESIZE A TEXT BOX

USE the presentation that is still open from the previous exercise.

1. Go to slide 2.
2. Click the **Insert** tab on the Ribbon.
3. Click **Text Box** in the Text group.
4. Drag to draw a text box under the *Divisional Breakdown* title.

5. Key the following items into the text box, placing each item on its own line:
   Sales
   Marketing
   Purchasing
   Production
   Distribution
   Customer Service
   Human Resources
   Product Development
   Information Technology
   Administration
6. Move the mouse pointer to the white square in the middle of the text box's right border. This is a resizing handle. The pointer changes to a double-headed arrow, as shown in Figure 3-27.

Figure 3-27

A text box with resizing handle selected

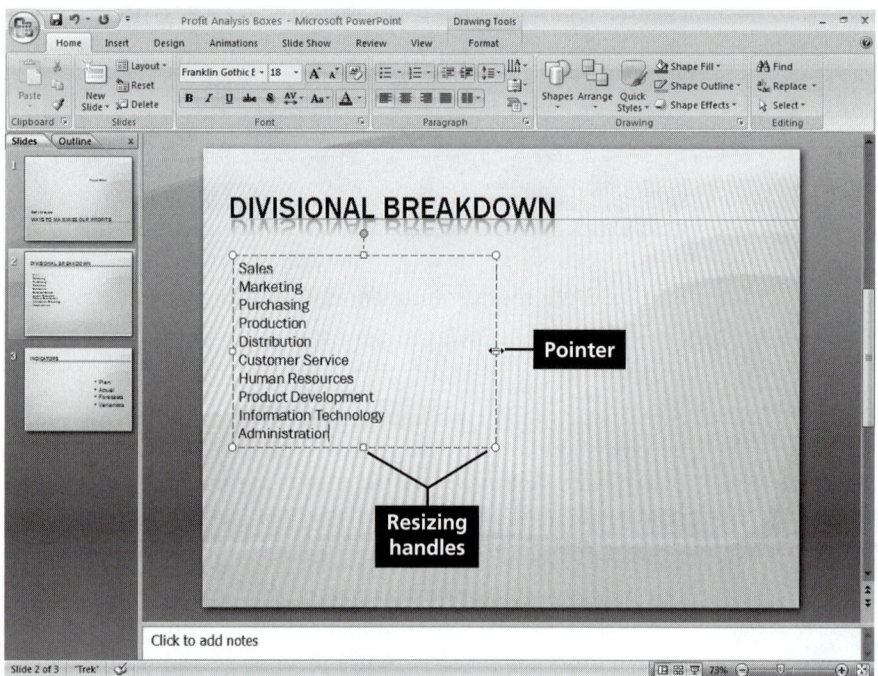

7. Click and hold down the mouse button.

TAKE NOTE A text box has eight resizing handles: one in each corner and one in the middle of each side.

8. Move the mouse pointer to the left until the text box's right border is close to the text (all entries should still be on a single line).
9. Release the mouse button. The text box resizes to a smaller size. Your slide should look like the one in Figure 3-28.

Figure 3-28

The resized text box

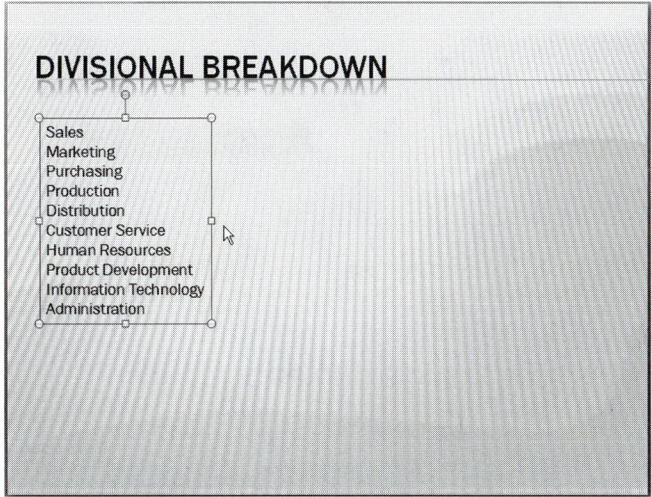

10. Click outside the text box to clear its border.

PAUSE. LEAVE the presentation open to use in the next exercise.

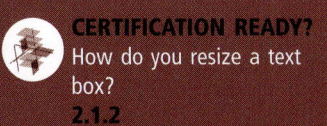

CERTIFICATION READY?
How do you resize a text box?
2.1.2

If the only object you have on your slide is a text box, you do not have to resize it. However, if you plan to add other objects, such as additional text boxes, WordArt, charts, pictures, and other items, you may want to resize text boxes so they do not consume too much space on your slides.

Setting Formatting Options for a Text Box

When you add a text box to a slide, you can see it because it has a resizing border around it. However, once you deselect the text box, you cannot see the text box itself, only its contents. You can use formatting options such as a Quick Style, a fill, or a border to make the text box more visible on the slide.

APPLYING A QUICK STYLE TO A TEXT BOX

PowerPoint's Quick Styles allow you to quickly format any text box or placeholder with a combination of fill, border, and effect formats to make the object stand out on the slide.

APPLY A QUICK STYLE TO A TEXT BOX

USE the presentation that is still open from the previous exercise.

1. Go to slide 1.
2. Click the *Fourth Coffee* text box to select it.
3. Click the **Quick Styles** button on the Home tab to display a gallery of Quick Styles.
4. Select the **Intense Effect – Accent 6** Quick Style, the last thumbnail in the last row. Click outside the text box to clear its border. The Quick Style formatting is applied to the text box, as shown in Figure 3-29.

TAKE NOTE

As you move the mouse pointer over the Quick Style thumbnails, your selected object shows how those formats would look if applied.

Figure 3-29

A Quick Style applied to a text box

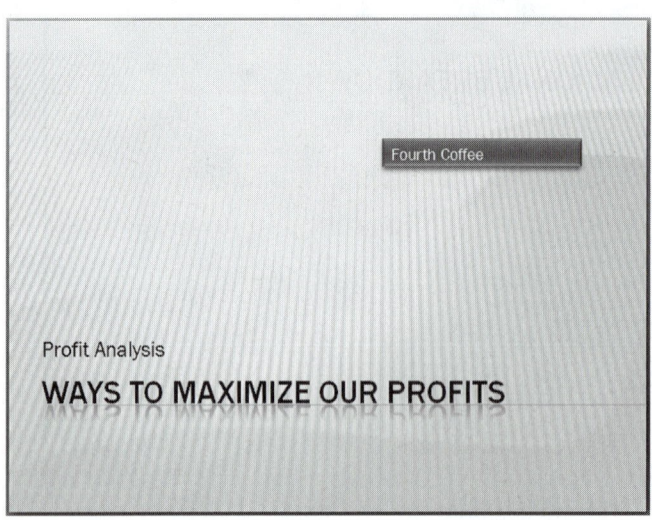

PAUSE. LEAVE the presentation open to use in the next exercise.

There are several advantages to using **Quick Styles** to format an object. Each Quick Style provides a number of formatting options that would take more time to apply separately. Quick Styles also give a professional appearance to slides. Using Quick Styles can also make it easy to format consistently throughout a presentation.

In this exercise, you applied a Quick Style to a text box, but you will find that PowerPoint also provides Quick Styles for other features such as tables, SmartArt graphics, charts, and pictures.

APPLYING FILL AND BORDER FORMATTING TO A TEXT BOX

If you want more control over formatting applied to a text box, you can use the Shape Fill and Shape Outline tools.

APPLY FILL AND BORDER FORMATTING TO A TEXT BOX

USE the presentation that is still open from the previous exercise.

1. Go to slide 2.
2. Click any item in the text box list. PowerPoint displays the text box border and sizing handles.
3. Click the **Shape Fill** drop-down arrow in the Drawing group. The Theme Colors palette for the text box fill color appears, as shown in Figure 3-30.

Figure 3-30

Choosing a color for a text box fill

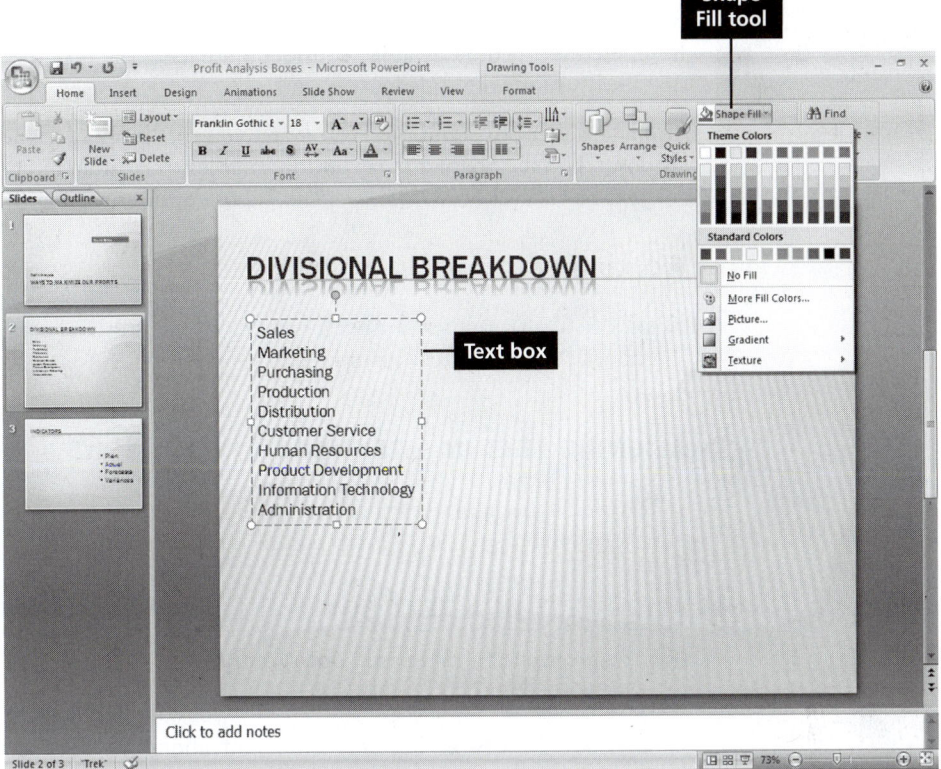

4. Click the **Light Yellow, Background 2, Darker 25%** theme color. PowerPoint formats the text box fill with this color.

5. Click the **Shape Outline** drop-down arrow. The Theme Colors palette for the text box border color appears.

6. Click the **Orange, Accent 1, Darker 25%** theme color. PowerPoint formats the text box border with this color.

7. Click the **Shape Outline** drop-down arrow again.

8. Click **Weight**. A menu with line weights appears.

9. Click **3 pt**. PowerPoint resizes the text box border to a 3-point border size.

10. Click outside the text box to clear its border. Your slide should look like the one in Figure 3-31.

Figure 3-31

The formatted text box

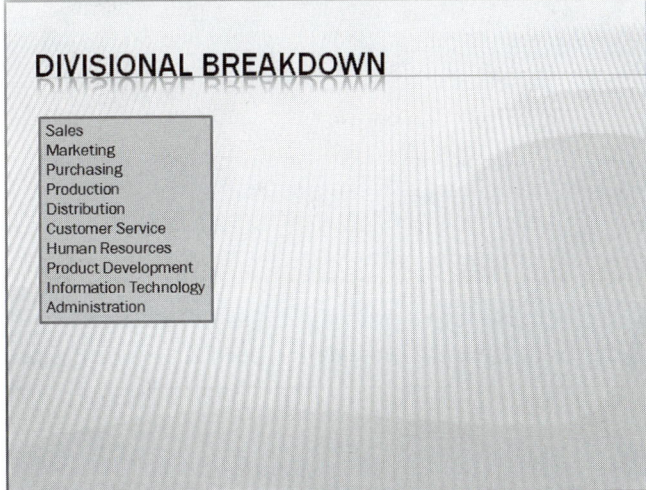

PAUSE. LEAVE the presentation open to use in the next exercise.

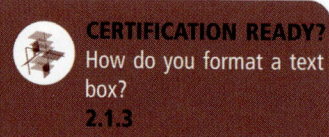

CERTIFICATION READY?
How do you format a text box?
2.1.3

Applying a fill color that contrasts with the text inside the box and with the slide background makes the text in a text box easy to read. If you choose not to use a fill in the text box (text boxes are not filled by default), consider boldfacing the text and enlarging it so that it shows up clearly against the slide background.

To make a text box stand out even more, you can apply special effects such as reflections or shadows. Use the Shape Effects button to access the different effects. You can also right-click the text box, select Format Shape, and choose options such as 3-D Format or 3-D Rotation.

Working with Text in a Text Box

You can format the text within a text box in a number of ways: adjust alignment, change text orientation, set text margins, and even set the text in columns.

ALIGNING TEXT IN A TEXT BOX

Text that appears in a text box can be aligned left, center, or right. In the following exercise, you align text to the center of the text box.

ALIGN TEXT IN A TEXT BOX

USE the presentation that is still open from the previous exercise.

1. On slide 2, click anywhere in the first line in the text box.
2. Click the **Center** button. PowerPoint aligns the text so that it is centered between the left and right border of the text box.
3. Select the rest of the text in the text box.
4. Click the **Center** button.
5. Click outside the text box to clear its border. Your slide should look like the one in Figure 3-32.

TAKE NOTE

If you resize a text box that has centered text, the text re-centers automatically based on the final size of the text box.

Figure 3-32

Text aligned in a text box

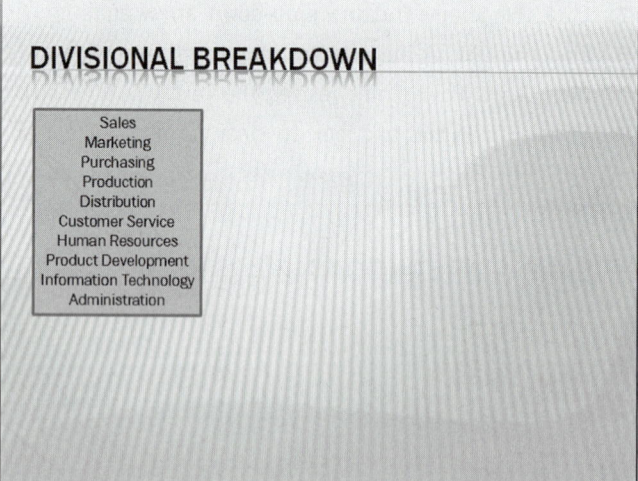

PAUSE. LEAVE the presentation open to use in the next exercise.

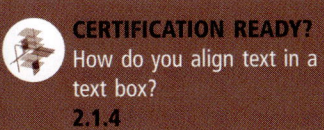

CERTIFICATION READY?
How do you align text in a text box?
2.1.4

You use the same alignment options in a text box that are available for a text placeholder: left, center, right, and justify. By default, PowerPoint aligns text in new text boxes to the left. If you align text to a different position, such as right, and then add a new paragraph by pressing Enter from that text, the new paragraph keeps the right-aligned formatting.

The Justify alignment option keeps long passages of text even on the left and right margins of a text box, similar to the way newspapers and many books align text. PowerPoint adds extra space between words if necessary to stretch a line to meet the right margin. This can result in a very "gappy" look that you can improve by adjusting font size and/or the width of the text box.

ORIENTING TEXT IN A TEXT BOX

You can change the text direction in a text box so that text runs from bottom to top or stacks one letter atop the other. This can make text in the text box more visually interesting. You can also change orientation by rotating the text box itself.

ORIENT TEXT IN A TEXT BOX

USE the presentation that is still open from the previous exercise.

1. Go to slide 1.
2. Select the *Fourth Coffee* text box.
3. Click the **Text Direction** drop-down arrow in the Paragraph group. A menu of text direction choices displays.
4. Click **Rotate all text 270°**. PowerPoint changes the orientation of the text in the text box to run from the bottom of the text box to the top, as shown in Figure 3-33.

Figure 3-33

The text in a different orientation

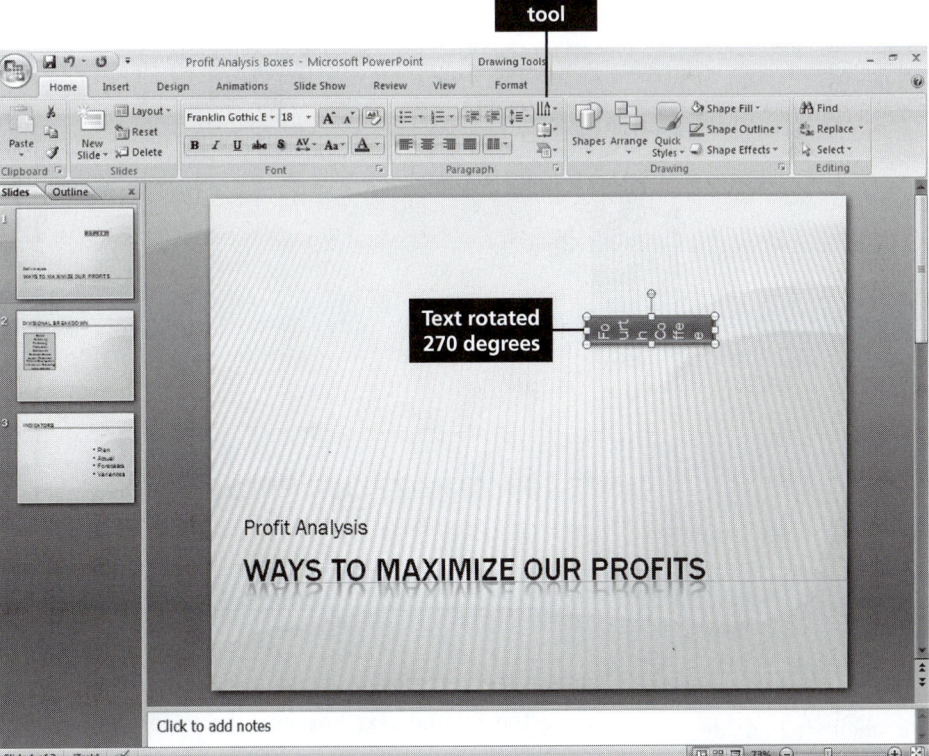

5. Resize the text box so the text appears in a single vertical column.
6. Increase the text size to 32 points. Resize the text box again if necessary so the text is on a single line.
7. Move the text box to the left side of the slide, above the subtitle.
8. Click outside the text box to clear its border. Your slide should look like the one in Figure 3-34.

Figure 3-34

The repositioned text box

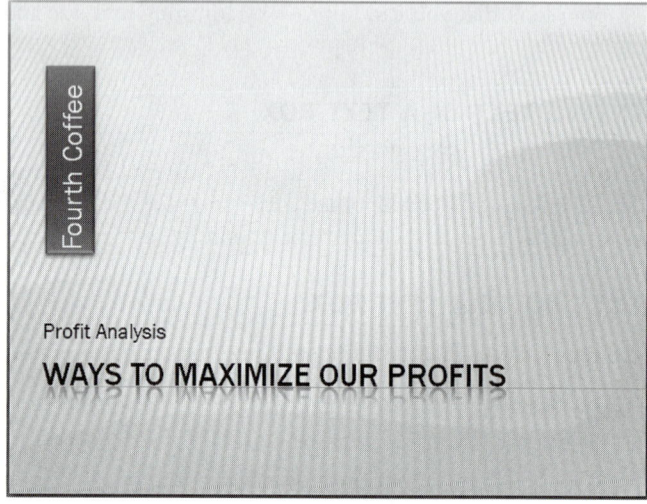

9. Draw another text box on slide 1 and key **Sales Dept.** in the text box.
10. Move the mouse to the round, green rotation handle at the top center of the text box. The mouse pointer changes to an open-ended circle with an arrow point.
11. Click and hold down the mouse button.
12. Move the mouse to the right so that the outline of the text box starts to rotate around its center, as shown in Figure 3-35.

Figure 3-35

Rotating a text box

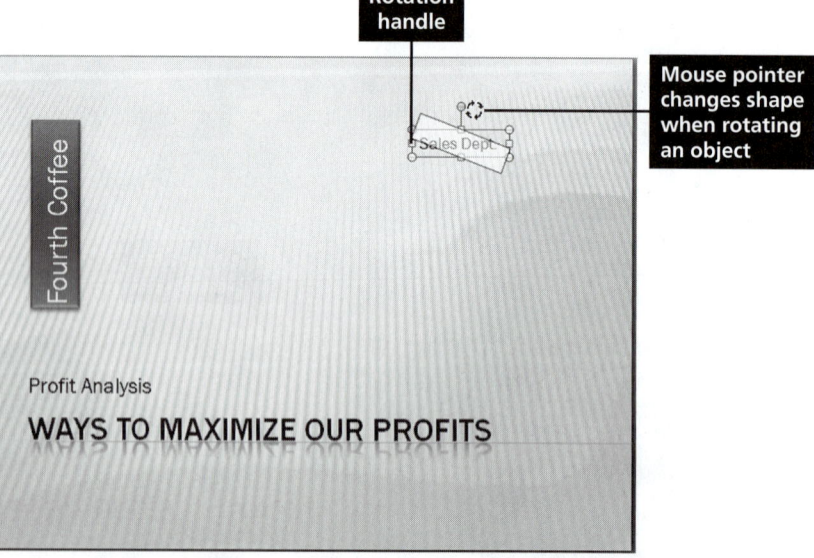

TAKE NOTE

When you drag an object's rotation handle, the mouse pointer turns into a small circle made of arrows.

13. Rotate the text box to about a 45-degree angle, then release the mouse button.
14. Move the rotated text box into the upper-right corner of the slide.
15. Click outside the text box to clear its sizing handles. Your slide should look like the one in Figure 3-36.

Figure 3-36

The rotated and repositioned text box

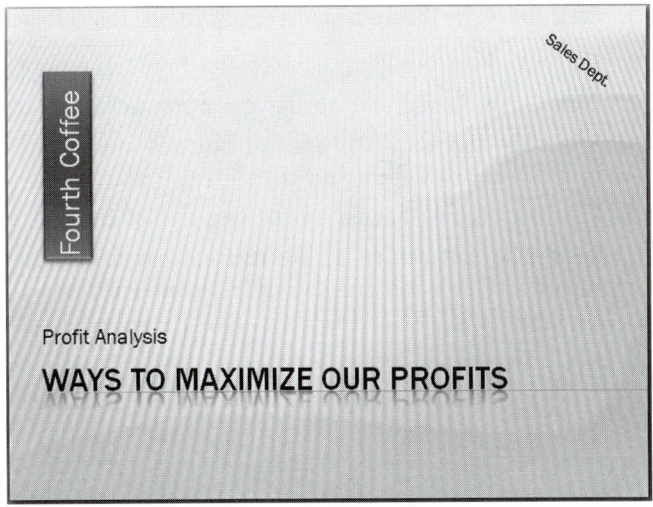

PAUSE. LEAVE the presentation open to use in the next exercise.

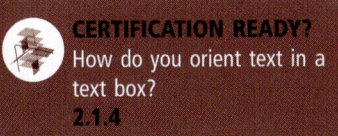

CERTIFICATION READY?
How do you orient text in a text box?
2.1.4

Orienting text boxes can be a design enhancement for your slides. For example, you might create a text box that includes your company name in it. Instead of drawing the text box horizontally on the slide, draw it so it is taller than wide and then choose one of the Text Direction button options to change text orientation. You can also rotate a text box or any placeholder for a special effect.

SETTING THE MARGINS IN A TEXT BOX

PowerPoint enables you to set the margins in a text box. Margins control the distance between the text and the outer border of the text box.

SET THE MARGINS IN A TEXT BOX

USE the presentation that is still open from the previous exercise.

1. Go to slide 3.
2. Select the text box on the right side of the slide.
3. Right-click inside the text box and click **Format Shape** on the shortcut menu. The Format Shape dialog box opens.
4. Click **Text Box** in the left pane of the Format Shape dialog box. Text box layout options appear, as shown in Figure 3-37.

Figure 3-37

Text box layout options

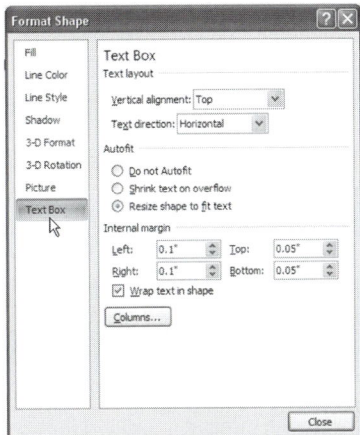

5. Click the ▲ in the Left spin control to set the left margin at **0.5"**.
6. Click the ▲ in the Right spin control to set the right margin at **0.5"**.
7. Click **Close**. PowerPoint applies the margin changes to the text box.
8. Select the top border of the text box and move the text box up so all of the text in the text box appears on the slide.
9. Grab the resizing handle on the left side of the text box.
10. Resize the text box so all the text appears readable on the slide. Your slide should look like the one shown in Figure 3-38.

Figure 3-38

Text box with new margins

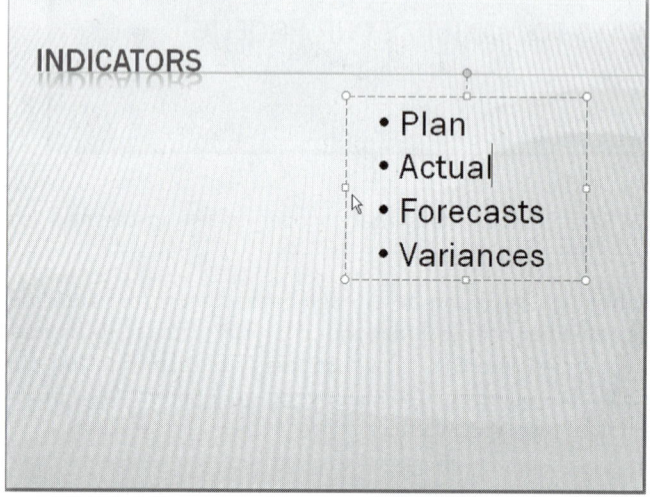

PAUSE. LEAVE the presentation open to use in the next exercise.

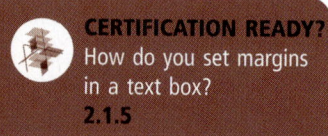

CERTIFICATION READY?
How do you set margins in a text box?
2.1.5

Resizing text box margins enables you to fine-tune text placement within a text box. For example, if you want text to appear 1 inch away from the left side of the text box, change the Left box to 1.0. You might want to do this if your slide design needs to have text align with other items placed on the slide. If you have chosen to format a text box or placeholder with a fill, increasing margins can also prevent the text from appearing to crowd the edges of the text box.

SETTING UP COLUMNS IN A TEXT BOX

Another way to format text in a text box is to format the text in columns. Columns can make text more readable.

SET UP COLUMNS IN A TEXT BOX

USE the presentation that is still open from the previous exercise.

1. Go to slide 2 and click inside the text box you formatted earlier.
2. Click the **Columns** drop-down arrow in the Paragraph group. A menu appears, as shown in Figure 3-39.

Figure 3-39

Setting up columns in a text box

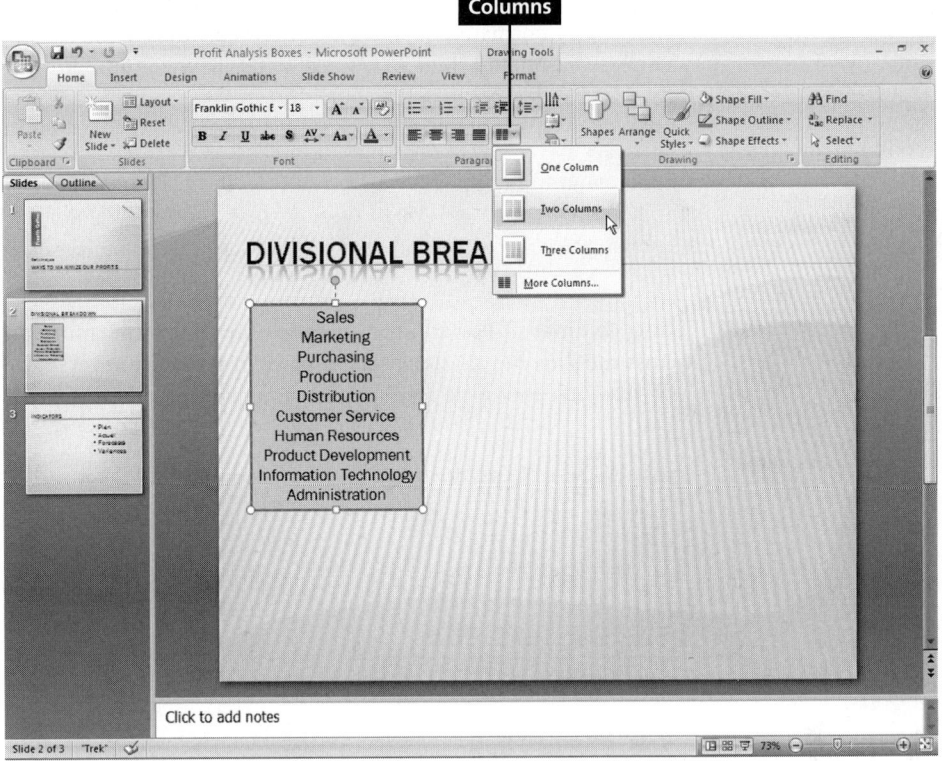

3. Click **Two Columns**. PowerPoint formats the list of items into two columns.

 If you need two lists on a slide but do not want to use columns, create two text boxes and position them side by side.

4. Drag the right sizing handle to the right so the text box contents are readable.
5. Drag the bottom resizing handle upward until an equal number of items appear in each column. You may need to resize the right side of the text box again. Each column should contain five lines of text, as shown in Figure 3-40.

Figure 3-40

The text box with two columns

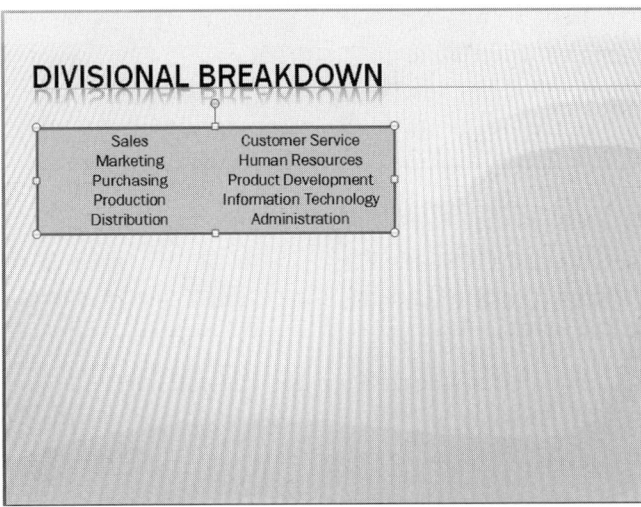

PAUSE. LEAVE the presentation open to use in the next exercise.

PowerPoint enables you to create columns in text boxes to help you format your text into columns of information. As you enter text or other items into a column, PowerPoint fills up the first column and then wraps text to the next column. You can create columns in any text box, placeholder, or shape.

TAKE NOTE

If the column choices in the Column drop-down menu do not meet your needs, click the More Columns option to display the Columns dialog box. Here you can set any number of columns and adjust the spacing between columns.

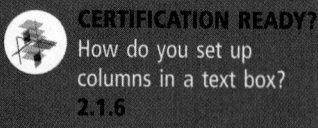

CERTIFICATION READY?
How do you set up columns in a text box?
2.1.6

Using columns in PowerPoint is a good way to present information you want to set up in lists across the slide but do not want to place in PowerPoint tables. Viewers of your presentation will have an easier time reading and remembering lists formatted into multiple columns.

Deleting a Text Box

Text boxes you no longer need on a slide can be deleted very easily in PowerPoint. In the following exercise, you delete a text box.

→ DELETE A TEXT BOX

USE the presentation that is still open from the previous exercise.

1. Go to slide 3.
2. Click in the text box under the slide title, then click the text box's border to select the text box, as shown in Figure 3-41. The text box's border is a solid line when selected.

Figure 3-41

Selecting a text box to delete

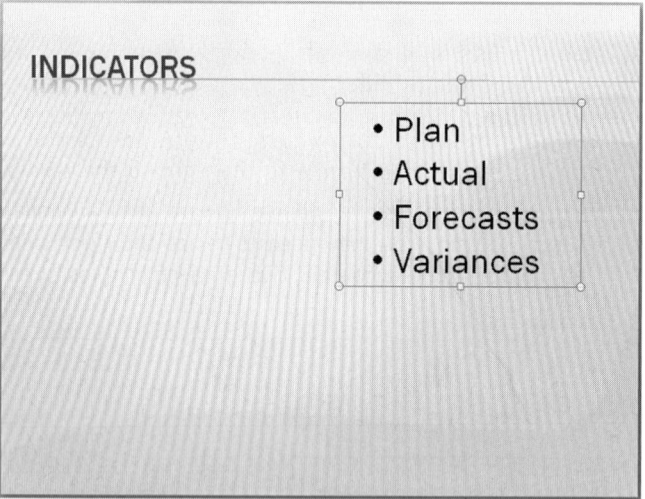

3. Press **Delete**. PowerPoint deletes the text box.
4. **SAVE** and **CLOSE** the file.

   STOP. CLOSE PowerPoint.

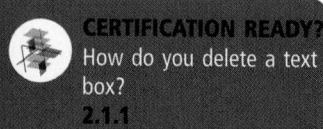

CERTIFICATION READY?
How do you delete a text box?
2.1.1

If you decide after you delete a text box that you want to undo your deletion, click the Undo button on the Quick Access Toolbar. You also can press Ctrl+Z to undo the deletion.

SUMMARY SKILL MATRIX

In This Lesson You Learned how to:
Choose Fonts and Font Sizes
Apply Font Styles and Effects
Change Font Color
Copy Character Formats with the Format Painter
Align Paragraphs
Set Paragraph Line Spacing
Create Numbered Lists
Work with Bulleted Lists
Insert a WordArt Graphic
Format a WordArt Graphic
Format Text with WordArt Styles
Add a Text Box to a Slide
Resize a Text Box
Set Formatting Options for a Text Box
Work with Text in a Text Box
Delete a Text Box

Knowledge Assessment

Fill in the Blank

Fill in each blank with the term or phrase that best completes the statement.

1. A(n) *placeholder* is a container for text or a picture on a slide.
2. A font *style* is an attribute such as boldface or italic.
3. The small white boxes on the borders of a text box are called *sizing handles*.
4. You can paint the background of a text box with a(n) *Fill* color.
5. The border of a WordArt character is called a(n) *Outline*.
6. A(n) *FONT* is sometimes also called a typeface.
7. *Justified* text is aligned to both the left and right margins of a text box.
8. A(n) *WordArt* object is text in the form of a graphic.
9. You should use a(n) *Numbered* list to show items in a specific order.
10. A(n) *bullet* is a small character, such as a dot or a square, that appears before an item in a list.

Multiple Choice

Circle the correct answer.

1. This PowerPoint feature lets you perform sophisticated formatting to text very quickly.
   a. **Quick Styles**
   b. Paragraph group
   c. Insert tab
   d. Line Spacing

2. You can select fonts and font sizes from the Ribbon or the _____.
   a. Quick Access Toolbar
   b. Format Painter
   c. **Mini toolbar**
   d. Shape Outline gallery

3. Which of the following is not a standard paragraph-alignment option?
   a. Left
   b. Center
   c. Right
   d. **Under**

4. Text attributes such as superscript and all caps are called _____.
   a. fonts
   b. **effects**
   c. bullets
   d. points

5. Most of PowerPoint's text placeholders automatically format text as a(n) _____ list.
   a. numbered
   b. **bulleted**
   c. sorted
   d. itemized

6. Each PowerPoint theme supplies bullet characters for up to _____ levels of bullets.
   a. 3
   b. 5
   c. 7
   d. **9**

7. The characters in a WordArt graphic include _____.
   a. **an outline and a fill**
   b. a bullet
   c. a shape and a shadow
   d. boldface and underlining

8. To apply a WordArt style to existing text on a slide, you must first _____.
   a. format the text with a Quick Style
   b. insert a text box
   c. **select the text**
   d. change the text's alignment

9. If you simply click the slide with the text box pointer, you create a text box in which text will not _____.
   a. appear
   b. fit
   c. wrap
   d. align

   p. 575

10. When you orient the text in a text box, you are changing the text's _____.
    a. alignment
    b. direction
    c. size
    d. font

Competency Assessment

Project 3-1: Blended Coffees

As director of marketing for Fourth Coffee, you have prepared a product brochure for new company employees. This year's brochure includes a new page of refreshments that you need to format. You will use Quick Styles to format the title and text placeholders.

GET READY. Launch PowerPoint if it is not already running.

The *Coffee Products* file is available on the companion CD-ROM.

1. **OPEN** the *Coffee Products* presentation.
2. Go to slide 2 and click anywhere in the slide title.
3. Click the **Quick Styles** button to display the Quick Styles gallery.
4. Click the **Moderate Effect – Accent 1** style.
5. Click in any of the bulleted product items.
6. Click the **Quick Styles** button.
7. Click the **Subtle Effect – Accent 1** style.
8. **SAVE** the presentation as *Coffee Products Brochure* and **CLOSE** the file.
   LEAVE PowerPoint open for the next project.

Project 3-2: Typecasting with Typefaces

As an account representative for the Graphic Design Institute, you are responsible for securing sales leads for your company's print and poster division. One way to do this is to send out a promotional flyer using a slide from a company PowerPoint presentation. As you select the slide, you notice that the fonts are not appropriate for your flyer. You need to modify both the font and size of the slide's text.

The *Graphic Designs* file is available on the companion CD-ROM.

1. **OPEN** the *Graphic Designs* presentation.
2. On slide 1, select all the text under the three photographs.
3. Click the **Font** drop-down arrow.
4. Click **Brush Script MT**.
5. Click the **Font Size** drop-down arrow.
6. Click **32**.
7. Click anywhere in the second paragraph (*Graphic Design Institute*).
8. Click the **Center** button in the Paragraph group.
9. Select the first paragraph of text, then click the **Format Painter** in the Clipboard group.

10. Go to slide 2, then drag the Format Painter pointer over the text on the right side of the slide.
11. **SAVE** the presentation as *Graphic Designs Final* and **CLOSE** the file.
    LEAVE PowerPoint open for the next project.

■ Proficiency Assessment

Project 3-3: Destinations

As the owner and operator of Margie's Travel, you are involved with many aspects of sales, marketing, customer service, and new products and services. Today you want to format the text in a slide presentation that includes new European destinations.

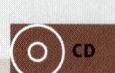

The *New Destinations* file is available on the companion CD-ROM.

1. **OPEN** the *New Destinations* presentation.
2. Go to slide 2 and select the slide's title text. Click the **Bold** button to make the title boldface.
3. Select all the text in the bulleted list. Click the **Align Text Left** button to align the list along the left side of the text placeholder.
4. With the list still selected, open the Bullets and Numbering dialog box. Change the bullets' color to **Orange, Accent 2**, then resize the bullets so they are 90% of the text's size.
5. Click the **Font Color** drop-down arrow, then change the list's font color to **Dark Green, Background 2, Lighter 80%**.
6. Click **Text Box** on the Insert tab, then click below the picture on the slide to create a nonwrapping text box.
7. In the text box, key **Companion Flies Free until Jan. 1!**
8. Click the **Quick Styles** button and apply the **Colored Outline – Accent 1** Quick Style to the text box.
9. **SAVE** the presentation as *New Destinations Final* and **CLOSE** the file.
    LEAVE PowerPoint open for the next project.

Project 3-4: Business To Business Imports

You are the lone marketing research person in your company, World Wide Importers. You often find exciting and potentially highly profitable new products that go overlooked by some of the senior staff. You need to draw attention to these products, and PowerPoint can help. Create a short presentation that uses WordArt to jazz up your presentation. This presentation will focus on precision equipment your company can start importing.

The *World Wide Importers* file is available on the companion CD-ROM.

1. **OPEN** the *World Wide Importers* presentation.
2. With slide 1 on the screen, open the WordArt gallery and select **Gradient Fill - Accent 1, Outline - White, Glow – Accent 2**.
3. In the WordArt text box that appears, key **World Wide Importers**. Reposition the text box so it is just above the subtitle and centered between the left and right edges of the slide.
4. In the WordArt Styles group, open the Text Fill color palette and click **Aqua, Accent 1, Darker 25%**.
5. Open the Text Effects menu and select the **Cool Slant** bevel effect.
6. Go to slide 2 and select all the text in the bulleted list.
7. Change the font size to **24**, then change the line spacing to **1.5**.

8. Click the **Numbering** button to convert the list into a numbered list.
9. Go to slide 3. Insert a text box under the slide's title. Key the following items into the text box, putting each item on its own line:

    Digital controls

    Heat sensors

    Laser guides

    Light sensors

    Motion detectors

    Pressure monitors

    Regulators

    Timing systems

10. Select all the text in the text box and change the font size to **24**.
11. Open the Quick Styles gallery and click **Colored Fill – Accent 4**.
12. Click the **Columns** button, then click **Two Columns**.
13. Resize the text box by dragging its sizing handles, as needed, so that four items appear in each column within the text box.
14. **SAVE** the presentation as *World Wide Importers Final* and **CLOSE** the file.

    LEAVE PowerPoint open for the next project.

■ Mastery Assessment

Project 3-5: Pop Quiz

As an instructor at the School of Fine Art, you decide to use a slide show to give beginning students the first pop quiz on art history. You need to finish the presentation by formatting the text and removing some unneeded text boxes.

The *Art History* file is available on the companion CD-ROM.

1. **OPEN** the *Art History* presentation.
2. On slides 2, 3, and 4, do each of the following:
   a. Format the slide's title with the **Intense Effect – Dark 1 Quick Style**.
   b. Convert the bulleted list of answers into a numbered list.
   c. Delete the text box (containing the correct answer) at the bottom of the slide.
3. **SAVE** the presentation as *Art History Final* and **CLOSE** the file.

   LEAVE PowerPoint open for the next project.

Project 3-6: Graphic Design Drafts

As the manager of the account representative that prepared the Graphic Designs slide, you want to put a few finishing touches on the slide before it is published. To protect against someone inadvertently printing the slide, you need to add a text box across the entire slide that announces the slide as a "Draft."

The *Graphic Designs Final* file is available on the companion CD-ROM.

1. **OPEN** the *Graphic Designs Final* presentation you completed in Project 3-2.
2. **SAVE** the presentation as *Graphic Designs Draft*.
3. Add a text box to the slide.
4. Key the word **DRAFT** into the text box.
5. Rotate the text box at a 45 degree angle across the center photo on the slide.

6. Enlarge the text to **88** points. Resize the text box as needed by dragging its sizing handles so the text fits properly inside the box.
7. **SAVE** and **CLOSE** the file.
   STOP. CLOSE PowerPoint.

INTERNET READY

Launch your browser and visit the Microsoft Web site at http://www.microsoft.com. On the Microsoft home page, click in the Search box, key the word *fonts*, then click the Search button. Look for pages on the Microsoft site that offer information about fonts; read the information to learn about how fonts are created and to find tips for using fonts wisely in your documents and presentations.

Designing a Presentation

4

LESSON SKILL MATRIX

Applying a Theme to a Presentation — 595	Students will learn how to apply a theme to a presentation.
Changing Theme Colors — 596	Students will learn how to change theme colors.
Changing Theme Fonts — 598	Students will learn how to change theme fonts.
Selecting a Theme Background — 599	Students will learn how to select a theme background.
Applying a Textured Background — 599	Students will learn how to apply a textured background.
Working with Different Layouts — 601	Students will learn how to work with different layouts.
Inserting a Date, Footer, and Slide Number — 603	Students will learn how to insert a date, footer, and slide number.
Adding a Hyperlink to a Slide — 605	Students will learn how to add a hyperlink to a slide.
Adding an Action to a Slide — 606	Students will learn how to add an action to a slide.
Testing Links in a Slide Show — 608	Students will learn how to test links in a slide show.
Applying a Transition — 609	Students will learn how to apply a transition.
Modifying a Transition — 610	Students will learn how to modify a transition.
Determining How Slides Will Advance — 611	Students will learn how to determine how slides will advance.
Using Built-In Animation — 612	Students will learn how to use built-in animation.
Modifying an Animation — 613	Students will learn how to modify an animation.
Creating a Customized Animation — 614	Students will learn how to create a customized animation.
Applying a Theme to a Slide Master — 618	Students will learn how to apply a theme to a slide master.
Changing a Slide Master's Background — 619	Students will learn how to change a slide master's background.
Adding New Elements to a Slide Master — 620	Students will learn how to add new elements to a slide master.

KEY TERMS
action
animation
footer
header
slide master
slide transition
target

593

Southridge Video is a small company that offers video services to the community, such as videography for special events, video editing services, and duplication and conversion services. As a sales representative for Southridge Video, you often present information on the company to those who are considering the use of professional-level video services. In this lesson, you will add design elements to a simple presentation to polish and improve its appearance. Themes, animations, and transitions provide visual interest that will convince new clients of your company's commitment to quality. You will also learn how to customize slide masters to make global changes to a presentation.

SOFTWARE ORIENTATION

Microsoft PowerPoint's Themes Gallery

PowerPoint's Themes gallery offers 20 unique designs you can apply to presentations to format the slides with colors, fonts, effects, and backgrounds. Figure 4-1 shows the Themes gallery.

Figure 4-1

The Themes gallery

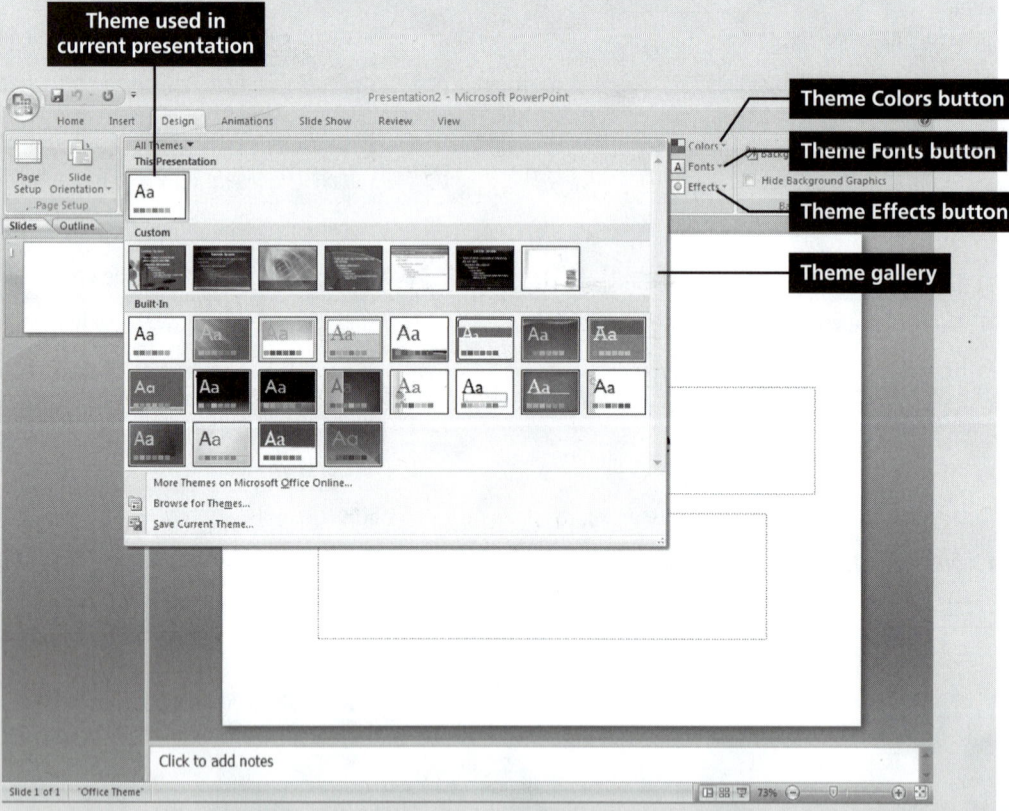

Use PowerPoint's built-in themes to give your presentation a polished, professional look without a lot of trial and error. Like Quick Styles, themes are designed to provide an immediate visual impact to a presentation.

Formatting Presentations with Themes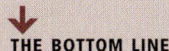

THE BOTTOM LINE Themes are new in PowerPoint 2007. Use a theme to quickly apply a unified set of colors, fonts, and effects to one or more slides in a presentation. You can modify a theme as desired to customize it for a particular presentation.

Applying a Theme to a Presentation

Select a theme from the Themes gallery to change the default "blank" formatting into a more visually striking slide show.

APPLY A THEME TO A PRESENTATION

GET READY. Before you begin these steps, be sure to launch Microsoft Office PowerPoint 2007.

The *Special Events* file is available on the companion CD-ROM.

1. Locate and open the *Special Events* presentation.
2. Click the **Design** tab and then click the **More** button in the Themes group. PowerPoint's available themes display in the Themes gallery, as shown in Figure 4-2.

Figure 4-2

The Themes gallery

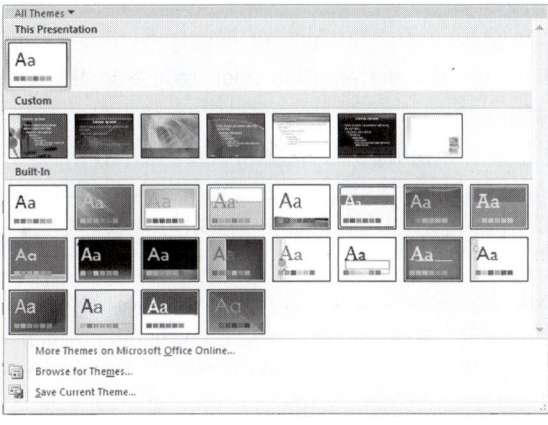

TAKE NOTE

The theme names are in alphabetical order in the gallery.

3. Point to any of the themes in the gallery. Notice that a ScreenTip displays the theme's name and the theme formats are instantly applied to the slide behind the gallery.
4. Point to the **Origin** theme to see its formats applied to the active slide, and then click the theme to apply it.
5. Scroll through the slides to see how the theme has supplied new colors, fonts, bullet symbols, and layouts. Slide 1 should resemble Figure 4-3.

Figure 4-3

Origin theme applied to slides

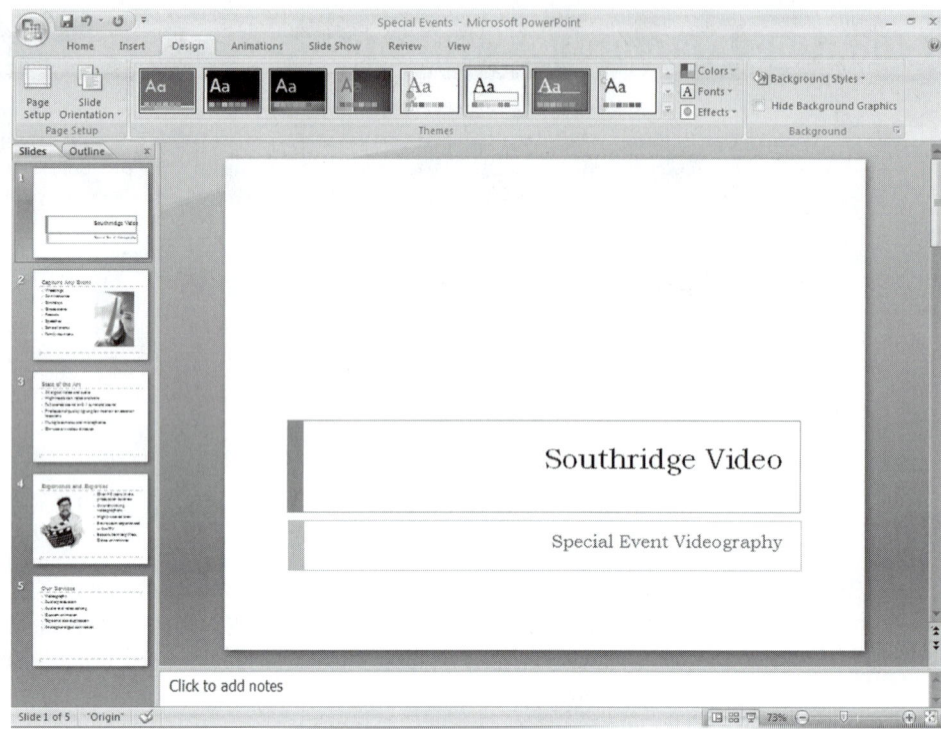

6. **SAVE** the presentation as *Special Events Final*.

PAUSE. LEAVE the presentation open to use in the next exercise.

A PowerPoint theme includes a set of colors designed to work well together, a set of fonts (one for headings and one for body text), special effects that can be applied to objects such as pictures or shapes, and often a graphic background. The theme also controls the layout of placeholders on each slide.

PowerPoint makes it easy to see how a theme will look on your slides by offering a *live preview*: As you move the mouse pointer over each theme in the gallery, that theme's formats display on the current slide. This formatting feature takes a great deal of guesswork out of the design process—if you don't like a theme's appearance, just move the pointer to a different theme or click outside the gallery to restore the previous appearance.

Clicking a theme applies it to all slides in a presentation. You can also apply a theme to a single slide or a selection of slides by making the selection, right-clicking the theme, and choosing Apply to Selected Slides. You can save any presentation you have customized as a new theme. Your custom themes display in the Custom area of the Themes gallery.

TAKE NOTE

The name of the current theme displays on the status bar to the right of the slide number information.

Changing Theme Colors

You can change theme colors by applying the colors of another theme or by creating a new theme color scheme.

⮕ CHANGE THEME COLORS

USE the presentation that is still open from the previous exercise.

1. Click the **Theme Colors** button in the Themes group. A gallery displays showing color palettes for all available themes.
2. Move the pointer over some of the color palettes to see the live preview of those colors on the current slide.
3. Click the **Aspect** theme color palette. The new colors are applied to the presentation, as shown in Figure 4-4.

Figure 4-4

The Aspect theme colors applied to all slides

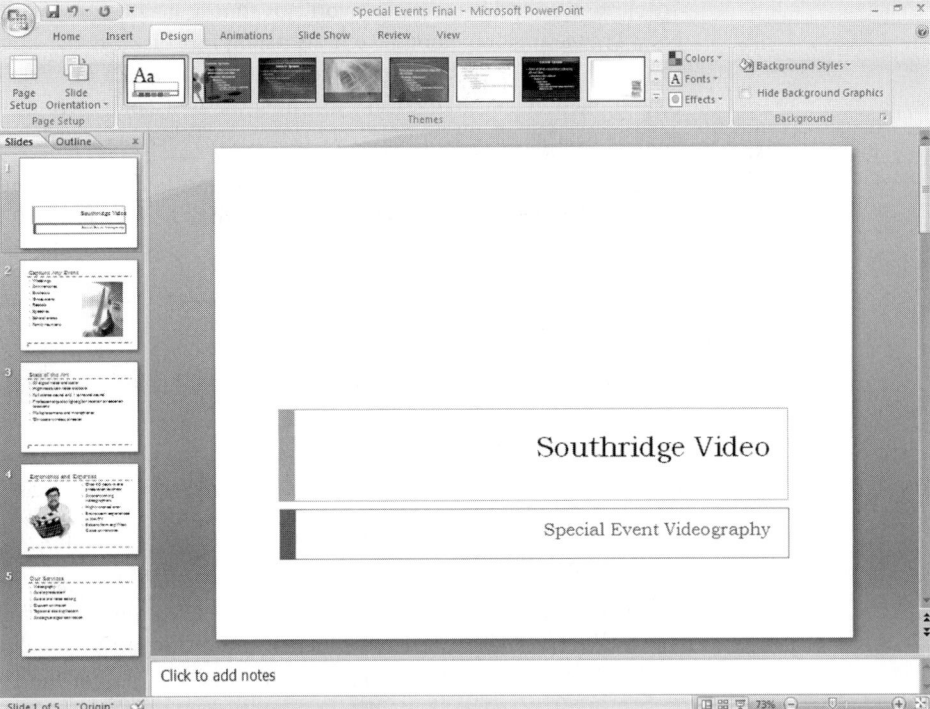

> **TAKE NOTE**
>
> Color palettes and font combinations are identified by theme name to make it easy to select them.

4. Click the **Theme Colors** button again, then click **Create New Theme Colors** at the bottom of the gallery. The dialog box shown in Figure 4-5 opens to allow you to replace colors in the current color palette.

Figure 4-5

The Create New Theme Colors dialog box

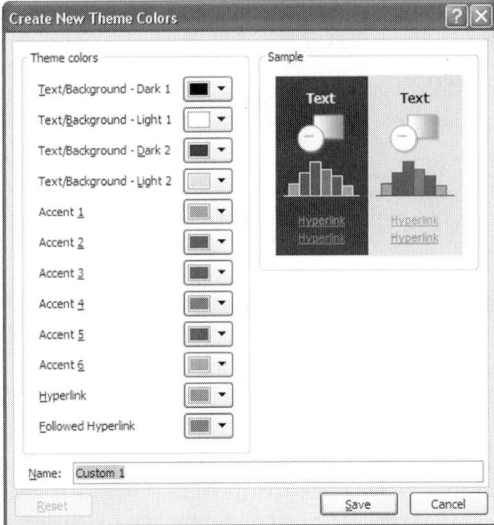

5. Click the drop-down arrow next to the light green color designated for Hyperlinks.
6. Click **Background 2, Lighter 25%** on the Theme Colors palette to change the color for hyperlinks to a medium gray.
7. Select the text in the **Name** box and key **Southridge** in its place. Click **Save** to save the new color palette.

   PAUSE. LEAVE the presentation open to use in the next exercise.

Although PowerPoint supplies specific colors for a theme, you do not have to use those colors if you prefer the colors of another theme. When you apply the colors from another theme, your current theme layout remains the same—only the colors of text and other elements change.

To create a unique appearance, you can choose new colors for theme elements in the Create New Theme Colors dialog box. This dialog box displays the theme's color palette and shows you what element each color applies to. A preview area shows the colors in use; as you change colors, the preview changes to show how the new colors work together. If you don't like the choices you have made, use the Reset button to restore the default colors.

You can save a new color scheme to make it available for use with any theme. Saved color schemes display at the top of the Theme Colors gallery in the Custom section.

Changing Theme Fonts

Each theme supplies a combination of two fonts to be applied to headings and text. You can select another set of theme fonts or create your own new combination.

⊙ **CHANGE THEME FONTS**

USE the presentation that is still open from the previous exercise.

1. Click the **Theme Fonts** button in the Themes group. A gallery displays showing font combinations for all available themes.
2. Move the pointer over some of the font combinations to see the live preview of those fonts on the current slide.
3. Click the **Trek** font combination to give a crisper look to the slide text. The new fonts are applied to the presentation, as shown in Figure 4-6.

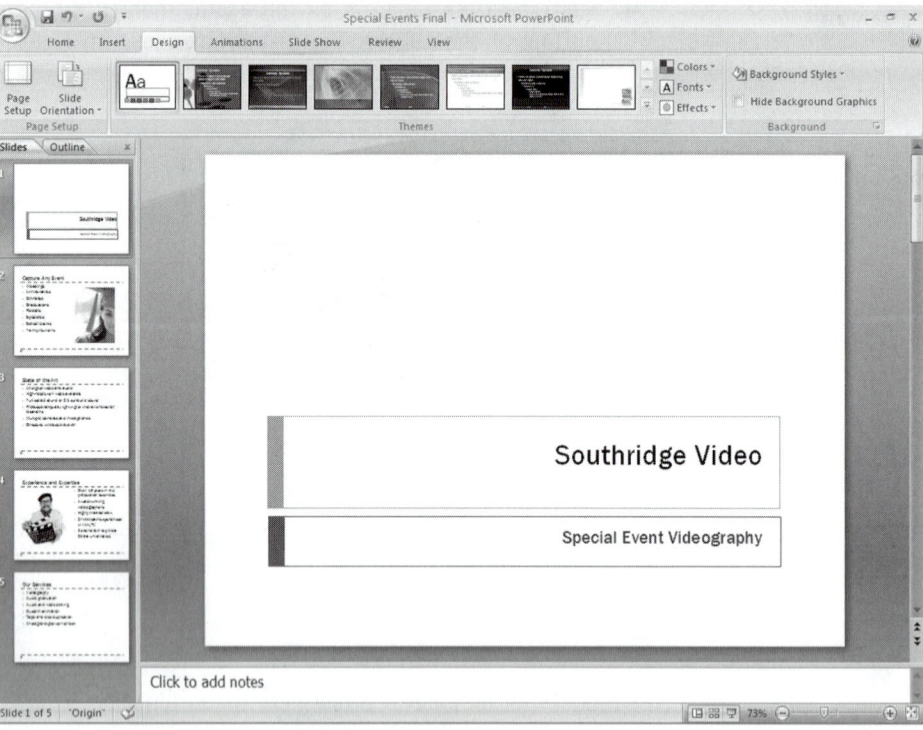

Figure 4-6

New fonts change the slides' appearance

PAUSE. Leave the presentation open to use in the next exercise.

PowerPoint supplies a wide variety of font combinations to allow you to choose among traditional serif fonts and contemporary sans serif fonts. The choice you make depends a great deal on the subject of your presentation and the impression you are trying to convey with your slides.

As with theme colors, you can select your own theme fonts and save them to be available to apply to any theme. Click Create New Theme Fonts at the bottom of the Theme Fonts gallery, select a heading font and body font, and then save the combination with a new name.

Changing Slide Backgrounds

THE BOTTOM LINE Themes provide a default background for all slides formatted with that theme. To customize a theme or draw attention to one or more slides, apply a different background.

Selecting a Theme Background

Use the Background Styles gallery to quickly apply a different background based on theme colors. You can apply a background to one or more selected slides or to all slides in the presentation.

➔ SELECT A THEME BACKGROUND

USE the presentation that is still open from the previous exercise.

1. Go to slide 1, if necessary.
2. Click the **Background Styles** button in the Background group. A gallery displays as shown in Figure 4-7, showing 12 background styles created using the theme's designated background colors.

Figure 4-7

Background Styles gallery

TAKE NOTE Rest the pointer on a background style to see its name and preview it on the current slide.

3. Right-click **Style 6**, then click **Apply to Selected Slides**. The background style is applied to slide 1 only.

   PAUSE. LEAVE the presentation open to use in the next exercise.

The Background Styles gallery allows you to choose from plain light or dark backgrounds and gradient backgrounds that gradually change from light to dark. Background colors are determined by the theme. Some background styles include graphic effects such as fine lines or textures over the entire background.

The area of the slide that is considered to be background can change depending on the theme. For example, the Aspect theme displays a shadowed graphic text box on top of the background, so the background displays as only a narrow border around some slide layouts.

Applying a Textured Background

Theme backgrounds are usually simple colors or color gradients. You can add more visual interest to a slide by changing the background to show a texture or even a picture.

APPLY A TEXTURED BACKGROUND

USE the presentation that is still open from the previous exercise.

1. With slide 1 still active, click the **Background Styles** button, then click **Format Background** at the bottom of the gallery. The Format Background dialog box opens, as shown in Figure 4-8.

Figure 4-8

The Format Background dialog box

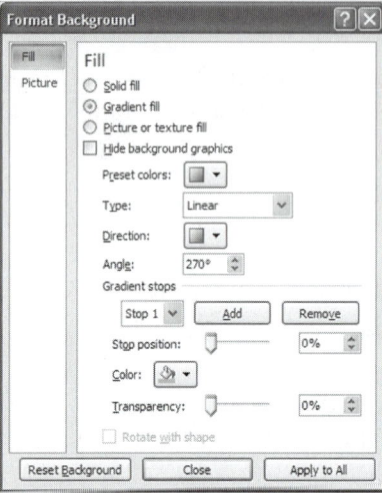

 Display the Format Background dialog box by right-clicking any blank area of the slide background and then clicking Format Background from the shortcut menu. Or, click the Background group's dialog box launcher.

2. Click **Picture or texture fill** in the right pane of the dialog box.
3. Click the **Texture** drop-down arrow to display a gallery of textures, as shown in Figure 4-9.

Figure 4-9

Texture gallery

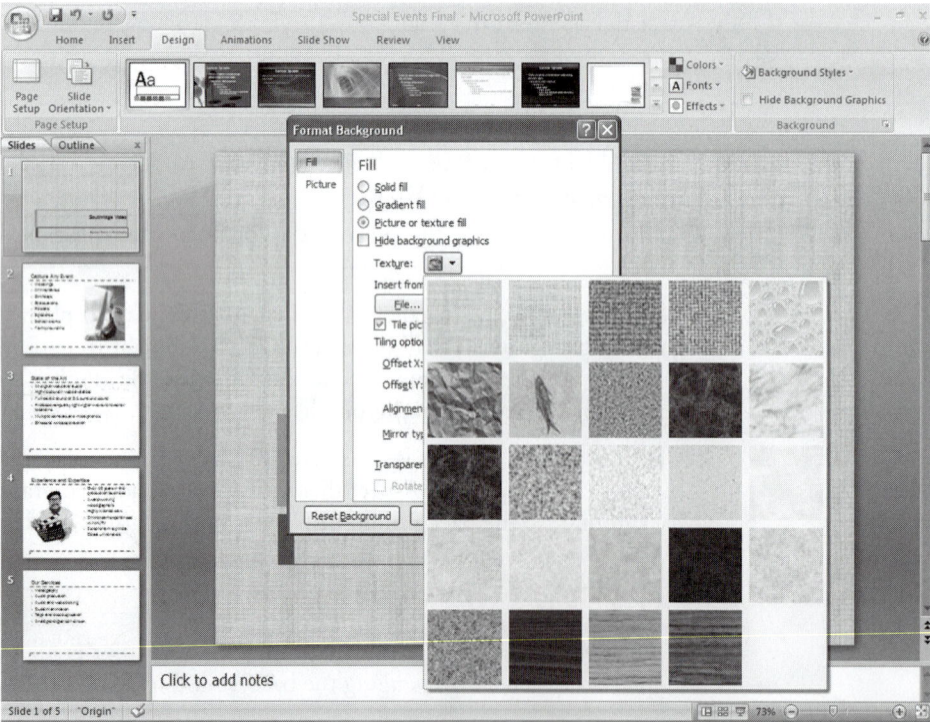

4. Click the **Stationery** texture, the fourth thumbnail in the first column, then click **Close**. The new texture gives slide 1 a brighter, warmer look.

PAUSE. LEAVE the presentation open to use in the next exercise.

Use the Format Background dialog box to create and modify any background, even a default theme background. You can apply a solid color or gradient fill, or select a picture or texture for the background. Options for each of these fill types allow you to modify the fill to suit your needs.

For any background choice, you can increase transparency to "wash out" the background so it doesn't overwhelm your text. For a gradient fill background, you can adjust the gradient by adding or removing colors. For a picture fill background, you can choose where to position a picture on the slide. For a texture, you can choose whether or not to tile the texture—position multiple copies of the texture over the slide background—or stretch the texture file over the whole slide.

By default, a new slide background created in this dialog box applies only to the current slide. Click the Apply to All button to apply the background to the entire presentation.

■ Working with Different Layouts

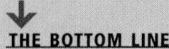

THE BOTTOM LINE

Slide layouts control the position of text and objects on a slide. Select a layout according to the content you need to add to it. If your current layout does not present information as you want it, you can change the layout.

➔ WORK WITH A DIFFERENT SLIDE LAYOUT

USE the presentation that is still open from the previous exercise.

1. Click the **Home** tab on the Ribbon.
2. Go to slide 5 and click **New Slide** in the Slides group. PowerPoint adds a new slide with the same layout as slide 5, Title and Content.
3. Key the title **Contact Information**.
4. Key the following information in the text placeholder:

   Address
       457 Gray Road
       North Hills, OH 45678
   Phone
       (513) 555-6543
   Fax
       (513) 555-5432

5. Turn off bullet formatting for the subordinate bullet items (the street address, phone number, and fax number). Your slide should look like Figure 4-10.

Figure 4-10

Add contact information to the slide

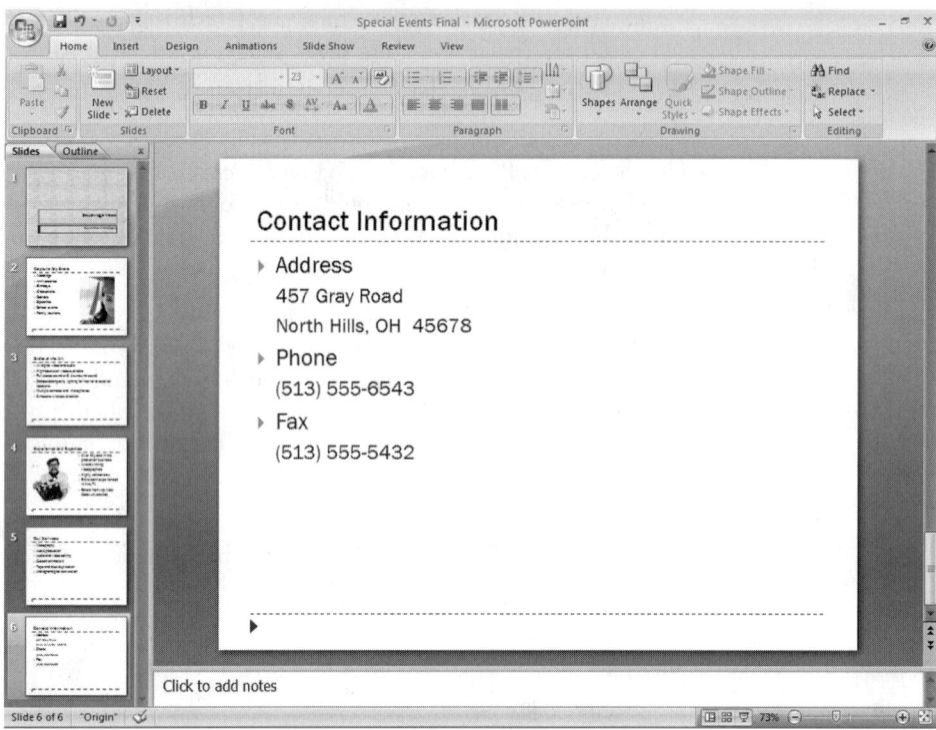

6. To make it easy to add an e-mail and Web site address in a separate placeholder, change the slide layout: Click the **Layout** button to display the slide layout gallery shown in Figure 4-11.

Figure 4-11

Slide layout gallery

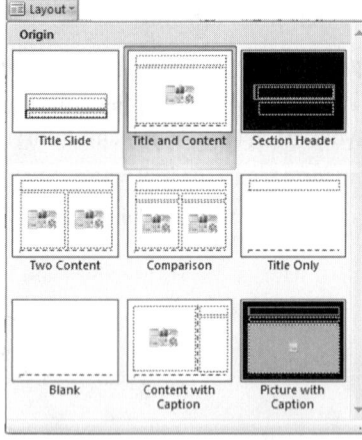

7. Click **Two Content** to change the layout to two side-by-side content placeholders.
8. In the second placeholder, key the following information:
   E-mail
       sales@southridgevideo.com

TAKE NOTE If you press the spacebar after keying an e-mail or Web address, PowerPoint automatically formats the text as a hyperlink.

Designing a Presentation | 603

9. Below the e-mail address, key the following information:

   Web site

   www.southridgevideo.com

   When you press Enter at the end of the Web address, PowerPoint formats the address as a hyperlink (formatting the address as gray, underlined text). Click the Undo button immediately to undo the formatting. You will learn how to insert an actual hyperlink into a slide later in this lesson.

10. Turn off the bullets for the subordinate e-mail address and Web address. Your slide should look similar to Figure 4-12.

Figure 4-12

E-mail and Web addresses added to the slide

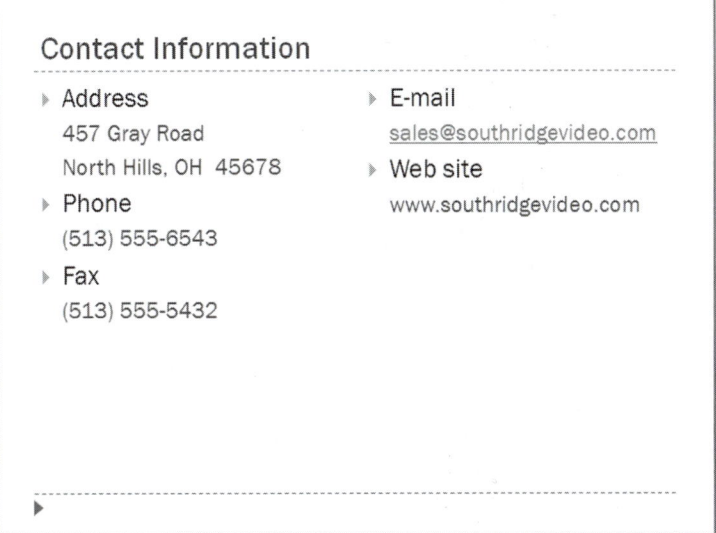

PAUSE. LEAVE the presentation open to use in the next exercise.

If you have applied a theme, the slide layout gallery shows available layouts with theme formats. Generally, several of the available layouts show the darker slide background supplied by the theme, which can add variety to a presentation while still coordinating with colors shown on other slides. If you have applied more than one theme to a presentation, the slide layout gallery shows available layouts from all themes so you can pick and choose among a greater variety of layout options.

All of PowerPoint's built-in themes offer a choice of nine layouts. PowerPoint's special purpose templates, however, may offer additional layouts required by the template's subject.

■ Inserting a Date, Footer, and Slide Numbers

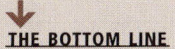
THE BOTTOM LINE

Adding a date, footer, and slide numbers to a presentation can help you identify and organize slides. In this exercise, you learn how to apply these useful elements to one or more slides.

➔ INSERT A DATE, FOOTER, AND SLIDE NUMBERS

USE the presentation that is still open from the previous exercise.

1. Click the **Insert** tab, and then click the **Header & Footer** button. The Header and Footer dialog box opens, as shown in Figure 4-13.

Figure 4-13

Header and Footer dialog box

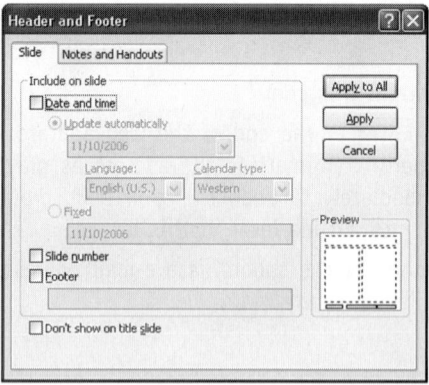

You can also open the Header and Footer dialog box by clicking the Date & Time button or the Slide Number button.

2. Click the **Date and time** check box, and then click **Update automatically** if necessary.
3. Click the **Slide number** check box.
4. Click the **Footer** check box and then key **Special Events** in the text box below the check box.
5. Click the **Don't show on title slide** check box.
6. Click **Apply to All** to apply the date, footer, and slide number to all slides except the title slide. Your slide 6 should look similar to Figure 4-14.

Figure 4-14

Slide number, footer, and date on a slide

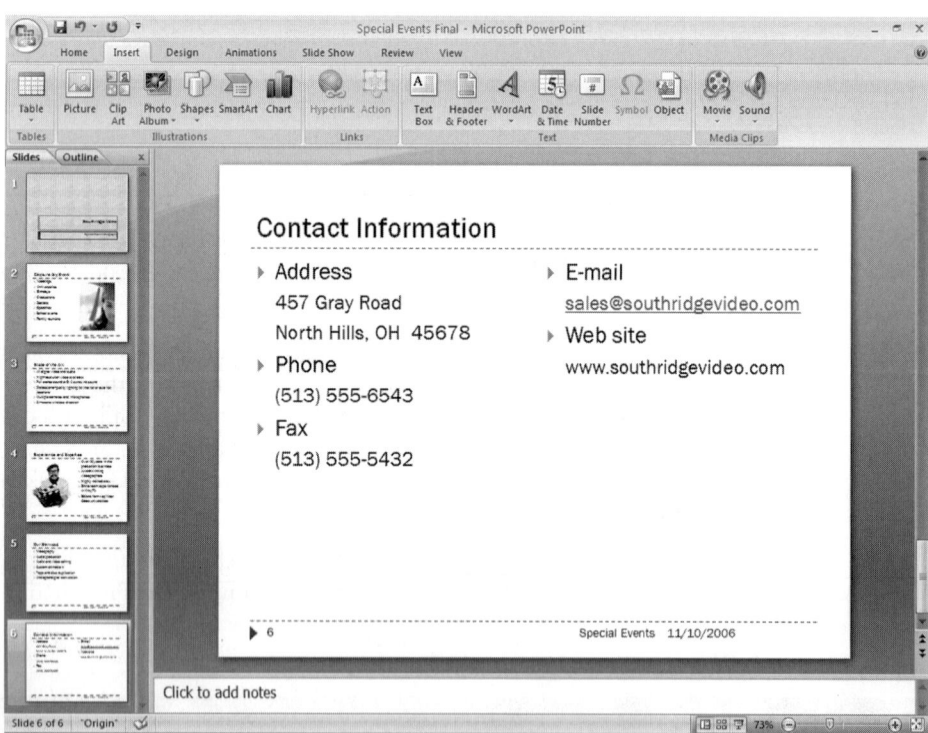

PAUSE. LEAVE the presentation open to use in the next exercise.

A *footer* is text that repeats at the bottom of each slide in a presentation. Use a footer to record the slide title, company name, or other important information that you want the audience to keep in mind as they view the slides.

You have two choices when inserting a date: A date that automatically updates changes to the current date each time the presentation is opened. A fixed date stays the same until you decide to change it. If it is important to indicate when slides were created or presented, use a fixed date.

Designing a Presentation | 605

You may have noticed that the Header and Footer dialog box has another tab, the Header tab. When you create notes pages and handouts, you can specify a *header* to appear at the top of every page. You can also create footers for notes pages and handouts.

■ Linking to Web Pages and Other Programs

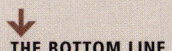
THE BOTTOM LINE

You can set up links on slides that allow you to jump from one slide to another or from a slide to a Web page. Action buttons allow you to quickly move from slide to slide, play sounds, or even run other programs. Links and action buttons contribute an element of interactivity to a presentation.

Adding a Hyperlink to a Slide

Use the Insert Hyperlink dialog box to set up links between slides or from slides to other targets.

ADD A HYPERLINK TO A SLIDE

USE the presentation that is still open from the previous exercise.

1. Go to slide 6, if necessary, and select the Web site address (*www.southridgevideo.com*).
2. Click the **Hyperlink** button on the Insert tab. The Insert Hyperlink dialog box opens, as shown in Figure 4-15.

Figure 4-15

Insert Hyperlink dialog box

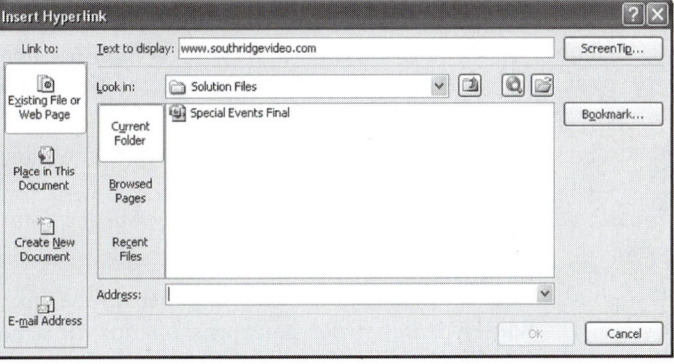

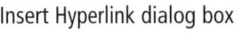
TAKE NOTE

If www.southridgevideo.com was already underlined when you selected it, the Edit Hyperlink dialog box will open instead.

3. Click in the **Address** box and key **http://www.southridgevideo.com** as the target of the link text.
4. Click **OK**. The Web site address is formatted with the theme's hyperlink color and an underline, as shown in Figure 4-16.

Figure 4-16

Text formatted as a hyperlink

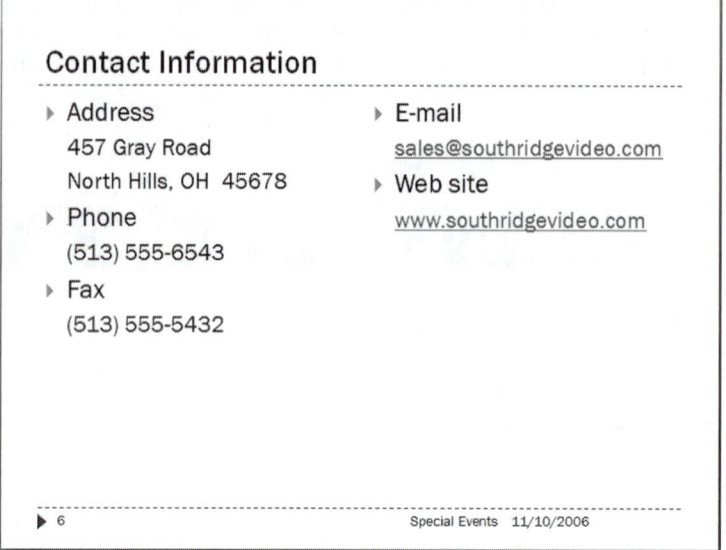

PAUSE. LEAVE the presentation open to use in the next exercise.

You can create links to a number of different types of *targets* using the Insert Hyperlink dialog box. The target is the page, file, or slide that opens when you click a link.

- Choose **Existing File or Web Page** to link to any Web page or any file on your system or network. Use the Look in box, the Browse the Web button, or the Browse File button to locate the desired page or file, or type the URL or path in the Address box.
- Choose **Place in This Document** to display a list of the current presentation's slides and custom shows. Click the slide or custom show that you want to display when the link is clicked.
- Choose **Create New Document** to create a link to a new document. You supply the path and the name for the new document and then choose whether to add content to the document now or later.
- Choose **E-mail Address** to key an e-mail address to which you want to link.

You can add hyperlinks to a slide in Normal view, but the links will work only in Slide Show view.

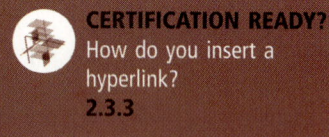

CERTIFICATION READY?
How do you insert a hyperlink?
2.3.3

If you need to change a link's target, click anywhere in the link and then click the Hyperlink button. The Edit Hyperlink dialog box opens, offering the same functionality as the Insert Hyperlink dialog box. You can remove a link by right-clicking the link and selecting Remove Hyperlink from the shortcut menu.

Adding an Action to a Slide

Use *actions* to perform tasks such as jumping to a new slide or starting a different program. Actions can be applied to text or shapes such as buttons.

ADD AN ACTION TO A SLIDE

ANOTHER WAY

The Shapes button is also available on the Home tab.

USE the presentation that is still open from the previous exercise.

1. Go to slide 5.
2. Click the **Shapes** button on the Insert tab to display a gallery of drawing shapes.
3. Click the **Action Button: Information** shape in the middle of the last row of shapes, as shown in Figure 4-17.

Figure 4-17

Select the Information action button shape

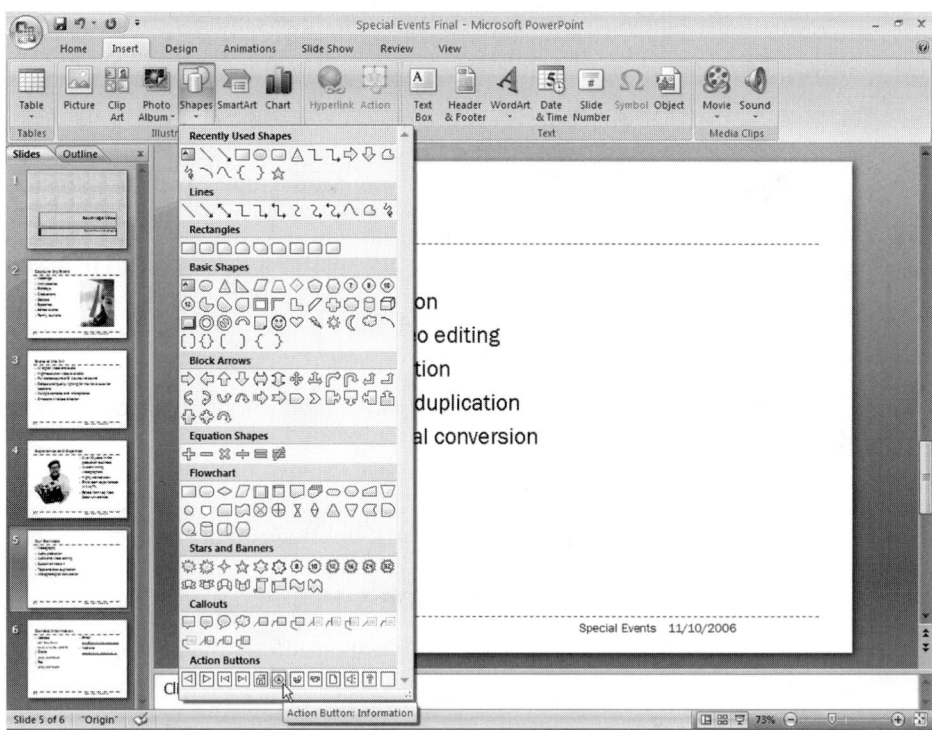

4. The pointer changes to a crosshair. Use the crosshair to draw a button shape near the bottom of the slide. As soon as you release the mouse button, the Action Settings dialog box opens.

5. Click **Hyperlink to** and then click the drop-down arrow of the box that displays *Next Slide*.

6. Scroll to the bottom of the list of possible link targets and click **Other File**. The Hyperlink to Other File dialog box opens.

The *Service Fees* file is available on the companion CD-ROM.

7. Navigate to the data files for this lesson, click the *Service Fees* file, and then click **OK**.

8. Click **OK** again to close the Action Settings dialog box. Your slide should look similar to Figure 4-18.

Figure 4-18

Action button on slide 5

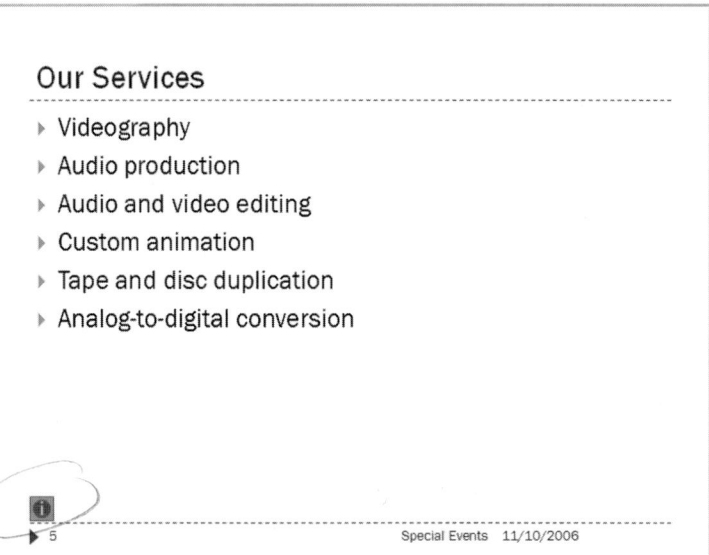

PAUSE. LEAVE the presentation open to use in the next exercise.

The Action Settings dialog box has two tabs that contain identical options. The default tab, Mouse Click, offers actions that will occur when you click the mouse pointer on the action item, such as the action button you drew in this exercise. The Mouse Over tab offers actions that will occur when you move the mouse pointer over the action item. It is therefore possible to attach two different actions to the same item. For example, you can specify that an action button will play a sound if you rest the mouse pointer on it and display a new slide if you click it.

Besides allowing you to set up links to specific slides or files, you can use action settings to run a particular program, run a macro, or perform an action with an object such as an embedded Excel worksheet. You can also play a sound from a list of default sounds or any sound file on your system.

As with hyperlink text, an action item works only in Slide Show view.

Testing Links in a Slide Show

Run a slide show to test the link and action you added in the previous exercises.

TEST LINKS IN A SLIDE SHOW

USE the presentation that is still open from the previous exercise.

1. **SAVE** the presentation and then press F5 to start the slide show from slide 1.
2. Click the mouse button to advance to slide 5 and then click the action button. An Excel worksheet opens, containing sample service fees, as shown in Figure 4-19.

Figure 4-19

The action button opens an Excel file

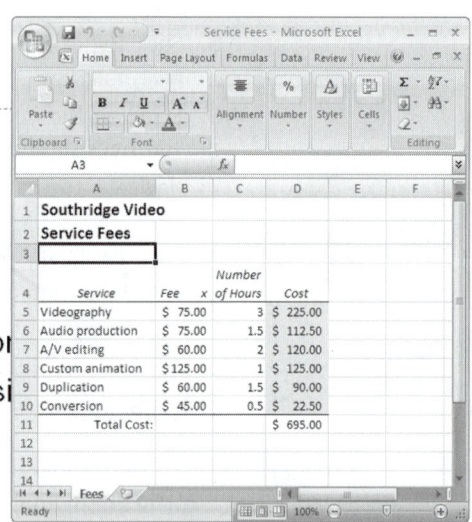

TROUBLESHOOTING

If you are prompted to enable PowerPoint to run an external program, click Enable and then continue with the exercise.

3. Close the Excel worksheet to return to Slide Show view.
4. Advance to slide 6 and click the Web site address, **www.southridgevideo.com**. Your Web browser opens and displays a Microsoft Web page.

TAKE NOTE

The Web site address you entered is a dummy address supported by Microsoft to allow you to practice creating links.

5. Close the Web browser and end the slide show.

   PAUSE. LEAVE the presentation open to use in the next exercise.

When you activate links or actions during a slide show, the target of the link or action displays in the full screen, like the slides in the slide show. If you open a Web browser using a link, you can use the Web browser's Back button to return to your slide.

Setting up Slide Transitions

THE BOTTOM LINE

Slide transitions supply another form of visual interest to slides and as such help to hold audience attention. PowerPoint offers over 50 different transitions that can be customized to create just the effect you want.

Applying a Transition

Transitions display in the Transition gallery on the Animations tab. Applying a transition is as simple as clicking one of the thumbnails in the gallery.

APPLY A TRANSITION

USE the presentation that is still open from the previous exercise.

1. Go to slide 1.
2. Click the **Animations** tab, and then click the **More** button for the Transition gallery. The gallery displays with the transition effects divided into categories, as shown in Figure 4-20.

Figure 4-20

The Transition gallery

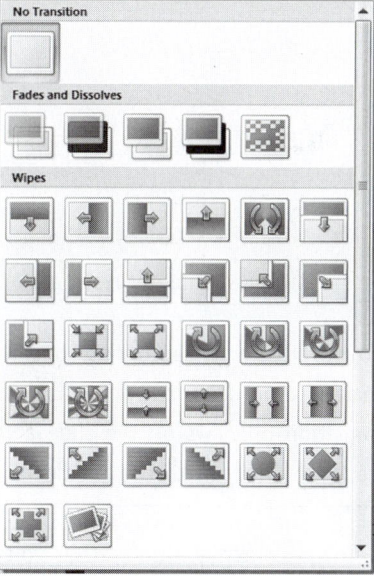

TAKE NOTE

You can click the star transition symbol or the Preview button on the Animations tab to preview the animation.

3. Point to several of the transitions in the gallery to see the live preview of the effect on slide 1.
4. Click **Fade Smoothly**, the first transition effect in the Fades and Dissolves section of the gallery. The star transition symbol displays under the slide number in the Slides tab.

   PAUSE. LEAVE the presentation open to use in the next exercise.

TAKE NOTE

You can apply transition effects in either Normal view or Slide Sorter view.

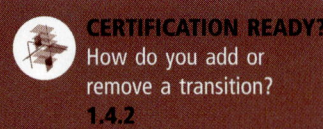

CERTIFICATION READY?
How do you add or remove a transition?
1.4.2

A *slide transition* is a special effect that occurs when one slide is being replaced by another during a slide show. Effects such as fades, dissolves, wipes, and covers hold audience attention until the next slide displays. You may want to choose transitions according to content, so that all section title slides, for example, have the same transition, or you can apply the Random transition to format each slide with a different transition.

By default, a transition is applied only to the current slide. You can also select several slides to apply the same transition or use the Apply To All button to apply the same transition effects to all slides in the presentation.

If you decide you don't want a transition, select the No Transition thumbnail in the Transition gallery. This option removes all transition formatting you have applied to the current slide.

Modifying a Transition

You have options for modifying a transition you have already applied: You can add a sound effect to the transition or change the transition speed.

 MODIFY A TRANSITION

USE the presentation that is still open from the previous exercise.

1. With slide 1 displayed, click the **Transition Sound** drop-down arrow. A menu of transition sounds displays, as shown in Figure 4-21.

Figure 4-21

Sound effects that can be applied to transitions

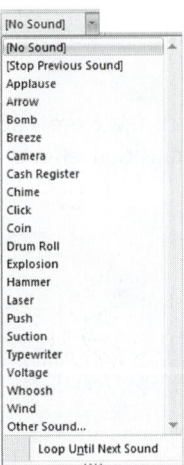

2. Preview several of the transition sounds by resting the mouse pointer on the sound name in the menu.
3. Click the **Applause** sound effect, an appropriate one for special events.
4. Click the **Transition Speed** drop-down arrow to display the speed options.
5. Click **Medium**. The transition previews on the slide at a slower speed.

   PAUSE. LEAVE the presentation open to use in the next exercise.

PowerPoint supplies a list of short, distinctive sound effects you can add to transitions, but you can also choose any sound file on your system by selecting Other Sound on the Transition Sound menu and then navigating to the sound file you want to use. When choosing a sound of your own, make sure the sound duration is short to avoid holding up the slides while the sound plays.

Take care when adding sound effects. Repeating a sound over and over can become irritating, as can playing many different sounds during the presentation. For best results, use sound sparingly to introduce significant content.

Designing a Presentation | 611

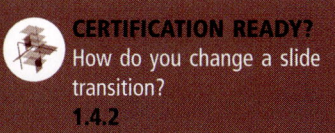

CERTIFICATION READY?
How do you change a slide transition?
1.4.2

By default, transitions are set to display at the Fast speed. If your projector system or computer has a fast processor speed, transitions can go by very quickly indeed. Changing transition speed allows the audience to enjoy the effects and gives you more time between slides to conclude remarks or prepare for the next topic.

Determining How Slides Will Advance

You can choose to control slide advance by clicking the mouse button to display the next slide, or you can have PowerPoint display slides automatically based on a specific time delay that you set. Automatic slide timings allow a presentation to run by itself in venues such as trade shows or kiosks.

→ DETERMINE HOW SLIDES WILL ADVANCE

USE the presentation that is still open from the previous exercise.

1. Click the **Automatically After** check box and then click the up spin control arrow ten times to set a slide timing of 00:10.
2. Click the **Apply To All** button to apply all transition effects to all slides.
3. Switch to Slide Sorter view. Notice that the slide timing displays under each slide, along with the star transition symbol, as shown in Figure 4-22.

Figure 4-22

Transition and timing symbols display in Slide Sorter view

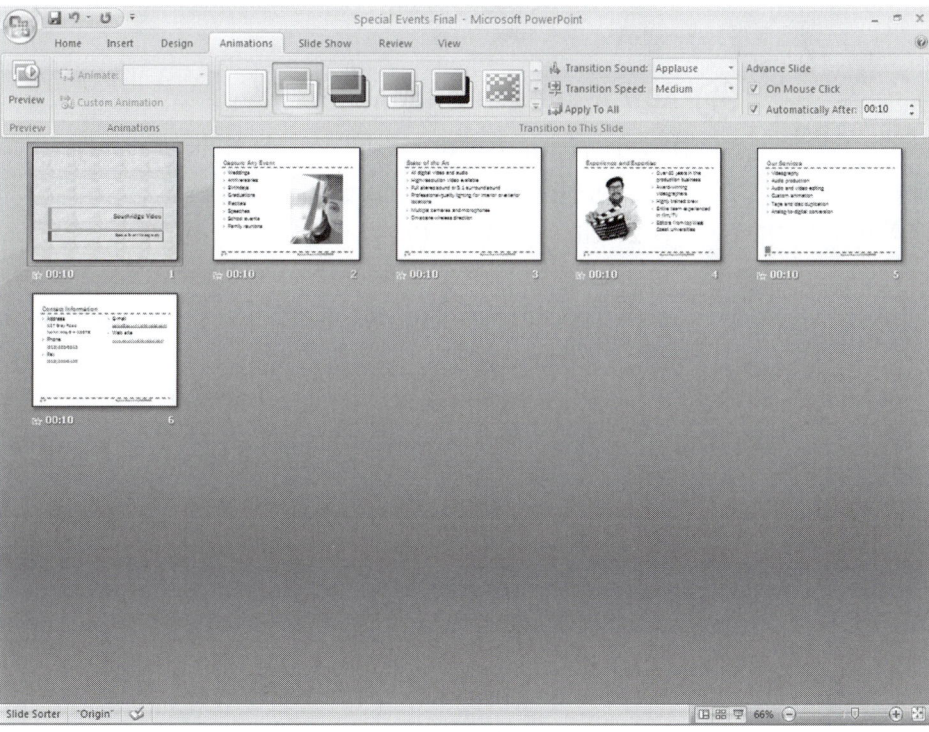

4. Click slide 2, hold down **Shift**, and then click slide 6 to select a group of slides. Click the **Transition Sound** drop-down arrow, and then click **[No Sound]** to remove the sound effect from transitions on these slides.
5. Press **F5** to start the slide show. Allow PowerPoint to control the slide advance. When you reach the end of the show, click the mouse button to return to Slide Sorter view.
6. Select all slides and click the **Automatically After** check box to remove the checkmark. You have turned off automatic slide timings.
7. **SAVE** your changes.

PAUSE. LEAVE the presentation open to use in the next exercise.

The default option for controlling slide advance is clicking the mouse (or pressing any of a number of keyboard keys) to move from one slide to the next. In some situations, however, you may want to have PowerPoint control the slide advance. If you intend to leave a presentation running by itself, for example, you must specify the amount of delay between slides to allow viewers time to read and understand slide content. You enter slide timings in seconds.

To have the best of both worlds, you can select both On Mouse Click and Automatically After. With both options checked, you can either wait for PowerPoint to advance the slides or click to advance if you're ready to go to the next slide before PowerPoint is.

Animating Your Slides

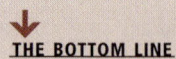

THE BOTTOM LINE

To add further visual interest to a presentation, add animations that control content using a variety of effects. For example, you can set all slide titles to fly in from the top or direct bullet items to appear one at a time. PowerPoint supplies some built-in animations that are simple to apply, or you can create custom animations to have more control over the animation effects.

Using Built-In Animations

PowerPoint supplies built-in animations that you can apply quickly to achieve interesting effects.

➲ **ADD A BUILT-IN ANIMATION**

USE the presentation that is still open from the previous exercise.

1. Switch to Normal view and go to slide 2.
2. Click the **Animations** tab to display it, if necessary.
3. Click anywhere in the text placeholder at the left side of the slide.
4. Click the **Animate** drop-down arrow in the Animations group to display the list of built-in animations, as shown in Figure 4-23.

To quickly return to Normal view with slide 2 active, double-click slide 2 in Slide Sorter view.

Figure 4-23

Menu of built-in animations

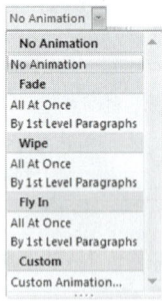

5. Click **By 1st Level Paragraphs** in the Fade section of the menu. The animation effect previews on the slide, displaying bullet items one by one.
6. Press F5 to start the slide show and advance to slide 2. Click to display the first bulleted item, and continue to click until you move to slide 3.

Designing a Presentation | 613

7. Press **Esc** to end the slide show to return to Normal view.

PAUSE. LEAVE the presentation open to use in the next exercise.

Animations are effects you apply to placeholders or other content to move the content in unique ways on the slide. Animations supply visual interest, but they also allow the presenter to control when content displays on the slide. Displaying content in a controlled fashion allows the audience to concentrate more completely on each bullet point or chart element.

PowerPoint's built-in animations can supply interesting effects with a minimum of fuss. You have a limited selection of animation options that are easy to apply, so it is possible to animate an entire presentation with only a few button clicks. Use the All At Once option to display all content of a placeholder or other object at one time. The By 1st Level Paragraphs option displays bullet items or other paragraphs one at a time.

CERTIFICATION READY?
How do you apply a built-in animation?
2.4.1

By default, built-in animations are set up to display when you click the mouse button. You can modify a built-in effect to have PowerPoint control the display of content, as well as adjust other options such as speed of the effect.

Modifying an Animation

While built-in animations provide quick effects, you may find that you need to modify those effects for your presentation. You use the Custom Animation task pane to modify built-in animations.

➔ MODIFY AN ANIMATION

USE the presentation that is still open from the previous exercise.

1. Go to slide 2 and click the **Custom Animation** button in the Animations group. The Custom Animation task pane opens, as shown in Figure 4-24. The built-in animation effect you applied in the last exercise displays in the effects list area of the task pane.

Figure 4-24

The Custom Animation task pane

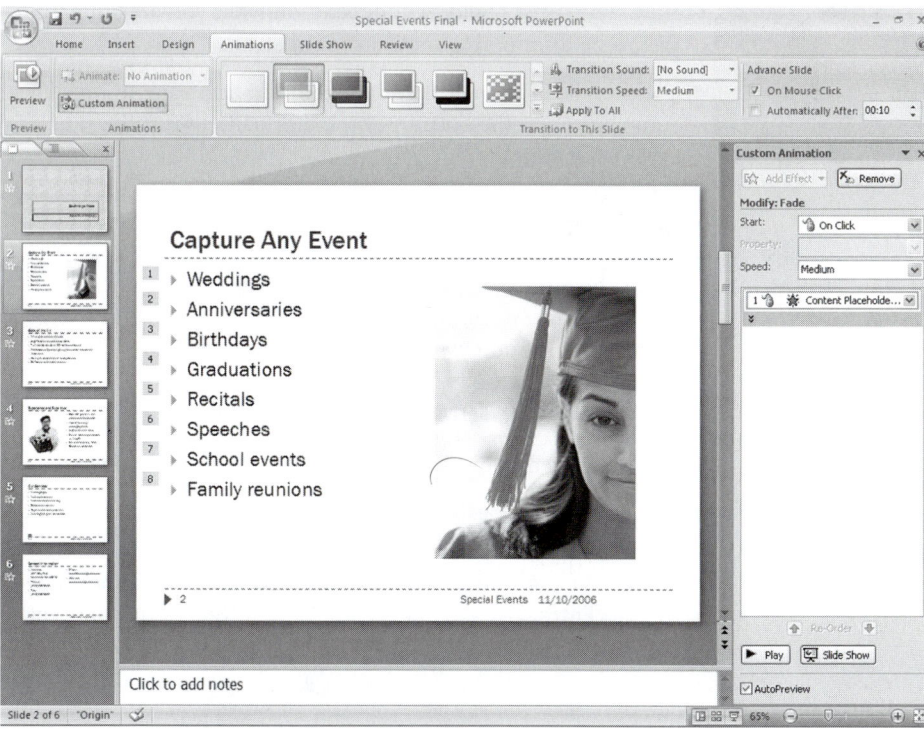

2. Click the **Content Placeholder 2** animation effect in the list area to select it.
3. Click the **Start** drop-down arrow near the top of the task pane and then click **After Previous**.
4. Click the Speed drop-down arrow and then click **Fast**. The modified effect previews on the slide.
5. Press F5 to start the slide show. Advance to slide 2 and notice that PowerPoint starts displaying the bullet items immediately after the transition has ended and controls their entry so you don't have to click the mouse.
6. Press Esc to end the show to return to Normal view. Leave the Custom Animation task pane open.

   PAUSE. LEAVE the presentation open to use in the next exercise.

Use the Custom Animation task pane to modify built-in animations or create new custom animations. The Custom Animation task pane displays buttons at the top of the pane for adding, changing, or removing an animation effect. Below the buttons are Start, Property, and Speed options that allow you to change how an object starts, how it plays, and how fast it occurs.

PowerPoint offers three options for starting an effect:

- **On Mouse Click** starts the effect when you click the mouse button. This gives you the most control over animations but can be tedious when you have to click repeatedly to display a bulleted list or the bars of a chart.
- **With Previous** starts the effect at the same time as the previous effect. Using this option can prevent delays from occurring between animations. You might use it, for example, for a text placeholder if you have also animated the title placeholder.
- **After Previous** starts the effect after the previous effect (either an animation or transition) has ended.

The Property option varies according to the effect; it may give you a choice of directions, for example, for objects that are flying in. You have five speed options, from Very Fast to Very Slow. The speed choice will depend on what you are animating. Your audience may find Very Fast to be disorienting for a text animation.

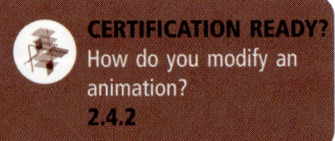

CERTIFICATION READY?
How do you modify an animation?
2.4.2

Use the Play button at the bottom of the task pane to preview animations. Use the Slide Show button at the bottom of the task pane to run the slide show from the current slide to check animations.

Creating a Customized Animation

For the most control over animations, select the effects and modify their settings yourself in the Custom Animation task pane. The Effect Options dialog box for an effect gives you further options for controlling the animation.

→ CREATE A CUSTOMIZED ANIMATION

USE the presentation that is still open from the previous exercise.

1. Go to slide 6 and select the left-hand text placeholder (click the outside border so it appears as a solid line).
2. In the Custom Animations task pane, click the **Add Effect** button, point to **Entrance**, and then click **More Effects**. The Add Entrance Effect dialog box opens, as shown in Figure 4-25.

Designing a Presentation | 615

Figure 4-25

Choose a new entrance effect from the Add Entrance Effect dialog box

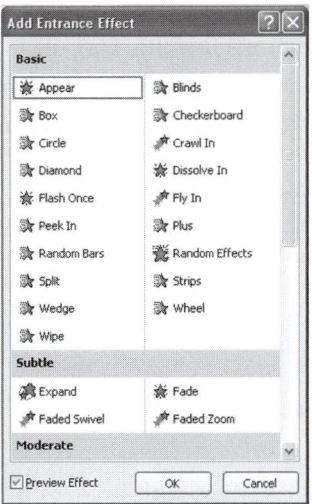

3. Click **Wipe** in the Basic area of the dialog box, and then click **OK**.
4. Click the **Start** drop-down arrow, then click **After Previous**.
5. Click the **Direction** drop-down arrow, then click **From Left**.
6. Click the **Speed** drop-down arrow, then click **Fast**.
7. Click the drop-down arrow at the right side of the content placeholder animation effect in the effects list. A shortcut menu displays.
8. Click **Effect Options** to open the Wipe dialog box, as shown in Figure 4-26.

Figure 4-26

The Wipe dialog box

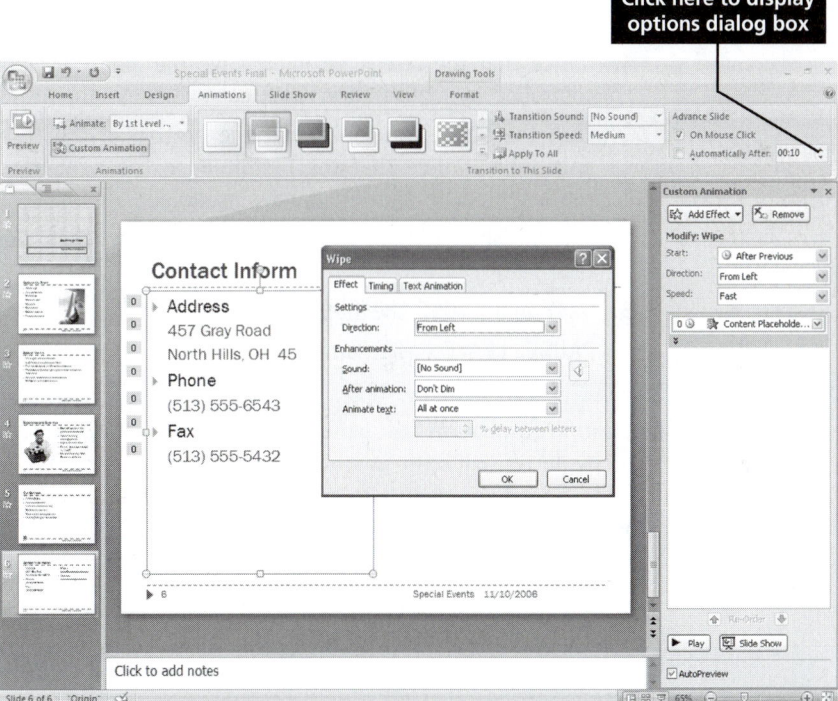

9. Click the **Text Animation** tab.
10. Click the **Group text** drop-down arrow, and then click **By 2nd Level Paragraphs**.
11. Click **OK**.
12. Click in **E-mail** in the right-hand placeholder. Add the **Wipe** entrance effect, start it **With Previous**, set the direction to **From Left**, and change the speed to **Fast**.

13. Open the Wipe effect options dialog box, click the **Text Animation** tab, and choose to group **By 2nd level paragraphs**. Click **OK**.
14. Click the double downward-pointing arrows in the blue bar below the Content Placeholder 3 effect to expand the effect so you can see the effects applied to all items in the placeholder, as shown in Figure 4-27.

Figure 4-27

Expand the effect

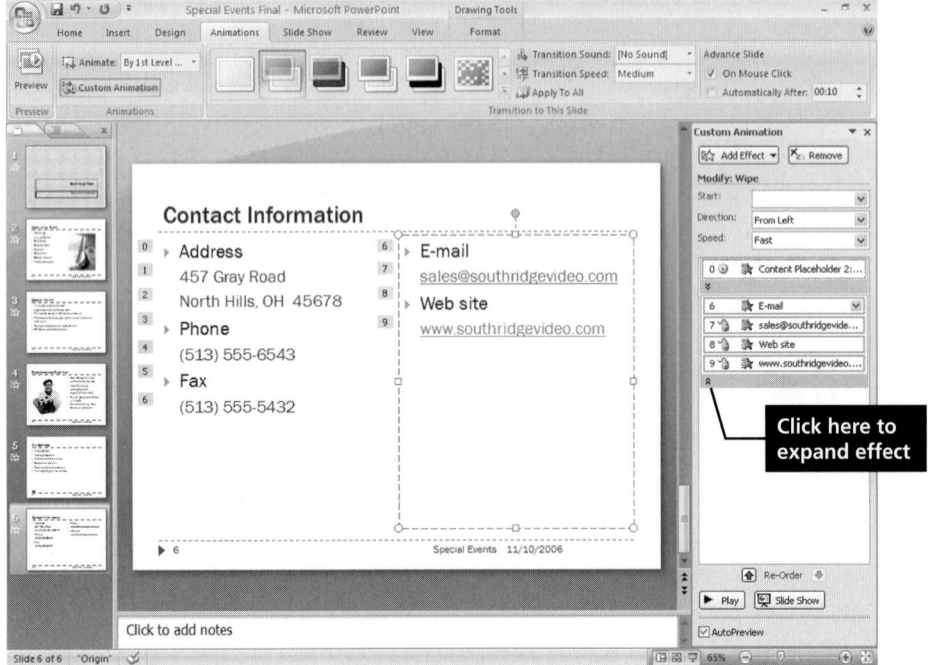

15. Notice that the last three items have the mouse symbol indicating that they are controlled by mouse click. Click each of these three lines, then click **After Previous**.
16. Click the Slide Show button at the bottom of the task pane to check the animation. Notice that the first item in the right-hand placeholder starts with the last item in the left-hand placeholder.
17. End the slide show to return to Normal view, then close the Custom Animation task pane.
18. **SAVE** and **CLOSE** the file.

    PAUSE. LEAVE PowerPoint open to use in the next exercise.

The Custom Animation task pane provides options for creating very sophisticated animation effects. By default, all built-in animations are entrance effects—they occur as content appears on a slide. When you choose to create a new custom animation, you can select from the following options:

- **Entrance** effects control how the object appears on the slide. Use these effects to add information to a slide.
- **Emphasis** effects control objects that already display on the slide. Use these effects to draw attention to existing slide content.
- **Exit** effects control how an object disappears from a slide. Use these effects to remove content from a slide.
- **Motion Path** effects cause an object such as a picture or placeholder to follow a path on the slide.

You can insert more than one animation on a slide. You can, for example, animate the slide title; text; pictures; and objects such as tables, SmartArt graphics, and charts. Animations are listed in the task pane as you apply them. You can reorder the list to control the order in which the animations occur. Numbers on the slide in the Slide pane show the order in which content is animated. If content is set to animate using With Previous or After Previous, these numbers are 0s to indicate that the content is automatically controlled.

If a placeholder contains more than one line of text, you can expand the effect in the effects list to apply separate settings to each item.

The amount of time available for animations depends on slide advance options. If you have not set an automatic advance time, animations proceed according to the speed you have set. If an automatic slide timing has been set, the animations take place within that time. If you decide to set slide timings, make sure you allow time for all animations to play at a reasonable speed.

You can set further options for any animation in the effect's Options dialog box. The tabs in this dialog box vary according to effect and what you are choosing to animate, but you always have Effect and Timing tabs to allow you to adjust properties and speed or delay for the effect.

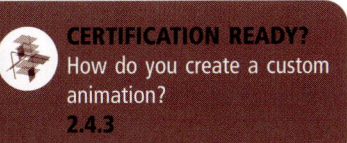

CERTIFICATION READY?
How do you create a custom animation?
2.4.3

Software Orientation

PowerPoint's Slide Master View

Slide Master view, shown in Figure 4-28, provides tools for modifying the master slides on which all of the current presentation's layouts and formats are based.

Figure 4-28

Slide Master view

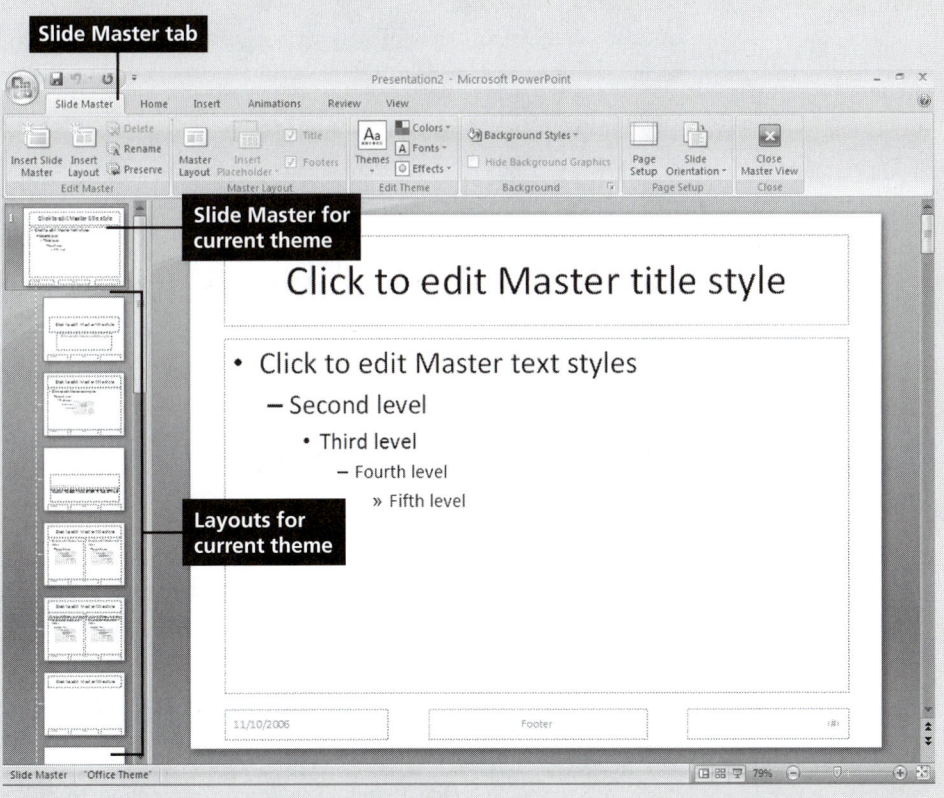

Use the tools on the Slide Master tab and the blank slide in the Slide pane to customize formats that will apply to all slides in a presentation. All layouts used in the current theme appear in the left pane so you can customize each layout as desired. Making a change to the Two Content layout, for example, will change all slides in the presentation that use that layout.

■ Customizing Slide Masters

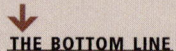
THE BOTTOM LINE

If you want to make design changes that will apply to many or all slides in a presentation, you can save a great deal of time by modifying the slide master rather than applying changes on each slide. Customizing a slide master makes it easy to apply changes consistently throughout a presentation.

Applying a Theme to a Slide Master

To customize a slide master, you use Slide Master view. Slide Master view has its own tab on the Ribbon to provide tools you can use to change the masters.

➔ APPLY A THEME TO A SLIDE MASTER

1. Locate and open the *Rates* presentation.
2. With slide 1 active, click the **View** tab.
3. Click the **Slide Master** button in the Presentation Views group. Slide Master view opens with the Title Slide Layout selected in the left pane, as shown in Figure 4-29.

The *Rates* file is available on the companion CD-ROM.

Figure 4-29

Slide Master view with the Title Slide layout selected

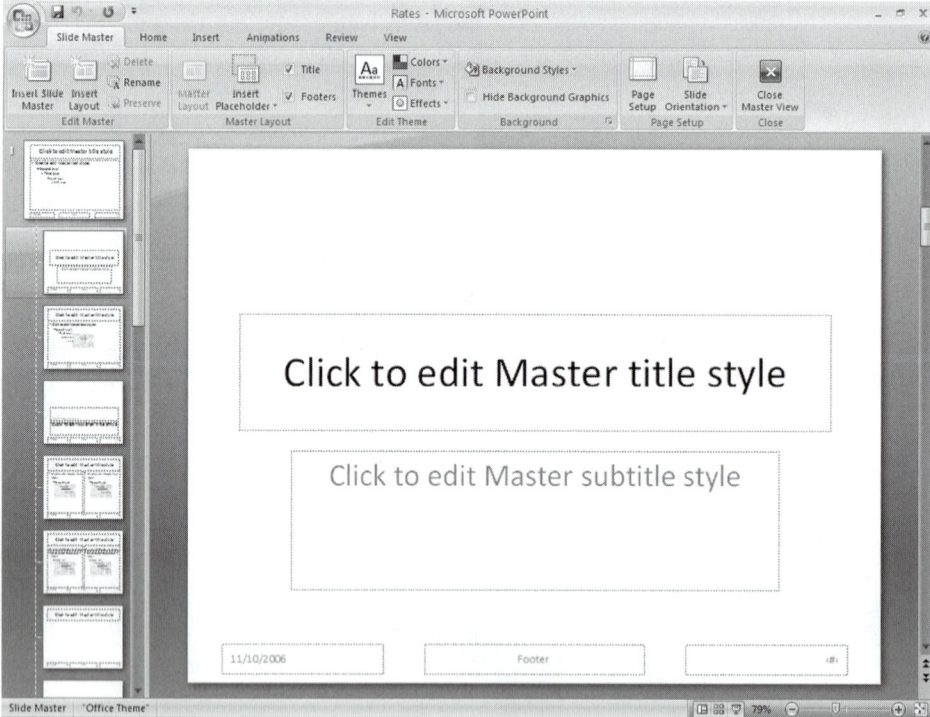

4. Click the first slide in the left pane, the slide master for the current theme.
5. Click the **Themes** button in the Slide Master tab's Edit Theme group.
6. Click the **Solstice** theme. The theme is applied to the slide master as well as all slide layouts in the left pane, as shown in Figure 4-30.

Figure 4-30

A new theme applied to the slide master and layouts

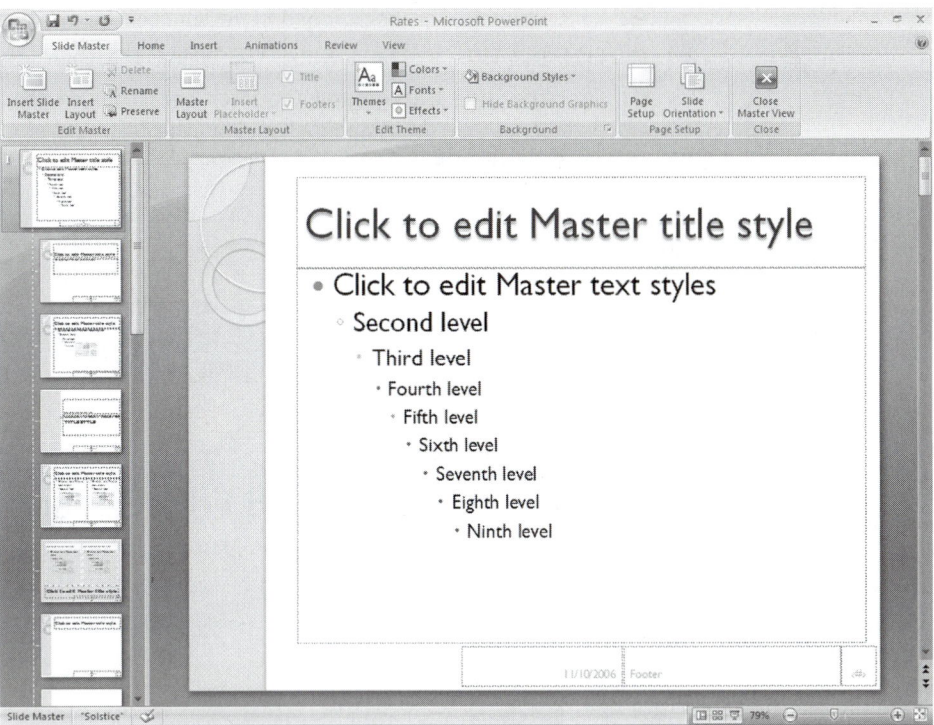

7. **SAVE** the presentation as *Rates Masters*.

   PAUSE. LEAVE the presentation open to use in the next exercise.

The *slide master* for a presentation stores information on the current theme, layout of placeholders, bullet characters, and other formats that affect all slides in a presentation. Slide Master view makes it easy to change formats globally for a presentation by displaying the slide master and all layouts available in the current presentation.

The slide master, displayed at the top of the left pane, looks like a blank Title and Content slide. To make a change to the master, edit it just the way you would edit any slide using tools on any of the Ribbon's tabs. For example, to change the font of the slide title, click the title, display the Home tab, and use the Font list to select a new font. Change bullet characters by clicking in any of the nine levels of bullets and then selecting a new bullet character from the Bullets and Numbering dialog box.

Some changes you make to the slide master display on the masters for other slide layouts. You can also click any of these layouts to display it in the Slide pane so you can make changes to that layout. Any changes you make to these layouts will display on slides that use those layouts. Your changed masters display in the slide layout gallery to be available when you create new slides.

Changing a Slide Master's Background

Change a slide master's background to quickly modify the background for all slides in the presentation. You can apply a different background style or hide background graphics to customize slide backgrounds.

CHANGE A SLIDE MASTER'S BACKGROUND

USE the presentation that is still open from the previous exercise.

1. With the slide master still selected in the left pane, click the **Background Styles** button in the Background group. The Background Styles gallery opens.

TAKE NOTE

Slide Master view shows two layouts—Title and Vertical Text and Vertical Title and Text—that are not available in the default slide layout gallery.

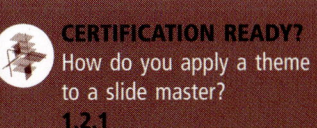

CERTIFICATION READY?
How do you apply a theme to a slide master?
1.2.1

2. Click **Style 6**. The background style changes for all layouts.
3. Click the **Title Master Layout**, just below the slide master in the left pane.
4. Click the **Hide Background Graphics** check box in the Background group. The white text panel and the graphic shapes at the left side of the slide are hidden, as shown in Figure 4-31.

Figure 4-31

Hide background graphics to change slide appearance

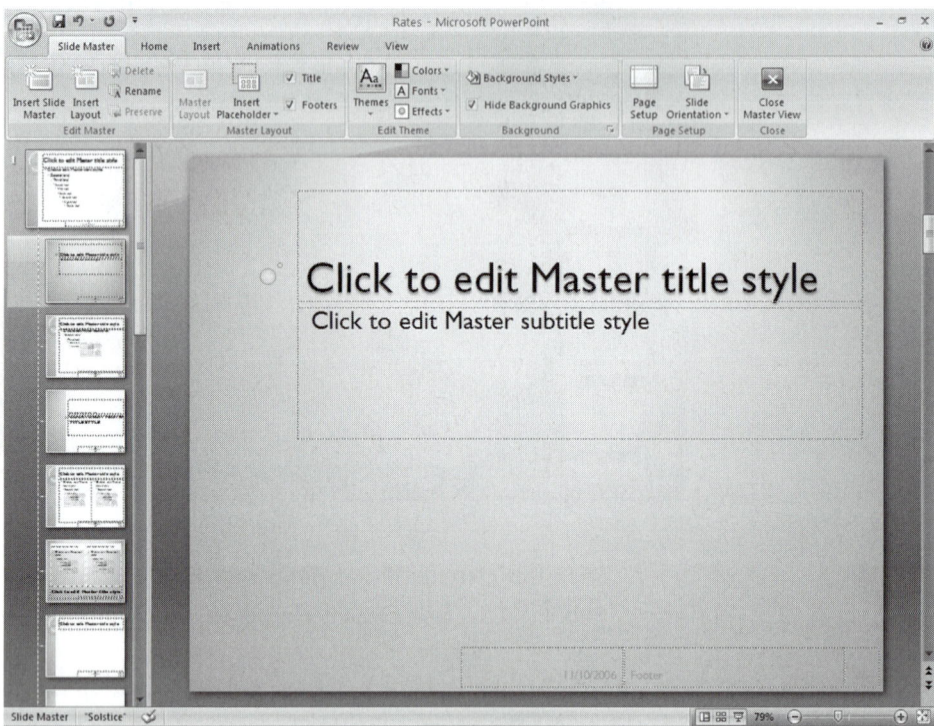

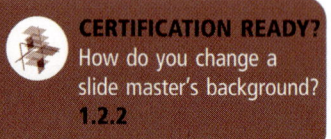

CERTIFICATION READY?
How do you change a slide master's background?
1.2.2

PAUSE. LEAVE the presentation open to use in the next exercise.

Changing the background of a slide master is the same process as changing the background of any slide in Normal view. Keep in mind that any changes you make to a specific slide master will display each time you use that master.

Adding New Elements to a Slide Master

If you add a picture or text to a slide master layout, it will display on all slides that use that layout. To allow the user to insert his or her own content, you can add a placeholder to a layout.

ADD A NEW ELEMENT TO A SLIDE MASTER

USE the presentation that is still open from the previous exercise.

1. Click the **Section Header Layout** in the left pane to display the Section Header master in the Slide pane.
2. Click the **Insert Placeholder** drop-down arrow in the Master Layout group, and then click **Text**. The pointer changes to a crosshair you can use to draw a new text placeholder.
3. Draw a placeholder in the upper-left corner of the slide. As soon as you release the mouse button, a list of bulleted text levels displays in the new text placeholder, as shown in Figure 4-32.

Figure 4-32

A new text placeholder on a slide master

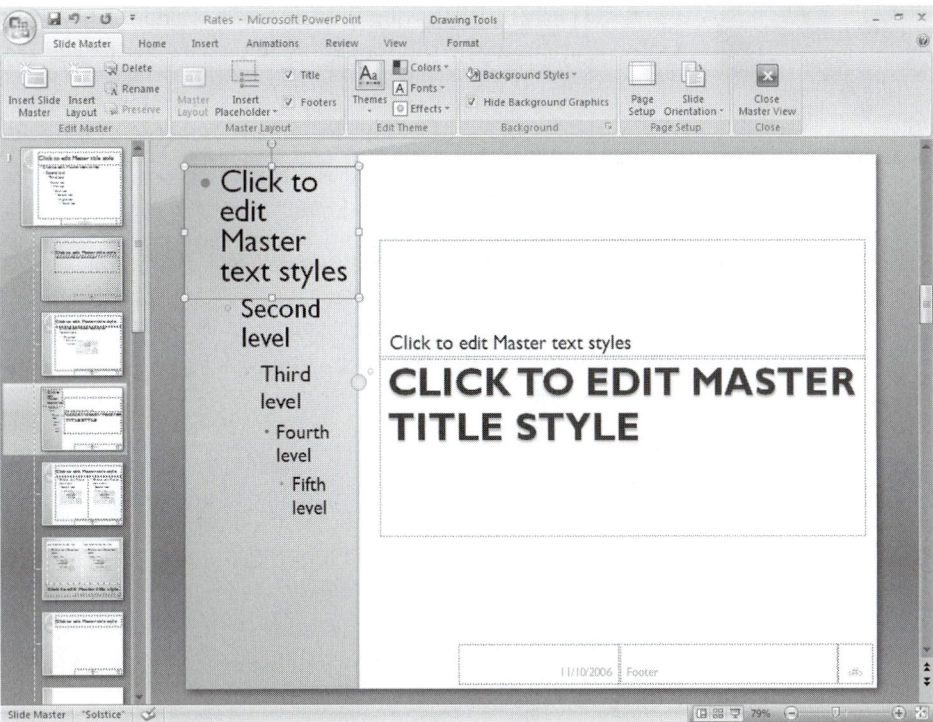

> **TAKE NOTE**
>
> The text in the placeholder still shows the hanging indent needed for a bulleted list. You can remove this indent using the Paragraph dialog box.

4. Select all text in the new placeholder and press [Delete] to remove the placeholder text.
5. Click the **Home** tab.
6. Turn off bullets for the new placeholder and change the text size of the placeholder to **18 point**.
7. Click the **Slide Master** tab, and then click the **Close Master View** button to return to Normal view.
8. Go to slide 1, if necessary, click the **Home** tab, and add a slide with the Section Header layout.
9. Key the slide title **Service Rates**.
10. Click in the new placeholder in the upper-left corner of the slide and key **As of [current date]**, replacing *[current date]* with a date such as 11/08/08.
11. **SAVE** and **CLOSE** the presentation.

    CLOSE PowerPoint.

If you need to create a number of slides with a layout different from any of the default layouts, you can create a new custom layout to your own specifications. Use the Insert Layout button on the Slide Master tab to insert a new layout in the layout list in the left pane of Slide Master view. You can then use tools in the Master Layout group to customize placeholders for your new layout. You can decide whether to display a title or the footer placeholders, and you can use the Insert Placeholder button to select from a number of standard placeholders, such as Text, Picture, Clip Art, or Table.

> **TAKE NOTE**
>
> Custom layouts remain in the presentation in which they are created.

If you have inserted a text placeholder, you should format the placeholder text the way you want text to appear on the slides. Apply formats using options on the Home tab.

When you have completed the custom layout, use the Rename button on the Slide Master tab to give the custom layout a meaningful name. It will then be available in the slide layout gallery any time you want to add a slide in that presentation.

In addition to creating your own custom layout, you can also insert another slide master into any presentation using the Insert Slide Master button on the Slide Master tab. When you insert

CERTIFICATION READY?
How do you add an element to a slide master?
1.3

a new slide master, PowerPoint displays a new default blank slide master and layouts. You can apply a different theme and formatting to the new master and layouts, allowing you considerable freedom when creating slides because you can draw on the layouts of both masters.

SUMMARY SKILL MATRIX

IN THIS LESSON YOU LEARNED HOW TO:
Apply a Theme to a Presentation
Change Theme Colors
Change Theme Fonts
Select a Theme Background
Apply a Textured Background
Work with Different Layouts
Insert a Date, Footer, and Slide Number
Add a Hyperlink to a Slide
Add an Action to a Slide
Test Links in a Slide Show
Apply a Transition
Modify a Transition
Determine How Slides Will Advance
Use Built-In Animation
Modify an Animation
Create a Customized Animation
Apply a Theme to a Slide Master
Change a Slide Master's Background
Add New Elements to a Slide Master

■ Knowledge Assessment

Fill in the Blank

Fill in each blank with the term or phrase that best completes the statement.

1. PowerPoint's _live preview_ feature lets you move the mouse pointer over items in a gallery to see instantly how formats look on the current slide.
2. To select a picture for a slide background, use the _Format Bkgrd_ dialog box.
3. A(n) _footer_ is text that repeats at the bottom of each slide in a presentation.
4. A(n) _transition_ is a special effect that occurs as one slide leaves the screen and another enters.
5. The _slide Master_ stores information about formats used on all slides in a presentation.

6. The _target_ is the page or slide that opens when you click a link.
7. _Animation_ can be used to control how an object enters or leaves the screen during a slide show.
8. You can create a(n) _header_ to appear at the top of every page of handouts.
9. To test links, you must be in _slideshow_ view.
10. Use a(n) _Action_ to play a sound file or open a file from another program.

Multiple Choice

Circle the correct answer.

1. A PowerPoint theme includes
    a. a palette of complementary colors
    b. a combination of fonts
    c. placeholder layouts
    d. all of the above *(p.596)*

2. A saved color scheme displays in the ___a___ *(p.598)*.
    a. Custom area of the Theme Colors gallery
    b. Built-In area of the Themes gallery
    c. My Colors area of the New Presentation dialog box
    d. Saved Colors area of the Theme Colors gallery

3. If you applied a texture that made it hard to read slide text, you could modify the effect by _____.
    a. changing the size of the texture tile
    b. changing the texture gradient
    c. changing the transparency of the texture
    d. changing the underlying slide color

4. PowerPoint's built-in themes offer a choice of _nine_ layouts.
    a. six
    b. nine
    c. twelve
    d. fifteen

5. If it is important to indicate what day slides were created, you should use a(n) _fixed_ date.
    a. automatically updating
    b. absolute
    c. numeric equivalent
    d. fixed

6. To link to a slide in the current presentation, choose ___a___ in the Insert Hyperlink dialog box.
    a. Existing File or Web Page
    b. Place in This Document
    c. Create New Document
    d. Show Current Slides

7. By default, transitions display at which speed?
   a. Slow
   b. Medium
   c. Fast
   d. Very Fast

8. To display the items in a placeholder one at a time, you would choose what animation option?
   a. All At Once
   b. One at a Time
   c. By Paragraph
   d. By 1st Level Paragraphs

9. To have the best control over when an animation plays, you would choose the _____ start option.
   a. On Mouse Click
   b. With Previous
   c. After Previous
   d. Either b or c

10. To remove objects from a slide's background, click the _____ check box.
    a. Hide All Slide Objects
    b. Suppress Graphics
    c. Hide Background Graphics
    d. Show Only Background

■ Competency Assessment

Project 4-1: Service with a Smile

You're the sales manager for a large chain of auto dealerships that prides itself on service and warranty packages that give customers a sense of security. The company, Car King, is rolling out a new line of extended warranties to offer its customers. You have created a presentation that details three levels of warranties. Now you need to improve the look of the slides to make customers take notice.

GET READY. Launch PowerPoint if it is not already running.

The *Warranty Plans* file is available on the companion CD-ROM.

1. **OPEN** the *Warranty Plans* presentation.
2. With slide 1 active, click the **New Slide** button to insert a new Title and Content slide.
3. Click the **Layout** button, and then click **Title Slide**.
4. Key the title **Car King** and the subtitle **Extended Warranty Plans**.
5. Drag the slide above slide 1 in the Slides tab so the title slide becomes the first slide.
6. Click the **Design** tab, and then click the **More** button to display the Themes gallery.
7. Click **Foundry** to apply this theme to all slides.
8. Click the **Theme Fonts** button, and then scroll down to locate and click the **Metro** theme fonts combination.
9. Click the **Theme Colors** button, and then click **Create New Theme Colors**.
10. Click the **Accent 1** drop-down arrow, then click the **Tan, Text 2, Darker 25%** color.
11. Click the **Accent 2** drop-down arrow, then click the **Tan, Text 2, Darker 50%** color.
12. Key **CarKing** as the color scheme name, and then click **Save**.
13. Go to slide 1, if necessary.
14. Click the **Background Styles** button, and then click **Style 7**.

Designing a Presentation | 625

15. SAVE the presentation as *Warranty Plans Final* and CLOSE the file.
    LEAVE PowerPoint open for the next project.

Project 4-2: Special Delivery

As a marketing manager for Consolidated Delivery, you have been asked to prepare and present information on the company's services to a prospective corporate client. You need to add some interactive features to a standard presentation to make your delivery especially interesting.

The *Messenger Service* file is available on the companion CD-ROM.

1. OPEN the *Messenger Service* presentation.
2. Go to slide 2 and select the text *Contact Consolidated* in the text box at the bottom of the slide.
3. Open the Insert Hyperlink dialog box, click **Place in This Document**, and then click **6. Our Numbers** in the list of slide titles. Click **OK**.
4. Go to slide 4 and click the WordArt graphic to select it.
5. Click the **Animations** tab, and then click the **Custom Animation** button to open the Custom Animation task pane.
6. Click the **Add Effect** button, point to **Emphasis**, and then click **Grow/Shrink**. Leave the default animation options in place and close the task pane.
7. Go to slide 5 and use the Shapes gallery on the Insert tab to select the **Information** action button.

The *Contract Plans* file is available on the companion CD-ROM.

8. Draw a button near the bottom of the slide and set the action to **Hyperlink to: Other File**. Select the file *Contract Plans*.
9. Go to slide 6, select the Web site address, and use the Insert Hyperlink dialog box to create a link to http://www.consolidatedmessenger.com.
10. Insert an automatically updating date, slide numbers, and the footer **Consolidated Messenger** on all slides except the title slide. (You may need to adjust the location of your action button on slide 5 after you add slide numbers and the footer.)
11. Press F5 to run the slide show from slide 1. Advance to slide 2 and test the link at the bottom of the slide. Slide 6 displays.
12. Right-click slide 6, point to **Go to Slide**, and then click **2 Our Services** to return to slide 2.
13. Advance to slide 4 and click the slide to see the emphasis animation take place.
14. Advance to slide 5 and click the action button to open the *Contract Plans* file. Close Microsoft Word to return to the slide show.
15. Advance to slide 6 and click the Web site link. Close the browser and end the slide show.
16. SAVE the presentation as *Messenger Services Links* and CLOSE the file.
    LEAVE PowerPoint open for the next project.

Proficiency Assessment

Project 4-3: Animated Speaker

You are an instructor at the School of Fine Art, and one of your supplementary tasks is to schedule and introduce speakers. You can add animations to a simple introductory slide to jazz up the presentation.

The *Speaker* file is available on the companion CD-ROM.

1. OPEN the *Speaker* presentation.
2. Select the slide title.

3. Apply the **Fly In** built-in animation.
4. Click in the bulleted list.
5. Apply the Fade **By 1st Level Paragraphs** built-in animation.
6. Open the Custom Animation task pane and modify the built-in animations as follows:
   a. For the title animation, change the start option to **With Previous**, the direction to **From Top**, and the speed to **Fast**.
   b. For the content placeholder animation, change the start option to **After Previous** and the speed to **Fast**.
7. Click the picture to select it and add the **Fade** entrance effect (you may have to go to the More Effects dialog box to locate this effect). Change the start option to **With Previous**.
8. With the picture effect still selected, click the **Re-Order Up** button at the bottom of the task pane to move the picture effect above the content placeholder effect so it will occur just after the title animation.
9. Click the **Slide Show** button to test the animations.
10. **SAVE** the presentation as *Speaker Animated* and **CLOSE** the file.
    LEAVE PowerPoint open for the next project.

Project 4-4: The Wild Blue Yonder, Revisited

As the Sales Manager for Blue Yonder Airlines, you have almost finished a presentation that you want to run at a regional travel exposition. You need to add transitions and set slide timings so the slides will run on their own.

The *Blue Yonder Introduction* file is available on the companion CD-ROM.

1. **OPEN** the *Blue Yonder Introduction* presentation.
2. Switch to Slide **Sorter** view and click the **Animations** tab.
3. Set a transition speed of **Medium**.
4. Click the **On Mouse Click** check box to deselect it, and then click **Automatically After**.
5. Set an advance timing of 10 seconds, and then apply these settings to all slides.
6. Select slide 1 and apply the **Fade Smoothly** transition.
7. Select slides 2 through 4 and apply the **Wipe Down** transition. Apply the **Wind** sound effect to slide 2 only.
8. Select slides 5 and 6 and apply the **Blinds Vertical** transition.
9. Apply the **Newsflash** transition to slide 7, and the **Fade Smoothly** transition to slide 8.
10. Run the slide show to view the transitions.
11. **SAVE** the presentation as *Blue Yonder Transitions* and **CLOSE** the file.
    LEAVE PowerPoint open for the next project.

■ Mastery Assessment

Project 4-5: The Art of the Biography

You work for the Editorial Director of Lucerne Publishing. She has asked you to fine-tune a presentation on new biographies she plans to deliver to the sales force. You want to make some global changes to the presentation by customizing the presentation's slide masters, and you need to create a new layout that you will use to introduce sections of biographies.

Designing a Presentation | 627

The *Biographies* file is available on the companion CD-ROM.

1. **OPEN** the *Biographies* presentation.
2. Switch to Slide Master view and apply a new theme of your choice to the slide master.
3. In the left pane, click the **Title and Content** layout and then click the **Insert Layout** button in the Edit Master group to insert a new layout.
4. Deselect **Title** in the Master Layout group to remove the title placeholder from the new layout.
5. Insert a text placeholder in the center of the slide. Delete the sample bulleted text, remove bullet formatting, and change font size to 40 point. Center the text in the placeholder.
6. Apply a new background style to this new layout.
7. Click the **Rename** button in the Edit Master group and key **Introduction** as the new layout name.
8. Close Slide Master view.
9. Insert a new slide after slide 1 using the Introduction layout. Key **American History** in the placeholder.
10. **SAVE** the presentation as *Biographies Masters* and **CLOSE** the file.

    LEAVE PowerPoint open for the next project.

Project 4-6: Adventure Works

You are a coordinator for Adventure Works, a company that manages outdoor adventures for children and teenagers. To introduce your programs, you have created a presentation to show at local schools and recreation centers. Finalize the presentation with design elements and effects that will catch the eye.

The *Adventures* file is available on the companion CD-ROM.

1. **OPEN** the *Adventures* presentation.
2. Apply a suitable theme to the presentation. Customize theme colors or fonts if desired.
3. Animate the bulleted text on slides 2, 3, and 4 using effects of your choice.
4. Apply transitions of your choice to all slides.
5. Set an automatic advance time that will allow plenty of time for animations and reading slide content, and apply it to all slides.
6. Run the slide show to make sure your timing is adequate.
7. **SAVE** the presentation as *Adventures Final* and **CLOSE** the file.

    STOP. CLOSE PowerPoint.

INTERNET READY

Have you ever wanted to create your own digital movies? Use an Internet search tool to locate information on digital video cameras. Select two that seem to offer quality for a reasonable price and make a list of their features. Create a new presentation with a theme of your choice, insert a title, and add a Comparison slide. List the two cameras you have researched in the subheading placeholders and key features for each camera in the text placeholders. Save the presentation with an appropriate name.

Circling Back

You are a sales representative for Contoso Food Services. You are preparing a brief presentation to introduce your company to the Food Services Committee at Trey College, in hopes of receiving a contract to provide food services for the campus dining hall.

Project 1: Create a Presentation

Begin by creating slides from a blank presentation. Then add slides from another presentation, rearrange the slides, and print the presentation.

GET READY. Launch PowerPoint if it is not already running.

1. Create a new, blank presentation.
2. On the title slide, key **Contoso Food Services** in the title placeholder.
3. Key **Trey College Proposal** in the subtitle placeholder.
4. Reuse slides 2–4 from the **Boilerplate** presentation.
5. Rearrange slides so that slide 2 becomes slide 3.
6. Print the presentation as slides in Grayscale mode.
7. **SAVE** the presentation as *Trey Proposal*.

   PAUSE. LEAVE PowerPoint and your presentation open for the next project.

The *Boilerplate* file is available on the companion CD-ROM.

Project 2: Format Your Presentation

Now that you have the bare bones of your presentation written, you can concentrate on formatting to improve the presentation's appearance. You will use WordArt, a theme, font styles, and other formatting options to give your slides punch.

USE the presentation that is open from the previous project.

1. Apply the Median theme, and then change theme colors to those for Office.
2. On slide 1, delete the title text and the title placeholder.
3. Create a WordArt graphic using the **Fill - Text 2, Outline - Background 2** style (the first one in the WordArt style gallery). Key the text **CONTOSO FOOD SERVICES**.
4. Make these changes to the WordArt graphic:
   a. Increase the font size so that the title stretches all the way across the slide, as shown in Figure 1. (Hint: Use the Increase Font Size button.)

Figure 1

Adjust the font size as shown

b. Change the WordArt fill to a gradient, using the **Linear Down** option in the Light Variations section of the Gradient gallery.

c. Change the WordArt outline color to **Dark Blue, Background 2, Lighter 80%**.

d. Apply the **Tight Reflection, touching** effect to the WordArt graphic.

5. Apply italics to the slide 1 subtitle.

6. Go to slide 2. Make these changes to the text in the right-hand placeholder:

   a. Select all text in the right-hand placeholder and change the font size to 24 point.

   b. Right-align the last three paragraphs in the quote (the attribution), and adjust line space so there is no extra space above these lines. (Hint: Choose Line Spacing Options at the bottom of the Line Spacing menu.)

   c. Use the Format Painter to copy formats from the quote paragraph and the quote attribution on slide 2 to the quote text and attribution on slide 3.

7. Go to slide 4. Insert a text box below the picture that is as wide as the picture and key the following text:

   Contoso Food Services is proud to serve institutions in fifteen states in this country and three Canadian provinces. Our reputation for quality is second to none.

8. Format the text box as follows:

   a. Center the text in the text box.

   b. Apply a Quick Style of your choice to the text box.

9. **SAVE** the presentation.

   PAUSE. LEAVE PowerPoint and your presentation open for the next project.

Project 3: Add Design Touches to Your Presentation

You are ready to do the final formatting and add the finishing touches to the presentation. You will adjust the slide master, add a slide, insert links, and set up transitions and animations.

1. Insert an automatically updating date and slide numbers that appear on all slides except the title slide. Notice that the date is partially obscured on slide 4 by the text box you added.

2. In Slide Master view, right-align the date in the date placeholder on the slide master. Close Slide Master view.

3. Insert a new slide at the end of the presentation using the **Two Content** layout.

4. Key the slide title **Contact Us**.

5. Insert the following contact information in the left-hand text placeholder. Format the information as desired.

   Mailing address:
   17507 Atlantic Blvd
   Boca Raton, FL   33456

   Phone:
   561 555 3663
   561 555 3664

6. Insert the following information in the right-hand text placeholder:

   E-mail:
   sales@contoso.com

   Web site:
   www.contoso.com

The *Pricing* file is available on the companion CD-ROM.

7. Create a hyperlink from the Web site text to the Web site at http://www.contoso.com.
8. Apply a different background style to slide 5 only to make it stand out.
9. Go to slide 3. Insert an Information action button above the date in the lower-right corner of the slide that links to the *Pricing* Excel file.
10. Go to slide 2. Animate the text on this slide as follows:
    a. Animate the bullet items in the left-hand text placeholder so that each item flies in from the bottom at a medium speed. Set the start option to **After Previous**.
    b. Animate the text in the right-hand placeholder to fade into view at a medium speed. The effect should start **After Previous**.
11. Apply the same animations to slide 3.
12. Go to slide 1. Apply the **Uncover Down** transition at **Medium** speed to all slides. Apply the **Chime** transition sound effect to slide 4 only.
13. Run the presentation in Slide Show view to test transitions, animations, and links.
14. **SAVE** your changes to the presentation.
15. **SAVE** the presentation as *Trey_2003* in the 97–2003 format, and then **CLOSE** the file.

    STOP. CLOSE PowerPoint.

Adding Tables, Charts, and SmartArt Graphics to Slides

LESSON SKILL MATRIX

Inserting a Table — 632	Students will learn how to insert a table.
Inserting an Excel Worksheet — 635	Students will learn how to insert an Excel worksheet.
Applying a Quick Style to a Table — 638	Students will learn how to apply a Quick Style to a table.
Inserting a Chart from a Content Placeholder — 639	Students will learn how to insert a chart from a content placeholder.
Choosing a Different Chart Type — 642	Students will learn how to choose a different chart type.
Applying a Different Chart Layout — 643	Students will learn how to apply a different chart layout.
Applying a Quick Style to a Chart — 645	Students will learn how to apply a Quick Style to a chart.
Inserting a SmartArt Diagram — 647	Students will learn how to insert a SmartArt diagram.
Applying a Quick Style to a SmartArt Diagram — 653	Students will learn how to apply a Quick Style to a SmartArt diagram.

You are an assistant director of ATM operations at Woodgrove Bank. Your job is to help oversee the placement and use of ATMs in your bank's branches and other locations. You often deliver presentations to bank officers to keep them up to date on ATM activities. The best way to organize information that has several related components is to use a table. Distributing information in rows and columns makes the data easy to read and understand. PowerPoint's charting capabilities allow you to communicate financial data in a visual way that makes trends and comparisons easy to understand. You also use SmartArt diagrams to explain your company's organization and standard processes to the newcomers. SmartArt diagrams provide an easy way to share complex information in the form of sophisticated graphics that clearly show relationships and processes. In this lesson, you will learn to use the table, chart, and SmartArt features of Microsoft Office PowerPoint 2007 to improve the readability and visual interest of your presentations.

KEY TERMS
assistant
chart
data marker
data series
embedded
linked
organization chart
subordinates
table
Text pane
top-level shape
worksheet

Software Orientation

A PowerPoint Table

Tables are designed to organize data in columns and rows, as shown in Figure 5-1.

Figure 5-1

A PowerPoint table and table tools on the Ribbon

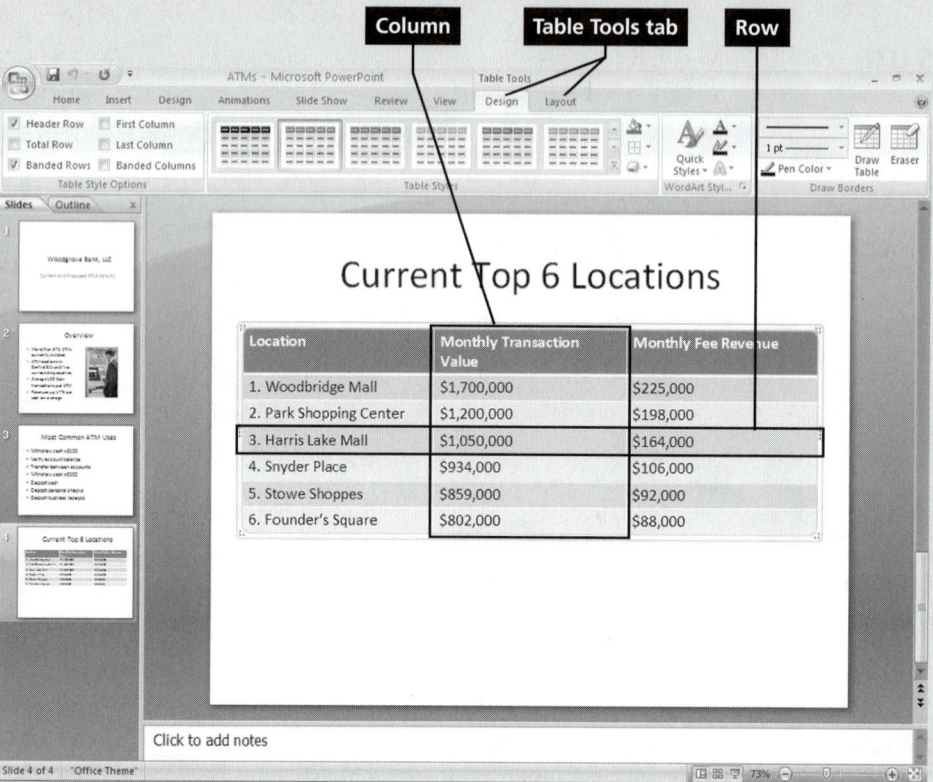

The Table Tools Design tab, shown above, and the Table Tools Layout tab provide tools for modifying and formatting a table. These tabs become active only when a table is selected.

Creating Tables

THE BOTTOM LINE

When you want to organize complex data on a slide, use a table. A table's column-and-row structure makes data easy to understand. If you need to organize numerical data that may be used in calculations, you can insert an Excel worksheet right on a slide and use Excel's tools to work with the data.

Inserting a Table

PowerPoint offers several ways to insert a table. The simplest is to click the Insert Table icon in any content placeholder.

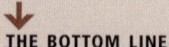 **INSERT A TABLE**

GET READY. Before you begin these steps, be sure to launch Microsoft Office PowerPoint 2007.

The *ATMs* file is available on the companion CD-ROM.

1. Locate and open the *ATMs* presentation.
2. Go to slide 4. Insert a new slide with the Title and Content layout.

Adding Tables, Charts, and SmartArt Graphics to Slides | 633

3. Key the slide title **Proposed ATM Locations**.
4. Click the **Insert Table** icon in the group of icons in the center of the content placeholder. The Insert Table dialog box opens, as shown in Figure 5-2.

Figure 5-2

The Insert Table dialog box

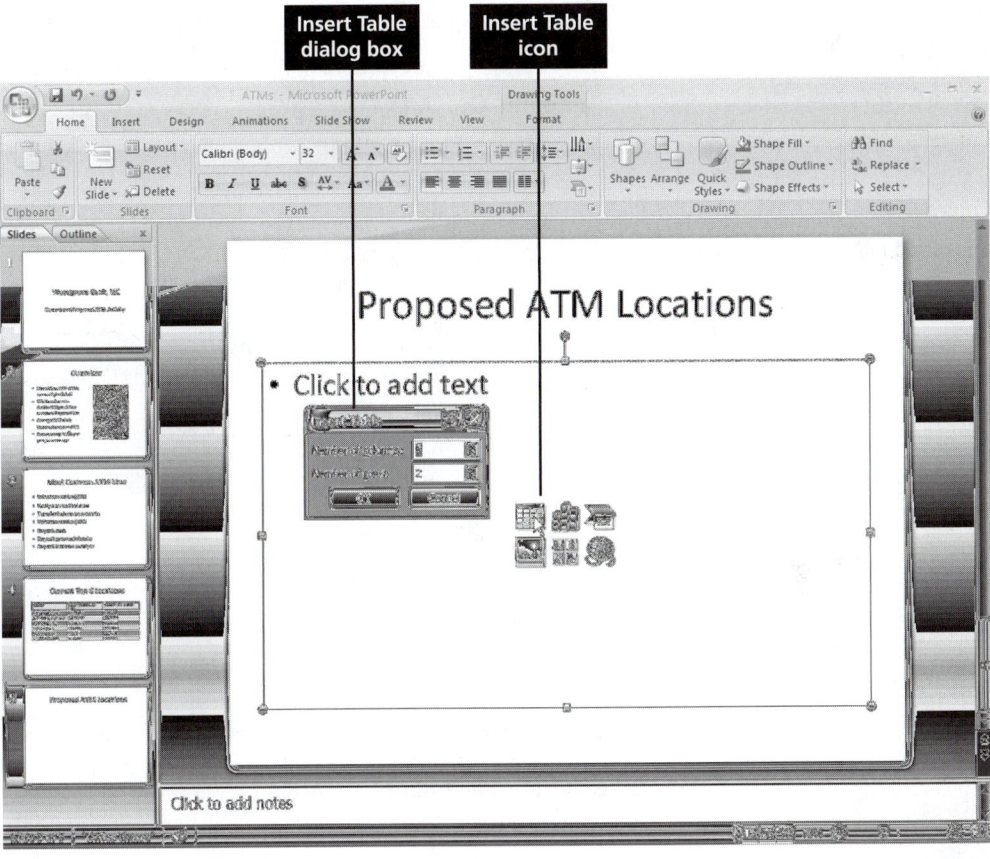

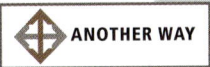 **ANOTHER WAY**   You can open the Insert Table dialog box by clicking the Table drop-down arrow on the Insert tab and then clicking Insert Table.

5. Key **3** to specify three columns, press **Tab**, and then key **6** to specify six rows. Click **OK**. PowerPoint creates the table in the content area, as shown in Figure 5-3. Notice that formats specified by the current theme have already been applied to the table.

Figure 5-3

A new table with three columns and six rows

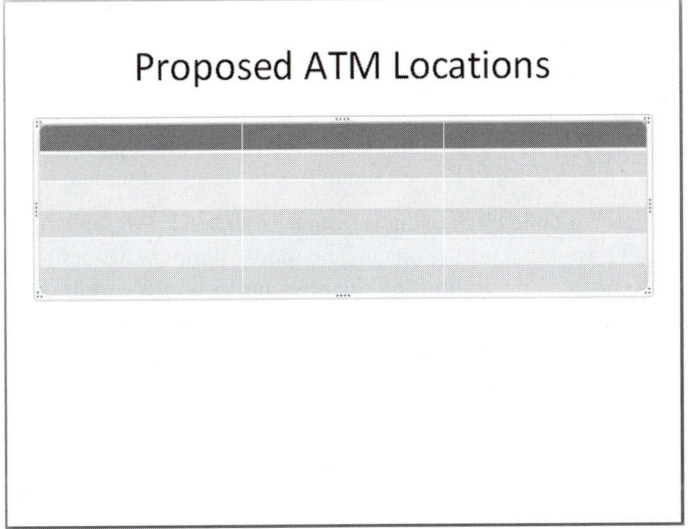

6. Click in the first table cell in the top row and key **Location**. Press Tab and key **Site Study Complete**. Press Tab and key **Nearest Competing ATM**.

7. Key the following information in the table cells, pressing **Tab** to move from cell to cell. Your table should look like Figure 5-4 when you complete it.

1. Springdale Cineplex	Yes	More than 2 miles
2. Glen Avenue BIG Foods	No	Three blocks
3. Findlay Market Square	Yes	One block
4. Center City Arena	Yes	One block
5. Williams State College	No	Half a mile

Figure 5-4

Completed table

Location	Site Study Complete	Nearest Competing ATM
Springdale Cineplex	Yes	More than 2 miles
Glen Avenue BIG Foods	No	Three blocks
Findlay Market Square	Yes	One block
Center City Arena	Yes	One block
Williams State College	No	Half a mile

Proposed ATM Locations

8. **SAVE** the presentation as **ATMs Final**.

   PAUSE. LEAVE the presentation open to use in the next exercise.

PowerPoint has automated the process of creating a ***table*** so that you can simply specify the number of columns and rows and then key data to achieve a professionally formatted result. By default, PowerPoint sizes a new table to fill the width of the content placeholder. If you have only a few columns, you may find the table a little too "spacious." You will learn later in this lesson how to adjust column widths and row heights to more closely fit the data you have entered.

Once you have become proficient with tables, you may want to use one of the other methods PowerPoint offers to create a new table: dragging over a grid of columns and rows to create a table or drawing the table from scratch.

To create a table by dragging, click the Table button on the Insert tab. PowerPoint displays a grid that you can drag over to select the desired number of columns and rows. As you drag, PowerPoint creates columns and rows in the content placeholder so you can easily see how your table will look. Release the mouse button to complete the table.

To create a table by drawing it from scratch, click the Table button drop-down arrow, then click Draw Table on the menu. The mouse pointer changes to a pencil pointer you can use to draw the table outline and the rows and columns within the table border. This option makes it easy to create a table that does not have a regular arrangement of columns and rows; if, for example, you need to create a table in which one column has three rows while an adjacent column has only one cell.

You can adjust a table's size by using the Height and Width options in the Table Size group on the Table Tools Layout tab. If you need to reposition a table on a slide, you can do so by simply dragging it into place using the light-blue table container outline.

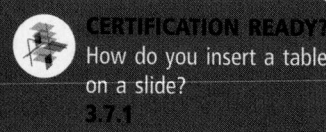

CERTIFICATION READY?
How do you insert a table on a slide?
3.7.1

Adding Tables, Charts, and SmartArt Graphics to Slides | 635

Inserting an Excel Worksheet

Microsoft Office 2007 allows for a great deal of integration among its programs. If you need to show numerical data on a slide, for example, you can insert an Excel worksheet directly on the slide and use it to manipulate data just as you would in Excel.

➔ INSERT AN EXCEL WORKSHEET

USE the presentation that is still open from the previous exercise.

1. Insert a new slide after the current slide (slide 5) with the Title Only layout.
2. Key the slide title **ATM Cost Analysis**.
3. Click the **Insert** tab, click the **Table** drop-down arrow, then click **Excel Spreadsheet**. PowerPoint creates a small Excel worksheet on the slide, as shown in Figure 5-5. Note that the PowerPoint Ribbon has been replaced by the Excel Ribbon.

Figure 5-5

A new Excel worksheet on a slide

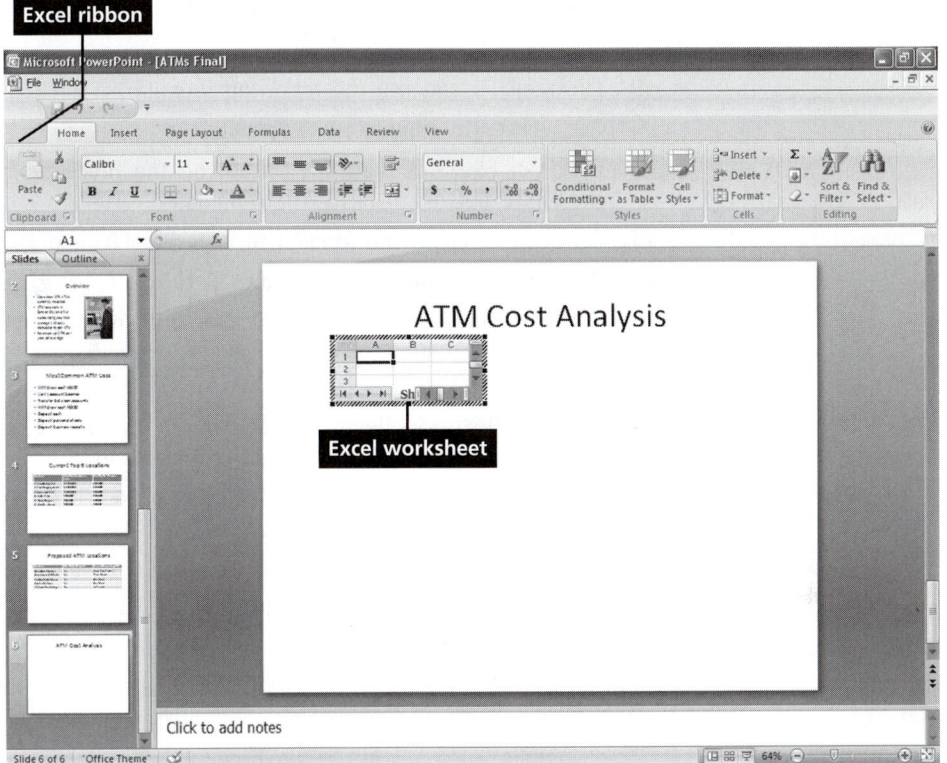

TAKE NOTE

When an Excel worksheet is open on the slide, you are actually working in Excel. To return to PowerPoint, click outside the worksheet.

4. Resize the worksheet object by dragging the lower-right corner handle diagonally to the right to display columns A through F and rows 1 through 10.

TROUBLESHOOTING

If your worksheet does not show lettered columns, click the Office button, click Excel Options, click Formulas, and remove the check mark from the R1C1 reference style check box.

5. Click the **Select All** area in the upper-left corner of the worksheet object, where the column headers and row headers intersect. The entire worksheet object is selected.
6. Click the **Font Size** drop-down arrow on the Home tab and click **18**.
7. Key data in the worksheet cells as shown in Figure 5-6. To adjust column widths, position the pointer on the border between columns and drag to the right until all data appears.

Figure 5-6

Key the data as shown

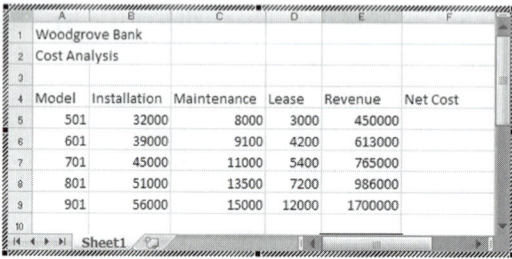

8. Click cell **F5** and key the following formula: **=E5−(B5+C5+D5)**.
9. Press **Enter** to complete the formula.
10. Click cell **F5**, click the **Copy** button on the Home tab, click cell **F6**, and click the **Paste** button to paste the formula.
11. Continue to paste the formula to cells **F7**, **F8**, and **F9**.
12. Drag over the numbers in columns B through F to select them.
13. Click the **Accounting Number Format** button in the Number group on the Home tab to apply a currency format. (Don't worry if some of the cells fill up with # signs.)
14. Click the **Decrease Decimal** button in the Number group twice to remove the decimal points and trailing zeros for the numbers.
15. Click cell **A1** and change the font size to **24**. Click the **Font Color** button and choose **Blue, Accent 1, Darker 25%**.
16. Adjust column widths again if necessary to present data clearly and attractively.
17. Click outside the worksheet object, and then click again to close the worksheet container. Your slide should look similar to Figure 5-7.

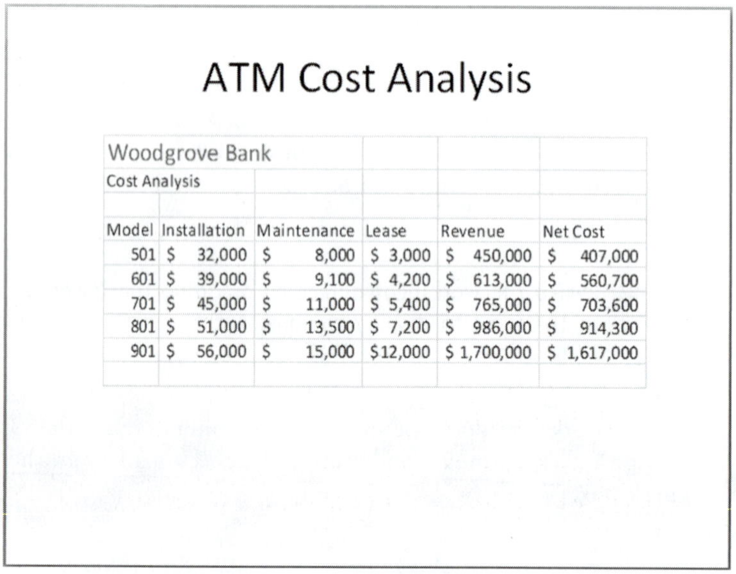

Figure 5-7

The completed Excel worksheet

ATM Cost Analysis

Woodgrove Bank
Cost Analysis

Model	Installation	Maintenance	Lease	Revenue	Net Cost
501	$ 32,000	$ 8,000	$ 3,000	$ 450,000	$ 407,000
601	$ 39,000	$ 9,100	$ 4,200	$ 613,000	$ 560,700
701	$ 45,000	$ 11,000	$ 5,400	$ 765,000	$ 703,600
801	$ 51,000	$ 13,500	$ 7,200	$ 986,000	$ 914,300
901	$ 56,000	$ 15,000	$ 12,000	$ 1,700,000	$ 1,617,000

18. **SAVE** the presentation.

PAUSE. LEAVE the presentation open to use in the next exercise.

Inserting an Excel *worksheet* gives you access to all of Excel's data manipulation and formatting tools. If you want to show Excel data on a slide and have not yet created the worksheet, it makes sense to create the worksheet directly on the PowerPoint slide. A worksheet you insert in this way is *embedded* on the slide—it is stored within the PowerPoint presentation but can be edited using the tools of its source application, Excel.

You can edit the embedded worksheet at any time by double-clicking the worksheet object to open it in Excel. You can remove the object by clicking it once to display the heavy, light-blue container border and then pressing Delete.

> **TAKE NOTE**
> You know a worksheet is open and ready to edit in Excel when it displays the heavy hatched border.

When you insert a worksheet using the Excel Spreadsheet command, the worksheet consists of only four visible cells. Drag the bottom or side sizing handle (or the lower-right corner handle) to reveal more cells. When you have finished inserting data, use these handles to adjust the border to hide empty cells that would otherwise show on the PowerPoint slide.

You can also resize a worksheet object by clicking it once to display the heavy, light-blue container border, then dragging a bottom, side, or corner of the container. This action enlarges or reduces the object itself; it does not change font size of the embedded data even though the text may look larger.

If you have already created an Excel worksheet and want to use the data on a slide, you have several additional options for getting it from Excel to PowerPoint:

- Select the data in Excel, copy it, and paste it on a PowerPoint slide. This action pastes the Excel data as a PowerPoint table that cannot be edited in Excel but can be modified like any other PowerPoint table.
- Select the data in Excel, copy it, click the Paste button drop-down arrow in PowerPoint, and select Paste Special. In the Paste Special dialog box, choose to paste the data as an Excel worksheet object. The data is then embedded on the slide just as when you used the Excel Spreadsheet command.
- Select the data in Excel, copy it, and open the Paste Special dialog box in PowerPoint. Choose to paste link the data as an Excel worksheet object. The data is then *linked* to the Excel worksheet so that if you make any change to the worksheet in Excel, the data on the slide will show that same change.
- Finally, you can click the Object button on the Insert tab to open the Insert Object dialog box. Here you can choose to create a new worksheet file or navigate to an existing file and paste or paste link it on the slide.

> **TAKE NOTE**
> The Insert Object dialog box allows you to create a number of objects other than worksheets. You can create formulas, Word documents in various versions, and even sound files.

You can use the same procedures to copy Excel charts to slides. When simply pasted on a slide, an Excel chart can be formatted using the same tools you use to work with a PowerPoint chart.

> **X REF**
> You will work with PowerPoint charts later in this lesson.

Formatting Tables

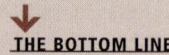 **THE BOTTOM LINE** PowerPoint provides default formats to all new tables so that they look good right from the start. You may want to modify formatting, however, because you do not like the default colors or you want a different look. Use the tools on the Table Tools Design tab to apply new formatting options.

Applying a Quick Style to a Table

PowerPoint tables are formatted by default with a Quick Style based on the current theme colors. You can choose another Quick Style to change color and shading formats.

APPLY A QUICK STYLE TO A TABLE

USE the presentation that is still open from the previous exercise.

1. Go to slide 5. Click anywhere in the table, then click the **Table Tools Design** tab.
2. Click the **More** button in the Table Styles group to display the Quick Styles gallery, as shown in Figure 5-8. Note that the table styles are organized into several groups—Best Match for Document, Light, Medium, and Dark.

Figure 5-8

Table Quick Styles gallery

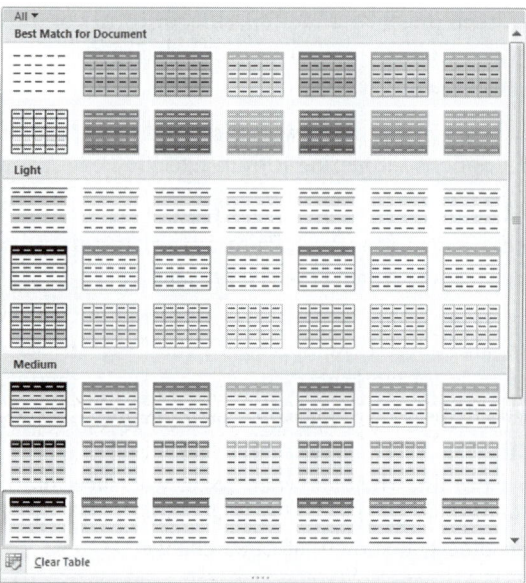

3. Click the **Themed Style 2–Accent 6** table style. This is a colorful alternative, but not exactly what you want.
4. Click the **More** button again, and then click the **Medium Style 3** style, a black and gray combination in the first column of the gallery.
5. **SAVE** the presentation and then **CLOSE** the file.

   PAUSE. LEAVE the presentation open to use in the next exercise.

Colors available for Quick Style formats are controlled by theme. If you apply a Quick Style and then change the theme, the Quick Style colors will adjust to those of the new theme.

You may on occasion want to remove all table formatting to present data in a simple grid without shading or border colors. You can remove formatting by clicking Clear Table at the bottom of the Quick Styles gallery. Once you have cleared formats, you can reapply them by selecting any table style.

Adding Tables, Charts, and SmartArt Graphics to Slides | 639

■ Software Orientation

A PowerPoint Chart

Charts can help your audience understand relationships among numerical values. Figure 5-9 shows a sample PowerPoint chart with some standard chart features labeled.

Figure 5-9

Components of a PowerPoint chart

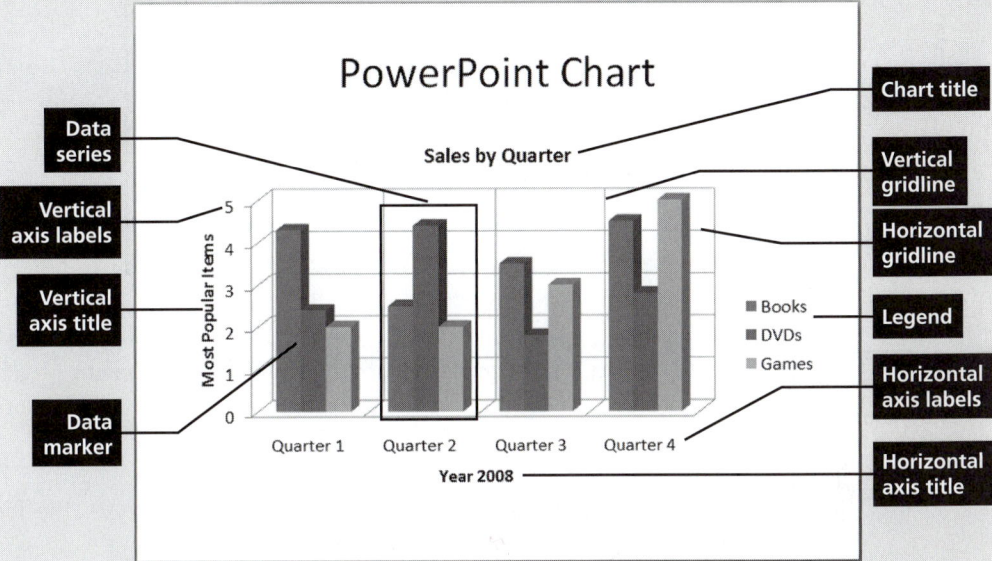

A PowerPoint chart can be as simple as a series of lines or two-dimensional columns, or it can provide a whole range of additional information, such as that shown in the chart above. Legends, titles, and gridlines can help present complex data so it can be easily understood.

■ Building Charts

THE BOTTOM LINE

You can create a chart in any content placeholder. PowerPoint and Excel work in tandem to streamline the operation of inserting and formatting the chart so that all you need to do is key the data for the chart. After you have inserted the chart, you can change the chart type or layout to display the data as you wish.

Inserting a Chart from a Content Placeholder

As with tables and other objects such as diagrams and pictures, the easiest way to insert a chart is to click the Insert Chart icon in any content placeholder. PowerPoint guides you the rest of the way to complete the chart.

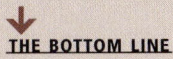

The **Revenues** file is available on the companion CD-ROM.

➔ INSERT A CHART

1. Locate and open the **Revenues** presentation.

2. Go to slide 3. Click the **Insert Chart** icon in the center of the content placeholder. The Insert Chart dialog box opens, as shown in Figure 5-10, showing chart types and subtypes.

Figure 5-10

Select a chart type and subtype

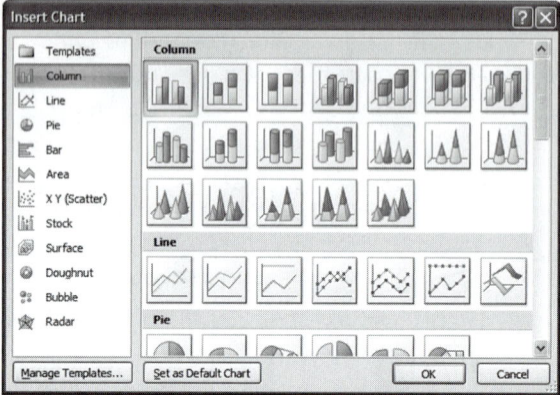

 **ANOTHER WAY** To insert a chart on a slide that does not have a content placeholder, click the Chart button on the Insert tab.

3. Click the **3-D Clustered Column** chart subtype (the fourth from the left in the top row of the dialog box).
4. Click **OK**. Microsoft Excel opens in a window to the right of the PowerPoint window, as shown in Figure 5-11. The PowerPoint slide displays a sample chart created from the sample data in the Excel window.

Figure 5-11

Creating a new chart requires Excel

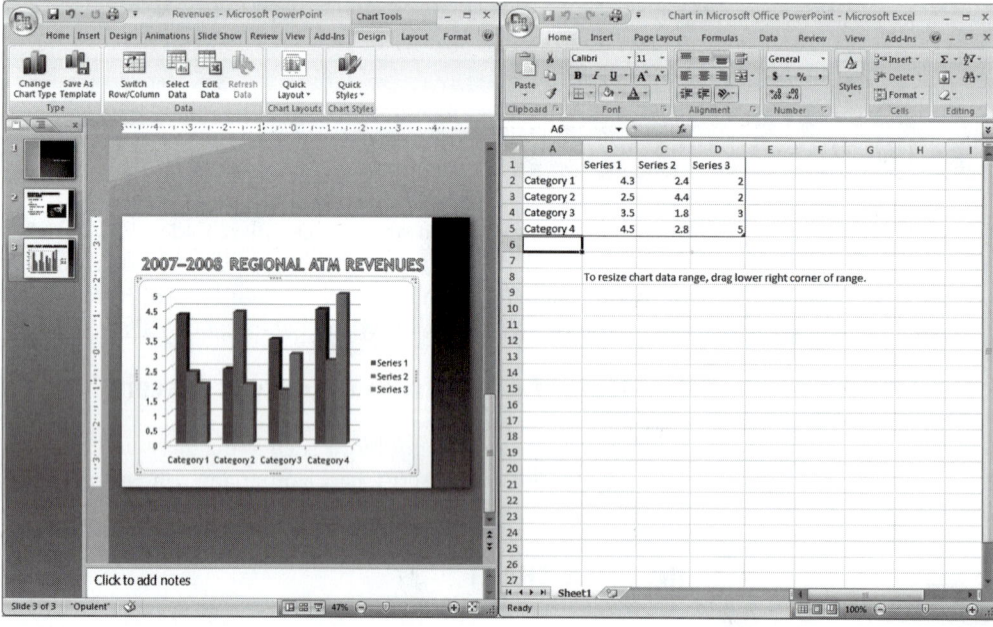

Adding Tables, Charts, and SmartArt Graphics to Slides | 641

In Excel, notice the bright-blue border that surrounds the data. This *range border* is used to indicate the data being charted. If the data you want to enter has more or fewer columns than the sample data, PowerPoint and Excel may not chart the data accurately unless you adjust this range border.

5. In Excel, click the sizing handle at the lower-right corner of the bright-blue range border. Drag to the left so that the border encloses the range A1:C5.
6. Drag over the cells that contain data in the Excel worksheet and press **Delete**. The chart disappears from the PowerPoint slide because you have removed the data that created it.
7. Click cell **B1** and key **2007**, press **Tab**, key **2008**, then press **Enter**. Notice that this data appears on the PowerPoint slide in the legend area.
8. Beginning in cell A2, key the following data in Excel to complete the chart. When you have entered the data, your screen should look like Figure 5-12.

District 1	$89,000	$102,000
District 2	$54,000	$62,000
District 3	$102,000	$118,000
District 4	$233,000	$267,000

Figure 5-12

Completed worksheet and chart

	A	B	C
		2007	2008
District 1		89000	102000
District 2		54000	62000
District 3		102000	118000
District 4		233000	267000

9. **SAVE** the presentation as *Revenues Final*.

   PAUSE. LEAVE the presentation open to use in the next exercise.

Charts are visual representations of numerical data. Chart features such as columns, bars, lines, or pie slices make it easy to understand trends or compare values. Once you have created a chart in PowerPoint, you can easily modify the data on which the chart is based, choose a different type of chart to display the data, change the layout of the chart, or modify its formats.

To take full advantage of PowerPoint 2007's charting capabilities, you must have Microsoft Excel installed. As you saw in the previous exercise, Excel opens to allow you to insert the data that creates the chart. If you do not have Excel installed, PowerPoint instead resorts to Microsoft Graph, the charting application used in previous versions of PowerPoint.

After you key the chart data, you can close Excel to restore the PowerPoint window to its full size. You can, if desired, save the Excel data if you want to work with it later in Excel, but you do not have to save before you close the worksheet. You can redisplay the Excel data any time you want to modify the data by clicking the Edit Data button on the PowerPoint Chart Tools Design tab.

PowerPoint assumes that you will want to key new data for a chart in the Excel worksheet, but you can also use existing Excel data to create a chart in PowerPoint. After Excel opens with the sample data worksheet, use Excel's Open command to open the workbook that contains the data you want to use. In PowerPoint, click the Select Data button to open the Select Data Source dialog box, shown in Figure 5-13.

Figure 5-13

The Select Data Source dialog box

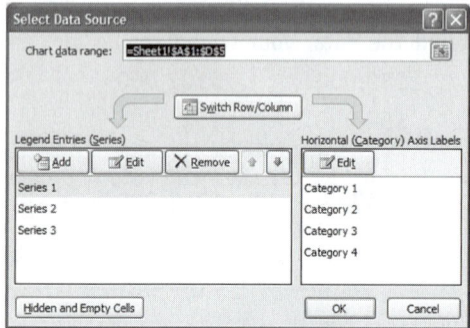

Activate the worksheet you want to use and then click the Collapse button in the Select Data Source dialog box to minimize the dialog box. Drag over the cells that contain the data you need for the chart, then click the Expand button to enlarge the dialog box. The Chart data range box should show the range of cells you want to use. Once you click OK, PowerPoint builds the chart from the specified data.

A somewhat simpler way to use data from an existing worksheet is simply to copy it and paste it in the Excel worksheet that appears when you create a new chart. You may need to adjust the range border to enclose the pasted data. You can do this by dragging the range border in Excel or by using the Select Data Source dialog box to specify the data range for the chart.

You have one other option for putting a chart on a slide: You can copy a chart that has already been created in Excel and paste it on the slide. An Excel chart that is simply pasted on the slide maintains a link to Excel by default so that if you modify the Excel chart, the chart on the slide is also modified. You can format a pasted chart the same way you format any PowerPoint chart.

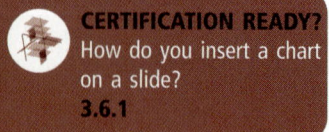

CERTIFICATION READY?
How do you insert a chart on a slide?
3.6.1

Choosing a Different Chart Type

If you decide that the chart type you have chosen does not display the data the way you want, you can choose a different chart type or subtype.

Adding Tables, Charts, and SmartArt Graphics to Slides | 643

➡ **CHOOSE A DIFFERENT CHART TYPE**

USE the presentation that is still open from the previous exercise.

1. Click the Excel window's **Close** button to close the data worksheet and restore the PowerPoint window to full size.
2. Click the **Change Chart Type** button in the Type group on the Chart Tools Design tab. The Insert Chart dialog box opens, showing the same options that appeared when you first created the chart.

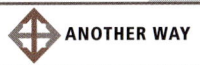 Right-click almost anywhere in a chart and then click Change Chart Type on the shortcut menu.

3. Click the **Clustered Cylinder** subtype (the first in the second row of column charts), and then click **OK**. The rectangular columns change to three-dimensional cylinders.

   PAUSE. LEAVE the presentation open to use in the next exercise.

In this exercise, you changed one subtype of a column chart to another column subtype. You can also change a chart from one type to another; for example, you can change a column chart to a bar chart without greatly affecting the visual display of information.

Not all chart types are interchangeable. Although you can, for instance, change your column chart to a line chart, the results would not be as informative in line format. And you cannot change a column chart to a pie chart without losing a great deal of information.

The default PowerPoint chart type is a column chart, and the sample Excel data is structured specifically for that type of chart. Other chart types, such as pie charts, may require data to be arranged in a different way, and if your data is not arranged that way, your chart will not display it correctly or completely.

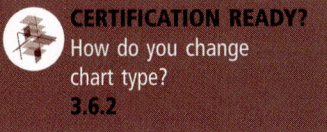
CERTIFICATION READY?
How do you change chart type?
3.6.2

If you apply a chart type that does not display your data as you want, use Undo to reverse the change and then try another type.

TROUBLESHOOTING Changing from a two-dimensional chart type to a three-dimensional one can yield unexpected results. For some chart types, PowerPoint may display the new chart type in a rotated, perspective view that you might not like. It is best to decide when you create the original chart whether you want it to use two or three dimensions, and then stick with those dimensions when making any change to the chart type.

Applying a Different Chart Layout

PowerPoint supplies several preformatted chart layouts that you can apply quickly to modify the default layout. These layouts may adjust the position of features such as the legend or add chart components such as titles and data labels.

APPLY A DIFFERENT CHART LAYOUT

USE the presentation that is still open from the previous exercise.

1. Click the **More** button in the Chart Layouts group on the Chart Tools Design tab. The Chart Layout gallery displays, as shown in Figure 5-14.

Figure 5-14

The Chart Layout gallery

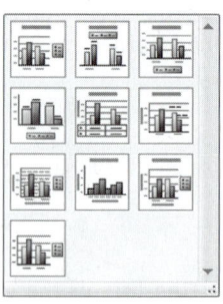

TAKE NOTE

The thumbnails in the Chart Layout gallery show in miniature the new layout and elements of the chart.

2. Click **Layout 1** in the gallery. The layout is modified to add the Chart Title element at the top of the chart.
3. Click the **Chart Title** placeholder, then drag over the text and press Delete.
4. Key **Revenues by District** in the chart title placeholder. Click outside the placeholder to close it. Your chart should look similar to Figure 5-15.

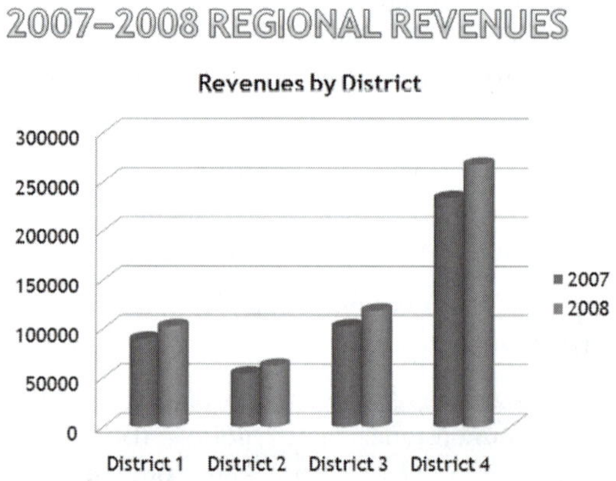

Figure 5-15

A chart title has been added to the chart

5. **SAVE** the presentation.

   PAUSE. LEAVE the presentation open to use in the next exercise.

PowerPoint charts can be customized in a very wide variety of ways by adding and removing chart elements such as titles, labels, and gridlines. If you do not want to take the time to add elements, PowerPoint's chart layouts can provide you with some standard appearance options to choose from. You will learn how to add elements yourself later in this lesson.

Adding Tables, Charts, and SmartArt Graphics to Slides | 645

✳ Workplace Ready

Choosing the Right Type of Chart

Each PowerPoint chart type is designed to present a specific type of data. When you create a chart, you should select the chart type that will best display your data. Some of the most commonly used chart types are described below.

- **Column charts:** Column charts are generally used for showing data changes over a period of time or for comparing items. Categories (such as Quarter 1 or 2008) display on the horizontal axis (the X axis), and values display on the vertical axis (the Y axis).
- **Bar charts:** Bar charts are used to compare individual items. They are especially useful when values are durations. Categories display on the vertical axis and values display on the horizontal axis.
- **Line charts:** Line charts are best used to display values over time or trends in data. Categories are usually evenly spaced items, such as months or years, and display on the horizontal axis.
- **Pie charts:** Pie charts are used to show the relationship of an individual category to the sum of all categories. Data for a pie chart consists of only a single column or row of data in the worksheet.
- **Area charts:** Area charts are used to show the amount of change over time as well as total value across a trend. Like a pie chart, an area chart can show the relationship of an individual category to the sum of all values.

You can learn more about chart types and subtypes and how they are designed to be used by consulting PowerPoint's Help files.

■ Formatting Charts with Quick Styles

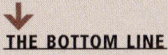 Chart Quick Styles provide instant formatting to change the look of a chart. A Quick Style can change colors and borders of data markers, apply effects to the data markers, and apply color to the chart or plot area.

Applying a Quick Style to a Chart

 APPLY A QUICK STYLE TO A CHART

USE the presentation that is still open from the previous exercise.

1. Go to slide 3 and click the chart to select it.
2. Click the **Chart Tools Design** tab.

3. Click the **More** button in the Chart Styles group. The Quick Styles gallery appears, as shown in Figure 5-16.

Figure 5-16

Chart Quick Styles gallery

4. Click **Style 7**. The data series' colors change to variations of another theme color. This is not quite dramatic enough for your purpose.
5. Click the **More** button again, and then click **Style 43**. This style applies new theme color, bevel effects, and different chart background colors, as shown in Figure 5-17.

Figure 5-17

The chart is more interesting with the new Quick Style applied

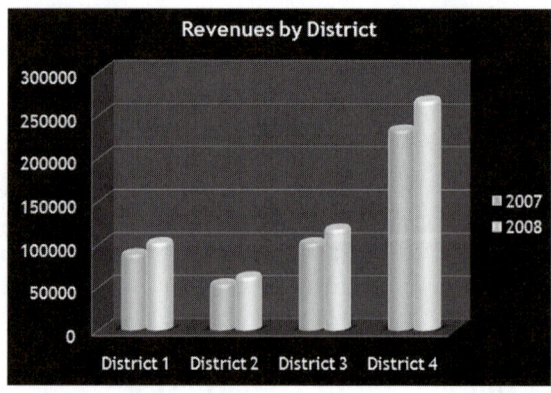

6. **SAVE** the presentation and then **CLOSE** the file.

   PAUSE. LEAVE PowerPoint open to use in the next exercise.

Use a Quick Style to format a chart if you do not have time to adjust formatting of chart elements such as *__data series__* or the individual *__data markers__* in a series. A data series consists of all the data points for a particular category, such as all the columns for Quarter 1 values. A data marker is one column or point in a series.

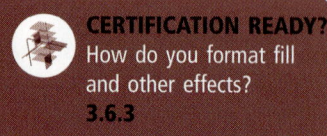

Chart Quick Styles give you six appearance options that you can vary by selecting specific theme colors or color combinations. Effects that are applied to the data series, such as bevels, are also applied in the legend.

Adding Tables, Charts, and SmartArt Graphics to Slides | 647

■ Software Orientation

Choosing a SmartArt Graphic

PowerPoint 2007 offers seven different types of SmartArt diagrams, with many layouts for each type. Figure 5-18 shows the dialog box that appears when you choose to insert a SmartArt diagram.

Figure 5-18

Choose a SmartArt Graphic dialog box

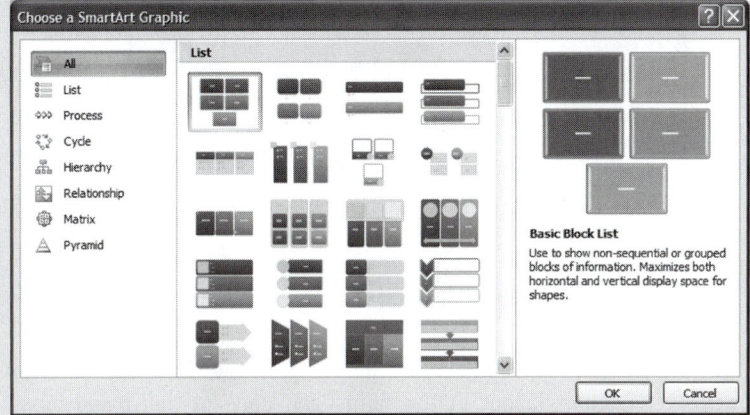

When you click a layout, the right pane of the dialog box shows you a close-up view of the selected layout and provides information on how to use the layout. The layout's description can help you decide whether the layout will be appropriate for your information.

■ Adding SmartArt to a Slide

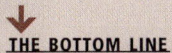

THE BOTTOM LINE Use the Insert SmartArt Graphic icon in any content placeholder to start a new diagram. After you have selected a type and a layout, you can add text to the diagram. PowerPoint also lets you use existing bullet items to create a SmartArt diagram.

Insert a SmartArt Diagram

Use an ***organization chart*** to show the relationships among personnel or departments in an organization. Organization charts are included in the Hierarchy type SmartArt layouts.

➔ INSERT AN ORGANIZATION CHART

GET READY. Before you begin these steps, make sure that your computer is on. Log on, if necessary.

1. Start PowerPoint, if the program is not already running.
2. Locate and open the **Woodgrove** presentation.
3. Go to slide 3, and click the **Insert SmartArt Graphic** icon in the center of the content placeholder. The Choose a SmartArt Graphic dialog box opens.

The ***Litware*** file is available on the companion CD-ROM.

 **ANOTHER WAY** To insert a SmartArt diagram on a slide that does not have a content placeholder, click the SmartArt button on the Insert tab.

4. Click **Hierarchy** in the type list at the left side of the dialog box. The layouts for the Hierarchy type display, as shown in Figure 5-19.

Figure 5-19

The Hierarchy layouts in the Choose a SmartArt Graphic dialog box

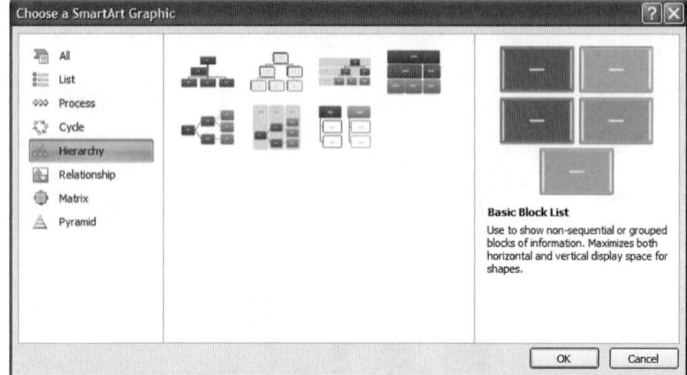

5. Click the first layout in the first row. Read the description of the Organization Chart layout in the right-hand pane of the dialog box.
6. Click **OK** to insert the diagram. The diagram and the fly-out Text pane appear on the slide, as shown in Figure 5-20.

Figure 5-20

A new, blank organization chart diagram

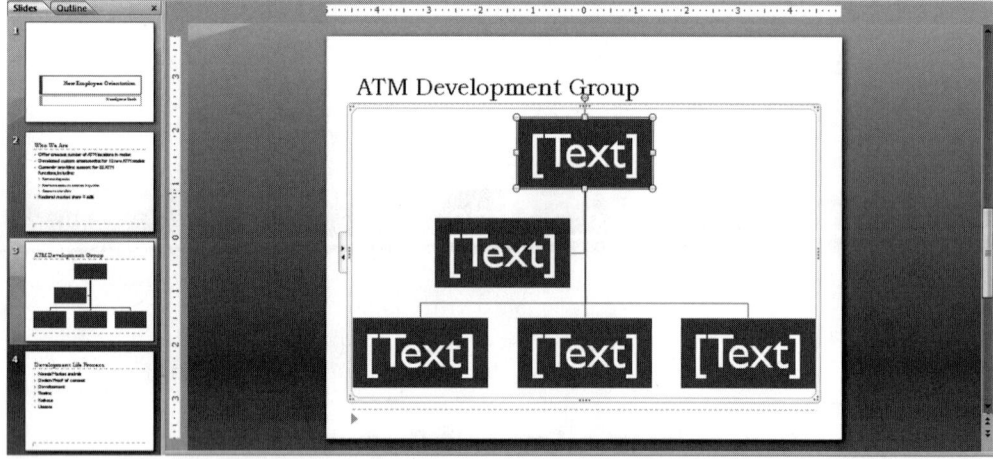

7. SAVE the presentation as *Woodgrove Final*.

   PAUSE. LEAVE the presentation open to use in the next exercise.

SmartArt diagrams are visual representations of information you want to communicate. SmartArt diagrams show items of related information in a graphical way that makes their relationships easy to understand. You can use SmartArt diagrams to present text information in a more visually interesting way than the usual bulleted or numbered formats.

Adding Tables, Charts, and SmartArt Graphics to Slides | 649

The Choose a SmartArt Graphic dialog box sorts its many layouts by types such as List, Process, Hierarchy, and so on. The following general descriptions of SmartArt types can help you choose a type:

- Use the **List** layouts to display information that does not have to be in a particular order.
- Use the **Process** layouts to show the steps in a process or timeline.
- **Cycle** layouts are useful for showing a continual process.
- **Hierarchy** layouts show levels of subordination.
- Use **Relationship** layouts to show connections between items.
- **Matrix** layouts show how parts relate to a whole.
- **Pyramid** layouts display relationships in terms of proportion, from largest at the bottom to smallest at the top.

When you are deciding on a layout, take into consideration the amount of text you want to use in the diagram. Some layouts are designed to handle only one or two words in a shape, while other layouts can accommodate longer text entries.

A new SmartArt diagram appears on the slide with empty shapes to which you add text (and in some cases, pictures) to create the final diagram. The appearance and position of these shapes are guided by the layout you chose, and shape color is controlled by the current theme.

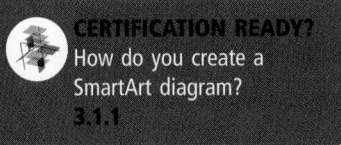

An organization chart, such as the one you just created, has some special terminology and layout requirements. In an organization chart, there can be only one ***top-level shape***—the person or department at the head of the organization. Persons or departments who report to the top-level entity are ***subordinates***. An ***assistant*** is a person who reports directly to a staff member and usually appears on a separate level.

ADD TEXT TO A SMARTART DIAGRAM

USE the presentation that is still open from the previous exercise.

1. If necessary, click next to the bullet at the top of the Text pane to place the insertion point there. Key **Ted Hicks** to enter the name in the top-level shape of the diagram. Notice that as you key the text in the Text pane, it appears in the top shape of the diagram.
2. Click in the bullet item below *Ted Hicks* in the Text pane, and then key **Rose Lang**. Rose Lang is an assistant to Ted Hicks and as such has an assistant shape on a level between the top-level shape and the subordinate shapes.
3. Click in the next bullet item in the Text pane and key **Marcus Short**. Marcus Short is a subordinate to Ted Hicks.
4. Click in the next bullet item and key **Ellen Camp**.

5. Click in the last bullet item and key **Pat Cramer**. Your diagram should look like Figure 5-21.

Figure 5-21

Names have been added to the organization chart

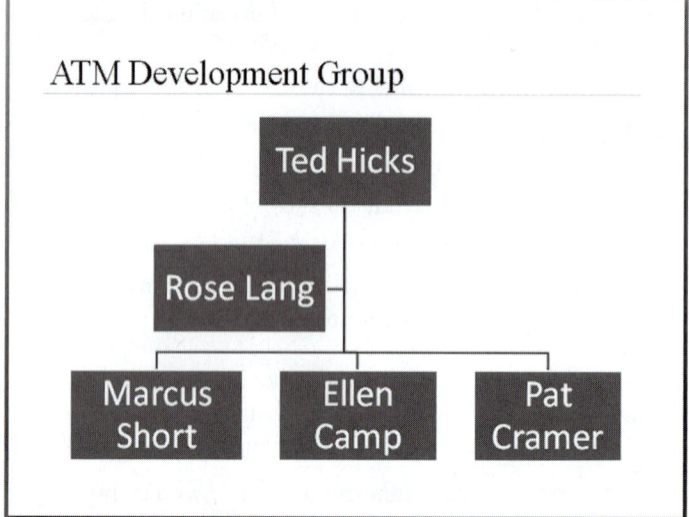

6. Click the **Close** button in the Text pane to hide it. You will complete the text entry by keying directly in the diagram shapes.
7. Click just to the right of the name *Hicks* in the top-level shape, press **Enter**, and key **Director**. Notice that the text size adjusts in all the shapes to account for the additional entry in the top-level shape.
8. Click after the name *Lang* in the assistant shape, press **Enter**, and key **Assistant Director**.
9. Key the title **Software Development** for Marcus Short, **ATM Programming** for Ellen Camp, and **New Model Support** for Pat Cramer. Your diagram should look similar to Figure 5-22.

Figure 5-22

Titles have been added to the organization chart

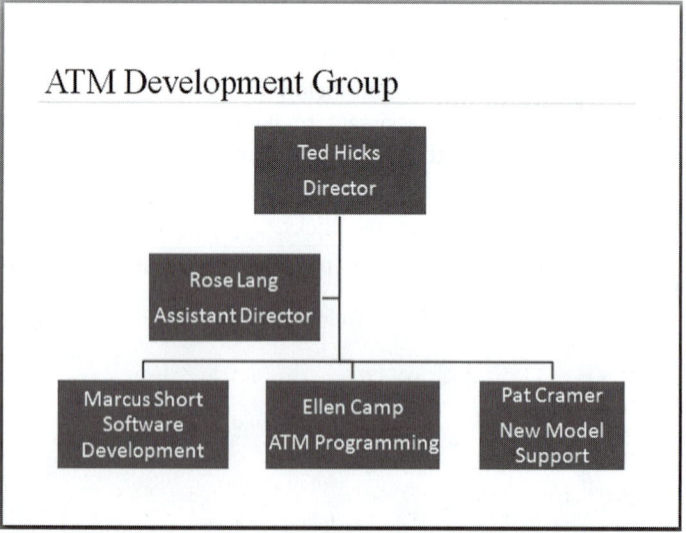

PAUSE. LEAVE the presentation open to use in the next exercise.

Text in a diagram appears either within a shape or as a bulleted list, depending on the diagram type and layout option. In the previous exercise, you inserted text only in shapes, because an organization chart does not offer the option of bulleted text. Figure 5-23 shows a list type diagram that contains both shape text and bulleted text.

Figure 5-23

Shape text and bulleted text in a diagram

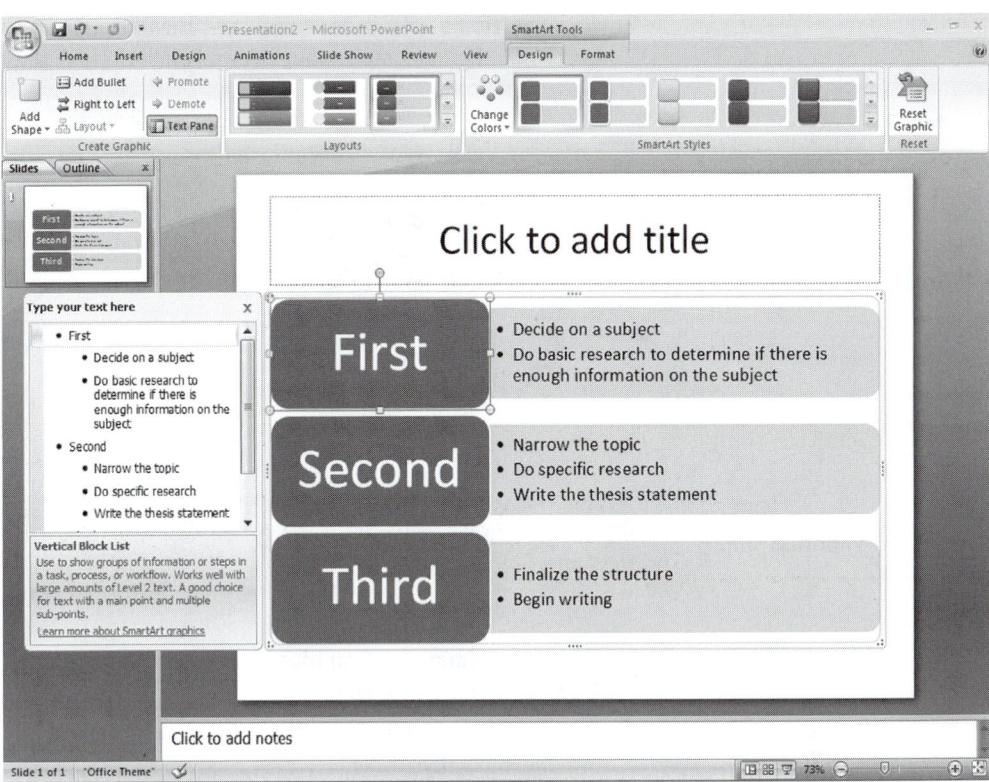

By default, PowerPoint displays the **Text pane** to the left of a new diagram. In the Text pane, shape text appears as the first-level bullet item and bulleted text is indented below the shape text, similar to the way several levels of bulleted text appear in a content placeholder.

You can use the Text pane to enter text, or you can enter text directly in each shape. Click next to a bullet in the Text pane or click any [Text] placeholder and begin typing. If you need more bullet items than are supplied in the default layout, press Enter at the end of the current bullet item to add a new one, or click the Add Bullet button in the Create Graphic group on the SmartArt Tools Design tab.

If you don't want to use the Text pane, you can close it to get it out of the way. To redisplay it, click the tab attached at the middle of the left container border or click the Text Pane button in the Create Graphic group on the SmartArt Tools Design tab. You can also right-click anywhere in the diagram and then click Show Text Pane on the shortcut menu.

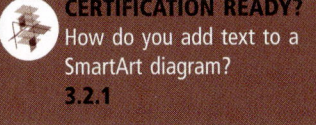

CERTIFICATION READY?
How do you add text to a SmartArt diagram?
3.2.1

As you enter text in the diagram, PowerPoint resizes the shapes to accommodate the longest line of text in the diagram. Font size is also adjusted for the best fit, and PowerPoint keeps the font size the same for all shapes.

TAKE NOTE

If you need to edit text you have entered in a diagram, you can click the text to activate it, then edit the text as necessary. You can also right-click a shape, click Edit Text on the shortcut menu, and then make the necessary changes.

Converting a Bulleted List to a Diagram

PowerPoint provides another way to create a SmartArt diagram: You can create a diagram from any bulleted list on a slide.

CONVERT A BULLETED LIST TO A DIAGRAM

USE the presentation that is still open from the previous exercise.

1. Go to slide 4 and click in the content placeholder.

2. Click the **Home** tab, if necessary, and then click the **Convert to SmartArt Graphic** button in the Paragraph group. PowerPoint displays the gallery shown in Figure 5-24.

Figure 5-24

The Convert to SmartArt gallery

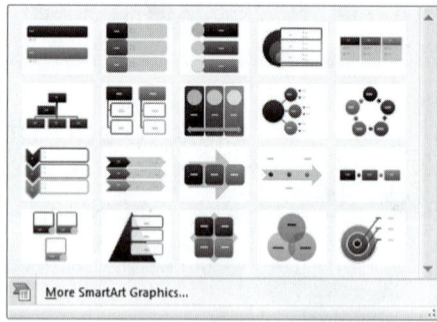

 **ANOTHER WAY** Right-click in a bulleted list, and then click Convert to SmartArt on the shortcut menu.

3. Click **More SmartArt Graphics** at the bottom of the gallery. The Choose a SmartArt Graphic dialog box opens.
4. Click **Cycle**, then click the **Block Cycle** layout. Read the description of how best to use the Block Cycle layout.
5. Click **OK**. The bulleted list is converted to a cycle diagram, as shown in Figure 5-25.

Figure 5-25

Bulleted list converted to a SmartArt diagram

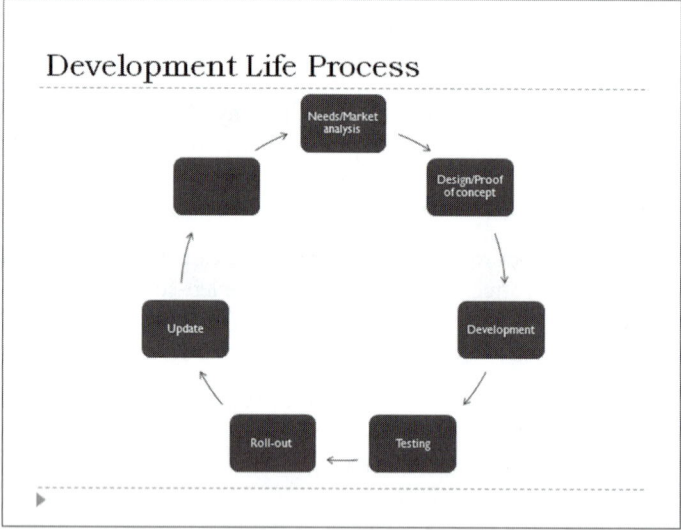

6. **SAVE** the presentation.

   PAUSE. LEAVE the presentation open to use in the next exercise.

As you work with slide text, you may realize that the information would work well as a SmartArt diagram. In this situation, you do not have to re-key the text in the SmartArt diagram shapes. Simply convert the bulleted list to a diagram. You can choose one of the common diagrams in the Convert to SmartArt gallery, or you can access the Choose a SmartArt Diagram dialog box to choose any diagram type or layout.

Adding Tables, Charts, and SmartArt Graphics to Slides | 653

CERTIFICATION READY?
How do you create a SmartArt diagram from bullet points?
3.1.2

You can use animation to make your diagram even more attention-getting. Use the Custom Animation task pane to apply animation effects to a SmartArt diagram. By default, a diagram is animated all at once, but you can use the SmartArt Animation tab in the effect's Options dialog box to change the way the parts of the diagram are animated.

■ Modifying SmartArt Graphics

THE BOTTOM LINE

Although a new SmartArt graphic makes an interesting visual statement on a slide in its default state, you will probably want to make some changes to the graphic to customize it for your use. Applying a Quick Style to a diagram is a quick way to completely change a diagram's appearance.

Applying a Quick Style to a SmartArt Diagram

As with other graphic objects, SmartArt diagrams can be quickly and easily formatted by applying a Quick Style. Quick Styles apply fills, borders, and effects to improve the appearance of the diagram's shapes.

APPLY A QUICK STYLE TO A SMARTART DIAGRAM

USE the presentation that is still open from the previous exercise.

1. Go to slide 3 and click once on the diagram to select it.
2. Click the **SmartArt Tools Design** tab to activate it if necessary.
3. Click the **More** button in the SmartArt Styles group. The SmartArt Quick Style gallery appears, as shown in Figure 5-26.

Figure 5-26

The SmartArt Quick Style gallery

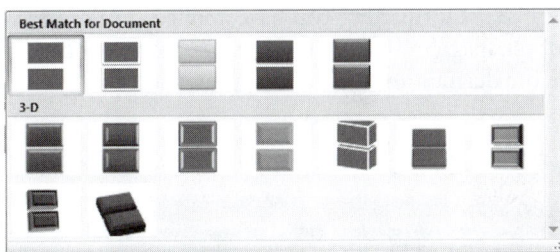

4. Click the **Intense Effect** style. PowerPoint applies the Quick Style.
5. Go to slide 4, click the diagram, and apply the same Quick Style. Your diagram should look similar to Figure 5-27.

Figure 5-27

A Quick Style applied to a diagram

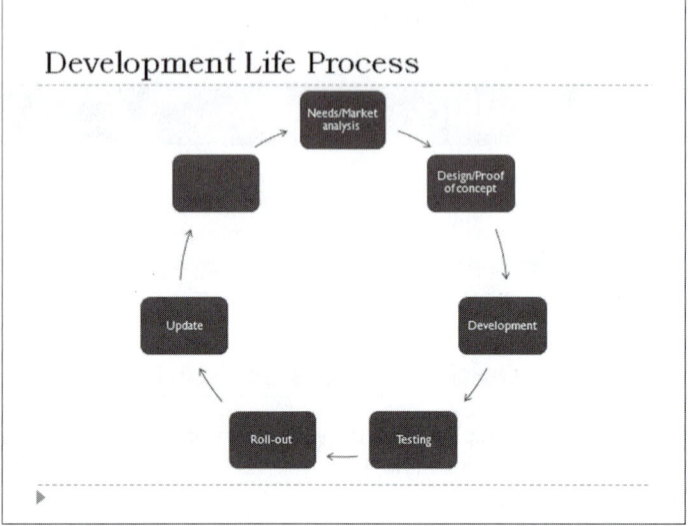

6. **SAVE** the presentation and then **CLOSE** the file.
   STOP. CLOSE PowerPoint

Quick Styles can instantly improve a new diagram by applying visual effects to the shapes. Review the results carefully, however, after applying a Quick Style. If your shapes contain several lines of text, some of the three-dimensional styles may obscure the text or cause it to run over on the edges—not a very attractive presentation.

If you do not like the formatting you have applied, you can easily revert to the original appearance of the diagram. Click the Reset Graphic button on the SmartArt Tools Design tab to restore the diagram to its default appearance.

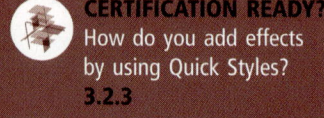

CERTIFICATION READY?
How do you add effects by using Quick Styles?
3.2.3

SUMMARY SKILL MATRIX

IN THIS LESSON YOU LEARNED HOW TO:
Insert a Table
Insert an Excel Worksheet
Apply a Quick Style to a Table
Insert a Chart from a Content Placeholder
Choose a Different Chart Type
Apply a Different Chart Layout
Apply a Quick Style to a Chart
Insert a SmartArt Diagram
Apply a Quick Style to a SmartArt Diagram

Adding Tables, Charts, and SmartArt Graphics to Slides

Knowledge Assessment

Matching

Match the term in Column 1 to its description in Column 2.

Column 1	Column 2
1. table (f)	a. panel in which you can key diagram text.
2. Draw Table (h)	b. a document used to manipulate numerical data.
3. Table Tools Design (g)	c. A single column on a chart that identifies one data point.
4. organization chart (i)	d. insert data so that it can be edited using its original application.
5. Text pane (a)	e. helps you resize a chart without distorting its appearance.
6. Paste Special (j)	f. an arrangement of columns and rows used to organize data.
7. data marker (c)	g. tab that allows you to apply a Quick Style to a table.
8. embedded (d)	h. option you can use to create a table outline and insert columns and rows where you want them.
9. shift key (e)	i. diagram that shows relationships among departments or personnel.
10. worksheet (b)	j. command that allows you to paste or paste link an object to a slide.

True / False

Circle T if the statement is true or F if the statement is false.

T **(F)** 1. The easiest way to create a table is to use the Insert Object button and then select the type of table to create.

(T) F 2. Text in a SmartArt diagram can appear either in a shape or in a bulleted list.

(T) F 3. Use a Cycle type diagram if you want to show a continual process. — p649

(T) F 4. You can copy and paste any Excel object to a PowerPoint slide.

T **(F)** 5. To take full advantage of PowerPoint 2007's charting capabilities, you must also have Microsoft Office Word 2007. *excel* — p641

(T) F 6. Click the Reset Graphic button on the SmartArt Tools Design tab to restore the diagram to its default appearance.

(T) F 7. The default PowerPoint chart type is a Column chart.

T **(F)** 8. Use the Blank Table option to quickly remove all formatting from a table. — p638

T **(F)** 9. If you want to show amount of change over time and total value across a trend, use a Pie chart. *(line chart)*

(T) F 10. By default, a new table is sized to fit the content placeholder in which it was created. — p634

Competency Assessment

Project 5-1: Job Fair

You work for Lucerne Executive Recruiters, a company that specializes in finding employees for a variety of clients. You are planning to give a brief presentation at a local job fair and need to prepare a slide that lists some currently available jobs for which you are recruiting candidates. You can use a table to display this information.

GET READY. Launch PowerPoint if it is not already running.

1. OPEN the *Jobs* presentation.
2. Go to slide 2, and click the **Insert Table** icon in the content placeholder.
3. Create a table with three columns and six rows.
4. Key the following information in the table.

Title	Company	Salary Range*
Senior Editor	Litware, Inc.	$30K - $42K
Sales Associate	Contoso Pharmaceuticals	$55K - $70K
District Manager	Tailspin Toys	$65K - $80K
Accountant	Fourth Coffee	$53K - $60K
Production Assistant	Fabrikam, Inc.	$38K - $45K

5. SAVE the presentation as *Jobs Final* and then CLOSE the file.

   LEAVE PowerPoint open for the next project.

The *Jobs* file is available on the companion CD-ROM.

Project 5-2: Making the Upgrade

You are a production manager at Tailspin Toys. You have been asked to give a presentation to senior management about anticipated costs of upgrading machinery in the assembly area. Because you want to sum the costs, you will use an Excel worksheet to present the information.

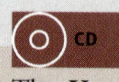

The *Upgrades* file is available on the companion CD-ROM.

1. OPEN the *Upgrades* presentation.
2. Go to slide 2, click the **Insert** tab, click the **Table** drop-down arrow, and then click **Excel Spreadsheet**.
3. Drag the lower-right corner handle of the worksheet object to reveal columns A through D and rows 1 through 7.
4. Key the following data in the worksheet. (Change the zoom size if desired to make it easier to see the data you are entering.)

Machine	Upgrade	Cost	Time Frame
Conveyor 2	New belt, drive	$28,000	30 days
Conveyor 3	Update software	$5,800	14 days
Drill Press 1	Replace	$32,000	30 days
Vacuum system	New pump, lines	$12,750	30 days
Docks 2 - 5	Doors, motors	$14,500	10 days

5. Click the Excel **Page Layout** tab, click the **Themes** button, and then click **Solstice** to apply the same theme to the worksheet that your presentation uses.
6. Adjust column widths by dragging or double-clicking column borders to display all data.
7. Click in cell **B7**, key **Total Costs**, and then press Tab.
8. Click the **Sum** button in the Editing group on the Home tab, then press Enter to complete the SUM function.

Adding Tables, Charts, and SmartArt Graphics to Slides | 657

9. Apply Quick Styles to the worksheet as follows:
   a. Select the column headings, then click the **Cell Styles** button in the Styles group on the Home tab.
   b. Click the **Accent5** style.
   c. Click the **Total Costs** cell, click the **Cell Styles** button, and click the **Accent1** style.
   d. Click the cell that contains the sum of costs, click the **Cell Styles** button, and click the **Total** style.
   e. Apply bold formatting to the column heads and the Total Costs cell.
10. Click the **Select All** area at the top left corner of the worksheet, then click the **Font Size** drop-down arrow and click **18**.
11. Select the entries in the *Time Frame* column, and click the **Center** button.
12. Click outside the worksheet twice to review your changes.
13. **SAVE** the presentation as *Upgrades Final* and then **CLOSE** the file.
    LEAVE PowerPoint open for the next project.

Proficiency Assessment

Project 5-3: Voter Turnout

You are a member of the Center City Board of Elections. You have been asked to create a presentation to deliver to the Board showing how turnout has varied in the city over the past four presidential elections. You can create a line chart to display this data clearly.

The *Turnout* file is available on the companion CD-ROM.

1. **OPEN** the *Turnout* presentation.
2. Go to slide 2, click the **Insert Chart** icon in the content placeholder, and then click **Line**. Click **OK** to accept the default subtype.
3. Key the following data in the Excel worksheet:

Year	Turnout
1992	0.62
1996	0.74
2000	0.49
2004	0.40

4. Delete the data in the Series 2 and Series 3 columns in the Excel worksheet, and then drag the range border by the lower-right handle until it encloses only the range A1:B5.
5. Close the Excel worksheet.
6. Click **Layout 12** in the Chart Layout gallery.
7. Click **Style 36** in the Quick Style gallery.
8. **SAVE** the presentation as *Turnout Final* and then **CLOSE** the file.
   LEAVE PowerPoint open for the next project.

Project 5-4: More Power

You are a financial analyst for City Power & Light. Senior managers have asked you to determine how much power sales increased from 2007 to 2008, based on customer types. You can compare rates of power sales using a bar chart.

1. Start a new, blank presentation and apply a theme of your choice.
2. Change the layout of the first slide to Title and Content, and key the slide title 2007–2008 Sales.
3. Create a Clustered Bar chart, and key the following chart data:

	Industrial	Commercial	Residential
2008	$3,010	$4,273	$5,777
2007	$2,588	$3,876	$4,578

4. Apply Layout 3 to the chart, and change the chart title to **Sales by Customer Type**.
5. Apply a Quick Style of your choice to the chart.
6. **SAVE** the presentation as *Power Sales* and then **CLOSE** the file.
   LEAVE PowerPoint open for the next project.

Mastery Assessment

Project 5-5: Corporate Reorganization

You are a director of operations at Fabrikam, Inc., a company that develops fabric treatments for use in the textile industry. Your company is undergoing reorganization, and you need to prepare a presentation that shows how groups will be aligned in the new structure. You can use SmartArt diagram to show the new organization.

The *Reorganization* file is available on the companion CD-ROM.

1. **OPEN** the *Reorganization* presentation.
2. Go to slide 2 and click the **Insert SmartArt Graphic** icon in the content placeholder.
3. Click the **Hierarchy** type, click the **Hierarchy** layout, and then click **OK**.
4. Click in the top-level shape and key **Operations**.
5. Click in the first second-level shape and key **Production**.
6. Click in the second second-level shape and key **R & D**.
7. Click in the first third-level shape and key **Manufacturing**.
8. Click in the remaining third-level shape (under *R & D*) and key **Quality Assurance**.
9. Display the SmartArt Quick Styles gallery and click the **Polished** style under the 3-D category.
10. **SAVE** the presentation as *Reorganization Final* and then **CLOSE** the file.
    LEAVE PowerPoint open for the next project.

Project 5-6: Tiger Tales

You are the owner of a karate studio that specializes in teaching youngsters. You are working on a presentation to give at local schools and after-school care centers. You want to add a diagram to your presentation to stress the importance of the proper attitude when learning karate.

The *Tigers* file is available on the companion CD-ROM.

1. **OPEN** the *Tigers* presentation.
2. Go to slide 3 and use the bulleted list to create a new SmartArt diagram using the Titled Matrix layout. Note that only the first bulleted item displays in the diagram.

Adding Tables, Charts, and SmartArt Graphics to Slides | 659

3. Apply a Quick Style of your choice.
4. **SAVE** the presentation as *Tigers Final* and then **CLOSE** the file.
   STOP. CLOSE PowerPoint.

INTERNET READY

You want to take a vacation over the winter holidays next year, but you have not yet decided whether to go skiing, enjoy the sun on a Caribbean island, or venture down under to Australia. Using Internet search tools, find several interesting ski packages in Canada and Europe, resort packages in the Caribbean, and lodgings in Sydney, Australia. Determine the local price for all these excursions. Create a PowerPoint presentation with a table that lists your possible destinations and dates of travel. Add a new slide and insert a worksheet. Enter the destinations and their costs and the conversion rate to convert local costs to dollars. Create formulas to convert costs so you can compare all package costs in U.S. dollars.

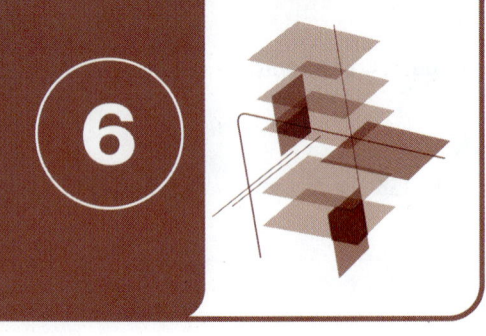

6 Adding Graphics and Media Clips to a Presentation

LESSON SKILL MATRIX

Inserting a ClipArt Picture — 662	Students will learn how to insert a ClipArt picture.
Inserting a Picture from a File — 665	Students will learn how to insert a picture from a file.
Using the Ruler, Gridlines, and Guides	Students will learn how to use the ruler, gridlines, and guides.
Rotating an Object — 669	Students will learn how to rotate an object.
Resizing Objects — 670	Students will learn how to resize objects.
Formatting a Picture with a Quick Style — 674	Students will learn how to format a picture with a Quick Style.
Adjusting a Picture's Color, Brightness, and Contrast — 675	Students will learn how to adjust a picture's color, brightness, and contrast.
Adding Special Effects to a Picture — 676	Students will learn how to add special effects to a picture.
Compressing the Images in a Presentation — 677	Students will learn how to compress the images in a presentation.
Drawing Lines — 678	Students will learn how to draw lines.
Inserting Basic Shapes — 680	Students will learn how to insert basic shapes.
Adding Text to Shapes — 681	Students will learn how to add text to shapes.
Formatting Shapes — 682	Students will learn how to format shapes.
Setting the Order of Objects — 684	Students will learn how to set the order of objects.
Aligning Objects with Each Other — 687	Students will learn how to align objects with each other.
Grouping Objects Together — 688	Students will learn how to group objects together.
Adding a Sound File to a Slide — 690	Students will learn how to add a sound file to a slide.
Adding a Movie to a Slide — 692	Students will learn how to add a movie to a slide.

Adding Graphics and Media Clips to a Presentation | 661

You are the director of promotions for the Baldwin Museum of Science. The museum is especially interested in attracting teachers and students to their permanent exhibits, so you have scheduled appearances at a number of high schools in your area, where you plan to present PowerPoint slide shows about the museum and various aspects of science. PowerPoint's graphics capabilities allow you to include and customize pictures, shapes, and movies to enliven your presentations. You can also add sounds to provide the finishing touch to a presentation.

KEY TERMS
aspect ratio
clip art
Clip Organizer
constrain
crop
gridlines
guides
keyword
order
rulers
scaling

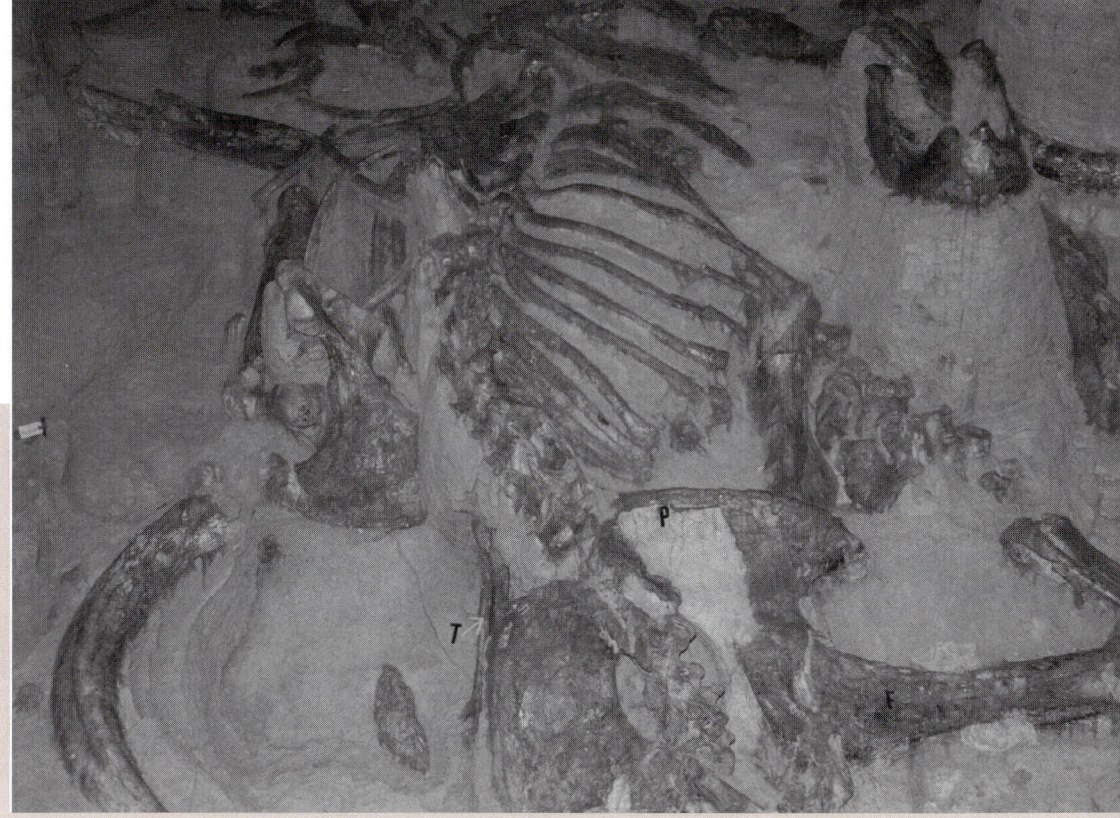

SOFTWARE ORIENTATION

Microsoft PowerPoint's Clip Art Task Pane

The Clip Art task pane, shown in Figure 6-1, allows you to search for graphic and multimedia content you can use to embellish and illustrate your slides. The gallery format of the task pane makes it easy to review content and choose a file to insert.

Figure 6-1

The Clip Art task pane

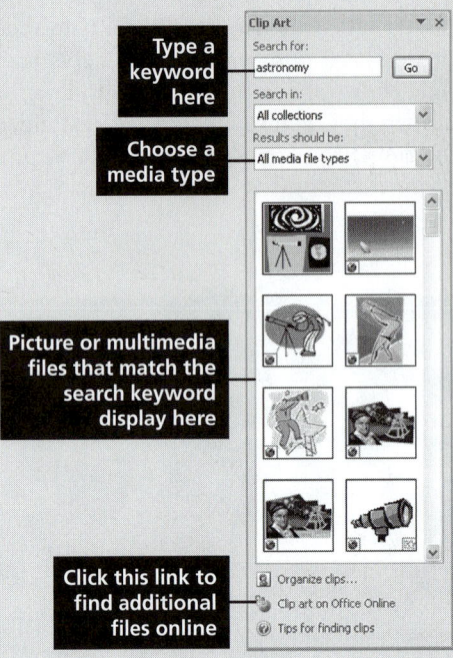

You can use the Clip Art task pane to locate and insert line drawings, photographs, animated graphics, and sound files. If you have a live Internet connection, you have access to thousands of files on the Office Online Web site.

■ Adding a Picture to a Slide

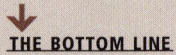
THE BOTTOM LINE

Pictures can be used to illustrate a slide's content or provide visual interest to help hold audience attention. You can insert clip art files that are installed with or accessed through Microsoft Office, or you can insert any picture with a compatible file format.

Inserting a Clip Art Picture

Microsoft Office clip art files include not only drawn graphics but photos and other multimedia objects. Use the Clip Art icon in any content placeholder to open the Clip Art task pane and search for clip art pictures.

CD

The *Exhibits* file is available on the companion CD-ROM.

➲ **INSERT A CLIP ART PICTURE**

GET READY. Before you begin these steps, be sure to launch Microsoft Office PowerPoint 2007.

1. Locate and open the *Exhibits* presentation.

Adding Graphics and Media Clips to a Presentation | 663

2. Go to slide 4 and click the **Clip Art** icon in the empty content placeholder. The Clip Art task pane opens, as shown in Figure 6-2.

Figure 6-2

The Clip Art task pane

ANOTHER WAY To insert clip art on a slide that does not have a content placeholder, click the Clip Art button on the Insert tab.

TAKE NOTE

The Clip Art task pane may show the keyword(s) used in the most recent search for clip art.

3. Select any existing text in the Search for box and press `Delete` to remove it.
4. Key **gears** in the Search for box.
5. Click the **Results should be** drop-down arrow, and remove checkmarks from all options *except* Photographs, as shown in Figure 6-3.

Figure 6-3

Choose to search for Photographs only

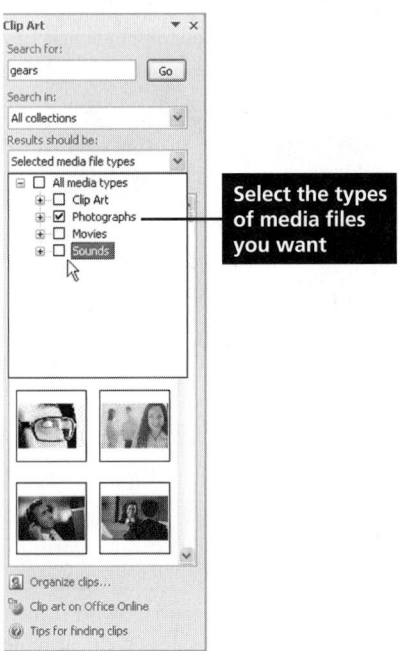

6. Click the **Go** button near the top of the task pane. PowerPoint searches for clip art photographs that match the keyword and displays them in the task pane.

7. Click the picture of gears shown in Figure 6-4, or one similar to it. The picture is inserted in the content placeholder. (The picture may not take up the entire placeholder.)

Figure 6-4

Select the photograph of gears

8. Click the **Close** button in the Clip Art task pane to close the pane. Your slide should look similar to Figure 6-5.

Figure 6-5

Clip art inserted in the content placeholder

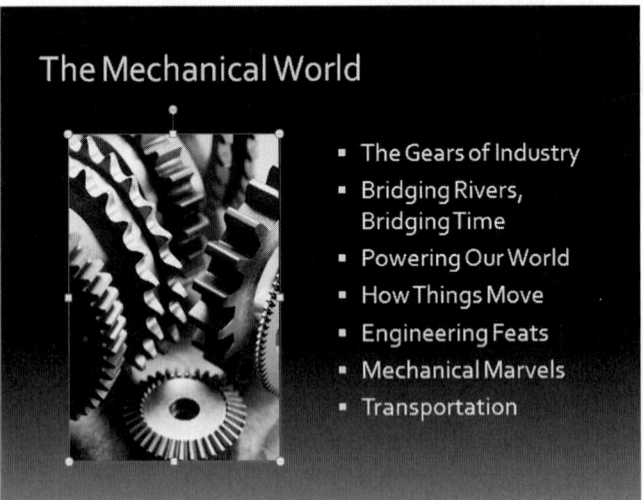

9. **SAVE** the presentation as *Exhibits Final*.

   PAUSE. LEAVE the presentation open to use in the next exercise.

Clip art is predrawn artwork in a wide variety of styles relating to a wide variety of topics. Microsoft Office supplies access to thousands of clip art graphics that you can insert in documents, worksheets, and databases as well as in PowerPoint presentations. To locate clip art graphics, you use a *keyword* search: In the Clip Art task pane, key a word that relates to the topic you want to illustrate, such as *gears* in the previous exercise.

Adding Graphics and Media Clips to a Presentation | 665

When you click the Go button, the graphics that appear may be stored on your system in the *Clip Organizer*, a series of folders with keyword names such as Nature and Animals that make it easy for you to locate specific graphic files. You can view files in the Clip Organizer, shown in Figure 6-6, by clicking the *Organize clips* link at the bottom of the Clip Art task pane.

Figure 6-6

The Clip Organizer stores pictures in folders

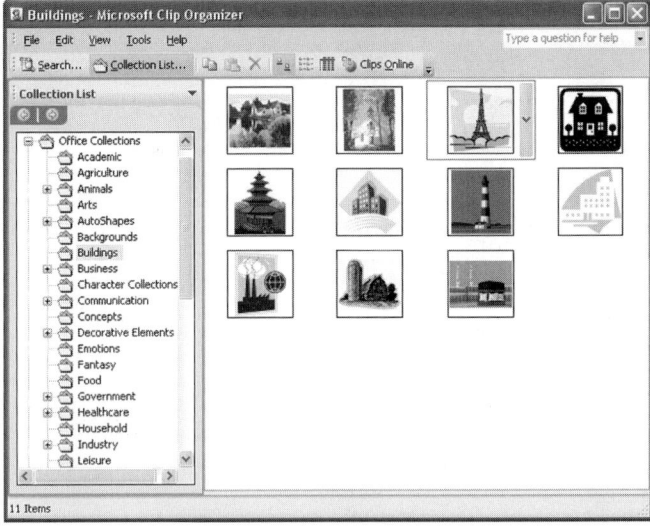

If you have a live Internet connection, PowerPoint will search not only the Clip Organizer on your computer but online graphic files as well and display all of them in the task pane. You can also go directly to the Office Online clip art Web site by clicking the *Clip art on Office Online* link at the bottom of the Clip Art task pane.

TAKE NOTE

If you find a clip you like on Office Online, you can download it to your computer. Office will store the clip in the Clip Organizer for future use.

Many clip art graphics are humorous in appearance and may not be suitable for corporate communications or presentations on serious topics. You can use the Clip Art task pane to search for photographs as well as clip art graphics. Photographs provide a more sophisticated and professional look for a presentation. The Clip Art task pane also allows you to search for movies and sound files. You will learn how to search for and insert these types of files later in this lesson.

When you insert clip art by using the Clip Art icon in a content placeholder to open the Clip Art task pane, PowerPoint will try to fit the graphic you select into the content placeholder. The graphic may not use up the entire placeholder area, depending on its size and shape. If you insert a graphic on a slide that doesn't have a placeholder, it will generally appear in the center of the slide. You can adjust the graphic's size and position, as you will learn later in this lesson.

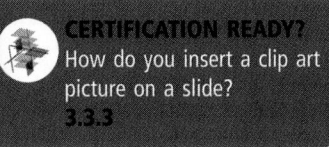

CERTIFICATION READY?
How do you insert a clip art picture on a slide?
3.3.3

If you decide you don't like a picture you have inserted, you can easily delete it. Click the picture to select it and then press Delete to remove it from the slide.

Inserting a Picture from a File

You do not have to rely on PowerPoint's clip art files to illustrate your presentation. You can locate many pictures available for free download on the Internet or create your own picture files using a digital camera.

 **INSERT A PICTURE FROM A FILE**

USE the presentation that is still open from the previous exercise.

1. Go to slide 3 and click the **Insert** tab to activate it.
2. Click the **Picture** button. The Insert Picture dialog box opens, as shown in Figure 6-7.

Figure 6-7

Locate a picture file in the Insert Picture dialog box

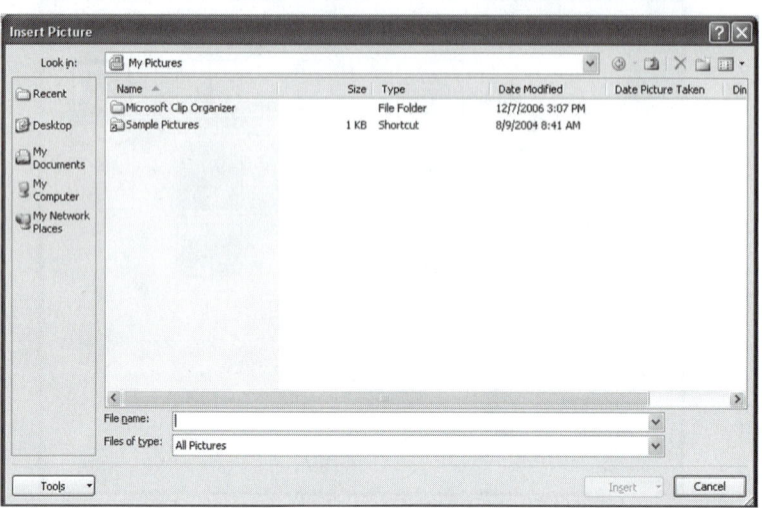

 **ANOTHER WAY**

Click the Insert Picture from File icon in any content placeholder to open the Insert Picture dialog box.

CD

The *Astronomy.jpg* file is available on the companion CD-ROM.

3. Navigate to the location of the data files for this lesson, click ***Astronomy.jpg***, and then click **Insert**. The picture appears on the slide, as shown in Figure 6-8.

Figure 6-8

The picture appears on the slide

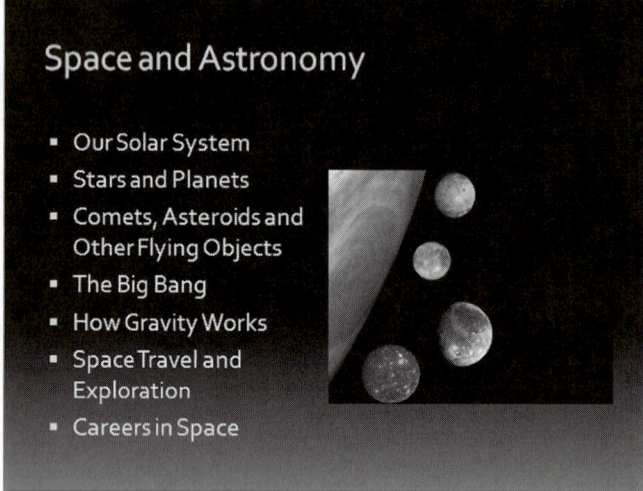

4. **SAVE** the presentation.

PAUSE. LEAVE the presentation open to use in the next exercise.

PowerPoint supports a variety of picture file formats, including GIF, JPEG, PNG, TIFF, BMP, and WMF. Be aware that graphic formats differ in the way they store graphic information, so some formats create larger files than others. GIF files, for example, are generally much smaller than TIFF files because they are limited to only 256 colors, but TIFF files show much greater detail.

If you take your own pictures using a digital camera, you do not have to worry about copyright issues, but you should pay attention to copyright permissions for pictures you locate from other sources. It is extremely easy to save any picture from a Web page to your system. If you are going to use the picture commercially, you need to contact the copyright holder, if there is one, and ask for specific permission to reuse the picture.

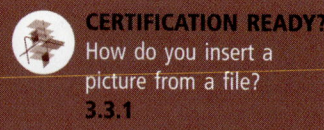 **CERTIFICATION READY?**
How do you insert a picture from a file?
3.3.1

Adding Graphics and Media Clips to a Presentation | 667

TAKE NOTE U.S. government sites such as NASA, the source of the picture you inserted in the previous exercise, make images available without requiring copyright permission.

■ Formatting Pictures

 PowerPoint provides many options for improving the appearance of pictures. You can reposition and resize them, rotate them, apply special effects such as Quick Styles, adjust brightness and contrast, and even recolor a picture for a special effect. If you do not like formatting changes you have made, you can reset a picture to its original appearance.

Using the Ruler, Gridlines, and Guides

The ruler, gridlines, and guides can help you position objects such as pictures so that they align with other objects on a slide and appear consistently throughout a presentation. You can move or copy guides to position them where you need them.

→ **USE THE RULER, GRIDLINES, AND GUIDES**

USE the presentation that is still open from the previous exercise.

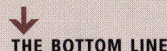

Right-click a slide outside of any placeholder, then click Ruler.

1. Go to slide 3 if necessary. Click the **View** tab to activate it, then click **Ruler** in the Show/Hide group if this option is not already selected. The vertical and horizontal rulers appear in the Slide pane.
2. Click **Gridlines** in the Show/Hide group. A grid of regularly spaced dots overlays the slide, as shown in Figure 6-9.

Figure 6-9

Rulers and gridlines

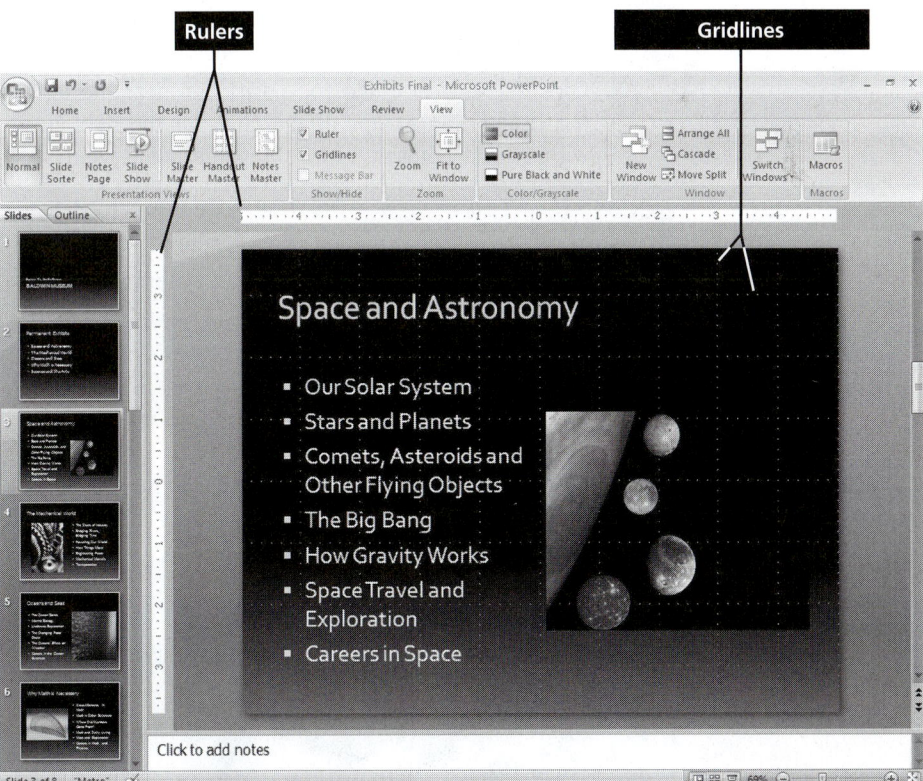

3. Right-click the current slide near the bottom of the slide (outside any placeholder), then click **Grid and Guides**. The Grid and Guides dialog box opens, as shown in Figure 6-10.

Figure 6-10

Grid and Guides dialog box

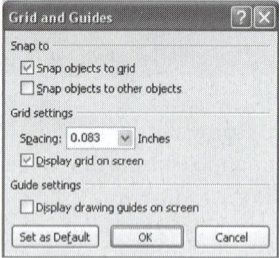

Press Alt+F9 to show or hide the guides.

4. Click **Display drawing guides on screen**, then click **OK**. The default vertical and horizontal drawing guides display, intersecting at the center of the slide.
5. The guides will be more useful for positioning pictures in this presentation, so you can turn off the gridlines: Click the **View** tab if necessary, and click **Gridlines** to remove the checkmark and hide the gridlines.
6. Click the text placeholder to activate it. You will use the placeholder's selection border to help you position guides.
7. Click the vertical guide above the slide title. You should see a ScreenTip that shows the current position of the guide, 0.0, indicating the guide is at the 0 inch mark on the horizontal ruler.
8. Drag the guide to the left until it aligns on the left border of the text placeholder. The ScreenTip should read 4.50 with a left-pointing arrow. Release the mouse button to drop the guide at that location.
9. Click the horizontal guide to the right of the planet picture and drag upward until the ScreenTip reads 1.67 with an upward-pointing arrow. Drop the guide. It should align with the capital letters in the text placeholder.
10. Click the vertical guide you positioned near the left edge of the slide, hold down **Ctrl**, and drag a copy of the guide to the right until the ScreenTip reads 4.50 with a right-pointing arrow. Drop the guide. Your slide should look like Figure 6-11.

Figure 6-11

Drawing guides positioned on the slide

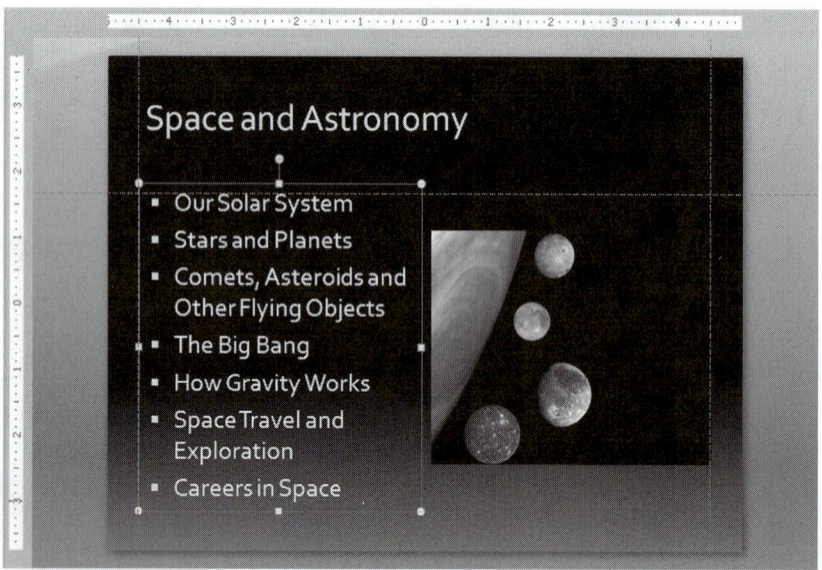

11. Go to slide 4, click the gear picture, and drag it until the upper-left corner of the picture snaps to the intersection of the vertical and horizontal guides. Your slide should look like Figure 6-12.

Figure 6-12

Picture repositioned using the guides

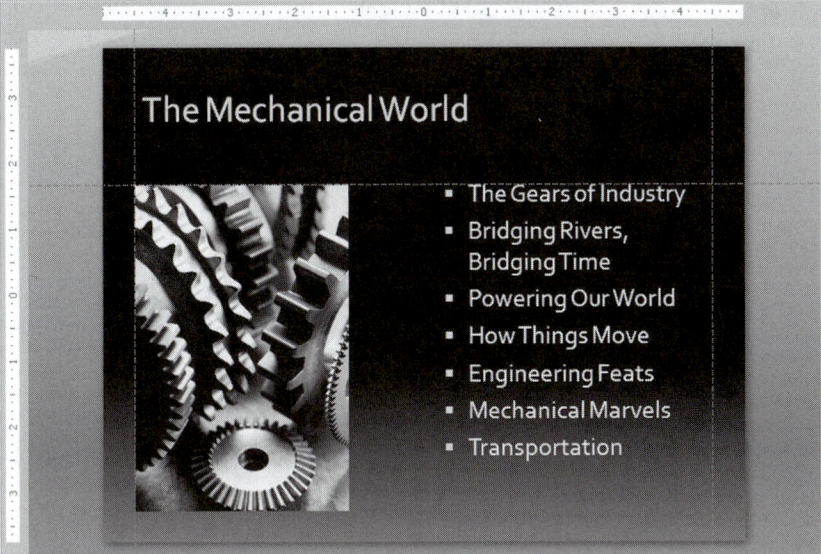

12. Go to slide 5 and drag the picture down and to the left so its upper-right corner snaps to the intersection of the guides.
13. Go to slide 6 and drag the picture up and to the left to snap to the intersection of the two guides.

   PAUSE. LEAVE the presentation open to use in the next exercise.

TAKE NOTE

You can adjust the spacing of the dots in the gridlines in the Grid and Guides dialog box.

In Normal view and Notes Page view, you can turn on PowerPoint's horizontal and vertical *rulers*, which help you measure the size of an object on the slide, as well as the amount of space between objects. As you move the pointer on a slide, short dotted lines show the pointer position on both the horizontal and vertical rulers. This allows you to be fairly precise when undertaking tasks such as resizing or cropping.

PowerPoint's drawing *guides* line up with measurements on the ruler to provide nonprinting guidelines you can use when positioning objects on a slide. You can move guides anywhere on the slide and copy them to create additional guides. To remove a guide, drag it off the slide.

PowerPoint also provides *gridlines*, a set of dotted horizontal and vertical lines that overlay the entire slide. Turn on gridlines when you want to arrange a number of objects on the slide or draw shapes to specific sizes.

CERTIFICATION READY?

How do you use guides to arrange pictures on a slide?

3.5.4

By default, objects "snap"—automatically align—to the gridlines even if the gridlines are not currently displayed. This feature can be helpful when you are positioning objects, but you may sometimes find that it hinders precise positioning. You can temporarily override the "snapping" by holding down Alt as you drag an object. Or, you can display the Grid and Guides dialog box and deselect the *Snap objects to grid* check box.

Rotating an Object

Rotate pictures to change their orientation on a slide. You can use the Rotate handle or a Ribbon option to rotate a picture or other object.

ANOTHER WAY

Click the Arrange button on the Home tab, click Rotate, and choose a rotation option.

 **ROTATE AN OBJECT**

USE the presentation that is still open from the previous exercise.

1. Go to slide 3, and click the picture to select it.
2. Click the **Picture Tools Format** tab, click **Rotate** in the Arrange group, and then click **Flip Horizontal**. The picture reverses its orientation so the planet is on the right and its moons are on the left, as shown in Figure 6-13.

Figure 6-13

The picture has been flipped horizontally

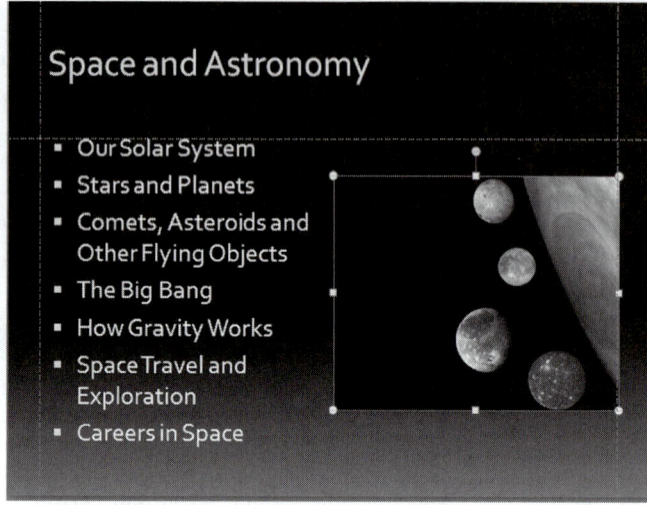

3. Drag the picture up into the upper-right corner of the slide, so that the top and right edges of the picture align with the top and right edges of the slide.

PAUSE. LEAVE the presentation open to use in the next exercise.

You have rotated objects already in this course, when you changed the orientation of text boxes in Lesson 3. Rotating and flipping can provide additional visual interest for a graphic or fit it more attractively on a slide.

PowerPoint offers some set rotation options, such as rotating right or left 90 degrees. For more control over the rotation, drag the green rotation handle or click More Rotation Options on the Rotate drop-down menu to open the Size and Position dialog box, where you can key a specific rotation amount.

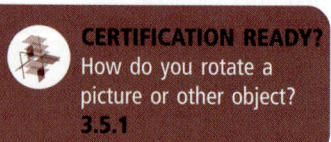**CERTIFICATION READY?**
How do you rotate a picture or other object?
3.5.1

Resizing Objects

You have several options for adjusting the size of a picture or other graphic object. You can crop an object to remove part of the object, drag a side or corner, specify exact measurements for an object, or scale it to a percentage of its original size.

CROP AN OBJECT

USE the presentation that is still open from the previous exercise.

1. Go to slide 4 and click the picture to select it.
2. Click the **Picture Tools Format** tab if necessary.
3. Click the **Crop** button in the Size group. The pointer changes to a crop pointer and crop handles appear around the edges of the picture.
4. Position the pointer on the top center crop handle and drag downward until the short dotted line on the vertical ruler is on the 0.5 inch mark, as shown in Figure 6-14.

Adding Graphics and Media Clips to a Presentation | 671

Figure 6-14

Drag the crop handle down to remove a portion of the picture

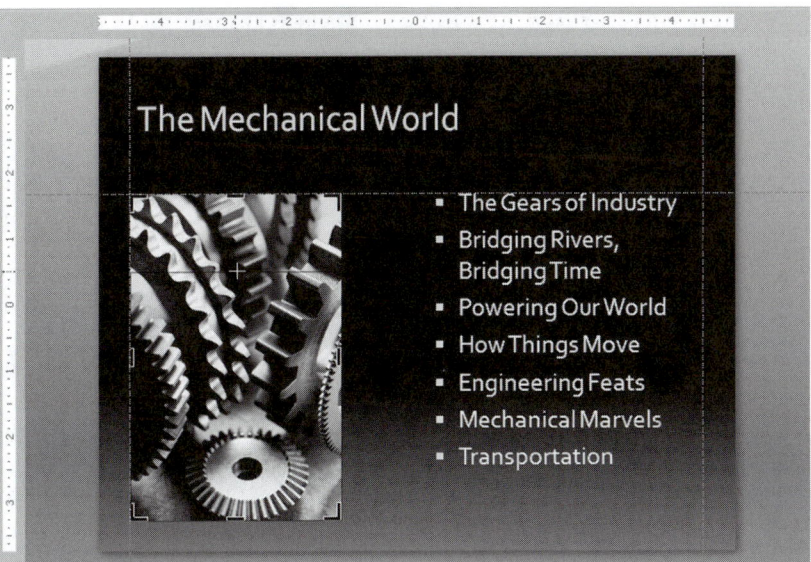

5. Release the mouse button, then click the **Crop** button again to complete the crop.
6. Move the cropped picture back up to the intersection of the two guides. Your slide should look similar to Figure 6-15.

Figure 6-15

The picture has been cropped and repositioned

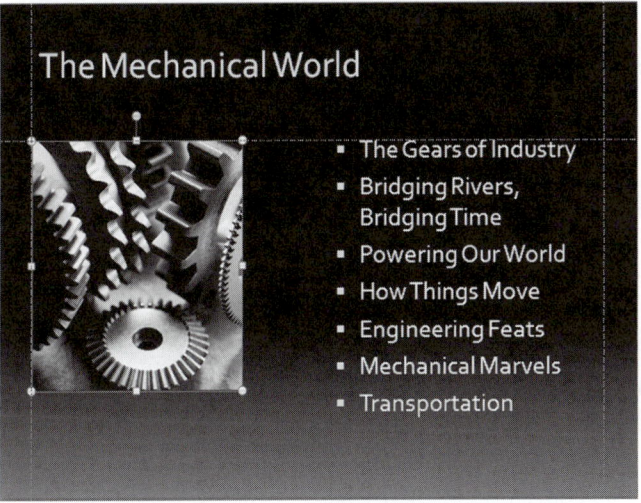

PAUSE. LEAVE the presentation open to use in the next exercise.

When you *crop* a picture, you remove a portion of the graphic that you think is unnecessary. Cropping allows you to focus attention on the most important part of a picture.

The portion of the picture you cropped is not deleted. You can restore the cropped material by using the crop pointer to drag outward to reveal the material that was previously hidden.

SIZE OR SCALE AN OBJECT

USE the presentation that is still open from the previous exercise.

1. Go to slide 3 and click the picture to select it.
2. Drag the lower-left corner of the picture diagonally until the short dotted line on the horizontal ruler is at 0 inches, as shown in Figure 6-16. (Don't worry that the slide title is partially covered; you'll fix this problem in a later exercise.)

Figure 6-16

Resize a picture by dragging a corner

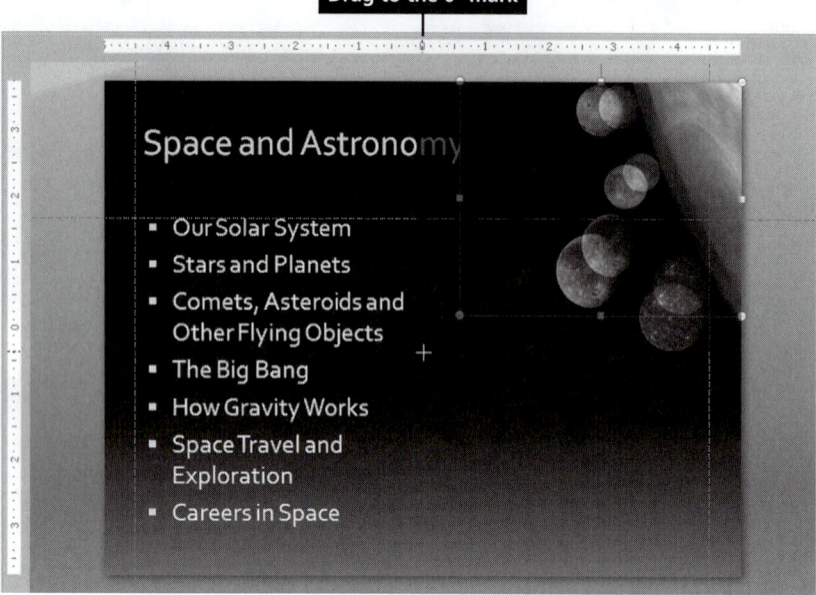

3. Go to slide 4 and click the picture to select it.
4. Right-click the picture, then click **Size and Position**. The Size and Position dialog box opens, as shown in Figure 6-17.

Figure 6-17

The Size and Position dialog box

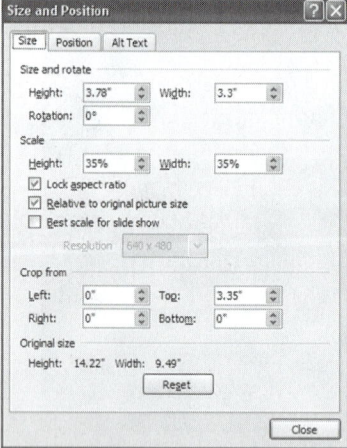

 ANOTHER WAY   You can open the Size and Position dialog box by clicking the dialog box launcher in the Size group on the Picture Tools Format tab.

5. Click the **Lock aspect ratio** check box to deselect this option. You can now specify the height and width independently.
6. In the Size and rotate area of the dialog box, click the **Height** up arrow until the height is 4.1 inches. Click the **Width** up arrow until the width is 4.2 inches.

Adding Graphics and Media Clips to a Presentation | 673

7. Click **Close** to close the dialog box. Your slide should look similar to Figure 6-18.

Figure 6-18

The picture has been resized

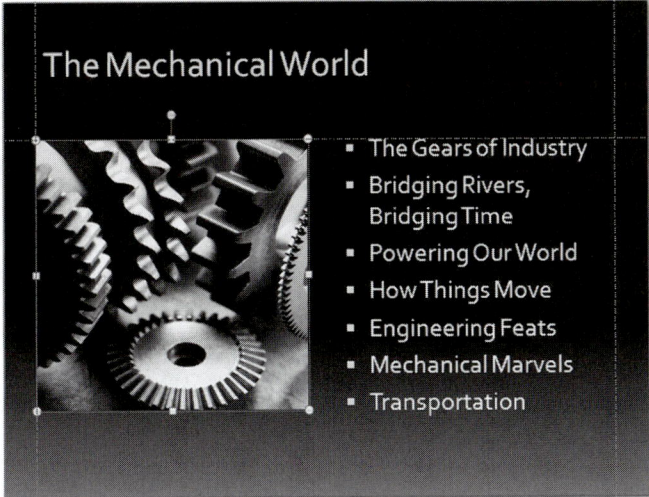

8. Go to slide 5 and click the picture to select it.
9. Click the **Picture Tools Format** tab if necessary, then click the **Width** down arrow in the Size group until the picture's width is 4.2 inches.
10. Drag the picture back over to the intersection of the two guides near the right edge of the slide.

    PAUSE. LEAVE the presentation open to use in the next exercise.

In this exercise, you learned three ways to adjust the size of a picture: by simply dragging a corner, by setting measurements in the Size and Position dialog box, and by setting a measurement in the Size group on the Picture Tools Format tab. You can use these options to resize any object on a slide.

Generally, you will want to maintain a picture's *aspect ratio* when you resize it. The aspect ratio is the relationship of width to height. By default, a change to the width of a picture is also applied to the height to maintain aspect ratio. For this reason, you adjusted only the width of the picture on slide 5; PowerPoint took care of adjusting the height to keep the picture in proportion.

Another way to maintain the current aspect ratio is to drag a corner of picture when resizing it. This action adjusts width and height at the same time.

TAKE NOTE

You can also easily distort a picture by dragging a side handle rather than a corner handle.

In some instances, you may want to distort a picture on purpose by changing one dimension more than the other. To do so, you must deselect the *Lock aspect ratio* check box in the Size and Position dialog box. You are then free to change width and height independently.

The Size and Position dialog box gives you a number of sizing and positioning options that can help you fine-tune pictures on slides.

- You can specify an exact height and width for the picture, as you did in this exercise, or a percentage of the original height or width. Specifying exact dimensions is generally referred to as *sizing*, and specifying a percentage of the original dimensions is called **scaling**. You can scale a picture larger or smaller than its original size.
- You can crop a picture using a precise measurement for any or all sides.
- You can reset the picture to its original appearance to remove any sizing or format changes you have made to it.

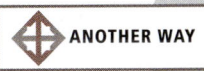 You can also restore a picture's original appearance by clicking the Reset Picture button in the Adjust group on the Picture Tools Format tab.

674 | Lesson 6

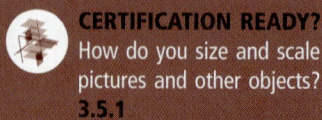

CERTIFICATION READY?
How do you size and scale pictures and other objects?
3.5.1

- You can use the Position tab in the Size and Position dialog box to key an exact location on the slide for an object, measuring from either the top left corner or the center of the slide.

Formatting a Picture with a Quick Style

PowerPoint provides a number of Quick Styles you can use to apply borders and other effects to pictures. Use Quick Styles to dress up your pictures or format them consistently throughout a presentation.

➔ **APPLY A QUICK STYLE TO A PICTURE**

USE the presentation that is still open from the previous exercise.

1. Go to slide 5 and click the picture to select it.
2. Click the **Picture Tools Format** tab if necessary.
3. Click the **More** button in the Picture Styles group. The Picture Styles gallery appears, as shown in Figure 6-19.

Figure 6-19

The Picture Styles gallery

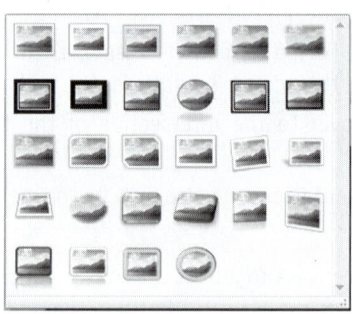

4. Click the **Soft Edge Oval** style. Your picture should look like the one in Figure 6-20.

Figure 6-20

The Quick Style gives the picture a very different look

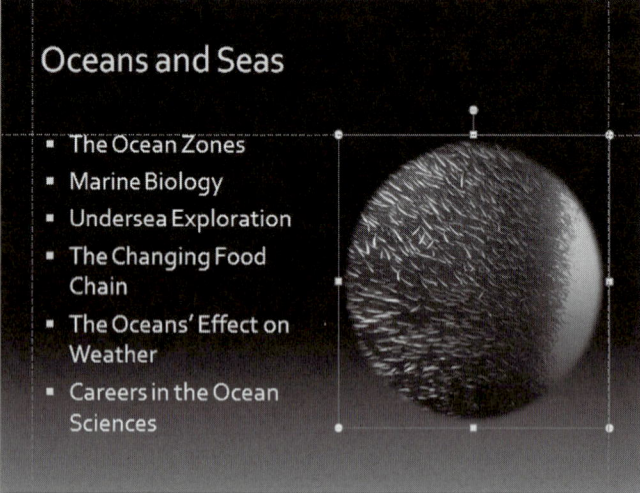

5. Press **Alt** + **F9** to hide the drawing guides.

   PAUSE. LEAVE the presentation open to use in the next exercise.

TAKE NOTE

The Quick Style picture borders are black or white by default, but you can apply any color to the border using the Picture Border button.

The picture Quick Styles give you a number of interesting ways to present pictures on your slides. You can easily apply styles with heavy borders, shadow and reflection effects, and different shapes such as ovals and rounded corners.

Adding Graphics and Media Clips to a Presentation | 675

CERTIFICATION READY?
How do you apply a Quick Style to a picture or other object?
3.4.1

If you have a number of pictures in a presentation, be careful not to apply too many different styles to the pictures. Using one or two styles throughout makes a presentation seem more unified and consistent.

Adjusting a Picture's Color, Brightness, and Contrast

You may need to modify a picture's appearance to make it show up well on a slide. This can be particularly important with pictures you insert from files. Use settings in the Adjust group to improve a picture.

ADJUST A PICTURE'S BRIGHTNESS AND CONTRAST

USE the presentation that is still open from the previous exercise.

1. Go to slide 6 and click the picture to select it. This picture is a bit dark.
2. Click the **Picture Tools Format** tab if necessary.
3. Click the **Brightness** button in the Adjust group, then click **+20%**. The picture becomes brighter.
4. Go to slide 5, right-click the picture, and click **Format Picture**. The Format Picture dialog box opens, as shown in Figure 6-21.

Figure 6-21

The Format Picture dialog box

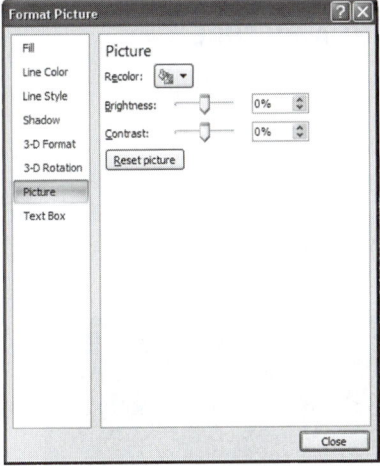

Open the Format Picture dialog box from the bottom of the Brightness or Contrast menu.

5. Click the **Brightness** up arrow to increase brightness to 15%.
6. Click the **Contrast** up arrow to increase contrast to 25%, and then click **Close**. The picture is now brighter and sharper than previously.

PAUSE. LEAVE the presentation open to use in the next exercise.

The Brightness and Contrast buttons in the Adjust group allow you to increase or decrease brightness and contrast in set intervals of 10 percent. For more control over brightness and contrast, use the Format Picture dialog box. As you adjust settings in the dialog box, the picture changes to show the modifications, making it easy to control final appearance.

The Adjust group and the Format Picture dialog box also offer the Recolor option. Use the Recolor gallery to apply grayscale, sepia, or one of the current theme colors to a selected picture to create a special effect, as shown in Figure 6-22.

Figure 6-22

The gears picture has been recolored

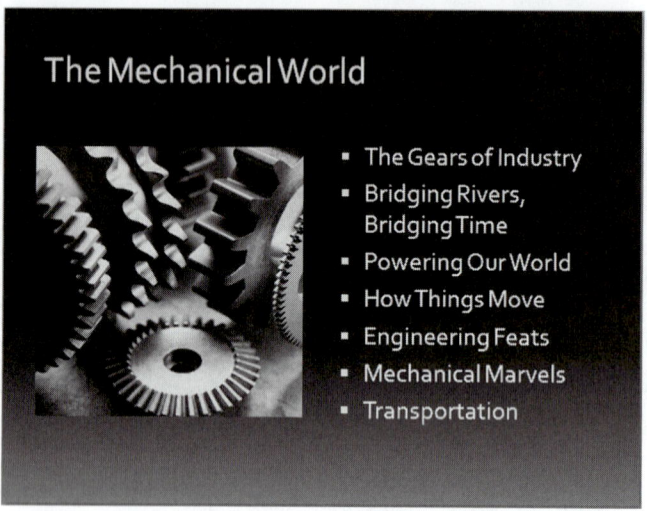

Adding Special Effects to a Picture

Use the Picture Effects options to apply Shadow, Reflection, Glow, and other effects to any picture in a presentation.

➔ ADD SPECIAL EFFECTS TO A PICTURE

USE the presentation that is still open from the previous exercise.

1. Go to slide 6 and click the picture to select it.
2. Click the **Picture Tools Format** tab if necessary.
3. Click **Picture Effects** in the Picture Styles group, point to **Soft Edges**, and then click **10 Point**. Your slide should look similar to Figure 6-23.

Figure 6-23

Soft edges effect applied to the picture

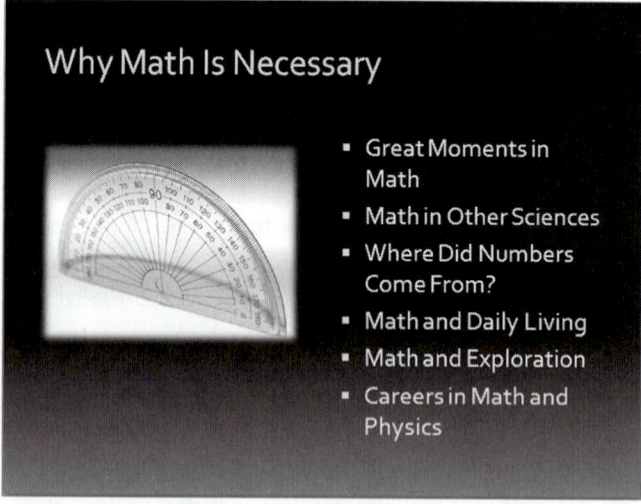

4. This is not quite the effect you want. Click **Picture Effects**, point to **Soft Edges**, and then click **No Soft Edges**.
5. Click **Picture Effects** again, point to **Reflection**, and then click **Tight Reflection, 4 pt offset**. Your picture should look like Figure 6-24.

Figure 6-24

The Reflection effect is a better option for this presentation

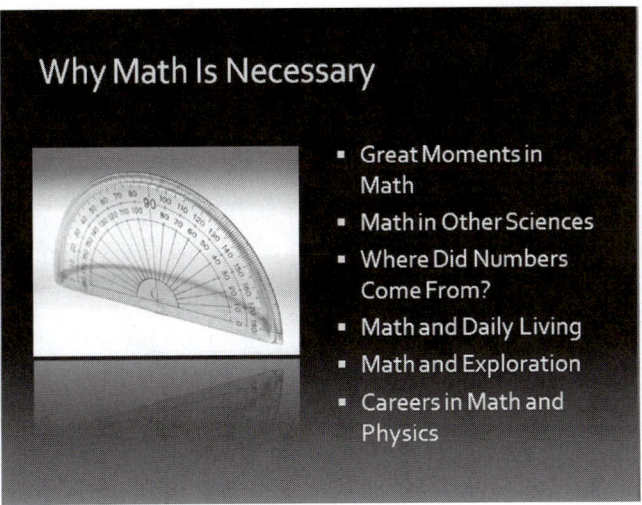

PAUSE. LEAVE the presentation open to use in the next exercise.

The effects offered on the Picture Effects gallery should be familiar by now, because you have applied similar effects to other objects such as tables, charts, and diagrams. You add and remove effects using the various submenus from the gallery.

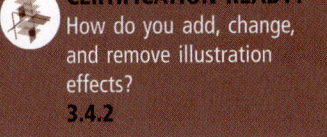

CERTIFICATION READY?
How do you add, change, and remove illustration effects?
3.4.2

Consider your background when choosing special effects for a picture (or any other object). Shadow effects will not have much impact on a dark background. Glow colors are designed to mix with the background color, so a dark background will make a glow less effective. Reflections, on the other hand, can look especially sharp on a dark background. In the previous exercise, the reflection also added height to the picture, helping it balance out the text placeholder on the right side of the slide.

Compressing the Images in a Presentation

Compressing images reduces the size of a presentation. This can make the presentation easier to store and speed up display if you have to work on a slow projector or computer system.

COMPRESS THE IMAGES IN A PRESENTATION

USE the presentation that is still open from the previous exercise.

1. Use a file management program such as My Computer to navigate to the current presentation. Use the Details view to check the size of the file.
2. In PowerPoint, click any picture in the presentation to select it, and then click the **Picture Tools Format** tab if necessary.
3. Click **Compress Pictures** in the Adjust group. The Compress Pictures dialog box opens.
4. Click the **Options** button in the dialog box. The Compression Settings dialog box opens, as shown in Figure 6-25.

Figure 6-25

Compression Settings dialog box

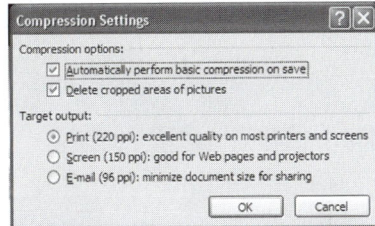

5. Click the **Screen (150 ppi)** option if necessary, then click **OK**.
6. Click **OK** again, and then **SAVE** the presentation. PowerPoint applies the compression settings you selected.
7. In My Computer, note the new file size of the presentation.

   PAUSE. LEAVE the presentation open to use in the next exercise.

When adding pictures to a presentation, you may need to consider the ultimate size of the presentation. Pictures will add considerably to the presentation's file size. This can make a large presentation difficult to store or work with.

The compression utility allows you to choose several options that can reduce file size. You can choose to delete the hidden portions of cropped pictures, for example. You can also choose a target output setting. If you know your slides will be presented on the Web or projected on a monitor, you can choose the Screen option. Presentations to be presented on a screen do not have to have the same quality as materials that might be printed because the monitor screen itself is limited in the quality it can display. Choose the E-mail option to reduce file size even further to improve transmission time when you are sharing a presentation by e-mail.

You can select a picture and then click the *Apply to selected pictures only* check box in the Compress Pictures dialog box. This allows you to compress some pictures while maintaining higher quality settings for others in the presentation.

Adding Shapes to Slides

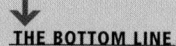

THE BOTTOM LINE PowerPoint offers sophisticated tools that allow you to create both basic and complex drawings. Use line tools and shapes to construct the drawing. You can easily add text to shapes to identify them and format the drawing using familiar fill, outline, and effects options.

Drawing Lines

PowerPoint supplies a number of different line tools so you can draw horizontal, vertical, diagonal, or free-form lines.

 DRAW LINES

USE the presentation that is still open from the previous exercise.

1. Go to slide 8. You will create a map on this slide to show potential visitors how to get to the museum. As you work, refer to Figure 8-26 for position of objects.
2. Click the **View** tab, and then click **Gridlines** to turn gridlines on.
3. Create the first street for the map as follows:
   a. Click the **Home** tab, then click the **Shapes** button (or the **More** button in the Drawing group) to display the gallery of drawing shapes.
   b. Click **Line** in the Line group. The pointer takes the shape of a crosshair.
   c. Locate the intersection of vertical and horizontal gridlines below the letter *n* in *John*, click at the intersection, and drag downward to create a vertical line three "blocks" long.

TAKE NOTE
You can also access the Shapes gallery on the Drawing Tools Format and insert tabs.

Adding Graphics and Media Clips to a Presentation | 679

4. Add the street name as follows:
   a. Click **Text Box** on the Insert tab, click anywhere on the slide, and key the text **Matthews Pike**.
   b. Click the outer border of the text box to select all content within the text box, and change the font size to **16**.
   c. Click **Arrange** in the Drawing group, point to **Rotate**, and click **Rotate Left 90°**.
   d. Move the rotated street name just to the left of the vertical line, as shown in Figure 8-26.
5. Click the **Line** tool again, hold down [Shift], and draw the diagonal line shown in Figure 8-26.
6. Click the **Line** tool again and draw the horizontal line shown in Figure 8-26.
7. Add the street name for the diagonal street as follows:
   a. Insert a text box anywhere on the slide, and key **Magnolia Parkway**.
   b. Change the font size to **16**.
   c. With the text box still selected, click **Arrange**, point to **Rotate**, and click **More Rotation Options**. The Size and Position dialog box opens.
   d. Key **-45** in the Rotate box, then click **Close**.
   e. Move the rotated text box to the right of the diagonal line, as shown in Figure 6-26.

Figure 6-26

The streets and street names have been added

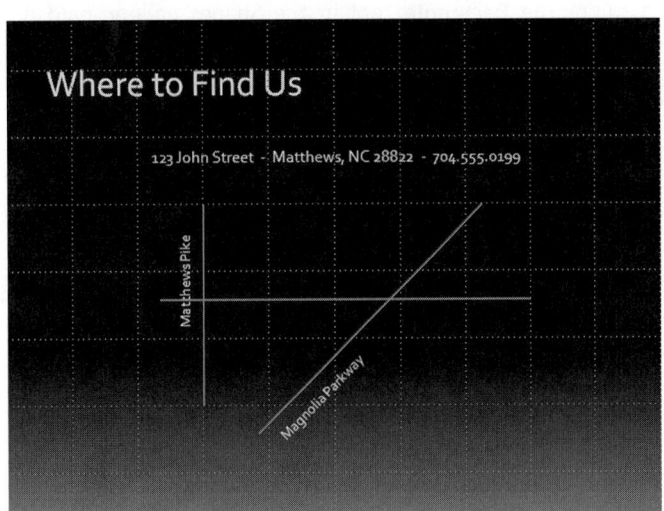

PAUSE. LEAVE the presentation open to use in the next exercise.

The Shapes gallery contains well over a hundred different shapes you can use to create drawings, from a simple rectangle to complex flowchart symbols. If you have worked with previous versions of PowerPoint, you may recognize many of these shapes as AutoShapes.

PowerPoint makes it easy to insert shapes by placing the Shapes gallery on three tabs: Insert, Home, and Drawing Tools Format. When a drawing shape is selected, the Drawing Tools Format tab is active and you can select another drawing tool from the Shapes gallery in the Insert Shapes group. If no shape is currently selected, you can use the Home tab or the Insert tab to select a drawing tool from the Shapes gallery.

To draw a shape with a shape tool, select the tool, click where you want to begin the shape, hold down the mouse button, and drag to make the shape the desired size.

You can use the Shift key to *constrain* some shapes to a specific appearance. For example:

- Hold down Shift while drawing a line to constrain it to a vertical, horizontal, or 45-degree diagonal orientation.
- Hold down Shift while drawing a rectangle to create a perfect square or while drawing an oval to create a perfect circle.
- Hold down Shift while drawing a triangle to create an equilateral triangle.

Selected shapes have sizing handles you can use to adjust the size of the object. Some complex shapes have yellow diamond adjustment handles that allow you to modify the shape. Drag a selected shape anywhere on a slide to reposition it.

Lines and other shapes take their color from the current theme. You can change color, as well as change outline and other effects, at any time while creating a drawing.

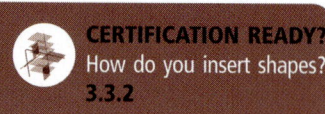

CERTIFICATION READY?
How do you insert shapes?
3.3.2

Inserting Basic Shapes

PowerPoint's many shape tools allow you to create multisided, elliptical, and even freeform shapes.

→ INSERT BASIC SHAPES

USE the presentation that is still open from the previous exercise. As you work, refer to Figure 8-27 to help you position and size objects.

1. Click the **Rectangle** tool in the Shapes gallery, hold down the mouse button, and drag to create the tall shape above the horizontal line shown in Figure 6-27.
2. With the shape still selected, click the **Drawing Tools Format** tab if necessary. Note the measurements in the Size group. If necessary, adjust the size so the shape is 1 inch high by 0.9 inches wide.
3. Click the **Rectangle** tool again and use it to create the wider rectangle shown in Figure 6-27. This shape should be 0.7 inch high by 1.2 inches wide.
4. Click the **Oval** tool in the Shapes gallery, hold down Shift, and draw the circle shown in Figure 6-27. This shape should be 1.2 inches high and wide.
5. Click the **Rectangle** tool and create a rectangle 0.7 inches high by 1 inch wide near the lower end of the diagonal street.
6. Click the shape's green rotate handle and drag to the right to rotate the shape so its right side is parallel to the diagonal road, as shown in Figure 6-27.
7. Click the **Freeform** tool in the Lines group in the Shapes gallery. Near the bottom of the slide (so you can easily see the line you are drawing), draw an irregular oval shape to represent a lake. The shape should be about 1.4 inches high and 1.5 inches wide.

TROUBLESHOOTING
When using the Freeform tool, if you return to the exact point at which you started drawing, PowerPoint will automatically close and fill the shape with color. If your shape does not fill, double-click to end it, click Undo, and start again.

8. Drag the lake shape to the right of the diagonal line, as shown in Figure 6-27.

Figure 6-27

Basic shapes have been added to the map

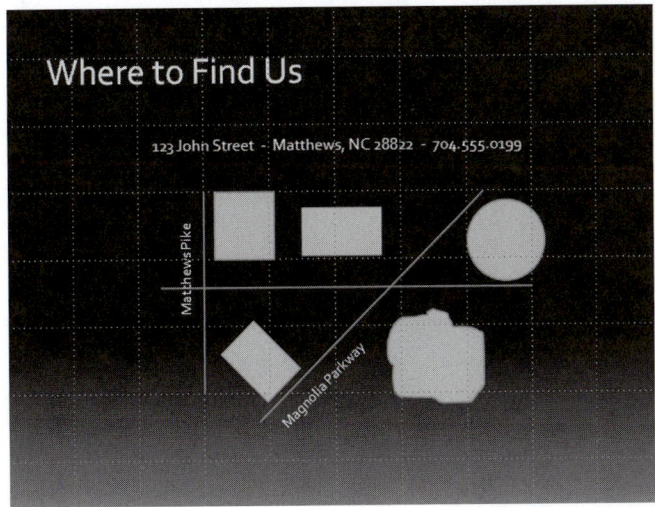

9. **SAVE** the presentation.

   PAUSE. LEAVE the presentation open to use in the next exercise.

When creating shapes, you can simply "eyeball" the size, use the rulers or gridlines to help you size, or use the Height and Width settings in the Size group on the Drawing Tools Format tab to scale the objects. Setting precise measurements can help you maintain the same proportions when creating objects of different shapes; for example, when creating circles and triangles that have to be the same height and width.

You can save yourself some time when drawing similar or identical shapes by copying shapes. Copy a selected shape, use Paste to paste a copy on the slide, then move or modify the copy as necessary. Or, select a shape, hold down the Ctrl key, and drag a copy of the shape to a new location.

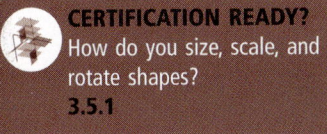

CERTIFICATION READY?
How do you size, scale, and rotate shapes?
3.5.1

If you are creating a drawing in which you want to show connections between objects, you can use connectors from the Lines group of the Shapes gallery. Connectors automatically snap to points on shape sides so you can easily draw an arrow, for instance, from one shape to another. As you reposition objects, the connectors remain attached and adjust as necessary to maintain the links between shapes.

Adding Text to Shapes

You can often improve a drawing by labeling the shapes to clearly state what they represent. In PowerPoint 2007, you can add text by simply clicking and keying.

➔ ADD TEXT TO SHAPES

USE the presentation that is still open from the previous exercise.

1. Click in the tall rectangle above the horizontal street, and then key **West Bank Center**.
2. Click in the wide rectangle shape, and then key **Baldwin Museum**.
3. Click in the circle shape, and then key **Miller Arena**.
4. Click in the rotated rectangle, and then key **Holmes College**. Note that the text is rotated as well.
5. Click in the freeform lake object, and then key **Magnolia Lake**.
6. Drag over the *Baldwin Museum* text to select it, then click the **Bold** button to boldface the text. Your map should look similar to Figure 6-28.

Figure 6-28

Text added to the shapes

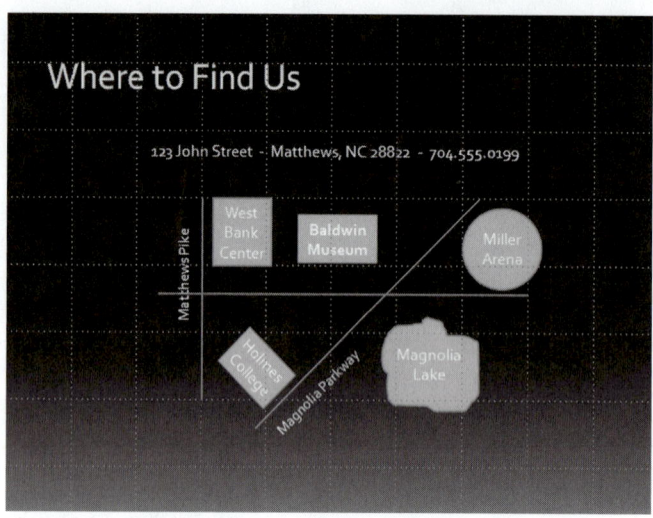

PAUSE. LEAVE the presentation open to use in the next exercise.

When you add text to a shape, the shape takes the function of a text box. PowerPoint automatically wraps text in the shape as in a text box; if the shape is not large enough to display the text, words will break up or the text will extend above and below the shape. You can solve this problem by resizing the shape or changing the text's point size.

> **TAKE NOTE**
> To adjust the way text appears in a shape, right-click the shape, click Format Shape, and access the Text Box settings.

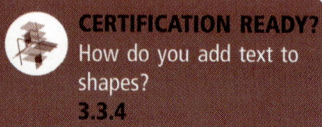

CERTIFICATION READY?
How do you add text to shapes?
3.3.4

You can use any text formatting options you like when adding text to shapes, just as when inserting text into a placeholder or text box. To select text in a shape to edit it, drag over it with the I-beam pointer.

Formatting Shapes

You format shapes using the Shape Fill, Shape Outline, and Shape Effects tools on the Drawing Tools Format tab. You can also apply Quick Styles to shapes for immediate impact.

➔ FORMAT SHAPES

USE the presentation that is still open from the previous exercise.

1. Format the *Matthews Pike* line and label:
   a. Click the vertical line that represents Matthews Pike, click the **Shape Outline** button, and then click the **Gold, Accent 3** theme color.

> **TAKE NOTE**
> You can use the Shape Outline button in the Drawing group on the Home tab or in the Shape Styles group on the Drawing Tools Format tab.

   b. Click the **Shape Outline** button again, point to **Weight**, and click **6 pt**.
   c. Click the outside border of the *Matthews Pike* text box to select all content in the text box, click the **Home** tab if necessary, click **Font Color**, and click **Black, Background 1**.
   d. With the text box still selected, click the **Shape Fill** button, and then click **White, Text 1**.

Adding Graphics and Media Clips to a Presentation | 683

2. Click the horizontal line and repeat steps 1a and 1b to format the line with the **White, Text 1, darker 35%** theme color and **6 pt** weight. (Don't worry about the street crossing over the *Matthews Pike* text box. You will fix this problem in a later exercise.)

3. Click the diagonal *Magnolia Parkway* line, click the **Shape Outline** button, point to **Weight**, and click **6 pt**.

4. Format the *Magnolia Parkway* text box following steps 1c and 1d to change text to black and the fill to white.

5. Format the other shapes as follows:
   a. Click the *West Bank Center* shape above the horizontal street, hold down **Shift**, and click each additional filled shape until all are selected. (Do *not* click any of the lines or the street name text boxes.)
   b. Click **Shape Outline**, and then click **No Outline**. You have removed outlines from the selected shapes.
   c. Click anywhere on the slide to deselect the selected shapes.
   d. Click the *West Bank Center* shape, click **Shape Fill**, and click **Periwinkle, Accent 5, Darker 25%**.
   e. Click the *Miller Arena* shape and fill with **Gold, Accent 3, Darker 25%**.
   f. Click the *Holmes College* shape and fill with **Pink, Accent 2, Darker 25%**.
   g. Click the *Magnolia Lake* shape and fill with **Turquoise, Accent 4, Darker 25%**.

6. You will use a Quick Style for the *Baldwin Museum* shape to make it stand out: Click the *Baldwin Museum* shape, display the Shape Styles gallery, and click **Intense Effect - Dark 1**.

7. Select all the filled shapes *except* the *Baldwin Museum* shape and the street name text boxes, click **Shape Effects**, point to **Bevel**, and click **Circle**. Your map should look similar to Figure 6-29.

Figure 6-29

The map has been formatted

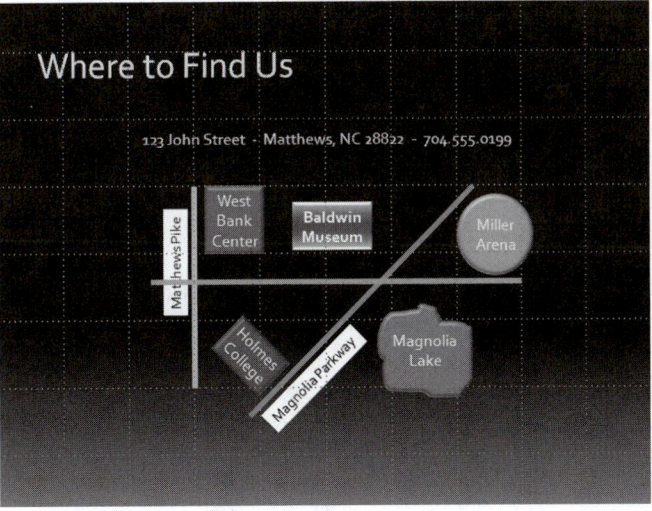

8. **SAVE** the presentation.

   PAUSE. LEAVE the presentation open to use in the next exercise.

You should be familiar by now with applying fills, outlines, and effects. You can format shapes using these options just as you formatted table cells, chart data markers, and SmartArt shapes.

Note that you can access fill, outline, and effect options from either the Home tab or the Drawing Tools Format tab. PowerPoint makes these options available on both tabs to minimize the amount of switching you have to do if you are also formatting text.

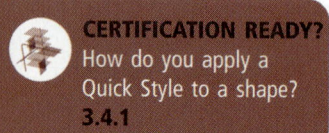

CERTIFICATION READY?
How do you apply a Quick Style to a shape?
3.4.1

Save time when applying the same kinds of formats to a number of objects by selecting all the objects that need the same formatting. You can then apply the format only once to modify all the selected objects. To select several objects, you use the Shift-click method: Click the first object you want to select, hold down the Shift key, and then click additional objects. If you select an object for your group by mistake, click it again to exclude it from the selection group.

Organizing Objects on a Slide

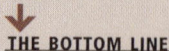

THE BOTTOM LINE

It is not uncommon to have to adjust the layout of objects you have added to slides. You may find that objects need to be reordered so they do not obscure other objects, or need to be aligned on the slide to present a neater appearance. You can also group objects together to make it easy to move or resize them all at once.

Setting the Order of Objects

As you applied formats to the lines in the map, you may have noticed that the lines are stacked on top of each other and the horizontal line appears to cross over a text box. You can adjust the order in which objects stack on the slide by using Arrange commands or the Selection and Visibility pane.

➔ **SET THE ORDER OF OBJECTS**

USE the presentation that is still open from the previous exercise.

1. Go to slide 3, and click the picture to select it.
2. Click the **Arrange** button on the Home tab, and then click **Send to Back**. The picture moves behind the slide title placeholder, as shown in Figure 6-30.

Figure 6-30

The picture moves behind the placeholder

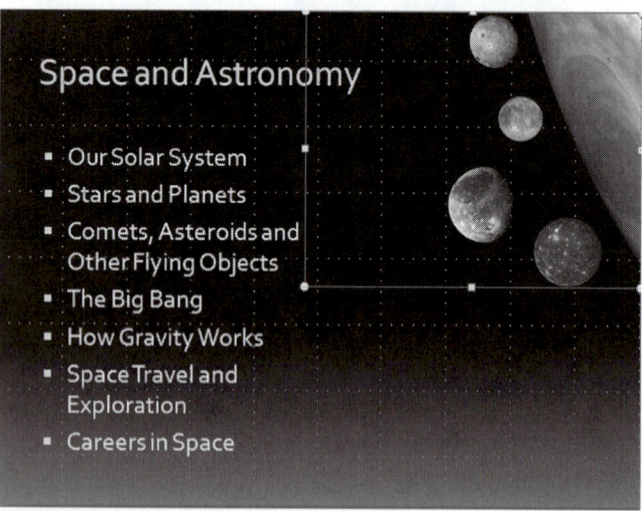

TAKE NOTE

The Arrange tools are available on both the Home tab and the Picture Tools Format tab.

3. Go to slide 8. Click the **Arrange** button, then click **Selection Pane**. The Selection and Visibility pane opens, as shown in Figure 6-31, showing the current slide content in the order in which it was created, from bottom to top.

Figure 6-31
The Selection and Visibility pane shows the current slide content

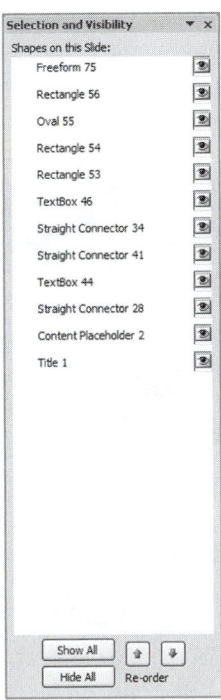

 **ANOTHER WAY** You can also display the Selection and Visibility pane by clicking Select on the Home tab, then clicking Selection Pane.

TROUBLESHOOTING Don't be concerned if the list in your Selection and Visibility pane doesn't exactly match the one shown in Figure 6-31. The order and numbering of objects in the pane can be affected by many actions.

4. Click the *Matthews Pike* street in the map to see how it is identified in the Selection and Visibility pane—it will have a name such as Straight Connector 4 and should be near the bottom of the list of objects. Then click the horizontal street line to see its name.

5. Click the *Matthew Pike* street line again to select it. Click the **Re-order** up arrow until the selected Straight Connector is above the horizontal Straight Connector in the Selection and Visibility pane. Notice that the gold line is now on top of the light gray line in the map.

6. Click the *Matthews Pike* text box and click the **Re-order** up arrow until the text box is on top of the horizontal gray line in the map.

7. Click the *Magnolia Parkway* street line and click the **Re-order** up arrow until the diagonal street is above the horizontal street in the map.

8. You have one more shape to add to the map: an arrow that labels the horizontal street as John Street and indicates that the street is one way. Click **Shapes** on the Home tab, click **Right Arrow** in the Block Arrows group, and draw a block arrow as shown in Figure 6-32. The arrow should be about 0.7 inches high and 5.2 inches wide.

Figure 6-32

Adding the block arrow to the map

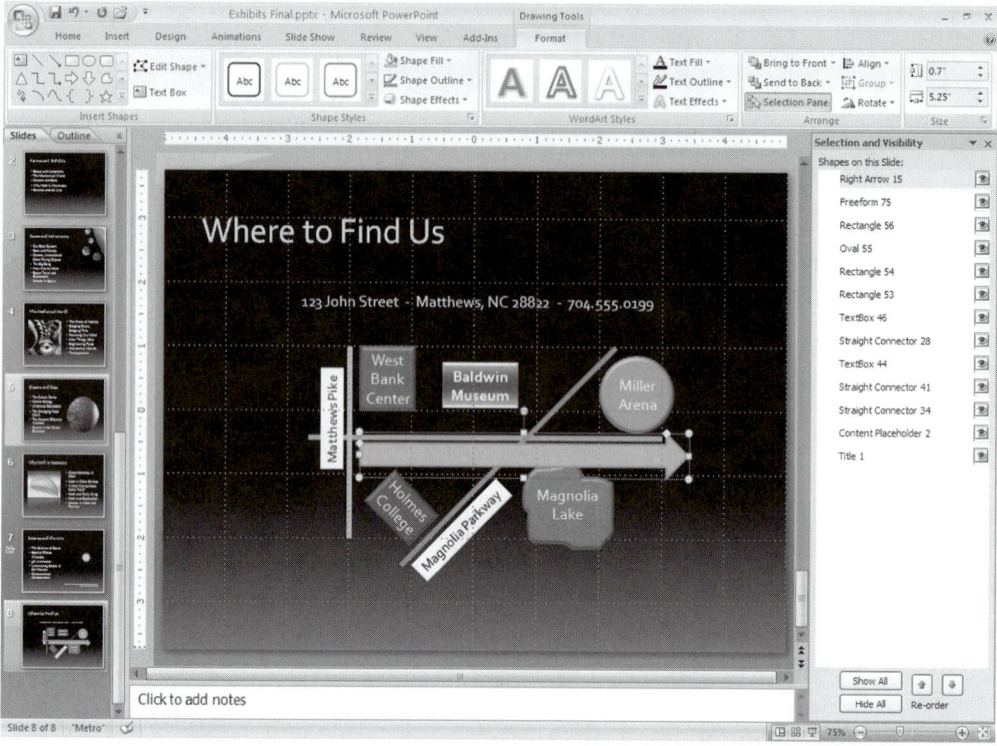

TAKE NOTE

Note that the Right Arrow object has been added at the top of the Selection and Visibility pane.

9. Remove the shape outline and fill the shape with **White, Text 1**.
10. Key **John Street**, press Tab twice, and key **ONE WAY**. You will not be able to see the text because it is white.
11. Click the outside border of the block arrow to select all content in the shape, click the **Home** tab, click **Font Color**, and click **Black, Background 1**.
12. Right-click a blank area of the block arrow (to the left of the words *John Street*, for example), point to **Send to Back**, and click **Send to Back**. The arrow moves behind all lines and shapes, as shown in Figure 6-33. Note the position of the Right Arrow object in the Selection and Visibility pane.

Figure 6-33

The block arrow has been moved behind all other objects

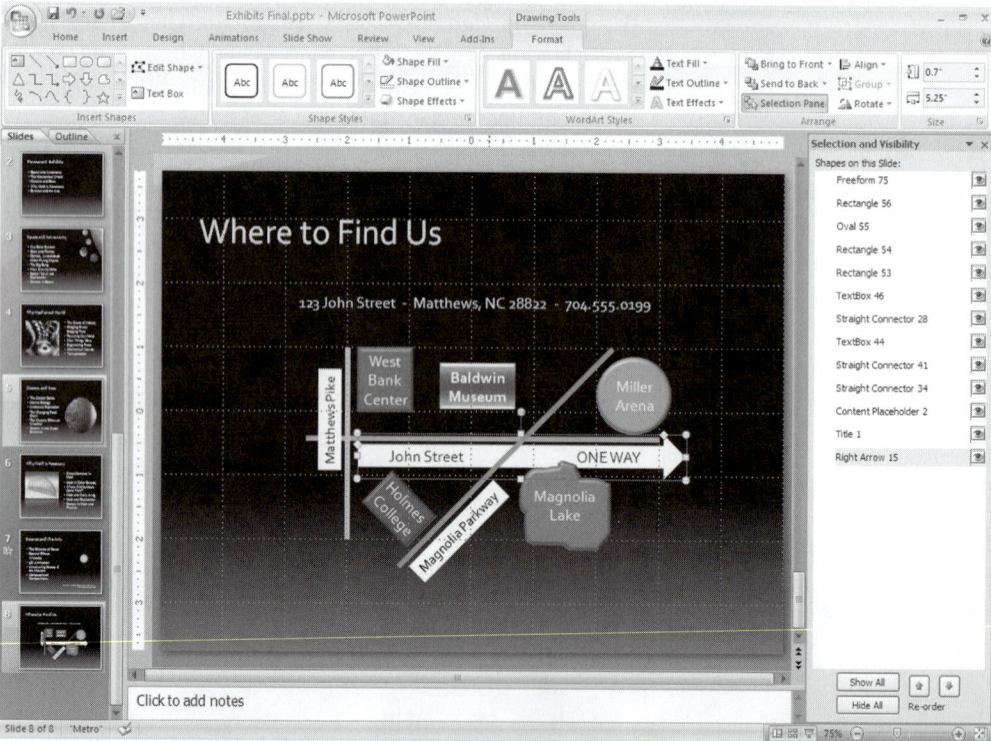

Adding Graphics and Media Clips to a Presentation | 687

13. Close the Selection and Visibility pane.
14. If any of your shapes obscures the text on the block right arrow, adjust their positions as necessary.

    PAUSE. LEAVE the presentation open to use in the next exercise.

Objects stack up on a slide in the order in which you created them, from bottom to top. If you insert a slide title on a slide, it will be the object at the bottom of the stack. The last item you create or add to the slide will be at the top of the stack. You can consider each object to be on an invisible layer in the stack.

As you have seen in the map exercises, some objects can obscure other objects because of the order in which you add them to the slide. You use the ***order*** options to reposition objects in the stack:

- **Bring to Front** moves the selected object to the front or top of the stack, on top of all other objects.
- **Bring Forward** moves an object one layer toward the front or top of the stack. Use this option if you need to position an object above some objects but below others.
- **Send to Back** moves an object all the way to the back or bottom of the stack, below all other objects.
- **Send Backward** moves an object one layer toward the back or bottom of the stack.

You can clearly see the stacking order of objects on a slide using the Selection and Visibility pane, new in PowerPoint 2007. This pane is similar to the Layers palette in a program such as Illustrator or Photoshop. It allows you to easily move objects up or down in the stacking order. You can click the visibility "eye" to hide objects that might be in your way as you work on another object—a handy feature when creating a complex drawing.

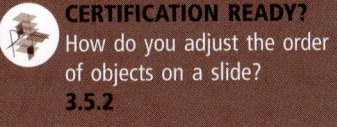

CERTIFICATION READY?
How do you adjust the order of objects on a slide?
3.5.2

If you do not want to use the Selection and Visibility pane, you can use options on the Home tab's Arrange button menu to reorder objects, or you can use buttons in the Drawing Tools Format tab in the Arrange group. You can also access these options readily by right-clicking an object and selecting the appropriate command from the shortcut menu.

TAKE NOTE Arrange options also display on other Format tabs, such as the Picture Tools Format and SmartArt Tools Format tabs.

Aligning Objects with Each Other

Your drawings will present a more pleasing appearance if similar items are aligned with each other or to the slide. Use PowerPoint's alignment options to position objects neatly.

ALIGN OBJECTS WITH EACH OTHER

USE the presentation that is still open from the previous exercise.

1. Click the **West Bank Center** shape, hold down **Shift**, and click the **Baldwin Museum** shape and the **Miller Arena** shape. These landmarks are all different distances from the *John Street* horizontal line but can be aligned for a neater appearance.
2. Click the **Drawing Tools Format** tab if necessary, click **Align**, and click **Align Bottom**. The shapes are now aligned at the bottom so they are the same distance from the horizontal line, as shown in Figure 6-34.

Figure 6-34

Objects have been aligned by their bottom edges

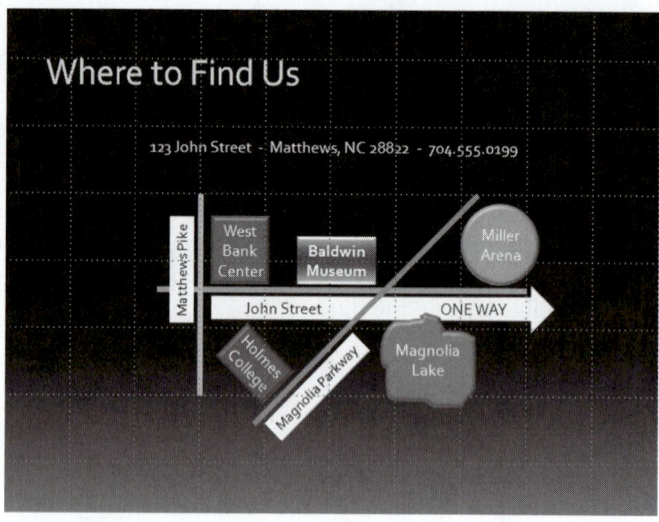

PAUSE. LEAVE the presentation open to use in the next exercise.

PowerPoint's alignment options allow you to line up objects on a slide both horizontally and vertically:

- Use **Align Left**, **Align Center**, or **Align Right** to align objects horizontally so that their left edges, vertical centers, or right edges are lined up with each other.
- Use **Align Top**, **Align Middle**, or **Align Bottom** to align objects vertically so that their top edges, horizontal centers, or bottom edges are lined up with each other.

You can also use distribute options to space objects evenly, either vertically or horizontally. This feature can be a great time-saver when you have a number of objects that you want to spread out evenly across a slide.

PowerPoint allows you to align (or distribute) objects either to each other or to the slide. If you select Align Selected Objects on the Align menu, PowerPoint will adjust only the selected objects. If you select Align to Slide, PowerPoint will rearrange objects using the entire slide area.

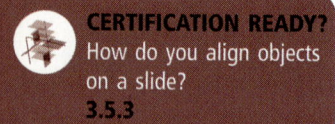

CERTIFICATION READY?
How do you align objects on a slide?
3.5.3

Grouping Objects Together

When a drawing consists of a number of objects, it can be tedious to move each one if you need to reposition the drawing. Grouping objects allows you to work with a number of objects as one unit.

→ GROUP OBJECTS TOGETHER

USE the presentation that is still open from the previous exercise.

1. Click the **Matthews Pike** text box, hold down [Shift], and click each of the other objects in the map until all are selected.
2. Click the **Drawing Tools Format** tab if necessary, click **Group**, and then click **Group**. All objects are surrounded by a single selection border, as shown in Figure 6-35.

Adding Graphics and Media Clips to a Presentation | 689

Figure 6-35

All elements of the map are grouped

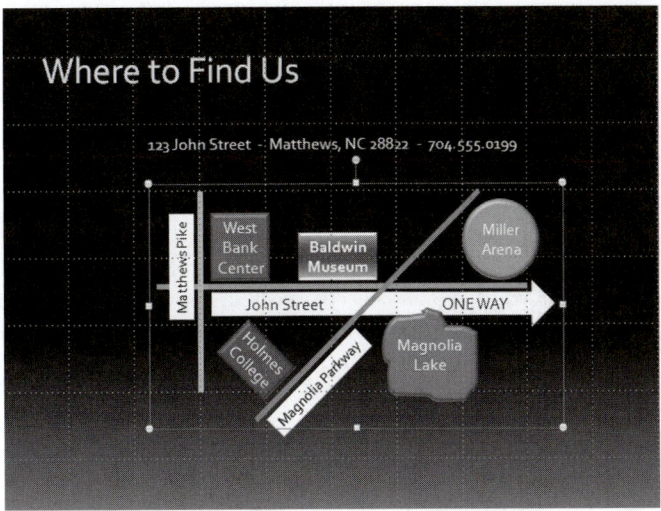

3. Click the **View** tab, then deselect **Gridlines** to hide the grid.
4. Click the **Drawing Tools Format** tab, click the **Align** button, and make sure that **Align to Slide** is selected.
5. Click the **Align** button again, and click **Align Center**. The grouped map is now centered horizontally on the slide, as shown in Figure 6-36.

Figure 6-36

The map is centered on the slide

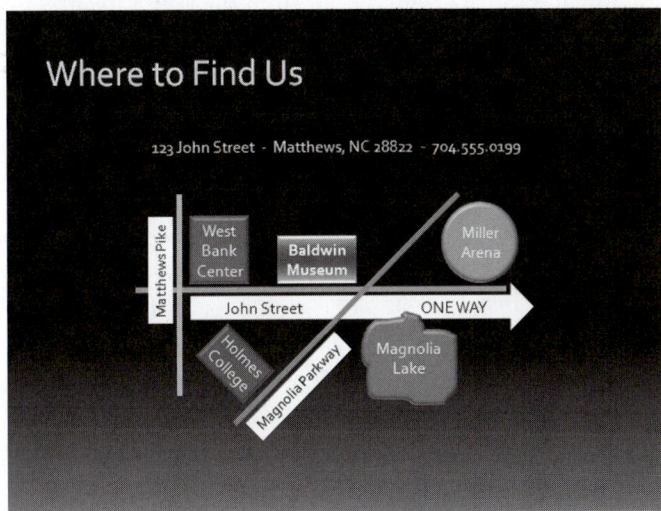

6. **SAVE** the presentation.

   PAUSE. LEAVE the presentation open to use in the next exercise.

If a drawing contains a number of objects, it makes sense to group the objects when you are finished with the drawing. You can more easily reposition a grouped object, and you can also apply formatting changes to all objects in a group much more quickly than by applying formats to each individual object. To select a group, click any object in the group.

If you find that you need to work further with one object in a group, you can simply click it to activate it. It remains part of the group while you modify it. If you need to remove objects or make sweeping changes to a group, you can use the Ungroup option to release the group

690 | Lesson 6

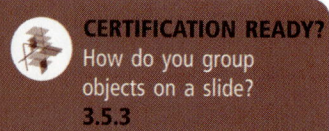

CERTIFICATION READY?
How do you group objects on a slide?
3.5.3

into its component parts. PowerPoint remembers the objects that are in the group so you can use Regroup if desired to restore the group.

If you are creating a very complex drawing, you can group portions of the drawing, then group those groups. This makes it easy to reuse portions of a drawing—simply ungroup the entire drawing, copy the group you need elsewhere, and regroup the whole.

TAKE NOTE

It is easy to miss an object when selecting parts of a complex drawing to create a group. To check that you have all objects selected, move the group. You will easily see if one or more objects do not move with the group. Undo the move, click the group, click any other objects that need to belong to the group, and issue the Group command again.

Adding Media Clips to a Presentation

THE BOTTOM LINE

Media clips include sounds and movies. You can add media clips to a presentation to present information or to support the mood or ambience of the presentation.

Adding a Sound File to a Slide

You can add sounds from files or from the Clip Organizer. PowerPoint allows you to specify when the sound will play and choose from other sound settings to control playback.

➔ **ADD A SOUND TO A SLIDE**

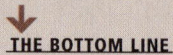

CD

The *Beethoven's Ninth.wma* file is available on the companion CD-ROM.

USE the presentation that is still open from the previous exercise.

1. Using a program such as My Computer, copy the **Beethoven's Ninth.wma** file from this lesson's data files and paste the copy in the folder in which you are storing solution files.
2. Go to slide 1 and then click the **Insert** tab.
3. Click **Sound** in the Media Clips group, then click **Sound from File**. The Insert Sound dialog box opens.
4. Navigate to the solution files for this lesson, click **Beethoven's Ninth**, and then click **OK**. A dialog box displays asking how you want to start the sound, as shown in Figure 6-37.

Figure 6-37

Choose how the sound will play

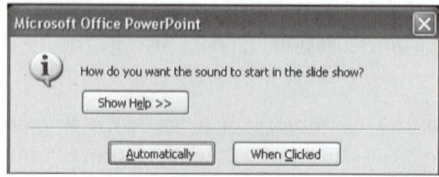

5. Click **Automatically**. A sound icon displays on the slide.
6. Drag the icon down to the lower-right corner of the slide, as shown in Figure 6-38.

Adding Graphics and Media Clips to a Presentation | 691

Figure 6-38

You can move the sound icon anywhere on the slide

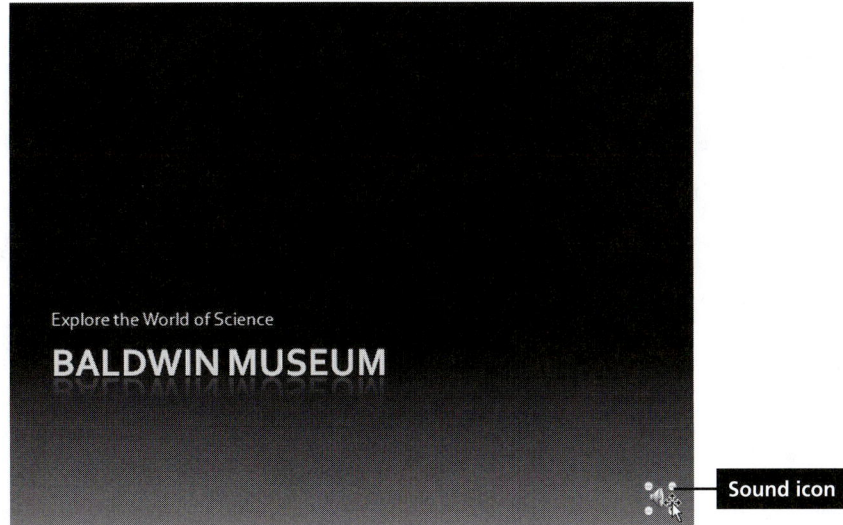

7. With the sound icon still selected, click the **Sound Tools Options** tab if necessary.
8. Click the **Play Sound** drop-down arrow in the Sound Options group, and then click **Play across slides**. This option allows a sound file to play even after you move to a new slide.
9. Press F5 to start the slide show from slide 1. The music starts playing. Click the mouse button to progress through the slides. The music will keep playing until you end the show.

    PAUSE. LEAVE the presentation open to use in the next exercise.

You have a number of options for adding sounds to a presentation:

- Use **Sound from File** if you have a sound file in a supported format that you want to insert. PowerPoint can handle AIFF, AU, MIDI, MP3, WAV, and WMA files.
- Use **Sound from Clip Organizer** to open the Clip Art task pane and search for a sound file the same way you searched for clip art. PowerPoint automatically selects Sounds in the *Results should be* list and displays sounds on your system. You can use a keyword search to find specific sounds.
- Use **Play CD Audio Track** to select a track or tracks to play during the presentation. You must have a CD in the computer's CD drive to play music this way during the presentation.
- Use **Record Sound** if you want to record your own sound to play on the slide. You must have a microphone to record the sound.

TAKE NOTE

You can also play a sound file while in Normal view by double-clicking the sound icon.

For best results, your system should have a sound card and speakers. Otherwise, sounds will play with the computer's default speaker, which generally isn't very powerful.

The Sound Tools Options tab provides a number of tools for working with a sound file. You can preview the sound, set its volume for the slide show, hide the sound icon during the slide show (don't use this option if you want to be able to play the sound by clicking on it during the presentation), loop the sound so it repeats until you stop it, adjust whether the sound plays automatically or when you click it, and adjust the maximum sound file size.

CERTIFICATION READY?
How do you insert media clips such as sounds?
2.3.4

Sound files can be either embedded in a presentation or linked to a presentation. Because only WAV files smaller than the default maximum sound file size can be embedded in a presentation, most sound files are actually linked to the presentation. For this reason, you should consider storing a presentation's sound files in the same folder with the presentation itself.

TROUBLESHOOTING

If you run a presentation and discover that objects such as sound files and movies will not play, chances are that PowerPoint cannot find the linked sound or movie file. You can reestablish the link by deleting the object that will not play and reinserting it from a known location.

Adding a Movie to a Slide

You can insert movies from files or movies from the Clip Organizer to add visual interest or information to a presentation.

➡ **ADD A MOVIE TO A SLIDE**

CD

The *Sunspot.mpeg* file is available on the companion CD-ROM.

USE the presentation that is still open from the previous exercise.

1. Using a program such as My Computer, copy the *Sunspot.mpeg* file from this lesson's data files and paste the copy in the folder in which you are storing solution files.
2. Go to slide 7 and click the **Insert Media Clip** icon in the content placeholder. The Insert Movie dialog box opens.
3. Navigate to the solution files for this lesson, click *Sunspot.mpeg*, then click **OK**.
4. Click **Automatically**. The first frame of the movie appears on the slide and the Movie Tools Options tab becomes active, as shown in Figure 6-39.

Figure 6-39

The movie file has been inserted on the slide

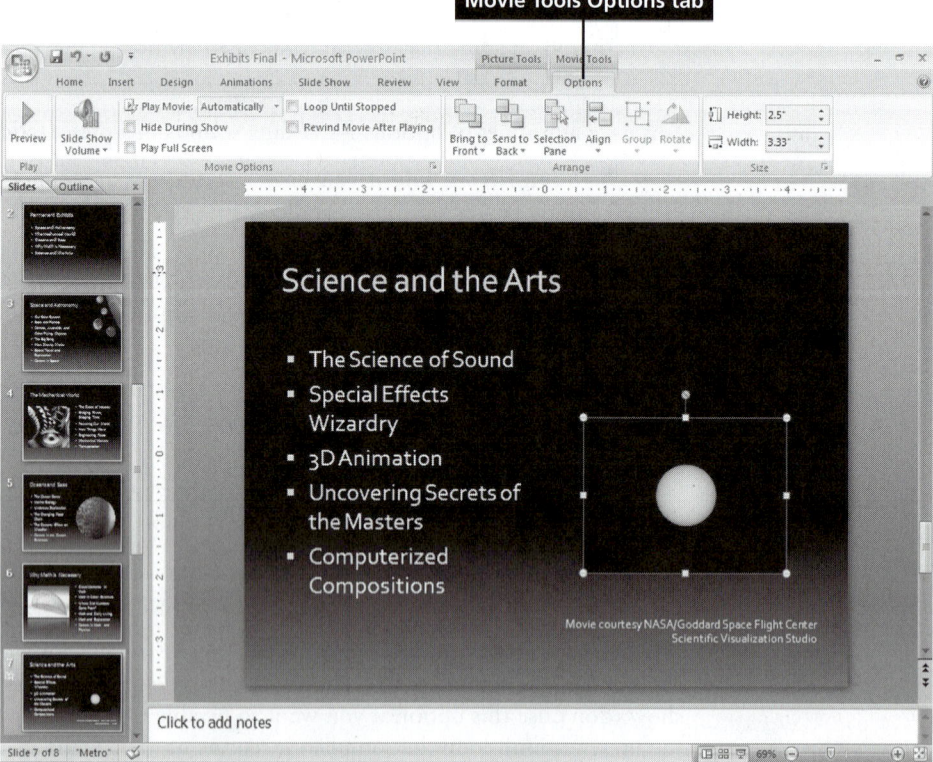

5. Press **Alt** + **F9** to display the drawing guides, and then drag the movie up and to the right so the upper-right corner snaps to the intersection of the two guides. Press **Alt** + **F9** again to hide the guides.
6. Click **Rewind Movie After Playing** in the Movie Options group on the Movie Tools Options tab.

Adding Graphics and Media Clips to a Presentation | 693

7. Press F5 to play the presentation from the beginning. When you reach slide 7, watch the movie, which shows an animation of the structure of a sunspot.
8. **SAVE** the presentation and **CLOSE** it.
   CLOSE PowerPoint.

> **TAKE NOTE**
> You can play a movie file while in Normal view by double-clicking the movie.

You have two options for inserting a movie on a slide:

- Use **Movie from File** if you have a movie file in a supported format that you want to insert. PowerPoint can handle ASF, AVI, MPEG, or WMV files.
- Use **Movie from Clip Organizer** to open the Clip Art task pane and search for a movie file the same way you searched for clip art. PowerPoint automatically selects Movies in the *Results should be* list and displays movies on your system. You can use a keyword search to find specific movies and search Office Online for more files.

Files identified as movies in the Clip Organizer are actually more like animated clip art graphics. They tend to be relatively small and cannot be significantly enlarged without a corresponding loss of quality. But they can still provide multimedia interest on a slide.

The Movie Tools Options tab provides some of the same options you find on the Sound Tools Options tab. In addition, you can choose to play the movie in the full screen during the slide show and rewind it back to the first frame after it finishes playing.

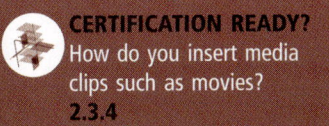

> **CERTIFICATION READY?**
> How do you insert media clips such as movies?
> 2.3.4

Like most sound files, movie files in formats other than WMF are generally linked to the presentation. For best results, store movie files in the same folder with their presentations.

SUMMARY SKILL MATRIX

IN THIS LESSON YOU LEARNED HOW TO:
Insert a ClipArt Picture
Insert a Picture from a File
Use the Ruler, Gridlines, and Guides
Rotate an Object
Resize Objects
Format a Picture with a Quick Style
Adjust a Picture's Color, Brightness, and Contrast
Add Special Effects to a Picture
Compress the Images in a Presentation
Draw Lines
Insert Basic Shapes
Add Text to Shapes
Format Shapes
Set the Order of Objects
Align Objects with Each Other
Group Objects Together
Add a Sound File to a Slide
Add a Movie to a Slide

Knowledge Assessment

Matching

Match the term in Column 1 to its description in Column 2.

Column 1

Column 2

1. order (h)
2. clip art (a)
3. guides (j)
4. constrain (f)
5. aspect ratio (b)
6. scaling (d)
7. keyword (c)
8. crop (i)
9. Clip Organizer (e)
10. gridlines (g)

a. predrawn graphics you can use to illustrate a slide
b. the relationship of width to height for a picture
c. a descriptive word or phrase you can use to search for specific types of objects
d. sizing to a percentage of the original size
e. series of folders in which pictures are stored on your computer
f. to force a drawing tool to create a shape such as a perfect square or circle
g. a series of vertical and horizontal dotted lines that help you align objects on a slide
h. to move one object behind or in front of another
i. to remove portions of a picture you don't need
j. nonprinting lines that you can move or copy to help you position objects on a slide

True / False

Circle T if the statement is true or F if the statement is false.

T **(F)** 1. When adding clip art to a slide, you are limited to the pictures stored on your computer. (P662)

(T) F 2. PowerPoint allows you to insert pictures that are stored in BMP format. (P666)

(T) F 3. As you move the pointer, a short dotted line also moves on both rulers.

T **(F)** 4. The Recolor option lets you select colors in a picture and replace them with other colors.

T **(F)** 5. One reason to compress pictures is to reduce the number of colors used. (P677)

(T) F 6. The color of a new shape is determined by the current theme.

T **(F)** 7. To add text to a shape, right-click the shape and then click Add Text and begin keying.

(T) F 8. If you want an object to be at the bottom of a stack of objects, you would use Send to Back. (P687)

(T) F 9. You can work with a single object in a group without having to ungroup all objects. (P689)

(T) F 10. A sound file in MP3 format will be linked to the presentation rather than embedded in it. (P691)

Competency Assessment

Project 6-1: Get the Picture

You are a recruiter for Woodgrove Bank, and you have prepared a presentation to be delivered at a local job fair. You need to locate a picture to illustrate one of the presentation's slides. You can use Microsoft Office clip art files to find a suitable picture.

GET READY. Launch PowerPoint if it is not already running.

The *Job Fair* file is available on the companion CD-ROM.

1. **OPEN** the *Job Fair* presentation.
2. Go to slide 5 and click the **Clip Art** icon in the right-hand content placeholder.
3. Key **business** as the keyword, click the **Results should be** drop-down arrow, and select only **Photographs**.
4. Review the results to find a photograph of a professionally dressed business person and then click a picture you like to insert it into the placeholder.
5. Use the Size options on the Picture Tools Format tab to resize the picture to be as wide as the text in the left-hand placeholder if necessary.
6. Click the **View** tab, then click **Gridlines**. Use the gridlines to align the top of the picture with the top of the text in the left-hand placeholder.
7. Click the picture to select it, click **Picture Effects** on the Picture Tools Format tab, point to **Shadow**, and click any shadow effect.
8. Hide the gridlines.
9. **SAVE** the presentation as *Job Fair Final*.

   LEAVE the presentation open for the next project.

Project 6-2: Final Touches

You have decided you need another picture in the Job Fair Final presentation. You have a picture file you think will work.

The *Building.jpg* file is available on the companion CD-ROM.

1. Go to slide 2 of *Job Fair Final* and click the **Insert Picture from File** icon in the right-hand content placeholder.
2. Navigate to the data files for this lesson, locate *Building.jpg*, click the file, and click **Insert**.
3. Right-click the picture and click **Size and Position**. In the Size and Position dialog box, scale the picture to 90% of its current height and width.
4. Press **Alt**+**F9** to display drawing guides. Click the slide title placeholder to display its border, then drag the vertical guide to the right to align with the right border of the slide title placeholder.
5. Drag the horizontal placeholder up to align with the capital letter in the first bulleted item in the left-hand placeholder.
6. Reposition the picture so that its upper-right corner snaps to the intersection of the two guides. Press **Alt**+**F9** to hide the guides.
7. Click the **More** button in the Picture Styles group on the Picture Tools Format tab, and then click the **Drop Shadow Rectangle** Quick Style.
8. Right-click the picture, click **Format Picture**, and change Brightness to 5% and Contrast to 10%.
9. Click **Compress Pictures** in the Adjust group on the Picture Tools Format tab, and then click **Options**.
10. Click **Screen (150 ppi)** if necessary, and then click **OK** twice.
11. **SAVE** the presentation and then **CLOSE** the file.

    LEAVE PowerPoint open for the next project.

Proficiency Assessment

Project 6-3: Go with the Flow

You are a professional trainer teaching a class on basic computer skills. For your class today, you need to explain the systems development life cycle (SDLC) to a group of students. You can use PowerPoint's drawing tools to create a flow chart that shows the process.

1. Create a new, blank presentation, and apply the Median theme.
2. Change the title slide to a Title Only slide, and key the slide title **Systems Development Life Cycle (SDLC)**.
3. Draw five rectangles stacked vertically on the slide. You do not have to worry about alignment or distribution at this point.
4. Key **Phase 1: Needs Analysis** in the top rectangle.
5. Add text to the remaining rectangles as follows:

   Phase 2: System Design

   Phase 3: Development

   Phase 4: Implementation

   Phase 5: Maintenance
6. Resize the shapes as necessary so that text fits on a single line.
7. Add connectors between the shapes as follows:
   a. Click the **Shapes** button to display the Shapes gallery, and click the **Elbow Arrow Connector** line in the Lines group.
   b. Move the crosshair pointer over the *Phase 1* shape to see the red connection points on all four sides of the shape.
   c. Click the red connection point at the bottom side of the shape, then drag down toward the next shape. When you see the red connection points on the second shape, click the one at the top center of the shape.
   d. Repeat these steps to create four connection arrows between the five shapes.
8. Click the **Elbow Arrow Connector**, click the right side connector point on the last shape, then drag upward and connect to the right side connector of the top shape.
9. **SAVE** the presentation as *SDLC Final*.

   LEAVE the presentation open for the next project.

Project 6-4: Final Flow

You have the basic flowchart structure on the slide. Now you need to modify and format it to improve its appearance.

1. Select the shape that has the most amount of text and check its size using the Size group of the Drawing Tools Format tab. (If desired, you can adjust the size upward or downward to round numbers.)
2. Use the Shift-click method to select the remaining four rectangles.
3. Set the width and height in the Size group to the measurements of the rectangle you checked in step 1. All rectangles should now be the same width and height.
4. Select all five rectangles, and use the **Align Left** option to align them with each other.
5. With all five rectangles still selected, use the **Distribute Vertically** option to equalize the space between the rectangles.
6. Apply a different Quick Style color to each rectangle. (Use the same effect for all rectangles, but vary the colors for each.)

Adding Graphics and Media Clips to a Presentation | 697

7. Select the vertical line connectors between shapes and apply a Quick Style that emphasizes the connectors; for example, **Moderate Line, Dark 1**. If any of the connectors do not quite touch the shape below, adjust the connector by dragging it to the red anchor point.
8. Click the connector that runs from the last shape to the first, change the line weight to **6 pt**, and drag the yellow diamond adjustment handle at the center of the shape to the right about one-quarter of an inch to give more room for the arrowhead at the top of the connector. Change the color of the connector to a darker theme color.
9. Group all drawing objects.
10. Use the **Align Center** option to center the grouped object on the slide.
11. **SAVE** the presentation and then **CLOSE** the file.

    LEAVE PowerPoint open for the next project.

■ Mastery Assessment

Project 6-5: Photo Flair

You are finalizing a presentation to introduce a speaker and want to do some work on the photo of the speaker you have included on a slide. You can use PowerPoint's picture tools to finalize the photo.

The *Speaker* file is available on the companion CD-ROM.

1. **OPEN** the *Speaker* presentation.
2. Go to slide 2 and select the picture.
3. Crop the picture to remove the coffee cup and newspaper at the right side of the picture.
4. Resize the photo so it is 4 inches high and align it with the top of the vertical line at the center of the slide.
5. Increase the contrast in the picture by 10%.
6. Draw a rectangle that exactly covers the picture. Remove the outline from the rectangle.
7. Click the ↓ twice and the → twice to slightly offset the shape from the picture, then send the shape behind the picture to act as a drop shadow.
8. Choose a new theme color for the rectangle shape that contrasts well with the picture but does not overwhelm it.
9. **SAVE** the presentation as *Speaker Final* and then **CLOSE** the file.

   LEAVE PowerPoint open for the next project.

Project 6-6: Media Support

Your Consolidated Courier presentation needs some additional pizzazz. You can insert media clips to add some life to the slides.

The *Messenger* file is available on the companion CD-ROM.

The *Town.mid* file is available on the companion CD-ROM.

1. **OPEN** the *Messenger* presentation.
2. Copy the sound file *Town.mid* to your solutions folder, and then insert this file on slide 1.
3. Choose to play the sound automatically, and then adjust settings so the sound file plays across slides.
4. Go to slide 5. Insert a movie from the Clip Organizer, using a keyword such as *airmail*, *world*, or *airplane* to convey the idea of global courier service.
5. Position the movie as desired on the slide.

6. Run the presentation in Slide Show view to check the sound file and view the animated graphic.
7. **SAVE** the presentation as *Messenger Final* and then **CLOSE** the file.
   STOP. CLOSE PowerPoint.

INTERNET READY

The local library has asked you to prepare a presentation for their book club, which is about to embark on a Famous Novels series of club meetings. The book club will read novels by Austen, Dickens, Melville, and Steinbeck this year. Using the Internet, research some basic facts about the lives of these four authors and locate and save pictures of each. Create a slide show to present the information you have gathered. On the first slide, use drawing tools to draw a stack or row of books with the names of the authors on the spines. Create a slide for each author and insert life details and the pictures you located. Adjust the pictures as necessary to be about the same size and location on each slide and use any picture formatting tools you like to improve the appearance of the pictures.

Delivering a Presentation

7

LESSON SKILL MATRIX

Selecting Slide Orientation – 700	Students will learn how to select slide orientation.
Setting Slide Size – 701	Students will learn how to set slide size.
Customizing Audience Handouts – 703	Students will learn how to customize audience handouts.
Omitting Selected Slides from a Presentation – 706	Students will learn how to omit selected slides from a presentation.
Creating a Custom Show – 708-712 (Rehears Timings)	Students will learn how to create a custom show.
Setting Up a Slide Show – 712	Students will learn how to set up a slide show.
Working with Presentation Tools – 713	Students will learn how to work with presentation tools.
Packaging a Presentation for Delivery – 718	Students will learn how to package a presentation for delivery.

You are an engineer for A. Datum Corporation, a contractor specializing in piledriving and heavy concrete construction. Your team has put together a bid on a large bridge construction project for the town of Center City, and you must present the bid package to the client. You will present a slide show for the client before reviewing the bid in detail. Your presentation will introduce your company and provide an overview of the bid itself. PowerPoint provides a number of tools that can help you set up your presentation, rehearse it, and then package it to use in the final presentation.

KEY TERMS
annotate
custom show
orientation

Adjusting Slide Orientation and Size

THE BOTTOM LINE Slides are generally displayed at a standard size and orientation. You can adjust orientation and size for special impact or to meet the requirements of a specific projection device or output option.

Selecting Slide Orientation

By default, slides are displayed so they are wider than they are tall. You can easily change this orientation by using the Page Setup dialog box or a Ribbon command.

➔ SELECT SLIDE ORIENTATION

GET READY. Before you begin these steps, be sure to launch Microsoft Office PowerPoint 2007.

1. Locate and open the *Bid* presentation.
2. Click the **Design** tab, and then click the **Page Setup** button in the Page Setup group. The Page Setup dialog box opens, as shown in Figure 7-1. Note the current width and height measurements at the left side of the dialog box.

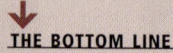

The *Bid* file is available on the companion CD-ROM.

Figure 7-1
Page Setup dialog box

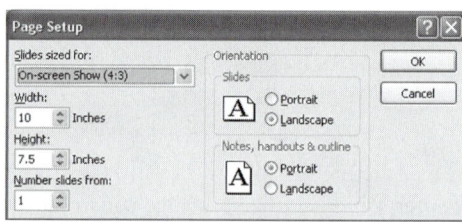

TAKE NOTE
You will see the result of this change to handout orientation later in this lesson.

3. Click **Portrait** in the Slides area of the dialog box. Note that the width and height measurements reverse.
4. Click **Landscape** in the Notes, handouts & outline area.
5. Click **OK**. The slides are now taller than they are wide, as shown in Figure 7-2.

Figure 7-2
The slides display in portrait orientation

Delivering a Presentation | 701

6. Click the **Slide Orientation** button in the Page Setup group, then click **Landscape**. The slides return to their default landscape orientation.
7. **SAVE** the presentation as **Bid Final**.

   PAUSE. LEAVE the presentation open to use in the next exercise.

Orientation refers to the direction material appears on a page when printed. A page printed in *landscape orientation* is wider than it is tall, like a landscape picture that shows a broad panorama view. A page printed in *portrait orientation* is taller than it is wide, like a portrait picture that focuses on a single upright figure.

Landscape orientation is the default choice for displaying and printing slides. You may want to change the orientation of a presentation for a special case; for instance, if you need to accommodate large graphics that have a portrait orientation or if you want to print slides at the same orientation as other materials.

You cannot mix landscape and portrait orientations in a single presentation, the way you can in a word processing document. All slides in a presentation must have the same orientation. However, if you need to display one or more slides in a different orientation, you can create a secondary presentation with the different orientation and then provide links between the main presentation and the secondary one. You can easily click the link during the slide show to jump to the secondary presentation and then click another link to return to your main presentation.

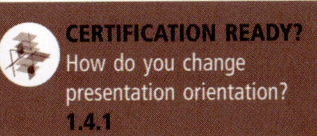

CERTIFICATION READY?
How do you change presentation orientation?
1.4.1

Presentation materials such as notes pages and handouts print in portrait orientation by default, because this orientation allows the most efficient placement of slide images and text on the page. Adjusting orientation for these materials allows you to fit more information across the longest axis of the page, a plus if you have a great many notes for each slide.

Setting Slide Size

Slides have a default size that you can change if you need to accommodate a particular kind of projection system or output. Use the Page Setup dialog box to adjust slide size.

➔ SET SLIDE SIZES

USE the presentation that is still open from the previous exercise.

1. Click the **Page Setup** button in the Page Setup group on the Design tab. The Page Setup dialog box opens. Note the width and height measurements for the default slide size.
2. Click the **Slides sized for** drop-down arrow, then click **On-screen Show (16:9)**. The width and height measurements change to reflect the new slide size.
3. Click **OK**. The slides are now much wider than they are tall, as shown in Figure 7-3.

Figure 7-3

Slides display at their new size

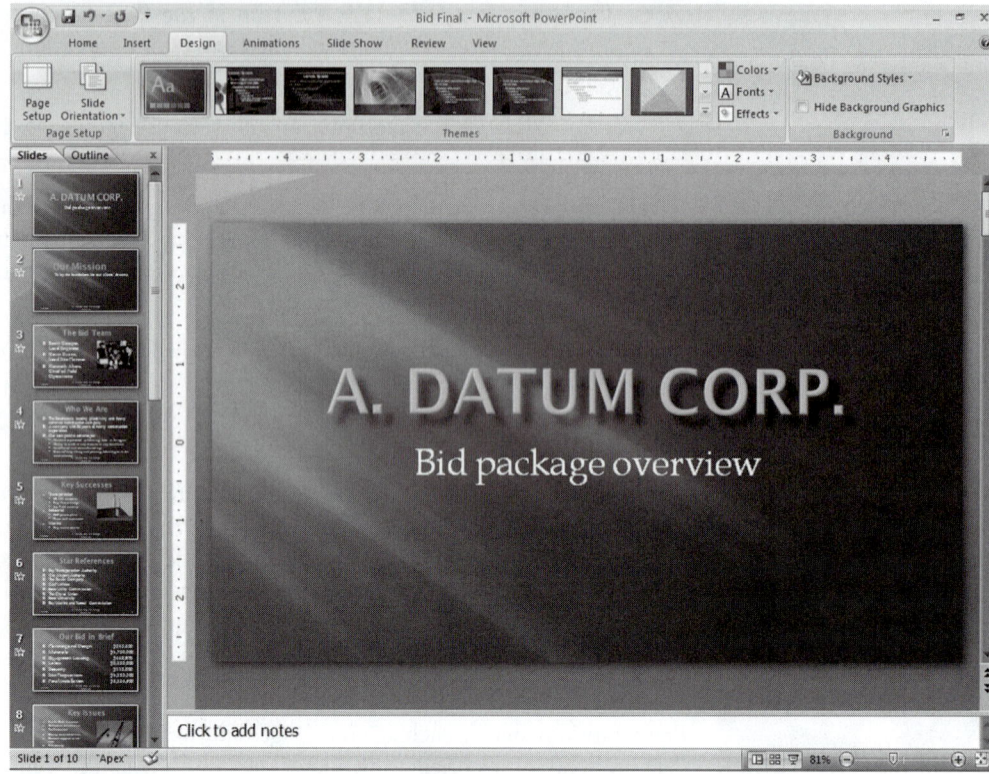

TAKE NOTE

The 16:9 option is an aspect ratio that is used for wide-screen monitors.

4. Click the **Page Setup** button again, click the **Slides sized for** drop-down arrow, then click **35mm Slides**.
5. Click **OK**. The slides are now the proper size to create slides that could be used in an old-style slide projector.
6. Click the **Page Setup** button again, click the **Slides sized for** drop-down arrow, then click **On-screen Show (4:3)**.
7. Click **OK**. The slides are now the default size again.
8. **SAVE** the presentation.

   PAUSE. LEAVE the presentation open to use in the next exercise.

Slides are sized by default at a 4:3 aspect ratio that allows them to be shown on a standard monitor without distortion. The *Slides sized for* drop-down list lets you choose from a number of other standard size options, including different screen aspect ratios, standard U.S. and European letter paper sizes, 35mm slides, overheads, and banners. Slide sizes apply to all slides in a presentation, not just the currently selected slide.

If you do not find a suitable size for a specific need, you can create a custom slide size. Adjust the width and height as desired in the Page Setup dialog box to create the custom slide size.

Besides allowing you to set slide size and orientation, the Page Setup dialog box lets you choose the starting number for slides in a presentation. This is useful if you are combining several separate presentations in one comprehensive slide show.

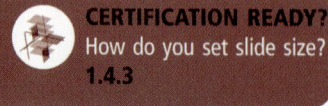

CERTIFICATION READY?
How do you set slide size?
1.4.3

Customizing Audience Handouts

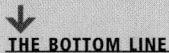

THE BOTTOM LINE

You can help your audience follow a presentation by giving them handouts, which show small versions of the slides arranged in various ways on a page. Handout layouts are controlled by a handout master, as slide appearance is controlled by the slide master. You can customize the handout master to create your own handout layout.

➔ CREATE A CUSTOMIZED HANDOUT MASTER

USE the presentation that is still open from the previous exercise.

1. Click the **Insert** tab, click **Header & Footer**, and click the **Notes and Handouts** tab.
2. Set up headers and footers as follows:
   a. Click in the **Date and time** check box, and make sure the Update automatically option is selected.
   b. Click the **Header** check box, and key the header **A. Datum Corporation**.
   c. Click the **Footer** check box, and key the footer **No Job Is Too Big for A. Datum**.
   d. Click **Apply to All**.
3. Click the **View** tab, and then click the **Handout Master** button in the Presentation Views group. Handout Master view opens as shown in Figure 7-4, with the header and footer you supplied in step 2.

Figure 7-4

Handout Master view

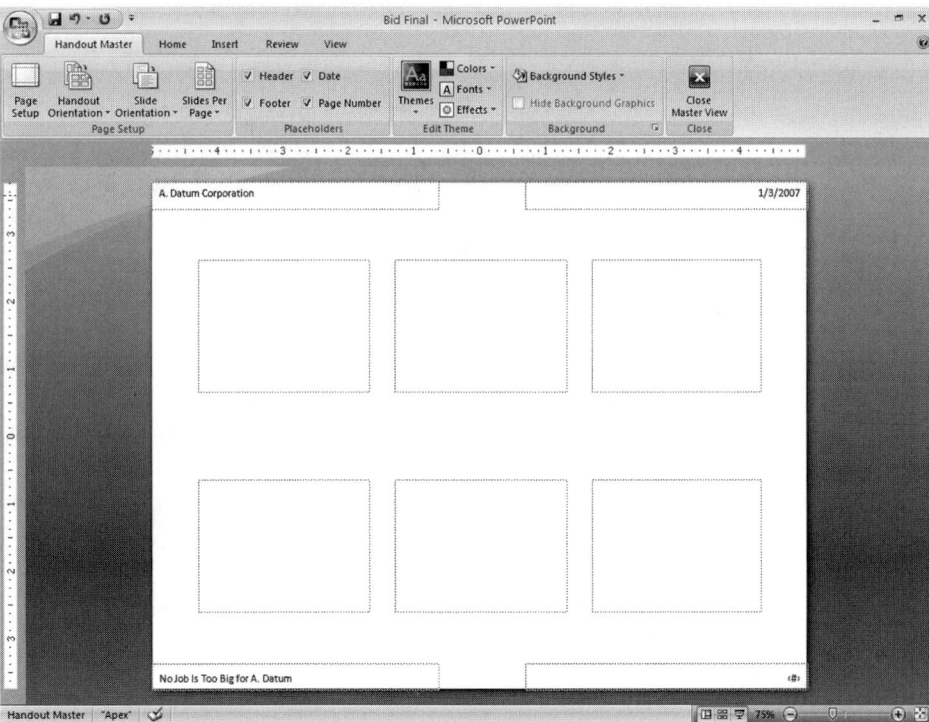

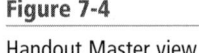

TAKE NOTE

The master displays in landscape orientation because you changed the orientation in a previous exercise.

4. Click the **Slides Per Page** button in the Page Setup group, then click **3 Slides**. The handout master displays the layout used to show three slides across the width of the page.

5. Click the **Insert** tab, click **Text Box**, and draw a text box above the center slide placeholder, the same width as the placeholder, as shown in Figure 7-5.

Figure 7-5

Add a text box to the handout placeholder

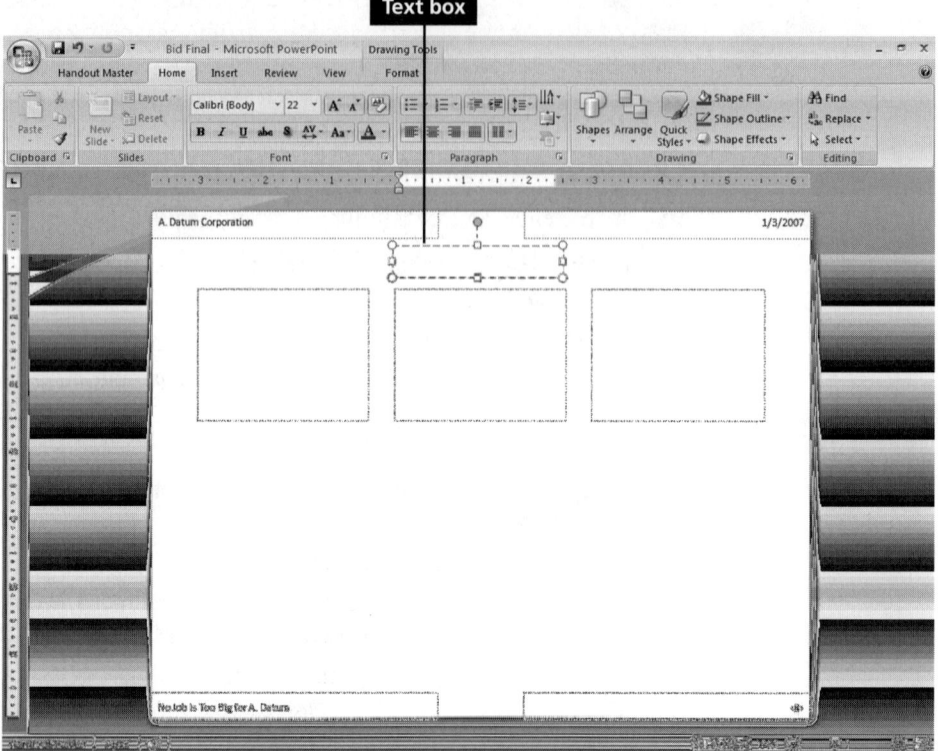

6. Key **Center City Bridge Project** in the text box.
7. Change the font size of the text box text to **18** if necessary, apply bold formatting, change the color to **Dark Blue, Text 2**, and center the text. Adjust the size of the text box as necessary to display the text on one line.
8. Click the outside border of the header placeholder in the upper-left corner of the master, hold down **Shift**, and click the date, footer, and page number placeholders.
9. Change the font size to **14**, apply bold formatting, and change the color to **Dark Blue, Text 2**.
10. Click the **Handout Master** tab, and then click the **Close Master View** button to exit Handout Master view.
11. Click the **Microsoft Office Button**, point to **Print**, and click **Print Preview**. In the Print What list, click **Handouts (3 Slides Per Page)**. Your customized handout master should resemble Figure 7-6.

Figure 7-6

Preview of the customized handout

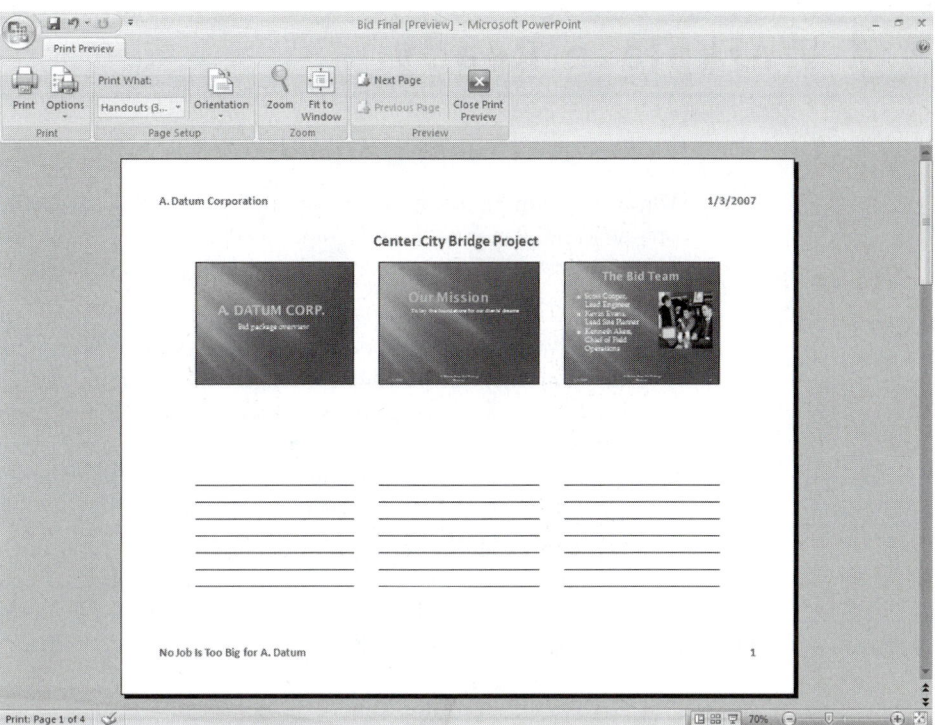

12. Click the **Next Page** button to see that the text box you added displays on each page of the handouts.
13. Click the **Print** button on the Print Preview tab to print the handouts.
14. Click the **Close Print Preview** button to return to Normal view.
15. **SAVE** the presentation.

    PAUSE. LEAVE the presentation open to use in the next exercise.

You can create handouts that show one, two, three, four, six, or nine slides on a page. If you make changes to any of these layouts, the changes are reflected on all other layouts. For example, the text box you added to the 3 Slides layout in the previous exercise also appears on the 1 Slide and 9 Slides layouts.

You cannot adjust the position or size of the slide placeholders in the handout master. You can, however, adjust both size and position of the Header, Date, Footer, and Page Number placeholders. You can also choose to hide some or all of these placeholders by deselecting their check boxes in the Placeholders group on the Handout Master tab.

The Handout Master tab allows you to change both slide orientation and handout orientation, using buttons in the Page Setup group. To further modify appearance of handouts, you can change theme colors and fonts (but not the current theme) and apply a different background style. You can format the Header, Date, Footer, and Page Number placeholders like any text box or placeholder using Quick Styles, fills, or outlines.

Note that you can also customize the Notes Page master in many of the same ways that you customize the handout master. Click the Notes Master button on the View tab to display the Notes Master tab. The Notes master allows you to adjust the size and position of the slide image as well as other placeholders on the page.

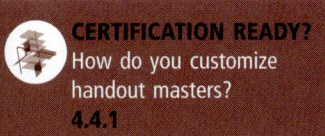

CERTIFICATION READY?
How do you customize handout masters?
4.4.1

✷ Workplace Ready

Ways to Present Slides

You have a number of options for projecting your slides when you are ready to give a presentation. The most popular options include projecting slides on a screen and displaying the slides on a computer monitor. You can also use new technology such as interactive whiteboards.

- **Projection options:** Slide projectors used to be noisy machines that shone bright light through 35mm slides to project the image on a screen. These projectors are still available, as is the technology to create 35mm slides from your PowerPoint files, but the most current projectors are digital devices that accept input from a computer. You can control the slide show from your computer monitor. When you use a digital projector, you project slides onto a screen.

- **Displaying slides on a computer monitor:** You do not need a projection device to present slides. You can display your presentation on a computer monitor, just as you do when using Slide Show view in PowerPoint. The computer monitor should be large enough for your audience to see the slide material clearly. Many computers allow you to connect more than one monitor to the video card, allowing you to use PowerPoint's Presenter view to control the slide show: The audience views the presentation on one monitor, while you use the other monitor to control the show.

- **Self-running or individual presentations:** You can also set up a presentation to run by itself on a monitor (see the *Setting Up the Slide Show* section later in this lesson), allow individuals to view a presentation on their own computers, or broadcast a presentation to viewers over the Internet.

- **Using an interactive whiteboard:** Interactive whiteboards allow you to project or display a presentation (or any other computer application) on a large white surface. The moderator can control slide display by simply touching the screen.

For best results in presenting slide shows from your computer, you should have a high-quality video card, sound card, and speakers. Quality sound and video components will make the most of multimedia files such as sounds and movies and allow transitions and animations to run smoothly.

If you do not have access to current technology, you can fall back on more traditional methods of presenting slides: You can submit PowerPoint files to photographic sources to prepare 35mm slides that can be used in standard slide projectors. You can also print slides onto clear film to create transparencies that can be used with overhead projectors.

■ Choosing Slides to Display

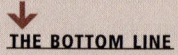
THE BOTTOM LINE

You may want to present only a portion of the slides you have prepared on a specific subject. You can select the slides to display by hiding slides or by creating a custom slide show.

Omitting Selected Slides from a Presentation

You can omit slides from a presentation by hiding them. Use the Hide Slide button or command to hide a slide so it won't appear during the presentation.

Delivering a Presentation | 707

→ OMIT A SLIDE FROM A PRESENTATION

USE the presentation that is still open from the previous exercise.

1. Go to slide 2, then click the **Slide Show** tab.
2. Click the **Hide Slide** button in the Set Up group. The slide is shaded on the Slides tab, as shown in Figure 7-7, and the slide number is surrounded by a box with a diagonal bar across it.

Figure 7-7

A hidden slide is shaded in the Slides tab

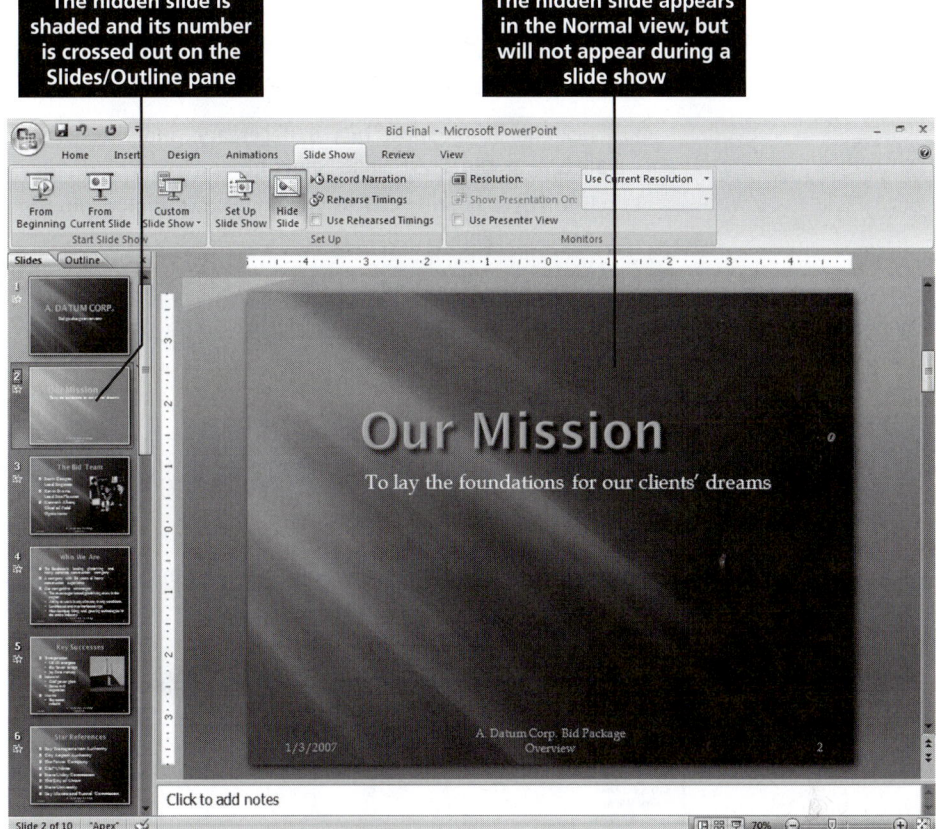

3. Press F5 to start the presentation from slide 1.
4. Click the mouse button and notice that slide 2, *Our Mission*, does not display—you go directly to slide 3, *The Bid Team*.

 Right-click a slide in the Slides tab or in Slide Sorter view, and click Hide Slide on the shortcut menu.

5. Press Esc to stop the slide show.

PAUSE. LEAVE the presentation open to use in the next exercise.

When you hide a slide, you can still see it in Normal view and Slide Sorter view. It is hidden only in Slide Show view, when you present the slides. You can unhide a slide using the same procedure you used to hide it.

 Another way to omit slides from a presentation is to set a range of slides to show in the Set Up Show dialog box, covered later in this lesson.

708 | Lesson 7

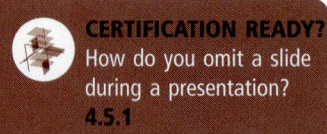

CERTIFICATION READY?
How do you omit a slide during a presentation?
4.5.1

If you find that you want to display a hidden slide during the presentation, you can show it using PowerPoint's presentation tools. You will learn more about controlling a presentation with these tools later in this lesson.

Creating a Custom Show

A comprehensive presentation may contain a number of slides that you can group to show to different audiences. You can create custom shows to organize groups of slides from a single presentation.

→ CREATE A CUSTOM SHOW

USE the presentation that is still open from the previous exercise.

1. Click the **Slide Show** tab, if necessary, and then click the **Custom Slide Show** button in the Start Slide Show group.
2. Click **Custom Shows**. The Custom Shows dialog box opens, as shown in Figure 7-8.

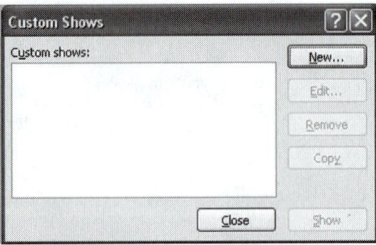

Figure 7-8

Custom Shows dialog box

3. Click the **New** button. The Define Custom Show dialog box opens, as shown in Figure 7-9.

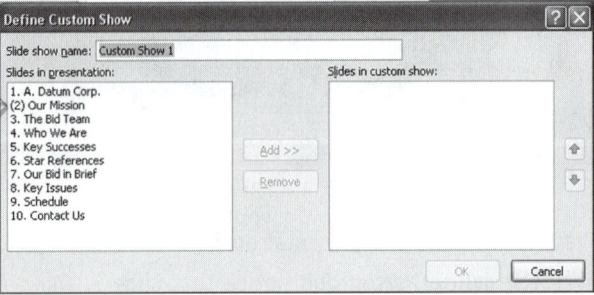

Figure 7-9

Define Custom Show dialog box

TAKE NOTE

The parentheses around slide 2's number indicate it is a hidden slide.

4. In the **Slide show name** box, key **Corporate Information**.
5. Click slide 2 in the *Slides in presentation* list, then click the **Add** button to place this slide in the *Slides in custom show* list.
6. Add slides 4, 5, and 6 to the custom show list. Your dialog box should look like Figure 7-10.

Figure 7-10

Four slides have been added to the custom show

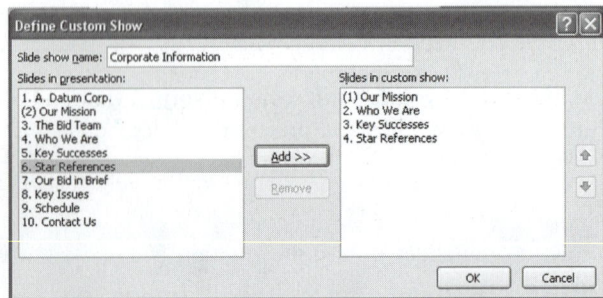

Delivering a Presentation | 709

> **ANOTHER WAY**
>
> You can quickly select more than one slide to add by clicking a slide in the list, holding down Shift, and then clicking additional slides.

   7. Click **OK**, then click **Show**. The custom show starts with the second slide you added (the first slide, slide 2, is still hidden).
   8. Click the mouse button to proceed through the slides of the custom show until the show ends.
   9. **SAVE** the presentation.

   PAUSE. LEAVE the presentation open to use in the next exercise.

Create *custom shows* to customize presentations for different groups using slides from a single presentation. A comprehensive year-end corporate review presentation, for example, might include information on the company as a whole as well as on the operations of each department. You could show all of the slides to the board of directors and use custom shows to present to each department the general company statistics and the information specific to that department. Custom shows allow you to focus attention on the material most relevant to a specific audience.

You select the slides for a custom show in the Define Custom Show dialog box. Add slide titles from the main presentation to the custom presentation. You can adjust the order in which the slides display in the custom show: Use the up and down arrows to the right of the *Slides in custom show* list to move a selected title up or down in the list.

> **TAKE NOTE**
>
> When you add slides to the *Slides in custom show* list, they are renumbered in the list, but the slide numbers on the slides do not change.

After you create a custom show, its name appears in the Custom Slide Show drop-down list, as well as in the Custom Shows dialog box. You can run the custom show from either list. You can also select the custom show in the Custom Shows dialog box and choose to edit the show, remove it, or copy it.

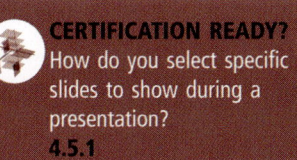

CERTIFICATION READY?
How do you select specific slides to show during a presentation?
4.5.1

You can create any number of custom shows in a presentation. When you set up a presentation for showing, you can specify that only the custom show slides will be presented. You can also choose to run the show while you are in Slide Show view.

■ Rehearsing Your Delivery

> **THE BOTTOM LINE**
>
> To make sure that your audience will have enough time to read and absorb the content on your slides, you can rehearse your delivery. After you rehearse, you have the option of saving your timings to use during your presentation.

➔ REHEARSE THE TIMING OF A PRESENTATION

USE the presentation that is still open from the previous exercise.

   1. Click the **Rehearse Timings** button in the Set Up group on the Slide Show tab. The slide show starts from slide 1 and the Rehearsal toolbar appears in the upper-left corner of the screen, as shown in Figure 7-11.   Q.3

Figure 7-11

The Rehearsal toolbar appears in Slide Show view

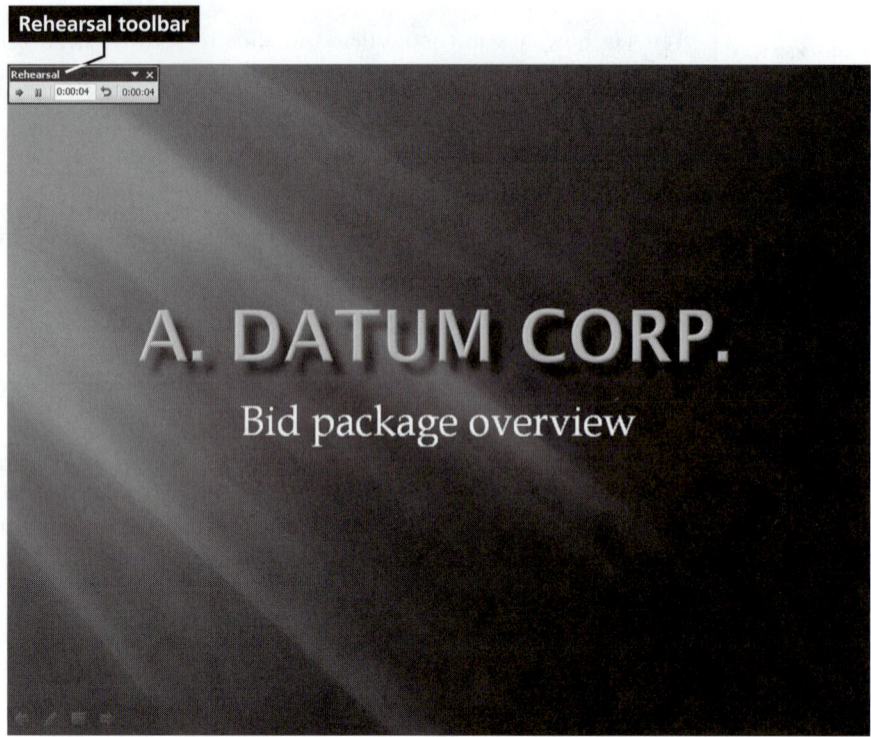

2. Read all the content on each slide, clicking the mouse button to display bullet items and advance slides.

3. When asked if you want to save the slide timings, click **Yes**. The presentation appears in Slide Sorter view, with the timing for each slide displayed below it, as shown in Figure 7-12.

Figure 7-12

Slide timings appear beneath each slide

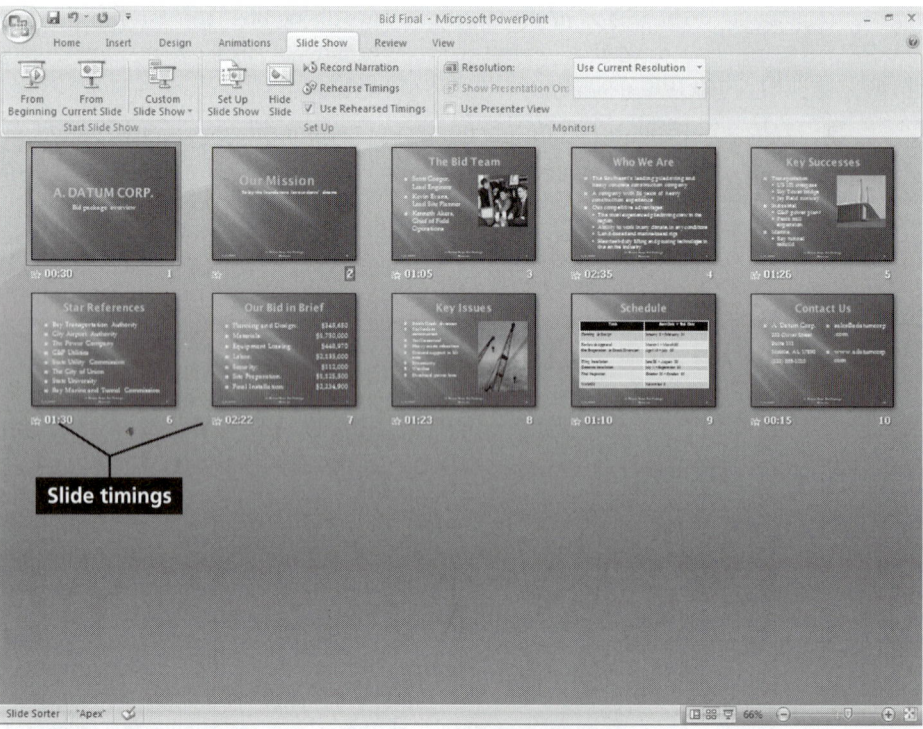

4. Press F5 to start the slide show again from slide 1. This time, let PowerPoint control the slides according to the rehearsal times you set.

Delivering a Presentation | 711

5. After three or four slides have displayed, press **Esc** to end the slide show. Switch to Normal view.
6. **SAVE** the presentation.

   PAUSE. LEAVE the presentation open to use in the next exercise.

When you rehearse a presentation, you read it just as if you were a member of the audience viewing the slides for the first time. Look at pictures, charts, and diagrams to read any information they supply.

Slide timings are particularly important if you intend to show the slides as a self-running presentation that viewers cannot control. You should allow plenty of time for viewers to read and understand the content on each slide. (You will learn more about self-running presentations in the next section.)

The Rehearsal toolbar that displays when you rehearse slides shows you how much time you have spent reading the current slide as well as the elapsed time for the entire presentation. You can pause the rehearsal if necessary, then resume it when you are ready to continue. You can also choose to start the time again for a particular slide.

Note that saving your rehearsed times applies timings to the slide that allow PowerPoint to control the slides for you. The presentation can run automatically without your having to click buttons to advance slides. If you have applied animations to slide objects, rehearsing will set the proper timing for those objects to display.

You do not have to save the slide timings after rehearsal if you do not want PowerPoint to control the slides for you. You can tell PowerPoint not to save the timings, or you can deselect Use Rehearsed Timings in the Set Up group on the Slide Show tab to remove slide timings.

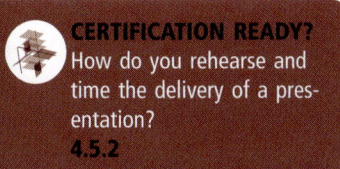

CERTIFICATION READY?
How do you rehearse and time the delivery of a presentation?
4.5.2

■ SOFTWARE ORIENTATION

The Set Up Show Dialog Box

When you are doing the final setup for a presentation, you have a number of decisions to make. The Set Up Show dialog box, shown in Figure 7-13, allows you to specify settings for any kind of show.

Figure 7-13

Set Up Show dialog box

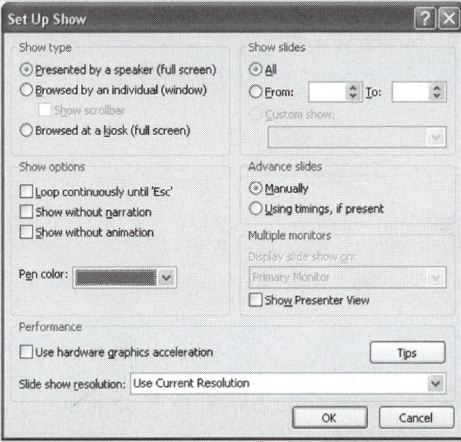

You can specify options such as how the presentation will be shown, what slides or custom show to present, how to advance slides, and whether to use more than one monitor. Choosing options in this dialog box is one of the last chores you'll complete before giving your presentation.

Setting Up a Slide Show

THE BOTTOM LINE

You will probably decide how to present your slides early in the process of creating the slide show. Use the Set Up Show dialog box to choose the final settings for the presentation type you have selected.

→ SET UP A SLIDE SHOW

USE the presentation that is still open from the previous exercise. Your boss has asked you to save a version of the presentation that can run unattended at a construction industry trade show.

1. **SAVE** the presentation as *Datum Custom*.
2. Adjust the slides for their new use as follows:
   a. Right-click slide 2 in the Slides pane, and then click **Hide Slide**. The slide is no longer hidden in this version of the presentation.
   b. Slide 2 does not have a timing because it was hidden when you rehearsed the other slides. Click the **Animations** tab, and then click the **Automatically After** up arrow four times to set 4 seconds as the timing for the slide.
   c. Click the **Insert** tab, click **Header & Footer**, and change the footer text to **A. Datum Corporation**. Click **Apply to All**.
3. Click the **Slide Show** tab, then click the **Set Up Slide Show** button in the Set Up group. The Set Up Show dialog box opens.
4. Click **Browsed at a kiosk (full screen)** in the Show type area. The *Loop continuously until 'Esc'* option is automatically selected and grayed out.
5. Click **Custom show** in the Show slides area. Your dialog box should look like the one in Figure 7-14.

Figure 7-14

Presentation is set up to run automatically

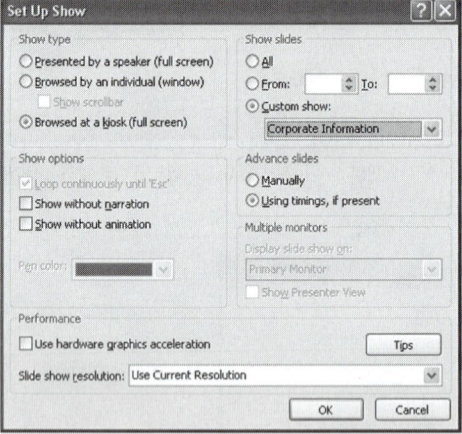

TAKE NOTE

The Corporate Information custom show is automatically selected because it is the only custom show in the presentation.

6. Click **OK**.
7. Press **F5** to start the presentation. Note that it starts with the first slide of your custom show, *Our Mission*.
8. Let the presentation run through all slides in the custom show until it displays the second slide (*Who We Are*) for the second time, then press **Esc**.
9. **SAVE** the presentation and then **CLOSE** the file.

   PAUSE. LEAVE PowerPoint running to use in the next exercise.

Delivering a Presentation | 713

The Set Up Show dialog box allows you to make a number of decisions about how slides display during a presentation. The first and most important decision to make is how the slides will be presented. The Show type area in the dialog box lists three show types that are most commonly used when presenting slides:

- **Presented by a speaker (full screen)** is the option to choose if the slides will be presented by a moderator (you or some other person) to a live audience. The slides will display at full screen size.
- **Browsed by an individual (window)** is the option to choose if you are preparing the presentation for a viewer to review on his or her own computer. The slides display within a window that contains a title bar with size/close controls. You can choose to also display a scrollbar to make it easy for the individual to scroll through the slides.
- **Browsed at a kiosk (full screen)** is the option to choose if you intend to have the presentation run unattended, with no moderator. This option is a standard choice for trade shows or other venues where the slides can loop indefinitely for viewers to watch as long as they desire.

The Show slides area of the dialog box allows you to specify a range of slides to show, or choose a custom show to limit the amount of information presented. You would most likely use these options if you are setting up a show to be browsed by an individual or at a kiosk.

If your slides have timings, you can specify that the show loop continuously until you press the Esc key (as you did in the previous exercise). This option is selected automatically if you choose to have slides browsed at a kiosk. If you have recorded narration for your slides or applied animations, you can choose whether to use those features in your final presentation.

 If you have a microphone attached to your computer, you can click the Record Narration button on the Slide Show tab and add voice narration to your slides.

If you have rehearsed a presentation to set slide timings, PowerPoint will select the *Using timings, if present* option by default. You can override this setting by selecting *Manually* if you want to control the slides and slide content yourself.

The Multiple monitors area of the dialog box provides support if you can attach more than one monitor to your computer. You can select which of your two monitors will display the slide show, and you can turn on Presenter view to help you control the presentation.

If you intend to make annotations on the slides, you can choose the color of the pen you will use to write with. You learn more about annotating in the next section.

CERTIFICATION READY?
How do you set slide show options?
4.5.5

The Set Up Show dialog box also allows you to control your system's performance. To increase the rate at which your screen displays slides, click *Use hardware graphics acceleration*. To improve graphic appearance, you can choose a higher resolution for the show, but be aware that the higher the resolution, the slower your system is likely to run.

■ Working with Presentation Tools

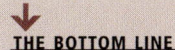 PowerPoint offers a number of tools you can use during a presentation to control the display of slides and mark directly on the slides if desired. You can use keyboard commands, mouse clicks, presentation tools, or menu commands to control the presentation. You can select from several marking options and colors to annotate your slides during the presentation.

USE PRESENTATION TOOLS

TAKE NOTE

You can find the file listed near the top of the Office menu's Recent Documents list.

1. **OPEN** the *Bid Final* presentation you worked with earlier in this lesson.
2. Click the **Slide Show** tab, and then click **Use Rehearsed Timings** to turn off slide timings so you can work more easily with presentation tools.
3. Click the **From Beginning** button in the Start Slide Show group on the Slide Show tab to start the presentation from slide 1. Move the pointer on the slide until you can see the presentation tools in the lower-left corner of the screen, as shown in Figure 7-15.

Figure 7-15

The presentation tools appear in the lower-left corner of each slide

4. Click the **Next** button (the right-pointing arrow at the far right of the tools). The next slide displays.
5. Click the **Previous** button (the left-pointing arrow at the far left of the tools).
6. Right-click anywhere on the slide to display the presentation shortcut menu, point to **Go to Slide**, and then click the hidden slide, **(2) Our Mission**, as shown in Figure 7-16. The hidden slide displays.

Figure 7-16

Displaying a hidden slide during a slide show

Delivering a Presentation | 715

ANOTHER WAY
To go to the next slide if it is hidden, press H.

7. Press **Page Down** to display the next slide.
8. Click the **Menu** button in the presentation tools (the second button from the right) to display a menu similar to the presentation shortcut menu, and then click **Last Viewed**. The slide you previously viewed (slide 2) displays.
9. Right-click the screen again, then click **End Show** on the presentation shortcut menu to end the presentation.

   PAUSE. LEAVE the presentation open to use in the next exercise.

PowerPoint allows you to use the tools that are most comfortable for you to go forward, backward, or to a specific slide. Table 7-1 summarizes the most popular navigation options in Slide Show view.

Table 7-1

Navigation options in Slide Show view

Action	Keyboard	Mouse	Shortcut Menu
Show the next slide or animation	N Enter Spacebar ✓ Page Down ✓ → ↓	left button	Next Advance
Show the previous slide or animation	P Page Up Backspace ← ↑		Previous Reverse
Go to last slide viewed			Last Viewed
Go to specific slide	Type slide number, press Enter		Go to Slide, select slide number
End show	Esc		End Show

TAKE NOTE
Consult PowerPoint's Help files to find many more keyboard shortcuts for controlling a presentation.

If you have chosen the *Browsed by an individual (window)* show type, the presentation tools at the lower-left corner of the screen do not display and you cannot use the mouse button to go to the next slide. You can use the keyboard options to go to the next or previous slide, or you can use the Next Slide and Previous Slide buttons on the scrollbar if you have chosen to display it. You can also right-click the slide and select Advance to move forward or Reverse to move backward through slides.

As you work with PowerPoint, you will find that you develop a feel for the navigation tools that you find easiest. It is often more efficient, for example, to use keyboard options because they can be quicker than right-clicking and then selecting an option from a shortcut menu.

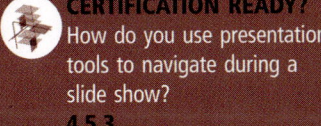
CERTIFICATION READY?
How do you use presentation tools to navigate during a slide show?
4.5.3

716 | Lesson 7

→ ANNOTATE SLIDES WITH THE PEN

USE the presentation that is still open from the previous exercise.

1. Press **F5** to start the presentation from slide 1, key **7**, and press **Enter**. Click the mouse button until all seven bullet items display on the slide.
2. Right-click the slide, point to **Pointer Options**, and click **Felt Tip Pen**. The pointer changes to a small, round, red pen pointer.
3. Right-click the slide, point to **Pointer Options**, and click **Ink Color**. Then click **Orange** in the Standard Colors palette.
4. Use the pen pointer to circle the value for labor, $2,135,000, as shown in Figure 7-17.

> **TROUBLESHOOTING**
>
> If you click too many times and advance to slide 8, press Page Up to return to slide 7.

Figure 7-17

Making an annotation on a slide

![Our Bid in Brief slide showing Planning and Design: $345,650; Materials: $1,750,000; Equipment Leasing: $448,970; Labor: $2,135,000 (circled); Security: $112,000; Site Preparation: $1,125,500; Final Installation: $2,234,900]

5. Click the **Menu** button in the presentation tools, point to **Screen**, and click **Black Screen**. The screen is blacked out so you can annotate without the distraction of the slide material.
6. Use the pen pointer to draw a large U. S. currency symbol, $, in the middle of the slide.
7. Right-click the slide, point to **Screen**, and click **Unblack Screen**. The slide background is restored and the annotation disappears.
8. Click the **Pointer Options** button in the presentation tools (the second tool from the left) and click **Arrow**. The arrow pointer is restored.
9. Press → to go to slide 8.
10. Press the spacebar eight times to display all eight bullet items.
11. Click the **Pointer Options** button in the presentation tools, then click **Highlighter**. Drag the highlighter pointer across the *Weather* bullet item to highlight it, as shown in Figure 7-18.

> **TAKE NOTE**
>
> While a pen pointer is active, you cannot use the mouse button to advance slides.

> **ANOTHER WAY**
>
> Press **Esc** to restore the arrow pointer.

Figure 7-18

Highlighting text on a slide

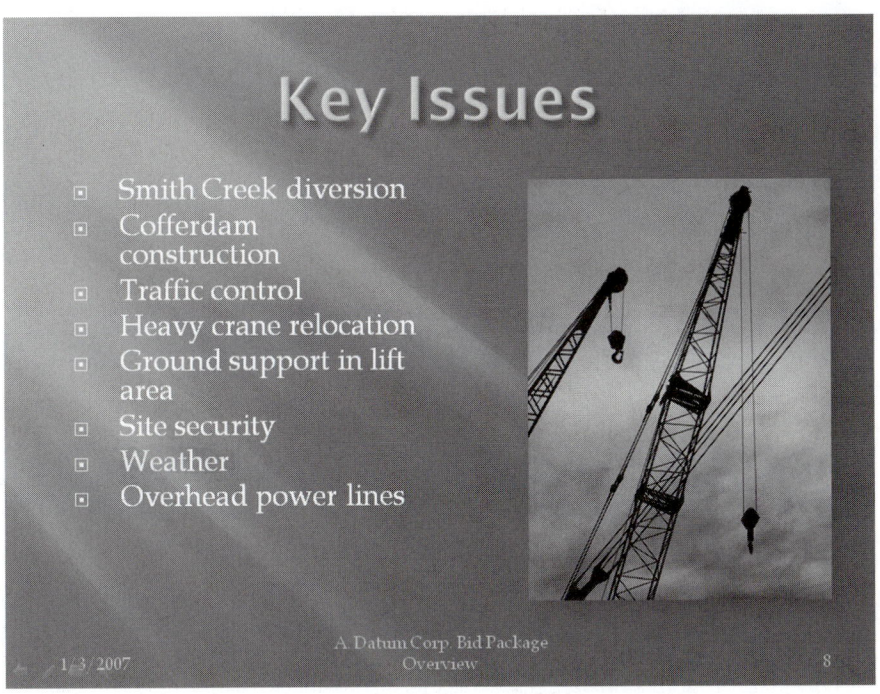

12. Click the **Pointer Options** button, then click **Erase All Ink on Slide**. The highlight you added is removed.

13. End the slide show. When asked if you want to keep your annotations, click **Discard**.

14. **SAVE** the presentation.

PAUSE. LEAVE the presentation open to use in the next exercise.

ANOTHER WAY

Press E to remove all annotations on a slide.

You can *annotate* slides by drawing or writing with the pointer to draw attention to text or other content on the slide. PowerPoint offers three different annotation pen options: Ball Point Pen, Felt Tip Pen, and Highlighter. These pen options have pointer sizes roughly corresponding to the actual writing instruments. You can change the ink color for any of the pen options.

You can erase any annotation you add to a slide. To remove a single annotation out of several on a slide, click the Eraser option on the Pointer Options submenu and then use the eraser pointer to click the annotation you want to remove. To remove all annotations on a slide, use the Erase All Ink on Slide command.

The Black Screen and White Screen options allow you to replace the current slide with a black or white screen that you can use for annotations or to cover the current material if you want to keep it under wraps while you are discussing some other issue.

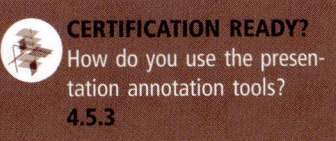

CERTIFICATION READY?

How do you use the presentation annotation tools?

4.5.3

If you choose to keep your annotations after ending the slide show, they display as shapes on the slides in Normal view. You can click any annotation in Normal view and press Delete to remove the annotation.

Packaging a Presentation for Delivery

THE BOTTOM LINE

You may need to transport your presentation materials to another computer to run your slide show. The Package for CD feature streamlines the process of packing up all the materials you need to show the presentation even if PowerPoint is not installed on the other computer.

PACKAGE A PRESENTATION FOR DELIVERY

USE the presentation that is still open from the previous exercise.

1. Click the **Slide Show** tab, if necessary, and then click **Use Rehearsed Timings** to restore the timings you set in a previous exercise.
2. Click the **Microsoft Office Button**, point to **Publish**, and click **Package for CD**.
3. Click **OK** when alerted that some files will be updated for use with the PowerPoint Viewer. The Package for CD dialog box opens, as shown in Figure 7-19.

Figure 7-19

Package for CD dialog box

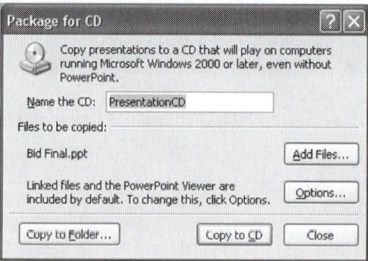

4. Delete the default CD name in the Name the CD text box, then key **Center City Bid**.
5. Click the **Options** button, and then click in the **Embedded TrueType fonts** check box to select the option.
6. Click **OK**.

   If you have the capability to save data on a CD, go to the next step. If you cannot write to a CD, go to step 8.

7. Create the CD package as follows:
   a. Click the **Copy to CD** button.
   b. Click **Yes** when asked if you want to link files. The Copying Files to CD message box shows the progress of the copy. When the copying is complete, the CD drive will open.
   c. When asked if you want to copy the files to another CD, click **No**.
   d. Click **Close**.
8. Copy the package to a folder on your system as follows:
   a. Click the **Copy to Folder** button. The Copy to Folder dialog box opens, as shown in Figure 7-20.

Figure 7-20

Copy to Folder dialog box

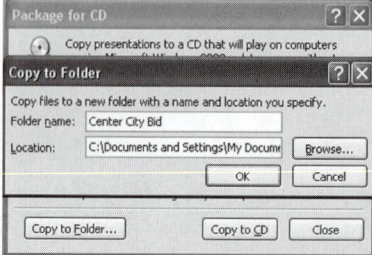

Delivering a Presentation | 719

    b. Click the **Browse** button. The Choose Location dialog box opens.

    c. Navigate to the folder in which you are storing your Lesson 10 solutions, and then click **Select**.

    d. Click **OK** and then click **Yes** when asked if you want to link files. The Copying Files to Folder dialog box shows the progress of the copy.

    e. Click **Close**.

9. Using a program such as My Computer, navigate to the CD or the folder where you stored your presentation.

10. Start the packaged presentation by clicking on the CD or by opening the Center City Bid folder on your system, double-clicking the **PPTVIEW.EXE** file, selecting **Bid Final**, and clicking **Open**. The presentation starts in Slide Show view.

11. End the show after several slides and close the PowerPoint Viewer.

12. **SAVE** the presentation and then **CLOSE** the file.

    CLOSE PowerPoint.

The Package for CD feature makes short work of packing up all the files you need to show your slides, no matter what kind of system you have to use to run the show. If the system you intend to use does not have PowerPoint, you can use the PowerPoint Viewer to run the presentation.

To make the process of storing files on a CD more efficient, you can choose to copy more than one presentation to the same CD. Click the Add Files button to open additional presentations. This feature can reduce the amount of wasted space that results if you copy a single presentation to a CD.

The Options dialog box that you can access from the Package for CD dialog box gives you additional choices for the packaging process.

- You can choose to create a Viewer Package, in which formats are updated to work with the PowerPoint Viewer, or an Archive Package in which your existing file formats are preserved. If you know the computer on which you intend to show the presentation has PowerPoint, select Archive Package to save file space on your CD.

- Use the *Select how presentations will play in the viewer* drop-down list to choose how to play presentations if you have more than one stored on a single CD. You can play presentations in order, play the first presentation automatically, allow the user to choose which presentation to play, or turn off the option that plays the CD automatically when you click it.

- Linked files, such as large movie and sound files, are included automatically, and you will normally want to retain this setting. You can, however, save the package without linked files if desired by deselecting this option.

- Embedding TrueType fonts is a good idea if you are not sure what fonts you might have access to on the system where you will run the presentation. Embedding fonts will add to file size but ensure the quality of your presentation's font appearance.

- You can specify a password to open or modify the presentation, and you can prompt PowerPoint to inspect the presentation for hidden or personal data you do not want to share.

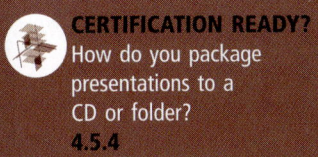

CERTIFICATION READY?
How do you package presentations to a CD or folder?
4.5.4

Besides using Package for CD to create materials to transport for a presentation, you can use this feature to archive presentations onto a CD or into folders for storage. The packaging process pulls together all the files you need for a presentation, so your stored presentation provides an excellent long-term backup for your work.

TAKE NOTE

Package for CD works only with CD formats. If you want to store a presentation on a DVD, you can save materials in a folder as in step 8 of the previous exercise and then use your system's DVD burning tools to copy the files to the DVD.

720 | Lesson 7

SUMMARY SKILL MATRIX

IN THIS LESSON YOU LEARNED HOW TO:
Select Slide Orientation
Set Slide Size
Customize Audience Handouts
Omit Selected Slides from a Presentation
Create a Custom Show
Set Up a Slide Show
Work with Presentation Tools
Package a Presentation for Delivery

■ Knowledge Assessment

Fill in the Blank

Fill in each blank with the term or phrase that best completes the statement.

P701 — 1. Use the __Page setup__ dialog box to adjust slide size.

P711 — 2. You can set up a presentation to run continuously until you press the __Esc__ key.

P709 — 3. Use the __Rehearsal__ toolbar to view timings as you rehearse a presentation.

4. __Orientation__ refers to the way information displays on a printed page.

5. To display a hidden slide during a presentation, click __Go To Slide__ on the shortcut menu and then click the hidden slide.

6. If the computer on which you will present your slides does not have PowerPoint, you can use the __PowerPoint viewer__ to show the presentation.

P703 — 7. Customize the __Handout Master__ to create your own handout layouts.

8. If you want to show your presentation on a screen, you can use a(n) __digital projector__ that accepts input from your computer.

9. When you __annotate__ slides, you use the pointer to draw or write.

10. Create a(n) __Custom show__ to organize several slides within a presentation into a group that can be shown separately.

Multiple Choice

Circle the correct answer.

1. A slide that is wider than it is tall is displayed in
   a. portrait orientation
   b. 4:3 orientation
   c. picture orientation
   d. landscape orientation

2. Which of the following is not a standard handout layout?
   a. 1 Slide
   b. 4 Slides
   c. 8 Slides
   d. 9 Slides

3. If you need to show slides on a wide-screen monitor, you might change their size to
   a. On-screen Show (16:9)
   b. On-screen Show (3:4)
   c. 35mm Slides
   d. Ledger Paper (11 × 17 in)

4. To prevent a slide from displaying during a presentation, select it and then choose
   a. Delete Slide
   b. Hide Slide
   c. Show/Hide Slide
   d. Conceal Slide

5. If you want to show only a selected series of slides from a presentation, the most efficient option is to
   a. hide each slide you do not want to use
   b. create an entirely new presentation and copy into it the slides you want to use
   c. create a custom show of the slides you want to show
   d. copy the presentation and then delete the slides you do not want to use

6. When you rehearse a presentation, you should
   a. skim over the content of each slide
   b. read the entire content of each slide and look carefully at pictures and diagrams
   c. allow yourself a set amount of time to view each slide regardless of its content
   d. look only at the slide titles

7. If you set up a slide show to be browsed by an individual, the slides display
   a. using the full screen
   b. in a virtual kiosk
   c. in a window with a title bar
   d. within the PowerPoint window

8. Which of the following is *not* a way to advance to the next slide during a presentation?
   a. press Home
   b. press the spacebar
   c. click the left mouse button
   d. press Page Down

9. A quick way to restore the arrow pointer after you have used it for drawing is to
   a. press End
   b. double-click the screen
   c. click the arrow pointer tool in the navigation tools
   d. press Esc

10. If you are not sure whether the computer you intend to use has PowerPoint, select the _____ option in the Package for CD Options dialog box.
    a. Archive Package
    b. Viewer Package
    c. Add Viewer
    d. Include Viewer

■ Competency Assessment

Project 7-1: Preparing to Fly

You are nearly ready to present the slide show for Blue Yonder Airlines. Use the tools you have learned about in this lesson to finalize the presentation and create handouts.

GET READY. Launch PowerPoint if it is not already running.

The *Airline* file is available on the companion CD-ROM.

1. **OPEN** the *Airline* presentation.
2. Click the **Design** tab, click the **Slide Orientation** button, and click **Landscape**.
3. Click the **Page Setup** button, click the **Slides sized for** drop-down arrow, and click **On-screen Show (4:3)**.
4. Click the **Slide Show** tab, then click the **Set Up Slide Show** button.
5. Choose the **Presented by a speaker** show type, deselect the **Loop continuously until 'Esc'** option, and choose to have slides advance **Manually**.
6. Click the **Insert** tab, click **Header & Footer**, and choose to display the date (update automatically), the header **Blue Yonder Airlines**, and page numbers for notes and handouts.
7. Click the **View** tab, then click **Handout Master** to open Handout Master view.
8. Center the header text and date in their placeholders, and right-align the page number in its placeholder. Close Handout Master view.
9. Hide the last slide in the presentation.
10. Click the **Microsoft Office Button**, click **Print**, and set the following print options:
    a. Choose to print handouts with four slides per page, in vertical order.
    b. Deselect the **Frame** option.
    c. Deselect the **Print hidden slides** option.
11. Print the handouts.
12. **SAVE** the presentation as *Airline Final* and then **CLOSE** the file.

LEAVE PowerPoint open for the next project.

Project 7-2: Twin Cities Crawl

You are ready to finalize the presentation you created to publicize the Twin Cities Gallery Crawl. You need to rehearse and set up the show and then package the presentation for delivery.

The *Galleries* file is available on the companion CD-ROM.

1. **OPEN** the *Galleries* presentation.
2. Click the **Slide Show** tab, and then click the **Rehearse Timings** button.
3. Read each slide. When the slide show ends, choose to save the rehearsed timings.
4. Click the **Set Up Slide Show** button, and set up the show to be browsed at a kiosk using the timings you saved to advance slides.
5. Click the **Microsoft Office Button**, point to **Publish**, and click **Package for CD**.

Delivering a Presentation | 723

6. Key the package name **Galleries**. If you can copy to a CD, click **Copy to CD** and complete the packaging process. If you cannot copy to a CD, click **Copy to Folder**, select the folder in which you are storing solutions for Lesson 10, and complete the packaging process.
7. Close the Package for CD dialog box.
8. **SAVE** the presentation as *Galleries Final* and then **CLOSE** the file.

    LEAVE PowerPoint open for the next project.

■ Proficiency Assessment

Project 7-3: Final Airline Check

You want to run through the Airline Final presentation before delivering it to make sure you are familiar with content and how to display it during the slide show.

1. **OPEN** the *Airline Final* presentation you created in Project 10-1.
2. Hide slide 7.
3. Press **F5** to view the presentation from slide 1.
4. Use the **Next** button in the presentation tools to move to slide 3.
5. Use the **Previous** button in the presentation tools to go backward to slide 1.
6. Right-click to display the shortcut menu, and use **Go to Slide** to jump to slide 4.
7. Right-click the slide, click **Pointer Options**, and select the highlighter.
8. Highlight the bullet items **Caribbean** and **Scuba**.
9. Restore the arrow pointer and press **Esc** to end the show. Choose not to save your annotations.
10. Rehearse timings for the presentation. When the presentation ends, save the slide timings.
11. Set up the slide show to use the slide timings you saved.
12. **SAVE** the presentation as *Airline Final Check* and then **CLOSE** the file.

    LEAVE PowerPoint open for the next project.

Project 7-4: Year-End Review

You are ready to do the final tweaking of the year-end review for Contoso's Human Resources department. You will create a custom show to send to Contoso's president and CEO, customize handouts for the year-end review meeting, and adjust slide size for printing.

The *Review* file is available on the companion CD-ROM.

1. **OPEN** the *Review* presentation.
2. Create a custom show named **Review Summary**. Include in the custom show slides 1, 3, 4, 6, 7, 9, 10, and 12.
3. Change the slide size to **Letter Paper (8.5x11 in)**.
4. Display a date that updates, the header **Contoso HR Year in Review**, and page numbers for all handouts and notes pages.
5. Display the handout master, and show the **3 Slides** layout.
6. Select the Header and Date placeholders, center the text in these placeholders, and adjust the vertical alignment in these placeholders to Middle. (Hint: Use Align Text on the Home tab to set Middle alignment.)
7. Reduce the width of each placeholder to 2.5 inches wide, and move the placeholders down about half an inch from the top of the page.
8. Center the Header placeholder over the slide image column, and center the Date placeholder over the empty column where the lines will appear to the right of the slide images. (You can check placement by displaying the handouts in Print Preview.)

9. Apply a Quick Style to the Header and Date placeholders. Boldface the text and adjust color if necessary to show up against the Quick Style formatting.
10. Print handouts with three slides per page.
11. **SAVE** the presentation as *Review Custom*.

    LEAVE the presentation open for the next project.

■ Mastery Assessment

Project 7-5: Review Final

You need to complete your preparation of the Review Custom presentation and test it before you send it to the HR executive staff.

1. Set the slides in the *Review Custom* presentation for normal screen 4:3 screen display.
2. Set up the slide show to display only the Review Summary custom show for an individual. Turn on the scrollbar option, and choose to advance slides manually.
3. Start the slide show from slide 1 and view the slides in the custom show, using keyboard options to advance slides.
4. **SAVE** the presentation as *Review Custom Final* and then **CLOSE** the file.

    LEAVE PowerPoint open for the next project.

Project 7-6: Museum Package

You are ready to package the presentation you created for the Baldwin Museum. This presentation contains linked sound and movie files that must be included with the presentation.

The *Museum* file is available on the companion CD-ROM.

1. **OPEN** the *Museum* presentation.
2. **SAVE** the presentation as *Museum Final*.
3. Open the Package for CD dialog box and name the new package **Museum Final**. Choose to embed TrueType fonts and make sure the **Linked files** option is selected.
4. Choose to copy the presentation files to a folder, and select the Lesson 7 solutions folder as the location to store the Museum Final folder. Be sure to click **Yes** when asked if you want to include linked files.
5. Close the Package for CD dialog box.
6. Navigate in My Computer to the Museum Final folder, open the PowerPoint Viewer, and open the *Museum Final* presentation.
7. Proceed through the slides, noting that the linked multimedia files play correctly.
8. **CLOSE** the PowerPoint Viewer, and then **CLOSE** *Museum Final*.

    STOP. CLOSE PowerPoint.

INTERNET READY

You have been asked to find out what kind of equipment you would need to project presentations in a medium-sized conference room using a computer to control the show. Using the Internet, research what type of digital projector and pull-down screen you would need to purchase. Read reviews if possible to locate several options for good-quality components that are not the most or least expensive on the market. Create a presentation with your suggestions in a table or diagram. You may also want to research interactive whiteboards as an alternative to the projector-and-screen combination.

Circling Back

You are a managing editor at Lucerne Publishing. You are preparing for an important meeting with the senior managing team, and you are producing a presentation that should serve two purposes: to show how you intend to grow the publishing plan for the coming year and to convince senior management to let you hire several new editors. You can use PowerPoint tools to focus attention on these two goals.

Project 1: Basic Formatting and Tables

In this project, you will open your draft presentation, apply a theme, and add both a table and an Excel worksheet to present data.

GET READY. Launch PowerPoint if it is not already running.

The *Opportunities* file is available on the companion CD-ROM.

1. OPEN the *Opportunities* presentation.
2. Apply the Origin theme.
3. Insert a date that updates automatically, slide numbers, and the footer **Editorial Opportunities**. Apply to all slides except the title slide.
4. Display the slide master and make these changes:
   a. Change the alignment of the date placeholder to right alignment.
   b. Boldface the slide titles.
   c. Change the color of the first-level bullet.
   d. Close Slide Master view.
5. Go to slide 4 and create a table that has three columns and six rows. Key the following data in the table:

Division	Current Year	Next Year
History	23	27
Science Fiction	19	23
Literature	12	16
Nonfiction	26	31
Lifestyle	38	43

6. Format the table with the **Light Style 3 – Accent 1** Quick Style.
7. Go to slide 3 and format the existing table to match the one you inserted on slide 4.
8. Go to slide 5 and insert an Excel worksheet. Key the following data in the worksheet:

Division	Current Year	Next Year
History	4.65	4.89
Science Fiction	3.77	4.01
Literature	8.92	9.15
Nonfiction	4.41	4.79
Lifestyle	3.59	3.95

9. In cell A8 of the worksheet, key **Average**. In cell B8, insert the formula =AVERAGE(B2:B6).
10. Copy the formula in cell B8 to cell C8.
11. Format the values in cells B8 and C8 as currency with two decimal places.
12. Format the worksheet as follows:
    a. Apply the Urban theme in Excel (you'll find the themes on the Page Layout tab in Excel).

b. Boldface the column headings.

c. Change the font of the worksheet cells to Corbel to match the text in the presentation. Change the font size to 18.

d. Adjust columns to display all data.

13. Adjust the size of the worksheet's hatched selection border to hide any empty rows or columns. Click outside the worksheet to deselect it.

14. SAVE the presentation as *Opportunities Final*.

PAUSE. LEAVE PowerPoint and your presentation open for the next project.

Project 2: Charting the Data

You are now ready to create a chart that shows the editorial workload for the current year and your projections for the next year. The chart will make it easy for your audience to compare the numbers.

USE the presentation that is open from the previous project.

1. Go to slide 6, and change the layout of the slide to Title and Content.
2. Click the **Insert Chart** icon in the content placeholder to begin a new chart. Select the Clustered Bar in 3D chart type.
3. Insert the following data in the chart worksheet:

Division	Current Year	Next Year
History	5.8	6.8
Science Fiction	6.3	7.6
Literature	4	5.3
Nonfiction	4.3	5.2
Lifestyle	5.4	6.1

4. Delete the unneeded sample data in column D and make sure the range border surrounds only the data you need for your chart. Close the worksheet.
5. Change the chart type to a 3-D Clustered Column chart.
6. Click on the four dots at the bottom center of the chart container and drag upward about half an inch to free up some room at the bottom of the slide.
8. Draw a text box below the chart and key the text ***Books per editor, based on current staffing**.
9. Resize the text box so that all text is on one line, and then apply a Quick Style to the text box that coordinates well with the chart. Change the font size to 12 pt.
10. SAVE the presentation.

PAUSE. LEAVE PowerPoint and your presentation open for the next project.

Project 3: Add Diagrams

You are ready to add SmartArt diagrams to display additional information about your organization and your department's work processes.

USE the presentation that is open from the previous project.

1. Go to slide 7 and click the **Insert SmartArt Graphic** icon in the content placeholder to start a new diagram.
2. Choose to create an organization chart and add text to the chart as follows:

   a. In the top-level box, key the name **Bill Bowen**, press Enter, and key the title **Managing Editor**.

Circling Back | 727

    b. In the assistant box, key **Eva Corets**, press **Enter**, and key **Chief Editorial Assistant**.

    c. In the second-level boxes, key the following names, titles, and departments:

Jo Berry	Dan Bacon	Jun Cao
Sr. Editor	Sr. Editor	Sr. Editor
History & Nonfiction	Science Fiction	Literature & Lifestyle

3. Apply a Quick Style to the diagram.
4. Boldface the text in the top-level shape.
5. Go to slide 8, and convert the bulleted list to a Vertical Process diagram.
6. Apply a Quick Style that matches the one you used on slide 7.
7. **SAVE** the presentation.

    PAUSE. LEAVE PowerPoint and your presentation open for the next project.

Project 4: Insert and Format a Picture

Now insert additional visual interest in the form of a picture. You will format the picture to improve its appearance.

USE the presentation that is open from the previous project.

1. Go to slide 2, and click the **Clip Art** icon in the content placeholder to open the Clip Art task pane.
2. Use the keyword *award* to search for a photograph of a trophy. You should find several if you have a live connection to the Internet. If do not find a gold trophy on a white background in your results, insert the picture *Award.jpg* in the placeholder.
3. Adjust the picture's brightness to +10% and contrast to +20%.
4. Apply the **Perspective Shadow, White** Quick Style.
5. Move the picture down so that it aligns at the bottom with the last line of text in the text placeholder.
6. Compress pictures in the presentation to the Screen setting.
7. **SAVE** the presentation.

    PAUSE. LEAVE PowerPoint and your presentation open for the next project.

The *Award.jpg* file is available on the companion CD-ROM.

Project 5: Prepare for Delivery

You are ready to apply transitions and animations to add interest during the presentation. It is also time to prepare handouts that your audience can use to follow the presentation as you deliver it.

USE the presentation that is open from the previous project.

1. Apply the **Wipe Down** transition at **Medium** speed to all slides.
2. Go to slide 2 and apply the **Fade By 1st Level Paragraphs** animation effect to the text in the content placeholder.
3. Open the handout master and make the follow changes:

    a. Display the **3 Slides** layout.

    b. Change the orientation of the handout page to **Landscape**.

    c. Close Handout Master view.

4. **PRINT** the handouts with three slides per page.
5. **SAVE** the presentation and then **CLOSE** the file.

    STOP. CLOSE PowerPoint.

Microsoft® Office
Access® 2007

Database Essentials

LESSON SKILL MATRIX

Navigating Access	Students will learn how to navigate Access.
Defining Table Fields	Students will learn how to define table fields.
Defining Data Types for Fields	Students will learn how to define data types for fields.
Defining Database Tables	Students will learn how to define database tables.

The School of Fine Art in Poughkeepsie, New York, is the brainchild of two professional artists—Shaun Beasley, a printmaker, and Jane Clayton, a sculptor. Last year, the new private high school opened with an enrollment of 12 students and with Jane and Shaun as the only full-time instructors. All academic and business records were maintained manually by the founders. This year, however, you were hired as an executive assistant to help them manage an increasing amount of information. Enrollment is climbing, new full-time faculty members are being hired, and the school is receiving scholarship funds from local patrons. With the help of an Access database, you will organize the school's academic and business data. In this lesson, you will learn basic database concepts and how to define data needs and types.

KEY TERMS
database
database management system (DBMS)
datasheet
data type
field
form
normal forms
normalization
object
primary key
query
record
redundant data
relational database
report
tab
table

Software Orientation

Microsoft Access' Opening Screen

Before you begin working in Microsoft Access, you need to be familiar with the primary user interface. In the next section, you will be asked to open a new blank database in Access. When you do so, a screen will appear that will be similar to the one shown in Figure 1-1.

Figure 1-1

Opening screen for new blank Access database

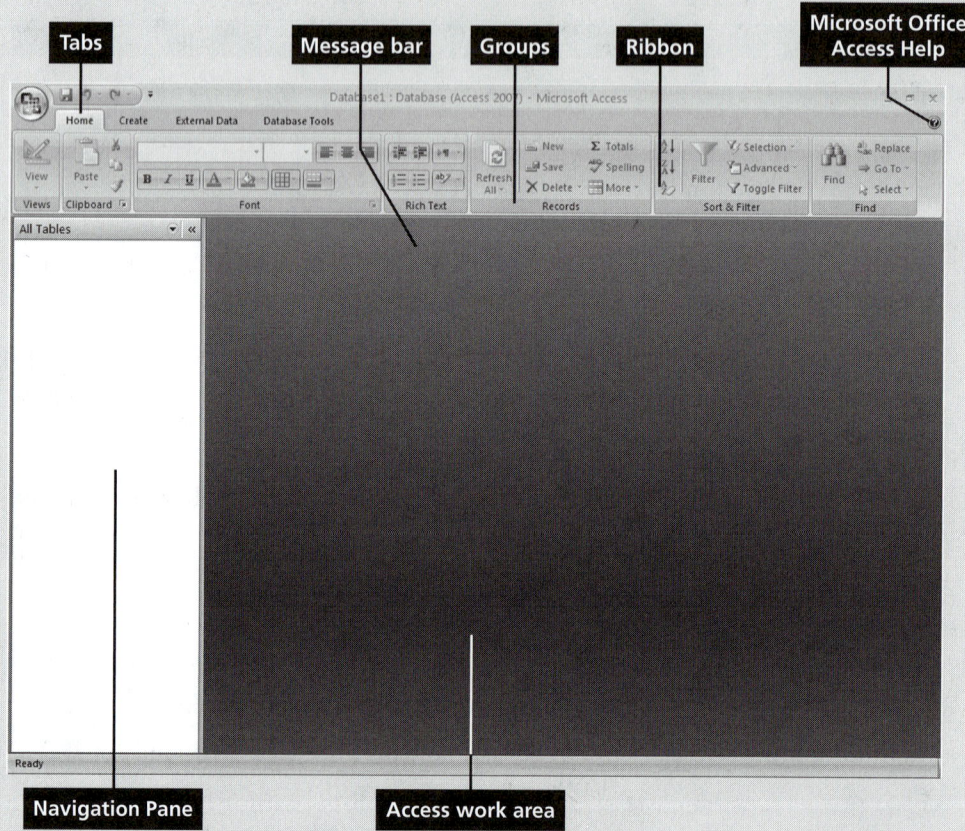

When you create a blank database in Microsoft Access, the opening screen provides you with a workspace in which to build a database. Understanding the screen elements helps orient you to important tools and information. The elements and features of your screen may vary if default settings have been changed or if other preferences have been set. Use this figure as a reference throughout this lesson as well as the rest of this book.

Working in the Access Window

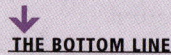

THE BOTTOM LINE

A database is a powerful tool for managing volumes of complex data. Before you can create a database, you need to understand its most basic elements. This section details important elements of the Getting Started with Microsoft Office Access screen. This lesson also introduces you to some of the elements in a database that help you organize data and navigate using the Navigation Pane, object tabs, and different views.

Navigating Access

When you start Access, you can choose from among several options for creating a new database or opening an existing saved database.

Database Essentials | 731

The *Student Information* database is available on the companion CD-ROM.

➔ DATABASE BASICS

GET READY. Before you begin these steps, be sure to turn on and/or log on to your computer.

1. Start Microsoft Access 2007.
2. The Getting Started with Microsoft Office Access page appears, as shown in Figure 1-2. Your screen may look slightly different, depending on your system.
3. Navigate to the data files for this lesson and open **Student Information**.

Figure 1-2

Getting Started with Microsoft Office Access page

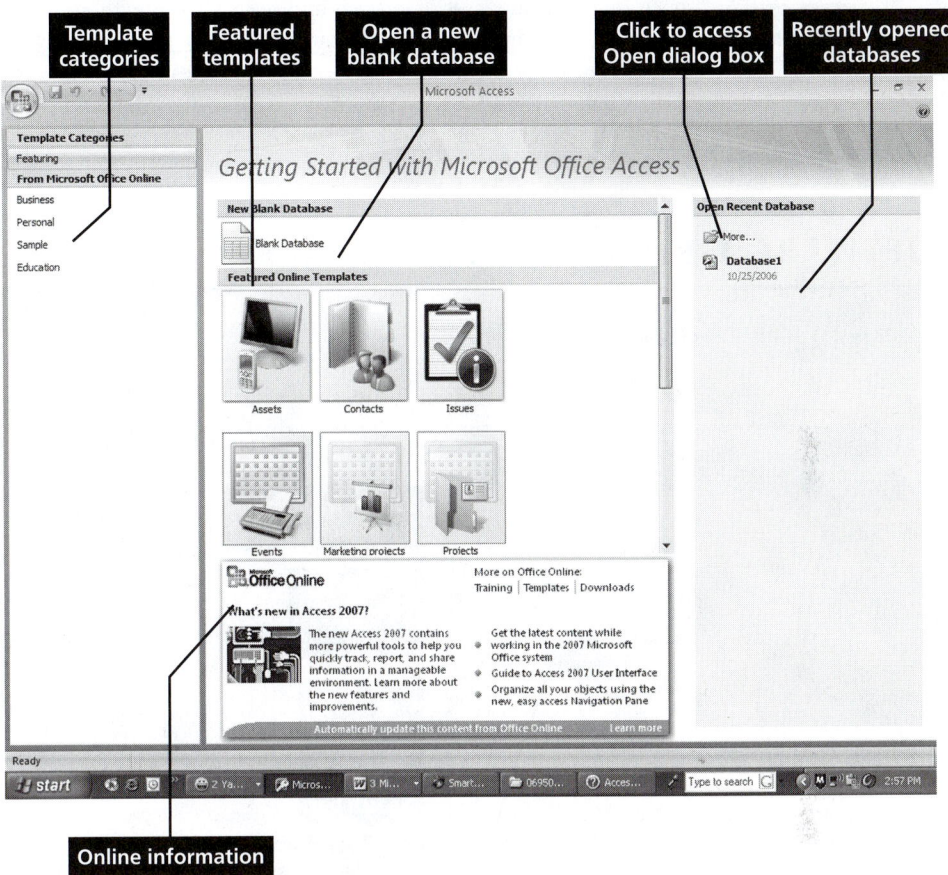

TROUBLESHOOTING As part of the Office Access 2007 security model, when you open a database outside of a trusted location, a tool called the Message Bar will appear to warn you that certain content has been disabled. If you know you can trust the database, click Options and then choose to enable the content in the dialog box that appears.

PAUSE. LEAVE the database open to use in the next exercise.

Any list you make for a specific purpose can be considered a simple database, even a grocery list. A *database* is a tool for collecting and organizing information. Databases can store information about people, products, orders, or anything else. For example, a phone book contains names, addresses, and phone numbers. As a database, it organizes large amounts of data and enables you to access it in a predictable way—usually by name in alphabetic order.

As you collect more data and it becomes more complex, your need to manage the data increases. A computerized *database management system (DBMS),* such as Microsoft Office Access, enables you to easily collect large volumes of data organized into categories of related information. This type of database enables you to store, organize, and manage your data, no matter how complex it is, and then retrieve and present it in various formats and reports.

The Getting Started with Microsoft Access screen appears whenever you start Access. From here, you can create a new blank database, create a database from a template, or open a recent database (if you have already created one). You can also access Microsoft Office Online for featured content and more information about the 2007 Microsoft Office system and Office Access 2007.

> **TAKE NOTE**
>
> Each time you start Access, you open a new instance of Access. You can only have one database open at a time in a single instance of Access. In other words, you cannot start Access, open one database, and then open another database without closing the first database. However, you can open multiple databases at the same time by opening another instance of Access. For example, to have two Access databases open, start Access and open the first Access database, and then start a new instance of Access and open the second database.

SOFTWARE ORIENTATION

Navigation Pane

By default, the Navigation Pane, shown in Figure 1-3, appears on the left side of the Access screen each time you create or open a database.

Figure 1-3

Navigation Pane

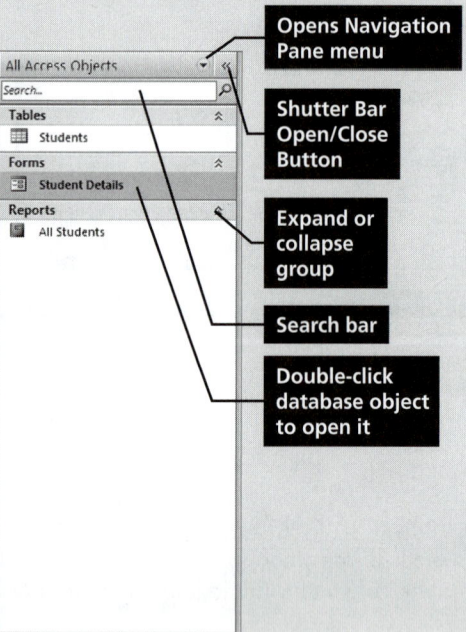

The Navigation Pane enables you to open, copy, and delete tables and other database objects. You will learn more about managing database objects such as forms, queries, and reports in later lessons of this book. For now, just familiarize yourself with the Navigation Pane. Use this figure as a reference throughout this lesson as well as the rest of this book.

USING THE NAVIGATION PANE

USE the database you used in the previous exercise.

1. In the Navigation Pane, double-click the **Students:Table** to display the table in the Access work area, as shown in Figure 1-4.

Figure 1-4

Table open in Access work area

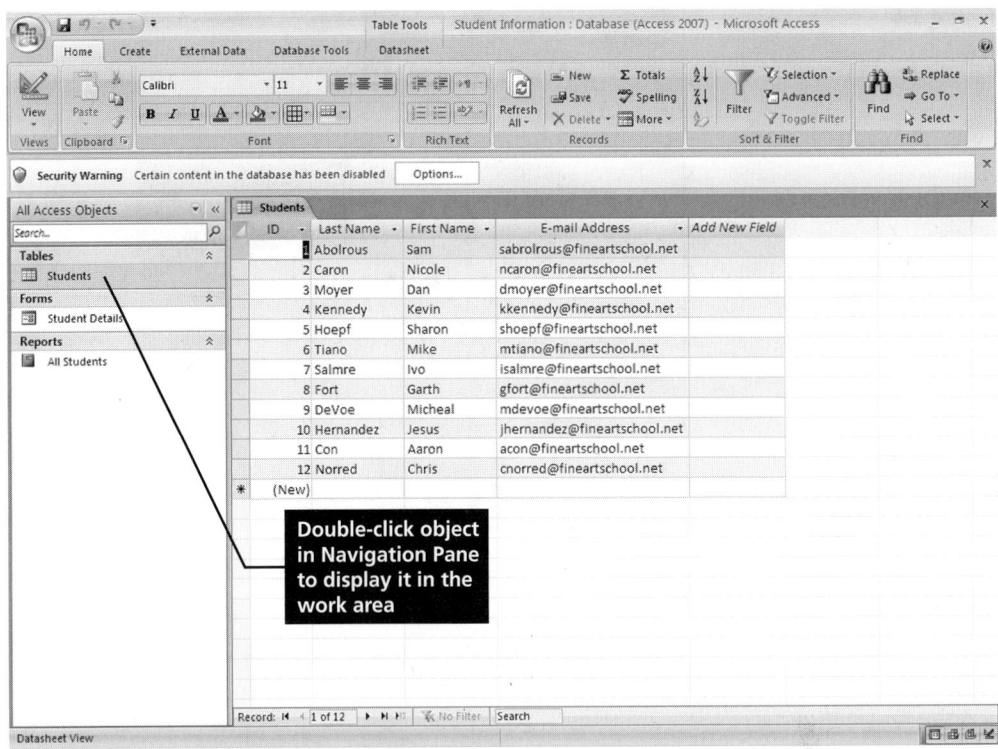

> **TAKE NOTE**
> The Navigation Pane replaces an older tool, the Database window, that appeared in earlier versions of Access.

2. Click the **down arrow** at the top of the Navigation Pane to display the menu, as shown in Figure 1-5.

Figure 1-5

Navigation Pane menu

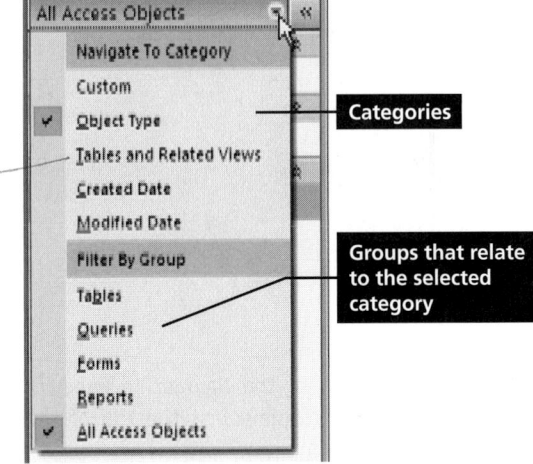

3. Click **Tables and Related Views**. The default group in this category is All Tables, which appears in the menu at the top of the Navigation Pane.
4. Right-click in the white area of the Navigation Pane to display a shortcut menu. Click **View By** and then **Details**, as shown in Figure 1-6.

Figure 1-6

Navigation Pane shortcut menu

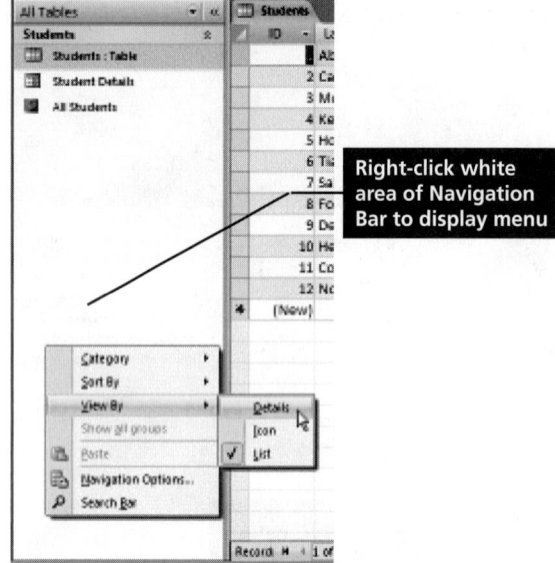

5. The database objects are displayed with details. Click the right side of the Navigation Pane and drag to make it wider so all the information can be read, as shown in Figure 1-7.

Figure 1-7

Widen the Navigation Pane

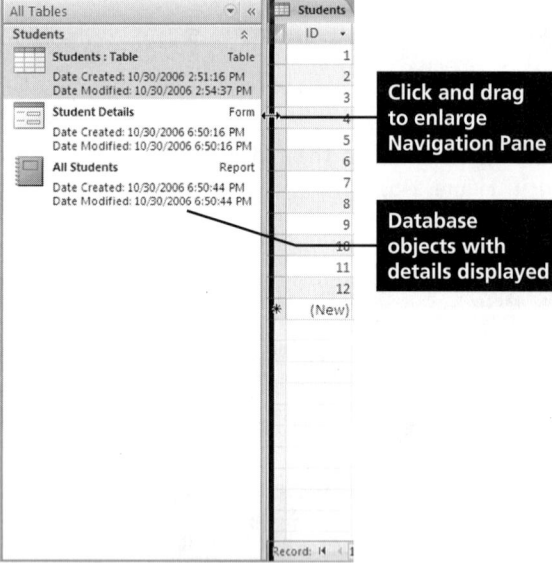

6. Right-click in the white area of the Navigation Pane. On the shortcut menu, click **Search Bar.** A search bar is displayed at the top of the Navigation Pane.
7. Display the Navigation Pane shortcut menu, click **View By** and then **List** to display the database objects in a list.
8. Click the **Shutter Bar Open/Close Button** to collapse the Navigation Pane. Notice it is not entirely hidden, as shown in Figure 1-8.

Figure 1-8

Navigation Pane collapsed

Navigation Pane collapsed

9. Click the **Shutter Bar Open/Close Button** to expand the Navigation Pane again.

   PAUSE. LEAVE the database open to use in the next exercise.

The Navigation Pane lists all the objects in your database. Some of the **objects,** which you will learn more about in later lessons, are described briefly in the following list:

- **Tables**—the most basic database object—store data in categories.
- **Queries** enable you to search and retrieve the data you have stored.
- **Forms** control data entry and data views. They provide visual cues that make data easier to work with.
- **Reports** present your information in ways that are most useful to you.

The Navigation Pane divides your database objects into categories, and those categories contain groups. The default category is Tables and Related Views, which groups the objects in a database by the tables to which they are related. You can change the category to Object Type, which groups database objects by their type—tables, forms, and so on.

To group your objects differently, select another category by using the menu at the top of the Navigation Pane. The menu is divided into two sections—the upper section contains categories, which display the predefined and custom categories for the database, and the lower section contains groups, which change based on the category selected. If the predefined categories and groups do not meet your needs, you can create custom ones.

For additional commands, right-click the white area of the Navigation Pane to display the shortcut menu to perform a variety of tasks. You can display the Search Bar to search for objects in large databases quickly. You can also change categories, sort the items in the pane, and show or hide the details for the objects in each group.

To expand or collapse the Navigation Pane, click the Shutter Bar Open/Close button. The pane is not entirely hidden when collapsed.

USING OBJECT TABS

USE the database you used in the previous exercise.

1. In the Navigation Pane, double-click **Details**. A new object tab opens to display the form, as shown in Figure 1-9.

Figure 1-9

Tab with form

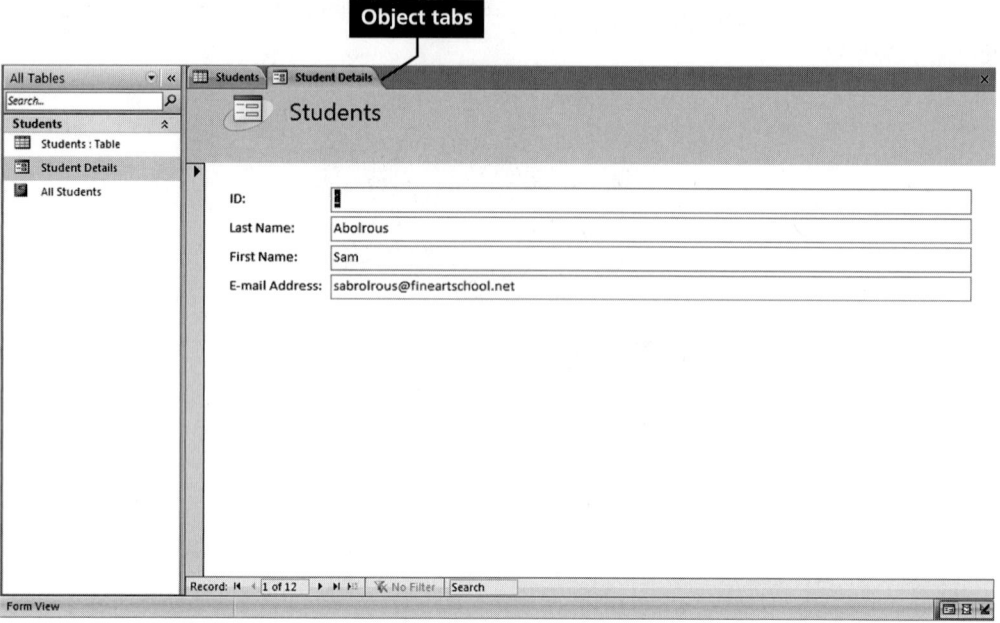

2. In the Navigation Pane, double-click **All Students**. A new object tab opens to display the report, as shown in Figure 1-10.

Figure 1-10

Tab with report

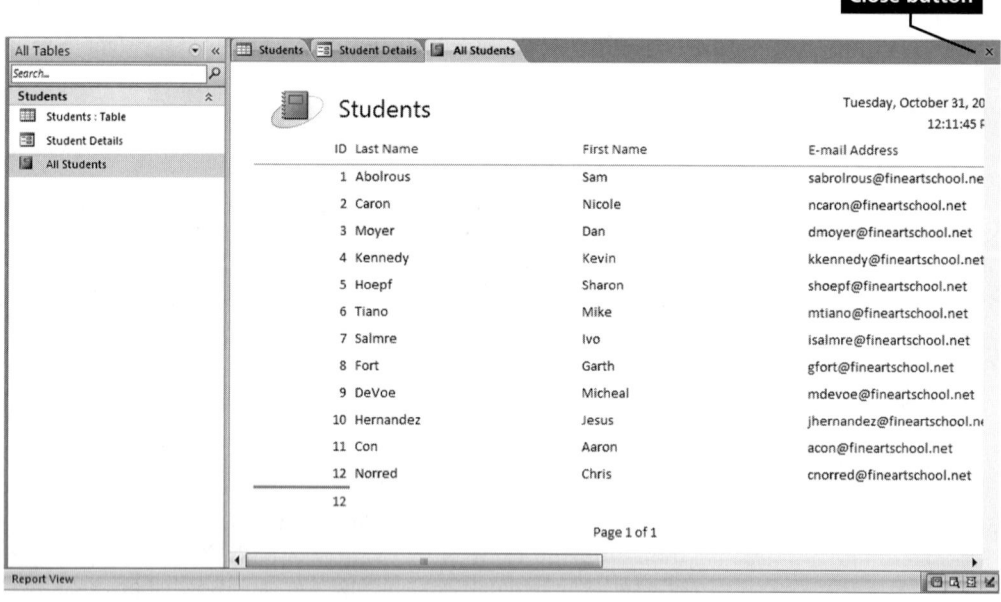

3. Click the **Close** button for the report tab to close it.

Database Essentials | 737

4. Right-click the **Student Details** tab to display the shortcut menu shown in Figure 1-11.

Figure 1-11

Tab shortcut menu

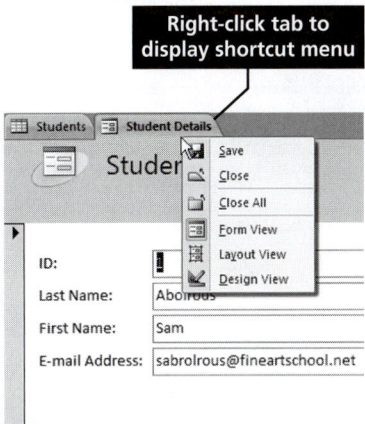

5. Click **Close** to close the form.

   PAUSE. LEAVE the database open to use in the next exercise.

When you create a database in Access, all the objects in that database—including forms, tables, reports, queries—are displayed in a single window separated by tabs. To move among the open objects, click a tab. Tabs help keep open objects visible and accessible.

To open a tab, double-click the object in the Navigation Pane. To close a tab, click its Close button. You can also right-click a tab to display the shortcut menu where you can save, close, close all, or switch views.

⊕ CHANGING VIEWS

USE the database you used in the previous exercise. The Students table should be displayed in the Access work area.

1. On the Home tab, in the Views group, click the **View** button's down arrow to display the menu shown in Figure 1-12.

Figure 1-12

View menu for a table

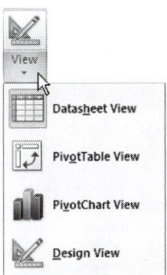

2. Click **Design View**. The table is displayed in Design View, as shown in Figure 1-13. Notice that the Design tab is now displayed on the Ribbon.

Figure 1-13

Table in Design View

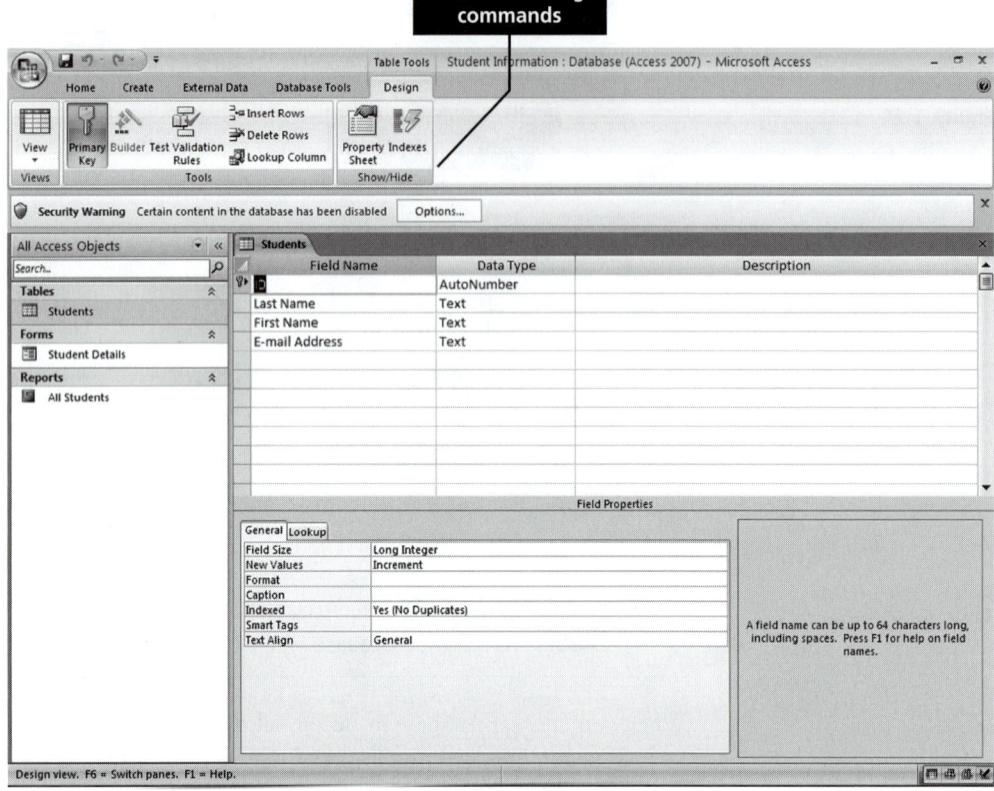

3. On the Design tab, in the Views group, click the View button's down arrow, and then click **Datasheet View**.
4. Click the **Datasheet** tab under the Table Tools tab on the Ribbon to display the contextual commands for that view, as shown in Figure 1-14.

Figure 1-14

Table in Datasheet View

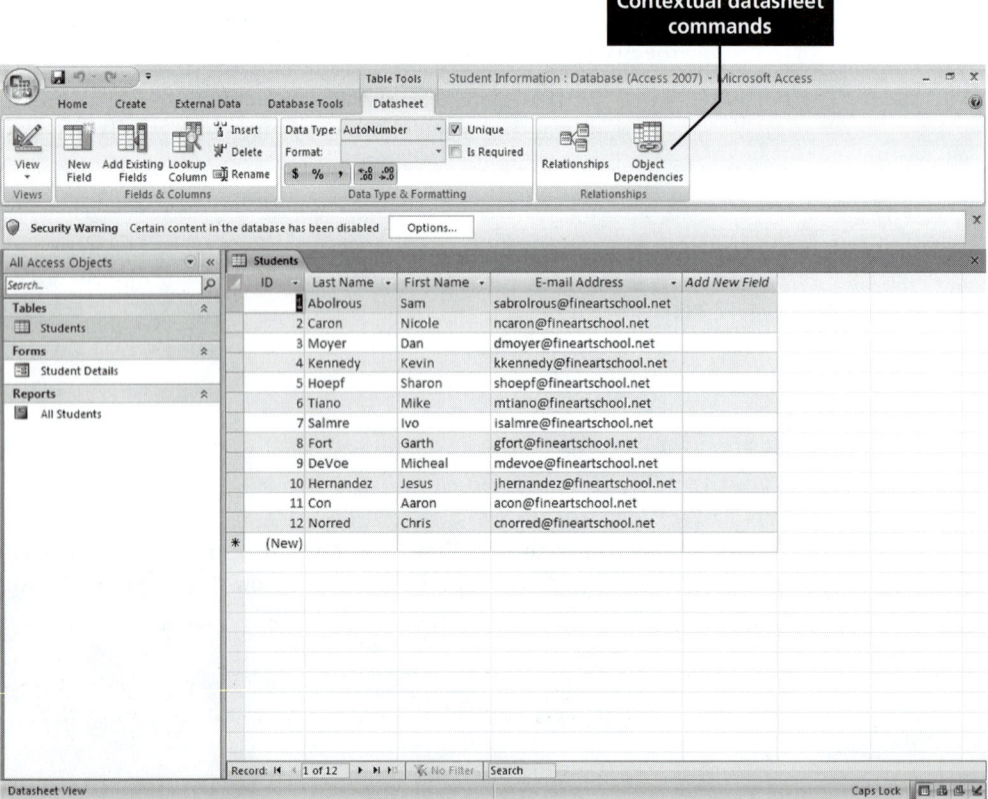

PAUSE. LEAVE the database open to use in the next exercise.

Each database object can be viewed several different ways. The main views for a table are Datasheet View and Design View. Datasheet View can be used to perform most table design tasks, so you will probably use it most often. A *datasheet* is the visual representation of the data contained in a table or of the results returned by a query.

To change the view, click the View button's down arrow and then choose a view from the menu. When you change views, the commands available on the Ribbon change to match the tasks you will be performing in that view. You will learn more about the Ribbon in the next section.

■ Defining Data Needs and Types

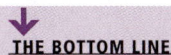

THE BOTTOM LINE   The first step in creating a database that achieves your goals and provides you with up-to-date, accurate information is to spend time planning and designing it.

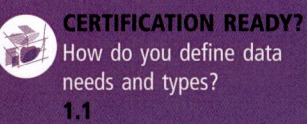

CERTIFICATION READY?
How do you define data needs and types?
1.1

Defining Table Fields

To define table fields, you establish which data needs to be stored in the table. Planning is an important part of creating a database. In this exercise, you will open a database that is further along in the process of being developed to see what a more advanced database looks like.

The ***Student Data*** database is available on the companion CD-ROM.

DEFINE TABLE FIELDS

1. **OPEN** the **Student Data** database from the data files for this lesson.
2. On the Student List form, click the ID for record **5** to display the details for Sharon Hoepf, as shown in Figure 1-15.

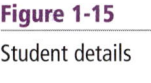

Figure 1-15

Student details

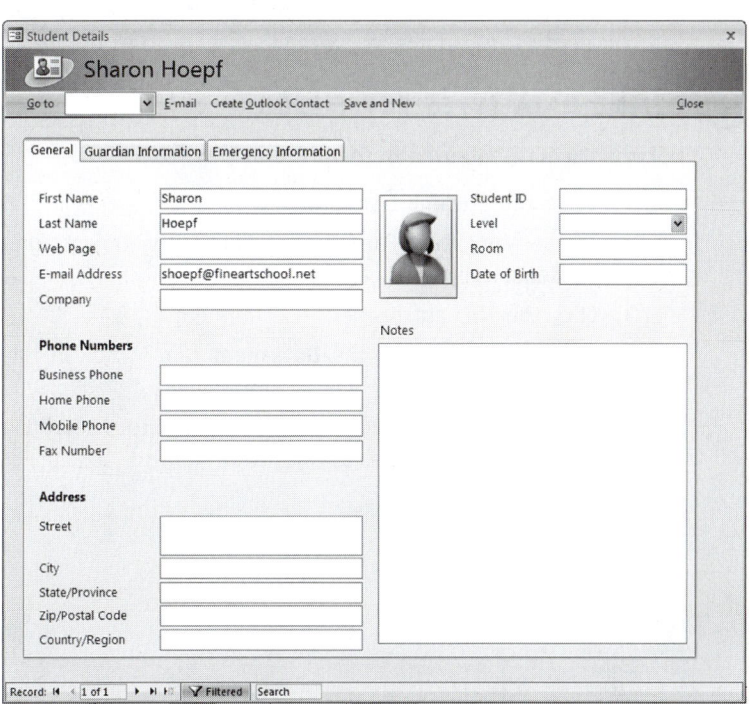

CERTIFICATION READY?
How do you define table fields?
1.1.1

3. Click the **Guardian Information** tab and then the **Emergency Information** tab. Each of the fields on these tabs is an example of the type of information that could be contained in a database table.
4. Click **Close** to close the details.
   PAUSE. LEAVE the database open to use in the next exercise.

When planning a database, the first step is to consider the purpose of your database. You need to design the database so that it accommodates all your data processing and reporting needs. You should gather and organize all the information that you want to include, starting with any existing forms or lists, and think about the reports and mailings you might want to create using the data.

Once you have decided how the information will be used, the next step is to categorize the information by dividing it into subjects such as Products or Orders, which become the tables in your database. Each table should only contain information that relates to that subject. If you find yourself adding extra information, create a new table.

In a database table, data is stored in rows and columns—similar in appearance to a spreadsheet. Each row in a table is called a *record*. Each column in a table is called a *field*. For example, if a table is named "Student List," each record (row) contains information about a different student and each field (column) contains a different type of information, such as last name or email address.

To create the columns within the table, you then need to determine what information you want to store in the table—such as Color, Year, or Cost. Break each piece of information into the smallest useful part—for example, use First Name and Last Name instead of just Name if you want to sort, search, calculate, or report using the separate pieces of information.

LOOKING AHEAD
You will learn more about defining and modifying a primary key in Lesson 3.

For each table, you will choose a primary key. A *primary key* is a column that uniquely identifies each row, such as Item Number.

Defining Data Types for Fields

When designing the database, you set a data type for each field (column) that you create to match the information it will store. Each data type has a specific purpose—for example, if you need to store dates, you would set the field to the Date/Time data type.

DEFINE DATA TYPES FOR FIELDS

USE the database you used in the previous exercise.

1. Close the Student List form.
2. In the Navigation Pane, in the Supporting Objects group, double-click the **Students** table to open it.
3. Click the **ID** field header.
4. On the Ribbon, click the **Datasheet** tab. Notice in the Data Type & Formatting group that the Data Type is AutoNumber.
5. Click the **down arrow** in the Format box to display the menu of formatting options for that type, as shown in Figure 1-16.

Figure 1-16

Format options for AutoNumber data type

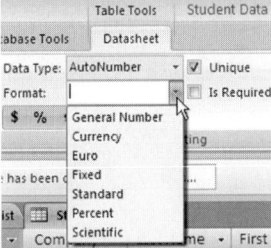

6. Click the **Last Name** header. Notice that the Data Type is Text and that no formatting options are available for that data type.
7. Scroll to the right and click the **Date of Birth** header.
8. Click the **down arrow** in the Format box to display the menu of formatting options for the Date/Time data type, as shown in Figure 1-17.

Figure 1-17

Format options for Date/Time data type

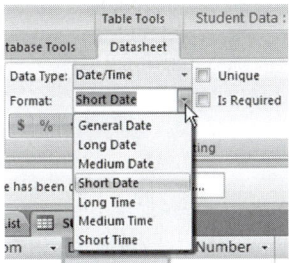

9. Scroll to the right and click the **Address** header.
10. In the Data Type box, click the **down arrow** and click **Text** to change the data type. When a warning message appears, click **Yes**.

> **TAKE NOTE** Be aware that changing a data type might cut off some or all of the data in a field, and in some cases may remove the data entirely.

11. Scroll to the far right and click the **Add New Field header.** In the Data Type box, click **Yes/No**.
12. Click the **down arrow** in the Format box to display the menu of formatting options for the Yes/No data type, as shown in Figure 1-18.

Figure 1-18

Format options for Yes/No data type

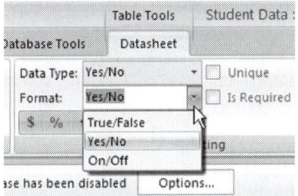

13. Click outside the menu to close it.

    PAUSE. LEAVE the database open to use in the next exercise.

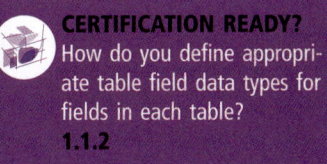

CERTIFICATION READY?
How do you define appropriate table field data types for fields in each table?
1.1.2

Each field in a table must be designated for a particular data type. A ***data type*** controls the type of data a field will contain—whether it is text, number, date/time, or some other type. Access provides ten different data types, each with its own purpose. The list in Table 1-1 describes the types of data that each field can be set to store.

Table 1-1

DATA TYPE	EXAMPLE	DESCRIPTION
Text	Last Name: Zimmerman Street: 6789 Walker Street	The most common data type for fields. Can store up to 255 characters of text, numbers, or a combination of both.
Memo	Comments: Student will make monthly payments on the 15th of each month of $247.	Allows you to store large amounts of text—up to 64,000 characters of text, numbers, or a combination (although if you use that much space, your database will run slowly).
Number	Age: 19	Stores numeric data that can be used in mathematical calculations.
Date/Time	Birthday: December 1, 1987	Stores date and/or time data.
Currency	Registration Fee: $50.00	Stores monetary data with precision to four decimal places. Use this data type to store financial data and when you don't want Access to round values.
AutoNumber	Student ID: 56	Unique values created by Access when you create a new record. Tables often contain an AutoNumber field used as the primary key.
Yes/No	Insurance? Yes	Stores Boolean (true or false) data. Access uses 1 for all Yes values and 0 for all No values.
OLE Object	Photo	Stores images, documents, graphs, and other objects from Office and Windows-based programs.
Hyperlink	Web addresses	Stores links to Web sites, sites or files on an intranet or Local Area Network (LAN), and sites or files on your computer.
Attachment	Any supported type of file	You can attach images, spreadsheet files, documents, charts, and other types of supported files to the records in your database, much like you attach files to email messages.

When you create a new field in a table and then enter data in it, Office Access 2007 automatically tries to detect the appropriate data type for the new column. For example, if you key a price, such as $10, Access recognizes the data as a price, and sets the data type for the field to Currency. If Access doesn't have enough information from what you enter to guess the data type, the data type is set to Text.

TAKE NOTE

The Number data type should only be used if the numbers will be used in mathematical calculations. For numbers such as phone numbers, use the Text data type.

LOOKING AHEAD

You will learn more about multivalued fields in Lesson 4.

When defining table fields, it will be important to define the appropriate data types for each. For example, if you are using a number, you should determine whether you need to use the Currency or Number data type. Or, if you need to store large amounts of text, you may need to use the Memo data type instead of Text. Most database management systems can store only a single value in a field, but with Microsoft Office Access 2007 you can create a field that holds multiple values, which may be appropriate in certain situations.

Defining Database Tables

CERTIFICATION READY?
How do you define tables in databases?
1.1.3

Tables are the most basic organizational element of a database. Not only is it important to plan the tables to hold the type of data you need, but also to plan how the tables and information will be connected.

DEFINE DATABASE TABLES

USE the database you used in the previous exercise.

1. On the Database Tools tab, in the Show/Hide section, click **Relationship** to display a visual representation of the relationship between the Students and Guardians tables, as shown in Figure 1-19.

Figure 1-19

Relationship between tables

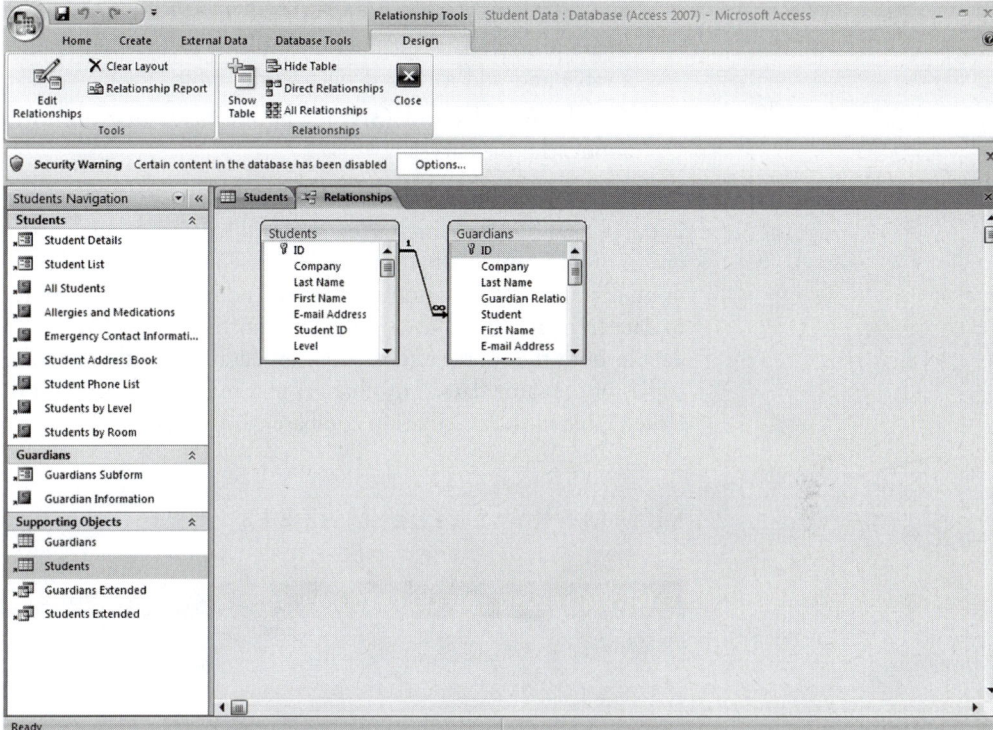

2. Close the Relationships tab.
3. Close the Students tab.

STOP. CLOSE the database.

In a simple database, you might only have one table, but most databases will have more. The tables you include in a database will be based on the data available. For example, a database of students might have a table for contact information, one for grades, and one for tuition and fees.

In database applications like Access, you can create a relational database. A ***relational database*** stores information in separate tables that are connected or linked by a defined relationship that ties the data together.

> **LOOKING AHEAD**
> You will learn more about table relationships in Lesson 3.

An important principle to consider when planning a database is to try to record each piece of information only once. Duplicate information, or ***redundant data,*** wastes space and increases the likelihood of errors. Relationships among database tables help ensure consistency and reduce repetitive data entry.

As you create each table, keep in mind how the data in the tables are related to each other. Enter test data and then add fields to tables or create new tables as necessary to refine the database. The last step is to apply data normalization rules to see if your tables are structured correctly and make adjustments as needed. ***Normalization*** is the process of applying rules to your database design to ensure that you have divided your information items into the appropriate tables.

Database design principles include standards and guidelines that can be used to determine if your database is structured correctly. These are referred to as ***normal forms***. There are five normal forms, but typically only the first three are applied, because that is usually all that is required. The following is a summary of the first three normal forms:

- **First Normal Form (1NF):** Break each field down into the smallest meaningful value, remove repeating groups of data, and create a separate table for each set of related data.
- **Second Normal Form (2NF):** Each nonkey column should be fully dependent on the entire primary key. Create new tables for data that applies to more than one record in a table and add a related field to the table.
- **Third Normal Form (3NF):** Remove fields that do not relate to, or provide a fact about, the primary key.

Data can be brought into an Access database in a number of ways, including linking and importing. When defining tables, you will have to decide whether data should be linked to or imported from external sources. When you import data, Access creates a copy of the data or objects in the destination database without altering the source. Linking lets you connect to data from another source without importing it, so that you can view and modify the latest data in both the source and destination databases without creating and maintaining two copies of the same data. Any changes you make to the data in the source are reflected in the linked table in the destination database, and vice versa.

SUMMARY SKILL MATRIX

IN THIS LESSON YOU LEARNED HOW TO:
Navigate Access
Define Table Fields
Define Data Types for Fields
Define Database Tables

■ Knowledge Assessment

Matching

Match the term in Column 1 to its description in Column 2.

Column 1

1. record (d)
2. field (f)
3. redundant data (c)
4. primary key (f)
5. database (j)
6. table (a)
7. query (e)

Column 2

a. most basic database object; stores data in categories
b. database object that presents information in a format that is easy to read and print
c. duplicate information in a database
d. row in a database table
e. database object that enables stored data to be searched and retrieved
f. column in a database that uniquely identifies each row
g. database object that simplifies the process of entering, editing, and displaying data

Database Essentials | 745

8. report (g.) h. column in a database table
9. form (j.) i. kind of information a field contains
10. data type (i.) j. tool for collecting and organizing information

True / False

Circle T if the statement is true or F if the statement is false.

T F 1. Any list you make for a specific purpose can be considered a simple database, even a grocery list.
T **F** 2. By default, the Navigation Pane appears on the right side of the Access screen each time you create or open a database.
T F 3. Forms, queries, and reports are examples of database objects.
T **F** 4. A query can be a database table, form, or report.
T **F** 5. A column that uniquely identifies each row in a database table is called the identification key.
T F 6. Microsoft Office Access is a database management system.
T F 7. In a database table, data is stored in rows and columns—similar in appearance to a spreadsheet.
T F 8. Each field in a table must be designated for a particular data type.
T **F** 9. An important principal to consider when planning a database is to try to record each piece of information as many times as possible for easy access.
T F 10. Normalization is the process of applying rules to your database design to ensure that you have divided your information items into the appropriate tables.

■ Competency Assessment

Project 1-1: Task List

The *task_list* database is available on the companion CD-ROM.

As a busy editor at Lucerne Publishing, you use Access to organize and manage your task list.

1. **OPEN** *Task_List* from the data files for this lesson.
2. Click the **Shutter Bar Open/Close Button** to display the Navigation Pane.
3. Click the **Contacts** group header in the Navigation Pane to display those database objects.
4. Click the **Supporting Objects** group header to display those database objects.
5. In the Supporting Objects group, double-click **Tasks** to open that table.
6. In the Tasks group, double-click **Tasks By Assigned To** to open that report.
7. **LEAVE** the database open for the next project.

Project 1-2: Database Views

While navigating through your database file, you find it helpful to use various views.

USE the database file that is open from the previous project.

1. Click to close the Task report in the Access work area.
2. Click to close the Tasks by Assigned to report.
3. With the Task List table still open, click the View button in the Views group of the Home tab and select Datasheet view.

4. Change the view to Layout view.
5. Close the Tasks table.
6. **CLOSE** the database.
   LEAVE Access open for the next project.

■ Proficiency Assessment

Project 1-3: Understanding Database Design

You work at Margie's Travel, a full-service travel agency that specializes in providing services to senior citizens. You plan to create a database of tours, cruises, adventure activities, group travel, and vacation packages geared toward seniors, but first you want to learn more about database design.

1. **OPEN** Access Help.
2. Search for *database design*.
3. Read the article about database design basics.
4. **OPEN** a new Word document.
5. List the steps that should be taken when designing a database with a short description of each.
6. **SAVE** the document as *database_design* and then **CLOSE** the file.
   LEAVE Access open for the next project.

Project 1-4: Planning Table Fields

You are a volunteer for the Tech Terrace Neighborhood Association that holds an annual March Madness 5K Run. In the past, all data has been kept on paper, but you decide it would be more efficient to create a database. Decide what fields would make sense for a table holding data about the runners.

1. Think about what fields would be useful in a database table that contains information about the runners in an annual 5K road race.
2. **OPEN** a new Word document.
3. In the document, key a list of the names of at least six possible field names.
4. **SAVE** the document as *race_fields* and keep the file open.
   LEAVE Access open for the next project.

■ Mastery Assessment

Project 1-5: Planning Data Types for Fields

Now that you have decided on what fields to use in a database table containing information about runners in an annual 5K road race, you need to determine what data type should be used for each field.

USE the document you used in the previous project.

1. Beneath the name of each possible field name for the table about runners in the annual 5K road race, key the data type that would be used with a short explanation of why you chose that type.
2. **SAVE** the document as *data_type* and then **CLOSE** the file.
   LEAVE Access open for the next project.

Project 1-6: Up to Speed with Access 2007

Your supervisor at Margie's Travel has suggested that you complete some additional training before you begin to create a database.

1. **OPEN** the Getting Started with Microsoft Office Access screen.
2. Use Access help to locate the demo training module called "Up to speed with Access 2007."
3. Watch the overview.
   CLOSE Access.

INTERNET READY

At the bottom of the Getting Started with Microsoft Office Access screen is an area called the Spotlight, as shown in Figure 1-20.

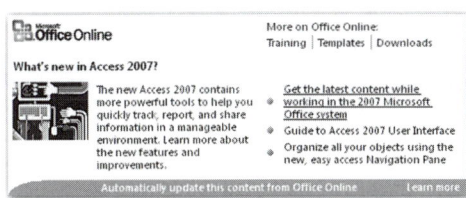

Figure 1-20
Spotlight

Use Access help to find out what this section offers and how to get the latest online content while working in Office 2007 by turning on automatic updates.

 # Workplace Ready

Working with Templates in Access

In today's business world, it can be overwhelming to keep up with the different types of data that a company needs to collect, organize, and report. Sales invoices, client contacts, employee files, vendor information—the list seems endless. You can customize the templates available in Access to meet your business needs and save the time it would take to create database objects from scratch.

In your position as the technical support director for the A. Datum Corporation, you are responsible for coordinating technical support for the company. You can streamline your work by downloading an Access template to use as a starting point and then modifying it to track critical data. Using the Issues database, you can set up, organize, and track technical service requests submitted by people in your organization. You can then assign, prioritize, and follow the progress of issues from start to finish.

The database template contains various predefined tables—such as Issues and Contacts—that you can use to enter data. Such tables may be functional just as they are. But, as you work, chances are that you will need to create tables that are more specific to the needs of your company.

The Issues database template, like all others in Microsoft Office Access 2007, also includes pre-designed forms, reports, and queries that can be used as they are. This not only saves time, but also enables you to see a complete database system developed by professionals so you can be sure you are capturing essential business information in a logical and efficient manner.

2 Create Database Tables

LESSON SKILL MATRIX

Using a Template to Create a Database —749	Students will learn how to use a template to create a database.
Creating a Blank Database —754	Students will learn how to create a blank database.
Creating a Table from a Template —757	Students will learn how to create a table from a template.
Creating a Table from Another Table —759	Students will learn how to create a table from another table.
Saving a Table —762	Students will learn how to save a table.

As an assistant curator at the Baldwin Museum of Science, you are responsible for the day-to-day management of the insect collection, including duties such as sorting and organizing specimens, as well as supervising the mounting and labeling of the insects. The insect collection catalog has never been transferred to an electronic database. Because you have experience with database management, part of your responsibility will be to create a database to store the information about the specimens and collections, as well as museum exhibits and events. In this lesson, you will learn how to create a blank database and how to use a template to create a database. You will also learn how to create a table from a template, how to create a table by copying the structure from another table, and how to save a database object.

748

Create Database Tables | 749

■ Software Orientation

Getting Started with Microsoft Office Access

Part of the Getting Started with Microsoft Office Access page, shown in Figure 2-1, provides options for creating a database.

Figure 2-1

Getting Started with Microsoft Office Access

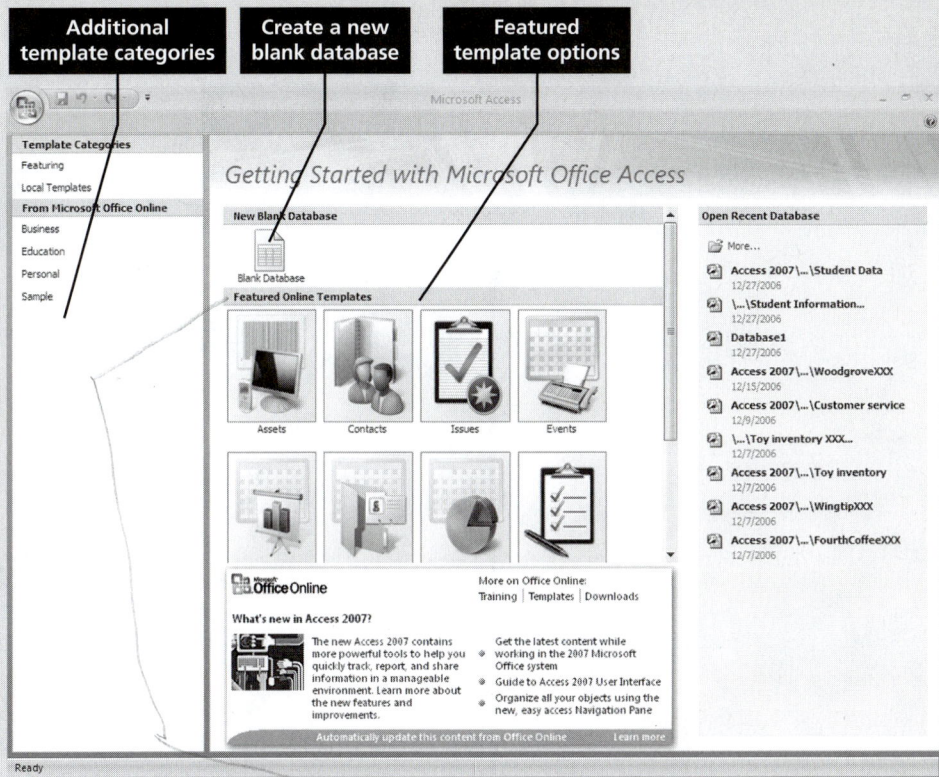

Several templates are displayed under Featured Online Templates, and more become available if you click one of the categories on the left. This is also where you can create a new, blank database. Use this figure as a reference throughout this lesson as well as the rest of this book.

■ Creating a Database

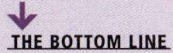

THE BOTTOM LINE

In Microsoft Office Access 2007, the process of creating a new database is easier than ever. You can create a database using one of the many templates available or by creating a new blank database.

Using a Template to Create a Database

CERTIFICATION READY?
How do you create databases?
2.1

If there is a template that fits your needs, that is usually the fastest way to create a database. Access offers a variety of templates to help get you started. Template databases can be used as is, or you can customize them to better suit your purposes.

USE A TEMPLATE TO CREATE A DATABASE

GET READY. Before you begin these steps, be sure that you are logged on to the Internet and launch Microsoft Access to display the Getting Started with Microsoft Office Access screen.

1. On the left of the Access window, in the From Microsoft Office Online section, click **Personal**.
2. In the list of Personal templates in the middle, click **Home inventory**. Your screen should look similar to Figure 2-2.

Figure 2-2

Personal templates

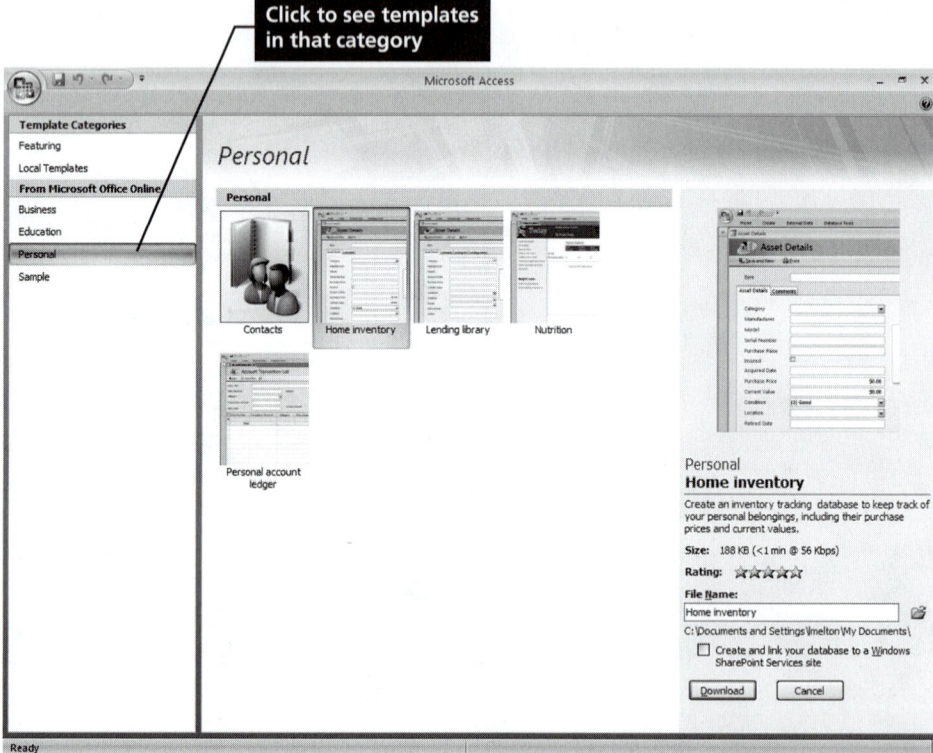

3. In the From Microsoft Office Online section on the left, click **Education**.
4. In the list of Education templates in the middle, click **Faculty**. Your screen should look similar to Figure 2-3.

Create Database Tables | 751

Figure 2-3

Education templates

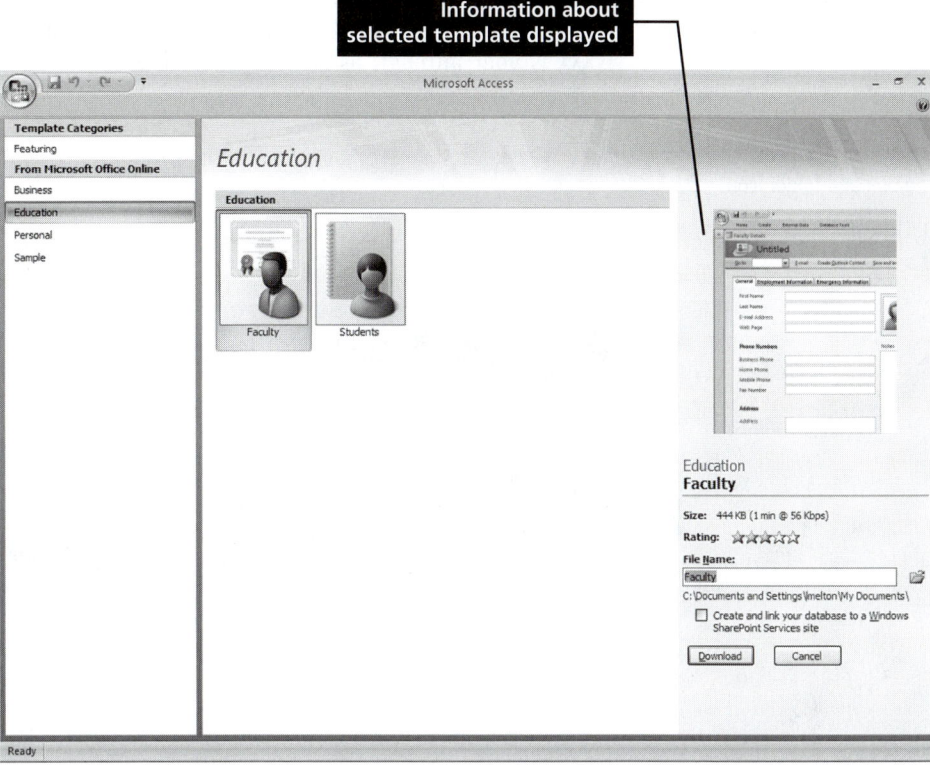

5. In the From Microsoft Office Online section on the left, click **Business**.
6. In the list of Business templates in the middle, click **Assets**. Your screen should look similar to Figure 2-4.

Figure 2-4

Business templates

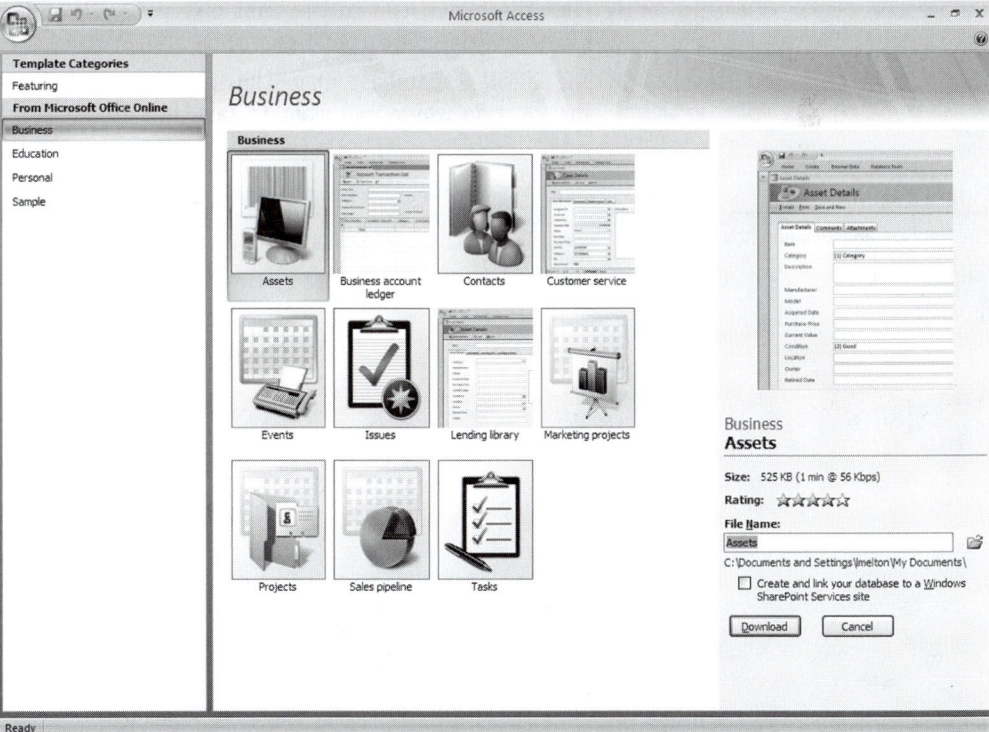

7. In the pane on the right, click in the File Name box and key your initials at the end of the suggested file name, so that the file name is now **AssetsXXX** (where XXX is your initials), as shown in Figure 2-5.

Figure 2-5

File Name box and folder icon

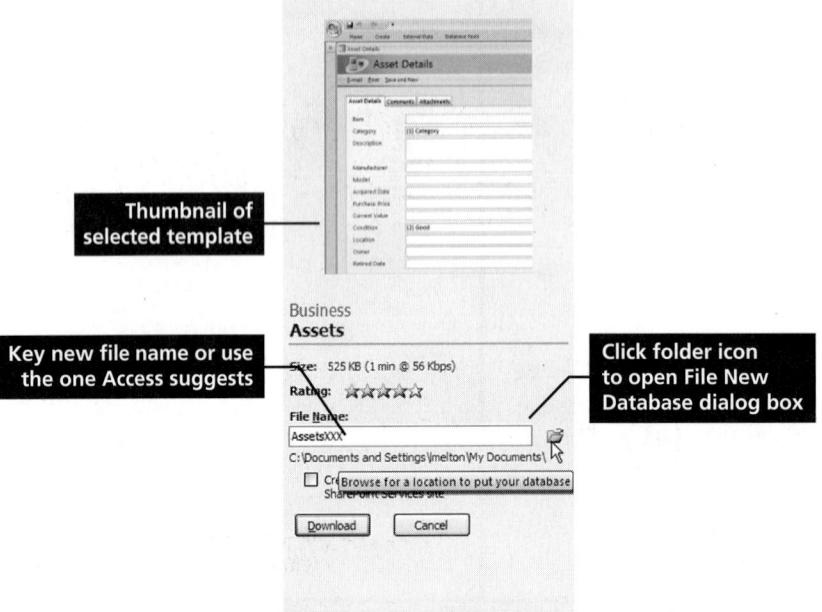

TAKE NOTE If you do not add an extension to your database file name, Access does it for you—for example, *AccessXXX.accdb*.

8. Click the folder icon to the right of the File Name box to browse for a location to store your database (see Figure 2-5).
9. The File New Database dialog box appears, as shown in Figure 2-6. Navigate to the location where you want to save the file and click **OK**.

Figure 2-6

File New Database dialog box

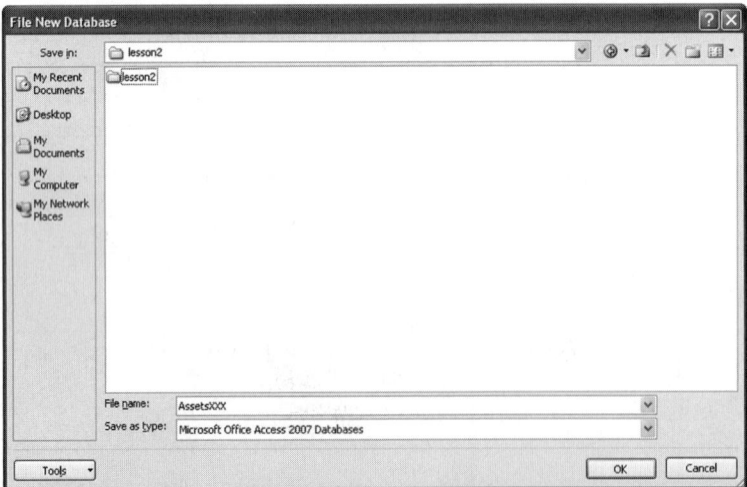

10. Click the **Download** button (see Figure 2-5). A dialog box shows that the template is being downloaded, as shown in Figure 2-7.

Figure 2-7

Downloading Template dialog box

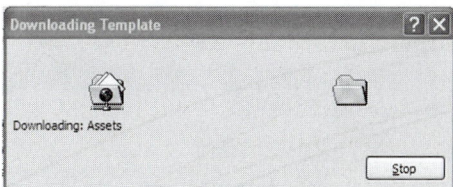

11. Access creates and then opens the database. A form is displayed in which you can begin entering data, as shown in Figure 2-8. Click to place the insertion point in the first cell of the Item field and key **Canon EOS Rebel 300D**.

Figure 2-8

Assets template database

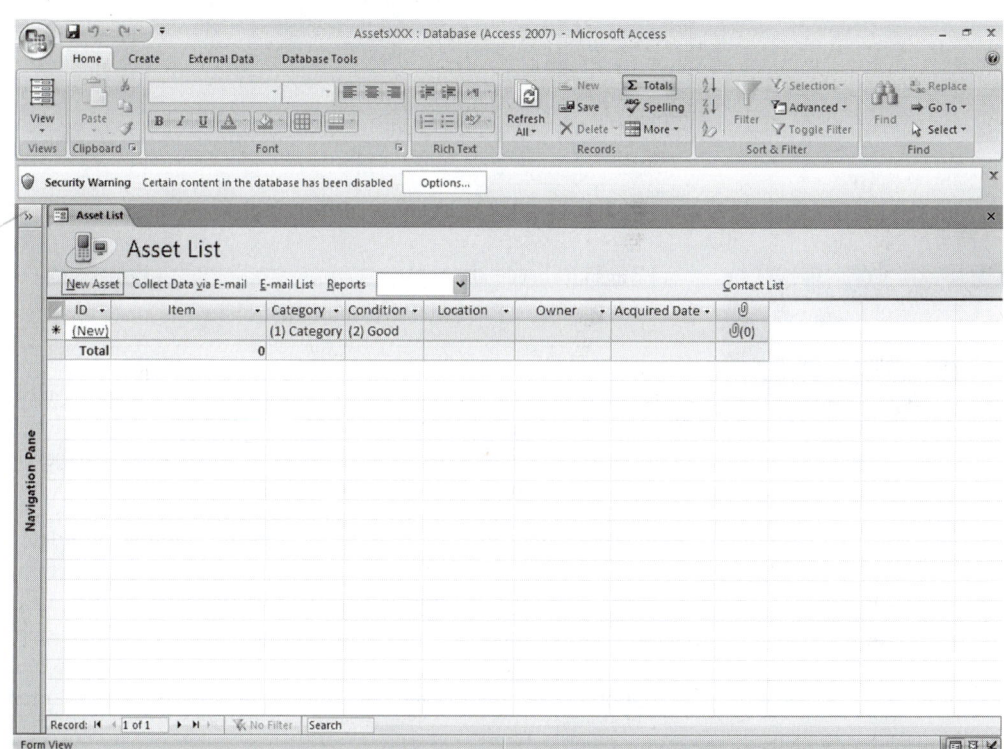

12. Click the **Shutter Bar Open/Close Button** to display the Navigation Pane, as shown in Figure 2-9, to see all the objects in the database.

Figure 2-9

Assets database with Navigation Pane displayed

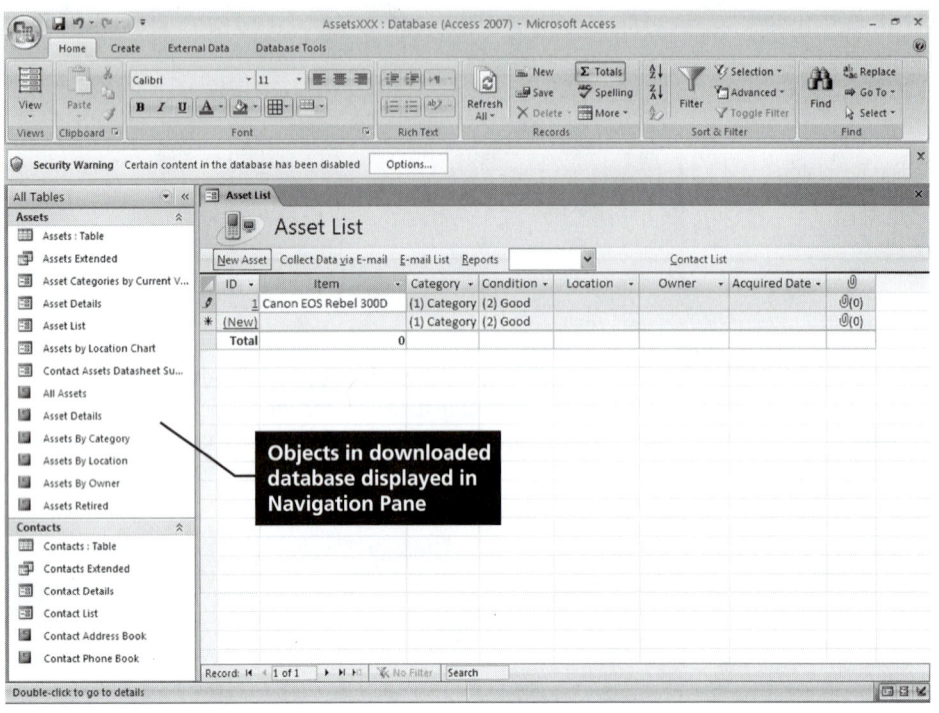

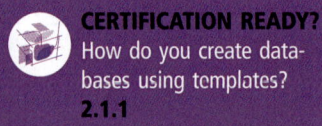

CERTIFICATION READY?
How do you create databases using templates?
2.1.1

13. **CLOSE** the database.

   PAUSE. LEAVE Access open to use in the next exercise.

A template is a ready-to-use database that contains all of the tables, queries, forms, and reports needed for performing a specific task. For example, templates are available that can be used to track issues, manage contacts, or keep a record of expenses. Some templates contain a few sample records to help demonstrate their use.

Several templates are displayed in the Featured Online Templates on the Getting Started with Microsoft Office Access or you can click a category on the left side of the Access window to view more options. Click the template you want to use, key a file name or use the one Access suggests, and select a location if you want to store the database in a location other than the default folder. Click Download (or click Create if not logged onto the Internet) to create and open the database, then begin entering data in the first empty cell on the form.

TAKE NOTE

Unless you choose a different folder, Access uses the following default locations to store your databases:
- Microsoft Windows Vista—*c:\Users\user name\Documents*
- Microsoft Windows Server 2003 or Microsoft Windows XP—*c:\Documents and Settings\user name\My Documents*

Creating a Blank Database

When you create a new blank database, Access opens a database that contains a table where you can enter data, but it creates no other database objects.

CREATE A BLANK DATABASE

GET READY. The Getting Started with Microsoft Office Access page should be on the screen from the previous exercise.

1. In the New Blank Database section, click the **Blank Database** icon. A Blank Database pane appears, as shown in Figure 2-10.

Figure 2-10

Blank Database pane

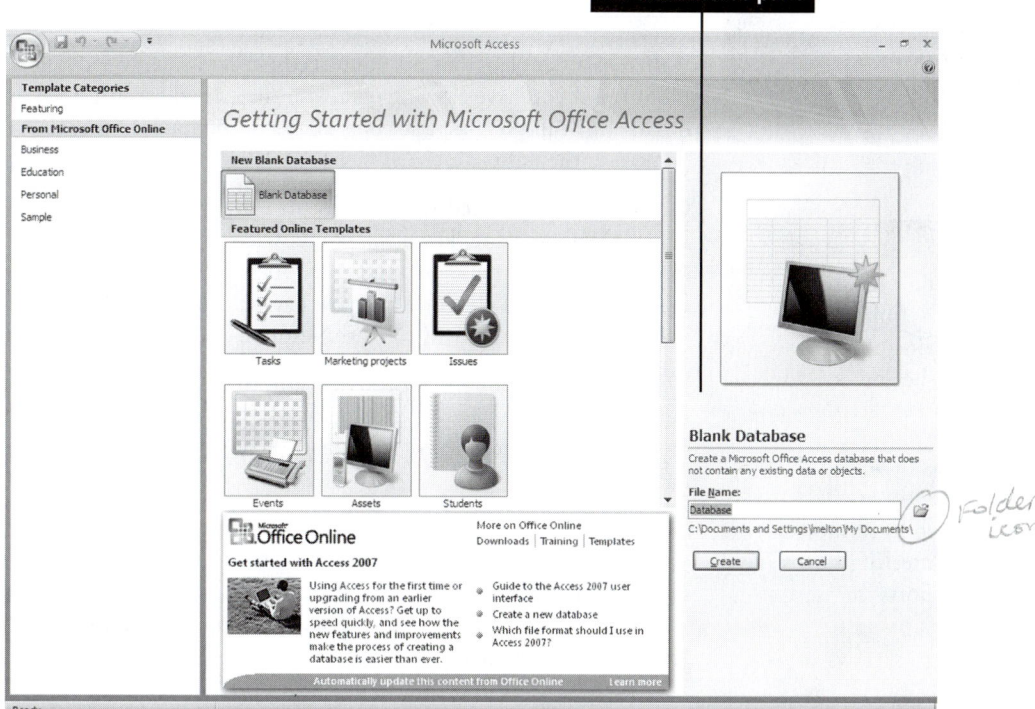

You can also create a new blank database by pressing Ctrl+N.

2. In the File Name box, key **BlankDatabaseXXX** (where XXX is your initials).
3. If you want to save the file in a location other than the one shown beneath the File Name box, click the folder icon and browse to a different location.
4. Click the **Create** button. A new blank database appears, as shown in Figure 2-11.

Figure 2-11

New blank database

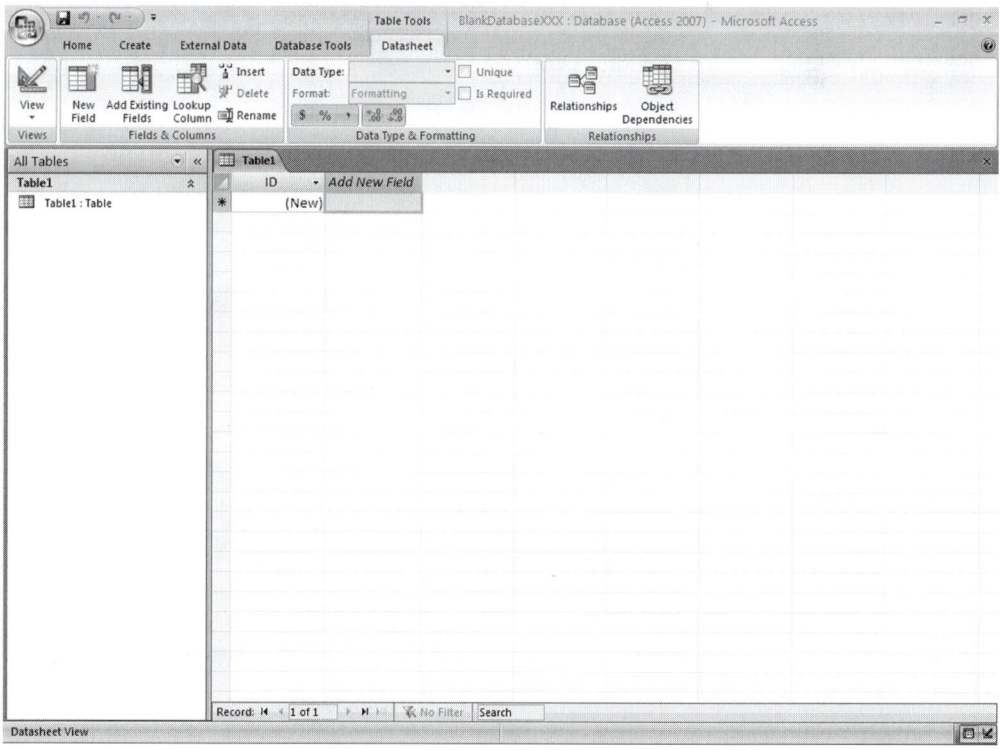

CERTIFICATION READY?
How do you create blank databases?
2.1.2

PAUSE. LEAVE the database open to use in the next exercise.

If there is a template that fits your needs, that is usually the fastest way to get a database started. However, if you have existing data, you may decide that it is easier to create a blank database because it would require a lot of work to adapt your existing data to the data structure already defined in the template.

On the Getting Started with Microsoft Office screen, click the Blank Database icon. In the Blank Database pane, key a file name, select a location to store the file, and click Create. Access creates the database, and then opens an empty table named Table1 in datasheet view. By default, Access creates a primary key field named "ID" for all new datasheets, and it sets the data type for the field to AutoNumber.

LOOKING AHEAD
You will learn more about defining and modifying a primary key in Lesson 3.

With the insertion point in the first empty cell, you can begin keying to add data. Entering data in Datasheet view is very similar to entering data into an Excel worksheet, except that data must be entered in contiguous rows and columns, starting at the upper-left corner of the datasheet.

LOOKING AHEAD
You will learn more about creating forms and reports in Lessons 5 and 6.

The table structure is created as you enter data. Anytime you add a new column to the table, a new field is defined. You do not need to format your data by including blank rows or columns, as you might do in an Excel worksheet, because that just wastes space in your table. The table merely contains your data. All visual presentation of that data will be done in the forms and reports that you design later.

SOFTWARE ORIENTATION

Tables Group Commands

The Tables group on the Create tab provides several commands you can use to insert a new table.

Figure 2-12
Tables Group Commands

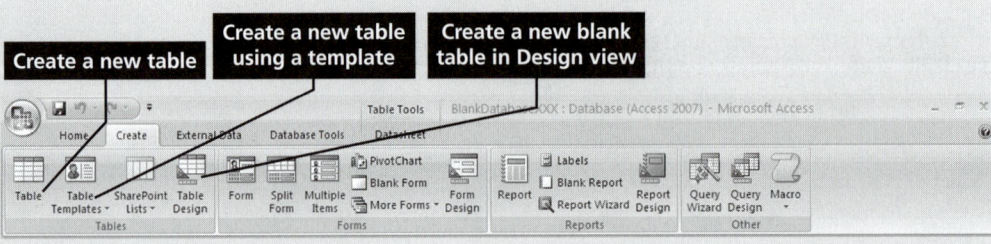

Use this figure as a reference throughout this lesson as well as the rest of this book.

Creating a Database Table

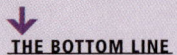
THE BOTTOM LINE

As you learned in the last exercise, when you create a new blank database, a new empty table is automatically inserted for you. You can also insert a new blank table into an existing database or use a table template to create a new table.

Create Database Tables | 757

Creating a Table from a Template

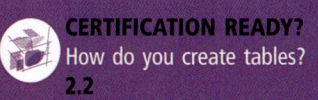

CERTIFICATION READY?
How do you create tables?
2.2

It is easy to create a new table using a table template. Table templates are available for common subjects such as contacts, issues, and tasks.

→ CREATE A TABLE FROM A TEMPLATE

USE the database that is open from the previous exercise.

1. On the Create tab, in the Tables group, click the **Table Templates** button to display the menu shown in Figure 2-13.

Figure 2-13

Table Templates menu

2. Click **Contacts**. A new table is created with fields for contacts, as shown in Figure 2-14.

Figure 2-14

New table for contacts

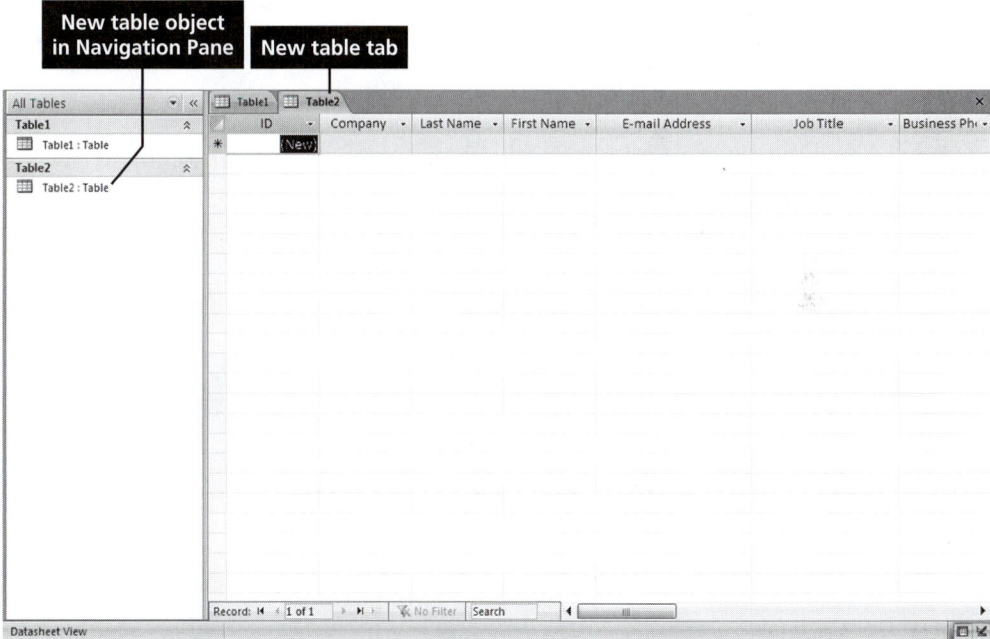

3. On the Table Templates menu, click **Tasks**. A new table is created with fields for tasks, as shown in Figure 2-15.

Figure 2-15

New table for tasks

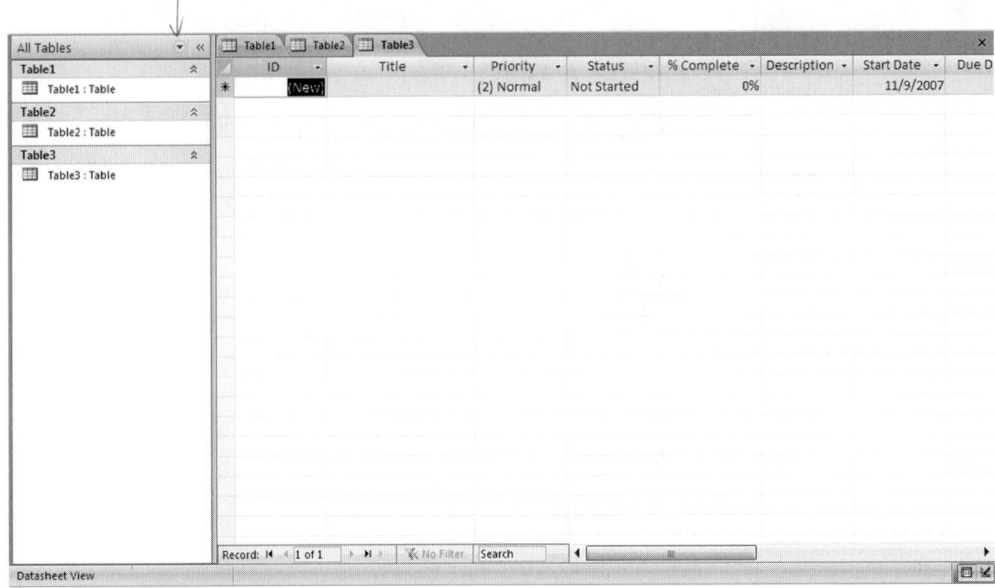

4. On the Table Templates menu, click **Issues**. A new table is created with fields for issues, as shown in Figure 2-16.

Figure 2-16

New table for issues

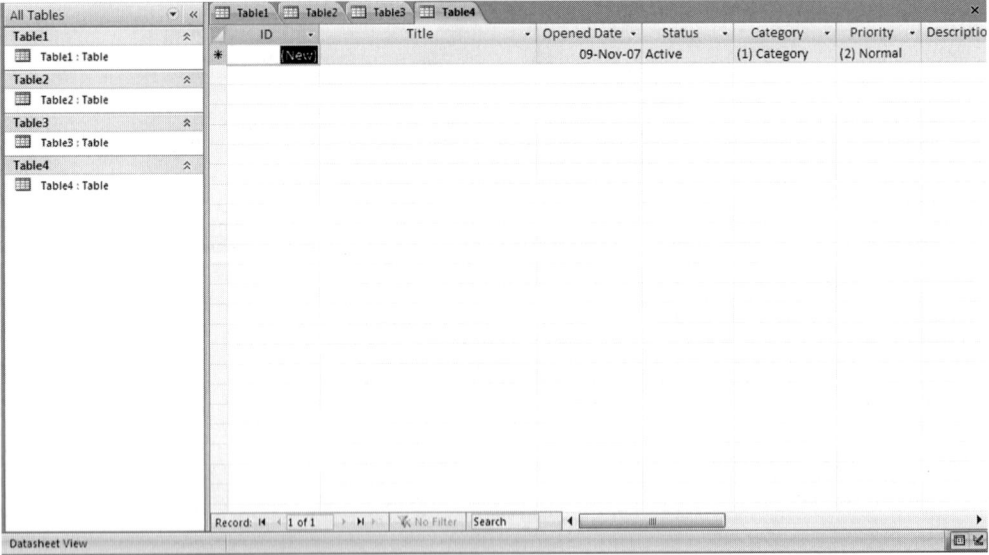

5. On the Table Templates menu, click **Events**. A new table is created with fields for events, as shown in Figure 2-17.

Figure 2-17

New table for events

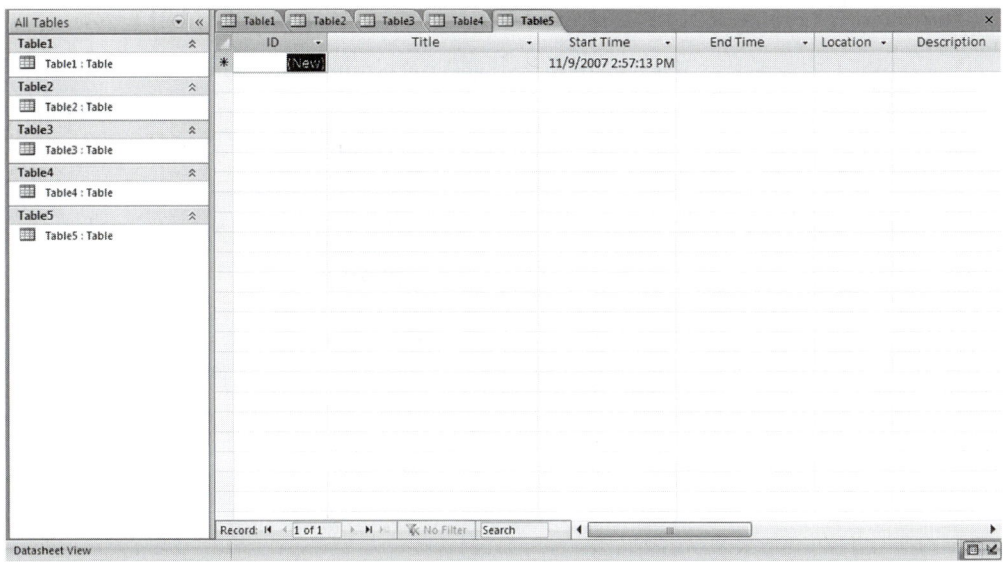

6. On the Table Templates menu, click **Assets**. A new table is created with fields for assets, as shown in Figure 2-18.

Figure 2-18

New table for assets

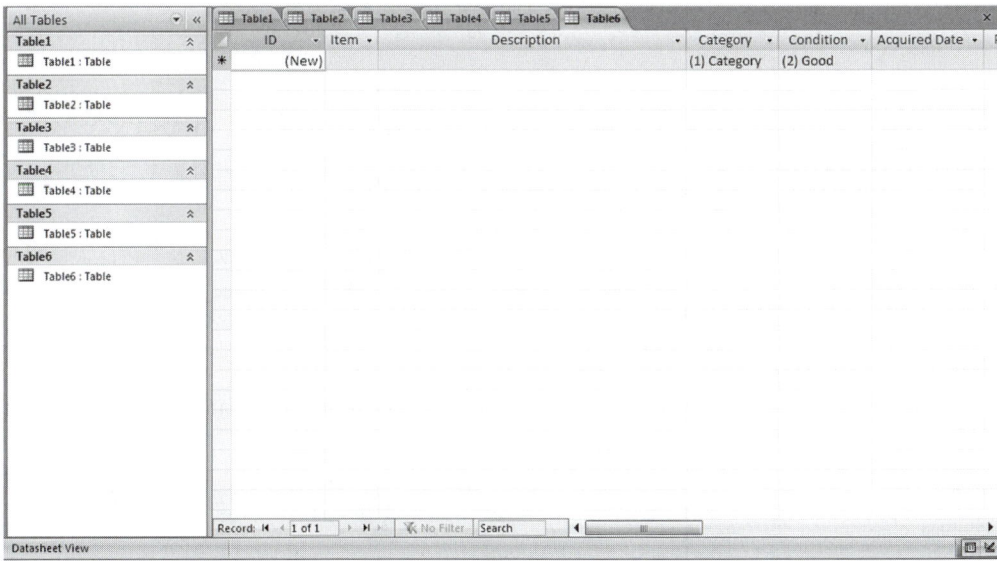

CERTIFICATION READY?
How do you create tables from templates?
2.2.3

PAUSE. LEAVE the database open to use in the next exercise.

To create a table for common subjects such as contacts, issues, and tasks, you might want to start with a table template. Open the database to which you want to add a table. On the Create tab, in the Tables group, click the Table Template button and then select an available template from the menu. A new table is inserted in the database, based on the table template that you chose, and you can begin keying data.

Creating a Table from Another Table

Another way to create a table is to copy the structure of an existing table using the Copy and Paste commands.

CREATING A TABLE FROM ANOTHER TABLE

USE the database that is open from the previous exercise.

1. On the Navigation Pane, right-click the **Table2: Table** database object to display the menu shown in Figure 2-19.

Figure 2-19

Database object menu

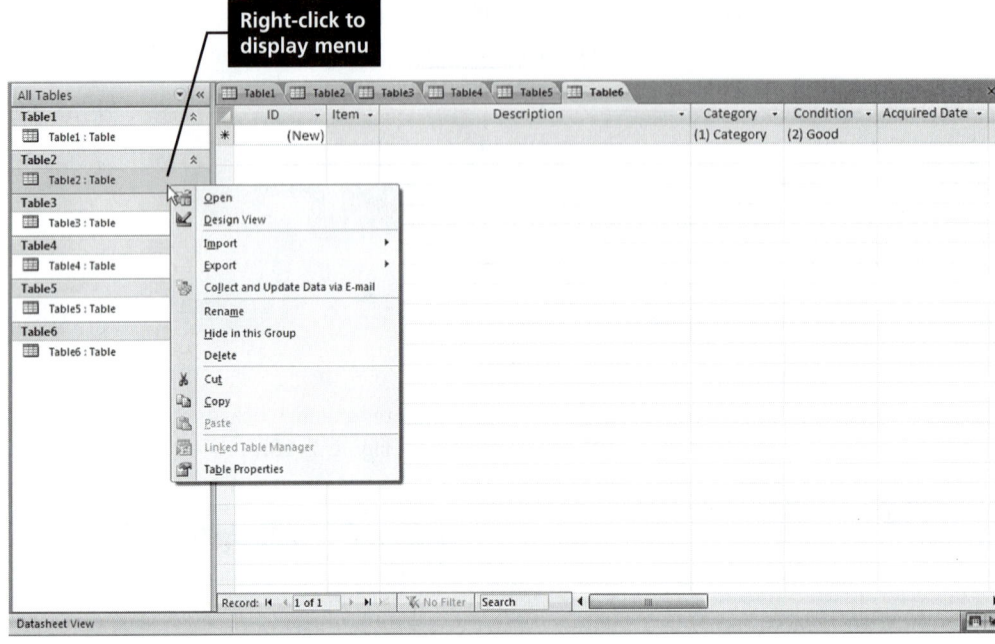

2. Click **Copy**.

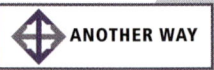 **ANOTHER WAY** You can also copy a database object by selecting it in the Navigation Pane and pressing Ctrl+C. Or on the Home tab, in the Clipboard group, click the Copy button.

3. Right-click in the Navigation Pane and click **Paste**, as shown in Figure 2-20.

Figure 2-20

Database object menu

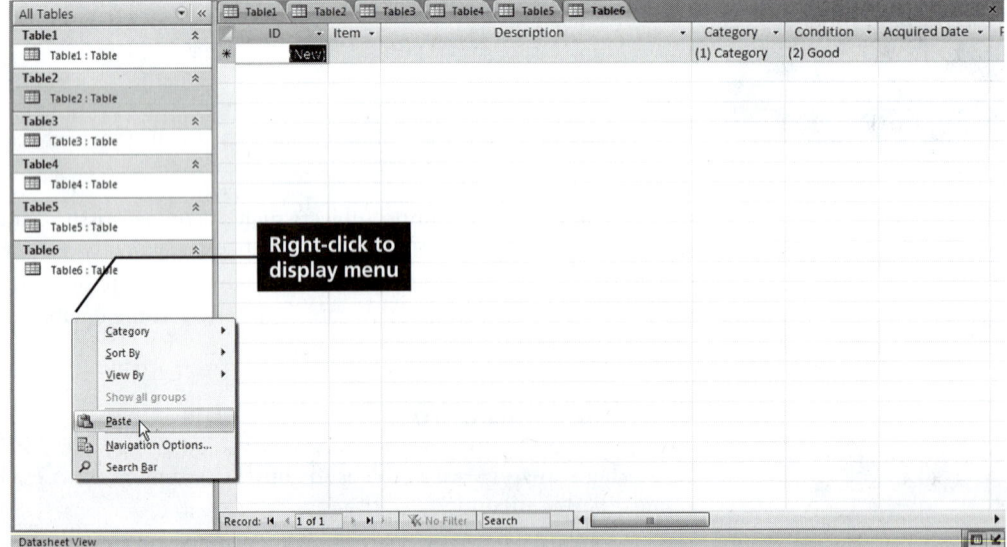

Create Database Tables | 761

ANOTHER WAY

You can also paste a database object by selecting the destination location in the Navigation Pane and pressing Ctrl+V. Or on the Home tab, in the Clipboard group, click the Paste button.

4. The Paste Table As dialog box appears, as shown in Figure 2-21. In the Table Name box, key **Assets**.

Figure 2-21

Paste Table As dialog box

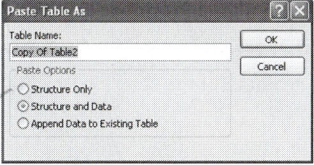

5. In the Paste Options section, select the **Structure Only** radio button.
6. Click **OK**.
7. The new table appears at the end of the list of database objects in the Navigation Pane, as shown in Figure 2-22.

Figure 2-22

New table copied from existing table

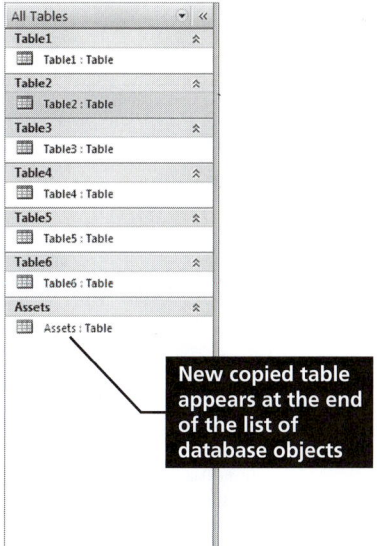

New copied table appears at the end of the list of database objects

CERTIFICATION READY?
How do you create tables by copying the structure of other tables?
2.2.2

8. Double-click **Assets: Table** to open the new table. Notice that the structure of the new table is the same as the table from which it was copied.

   PAUSE. LEAVE the database open to use in the next exercise.

Another way to create a table is to copy the structure of an existing table and paste it into the database. You can copy a database object and paste it in the same database or into a different database that is open in another instance of Access.

Select the table in the Navigation Pane, right-click, and choose Copy. To paste, select the destination location, right-click, and choose Paste. In the Paste Table As dialog box, key a name for the new table. To paste just the structure of the table, click Structure Only. To also paste the data, click Structure and Data.

LOOKING AHEAD

You will learn more about defining table relationships in Lesson 3.

When you add a new table to an existing database, that new table stands alone until you relate it to your existing tables. For example, say you need to track orders placed by a distributor. To do that, you add a table named Distributor Contacts to a sales database. To take advantage of the power that a relational database can provide—to search for the orders placed by a given contact, for example—you must create a relationship between the new table and any tables that contain the order data.

Saving a Database Object

THE BOTTOM LINE

Access automatically saves data that you have entered any time you move to a new record; close an object or database; or quit the application. But you will need to save the design of a table, or any other database object, after it is created.

Saving a Table

After you have created a table or other database object, you should save it with a descriptive name, such as Inventory Parts or Contacts.

SAVE A TABLE

USE the database that is open from the previous exercise.

1. Right-click on the **Table2 tab** to display the shortcut menu, as shown in Figure 2-23.

Figure 2-23

Shortcut menu

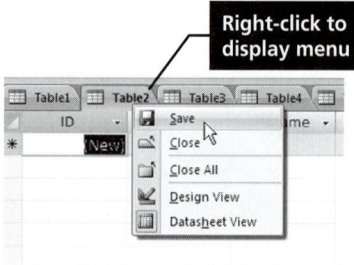

2. Click **Save**. The Save As dialog box appears, as shown in Figure 2-24.

Figure 2-24

Save As dialog box

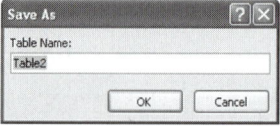

ANOTHER WAY

You can also save a table by pressing Ctrl+S.

3. In the Table Name box, key **Contacts**.
4. Click **OK**.
5. Click the **Table3 tab** to display that table.
6. Click the **Office Button** and click **Save** to display the Save As dialog box.
7. In the Table Name box, key **Tasks**.
8. Click **OK**.
9. Click the **Table4 tab** and save the table as **Issues**.
10. Click the **Table5 tab** and save the table as **Events**.
11. Click the **Table6 tab** and save the table as **Exhibits**.
12. **CLOSE** the database.
    CLOSE Access.

After you add fields to a table, you should save its design. When you save a new table for the first time, give it a name that describes the information it contains. You can use up to 64 characters (letters or numbers), including spaces. For example, you might name a table Orders 2007, Clients, or Tasks.

To save a table, click the Office Button and then click Save. Or you can right-click the table tab and then click Save on the shortcut menu. In the Save As dialog box, type a descriptive name for the table.

You do not need to save new data that you enter. Access automatically saves a record when you move to a different record or close the object or database.

Access also automatically saves changes to your data whenever you quit the program. However, if you have made changes to the design of any database objects since you last saved them, Access asks whether you want to save these changes before quitting.

SUMMARY SKILL MATRIX

In this lesson you learned how to:
Use a Template to Create a Database
Create a Blank Database
Create a Table from a Template
Create a Table from Another Table
Save a Table

■ Knowledge Assessment

Fill in the Blank

Complete the following sentences by writing the correct word or words in the blanks provided.

1. You can create a database using one of the many templates available or by creating a new ____blank____ database.

2. By default, Access creates a(n) __Primary Key__ field named "ID" for all new datasheets. p. 756

3. Entering data in Datasheet view is very similar to entering data in a(n) __Excel Worksheet__. p. 756

4. Table __templates__ p. 759 are available for common subjects such as contacts, issues, and tasks.

5. One way to create a table is to copy the __structure__ of an existing table and paste it into the database.

6. When you add a new table to an existing database, that new table stands alone until you __relate__ p. 761 it to your existing tables.

7. You can use up to __64__ characters (letters or numbers), including spaces, to name a database object.

8. Several options for creating a database are provided on the __Getting Started MS off. Access__ page.

9. When you find a template that you want to use, click the __Table Template__ button for Access to create and open the database.

10. After you add __fields__ to a table, you should save its design.

Multiple Choice

Select the best response for the following statements.

1. A template is
   a. a database to manage contacts.
   b. where a database is stored.
   c. two tables linked together.
   d. a ready-to-use database.

2. When you create a new blank database, Access opens a database that contains
   a. one of each type of database object.
   b. a table.
   c. sample data.
   d. a template.

3. To save a database file in a location other than the default, click the
   a. folder icon.
   b. blank database icon.
   c. file name button.
   d. Help button.

4. The table structure is created when you
   a. format the data.
   b. enter data.
   c. insert blank rows and columns.
   d. switch to Design view.

5. The Tables group commands are located on which tab?
   a. Home
   b. Create
   c. Database Tools
   d. Datasheet

6. To copy a table, you must first select it in
   a. the Clipboard.
   b. Microsoft Office Online.
   c. the Navigation Pane.
   d. Datasheet view.

7. When you paste a table, which dialog box is displayed?
   a. Table Structure
   b. Copy Table
   c. Paste Data
   d. Paste Table As

8. After you have created a table or other database object, you should
   a. save it with a descriptive name.
   b. copy it to create a backup.
   c. link it to an external data source.
   d. insert a blank column at the end.

Create Database Tables | 765

9. When you quit the program, Access automatically
   a. creates a link between all tables.
   b. leaves the Navigation Pane open.
   c. saves the data.
   d. renames the file.
10. Which is *not* a way to create a new database table?
    a. Use a table template.
    b. Choose Create on the Table menu.
    c. Copy the structure of another table.
    d. Create a new blank database.

■ Competency Assessment

Project 2-1: Contacts Database

You want to use Access to store, organize, and manage the contact information for the wholesale coffee suppliers used by Fourth Coffee, where you work as a buyer for the 15 stores in the northeast region. Use a template to create a database for the contacts.

GET READY. Launch Access if it is not already running.

1. In the Business template category, select the **Contacts** database.
2. Key *ContactsXXX* (where XXX is your initials) in the File Name box.
3. If necessary, click the folder icon and choose a different location for the file.
4. Click **Download** (or click **Create** if not logged onto the Internet) to create and open the database.
5. Click the **Shutter Bar Open/Close Button** to open the Navigation Pane.
6. Click the **Supporting Objects** header to display the database objects in that group.
7. Right-click the **Contacts** table to display the menu and click **Copy**.
8. Right-click in the white area of the Navigation Pane and click **Paste** on the menu.
9. In the Paste Table As dialog box, key **Suppliers**.
10. Click the **Structure Only** radio button.
11. Click **OK**.
12. **CLOSE** the database.

    LEAVE Access open for the next project.

Project 2-2: Database for Polling Sites

As a volunteer precinct captain, you are responsible for coordinating the polling sites for the upcoming general and special elections. You decide to create a database to store the necessary information.

1. On the Getting Started with Microsoft Office Access page, click the **Blank Database** icon.
2. In the Blank Database pane on the right, key **VotingXXX** (where xxx is your initials) in the File Name box.
3. If necessary, click the folder icon and choose a different location for the file.
4. Click the **Create** button.
5. Right-click the **Table1 tab** and click **Save**.
6. In the Save As dialog box, key **Locations**.
7. Click **OK**.

   LEAVE Access open for the next project.

Proficiency Assessment

Project 2-3: Adding Tables

You need to add some tables to the voting database that you just created for information about polling sites.

USE the database that is open from the previous project.

1. Use the Table Templates to create a table for contacts.
2. Name the table **Officials**.
3. Copy the structure of the Officials table to create a new table.
4. Name the new table **Volunteers**.
5. **CLOSE** the database.

   LEAVE Access open for the next project.

Project 2-4: Nutrition Tracker

You have become health conscious and want to track your activity, exercise, and food logs using Access.

1. If necessary, log on to the Internet.
2. In the Personal category, download the Nutrition template with the file name **Nutrition XXX** (where xxx is your initials).

> **TROUBLESHOOTING**
> If this template is not available, you may have to click "Automatically update this content from Office Online" on the Getting Started with Microsoft Office Access page.

> **TROUBLESHOOTING**
> If you are asked to enable the content, click the Options button on the Message Bar. In the dialog box, click Enable this content and then click OK.

3. Key your information in the My Profile form that is displayed to see your body mass index and recommended calorie consumption. (If the My Profile form is not displayed, open it first.)
4. Click **OK**.
5. Open the Tips table to view the tips stored in the database.
6. Explore the other useful forms and information available.
7. **CLOSE** the database.

   LEAVE Access open for the next project.

Mastery Assessment

Project 2-5: Northwind Traders

You have just joined the sales force at Northwind Traders. To familiarize yourself with the information available in the company database, open the file and browse through the objects.

1. In the Sample category, download the Northwind 2007 database using the name **Northwind 2007 XXX** (where XXX is your initials).
2. Enable the content.
3. Log in as a sales representative, Jan Kotas, by selecting that name from the Select Employee dropdown menu and clicking the Log In button.
4. Open the Navigation Pane and open each group to view all the objects that are part of the database.

5. **CLOSE** the database.

LEAVE Access open for the next project.

Project 2-6: Customer Service Database

Southridge Video has a large membership of customers that rent new release and film library movies, as well as video games. As the store manager, customer complaints are directed to you. Create an Access database for the purpose of tracking customer service issues.

1. Choose a template to create a database called **SouthridgeXXX** (where xxx is your initials) that will store information about customer service issues.
2. **CLOSE** the database.

   CLOSE Access.

INTERNET READY

If you can't find a template that fits your needs on the Getting Started with Microsoft Office Access page, you can explore the Office Online Web site for a larger selection. Near the bottom of the Getting Started with Microsoft Office Access page, under More on Office Online, click Templates to display the Templates Homepage, as shown in Figure 2-25.

Figure 2-25

Templates Homepage

3 Work with Tables/Database Records

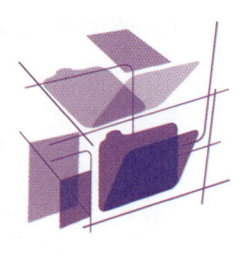

LESSON SKILL MATRIX

Navigating Using the Keyboard — 769	Students will learn how to navigate using the keyboard.
Navigating Using Navigation Buttons — 770	Students will learn how to navigate using navigation buttons.
Entering, Editing, and Deleting Records — 771	Students will learn how to enter, edit, and delete records.
Defining and Modifying a Primary Key — 773	Students will learn how to define and modify a primary key.
Defining and Modifying a Multi-field Primary Key — 774	Students will learn how to define and modify a multi-field primary key.
Finding and Replacing Data — 775	Students will learn how to find and replace data.
Attaching and Detaching Documents — 777	Students will learn how to attach and detach.
Sorting Data Within a Table — 779	Students will learn how to sort data within a table.
Filtering Data Within a Table — 781	Students will learn how to filter data within a table.
Removing a Filter — 783	Students will learn how to remove a filter.
Defining Table Relationships — 785	Students will learn how to define table relationships.
Modifying Table Relationships — 786	Students will learn how to modify table relationships.
Printing Table Relationships — 787	Students will learn how to print table relationships.

KEY TERMS
ascending
composite key
descending
filter
foreign key
innermost field
input mask
outermost field
referential integrity
sort
wildcard

Work with Tables/Database Records | 769

Fourth Coffee is a national chain of coffee shops. A new store recently opened in your neighborhood. You were able to get a part-time job working in the office, helping the office manager organize data on the computer. In addition to being a traditional neighborhood coffee shop, the store has also started selling coffees to companies for use at their business sites. It is your job to manage the inventory, customers, and order tables in Access. In this lesson, you will learn to navigate among records; enter, edit, and delete records; find and replace data; sort and filter data; attach and detach documents; and define, modify, and print table relationships.

■ Navigating Among Records

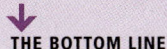
THE BOTTOM LINE

Database tables are usually large, which is why they are so useful. When a table contains many records and fields, it is important to be able to navigate among them.

Navigating Using the Keyboard

Access users who prefer using the keyboard to navigate records can press keys and key combinations to move among records in Datasheet view. If you prefer to use the mouse, you can move among records by clicking the navigation buttons.

➔ **NAVIGATE AMONG RECORDS USING THE KEYBOARD**

GET READY. Before you begin these steps, be sure to turn on and/or log on to your computer and start Access.

The *Fourth Coffee* database is available on the companion CD-ROM.

1. **OPEN** *Fourth Coffee* from the data files for this lesson.
2. Click the **Office Button**, point to Save As, and select **Access 2007 Database.**
3. Key **FourthCoffeeXXX** (where XXX is your initials) in the File name box. Find the location where you will save the solution files for this lesson and click **Save**.
4. In the Navigation Pane, double-click **Coffee Inventory: Table** to open the table.
5. Notice that the first cell of the first record is selected.
6. Press the [Down Arrow] key to move down to the next row. Notice that the cell is selected.
7. Press the [Right Arrow] key to move to the Product Name field.
8. Press the [Tab] key to move to the next cell.
9. Press the [Tab] key to move to the next cell.
10. Press the [Tab] key to move to the next row.
11. Press [Ctrl + Down Arrow] to move to the current field of the last record.
    PAUSE. LEAVE the database open to use in the next exercise.

In Datasheet view, you can navigate among records using the up, down, left, and right arrow keys to move to the field you want. You can also use the Tab key to move from field to field in a record and from the last field in a record to the first field of the next record.

Table 3-1 lists keys and key combinations for moving among records.

Table 3-1

Keyboard Commands for Navigating Records

PRESS	TO MOVE
Tab or Right Arrow	To the next field
End	To the last field in the current record
Shift + Tab or Left Arrow	To the previous field
Home	To the first field in the current record
Down Arrow	To the current field in the next record
Ctrl + Down Arrow	To the current field in the last record
Ctrl + End	To the last field in the last record
Up Arrow	To the current field in the previous record
Ctrl + Up Arrow	To the current field in the first record
Ctrl + Home	To the first field in the first record

CERTIFICATION READY?
How do you navigate among records?
3.2

Navigating Using Navigation Buttons

Access users who prefer to use the mouse can move among records by clicking the navigation buttons.

NAVIGATE AMONG RECORDS USING NAVIGATION BUTTONS

USE the database open from the previous exercise.

1. Click the **First record** button, shown in Figure 3-1. The selection moves to the first record.

Figure 3-1

Record navigation buttons

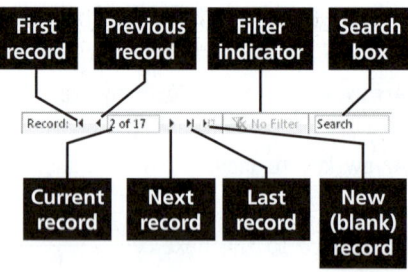

2. Click the **Next record** button. The selection moves to the next record.
3. Select the number *2* in the **Current Record** box. Key **5** and press Enter. The selection moves to the fifth record.
4. Click the **Search** box to position the insertion point. Key **sunrise** into the Search box. Notice that the selection moves to the first occurrence of the word *Sunrise*.
5. Press Enter. The selection moves to the next occurrence of the word *Sunrise*.
6. Click the **New (blank) record** button.

   PAUSE. LEAVE the database open to use in the next exercise.

Work with Tables/Database Records | 771

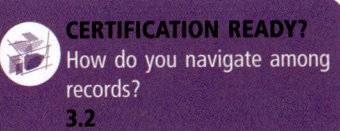

CERTIFICATION READY?
How do you navigate among records?
3.2

The record navigation buttons are displayed at the bottom of the screen in Datasheet view. Click the First, Previous, Next, Last, and New (blank) Record buttons to go to those records. Key a record number into the Current Record box and press Enter to go to that record. Key data into the Search box to find a match in the table. The Filter Indicator shows whether a filter has been applied to the table.

■ Entering, Editing, and Deleting Records

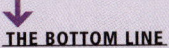
THE BOTTOM LINE

Databases are constantly changing. New data is added, and old data is updated or deleted. Keeping a database up-to-date and useful is an ongoing process. You can easily enter data by positioning the insertion point in the cell where you want to add data and begin keying. Select existing data to edit or delete it.

➔ ENTER, EDIT, AND DELETE RECORDS

USE the database you used in the previous exercise.

1. The insertion point should be positioned in the first field of the new, blank row at the bottom of the datasheet, as shown in Figure 3-2. Notice the asterisk in the record selector, which indicates that this is a new record, ready for data.

Figure 3-2

Blank record in Datasheet view

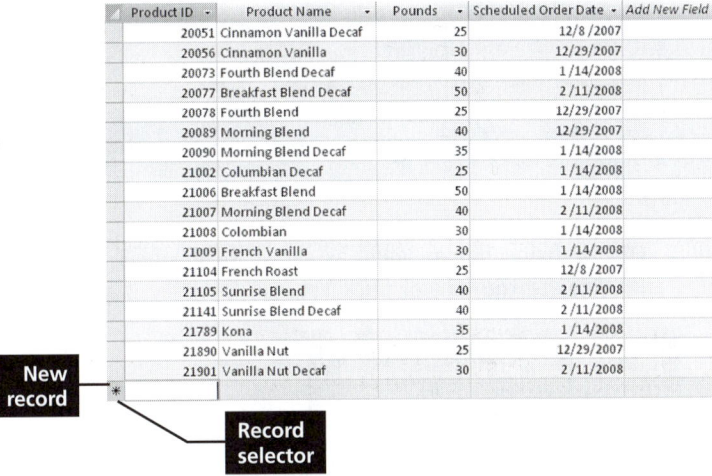

2. Key **21905** and press Tab. Notice that the asterisk has changed to a pencil icon, as shown in Figure 3-3, indicating that the record is being edited.

Figure 3-3

Enter data into a record

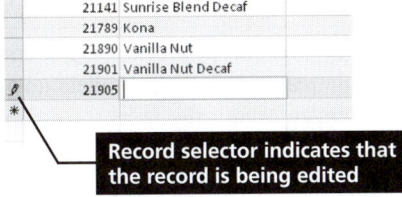

3. Key **Hazelnut** and press Tab.
4. Key **30** and press Tab.
5. Key **02112008** and press Enter. Notice that the input mask, shown in Figure 3-4, requires that the date be keyed exactly as formatted.

Figure 3-4

Input mask

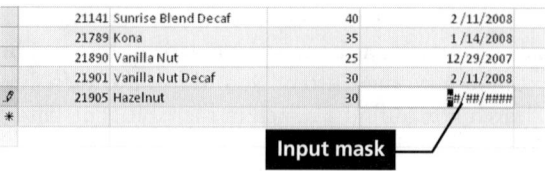

6. Select **sunrise** in the Search box and key **Kona** to locate the Kona record.
7. Select **Kona** in the record to position the blinking insertion point there. Key **Hawaiian** and press Tab.
8. Click the **Undo** button on the Quick Access Toolbar.
9. Press Tab. Key **12292007** and press Tab.
10. Click the **Select All** button to the left of the Product ID field of the first record, *20051*.
11. On the Home tab, in the Records group, click the arrow beside the Delete button. Select **Delete Record** from the menu, as shown in Figure 3-5.

Figure 3-5

Delete menu

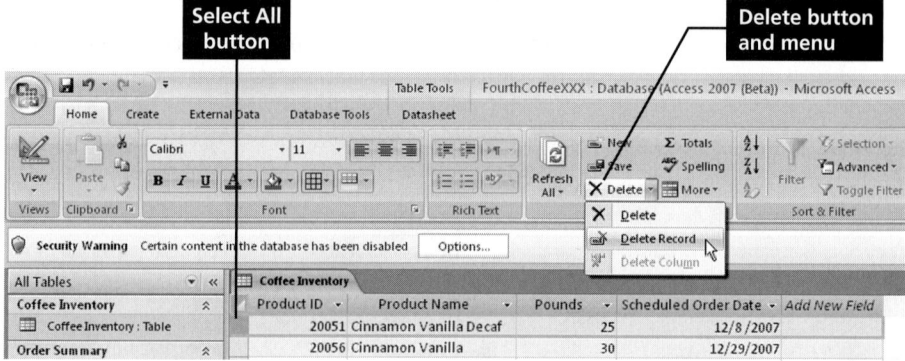

12. A dialog box appears, as shown in Figure 3-6, asking if you are sure you want to delete the record. Click **Yes**.

Figure 3-6

Microsoft Office Access Dialog box

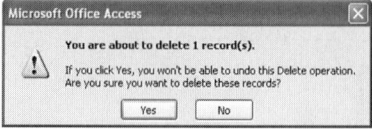

13. Notice that the Undo button on the Quick Access Toolbar is not available because you cannot undo a deletion. **CLOSE** the table.

PAUSE. LEAVE the database open to use in the next exercise.

In Datasheet view, position the insertion point in the first empty cell of a record and begin keying to add data. Continue entering data field by field and row by row. After you enter data and move to a new field, Access automatically saves the data in the table.

As you enter data, remember that each field in a table is formatted with a specific data type, so you must enter that kind of data in the field. If you do not, you will get an error message. For example, if a field is formatted to accept numbers, you cannot enter text.

Sometimes fields may contain an ***input mask***, which is a set of placeholder characters that force you to enter data in a specific format. For example, an input mask for a date might look like this: *xx/xx/xxxx*. All dates in that field must be entered in that format or you will get an error message. Input masks help maintain consistency and prevent users from entering invalid data.

Work with Tables/Database Records | 773

To insert a new record, select any record in the table and click the New button on the Home tab in the Records group. You can also right-click a selected record and select New Record from the shortcut menu. A new record is added to the end of the table.

To delete information from a field, select it and press the Delete key or click the Delete button on the Home tab in the Records group. If you change your mind after you delete information from a field, you can undo the action by clicking the Undo button on the Quick Access Toolbar.

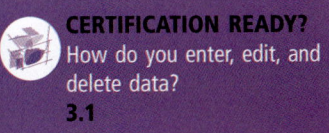

You can also delete an entire record or several records at once from a database. Just select the row or rows and press the Delete key or click the Delete button on the Home tab in the Records group. You can also right-click and select Delete Record from the shortcut menu. After you delete a record, you cannot undo it.

An easy way to select an entire record is to click the Select All button, which is a square to the left of a record. If you need to select other records above or below it, you can drag the mouse up or down to include those in the selection. To delete one or more selected records, right-click the Select All button and choose Delete Record from the shortcut menu.

To delete a record without selecting it, place the cursor in one of the fields of a record and click the Delete menu on the Home tab in the Records group. Select Delete Record from the menu.

■ Creating and Modifying Primary Keys

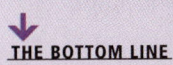

A primary key identifies a record or row in a table. Customer IDs, serial numbers, or product IDs usually make good primary keys. Each table should have a primary key, and some tables might have two or more. When you divide information into separate tables, the primary keys help Access bring the information back together again.

Defining and Modifying a Primary Key

A field designated as the primary key should uniquely identify each record, never be empty, and never change.

⬇ **DEFINE AND MODIFY A PRIMARY KEY**

USE the database you used in the previous exercise.

1. **OPEN** the **Order Summary** table.
2. On the Home tab, in the Views group, click the arrow on the View menu. Select **Design View**.
3. Click the **Select All** box beside the Order ID row to select the row.

774 | Lesson 3

4. On the Design tab, in the Tools group, click the **Primary Key** button. The Primary Key button is pushed in and appears orange. A key icon is displayed on the Order ID row to designate the field as a primary key, as shown in Figure 3-7.

Figure 3-7

Primary key

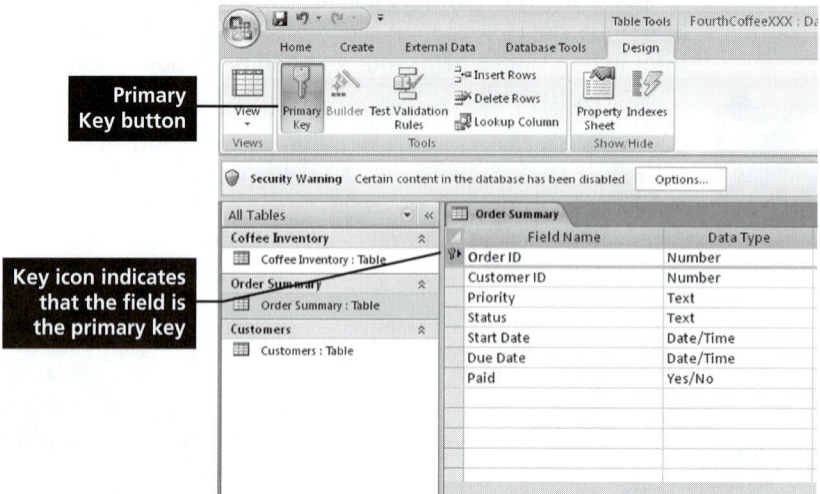

5. With the Order ID row still selected, click the **Primary Key** button. The button changes back to its original color, and the key icon in the Order ID row is removed.

 To add or remove the primary key from a field, you can also select the row, right-click, and select Primary Key from the shortcut menu.

PAUSE. LEAVE the table open to use in the next exercise.

As you learned in Lesson 1, a primary key is a column that uniquely identifies each row, such as Item Number.

You just defined a primary key in an existing table using Design view. Now that it is defined, you can use the primary key in other tables to refer back to the table with the primary key. When a primary key from one table is used in another table, it is called the *foreign key*. The foreign key is used to reference the data from the primary key to help avoid redundancy.

You can modify a primary key by deleting it from one field and adding it to another field. To delete a primary key in Design view, select the row and click the Primary Key button to remove it.

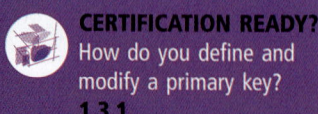

CERTIFICATION READY?
How do you define and modify a primary key?
1.3.1

When you create a new database, Access creates a primary key field named "ID" by default and sets the data type for the field to AutoNumber. If you don't have a field in an existing database that you think will make a good primary key, you can use a field with the AutoNumber data type. It doesn't contain factual information (such as a telephone number) about a record and it is not likely to change.

Defining and Modifying a Multi-field Primary Key

Some tables might have multiple primary keys.

➔ **DEFINE AND MODIFY A MULTI-FIELD PRIMARY KEY**

USE the database open from the previous exercise.

1. Press and hold the **CTRL** key.

Work with Tables/Database Records | 775

2. Click the **Select All** button beside the **Paid** row. Continue to hold down the **CTRL** key and click the **Order ID** selection button. Both fields should be selected, as shown in Figure 3-8. If not, continue to hold the **CTRL** key and click the **Paid** selection button again.

Figure 3-8

Primary key

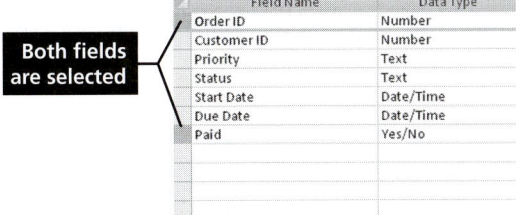

Both fields are selected

3. On the Design tab, in the Tools group, click the **Primary Key** button. A key icon should be displayed beside each of the two fields.
4. With the rows still selected, click the **Primary Key** button again to remove the primary key designation from both the fields.
5. Click in any field to remove the selection.
6. Click the **Select All** button beside the **Order ID** row. Drag down to the next row, the **Customer ID** row, to select it as well.
7. On the Design tab, in the Tools group, click the **Primary Key** button. Both rows should have a key displayed beside them.
8. Click the **Save** button on the Quick Access Toolbar.
9. **CLOSE** the Design view.

   PAUSE. LEAVE the database open to use in the next exercise.

CERTIFICATION READY?
How do you define and modify a multi-field primary key?
1.3.2

In some cases, you may want to use two or more fields that, together, provide the primary key of a table. For example, in the Order Summary table, you used the Order ID and the Customer ID as primary keys. Two or more primary keys in a table are called the ***composite key.***

As you just practiced, you can modify the primary keys by changing which fields are defined as the primary keys. In Design view, select the rows you want to designate as primary keys and click the Primary Key button.

To remove multiple primary keys, select the rows and click the Primary Key button.

■ Finding and Replacing Data

THE BOTTOM LINE

A big advantage of using a computer database rather than paper and pencil for recordkeeping is the ability to quickly search for and/or replace data. These features may be accessed from the Find and Replace dialog box. The Find and Replace commands in Access work very much like those you've probably used in Word or other Office applications. You can use the Find command to search for specific text in a table or to move quickly to a particular word or number in the table. The Replace command can be used to automatically replace a word or number with another.

➔ FIND AND REPLACE DATA

USE the database open from the previous exercise.

1. **OPEN** the **Customers** table.

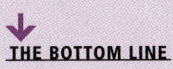

2. On the Home tab, in the Find group, click the **Find** button. The Find and Replace dialog box appears with the Find tab displayed.

3. Click the **Replace** tab in the Find and Replace dialog box.
4. Key **Elm** into the Find What box.
5. Key **Little Elm** into the Replace With box.
6. Click the down arrow beside the Look in menu and select **customers**, so that the entire database will be searched instead of just the Customer ID field.
7. Click the down arrow beside the Match menu and select **Any Part of Field** to broaden the search. See Figure 3-9.

Figure 3-9

Find and Replace dialog box

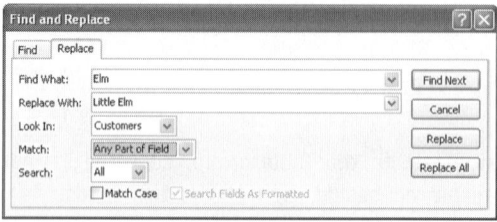

8. Click the **Find Next** button. Access searches the table and finds and selects the word *Elm*.
9. Click the **Replace** button. Access replaces *Elm* with *Little Elm*.
10. Click the **Find Next** button. Access finds *Elm* in the new text that was just inserted.
11. Click **Find Next** again. Access displays a message saying that no more occurrences of the word have been found. Click **OK**.
12. Click **Cancel** to close the dialog box.
13. Press Down Arrow to remove the selection and allow Access to save the change.
14. **CLOSE** the table.

    PAUSE. LEAVE the database open to use in the next exercise.

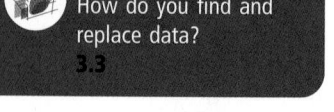

CERTIFICATION READY?
How do you find and replace data?
3.3

ANOTHER WAY

To open the Find tab in the Find and Replace dialog box using the keyboard, press Ctrl+F. To open the Replace tab, press Ctrl+H.

In the Find and Replace dialog box, key the text or numbers that you want to search for into the Find What box and click Find Next to locate the record containing the data. If you want to replace the data, key the new data into the Replace With box and click Replace or Replace All.

TAKE NOTE

When replacing data, it is usually a good practice to click Replace instead of Replace All so that you can confirm each replacement to make sure that it is correct.

The Find and Replace dialog box searches only one table at a time; it does not search the entire database. The Look In menu allows you to choose to search by field or to search the entire table. By default, Access searches the field that was selected when you opened the Find and Replace dialog box. If you want to search a different field, select the field while the dialog box is open; you don't have to close it first.

In the Match menu, you can specify where you want Access to look in a field. Select Any Part of Field for the broadest search.

Sometimes Access selects the Search Fields As Formatted checkbox. When it does, do not clear the checkbox, or your search probably will not return any results.

Click the Match Case box to search for text with the same uppercase and/or lowercase capitalization of text.

Work with Tables/Database Records | 777

You can use *wildcard* characters to find words or phrases that contain specific letters or combinations of letters. Key a question mark (?) to represent a single character—for example, keying b?t will find *bat*, *bet*, *bit*, and *but*. Key an asterisk (*) to represent a string of characters—for example, m*t will find *mat*, *moment*, or even *medium format*.

If you key a wildcard character in the Replace With box, Access will insert that character just as you keyed it.

TAKE NOTE

If you want to use the Find and Replace dialog box to search for characters that are used as wildcards, such as a question mark, you must enclose that character in brackets, for example, [?]. Follow this rule when searching for all wildcard characters except exclamation points (!) and closing brackets (]).

Attaching and Detaching Documents

THE BOTTOM LINE

Access 2007 allows you to attach documents, such as Word documents or photo files, to records in a database. For example, the human resources department of a large company could keep a photo, a resume, and employee evaluation documents with each employee record. These attached files can also be easily detached, if necessary. The Attachments dialog box allows you to manage the documents attached to records.

ATTACH AND DETACH DOCUMENTS **NEW FEATURE**

USE the database open from the previous exercise.

1. **OPEN** the **Order Summary** table.
2. Click the header row of the Due Date field to select it.
3. On the Datasheet tab, in the Fields & Columns group, click the **New Field** button. The Field Templates menu appears.
4. Double-click **Attachment** under Basic Fields, as shown in Figure 3-10. The Attachment field is inserted in the table.

Figure 3-10

Field Templates menu

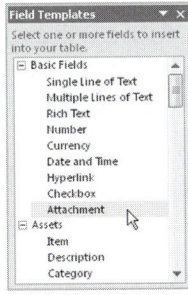

5. Click the **Close** button to close the Field Templates box.
6. Double-click the first row of the Attachments field. The Attachments dialog box appears.
7. Click the **Add** button. Navigate to the data files for this lesson and select *invoice100.docx*. Click **Open**. The document appears in the Attachments dialog box, as shown in Figure 3-11.

Figure 3-11

Attachments dialog box

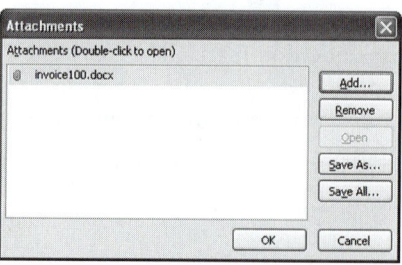

8. Click **OK**. The number of attachments in the first record changes to 1, as shown in Figure 3-12.

Figure 3-12

Attachments field

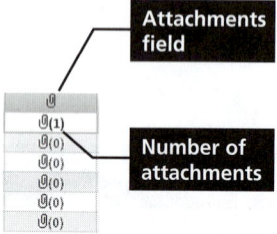

9. Double-click the attachment number. The Attachments dialog box appears.
10. Click the **Open** button. The attachment opens in Microsoft Word.
11. Click the **Close** button to close the invoice document.
12. Click the Access button on the taskbar to return to Access.
13. In the Attachments dialog box, click the **Remove** button and click **OK**. The attachment is removed from the record.
14. **CLOSE** the Order Summary table.

   PAUSE. LEAVE the database open to use in the next exercise.

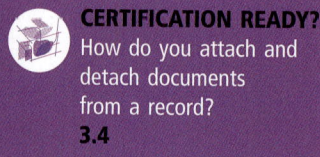

CERTIFICATION READY?
How do you attach and detach documents from a record?
3.4

TAKE NOTE
You can only attach files to databases created in Access 2007. You cannot share attachments with a database created in an earlier version of Access.

Before you can start attaching documents, you must create a field in a table and format it with the Attachment data type. You can add the field in Datasheet view or in Design view. Access displays a paper clip icon in the header row and in every record in the field along with a number in parentheses indicating the number of attached files in the field.

Double-click the record in the Attachments field to display the Attachments dialog box where you can add, remove, open, or save multiple attachments, such as images, documents, and spreadsheets, for a single record.

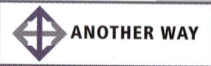 **ANOTHER WAY**
You can also right-click in the Attachments field to display a shortcut menu. Select Manage Attachments from the menu to display the Attachments dialog box.

If the program that was used to create the attached file is installed on your computer, you can open and edit the file using that program. For example, if you open a Word resume that is attached to a record, the Word program starts and you view the document in Word. If you do not have the program that was used to create a file, Access prompts you to choose a program you do have to view the file.

You can save attached files to your hard disk or network drive so that you can save changes to documents there before saving them to the database.

Sorting and Filtering Data Within a Table

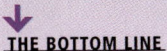

THE BOTTOM LINE

It is often helpful to display data in order or to display similar records. Sorting allows you to order records. For example, an office contact list that displays employees in alphabetical order by last name would help the user find information for a particular employee quickly. If you wanted to view only the records of employees in a particular department, you could create a filter to display only those records.

SOFTWARE ORIENTATION

Sort & Filter Group

The Sort & Filter group is located on the Home tab in the Ribbon.

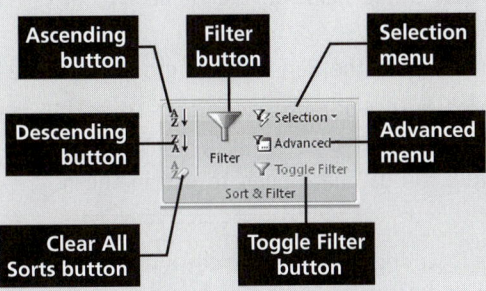

Figure 3-13

Sort & Filter Group

Use the Sort & Filter group of commands to sort and filter records in tables.

Sorting Data Within a Table

Sorting within a table displays all the records in the table in the order that you select. You can easily sort by one or more fields to achieve the order that you want.

→ SORT DATA WITHIN A TABLE

USE the database you used in the previous exercise.

1. **OPEN** the **Customers** table.
2. Click the header row of the Customer ID field to select it.
3. Right-click in the field to display the shortcut menu, shown in Figure 3-14. Select **Sort Largest to Smallest**.

Figure 3-14

Shortcut menu

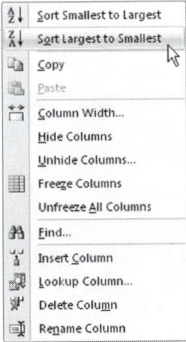

4. The data is sorted and an arrow is inserted in the header row, as shown in Figure 3-15, indicating that the data is displayed in sort order.

Figure 3-15

Sorted data

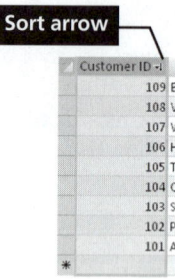

5. On the Home tab, in the Sort & Filter group, click the **Clear All Sorts** button. The sort is removed from the Customer ID field.
6. Select the First Name field. On the Home tab, in the Sort & Filter group, click the **Ascending** button.
7. Select the **Last Name** field. On the Home tab, in the Sort & Filter group, click the **Ascending** button.
8. On the Home tab, in the Sort & Filter group, click the **Clear All Sorts** button.
9. **CLOSE** the table. If a pop-up screen appears asking if you want to save changes to the table, click **No.**

   PAUSE. LEAVE the database open to use in the next exercise.

CERTIFICATION READY?
How do you sort data within a table?
5.1.1

To *sort* data means to arrange it alphabetically, numerically, or chronologically. Access can sort text, numbers, or dates in ascending or descending order. *Ascending* order sorts data from beginning to end, such as from A to Z, 1 to 10, and January to December. *Descending* order sorts data from the end to the beginning, such as from Z to A, 10 to 1, and December to January.

To sort text, numbers, dates, or other data types in a column, you first need to select the column. Then click the Ascending or Descending button in the Sort & Filter group of the Home tab. You can also right-click a selected column and choose a Sort command from the shortcut menu. The available sort commands in the shortcut menu vary depending on the type of data in the column, as shown in Table 3-2.

Table 3-2

Sort Commands on the shortcut menu

TYPE OF DATA	SORT COMMAND ON THE SHORTCUT MENU
Number, Currency, or AutoNumber	Sort Smallest to Largest / Sort Largest to Smallest
Text, Memo, or Hyperlink	Sort A to Z / Sort Z to A
Yes/No	Sort Selected to Cleared / Sort Cleared to Selected
Date/Time	Sort Oldest to Newest / Sort Newest to Oldest

Work with Tables/Database Records | 781

You can also sort records on multiple fields. When you are using multiple fields, determine which order you want them to be sorted in. The primary sort field is called the ***outermost field***. A secondary sort field is called an ***innermost field.*** For example, if you want to sort a contact list so that each employee's last name is sorted primarily and first name is sorted secondarily, Last Name would be the outermost field and First Name would be the innermost field. In your completed sort, Wright, David, would be listed before Wright, Steven, in an A to Z sort. When designating the sort order, however, you select the innermost field first and choose the type of sort you want from the shortcut menu. Then select the outermost field and select the type of sort that you want.

After you sort one or more columns, Access inserts sort arrows in the header row to show that the field is sorted. These sort commands remain with the table until you remove them. When you want to remove a sort order, click the Clear All Sorts button from the Sort & Filter group on the Home tab. This removes the sorting commands from all the fields in the table. In a table with more than one sorted fields, you cannot remove just one sort.

Filtering Data Within a Table

When you apply a filter, Access displays only the records that meet your filter criteria; the other records are hidden from view.

FILTER DATA

USE the database you used in the previous exercise.

1. **OPEN** the **Coffee Inventory** table. 
2. Select the **Product Name** field. On the Home tab, in the Sort & Filter group, click the **Filter** button. A menu appears.
3. Point to **Text Filters**. A second menu appears. Select **Contains**, as shown in Figure 3-16.

Figure 3-16

Filter menu

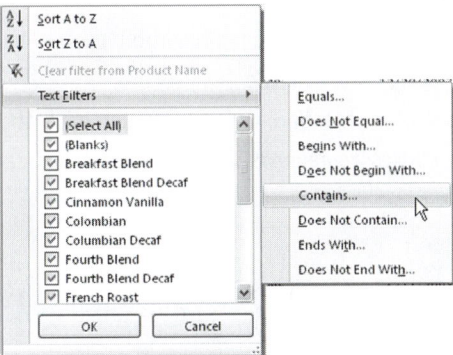

4. The Custom Filter box appears. Key **Decaf**, as shown in Figure 3-17, and click **OK**. Notice that only the records containing the word *Decaf* are displayed, and a filter icon is displayed in the header row of the field, as shown in Figure 3-18.

Figure 3-17

Custom filter box

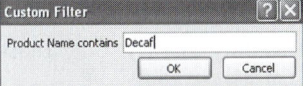

Figure 3-18

Filtered records

5. Click the **Toggle Filter** button to display the records without the filter.
6. In the second record in the Product Name field, double-click the word *Decaf* to select it.
7. Right-click to display the shortcut menu. Select **Does Not Contain "Decaf"**, as shown in Figure 3-19. Notice that the records are filtered to show only those that do not contain the word *Decaf*.

Figure 3-19

Shortcut menu

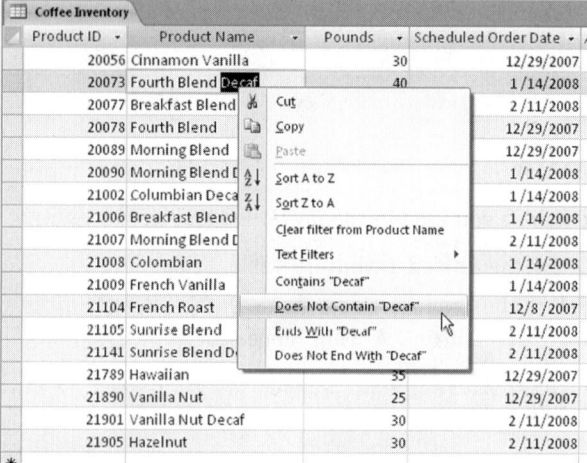

8. Click the **Filtered** button on the Navigation button bar.
9. Click in the **Pounds** field of the first record.
10. On the Home tab, in the Sort & Filter group, click the **Filter** button.
11. Click the checkboxes to remove the checkmarks beside **30**, **35**, **40**, and **50**, as shown in Figure 3-20.

Figure 3-20

Filter menu

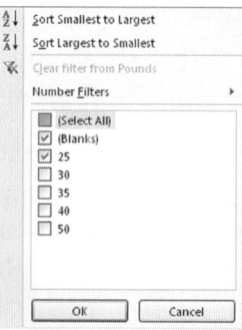

12. Click **OK**. Access filters the records to show only those containing the number 25.
13. Click the **Toggle Filter** button.
14. In the Date field of the second row, select **1/14/2008**.
15. On the Home tab, in the Sort & Filter group, click the **Selection** button. A menu appears.

Work with Tables/Database Records | 783

16. Select **On or After 1/14/2008**, as shown in Figure 3-21. The data is filtered.

Figure 3-21

Selection menu

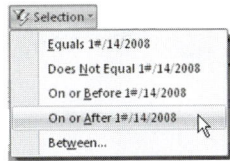

17. In the Pounds field of the seventh row, select **30**.
18. On the Home tab, in the Sort & Filter group, click the **Selection** button. Select **Less Than or Equal to 30**. The records are filtered.

    PAUSE. LEAVE the database open to use in the next exercise.

CERTIFICATION READY?
How do you filter data within a table?
5.2.1

A *filter* is a set of rules for determining which records will be displayed. Once the filtered records are displayed, you can edit and navigate the records just as you would without a filter applied.

You just practiced creating filters in several different ways.

You clicked the Filter button to view a menu of filtering choices, and you right-clicked fields to access context-related menus. The commands available on the menus vary, depending on the type of field or data selected. You also selected data and chose filters from the Selection menu.

TAKE NOTE

Only one filter can be applied per column. When you apply a filter to a column that is already filtered, the previous filter is removed and the new filter is applied.

The Toggle Filter button in the Sort & Filter group on the Home tab lets you temporarily remove a filter and switches you back to the original view. Click the toggle button again to return to the filtered view. In the same way, you can click the Filtered/Unfiltered button on the navigator bar at the bottom of the page to switch between filtered and unfiltered views.

Filters remain in effect until you close the object. You can switch between views, and the filter settings will stay in effect. To make the filter available the next time you open the object, save the object before closing it.

Removing a Filter

After applying a filter, you may need to return to records not displayed by the filter. The Toggle Filter button lets you switch between viewing the filtered records and viewing the table without the filter. When you are finished using the filter, you can permanently remove it.

➔ REMOVE A FILTER

USE the table you used in the previous exercise.

1. Select the Pounds field. On the Home tab, in the Sort & Filter group, click the **Filter** button. A menu appears.
2. Select **Clear Filter from Pounds**, as shown in Figure 3-22.

Figure 3-22

Filter menu

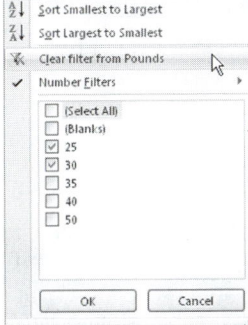

3. On the Home tab, in the Sort & Filter group, click the **Advanced** button. A menu appears.

Figure 3-23

Advanced menu

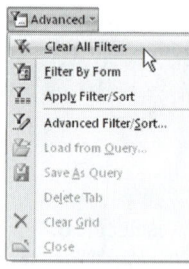

4. Select **Clear All Filters** from the menu, as shown in Figure 3-23.

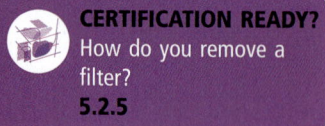

CERTIFICATION READY?
How do you remove a filter?
5.2.5

5. **SAVE** and **CLOSE** the table.

PAUSE. LEAVE the database open to use in the next exercise.

If you want to permanently remove a filter from a single field, select the field and click the Filter button on the Sort & Filter group on the Home tab. From the menu, select Clear filter from field name.

To clear all filters from all fields, click the Advanced button from the Sort & Filter group on the Home tab. From the menu, select Clear All Filters. When you clear a filter, it is gone. You can no longer apply it again by clicking the Toggle Filter button.

■ Understanding Table Relationships

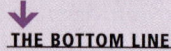
THE BOTTOM LINE

As you have already learned, most databases have more than one table. Creating relationships among these tables allows Access to bring that information back together again so that you can display information from several tables at once. This is why it is a good idea to define table relationships before you start creating reports and queries.

■ SOFTWARE ORIENTATION

Relationship Tools on the Ribbon

When you click the Relationships button on the Datasheet tab, the Relationship window appears and the Relationship Tools are displayed in the Ribbon, as shown in Figure 3-24.

Figure 3-24

Relationship Tools

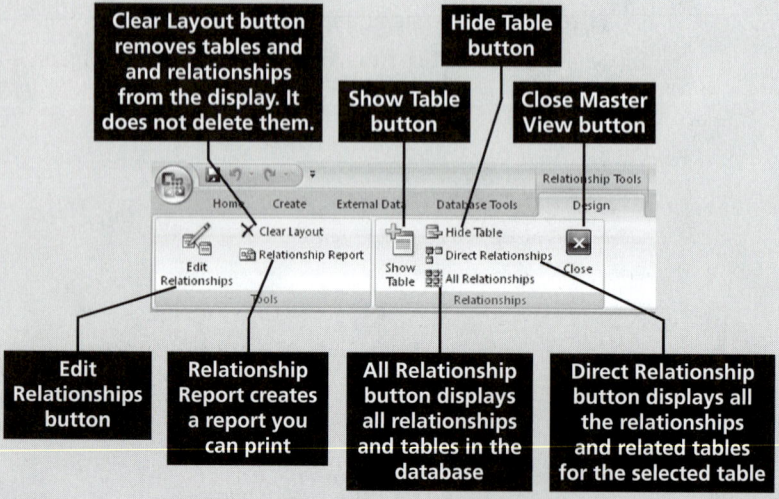

Use the Relationship Tools to define and modify table relationships.

Defining Table Relationships

In relational database applications like Access, you can store information in separate tables that are connected by a defined relationship that ties the data together. To create that relationship, you place common fields in tables and define the relationships between the tables.

→ DEFINE TABLE RELATIONSHIPS

USE the database you used in the previous exercise.

1. On the Database Tools tab in the Show/Hide group, click the **Relationships** button. The Relationships view appears with the Customers table represented.
2. Click the **Show Table** button. The Show Table dialog box appears, as shown in Figure 3-25.

Figure 3-25

Show Table dialog box

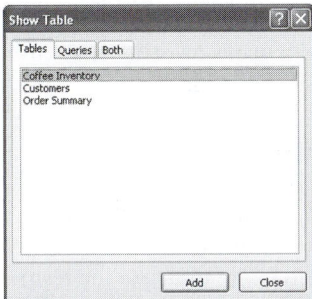

3. Select **Order Summary** and click **Add.**
4. Click **Close**. The two tables are represented in Relationship view.
5. Click the **Customer ID** field in the Customers table and drag it to the Customer ID field of the Order Summary table and release the mouse button. The Edit Relationship dialog box appears, as shown in Figure 3-26.

Figure 3-26

Edit Relationship dialog box

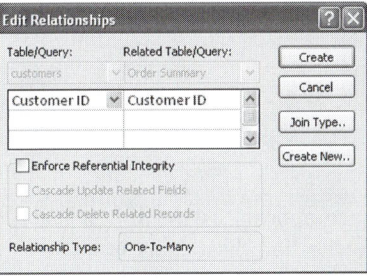

6. Click **Create**. The one-to-many table relationship of the Order Summary and the Customers Table is displayed, as shown in Figure 3-27.

Figure 3-27

One-to-many relationship

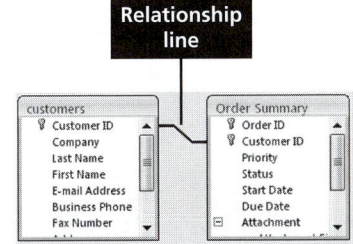

CERTIFICATION READY?
How do you define table relationships?
1.2.1

PAUSE. LEAVE the database open to use in the next exercise.

You can define a table relationship in the Relationships window.

Common fields used in different tables do not have to have the same names, but they usually do. They must have the same data type, though.

You can create three types of relationships: one-to-one, one-to-many, and many-to-many.

In a one-to-one relationship, both tables have a common field with the same data. Each record in the first table can only have one matching record in the second table, and each record in the second table can have only one matching record in the first table. This type of relationship is not common, because information related in this way is usually stored in the same table.

A one-to-many relationship is more common, because each record in the first table can have many records in the second table. For example, in a Customers table and an Orders table, one customer could have many orders. The Customer ID would be the primary key in the Customers table (the one) and the foreign key in the Orders table (the many).

In a third type of relationship, called a many-to-many relationship, many records in the first table can have many records in the second table.

Modifying Table Relationships

A table relationship is represented by the line that connects the tables in the Relationship window. To modify the relationship, you can double-click the line to display the Edit Relationships dialog box or delete the line to delete the relationship.

MODIFY TABLE RELATIONSHIPS

USE the database you used in the previous exercise.

1. Right-click the center section of the line connecting the two tables. A menu appears, as shown in Figure 3-28.

Figure 3-28

Edit/Delete menu

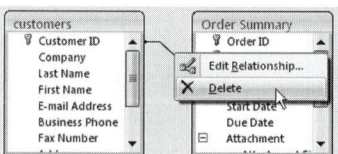

2. Select **Delete**. A message appears asking if you are sure you want to delete the relationship. Click **Yes**. The line disappears.
3. Select the **Customer ID** field in the first table. Drag the mouse to the Customer ID field in the second table and release the mouse button. The Edit Relationships dialog box appears.
4. Click the **Create** button. A line appears, creating the relationship.
5. Double-click the center section of the line. The Edit Relationships dialog box appears again, listing the tables and the Customer ID fields on each side.

Work with Tables/Database Records | 787

6. Click the **Enforce Referential Integrity** box and click **OK**. The line appears thicker, with the number 1 beside the first table and the infinity symbol (∞) beside the second, as shown in Figure 3-29.

Figure 3-29

Relationship displaying enforced referential integrity

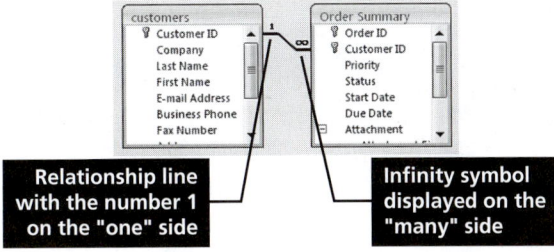

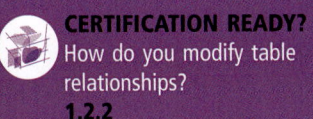

CERTIFICATION READY?
How do you modify table relationships?
1.2.2

PAUSE. LEAVE the database open to use in the next exercise.

When you want to change the table relationship, you can double-click the line connecting the tables or click the Edit Relationships command in the Tools group. The Edit Relationships dialog box allows you to change a table relationship. You can change the tables on either side of the relationship or the fields on either side. You can also set the join type or enforce referential integrity and choose a cascade option.

Referential integrity prevents orphan records. An orphan record is a record in one table that references records in another table that no longer exist. You can enforce referential integrity by clicking the Enforce Referential Integrity button in the Edit Relationships dialog box. Once this feature is turned on, Access will not allow any operation that violates referential integrity.

When you enforce referential integrity between tables, the line connecting the tables becomes thicker. The number 1 is also displayed on the line on the one side of the relationship and an infinity symbol (∞) appears on the other side.

To remove a table relationship, you must delete the relationship line. You can select the line by pointing to it and clicking it. When the relationship line is selected, it appears thicker. Press the Delete key to delete the line and remove the relationship or right-click the line to display the delete menu.

Printing Table Relationships

You may want to print out a table relationship to save for your records or to discuss with a colleague. The Relationship Report command makes this easy.

→ **PRINT TABLE RELATIONSHIPS**

USE the database you used in the previous exercise.

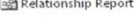

1. Click the **Relationship Report** button. The report is created and the Print Preview tab appears, as shown in Figure 3-30.

Figure 3-30

Print preview of Relationship Report

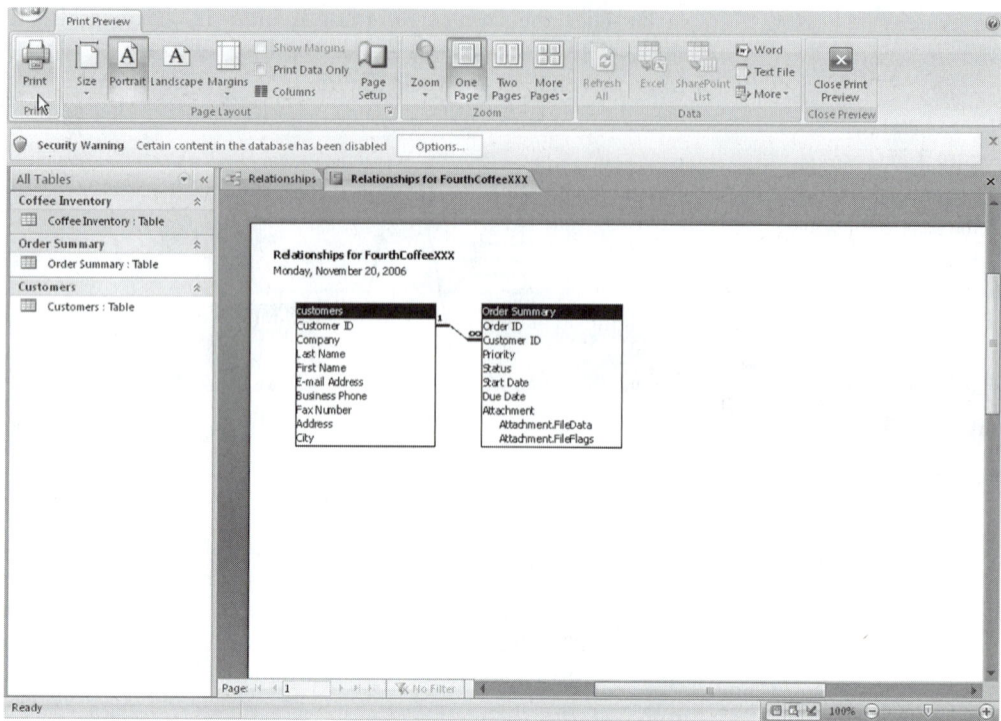

2. Click the **Print** button. The Print dialog box appears, allowing you to select the printer you want to use.
3. Click **OK**.
4. Click the **Close** button to close the Relationships for FourthCoffee tab. A message appears asking if you want to save changes to the report. Click **No**.
5. **CLOSE** the Relationships tab.

   STOP. CLOSE the database.

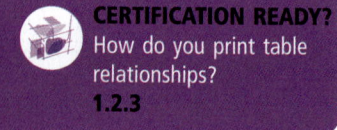

CERTIFICATION READY?
How do you print table relationships?
1.2.3

You printed a table relationship using the Relationship Report command. When you chose to print the report, the Print Preview tab appeared with options for viewing and printing the report. After you make any changes to the layout of the report, click the Print button to start printing. After printing the report, you can choose to save it.

Work with Tables/Database Records | 789

SUMMARY SKILL MATRIX

IN THIS LESSON YOU LEARNED HOW TO:
Navigate Using the Keyboard
Navigate Using Navigation Buttons
Enter, Edit, and Delete Records
Define and Modify a Primary Key
Define and Modify a Multi-field Primary Key
Find and Replace Data
Attach and Detach Documents
Sort Data Within a Table
Filter Data Within a Table
Remove a Filter
Define Table Relationships
Modify Table Relationships
Print Table Relationships

■ Knowledge Assessment

Matching

Match the term in Column 1 to its description in Column 2.

Column 1

1. foreign key (e)
2. composite key (h)
3. input mask (j)
4. referential integrity (a)
5. wildcards (i)
6. ascending order (b)
7. descending order (c)
8. filter (f)
9. sort (d)
10. innermost field (g)

Column 2

a. to prevent orphan records, to ensure that records do not reference other records that no longer exist
b. sorts data from beginning to end
c. sorts data from end to beginning
d. to arrange data alphabetically, numerically, or chronologically
e. a primary key from one table that is used in another table
f. a set of rules for determining which records will be displayed
g. the secondary sort field in a multi-field sort
h. two or more primary keys in a table
i. characters used to find words or phrases that contain specific letters or combinations of letters
j. a set of placeholder characters that force you to enter data in a specific format

True / False

Circle T if the statement is true or F if the statement is false.

T F 1. You can use the Navigation buttons to search for data in a table.

T **F** 2. You can enter any kind of data into any field.

T F 3. After you enter data and move to a new field, Access automatically saves the data for you in the table.

T **F** 4. After you delete a record, you can click the Undo button to bring it back.

T **F** 5. The Find and Replace dialog box searches all the tables in a database at one time.

T F 6. An AutoNumber field will usually make a good primary key.

778 - **T** F 7. Before you can attach a document, there must be a field in a table formatted with the Attachment data type.

781 - **T** F 8. The outermost field is the primary sort field in a multi-field sort.

783 - T **F** 9. The Toggle Filter button lets you permanently remove a filter and switches you back to the original view. *Temporarily*

T F 10. In a one-to-many relationship, each record in the first table can have many records in the second table. *only one matching record*

■ Competency Assessment

Project 3-1: Charity Event Contacts List

You are working as an intern for Woodgrove Bank. Part of your job is helping your supervisor organize a charity event. Use an Access table to create a contacts list that your supervisor will use to make calls to local businesses requesting sponsorships and donations for the event.

GET READY. Launch Access if it is not already running.

1. **OPEN** the *Charity Event* database.
2. Save the database as *Charity EventXXX* (where XXX is your initials).
3. Open the **Contacts** table.
4. Enter the records shown in the following table.

ID	Company	Last Name	First Name	Business Phone
17	Trey Research	Tiano	Mike	469-555-0182
18	Fourth Coffee	Culp	Scott	469-555-0141
19	Wingtip Toys	Baker	Mary	972-555-0167
20	Margie's Travel	Nash	Mike	972-555-0189

5. Click the **View** menu and choose **Design** view.
6. Select the **ID** row. On the Design tab, on the Tools menu, click the **Primary Key** button.
7. Save the design of the table and return to Datasheet view.
8. On the Home tab, in the Find group, click the **Find** button. The Find and Replace dialog box appears. Key **0177** into the Find What box.
9. Select **Contents** from the Look In menu and select **Any Part of Field** in the Match menu.
10. Click the **Replace** tab. Key **0175** into the Replace With box.
11. Click **Find Next** and then click **Replace**.

The *Charity Event* database is available on the companion CD-ROM.

Work with Tables/Database Records | 791

12. Click **Cancel** to close the dialog box.
13. Select the **Lucern Publishing** record.
14. On the Home tab, in the Records group, click the **Delete** button. Click **Yes** to delete the record.
15. **CLOSE** the database.

    LEAVE Access open for the next project.

Project 3-2: Angels Project Wish List

The four kindergarten classes at the School of Fine Art have adopted one boy and one girl "angel" from the community. Children from the classes may purchase holiday gifts for their angels. As an office assistant at the school, you are working with the Angel Project staff to organize information about each angel.

1. **OPEN** *Angels* from the data files for this lesson.
2. **SAVE** the database as *AngelsXXX*, where XXX is your initials.
3. **OPEN** the List table.
4. Select the **Gender** field. On the Home tab, in the Sort & Filter group, click the **Ascending** button.
5. Select the **Age** field. On the Home tab, in the Sort & Filter group, click the **Descending** button.
6. On the Home tab, in the Sort & Filter group, click the **Clear All Sorts** button.
7. In the Gender field, select the **M** in the first record.
8. On the Home tab, in the Sort & Filter group, click the **Selection** button and select **Equals "M"**.
9. On the Home tab, in the Sort & Filter group, click the **Toggle Filter** button.
10. Select the **Wants** field. On the Home tab, in the Sort & Filter group, click the **Filter** button. Select **Text Filters** from the menu, select **Contains** from the next menu, and key **Bike** in the Custom Filter dialog box.
11. On the Home tab, in the Sort & Filter group, click the **Advanced** button and select **Clear All Filters** from the menu.

    LEAVE Access open for the next project.

The *Angels* database is available on the companion CD-ROM.

■ Proficiency Assessment

Project 3-3: Angel Project Contact Information

1. The Angel database should be open on your screen.
2. **OPEN** the **Contact Information** table.
3. Enter the following new records.

ID	Last Name	First Name	Parent's Name	Address	City	State	Zip Code	Home Phone
15	Wright	Steven	Kevin	2309 Monroe Ct	Marietta	GA	34006	770-555-0142
16	Cook	Cathan	Patrick	1268 Oak Dr	Marietta	GA	34006	770-555-0128

4. Switch to Design view. Remove the primary key from the Home Phone field and define the ID field as the primary key.
5. Save the design and return to Datasheet view.

6. Select the ID field and sort it in ascending order.
7. On the Datasheet tab, in the Relationships group, click the **Relationships** button.
8. Create a one-to-one relationship between the ID field of the List table and the ID field of the Contact Information table.
8. **SAVE** the relationships view and **CLOSE** it.
9. **CLOSE** the tables and the database.

   LEAVE Access open for the next project.

Project 3-4: Wingtip Toys Inventory Table

Wingtip Toys, a small manufacturer of wooden toys, has kept most of its records on paper for the last 20 years. The business has recently expanded, and you have been hired to help the company transfer its entire inventory and other administrative data to Office 2007. Edit the table to include all the latest handwritten data you've found.

The *Wingtip Toys* database is available on the companion CD-ROM.

1. **OPEN** the *Wingtip Toys* database and save it as *WingtipXXX*, where XXX is your initials.
2. **OPEN** the *Inventory* table.
3. On the Home tab, in the Find group, click the **Replace** button to display the Find and Replace dialog box. Change the following prices:

   Find all **14.99** and replace with **29.99**
   Find all **16.99** and replace with **34.99**
   Find all **15.99** and replace with **30.99**
   Find all **24.99** and replace with **34.99**

4. Delete the following records from the database:

   ID = 13
   ID = 19
   ID = 16

5. Edit the following records:

   ID = 30, change the number of items in stock to 3
   ID = 28, change the number of items in stock to 6
   ID = 6, change the number of items in stock to 4

6. Select the **In Stock** field and create a filter to display all the records with a value less than or equal to 10 in the field.
7. Remove the filter.
8. **CLOSE** the table.
9. **CLOSE** the database.

   LEAVE Access open for the next project.

■ Mastery Assessment

Project 3-5: Soccer Roster

As coach of your son's soccer team, you have created a database in which to store information about the team. Enter, edit, and delete records to update it.

The *Soccer* database is available on the companion CD-ROM.

1. **OPEN** the *Soccer* database from the data files for this lesson.
2. **SAVE** the database as *SoccerXXX*, where XXX is your initials.
3. **OPEN** the *Roster* table.

4. Enter the following record for a new player:

   Eric Parkinson, 806-555-0170, uniform number 9

5. One player has quit the team, Russell King. Replace his data with the data for the following new player:

   George Jiang, 806-555-0123, uniform number 4

6. In the **Size** field, enter **XS** for each player, except for uniform numbers 4, 6, and 7, which should be size **S**.
7. Create an Attachment field and attach the Word document *medicalalert.docx* to the record for Garrett Young.
8. Define the Uniform field as the primary key.
9. **SAVE** the table design and **CLOSE** the database.

   LEAVE Access open for the next project.

The *medicalalert* document is available on the companion CD-ROM.

Project 3-6: Donations Table

Donations are starting to come in for Woodgrove Bank's charity event. Track the donation commitments received.

1. **OPEN** the *CharityEventXXX* database.
2. **OPEN** the **Donations** table.
3. Create a filter to display the items in the Needs field without Commitments from a company.
4. Clear the filter.
5. Use Find and Replace to find each occurrence of the word *Company* in the Needs field and replace it with the word *Volunteer*.
6. Create a relationship between the ID field in the Contacts table and the Committed Company ID in the Donations table.
7. Print the relationship.
8. **CLOSE** the relationship without saving.
9. **CLOSE** the tables.
10. **CLOSE** the database.

    CLOSE Access.

The *charity event* database is available on the companion CD-ROM.

INTERNET READY

Search the Internet for at least five coffee shops in your area or a favorite city of your choice. Draw a table on paper or in a Word document with fields for the Company Name, Location, Phone Number, and Hours of Operation. Insert data for the five coffee shops you found. If you feel ready for a challenge, create the table in a new database.

4 Modify Tables and Fields

LESSON SKILL MATRIX

Modifying Table Properties — 795	Students will learn how to modify table properties.
Renaming a Table — 797	Students will learn how to rename a table.
Deleting a Table — 798	Students will learn how to delete a table.
Modifying Field Properties — 800	Students will learn how to modify field properties.
Creating and Deleting Fields — 807	Students will learn how to create and delete fields.
Creating and Modifying Multi-valued Fields — 811	Students will learn how to create and modify multi-valued fields.
Creating and Modifying Attachment Fields — 817	Students will learn how to create and modify attachment fields.

Margie's Travel is a full-service travel agency that specializes in sports-event travel packages. The company offers both individual and group travel packages to many of the leading sports events throughout the country. The travel packages can be customized to include plane tickets, event tickets, event transportation, hotel accommodations, official event souvenirs, and on-site staff assistance. As an assistant event coordinator, you are responsible for gathering information about a variety of events; you use Access to store the necessary data. In this lesson, you will learn how to modify table properties; rename a table; delete a table; modify field properties; and create and modify fields—including multi-value and attachment fields.

KEY TERMS
multi-valued field
validation rule
validation text
zero-length string

Modify Tables and Fields | 795

Modifying a Database Table

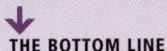 **THE BOTTOM LINE**

After a table has been created, you may need to modify it. You can make many changes to a table—or other database object—using its property sheet. You can also rename or delete a table, but keep in mind that such a change could possibly break the functionality of the database, because in a relational database the various components work together.

Modifying Table Properties

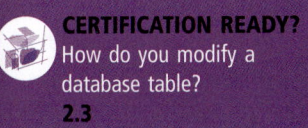

CERTIFICATION READY?
How do you modify a database table?
2.3

You can set properties that control the appearance or behavior characteristics for an entire table in the table's property sheet.

MODIFY TABLE PROPERTIES

GET READY. Before you begin these steps, be sure to launch Microsoft Access.

1. **OPEN** the *Events* database from the data files for this lesson.
2. **SAVE** the database as *EventsXXX* (where XXX is your initials).
3. Click the **Close 'Event List'** button to close that form.
4. In the Navigation Pane, double-click **Events** to open that table.
5. On the Home tab, in the Views group, click the **Views** button and then click **Design View**.
6. On the Design tab, in the Show/Hide group, click **Property Sheet**. The property sheet appears on the right of the Access window, as shown in Figure 4-1.

The *Events* database is available on the companion CD-ROM.

Figure 4-1

Property sheet displayed

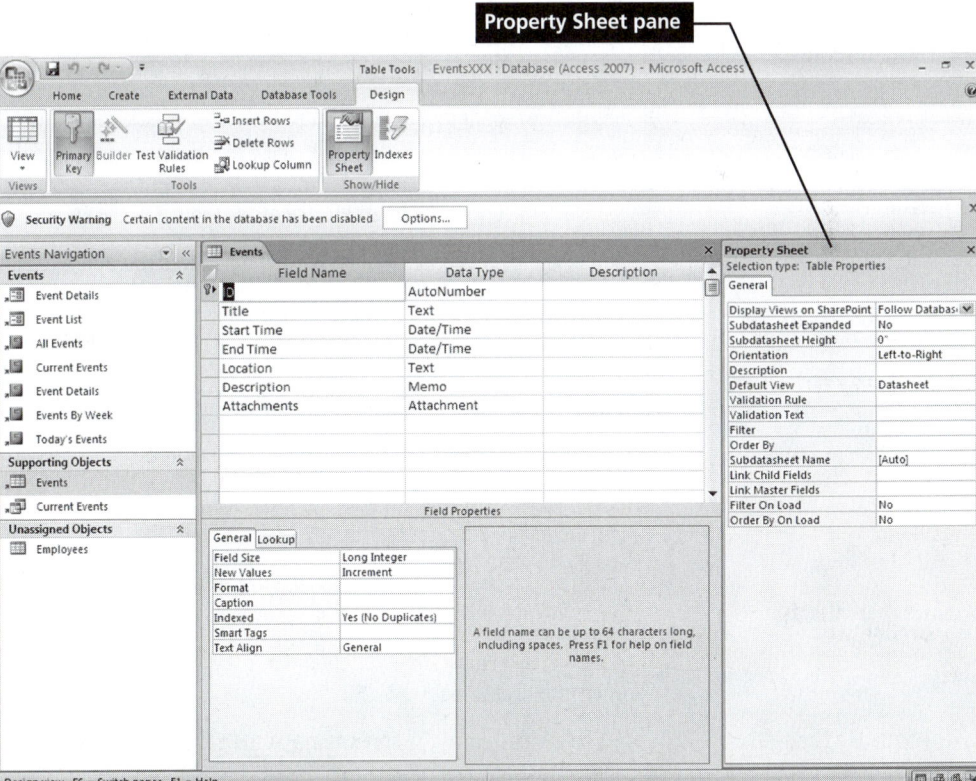

 **ANOTHER WAY**

You can also press Alt+Enter to display the property sheet for an object.

7. Place the insertion point in the property box for Description.
8. Press **Shift** + **F2** to open the Zoom box, shown in Figure 4-2.

Figure 4-2

Zoom box

9. Key **Most popular events for 2008**.
10. Click **OK**.
11. Click the **Close** button on the property sheet to close it.
12. Click the **Office Button** and click **Save**.
13. **LEAVE** the database open.

PAUSE. LEAVE Access open to use in the next exercise.

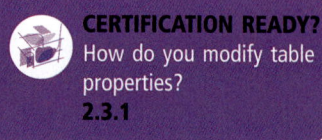

CERTIFICATION READY?
How do you modify table properties?
2.3.1

Table 4-1

Table Properties

To set the properties for a table, open the table in Design view. On the Design tab, in the Show/Hide group, click Property Sheet. Click the box for the property you want to set and key a setting for the property. Table 4-1 lists the available table properties and what they control.

Use this table property	To
Display Views on SharePoint	Specify whether forms and reports associated with the table should be available on the View menu in Windows SharePoint Services if the database is published to a SharePoint site.
Subdatasheet Expanded	Set whether to expand all subdatasheets when you open the table.
Subdatasheet Height	Specify whether to expand to show all available subdatasheet rows (default) when opened or to set the height of the subdatasheet window to show when opened.
Orientation	Set the view orientation, according to whether your language is read left-to-right or right-to-left.
Description	Provide a description of the table.
Default View	Set Datasheet, PivotTable, or PivotChart as the default view when you open the table.
Validation Rule	Supply an expression that must be true whenever you add a record or change a record.
Validation Text	Enter text that appears when a record violates the Validation Rule expression.
Filter	Define criteria to display only matching rows in Datasheet view.
Order By	Select one or more fields to specify the default sort order of rows in Datasheet view.
Subdatasheet Name	Specify whether a subdatasheet should appear in Datasheet view, and, if so, which table or query should supply the rows in the subdatasheet.
Link Child Fields	List the fields in the table or query used for the subdatasheet that match this table's primary key field(s).
Link Master Fields	List the primary key field(s) in this table that match the child fields for the subdatasheet.
Filter On Load	Automatically apply the filter criteria in the Filter property (by setting to Yes) when the table is opened in Datasheet view.
Order By On Load	Automatically apply the sort criteria in the OrderBy property (by setting to Yes) when the table is opened in Datasheet view.

If you want more space to enter or edit a setting in the property box, press Shift+F2 to display the Zoom box. Because you have made changes to the design of the table, you will need to save the changes before closing the database.

Renaming a Table

Think carefully before you rename a table. If existing database objects, such as queries or reports, use data from that table, the name modification might break the functionality of the database.

→ RENAME A TABLE

USE the database that is open from the previous exercise.

1. On the Create tab, in the Tables group, click the **Table Templates** button and click **Events** to create a new table.
2. Click **Table1** in the Navigation Pane and press F2. A message appears that states that you cannot name the table while it is open, as shown in Figure 4-3.

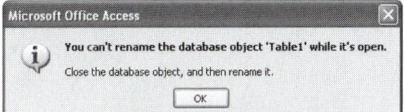

Figure 4-3
Can't rename table message

3. Click the **Close 'Table1'** button. A message appears asking if you want to save the design changes, as shown in Figure 4-4.

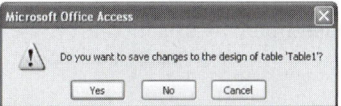

Figure 4-4
Save design changes message

4. Click **Yes**. The Save As dialog box appears, as shown in Figure 4-5.

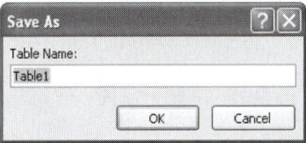

Figure 4-5
Save As dialog box

5. Click **OK** to save the table as Table1.
6. Right-click **Table1** in the Navigation Pane to display the menu shown in Figure 4-6.

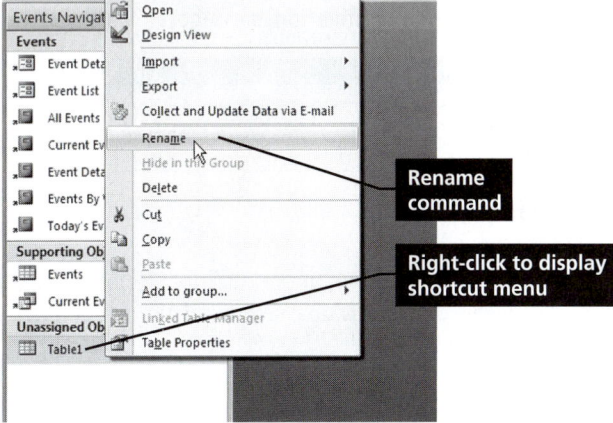

Figure 4-6
Rename command on table shortcut menu

Figure 4-7
Table name selected for renaming

7. Click **Rename**. The table name is now selected for renaming, as shown in Figure 4-7.

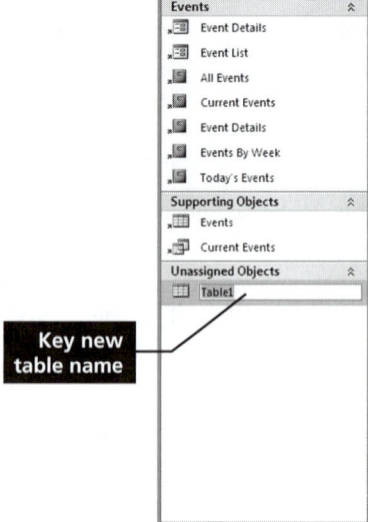

ANOTHER WAY

You can also select a database object in the Navigation Pane and press F2 to rename it.

CERTIFICATION READY?
How do you rename a table?
2.3.3

8. Key **Racing Events** and press **Enter**. The table has been renamed.
9. **LEAVE** the database open.

   PAUSE. LEAVE the database open to use in the next exercise.

To rename a table or other database object, you must first close it. In the Navigation Pane, locate and right-click the object that you want to rename, and then click Rename. Or, select the table in the Navigation Pane, press F2, key a new name, and press Enter.

Deleting a Table

If you delete a database table, you cannot undo the action, so you will be asked to confirm the deletion first.

DELETE A TABLE

USE the database that is open from the previous exercise.

1. Right-click the **Racing Events** table in the Navigation Pane and click **Delete** on the shortcut menu. A confirmation message appears, as shown in Figure 4-8.

Figure 4-8
Delete table confirmation message

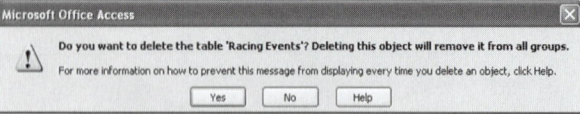

2. Click **Yes** to delete the table.

TAKE NOTE

If the table was related to one or more additional tables, Access would ask if you wanted to delete those relationships before deleting the table.

CERTIFICATION READY?
How do you delete a table?
2.3.4

3. **LEAVE** the database open.

   PAUSE. LEAVE the database open to use in the next exercise.

To delete a table or other database object, right-click it in the Navigation Pane and click Delete. Or, select the table in the Navigation Pane and press Delete.

Modify Tables and Fields | 799

Deleting an entire table is not a complex process; however, remember that when you delete an entire table you might break the functionality of your database. In addition, you lose all the data in the deleted table permanently. For those reasons, you should always back up your database before you delete a table.

 Another way to remove data is to delete information from individual records or delete entire records from a table, as you learned in Lesson 3.

Software Orientation

Field Properties

Some field properties are available in Datasheet view, but to access the complete list of field properties you must use Design view. An example of field properties for a table in Design view is shown in Figure 4-9.

Figure 4-9

Field properties

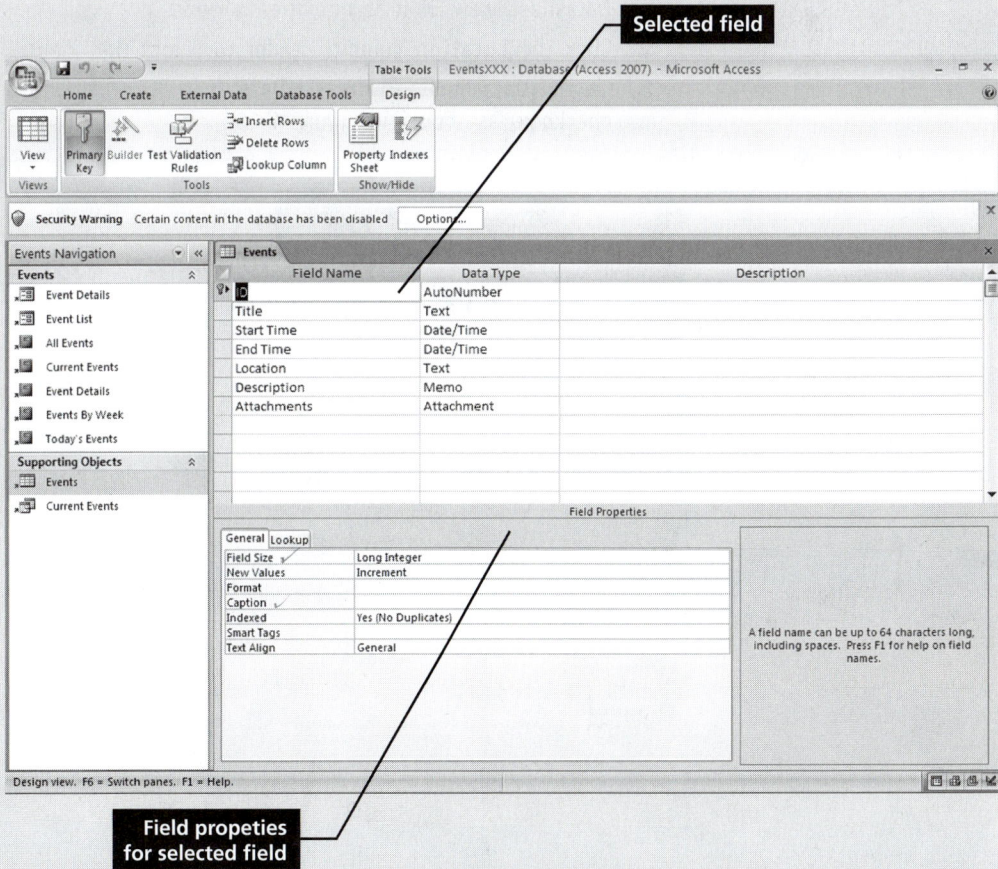

Use this Figure as a reference throughout this lesson as well as the rest of this book.

Creating Fields and Modifying Field Properties

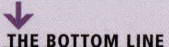
THE BOTTOM LINE

A field has certain defining characteristics, such as a name that uniquely identifies the field within a table and a data type that's chosen to match the information to be stored. Every field also has an associated group of settings called *properties* that define the appearance or behavior of the field. In this section, you will learn how to create fields and modify field properties.

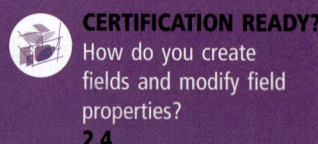
CERTIFICATION READY?
How do you create fields and modify field properties?
2.4

Modifying Field Properties

You can control the appearance of information, prevent incorrect entries, specify default values, speed up searching and sorting, and control other appearance or behavior characteristics by setting or modifying field properties. For example, you can format numbers to make them easier to read or you can define a validation rule that must be satisfied for information to be entered in a field.

→ **SET A FIELD PROPERTY IN DATASHEET VIEW**

USE the database that is open from the previous exercise.

1. Double-click the **Events** table in the Navigation Pane to open the table in Datasheet view, if it is not already open.
2. Click the **Location** column header to select that field.
3. On the Datasheet tab, in the Data Type & Formatting group, click the **Is Required** checkbox, as shown in Figure 4-10.

Figure 4-10

Set field property in Datasheet view

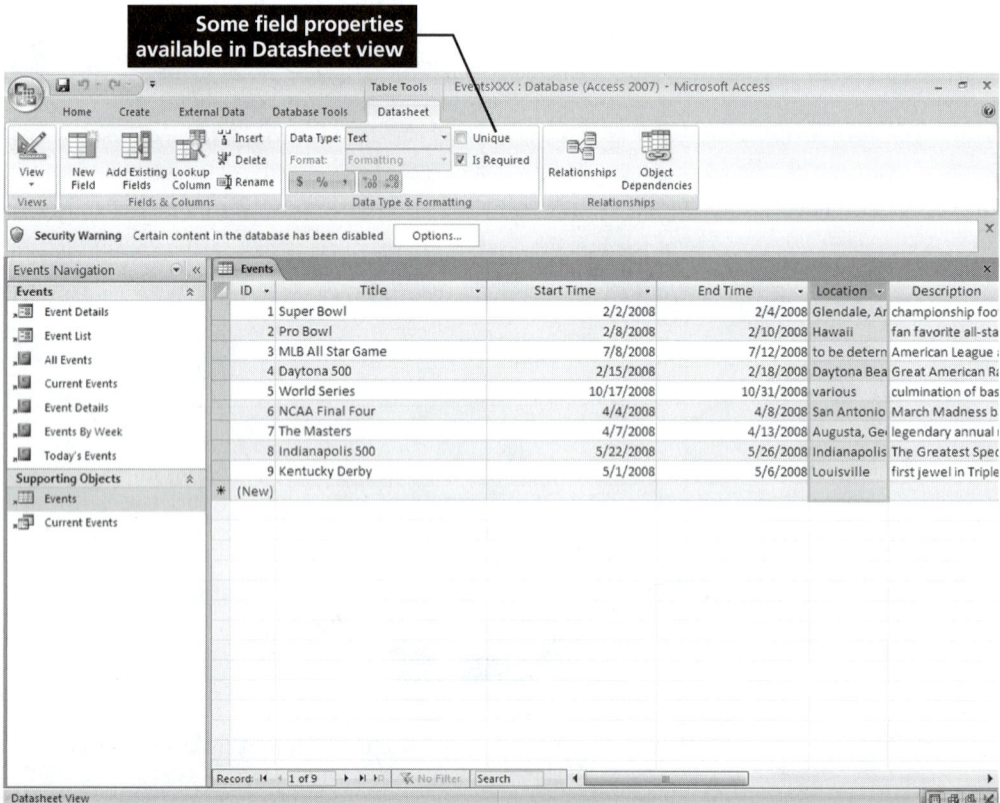

PAUSE. LEAVE the database open to use in the next exercise.

Access uses the field property settings when you view and edit data. For example, the Format, Input Mask, and Caption properties affect how your information appears in table and query datasheets. In addition, any controls on new forms and reports that are based on the fields in the table inherit these same property settings by default.

To set a field property in Datasheet view, open the table in Datasheet view. Click in the field for which you want to set the property. On the Datasheet tab, in the Data Type & Formatting group, select the Unique checkbox to require the values in the field to be unique for all the records in the table. Or, select the Is Required checkbox to make this a required field where all instances of this field must contain a value.

You can set only a few of the available field properties in Datasheet view. To set additional field properties, you must open the table in Design view.

 DEFINE TEXT LENGTH

USE the database that is open from the previous exercise.

1. On the Home tab, in the Views group, click the **View** button and click **Design View**.
2. In the Field Name column in the upper portion of the table design grid, click in the **Title** cell.
3. In the Field Size row in the lower portion of the table design grid, select **150** in the property box and key **175** to change the maximum number of characters you can enter.

TAKE NOTE To define the text length for a field, modify the Field Size property. The maximum number of characters you can enter into a field is 255.

PAUSE. LEAVE the database open to use in the next exercise.

To set field properties in Design view, open the table in Design view. In the upper portion of the table design grid, click the field for which you want to set properties. The properties for this field are displayed in the lower portion of the table design grid.

Click the box for the field property you want to set. Alternatively, you can press F6 and then move to the property by using the arrow keys. Type a setting for the property or, if an arrow appears at the right side of the property box, click the arrow to choose from a list of settings for the property.

Table 4-2 lists the available field properties.

Table 4-2
Field Properties

Use this field property	To
Field Size	Set the maximum size for data stored as a Text, Number, or AutoNumber data type.
Format	Customize the way the field appears when displayed or printed.
Decimal Places	Specify the number of decimal places to use when displaying numbers.
New Values	Set whether an AutoNumber field is incremented or assigned a random value.
Input Mask	Display editing characters to guide data entry.
Caption	Set the text displayed by default in labels for forms, reports, and queries.
Default Value	Automatically assign a default value to a field when new records are added.
Validation Rule	Supply an expression that must be true whenever you add or change the value in this field.
Validation Text	Enter text that appears when a value violates the Validation Rule expression.
Required	Require that data be entered in a field.
Allow Zero Length	Allow entry (by setting to Yes) of a zero-length string ("") in a Text or Memo field.
Indexed	Speed up access to data in this field by creating and using an index.
Unicode Compression	Compress text stored in this field when a large amount of text is stored (> 4,096 characters).
IME Mode	Specify an Input Method Editor, a tool for using English versions of Access with files created in Japanese or Korean versions of Access.
IME Sentence Mode	Specify the type of data you can enter by using an Input Method Editor.
SmartTags	Attach a smart tag to this field.
Append Only	Allow versioning (by setting to Yes) of a Memo field.
Text Format	Choose Rich Text to store text as HTML and allow rich formatting. Choose Plain Text to store only text.
Text Align	Specify the default alignment of text within a control.
Precision	Specify the total number of digits allowed, including those both to the right and the left of the decimal point.
Scale	Specify the maximum number of digits that can be stored to the right of the decimal separator.

Modify Tables and Fields | 803

  DEFINE INPUT MASKS FOR FIELDS

USE the database that is open from the previous exercise.

1. In the Field Name column in the upper portion of the table design grid, click in the **Start Time** cell.
2. Click the **Input Mask** property box in the lower portion of the table design grid to display the Input Mask Wizard button on the far right of the cell, as shown in Figure 4-11.

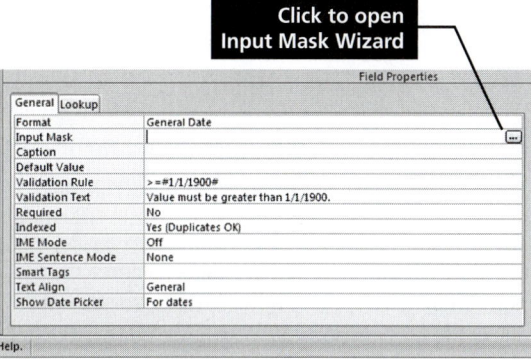

Figure 4-11

Input Mask Wizard button

3. Click the **Input Mask Wizard button**. A message appears asking if you want to save the table now, as shown in Figure 4-12.

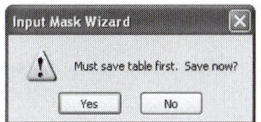

Figure 4-12

Input Mask Wizard message

4. Click **Yes** to display the Input Mask Wizard, as shown in Figure 4-13.

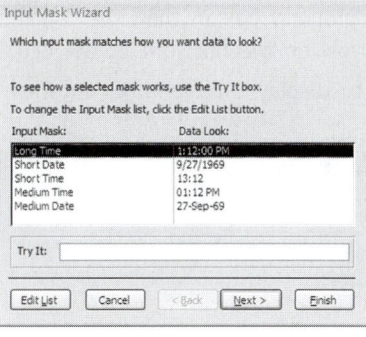

Figure 4-13

Input Mask Wizard

5. Click **Medium Date** and then click **Next>**. The next screen in the Input Mask Wizard appears, as shown in Figure 4-14.

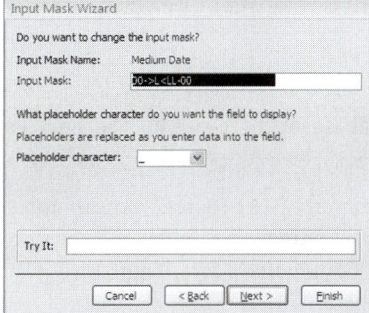

Figure 4-14

Input Mask Wizard, next screen

804 | Lesson 4

6. Click **Next** to display the final Input Mask Wizard screen, as shown in Figure 4-15.

Figure 4-15

Input Mask Wizard, final screen

7. Click **Finish**. The input mask appears in the Input Mask row.

PAUSE. LEAVE the database open to use in the next exercise.

You use an input mask whenever you want users to enter data in a specific way. An input mask can require users to enter dates in a specific format, for example, DD-MM-YYYY, or telephone numbers that follow the conventions for a specific country or region. An input mask is helpful because it can prevent users from entering invalid data (such as a phone number in a date field). In addition, input masks can ensure that users enter data in a consistent way.

You can add input masks to table fields by running the Input Mask Wizard or by manually entering masks in the Input Mask field property. In this exercise, you specified that dates in the Start Time field be entered in Medium Date format, following the required pattern, *24-Sep-69*.

➔ ALLOW ZERO LENGTH

USE the database that is open from the previous exercise.

1. In the Field Name column in the upper portion of the table design grid, click in the **Description** cell.
2. Click the **Zero Length** property box in the lower portion of the table design grid to display the down arrow on the far right of the cell.
3. Click the **down arrow** to display the menu, as shown in Figure 4-16.

Figure 4-16

Zero Length property menu

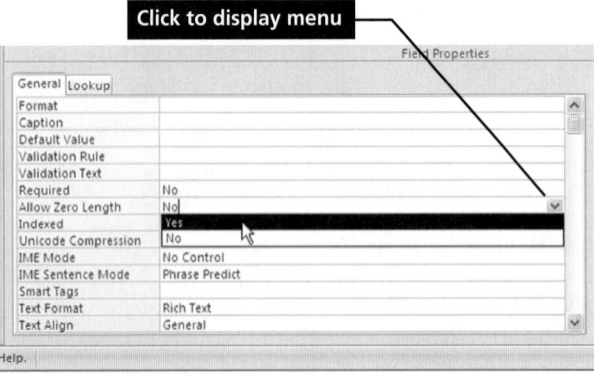

4. Click **Yes**.

PAUSE. LEAVE the database open to use in the next exercise.

When the Zero Length field property is set to Yes, you can enter zero-length strings in a field. A ***zero-length string*** contains no characters; you use the string to indicate that you know no value exists for a particular field. You enter a zero-length string by typing two double quotation marks with no space between them ("").

Modify Tables and Fields | 805

 SET MEMO FIELD AS APPEND ONLY

USE the database that is open from the previous exercise.

1. In the Field Name column in the upper portion of the table design grid, the **Description** cell should be selected.
2. Click the **Append Only** property box in the lower portion of the table design grid to display the down arrow on the far right of the cell.
3. Click the **down arrow** to display the menu and click **Yes**.

   PAUSE. LEAVE the database open to use in the next exercise.

> **TAKE NOTE**
>
> By default, when you try to position the pointer in a Memo field with the Append Only property enabled, Access hides the text.

A field's data type determines the properties you can set. For example, the Append Only property applies only to a field that is set to the Memo data type. You cannot set this property on a field with any other data type.

You use a Memo field when you need to store large amounts of text in a database. When the Append Only field is enabled, users can add data to the Memo field, but they cannot change or remove existing data.

 SET DATA VALIDATION RULES

USE the database that is open from the previous exercise.

1. In the Field Name column in the upper portion of the table design grid, click the **End Time** cell.
2. Click the **Validation Rule** property box in the lower portion of the table design grid to display the Expression Builder button on the far right of the cell, as shown in Figure 4-17.

Figure 4-17

Expression Builder button

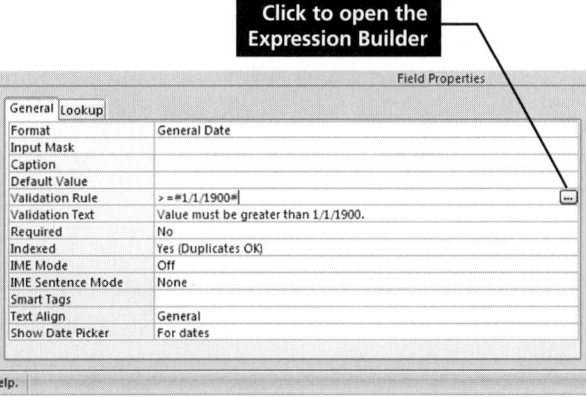

3. Click the **Expression Builder button** to display the Expression Builder dialog box, as shown in Figure 4-18.

Figure 4-18

Expression Builder dialog box

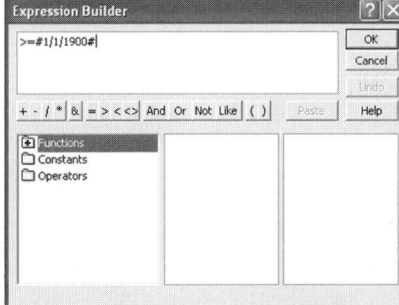

4. Select the number **1900** and replace it by keying **2006**.
5. Click **OK**.
6. Click the **Validation Text** property box in the lower portion of the table design grid.
7. Select the number **1900** and replace it by keying **2006**. The property boxes should look like those shown in Figure 4-19.

Figure 4-19

Modified Validation field properties

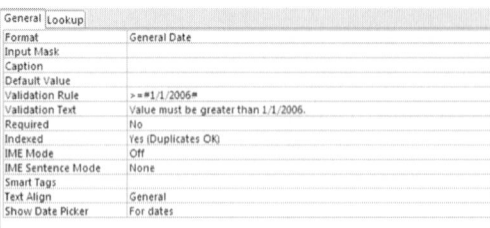

PAUSE. LEAVE the database open to use in the next exercise.

Validation rules restrict what users can enter into a given field and also help to ensure that your database users enter the proper types or amounts of data. A ***validation rule*** is an expression that limits the values that can be entered in the field. The maximum length for the Validation Rule property is 2,048 characters. For example, if the field contains a date, you can require that the date entered in the field be later than January 1, 1964.

When data is entered that violates the rule defined for the field, you can use the Validation Text property to specify the resulting error message. ***Validation text*** specifies the text in the error message that appears when a user violates a validation rule. For example, the error message could say "Please enter a date that is later than January 1, 1964." The maximum length for the Validation Text property is 255 characters.

Data can be validated in several ways, and you will often use multiple methods to define a validation rule. Each of the following can be used to ensure that your users enter data properly:

- **Data types**—When you design a database table, you define a data type for each field in the table, and that data type restricts what users can enter. For example, a Date/Time field accepts only dates and times, a Currency field accepts only monetary values, and so on.
- **Field sizes**—Field sizes provide another way to validate text. For example, if you create a field that stores first names, you can set it to accept a maximum of 15 characters. This can prevent a malicious user from pasting in large amounts of text into the field. It could also prevent an inexperienced user from mistakenly entering a first, middle, and last name in a field designed only to hold a first name.
- **Table properties**—Table properties provide very specific types of validation. For example, you can set the Required property to Yes, and, as a result, force users to enter a value in a field.
- **Field properties**—You can also use field properties, such as the Validation Rule property, to require specific values, and the Validation Text property, to alert your users to any mistakes. For example, entering a rule such as >1 and <100 in the Validation Rule property forces users to enter values between 1 and 100. Entering text such as "Enter values between 1 and 100" in the Validation Text property tells users when they have made a mistake and how to fix the error.

As you already learned in this lesson, the Input Mask field property is another way to validate data by forcing users to enter values in a specific way. For example, an input mask can force users to enter dates in a European format, such as 2008.07.10.

Modify Tables and Fields | 807

➔ **ENTER CAPTIONS**

USE the database that is open from the previous exercise.

1. In the Field Name column in the upper portion of the table design grid, click the **Location** cell.
2. Click the **Caption** property box in the lower portion of the table design grid.
3. Key **To be announced**.

PAUSE. LEAVE the database open to use in the next exercise.

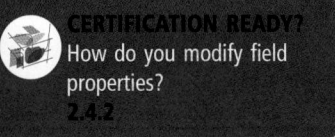

CERTIFICATION READY?
How do you modify field properties?
2.4.2

The Caption property field specifies the text displayed by default in labels for forms, reports, and queries. This property is used in the Text field. The maximum length for the Caption property is 255 characters. If you don't specify a caption to be displayed, the field name is used as the label.

■ **SOFTWARE ORIENTATION**

Fields & Columns Group

When creating fields, you will use the Fields & Columns group on the Datasheet tab, which is shown in Figure 4-20. You can use these commands to create a new field, add an existing field, or insert a lookup column, as well as insert, delete, or rename columns.

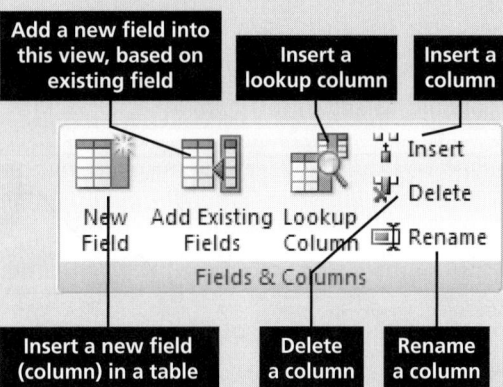

Figure 4-20
Fields & Column group

Use this figure as a reference throughout this lesson as well as the rest of this book.

Creating and Deleting Fields

Fields can be created in several different ways. You can add fields to a table in Datasheet view, add fields with a field template, or add a field from another table.

➔ **CREATE FIELDS**

USE the database that is open from the previous exercise.

1. On the Home tab, in the Views group, click the **View** button and click **Datasheet View**. Save the table, if required. If you get a message about data integrity, click **OK**.

2. Scroll to the right of the Events table to display the last column and click in the first cell below the Add New Field header, as shown in Figure 4-21.

Figure 4-21

Add New Field column

3. Key **Yes** and press **Enter**. A new field named *Field1* is added, and the Add New Field column becomes the last column in the table, as shown in Figure 4-22.

Figure 4-22

New field created

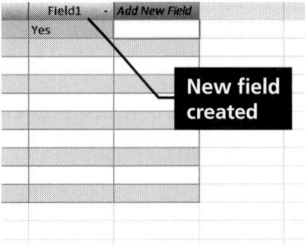

4. Right-click the **Field1** column header to display the shortcut menu and click **Rename Column**, as shown in Figure 4-23.

Figure 4-23

Column shortcut menu

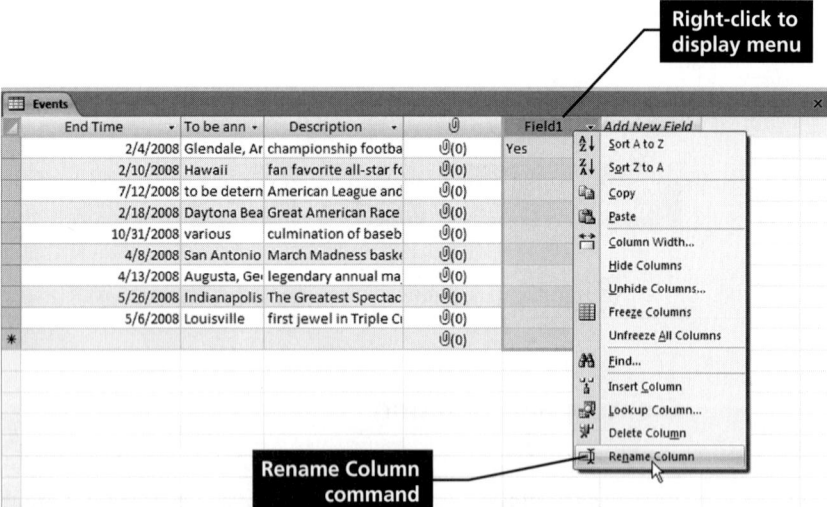

5. Key **On-site staff?** as the column name.
6. On the Datasheet tab, in the Fields & Columns group, click **New Field** to display the Field Templates pane, which is shown in Figure 4-24.

Modify Tables and Fields | 809

Figure 4-24

Field Templates pane

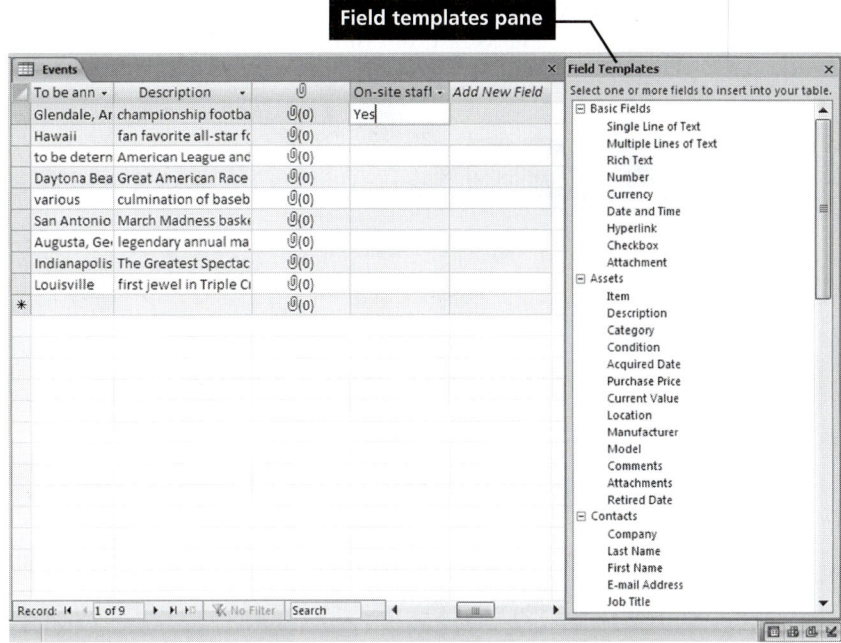

7. In the Basic Fields category, double-click **Checkbox**. A new field with checkboxes is created in the table, as shown in Figure 4-25.

Figure 4-25

Checkbox field created

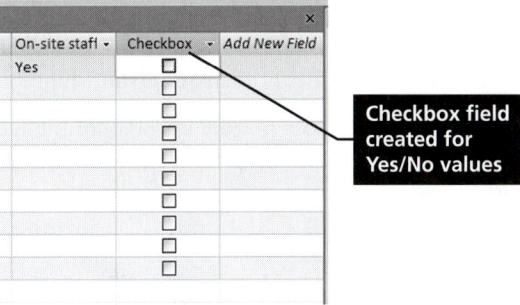

You can select more than one field in the Field Templates pane and then drag them to the table. When the insertion line appears, drop the fields into position.

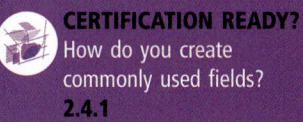

CERTIFICATION READY?
How do you create commonly used fields?
2.4.1

8. On the Datasheet tab, in the Fields & Columns group, click the **Rename** button.
9. Key **Souvenirs** and press **Enter**.
10. Click **Close** to close the Field Templates pane.

   PAUSE. LEAVE the database open to use in the next exercise.

The last column in a table in Datasheet view has an Add New Field column in which you can add a field simply by keying information in that column. Rename the field by right-clicking the column head, choosing Rename Column from the menu, and keying a new name.

Sometimes it is easier to choose from a predefined list of fields than to manually create a field. Access comes with a set of built-in field templates that can save you considerable time when creating fields. A field template is a predefined set of characteristics and properties that describes a field, including a field name, a data type, and a number of other field properties.

To create a new field using a field template, display the Field Templates pane, and then double-click a field template or drag and drop one or more templates to the table that is opened in Datasheet view.

If you are using a database that contains multiple tables, you can add a field from an existing table using the Field List, shown in Figure 4-26.

Figure 4-26

Field list

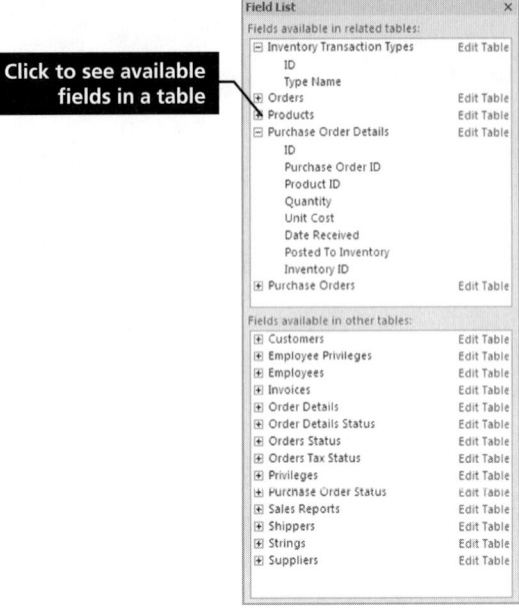

On the Datasheet tab, in the Fields & Columns group, click Add Existing Fields. The Field List pane appears; it lists all of the other tables in your database in two categories: fields available in related tables and fields available in other tables. The first category lists all of the tables with which the table you have open has a relationship. The second category lists all of the tables with which your table does not have a relationship.

Click the plus sign (+) next to a table to see a list of all of the fields available in that table. To add a field to your table, drag and drop the field you want from the Field List pane to the table in Datasheet view.

→ DELETE A FIELD

USE the database that is open from the previous exercise.

1. Click the column header for the **Attachment** field, located between the *Description* field and the *On-site staff?* field.
2. Right-click in the column to display the shortcut menu and click **Delete Column**, as shown in Figure 4-27.

Figure 4-27

Delete Column command on field shortcut menu

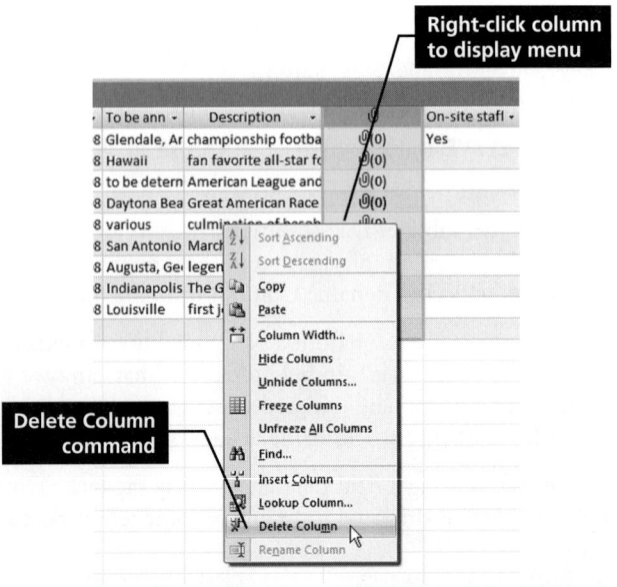

 **ANOTHER WAY**

You can also delete a field by clicking the Delete button on the Datasheet tab in the Fields & Columns group.

Modify Tables and Fields | 811

3. A message appears, as shown in Figure 4-28. Click **Yes**.

Figure 4-28

Delete field message

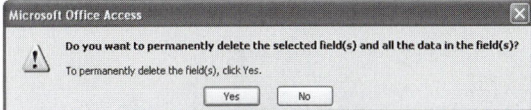

4. A confirmation message appears, as shown in Figure 4-29. Click **Yes**. The field is deleted.

Figure 4-29

Delete field confirmation message

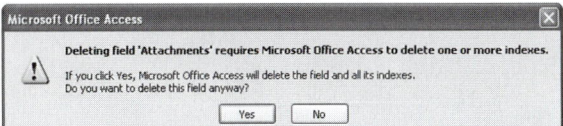

PAUSE. LEAVE the database open to use in the next exercise.

Before you delete a column from a datasheet, remember that doing so deletes all the data in the column and that the action cannot be undone. For that reason, you should back up the table before you delete the column. Before you can delete a primary key or a lookup field, you must first delete the relationships for those fields.

To delete a field in Datasheet view, select the column, right-click, and then click Delete Column from the shortcut menu. Or, on the Datasheet tab in the Fields & Columns group, click the Delete button. You will see a confirmation message asking if you are sure you want to delete the column and all the data.

 You can also delete a field in Design view by selecting the field (row) that you want to delete and clicking Delete Rows on the Design tab, in the Tools group.

Creating and Modifying Multi-valued Fields

In Office Access 2007, it is possible to create a multi-valued field that lets you select more than one choice from a list, without having to create a more advanced database design.

⊙ CREATE A MULTI-VALUED FIELD

USE the database that is open from the previous exercise.

1. Place the insertion point in the first cell of the table. On the Datasheet tab, in the Field & Column group, click the **Lookup Column** button. The Lookup Wizard appears, as shown in Figure 4-30.

Figure 4-30

Lookup Wizard

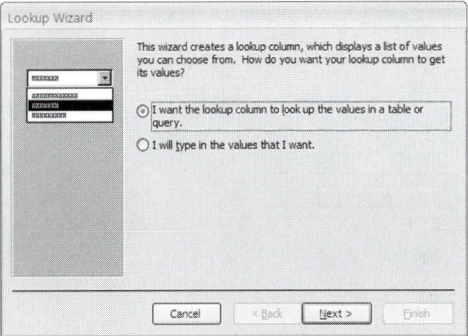

2. Click **Next>** to display the next screen in the Lookup Wizard, as shown in Figure 4-31.

Figure 4-31

Lookup Wizard, second screen

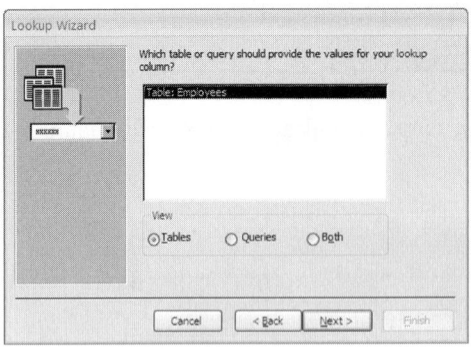

3. Click **Next>** to display the next screen in the Lookup Wizard, as shown in Figure 4-32.

Figure 4-32

Lookup Wizard, third screen

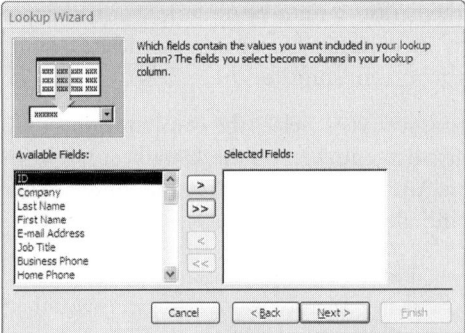

4. In the Available Fields list, select **Last Name**, then click the > button to move it to the Selected Fields box.
5. In the Available Fields list, select **First Name**, then click the > button to move it to the Selected Fields box.
6. Click **Next>** to display the next screen in the Lookup Wizard.
7. Click the down arrow in the first box and click **Last Name**, as shown in Figure 4-33.

Figure 4-33

Lookup Wizard, fourth screen

Modify Tables and Fields | 813

8. Click **Next>** to display the next screen in the Lookup Wizard, as shown in Figure 4-34.

Figure 4-34

Lookup Wizard, fifth screen

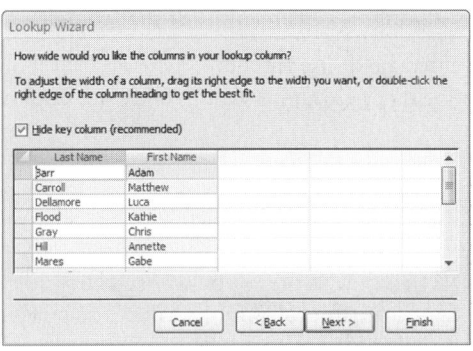

9. Click **Next>** to display the final screen in the Lookup Wizard, as shown in Figure 4-35.

Figure 4-35

Lookup Wizard, final screen

10. In the *What label would you like for your lookup column?* box, key **Coordinator**.
11. Click the **Finish** button. A new column named Coordinator appears at the beginning of the table. Click the down arrow to display the list of names, as shown in Figure 4-36.

Figure 4-36

Lookup column

12. Click **Flood/Kathie** on the list to choose that value for the field.

   PAUSE. LEAVE the database open to use in the next exercise.

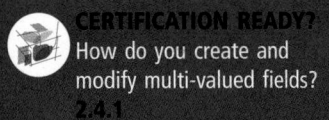

CERTIFICATION READY?
How do you create and modify multi-valued fields?
2.4.1

In most database management systems, including earlier versions of Microsoft Access, a field can store only a single value. But in Microsoft Office Access 2007, you can create a field that holds multiple values, such as a list of employees that you have assigned to a particular event. You can use a ***multi-valued field*** to select more than one value from a list.

Use a multi-valued field when you want to store multiple selections from a list of choices that is relatively small. It is also appropriate to use a multi-valued field when you will be integrating your database with Windows SharePoint Services—for example, by exporting an Access table to a SharePoint site or linking to a SharePoint list that contains a multi-valued field type.

To create the multi-valued field, use the Lookup Wizard in table Design view. On the Datasheet tab, in the Fields & Columns group, click the Lookup Column button to start the Lookup Wizard.

> **TROUBLESHOOTING**
>
> Consider using a multi-valued field only when you are relatively sure that your database will not be moved to a Microsoft SQL Server at a later date. An Access multi-valued field is upsized to SQL Server as a memo field that contains a delimited set of values. Because SQL Server does not support a multi-valued data type, additional design and conversion work might be needed.

➔ MODIFY A MULTI-VALUED FIELD

USE the database that is open from the previous exercise.

1. On the Home tab, in the Views group, click the **View** button and click **Design View**.
2. Place the insertion point in the **Coordinator** cell in the upper portion of the table design grid and click the **Lookup** tab in the lower portion of the table design grid to display the Lookup field properties, as shown in Figure 4-37.

Figure 4-37

Lookup field properties

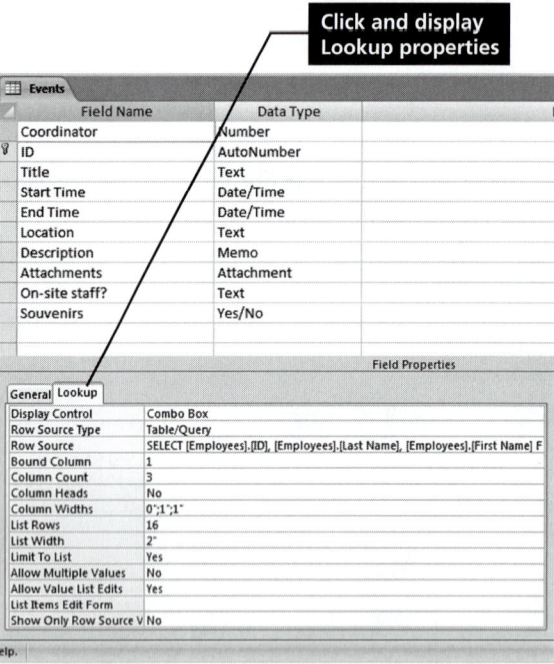

3. Click in the Allow Multiple Values property box, then click the **down arrow** on the right side, and click **Yes**. A message appears, as shown in Figure 4-38.

Figure 4-38

Change lookup column message

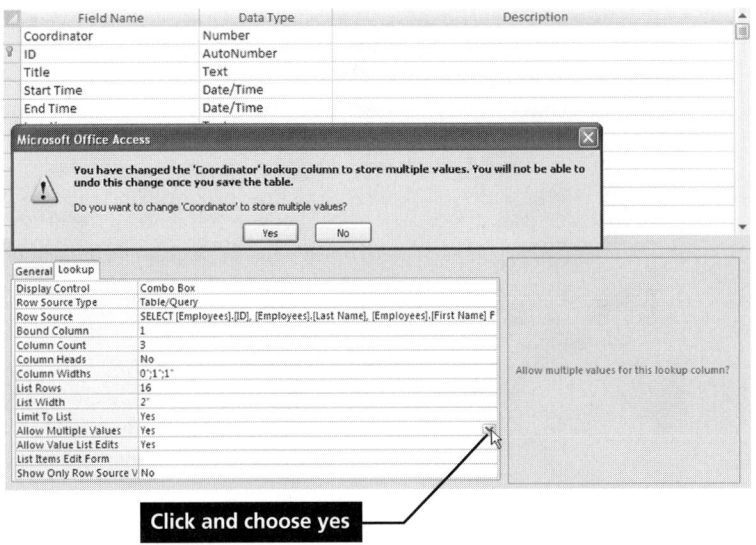

4. Click **Yes**.
5. On the Home tab, in the Views group, click the **View** button and click **Datasheet View**.
6. Click **Yes** to save the table.
7. Click the down arrow in the second cell of the Coordinator column to display the list, as shown in Figure 4-39.

Figure 4-39

Lookup column list

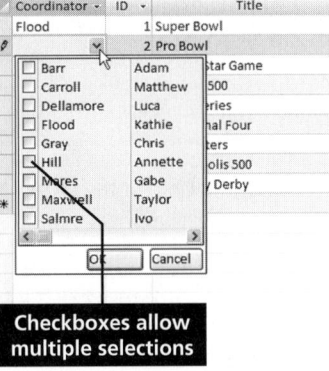

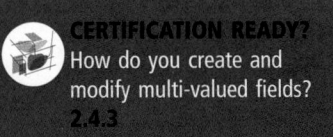

CERTIFICATION READY?
How do you create and modify multi-valued fields?
2.4.3

8. Notice the list now allows multiple values by providing checkboxes. Click to select the checkboxes for **Adam Barr** and **Annette Hill**.
9. Click **OK**.

PAUSE. LEAVE the database open to use in the next exercise.

To modify the lookup field properties, you can view and change them in the bottom pane of Design view under Field Properties. To see the properties specifically related to the lookup column, click the Lookup tab. Table 4-3 shows the properties you can set for the Lookup field properties.

Table 4-3

Lookup Field Properties

Set this property	To
Display Control	Set the control type to Check Box, Text Box, List Box, or Combo Box. Combo Box is the most common choice for a lookup column.
Row Source Type	Choose whether to fill the lookup column with values from another table or query or from a list of values that you specify.
Row Source	Specify the table, query, or list of values that provides the values for the lookup column. When the Row Source Type property is set to Table/Query or Field List, this property should be set to a table or query name or to a SQL statement that represents the query. When the Row Source Type property is set to Value List, this property should contain a list of values separated by semicolons.
Bound Column	Specify the column in the row source that supplies the value stored by the lookup column. This value can range from 1 to the number of columns in the row source.
Column Count	Specify the number of columns in the row source that can be displayed in the lookup column. To select which columns to display, provide a column width in the Column Widths property.
Column Heads	Specify whether to display column headings.
Column Widths	Enter the column width for each column. If you don't want to display a column, such as an ID column, specify 0 for the width.
List Rows	Specify the number of rows that appear when you display the lookup column.
List Width	Specify the width of the control that appears when you display the lookup column.
Limit To List	Choose whether you can enter a value that isn't in the list.
Allow Multiple Values	Specify whether the lookup column employs a multi-valued field and allows multiple values to be selected.
Allow Value List Edits	Specify whether you can edit the items in a lookup column that is based on a value list. When this property is set to Yes and you right-click a Lookup field that is based on a single column value list, you will see the Edit List Items menu option. If the lookup field has more than one column, this property is ignored.
List Items Edit Form	Name an existing form to use to edit the list items in a lookup column that is based on a table or query.
Show Only Row Source Values	Show only values that match the current row source when Allow Multiple Values is set to Yes.

Modify Tables and Fields | 817

Creating and Modifying Attachment Fields

Attachment fields are used to add one or more pieces of data, such as files or graphics, to the records in your database.

➔ CREATE AND MODIFY ATTACHMENT FIELDS

USE the database that is open from the previous exercise.

1. Scroll to the end of the table and click the **Add New Field** header.
2. On the Datasheet tab, in the Data Type & Formatting group, click the **down arrow** in the Data Type box to display the menu.
3. Click **Attachment**. A new column is inserted with a paper clip icon in the header, as shown in Figure 4-40.

Figure 4-40

Attachments field created

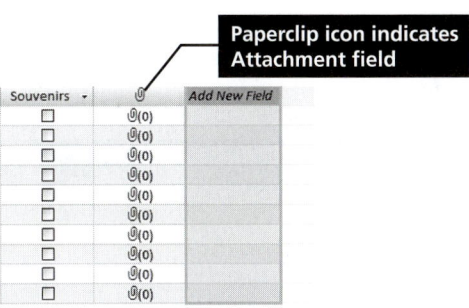

TAKE NOTE

Once a field has been set to the Attachment data type, it cannot be converted to another data type.

4. Double-click on the first cell in the Attachment column to open the Attachments dialog box, as shown in Figure 4-41.

Figure 4-41

Attachment dialog box

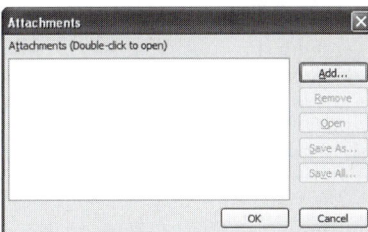

5. Click the **Add** button. The Choose File dialog box opens, as shown in Figure 4-42.

Figure 4-42

Choose File dialog box

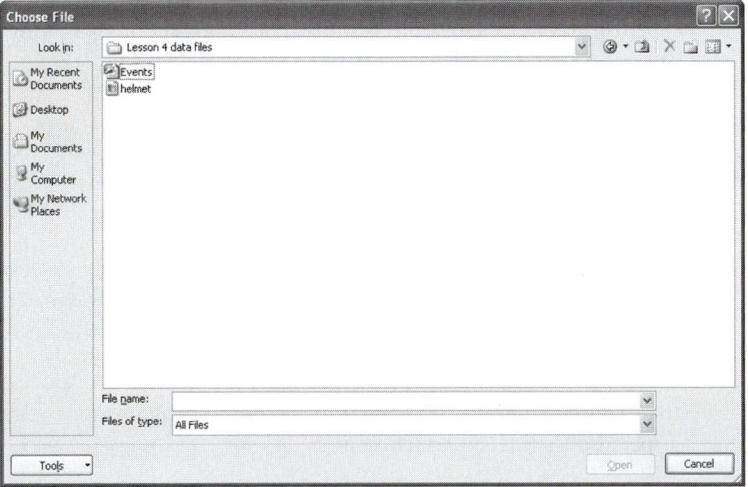

6. Navigate to the data files for this lesson and select the helmet image file. Click **Open**. The file is added to the Attachment dialog box.
7. Click **OK** to close the Attachment dialog box and attach the file to the record, as shown in Figure 4-43.

Figure 4-43

Record with file attached

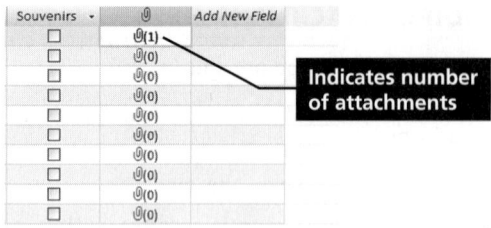

The *helmet.jpg* image file is available on the companion CD-ROM.

8. Double-click the attachment field in the record that has the file attachment. The Attachment dialog box opens.
9. Double-click *helmet.jpg*. The image file opens in a program that will display it, as shown in Figure 4-44.

Figure 4-44

Opened image file attachment

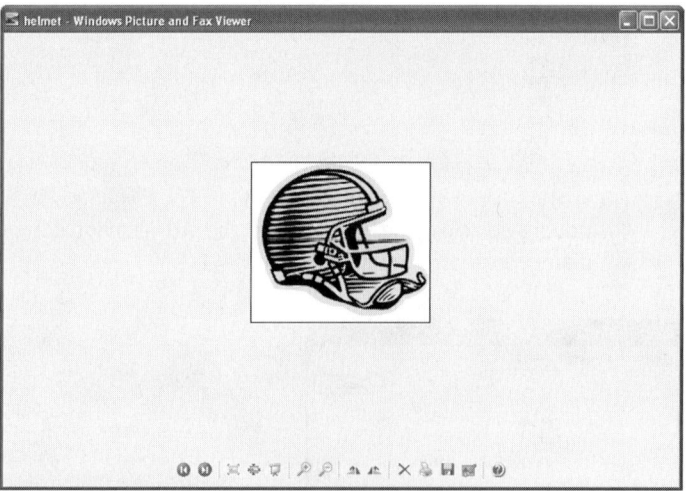

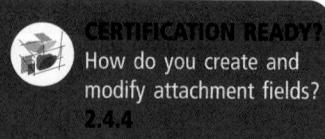

CERTIFICATION READY?
How do you create and modify attachment fields?
2.4.4

10. Close the photo-viewing program. Click **Cancel** to close the Attachments dialog box.
    STOP. CLOSE the database.

You can use attachments to store several files in a single field, and you can even store multiple types of files in a field. For example, you can store images along with files created with word processing or spreadsheet programs.

TAKE NOTE

You can attach a maximum total of 2 gigabytes of data, but each individual file cannot exceed 256 megabytes in size.

Attachments are useful because they store data efficiently. Access stores the attached files in their native formats and, if the program that was used to create the attached file is installed on your computer, you can open and edit the attached files in that program.

To add an Attachment field in Datasheet view, click the Add New Field column header. On the Datasheet tab, in the Data Type & Formatting group, click the down arrow next to Data Type, and then click Attachment.

Modify Tables and Fields | 819

 You can also add an Attachment field in Design view by selecting a blank row, keying a name for the Attachment field, and clicking Attachment under Data Type in the same row.

Access sets the data type for the field to Attachment and places a paperclip icon in the header row of the field. By default, you cannot enter text into the header row of Attachment fields. Use the Attachments dialog box to add, edit, and manage attachments. You can open the dialog box directly from the attachment field in a table by double-clicking the field.

By default, each field in a relational database contains only one piece of data. However, even though you can attach more than one file to a field, this does not break the rules of database design, because as you attach files to a record Access 2007 creates one or more system tables and uses those tables behind the scenes to normalize your data. You cannot view or work with those tables.

SUMMARY SKILL MATRIX

IN THIS LESSON YOU LEARNED HOW TO:
Modify Table Properties
Rename a Table
Delete a Table
Modify Field Properties
Create and Delete Fields
Create and Modify Multi-valued Fields
Create and Modify Attachment Fields

■ Knowledge Assessment

Fill in the Blank

Complete the following sentences by writing the correct word or words in the blanks provided.

p.795 1. _renaming_ or _deleting_ a table could possibly break the functionality of the database.

p.796 2. If you want more space to enter or edit a setting in the property box, press Shift+F2 to display the _Zoom_ box.

p.804 3. A(n) _Zero-length string_ contains no characters, and you use it to indicate that you know no value exists for a field.

4. _Validation Text_ specifies the text in the error message that appears when users violate a validation rule.

5. The _Caption_ property field specifies the text displayed by default in labels for forms, reports, and queries.

6. When creating fields, use the commands in the ___Fields___ (Fields + columns) group on the Datasheet tab.
7. A(n) ___Field Template___ is a predefined set of characteristics and properties that describes a field.
8. To add a field to your table, drag and drop the field you want from the ___Field List___ pane to the table in Datasheet view.
9. You can use ___Attachment___ to store several files in a single field.
10. By default, each field in a(n) ___relational___ database contains only one piece of data.

Multiple Choice

Select the best response for the following statements or questions.

1. To rename a table or other database object, first
   a. save it.
   b. close it.
   c. rename it.
   d. open it.

2. If you delete a database table,
   a. you cannot undo the action.
   b. click Undo to restore the table.
   c. it is still available in the Navigation Pane.
   d. the data is transferred to the Clipboard.

3. A complete list of field properties is available in
   a. the Navigation Pane.
   b. Datasheet view.
   c. Design view. (P.799)
   d. all of the above.

4. Which of the following is *not* a field property?
   a. Column Template
   b. Field Size
   c. Caption
   d. Allow Zero Length

5. Which field property requires users to enter data in a specific format?
   a. Validation Text
   b. Default Value
   c. Required
   d. Input Mask

6. The Append Only property applies only to a field that is set to
   a. Memo.
   b. Number.
   c. Currency.
   d. Text.

7. Which of the following is *not* a way to validate data?
   a. Data type
   b. Field sizes
   c. Filtering
   d. Field properties

8. The Caption field property is used for which field?
   a. Text
   b. Attachment
   c. Date/Time
   d. Hyperlink

9. Which type of field allows you to select more than one choice from a list?
   a. Attachment
   b. Multi-valued
   c. Caption
   d. Validation

10. A paperclip icon in the header row indicates what type of field?
    a. Attachment
    b. Input mask
    c. Caption
    d. Memo

Competency Assessment

Project 4-1: Home Inventory

You decide to use Access to create a home inventory database for insurance purposes. To include all the information you want, you need to add several fields to the existing table.

GET READY. Launch Access if it is not already running.

The *Home inventory* database file is available on the companion CD-ROM.

1. OPEN *Home inventory* from the data files for this lesson.
2. SAVE the database as *Home inventory XXX* (where XXX is your initials).
3. Close the Home Inventory List form that is open.
4. In the Navigation Pane, double-click the **Assets** table to open it.
5. Scroll to the end of the table and click in the cell below the Add New Field header.
6. On the Datasheet tab, in the Data Type & Formatting group, click the down arrow in the Data Type box and click **Yes/No**. A column named **Field1** is created.
7. On the Datasheet tab, in the Fields & Columns group, click the **Rename** button.
8. Key **Insured** to rename the Field1 column.
9. Click in the cell below the Add New Field header.
10. On the Datasheet tab, in the Data Type & Formatting group, click the down arrow in the Data Type box and click **Attachment** to create an attachment field.
11. **CLOSE** the database.

LEAVE Access open for the next project.

Project 4-2: Customer Service

You are employed in the customer service department at City Power & Light. Each call that is received is recorded in an Access database. Because you know how to modify tables and fields, your supervisor asks you to add a lookup column to the Calls table to record the customer service representative who receives the call.

1. **OPEN** *Customer service* from the data files for this lesson.
2. **SAVE** the database as *Customer serviceXXX* (where XXX is your initials).
3. Close the Case List form that is open.
4. In the Navigation Pane, open the Supporting Objects group and double-click the **Calls** table to open it. Place the insertion point in the first cell of the table.
5. On the Datasheet tab, in the Field & Column group, click the **Lookup Column** button. The Lookup Wizard appears.
6. Click **Next>** to display the next screen in the Lookup Wizard.
7. Select **Table: Employees** and click **Next>**.
8. In the Available Fields list, select **First Name**, then click the **>** button to move it to the Selected Fields box.
9. In the Available Fields list, select **Last Name**, then click the **>** button to move it to the Selected Fields box.
10. Click **Next>** to display the next screen in the Lookup Wizard.
11. Click the down arrow in the first box and click **Last Name**.
12. Click **Next>** to display the next screen in the Lookup Wizard.
13. Click **Next>** again to display the final screen in the Lookup Wizard.
14. In the *What label would you like for your lookup column?* box, key **Service Rep**.
15. Click the **Finish** button. A new column named Service Rep appears at the beginning of the table.
16. Click the down arrow and choose **Clair/Hector** from the list.
17. **LEAVE** the database open for the next project.

    LEAVE Access open for the next project.

> **CD**
>
> The *Customer service* database file is available on the companion CD-ROM.

■ Proficiency Assessment

Project 4-3: Modify Field Properties

Your supervisor at City Power & Light asks you to make some modifications to the field properties in the Calls table of the customer service database.

USE the database that is open from the previous project.

1. Switch to **Design View**.
2. Display the Lookup field properties for the **Service Rep** field.
3. Change the Allow Multiple Values property to **Yes** and confirm the change.
4. Display the General field properties for the **Call Time** field.
5. Change the Validation Rule property so that the value must be greater than **1/1/2000**.
6. Change the Validation Text property to say "Please enter a value that is greater than 1/1/2000."
7. Display the General field properties for the **Caller** field.
8. Change the Field Size property to **60**.
9. Display the General field properties for the **Notes** field.

Modify Tables and Fields | 823

10. Change the Allow Zero Length property to **Yes**.
11. Change the Append Only property to **Yes**.
12. Save the table. If a data integrity message appears, click **No**.
13. **CLOSE** the database.

    LEAVE Access open for the next project.

Project 4-4: Modify Database Tables

You work as the operations manager at Alpine Ski House and decide to increase your efficiency by using Access to plan the annual race events. You have started to create a database to manage the events sponsored by the company, but need to modify the tables.

The *Alpine* database file is available on the companion CD-ROM.

1. **OPEN** *Alpine* from the data files for this lesson.
2. Save the database as *AlpineXXX* (where XXX is your initials).
3. Close the Event List form that is open.
4. Delete the Nordic Events table and confirm the action.
5. Rename the World Cup table to **Championships**.
6. Open the Events table and switch to Design view.
7. Display the property sheet.
8. In the Description property box, key **Annual events**.
9. **CLOSE** the database.

    LEAVE Access open for the next project.

■ Mastery Assessment

Project 4-5: Changing List Items

You are the owner of Coho Vineyard & Winery, a growing company that is converting all of its data from spreadsheets to Access. You created a table using the Assets table template, but need to make some modifications before you enter information in the database. Because you have not made changes to list items before, you might need to use Access Help.

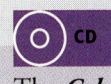
The *Coho* database file is available on the companion CD-ROM.

1. **OPEN** *Coho* from the data files for this lesson.
2. Save the database as *Coho XXX* (where XXX is your initials).
3. Open the **Red Wine** table and switch to Design view.
4. Display the Lookup properties for the Category field.
5. Change the **Allow Value List Edits** property to **Yes**.
6. Place the insertion point in the Row Source property box and click the button on the right side to display the Edit List Items dialog box.
7. Set the list items as follows:

    (1) **Merlot**
    (2) **Cabernet**
    (3) **Shiraz**
    (4) **Zinfandel**

8. Change the default value to **(1) Merlot**.
9. Change the name of the Category column to **Type**.
10. Change the name of the Condition column to **Country**.
11. Display the Lookup properties for the Country field.

12. Change the **Allow Value List Edits** property to **Yes**.
13. Display the Edit List Items dialog box for the Country field and set them as follows:
    (1) **Chile**
    (2) **France**
    (3) **South Africa**
    (4) **Spain**
    (5) **United States**
14. Change the default value to **(1) Chile**.
15. **SAVE** the table and switch to Datasheet view.
16. **CLOSE** the database.
    LEAVE Access open for the next project.

Project 4-6: Lending Library

You have an extensive personal library that friends and family frequently ask to share. To keep track of all your books, you decide to use Access to create a lending library database.

1. **OPEN** *Lending library* from the data files for this lesson.
2. **SAVE** the database as *Lending library XXX* (where XXX is your initials).
3. Use the skills you have learned in this lesson to make any changes that you think would be useful to the tables or field properties.
4. **CLOSE** the database.
   CLOSE Access.

The *Lending library* database is available on the companion CD-ROM.

Modify Tables and Fields | 825

INTERNET READY

A number of online resources can provide solutions to challenges that you might face during a typical workday. Search the Microsoft site for Work Essentials, shown in Figure 4-45.

Figure 4-45

Work Essentials site

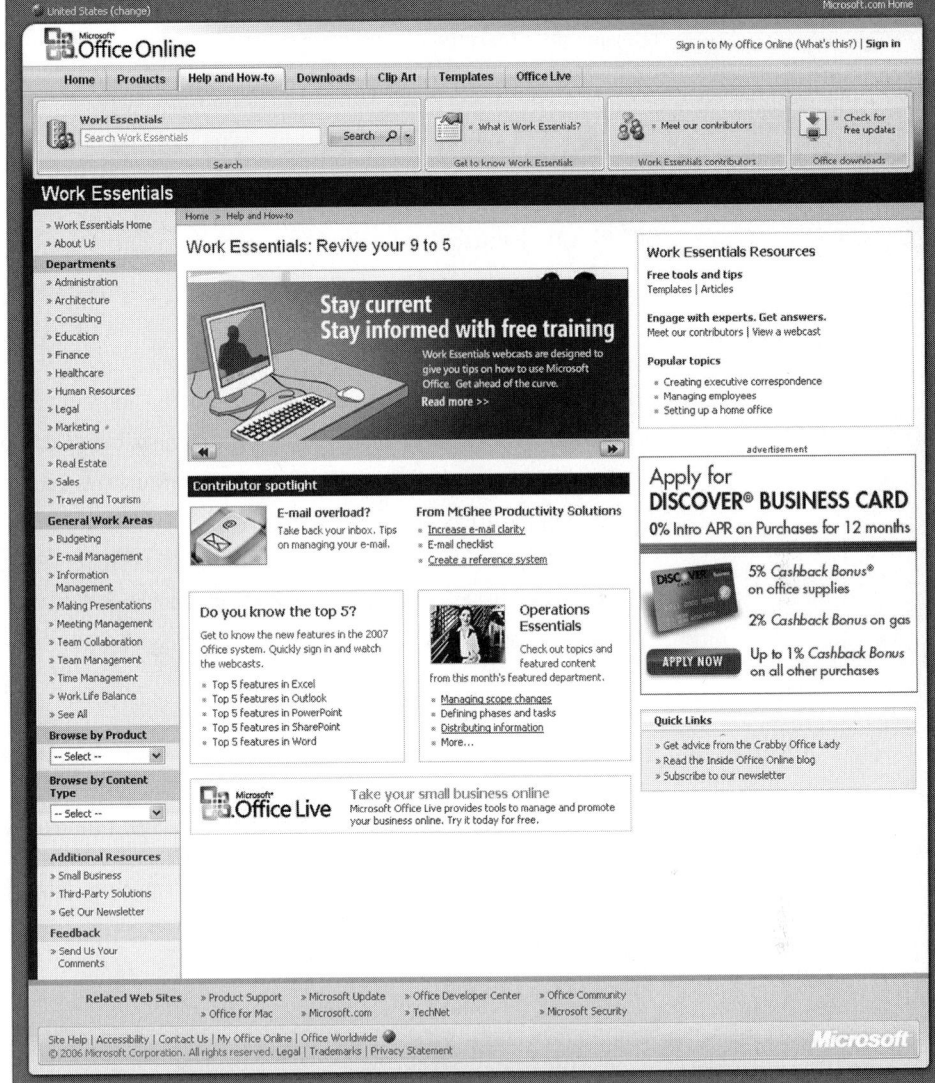

Work Essentials is a place where you can find information on how to use Microsoft Access efficiently to perform typical business tasks and activities. Explore the resources and content that Work Essentials offers to discover tools or solutions that could be useful on the job and ways you could use the site to be more productive.

Circling Back

You are a real estate agent and have recently opened your own office—Woodgrove Real Estate—with several other licensed agents. Because you are the one who is most knowledgeable about computers, you will be responsible for keeping track of the listings and other relevant information. You will use Access to begin developing the database that will be used by everyone in the office.

Project 1: Create a Database and Tables

After sketching out a plan on paper, you are ready to begin creating the database and tables.

GET READY. Launch Access if it is not already running.

1. In the New Blank Database section, click the **Blank Database icon.** A Blank Database pane appears.
2. In the File Name box, key **WoodgroveXXX** (where XXX is your initials).
3. Click the folder icon and browse to the location where you want to store the file.
4. Click the **Create** button to create a new blank database.
5. Right-click **Add New Field** and click **Rename Column** on the shortcut menu.
6. Key **Address** and press Enter.
7. Add new columns named **Bedrooms**, **Bathrooms**, **Square Feet**, and **Price**.
8. Click the **Microsoft Office Button** and click **Save**.
9. In the Save As dialog box, key **Listings** as the table name and click **OK**.
10. On the Create tab, in the Tables group, click the **Table Templates** button, and click **Contacts** to create a new table.
11. Right-click the **Company** field header and click **Delete Column** on the shortcut menu.
12. Delete the Job Title, Business Phone, Fax Number, Address, City, State/Province, ZIP/Postal Code, Country/Region, Web Page, Notes, and Attachment columns. (If you get a message asking if you want to delete all indexes for the ZIP column, click **Yes**.)
13. Save the table as **Agents**.

    PAUSE. LEAVE the database open to use in the next project.

Project 2: Modify Tables and Fields

Now that you have created the tables for your database, you need to modify them to suit your needs.

USE the database that is open from the previous project. The Agents table should be displayed.

1. On the Home tab, in the Views group, click **Design** view.
2. On the Home tab, in the Show/Hide group, click **Property Sheet**.
3. In the Description property box, key **Agent contact information**.
4. Click **Close** to close the property sheet.
5. In the upper portion of the table design grid, click the **E-mail Address field**. In the field properties on the bottom, click in the Required property box and set it to **Yes**.
6. **SAVE** the table and switch back to **Datasheet** view.
7. Click the **Listings** table tab to switch to that table. Place the insertion point in the **Price** column.

8. On the Datasheet tab, in the Data Type & Formatting group, click the **down arrow** in the Data Type box and click **Number**.
9. In the Format box, click the **down arrow** and choose **Currency**.
10. Change the data type/format on the Bedrooms, Bathrooms, and Square Feet fields to **Number/General Number**.
11. Click the **Add New Field** column. Choose **Attachment** as the data type to create an attachment column.
12. **SAVE** the table.
    PAUSE. LEAVE the database open for the next project.

Project 3: Create Forms and Enter Data

Now it is time to enter data into your database. First you create a form to make this task easier.

USE the database that is open from the previous project. The Listings table should be displayed.

1. On the Create tab, in the Forms group, click the **More Forms** button.
2. Click **Datasheet** to create a datasheet form.
3. Click the **Microsoft Office Button** and click **Save**.
4. In the Save As dialog box, key **Listings** as the form name and click **OK**.
5. Use the form to enter data into the Listings table, as shown in Figure 1.

Figure 1

Listings data

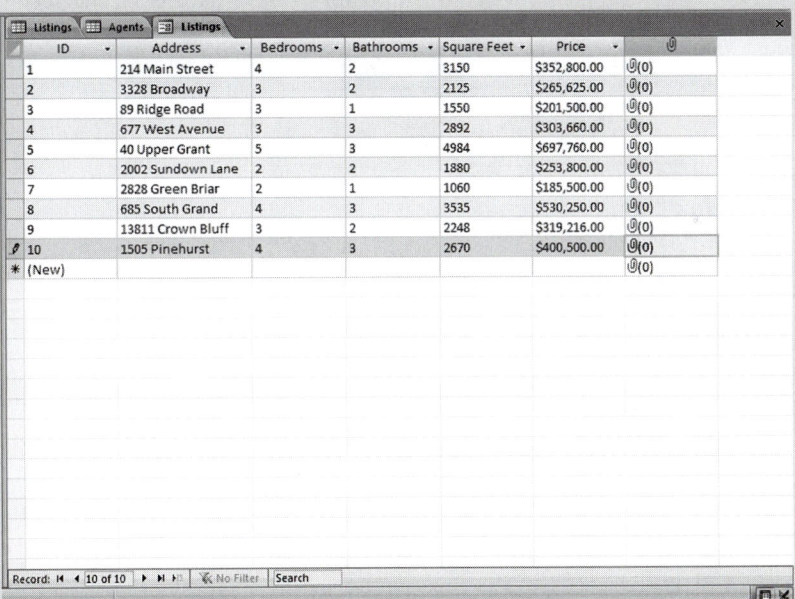

6. Display the **Agents** table.
7. On the Create tab, in the Forms group, click the **Form** button.
8. Save the form as **Agents**.

9. Switch to Form view and use the form to enter the data shown in Figure 2.

Figure 2

Agents data, record 1

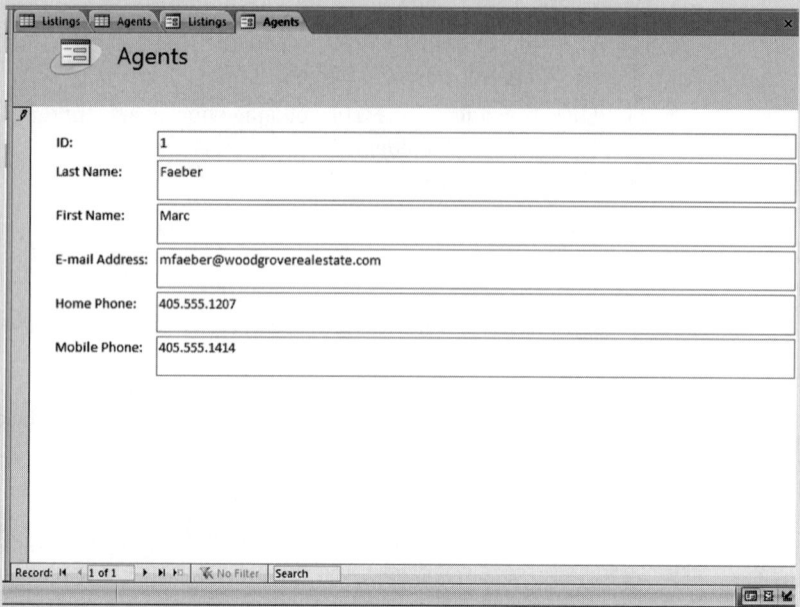

10. Click the **Next record** button on the record navigator.
11. Enter the data shown in Figure 3 as the second record.

Figure 3

Agents data, record 2

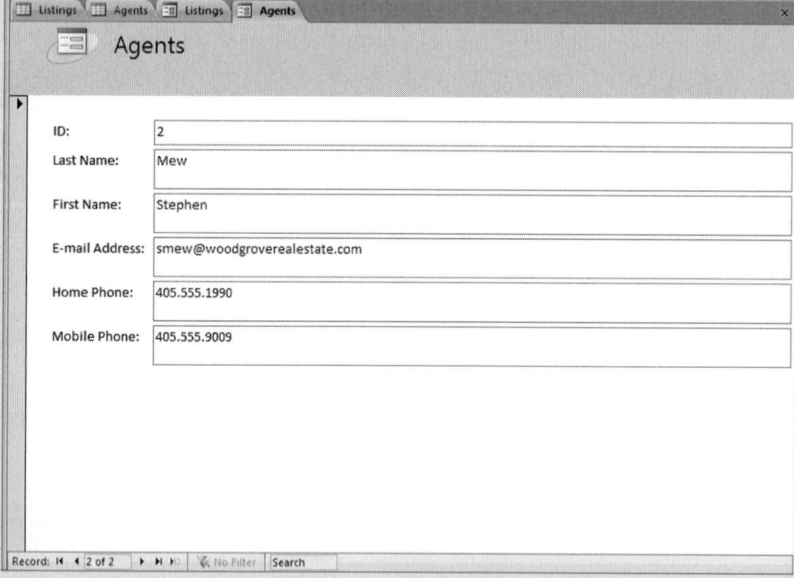

12. Enter the data shown in Figure 4 as the third record.

Figure 4

Agents data, record 3

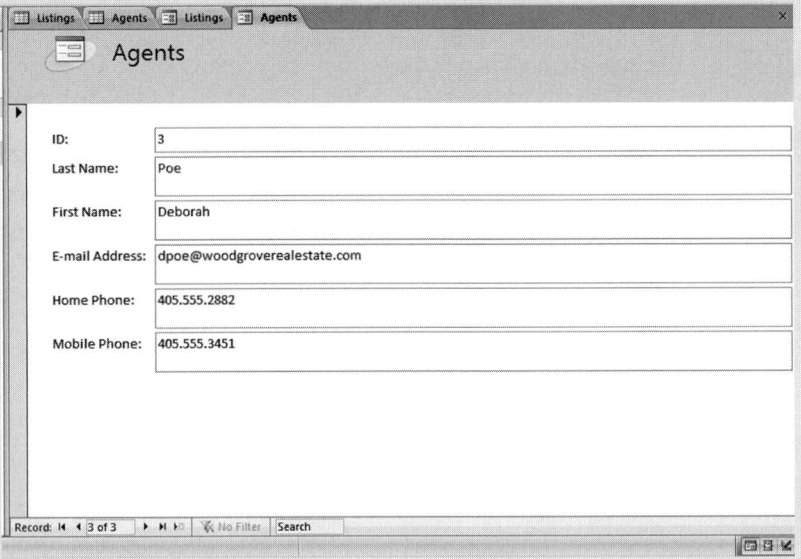

13. **CLOSE** the Agents form and the Listings form.

    PAUSE. LEAVE the database open for the next project.

Project 4: Add Attachments and Create a Lookup Field

You have begun to use the database and realize it would be helpful for the Listings table to include the listing agent. Create a lookup field with this information and attach photos for some of the houses.

USE the database that is open from the previous project

1. In the Listings table, double-click the **Attachment field for the fourth record** (677 West Avenue).
2. In the Attachments dialog box, click **Add**.
3. Navigate to the data files for this lesson, select *677_West_Avenue*, and click **Open**.
4. In the Attachments dialog box, click **OK**.
5. Attach the photo named *2002_Sundown_Lane* to the sixth record.
6. **CLOSE** the Listings form.
7. Display the Listings table and place the insertion point in the Add New Field column.
8. On the Datasheet tab, in the Fields & Columns group, click the **Lookup Column** button.
9. Click **Next>** twice.
10. Click **Last Name** and then click the **>** button to move it to the Selected Fields box.
11. Click **Next>** three times.
12. Key **Listing Agent** as the title for your lookup column.
13. Click **Finish**.
14. **SAVE** the **Listings** table.

    PAUSE. LEAVE the database open for the next project.

The *677_West_Avenue* file is available on the companion CD-ROM.

The *2002_Sundown_Lane* file is available on the companion CD-ROM.

Project 5: Modify a Form

Now that you have a lookup field, you want to add it to your form and use it to enter additional information.

USE the database that is open from the previous project.

1. Display the Listings form and switch to Design view.
2. Click the Field1 field on the design grid and press **Delete**.
3. On the Design tab, in the Tools group, click **Add Existing Fields**.
4. In the Fields available for this view box, click **Listing Agent** and drag it to the form below the Price field.
5. Close the Field List and switch to Datasheet view.
6. In the Listing Agent column click the down arrow and select the last name for each record, as shown in Figure 5.

Figure 5

Listing agents

7. **CLOSE** the form.
8. **CLOSE** the database.
   CLOSE Access.

Create Forms

5

LESSON SKILL MATRIX

Creating a Simple Form — 832	Students will learn how to create a simple form.
Creating a Form in Design View — 832	Students will learn how to create a form in Design View.
Creating a Form in Layout View — 836	Students will learn how to create a form in Layout View.
Creating a Datasheet Form — 837	Students will learn how to create a datasheet form.
Applying AutoFormat — 840	Students will learn how to apply AutoFormat.
Sorting Data Within a Form — 842	Students will learn how to sort data within a form.
Filtering Data Within a Form — 844	Students will learn how to filter data within a form.

You are the owner of the Graphic Art Institute, a small fine-arts gallery dedicated to presenting challenging and contemporary visual arts and educational programs. The current exhibition is successfully underway; you are now calling for submissions for the next exhibition—a juried art show featuring photographic work from the local region. The competition is open to all regional artists who use photographic processes in their work. This particular event will be open to digital submissions. As each submission is received, you will enter the artist and image information into an Access database for easy retrieval. In this lesson, you will learn how to create forms using a variety of methods; how to apply an AutoFormat to a form; and how to sort and filter data within a form.

KEY TERMS
AutoFormat
Blank Form tool
common filter
filter by form
Form Design button
Form tool
Form Wizard

Software Orientation

Forms Group

The Forms group, as shown in Figure 5-1, is located on the Create tab in the Ribbon and can be used to create a variety of forms.

Figure 5-1

Forms group

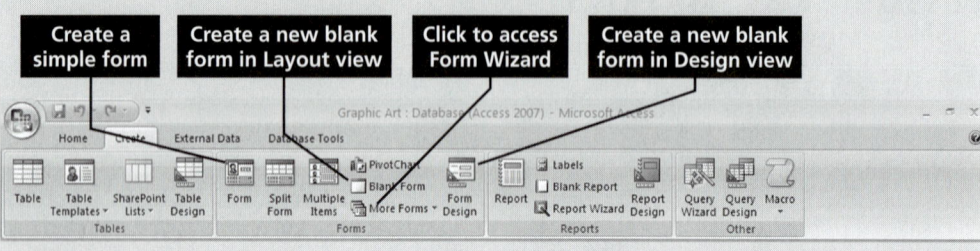

Use this figure as a reference throughout this lesson as well as the rest of this book.

Creating Forms

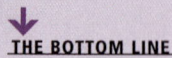
THE BOTTOM LINE

A form is a database object that you can use to enter, edit, or display data from a table or query. Forms can be used to control access to data by limiting which fields or rows of data are displayed to users. For example, certain users might need to see only certain fields in a table. Providing those users with a form that contains just those fields makes it easier for them to use the database. Think of forms as windows through which people see and reach your database in a more visually attractive and efficient way.

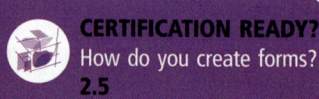
CERTIFICATION READY?
How do you create forms?
2.5

Creating a Simple Form

You can use the Form tool to create a form with a single mouse-click.

CREATE A SIMPLE FORM

GET READY. Before you begin these steps, be sure to launch Microsoft Access.

1. **OPEN** the *Graphic Art* database from the data files for this lesson.
2. **SAVE** the database as *Graphic Art XXX* (where XXX is your initials).
3. In the Navigation Pane, click the **Photo Exhibit** table.
4. On the Create tab, in the Forms group, click the **Form** button. Access creates the form and displays it in Layout view, as shown in Figure 5-2. Your form may be slightly different.

CD

The *Graphic Art* database file is available on the companion CD-ROM.

Figure 5-2

Simple form

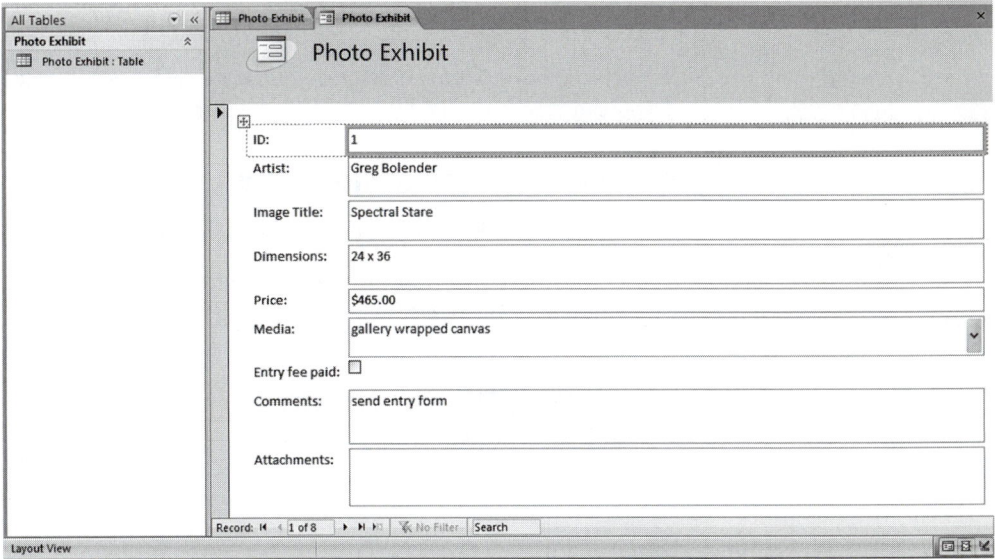

5. Click the **Office Button** and click **Save**. The Save As dialog box appears, as shown in Figure 5-3.

Figure 5-3

Save As dialog box

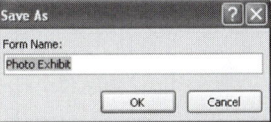

TAKE NOTE
You can use the record navigation buttons at the bottom of a form to navigate among the form's records, just as you used them to navigate among records in a table in Lesson 3.

6. Click **OK** to accept the *Photo Exhibit* form name suggested by Access. The form name appears in the Navigation Pane.
7. Click the **Close 'Photo Exhibit'** button to close the form.
8. **LEAVE** the database open.

    PAUSE. LEAVE Access open to use in the next exercise.

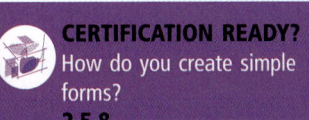

CERTIFICATION READY?
How do you create simple forms?
2.5.8

To use the ***Form tool*** to create a simple form, first click the table in the Navigation Pane that contains the data you want to see on the form. On the Create tab, in the Forms group, click Form. When you use this tool, all the fields from the underlying data source are placed on the form.

Access creates the form and displays it in Layout view. You can begin using the new form immediately, or you can modify it in Layout view or Design view to better suit your needs.

To save your form design, click the Office Button and click Save. Key a name in the Form Name box and click OK. After you save your form design, you can run the form as often as you want. The design stays the same, but you see current data every time you view the form. If your needs change, you can modify the form design or create a new form that is based on the original.

834 | Lesson 5

Creating a Form in Design View

Click the Form Design button to quickly create a new blank form in Design view where you can view a detailed structure of the form.

➔ CREATE A FORM IN DESIGN VIEW

USE the database that is open from the previous exercise.

1. On the Create tab, in the Forms group, click the **Form Design** button. A new blank form is created in Design view, as shown in Figure 5-4.

Figure 5-4

New blank form in Design view

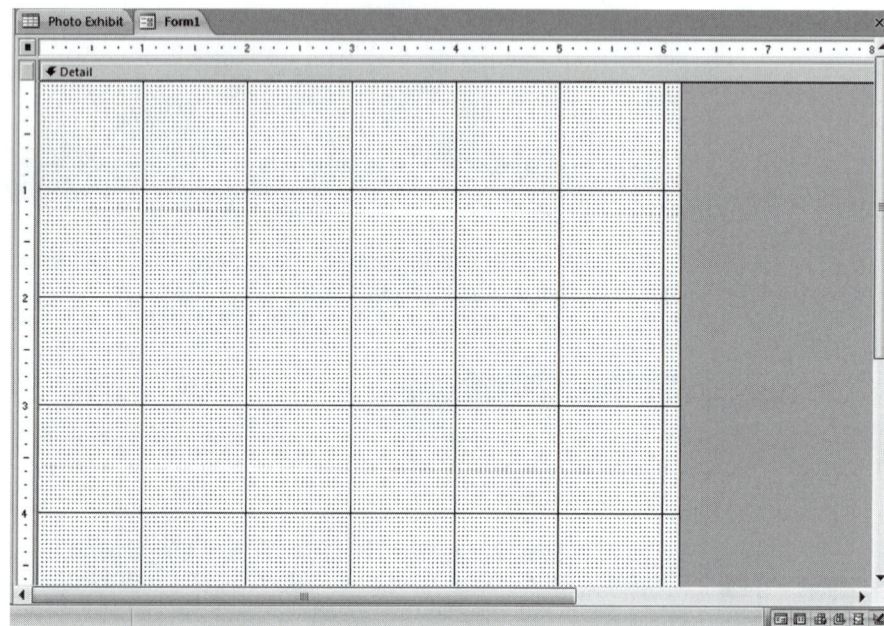

 **ANOTHER WAY**

You can also display the Field List pane by clicking Alt+F8.

2. On the Design tab, in the Tools group, click the **Add Existing Fields** button. The Field List pane appears, as shown in Figure 5-5.

Figure 5-5

Field List pane

3. In the list of fields, double-click **Artist** to add it to the form.
4. Double-click **Image Title** to add it to the form.
5. Double-click **Price** to add it to the form. Your form should look similar to Figure 5-6.

Figure 5-6

Fields inserted in Design view

ANOTHER WAY

You can also click the field name and drag it onto the form to add a field.

6. Click the **Office Button** and click **Save**.
7. In the Save As dialog box, key **Photo Label**, and click **OK**.
8. On the Design menu, in the Views group, click the **View** button and click **Form View** to display form in Form view, as shown in Figure 5-7.

Figure 5-7

Form view

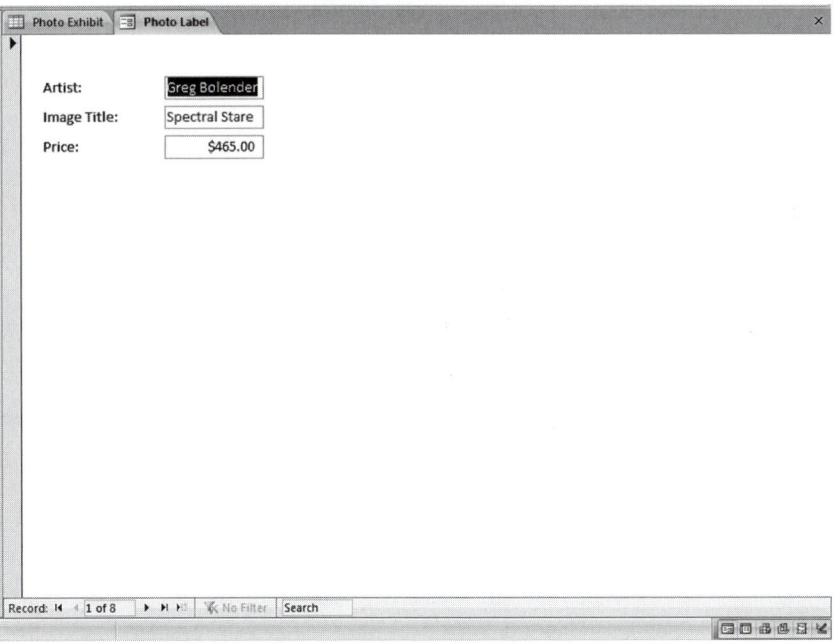

9. Click the **Close** button to close the Field List.
10. Click the **Close 'Photo Label'** button to close the form.
11. **LEAVE** the database open.

    PAUSE. LEAVE the database open to use in the next exercise.

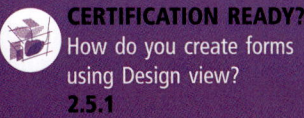

CERTIFICATION READY?

How do you create forms using Design view?

2.5.1

When you click the **Form Design button**, a new blank form is created in Design view. Design view gives you a more detailed view of the structure of your form than Layout view. The form is not actually running when it is shown in Design view, so you cannot see the underlying data while you are making design changes.

You can fine-tune your form's design by working in Design view. To switch to Design view, right-click the form name in the Navigation Pane and then click Design View. You can add new controls and fields to the form by adding them to the design grid, plus the property sheet gives you access to a large number of properties that you can set to customize your form.

Creating a Form in Layout View

Click the Blank Form button to quickly create a new blank form in Layout view with which you can make design changes to the form while viewing the underlying data.

CREATE A FORM IN LAYOUT VIEW

USE the database that is open from the previous exercise.

1. On the Create tab, in the Forms group, click the **Blank Form** button. A new blank form is created in Layout view, with the Field List displayed, as shown in Figure 5-8.

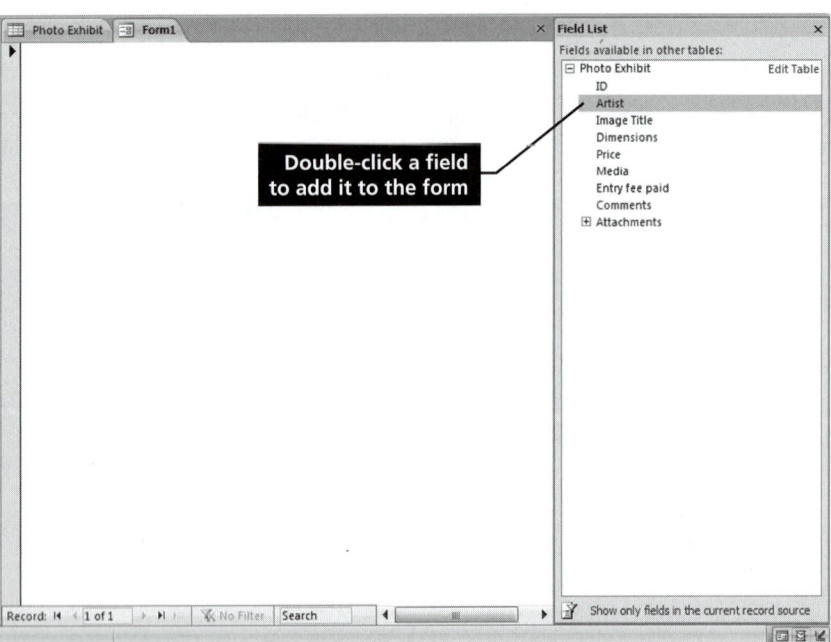

Figure 5-8

New blank form in Layout view

2. In the list of fields, double-click **Image Title** to add it to the form.
3. Double-click **Dimensions** to add it to the form.
4. Double-click **Media** to add it to the form. Your form should look similar to Figure 5-9.

Figure 5-9

Fields inserted in Layout view

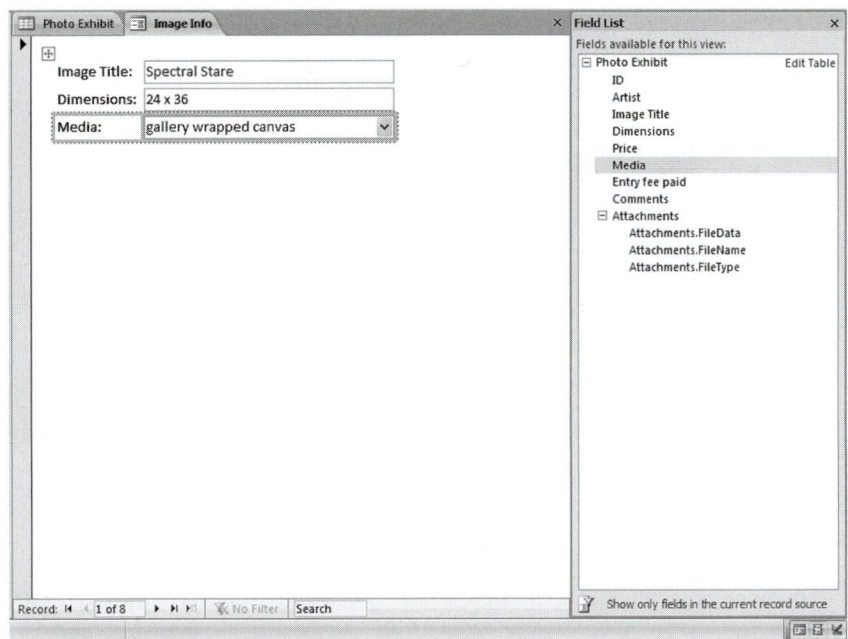

5. Click the **Office Button** and click **Save**.
6. In the Save As dialog box, key **Image Info**, and click **OK**.
7. Click the **Close** button to close the Field List.
8. Click the **Close 'Image Info'** button to close the form.
9. **LEAVE** the database open.

   PAUSE. LEAVE the database open to use in the next exercise.

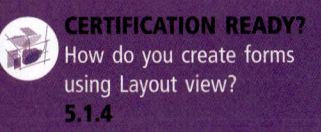

CERTIFICATION READY?
How do you create forms using Layout view?
5.1.4

If other form-building tools do not fit your needs, you can use the Blank Form tool to create a form. The **Blank Form tool** creates a new form in Layout view. This can be a very quick way to build a form, especially if you plan to put only a few fields on your form.

On the Create tab, in the Forms group, click the Blank Form button. Access opens a blank form in Layout view, and displays the Field List pane. To add a field to the form, double-click it or drag it onto the form. In Layout view, you can make design changes to the form while it is displaying data.

 **TAKE NOTE**

To add more than one field at a time, press CTRL and click several fields; then, drag them all onto the form at once.

Creating a Datasheet Form

A datasheet form looks very similar to the table upon which it is based and provides a way to enter data using columns and rows.

➔ CREATE A DATASHEET FORM

USE the database that is open from the previous exercise.

1. On the Create tab, in the Forms group, click the **More Forms** button to display the menu shown in Figure 5-10.

Figure 5-10

More Forms menu

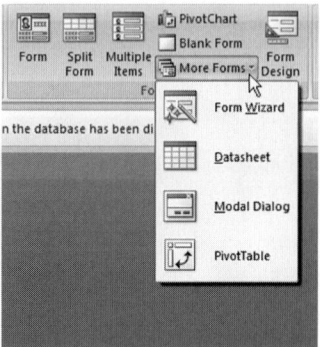

2. Click **Form Wizard** to display the Form Wizard, as shown in Figure 5-11.

Figure 5-11

Form Wizard

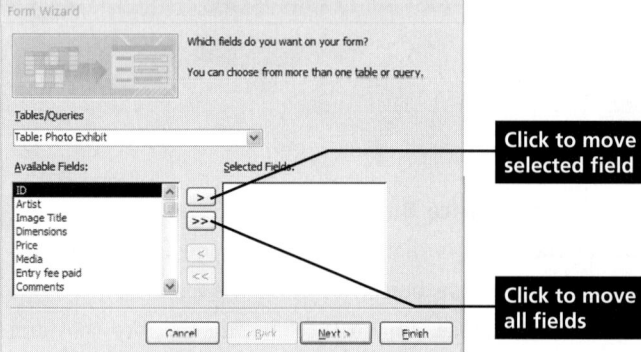

3. Click the **>>** button to move all the fields from the Available Fields box to the Selected Fields box.
4. Click the **Next>** button to move to the next page in the Form Wizard, shown in Figure 5-12.

Figure 5-12

Form Wizard, page 2

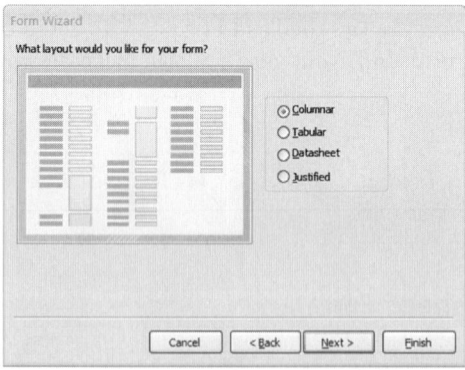

5. Click **Datasheet** as the layout for the form.
6. Click the **Next>** button to move to the next page in the Form Wizard, as shown in Figure 5-13.

Figure 5-13

Form Wizard, page 3

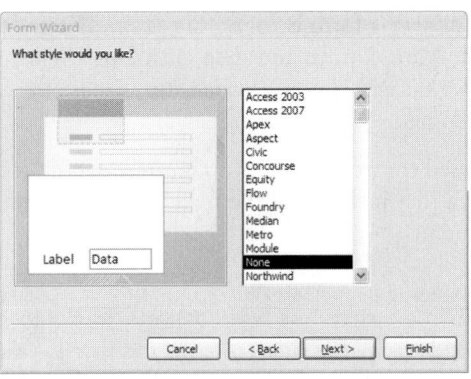

7. Click **None** as the style.
8. Click the **Next>** button to move to the final page in the Form Wizard, as shown in Figure 5-14.

Figure 5-14

Form Wizard, final page

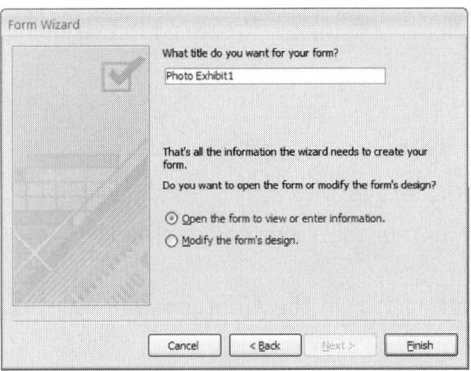

9. Key **Photo Details** as the title of the form.
10. Click the **Finish** button. A datasheet form appears, as shown in Figure 5-15.

Figure 5-15

Datasheet form

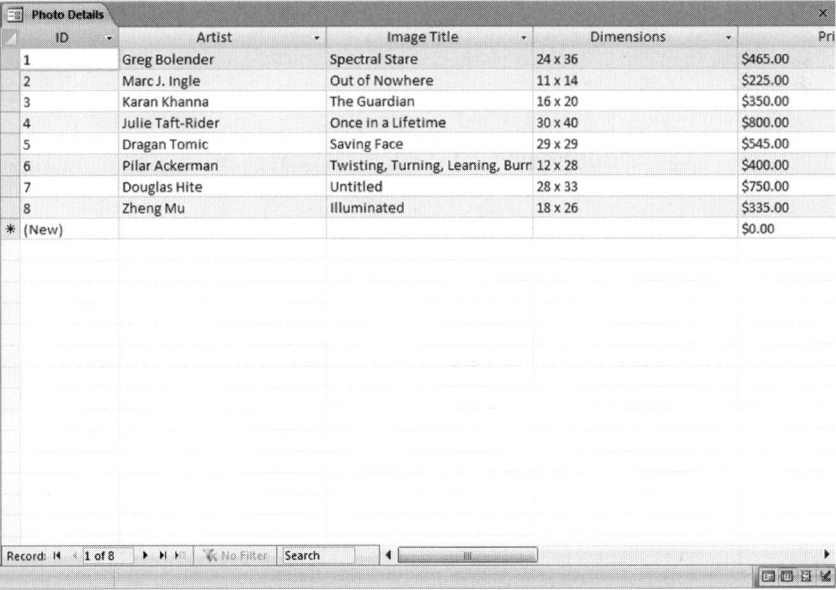

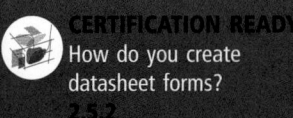

CERTIFICATION READY?
How do you create datasheet forms?
2.5.2

11. Click the **Close 'Photo Details'** button to close the form.

PAUSE. LEAVE the database open to use in the next exercise.

Another method of building a form is to use the ***Form Wizard*** tool. On the Create tab, in the Forms group, click More Forms, and then click Form Wizard. The Form Wizard allows you to select the fields that will appear on the form, choose the form layout, and also choose a predefined style, if desired.

In this exercise, you used the Form Wizard to create a datasheet form. Another way to quickly create a datasheet form that includes all the fields from the selected table is to click Datasheet on the More Forms menu.

TAKE NOTE To include fields from more than one table on your form, do not click Next or Finish after you select the fields from the first table on the first page of the Form Wizard. Instead, repeat the steps to select another table, and click any additional fields that you want to include on the form before continuing.

Applying AutoFormat

The AutoFormat command applies a predefined format to a form or report.

→ APPLY AUTOFORMAT

USE the database that is open from the previous exercise.

1. Double-click the **Image Info** form in the Navigation Pane to open it.
2. On the Home tab, in the Views group, click the **View** button, and click **Layout View**.
3. On the Formatting tab, in the AutoFormat group, click the **More** button, shown in Figure 5-16.

Figure 5-16

AutoFormat group

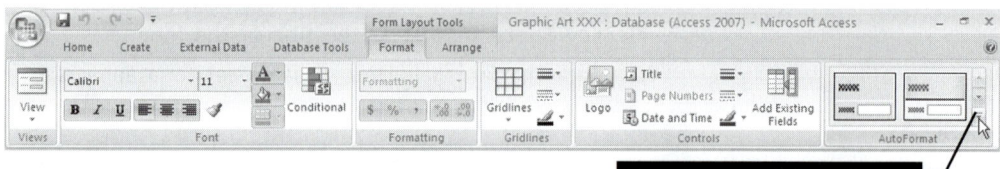

More button. Click to display gallery of AutoFormat styles

4. A gallery of format options appears, as shown in Figure 5-17.

Figure 5-17

AutoFormat options

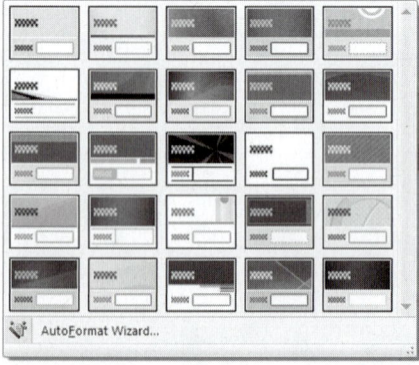

5. Click **AutoFormat Wizard...** at the bottom of the gallery to display the AutoFormat dialog box, shown in Figure 5-18.

Figure 5-18

AutoFormat dialog box

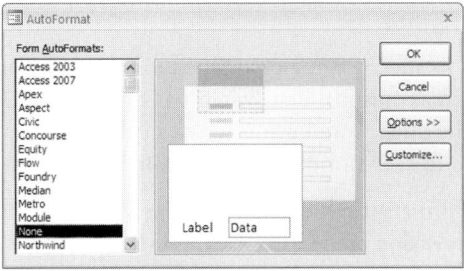

6. In the Form AutoFormats list, scroll down and click **Verve**.
7. Click the **Options>>** button. The Attributes to Apply box appears at the bottom of the dialog box.
8. Click the **Borders** checkbox to deselect it. The dialog box should look similar to Figure 5-19.

Figure 5-19

AutoFormat Attributes to Apply

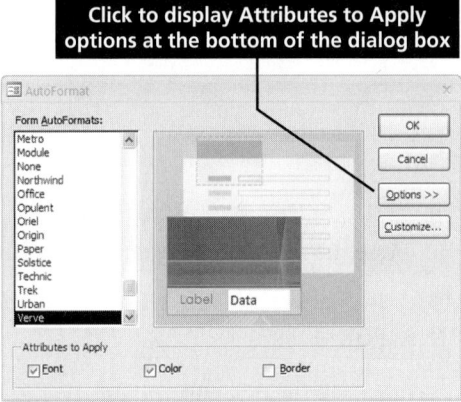

9. Click **OK**. The Image Info form now looks similar to Figure 5-20.

Figure 5-20

Form with AutoFormat applied

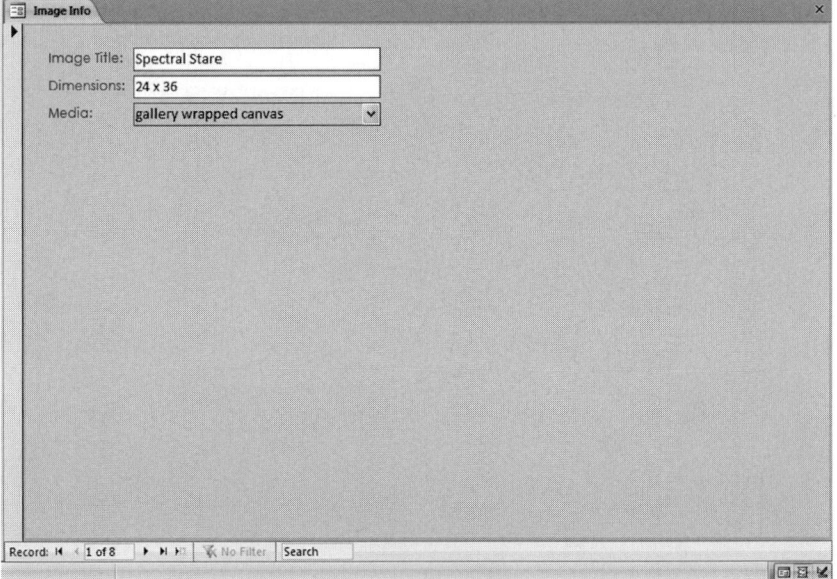

842 | Lesson 5

CERTIFICATION READY?
How do you apply AutoFormats to forms and reports?
2.7.7

10. Click **Close 'Image Info'** to close the form. When asked if you want to save the changes, click **Yes**.

PAUSE. LEAVE the database open to use in the next exercise.

The **AutoFormat** command applies a predefined format that you select to a form or report. To access the AutoFormat options, first switch to Layout view. On the Formatting tab, in the AutoFormat group, click the More button to see a gallery of format styles from which to choose. You can point to each option to see the name of that format.

To manage the AutoFormats, click the AutoFormat Wizard at the bottom of the gallery to open the AutoFormats dialog box. Click the Options button to select which attributes—font, color, and border—that you want to apply. Click the Customize button to display options shown in Figure 5-21 that allow you to create, update, or delete an AutoFormat.

Figure 5-21

Customize AutoFormat dialog box

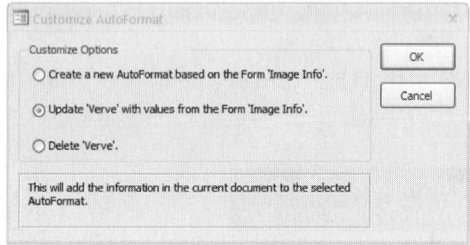

Sorting Data Within a Form

Sorting data in a form can help make it much more effective and easy to use. Sorting helps users review and locate the records they want without having to browse the data.

→ SORT DATA WITHIN A FORM

USE the database that is open from the previous exercise.

1. Double-click the **Photo Label** form in the Navigation Pane to open it in Form view.
2. Right-click the **Price** field to display the shortcut menu shown in Figure 5-22.

Figure 5-22

Price field shortcut menu

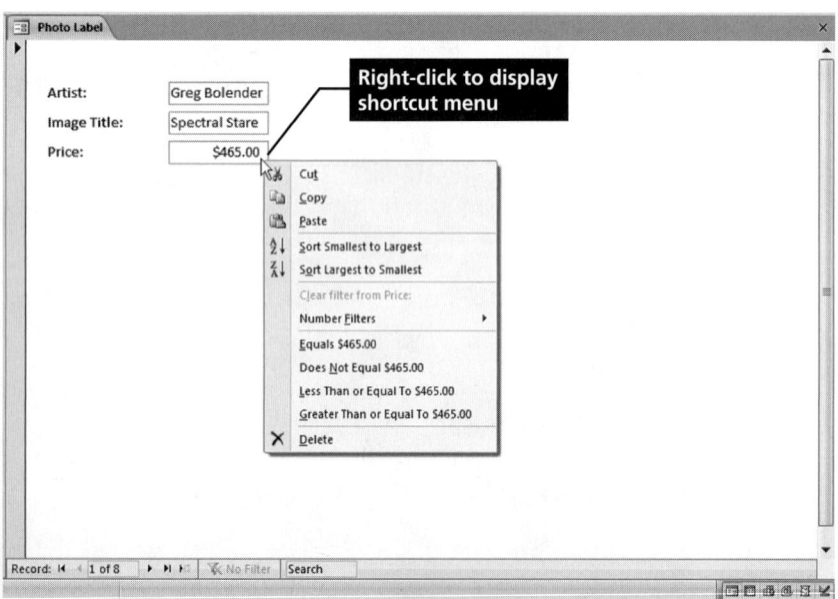

3. Click **Sort Smallest to Largest**. The form is sorted by price from smallest to largest. The record with the smallest price is displayed first, as shown in Figure 5-23.

Figure 5-23

Form sorted by price

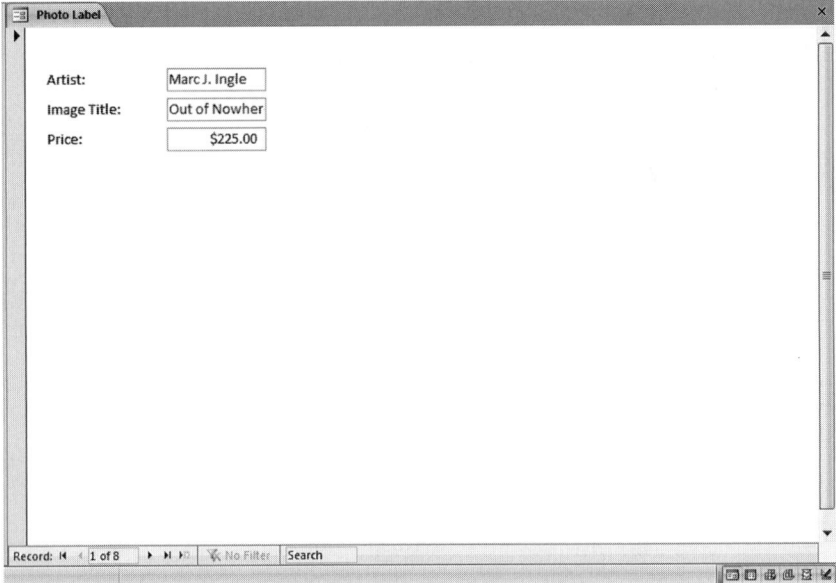

 **ANOTHER WAY**   You can also sort on a field by selecting it and clicking the Ascending or Descending button on the Home tab in the Sort & Filter group.

4. Click the **Next record** button on the record navigator at the bottom of the form. Continue clicking through all the records to see the records in order according to price.
5. On the Home tab, in the Sort & Filter group, click the **Clear All Sorts** button.
6. Click **Close 'Photo Label'** to close the form.

   PAUSE. LEAVE the database open to use in the next exercise.

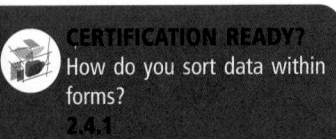

CERTIFICATION READY?
How do you sort data within forms?
2.4.1

Data can be sorted in the Form view of a form. The order that is chosen when a form is designed becomes that object's default sort order. But when viewing the form, users can sort the records in whatever way is most useful. You can sort the records in a form on one or more fields.

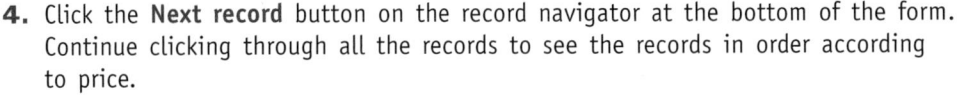 **TAKE NOTE**   You cannot sort on a field that contains attachments. When sorting on a field with the Yes/No data type, a value of "Yes," "True," or "On" is considered "Selected"; a value of "No," "False," or "Off" is considered "Cleared."

Identify the fields on which you want to sort. To sort on two or more fields, identify the fields that will act as the innermost and outermost sort fields. Right-click anywhere in the column corresponding to the innermost field, and click one of the sort commands. The commands vary based on the type of data that is in the selected field. Repeat the process for each sort field, ending with the outermost sort field. The records are rearranged to match the sort order.

 REF   You already learned how to sort data within a table in Lesson 3. Sorting in a form is very similar.

The last-applied sort order is automatically saved with the form. If you want it automatically applied the next time you open the form, make sure the Order By On Load property of the form is set to Yes. Remember that you cannot remove a sort order from just a single field. To remove sorting from all sort fields, on the Home tab, in the Sort & Filter group, click Clear All Sorts.

Filtering Data Within a Form

To find one or more specific records in a form, you can use a filter. A filter limits a view of data to specific records without requiring you to alter the design of the form.

➔ FILTER DATA WITH COMMON FILTERS

USE the database that is open from the previous exercise.

1. Double-click the **Photo Exhibit** form in the Navigation Pane to open it in Form view.
2. Right-click the **Media** field to display the shortcut menu and click **Text Filters**, as shown in Figure 5-24.

Figure 5-24

Media field text filters

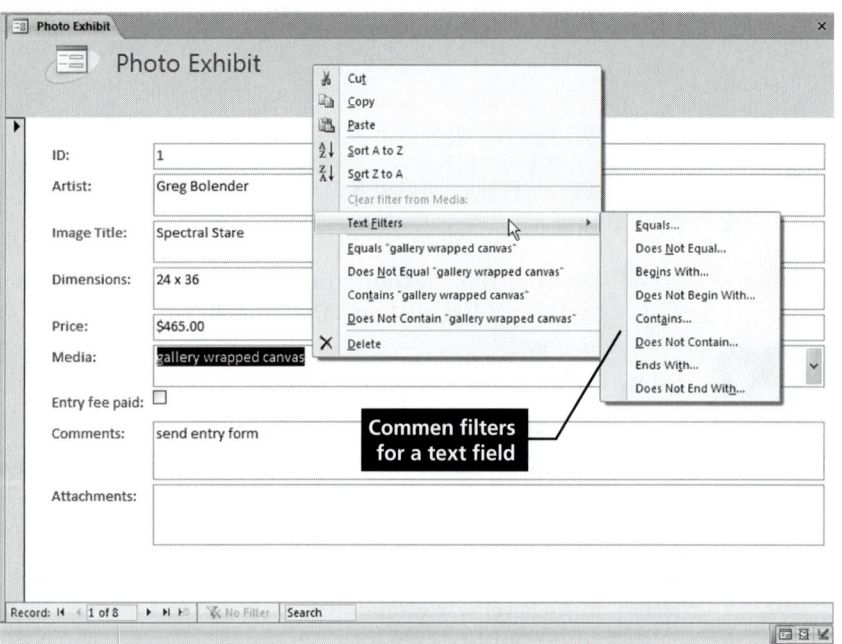

3. Click **Contains...** to display the Custom Filter dialog box, as shown in Figure 5-25.

Figure 5-25

Custom Filter dialog box

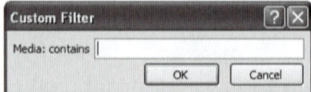

4. In the **Media: contains** box, key **print**, and click **OK**.
5. Click the **Next record** button on the record navigator at the bottom of the form. Continue clicking to see the five records that contain the word "print" in the Media field.
6. Right-click the **Price** field to display the shortcut menu and click **Number Filters**, as shown in Figure 5-26.

Figure 5-26

Price field number filters

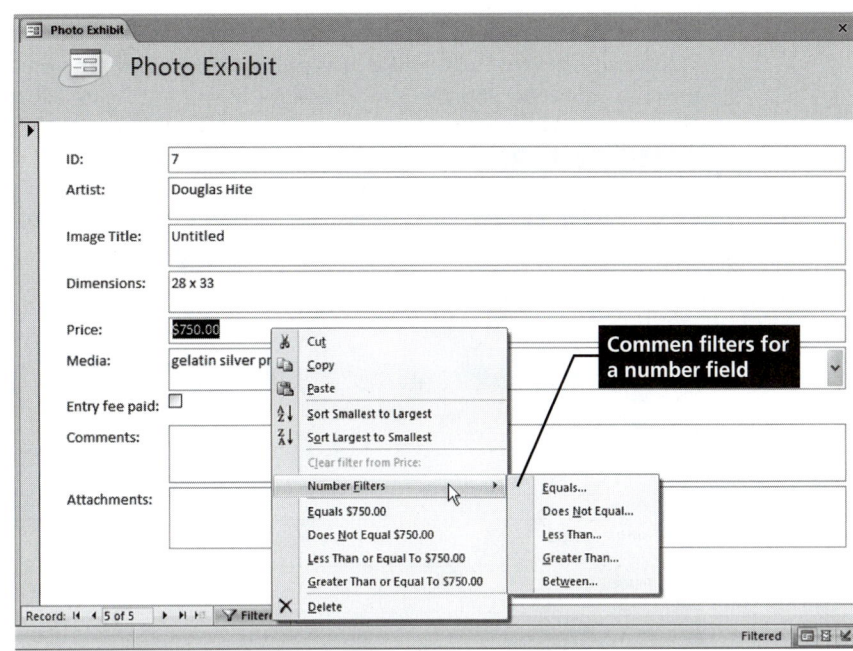

7. Click **Less Than...** to display the Custom Filter dialog box shown in Figure 5-27.

Figure 5-27

Custom Filter dialog box

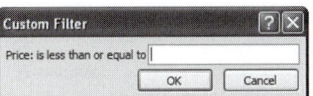

8. In the **Price: is less than or equal to** box, key **500**, and click **OK**.
9. Click the **Next record** button on the record navigator at the bottom of the form. Continue clicking to see the three photos that use print media and are less than $500.
10. On the Home tab, in the Sort & Filter group, click the **Advanced** button to display the menu shown in Figure 5-28.

Figure 5-28

Advanced button menu

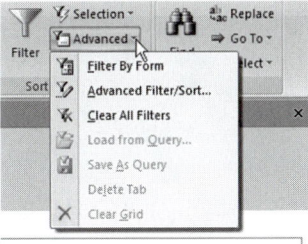

CERTIFICATION READY?
How do you filter data within forms?
5.2.4

11. Click **Clear All Filters**.

PAUSE. LEAVE the database open to use in the next exercise.

You already learned how to filter data within a table in Lesson 3. Filtering in a form using common filters is very similar.

Filters are easy to apply and remove. *Common filters* are built into every view that displays data. The filters available depend on the type and values of the field. When you apply the filter, only records that contain the values that you are interested in are included in the view. The rest are hidden until you remove the filter.

Filter settings remain in effect until you close the form, even if you switch to another view. If you save the form while the filter is applied, it will be available the next time that you open the form. To permanently remove a filter, on the Home tab, in the Sort & Filter group, click the Advanced button and click Clear All Filters.

Although only a single filter can be in effect for any one field at any one time, you can specify a different filter for each field that is present in the view. In addition to the ready-to-use filters for each data type, you can also filter a form by completing a form called Filter by Form.

FILTER BY FORM

USE the database that is open from the previous exercise.

1. On the Home tab, in the Sort & Filter group, click the **Advanced** button and click **Filter by Form**. A form filter appears, as shown in Figure 5-29.

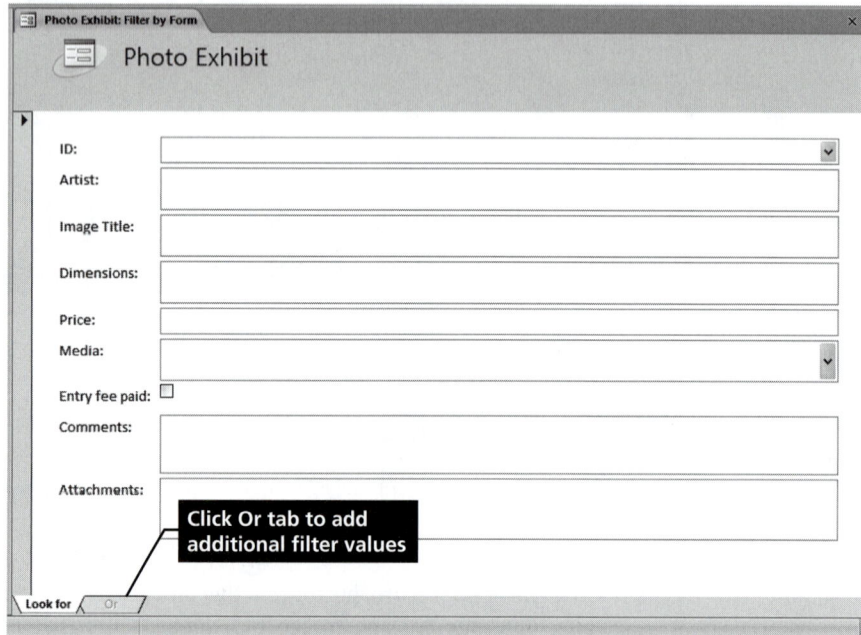

Figure 5-29

Form filter

2. Place the insertion point in the **Dimensions** box and click the **down arrow** on the right to display the list of options shown in Figure 5-30.

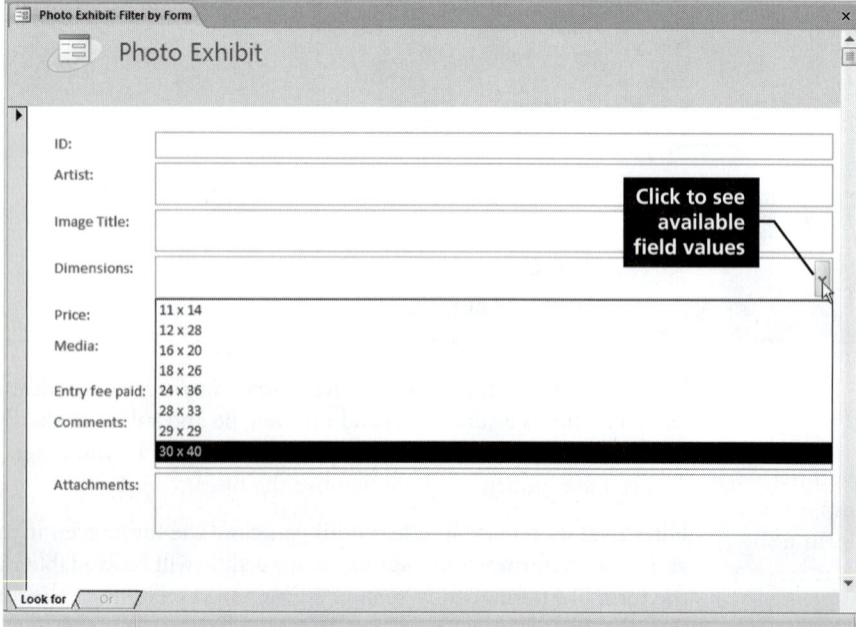

Figure 5-30

Form filter field options

3. Click **30 × 40**.
4. Click the **Or** tab at the bottom of the form.
5. Place the insertion point in the **Dimensions** box, click the **down arrow**, and then click **12 × 28**.
6. On the Home tab, in the Sort & Filter group, click the **Toggle Filter** button to apply the filter. The records containing either the dimensions 30 × 40 or 12 × 28 are displayed, as shown in Figure 5-31.

Figure 5-31

Form filter results

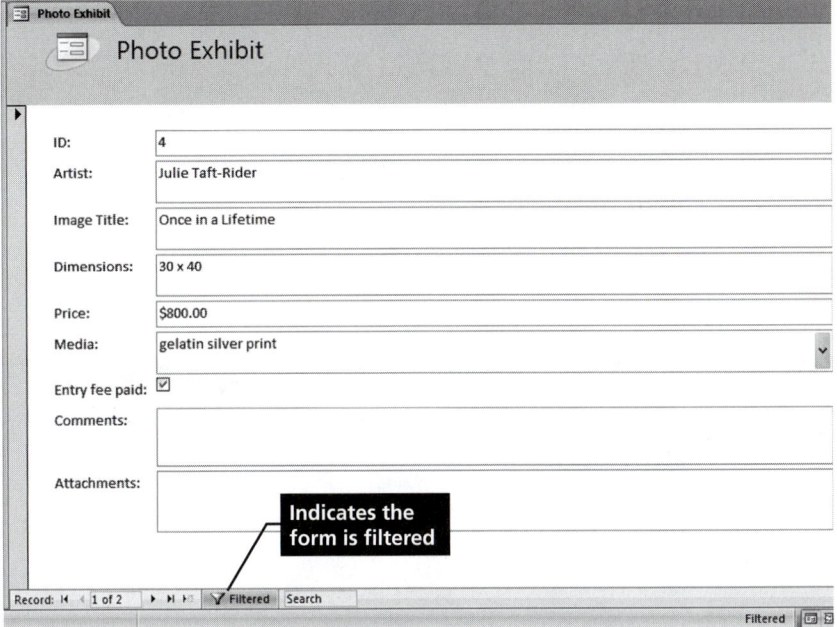

7. Click the **Next record** button on the record navigator at the bottom of the form to see the second record in the form filter results.
8. On the Home tab, in the Sort & Filter group, click the **Toggle Filter** button again to remove the filter.
9. On the Home tab, in the Sort & Filter group, click the **Advanced** button and click **Clear All Filters**.
10. Click the **Office Button** and click **Close Database**.
    STOP. CLOSE Access.

CERTIFICATION READY?
How do you filter data within forms?
5.2.4

TAKE NOTE*

If you want a field value to operate as a filter that is independent of other field values, you must enter that value on the Look for tab and each Or tab. In other words, the Look for tab and each Or tab represents an alternate set of filter values.

Filter by form is useful when you want to filter on several fields in a form or if you are trying to find a specific record. Access creates a blank form that is similar to the original form, you then complete as many of the fields as you want. When you are done, Access finds the records that contain the specified values.

Open the form in Form view and make sure the view is not already filtered by verifying that either the Unfiltered or the dimmed No Filter icon is present on the record selector bar. On the Home tab, in the Sort & Filter group, click Advanced, and then click Filter by Form. Click the down arrow in a field to display the available values.

Enter the first set of values on the Look for tab, then click the Or tab and enter the next set of values. Each time you click the Or tab, Access creates another Or tab so you can continue to add additional filter values if you want. Click the Toggle Field button to apply the filter. The filter returns any record that contains all of the values specified on the Look for tab, or all of the values specified on the first Or tab, or all of the values specified on the second Or tab, and so on.

SUMMARY SKILL MATRIX

IN THIS LESSON YOU LEARNED HOW TO:
Create a Simple Form
Create a Form in Design View
Create a Form in Layout View
Create a Datasheet Form
Apply AutoFormat
Sort Data Within a Form
Filter Data Within a Form

Knowledge Assessment

Matching

Match the term in Column 1 to its description in Column 2.

Column 1

1. Form Wizard — e
2. Form Design button — d
3. AutoFormat command — c
4. Blank Form button — j
5. form — h
6. Filter by Form — a
7. sorting — i
8. Form tool — b
9. common filters — g
10. filter — f

Column 2

a. useful when you want to filter on several fields in a form or if you are trying to find a specific record
b. creates a simple form with a single mouse-click
c. applies a predefined format that you select to a form or report
d. quickly creates a new blank form in Design view
e. allows you to select fields for the form, choose the form layout, and also choose a predefined style
f. limits a view of data to specific records without requiring you to alter the design of the form
g. built into every view that displays data
h. database object that you can use to enter, edit, or display data from a table or a query
i. helps users review and locate records without having to browse the data
j. quickly creates a new blank form in Layout view

True / False

Circle T if the statement is true or F if the statement is false.

T **F** 1. The Forms group is located on the Home tab in the Ribbon.

T F 2. Forms can be used to control access to data, such as which fields or rows of data are displayed.

T F 3. After you save your form design, you can run the form as often as you want.
T F 4. Layout view gives you a more detailed view of the structure of your form than Design view.
T F 5. Using the Blank Form tool is a very quick way to build a form, especially if you plan to put only a few fields on your form.
T F 6. To access the AutoFormat options, first switch to Form view.
T F 7. You cannot remove a sort order from just a single field.
T F 8. The filters available depend on the field's data type and values.
T F 9. To filter by form, first switch to Design view.
T F 10. When using the Form Wizard, you can only include fields from one table.

Competency Assessment

Project 5-1: Form Wizard

As a travel agent at Margie's Travel, you need an easy way to input data about events into the database. You decide to use the Form Wizard to create a datasheet form that has a preformatted style.

GET READY. Launch Access if it is not already running.

The *Travel Events* database file is available on the companion CD-ROM.

1. **OPEN** *Travel Events* from the data files for this lesson.
2. **SAVE** the database as *Travel Events XXX* (where XXX is your initials).
3. On the Create tab, in the Forms group, click the **More Forms** button, and click **Form Wizard**.
4. Click the **>>** button to move all the fields from the Available Fields box to the Selected Fields box.
5. Click the **Next>** button to move to the next page in the Form Wizard.
6. Click **Datasheet** as the layout for the form.
7. Click the **Next>** button to move to the next page in the Form Wizard.
8. Click **Module** as the style.
9. Click the **Next>** button to move to the final page in the Form Wizard.
10. Key **Event Details** as the title of the form.
11. Click the **Finish** button to create a datasheet form.
12. On the Home tab, in the Views group, click the **View** button, and click **Form View**.
13. Click the **'Close Event Details'** button to close the form.
14. **CLOSE** the database.

LEAVE Access open for the next project.

Project 5-2: Used Games Forms

The *Games inventory* database file is available on the companion CD-ROM.

You are the manager at Southridge Video. To expand the store, you have recently started taking used games in trade. You store information about each title in an Access database. You decide to create some forms to help you use the database more efficiently.

1. **OPEN** *Games inventory* from the data files for this lesson.
2. SAVE the database as *Games inventory XXX* (where XXX is your initials).
3. In the Navigation Pane, double-click **Games: Table** to open the table.

4. On the Create tab, in the Forms group, click the **Form** button to create a simple form and display it in Layout view.
5. Click the **Office Button** and click **Save**.
6. In the Save As dialog box, click **OK** to accept the *Games* form name suggested by Access.
7. Click the **Close 'Games'** button to close the form.
8. On the Create tab, in the Forms group, click the **Form Design** button to create a new blank form in Design view.
9. On the Design tab, in the Tools group, click the **Add Existing Fields** button to display the Field List pane.
10. Click the **+** next to Games to list the available fields.
11. Double-click **Title** to add it to the form.
12. Double-click **Rating** to add it to the form.
13. Double-click **Platform** to add it to the form.
14. Click the **Office Button** and click **Save**.
15. In the Save As dialog box, key **Game Rating**, and click **OK**.
16. Click the **Close** button to close the Field List.
17. On the Design menu, in the Views group, click the **View button** and click **Form View** to display form in Form view.
18. Click the **Close 'Game Rating'** button to close the form.
19. **LEAVE** the database open for the next project.

    LEAVE Access open for the next project.

Proficiency Assessment

Project 5-3: Sort and Filter Games

A customer comes into Southridge Video and asks about game publishers and the availability of a particular game. Sort and filter data in the forms you created to get the information that you need.

USE the database that is open from the previous project.

1. In the Navigation Pane, double-click the **Games** form to open it.
2. Right-click the **Publisher** field to display the shortcut menu.
3. Click **Sort A to Z** to sort the form by publisher name in alphabetic order.
4. Navigate to **record 3**, titled *Marvel: Ultimate Alliance*.
5. Right-click the **Title** field and click **Equals "Marvel: Ultimate Alliance"**.
6. Click the **Next record** button on the record navigator at the bottom of the form to see all the versions of the game with that name.
7. On the Home tab, in the Sort & Filter group, click the **Clear All Sorts** button.
8. **CLOSE** the database.

    LEAVE Access open for the next project.

Project 5-4: Toy Inventory

Your brother owns Wingtip Toys and recently started keeping a list of the store inventory in an Access database. He wants to add a form to the database and asks for your help. Add a simple form and then show him how to sort and apply filters.

The *Toy inventory* database file is available on the companion CD-ROM.

1. **OPEN** *Toy inventory* from the data files for this lesson.
2. Save the database as *Toy inventory XXX* (where XXX is your initials).
3. Open **Inventory: Table**.
4. Use the **Form** tool to create a simple form.
5. Format it using the **Trek** style AutoFormat option.
6. Save the form as **Inventory**.
7. Sort the **In Stock** field from **Largest to Smallest**.
8. Sort the **Description** field from **A to Z**.
9. Run a filter that finds all the records where the **Price** field is **between $50 and $100**.
10. Clear all sorts and filters.
11. Create a filter by form to find all the records that have two items in stock.
12. **CLOSE** the form and close the database.

    LEAVE Access open for the next project.

■ Mastery Assessment

Project 5-5: Red Wines

The Coho Vineyard has started a monthly wine club. Each month features a red wine hand-picked for its unique label and diverse style. Information about the monthly club selections is stored in an Access database; you will create forms so that you can retrieve the data in a useful way.

The *Red Wine* database file is available on the companion CD-ROM.

1. Open the *Red Wine* database from the data files for this lesson.
2. Save the database as *Red Wine XXX* (where XXX is your initials).
3. Create a simple form that contains all the fields in the Club Selections table and name it **Club Wines**.
4. Use the Form Design button to create a form named **Wine Details** that looks like the one shown in Figure 5-32 when displayed in Form view.

Figure 5-32

Wine Details form

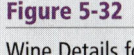

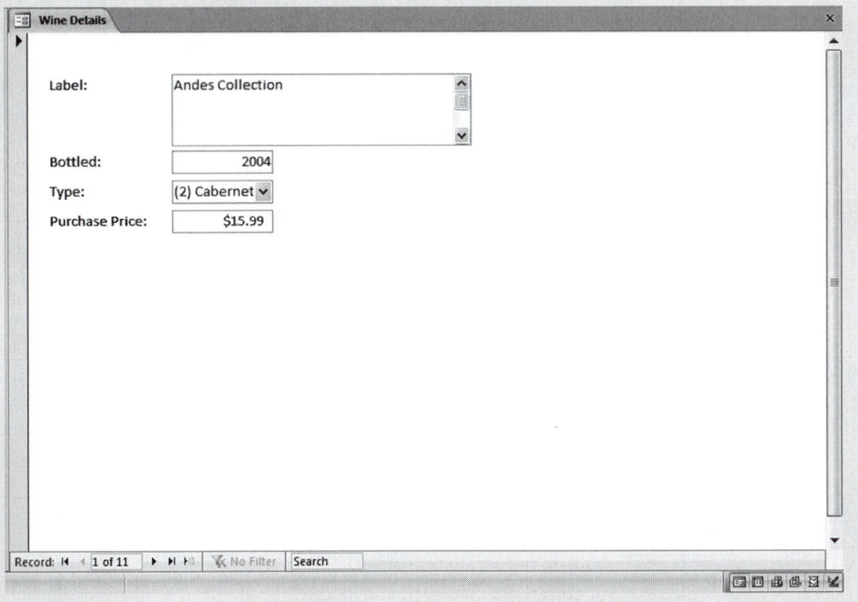

5. **CLOSE** the database.
   LEAVE Access open for the next project.

Project 5-6: Personal Contacts

Your address book is becoming outdated, and you decide to transfer all the current information about friends and family to an Access database. Input the data and then create forms to manage it efficiently.

1. **OPEN** *Personal Contacts* from the data files for this lesson.
2. **SAVE** the database as *Personal Contacts XXX* (where XXX is your initials).
3. Input as much contact information as you have about at least five friends or family members.
4. Create at least two forms that help you input, sort, or filter the data in a useful way. Use AutoFormats to improve the look of the forms.
5. **CLOSE** the database.
   STOP. CLOSE Access.

The *Personal Contacts* database file is available on the companion CD-ROM.

INTERNET READY

Microsoft has numerous online resources available to provide solutions, services, and support for whatever business needs you may have. If you are in small business, a helpful site is the Microsoft Small Business Center. Here, you can find advice, products, tools, and information tailored to small businesses. Search the Microsoft site for the Small Business Center, shown in Figure 5-33.

Figure 5-33

Microsoft Small Business Center

Explore the resources offered on the site. In the Articles & Research section, choose a topic about which you would like to know more, and read an article that interests you.

Create Reports

LESSON SKILL MATRIX

Creating a Simple Report – 854	Students will learn how to create a simple report.
Using the Report Wizard – 856	Students will learn how to use the report wizard.
Creating a Report in Design View – 859	Students will learn how to create a report in Design View.
Applying AutoFormat – 861	Students will learn how to apply AutoFormat.
Sorting Data Within a Report – 862	Students will learn how to sort data within a report.
Filtering Data Within a Report – 864	Students will learn how to filter data within a report.

Alpine Ski House is a small mountain lodge that features cross-country skiing in the winter and hiking in the summer. As an administrative assistant for Alpine Ski House, you take care of many of the administrative duties for the innkeepers, including reservations, billing, and recordkeeping. You have recently started using Access to keep track of customers and reservations at the lodge. In this lesson, you will learn three different ways to create reports for the lodge. You will also learn to apply Auto Formats to reports as well as sort and filter report data.

KEY TERMS
record source
report

SOFTWARE ORIENTATION

Reports Group

The Reports group is located on the Create tab in the Ribbon, as shown in Figure 6-1.

Figure 6-1

Reports group

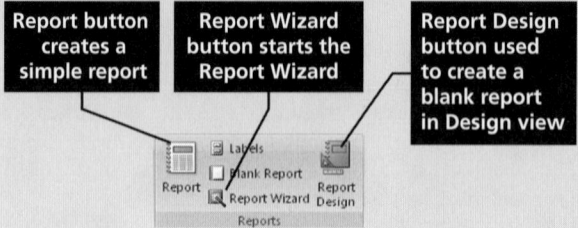

Use the Reports group of commands to create reports.

Creating Reports

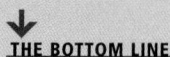

THE BOTTOM LINE

Reports display data pulled from tables and queries. You can create a report using the Report button, the Report Wizard, or Design view, depending on the amount of customization desired. After creating a report, you can apply an AutoFormat to create an instant professional look. You can also sort and filter data in a report to display the records to suit your needs.

Creating a Simple Report

You can use Access 2007 to create simple or complex reports. When creating a complex report, you might spend quite a bit of time choosing which fields you want to include from various tables or queries. That is fine when you need such a report, but when you need a simple display of all the fields in a table or query you can use the Report button to create a simple report.

→ **CREATE A REPORT**

GET READY. Before you begin these steps, be sure to turn on and/or log on to your computer and start Access.

1. OPEN *AlpineSkiHouse* from the data files for this lesson.
2. Save the database as *AlpineSkiHouseXXX* (where XXX is your initials).
3. In the Navigation Pane, click the **Rooms** table to select it. This is your record source.
4. On the Create tab, in the Reports group, click the **Report** button. The report appears in Layout view, as shown in Figure 6-2. Notice the Report Layout tools that appear in the Ribbon.

The *AlpineSkiHouse* database is available on the companion CD-ROM.

Figure 6-2

Simple report

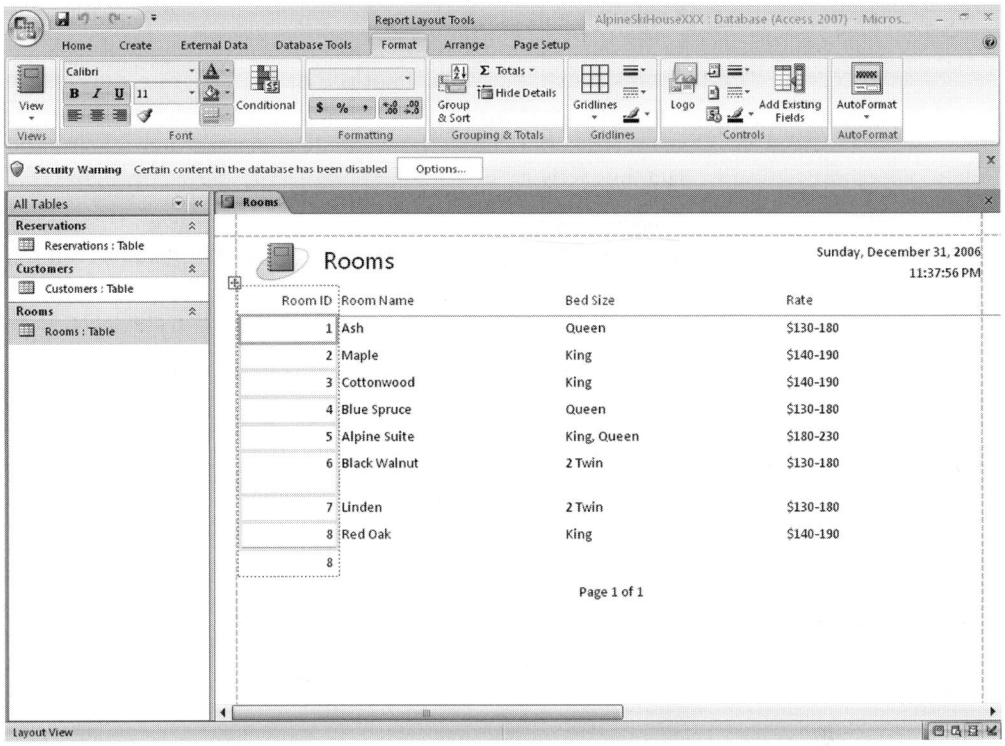

5. Click the **Room ID** header to select it. Position the pointer over the right border until you see a double-sided arrow. Click and drag to the left, resizing the column to remove excess white space.
6. Resize the other columns until your screen looks similar to Figure 6-3.

Figure 6-3

Report with resized columns

7. Click the **Save** button on the Quick Access Toolbar. The Save As dialog box appears with *Rooms* in the Report Name box. Click **OK**. Notice that the Rooms report is listed in the Navigation Pane.
8. Click the **Close** button to close the Rooms report.
   PAUSE. LEAVE the database open to use in the next exercise.

A *report* is a database object that is used to organize and display data from tables and queries. Reports are commonly used as formatted hard copies of table or query data. You can modify a report's design, but you cannot add or edit data in a report. The purpose of a report is to allow users to view data, not edit it. For example, a supervisor might ask you to create a sales report that is filtered to show only one region's sales. The supervisor does not need to edit the data, just view it.

A report's *record source* is the table or query that provides the data used to generate a report. Before you can create a report, you need to define the record source by clicking in the Navigation Pane on the table or query on which you want to base the report. Then, click the Report button and a report is generated based on the table or query you selected.

You can edit, print, or save and close a report. You should save a report's design if you are likely to use it again. To save a report, click the Save button on the Microsoft Office Button or in the Quick Access Toolbar. If you click the Close button without saving, Access will display a dialog box asking if you want to save it. Once it is saved, the report is listed in the Navigation Pane. You can open it and modify in the future or create a new report based on the original.

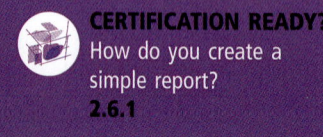

CERTIFICATION READY?
How do you create a simple report?
2.6.1

The next time you run the report, the design will be the same, but the data will be different if the data in the table or query has been updated.

Using the Report Wizard

> You are probably already familiar with the way a "wizard" works. The Report Wizard displays a series of questions about the report you want and then it creates the report for you based on your answers. The Report Wizard knows what makes a good report, so the questions are designed to help you create a professional report with little effort.

➔ USE THE REPORT WIZARD

USE the database you used in the previous exercise.

1. On the Create tab, in the Reports group, click the **Report Wizard** button. The first screen of the Report Wizard appears.
2. Make sure the **Rooms** table is selected in the Tables/Queries menu.
3. Click the double right arrow **>>** button to move all the fields into the Selected Fields list.
4. Click the **Room ID** field to select it and click the **<** left arrow button to move it back to the Available Fields list, as shown in Figure 6-4. Click the **Next** button.

Figure 6-4

The Report Wizard Fields screen

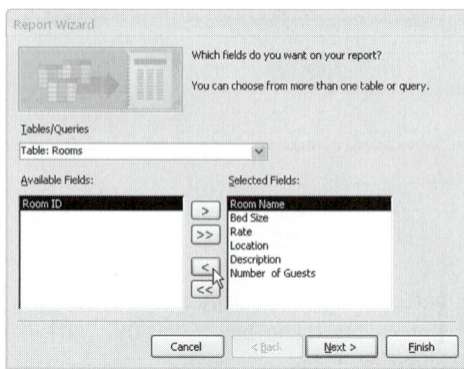

5. Click the **Location** field to select it and click the **>** right arrow button to add it as a grouping level, as shown in Figure 6-5.

Figure 6-5

The Report Wizard Grouping screen

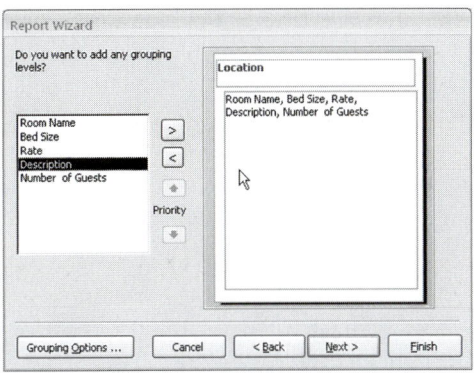

6. Click the **Next** button.
7. Select **Room Name** from the fields menu to sort in ascending order, as shown in Figure 6-6, and click the **Next** button.

Figure 6-6

The Report Wizard Sort screen

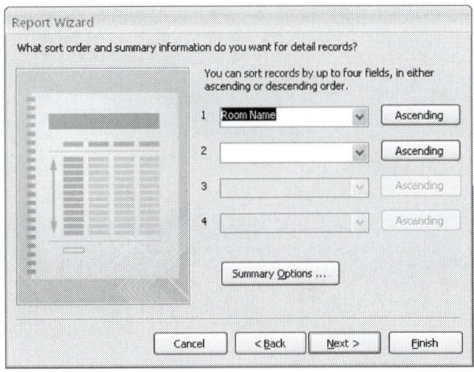

8. In the Layout section, click the **Outline** button. In the Orientation section, click the **Landscape** button, as shown in Figure 6-7. Click **Next**.

Figure 6-7

The Report Wizard Layout screen

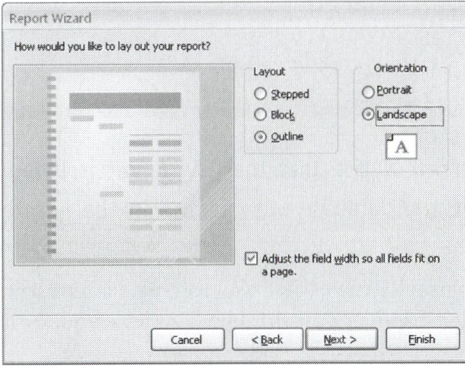

9. Click **Flow** in the styles list, as shown in Figure 6-8, and click **Next**.

Figure 6-8

The Report Wizard Style screen

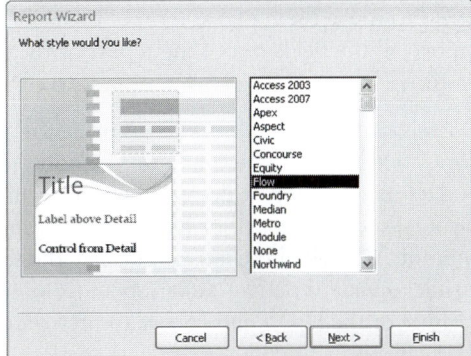

10. Key **Rooms Wizard** as the title of the report, as shown in Figure 6-9.

Figure 6-9

The Report Wizard Title screen

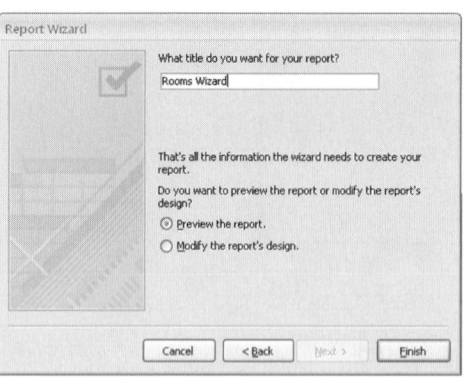

11. Click **Finish**. The Rooms Wizard report appears on the screen, as shown in Figure 6-10.

Figure 6-10

The Rooms Wizard report

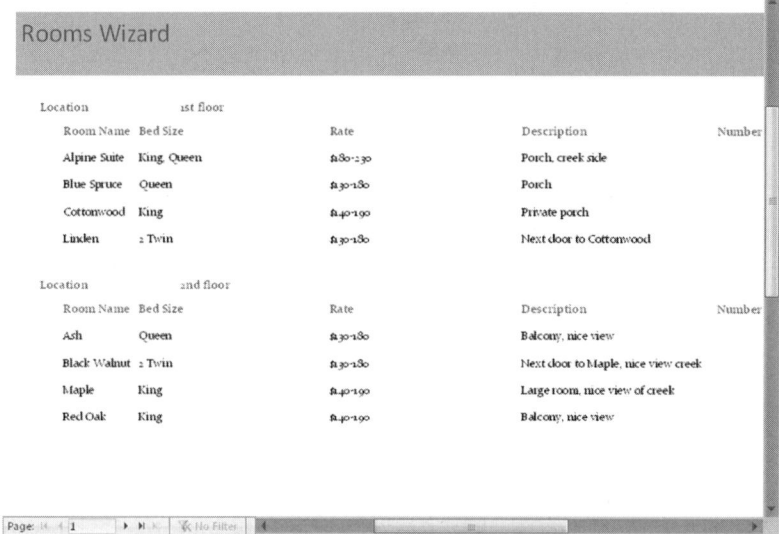

12. CLOSE the report. Notice that the new report is listed in the Navigation Pane.

PAUSE. LEAVE the database open to use in the next exercise.

The Report Wizard is usually the easiest way to create a report when you want to choose which fields to include. It guides you through a series of questions and then generates a report based on your answers.

The Report Wizard allows you to include fields from more than one table or query. You can click the double right arrow button (>>) to include all the fields in the report or click the single right arrow button (>) to move them one at a time. Likewise, you can click the double left arrow button (<<) to move all the fields out of the report or the single left arrow button (<) to move them one at a time.

You can specify group levels, as when you displayed all of the first floor rooms together and all of the second floor rooms together in the Room Wizard report. You can also choose up to four fields on which to sort data in ascending or descending order. On the layout screen, you can choose from various layouts, such as stepped or tabular, depending on the data and the choices you have made to this point. You can also choose to display the report in portrait or landscape orientation. Access provides a wide variety of design styles from which to choose. On the last screen, you can key a name for the report and choose to preview or modify the report.

Create Reports | 859

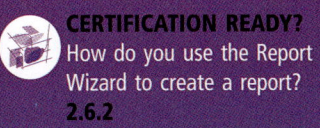

CERTIFICATION READY?
How do you use the Report Wizard to create a report?
2.6.2

If you want to skip steps such as Sorting or Grouping, click the Next button to go to the next screen. You can click the Finish button anytime it is available to create the report with the choices you have specified.

Creating a Report in Design View

When you want a customized report, you can create it in Design view, which offers you many options for creating the report exactly the way you want it.

→ CREATE A REPORT IN DESIGN VIEW

USE the database you used in the previous exercise.

1. If necessary, click the Rooms table in the Navigation Pane to select it.
2. On the Create tab, in the Reports group, click the **Report Design** button. A new blank report is displayed in Design view, as shown in Figure 6-11.

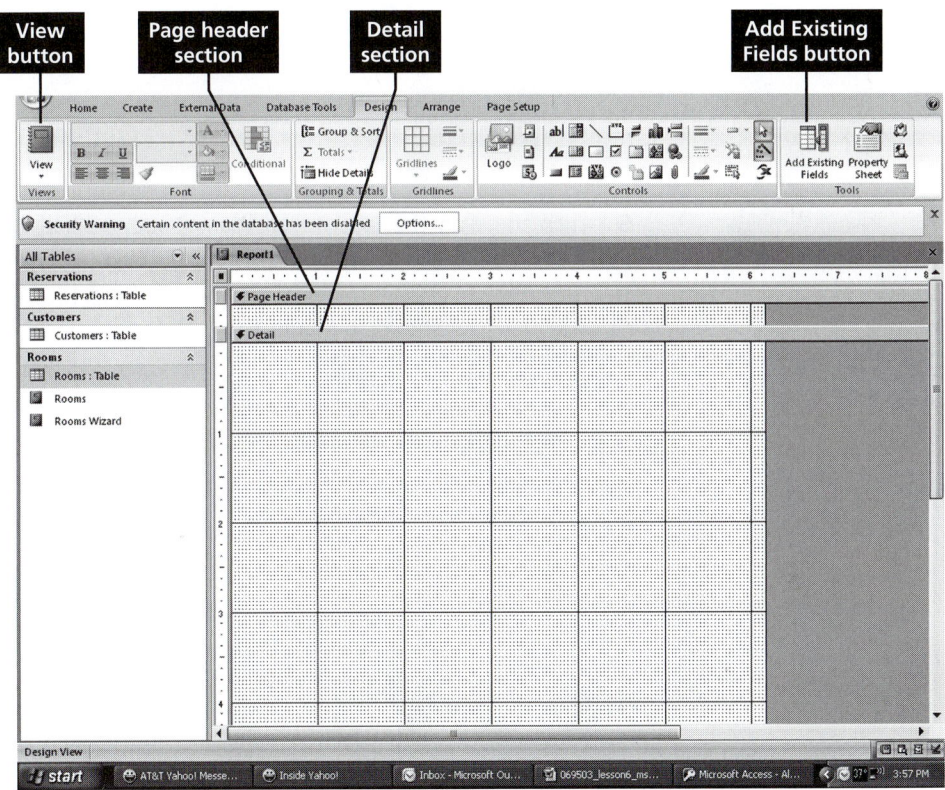

Figure 6-11
New blank report in Design view

3. If the Fields List is not already displayed, on the Design tab, in the Tools group, click the **Add Existing Fields** button. The Fields List appears.

4. Click the plus (+) box beside **Rooms** to display the fields in the table, as shown in Figure 6-12.

Figure 6-12
Fields List pane

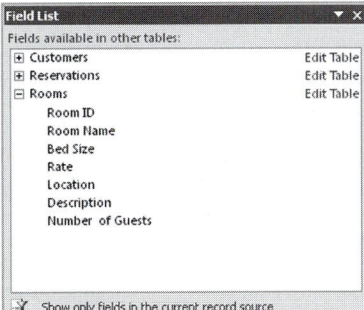

5. Double-click **Room ID**. The field is inserted onto the design grid.
6. Double-click **Room Name**, **Bed Size**, and **Rate**.
7. Click the **Close** button on the Field List pane.
8. Click the **Bed Size** label. The border around the label changes to orange, indicating it is selected. Position the insertion point over the top orange border until the pointer changes to a four-sided arrow, as shown in Figure 6-13.

Figure 6-13

Move pointer

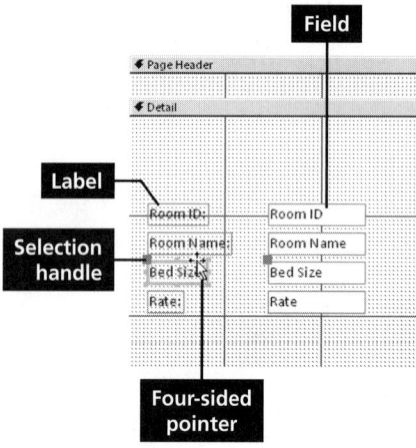

9. Click and drag the label to position about one-half inch to the right of the Room ID field and release the mouse button. The field moved along with the label.
10. In the same manner, move the **Rate** label and field to position below the Bed Size field, as shown in Figure 6-14.

Figure 6-14

Moved fields

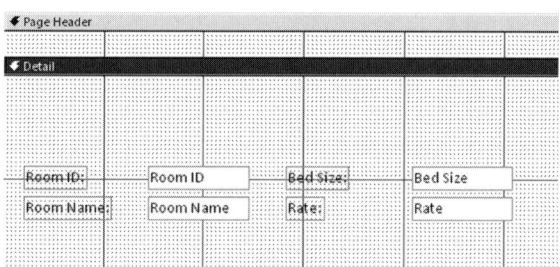

11. Click the **Room ID** field to select it. Position the mouse pointer on the square handle in the middle of the right-side border. Click and drag the field to the left to decrease the size by about one-quarter inch.
12. On the Home tab, in the Views group, click the **View** button and select **Report View** from the menu. The report is shown in Report View. Scroll down to see all the records.
13. Click the **Save** button on the Quick Access Toolbar.
14. Key **Report Design** in the Report Name box and click **OK**.
15. **CLOSE** the report.

    PAUSE. LEAVE the table open to use in the next exercise.

In the previous exercise, you created a very basic report in Design view. Design view gives you the most options for creating a report, because it shows you the underlying structure of the report. It also provides you with more design tools and capabilities.

In Design view, a report is displayed on a design grid with sections. The sections include the following:

- **Report Header:** This section is printed once at the beginning of every report. This is a good place to include a logo, a date, or information that might normally appear on a cover page.
- **Page Header:** This section is printed at the top of every page of a report, so it would be good place to include the report title.
- **Group Header:** This section is printed at the beginning of a group. It is a good place to include the group name.
- **Detail:** This section includes the body of the report. It is printed once for every row in a record source.
- **Group Footer:** This section is printed at the end of a group. It may include summary information for the group.
- **Page Footer:** This section is printed at the bottom of every page of a report, so it would be a good place to include information such as a page number.
- **Report Footer:** This section is printed once at the end of every report. This is a good place for report totals.

To add fields to the report design, you can display the Field List pane by clicking the Add Existing Fields button. Double-click a field in the Field List to add it to the design grid, or you can drag the field to a location on the grid.

TAKE NOTE
You can add more than one field to a report design at once. Hold down the **CTRL** key and click the fields you want, and then drag the selected fields onto the report.

If you need to move a field on the grid, click the field to select it and then position the pointer on the border until you see a four-sided arrow. Then, drag to the new location. To change the size of a field, click and drag a selection handle.

To see what your report will look like, click the View button on the Views group and select Report from the menu.

CERTIFICATION READY?
How do you create a report in Design view?
2.6.3

Applying AutoFormat

An AutoFormat applies a set of predefined fonts, colors, and design to a report. The instant formatting can quickly give your report the professional look you want.

⇨ APPLY AUTOFORMAT

USE the database open from the previous exercise.

1. **OPEN** the **Rooms** report.
2. On the Home tab, in the Views group, click the **View** button. Select **Layout view** from the menu.
3. On the Format tab, in the AutoFormat group, click the **AutoFormat** button. A menu of predefined report formats appears.
4. Click the **Metro** design, as shown in Figure 6-15. The format is applied to the report.

Figure 6-15

AutoFormat menu

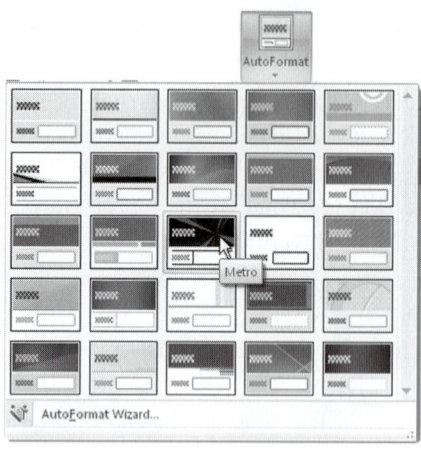

5. On the Format tab, in the AutoFormat group, click the **AutoFormat** button. Select **AutoFormat Wizard** from the menu. The AutoFormat dialog box appears.

6. Click **Module** in the Report AutoFormats list, as shown in Figure 6-16, and click **OK.** The new format is applied.

Figure 6-16

AutoFormat dialog box

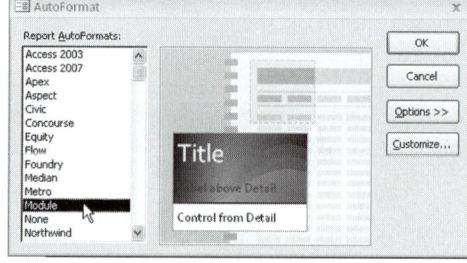

CERTIFICATION READY?
How do you apply AutoFormat to a report?
2.7.7

7. **SAVE** the report.

PAUSE. LEAVE the report open to use in the next exercise.

An AutoFormat is a predefined format that you can apply to any report in Layout view. The AutoFormat menu displays a variety of designs. After you click the design you want, it is applied to the report.

Select the AutoFormat Wizard command to display the AutoFormat dialog box. You can select a design from the list displayed. You can also format options and customize an AutoFormat. You can create a new AutoFormat based on the current report, update the AutoFormat design with values from the current report, or delete the AutoFormat design.

Sorting Data Within a Report

Sorting organizes data in a particular order, such as alphabetic order or from smallest to largest numbers. For example, you can sort a customer list in alphabetic order by last name or by customer ID number. You can sort data by clicking the buttons on the Ribbon, right-clicking and choosing commands from the shortcut menu, or by using the Group, Sort, and Total pane.

→ SORT DATA WITHIN A REPORT

USE the report open from the previous exercise.

1. On the Home tab in the Views group, click the **View** button. Select **Layout** from the menu.
2. Click the **Room Name** header.

3. On the Home tab, in the Sort & Filter group, click the **Ascending** button. The column is sorted in ascending alphabetic order.
4. On the Home tab, in the Sort & Filter group, click the **Clear All Sorts** button. The Sort is cleared.
5. Right-click the **Room Name** header. The shortcut menu appears.
6. Select **Sort Z to A**, as shown in Figure 6-17. The column is sorted.

Figure 6-17

Shortcut menu

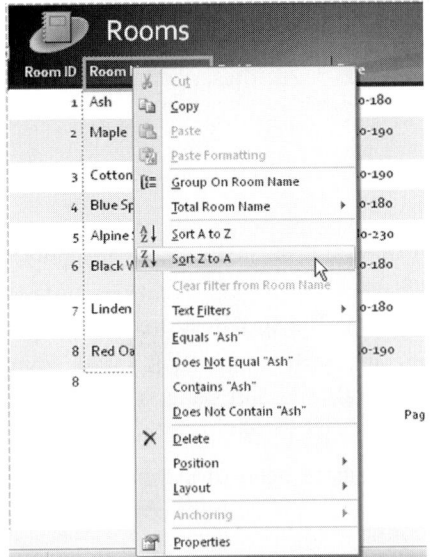

7. On the Home tab, in the Sort & Filter group, click the **Clear All Sorts** button. The Sort is cleared.
8. On the Formatting tab, in the Grouping & Totals group, click the **Group & Sort** button. The Group, Sort, and Total pane appears at the bottom of the screen, as shown in Figure 6-18.

Figure 6-18

Group, Sort, and Total pane

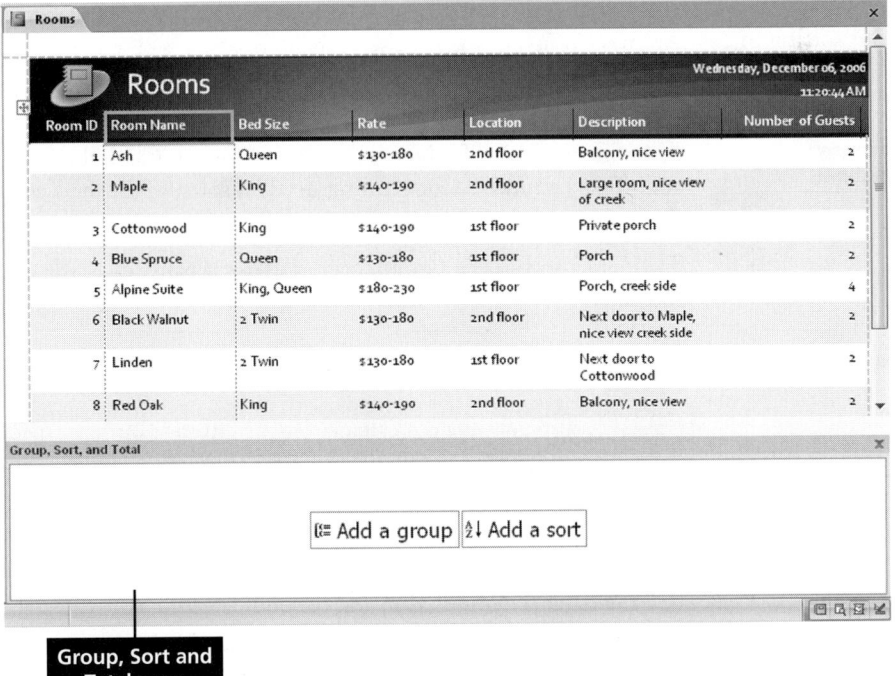

9. Click the **Add a Sort** button in the Group, Sort, and Total pane.
10. Click the **Room Name** field in the fields list. Notice that the field was sorted in ascending order by default and a line was added describing the sort.
11. Click the down arrow beside **with A on top** and select **with Z on top** from the menu, as shown in Figure 6-19. The field is sorted in descending order.

Figure 6-19

Sort displayed in the Group, Sort, and Total pane

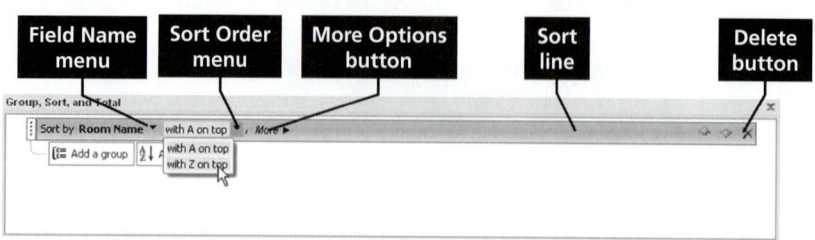

12. Click the **More Options** button in the Sort line. Notice the options available for customizing a sort.
13. Click the **Delete** button. The sort is cleared.
14. On the Formatting tab, in the Grouping & Totals group, click the **Group & Sort** button. The Group, Total, and Sort pane is removed.
15. **SAVE** the table.

    PAUSE. LEAVE the database open to use in the next exercise.

CERTIFICATION READY?
How do you sort data within a report?
5.1.3

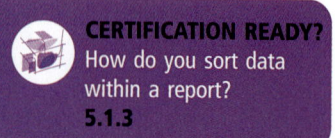

X REF

Lesson 3 has more information about sorting in a table.

X REF

Lesson 5 has more information about sorting in a form.

LOOKING AHEAD

Lesson 8 has more information about sorting in a query.

Sorting data in a report is similar to sorting in a table. In Layout view, select the field you want to sort and click the Ascending or Descending button on the Home tab, in the Sort & Filter group. Click the Clear All Sorts button to remove the sort orders. You can sort as many fields as you like one at a time.

You can also easily sort data by right-clicking in a field and choosing the type of sort you want from the shortcut menu. The sort commands in the shortcut menu vary depending on the type of data in the field. For text, you will choose Sort A to Z or Sort Z to A; for numbers, you will choose Sort Smallest to Largest or Sort Largest to Smallest; and for dates, you will choose Sort Oldest to Newest or Sort Newest to Oldest.

The Group, Sort, and Total pane gives you more sorting options. You can use the pane to specify the sort order or to view the results of sorting using the shortcut menu. To specify a sort, click the Add a Sort button and select a field from the pop-up menu. Click the drop-down menu to specify the type of sort you want. Click the More Options button to display additional commands for creating detailed sorts. Click the Less Options button to return to the basic sorting options.

To delete a sort in the Group, Sort, and Total pane, click the Delete button at the end of the sort line.

Filtering Data Within a Report

A filter displays only data that meet the criteria you have specified and hides the rest. It does not modify the table data or the design of the report. After you remove a filter, all the records are displayed again.

FILTER DATA WITHIN A REPORT

USE the database you used in the previous exercise.

1. Click the **Location** header to select it.
2. On the Home tab, in the Sort & Filter group, click the **Filter** button. A menu appears.

3. Point to **Text Filters**. A second menu appears. Select **Begins with...**, as shown in Figure 6-20.

Figure 6-20

Shortcut menu

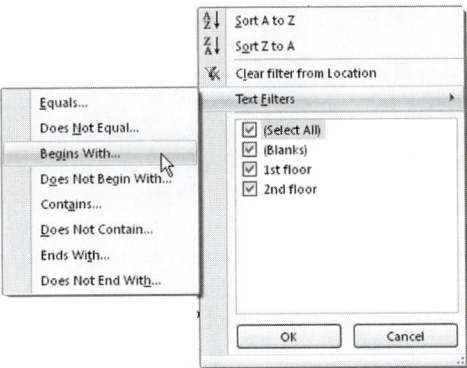

4. Key **1** into the Custom Filter box and click **OK**. The data is filtered to show only the rooms on the first floor.
5. Click the **Toggle Filter** button.
6. In the Bed Size field, click **King** in the second row.
7. On the Home tab, in the Sort & Filter group, click the **Selection** button. Select **Equals "King"** from the menu. The data is filtered to show only the rooms with King size beds.
8. Right-click the **Bed Size** header. A shortcut menu appears. Notice that the Equals "King" filter and the other filters from the Selection menu are also available in the shortcut menu, shown in Figure 6-21.

Figure 6-21

Shortcut menu

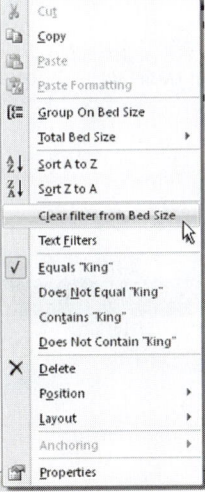

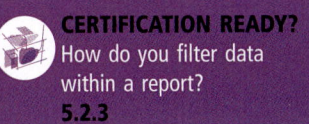

CERTIFICATION READY?
How do you filter data within a report?
5.2.3

9. Select **Clear filter from Bed Size** from the menu. The filter is cleared.
10. **SAVE** and **CLOSE** the table. **CLOSE** the database.
    STOP. CLOSE Access.

Filtering data in Layout view of a report is very similar to filtering data in a table. You can apply common filters using the commands on the Sort & Filter group or by right-clicking a field and choosing a filter from the shortcut menu. The filters available on the shortcut menu vary depending on the type of data in the field.

Only one filter can be applied to a field at a time. However, you can specify a different filter for each field.

You can toggle between filtered and unfiltered views using the Toggle Filter button. You just practiced removing a filter from a field by right-clicking in the field and selecting the *Clear filter from field name* command. To remove all filters permanently, select the Clear All Filters command on the Advanced menu in the Sort & Filter group.

TAKE NOTE

If you save a report (or other object) while a filter is applied, it will be available the next time that you open the report. If you want to open the report and see the filter already applied, set the FilterOnLoad property setting to Yes.

You can also filter by selection in a report. If you want to view only the reservations for 12/13/07, select that date in the Check-in field and click the Selection button. That date will appear in the menu, so that you can choose Equals 12/13/07, Does Not Equal 12/13/07, and so on. You can also access these commands on the shortcut menu by right-clicking the value.

TAKE NOTE

If you need to apply a filter that is not in the common filters list, you can write an advanced filter using the Advanced Filter/Sort command on the Advanced menu. You will need to be familiar with writing expressions, which are similar to formulas, and be familiar with the criteria that you specify when designing a query.

Lesson 3 has more information about filtering records in a table.

Lesson 5 has more information about filtering data within a form.

LOOKING AHEAD
Lesson 7 has more information about filtering data within a query.

SUMMARY SKILL MATRIX

IN THIS LESSON YOU LEARNED HOW TO:
Create a Simple Report
Use the Report Wizard
Create a Report in Design View
Apply AutoFormat
Sort Data Within a Report
Filter Data Within a Report

Knowledge Assessment

Matching

Match the term in Column 1 to its description in Column 2.

Column 1	Column 2
1. report **d**	**a.** organizes data in a particular order
2. record source **f**	**b.** displays data that meets the criteria you have specified and hides the rest
3. Report Wizard **h**	**c.** a list of available fields for adding to a report
4. Field List pane **c**	**d.** a database object that is used to organize and display data from tables and queries
5. Detail **i**	**e.** removes all sort orders
6. AutoFormat **j**	**f.** the table or query that provides the data used to generate a report
7. Sort **a**	**g.** the way a report is displayed in Design view
8. Filter **b**	**h.** guides you through a series of questions and then generates a report based on your answers
9. design grid **g**	**i.** the section of a report that includes the body of the report
10. Clear All Sorts **e**	**j.** a predefined format that you can apply to any report in Layout view

True / False

Circle T if the statement is true or F if the statement is false.

T F 1. A simple report contains all the records in a table or query.

T **F** 2. You can edit the data in a report.

T **F** 3. Click the Report button to define a record source.

T F 4. In the Report Wizard, you can skip steps such as Sorting or Grouping by clicking the Next button.

T F 5. You can drag a field from the Field List pane to the design grid to add it to the report.

T **F** 6. Layout view gives you the most options for creating a report, because it shows you the underlying structure of the report.

T **F** 7. AutoFormat resizes column widths for you.

T F 8. You can save a filter with a report.

T F 9. You can use the Group, Sort, and Total pane to specify sort order or view the results of sorting using the shortcut menu.

T **F** 10. The Toggle Filter button removes a filter permanently.

Competency Assessment

Project 6-1: Soccer Team Report

You need a copy of the soccer team's roster that you can print and take with you to work. Create a simple report and apply an AutoFormat.

GET READY. Launch Access if it is not already running.

The Soccer Team database is available on the companion CD-ROM.

1. Open the *SoccerTeam* database.
2. Save the database as *SoccerTeamXXX* (where XXX is your initials).
3. Click the **Roster** table to select it.
4. On the Create tab, in the Reports group, click the **Report** button. A new report is created.
5. Resize each field so that all fields fit on one page.
6. On the Format tab, in the AutoFormat group, click the **AutoFormat** button.
7. Select the purple format in the fourth row named **Opulent**.
8. Click the **Save** button on the Quick Access Toolbar. The Save As dialog box appears with the name *Roster* in it. Click **OK** to accept that name for the report.
9. **CLOSE** the report.
10. **CLOSE** the database.

    LEAVE Access open for the next project.

Project 6-2: Fourth Coffee Inventory Report

In your job at Fourth Coffee, you are responsible for maintaining the coffee inventory. Create a report to view the inventory and prepare for the next order.

The Coffee database is available on the companion CD-ROM.

1. **OPEN** *Coffee* from the data files for this lesson.
2. **SAVE** the database as *CoffeeXXX* (where XXX is your initials).
3. Click the **Coffee Inventory Table** in the Navigation Pane to select it.
4. On the Create tab, in the Reports group, click the **Report Wizard** button. The first Report Wizard screen appears.
5. Click the double arrow >> to move all the fields to the Selected Fields list and click **Next**.
6. On the grouping screen, click the **Scheduled Order Date** field, click the > arrow, and click **Next**.
7. On the sorting screen, click the down arrow on the menu, select **Pounds**, and click **Next**.
8. Keep the defaults as is on the layout screen and click **Next**.
9. On the style screen, click **Paper**, and click **Next**.
10. Click **Finish**. The report is created.
11. **CLOSE** the report.
12. **CLOSE** the database.

    LEAVE Access open for the next project.

Proficiency Assessment

Project 6-3: Alpine Ski House Reservations Report

Every week is different at the Alpine Ski House. Sometimes the lodge is full of guests, and sometimes only a few rooms are occupied. Create a report to show the innkeepers what to expect in the coming weeks.

The *AlpineHouse* database is available on the companion CD-ROM.

1. **OPEN** the *AlpineHouse* database.
2. **SAVE** it as *AlpineHouseXXX* (where XXX is your initials).
3. Use the Report Wizard to create a report using the Room, Check-in Date, and Check-out Date fields.
4. Group the report by Room and sort it in ascending order by Check-in Date.
5. Use stepped and portrait layout and apply the Foundry format.
6. Name the report **December Reservations** and finish the wizard.
7. Switch to Layout view and increase the width of the Room field.
8. **SAVE** and **CLOSE** the table.
9. **CLOSE** the database.

   LEAVE Access open for the next project.

Project 6-4: Wingtip Toys Design View Report

The manufacturing department at Wingtip Toys needs summary information about each toy in inventory. Create a report in Design view that will display the requested information.

The *Wingtip Toys* database is available on the companion CD-ROM.

1. **OPEN** *Wingtip Toys* and save it as *WingtipToysXXX* (where XXX is your initials).
2. Click the **Inventory** table in the Navigation Pane to select it.
3. On the Create tab, in the Reports group, click the **Report Design** button.
4. On the Design tab, in the Tools group, click the **Add Existing Fields** button. The Field List pane appears.
5. Position the fields onto the design grid, as shown in Figure 6-22. Adjust field widths as shown.

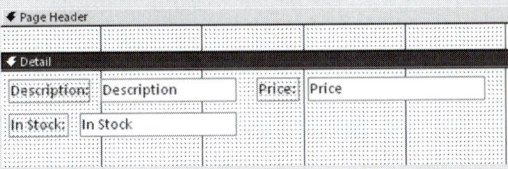

Figure 6-22
Wingtip Toys report in Design view

6. Save the report as **Toy Summary**.
7. **CLOSE** the report.

   LEAVE the database open for the next project.

Mastery Assessment

Project 6-5: Filter and Sort a Wingtip Toys Report

A large order was recently filled, and now the inventory at Wingtip Toys is quite low on some items. Create a report that displays this information.

The *WingtipToysXXX* database should be open.

1. Define the **Inventory** table as the record source for a new report.
2. Create a simple report.
3. Apply the **Equity** AutoFormat to the new report.
4. Sort the report in ascending order by the Description field.
5. Click the first row of the **In Stock** field, which contains the number 10.
6. Filter by selection to display the toys with 10 or fewer items in stock.
7. Click the **In Stock** field header and sort the field in ascending order.
8. Clear all sorts.
9. Clear all filters.
10. **SAVE** the report as **Inventory**.
11. **CLOSE** the report.
12. **CLOSE** the database.
    LEAVE Access open for the next project.

Project 6-6: Angel Project Report

The school Angel Project has begun. Information for the boy angels needs to be distributed to the boys in the kindergarten classes, and the girl angels' information needs to be distributed to the girls. Create a report with filters that displays the boy and girl information separately.

The *AngelProject* database is available on the companion CD-ROM.

1. **OPEN** the *AngelProject* database.
2. Save the database as **AngelProjectXXX** (where XXX is your initials).
3. Define the List table as the record source for a new report.
4. Use the Report Wizard to create a report with all the fields.
5. Skip the grouping and sorting screens, and choose a tabular, portrait layout and the Trek format.
6. Name the report **Angel Needs and Wants.**
7. Switch to Layout view and adjust field widths as necessary so that all data fits on the screen and on one page.
8. Display the Group, Sort, and Total pane.
9. Sort the report in ascending order by Age.
10. Create a filter to show only the information for the males.
11. Toggle the filter and create a new filter to show only the information for the females.
12. **SAVE** and **CLOSE** the report.
13. **CLOSE** the database.
    CLOSE Access.

INTERNET READY

Search the Internet for at least five dream vacation packages and create a database table that lists each hotel's location, name, cost, and favorite amenities or activities. After creating the table, use the Report Wizard to create a professional looking report that displays your data.

Create and Modify Queries

LESSON SKILL MATRIX

Creating a Query from a Table	Students will learn how to create a query from a table.
Creating a Query from Multiple Tables	Students will learn how to create a query from multiple tables.
Adding a Table to a Query	Students will learn how to add a table to a query.
Removing a Table from a Query	Students will learn how to remove a table from a query.
Sorting Data Within a Query	Students will learn how to sort data within a query.
Filtering Data Within a Query	Students will learn how to filter data within a query.

You work for Northwind Traders, a mountain-climbing apparel company dedicated to producing high-quality and technically innovative products. The company has a program called Industry Friends that offers discount purchasing privileges for employees and other outdoor professionals and friends who qualify. As operations coordinator, you are responsible for approving applications for the program and entering related information into the database. You often need to pull specific data from the database. In this lesson, you will learn how to create queries from a single table—including a simple query and a find duplicates query—and how to create queries from multiple tables, including a find unmatched query. You will learn how to modify a query by adding a table, removing a table, and adding criteria to a query. You will also learn how to sort and filter data within a query.

KEY TERMS
field list
parameter query
query criterion
recordsource
select query

872 | Lesson 7

Software Orientation

Other Group

The Other group on the Create tab, as shown in Figure 7-1, contains the commands used to create queries. The Query Wizard button launches the Query Wizard, which helps you to create a simple query, a crosstab query, a find duplicates query, or a find unmatched query. The Query Design button creates a new, blank query in Design view.

Figure 7-1

Other group

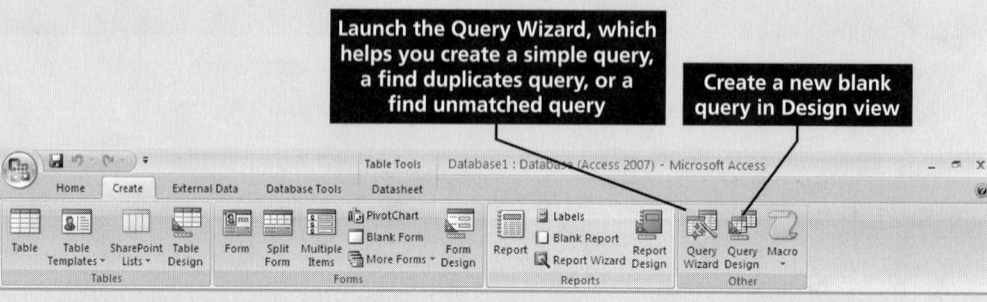

Use this figure as a reference throughout this lesson as well as the rest of this book.

Creating a Query

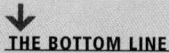

THE BOTTOM LINE

A query is a set of instructions used for working with data. Creating a query is like asking the database a question. Running a query performs these instructions and provides the answers. The results that a query returns can be sorted, grouped, or filtered. A query can also create, copy, delete, or change data.

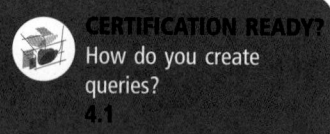

CERTIFICATION READY?
How do you create queries?
4.1

Creating a Query from a Table

When one table will provide the information that you need, you can create a simple select query using the Query Wizard. You can also use a query to find records with duplicate field values in a single table.

The *Northwind* database file is available on the companion CD-ROM.

→ **CREATE A SIMPLE QUERY**

GET READY. Before you begin these steps, be sure to launch Microsoft Access.

1. **OPEN** the *Northwind* database from the data files for this lesson.
2. **SAVE** the database as *NorthwindXXX* (where XXX is your initials).
3. On the Create tab, in the Other group, click the **Query Wizard** button. The New Query dialog box appears, as shown in Figure 7-2.

Create and Modify Queries | 873

Figure 7-2

New Query dialog box

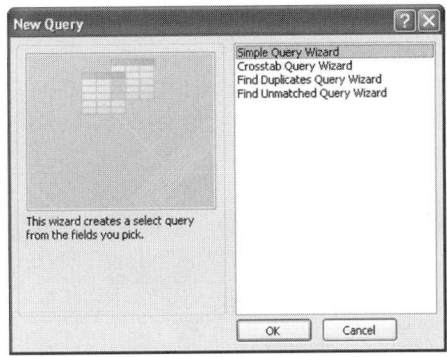

4. Click **Simple Query Wizard** and then click **OK**. The Simple Query Wizard appears, as shown in Figure 7-3.

Figure 7-3

Simple Query Wizard, screen 1

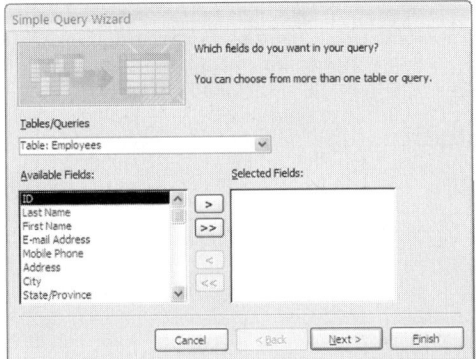

5. In the Tables/Queries dropdown list, **Table: Employees** should be selected. If it is not, select it.
6. Under Available Fields, double-click **Last Name**, **First Name**, **E-mail Address**, **Mobile Phone**, and **Position** to move them to the *Selected Fields* box.

> **TAKE NOTE**
>
> To remove a field from the Selected Fields box, double-click the field. This moves it back to the Available Fields box.

7. Click the **Next >** button. The second screen in the Simple Query Wizard appears, as shown in Figure 7-4.

Figure 7-4

Simple Query Wizard, screen 2

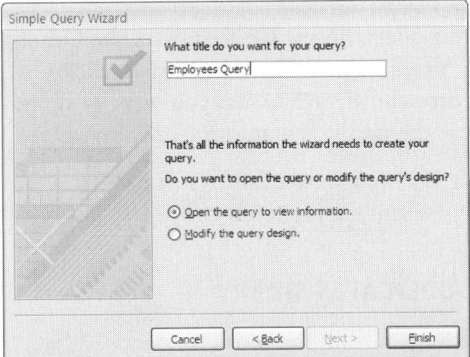

8. Name the query **Employees Contact Query**. *Open the query to view information* should be selected.

9. Click the **Finish** button. The Employees Contact Query is displayed, as shown in Figure 7-5. The results show all of the records, but show only the five fields that you specified in the query wizard.

Figure 7-5

Simple select query

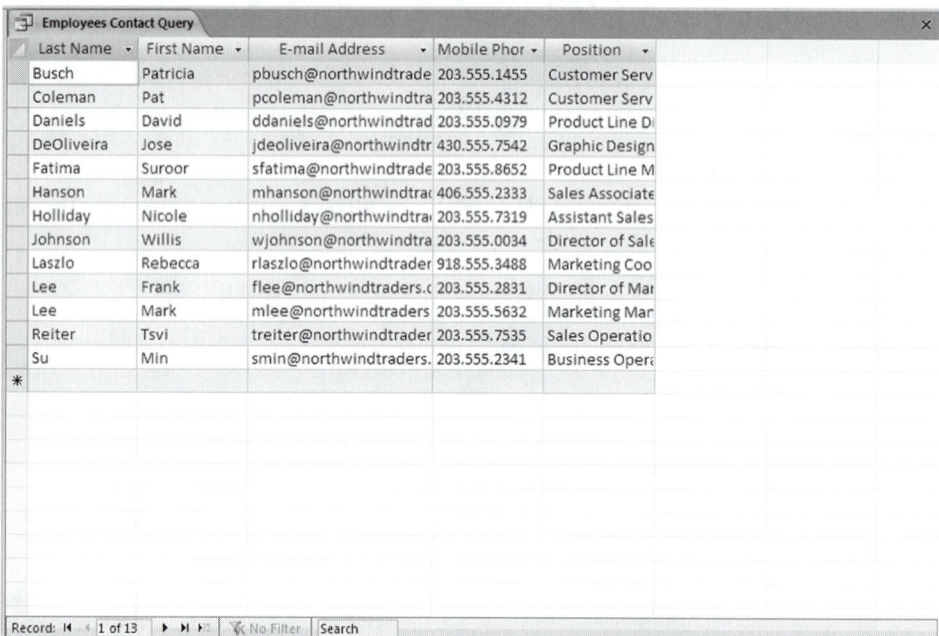

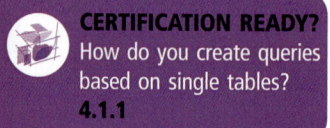

CERTIFICATION READY?
How do you create queries based on single tables?
4.1.1

10. Click the **Close 'Employees Contact Query'** button to close the query.

    PAUSE. LEAVE Access open to use in the next exercise.

In this activity, you created a simple select query that searched the data in a single table. A *select query* is the most basic type of Access query. It creates subsets of data that you can use to answer specific questions or to supply data to other database objects. The data is displayed in Datasheet view without being changed.

A query is a powerful and versatile database tool. Queries differ from sort or filter commands because they can be saved for future use and can extract data from multiple tables or queries.

A query can get its data from one or more tables, from existing queries, or from a combination of the two. The tables or queries from which a query gets its data are referred to as its *recordsource*.

To create a simple select query, on the Create tab, in the Other group, click the Query Wizard button. Click Simple Query Wizard and then click OK. Specify the table you want to use as the recordsource and the fields that you want to show. Name the query and click Finish. When you close the query, it is automatically saved.

To run a query after it has been created, simply double-click it in the Navigation pane to open it in Datasheet view and see the results.

➔ CREATE A FIND DUPLICATES QUERY

USE the database that is open from the previous exercise.

1. On the Create tab, in the Other group, click the **Query Wizard** button. The New Query dialog box appears.

2. Click **Find Duplicates Query Wizard** and then click **OK**. The Find Duplicates Query Wizard appears, as shown in Figure 7-6.

Figure 7-6

Find Duplicates Query Wizard, screen 1

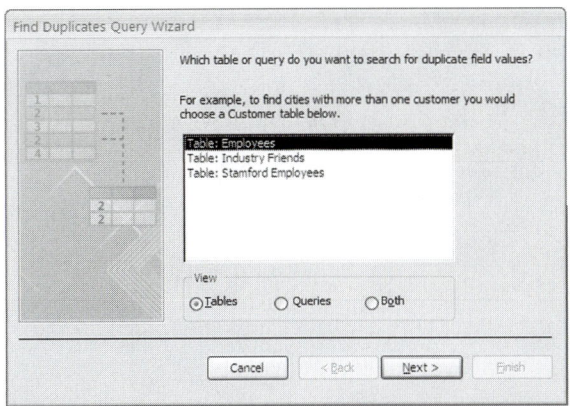

3. Click **Table: Industry Friends** and then click **Next>**. The next screen in the Find Duplicates Query Wizard appears, as shown in Figure 7-7.

Figure 7-7

Find Duplicates Query Wizard, screen 2

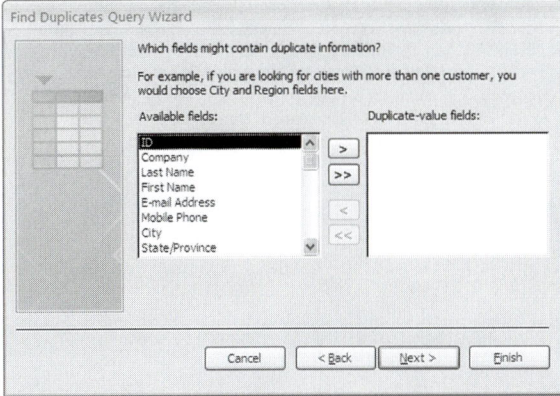

4. Double-click **Last Name**, **First Name**, and **E-mail Address** to move them to the *Duplicate-value fields* box.
5. Click **Next >** to display the next screen in the Find Duplicate Query Wizard, shown in Figure 7-8.

Figure 7-8

Find Duplicates Query Wizard, screen 3

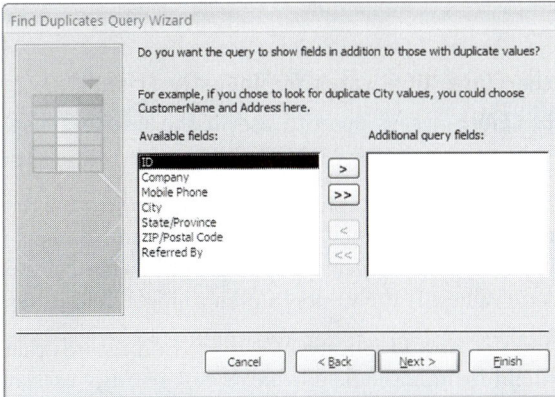

6. Double-click **Company** and **Referred By** to move them to the *Additional query fields* box.
7. Click **Next >** to display the final screen in the Find Duplicate Query Wizard, shown in Figure 7-9.

Figure 7-9

Find Duplicates Query Wizard, final screen

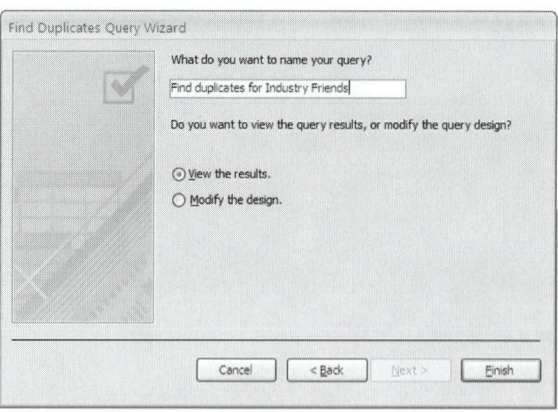

8. Name the query **Duplicates for Industry Friends** and click **Finish**. The query showing duplicate records in the table is displayed, as shown in Figure 7-10.

Figure 7-10

Duplicates for Industry Friends query

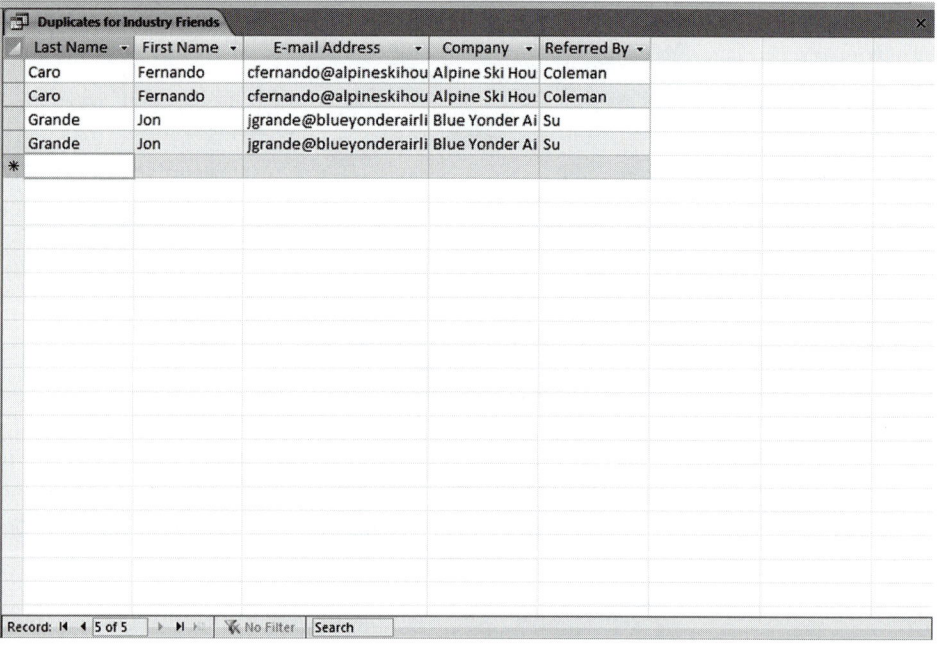

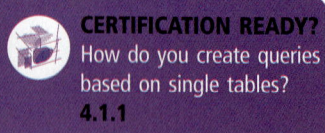

CERTIFICATION READY?
How do you create queries based on single tables?
4.1.1

9. Click the **Close 'Duplicates for Industry Friends'** button to close the query.

   PAUSE. LEAVE Access open to use in the next exercise.

As a general rule, duplicate data should be eliminated from a database whenever possible to reduce costs and increase accuracy. The first step in this process is finding duplicate data. Two or more records are considered duplicates only when all the fields in your query results contain the same values. If the values in even a single field differ, each record is unique.

You can also use the Find Duplicates Wizard to find records that contain *some* matching field values. You should include the field or fields that identify each record uniquely, typically the primary key. The query returns matching records where the values in the specified fields match character for character.

Creating a Query from Multiple Tables

If the data you need is spread out in more than one table, you can build a query that combines information from multiple sources. You can also create a query that finds records in one table that have no related records in another table.

➔ CREATE A QUERY FROM MULTIPLE TABLES

USE the database that is open from the previous exercise.

1. In the Navigation pane, double-click **Employees: Table** to open the table.
2. On the Datasheet tab, in the Relationships group, click the **Relationships** button to display the table relationship, as shown in Figure 7-11.

Figure 7-11

Relationships for Employees table

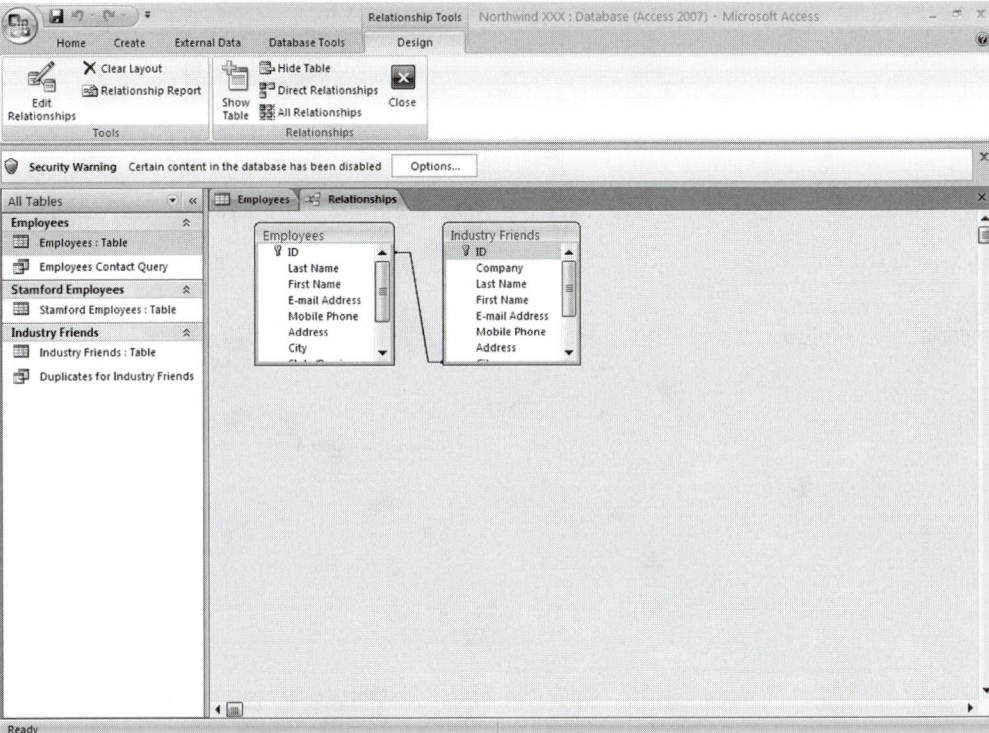

3. Click the **Close 'Relationships'** button to close the Relationship window and click the **Close 'Employees'** button to close the Employees table.
4. On the Create tab, in the Other group, click the **Query Wizard** button to display the New Query dialog box.
5. Click **Simple Query Wizard** and then click **OK** to display the Simple Query Wizard.
6. In the Tables/Queries dropdown list, click **Table: Industry Friends.**
7. Under Available Fields, double-click **Last Name**, **First Name**, and **Referred By** to move them to the *Selected Fields* box.
8. In the Tables/Queries dropdown list, click **Table: Employees.**
9. Under Available Fields, double-click **Position** and then **E-mail Address** to move them to the *Selected Fields* box.
10. Click the **Next >** button to display the next screen, shown in Figure 7-12. Detail query should be selected.

Figure 7-12

Simple Query Wizard for multiple tables

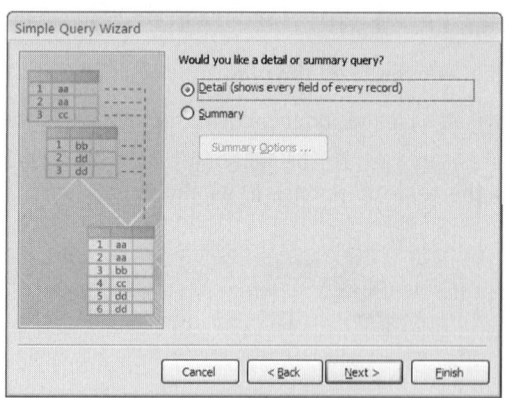

11. Click the **Next >** button to display the final screen, shown in Figure 7-13.

Figure 7-13

Simple Query Wizard for multiple tables, final screen

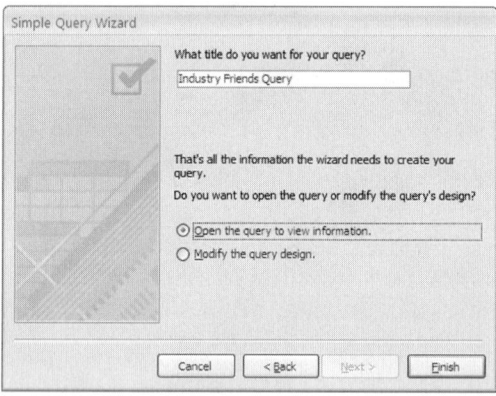

12. Click the **Finish** button to accept the suggested name and display the query, shown in Figure 7-14. This query shows the position and e-mail address of the employee who referred each industry friend.

Figure 7-14

Industry Friends query

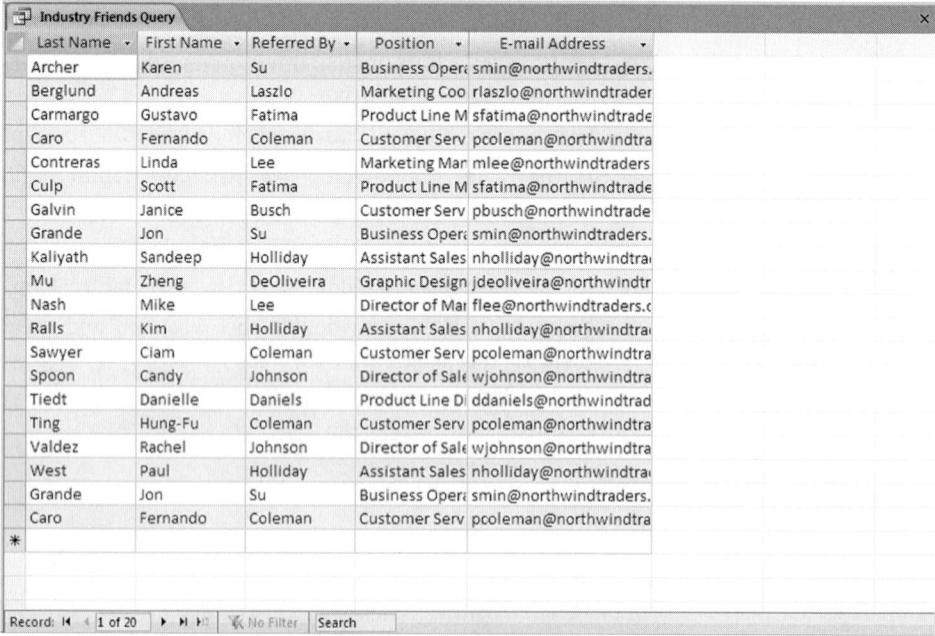

CERTIFICATION READY?
How do you create queries based on more than one table?
4.1.2

13. Click the **Close 'Industry Friends Query'** button to close the query.

PAUSE. LEAVE the database open to use in the next exercise.

Sometimes using data from a related table would help make the query results clearer and more useful. For example, in this activity, you could pull the name of the industry friends and the employee who referred them from one table. But to get additional information about the referring employees, you need to pull data from the related Employee table.

When you need to include multiple tables in your query, you can use the Simple Query Wizard to build a query from a primary table and a related table. The process is similar to creating a query from a single table, except that you include fields from additional tables.

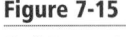

REF

You learned about defining and modifying table relationships in Lesson 3.

Before creating a query from multiple tables, you must first ensure that the tables have a defined relationship in the Relationships window. A relationship appears as a line connecting the two tables on a common field. You can double-click a relationship line to see which fields in the tables are connected by the relationship.

FIND UNMATCHED RECORDS

USE the database that is open from the previous exercise.

1. On the Create tab, in the Other group, click the **Query Wizard** button. The New Query dialog box appears.
2. Click **Find Unmatched Query Wizard** and then click **OK**. The Find Unmatched Query Wizard appears, as shown in Figure 7-15.

Figure 7-15

Find Unmatched Query Wizard, screen 1

3. **Table: Employees** should be selected. Click the **Next >** button to display the next screen in the Find Unmatched Query Wizard, shown in Figure 7-16.

Figure 7-16

Find Unmatched Query Wizard, screen 2

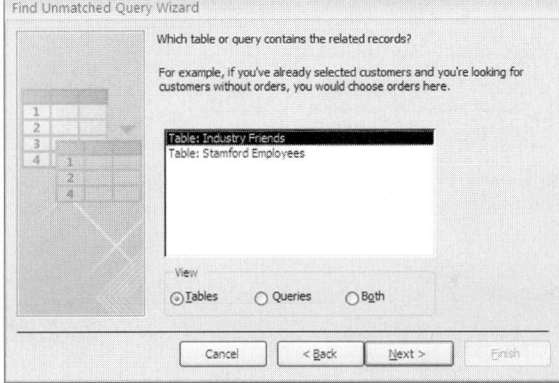

4. Select **Table: Stamford Employees**. Click the **Next >** button to display the next screen in the Find Unmatched Query Wizard, shown in Figure 7-17.

Figure 7-17

Find Unmatched Query Wizard, screen 3

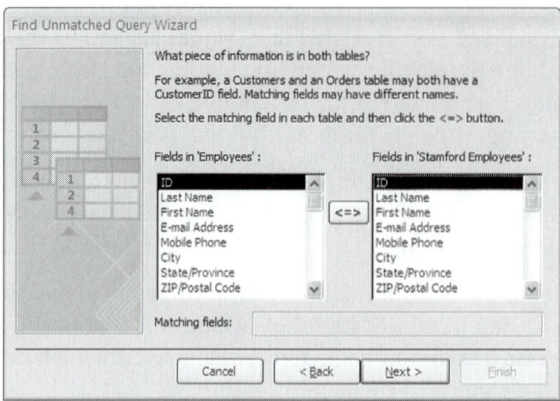

5. Click **E-mail Address** in the Fields in 'Employees' list. Click **E-mail Address** in the Fields in 'Stamford Employees' list. Click the **<=>** button to display them in the Matching fields box.

6. Click the **Next >** button to display the next screen in the Find Unmatched Query Wizard, shown in Figure 7-18.

Figure 7-18

Find Unmatched Query Wizard, screen 4

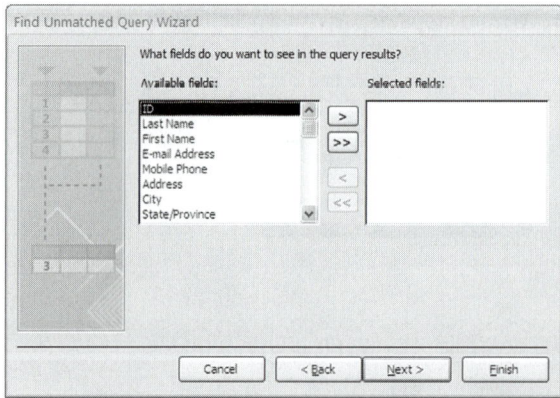

7. In the Available fields box, double-click **Last Name**, **First Name**, **Position**, and **City** to move them to the *Selected fields* box.

8. Click the **Next >** button to display the final screen in the Find Unmatched Query Wizard, shown in Figure 7-19.

Figure 7-19

Find Unmatched Query Wizard, final screen

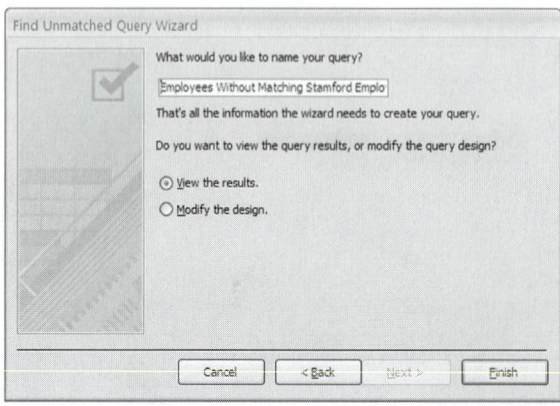

Create and Modify Queries | 881

9. Name the query **Non-Stamford Employees** and click the **Finish** button. The query is displayed, as shown in Figure 7-20.

Figure 7-20

Non-Stamford Employees query

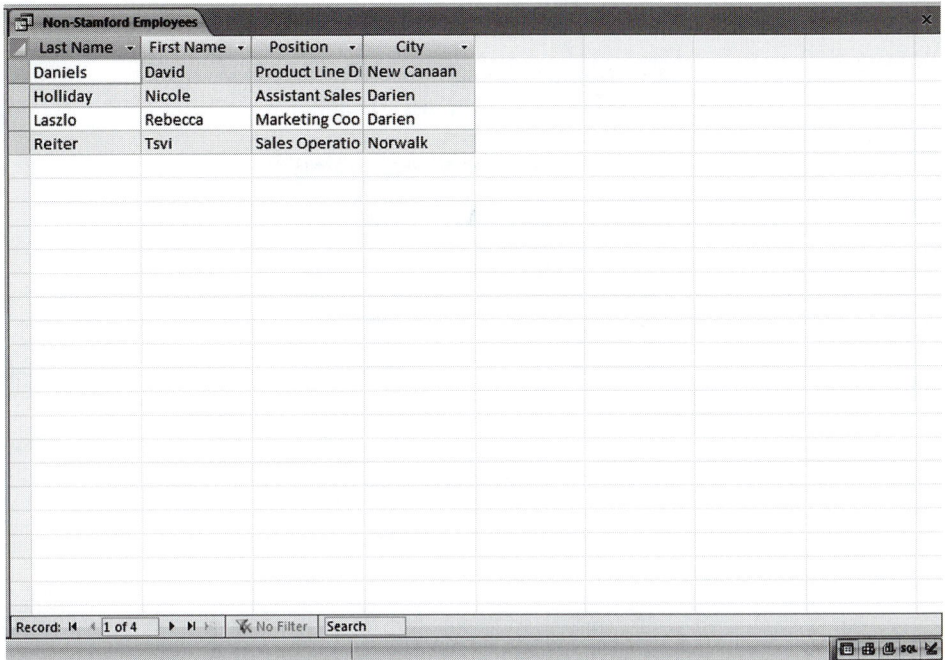

10. Click the **Close 'Non-Stamford Employees'** button to close the query.

    PAUSE. LEAVE the database open to use in the next exercise.

CERTIFICATION READY?
How do you create queries based on more than one table?
4.1.2

To view only the records in one table that do not have a matching record in another table, you can create a Find Unmatched query. In the activity above, you created a query that displayed all the employees who do not live in Stamford.

On the Create tab, in the Other group, click Query Wizard and then click Find Unmatched Query Wizard to start the wizard. In this activity, once you have created a find unmatched query, it returns four records in the Employees table that do not have overlapping records in the Stamford Employees table.

Software Orientation

Design Tab

By switching to Design view, you can access all the tools needed to modify your query on the Design tab, shown in Figure 7-21.

Figure 7-21

Design tab

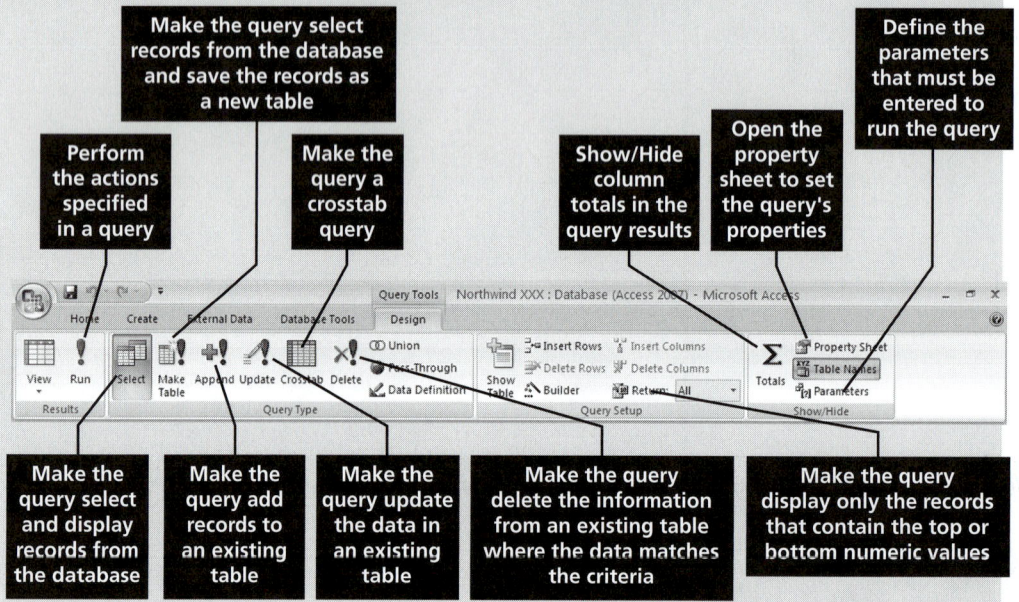

Use this figure as a reference throughout this lesson as well as the rest of this book.

Modifying a Query

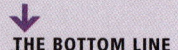

THE BOTTOM LINE — A query can be modified in Design view, regardless of how it was created. You can add or remove a table, add or remove fields, or add criteria to refine query results.

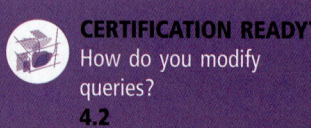

CERTIFICATION READY?
How do you modify queries?
4.2

Adding a Table to a Query

The Show Table dialog box is used to add a table to a query in Design view.

ADD A TABLE TO A QUERY

USE the database that is open from the previous exercise.

1. Double-click the **Industry Friends** query in the Navigation pane to open it.
2. On the Home tab, in the Views menu, click the **View** button and then click **Design View**. The query appears in Design view, as shown in Figure 7-22.

Create and Modify Queries | 883

Figure 7-22

Query in Design view

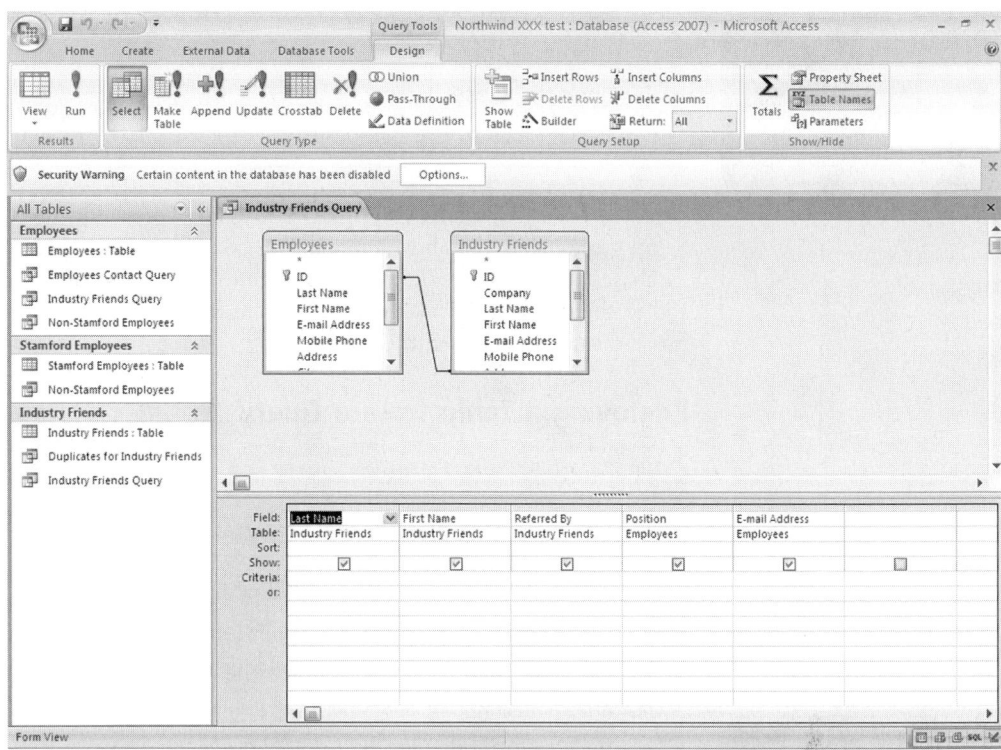

3. On the Design tab, in the Query Setup group, click the **Show Table** button to display the Show Table dialog box, shown in Figure 7-23.

Figure 7-23

Show Table dialog box

4. Click **Industry Friends** and click the **Add** button. A second copy of the Industry Friends table is added to the query, as indicated by the "1" in the title, as shown in Figure 7-24.

Figure 7-24

Second copy of table in a query

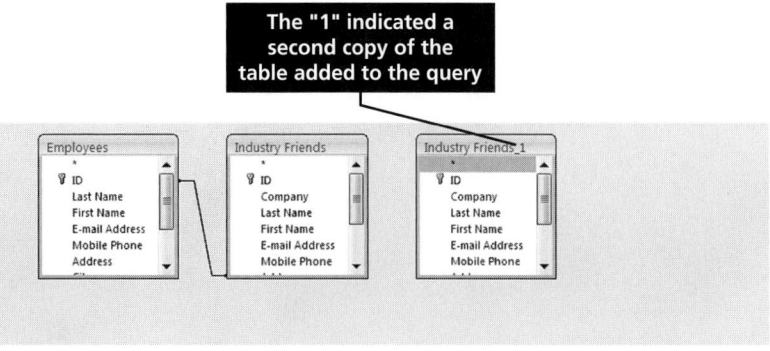

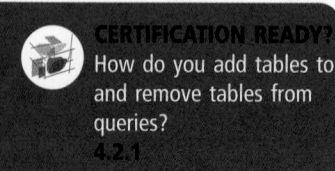

CERTIFICATION READY?
How do you add tables to and remove tables from queries?
4.2.1

5. Click **Stamford Employees** and click the **Add** button. The table is added to the query.
6. Click the **Close** button.

   PAUSE. LEAVE the database open to use in the next exercise.

To add a table to a query, you must be in Design view. On the Design tab, in the Query Setup group, click the Show Table dialog box. There is a tab that contains the tables in the database, a tab with the queries, and a tab that displays both. Select the object you want to add to the query and click the Add button. If you add a second copy of a table to the query, it is indicated by a "1" in the title.

Removing a Table from a Query

A table can be removed from a query in Design view.

→ REMOVE A TABLE FROM A QUERY

USE the database that is open from the previous exercise.

1. Click anywhere in the **Industry Friends_1** field list.
2. Press the [Delete] key to remove the table.
3. Click anywhere in the Stamford Employees field list.
4. Press the [Delete] key to remove the table.
5. Click the **Close 'Industry Friends'** button to close the query. If a message asks you if you want to save the changes, click **Yes**.

   PAUSE. LEAVE the database open to use in the next exercise.

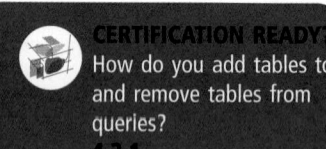

CERTIFICATION READY?
How do you add tables to and remove tables from queries?
4.2.1

To remove a table from a query, first open the query in Design view. In the upper part of query Design view, select the table you want to remove by clicking anywhere in its field list—a ***field list*** is a window that lists all the fields in the underlying record source or database object—then press the Delete key. The table is removed from the query, but it is not deleted from the database.

Adding Criteria to a Query

Not all queries must include criteria, but if you are not interested in seeing all the records that are stored in the underlying recordsource, you can add criteria to a query when designing it.

→ ADD CRITERIA TO A QUERY

USE the database that is open from the previous exercise.

1. In the Navigation pane, double-click the **Employees Contact Query** to open it.
2. On the Home tab, in the Views group, click the **View** button and click **Design View**.
3. In the Criteria row of the Position field, key **Like "*Manager*"**, as shown in Figure 7-25.

Figure 7-25

Query criterion

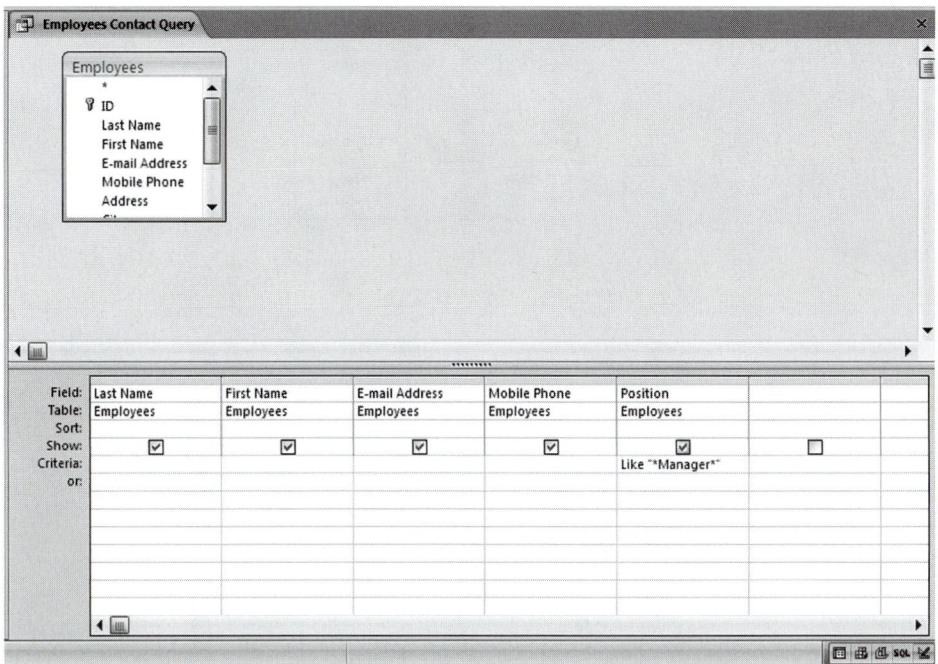

4. On the Design tab, in the Results group, click the **View** button and click **Datasheet View**. The query results display all records with "Manager" in the position field, as shown in Figure 7-26.

Figure 7-26

Results with query criteria applied

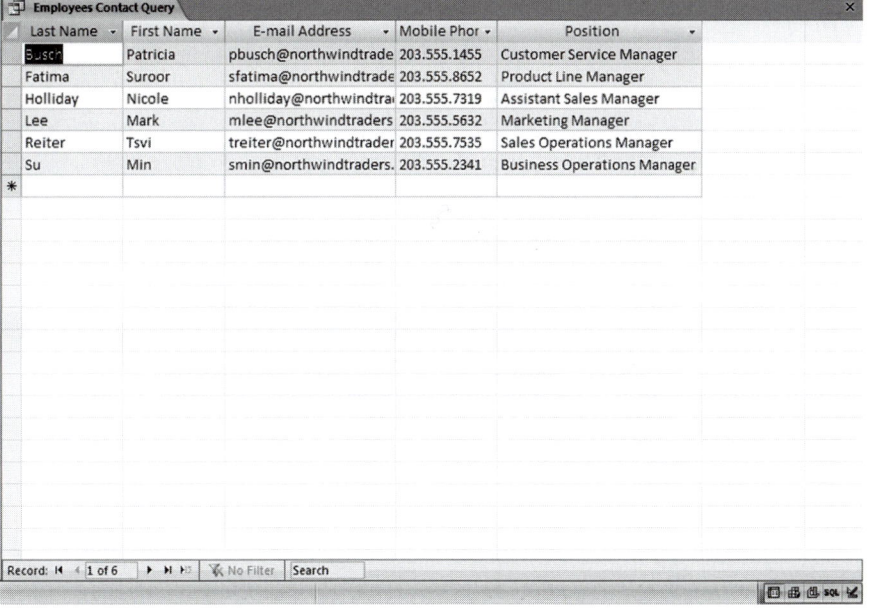

5. Click the **Close 'Employees Contact Query'** button to close the query. When prompted to save, click **Yes**.
6. In the Navigation pane, double-click the **Non-Stamford Employees Query** to open it.
7. On the Home tab, in the Views group, click the **View** button and click **Design View**.
8. In the Criteria row of the Position field, key **[City?]**, as shown in Figure 7-27.

Figure 7-27

Parameter query criteria

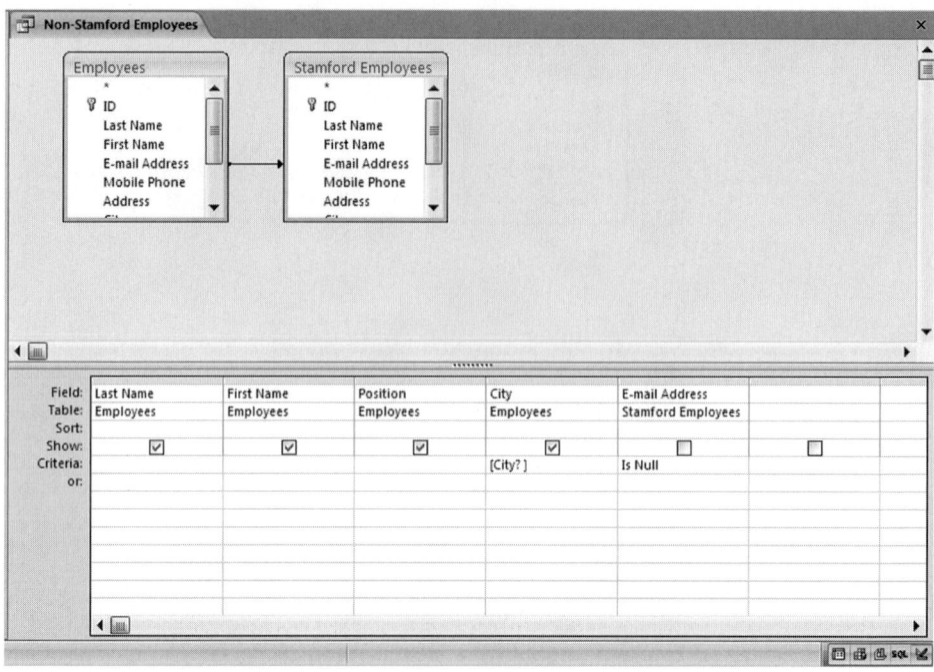

9. On the Home tab, in the Views group, click the **View** button and click **Datasheet View**. The prompt appears in the Enter Parameter Value dialog box, as shown in Figure 7-28.

Figure 7-28

Parameter query prompt dialog box

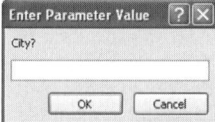

10. Key **Darien** in the City? box.
11. Click **OK**. The records for non-Stamford employees who live in Darien are displayed in the results, as shown in Figure 7-29.

Figure 7-29

Parameter query results

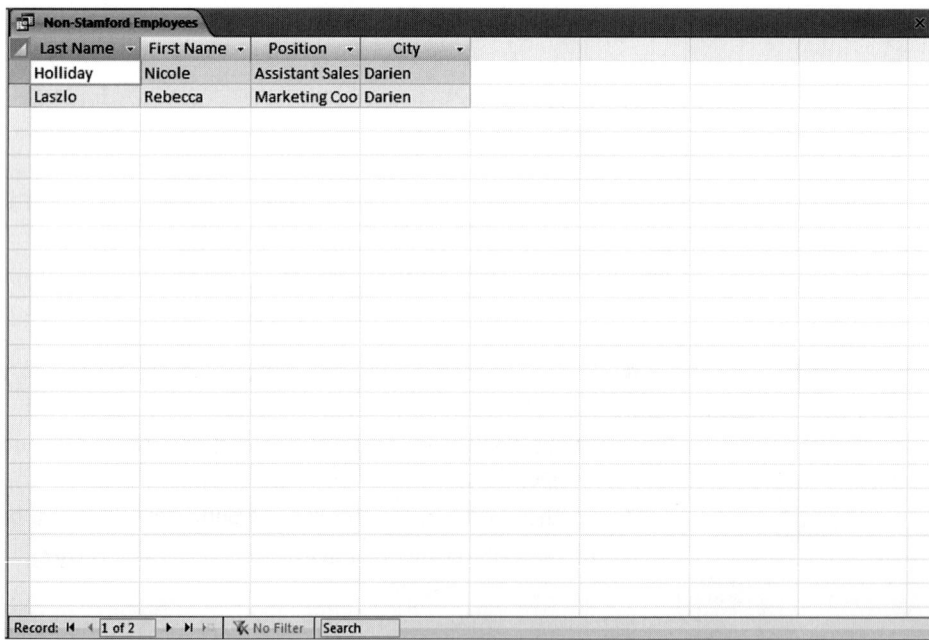

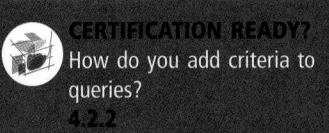

CERTIFICATION READY?
How do you add criteria to queries?
4.2.2

12. Click the **Close 'Non-Stamford Employees'** button to close the query. When prompted to save, click **Yes**.

    PAUSE. LEAVE the database open to use in the next exercise.

A *query criterion* is a rule that identifies the records that you want to include in the query result. To specify one or more criteria to restrict the records returned in the query results, open the query in Design view. Select the field and type the condition that you want to specify in the Criteria row. To see the results, switch to Datasheet view.

A criterion is similar to a formula. Some criteria are simple and use basic operators and constants. Others are complex and use functions, special operators, and include field references. Criteria can look very different from each other, depending on the data type of the field to which they apply and your specific requirements.

Table 7-1 shows some sample criteria and explains how they work. Table 7-2 shows the query results that are returned when specific criterion is used.

Table 7-1

Criteria examples

Criteria	Description
>25 and <50	This criterion applies to a Number field, such as Inventory. It includes only those records where the Inventory field contains a value greater than 25 and less than 50.
DateDiff ("yyyy", [BirthDate], Date()) > 21	This criterion applies to a Date/Time field, such as BirthDate. Only records where the number of years between a person's birth date and today's date is greater than 21 are included in the query result.
Is Null	This criterion can be applied to any type of field to show records where the field value is null.

Table 7-2

Query result examples

To include records that...	Use this criterion	Query result
Exactly match a value, such as Manager	"Manager"	Returns records where the given field is set to Manager.
Do not match a value, such as Chicago	Not "Chicago"	Returns records where the given field is set to a value other than Chicago.
Begin with the specified string, such as B	Like B*	Returns records for the given field where the value starts with "B," such as Boston, Bakersfield, and so on.
Do not begin with the specified string, such as B	Not Like B*	Returns records for the given field where the value starts with a character other than "B."
Contain the specified string, such as Sales	Like "*Sales*"	Returns records for the given field that contain the string "Sales."
Do not contain the specified string, such as Sales	Not Like "*Sales*"	Returns records for the given field that do not contain the string "Sales."

You can also run a ***parameter query***, in which the user interactively specifies one or more criteria values. This is not a separate query; it extends the flexibility of another type of query, such as a select query, by prompting the user for a value when it is run.

Sorting and Filtering Data Within a Query

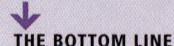
THE BOTTOM LINE

Sorting and filtering data within a query allows you to display only the records you want and/or only in a particular order.

Sorting Data Within a Query

Sorting data in a query can help organize data efficiently and make it easier for users to review and locate the records they want without having to browse the data.

XREF

You learned about sorting data within a table in Lesson 3, sorting data within a form in Lesson 5, and sorting data within a report in Lesson 6.

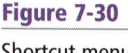
SORT DATA WITHIN A QUERY

USE the database that is open from the previous exercise.

1. In the Navigation pane, double-click the **Industry Friends Query** to open it.
2. Right-click the **Referred by** field to display the shortcut menu shown in Figure 7-30.

Figure 7-30

Shortcut menu

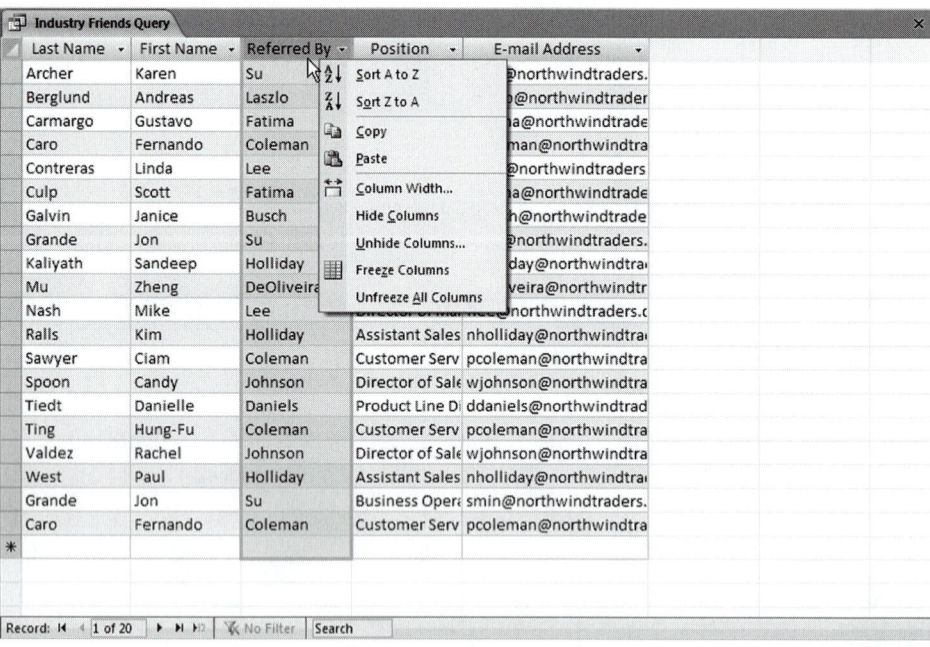

3. Click **Sort A to Z**. The field is sorted in alphabetic order from A to Z, as shown in Figure 7-31.

Figure 7-31

Sorted query

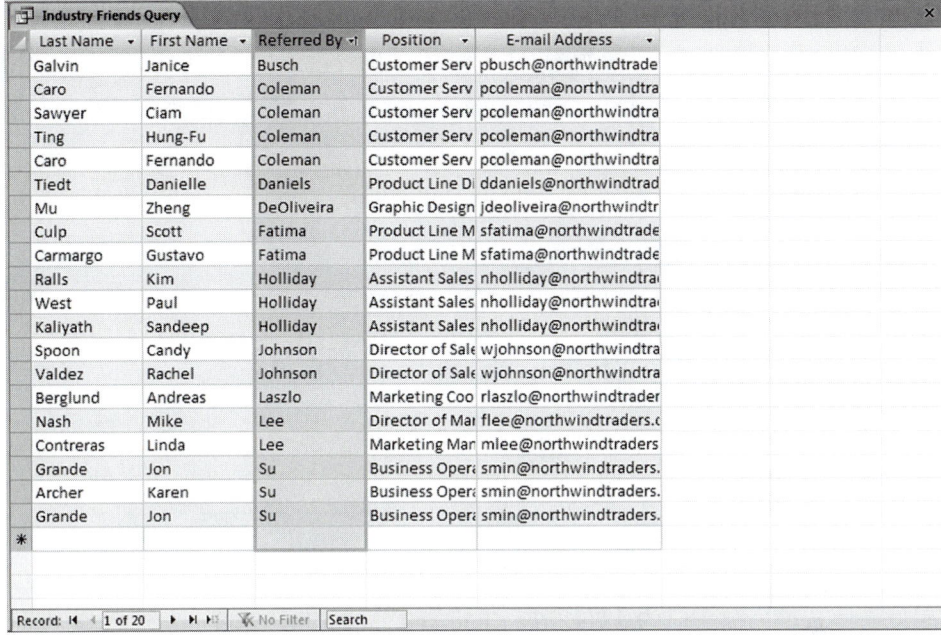

4. On the Home tab, in the Sort & Filter group, click the **Clear All Sorts** button.
5. On the Home tab, in the Sort & Filter group, click the **Advanced** button to display the menu shown in Figure 7-32.

Figure 7-32

Advanced menu

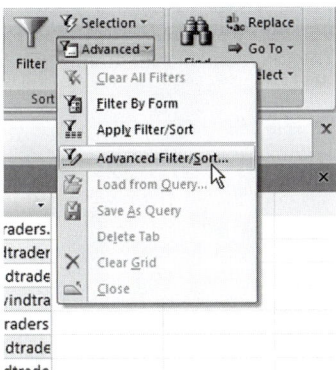

6. Click **Advanced Filter/Sort**. An Industry Friends QueryFilter1 tab appears, as shown in Figure 7-33.

Figure 7-33

Industry Friends QueryFilter1 tab

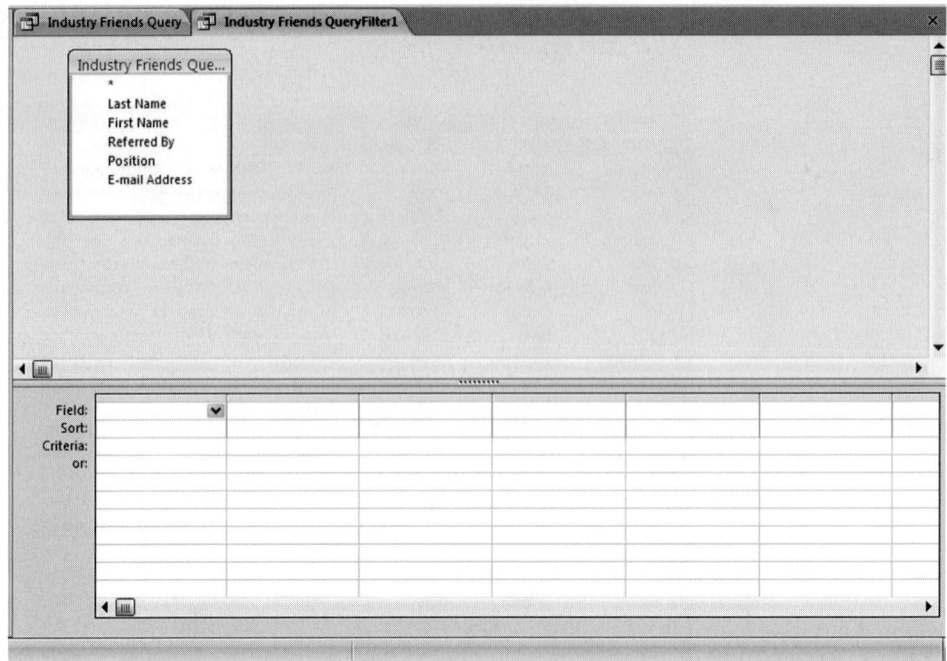

7. Click the **Field cell** in the first column, click the **down arrow**, and click **Referred by** on the dropdown menu.
8. Click the **Sort cell** in the first column, click the **down arrow**, and click **Ascending** on the dropdown menu.
9. Click the **Field cell** in the second column, click the **down arrow**, and click **Last Name** on the dropdown menu.
10. Click the **Sort cell** in the second column, click the **down arrow**, and click **Ascending** on the dropdown menu. Your screen should look similar to Figure 7-34.

Figure 7-34

Advanced sort criteria

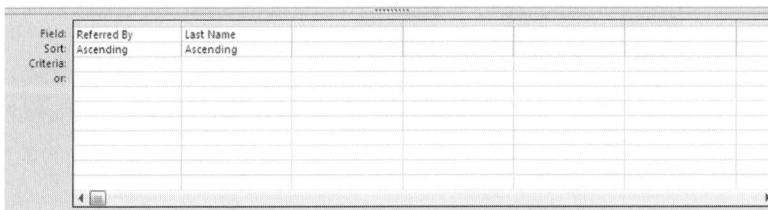

11. On the Home tab, in the Sort & Filter group, click the **Advanced** button and click **Apply Filter/Sort**. The query is sorted by the Referred by field in ascending order and then by the Last Name field in ascending order, as shown in Figure 7-35.

Create and Modify Queries | 891

Figure 7-35

Sorted query

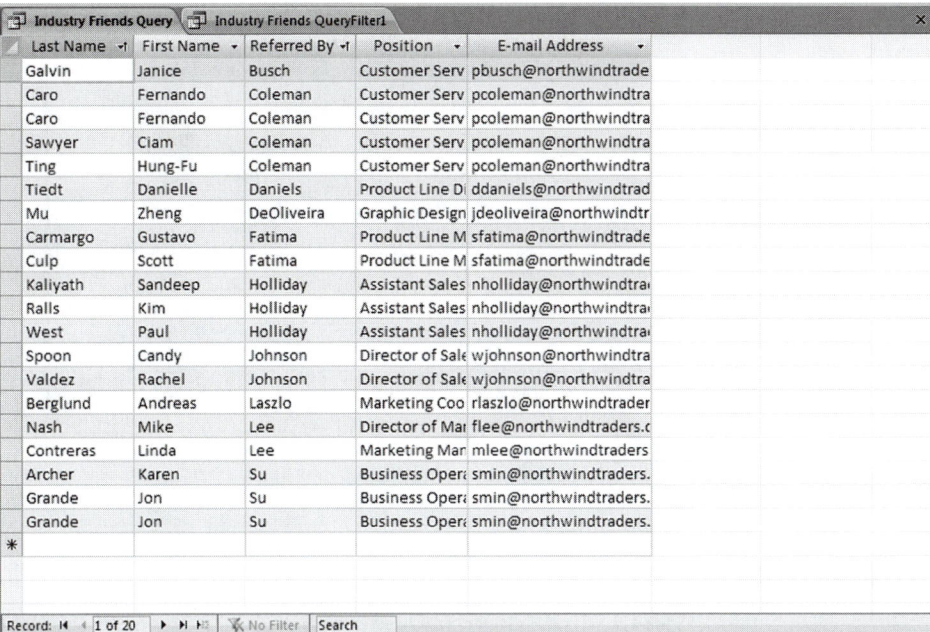

CERTIFICATION READY?
How do you sort data within queries?
5.1.2

12. On the Home tab, in the Sort & Filter group, click the **Clear All Sorts** button.

PAUSE. LEAVE the database open to use in the next exercise.

Data can be sorted in the Datasheet view of a query. Right-click the field on which you want to sort and click the sort order you want—ascending or descending—from the shortcut menu. The records are rearranged to match the sort order.

TAKE NOTE

The same tab is used to perform an advanced filter for the query.

To sort by more than one field, on the Home tab, in the Sort & Filter group, click the Advanced button and click Advanced Filter/Sort to open up a tab where you can specify more than one field to sort by and the sort order.

Filtering Data Within a Query

A filter limits a view of data to specific records without requiring you to alter the design of the underlying query.

You learned about filtering data within a table in Lesson 3, filtering data within a form in Lesson 5, and filtering data within a report in Lesson 6.

➔ FILTER DATA WITHIN A QUERY

USE the database that is open from the previous exercise. The Industry Friends Query should be open.

1. Click the **Position header** to select the field.
2. On the Home tab, in the Sort & Filter group, click the **Filter** button. A menu appears on the field, as shown in Figure 7-36.

Figure 7-36

Filter menu

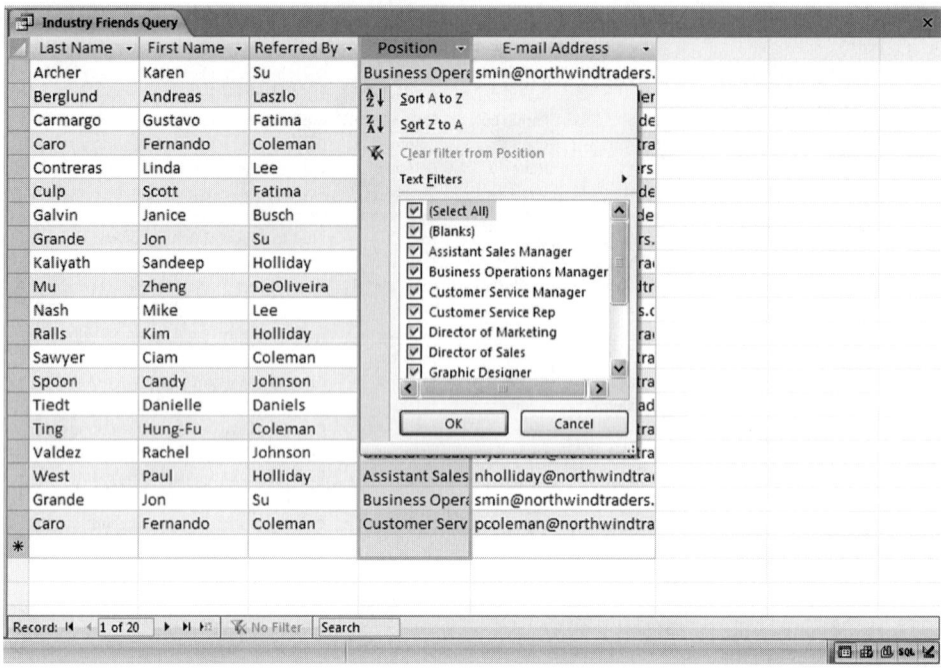

3. Click **Text Filters** and click **Contains** on the submenu. A Custom Filter dialog box appears, as shown in Figure 7-37.

Figure 7-37

Custom Filter dialog box

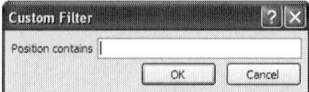

4. In the Position contains box, key **Marketing** and click **OK**. The records are filtered to show only those containing the word "Marketing" in the Position field, as shown in Figure 7-38.

Figure 7-38

Filtered query

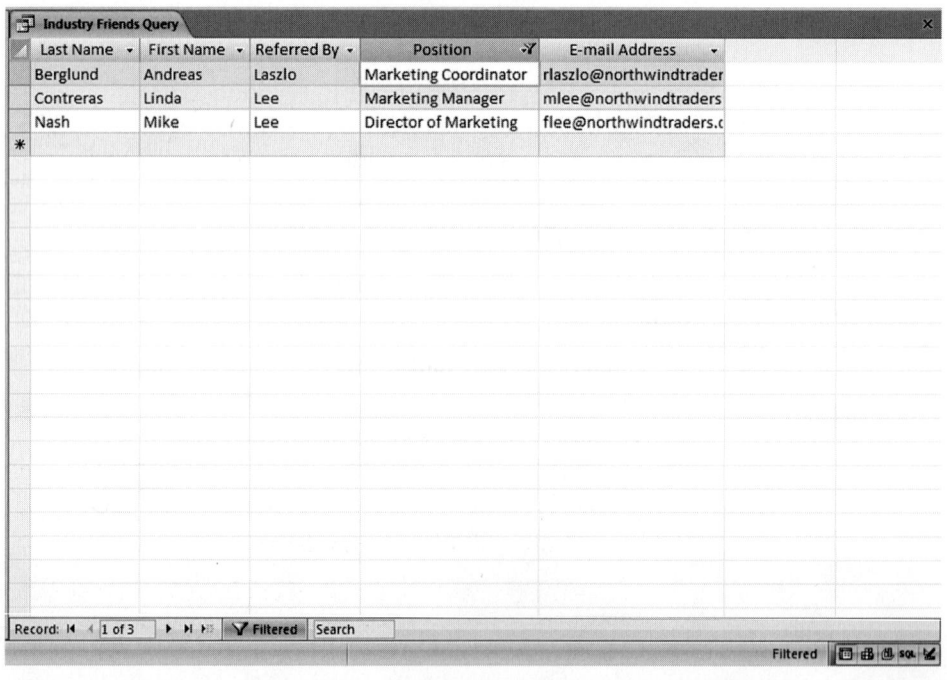

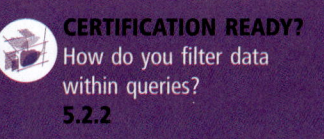

CERTIFICATION READY?
How do you filter data within queries?
5.2.2

5. On the Home tab, in the Sort & Filter group, click the **Toggle Filter** button to remove the filter.
6. Click the **Close 'Industry Friends Query'** to close the query and click **Yes** to save changes when prompted.
7. **CLOSE** the database.
   CLOSE Access.

If the criteria are temporary or change often, you can filter the query result instead of frequently modifying the query criteria. A filter is a temporary criterion that changes the query result without altering the design of the query.

Click the field you want to filter. On the Home tab, in the Sort & Filter group, click the Filter button. The filters available depend on the type and values of the field. When you apply the filter, only records that contain the values that you are interested in are included in the view. The rest are hidden until you remove the filter by clicking the Toggle Filter button.

SUMMARY SKILL MATRIX

IN THIS LESSON YOU LEARNED HOW TO:
Create a Query from a Table
Create a Query from Multiple Tables
Add a Table to a Query
Remove a Table from a Query
Sort Data Within a Query
Filter Data Within a Query

■ Knowledge Assessment

Fill in the Blank

Complete the following sentences by writing the correct word or words in the blanks provided.

1. The Other group on the _Create_ tab contains the commands used to create queries.
2. The _Query Design_ button creates a new, blank query in Design view.
3. A(n) _Sel. Query_ is the most basic type of Access query.
4. The tables or queries from which a query gets its data are referred to as its _Record Source_.
5. To run a query after it has been created, double-click it in the Navigation pane to open it in _datasheet_ view and see the results.
6. Two or more records are considered _Duplicate_ only when all the fields in your query results contain the same values.
7. When you need to include multiple tables in your query, use the _Simple Query_ Wizard to build a query from a primary table and a related table.

8. To view only the records in one table that don't have a matching record in another table, you can create a _find Unmatched_ query.

9. By switching to _design_ view, you can access all the tools needed to modify your query.

10. A(n) _field List_ is a window that lists all the fields in the underlying record source or database object.

Multiple Choice

Select the best response for the following statements or questions.

1. Creating a query is like
   a. sorting the data.
   b. asking the database a question. ✓
   c. creating a new table.
   d. opening an existing database.

2. The results that a query returns can be
   a. sorted.
   b. grouped.
   c. filtered.
   d. all of the above. ✓
   e. none of the above.

3. When one table will provide the information that you need, you can create a
   a. recordsource.
   b. simple select query. ✓
   c. query criterion.
   d. parameter query.

4. Which query cannot be created using the Query Wizard?
   a. Parameter query ✓
   b. Simple query
   c. Find duplicates query
   d. Find unmatched query

5. Queries are different from sort or filter commands because they can be
   a. applied to multiple fields.
   b. saved. ✓
   c. modified.
   d. used on forms.

6. A query can get its data from
   a. one or more tables.
   b. existing queries.
   c. a combination of a and b.
   d. all of the above ✓
   e. none of the above.

7. To find records that contain matching field values, you can create a query using which wizard?
   a. Find Matching
   b. Matching Fields
   c. Duplicate Records
   d. Find Duplicates

8. Before creating a query from multiple tables, you must first ensure that the tables have
   a. unmatched records.
   b. a defined relationship.
   c. a filter applied.
   d. no related records.

9. To add a table to a query, you must be in what view?
   a. SQL
   b. Datasheet
   c. PivotTable
   d. Design

10. A rule that identifies the records that you want to include in the query result is called a
    a. parameter query.
    b. query criterion.
    c. select query.
    d. field list.

■ Competency Assessment

Project 7-1: Games Select Query

As the manager at Southridge Video, you have stored information in an Access database about each used game that the store has taken in trade. Now that you know how to create queries, you decide to create a select query to list the title, rating, and category, which are the fields that you most often need to view.

The *Games* database file is available on the companion CD-ROM.

GET READY. Launch Access if it is not already running.

1. **OPEN** *Games* from the data files for this lesson.
2. **SAVE** the database as *GamesXXX* (where XXX is your initials).
3. On the Create tab, in the Other group, click the **Query Wizard** button to display the New Query dialog box.
4. Click **Simple Query Wizard** and then click **OK**.
5. In the Tables/Queries dropdown list, **Table: Games** should be selected.
6. Under Available Fields, double-click **Title**, **Rating**, and **Category** to move them to the *Selected Fields* box.
7. Click the **Next >** button. The second screen in the Simple Query Wizard appears.
8. Name the query **Games Query**. *Open the query to view information* should be selected.
9. Click the **Finish** button.

10. Click the **Close 'Games Query'** button to close the query.
11. **LEAVE** the database open for the next project.
    LEAVE Access open for the next project.

Project 7-2: Find Duplicates Query

You have taught the night manager at Southridge Video how to enter used game information into the database, but you have not yet developed a reliable system for determining if the game has already been entered. You are concerned there may be duplicate records. Create a find duplicates query to determine if there are duplicates.

USE the database that is open from the previous project.

1. On the Create tab, in the Other group, click the **Query Wizard** button.
2. In the New Query dialog box, click **Find Duplicates Query Wizard** and then click **OK**.
3. Click **Table: Games** and then click **Next >**. The next screen in the Find Duplicates Query Wizard appears.
4. Double-click **Title**, **Platform**, and **Publisher** to move them to the *Duplicate-value fields* box.
5. Click **Next >** to display the next screen in the Find Duplicates Query Wizard.
6. Double-click **Category** to move it to the *Additional query fields* box.
7. Click **Next >** to display the final screen in the Find Duplicates Query Wizard.
8. Name the query **Duplicates for Games** and click **Finish** to display the query showing duplicate records in the table.
9. Click the **Close 'Duplicates for Games'** button to close the query.
10. **CLOSE** the database.
    LEAVE Access open for the next project.

■ Proficiency Assessment

Project 7-3: Create a Query from Multiple Tables

Information about each selection for the Coho Vineyard monthly wine club is stored in an Access database. Information about red wine and white wine is stored in separate tables. In your position as customer service rep, it would be useful to be able to query information from both tables.

The *Club Wines* database file is available on the companion CD-ROM.

1. **OPEN** *Club Wines* from the data files for this lesson.
2. **SAVE** the database as *Club WinesXXX* (where XXX is your initials).
3. Open the **Red Wines: Table**.
4. Open the Relationships window to ensure there is a relationship between the red and white wine tables. **CLOSE** the Relationships window.
5. Start the Query Wizard and choose **Simple Query Wizard**.
6. In the Tables/Queries dropdown list, click **Table: Red Wines**.
7. Move the **Bottled**, **Label**, and **Type** fields to the **Selected Fields** box.
8. In the Tables/Queries dropdown list, click **Table: White Wines**.
9. Move the **Bottled**, **Label**, and **Type** fields to the **Selected Fields** box.
10. Click the **Next >** button.
11. Click the **Next >** button and name the query **Wines Query**.
12. Click the **Finish** button.

13. Review the information in the query and then close it.
14. LEAVE the database open for the next project.
    LEAVE Access open for the next project.

Project 7-4: Find Unmatched Query

A red wine and a white wine should be selected for each month. To determine if there are any records in the red wine table that don't have a matching record in the white wine table, you decide to create a find unmatched query.

USE the database that is open from the previous project.

1. Start the Query Wizard and choose Find Unmatched Query Wizard.
2. Table: Red Wines should be selected. Click the Next >.
3. Select Table: White Wines and click the Next > button.
4. Click ID in the Fields in 'Red Wines' list. Click ID in the Fields in 'White Wines' list. Click the <=> button to display them in the Matching fields box.
5. Click the Next > button.
6. Move the Month?, Bottled, Label, and Type fields to the Selected fields box.
7. Click the Next> button and name the query.
8. Name the query Unmatched Month and click the Finish button to display the query.
9. CLOSE the query.
10. CLOSE the database.
    LEAVE Access open for the next project.

■ Mastery Assessment

The *Sports Events* database file is available on the companion CD-ROM.

Project 7-5: Query

In your job as a travel agent at Margie's Travel, a client has asked you to provide a list of all the travel packages available to sporting events that start in the month of April or May. You will add criteria to a query to get this information from the database.

1. Open Sports Events from the data files for this lesson.
2. Save the database as Sports EventsXXX (where XXX is your initials).
3. Open the Events query and switch to Design view.
4. Add criteria that will query the database for all events that start between 4/1/2008 and 5/31/2008.
5. Run the query.
6. CLOSE the query and save the design when prompted.
7. CLOSE the database.
   LEAVE Access open for the next project.

Project 7-6: Parameter Query

The *Toys* database file is available on the companion CD-ROM.

Your brother, who owns Wingtip Toys, wants to be able to pull data from his toy inventory and asks for your help in creating a query. He wants to be able to query the database for toys for specific ages when prompted, so you show him how to create a parameter query.

1. OPEN Toys from the data files for this lesson.
2. SAVE the database as ToysXXX (where XXX is your initials).

3. Create a simple query named **Inventory Query** that contains all the available fields, except the ID field.
4. Create a parameter query on the For Ages field that gives you the prompt shown in Figure 7-39 when the query is run.

Figure 7-39

Enter Parameter Value prompt

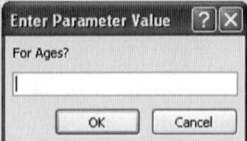

5. Query the database for all the toys for ages 10-14 years.
6. **CLOSE** the query and save when prompted.
7. **CLOSE** the database.
   CLOSE Access.

INTERNET READY

Blogs can be a fun way to pass time, but they can also be a great source of business information. If you enjoy blogs, check out some of the business-related blogs available, such as The Microsoft Connections Blog, shown in Figure 7-40. The URL for this blog is: *http://blogs.msdn.com/conblog/default.aspx*. Search for information on mail merges or another topic of interest to you and see what you can find.

Figure 7-40

The Microsoft Connections Blog

Database Tools

LESSON SKILL MATRIX

Backing Up a Database	Students will learn how to back up a database.
Compacting and Repairing a Database	Students will learn how to compact and repair a database.
Configuring Database Options	Students will learn how to configure database options.
Encrypting a Database	Students will learn how to encrypt a database.
Identifying Object Dependencies	Students will learn how to identify object dependencies.
Using the Database Documenter	Students will learn how to use the database documenter.
Using the Linked Table Manager	Students will learn how to use the linked table manager.
Splitting a Database	Students will learn how to split a database.

Fabrikam, Inc. is a furniture manufacturer that supplies new lines, or collections, of furniture to showrooms each season. As an intern in the office, you help maintain the records related to the furniture collections and the showrooms that sell them for your company. Your supervisor is concerned about the maintenance, security, and the overall integrity of the database files, so your assignment is to safeguard these files. In this lesson, you will learn to back up a database and to compact and repair a database. You will also learn to use database tools to configure database options, encrypt a database, identify object dependencies, document a database, refresh linked tables, and split a database.

KEY TERMS
back-end file
backup
Database Documenter
Database Splitter
decrypting
encrypting
front-end file
Linked Table Manager
object dependencies

Maintaining a Database

THE BOTTOM LINE

You can maintain some important aspects of a database by using the Manage menu on the Office Button. Though they might not seem as important as the actual data in your database, these commands allow you to provide protection of all the data in the file, and that is important. You can create a backup copy of your database and compact and repair the database.

Backing Up a Database

After all the work you have put into a database, you start to depend on being able to access and update the data and the information in it on a regular basis. To protect your work, it is a good idea to back up a database. Essentially, you are making another copy of the database that you can store on your computer, on a network drive, or in another safe location to prevent the loss of your data.

BACKUP A DATABASE

GET READY. Before you begin these steps, be sure to turn on and/or log on to your computer and start Access.

1. **OPEN** *Fabikam* from the data files for this lesson.
2. Save the database as *FabrikamXXX* (where XXX is your initials).
3. Click the **Office Button** and point to **Manage**. The Manage this database menu appears, as shown in Figure 8-1.

The *Fabrikam* database is available on the companion CD-ROM.

Figure 8-1

Manage This Database menu

4. Click **Back Up Database**. The Save As dialog box appears, as shown in Figure 8-2. Notice that Access automatically adds the current date to the end of the filename.

Figure 8-2

Save As dialog box

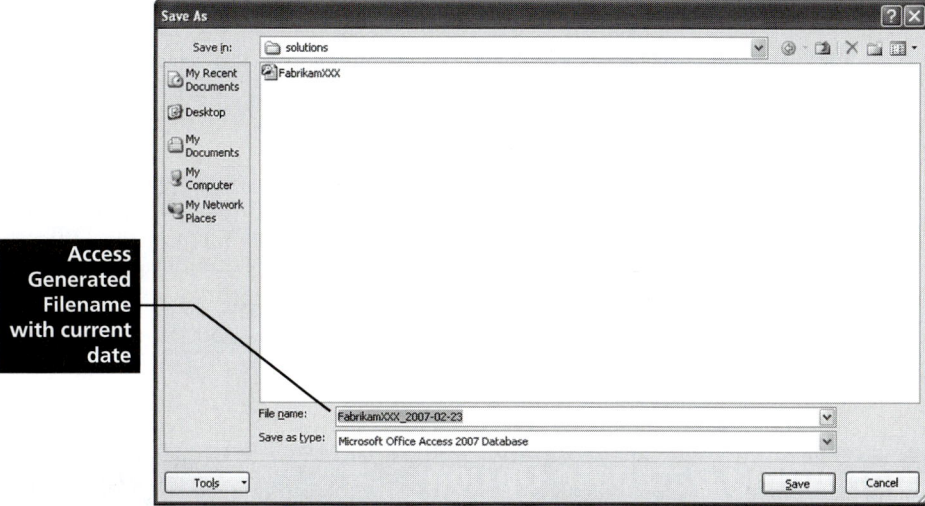

5. Click the **Save** button to accept the generated filename.

PAUSE. LEAVE the database open to use in the next exercise.

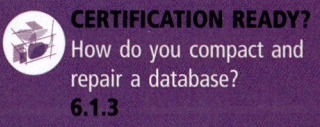

CERTIFICATION READY?
How do you back up a database?
6.1.2

A ***backup*** is a copy of a file. It is a good idea to create backup files of all your databases and continue to back them up on a regular basis.

You can store a backup copy in the same place as your original file is, such as on your computer. However, if something happened to your computer, both files would be affected. A better solution is to save a backup copy to a network drive or removable media that is stored in a different physical location. For example, some companies that maintain sensitive client data have elaborate backup processes in place to store backup copies on computers or other media off premises in another part of the city or in another part of the country. If an entire office building is destroyed by fire or a city is involved in a natural disaster, the backup files containing client data are safe in another location. It is a good idea to consider the appropriate precautions needed for even a small company's data.

When backing up a database, Access automatically adds the date to the filename. You can keep this filename as an identifier for the backup file or change the filename to something else. Just keep in mind that you need a new name or location so that you aren't just overwriting your original file. In the Save In box, choose the location where you want to save the file.

Compacting and Repairing a Database

The Compact and Repair command optimizes files and fixes minor problems in the file structure that may result from normal, everyday use of a database file.

COMPACT AND REPAIR A DATABASE

USE the database open from the previous exercise.

1. Click the **Office Button**, point to Manage, and select **Compact and Repair Database.** Access compacts and repairs the database.

PAUSE. LEAVE the database open to use in the next exercise.

CERTIFICATION READY?
How do you compact and repair a database?
6.1.3

As records or objects in a database are deleted, the empty space within the file might not be replaced right away, leaving the file fragmented or with large empty spaces within the file structure. In databases with many records and objects, these issues can affect the database's performance over time. In the same way, minor errors can occur in any file, especially when it is shared by many different users on a network drive. Using the Compact and Repair command on a regular basis will help to optimize the file and repair minor problems before they become major ones.

Before you use this command on a shared file, make sure no one else has the file open.

TAKE NOTE

You can set Access to compact a database every time you close it. On the Office Button menu, click the Access Options button and select Current Database. Click the Compact On Close checkbox and click OK.

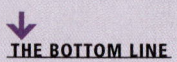

TROUBLESHOOTING

If Access detects a problem with a file, or if you suspect a problem, the Office Diagnostics program may help repair the file. On the Office Button menu, click the Access Options button and select Resources. Click the Diagnose button and click OK. It is a good idea to search Access Help for more information about the Office Diagnostics program and any special precautions you should take before running the program.

■ Configuring Database Options

THE BOTTOM LINE

The Access Options dialog box provides many ways to customize Access. From changing popular options to specific or advanced options for databases, you can specify many options for customizing your copy of Access for the way you use it on a daily basis.

Through the Access Options dialog box, you can enable error checking, show/hide the Navigation pane, and select a startup display form.

The *FabrikamInc* database is available on the companion CD-ROM.

➲ CONFIGURE DATABASE OPTIONS

OPEN *FabrikamInc* from the data files for this lesson.

1. Save the database as **FabrikamIncXXX** (where XXX is your initials).
2. Click the **Office Button** and click the **Access Options** button. The Access Options dialog box appears.
3. Click the **Current Database** button on the left to display the Current Database section of the Access Options dialog box, as shown in Figure 8-3.

Figure 8-3

Access Options dialog box

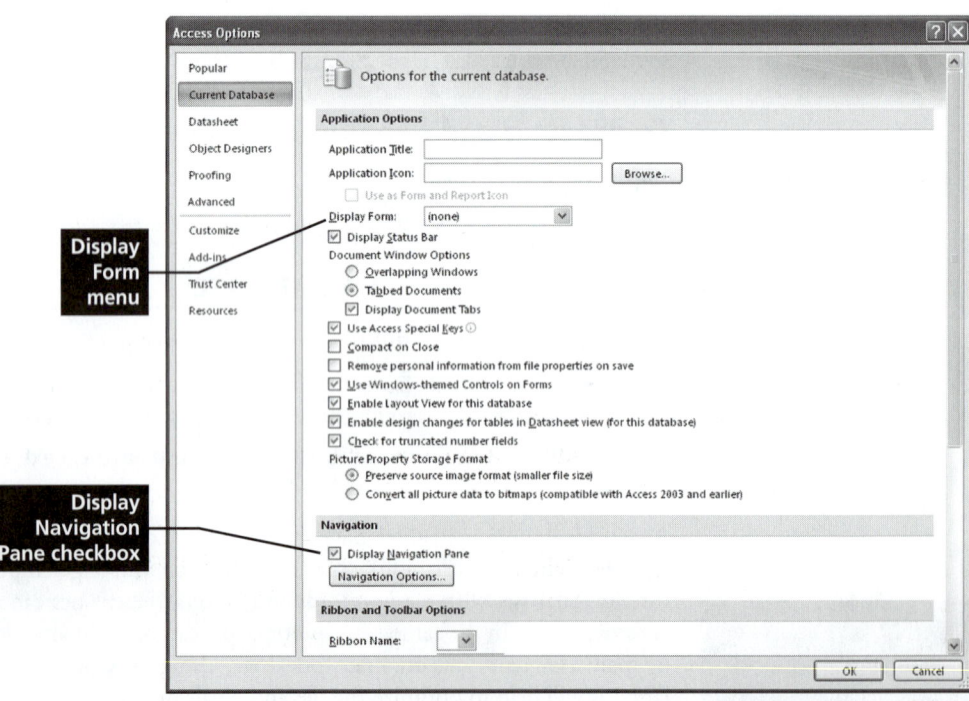

4. In the Application Options section, click the down arrow beside Display Form and select **Showroom Contact Form** from the menu.
5. In the Navigation section, notice that the Display Navigation Pane is turned on by default.
6. Click the **Display Navigation Pane** checkbox to remove the checkmark and click **OK**. A Microsoft Office Access dialog box appears, as shown in Figure 8-4, saying you need to close and reopen the database for the changes to take affect.

Figure 8-4

Microsoft Office Access dialog box

7. Click **OK**.
8. **CLOSE** the database.
9. Open the *FabrikamIncXXX* database. Notice that the Navigation pane is not visible and the Showroom Contact Form is displayed, as shown in Figure 8-5.

Figure 8-5

Showroom Contact form

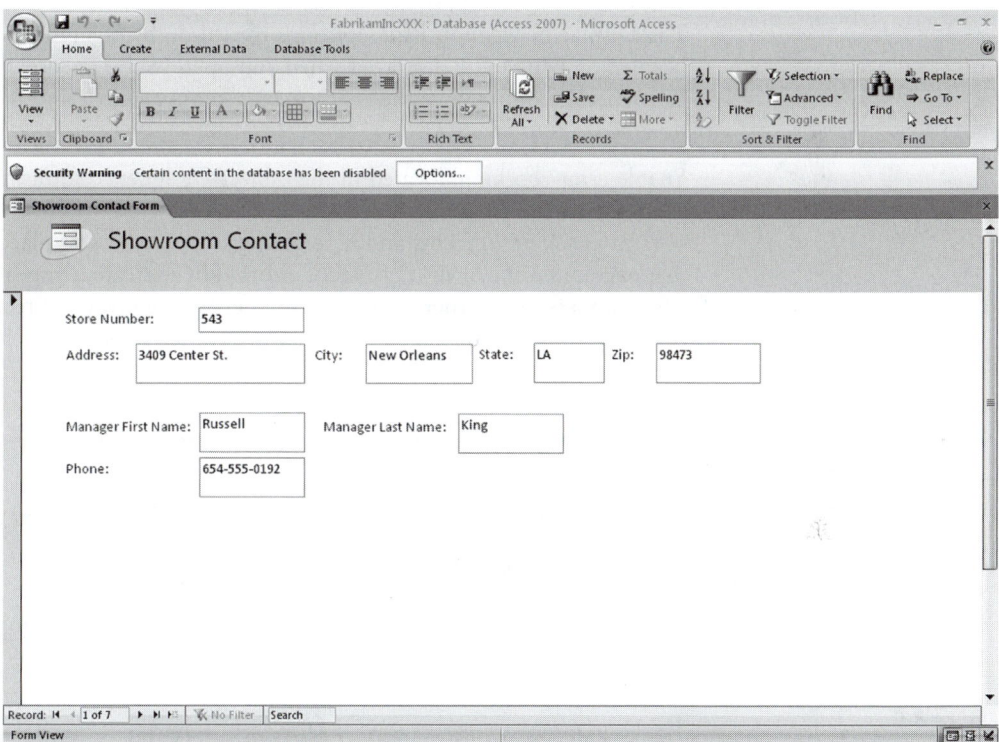

10. Click the **Office Button** and click the **Access Options** button.
11. Click the **Current Database** button on the left.
12. In the Application Options section, click the down arrow beside Display Form and select **None** from the menu.
13. In the Navigation pane section, click the **Display Navigation Pane** checkbox to insert a checkmark.
14. Click the **Navigation Options** button. The Navigation Options dialog box appears. Notice the grouping and display options available and click **Cancel**.
15. Click the **Object Designers** button on the left.

904 | Lesson 8

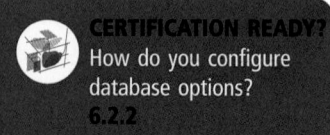

CERTIFICATION READY?
How do you configure database options?
6.2.2

16. Scroll to the bottom of the window to see the Error checking section. The Enable Error Checking options are turned on by default.
17. Click **OK**. The Microsoft Access dialog box appears again.
18. Click **OK**.
19. **CLOSE** the database.
20. **OPEN** the *FabrikamIncXXX* database. Notice the Navigation pane is displayed and the form is not.

    PAUSE. LEAVE the report open to use in the next exercise.

The Access Options dialog box lets you customize certain aspects of Access and your databases. The Access Options dialog box has 10 sections of customizable options, including Popular, Current Database, Datasheet, Object Designers, Proofing, and Advanced. In the previous exercise, you used the Current Database options to set a display form and hide the Navigation pane.

If you want a form to be displayed automatically when you open a database, the Display Form menu lets you choose from available forms in the database. You can choose none if you do not wish to display a form.

The Display Navigation Pane option is turned on by default, but if you don't want the Navigation pane to be displayed when you open your database, click the Display Navigation Pane checkbox to remove the check mark. You must close and reopen the current database for these settings to take effect.

Enable error checking, located in the Object Designers options, is another feature you can change. Error checking is on by default, but you can clear the checkbox to disable all types of error checking in forms and reports. For example, Access places error indicators in controls that encounter one or more types of errors. The indicators appear as triangles in the upper-left or upper-right corner of the control, depending on text direction. The default indicator color is green, but you can change that to another color if you choose.

■ SOFTWARE ORIENTATION

Database Tools Tab

The Database Tools tab on the Ribbon contains advanced commands for maintaining documents, as shown in Figure 8-6.

Figure 8-6

Database Tools tab

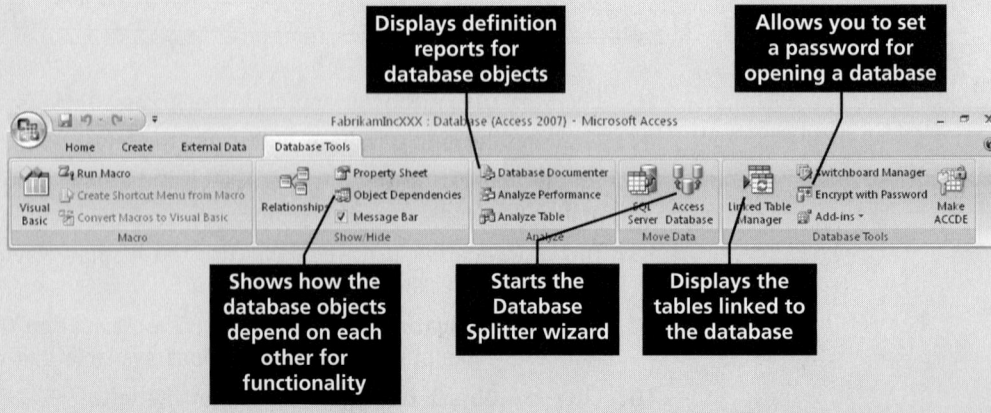

Use this figure as a reference throughout this lesson as well as the rest of this book.

Using Database Tools

THE BOTTOM LINE

The Database Tools tab has advanced commands for maintaining databases. These tools allow you to encrypt and decrypt a database, identify object dependencies, create object reports with the Database Documenter, refresh links with the Linked Table Manager, and split a database.

Encrypting a Database

When you need to protect a database from unauthorized users, you can encrypt it with a password and only provide that password to authorized users. Encrypting a database can provide security for sensitive data. You can use the decrypt database command to change the password on a regular basis or to remove it.

→ ENCRYPT AND DECRYPT A DATABASE

USE the database open from the previous exercise.

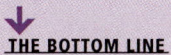

1. On the Database Tools tab, in the Database Tools group, click the **Encrypt with Password** button. The Microsoft Office Access message box appears saying you must open the database in Exclusive mode, as shown in Figure 8-7.

Figure 8-7

Microsoft Office Access Message box

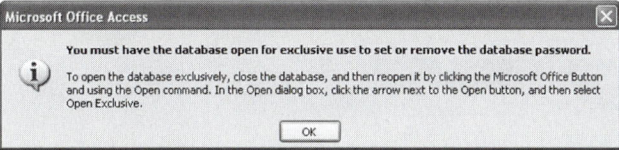

2. Click **OK**.
3. **CLOSE** the database.
4. Click the **More** link in the Open Recent Database list. The Open dialog box appears.
5. Navigate to the data files for this lesson and select **FabrikamIncXXX**.
6. Click the down arrow on the **Open** button and select **Open Exclusive** from the menu, as shown in Figure 8-8. FabrikamXXX opens in exclusive mode.

Figure 8-8

Open menu

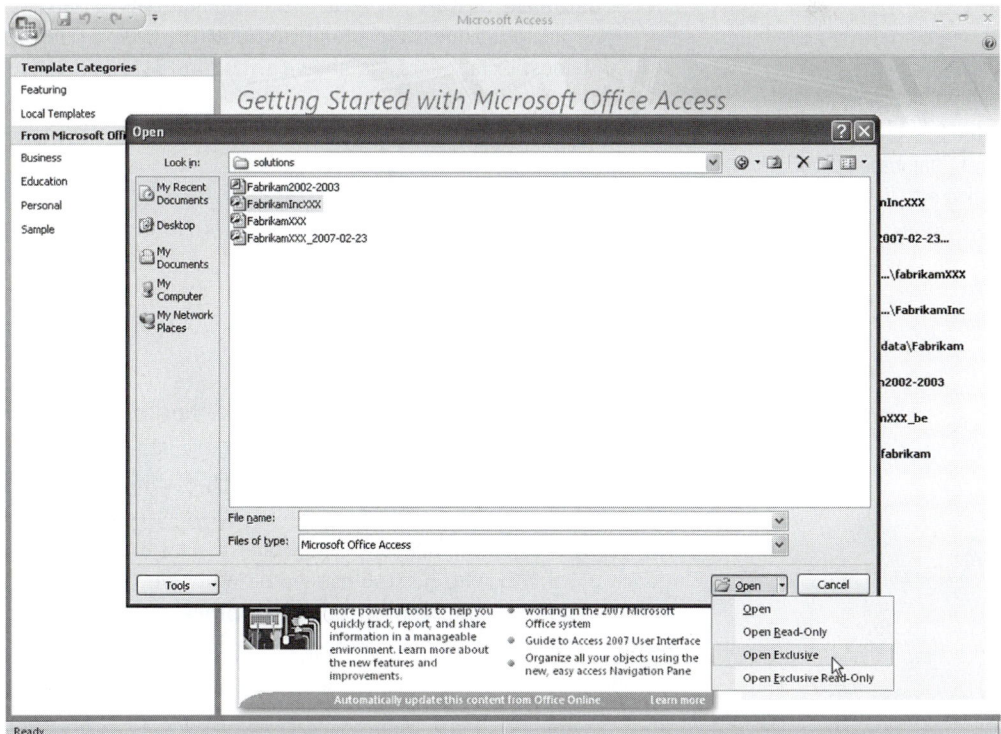

7. On the Database Tools tab, in the Database Tools group, click the **Encrypt with Password** button. The Set Database Password dialog box appears, as shown in Figure 8-9.

Figure 8-9

Set Database Password dialog box

8. Key **$Fabrikam09fc** in the Password box.

 Be careful to key the passwords exactly as printed throughout this exercise to avoid error messages.

9. Key **$Fabrikam09fc** in the Verify box.
10. Click **OK**. The database is now encrypted with a password.
11. **CLOSE** the database.
12. **OPEN** the database in Exclusive mode again. The Password Required dialog box appears, as shown in Figure 8-10.

Figure 8-10

Password Required dialog box

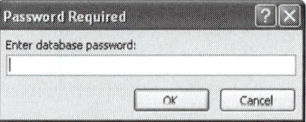

 You only need to open the database in Exclusive mode if you are going to set or unset a password. The database will be protected with the password in any mode.

13. Key **$Fabrikam09fc** and click **OK**. The database opens.
14. On the Database Tools tab, in the Database Tools group, click the **Decrypt Database** button. (If you hadn't opened the database in Exclusive mode, you would get a message prompting you to do so.) The Unset Database Password dialog box appears, as shown in Figure 8-11.

Figure 8-11

Unset Database Password dialog box

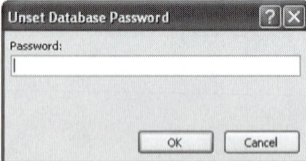

15. Key **$Fabrikam09fc** and click **OK**.
16. **CLOSE** the database.
17. **OPEN** the database in regular mode. Notice that a password is no longer required to open the file.

    PAUSE. LEAVE the database open to use in the next exercise.

Encrypting a database means to scramble the data in a way that can only be reconverted by an authorized user who has the password. When you use a database password to encrypt a database, you make all data unreadable by other tools and you force users to enter a password to use the database.

To encrypt a database, you first need to open it in Exclusive mode.

It is very important for you to remember your password, because if you forget it Microsoft cannot retrieve it for you. Write down the password and store it in a safe location.

TAKE NOTE

Use strong passwords that combine uppercase and lowercase letters, numbers, and symbols. Weak passwords do not mix these elements. Strong password: W5!dk8. Weak password: CAR381. Passwords should be 8 or more characters in length. A pass phrase that uses 14 or more characters is better.

When you open an encrypted database, the Password Required dialog box appears where you key the password. Passwords are case sensitive, meaning you can use uppercase and lowercase letters as well as numbers and symbols, but you must enter them exactly as they were entered when the password was set in order for there to be a match.

CERTIFICATION READY?
How do you encrypt a database?
6.2.1

Decrypting a database is removing the password from a file that has been encrypted. If you want to remove a password, open the database in Exclusive mode, then click the Decrypt Database button from the Database Tools group and key the password in the Unset Database Password dialog box exactly as it was entered to encrypt the database.

Identifying Object Dependencies

The Object Dependencies task pane helps you manage a database by displaying how all its components interact. This can be helpful if you want to delete a table or form. You will be able to see which other objects may also need to be changed so that they will still function without the deleted table.

→ **IDENTIFY OBJECT DEPENDENCIES**

USE the database open from the previous exercise.

1. Click the **Produce Placements Table** in the Navigation pane to select it.

2. On the Database Tools tab, in the Show/Hide group, click the **Object Dependencies** button. The **Object Dependencies pane** displays dependency information for the selected table, as shown in Figure 8-12. Notice that the *Objects that depend on me* button is selected.

Figure 8-12

Object Dependencies task pane

CERTIFICATION READY?
How do you identify object dependencies?
6.2.4

3. Click the **Objects that I depend on** button. Notice the changes in the Reports section.
4. Click the **Objects that depend on me** button. Click the **plus sign (+)** beside the Showroom Contact table to see the tables and forms that depend on the Showroom Contact table.
5. Click the **Showroom Contact** link to display it in Design view where you could make any necessary changes regarding dependencies.
6. **CLOSE** the Object Dependencies pane.

   PAUSE. LEAVE the database open to use in the next exercise.

Object dependencies describe how objects in a database rely on other components to function properly. The Object Dependencies task pane displays how database objects, such as tables or forms, use other objects. This process helps keep databases running smoothly by preventing errors that could result when changes or deletions are made to objects in a database. The Object Dependencies task pane works only for tables, forms, queries, and reports in an Access database.

Using the Database Documenter

The Database Documenter provides detailed information about a database and presents it as a report that can be printed. Use the Database Documenter when you need to have a printed record of this information, such as for record-keeping purposes or as insurance in case you have to re-create the database or object.

➔ USE THE DATABASE DOCUMENTER

USE the database open from the previous exercise.

1. On the Database Tools tab, in the Analyze group, click the **Database Documenter** button. The Documenter dialog box appears, as shown in Figure 8-13.

Figure 8-13

Documenter dialog box

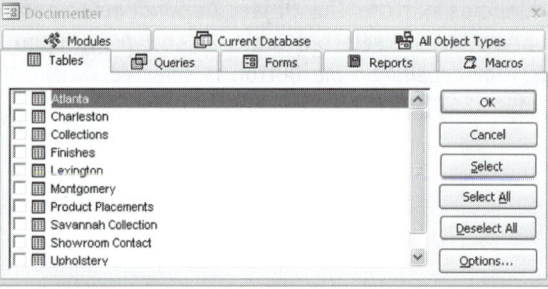

2. Click the **All Object Types** tab.
3. Click the **Tables** tab.
4. Click the **Showroom Contact** checkbox.

Database Tools | 909

5. Click the **Options** button. The Print Table Definition dialog box appears, as shown in Figure 8-14.

Figure 8-14

Print Table Definition dialog box

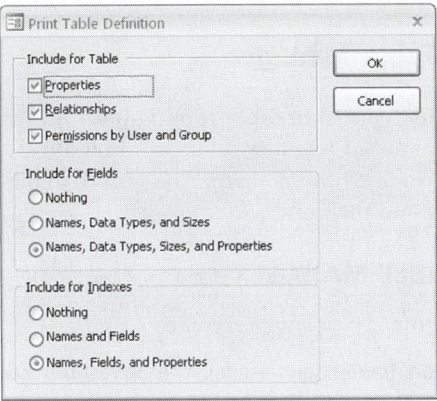

6. Click **OK**.
7. Click **OK**. The Object Definition report appears in Print Preview.
8. Click the **Zoom magnifying glass pointer** to view the report, as shown in Figure 8-15. At this point, you could print the report or make any changes to the layout and then print it.

Figure 8-15

Object Definition report

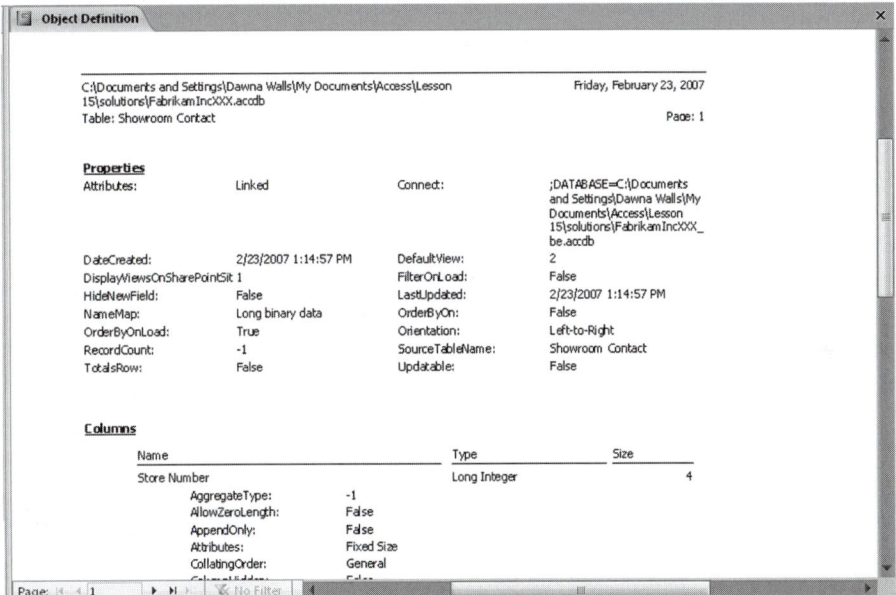

9. Click the **Last Page** button on the record navigation bar to move to page 4. Notice the relationship diagram included in the report.
10. Click the **Close Print Preview** button.

   PAUSE. LEAVE the database open to use in the next exercise.

The ***Database Documenter*** creates a report that shows details, or definitions, about a selected object and opens it in Print Preview. You can view the properties for a form, which are details about a file that describe or identify it, as well as properties for each section of the form and each label, button, or control on the form. The Documenter dialog box contains tabs for each type of object, as well as a tab that displays all objects. Select the object whose definitions you want to view or print. The Options button lets you further specify which features of the object you want to view the definitions for.

CERTIFICATION READY?
How do you use the Database Documenter?
6.2.6

910 | Lesson 8

> **TAKE NOTE** Some object definitions can be several pages long, so it is a good idea to check the length of the report before printing.

Using the Linked Table Manager

You can import and link data from other applications into your Access 2007 databases. If these linked files get moved to a new folder or other location, the Access database you are using might have trouble finding them. The Linked Table Manager identifies these broken paths and refreshes the links.

→ USE THE LINKED TABLE MANAGER

USE the database open from the previous exercise.

1. In the Navigation pane, double-click the **Savannah Collection** table, which has been imported from Excel. A message appears saying that Access cannot find the file. Click **OK**.
2. On the Database Tools tab, on the Database Tools group, click the **Linked Table Manager** button. The Linked Table Manager dialog box appears, as shown in Figure 8-16.

Figure 8-16

Linked Table Manager dialog box

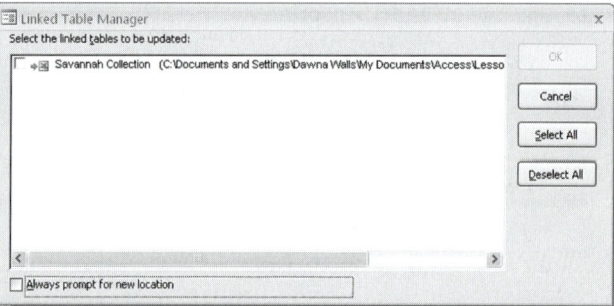

3. Click the **Savannah Collection** checkbox.
4. Click the **Always prompt for new location** checkbox and click **OK**. The Select New Location of Savannah Collection dialog box appears.
5. Navigate to the data files for this lesson on the companion CD-ROM. Open the New Collections folder, and click the **savannah** excel file, as shown in Figure 8-17.

Figure 8-17

Select new location of Savannah Collection

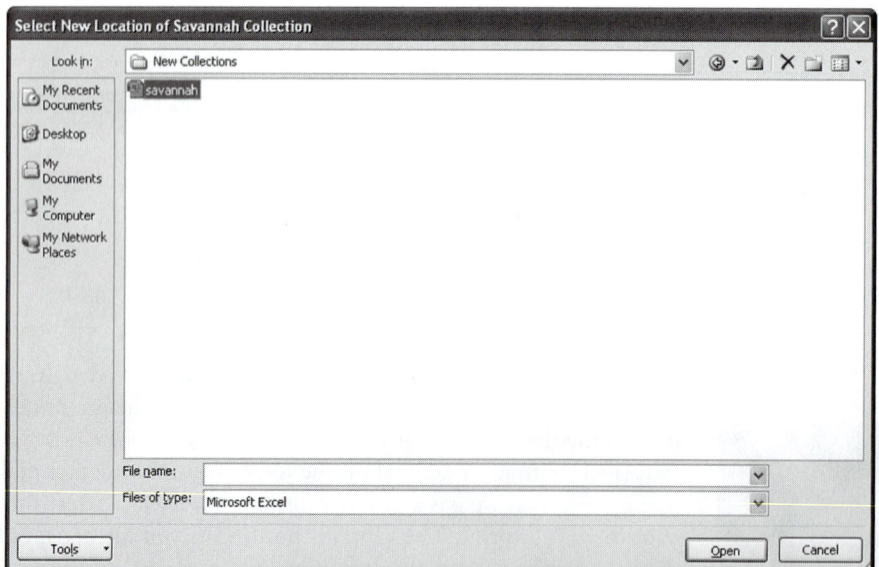

Database Tools | 911

6. Click **Open**. The Linked Table Manager dialog box appears, as shown in Figure 8-18.

Figure 8-18

Linked Table Manager dialog box

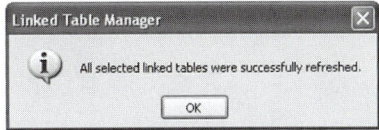

7. Click **OK**.
8. Click the **Close** button.
9. In the Navigation pane, double-click the **Savannah Collection** table, notice it opens this time.
10. **CLOSE** the **Savannah Collection** table.

   PAUSE. **LEAVE** Access open to use in the next exercise.

The *Linked Table Manager* lists the paths to all currently linked tables and refreshes any links for tables that have moved. If several selected tables have moved to the new location that you specify, the Linked Table Manager searches that location for all selected tables and updates all links in one step. The Linked Table Manager does not move database or table files, it just helps you locate them if they have moved and refreshes that path.

CERTIFICATION READY?
How do you use the Linked Table Manager?
6.2.6

You can refresh table links one at a time, if you know that only one has been moved, or you can click the Select All button in the Linked Table Manager to refresh all the links at once.

The Always prompt for new location lets you find the file and specify its new location.

Splitting a Database

It can be difficult for many people to use the data in a database at the same time. Synchronizing data can be difficult and time consuming. To avoid slowing down the network because of constant changes being made to a database, the Database Splitter wizard can split the database in two.

 **SPLIT A DATABASE**

USE the database open from the previous exercise.

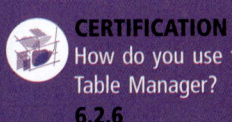

1. On the Database Tools tab, in the Move Data group, click the **Access Database** button. The Database Splitter Wizard appears, as shown in Figure 8-19.

Figure 8-19

Database Splitter Wizard

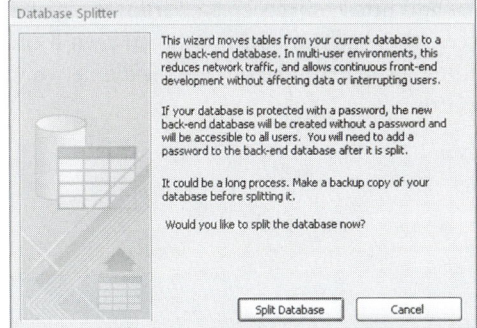

2. Click the **Split Database** button. The Create Back-end Database dialog box appears, as shown in Figure 8-20.

Figure 8-20

Create Back-end Database dialog box

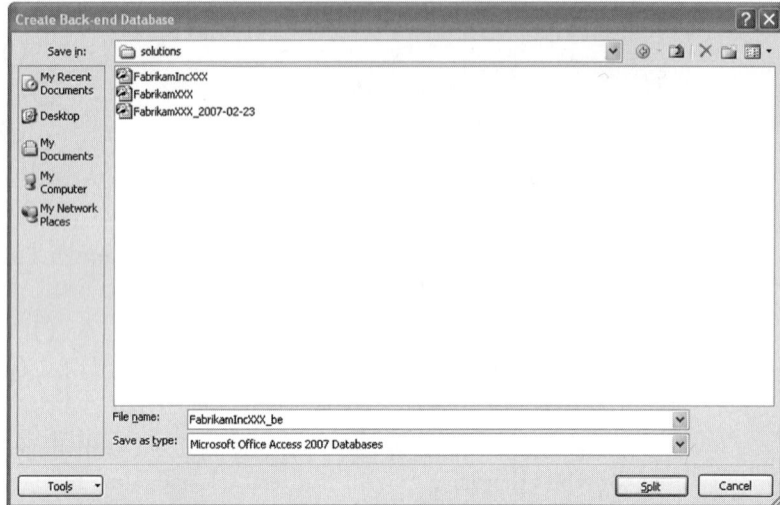

3. Navigate to the location where you want to save the back-end file and click **Split**. After a few moments, the Database Splitter dialog box appears, as shown in Figure 8-21.

Figure 8-21

Database Splitter dialog box

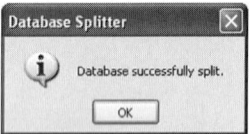

4. Click **OK**.
5. **CLOSE** the database.
6. **OPEN** *FabrikamXXX_be*. Notice that it contains only the tables for the database.
7. **CLOSE** the database.
   CLOSE Access.

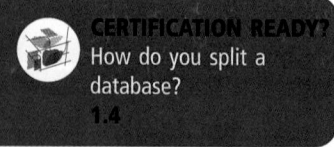

CERTIFICATION READY?
How do you split a database?
1.4

The *Database Splitter* is a wizard that splits a database for you. You can split a database into two files: one that contains the tables, called the ***back-end file***, and one that contains the queries, forms, reports, and other objects created from the tables, called the ***front-end file***. Users who need to access the data can customize their own forms, reports, pages, and other objects while maintaining a single source of data on the network. It is a good idea to back up the database before splitting it.

SUMMARY SKILL MATRIX

In this lesson you learned how to:
Back Up a Database
Compact and Repair a Database
Configure Database Options
Encrypt a Database
Identify Object Dependencies
Use the Database Documenter
Use the Linked Table Manager
Split a Database

Knowledge Assessment

Matching

Match the term in Column 1 to its description in Column 2.

Column 1

1. backup — h
2. back-end file — i
3. front-end file — a
4. database properties — b
5. Database Splitter — j
6. Linked Table Manager — c
7. encrypting — d
8. object dependencies — f
9. Database Documenter — g
10. decrypting — e

Column 2

a. in a split database, the file that contains the queries, forms, reports, and other objects created from the tables

b. details about a file that describe or identify it

c. lists the paths to all currently linked tables and refreshes the links to any tables that have moved

d. to scramble data in a way that can only be reconverted by an authorized user who has the correct password

e. removing the password from an encrypted file

f. describe how objects in a database are dependent on or rely on other components to function properly

g. creates a report that shows details, or definitions, about a selected object and opens it in Print Preview

h. a copy of a database file

i. the file that contains the tables in a split database

j. a wizard that splits a database for you

True / False

Circle T if the statement is true or F if the statement is false.

T **F** 1. Backing up files on a regular basis is really not necessary.
T F 2. When you back up a database, Access automatically adds the date to the filename.
T **F** 3. Compacting and repairing a database leaves the file fragmented.
T F 4. database properties can be viewed in a Database Documenter report.
T **F** 5. The .accdb extension is for the Access 2002-2003 file format.
T F 6. Access Options allow you to customize Access.
T **F** 7. If you forget a password for a database, Microsoft can retrieve it for you.
T F 8. You can print a report from the Database Documenter.
T **F** 9. The Linked Table Manager moves databases and tables then refreshes the path.
T F 10. It is a good idea to back up a database before splitting it.

■ Competency Assessment

Project 8-1: Compact and Repair the Blue Yonder Database

As an investor relations specialist for Blue Yonder Airlines, you need to maintain and safeguard the databases that you use. Compact and repair the Income and Expenses database.

The *BlueYonder* database is available on the companion CD-ROM.

GET READY. Launch Access if it is not already running.

1. Open the *BlueYonder* database from the data files for this lesson.
2. Save the database as *BlueYonderXXX* (where XXX is your initials).
3. Click the Office Button, point to Manage, and select **Compact and Repair Database**.

   CLOSE the database.

Project 8-2: Back Up and Split the WingTip Database

As part of your maintenance of database files at WingTip Toys, you decide to create a backup of a database and split it so that others in the company can create their own forms and reports using the data in the tables.

The *Wingtip* database is available on the companion CD-ROM.

GET READY. Launch Access if it is not already running.

1. **OPEN** the *Wingtip* database from the data files for this lesson.
2. Save the database as *WingtipXXX* (where XXX is your initials).
3. Click the Office Button, point to Manage, and select **Back Up Database**.
4. Use the generated file name with the date and click **Save**.
5. On the Database Tools tab, in the Move Data group, click the **Access Database** button.
6. Click the **Split database** button.
7. Accept the *WingtipXXX_be* file name and click **Split**.
8. Click **OK**.

   CLOSE the database.

Proficiency Assessment

Project 8-3: Encrypt the Blue Yonder Database

Create a password to protect the data in the Income and Expenses database.

USE the *BlueYonderXXX* database that you saved in a previous exercise.

1. OPEN the *BlueYonderXXX* database in Exclusive mode.
2. On the Database Tools tab, in the Database Tools group, click the **Encrypt with Password** button.
3. Key **#1BlueYonder$87** in the Password box.
4. Key **#1BlueYonder$87** in the Verify box.
5. Click **OK**.
6. **CLOSE** the database.
7. Open the database in regular mode.
8. Key **#1BlueYonder$87** in the Password box.
9. Open the **Database Documenter**.
10. Select the **Income & Expenses Summary** table and click **OK** to view the report.
11. Print the report.
12. Close **Print Preview**.

    CLOSE the database.

The *Lucerne* database is available on the companion CD-ROM.

Project 8-4: Save the Lucerne Database in a Previous File Format

OPEN the *Lucerne* database from the data files for this lesson.

1. Save the database in the Access 2002-2003 Database file format with the file name *Lucerne2002-2003*.

   CLOSE the database.

Mastery Assessment

Project 8-5: Decrypt and Back Up the Blue Yonder Database

Password protection for the Blue Yonder Income and Expenses database is no longer necessary. Remove the encryption.

USE the *BlueYonderXXX* database that you saved in a previous exercise.

1. Remove the encryption with a password from the Blue Yonder database.
2. Create a backup file for the database using the generated file name. Save it in the same location as the original version.

   CLOSE the database.

Project 8-6: Refresh Links and View Object Dependencies in the Humongous Database

An assistant at Humongous Insurance has moved some files around on the computer you share. Use the Linked Tables Manager to refresh a link to an Excel file that has been imported.

OPEN *HumongousInsurance* from the data files for this lesson.

The *Humongous Insurance* database is available on the companion CD-ROM.

1. Save the database as *HumongousInsuranceXXX* (where XXX is your initials).
2. Refresh the link for the **Benefit Providers** Excel file, located on the companion CD-ROM, using the Linked Table Manager.
3. View the Object Dependencies Information for the Part-time Employees Table.
4. **SAVE** the database.
   CLOSE Access.

INTERNET READY

On the Office Button menu, click the Access Options button to launch the Access Options dialog box. Click the Trust Center button on the left. In the Security & more section, click the Microsoft Trustworthy Computing link and read the online article. Browse other links that interest you at the Trust Center.

Circling Back

Woodgrove Real Estate is growing and adding more listings. Your office has added another real estate agent and has begun listing commercial properties as well as residential ones. The database you created has been a great way to keep track of all the listings and other relevant information. As you learn more about Access, you begin using it for a wider variety of tasks.

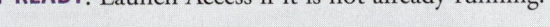 Project 1: Create and Format a Report

You want to create a report to display data about each agent's listings. Use the Report Wizard and then switch to Design view to make changes to the format and add a control.

GET READY. Launch Access if it is not already running.

The *Real Estate* file is available on the companion CD-ROM.

1. **OPEN** the *Real Estate* database from the data files for this lesson.
2. **SAVE** the database as *Real Estate XXX* (where XXX is your initials).
3. On the Create tab, in the Reports group, click the **Report Wizard** button.
4. In the Tables/Queries menu, choose **Table: Listings**.
5. Click the **double right arrow >>** button to move all the fields into the Selected Fields list.
6. Click the **ID** field to select it and click the **left arrow <** button to move it back to the Available Fields list.
7. Click the **Next** button.
8. Click the **Listing Agent** field to select it and click the **right arrow >** button to add it as a grouping level.
9. Click the **Next** button.
10. Select **Price** from the fields menu to sort in Ascending order and click the **Next** button.
11. In the Layout section, click the **Outline** button. In the Orientation section, click the **Landscape** button. Click **Next**.
12. Click **Paper** in the styles list and click **Next**.
13. Key **Listings Report** as the title of the report.
14. Click **Finish** to display the Listings Report.
15. On the Print Preview tab, in the Close Preview group, click the **Close Print Preview** button to display the report in Design view.
16. In the Listing Agent Header section, click and drag the **right border of the Listing Agent field** to make it smaller.
17. Click and drag the **right border of the Price field** to make it larger.
18. Click and drag the **right border of the Price field** to make it smaller.

19. On the Design tab, in the Views group, click the **View** button and click **Report View**. Your report should look similar to Figure 1.

Figure 1

Listings report

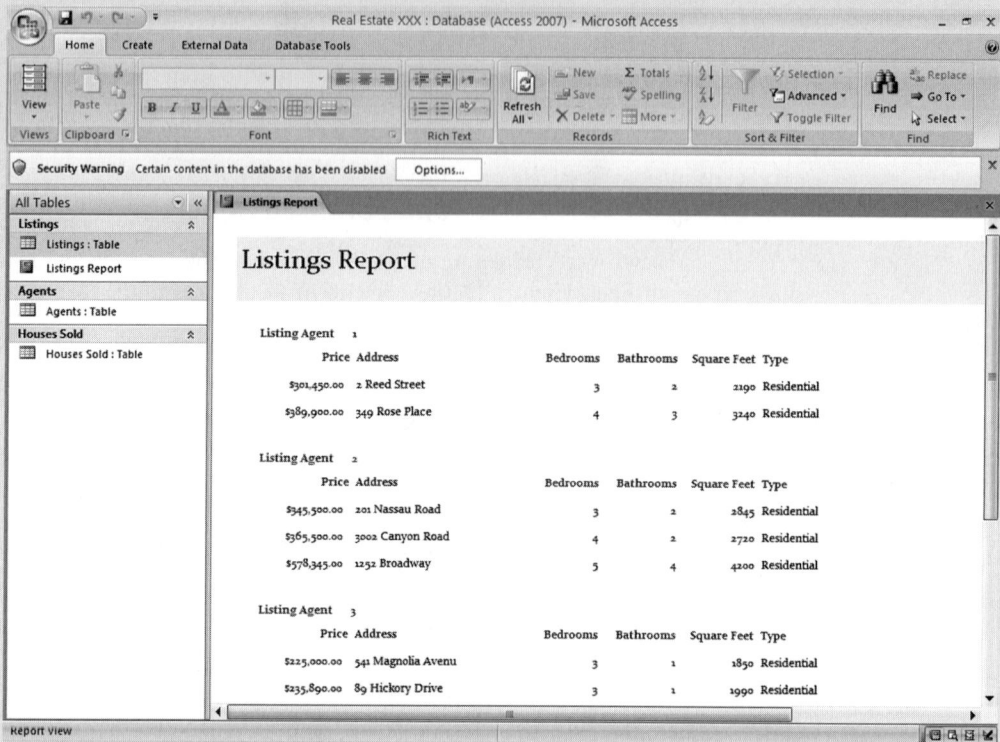

20. Click the **Close 'Listings Report'** button to close the report and save the changes when prompted.

   PAUSE. LEAVE the database open to use in the next project.

Project 2: Create and Modify Queries

You want to query the database to find all the houses that closed in June. Create a query using the Query Wizard and then add criteria to get the information you need.

USE the database that is open from the previous project.

1. On the Create tab, in the Other group, click the **Query Wizard** button to display the New Query dialog box.
2. Click **Simple Query Wizard** and then click **OK** to display the Simple Query Wizard.
3. In the Tables/Queries dropdown list, click **Table: Houses Sold**.
4. Under Available Fields, double-click **Listing Agent**, **Address**, **Selling Price**, and **Closing Date** to move them to the Selected Fields box.
5. Click the **Next >** button to display the next screen. Detail query should be selected.
6. Click the **Next >** button to display the final screen.
7. Click the **Finish** button to display the query.
8. On the Home tab, in the Views group, click the **View** button and click **Design View**.
9. In the Criteria row of the Closing Date field, key **Between #6/1/2008# And #6/30/2008#**.
10. On the Design tab, in the Results group, click the **View button** and click **Datasheet View** to display the query results of all records for houses that closed in June.

11. Right-click the **Closing Date field header** and choose **Sort Oldest to Newest** on the menu. Your query should look similar to Figure 2.

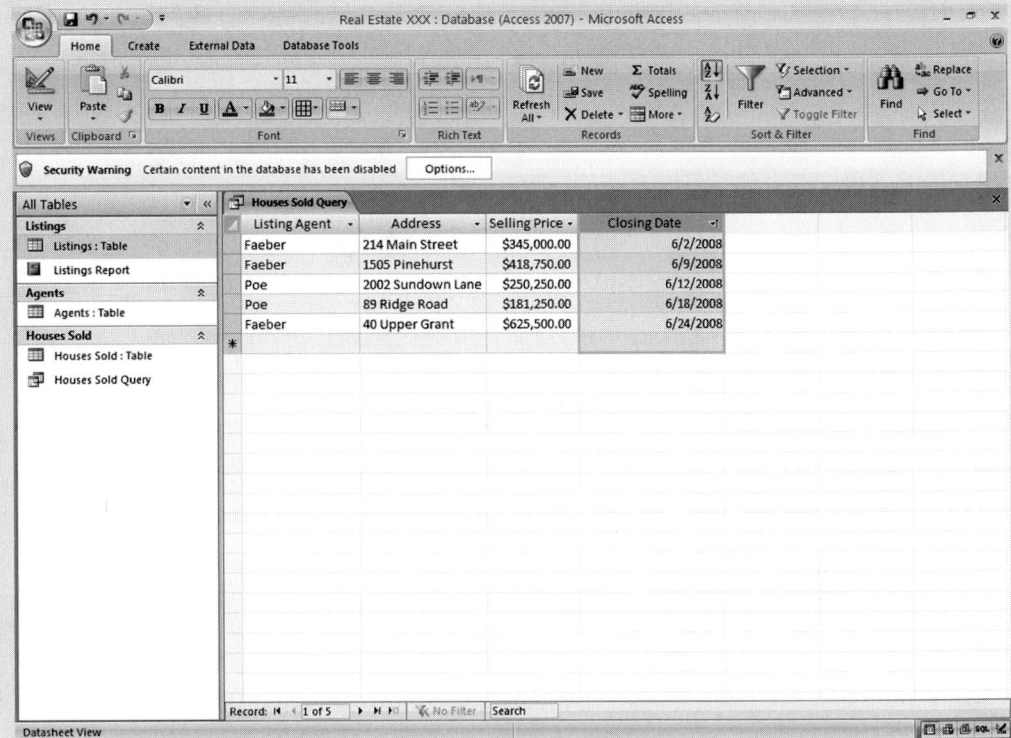

Figure 2

Query results

12. Click the **Close 'Houses Sold Query'** button to close the query. When prompted to save, click **Yes**.

    PAUSE. LEAVE the database open for the next project.

Project 3: Sum Table Data

You want to know the total value of the current listings. Open the table and add a Totals Row to get this information.

USE the database that is open from the previous project.

1. **OPEN** the **Listings** table.
2. On the Home tab, in the Records group, click the **Totals** button. The Totals Row appears below the asterisk (*) row.
3. Click the **down arrow** in the Price column of the Totals Row. Select **Sum** from the menu. Your screen should look similar to Figure 3.

Figure 3

Totals row

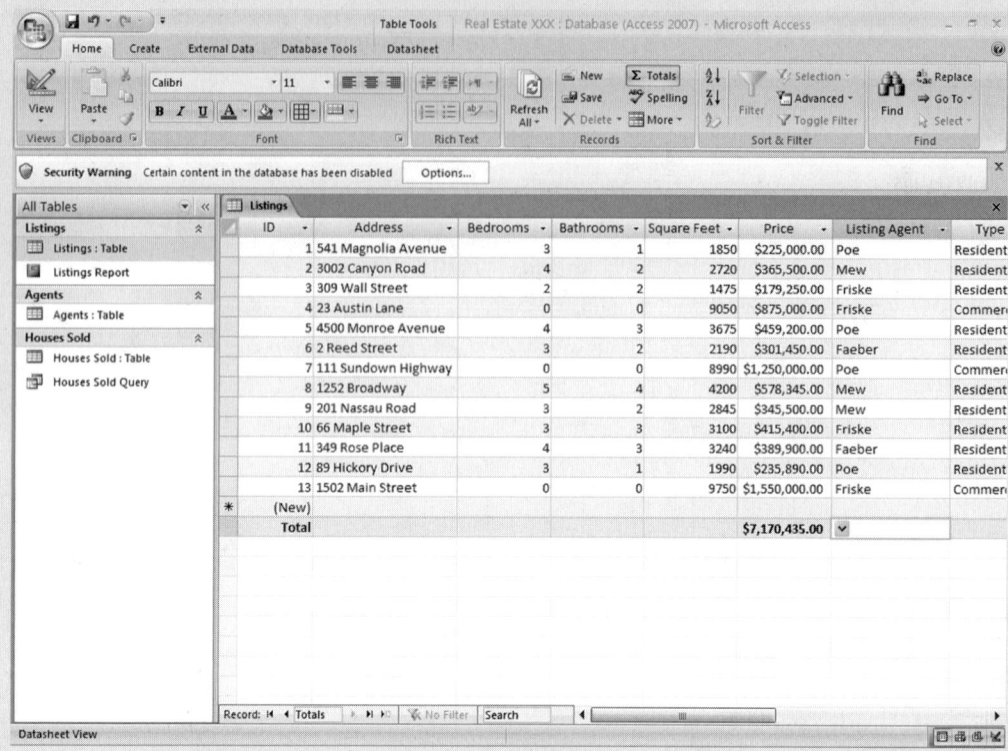

4. On the Home tab, in the Records group, click the **Totals** button to hide the Totals Row.
5. On the Home tab, in the Records group, click the **Totals** button again. The Totals Row reappears.
6. **SAVE** and **CLOSE** the table.

   PAUSE. LEAVE the database open for the next project.

Project 4: Maintain, Back Up, and Split a Database

You regularly perform routine maintenance on the database to ensure data integrity. You decide to split the database into two files to reduce network traffic, but after all the work you have put into the database you first want to protect your work by backing it up to prevent data loss.

USE the database that is open from the previous project.

1. Click the **Office Button**, point to **Manage**, and click **Compact and Repair Database**. Access compacts and repairs the database.
2. Click the **Office Button**, point to **Manage**, and click **Back Up Database** to display the Save As dialog box. Access automatically adds the current date to the end of the filename.
3. Click the **Save** button to accept the generated filename.
4. On the Database Tools tab, in the Move Data group, click the **Access Database** button to display the Database Splitter Wizard.
5. Click the **Split Database** button to display the Create Back-end Database dialog box.

6. Navigate to the location where you want to save the back-end file and click **Split**. After a few moments, the Database Splitter dialog box appears.
7. Click **OK**.
8. **CLOSE** the database.
9. **OPEN** *Real Estate XXX_be*. Notice that it contains only the tables for the database.
10. **CLOSE** the database.
    STOP. CLOSE Access.

Workplace Ready

Collaborating using Windows SharePoint Services

As a purchase order manager for Coho Vineyard and Winery, you use Access to organize and manage all purchase-related data, such as purchase status, vendor and supplier information, and activity logs. You use the database to quickly track activities, print purchase orders, and create summary reports.

Microsoft Office Access 2007 also allows you to share this information with colleagues by moving Access files to a Windows SharePoint Services Web site. In this way, your team can communicate, share documents, and work together on projects by interacting with published files through a browser. Using Windows SharePoint Services, you can easily transfer your local data to a server where it can be managed, kept secure, and backed up at regular intervals. You can track records and view when data was created, edited, and deleted, and by whom. You can set data access permissions for various users and also recover deleted information using the Recycle Bin feature.

Microsoft® Office
Outlook® 2007

Getting to Know Outlook

LESSON SKILL MATRIX

Using the On-Screen Tools	Students will learn how to use the On-Screen Tools.
Changing Outlook's View	Students will learn how to change Outlook's view.
Working with the Reading Pane	Students will learn how to work with the Reading Pane.
Viewing, Hiding, and Minimizing the To-Do Bar	Students will learn how to view, hide, and minimize the To-Do Bar.
Customizing the To-Do Bar	Students will learn how to customize the To-Do Bar.

Adventure Works is a luxurious resort located in Ohio. During the summer, activities such as kayaking, canoeing, hiking, and horseback riding are available. In the winter months, visitors enjoy skiing, snowshoeing, and sleigh rides. Partners Mindy Martin and Jon Morris own and operate Adventure Works. They work hard to ensure that guests enjoy their stay. Employees are well-trained and well-treated professionals. For one week every year, Mindy and Jon close the resort to guests and open the facilities to employees and their families.

KEY TERMS
folder
item
Navigation pane
Reading pane
To-Do Bar

Software Orientation

Microsoft Outlook's Opening Screen

Before you begin working in Microsoft Outlook, you need to be familiar with the primary user interface. When you first launch Microsoft Outlook, you will see a screen similar to that shown in Figure 1-1.

Figure 1-1

Outlook opening screen

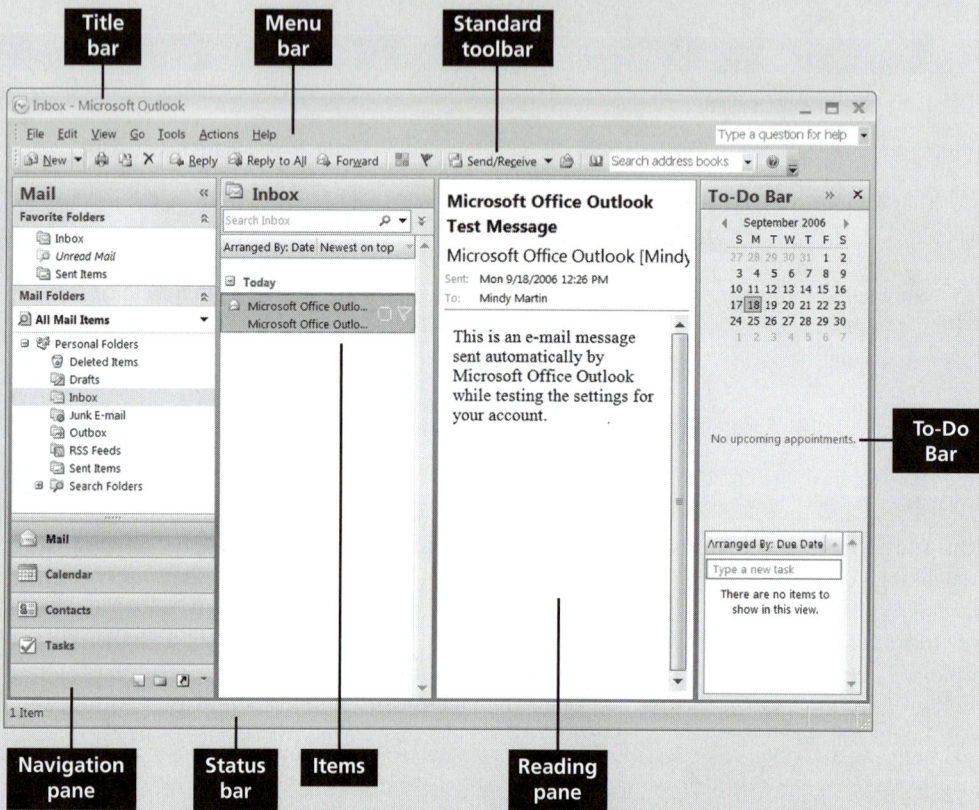

The elements and features of this screen are typical for Microsoft Outlook. Your screen may vary if default settings have been changed or if other preferences have been set. Use this figure as a reference throughout this lesson as well as the rest of this book.

Working in the Outlook Window

THE BOTTOM LINE

Outlook has a variety of tools that help you organize your communication and manage your time.

If you need to send a message to a vendor making a late delivery, look up an old friend's phone number, or schedule a staff meeting, Outlook provides the tools that will save time and make your job easier. Refer to Figure 1-1 to view the Outlook window you see when you launch Outlook.

Getting to Know Outlook | 927

Using the On-Screen Tools

Outlook's on-screen tools enable you to access the information you need.

These include menu commands and buttons that help you to navigate through Outlook's components. As you click buttons or select menu commands, the components in the Outlook window change to display the information you requested or provide space to enter new information.

> **ANOTHER WAY**
>
> You also can select the component from the Go menu or use the keyboard shortcut listed next to each component in the Go menu.

USE THE ON-SCREEN TOOLS

GET READY Before you begin these steps, be sure to turn on or log on to your computer.

1. Start Microsoft Office Outlook.
2. Click the **Calendar** button in the Navigation pane, as shown in Figure 1-2. The calendar is displayed.

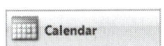

Figure 1-2

Calendar button in the Navigation pane

3. Click the **Contacts** button in the Navigation pane, as shown in Figure 1-3. Information about the contacts stored in Outlook is displayed.

Figure 1-3

Contacts button in the Navigation pane

4. Click the **Tasks** button in the Navigation pane, as shown in Figure 1-4. Information about your current tasks and your to-do list are displayed.

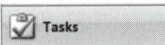

Figure 1-4

Tasks button in the Navigation pane

5. Click the **Notes** button in the Navigation pane, as shown in Figure 1-5. Any notes already entered are displayed.

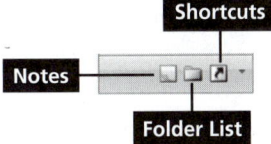

Figure 1-5

Notes, Folder List, and Shortcuts buttons in the Navigation pane

6. Click the **Folder List** button in the Navigation pane, as shown in Figure 1-5. The list of folders is displayed in the upper area of the Navigation pane.
7. Click the **Shortcuts** button in the Navigation pane, as shown in Figure 1-5. Any shortcuts already created are displayed in the upper area of the Navigation pane.
8. Click the **Minimize** button at the top of the Navigation pane, as shown in Figure 1-6. The Navigation pane is displayed as a vertical strip on the left side of the Outlook window.

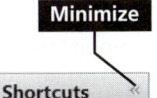

Figure 1-6

Minimize the Navigation pane

9. Click the **Expand** button at the top of the minimized Navigation pane, as shown in Figure 1-7. The Navigation pane is restored to its previous size and location.

Figure 1-7

Expand the Navigation pane

10. Click the **Mail** button in the Navigation pane, as shown in Figure 1-8. The window should return to the default view displayed when you launched Outlook.

Figure 1-8

Mail button in the Navigation pane

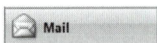

PAUSE. LEAVE Outlook open to use in the next exercise.

In the previous exercise, you took a quick look at the Outlook components by using the Navigation pane. The following table describes the basic function of each on-screen tool used to access Outlook's components. More detailed information about using the components is available in the following sections of this lesson and the remaining lessons.

ON-SCREEN TOOL	DESCRIPTION
Item	An *item* is a record stored in Outlook. A message, appointment, contact, task, or note is an item in Outlook.
Menu bar	The Menu bar contains the menus and commands available in Outlook.
Navigation pane	The **Navigation pane** provides access to the Outlook components, such as the Contacts and the Calendar. In Outlook 2007, you can free up additional space by minimizing the Navigation pane. The navigation elements are still available when the Navigation pane is minimized.
Reading pane	The **Reading pane** displays the text of a selected email message.
Standard toolbar	The Standard toolbar contains buttons that access frequently used commands.
Status bar	The Status bar identifies the number of items in the active component. For example, when the Contacts component is active, the number of contacts stored is displayed in the Status bar.
Title bar	The Title bar identifies the application and the active component. For example, when the Calendar is active, the Title bar says "Calendar—Microsoft Outlook."
To-Do Bar	The **To-Do Bar** is a new feature that summarizes information about appointments and tasks.

Changing Outlook's View

Every Outlook component has multiple viewing options.

To help you accomplish each task, the Outlook components provide specific information in the Outlook window. For example, the Contacts component provides the names, addresses, and phone numbers for the individuals and companies you contact. The Calendar tracks your appointments and meetings. Mail enables you to send and receive email messages.

Outlook stores and organizes many of the little pieces of information that form the core of your daily activities. In a single day, you might meet with the design team at 9:00; negotiate a deal with a new supplier at 10:00; have lunch with the Vice President of Marketing at 12:30; call several associates to discuss a new design concept; send a message to the vice president's office confirming details about the new design; attend a department meeting at 3:00, when your promotion to department head is announced; and scoot out the door at 5:15 to pick up your daughter from soccer practice. What part did Outlook play in those activities? You used Outlook to schedule the meetings, look up the phone numbers, send the email message, and set up the reminders that helped you arrive on time for every meeting. You used Outlook's Calendar, Mail, and Contacts components to keep you on top of everything. That promotion was well deserved!

In the previous exercise, you used the on-screen tools to move through the Outlook components. In this exercise, you will access the Outlook components again and see some of the viewing options available in each one. Don't worry about using the components yet. The components you use most frequently are covered in more detail in the following lessons. Shortcuts and the Journal are not frequently used, and they are not covered in this book.

CHANGE OUTLOOK'S VIEW

GET READY. Before you begin these steps, be sure that Microsoft Outlook is running.

1. If necessary, click the **Mail** button in the Navigation pane to display the Mail folder, as shown in Figure 1-9.

Figure 1-9

Mail folder

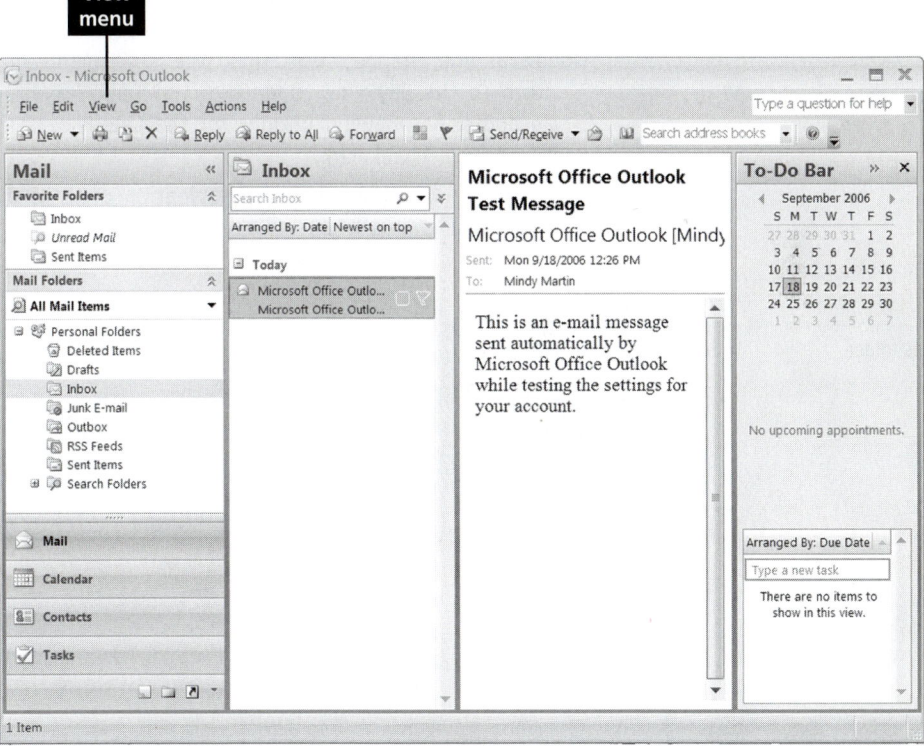

2. Open the View menu. Point to **Arrange By** to see the basic viewing options for the Mail folder. Point to **Current View** to see additional viewing options. The options currently active are identified by a checkmark.

3. Click the **Calendar** button in the Navigation pane to display the Calendar folder, and click the Day button above the calendar as shown in Figure 1-10. The view showing today's date is displayed.

Figure 1-10

Calendar folder

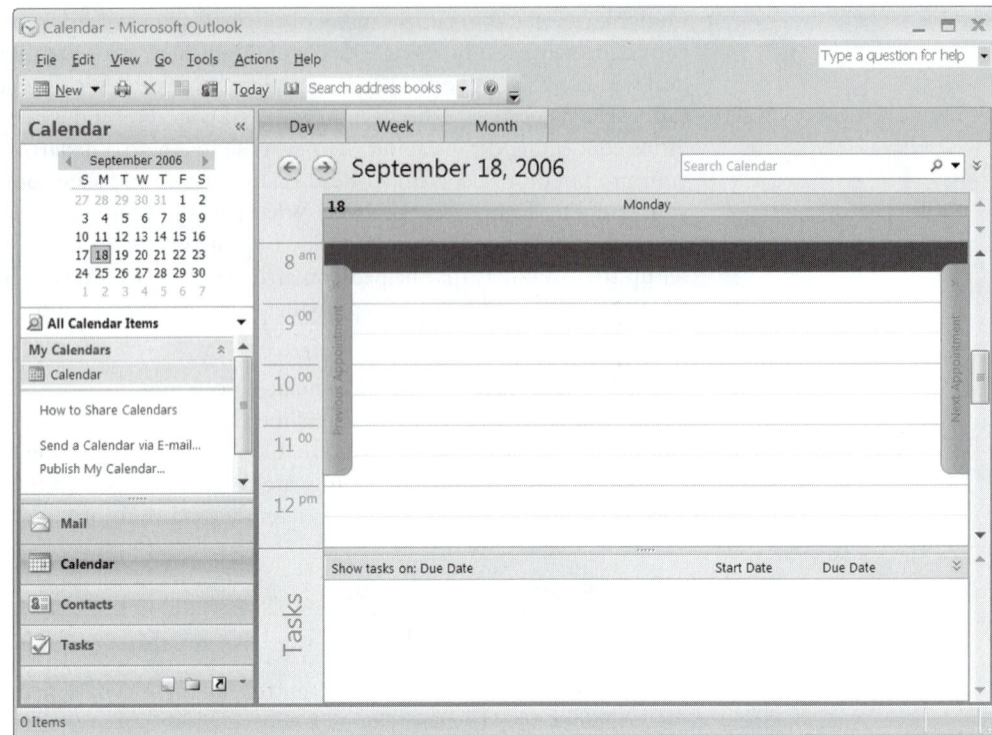

 **ANOTHER WAY**

You can also click the Day, Week, and Month buttons below the Standard toolbar to change the view.

4. Open the **View** menu. The Day option is currently selected. In the View menu, click the **Work Week**, **Week**, and **Month** options. Note the changes in the Outlook window as you change views. Open the **View** menu again and click the **Day** option to return to the day view. Open the **View** menu again and point to **Current View** to see additional viewing options for the Calendar. The options currently active are identified by a checkmark.

5. Click the **Contacts** button in the Navigation pane to display the Contacts folder, as shown in Figure 1-11.

Figure 1-11

Contacts folder

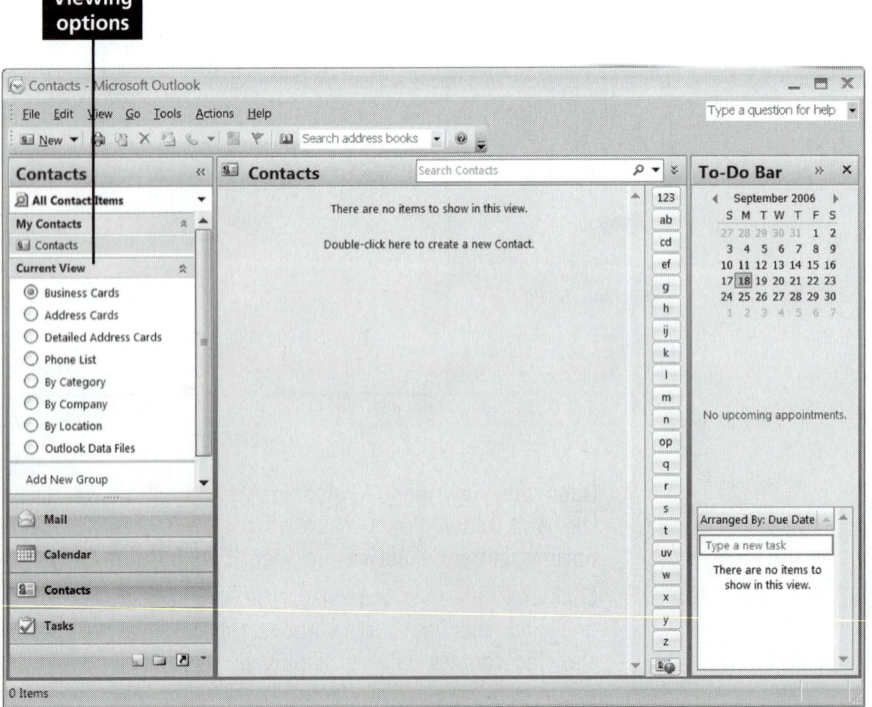

Getting to Know Outlook | 931

6. Open the **View** menu. Point to **Current View** to see the viewing options. The options currently active are identified by a checkmark. Note that the same options listed in the Current View menu are displayed in the Navigation pane.

7. Click the **Tasks** button in the Navigation pane to display the Tasks folder, as shown in Figure 1-12.

Figure 1-12

Tasks folder

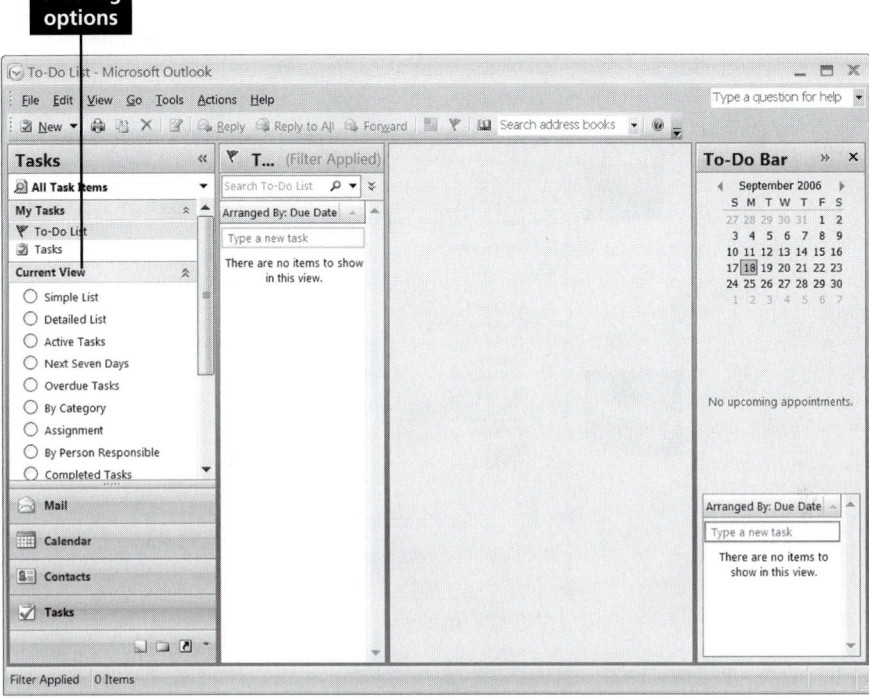

8. Open the **View** menu. Point to **Current View** to see the viewing options. The options currently active are identified by a checkmark. Note that the same options listed in the Current View menu are displayed in the Navigation pane.

9. Click the **Notes** button in the Navigation pane to display the Notes folder, as shown in Figure 1-13.

Figure 1-13

Notes folder

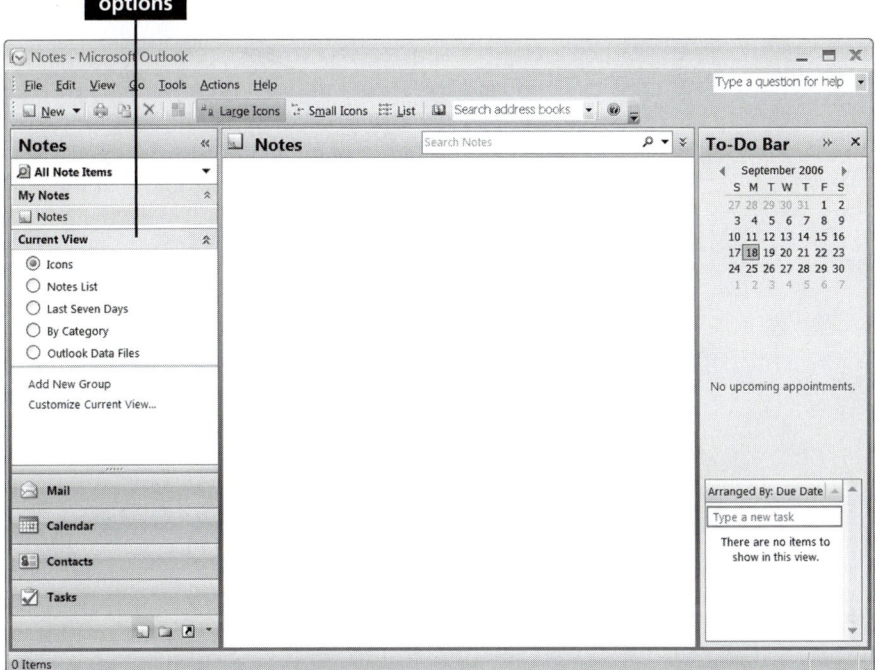

10. Open the **View** menu. Point to **Current View** to see the viewing options. The options currently active are identified by a checkmark. Note that the same options listed in the Current View menu are displayed in the Navigation pane.

11. Click the **Folder List** button in the Navigation pane to display the Folder List in the upper area of the Navigation pane, as shown in Figure 1-14. Note that the Notes folder is highlighted in the Folder List and the main portion of the Outlook window still displays the Notes folder. Clicking the Folder List button only affects the information displayed in the Navigation pane.

Figure 1-14

Folder List and Notes folder displayed

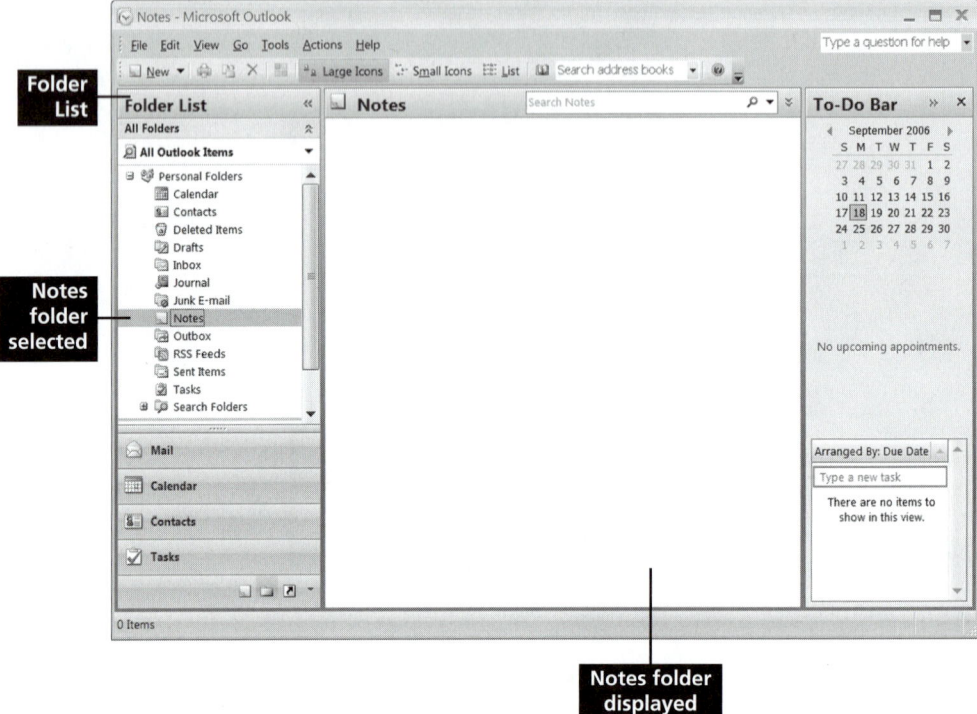

12. Click the **Mail** button in the Navigation pane to return to the default view displayed when Outlook is launched.

    PAUSE. LEAVE Outlook open to use in the next exercise.

Outlook components are commonly called *folders,* because the items are organized into folders. For example, when you click the Mail button, Outlook's Mail component, or Mail folder, is displayed. This becomes more obvious when you display the Folder List, as shown in Figure 1-14. Every Outlook component is a folder in the Folder List. If you create folders in the future to further organize your Outlook items, the folders you create will also be displayed in the Folder List.

In the previous exercise, you displayed each of the commonly used Outlook folders. The following table briefly describes how these Outlook folders are used.

Getting to Know Outlook | 933

Folder	Description
Calendar	The Calendar folder contains a calendar and appointment book to help you keep track of your schedule.
Contacts	The Contacts folder stores contact information about individuals, groups, and companies.
Folder List	The Folder List identifies all of your Outlook folders. If your company or organization uses Microsoft Exchange Server, public folders you can access also are listed.
Mail	The Mail folder contains your email messages. Folders in the Mail folder include your Inbox (messages received), Sent Items (messages sent), Outbox (messages waiting to be sent), and Junk E-mail (unwanted messages you received that were not directed to another folder).
Notes	The Notes folder stores small pieces of information on electronic sticky notes. Notes can be forwarded as email messages.
Tasks	The Tasks folder displays tasks assigned to you.

■ Personalizing Outlook

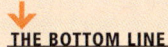

You can arrange the elements on the Outlook window to fit your needs.

Resize, rearrange, hide, or display Outlook components to create an environment that meets your requirements. Reposition the Reading pane. Hide components you don't use. Expand panes that contain critical information you need to see.

Working with the Reading Pane

Show, hide, or move the Reading pane.

Arrange the Reading pane to fit your needs. Do you get a lot of long email messages? Display the Reading pane vertically on the right to display the most text possible. Perhaps the messages you receive contain a lot of information in the item listing area. Display the Reading pane horizontally.

➔ WORK WITH THE READING PANE

GET READY. Before you begin these steps, be sure that Microsoft Outlook is running.

1. If necessary, click the **Mail** button in the Navigation pane to display the Mail folder.

2. Click the **View** menu, point to **Reading Pane**, and select the **Bottom** option. The Reading pane is displayed horizontally, across the bottom of the message viewing area, as shown in Figure 1-15.

Figure 1-15

Reading pane displayed in the bottom position

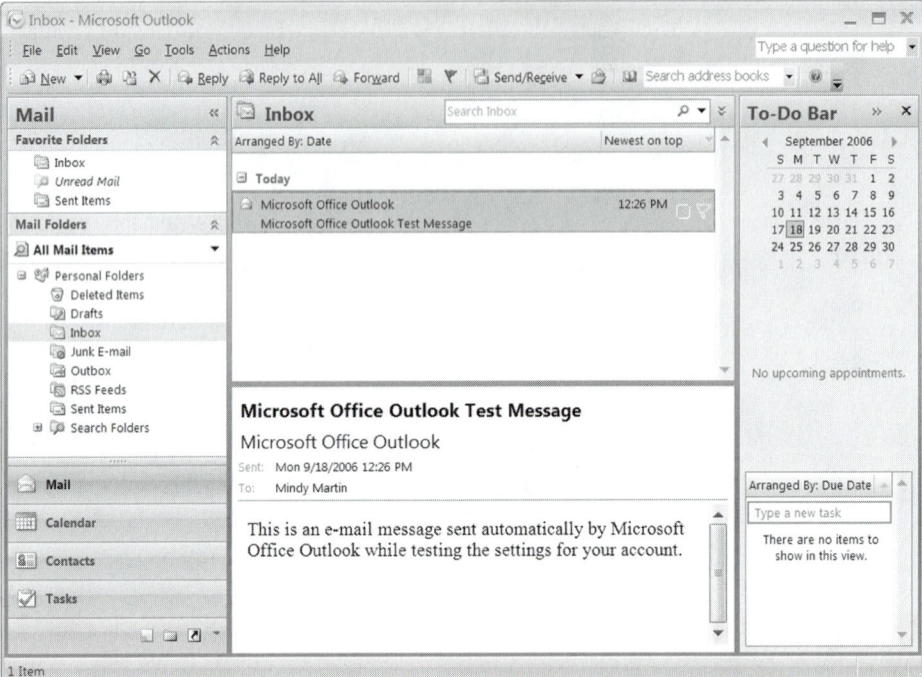

3. Click the **View** menu, point to **Reading Pane**, and select the **Off** option. The Reading pane is hidden, as shown in Figure 1-16.

Figure 1-16

Reading pane is hidden

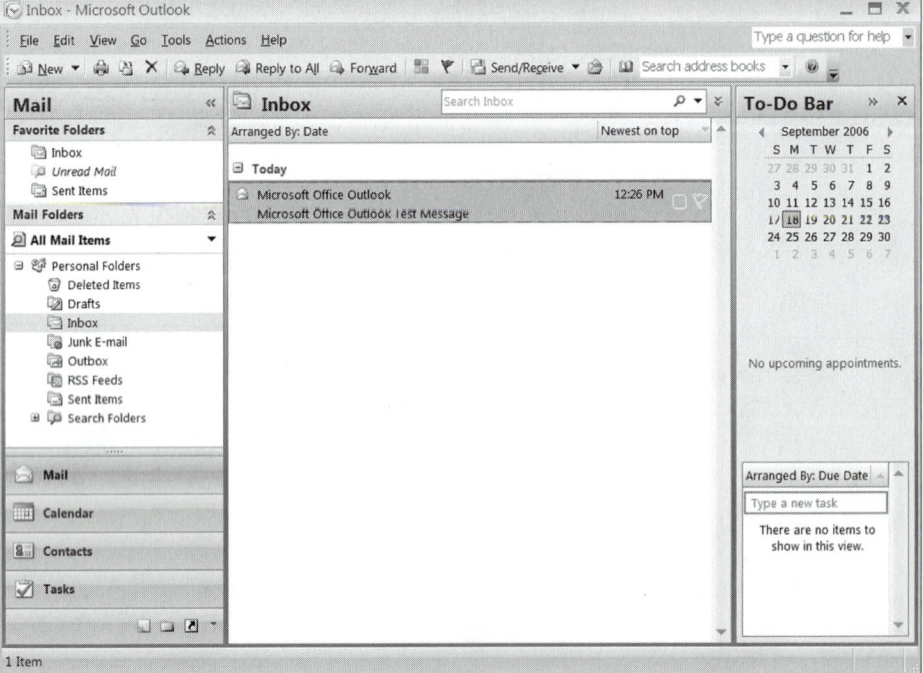

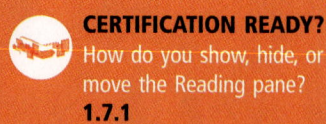

CERTIFICATION READY?
How do you show, hide, or move the Reading pane?
1.7.1

4. Click the **View** menu, point to **Reading Pane**, and select the **Right** option. The Reading pane is displayed in its default position on the right.

PAUSE. LEAVE Outlook open to use in the next exercise.

Getting to Know Outlook | 935

Viewing, Hiding, and Minimizing the To-Do Bar

The To-Do Bar is a new feature in Outlook 2007. It summarizes the current items that need your attention. You can show, hide, or minimize the To-Do Bar.

➔ VIEW, HIDE, AND MINIMIZE THE TO-DO BAR

GET READY. Before you begin these steps, be sure that Microsoft Outlook is running.

1. If necessary, click the **Mail** button in the Navigation pane to display the Mail folder.
2. Click the **View** menu, point to **To-Do Bar**, and select the **Minimized** option. The To-Do Bar is minimized to a slim pane on the right side of the Outlook window, as shown in Figure 1-17.

Figure 1-17

Minimized To-Do Bar

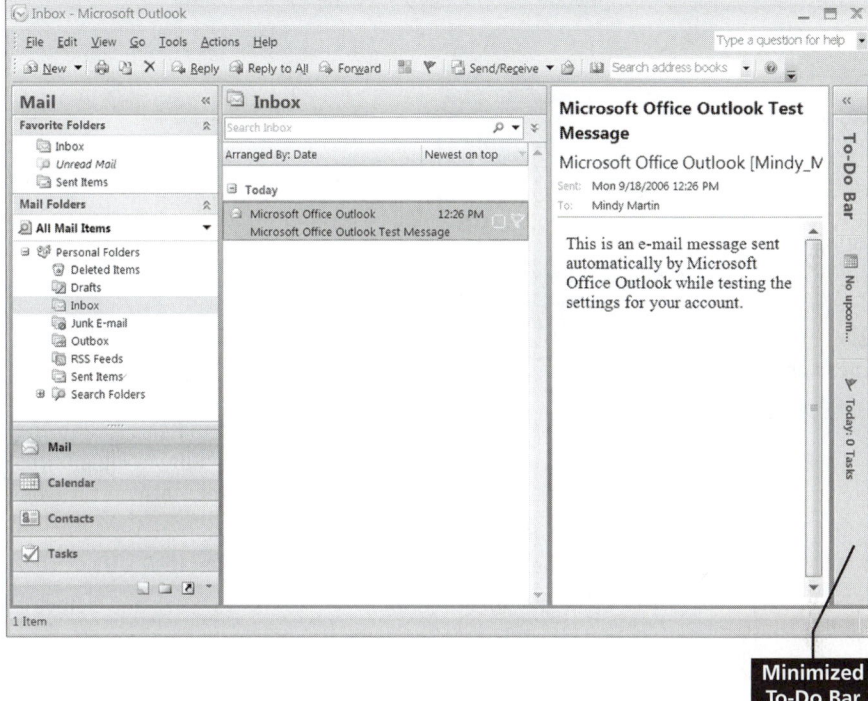

3. Click the View menu, point to **To-Do Bar**, and select the **Off** option. The To-Do Bar is hidden.
4. Click the **View** menu, point to **To-Do Bar**, and select the **Normal** option. The To-Do Bar is restored to its original size and position.

   PAUSE. LEAVE Outlook open to use in the next exercise.

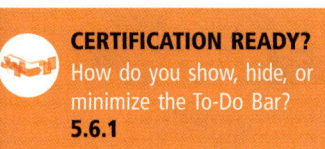

CERTIFICATION READY?
How do you show, hide, or minimize the To-Do Bar?
5.6.1

In the previous exercise, you hid, minimized, and expanded the To-Do Bar. In the next exercise, you will customize the To-Do Bar for your use.

Customizing the To-Do Bar

You can select the elements to include on the new To-Do Bar.

The To-Do Bar summarizes the current Outlook items that need some follow-up. With a single glance, you can see your appointments, tasks, and email messages that require some action.

CUSTOMIZE THE TO-DO BAR

GET READY. Before you begin these steps, be sure that Microsoft Outlook is running.

1. If necessary, click the **Mail** button in the Navigation pane to display the Mail folder and verify that the To-Do Bar is displayed.
2. Click the **View** menu, point to **To-Do Bar**, and select **Options**. The To-Do Bar Options dialog box is displayed, as shown in Figure 1-18.

Figure 1-18

To-Do Bar Options dialog box

 **ANOTHER WAY**

You can also show or hide the To-Do Bar by opening the View menu and selecting the To-Do Bar.

3. Examine the options. The checkmark indicates that the element is currently displayed. The numbers indicate the number of months you want to display in the Date Navigator and the number of appointments to be displayed.
4. Click the **Show Task List** checkbox and click the **OK** button. The dialog box closes and the Task List is removed from the To-Do Bar.
5. Click the **View** menu, point to **To-Do Bar**, and select the **Task List** option. The Task List is displayed on the To-Do Bar.

   PAUSE. CLOSE outlook.

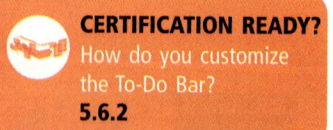

CERTIFICATION READY?
How do you customize the To-Do Bar?
5.6.2

In the previous exercise, you customized the To-Do Bar by selecting the elements to be displayed. The following table describes the elements in the To-Do Bar so you can decide which elements you want to use.

TO-DO BAR ELEMENT	DESCRIPTION
Appointments	The Appointments element displays appointments scheduled in Outlook. You can select the number of appointments to be displayed.
Date Navigator	The Date Navigator displays a small calendar. You can select the number of months to be displayed.
Task Input Panel	Key new tasks into the Task Input Panel.
Task list	The task list displays the tasks that have been assigned to you.

SUMMARY SKILL MATRIX

IN THIS LESSON YOU LEARNED HOW TO:
Use the On-Screen Tools
Change Outlook's View
Work with the Reading Pane
View, Hide, and Minimize the To-Do Bar
Customize the To-Do Bar

Knowledge Assessment

Matching

Match the term with its definition.

- **a.** desktop shortcut
- **b.** folder
- **c.** item
- **d.** launch
- **e.** Reading pane
- **f.** maximize
- **g.** minimize
- **h.** Navigation pane
- **i.** Title bar
- **j.** To-Do Bar

____C____ 1. A record stored in Outlook

____G____ 2. Reduce the size of a pane or window

____J____ 3. New feature that summarizes information about appointments and tasks

____D____ 4. Start running an application

____B____ 5. Common name for Outlook components

____F____ 6. Restore a minimized pane or window

____H____ 7. Provides access to the Outlook components, such as the Contacts and Calendar

____E____ 8. Displays the text of a selected email message

____I____ 9. Identifies the application and the active component

____A____ 10. An icon placed on the Windows desktop that launches an application, opens a folder, or opens a file

True/False

Circle T if the statement is true or F if the statement is false.

T F 1. Items such as messages, appointments, contacts, tasks, and notes are stored as records in Outlook.

T F 2. The To-Do Bar is a new feature in Outlook 2007.

T **F** 3. Select a component from the Go menu to minimize the component.

T **F** 4. The Status bar identifies the application and the active component.

T F 5. In Outlook, messages, appointments, contacts, tasks, and notes are called items.

T **F** 6. The Viewing pane displays the text of a selected email message.

T F 7. The Calendar folder contains an appointment book.

T F 8. The Reading pane can be hidden.
T F 9. In the To-Do Bar, you can see your appointments, tasks, and email messages that require some action.
T F 10. The Date Navigator in the To-Do Bar can only display one month.

■ Competency Assessment

Project 1-1: View the Outlook Menus

Become familiar with the Outlook menus.

GET READY. Before you begin these steps, be sure that Microsoft Outlook is running.

1. If necessary, click the **Mail** button in the Navigation pane to display the Mail folder and verify that the To-Do Bar is displayed.
2. Click the **File** menu. Point to each option in the File menu.
3. Click the **Edit** menu. Point to each option in the Edit menu.
4. Click the **View** menu. Point to each option in the View menu.
5. Click the **Go** menu. Point to each option in the Go menu.
6. Click the **Tools** menu. Point to each option in the Tools menu.
7. Click the **Actions** menu. Point to each option in the Actions menu.
8. Click the **Help** menu. Point to each option in the Help menu.

   LEAVE Outlook open for the next project.

Project 1-2: Use the Folder List

Use the Folder List to display the Outlook folders.

1. Click the **Folder List** button in the Navigation pane. The Folder List is displayed in the upper area of the Navigation pane.
2. Click the **Calendar** folder in the Folder List. The Calendar is displayed.
3. Click the **Contacts** folder in the Folder List. The Contacts folder is displayed.
4. Click the **Folder List** button again. Click the **Deleted Items** folder in the Folder List. The Deleted Items folder is displayed. Any deleted Outlook items are stored here until this folder is emptied.
5. Right-click the **Deleted Items** folder in the Folder List. Note the Empty "Deleted Items" Folder option. Selecting this option permanently deletes these items.
6. Click the **Inbox** folder in the Folder List. By default, the Inbox folder contains any email messages you have received.
7. Click the **Notes** folder in the Folder List. The Notes folder is displayed.
8. Click the **Tasks** folder in the Folder List. The Tasks folder is displayed.
9. Click the **Mail** button in the Navigation pane to return to Outlook's default view.

   LEAVE Outlook open for the next project.

■ Proficiency Assessment

Project 1-3: Use Keyboard Shortcuts to View Outlook Folders

The main Outlook folders can be accessed by keyboard shortcuts. Use the shortcuts to display the folders.

Getting to Know Outlook | 939

1. Identify the keyboard shortcuts used to display the Mail, Calendar, Contacts, Tasks, Notes, and Folder List components.
2. Use the keyboard shortcuts to display the Outlook components.
   LEAVE Outlook open for the next project.

Project 1-4: Customize the To-Do Bar

Change the number of months and appointments displayed in the To-Do Bar.

1. If necessary, click the **Mail** button in the Navigation pane to display the Mail folder and verify that the To-Do Bar is displayed.
2. Display the options for Outlook's To-Do Bar.
3. Change the options to display two months and five appointments.
4. Return to the main Outlook window to see the changes in the To-Do Bar.
5. Display the options for Outlook's To-Do Bar again.
6. Change the options to the default values to display one month and three appointments.
7. Return to the main Outlook window to see the changes in the To-Do Bar.
   LEAVE Outlook open for the next project.

■ Mastery Assessment

Project 1-5: Identify the New Features in Outlook 2007

The To-Do Bar discussed in this lesson is only one of many new features in Outlook 2007.

1. Use Microsoft Office Outlook Help to investigate the new features in Outlook 2007.
2. Identify the new features that could affect how you use Outlook 2007.
   LEAVE Outlook open for the next project.

Project 1-6: Customize the Outlook Window

The panes inside the Outlook window can be resized like the panes in most Microsoft Office products.

1. If necessary, click the **Mail** button in the Navigation pane to display the Mail folder and verify that the To-Do Bar is displayed.
2. Using the mouse, hover over a border between two panes. When the pointer icon changes, drag the border to resize the pane.
3. Adjust the size of all the panes.
4. Close Outlook. Launch Outlook. The resized panes should be displayed.
   CLOSE Outlook.

> **INTERNET READY**
>
> **U**nfortunately, you might not be the only user on your computer. You might share your computer with a coworker at the office or a family member at home. How can you keep your email private without requiring passwords or a series of arcane gestures and dance steps? Create an email profile. Use the Internet or Microsoft Office Outlook Help to investigate the benefits and limitations of an email profile.

2 Email Basics

LESSON SKILL MATRIX

Sending a Message — 943	Students will learn how to send a message.
Resending a Message — 944	Students will learn how to resend a message.
Saving a Copy of a Sent Message in a Different Location — 946	Students will learn how to save a copy of a sent message in a different location.
Automatically Previewing Messages — 947	Students will learn how to automatically preview messages.
Sending a Reply to a Message — 948	Students will learn how to send a reply to a message.
Forwarding a Message — 949	Students will learn how to forward a message.
Attaching a File to a Message — 951	Students will learn how to attach a file to a message.
Previewing an Attachment in Outlook — 952	Students will learn how to preview an attachment in Outlook.
Saving an Attachment to a Specific Location — 953	Students will learn how to save an attachment to a specific location.
Opening an Attachment — 954	Students will learn how to open an attachment.
Creating a Personal Signature — 956	Students will learn how to create a personal signature.
Adding a Signature to a Single Message — 958	Students will learn how to add a signature to a single message.
Adding a Signature to All Outgoing Messages — 959	Students will learn how to add a signature to all outgoing messages.
Creating an Internal Out of Office Message — 959	Students will learn how to create an internal out of office message.
Creating an External Out of Office Message — 960	Students will learn how to create an external out of office message.

KEY TERMS
attachment
AutoComplete
AutoPreview
signature
subject

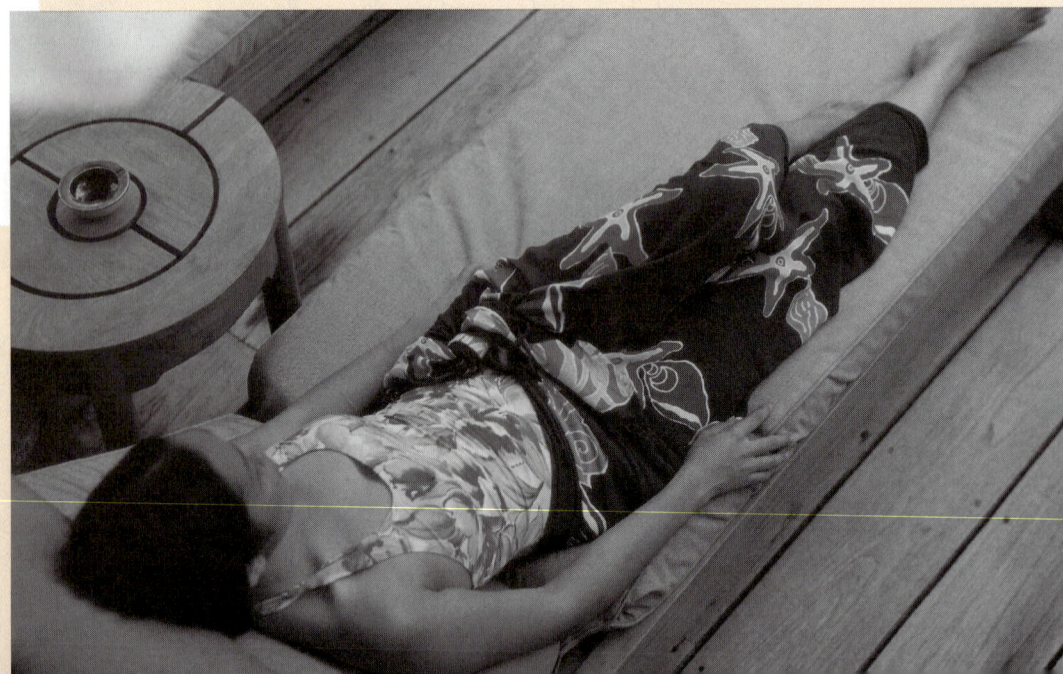

Email Basics

Mindy Martin and Jon Morris own and operate Adventure Works, a luxury resort in Ohio. They stay busy throughout the day. Frequently, they work different shifts to stay on top of the activities that occur at different times of the day. Sometimes, they rely on email to keep each other informed.

SOFTWARE ORIENTATION

Microsoft Outlook's Message Window

Email is the most frequently used Outlook component. The message window, shown in Figure 2-1, is familiar to every Outlook user.

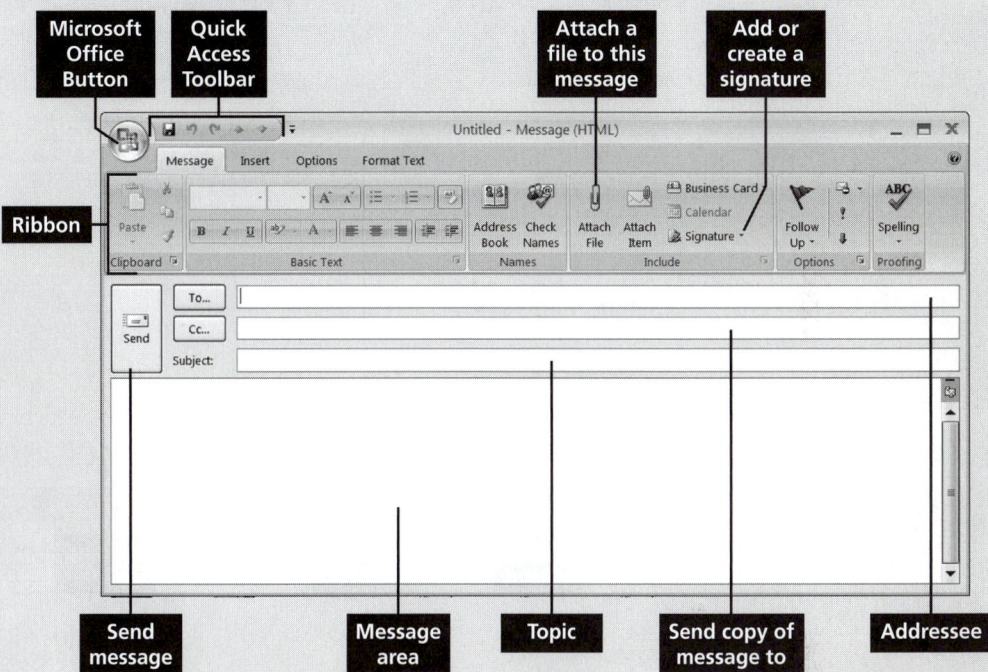

Figure 2-1
Outlook's Message window

Many of the elements in the Message window are familiar to you if you use Microsoft Word 2007. The editor used to create messages in Outlook is based on Microsoft Word 2007. Your screen may vary if default settings have been changed or if other preferences have been set. Use this figure as a reference throughout this lesson as well as the rest of this book.

Creating and Sending Messages

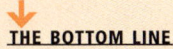
THE BOTTOM LINE

Creating and sending messages are the most common user activities in Outlook. Sending an email message is easier than addressing and mailing a letter. An email message can be sent to one or more recipients, resent if necessary, and saved for future reference.

Composing a Message

Microsoft Outlook's email component is a full-featured composition tool that provides many of the same functions found in Microsoft Word.

Keying, copying, cutting, and deleting text in an Outlook message are identical to these same functions in Microsoft Word 2007. Formatting and spellchecking text also are similar.

COMPOSE A MESSAGE

GET READY. Before you begin these steps, be sure to launch Microsoft Outlook.

1. If necessary, click the **Mail** button in the Navigation pane to display the Mail folder, as shown in Figure 2-2.

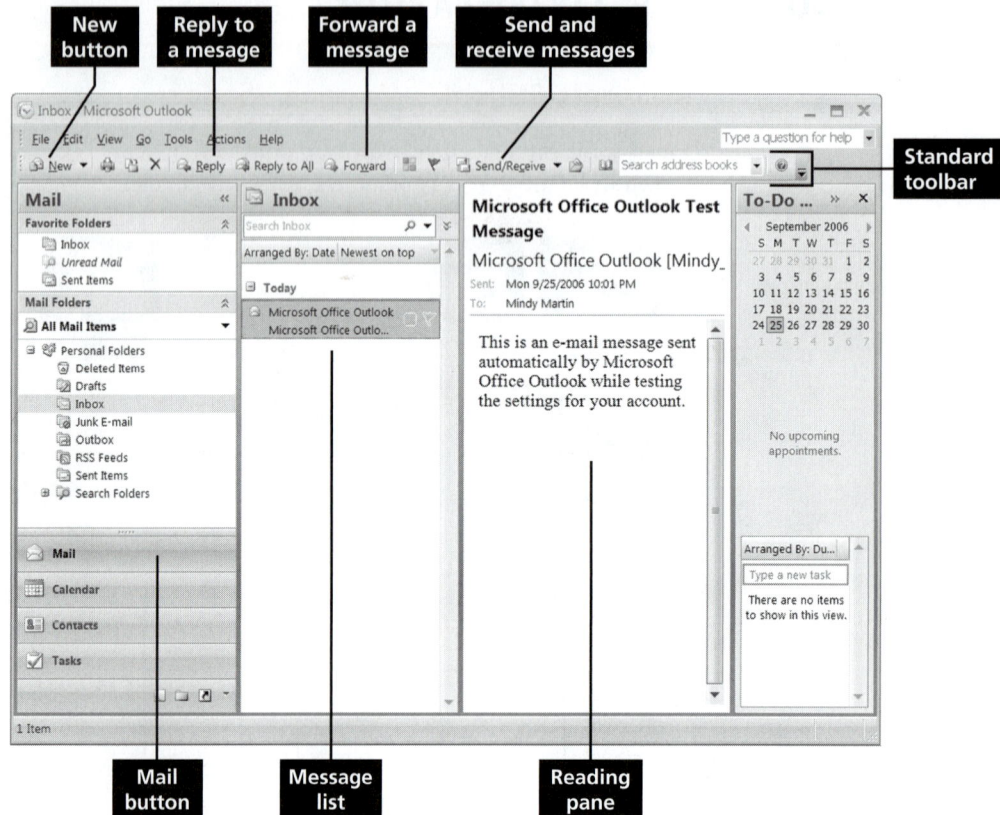

Figure 2-2

Outlook's opening screen

2. Click the **New** button in the Standard toolbar. The Message window is displayed.
3. Click the message area.
4. Key today's date in month–day–year format. For example, key **September 7, 2006**. As you begin to key the name of the month, Outlook will display the name of the month. Press **Enter** to accept the suggested month or continue keying the letters to ignore the suggestion. This is the **AutoComplete** function. It helps you quickly enter the names of the months and days of the week. AutoComplete cannot be turned off.
5. Press **Enter** twice to move to the next line and add a blank line.
6. Key **Hi Jon**, and press **Enter**. Press **Enter** again to add a blank line.
7. Key **Blue Yonder Airlines is running a contest in January. The winner gets free round-trip airfare to Cincinnati. Terry Crayton, a marketing assistant at Blue Yonder, asked if we would be interested in offering a free weekend at Adventure Works as part of the prize. What do you think?**
8. Press **Enter** twice to end the paragraph and insert a blank line.
9. Key **Let me know**, and press **Enter**.
10. Key your name, and press **Enter**.

   PAUSE. LEAVE the message open to use in the next exercise.

Regardless of the tool you use, the task of writing a message is the same. In normal business correspondence, you would be more formal in addressing the correspondence. However, this example is just a quick note between the partners at Adventure Works.

Sending a Message

Addressing an email message is similar to addressing a letter. In seconds, you can send an email message to one or more recipients.

SEND A MESSAGE

USE the message you created in the previous exercise.

1. Click the **To** field. Key **someone@example.com** or key the email address of a friend or coworker. To send the message to more than one recipient, key a semicolon (;), and then key another email address.
2. Click the **Subject** field. Key **Blue Yonder Airlines contest**, as shown in Figure 2-3.

Figure 2-3

Message ready to be sent

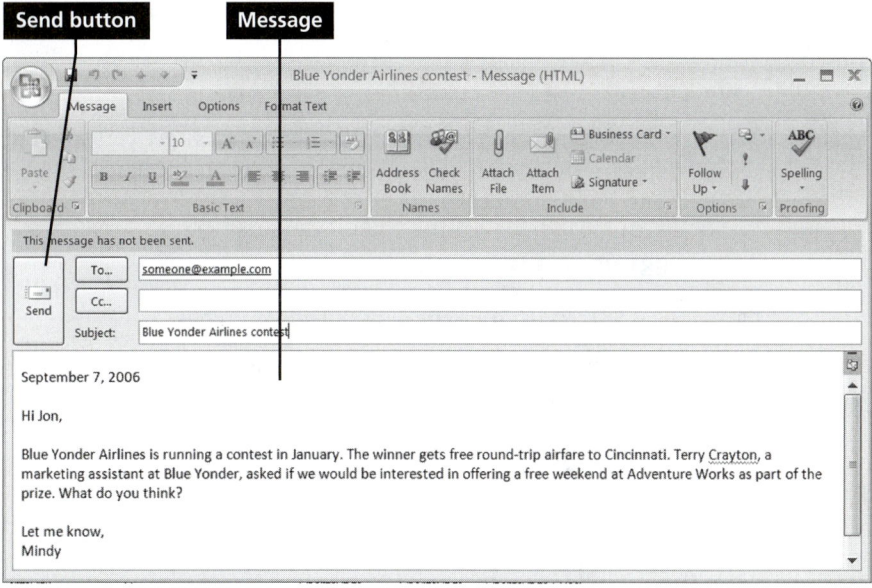

TROUBLESHOOTING

Someone@example.com is an address owned by Microsoft Corporation. Because this is not a real email address, you will receive an error message or a message thanking you for using Microsoft products.

3. Click the **Send** button. The Message window closes, and the message is moved to the Outbox. If your computer is connected to the Internet, the message is sent to the addressee. If your computer is not connected to the Internet, the message will remain in the Outbox until an Internet connection is made and the message can be sent.

PAUSE. LEAVE Outlook open to use in the next exercise.

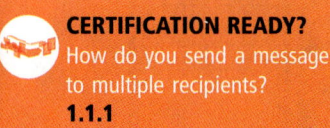

CERTIFICATION READY?
How do you send a message to multiple recipients?
1.1.1

In the previous exercise, you used the Message window to compose and send an email message. The To, Cc, Subject, and message area are elements found in Microsoft Outlook. The Ribbon, the Microsoft Office Button, and the Quick Access Toolbar, shown in Figure 2-1.

The following table describes the function of each element in the Message window.

ELEMENT	DESCRIPTION
Cc	The Cc field is optional. You can send a message without entering anything in the Cc field. Generally, you would use this to send a copy of the message to individuals who you think should be informed about the message content, but you don't expect the person receiving a copy to take any action.
Message area	Key the content of the message in the message area.
Subject	Key a brief description of the information in the message. The **Subject** tells the recipient what the message is about and makes it easier to find the message later.
To	Key the name or email address of the person or people who will receive the message you are sending. To send the message to several addressees, key a semicolon after a name before adding the next addressee.

Resending a Message

Occasionally, you may want to resend a message. Perhaps you want to send the same message to additional recipients or the recipient has accidentally deleted the message and needs another copy.

RESEND A MESSAGE

USE the message you sent in the previous exercise.

1. In the Navigation pane, click the **Sent Items** folder. The email messages you sent will be listed as items in the Sent Items folder, as shown in Figure 2-4.

Figure 2-4

Sent Items folder

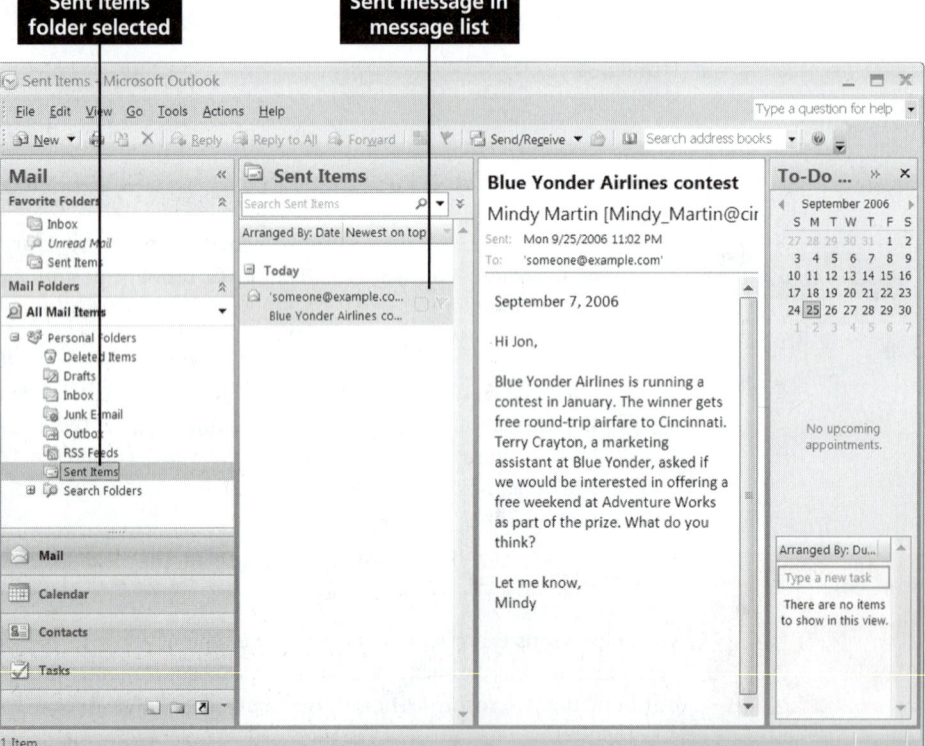

Email Basics | 945

TROUBLESHOOTING If your computer has not been connected to the Internet since you started this lesson, the messages you sent will still be in the Outbox. Outgoing messages are moved to the Outbox when you click the Send button. They are moved to the Sent Items folder when you connect to the Internet and the messages are sent.

2. In the list of items that have been sent, double-click the message you sent in the last exercise. The message is displayed in a new window, as shown in Figure 2-5. The title bar of the new window is the subject of the message.

Figure 2-5

Sent message

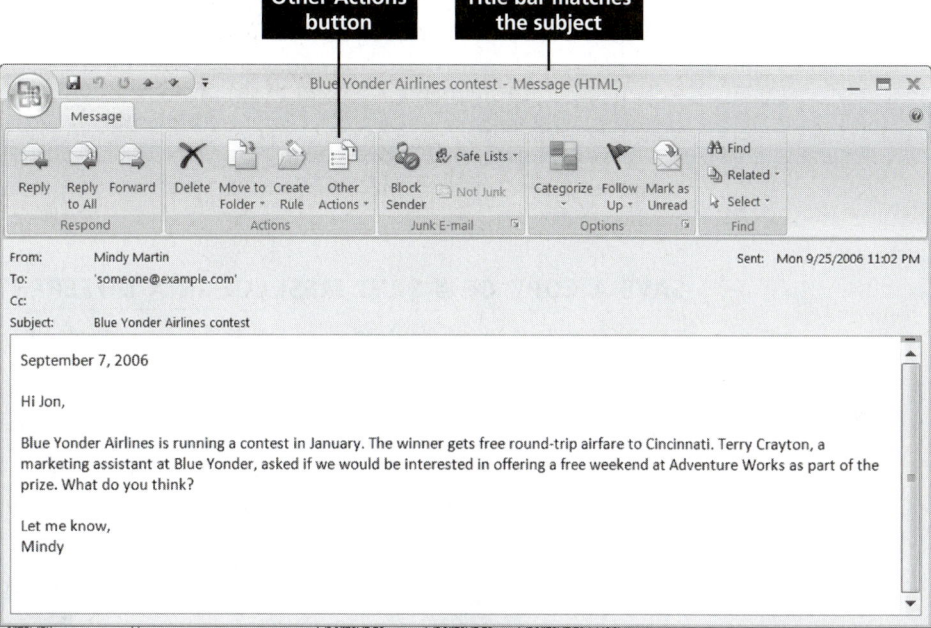

3. Click the **Other Actions** button in the Actions group on the Ribbon. Select the **Resend This Message** option. This opens the message in a new window. It enables you to key additional addresses and edit the content of the message.

4. Click after the addressee in the To field. Key a semicolon (;) and an additional email address, as shown in Figure 2-6. For this exercise, use your email address as the addressee.

Figure 2-6

Message ready to be resent

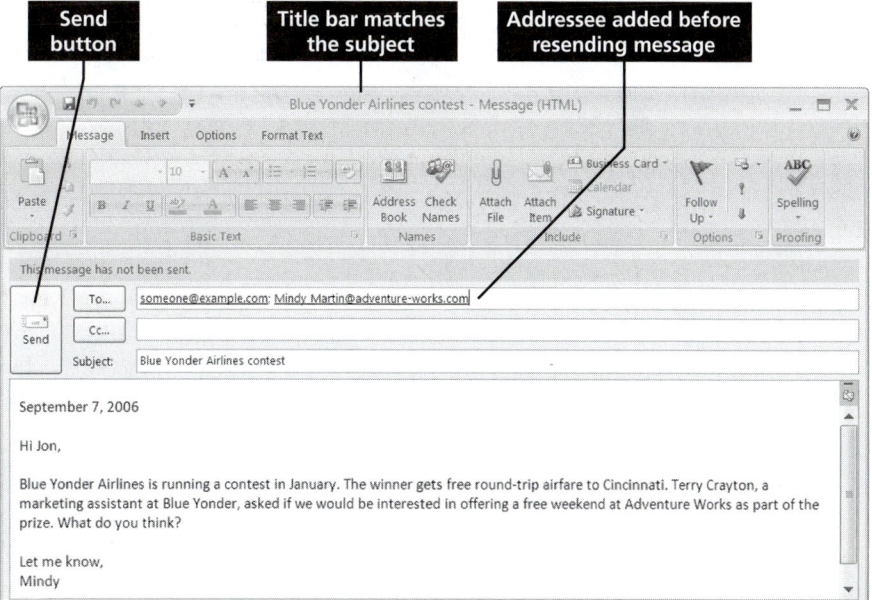

946 | Lesson 2

CERTIFICATION READY?
How do you resend a message?
1.1.3

5. Click the **Send** button. The Message window closes, and the message is moved to the Outbox. The message is sent when your computer is connected to the Internet.
6. Close the Message window that was displayed when you double-clicked the sent item.
7. In the Navigation pane, click the **Inbox** folder. The Inbox is displayed.

   PAUSE. LEAVE Outlook open to use in the next exercise.

In the previous exercise, you resent a message. When you resend a message, you can delete the original addressee, add new addressees, and edit the message content.

Saving a Copy of a Sent Message in a Different Location

By default, sent messages are saved in the Sent Items folder. You might want to save a copy of a message in a different location. For example, you can keep messages about a specific project in a different folder. Or, you can keep correspondence with a specific individual in a separate folder. Organizing your messages can help you stay on top of a hectic day.

➔ SAVE A COPY OF A SENT MESSAGE IN A DIFFERENT LOCATION

GET READY. Before you begin these steps, be sure to launch Microsoft Outlook.

1. Click the **New** button in the Standard toolbar. The Message window is displayed.
2. Click the **To** field. Key the email address of a friend or coworker.
3. Click the **Subject** field. Key **Different Save Location**.
4. Click the **Options** tab on the Ribbon, as shown in Figure 2-7.

Figure 2-7

New message to be saved in a different location

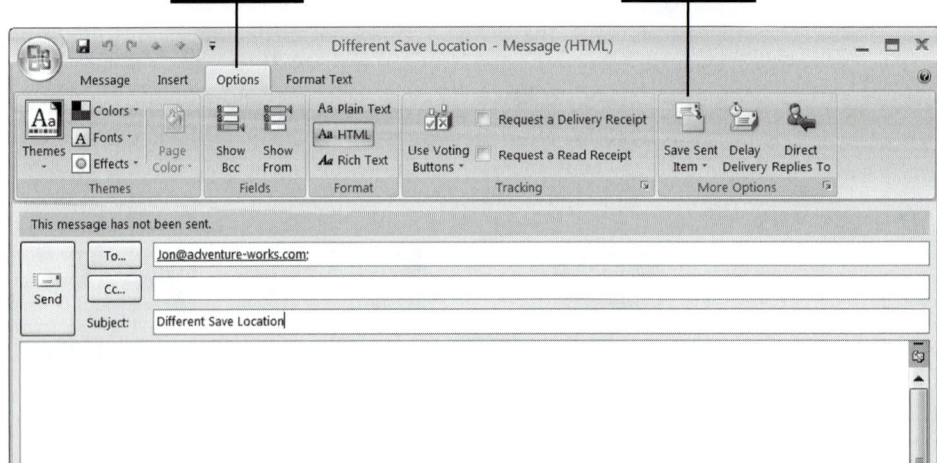

Email Basics | 947

5. Click the **Save Sent Item** button and select the **Other Folder** option. The Select Folder dialog box is displayed, as shown in Figure 2-8.

Figure 2-8

Select Folder dialog box

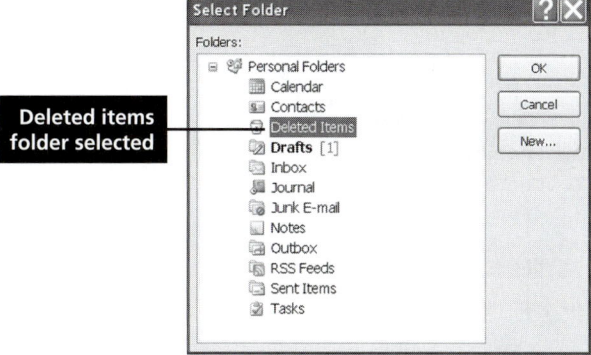

6. Select the **Deleted Items** folder, and click **OK** to close the dialog box.

TROUBLESHOOTING Normally, you will create a new folder or save the message to a folder you created earlier. That isn't necessary for this exercise.

You will learn more about creating and using folders in Lesson 3.

7. Click the **Send** button. The Message window closes, and the message is moved to the Outbox. The message is sent when your computer is connected to the Internet.
8. In the main Outlook window, click the **Deleted Items** folder in the Navigation pane. The message will be displayed in the Deleted Items folder when it has been sent.
9. Click the **Inbox** in the Navigation pane.

    PAUSE. LEAVE Outlook open to use in the next exercise.

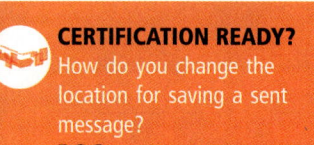
CERTIFICATION READY?
How do you change the location for saving a sent message?
5.3.3

Save sent messages in different folders determined by the message content or addressee. Later, you will learn to create rules that automatically move messages to different folders.

Reading and Replying to Messages

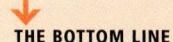
THE BOTTOM LINE When you receive an email message, you naturally want to read it and send a reply. Outlook enables you to preview and reply to a message with a few mouse clicks.

Automatically Previewing Messages

If you return to your desk after a meeting to find 20 messages in your Inbox and another meeting to attend in 5 minutes, it's impossible to read all the messages and still get to the meeting on time. Use **AutoPreview** to view the first three lines of every message in the message list.

AUTOMATICALLY PREVIEW MESSAGES

GET READY. Outlook must be running to turn on the AutoPreview option.

1. Click the **View** menu. Select the **AutoPreview** option. The first three lines of text in each message are displayed, as shown in Figure 2-9.

Figure 2-9

AutoPreview messages

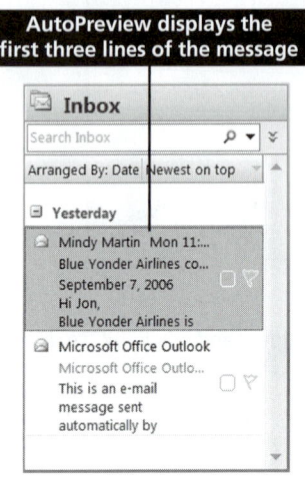

 **CERTIFICATION READY?**
How do you automatically preview messages?
1.7.2

2. Click the **View** menu. Select the **AutoPreview** option. This turns off the AutoPreview function.

   PAUSE. LEAVE Outlook open to use in the next exercise.

AutoPreview requires more space in the message list. Therefore, you probably want to turn off the feature most of the time.

Sending a Reply to a Message

Every message doesn't require a reply, but many messages need a response of some type. When you use the Reply function, your response is automatically addressed to the person who sent the message to you.

 SEND A REPLY TO A MESSAGE

USE the message you received when you sent a message to yourself in a previous exercise.

1. In the Inbox, click the message with the subject "Blue Yonder Airlines contest." The message is selected.

TAKE NOTE* If you click the Reply to All button on the Standard toolbar, the reply will be sent to the sender and everyone who received the original message.

2. Click the **Reply** button on the Standard toolbar. The message is displayed in a new window, as shown in Figure 2-10. Note that the To and Subject fields are already filled. In the Subject field, the text "RE:" was inserted before the original subject line. "RE:" tells the recipient that the message is a reply about the Blue Yonder Airlines contest topic. The original message is included at the bottom of the window. It is sent as part of the reply.

Figure 2-10

Reply to a message you received

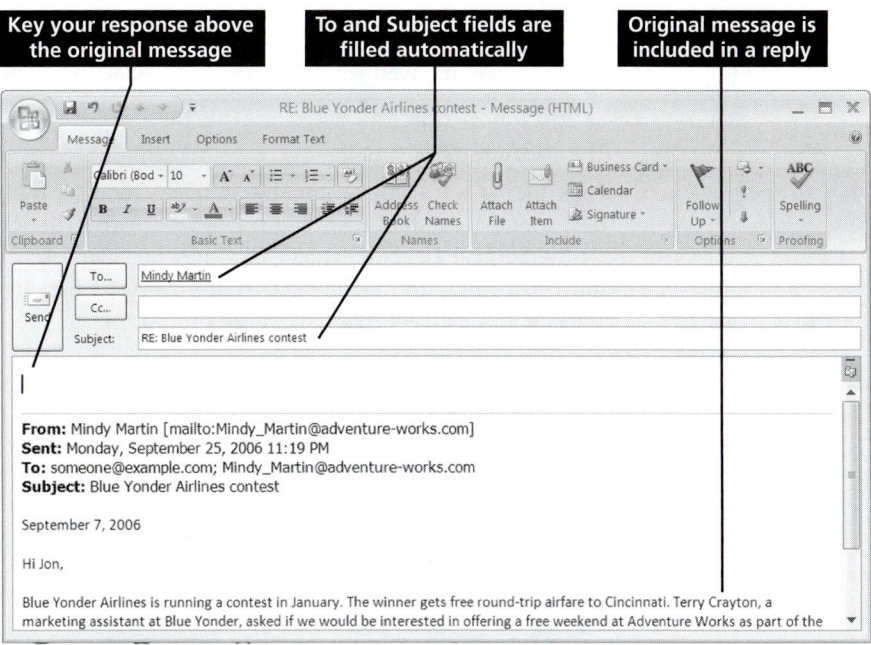

3. Key **The contest could be a good idea. Let's set up a meeting.**
4. Press **Enter**. Click the **Send** button. The Message window closes, and the reply is moved to the Outbox. The message is sent when your computer is connected to the Internet.

   PAUSE. LEAVE Outlook open to use in the next exercise.

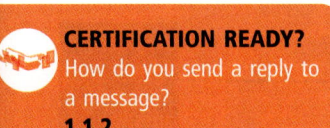

CERTIFICATION READY?
How do you send a reply to a message?
1.1.2

When a reply has been sent, the icon next to the original message is changed. An arrow pointing left, as shown in Figure 2-11, indicates that you replied to the message. When you view the main Outlook window, this icon tells you which messages you have answered.

Figure 2-11

Icon indicates a reply was sent

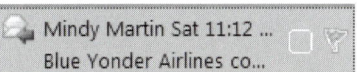

■ Forwarding a Message

THE BOTTOM LINE

Outlook enables you to forward a message you received to another person or several people.

Occasionally, you receive a message that should be sent to additional people. Outlook's Forward function is a quick method of sending the message to additional people without re-creating the original message.

FORWARD A MESSAGE

USE the message you received when you sent a message to yourself in a previous exercise.

1. In the Inbox, click the message with the subject "Blue Yonder Airlines contest." The message is selected.
2. Click the **Forward** button on the Standard toolbar. The message is displayed in a new window, as shown in Figure 2-12. Note that the Subject field is already filled. In the Subject field, the text "FW:" has been inserted before the original subject line. "FW:" tells the recipient that the message has been forwarded by the sender. The original message is included at the bottom of the window.

Figure 2-12

Forward a message you received

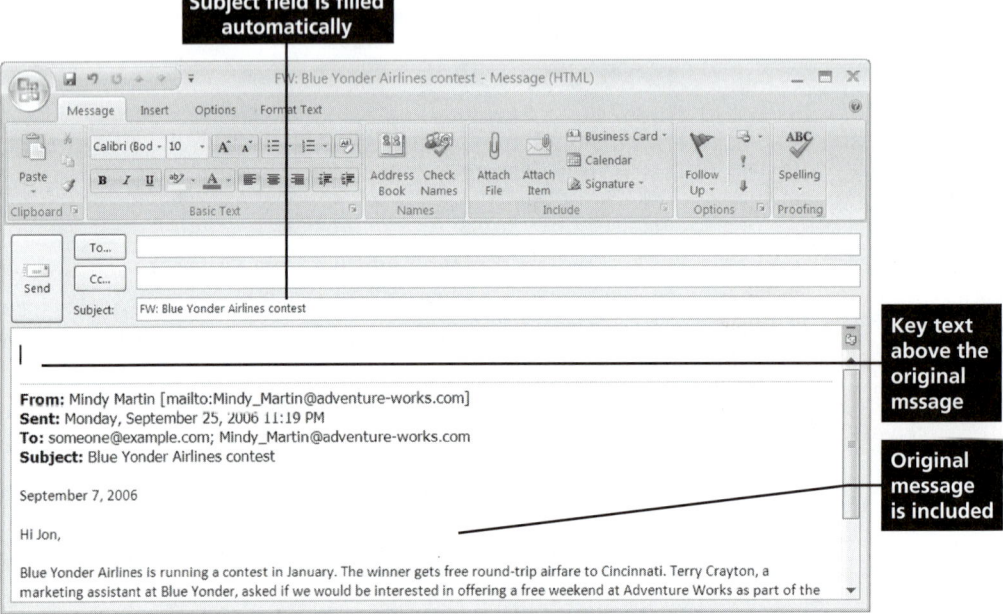

3. In the To field, key **someone@example.com**.
4. Click the message area above the original message. Key **What is the value of the airfare and weekend at Adventure Works?**
5. Press **Enter**. Key your name.
6. Click the **Send** button. The Message window closes, and the message is moved to the Outbox. The message is sent when your computer is connected to the Internet.

   PAUSE. LEAVE Outlook open to use in the next exercise.

CERTIFICATION READY?
How do you forward a message?
1.1.4

When a message has been forwarded, the icon next to the original message is changed. An arrow pointing right, as shown in Figure 2-13, indicates that you forwarded the message.

Figure 2-13

Icon indicates the message was forwarded

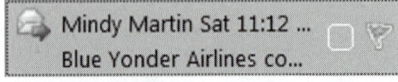

Working with Attachments

THE BOTTOM LINE — *Attachments* are files sent as part of an email message. An attachment is a convenient way to send pictures, spreadsheets, and other types of files.

Attaching a File to a Message

Do you need to submit a five-page report to your supervisor at the home office? Perhaps you have a new product brochure to distribute to all the sales representatives, or you want to share a picture of your new puppy with a friend. Attach the file to an email message and send it.

→ **ATTACH A FILE TO A MESSAGE**

GET READY. Outlook must be running.

1. Click the **New** button on the Standard toolbar. A new Message window is displayed.
2. In the To field, key your email address. You will send this message to yourself so you can use the attachment in the following exercises.
3. In the Subject field, key **Stained glass window attached**.
4. Click the message area. Key **Hi Josh,** and press [Enter] twice.
5. Key the following note: **I attached a picture of the stained glass window that was broken yesterday. We can't accept reservations for the suite until the window is replaced, so we need a new window as soon as possible. Please provide an estimated completion date and price**. Press [Enter] twice.
6. Key **Thanks**, and press [Enter].
7. Key your name.
8. Click the **Attach File** button on the Ribbon, shown previously in Figure 2-1. The Insert File dialog box is displayed.
9. Navigate to the data files for this lesson. Click the **Window** file, and click the **Insert** button. The Insert dialog box is closed, and the Window file is listed in the Attached field, as shown in Figure 2-14.

CD — The *Window* image file is available on the companion CD-ROM.

Figure 2-14

Sending an attachment

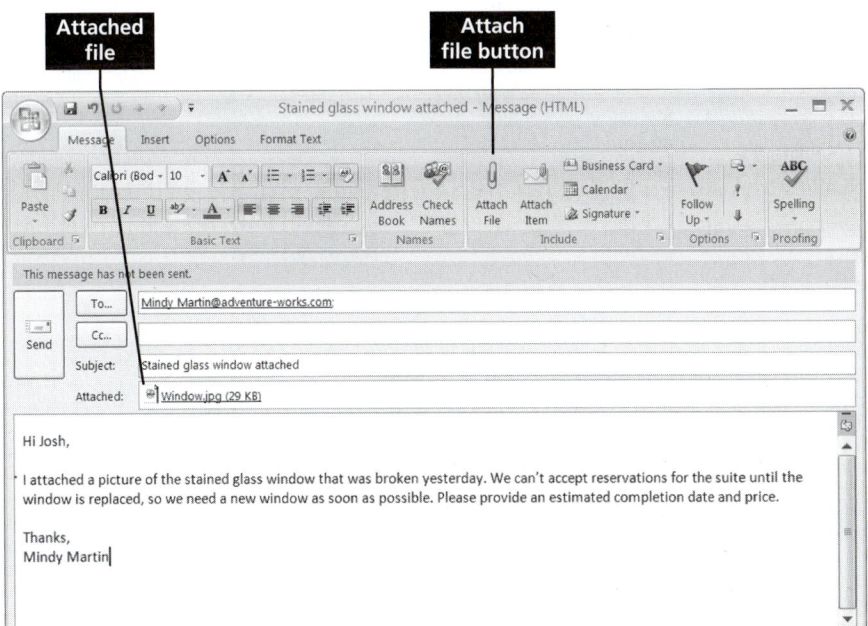

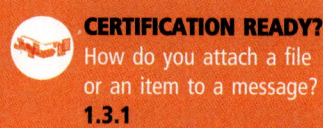

CERTIFICATION READY?
How do you attach a file or an item to a message?
1.3.1

10. Click the **Send** button. The Message window closes, and the message is moved to the Outbox. The message is sent when your computer is connected to the Internet.
    PAUSE. LEAVE Outlook open to use in the next exercise.

An attachment can be a file or an Outlook item, such as a contact, a note, or a task. When you attach a file to a message, the filename, size, and an icon representing the file are displayed in the Attached field. If you attach more than one file, the files are listed separately in the Attached field.

To attach an Outlook item, click the Attach Item button on the Ribbon. The Insert Item dialog box is displayed. In the Look In list, select the Outlook folder containing the item. In the Items list, click the Outlook item to be attached and click OK. The Insert Item dialog box is closed, and the item is listed in the Attached field of the email message.

Previewing an Attachment in Outlook

Outlook's new Attachment Previewer enables you to view attachments in the Reading pane. Without the need to save and open an attachment, you can make critical decisions quickly and efficiently.

Note: For some types of files, you may be asked if you want to preview the file before the attachment is displayed.

→ PREVIEW AN ATTACHMENT

USE the message with the attachment you received when you sent a message to yourself in the previous exercise.

1. If the message with the Window attachment has not arrived yet, click the **Send/Receive** button on the Standard toolbar to check for new messages. The paper clip icon with the message, as shown in Figure 2-15, indicates that the message has an attachment.

Figure 2-15

Message with attachment received

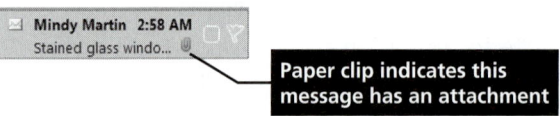

2. Click the message. The message is displayed in the Reading pane, as shown in Figure 2-16.

Figure 2-16

Reading pane containing the message with an attachment

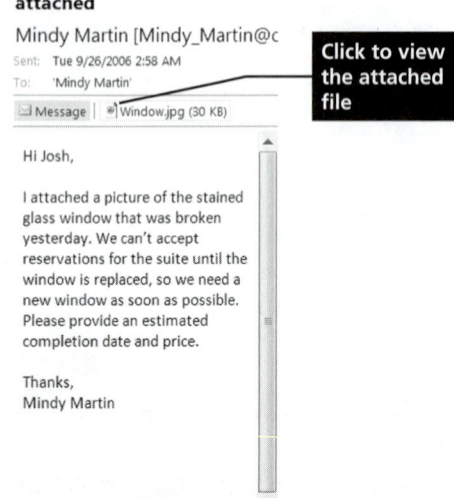

3. In the Reading pane, click the attachment's filename. The attachment is displayed in the Reading pane, as shown in Figure 2-17. For some types of files, you may be asked if you want to preview the file before the attachment is displayed.

Figure 2-17

Attachment displayed in the Reading pane

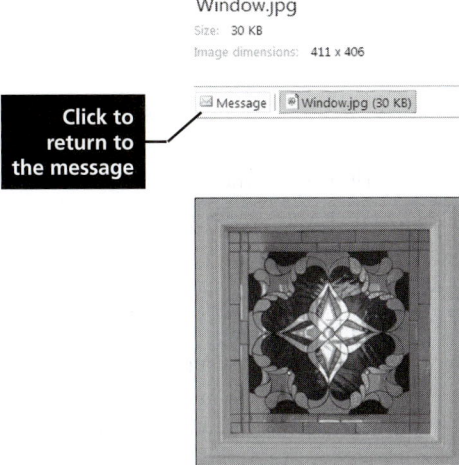

For your protection, all scripts, macros, and ActiveX controls are disabled in a previewed document.

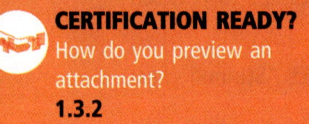

CERTIFICATION READY?
How do you preview an attachment?
1.3.2

4. In the Reading pane, click the Message icon to close the preview and display the message.

    PAUSE. LEAVE Outlook open to use in the next exercise.

Outlook comes with several previewers. Additional previewers are available through Microsoft's Web site.

Saving an Attachment to a Specific Location

Attachments can be saved before or after previewing the attachment. Attachments can be saved from the message list, from the Reading pane, and from an open message. In the following three exercises, you will save an attachment from each location.

SAVE AN ATTACHMENT FROM THE MESSAGE LIST

USE the message with the attachment you received when you sent a message to yourself in a previous exercise.

1. In the message list, click the message with the subject "Stained glass window attached," if necessary.
2. Click the **File** menu, point to **Save Attachments**, and select **Window.jpg**. The Save Attachment dialog box is displayed. By default, the My Documents folder is displayed.
3. Create a new folder named **Outlook Solutions Lesson 02** in the My Documents folder.
4. In the File name field, change the name of the file to *Window from message list*. Click the **Save** button.

    PAUSE. LEAVE Outlook open to use in the next exercise.

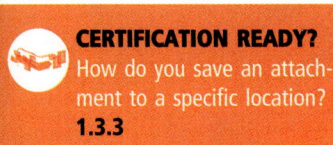

CERTIFICATION READY?
How do you save an attachment to a specific location?
1.3.3

In the previous exercise, you created a folder and saved an attachment from the message list. In the next exercise, you will not create a new folder. You will save the attachment from the Reading pane.

SAVE AN ATTACHMENT FROM THE READING PANE

USE the message with the attachment you received when you sent a message to yourself in a previous exercise.

1. In the message list, click the message with the subject "Stained glass window attached," if necessary.
2. In the Reading pane, right-click the *Window.jpg* attachment.
3. Select *Save As* on the shortcut menu. The Save Attachments dialog box is displayed.
4. If necessary, navigate to the *Outlook Solutions Lesson 02* folder you created in the previous exercise.
5. In the File name field, change the name of the file to *Window from Reading pane*. Click the *Save* button.

   PAUSE. LEAVE Outlook open to use in the next exercise.

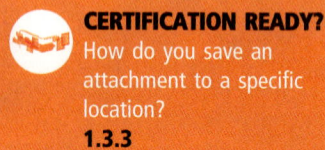

CERTIFICATION READY?
How do you save an attachment to a specific location?
1.3.3

In the previous exercise, you saved an attachment from the Reading pane to a folder you created earlier. In the next exercise, you will save an attachment from an open message.

SAVE AN ATTACHMENT FROM AN OPEN MESSAGE

USE the message with the attachment you received when you sent a message to yourself in a previous exercise.

1. In the message list, double-click the message with the subject "Stained glass window attached." The message is opened in a new window.
2. In the new window, right-click the *Window.jpg* attachment.
3. Select *Save As* on the shortcut menu. The Save Attachments dialog box is displayed.
4. If necessary, navigate to the *Outlook Solutions Lesson 02* folder you created in the previous exercise.
5. In the File name field, change the name of the file to *Window from open message*. Click the *Save* button.
6. Click the *Close* button in the upper-right corner of the open message window. The message is closed.

   PAUSE. LEAVE Outlook open to use in the next exercise.

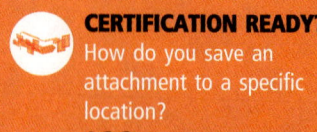

CERTIFICATION READY?
How do you save an attachment to a specific location?
1.3.3

In the previous exercise, you saved an attachment from an open message. Now you have saved an attachment from the message list, from the Reading pane, and from an open message.

Opening an Attachment

Just as you can save an attachment from the message list, the Reading pane, and an open message, you can also open an attachment from these locations. In the following three exercises, you will open an attachment from each location.

Email Basics | 955

OPEN AN ATTACHMENT FROM THE MESSAGE LIST

USE the message with the attachment you received when you sent a message to yourself in a previous exercise.

1. In the message list, right-click the message with the subject "Stained glass window attached," if necessary.
2. In the shortcut menu, click **View Attachments** and select **Window.jpg**. The Opening Mail Attachment dialog box is displayed, as shown in Figure 2-18.

TROUBLESHOOTING If you opened this type of attachment in the past, the Opening Mail Attachment dialog box may not be displayed.

Figure 2-18

Opening Mail Attachment dialog box

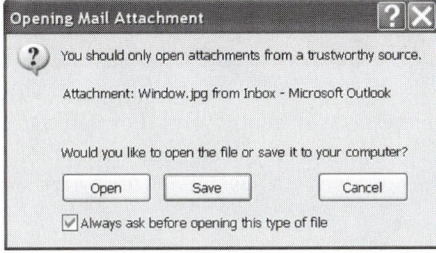

TROUBLESHOOTING It is safer to save an attachment and scan the file with an antivirus software program before opening an attachment. Do not open attachments from unknown sources.

CERTIFICATION READY?
How do you open a message attachment?
1.3.4

3. Click **Open**. The application designated to open .jpg files on your computer is used to open the application.
4. Close the Window file and exit the application used to open the file, if necessary.
   PAUSE. LEAVE Outlook open to use in the next exercise.

In the previous exercise, you opened an attachment from the message list. In the next exercise, you will open the attachment from the Reading pane.

OPEN AN ATTACHMENT FROM THE READING PANE

USE the message with the attachment you received when you sent a message to yourself in a previous exercise.

1. In the message list, click the message with the subject "Stained glass window attached," if necessary.
2. In the Reading pane, double-click the attachment. The Opening Mail Attachment dialog box is displayed. Refer to Figure 2-18.

CERTIFICATION READY?
How do you open a message attachment?
1.3.4

3. Click **Open**. The application designated to open .jpg files on your computer is used to open the application.
4. Close the Window file and exit the application used to open the file, if necessary.
   PAUSE. LEAVE Outlook open to use in the next exercise.

In the previous exercise, you opened an attachment from the Reading pane. In the next exercise, you will open the attachment from an open message.

OPEN AN ATTACHMENT FROM AN OPEN MESSAGE

USE the message with the attachment you received when you sent a message to yourself in a previous exercise.

1. In the message list, double-click the message with the subject "Stained glass window attached." The message is opened in a new window.

956 | Lesson 2

2. In the new window, right-click the **Window.jpg** attachment. Click **Open** on the shortcut menu. The Opening Mail Attachment dialog box is displayed. Refer to Figure 2-18.
3. Click **Open**. The application designated to open .jpg files on your computer is used to open the application.
4. Close the Window file and exit the application used to open the file, if necessary.

PAUSE. LEAVE Outlook open to use in the next exercise.

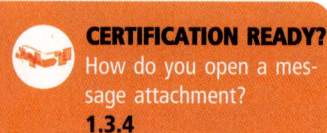

CERTIFICATION READY?
How do you open a message attachment?
1.3.4

In the previous exercise, you opened an attachment from an open message. Now you have opened an attachment from the message list, from the Reading pane, and from an open message.

■ Personalizing Messages

THE BOTTOM LINE

You can personalize your messages in many ways. Formatting, colors, and images probably come to mind first. However, the signature is one of the most useful places to personalize your messages.

Creating a Personal Signature

A *signature* is text or images that are automatically placed at the end of your outgoing messages. A signature can be as fancy or as plain as you like.

→ **CREATE A PERSONAL SIGNATURE**

GET READY. Outlook must be running to create a signature.

1. Click **New** on the Standard toolbar. A new message window is displayed. By default, the Message tab of the Ribbon is displayed.
2. In the Include group on the Ribbon, click **Signature** and select **Signatures**. The Signatures and Stationery dialog box is displayed, as shown in Figure 2-19.

Figure 2-19

Signatures and Stationery dialog box

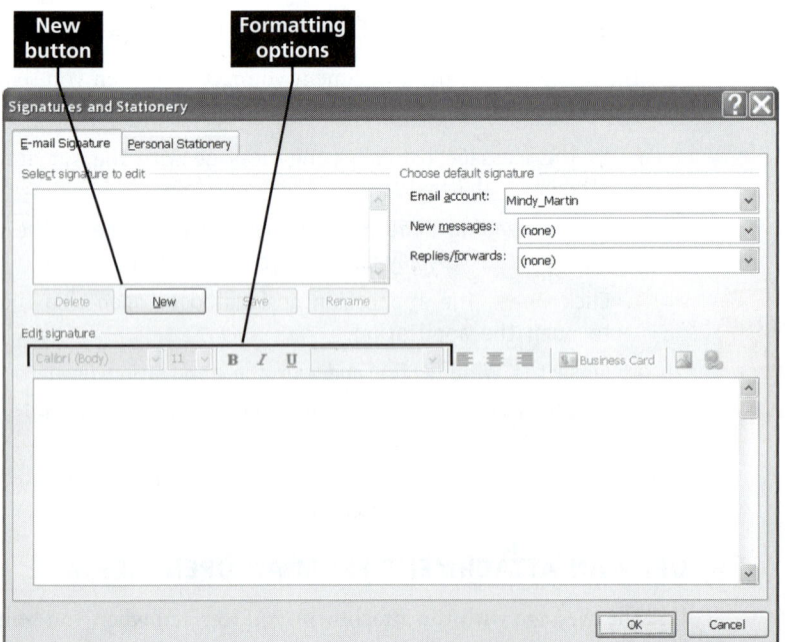

TAKE NOTE If you share your email account with other users or additional Outlook profiles have been created, signatures created by other users may be listed in the Signatures and Stationery dialog box.

3. Click the **New** button. The New Signature dialog box is displayed, as shown in Figure 2-20.

Figure 2-20
New Signature dialog box

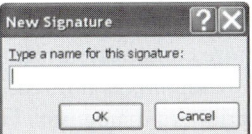

4. Key **Lesson 2** in the *Type a name for this signature* field and click **OK**. The New Signature dialog box is closed, and Lesson 2 is highlighted in the Select signature to edit list box.

5. Click in the empty **Edit signature** box. Any changes you make here are applied to the selected Lesson 2 signature. If additional signatures were listed, you could select a different signature and make changes to it.

6. Key your name and press **Enter**. Key your title and press **Enter**. Key your email address and press **Enter** twice. Key the name of your company and press **Enter**. Key the Web address of your company and press **Enter**. If you do not have a title, company, or company Web site, key the information that applies to you.

TROUBLESHOOTING If formatting has been applied to your email messages or other signatures, the same formatting might be applied to the signature as you key the text. You can change the formatting after you key the signature.

7. Select all the text in the signature. Select the **Ariel** font. Select the font size **10**. Select the color **Blue**.

8. Select your name. Click **Bold** and **Italic**. Change the font size to **12**, as shown in Figure 2-21.

Figure 2-21
New signature

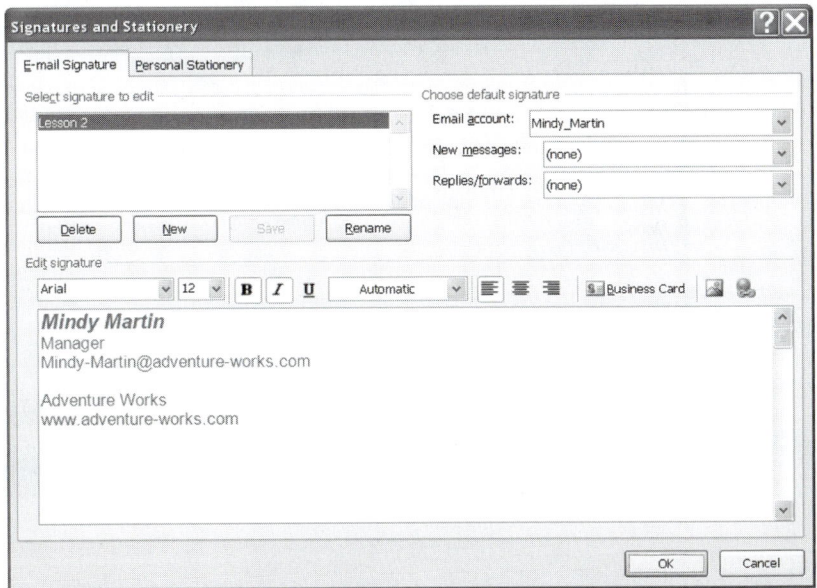

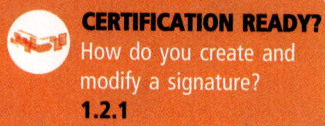

CERTIFICATION READY?
How do you create and modify a signature?
1.2.1

9. Verify that **(none)** is still selected in the New messages and Replies/forwards fields. Click **OK**. The dialog box is closed, and the signature is saved. Close the Message window.

   PAUSE. LEAVE Outlook open to use in the next exercise.

In the previous exercise, you created a simple signature that provides valuable information. It contains your name, title, email address, company name, and the company's Web address. You also may want to include your phone number, your department, and your company's mailing address in your signature.

Although you can include images and more complicated formatting, the formatting you can do in the Signatures and Stationery dialog box is limited. For example, you can't resize an image in the Signatures and Stationery dialog box. However, you can open a new message, use the formatting tools in the new Message window to create a signature you like, cut the signature, and paste it into the Signatures and Stationery dialog box as a new signature.

Adding a Signature to a Single Message

You can choose to add a signature to an individual message. This enables you to create and use more than one signature.

➔ ADD A SIGNATURE TO A SINGLE MESSAGE

GET READY. Outlook must be running to create a new message.

1. Click **New** on the Standard toolbar. A new message window is displayed.
2. In the message area, key **I'm testing my new signature**. Press **Enter** twice.
3. In the Include group on the Ribbon, click **Signature** and select **Lesson 2**. The signature is inserted into the message, as shown in Figure 2-22.

Figure 2-22

Message using new signature

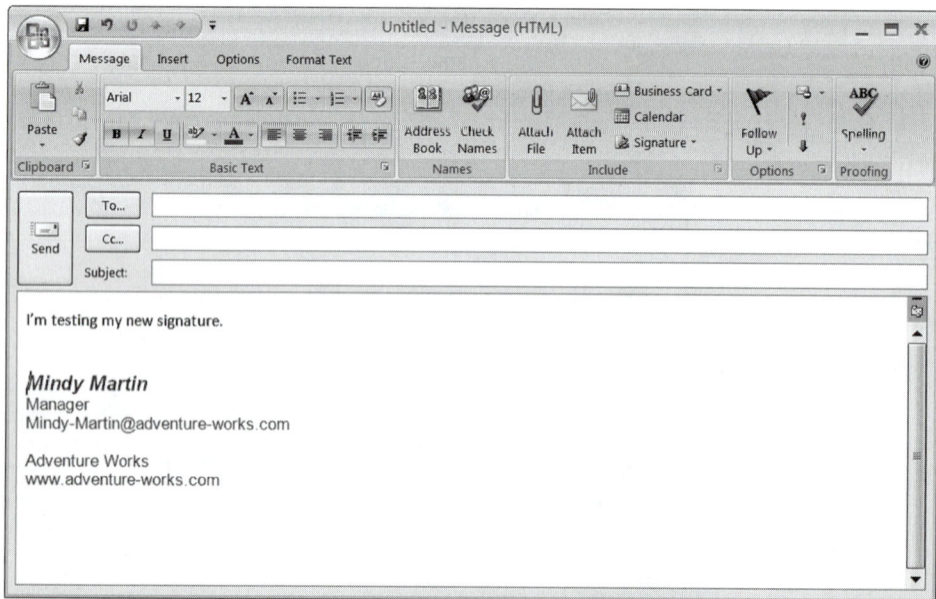

4. Click the **To** field and key your email address.
5. Click the **Subject** field and key *Testing signature in a single message*. Click the **Send** button.
6. If the message has not been received, click the **Send/Receive** button.
7. Click the message in the message list. Click the **File** menu and select the **Save As** option. The Save As dialog box is displayed.
8. Navigate to the **Outlook Solutions Lesson 02** folder and click the **Save** button. The message is saved as *Testing signature in a single message.htm*.

   PAUSE. LEAVE Outlook open to use in the next exercise.

In the previous exercise, you inserted your new signature into a single message. Create several signatures. This enables you to select the signature to match the message. When you send a personal message, use a signature that includes a picture from your favorite sport or a photo of your new puppy. When you send a business message, use a signature that includes your business information.

Adding a Signature to All Outgoing Messages

If you primarily use your email account for the same type of email (business or personal), you can select a signature that is automatically inserted into every outgoing message. This gives you a quick consistent way to insert your signature.

→ **ADD A SIGNATURE TO ALL OUTGOING MESSAGES**

GET READY. Outlook must be running to create a new message.

1. Click **New** on the Standard toolbar. A new message window is displayed.
2. In the Include group on the Ribbon, click **Signature** and select **Signatures**. The Signatures and Stationery dialog box is displayed.
3. In the New Messages field, select **Lesson 2**, if necessary. Click **OK**. The Lesson 2 signature will automatically be added to every outgoing message. Close the message window.

   PAUSE. LEAVE Outlook open to use in the next exercise.

Even if you use your email account to send business and personal messages, you can save time by automatically adding a signature. Half of the time, the automatic signature will be the correct one. When it isn't correct, delete it from the message and insert the correct signature.

■ Working with Automated Replies

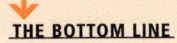
THE BOTTOM LINE When you're out of the office, you will still receive email messages. You can automatically send a reply informing the addressee that you are out of the office.

Creating an Internal Out of Office Message

If you use a Microsoft Exchange Server email account, you can use the improved Out of Office Assistant to send an automated message informing coworkers that you are out of the office.

CREATE AN INTERNAL OUT OF OFFICE MESSAGE

GET READY. You must use a Microsoft Exchange Server account to complete this exercise.

1. Click the **Tools** menu and select the **Out of Office Assistant** option. The Out of Office Assistant dialog box is displayed.
2. Click the **Send Out of Office auto-replies** option.
3. Click the **Only send during this time range** option. Select **12:00 AM** tomorrow as the Start time. Select **12:00 AM** the following day as the End time.
4. Click the **Inside My Organization** tab, if necessary. Key **I am out of the office today. I'll respond to your message tomorrow.**
5. Click **OK**. The dialog box is closed. The Out of Office message will be sent when you receive messages from other email accounts in your organization.

   PAUSE. LEAVE Outlook open to use in the next exercise.

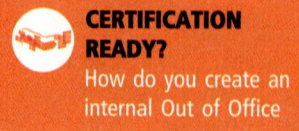

CERTIFICATION READY?
How do you create an internal Out of Office

Improvements to the Out of Office Assistant include additional formatting options, the ability to set the dates that you will be out of the office, and the ability to send an Out of Office message to correspondents outside of your organization.

In the previous exercise, you prepared a message to be sent as a reply to emails received from other members of your organization. In the next exercise, you will prepare an Out of Office message to be sent as a reply to messages sent by email accounts outside your organization.

Creating an External Out of Office Message

If you use a Microsoft Exchange Server email account, you can use the improved Out of Office Assistant to send an automated message informing people outside your organization that you are out of the office.

 CREATE AN EXTERNAL OUT OF OFFICE MESSAGE

GET READY. You must use a Microsoft Exchange Server account to complete this exercise.

1. Click the **Tools** menu and select the **Out of Office Assistant** option. The Out of Office Assistant dialog box is displayed.
2. Click the **Send Out of Office auto-replies** option.
3. Click the **Only send during this time range** option. Select **12:00 AM** tomorrow as the Start time. Select **12:00 AM** the following day as the End time.
4. Click the **Outside My Organization** tab. In the text entry area, key **I am out of the office today. I'll respond to your message tomorrow.**
5. Click **OK**. The dialog box is closed. The Out of Office message will be sent when you receive messages from email accounts outside your organization.

   CLOSE Outlook.

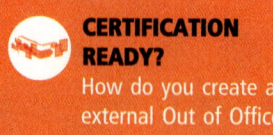

CERTIFICATION READY?
How do you create an external Out of Office

SUMMARY SKILL MATRIX

IN THIS LESSON YOU LEARNED HOW TO:

Send a Message

Resend a Message

Save a Copy of a Sent Message in a Different Location

Automatically Preview Messages

Send a Reply to a Message

Forward a Message

Attach a File to a Message

Preview an Attachment in Outlook

Save an Attachment to a Specific Location

Open an Attachment

Create a Personal Signature

Add a Signature to a Single Message

Add a Signature to All Outgoing Messages

Create an Internal Out of Office Message

Create an External Out of Office Message

■ Knowledge Assessment

Matching

Match the term with its definition.

a. attachment
b. AutoComplete
c. AutoPreview
d. forward
e. macros
f. Cc
g. reply
h. Message area
i. signature
j. subject

____b____ 1. Automatically completes the names of the months and days of the week

____h____ 2. Where the content of a message is keyed.

____f____ 3. Optional field.

____i____ 4. Text or images that are automatically placed at the end of your outgoing messages

____a____ 5. File sent as part of an email message

____c____ 6. Displays the first three lines of every message in the message list

____e____ 7. Disabled in previewed documents for your protection.

____g____ 8. Respond to a message you received by sending a message back to the sender

____j____ 9. Topic of a message

____d____ 10. Send a message you received to another email account

True/False

Circle T if the statement is true or F if the statement is false.

T **(F)** 1. Use the AutoComplete function to insert your signature before you send a message.
T **(F)** 2. A message is moved to the Sent Items folder when you click the Send button.
(T) F 3. Use the Message window to compose and send an email message.
T **(F)** 4. You must fill in the Cc field before a message can be sent.
(T) F 5. Outlook disables all scripts, macros, and ActiveX controls in previewed messages.
T **(F)** 6. To send a message to several recipients, key a colon (:) after a name before adding the next addressee
(T) F 7. When you send a reply, the text "RE:" is inserted before the original subject line.
(T) F 8. Outlook's Forward function is a quick method of sending the message to additional people without re-creating the original message.
(T) F 9. The paper clip icon indicates that a message has an attachment.
T **(F)** 10. An image can't be included in a signature.

■ Competency Assessment

Project 2-1: Send an Email Message to a Friend

Send an email message to a friend inviting him to lunch tomorrow.

GET READY. Launch Outlook if it is not already running.

1. On the Standard toolbar, click the **New** button to open a new Message window.
2. Key a friend's email address in the To field. If you are not completing these exercises with a friend or coworker, key your email address in the To field. This will give you a message to reply to in the next exercise.
3. In the Subject field, key **Lunch tomorrow?**
4. Click in the message area. Key **Hi**, and press **Enter** twice.
5. Key **How about lunch tomorrow?** Press **Enter** twice. Key your name.
6. Click the **Send** button.

LEAVE Outlook open for the next project.

Project 2-2: Reply to a Friend's Email Message

Complete Project 2-1 before starting this project.

1. If the message sent in Project 2-1 has not arrived, click the **Send/Receive** button on the Standard toolbar.
2. In the message list, click the message sent in Project 2-1.
3. Click the **Reply** button on the Standard toolbar.v
4. Key **I'll pick you up at 1:00 PM. Don't be late!** Press **Enter** twice. Key your name.
5. Click the **Send** button.
6. Click the **Send/Receive** button on the Standard toolbar.
7. In the message list, click the reply message.
8. Click the **File** menu and select the **Save As** option. The Save As dialog box is displayed.

9. Navigate to the **Outlook Solutions Lesson 02** folder. Click the **Save** button. The message is saved as **RE Lunch tomorrow.htm**.

   LEAVE Outlook open for the next project.

■ Proficiency Assessment

Project 2-3: Send an Attachment

The last guest in the best suite at Adventure Works accidently broke the stained glass window in the suite. You must replace the window before you can accept any reservations for the suite.

> **TROUBLESHOOTING** The email adddresses provided in these projects belong to unused domains owned by Microsoft. When you send a message to these addresses, you will receive an error message stating that the message could not be delivered. Delete the error messages when they arrive.

The **Window** image file is available on the companion CD-ROM.

1. Create a new email message to Nancy Anderson at the Graphic Design Institute. Nancy's email address is Nancy@graphicdesigninstitute.com. Ask Nancy if she can design a window similar to the stained glass window that was broken. Ask Nancy how long the project will take and how much it will cost.
2. Attach the **Window.jpg** file located in the data files for this lesson.
3. Send the message.

   LEAVE Outlook open for the next project.

Project 2-4: Resend a Message

Complete Project 2-3 before starting this project.

1. You need more than one estimate, but you don't want to key all the information again. In the Sent Items folder, open the message you sent in Project 2-3.
2. Use the Resend function to create a new message.
3. Change the message so it can be sent to Michael Entin at the School of Fine Art. His email address is Michael@fineartschool.net.
4. Send the message.

   LEAVE Outlook open for the next project.

■ Mastery Assessment

Project 2-5: Send a Message Using Stationery

You work for the Adventure Works resort. Mindy Martin, one of the owners, asked you to select stationery to be used when messages are sent to guests from resort employees.

1. Open a new message.
2. Open the Signatures and Stationery dialog box. Click the **Theme** button on the Personal Stationery tab. Select the Clear day stationery theme.
3. Close the current message without saving a draft.
4. Open a new message. The stationery theme will be applied. If necessary, insert the Lesson 2 signature.
5. **SAVE** the unsent new message using the stationery as **Project 2-5.htm** in the Outlook Solutions Lesson 02 folder.

6. Close the message without completing or sending it.
   LEAVE Outlook open for the next project.

Project 2-6: Create a Signature

Mindy Martin, one of the owners of the Adventure Works resort, was pleased with the stationery you selected for outgoing email messages. She asked you to create a signature that uses the Window image.

1. Open a new message.
2. Use the formatting tools in the New Message window to create an attractive signature using the Window image. Insert the *Window* image and resize it to fit in the signature. Use a table to position the elements in the message. Do not display the table's borders.
3. Cut the new signature from the message and paste it into a new signature in the Signatures and Stationery dialog box.
4. Create a new message using the new signature.
5. **SAVE** the unsent new message using the new signature as *Project 2-6.htm* in the Outlook Solutions Lesson 02 folder.
   CLOSE Excel.

The *Window* image file is available on the companion CD-ROM.

INTERNET READY

Many people use images in their stationery or signature. It is tempting to download an image from a Web site to use in your email messages. However, the images used on the Internet are protected by copyright laws. If you don't have an image you created to use in your signature, visit www.microsoft.com. Microsoft provides a large library of clip art that can be downloaded and used in your documents.

Managing Mail with Folders

3

LESSON SKILL MATRIX

Creating and Moving a Mail Folder — 966	Students will learn how to create and move a mail folder.
Deleting and Restoring a Folder — 968	Students will learn how to delete and restore a folder.
Moving Messages to a Different Folder — 969	Students will learn how to move messages to a different folder.
Emptying the Deleted Items Folder — 971	Students will learn how to empty the deleted items folder.
Archiving Outlook Items — 971	Students will learn how to archive Outlook items.

Mindy Martin, Adventure Works' co-owner, started using Outlook two months ago. She was amazed to see that her Inbox currently contains 180 messages. Clearly, she needs some way to organize them. After a bit of thought, she decides to mimic the organization she uses with her paper documents. She begins creating folders for the main categories of vendors, events, and guests.

KEY TERMS
archive
AutoArchive
Deleted Items folder
Drafts folder
Inbox folder
Junk E-mail folder
Outbox
restore
retention rules
Sent Items folder

Software Orientation

Microsoft Outlook's Folder List

The Folder List, shown in Figure 3-1, provides a complete list of your existing Outlook folders. It includes a folder for each Outlook component, such as the Calendar and Notes.

Figure 3-1

Folder List

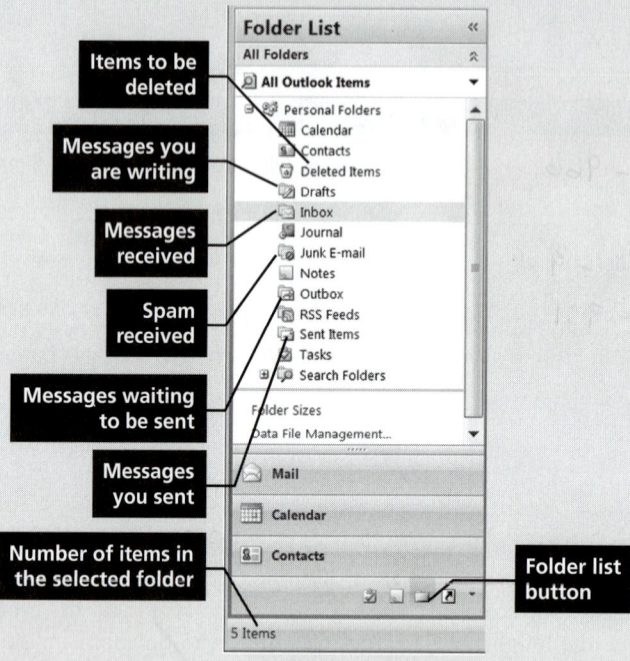

Although the Folder List includes every component, you will normally work only with the mail folders identified in Figure 3-1. The status bar at the bottom of the Outlook window displays the number of items in the selected folder. Create new folders to organize Outlook items by projects or individuals.

■ Working with Folders

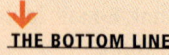
THE BOTTOM LINE

How often do you wander around your house looking for your car keys? If your answer is "rarely," you are already in the habit of putting things away so you know where to find them later. Organize your Outlook items in folders for the same reason. Items are easier to find when you put them away.

Creating and Moving a Mail Folder

In your office, new documents arrive in your Inbox regularly. You look at the document, perform the associated tasks, and file the paper in a folder you labeled for that type of item. You don't place it back in your Inbox. If you piled up all your documents in your Inbox, in a few weeks or months you would have a stack of paper that was several inches tall. In the same way, you don't want to keep all your messages in your Inbox in Microsoft Outlook.

Managing Mail with Folders | 967

 ANOTHER WAY

To create a new folder, right-click any folder in the folder list and select **New Folder**.

CREATE AND MOVE A MAIL FOLDER

GET READY. Before you begin these steps, be sure to launch Microsoft Outlook.

1. Click the **Folder List** button in the bottom of the Navigation pane to display the Folder List shown in Figure 3-1.
2. Click the arrow next to **New** in the Standard toolbar. Click **Folder**. The Create New Folder dialog box is displayed, as shown in Figure 3-2. The folder that was selected in the Folder List is currently selected in the dialog box.

Figure 3-2

Create New Folder dialog box

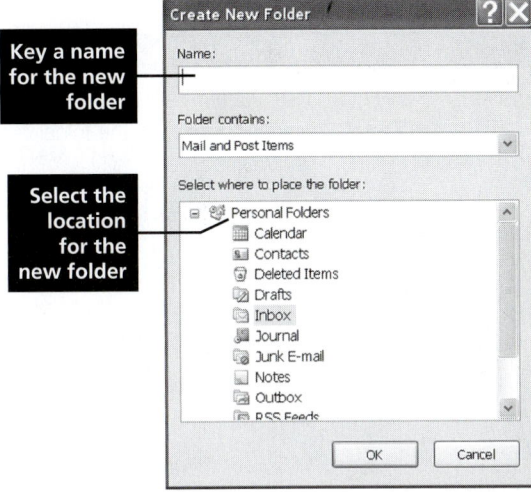

3. In the Name field, key **Lesson 3** to identify the new folder. When creating a folder, use a name that identifies its contents. Don't use abbreviations that you won't remember next week or six months from now.
4. Click **Personal Folders**. This determines the location where the new folder will be placed when it is created. If you do not have the correct location selected, you can move the new folder later.
5. Click the **OK** button to close the dialog box and create the folder. The new folder is added to the Folder List.
6. Click the **Lesson 3** folder to select it and then drag the folder down and drop it in the Notes folder. A plus sign (+) is displayed next to the Notes folder, indicating that it contains a folder.
7. Click the **plus sign** (+) next to the Notes folder. The Folder List expands to display the Lesson 3 folder, as shown in Figure 3-3.

Figure 3-3

New folder created and moved into the Notes folder

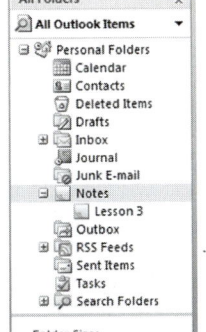

 **CERTIFICATION READY?**
How do you create and move a mail folder?
5.3.1

8. Drag the **Lesson 3** folder and drop it on the Personal Folders icon in the Folder List. The Lesson 3 folder is placed alphabetically in the Personal Folders list, and the plus sign (+) is removed from the Notes folder.

PAUSE. LEAVE Outlook open to use in the next exercise.

Outlook provides several default mail folders that meet your most basic organizational needs. Table 3-1 identifies the default mail folders and describes their content.

Table 3-1

Default mail folders

Folder	Description
Deleted Items	Deleted items are held in this folder until the folder is emptied. Emptying the folder removes the items from your computer.
Drafts	Outlook messages you write but haven't sent are stored in this folder. You can return to a draft later to complete and send the message. If you close a message without sending it, a dialog box will ask if you want to save the draft. Click Yes to save the draft. Click No to discard the draft.
Inbox	By default, new messages to you are placed in this folder when they arrive.
Junk E-mail	Messages identified as spam are placed in this folder when they arrive.
Outbox	Outgoing messages are held in this folder until you are connected to the Internet. When an Internet connection is detected, the message is sent.
RSS Feeds (NEW FEATURE)	Really Simple Syndication (RSS) is a new Outlook 2007 feature that allows you to subscribe to content from a variety of Web sites offering the service. RSS is not covered in this book. Use Outlook's Help feature to find more information on RSS.
Sent Items	Items are automatically moved to this folder after they have been sent.

Deleting and Restoring a Folder

TROUBLESHOOTING

If you delete an item from the Deleted Items folder, the item is removed from your computer.

Because you can create new Outlook folders, you need the ability to delete folders. Delete a folder created accidentally or a folder you no longer need. Folders you delete are moved to the Deleted Items folder. Items in the Deleted Items folder are still on your computer. You can *restore* these items, that is, make them available for use again, by moving them out of the Deleted Items folder.

➡ **DELETE AND RESTORE A FOLDER**

GET READY. Before you begin these steps, be sure to launch Microsoft Outlook.

1. If necessary, click the **Folder List** button in the Navigation pane to display the complete list of Outlook folders.

TROUBLESHOOTING

Do not delete the default Outlook folders.

Managing Mail with Folders | 969

2. Right-click the **Lesson 3** folder created in the previous exercise. Click **Delete "Lesson 3"** from the shortcut menu. A warning dialog box is displayed, as shown in Figure 3-4.

Figure 3-4

Deleting a folder

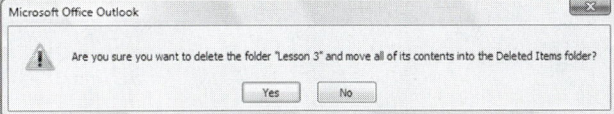

3. Click **Yes** to close the warning dialog box. The Lesson 3 folder is moved to the Deleted Items folder. It will not be removed from your computer until the Deleted Items folder is emptied.
4. In the Folder List, click the **plus sign** (+) next to the Deleted Items folder. The Lesson 3 folder is displayed in the Folder List.
5. Drag the **Lesson 3** folder and drop it on the Personal Folders icon in the Folder List. The Lesson 3 folder is placed in the Personal Folders, and the plus sign (+) is removed from the Deleted Items folder. The Lesson 3 folder has been restored, and it is now available for use.

   PAUSE. LEAVE Outlook open to use in the next exercise.

In the previous exercise, you deleted a folder you created earlier. Because deleted Outlook items are held in the Deleted Items folder until the folder is emptied, you were able to restore the Lesson 3 folder to the Personal Folders so it could be used again.

■ Moving Messages to a Different Folder

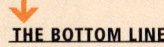
THE BOTTOM LINE

Messages arrive in the Inbox. Messages you send are stored in the Sent Items folder. To effectively organize your messages, create new folders for projects or individuals and move the related messages into the new folders.

MOVE MESSAGES TO A DIFFERENT FOLDER

GET READY. Before you begin these steps, be sure to launch Microsoft Outlook.

1. If necessary, click the **Mail** button in the Navigation pane to display the Mail folder.
2. Click the **New** button in the Standard toolbar. The Message window is displayed. By default, the Message tab is selected.
3. In the To field, key your email address. In the Subject field, key **Sample Message for Lesson 3**.
4. In the message area, key **Sample Message for Lesson 3**.
5. Click the **Send** button. The message is moved to the Outbox, and it is sent when your computer is connected to the Internet.
6. Return to your Inbox, if necessary. Click the **Send/Receive** button if the message has not arrived yet. Because the message was sent to your email address, the message is moved to the Sent Items folder *and* it arrives in your Inbox. You will move both copies of the message into the Lesson 3 folder.
7. Right-click the **Sample Message for Lesson 3** message that just arrived in your Inbox. Click **Move to Folder** on the shortcut menu. The Move Items dialog box is displayed, as shown in Figure 3-5.

ANOTHER WAY

To move a message, you can drag the message from the message list and drop it on a folder in the Navigation pane.

Figure 3-5

Move Items dialog box

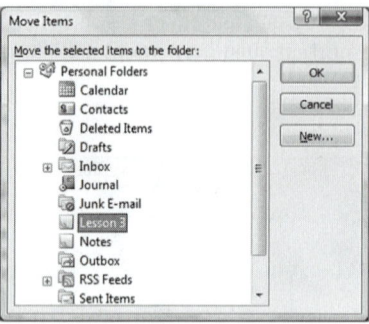

8. Click the Lesson 3 folder in the dialog box, if necessary. Click the OK button to close the dialog box and move the received message from the Inbox to the Lesson 3 folder.

9. Click the Sent Items folder in the Folder List. A list of the messages you sent is displayed in the message list.

10. Right-click the Sample Message for Lesson 3 message. Click Move to Folder on the shortcut menu. The Move Items dialog box is displayed.

11. Click the Lesson 3 folder in the dialog box, if necessary. Click the OK button to close the dialog box and move the sent message from the Sent Items folder to the Lesson 3 folder.

12. Click the Lesson 3 folder in the Folder List. The two messages you moved are displayed in the message list, as shown in Figure 3-6.

Figure 3-6

Messages moved to the Lesson 3 folder

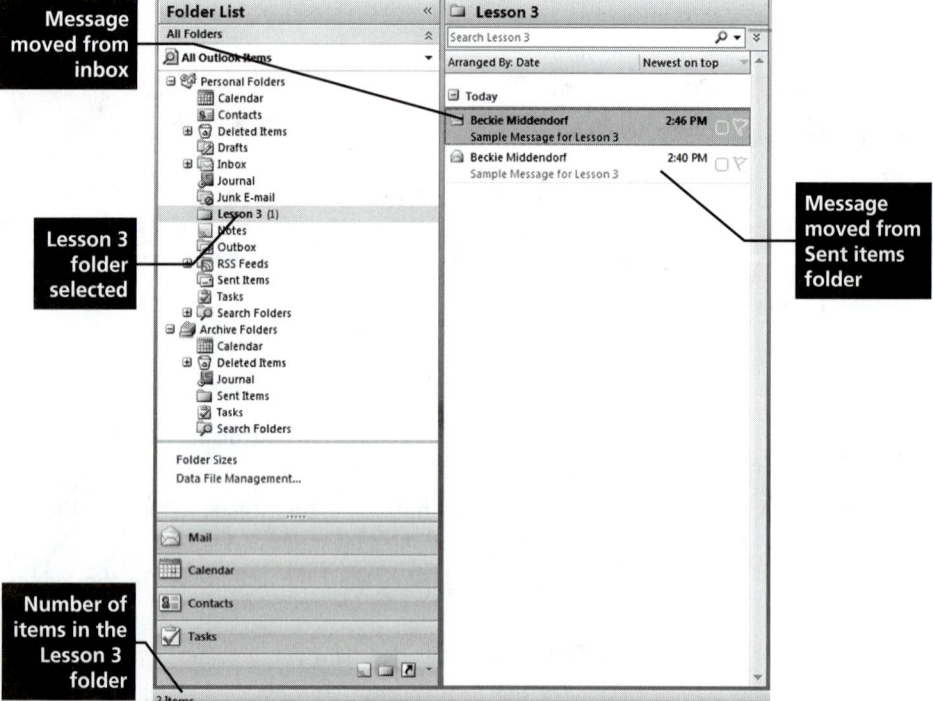

PAUSE. LEAVE Outlook open to use in the next exercise.

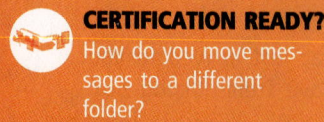

CERTIFICATION READY?
How do you move messages to a different folder?
5.3.2

In the previous exercise, you sent and received a message. When the message arrived in your Inbox, you moved the message to the Lesson 3 folder. It is a good idea to organize messages into folders based on projects or senders.

Managing Mail with Folders | 971

Deleting and Archiving Outlook Items

THE BOTTOM LINE To maintain your folders, you should delete or archive old items. This prevents you from keeping old items past the date when they are useful.

Emptying the Deleted Items Folder

When you delete an Outlook item, it is moved to the Deleted Items folder. It is held in the Deleted Items folder until the folder is emptied. Emptying the Deleted Items folder removes its contents from your computer. The same procedure can be used to empty the Junk E-mail folder.

→ EMPTY THE DELETED ITEMS FOLDER

GET READY. Before you begin these steps, be sure to launch Microsoft Outlook.

1. If necessary, click the **Mail** button in the Navigation pane to display the Mail folder.
2. Right-click the **Deleted Items** folder in the Folder List. Click **Empty "Deleted Items" Folder** on the shortcut menu. A warning dialog box is displayed, as shown in Figure 3-7.

Figure 3-7

Emptying the Deleted Items folder

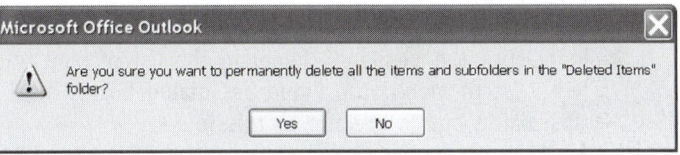

3. Click the **OK** button to remove the items from your computer.

PAUSE. LEAVE Outlook open to use in the next exercise.

CERTIFICATION READY?
How do you empty the Deleted Items folder?
5.3.4

In the previous exercise, you emptied the Deleted Items folder. When you delete an Outlook item, it is not immediately removed from your computer. It is stored in the Deleted Items folder until the folder is emptied. Emptying the Deleted Items folder removes the items from your computer.

Archiving Outlook Items

It is easy to accumulate messages. Some messages are no longer related to your current projects, but you don't want to delete them. Also, some companies or departments have to follow *retention rules* that determine the length of time correspondence must be kept. To *archive* a message, you store it in a separate folder, reducing the number of messages in the folders you use most often. You can still access archived messages in Outlook. By default, items are archived automatically using the **AutoArchive** function, but you can change the AutoArchive settings and manually archive items.

→ ARCHIVE OUTLOOK ITEMS

GET READY. Before you begin these steps, be sure to launch Microsoft Outlook.

1. If necessary, click the **Mail** button in the Navigation pane to display the Mail folder. Click any mail folder.
2. Click the **Tools** menu and click **Options**. The Options dialog box is displayed.

3. Click the **Other** tab and click the **AutoArchive** button. The AutoArchive dialog box is displayed, as shown in Figure 3-8. This dialog box displays the AutoArchive options that are currently active.

Figure 3-8

AutoArchive dialog box

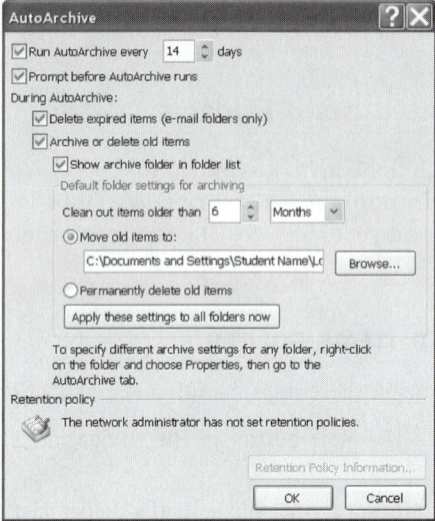

4. Click the **Cancel** button to close the AutoArchive dialog box without making any changes. Click the **Cancel** button to close the Options dialog without making any changes.

5. Right-click the **Lesson 3** folder in the list of mail folders. Click **Properties** on the shortcut menu. The Properties dialog box is displayed. The information in this dialog box is specific to this folder.

6. Click the **AutoArchive** tab. The automatic archive settings for the Lesson 3 folder are displayed, as shown in Figure 3-9. Currently, this folder is not included in the AutoArchive process.

Figure 3-9

Default archive properties for the Lesson 3 folder

7. To change the AutoArchive settings for the Lesson 3 folder, click the **Archive this folder using these settings** option. This activates the dimmed options in this category.

8. In the *Clean out items older than* field, change the value to **1** and change the time period to **days**. Click the **Apply** button to apply the changes. Click the **OK** button to close the dialog box. Normally, you will set a longer time period.

9. To run the Archive process, click the **File** menu and click **Archive**. The Archive dialog box is displayed, as shown in Figure 3-10.

Figure 3-10

Archive dialog box

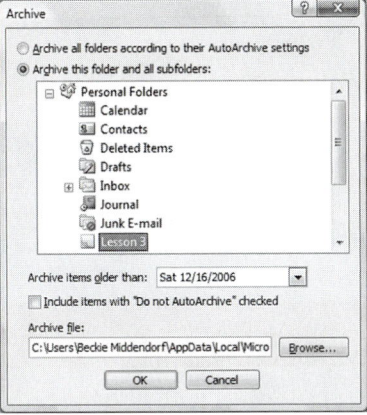

10. In the *Archive items older than* field, click **tomorrow's date** so the messages you worked with today are included in the archive process.

11. Click the **OK** button. If you did not have archive folders because the archive process had not been run before, archive folders will be created. If the archive folders exist, the Lesson 3 folder will be added to the archive folders.

12. Click **Yes** to close the warning message. The warning message is displayed because you selected a future date. Normally, you will select a date in the past, so you won't see this warning message. In this exercise, you selected a future date to ensure that the messages created earlier in this lesson are moved to the archive folder.

13. Click the **Lesson 3** archive folder. The messages have been moved from the active Lesson 3 folder to the archived Lesson 3 folder.

14. To clean up your folders from the changes in this lesson, delete the **Lesson 3** folder in the Personal Folders and delete the **Lesson 3** folder in the Archive Folders. Empty the Deleted Items folder.

    CLOSE Outlook.

> **TROUBLESHOOTING**
>
> This process archives every folder that has the archive setting selected. If this is the first time you have archived your folders or you have many messages in folders that get archived, there might be a short delay until the process is complete.

> **TROUBLESHOOTING**
>
> Check your state and company retention policies before deleting any business-related messages.

In the previous exercise, you viewed your AutoArchive settings, added archive settings to a new folder, and manually archived a folder. At the end of the exercise, you deleted the Lesson 3 folder from the Personal Folders and the Archive Folders.

SUMMARY SKILL MATRIX

IN THIS LESSON YOU LEARNED HOW TO:
Create and Move a Mail Folder
Delete and Restore a Folder
Move Messages to a Different Folder
Empty the Deleted Items Folder
Archive Outlook Items

■ Knowledge Assessment

Fill in the Blank

Complete the following sentences by writing the correct word or words in the blanks provided.

1. Spam is stored in the _Junk Email Folder_ when it arrives.
2. _Retention Rules_ determine the length of time correspondence should be kept.
3. By default, new messages are placed in the _Inbox folder_ when they arrive.
4. A deleted item can be _restored/held_ until it is completely removed from your computer.
5. _Archive_ your messages in a separate folder to reduce the number of messages stored in your active folders.
6. Messages you send are stored in the _Outbox Folder_ until your computer is connected to the Internet.
7. The _AutoArchive_ function automatically archives messages.
8. Messages are automatically moved to the _Sent Items Folder_ after they are sent.
9. Messages you delete are stored in the _Deleted Items Folder_ until it is emptied.
10. The _Drafts Folder_ contains messages you have written but not sent.

Multiple Choice

Circle the correct choice.

1. What do you use to organize Outlook items?
   A. Archives
   B. Folders
   C. Search criteria
   D. Number of items

2. By default, where does email arrive?
   A. Inbox
   B. Outbox
   C. Junk E-Mail
   D. Sent Items

3. Which folders are displayed when you click the Folder List button in the Navigation pane?
   A. Mail folders
   B. Archive folders
   C. Personal folders
   D. All of the above

4. What should you consider when naming a folder?
   A. Use abbreviations to shorten the name
   B. The date the folder was created
   C. The content of the folder
   D. Use your initials so other users know you created the folder

5. Which folder is *not* one of the default Outlook folders?
   A. Outbox
   B. My Mail
   C. Drafts
   D. Sent Items

6. How do you restore a folder?
   A. Delete the folder
   B. Archive the folder
   C. Move the folder to the Personal Folders in the Folder List
   D. Delete items from the folder

7. How do you remove an Outlook item from your computer?
   A. Empty the Deleted Items folder
   B. Move the item to the Deleted Items folder
   C. Select the item and press the Delete key
   D. Delete the item and close Outlook

8. What company policies determine how long correspondence should be kept?
   A. Archival regulations
   B. Retention rules
   C. AutoArchive policy
   D. Correspondence policies

9. What attribute does AutoArchive use to determine which messages should be archived?
   A. Size
   B. Sender
   C. Attachments
   D. Date

10. How does AutoArchive identify which folders should be archived?
    A. Folder size
    B. Folder name
    C. Folder properties
    D. Folder location

■ Competency Assessment

Project 3-1: Create a Mail Folder

The Alpine Ski House is just a brisk walk away from Adventure Works. Joe Worden, Mindy Martin's cousin, is the owner of the Alpine Ski House. As the name implies, the Alpine Ski House sells ski equipment. However, the Alpine Ski House needs to attract and hold local customers when it isn't ski season. Joe started a ski club for local residents. During the off-season, club members meet to hike, bike, and exercise together to stay in shape for skiing. As the ski club becomes more active and gains more members, Joe decides he needs to organize his ski club messages.

GET READY. Launch Outlook if it is not already running.

1. Click the **Folder List** button in the Navigation pane to display the Folder List.
2. Click the arrow next to **New** in the standard toolbar. Click **Folder**. The Create New Folder dialog box is displayed.
3. In the Name field, key **Ski Club** to identify the new folder.
4. Click **Personal Folders**.
5. Click the **OK** button to close the dialog box and create the folder.

   LEAVE Outlook open for the next project.

Project 3-2: Move a Message into the Ski Club Folder

Joe Worden of the Alpine Ski House is planning a hike for the ski club members. Send a message about the hike and move the message to the Ski Club folder.

1. If necessary, click the **Mail** button in the Navigation pane to display the Mail folder.
2. Click the **New** button in the Standard toolbar. The Message window is displayed. By default, the Message tab is selected.
3. In the To field, key your email address. In the Subject field, key **Ski Club Hike Saturday!**
4. In the message area, key the following message:

   Hi Ski Club members! (Press Enter twice.)

   This is just a reminder. We'll be hiking the Mountain Dancer trail this Saturday. Meet in the Mountain Dancer camp site. Bring sandwiches for lunch and plenty of water for the hike. The weather forecast says it will be hot, hot, hot! Be sure you stay hydrated! (Press Enter twice.)

   I'll see you Saturday at 9 AM! Call by Friday afternoon if you can't make it for the hike! (Press Enter twice.)

   Joe Worden (Press Enter.)

   Alpine Ski House (Press Enter.)

5. Click the **Send** button. The message is moved to the Outbox, and it is sent when your computer is connected to the Internet.
6. Return to your Inbox if necessary. Click the **Send/Receive** button if the message has not arrived yet.
7. Right-click the **Ski Club Hike Saturday!** message that just arrived in your Inbox. Click **Move to Folder** on the shortcut menu. The Move Items dialog box is displayed.
8. Click the **Ski Club** folder in the dialog box, if necessary. Click the **OK** button to close the dialog box and move the received message from the Inbox to the Ski Club folder.

   LEAVE Outlook open for the next project.

■ Proficiency Assessment

Project 3-3: Change the AutoArchive Settings for the Ski Club Folder

The ski club holds an event every month. Joe decided he wants to archive messages that are older than two months.

1. Right-click the **Ski Club** folder in the list of mail folders. Click **Properties** on the shortcut menu. The Properties dialog box is displayed.
2. Click the **AutoArchive** tab to view the automatic archive settings.
3. Click the **Archive this folder using these settings** option.
4. In the *Clean out items older than* field, change the value to **2** and change the time period to **months**, if necessary. Click the **Apply** button to apply the changes. Click the **OK** button to close the dialog box.

   LEAVE Outlook open for the next project.

Project 3-4: Manually Archive the Ski Club Folder

It isn't really time to archive the Ski Club folder, but Joe decides to run the archive process manually anyway.

1. Click the **File** menu and click **Archive**. The Archive dialog box is displayed.
2. In the *Archive items older than* field, click **tomorrow's date** so the message you worked with today is included in the archive process.
3. Click the **OK** button to run the archive process. Click **Yes** in the warning box. A warning message is displayed because you selected a future date.
4. Click the **Ski Club** archive folder. The messages have been moved from the active Ski Club folder to the archived Ski Club folder.

   LEAVE Outlook open for the next project.

■ Mastery Assessment

Project 3-5: Delete and Restore the Ski Club Folder

Joe Worden thought about the ski club while he sipped his coffee. With only one event per month, perhaps it wasn't necessary to create a folder just for the ski club.

1. If necessary, click the **Folder List** button in the Navigation pane to display the complete list of Outlook folders.
2. Right-click the **Ski Club** folder created in a previous project. Click **Delete** "Ski Club" from the shortcut menu. A warning dialog box is displayed.
3. Click **Yes** to close the warning dialog box. The Ski Club folder is moved to the Deleted Items folder. Now that the folder is deleted, Joe decides he should keep the folder.
4. In the Folder List, click the **plus sign** (+) next to the Deleted Items folder.
5. Drag the **Ski Club** folder and drop it on the Personal Folders icon in the Folder List. The Ski Club folder has been restored, and it is now available for use.

   LEAVE Outlook open for the next project.

Project 3-6: **Permanently Delete the Ski Club Folder**

This time, Joe is sure he wants to delete the Ski Club folder. If the correspondence about the club increases, he can always create the folder again.

1. Right-click the **Ski Club** folder created in a previous project. Click **Delete "Ski Club"** from the shortcut menu. A warning dialog box is displayed.
2. Click **Yes** to close the warning dialog box. The Ski Club folder is moved to the Deleted Items folder.
3. Right-click the **Ski Club** archive folder. Click **Delete "Ski Club"** from the shortcut menu. A warning dialog box is displayed.
4. Click **Yes** to close the warning dialog box. The Ski Club archive folder is moved to the Deleted Items folder.
5. Right-click the **Deleted Items** folder in the Folder List. Click **Empty "Deleted Items" Folder** on the shortcut menu. A warning dialog box is displayed.
6. Click the **OK** button to remove the items from your computer.

   CLOSE Outlook.

INTERNET READY

Find a business on the Internet that is similar to the Alpine Ski House. Make a list of the Outlook folders you would suggest for the owner.

Processing Messages with Rules

LESSON SKILL MATRIX

Creating a Rule to Move Messages from a Template	Students will learn how to create a rule to move message from a template.
Running a Rule	Students will learn how to run a rule.
Creating a Rule to Categorize Messages from a Selected Message	Students will learn how to create a rule to categorize messages from a selected message.
Creating a Rule to Forward a Message by Copying an Existing Rule	Students will learn how to create a rule to forward a message by copying an existing rule.
Creating a Rule to Delete Messages from Scratch	Students will learn how to create a rule to delete messages from scratch.
Sequencing Rules	Students will learn how to sequence rules.
Turning Off a Rule	Students will learn how to turn off a rule.
Deleting a Rule	Students will learn how to delete a rule.

Mindy Martin is a co-owner of Adventure Works, a luxury resort near Cincinnati, Ohio. As with any business, a steady stream of information goes in and out of her office. Reservations, schedules, vendor orders, maintenance requests, and menus for the resort's restaurant are only a small sample of the information flying in and out of Mindy's email folders. To keep things straight, Mindy uses message rules to organize her messages as they arrive.

KEY TERMS
action
condition
exception
rule
template
Wizard

Software Orientation

Microsoft Outlook's Rules and Alerts Window

Message rules are displayed in the Rules and Alerts dialog box, as shown in Figure 4-1.

Figure 4-1

Outlook's Rules and Alerts window

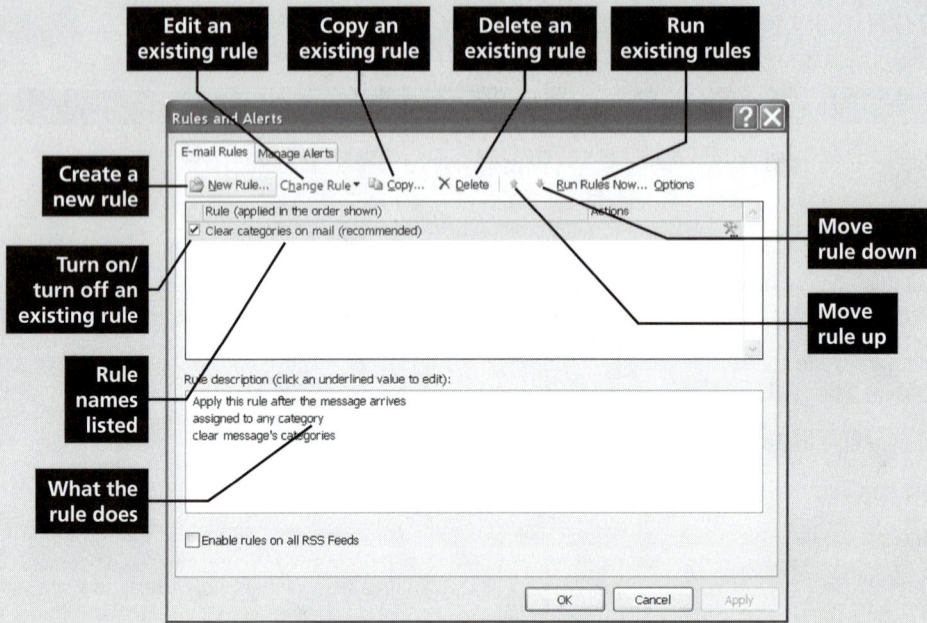

The rules that help you organize your messages are displayed in the Rules and Alerts window. In this window, you can edit existing rules, create new rules, enable rules, and disable rules.

Using Rule Templates

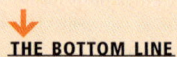
THE BOTTOM LINE

Using a template is the easiest method for creating a new rule. A ***template*** is an existing rule provided by Outlook that contains specific pieces of information that can be customized to create new rules. Usually, it is easier to use a template to create a rule than it is to create one from scratch.

Creating a Rule to Move Messages from a Template

A ***rule*** defines an action that happens automatically when messages are received or sent. Moving messages to specific folders to group related messages when they arrive is a basic method of organizing your messages. You can place messages about your active projects in project folders. You can place messages from vendors in separate folders. Create and use as many folders as you need to keep organized.

CREATE A RULE TO MOVE MESSAGES FROM A TEMPLATE

GET READY. Before you begin these steps, be sure to launch Microsoft Outlook.

1. If necessary, click the **Mail** button in the Navigation pane to display the Mail folder. Then, right-click **Personal Folders** in the Folders List, and click **New Folder** in the shortcut menu. The Create New Folder dialog box is displayed.

Processing Messages with Rules | 981

2. In the Name field, key **Lesson 4 Schedules**. If necessary, click **Personal Folders** in the *Select where to place the folder* section. Click **OK** to create the folder and close the dialog box. You will create a rule to move messages into this folder.

3. Click the **Tools** menu, and click the **Rules and Alerts** option. The Rules and Alerts window shown in Figure 4-1 is displayed. Click the **New Rule** button. The Rules Wizard window is displayed, as shown in Figure 4-2. A ***Wizard*** consists of steps that walk you through completing a process in Microsoft Office applications.

Figure 4-2

Rules Wizard window with default selections

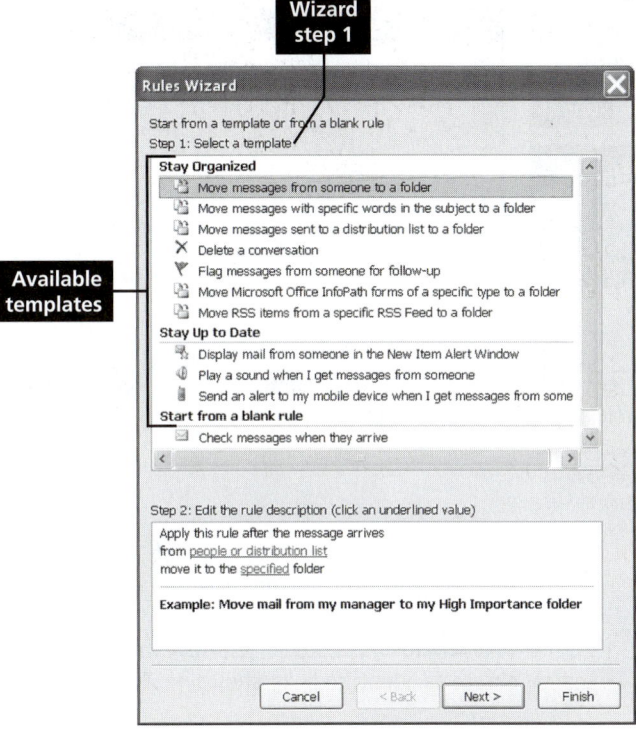

4. In the *Stay Organized* category, click **Move messages with specific words in the subject to a folder**. This rule will move messages about the selected topic. The rule description in the lower area of the window changes, as shown in Figure 4-3.

Figure 4-3

Rules Wizard window with template to move messages selected

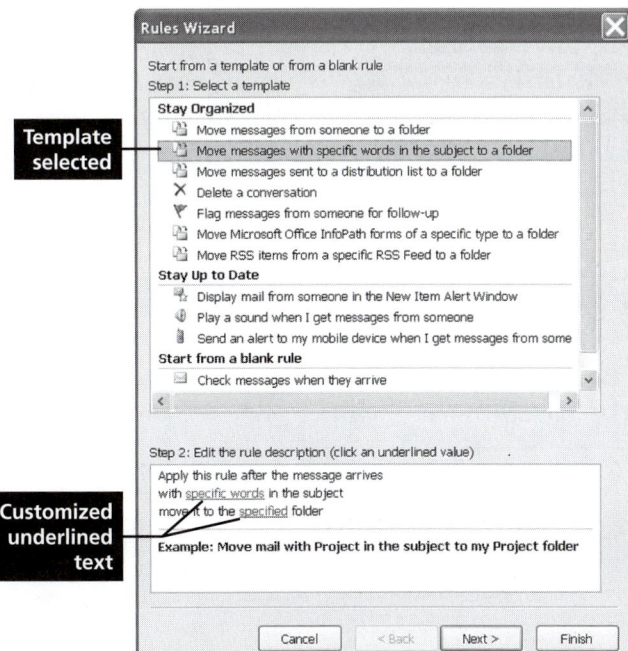

TROUBLESHOOTING To ensure that a rule looking for a specific subject moves the messages, the subject line must contain the exact words.

5. In the *Step 2* area, click **specific words**. The Search Text window is displayed, as shown in Figure 4-4.

Figure 4-4

Search Text window

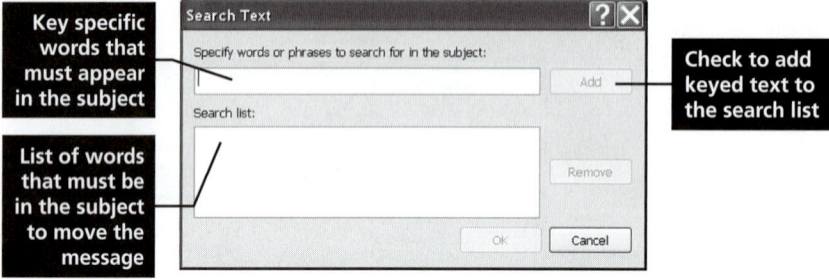

TAKE NOTE In this exercise, you used a single phrase as the search text. To add more words or phrases to the search list, key the text into the Search Text window and click the Add button.

6. In the *Specify words or phrases to search for in the subject* field, key **Lesson 4 Schedule**. Click the **Add** button. The *Lesson 4 Schedule* phrase is enclosed by quotation marks and added to the search list for this rule. Click **OK** to close the Search Text window. The Rules Wizard window is displayed. The Lesson 4 Schedule search phrase is identified, as shown in Figure 4-5.

Figure 4-5

Rules Wizard window with the search phrase identified

Processing Messages with Rules | 983

7. In the *Step 2* area of the Rules Wizard window, click **specified** to identify the destination folder. The Folder List is displayed in the Rules and Alerts window, as shown in Figure 4-6.

Figure 4-6

Select the destination folder

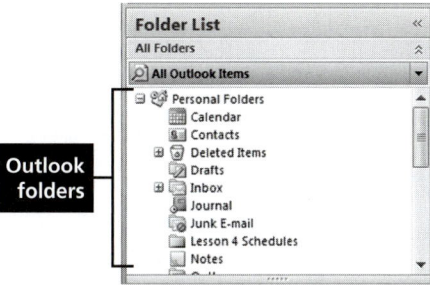

8. Click the **Lesson 4 Schedules** folder, and click **OK**. The specified destination folder is identified in the Rules Wizard window, as shown in Figure 4-7.

Figure 4-7

Rules Wizard window with the destination folder identified

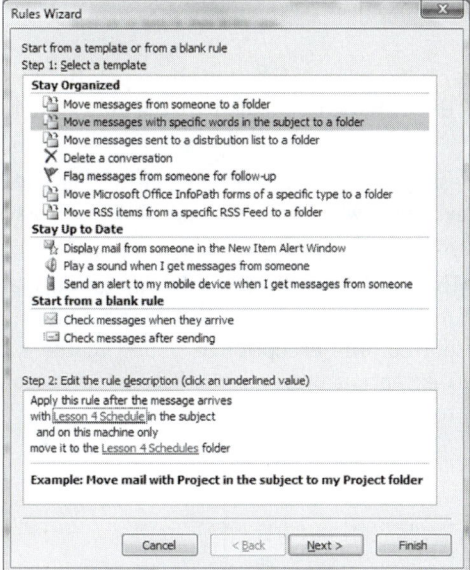

9. Click the **Next** button to continue the Wizard. Under *Step 1: Select condition(s)*, you will see a list of conditions that can be added to the rule. You don't want to add conditions to this rule, so click the **Next** button to continue the Wizard. Under *Step 1: Select action(s)*, you will see a list of actions that can be taken. You don't want to add actions to this rule, so click the **Next** button to continue the Wizard. A list of exceptions to the rule is displayed, as shown in Figure 4-8.

Figure 4-8

Rules Wizard window with exceptions that can be added to the rule

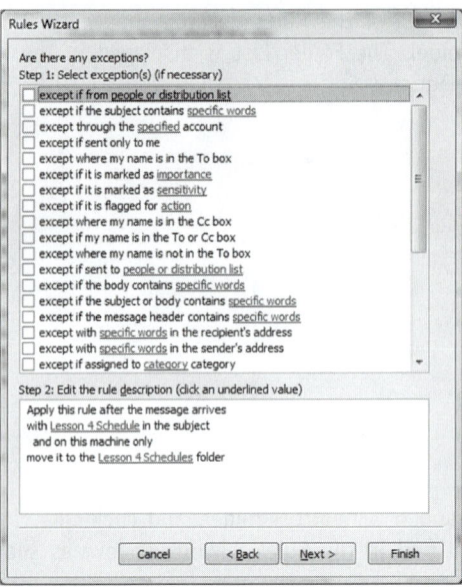

10. Click the **except if the subject contains specific words** checkbox. This option is second on the list. Text is added to the rule description at the bottom of the Rules Wizard window.

11. In the rule description area at the bottom of the window, click **specific words**. The Search text window shown in Figure 4-4 is displayed.

12. In the *Specify words or phrases to search for in the subject* field, key **RE:**. Click the **Add** button. The *RE:* text is enclosed by quotation marks and added to the search list for this rule. Click **OK** to close the Search Text window. The Rules Wizard window is displayed. The exception is added to the rule, as shown in Figure 4-9. Making RE: an exception prevents replies to the Lesson 4 Schedule messages from being moved to the destination folder.

Figure 4-9

Rules Wizard window with exception added to the rule

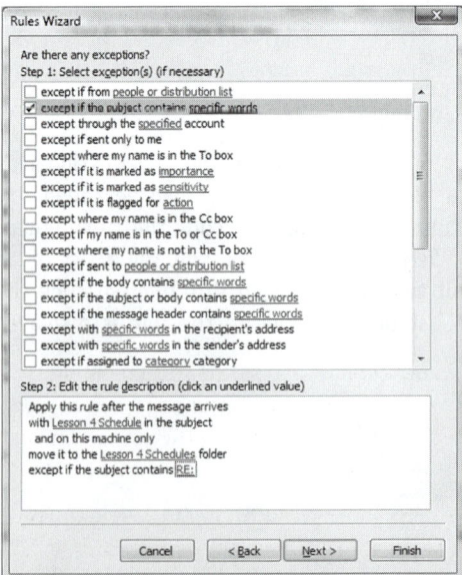

13. Click the **Next** button to continue the Wizard. The rule is displayed for your approval, as shown in Figure 4-10.

Figure 4-10

Rules Wizard window with rule displayed for approval

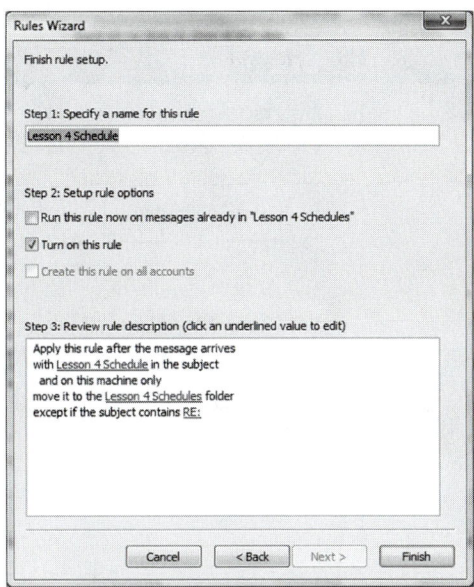

14. Examine the rule carefully to verify that it is correct. Click the **Finish** button. The new rule is displayed in the Rules and Alerts window, as shown in Figure 4-11.

Figure 4-11

Rules and Alerts window with the new rule displayed

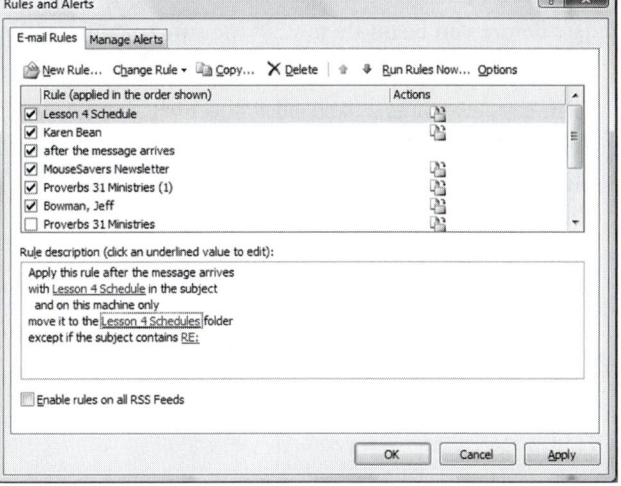

CERTIFICATION READY?
How do you create a rule to move messages?
5.5.1

15. Click the **OK** button to close the Rules and Alerts window.

PAUSE. LEAVE Outlook open to use in the next exercise.

In the previous exercise, you used a Wizard to create a new rule to move arriving messages about a specific subject to a selected destination folder. Using the wizard to create a new rule simplifies the process. If you try to advance to the next step without completing the current step, an error message is displayed. It instructs you to finish the current step.

A rule consists of three parts: a condition, an action, and an exception. In simple terms, a rule says **if A** happens (the condition) **then B** (the action) **unless C** (the exception.) Table 4-1 describes the parts of a rule.

Table 4-1

Parts of a rule

PART	DESCRIPTION
Condition	The *condition* identifies the characteristics used to determine the messages affected by the rule. Use caution when you define the conditions. If your conditions are too broad, the rule will affect more messages than intended. If your conditions are too narrow, the rule will not identify messages that should be affected.
Action	The *action* determines what happens when a message meets the conditions defined in the rule. For example, the message can be moved, forwarded, or deleted.
Exception	The *exception* identifies the characteristics used to exclude messages from being affected by the rule.

Running a Rule

Rules run automatically when new messages arrive. You can also run rules manually to test them. Send yourself a message that meets the rule's conditions. Verify that the action is carried out as intended.

➔ RUN A RULE

GET READY. Before you begin these steps, be sure to complete the previous exercise creating a rule.

1. Click the **Tools** menu, and click the **Rules and Alerts** option. The Rules and Alerts window shown in Figure 4-1 is displayed.
2. Click the **Run Rules Now** button. The Run Rules Now dialog box is displayed, as shown in Figure 4-12.

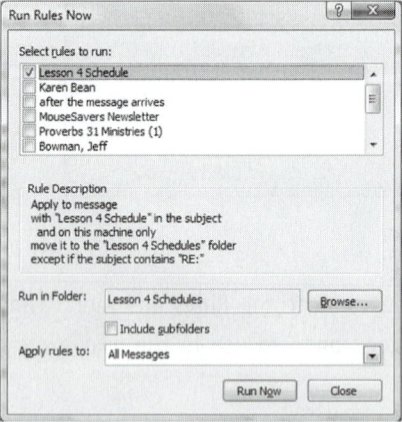

Figure 4-12

Run Rules Now dialog box

3. In the *Select rules to run* section, click the **Lesson 4 Schedule** checkbox. Click the **Run Now** button. Because you don't have any messages that meet the condition, no action is taken. To test this rule, you need to receive a message that meets the condition.

Processing Messages with Rules | 987

4. Click the **Close** button, and click the **OK** button to return to the main Outlook window.
5. Click the **New** button in the Standard toolbar. The Message window is displayed.
6. Click the **To** field. Key your email address.
7. Click the **Subject** field. Key **Lesson 4 Schedule**. When this message arrives, it will meet the condition defined in the Lesson 4 Schedule rule.
8. In the message area, key **Lesson 4 Schedule rule test**.
9. Click the **Send** button. The message is moved to the Outbox and sent when the computer is connected to the Internet.
10. If necessary, click the **Send/Receive** button to receive the message. When the message arrives, the rule runs automatically and places the message in the Lesson 4 Schedules folder, as shown in Figure 4-13.

Figure 4-13

Rule moved the received message

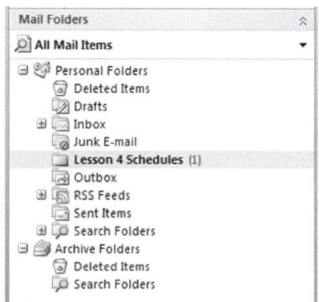

PAUSE. LEAVE Outlook open to use in the next exercise.

After creating a rule, test the rule to verify that it works. For example, to test the rule created in the previous exercise you sent a message with *Lesson 4 Schedule* as the subject to yourself. Over time, you might need to add conditions to the rule because everyone who sends schedules to you does not use the correct subject. You can add a condition such as the *Lesson 4 Schedule* phrase in the body of the message or add a condition identifying any message with the word *schedule* in the subject.

■ Creating and Editing Rules

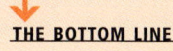
THE BOTTOM LINE

In many situations, creating a rule from a template is one of the easiest methods for creating a rule. However, rules can be created in a number of different ways. You can create a rule from an existing message or copy an existing rule and edit one or more of the rule's components. If a rule is simple, it can be created quickly from scratch.

Creating a Rule to Categorize Messages from a Selected Message

Repeating the same action over and over is one of the most common reasons for creating a rule. The next time you select a message on which you plan to perform an often-repeated action, use the message to create a rule. For example, categorizing messages is a common organizational task. A rule can automate this repetitive task.

988 | Lesson 4

➡ **CREATE A RULE TO CATEGORIZE MESSAGES FROM A SELECTED MESSAGE**

USE the message you sent in the previous exercise.

1. In the Navigation pane, click the **Lesson 4 Schedules** folder. One message is in the folder. It is highlighted in the Message List.
2. Right-click the message. Click **Create Rule** on the shortcut menu. The Create Rule dialog box is displayed, as shown in Figure 4-14. The characteristics of the selected message are displayed in the dialog box.

Figure 4-14

Create Rule dialog box

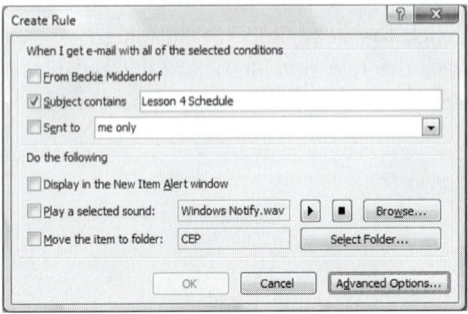

3. Click the **Subject contains** checkbox. The field contains *Lesson 4 Schedule*, the subject of the selected message. Click the **Advanced Options** button to specify additional rule components. The Rules Wizard window is displayed.
4. The condition about the message's subject is already selected. Click the **Next** button. The Rules Wizard window lists the available actions for the rule. Actions based on the selected message are displayed at the top of the list. Click the **assign it to the category category** checkbox. The selected action is moved to the lower area of the window, as shown in Figure 4-15.

Figure 4-15

Rules Wizard window with available actions based on the selected message

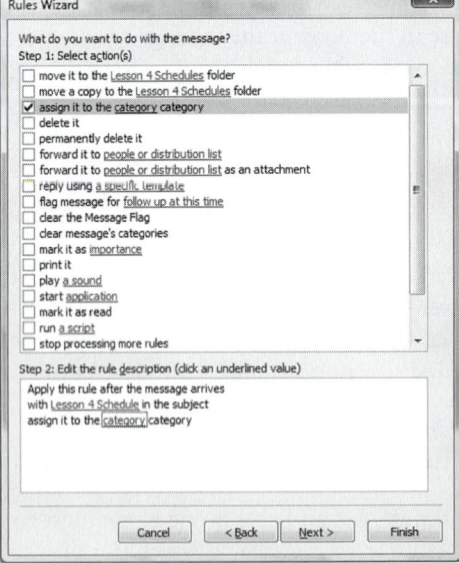

Processing Messages with Rules | 989

 Color Category is a new feature in Outlook 2007. You can find more information on Color Categories in Lesson 10.

5. In the *Step 2: Edit the rule description* area, click the underlined **category**. The Color Categories dialog box is displayed, as shown in Figure 4-16.

Figure 4-16

Color Categories dialog box

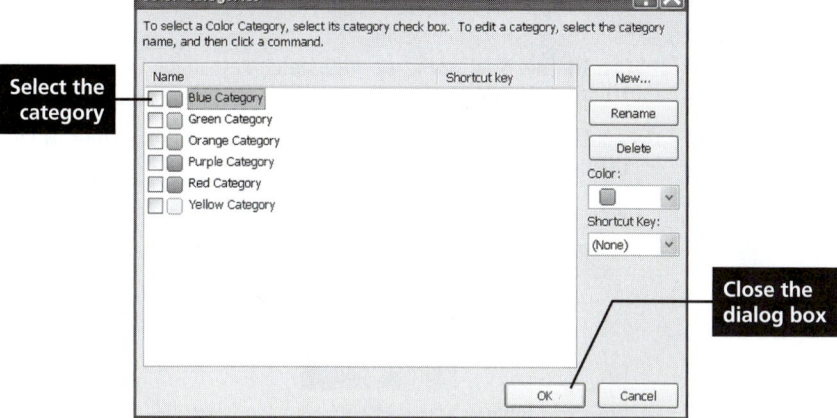

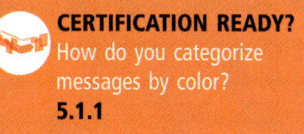

TAKE NOTE*

You can rename categories, but it isn't necessary in this lesson.

CERTIFICATION READY?
How do you categorize messages by color?
5.1.1

6. Click the **Blue Category** checkbox. Click **OK**. If a Rename Category window is displayed, click the **No** button. The Color Categories dialog box is closed, and you are returned to the Rules Wizard window.

7. The condition and action for the rule are complete. You don't want to identify any exceptions. Click the **Finish** button. The rule is saved. The Rules Wizard window is closed, and you are returned to the main Outlook window. In the following steps, you will rename and test the new rule.

8. Click the **Tools** menu and click the **Rules and Alerts** option. The Rules and Alerts dialog box is displayed, as shown in Figure 4-17. The new rule you just created is identified as *Lesson 4 Schedule (1)*. The name was inherited from the rule already applied to the message when you selected the message.

Figure 4-17

Rule created from a selected message

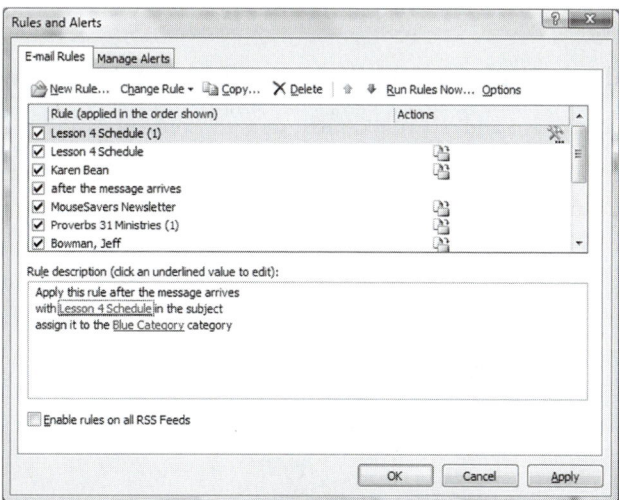

990 | Lesson 4

9. If necessary, select the **Lesson 4 Schedule (1)** rule. Click the **Change Rule** button, and click the **Rename Rule** option. The Rename dialog box is displayed, as shown in Figure 4-18.

Figure 4-18
Rename a rule

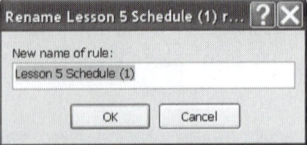

10. In the *New name of rule* field, key **Blue Lesson 4 Schedule**. Click **OK**. The Rename dialog box is closed. The name of the rule has been changed.
11. Click the **Run Rules Now** button. The Run Rules Now dialog box is displayed.
12. Click the **Blue Lesson 4 Schedule** checkbox. Click the **Run Now** button.
13. Click the **Close** button. Click **OK** to return to the main Outlook window. In the Messages List, the Blue Category has been assigned to the message. See Figure 4-19.

Figure 4-19
Blue Category assigned to a message

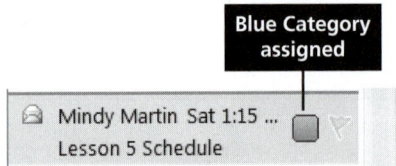

PAUSE. LEAVE Outlook open to use in the next exercise.

CERTIFICATION READY?
How do you create a rule to categorize messages?
5.5.2

Creating a rule from a selected message has advantages. As you create the rule, the characteristics of the selected message are offered as rule components. This saves time and increases the rule's accuracy.

Creating a Rule to Forward a Message by Copying an Existing Rule

Forwarding messages is another common task that can be performed by a rule. When many of the rule components are similar to an existing rule, you can copy the existing rule to create the new rule.

➔ **CREATE A RULE TO FORWARD A MESSAGE BY COPYING AN EXISTING RULE**

USE the message and the rule created in a previous exercise.

1. Click the **Tools** menu. Click the **Rules and Alerts** option. The Rules and Alerts window shown in Figure 4-1 is displayed.
2. Click the **Blue Lesson 4 Schedule** rule. Click the **Copy** button. The Copy rule to dialog box is displayed, as shown in Figure 4-20.

Figure 4-20
Copying a rule

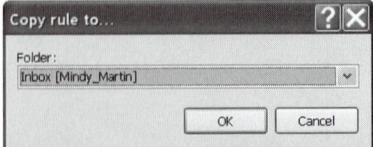

 Processing Messages with Rules | 991

TAKE NOTE *If your Outlook profile accesses more than one email account, you can choose the Inbox affected by the rule. Refer to Outlook's Help for more information about Outlook profiles.*

3. Click **OK**. This identifies the Inbox affected by the rule. A copy of the selected rule is created and added to the list of rules, as shown in Figure 4-21.

Figure 4-21

Copied rule created

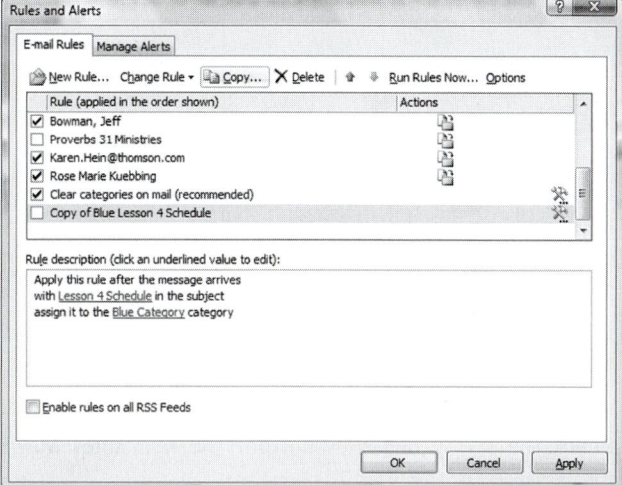

4. Select the **Copy of Blue Lesson 4 Schedule** rule, if necessary. Click the **Change Rule** button, and click **Rename Rule**. The Rename dialog box is displayed.

5. In the *New name of rule* field, key **Forward Lesson 4 Schedule**. Click **OK**. The dialog box is closed, and the rule's name is changed.

6. With the Forward Lesson 4 Schedule rule selected, click the **Change Rule** button, and click the **Edit Rule Settings** option. The Rules Wizard window is displayed.

7. The condition about the message's subject is already selected. Click the **Next** button. The Rules Wizard window lists the available actions for the rule.

8. Click the **assign it to the category category** checkbox to deselect the action. Click the **forward it to people or distribution list** checkbox. The *forward it to people or distribution list* action is moved to the rule description in the lower area of the Rules Wizard window.

9. In the *Step 2: Edit the rule description* area, click the underlined **people or distribution list** text. The Rule Address dialog box is displayed.

 REF Rather than keying an email address into the To field, you can select a person from your Outlook Contacts. You will learn more about contacts in Lesson 5.

10. In the To field, key the email address of a friend or coworker. Click the **OK** button to close the dialog box. The Rules Wizard window is updated, as shown in Figure 4-22.

Figure 4-22

Rule to forward messages

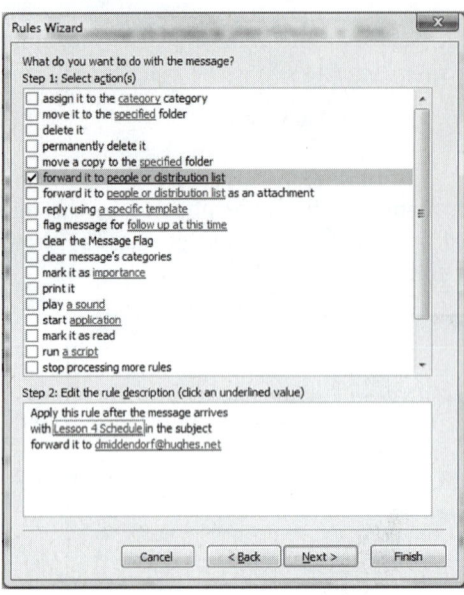

11. This rule does not have exceptions. Click the **Finish** button to save the rule and return to the Rules and Alerts window.
12. Click the **Forward Lesson 4 Schedule** checkbox to turn on the rule.
13. Click the **Run Rules Now** button. The Run Rules Now dialog box is displayed.
14. Click the **Forward Lesson 4 Schedule** checkbox. Click the **Run Now** button.
15. Click the **Close** button. Click **OK** to return to the main Outlook window. The forwarded message is listed in the Sent Items folder.

    PAUSE. LEAVE Outlook open to use in the next exercise.

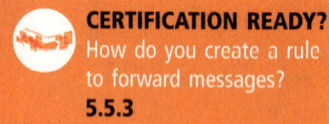

CERTIFICATION READY?
How do you create a rule to forward messages?
5.5.3

So far, you have created a rule to move a message, a rule to assign a category, and a rule to forward messages. Rather than creating three separate rules, you could create a single rule that performs all three actions.

How do you decide which actions can be combined into a single rule? You can turn individual rules on and off. If you turn off a rule with several actions, none of the actions are performed. When you combine actions into a single rule, don't include components that you might need to turn off separately.

Suppose that Jon, the addressee for the forwarded messages, goes on a two-week business trip followed by a two-week vacation in Hawaii. He asked you to stop forwarding schedules to him for four weeks. If the three actions were combined into one rule, you would need to create new rules or edit the combined rule so that the messages are still moved and categorized, but *not* forwarded to Jon. If you keep the forwarded action in a separate rule, you can turn off the forwarding rule until Jon returns with a tan and too many vacation photos.

Creating a Rule to Delete Messages from Scratch

Some rules are simple to write. You want to find messages that meet one condition and perform one action without exceptions. For example, a simple rule might be "Delete all the messages in the Blue Category." You can quickly create simple rules like this from scratch.

CREATE A RULE TO DELETE MESSAGES FROM SCRATCH

USE the message you sent in the previous exercise.

1. Click the **Tools** menu, and click the **Rules and Alerts** option. The Rules and Alerts window shown in Figure 4-1 is displayed.
2. Click the **New Rule** button. The Rules Wizard window is displayed, as shown in Figure 4-23.

Figure 4-23

Creating a rule from scratch

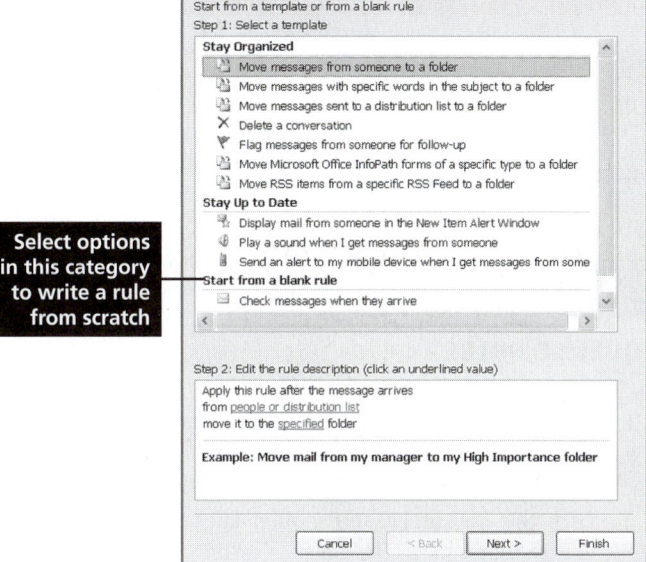

3. In the *Start from a blank rule* section, click **Check messages when they arrive**. This identifies when the rule will run automatically. Click the **Next** button to continue creating the rule.

TAKE NOTE
> To delete all messages from a specific sender, select the *from people or distribution list* condition in the Step 1 area. In the Step 2 area, click *people or distribution list*. Then, you can key the sender's email address into the From field and click OK to continue creating the rule.

4. In this Rules Wizard window, you identify the conditions of the rule. Click **with specific words in the subject**. This rule will identify messages about the selected topic.
5. In the *Step 2* area, click **specific words**. The Search Text window is displayed.
6. In the *Specify words or phrases to search for in the subject* field, key **Lesson 4 Schedule**. Click the **Add** button. The *Lesson 4 Schedule* phrase is enclosed by quotation marks and added to the search list for this rule. Click **OK** to close the Search Text window. The Rules Wizard window is displayed. The *Lesson 4 Schedule* search phrase is identified. Click the **Next** button to continue creating the rule.
7. Available actions are listed in the Rules Wizard window. Click the **delete it** checkbox. You don't want to add any additional conditions, actions, or exceptions. Click the **Finish** button. The rule is complete: When a message arrives with *Lesson 4 Schedule* in the subject, delete it.
8. Select the **Lesson 4 Schedule (1)** rule, if necessary. Click the **Change Rule** button, and click **Rename Rule**. The Rename dialog box is displayed.
9. In the *New name of rule* field, key **Delete Lesson 4 Schedule**. Click **OK**. The dialog box is closed, and the rule's name is changed.

994 | Lesson 4

CERTIFICATION READY?
How do you create a rule to delete messages?
5.5.4

10. Click the **Delete Lesson 4 Schedule** checkbox to clear the checkbox. Click the **OK** button to close the Rules and Alerts window.
    PAUSE. LEAVE Outlook open to use in the next exercise.

In the previous exercise, you created a rule from scratch. This is the best method to create simple rules with one condition, one action, and no exceptions.

■ Managing Rules

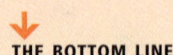

THE BOTTOM LINE

Rules manage your messages. To manage your rules, change their sequence or turn them on or off.

Sequencing Rules

The sequence in which rules are processed can be important. For example, you can change the importance of a message before forwarding it to a coworker. Also, you want to forward a message before you delete it.

→ **SEQUENCE RULES**

USE the rules you created in the previous exercises.

1. Click the **Tools** menu, and click the **Rules and Alerts** option. The Rules and Alerts window shown in Figure 4-1 is displayed.
2. Click the **Delete Lesson 4** rule. Click the **Move Down** button (blue arrow pointing down) four times. The *Delete Lesson 4 Schedule* rule is last on the list of rules.
3. Click the **Clear categories on mail (recommended)** rule. Click the **Move Up** button (blue arrow pointing up) two times. The sequence of your rules should match the rule sequence in Figure 4-24.

Figure 4-24

Sequenced rules

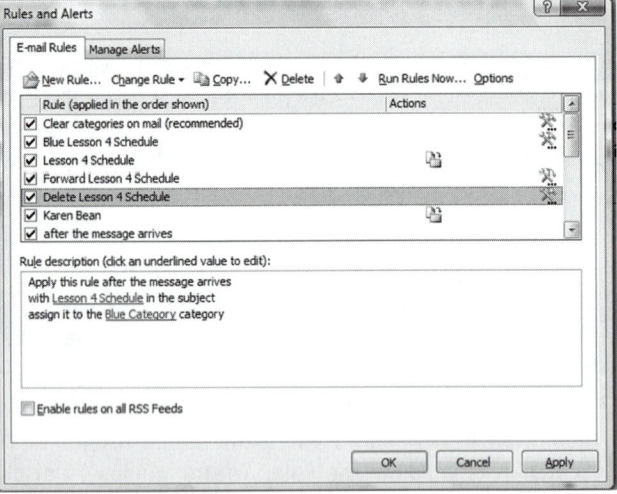

4. Click OK to save the changes and close the Rules and Alerts window.
    PAUSE. LEAVE Outlook open to use in the next exercise.

In the previous exercise, you moved two rules. The *Clear categories on mail (recommended)* rule is first on the list of rules. This clears the categories of the arriving message so you can apply your own category in the *Blue Lesson 4 Schedule* rule.

Turning Off a Rule

> In the Rules and Alerts window, the checkbox in front of the rule's name controls its status. A rule is either off or on. If a rule is on, the checkbox in front of the rule is filled. If a rule is off, the checkbox in front of the rule is empty.

➔ TURN OFF A RULE

USE the rules you created in the previous exercises.

1. Click the **Tools** menu, and click the **Rules and Alerts** option. The Rules and Alerts window shown in Figure 4-1 is displayed.
2. Click the **Delete Lesson 4 Schedule** checkbox so the checkbox is empty.
3. Click **OK** to save the changes and close the Rules and Alerts window.
   PAUSE. LEAVE Outlook open to use in the next exercise.

Turning off a rule rather than deleting it enables you to turn on the rule if it is needed later. It also enables you to keep a rule turned off and run it at a time of your choice.

Deleting a Rule

> Turning off a rule rather than deleting it has advantages. However, if you created a rule that you will not use again, delete it. This keeps your list of rules organized and reduces confusion caused by a long list of old rules that are not used.

➔ DELETE A RULE

USE the rules you created in the previous exercises.

1. Click the **Tools** menu, and click the **Rules and Alerts** option. The Rules and Alerts window shown in Figure 4-1 is displayed.
2. Click the **Delete Lesson 4 Schedule** rule. Click the **Delete** button. Click **Yes** in the dialog box.
3. Click **OK** to save the changes and close the Rules and Alerts window.
4. To clean up your folders from the changes in this lesson, delete the **Lesson 4 Schedules** folder in the Personal Folders, and delete the rules created in this lesson. The rules to delete include *Blue Lesson 4 Schedule, Lesson 4 Schedule,* and *Forward Lesson 4 Schedule*. Do not delete the *Clear categories on mail (recommended)* rule. Empty the Deleted Items folder.
   CLOSE Outlook.

CERTIFICATION READY?
How do you delete a rule?
5.5.1

Use caution when deleting a rule rather than disabling it. You don't want to spend time recreating a rule that you carelessly deleted. Managing your rules also manages your messages.

Summary Skill Matrix

In This Lesson You Learned how to:
Create a Rule to Move Messages from a Template
Run a Rule
Create a Rule to Categorize Messages from a Selected Message
Create a Rule to Forward a Message by Copying an Existing Rule
Create a Rule to Delete Messages from Scratch
Sequence Rules
Turn Off a Rule
Delete a Rule

■ Knowledge Assessment

Fill in the Blank

Complete the following sentences by writing the correct word or words in the blanks provided.

1. _____ manage your messages.
2. A(n) _____ is taken only if the conditions are met.
3. Many rules do not have _____.
4. A(n) _____ walks you through a process.
5. The first part of a rule is the _____.
6. A(n) _____ provides structure for a rule.
7. A(n) _____ is easy to see because it is colored.
8. The _____ of the rules changes when you move a rule up or down.
9. An existing rule can be _____ to create a new rule.
10. A rule has _____ parts.

Multiple Choice

Circle the correct choice.

1. What window enables you to add steps in a rule?
   A. Rules and Alerts
   B. Rules Wizard
   C. Steps
   D. New Rule

2. How does a rule identify the messages it affects?
   A. Actions
   B. Cues
   C. Conditions
   D. Phrases

3. What part of a rule is not required?
   A. Actions
   B. Conditions
   C. Exceptions
   D. All of the above

4. What happens if a rule's conditions are too broad?
   A. The rule will affect more messages than intended.
   B. The rule will affect fewer messages than intended.
   C. The rule will not run.
   D. The affected messages are deleted.

5. How do you test a rule?
   A. Read the rule.
   B. Create a message that meets the rule's exceptions.
   C. Create a separate folder for testing.
   D. Run the rule manually.

6. Why would you use an existing message to create a rule?
   A. The message is part of the rule.
   B. The message is not affected by the rule.
   C. Only the selected message is affected by the rule.
   D. The message's characteristics are used to create the rule.

7. Why would you copy an existing rule to create a new rule?
   A. Many of the new rule's characteristics are similar to the existing rule.
   B. The new rule replaces the existing rule.
   C. The existing rule does not work correctly.
   D. This process tests the existing rule.

8. How do you decide which actions can be combined in a single rule?
   A. The conditions are the same for all of the actions.
   B. The exceptions are the same for all the actions.
   C. A rule with combined actions is easier to write.
   D. The actions won't need to be turned off separately.

9. Why would you change the sequence of your rules?
   A. Rules should be in alphabetic order.
   B. Short rules should be processed first.
   C. Some actions should be performed before others.
   D. Rules should be processed in the order they were created.

10. Why would you turn off a rule?
    A. The rule is no longer needed.
    B. The rule should only be run periodically.
    C. You don't want the rule to run automatically.
    D. All of the above

Competency Assessment

Project 4-1: Create Folders and Messages to Test Rules

Jack Creasey owns a small Internet-based gift shop with a big name. World-Wide Importers sells a variety of crafted objects created by small crafters across the country and one vendor in Canada, justifying the "World-Wide" portion of his company's name. Jack regularly receives pictures of crafted items from his suppliers and sends invoices to customers who buy his products. Jack decided to create rules to manage his messages automatically. First, he needs to create two folders and a message.

GET READY. Launch Outlook if it is not already running.

1. If necessary, click the **Mail** button in the Navigation pane to display the Mail folder.
2. Right-click **Personal Folders** in the Folders List. Click **New Folder** in the shortcut menu. The Create New Folder dialog box is displayed.
3. In the Name field, key **P4 Products**. If necessary, click **Personal Folders** in the *Select where to place the folder* section. Click **OK** to create the folder and close the dialog box. You will create a rule to move messages into this folder.
4. Right-click **Personal Folders** in the Folders List. Click **New Folder** in the shortcut menu. The Create New Folder dialog box is displayed.
5. In the Name field, key **P4 Invoices**. If necessary, click **Personal Folders** in the *Select where to place the folder* section. Click **OK** to create the folder and close the dialog box.
6. Click the **New** button in the Standard toolbar. The Message window is displayed.
7. Click the **To** field. Key your email address.
8. Click the **Subject** field. Key **New ceramic statue!**
9. In the message area, key **Take a look at this new flying pig birdfeeder! It's sure to be a big hit!**
10. Click the **Attach File** button. Navigate to the data folders for this lesson. Click the *Flying Pig Birdfeeder* file, and click the **Insert** button.
11. Click the **Send** button. The message is moved to the Outbox and sent when the computer is connected to the Internet.

    LEAVE Outlook open for the next project.

The *Flying Pig Birdfeeder* image is available on the companion CD-ROM.

Project 4-2: Create a Rule from Scratch to Categorize Messages

Jack wants to create a rule that categorizes the messages he sends with "Invoice" in the Subject field. Assign the messages to the Yellow Category. Complete Project 4-1 before starting this project.

1. Click the **Tools** menu, and click the **Rules and Alerts** option. The Rules and Alerts window is displayed.
2. Click the **New Rule** button. The Rules Wizard window is displayed.
3. In the *Start from a blank rule* section, click **Check messages after sending**. Click the **Next** button.
4. In the *Step 1: Select condition(s)* area, click the **with specific words in the subject** checkbox.
5. In the *Step 2* area, click **specific words**. The Search Text window is displayed.
6. In the *Specify words or phrases to search for in the subject* field, key **Invoice**. Click the **Add** button. *Invoice* is enclosed by quotation marks and added to the search list for this rule. Click **OK** to close the Search Text window.

Processing Messages with Rules | 999

7. In the Rules Wizard window, click the **Next** button.
8. In the *Step 1: Select action(s)* area, click the **assign it to the category category** checkbox.
9. In the *Step 2* area, click the underlined **category**.
10. Click the **Yellow Category** checkbox. Click **OK**. If a Rename Category window is displayed, click the **No** button. The Color Categories dialog box is closed, and you are returned to the Rules Wizard window.
11. In the Rules Wizard window, click the **Finish** button. The new Invoice rule is listed in the Rules and Alerts window. Click **OK** to close the Rules and Alerts window.

    LEAVE Outlook open for the next project.

■ Proficiency Assessment

Project 4-3: Test a Rule

To test the Invoice rule, Jack sends a message to himself with the word "Invoice" in the Subject field. Complete Project 4-1 before starting this project.

1. Create a new message addressed to yourself.
2. In the Subject field, key **Invoice**.
3. In the message area, key **Testing**.
4. Send the message.
5. Click the **Sent Items** folder. Verify that the Invoice message in the Sent Items folder was assigned to the Yellow Category.
6. Click the **Inbox**. When the *Invoice* message arrives, it is not assigned to the Yellow Category because categories are cleared for arriving messages by the *Clear categories on mail (recommended)* rule.
7. Click the **Tools** menu, and click the **Rules and Alerts** option. The Rules and Alerts window is displayed.
8. Click the **Invoice** checkbox to clear the checkbox. This turns off the Invoice rule. Click **OK** to close the Rules and Alerts window.

    LEAVE Outlook open for the next project.

Project 4-4: Use a Template to Create a Rule that Moves Messages

Jack wants to move messages about invoices into the P4 Invoices folder. Complete Projects 4-1 and 4-3 before starting this project.

1. Open the Rules and Alerts window.
2. Click the **New Rule** button. The Rules Wizard window is displayed.
3. In the *Stay Organized* category, click **Move messages with specific words in the subject to a folder**.
4. In the *Step 2* area, click **specific words**. The Search Text window is displayed.
5. In the *Specify words or phrases to search for in the subject* field, key **Invoice**. Click the **Add** button. Click **OK** to close the Search Text window.
6. In the *Step 2* area of the Rules Wizard window, click **specified** to identify the destination folder.
7. Click the **P4 Invoices** folder, and click **OK**.
8. Click the **Finish** button.

9. In the Rules and Alerts window, click **Change Rule**, and click the **Rename Rule** option. Key **Move Invoices** in the *New name of rule* field.
10. Close the dialog boxes and return to the main Outlook window.
11. If necessary, click the **Send/Receive** button to receive the Invoice message sent in Project 4-3. The rule is run automatically when messages are received, so skip to step 13.
12. If the Invoice message was already received before you created the Move Invoices rule, click the **Tools** menu, and click the **Rules and Alerts** option. The Rules and Alerts window is displayed. Click the **Run Rules Now** button. In the Run Rules Now dialog box, click the **Move Invoices** checkbox so the checkbox is filled, and click the **Run Now** button. Close the dialog boxes and return to the main Outlook window.
13. Click the **P4 Invoices** folder to verify that the received Invoice message was moved to the P4 Invoices folder.
14. Click the **Move Invoice** checkbox to clear the checkbox in the Rules and Alerts window. This turns off the Invoice rule. Click **OK** to close the Rules and Alerts window.

    LEAVE Outlook open for the next project.

■ Mastery Assessment

Project 4-5: Use a Message to Create a Rule that Moves Messages

Suppliers frequently send pictures of new products to Jack. He wants to move these messages to the P4 Products folder. Complete Project 4-1 before starting this project.

1. In the Inbox, right-click the **New ceramic statue!** message, and click **Create Rule** on the shortcut menu.
2. In the Create Rule dialog box, click the **Subject contains** checkbox. Click in the *Subject contains* field and modify the value to the single word *New*.
3. Click the **Move to folder** checkbox and select **P4 Products** as the destination folder.
5. Click the **OK** button. In the Success dialog box, click the checkbox to run the rule. Click the **OK** button to close the Success dialog box.
6. Click the **P4 Products** folder to verify that the *New ceramic statue!* message was moved to the P4 Products folder.
7. Change the name of the rule you just created to **Move Products**.
8. Turn off the Move Products rule. Close the Rules and Alerts window and return to the main Outlook window.

    LEAVE Outlook open for the next project.

Project 4-6: Copy a Rule to Create a New Rule Assigning a Category

Jack wants to apply a Color Category to the arriving messages that have attachments. He can copy the Move Products rule and edit the action to move the messages. Complete Projects 4-1 and 4-5 before starting this project.

1. In the Rules and Alerts window, click the **Move Products** rule. Click the **Copy** button. In the *Copy rule to* dialog box, verify that your Inbox is selected and click **OK**.
2. Scroll down to select the new rule, if necessary. Change the name of the rule to *Categorize Products*.

3. Click **Change Rule**, and then click **Edit Rule Settings**. The Rules Wizard window is displayed.
4. You don't want to change the conditions, so continue the Wizard to the list of actions.
5. Turn off the *move it to the specified folder* action. Click the **assign it to the category category** checkbox.
6. In the *Step 2* area, select the **Purple Category**.
7. Click the **Finish** button.
8. In the Rules and Alerts window, move the rules to place them in the following sequence:

   Clear categories on mail (recommended)

   Categorize Products

   Move Products

   Invoice

   Move Invoices
9. Activate and run all the rules for Projects 4-1 to 4-6. After running the rules, your folders should contain the following items:

   P4 Invoices folder: *Invoice* message without an assigned category

   P4 Products folder: *New ceramic statue!* message assigned to the Purple Category

   Sent Items: Sent *Invoice* message assigned to the Yellow Category
10. To clean up after completing these projects, delete the P4 Invoices and P4 Products folders. Delete the Categorize Products, Move Products, Invoice, and Move Invoices rules.

    CLOSE Outlook.

INTERNET READY

Another common way to organize messages is based on the sender. Create an email account with a free Website such as Yahoo.com. Create a rule to manage messages from the Web-based account. Test the rule by sending a message from the Web-based account to your Outlook account.

5 Contact Basics

LESSON SKILL MATRIX

Creating a Contact from a Blank Contact — 1004	Students will learn how to create a contact from a blank contact.
Creating a Contact from an Existing Contact — 1006	Students will learn how to create a contact from an existing contact.
Modifying Contact Information — 1007	Students will learn how to modify contact information.
Sending a Contact as an Attachment — 1008	Students will learn how to send a contract as an attachment.
Saving a Contact Received as a Contact Record — 1009	Students will learn how to save a contact received as a contact record.
Creating a Contact from a Message Header — 1011	Students will learn how to create a contact from a message header.
Viewing and Deleting Contacts — 1012	Students will learn how to view and delete contacts.
Creating a Distribution List — 1013	Students will learn how to create a distribution list.
Modifying a Distribution List — 1015	Students will learn how to modify a distribution list.

Like many business executives, Mindy Martin will tell you that *who* you know is just as important as *what* you know. Mindy refers to Outlook's contact information dozens of times every day. She calls, writes, and sends messages to suppliers, guests, and other business organizations. Direct contact with the right people can avoid problems or solve small problems before they become catastrophes.

KEY TERMS
contact
Contacts folder
distribution list
duplicate contact
message header
ScreenTip
spoofing

Contact Basics | 1003

■ Software Orientation

Microsoft Outlook's Contacts Window

The main Contact window displays basic information about the contacts in your Contacts folder, as shown in Figure 5-1.

Figure 5-1

Outlook's Contacts folder

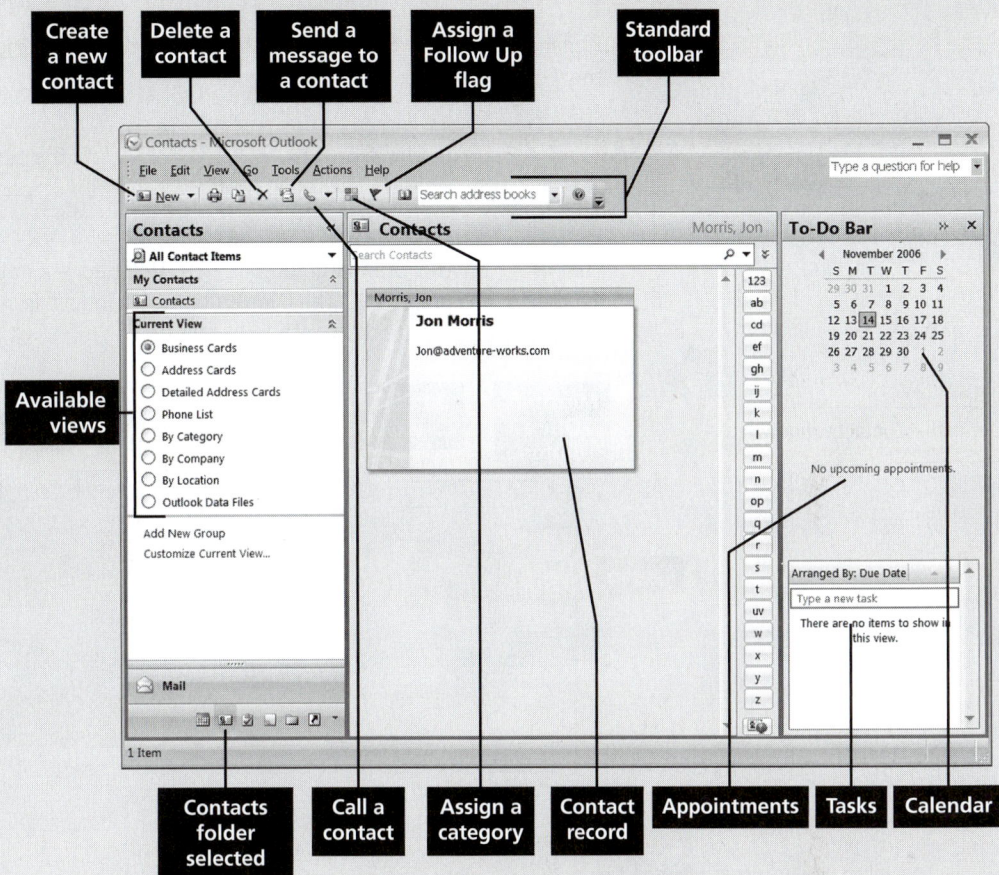

The Contacts folder enables you to organize and maintain information about the individuals and businesses you communicate with regularly. In this window, you can select a contact record, create a new contact record, view appointments, view tasks, send a message to a contact, call a contact, assign a contact to a category, and assign a follow-up flag to a contact.

■ Creating and Modifying Contacts

THE BOTTOM LINE
A ***contact*** is a collection of information about a person or company. The ***Contacts folder*** is an electronic organizer that enables you to create, view, and edit contact information.

TAKE NOTE*
Contacts can be added in many different ways. For example, Mindy Martin's Contacts folder contains a contact for Jon Morris. The contact for Jon was created automatically when Jon and Mindy exchanged digital signatures.

Creating a Contact from a Blank Contact

You can use a variety of methods to create contacts. The most basic method of creating a contact is opening a new contact and keying the information into the Contact window.

CREATE A CONTACT FROM A BLANK CONTACT

GET READY. Before you begin these steps, be sure to launch Microsoft Outlook.

1. If necessary, click the **Contacts** button in the Navigation pane to display the Contacts folder shown in Figure 5-1.

TAKE NOTE* The Standard toolbar in the Contacts folder differs from the Standard toolbar in the Mail folder. The options on the toolbars reflect the actions you can take in the folder.

2. Click **New** on the Standard toolbar. The Untitled – Contact window is displayed, as shown in Figure 5-2. The blank Contact window is ready to store data for a new contact.

Figure 5-2

Untitled – Contact window

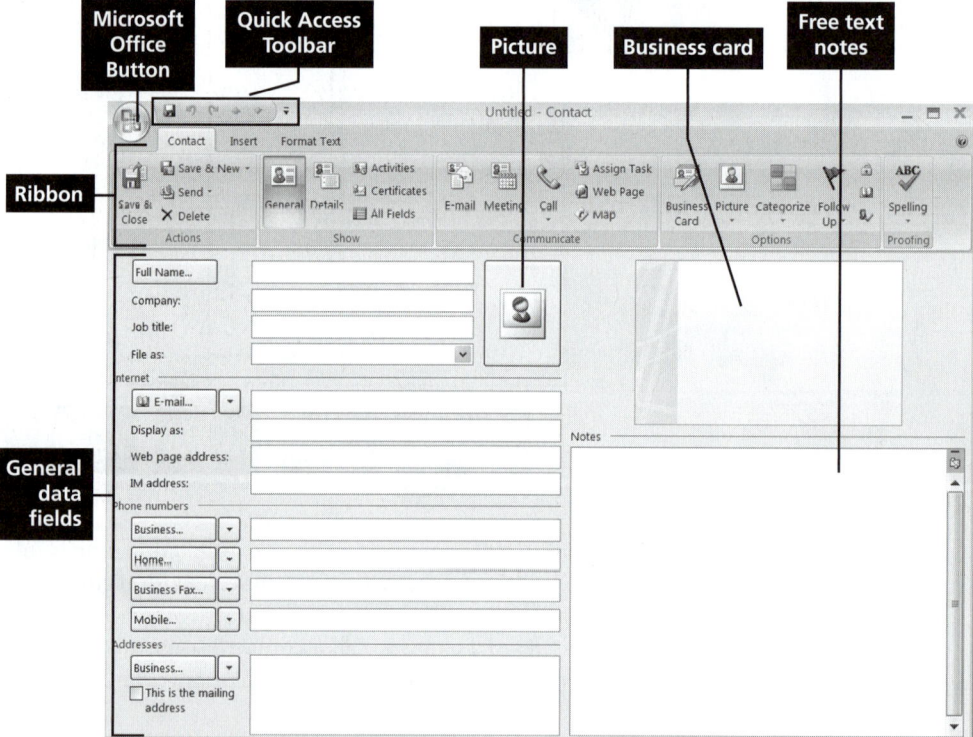

3. Move your mouse over each button in the Ribbon on the new Contact window. The Ribbon is a new feature in Outlook 2007. *ScreenTip* providing a brief description of an item's purpose is displayed as the mouse hovers over each button.

4. Click the **Full Name** field, if necessary. Key **Gabe Mares** and press Tab. The insertion point moves to the Company field. The *File as* field is automatically filled with *Mares, Gabe,* and *Gabe Mares* is displayed in the business card. The name of the window is changed to Gabe Mares – Contact.

5. In the Company field, key **Wingtip Toys** and press Tab. The insertion point moves to the *Job title* field. The company's name is added to the business card.

6. In the *Job title* field, key **Software Support Manager** and press Tab. Gabe's job title is added to the business card. The insertion point moves to the *File as* field, highlighting the current value.

7. Click the dropdown arrow in the *File as* field. A short list of alternative ways of filing the contact is displayed. Some methods use the company name to file the contact. Other alternatives file the contact by the contact's first name. Release the mouse button without selecting a different option.

TROUBLESHOOTING The email addresses provided in these exercises belong to unused domains owned by Microsoft. When you send a message to these addresses, you will receive an error message stating that the message could not be delivered. Delete the error messages when they arrive.

8. Click the **E-mail** field. Key **Gabe@wingtiptoys.com** and press `Tab`. The *Display as* field is automatically filled, and Gabe's email address is added to the business card.
9. You don't want to change the way Gabe's email address is displayed, so press `Tab`. The insertion point moves to the *Web page address* field.
10. In the *Web page address* field, key **www.wingtiptoys.com**.
11. Below the *Phone numbers* heading, click the **Business** field. When you move the insertion point out of the *Web page address* field, the Web page address is automatically added to the business card. Key **6155551205**.
12. Below the Addresses heading, click the **Business** field. Key **7895 First Street**. Press `Enter`. Key **Nashville, TN 76534**. Press `Tab`. The business card is automatically updated. The Gabe Mares–Contact window is displayed in Figure 5-3.

TAKE NOTE
It isn't necessary to key spaces or parentheses in phone numbers. Outlook automatically formats phone numbers when the insertion point leaves the field.

Figure 5-3
Gabe Mares – Contact window

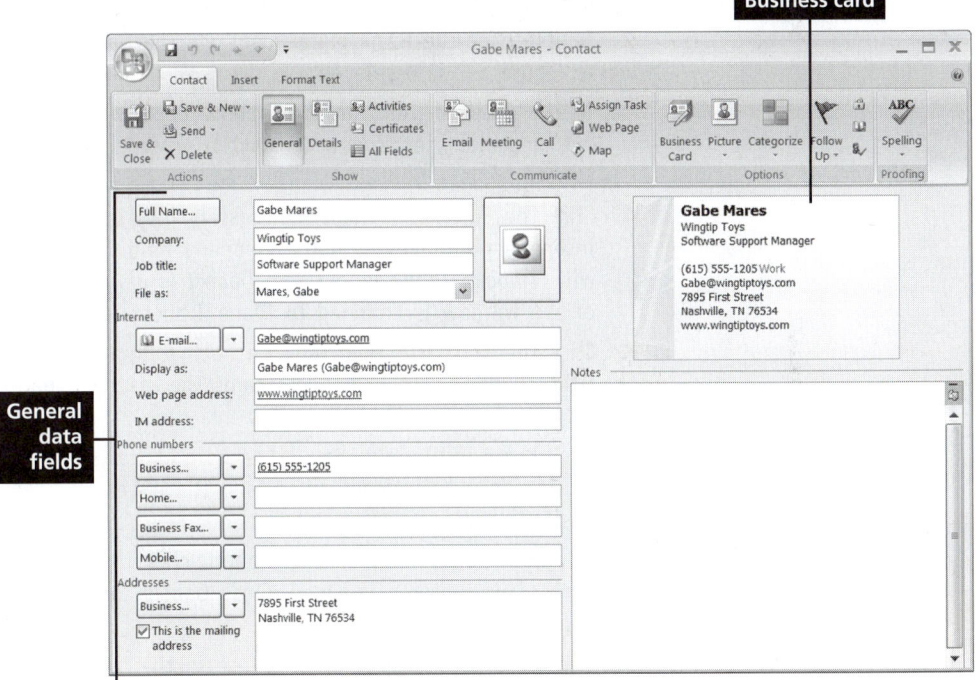

TROUBLESHOOTING If you press Tab in the Address field before keying at least two lines of text, the Check Address dialog box is displayed. Because Outlook expects at least two lines of text in an address, the text you have already keyed might be displayed in the wrong fields in the Check Address dialog box. Click the Cancel button to close the dialog box and continue keying the address.

13. In the Actions group on the Ribbon, click the **Save & Close** button. Gabe Mares' contact information is saved, and you are returned to the main Contacts window.

   PAUSE. LEAVE Outlook open to use in the next exercise.

TAKE NOTE In a contact record, using the postal abbreviation for a state makes it easier to use the information in a mailing list or other data exports.

In the previous exercise, you keyed the basic information for a contact. You do not have to key information into every field. To save contact information, you should have a value in the *File as* field. If the *File as* field is empty, a warning message is displayed when you try to save the contact. The warning tells you that the *File as* field is empty and asks if you want to save the contact with an empty *File as* field. If you save the contact, it will be placed before any other contacts saved with a value in the *File as* field, because a blank is sorted as a value that occurs before any other value.

CERTIFICATION READY?
How do you create a contact from a blank contact?
4.1.1

Creating a Contact from an Existing Contact

Often, you will have several contacts who work for the same company. Rather than keying the same data for a new contact, you can create the new contact from the existing contact.

CREATE A CONTACT FROM AN EXISTING CONTACT

GET READY. Before you begin these steps, be sure to complete the previous exercise creating a contact.

1. If necessary, click the **Contacts** button in the Navigation pane to display the Contacts folder shown in Figure 5-1.
2. Double-click the **Gabe Mares** contact. The Gabe Mares – Contact window shown in Figure 5-3 is displayed.
3. In the Actions group on the Ribbon, click the **Save & New** arrow. In the dropdown list of options, click **New Contact from Same Company**. A new window titled Wingtip Toys – Contact is displayed.
4. Click the **Full Name** field if necessary. Key **Diane Tibbott** and press [Tab]. The insertion point moves to the Company field. The *File as* field is automatically filled with *Tibbott, Diane*, and *Diane Tibbott* is displayed in the business card. The name of the window is changed to Diane Tibbott – Contact.
5. Click the **Job title** field. Key **Marketing Representative** and press [Tab]. Diane's job title is added to the business card. The insertion point moves to the *File as* field, highlighting the current value.
6. Click the **E-mail** field. Key **Diane@wingtiptoys.com** and press [Tab]. The *Display as* field is automatically filled, and Diane's email address is added to the business card.
7. In the Actions group on the Ribbon, click the **Save & Close** button. Diane Tibbott's contact information is saved. Close Gabe's contact record to return to the main Contacts window.

PAUSE. LEAVE Outlook open to use in the next exercise.

CERTIFICATION READY?
How do you create a contact from an existing contact?
4.1.1

When you create a new contact for a person from the same company, the company name, File as, Website, phone number, and address are carried over to the new contact. The name, job title, and email address are not carried over to the new contact, because these fields will usually differ between contacts, even though they work for the same company.

Modifying Contact Information

People move. They change jobs. They retire. To keep the information in your Contacts folder current, you will need to modify the information for existing contacts. You can modify an existing contact and save it as a new contact rather than overwriting the existing contact.

Contact Basics | 1007

➔ MODIFY CONTACT INFORMATION

GET READY. Before you begin these steps, be sure to complete the first exercise creating a contact for Gabe Mares.

1. If necessary, click the **Contacts** button in the Navigation pane to display the Contacts folder shown in Figure 5-1.
2. Double-click the **Gabe Mares** contact. The Gabe Mares – Contact window shown in Figure 5-3 is displayed.
3. Click the following fields and replace the existing values with the new values.

Company	**Tailspin Toys**
Job title	**Software Development Manager**
E-mail	**Gabe@tailspintoys.com**
Web page address	**www.tailspintoys.com**
Business phone number	**6155550195**
Business address	**5678 Park Place**
	Nashville, TN 76502

4. In the Actions group on the Ribbon, click the **Save & Close** button. The modified contact information is saved, and you are returned to the main Contacts window.
5. Double-click the **Diane Tibbott** contact. The Diane Tibbott – Contact window is displayed.
6. Click the **Job title** field. Select the existing value, key **Software Support Manager**, and press . Diane's job title is modified on the business card.
7. In the Actions group on the Ribbon, click the **Save & Close** button. The modified contact information is saved, and you are returned to the main Contacts window.
8. Compare your Contacts folder to Figure 5-4.

ANOTHER WAY

To open a contact, right-click the *contact* in the Contacts folder and click *Open* on the shortcut menu.

Figure 5-4

Modified contacts

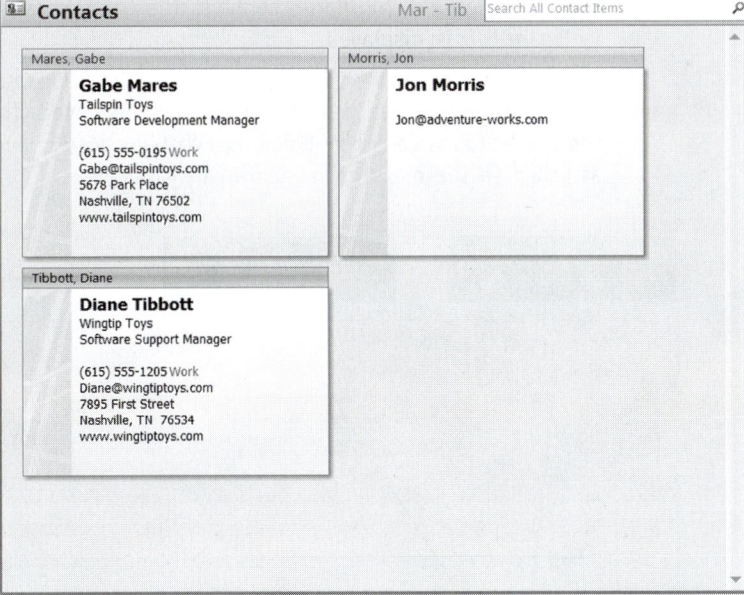

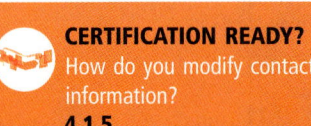

CERTIFICATION READY?
How do you modify contact information?
4.1.5

PAUSE. LEAVE Outlook open to use in the next exercise.

In the previous exercise, you updated the information for two contacts. The following changes occurred.

- Gabe Mares left Wingtip Toys. He was hired by Tailspin Toys as the Software Development Manager. Most of his contact information has changed.
- Diane Tibbott was promoted to Gabe's previous position as Software Support Manager. Her email address and phone number remain the same. Only her title has changed. The corner office with a view that came with the promotion is not part of her contact information.

■ Sending and Receiving Contacts

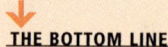
THE BOTTOM LINE

It is easy to exchange contact information via email. You can send and receive contacts as attachments. Every time you send a message, you are sending your contact information. In Outlook, you can create a contact for the sender of any message you receive.

Sending a Contact as an Attachment

You already know that you can send documents and files as attachments. You can also send a contact as an attachment.

→ SEND A CONTACT AS AN ATTACHMENT

GET READY. Before you begin these steps, be sure to complete the first exercise creating a contact for Gabe Mares.

1. If necessary, click the **Contacts** button in the Navigation pane to display the Contacts folder shown in Figure 5-1.
2. Double-click the **Gabe Mares** contact. The Gabe Mares – Contact window shown in Figure 5-3 is displayed.
3. In the Actions group on the Ribbon, click the **Send** button. Click the **In Outlook Format** option. A new message window is displayed. In the Subject field, the topic is automatically identified as FW: Gabe Mares, and Gabe's contact record is attached to the message, as shown in Figure 5-5.

Figure 5-5

Sending a contact as an attachment

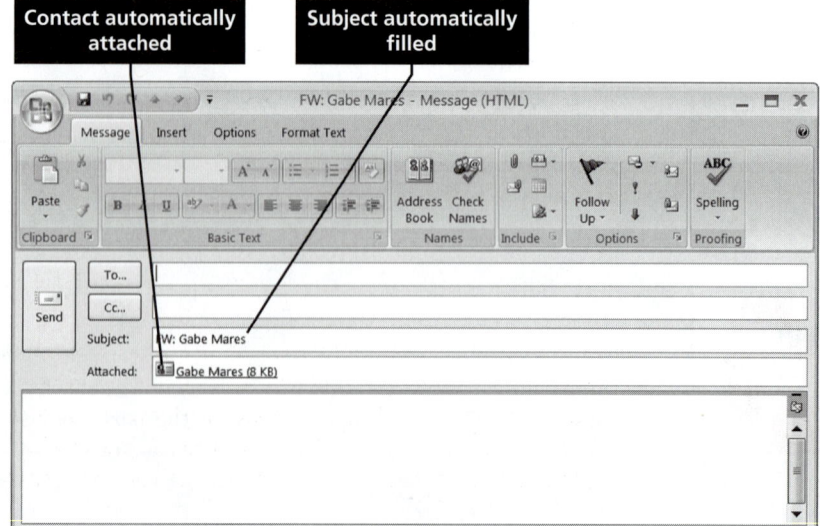

TROUBLESHOOTING If a message is displayed stating that you must save the original item, click *OK* to continue.

4. In the message area, key **Gabe Mares' contact information is attached.**
5. In the To field, key your email address.

TAKE NOTE When you send contact information, any text in the Notes area of the contact record and items attached to the contact record are also sent. Before you send the contact record, delete any information in the Notes area and attachments that you don't want the recipient to see.

6. Click the **Send** button. The message is moved to the Outbox, and it is sent when your computer is connected to the Internet.
7. **CLOSE** the Gabe Mares - Contact window.

   PAUSE. LEAVE Outlook open to use in the next exercise.

In the previous exercise, you sent contact information directly from the Contacts folder as an attachment to a message. This enables you to send contact information without keying it as text in a message.

TROUBLESHOOTING If the recipient does not use Outlook 2007, the contact information might not be displayed correctly and the recipient might not be able to create a contact from the attachment.

You will learn more about electronic business cards in Lesson 6.

Saving a Contact Received as a Contact Record

When you request contact information from a coworker's Contacts folder, the coworker can send the information as a business card or a contact record in Outlook format. If the contact record is sent in Outlook format, you can open the attachment, view the information, and save it as a contact record.

 SAVE A CONTACT RECEIVED IN OUTLOOK FORMAT

USE the FW: Gabe Mares message sent in the previous exercise.

1. If necessary, click the **Mail** button in the Navigation pane to display the Mail folder. If the FW: Gabe Mares message has not arrived yet, click the **Send/Receive** button on the Standard toolbar.
2. Click the **FW: Gabe Mares** message. The message is displayed in the Reading pane.
3. In the Reading pane, right-click the **Gabe Mares** attachment. Click **Open** on the shortcut menu. The attachment opens in the Gabe Mares – Contact window.
4. In the Actions group on the Ribbon, click the **Save & Close** button. Because you received this contact information at the same email address used to send the contact information, the contact record is already in your Contacts folder. Therefore, Outlook detects that this is a ***duplicate contact***. The Duplicate Contact Detected window shown in Figure 5-6 is displayed. If the contact record was not a duplicate, the contact would be saved without any further action needed.

Figure 5-6

Duplicate Contact Detected window

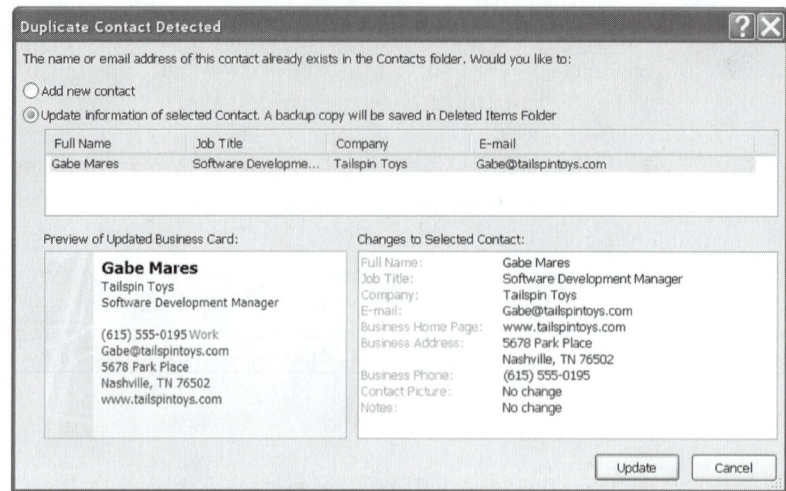

5. You want to create a new contact, so select the **Add new contact** option at the top of the window, and click the **Add** button at the bottom of the window. The Duplicate Contact Detected window is closed, the contact record is created, and you are returned to the Mail folder.

6. Click the **Contacts** button in the Navigation pane to display the Contacts folder. Now, you have the original Gabe Mares contact record you created by keying the data and the Gabe Mares contact record you created from the attachment. Your Contacts folder should be similar to Figure 5-7.

Figure 5-7

Duplicate contact record created

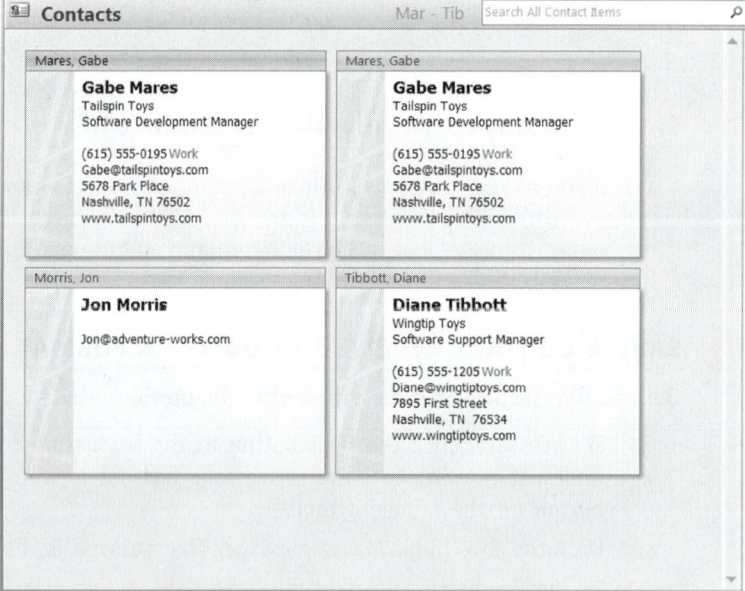

PAUSE. LEAVE Outlook open to use in the next exercise.

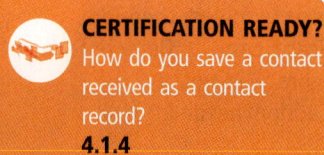

CERTIFICATION READY?
How do you save a contact received as a contact record?
4.1.4

In the previous exercise, you saved a contact in Outlook format that was sent to you as an attachment. You used the same account in an earlier exercise to send the contact record. Therefore, when you received the contact record Outlook recognized it as a duplicate of an existing contact. If this had been a new contact record that you did not have in your Contacts folder, you would have been finished after you clicked the Save & Close button.

Contact Basics | 1011

Creating a Contact from a Message Header

Every message you send automatically contains your contact information in the message header. The *message header* is the text automatically added at the top of a message. The message header contains the sender's email address, the names of the servers used to send and transfer the message, the subject, the date, and other basic information about the message. You can use the message header to create a contact record in your Contacts folder for the message's sender.

➔ CREATE A CONTACT FROM A MESSAGE HEADER

USE the FW: Gabe Mares message sent in a previous exercise.

1. If necessary, click the **Mail** button in the Navigation pane to display the Mail folder.
2. Click the **FW: Gabe Mares** message. The message is displayed in the Reading pane.
3. In the Reading pane, right-click the sender's name or email address. Click the **Add to Outlook contacts** option on the shortcut menu. A contact window containing the sender's name and email address is displayed, as shown in Figure 5-8. Because you sent the FW: Gabe Mares message, it is your contact information in the Contact window.

Figure 5-8

Creating a contact from a message header

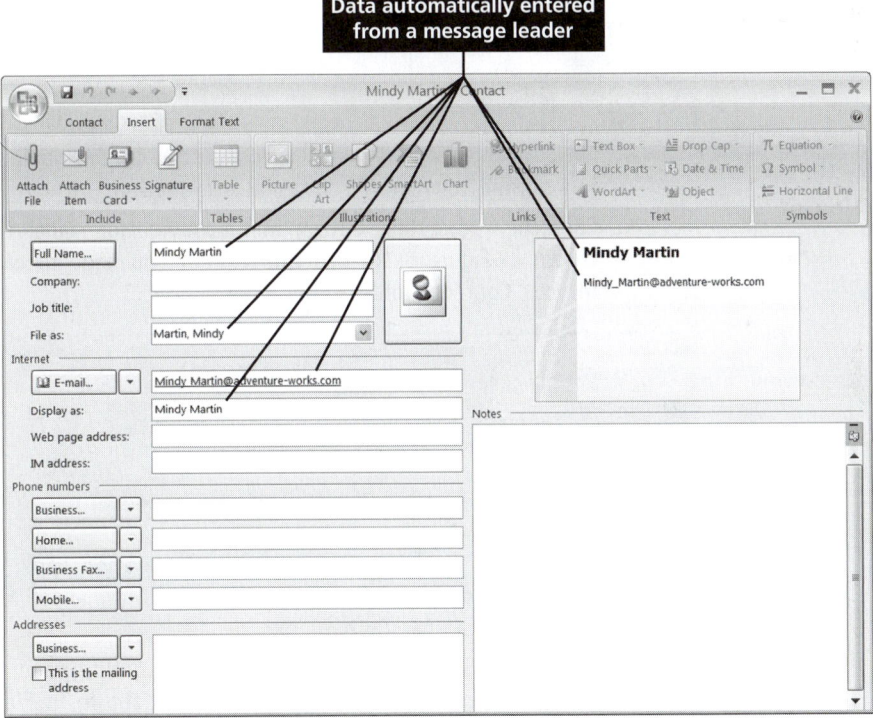

4. In the Actions group on the Ribbon, click the **Save & Close** button. The contact record is created, and you are returned to the Mail folder.
5. Click the **Contacts** button in the Navigation pane to display the Contacts folder. Now, you have the original Gabe Mares contact record you created by keying the data, the Gabe Mares contact record you created from the attachment, Diane Tibbott's contact record created from Gabe's record, and your contact record created from a message header.

   PAUSE. LEAVE Outlook open to use in the next exercise.

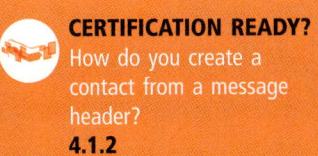

CERTIFICATION READY?
How do you create a contact from a message header?
4.1.2

In the previous exercise, you created a contact from a message header. Although a message header contains important information, it is important to note that false information can be provided in the message header. This is known as *spoofing*. Many junk messages contain false information in the message header.

Viewing and Deleting Contacts

THE BOTTOM LINE — By default, contacts are displayed as business cards. However, other views are available. Select a different view to focus on specific information. Prevent clutter in your Contacts folder. When a contact is no longer useful or you found a duplicate contact, delete the contact record.

VIEW AND DELETE CONTACTS

USE the contacts you created in the previous exercises.

1. If necessary, click the **Contacts** button in the Navigation pane to display the Contacts folder shown in Figure 5-1. This is the Business Cards view. It is the only view that displays any graphics on the business card.

2. Click the **Address Cards** button in the Navigation pane. The view is modified, as shown in Figure 5-9. Job title and company information is hidden. Any graphics on the Business Card view are also hidden. The address cards contain only text.

Figure 5-9

Contact in Address Cards view

3. Click the **Detailed Address Cards** button in the Navigation pane. The view is modified to display additional information.

4. Click the **Phone List** button in the Navigation pane. The view is modified, as shown in Figure 5-10. Use this view if you need to call several contacts in your Contacts folder.

Figure 5-10

Contacts in Phone List view

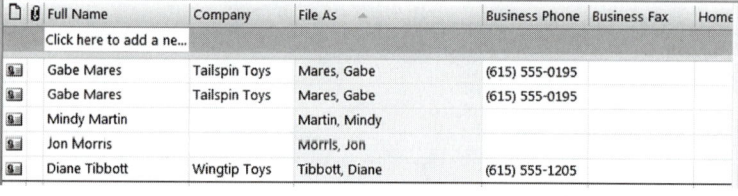

X REF

You will learn more about categories in Lesson 10.

5. Click the **By Category** button in the Navigation pane. The view is modified to group the contacts by category. Use this view if you need to see all the contacts assigned to a specific category.

6. Click the **By Company** button in the Navigation pane. The view is modified to group the contacts by company name, as shown in Figure 5-11. Use this view to see all the contacts working for a specific company.

Figure 5-11

Contacts grouped by company name

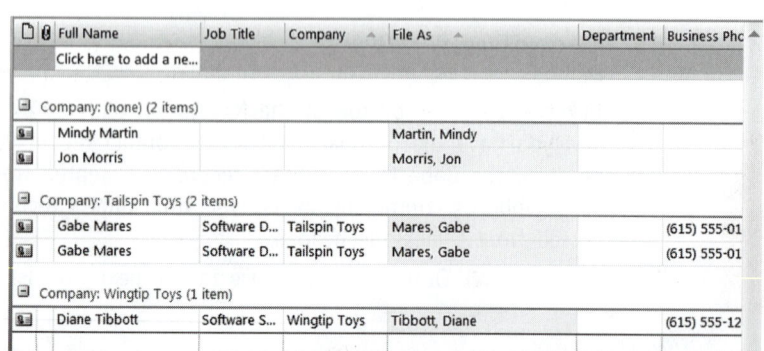

X REF

You will learn more about Outlook data files in Lesson 10.

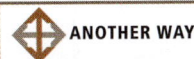

ANOTHER WAY

To delete a contact record, right-click the contact and click Delete on the shortcut menu.

7. Click the **By Location** button in the Navigation pane. The view is modified to group the contacts by country/region. Use this view to see contacts with an address in a particular area. This is more useful if your contacts are not located in the same geographic area.

8. Click the **Outlook Data Files** button in the Navigation pane. The view is modified to display the contacts as they would appear in a data file.

9. Click the **Business Cards** button in the Navigation pane to return to the default view of the contacts.

10. Click the first **Gabe Mares** contact record. On the Standard toolbar, click the **Delete** button. The contact record is moved to the Deleted Items folder. It will not be removed from your computer until the Deleted Items folder is emptied.

   PAUSE. LEAVE Outlook open to use in the next exercise.

Because several views are available, select the view that targets the information you need to see. When you are viewing contact records, you can minimize the clutter by deleting contacts that are no longer useful or duplicates that have been accidentally created.

■ Creating and Modifying a Distribution List

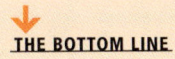

THE BOTTOM LINE

A *distribution list* is a group of individual contacts saved together as a single contact. A distribution list simplifies the task of regularly sending the same message to a group of people. For example, suppose that you manage a group of seven sales representatives. Every week, you send every sales representative a message that summarizes the sales revenue for the previous week and sets the sales goals for the current week. To address the message, you must select seven email addresses. If you create a distribution list, you can add the seven individual contacts to the distribution list. Next week, you can use the distribution list as the address for the sales message. You make one selection in the To field to send the message to the seven members of the distribution list.

Creating a Distribution List

To create a distribution list, you create a contact that is identified as a distribution list. Then you select the members of the distribution list and save the distribution list. To send a message to all the members of the distribution list, simply select the distribution list as the recipient.

➔ CREATE A DISTRIBUTION LIST

USE the contacts you created in the previous exercises.

1. If necessary, click the **Contacts** button in the Navigation pane to display the Contacts folder shown in Figure 5-1.

2. On the Standard toolbar, click the **New** arrow to display the dropdown menu. Click the **Distribution List** option. The Untitled – Distribution List window is displayed, as shown in Figure 5-12. The Members button in the Show group on the Ribbon is selected.

Figure 5-12

Untitled – Distribution List window

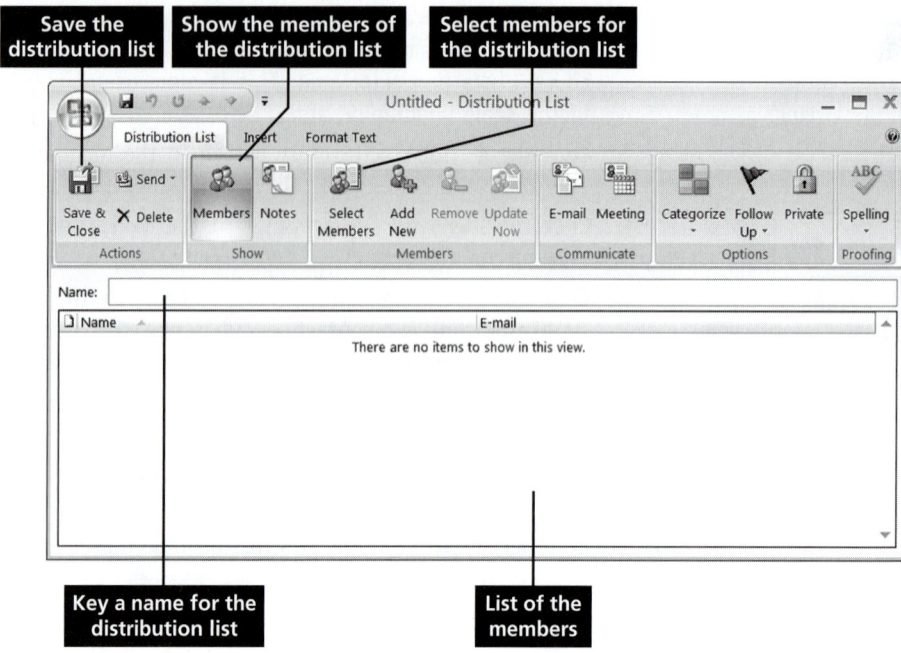

3. In the Members group on the Ribbon, click the **Select Members** button. The Select Members: Contacts window is displayed, as shown in Figure 5-13. The contacts in your Contacts folder are listed. The first contact is already selected.

Figure 5-13

Select Members: Contacts window

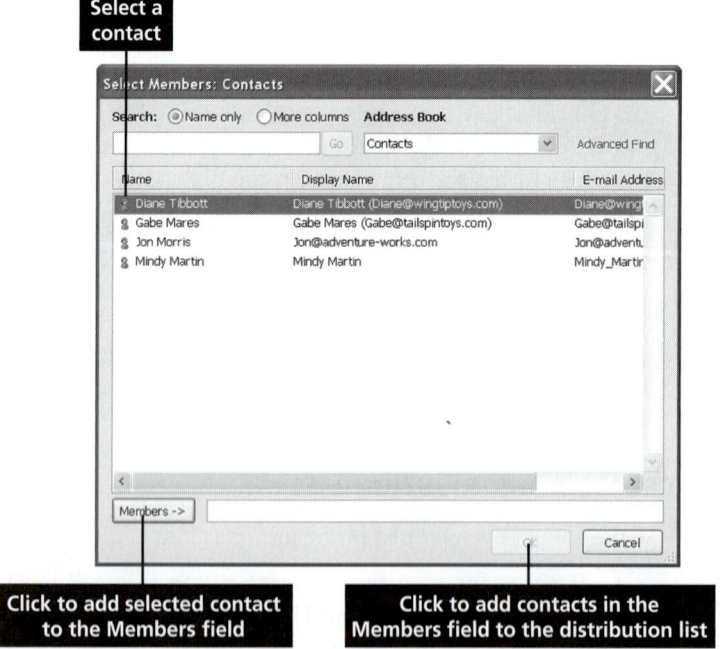

4. Because the first contact you want to include in the distribution list is already selected, click the **Members** button. The contact's name is added to the Members field at the bottom of the window.

5. Click the **second contact** in the list. Click the **Members** button. The second contact is added to the Members field.

6. Click the **third contact** on the list. Click the **Members** button. The third contact is added to the Members field.

7. Click **OK**. The Select Members: Contacts window is closed, and you are returned to the Untitled – Distribution List window. The four contacts are listed in the lower area of the window.
8. Click the **Name** field. Key **Wingtip Toys List**. This name is used to identify the distribution list in the Contacts folder.
9. Click the **Save & Close** button. The distribution list is saved. The window is closed, and you are returned to the Contacts folder. The Wingtip Toys List contact is displayed, as shown in Figure 5-14.

Figure 5-14

Distribution list created

TAKE NOTE* When you view the distribution list in the Contacts folder, the list of members is not visible. To see the list of members, open the contact record.

PAUSE. LEAVE Outlook open to use in the next exercise.

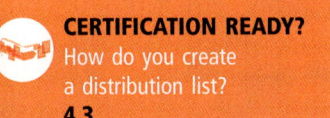

CERTIFICATION READY?
How do you create a distribution list?
4.3

In the previous exercise, you created a distribution list that contains all of your contacts. Normally, a distribution list contains multiple members, but it won't contain all of your contacts.

Modifying a Distribution List

Any distribution list used over time will eventually require changes. In fact, the distribution list you just created already requires a change.

➔ MODIFY A DISTRIBUTION LIST

USE the contacts you created in the previous exercises.

1. If necessary, click the **Contacts** button in the Navigation pane to display the Contacts folder shown in Figure 5-1.
2. Double-click the **Wingtip Toys List** contact. The Wingtip Toys List – Distribution List window is displayed.
3. Click **Gabe's name** in the lower area of the window. In the Members group on the Ribbon, click the **Remove** button. Gabe is removed from the distribution list.
4. In the list of members, double-click your name. Your contact record is displayed.
5. Click the **Company** field. Key the name of your company.
6. Click the **Save & Close** button in your contact window. Your modified contact record is saved and closed.
7. Click the **Save & Close** button in the distribution list window. The distribution list is saved. The window is closed, and you are returned to the Contacts folder.

8. Double-click the **Wingtip Toys List** contact to reopen it. The Wingtip Toys List – Distribution List window is displayed.

9. In the Communicate group on the Ribbon, click the **E-mail** button. A blank Message window is displayed. In the To field, the Wingtip Toys List contact is automatically entered, as shown in Figure 5-15. The rest of the fields are empty.

Figure 5-15

Message addressed to the distribution list created

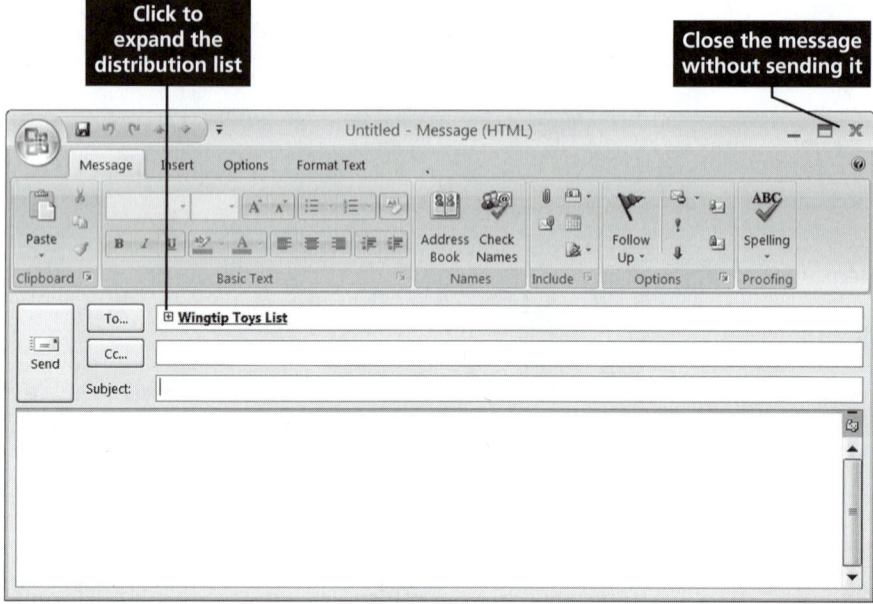

10. Click the **plus sign** in the To field. A warning box is displayed stating that the list will be replaced with its members. Click **OK**. The individual addressees are displayed in the To field.

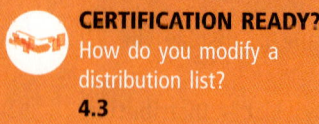

It is not necessary to expand the distribution list in a message. You expanded the distribution list in this exercise for demonstration purposes.

CERTIFICATION READY?
How do you modify a distribution list?
4.3

11. Click the **Close** button to close the message without sending it. Do not save changes to the message.

   CLOSE Outlook.

When you created the Wingtip Toys distribution list, you included Gabe Mares. However, he works for Tailspin Toys now. In the previous exercise, you removed Gabe from the distribution list. You also accessed and modified your contact record through the distribution list. Finally, you created a message that could be sent to the members of the distribution list. After all, sending a message to multiple recipients quickly and easily is the purpose of creating and maintaining a distribution list.

Summary Skill Matrix

In This Lesson You Learned how to:
Create a Contact from a Blank Contact
Create a Contact from an Existing Contact
Modify Contact Information
Send a Contact as an Attachment
Save a Contact Received as a Contact Record
Create a Contact from a Message Header
View and Deleting Contacts
Create a Distribution List
Modify a Distribution List

Knowledge Assessment

Fill in the Blank

Complete the following sentences by writing the correct word or words in the blanks provided.

1. The <u>Contacts Folder</u> is an electronic organizer that enables you to create, view, and edit contact information.
2. Like documents and files, contact information can be sent as a(n) <u>Attachment</u>.
3. The text automatically added at the top of a message is the <u>Message Header</u>.
4. A(n) <u>Contact</u> is a collection of information about a person or company.
5. The default view in the Contacts folder is the <u>Business Card</u> view.
6. A(n) <u>Screen Tip</u> provides a brief description of an item's purpose.
7. If you try to add a contact that already exists in your Contacts folder, Outlook detects a(n) <u>Duplicate Contact</u>.
8. Providing false information in a message header is called <u>Spoofing</u>.
9. A(n) <u>Distribution List</u> is a group of individual contacts saved together as a single contact.
10. Contact records in a distribution list are known as <u>Members</u> of the distribution list.

Multiple Choice

Circle the correct choice.

1. What window is displayed when the mouse hovers over a button?
    A. the contact's name
    B. Online Help
    C. ScreenTip
    D. enlarged view of the button

2. Which field should contain a value when you save a contact?
   A. File as
   B. Display as
   C. Full Name
   D. E-mail

3. What value is not carried over to the new contact when you create a new contact record from the same company?
   A. Address
   B. Website
   C. Phone number
   D. Email address

4. A duplicate contact should be
   A. created for every contact.
   B. displayed before the original contact.
   C. deleted.
   D. modified.

5. When you key a phone number in a contact record,
   A. key the parentheses around the area code.
   B. don't key the area code.
   C. key a hyphen between each group of numbers.
   D. don't key spaces in the number.

6. Which of the following is a way to create a contact record?
   A. Key information into a blank contact record.
   B. Modify an existing contact record and save it as a new contact.
   C. Create a contact from a message header.
   D. All of the above

7. What does a recipient need to save a contact received in Outlook format?
   A. Outlook 2007
   B. Existing contact records
   C. Any email program
   D. All of the above

8. What provides the information to create a contact from any message you receive?
   A. The attachment
   B. The subject
   C. The message header
   D. The Subject field

9. How many views are available in the Contacts folder?
   A. Eight
   B. One
   C. It depends on the number of contact records you have saved
   D. Five

10. How can you simplify the task of regularly sending messages to the same group of contacts?
    A. Resend the message to each contact.
    B. Use nicknames for the contacts.
    C. Set a predetermined time for sending the messages.
    D. Create a distribution list.

Competency Assessment

Project 5-1: Create Contacts from Blank Contacts

Gabe Mares recently started a new job at Tailspin Toys. As part of the training program, he will be travelling to different divisions to examine their procedures. At his first stop in Pittsburgh, PA, Gabe collected contact information for the team leader.

GET READY. Launch Outlook if it is not already running.

1. If necessary, click the **Contacts** button in the Navigation pane to display the Contacts folder.
2. Click **New** on the Standard toolbar. The Untitled – Contact window is displayed.
3. Click the **Full Name** field if necessary. Key **Mandar Samant** and press **Tab**.
4. In the Company field, key **Tailspin Toys** and press **Tab**.
5. In the *Job title* field, key **Software Development Team Lead** and press **Tab**.
6. Click the **E-mail** field. Key **Mandar@tailspintoys.com** and press **Tab**.
7. In the *Web page address* field, key **www.tailspintoys.com**.
8. Below the *Phone numbers* heading, click the **Business** field. Key **4125551117**. Press **Tab**.
9. Below the Addresses heading, click the **Business** field. Key **4567 Broadway**. Press **Enter**. Key **Pittsburgh, PA 14202**. Press **Tab**.
10. In the Actions group on the Ribbon, click the **Save & Close** button.

LEAVE Outlook open for the next project.

Project 5-2: Create a Contact from a Contact at the Same Company

While Gabe was in Pittsburgh, he interviewed a software developer in Mandar Samant's team. Although Gabe doesn't usually contact developers directly, he wants to save her contact information in case an opening occurs as a team leader.

1. If necessary, click the **Contacts** button in the Navigation pane to display the Contacts folder.
2. Double-click the **Mandar Samant** contact. The contact window is displayed.
3. In the Actions group on the Ribbon, click the **Save & New** arrow. In the dropdown list of options, click **New Contact from Same Company**.
4. Click in the **Full Name** field if necessary. Key **Jamie Reding** and press **Tab**.
5. In the *Job title* field, key **Software Developer** and press **Tab**.
6. In the *E-mail* field, key **Jamie@tailspintoys.com** and press **Tab**.
7. In the *Notes* field, key **Potential team lead**.
8. In the Actions group on the Ribbon, click the **Save & Close** button.
9. **CLOSE** the Mandar Samant contact record without saving changes.

LEAVE Outlook open for the next project.

Proficiency Assessment

Project 5-3: Modify Contact Information

Two months later, Jamie Reding was promoted to a team leader in the Pittsburgh office. Gabe modified her contact information.

1. If necessary, click the **Contacts** button in the Navigation pane to display the Contacts folder.
2. Double-click the **Jamie Reding** contact. The contact window is displayed.
3. Click the **Job title** field. Change her title to **Software Development Team Lead** and press **Tab**.
4. Click the **Notes** field. Change the text to **Monitor her progress**.
5. In the Actions group on the Ribbon, click the **Save & Close** button.
   LEAVE Outlook open for the next project.

Project 5-4: Send a Contact as an Attachment

Gabe's manager asked for information about a team leader for a new project. Gabe sends Jamie's contact record.

1. If necessary, click the **Contacts** button in the Navigation pane to display the Contacts folder.
2. Double-click the **Jamie Reding** contact. The Contact window is displayed.
3. In Actions group on the Ribbon, click the **Send** button. If a message is displayed stating that you must save the original item, click **OK** to continue. Click the **In Outlook Format** option.
4. Click the **To** button. In the Select Names: Contacts window, click your contact record. Click the **To** button. Click **OK**.
5. Click in the message area. Key **The contact information you requested is attached**.
6. Click the **Send** button.
7. **CLOSE** Jamie Reding's contact record without saving changes.
   LEAVE Outlook open for the next project.

Mastery Assessment

Project 5-5: Create a Distribution List

Gabe sends several messages to the team leaders each day. To simplify the task, Gabe creates a distribution list.

1. If necessary, click the **Contacts** button in the Navigation pane to display the Contacts folder.
2. On the Standard toolbar, click the **New** arrow and then click the **Distribution List** option on the shortcut menu.
3. In the Members group on the Ribbon, click the **Select Members** button.
4. Add all the Tailspin Toys employees to the Members field, including Gabe, and click **OK**.
5. Name the distribution list **Tailspin Team Leaders**.
6. Click the **Save & Close** button.
   LEAVE Outlook open for the next project.

Project 5-6: Modify a Distribution List

Gabe was not surprised to determine that the Tailspin Team Leaders distribution list needs to be changed. Gabe needs to remove himself from the distribution list and add Diane Tibbott. Diane just accepted the position of Software Development Team Lead for Tailspin Toys. She will work in the Nashville office with Gabe.

1. If necessary, click the **Contacts** button in the Navigation pane to display the Contacts folder.
2. Use Gabe's contact record to create a new contact record from the same company for Diane Tibbott. Use the following information.

Full Name	**Diane Tibbott**
Job title	**Software Development Team Lead**
E-mail	**Diane@tailspintoys.com**

3. Delete Diane Tibbott's outdated contact record from Wingtip Toys.
4. Open the **Tailspin Team Leaders** contact record.
5. Click **Gabe Mares** in the list of members and click the **Remove** button.
6. Click the **Select Members** button. In the Select Members: Contacts window, add Diane Tibbott to the Members field and click **OK**.
7. **SAVE** the changes to the distribution list.

   CLOSE Outlook.

INTERNET READY

Looking for a new job with better pay, the right amount of travel, better hours, and a larger office? Use the Internet. Research some companies that interest you. Create contact records for the Human Resources offices in those companies.

Circling Back

Kim Ralls was promoted to Shift Supervisor and transferred to the downtown office at City Power & Light. Although Kim was transferred, her computer and other equipment did not move with her. She needs to set up Outlook 2007 with her signature, new rules and contacts to help her manage her new responsibilities. She also needs to update her electronic business card to display her new title and contact information.

Project 1: Signature

Kim needs to create a signature for email messages. She asked you to use a graphic she likes.

GET READY. Launch Outlook if it is not already running.

1. Click the **New** button. A new message window is opened.
2. Click in the message area. Click the **Insert** tab on the Ribbon.
3. Click the **Table** button in the Tables group. Click the second square in the fifth row of boxes in the drop-down list. An empty table with two columns and five rows is inserted in the message area.
4. Select all the cells in the first column of the table.
5. Click the **Layout** tab in the Ribbon. Because table cells are selected, the displayed layout options on the Ribbon apply to tables.
6. Click the **Merge Cells** button in the Merge group on the Ribbon. The cells in the first column are merged.
7. Click in the merged cell. Click the **Insert** tab on the Ribbon.
8. Click the **Picture** button in the Illustrations group. Select the *Sun.gif* file in the Data files. Click the **Insert** button on the dialog box. The image is inserted, but it is much too large to use in a signature. The image is automatically selected in the table.

The *Sun* image is available on the companion CD-ROM.

9. With the picture still selected, click the **Size** button, and then click the **Size Dialog Box Launcher**. The Size dialog box is displayed.
10. In the Scale area, click the **Lock aspect ratio** checkbox to select the option if necessary. This option will keep the image in proportion as you resize it.
11. Click in the Height box. Key **5%**, and press Tab. Click the **Close** button to return to the message window. The sun image has been resized.
12. Drag the vertical center **border** of the table to the left so the first column is barely wider than the sun image.
13. Click in the first row of the second column. Key **Kim Ralls**.
14. Click in the second row of the second column. Key **Kim Ralls, Shift Supervisor**.
15. Click in the third row of the second column. Key **City Power and Light**.
16. Click in the fourth row of the second column. Key **www.cpl.com**.
17. Click in the fifth row of the second column. Key **800-555-8734 or Kim@cpl.com**.
18. Select all the text in the table. Click the **Message** tab if necessary. In the Basic Text group, change the font to **Verdana**. (Use Arial font if you don't have Verdana.)
19. Select **Kim's name** in the first row of the second column. Change the font to **Freestyle Script**. (If you don't have Freestyle Script font, use any font that looks like handwriting or leave the font unchanged.)

20. Increase the font size of **Kim's** name to **20** and click the **Bold** button.
21. Select all the **text** in the table. Click the **Font Color** arrow. Click **More Colors**. In the displayed colors, click a **dark red** shade that coordinates with the color of the sun image. Click **OK** to close the dialog box.
22. Drag the right **border** of the table to the left so that the second column is barely wider than the widest text in the column.
23. Click the **sun** image. Click the **Table Tools** option displayed above the menu. Click the **Layout** tab. Click the **Align Center** button in the Alignment group.
24. Select the **table**. Click the **Design** tab. In the Table Styles group, click the **Borders** arrow. Click the **No Border** option.
25. With the table selected, press **Ctrl + C** to copy the table.
26. Click the **Message** tab. In the Include group, click the **Signature** button. Click the **Signatures** option to display the Signatures and Stationery dialog box.
27. Click the **New** button. The New Signature dialog box is displayed.
28. Key **KR Project 1** and click **OK** to return to the Signatures and Stationery dialog box.
29. Click in the Edit signature area. Press **Ctrl + V** to paste the new signature into the box. Click the **OK** button to return to the message window.

    LEAVE Outlook and the message window open for the next project.

Project 2: Create Mail and Contacts Folders

Kim starts the process of customizing Outlook 2007 to meet her needs by creating new folders. One mail folder will contain messages about requests for new service. Another folder will contain contact information for the CP&L service technicians responsible for establishing service at new homes and businesses.

GET READY. Launch Outlook if it is not already running.

1. Click the **Folder List** button in the bottom of the Navigation pane to display the Folder List.
2. Click the arrow next to **New** in the standard toolbar. Click **Folder**. The Create New Folder dialog box is displayed.
3. In the Name field, key **New Service** to identify the new folder. Verify that **Mail and Post Items** is selected in the *Folder contains* field. If necessary, click **Personal Folders** in the *Select where to place the folder* list. Click **OK** to create the folder.
4. Click the arrow next to **New** in the standard toolbar. Click **Folder**. The Create New Folder dialog box is displayed.
5. In the Name field, key **New Service Techs** to identify the new folder. Select **Contact Items** in the *Folder contains* field. If necessary, click **Contacts** in the *Select where to place the folder* list. Click **OK** to create the folder.

    LEAVE Outlook open for the next project.

Project 3: Create a Rule

Kim receives messages requesting new service from the Customer Service department. Messages could come from a dozen different Customer Service representatives. However, the Subject field for every message contains the words "New Service Request." Kim decided to create a rule moving all of the requests to the New Service folder.

USE the New Service folder created in the previous project. Your computer must be connected to the Internet to test the rule at the end of this project.

1. If necessary, click the **Mail** button in the Navigation pane to display the Mail folder.
2. Click the **Tools** menu, and click the **Rules and Alerts** option. The Rules and Alerts window is displayed. Turn off all rules except the *Clear categories on mail* rule.
3. Click the **New Rule** button. The Rules Wizard window is displayed.
4. In the *Stay Organized* category, click **Move messages with specific words in the subject to a folder**.
5. In the *Step 2* area, click **specific words**. The Search Text window is displayed.
6. In the *Specify words or phrases to search for in the subject* field, key **New Service Request**. Click the **Add** button. Click **OK** to close the Search Text window. The Rules Wizard window is displayed.
7. In the *Step 2* area of the Rules Wizard window, click **specified** to identify the destination folder. The Folder List is displayed in the Rules and Alerts window.
8. Click the **New Service** folder, and click **OK**. The specified destination folder is identified in the Rules Wizard window. Click the **Next** button to continue the Wizard.
9. Click the **Next** button twice to continue the Wizard without modifying conditions or actions.
10. Under *Select exceptions*, click the **except if the subject contains specific words** checkbox. Text is added to the rule description at the bottom of the Rules Wizard window.
11. In the rule description area, click **specific words**. The Search text window is displayed.
12. In the *Specify words or phrases to search for in the subject* field, key **RE:**. (Be sure to include the colon in the specified words or any message subject containing the letters *re* will be an exception.) Click the **Add** button. The *RE:* text is enclosed by quotation marks and added to the search list for this rule. Click **OK** to close the Search Text window. The Rules Wizard window is displayed.
13. Click the **Next** button to continue the Wizard. The rule is displayed for your approval. Examine the rule carefully to verify that it is correct. Click the **Finish** button. The new rule is displayed in the Rules and Alerts window. Verify that the only active rules are the *New Service Request* and *Clear categories on mail* rules. Click the **OK** button to close the Rules and Alerts window.
14. Click the **New** button to display a new Message window. Address the message to your email address. In the Subject field, key **New Service Request**. Send the message. Create and send a second message to your email address using **RE: New Service Request** in the Subject field.
15. Click the **Send/Receive** button, if necessary, to receive the messages. Verify that the New Service Request message was moved to the New Service folder and the RE: New Service Request message remained in the Inbox.
16. Click the **Tools** menu, and click the **Rules and Alerts** option. The Rules and Alerts window is displayed. Turn off all rules except the *Clear categories on mail* rule. Click **OK** to close the Rules and Alerts window.

    LEAVE Outlook open for the next project.

Project 4: Create Contact Records

Kim needs to create contact records for herself and the two new Service Technicians in her department.

USE the New Service Techs folder created in the first project.

1. If necessary, click the **Contacts** button in the Navigation pane to display the Contacts folder. Under My Contacts in the Navigation pane, click **New Service Techs** to open the new folder created in Project 1.
2. Click **New** on the Standard toolbar to display a blank Contact window.
3. Click the *Full Name* field, if necessary. Key **Kim Ralls** and press **Tab**.
4. In the *Company* field, key **City Power & Light** and press **Tab**.
5. In the *Job title* field, key **Shift Supervisor** and press **Tab**.

> **TROUBLESHOOTING** The email addresses provided in these projects belong to unused domains owned by Microsoft. When you send a message to these addresses, you will receive an error message stating that the message could not be delivered. Delete the error messages when they arrive.

6. Click the *E-mail* field. Key **Kim@cpandl.com** and press **Tab**.
7. In the *Web page address* field, key **www.cpandl.com**.
8. Below the *Phone numbers* heading, click the **Business** field. Key **2175559821**.
9. Below the Addresses heading, click the **Business** field. Key **324 Main Street**. Press **Enter**. Key **Springfield, IL 68390**. Press **Tab**.
10. In the Actions group on the Ribbon, click the **Save & New** arrow. In the dropdown list of options, click **New Contact from Same Company**.
11. Click the *Full Name* field, if necessary. Key **Jay Henningsen** and press **Tab**. Click the *Job title* field. Key **New Service Technician** and press **Tab**. Click the *E-mail* field. Key **Jay@cpandl.com** and press **Tab**.
12. In the Actions group on the Ribbon, click the **Save & New** arrow. In the dropdown list of options, click **New Contact from Same Company**.
13. Click the *Full Name* field, if necessary. Key **Julia Moseley** and press **Tab**. Click the *Job title* field. Key **New Service Technician** and press **Tab**. Click the *E-mail* field. Key **Julia@cpandl.com** and press **Tab**.
14. In the Actions group on the Ribbon, click the **Save & Close** button.
15. **CLOSE** any open contact records.

    CLOSE Outlook.

6 Advanced Contact Management

LESSON SKILL MATRIX

Editing an Electronic Business Card	Students will learn how to edit an electronic business card.
Sending an Electronic Business Card	Students will learn how to send an electronic business card.
Creating a Contact from an Electronic Business Card	Students will learn how to create a contact from an electronic business card.
Using an Electronic Business Card in a Signature	Students will learn how to use an electronic business card in a signature.
Searching for Contacts	Students will learn how to search for contacts.
Searching for Items Related to a Contact	Students will learn how to search for items related to a contact.
Creating a Custom Search Folder	Students will learn how to create a custom search folder.
Creating a Secondary Address Book for Personal Contacts	Students will learn how to create a secondary address book for personal contacts.
Importing a Secondary Address Book from a File	Students will learn how to importing a secondary address book from a file.

The Marketing department at Tailspin Toys is holding a contest that is open to all employees. To compete, employees must design an electronic business card. Gabe Mares, the Software Development Manager, wasn't planning to enter the contest. However, he had an idea for an electronic business card that he couldn't resist. He thumbed through the Tailspin Toys catalog until he found the perfect picture for his design. After all, who can resist a teddy bear?

KEY TERMS
address book
Categorized Mail
electronic business cards
import
Large Mail
Search Folder
secondary address book
Unread Mail
virtual folder

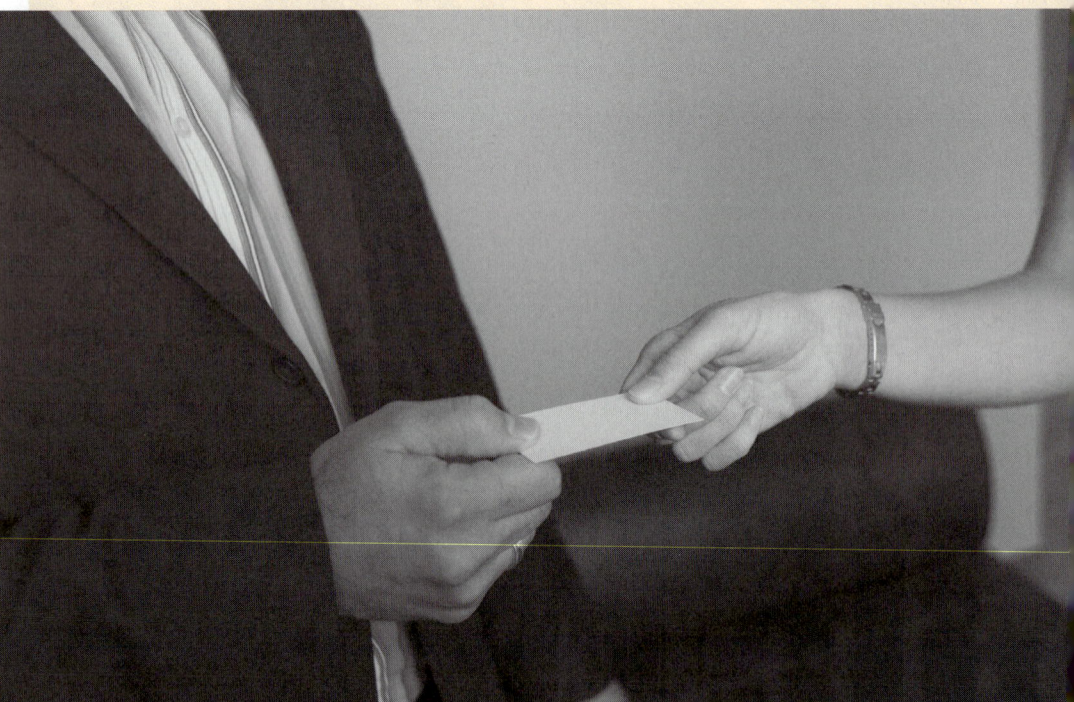

Advanced Contact Management | 1027

Software Orientation

Microsoft Outlook's Edit Business Card Window

The default view in the Contacts folder is the Business Cards view. It displays all of the contacts in your Contacts folder as business cards. By default, the text appears on the right and the left side of the card contains a gray bar, as shown in Figure 6-1.

Figure 6-1

Outlook's Edit Business Card window

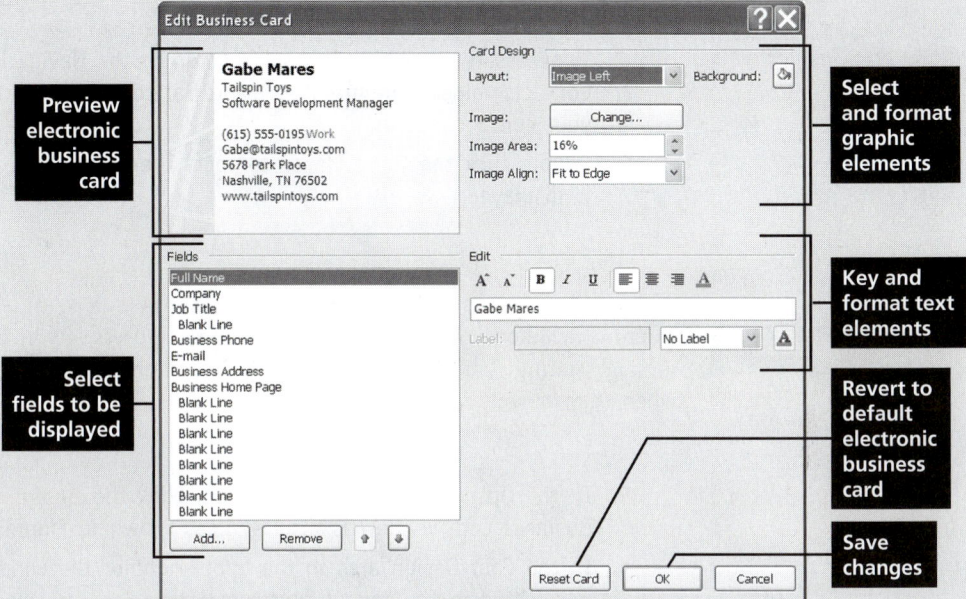

Use the Edit Business Card window to create a business card that fits your company image. Refer to Figure 6-1 as you complete the following exercises.

■ Using Electronic Business Cards

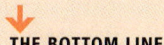

THE BOTTOM LINE

The electronic business card is a new feature in Outlook 2007. ***Electronic business cards*** are the digital version of paper business cards. They can be sent as attachments, used as signatures, and used to create a contact record. Because the default view in the Contacts folder displays the electronic business cards, it is important to design an electronic business card that is memorable and easy to find when several electronic business cards are displayed on the screen.

Editing an Electronic Business Card

"Here's my card. Give me a call sometime." How many times have you shaken hands and exchanged business cards with new contacts? Electronic business cards are the paperless version of the business cards you currently have stashed in your wallet, falling out of your address book, choking your Rolodex, and marking the page in the latest novel you're reading.

EDIT AN ELECTRONIC BUSINESS CARD

GET READY. Before you begin these steps, be sure to launch Microsoft Outlook. The Greg Mares contact record was created in Lesson 5.

> **TAKE NOTE*** An electronic business card is created automatically when you create a contact. It is basically another view of the contact record. If you delete the electronic business card, you delete the contact. Changes made to the information on the electronic business card are changed for the contact as well.

1. If necessary, click the **Contacts** button in the Navigation pane to display the Contacts folder. Minimize the To-Do Bar to provide additional room to display your contact records.
2. Double-click the **Gabe Mares** contact. The Gabe Mares – Contact window is displayed.

> **TROUBLESHOOTING** The email addresses provided in these exercises belong to unused domains owned by Microsoft. When you send a message to these addresses, you will receive an error message stating that the message could not be delivered. Delete the error messages when they arrive.

3. In the Options group on the Ribbon, click the **Business Card** button. The Edit Business Card window is displayed, as shown in Figure 6-1.
4. In the Card Design area in the upper-right of the window, verify that **Image Left** is selected in the Layout field and **Fit to Edge** is selected in the Image Align field. This defines the position of the graphic. Currently, the graphic is the default gray bar.
5. Click the **Change** button. The Add Card Picture dialog box is displayed. Navigate to the data files for this lesson. Click the *bear side* file and click **OK**. The bear image is added to the card preview.

 The *bear side* image is available on the companion CD-ROM.

6. In the Card Design area, click the **Image Area** field. Change the value to **25%**, if necessary. In the card preview, the image area widens to 25% of the card's width.
7. In the Card Design area, click the **Image Align** field. In the dropdown list, click **Bottom Center**. In the card preview, the image is resized and repositioned.
8. In the Card Design area, click the **Image Align** field. In the dropdown list, click **Fit to Edge**. In the card preview, the image is resized and placed in its original position.
9. In the Fields area, click **Business Home Page** in the list of fields. Click the **Add** button. In the dropdown menu, point to **Internet Address** and then click **IM Address**. IM Address is added to the list of fields. The IM Address field is used for an instant messaging address.

Advanced Contact Management | 1029

10. With IM Address selected in the list of fields, click the empty field in the Edit area. Key **GabeTailspinToys**, as shown in Figure 6-2.

Figure 6-2

Modified Edit Business Card window

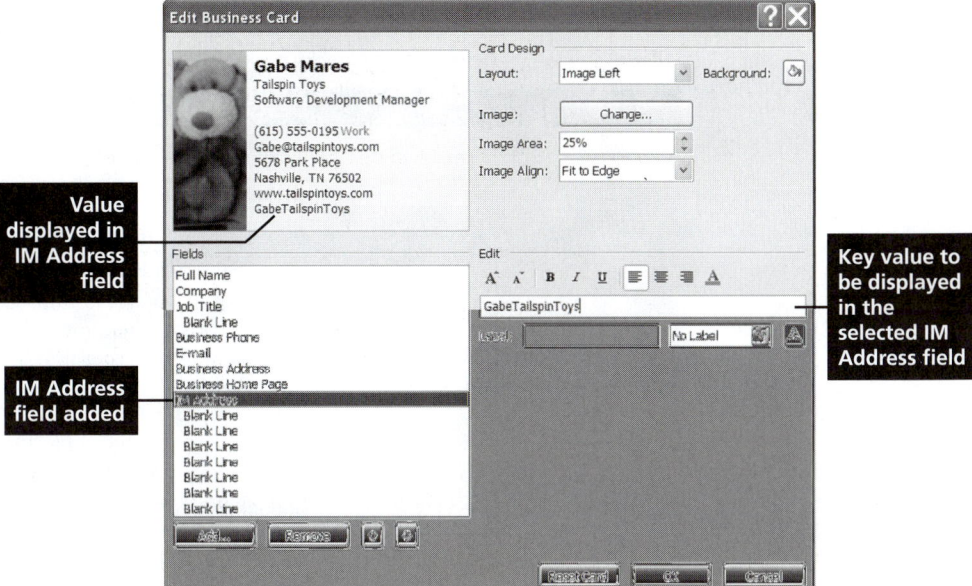

11. Click **OK**. The Edit Business Card window is closed. Click the **Save & Close** button to return to the Contacts folder. Gabe's business card is displayed, as shown in Figure 6-3.

Figure 6-3

Modified business card

> **CERTIFICATION READY?**
> How do you edit an electronic business card?
> 4.2.1

PAUSE. LEAVE Outlook open to use in the next exercise.

In the previous exercise, you modified the default electronic business card to create a memorable business card that can easily be picked out of the crowd of electronic business cards many users store in their Contacts folders. Gabe wants to present an image of fun and safety for Tailspin Toys. A teddy bear presents that image.

The Edit Business Card window has four separate areas, as identified in Table 6-1. The four areas work together to provide a flexible tool that can create an amazing variety of customized electronic business cards.

Table 6-1

Edit Business Card window

Area	Description
Preview	View the effect of the changes you make.
Fields	Identify the fields you want to display on the electronic business card. Use the Add button to insert a new field. Select a field in the list and click the Remove button to delete a field. To move a field up or down on the card, select the field and click the Move Field Up (Up arrow) button or the Move Field Down (Down arrow) button .
Card Design	Insert and position a graphic or select a background color for the card. Position the image and define the amount of the card that can be used for the graphic. Graphics cannot be edited in Outlook 2007. The image must be ready to be placed before it is used in the electronic business card.
Edit	Key the value to be displayed in the field. Limited text formatting options are available.

Sending an Electronic Business Card

Electronic business cards can be shared with others. Insert one or more business cards in a message and click the Send button.

 SEND AN ELECTRONIC BUSINESS CARD

USE the Gabe Mares contact record.

1. If necessary, click the **Mail** button in the Navigation pane to display the Mail folder.
2. Click the **New** button in the Standard toolbar. The Message window is displayed. By default, the Message tab is selected.
3. Click the **To** field. Key your email address.
4. Click the **Subject** field. Key **Business cards attached**.
5. Click in the message area. Key **I attached the electronic business cards you requested.** Press **Enter**.
6. In the Include group on the Ribbon, click the **Insert Business Card** button. A dropdown list is displayed.
7. Click **Other Business Cards** in the dropdown list. The Insert Business Card window is displayed, as shown in Figure 6-4.

 If the contact name is displayed in the dropdown list, you can click the name to insert the electronic business card.

Advanced Contact Management | 1031

Figure 6-4

Insert Business Card window

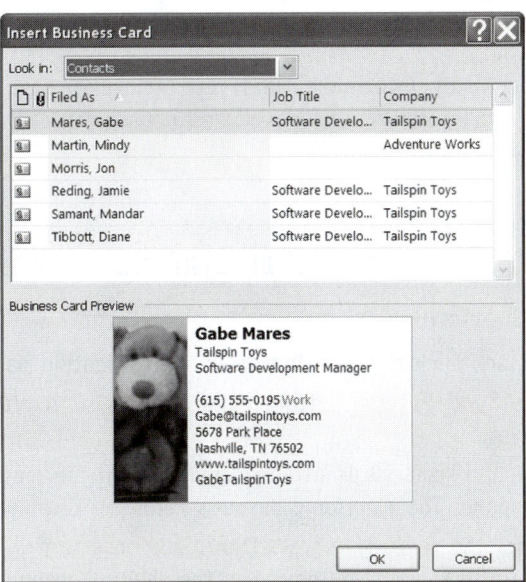

8. Click the **Gabe Mares** contact. Press **Ctrl** and click the **Diane Tibbott** contact. Click **OK**. The electronic business cards are inserted into the message. In the Attached field, the contact records are attached as .vcf files, as shown in Figure 6-5.

Figure 6-5

Electronic business cards inserted into a message

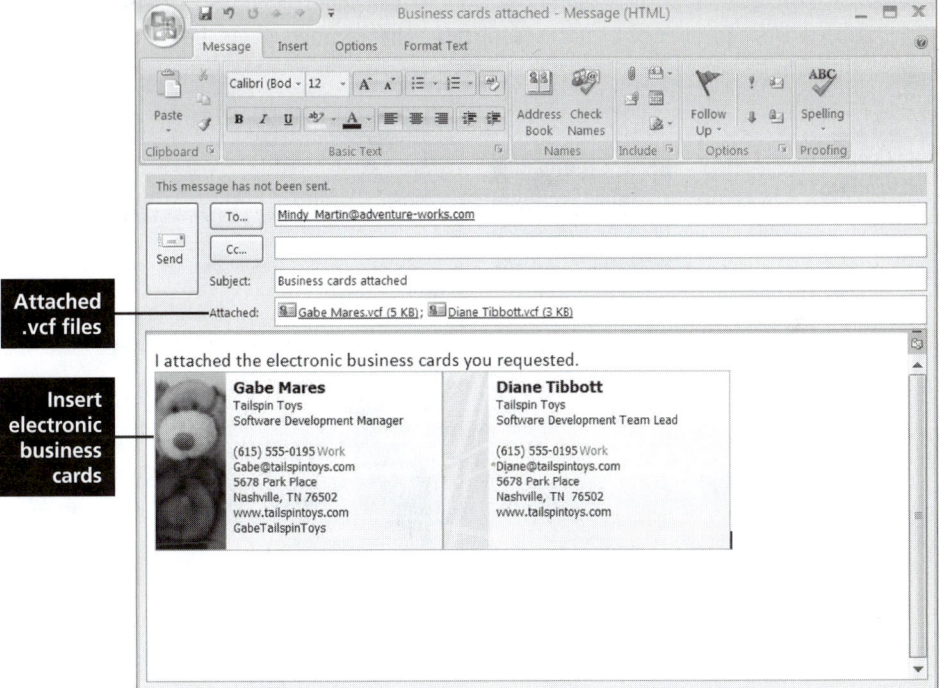

CERTIFICATION READY?
How do you send an electronic business card to others?
4.2.2

9. Click the **Send** button.

PAUSE. LEAVE Outlook open to use in the next exercise.

In the previous exercise, you sent an electronic business card in a message. Outlook 2007 users will be able to create contact records from the electronic business records. Users of other email applications will be able to get the contact information from the .vcf files that were automatically created by Outlook and attached to the message when you inserted the electronic business cards.

You can find more information on other methods of creating contacts in Lesson 5.

Creating a Contact from an Electronic Business Card

When you receive an electronic business card, you can use the card to create a contact record. All of the information on the electronic business card and the card's appearance are saved in your Contacts folder.

CREATE A CONTACT FROM AN ELECTRONIC BUSINESS CARD

USE the message you sent in the previous exercise.

1. If necessary, click the **Mail** button in the Navigation pane to display the Mail folder.
2. Click the **Send/Receive** button if the *Business cards attached* message has not arrived yet.
3. Click the **Business cards attached message** in the message list to display it in the Reading pane. The electronic business cards are displayed in the message body.
4. Right-click the **Gabe Mares electronic business card** in the message body. Click the **Add to Outlook Contacts** option in the shortcut menu. A Gabe Mares – Contact window is displayed that contains the information displayed on the electronic business card, including the preview image of the card.
5. Click the **Save & Close** button in the Actions group on the Ribbon. Because you received this contact information at the same email address used to send the contact information, the contact record is already in your Contacts folder. Therefore, Outlook detects that this is a duplicate contact, and the Duplicate Contact Detected window shown in Figure 6-6 is displayed. If the contact record was not a duplicate, the contact would be saved without any further action needed.

Figure 6-6

Duplicate Contact Detected window

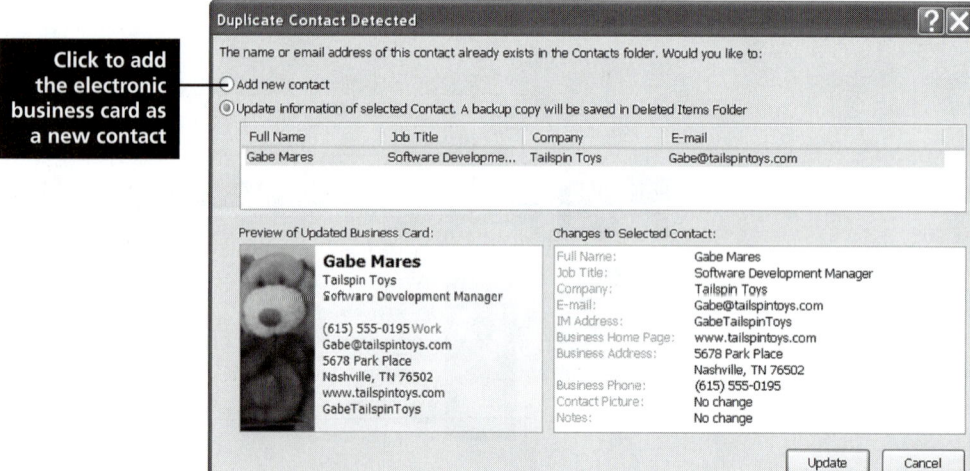

6. You want to create a new contact, so select the **Add new contact** option at the top of the window and click the **Add** button at the bottom of the window. The Duplicate Contact Detected window is closed, the contact record is created, and you are returned to the Mail folder.
7. Click the **Contacts** button in the Navigation pane to display the Contacts folder. Now, you have the original Gabe Mares contact record and the Gabe Mares contact record you created from the electronic business card in the message.

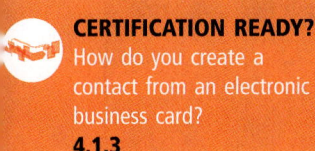

CERTIFICATION READY?
How do you create a contact from an electronic business card?
4.1.3

8. In the Contacts folder, click the first **Gabe Mares contact record** and click the **Delete** button in the Standard toolbar. The contact record is moved to the Deleted Items folder. It will not be removed from your computer until the Deleted Items folder is emptied.

PAUSE. LEAVE Outlook open to use in the next exercise.

In the previous exercise, you created a contact from an electronic business card you received in a message. However, you used the same email account in an earlier exercise to send the electronic business card. Therefore, when you tried to create a contact Outlook recognized it as a duplicate of an existing contact. If this had been a new contact record that you did not have in your Contacts folder, you would have been finished after you clicked the Save & Close button.

Normally, when you receive a duplicate record you will use the received information to update the contact in your Contacts folder. You can compare the information in your contact record with the information sent to you in the message. Before you update contact information, be sure that the new data is accurate.

 ## Using an Electronic Business Card in a Signature

A signature can be added automatically in every message you send. Include your electronic business card in your signature to provide an easy way for the recipient to add the contact to the Contacts folder.

 ### USE AN ELECTRONIC BUSINESS CARD IN A SIGNATURE

X REF

You can find more information on creating signatures in Lesson 2.

USE the Gabe Mares electronic business card you modified in a previous exercise.

1. If necessary, click the **Mail** button in the Navigation pane to display the Mail folder.
2. Click the **New** button in the Standard toolbar. The Message window is displayed. By default, the Message tab is selected.
3. Click the **Signature** button in the Include group on the Ribbon. In the dropdown list, click **Signatures**. The Signatures and Stationery window is displayed.
4. Click the **New** button to create a new signature. The New Signature dialog box is displayed.
5. To name the new signature, key **Gabe** into the *Type a name for this signature* field. Click **OK**. The New Signature dialog box is closed, and Gabe is highlighted in the *Select signature to edit* list box.
6. Click in the empty **Edit signature** box. Key **Gabe Mares** and press [Enter]. Key **Software Development Manager** and press [Enter]. Key **Tailspin Toys** and press [Enter]. Key **Gabe@tailspintoys.com** and press [Enter].
7. Click the **Insert Business Card** button above the Edit Signature box. The Insert Business Card window in Figure 6-4 is displayed.
8. Click the **Gabe Mares contact record** and click **OK**. The electronic business card is inserted into the signature, as shown in Figure 6-7.

Figure 6-7

Signature containing an electronic business card

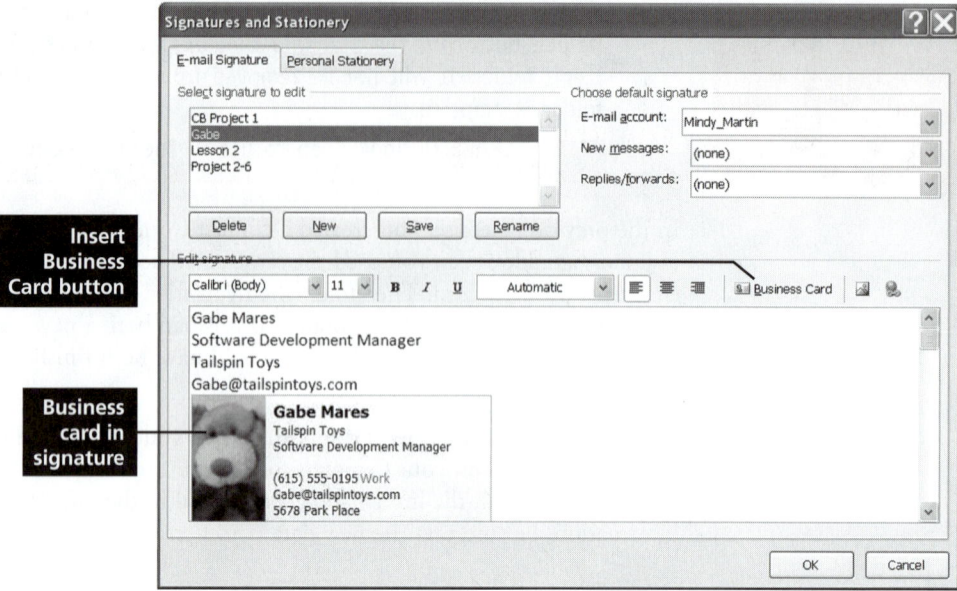

9. Click **OK** to close the Signatures and Stationery window.
10. In the Message window, click the **To** field, if necessary, and then key your email address.
11. In the Subject field, key **New Signature Test**.
12. In the message body, key **Testing new signature** and press **Enter**.
13. In the Include group on the Ribbon, click the **Signature** button and then click **Gabe**. The signature is inserted into the message, as shown in Figure 6-8.

Figure 6-8

Message containing Gabe signature

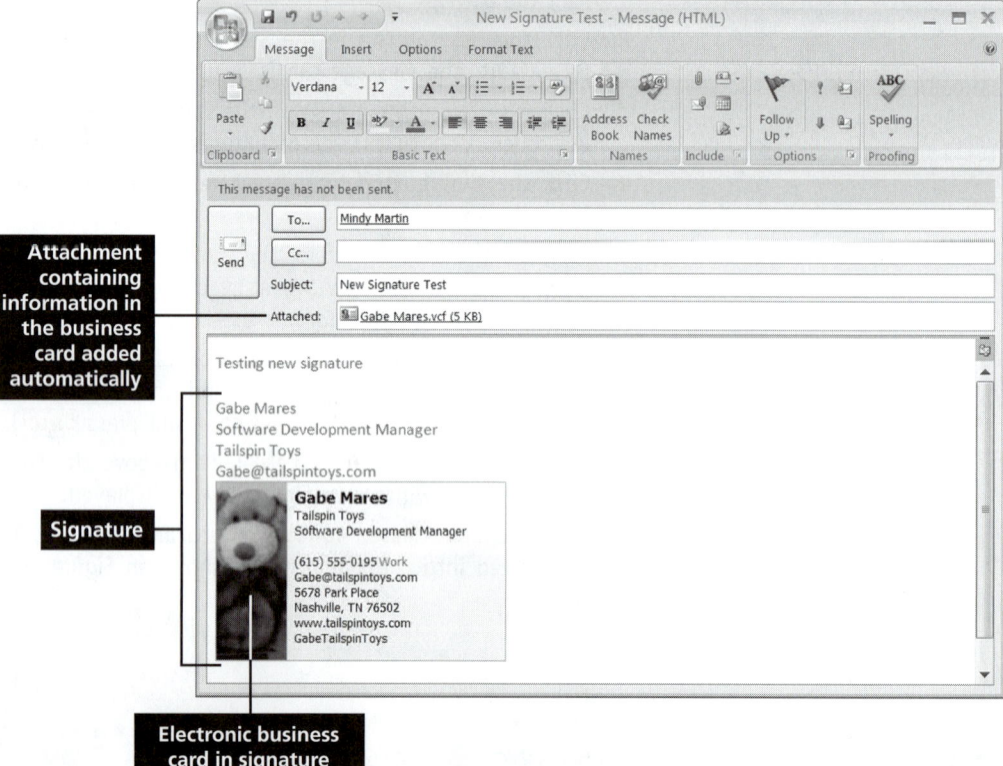

 **Advanced Contact Management | 1035**

CERTIFICATION READY?
How do you use an electronic business card as an automatic signature in messages?
4.2.3

14. Click the **Send** button.

PAUSE. LEAVE Outlook open to use in the next exercise.

In the previous exercise, you created a signature containing an electronic business card. Any recipient using Outlook 2007 can create a contact directly from the electronic business card.

Recipients using other email programs might not be able to view the electronic business card or save it as a contact record. Outlook automatically attaches the .vcf file containing the contact information. However, you can key the contact information into the signature so that it is displayed in the message. You can also delete the attachment before sending the message. Some people avoid opening messages with attachments. Deleting the attachment prevents the recipient from ignoring your message simply because it has an attachment.

■ Finding Contact Information

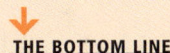

Memory can be unreliable. How often have you recognized a face but couldn't match it to a name? Or you remembered that nice woman who just moved into the office down the hall, but you can't remember the name of her company? Outlook's search features can help you. Use the information you know to find the information you can't remember.

Searching for Contacts

When you search the Contacts folder, you can use any information in a contact record to identify a particular contact or several contacts. You can search for contacts containing text such as Diane, Pittsburgh, or Lead. Using the new Instant Search feature, matching contacts are displayed as they are found.

→ SEARCH FOR CONTACTS

GET READY. Before you begin these steps, be sure to launch Microsoft Outlook. Instant Search must be enabled. The contacts used in this exercise were entered in Lesson 5.

1. If necessary, click the **Contacts** button in the Navigation pane to display the Contacts folder.
2. In the Instant Search box, key **Pittsburgh**. As you key the search text, Outlook displays the matching contacts, as shown in Figure 6-9. The two contacts located in Pittsburgh are displayed.

Figure 6-9

Search for contacts

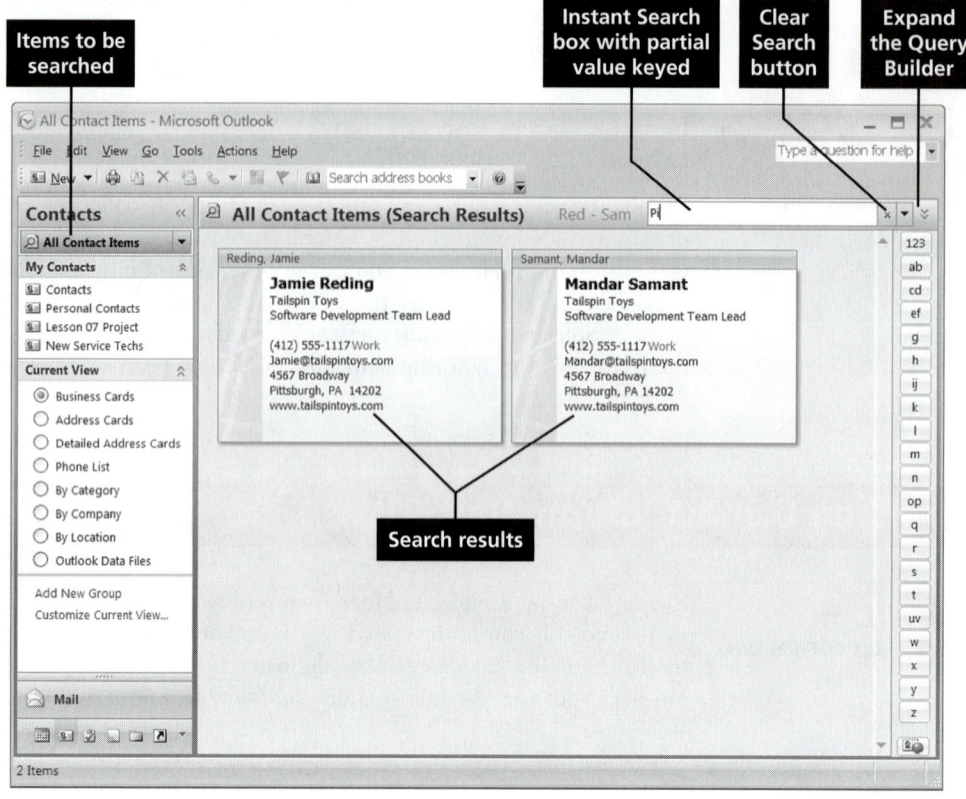

3. Click the **Expand the Query Builder** button. The Query Builder is expanded, as shown in Figure 6-10.

Figure 6-10

Expanded Query Builder

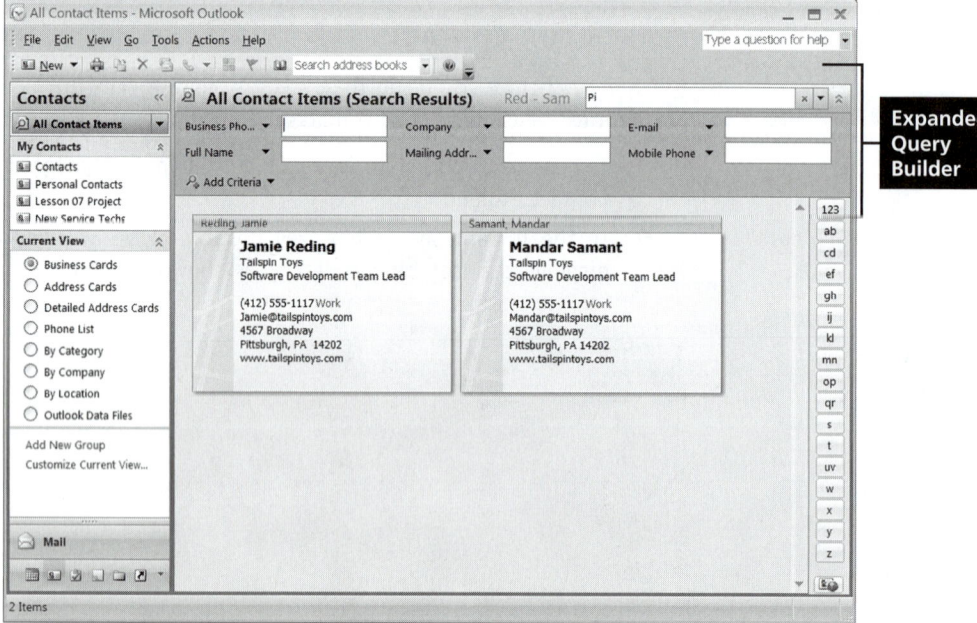

TROUBLESHOOTING The size and layout of the Query Builder depend on the size and resolution of your monitor and the amount of the screen occupied by the Outlook application.

Advanced Contact Management | 1037

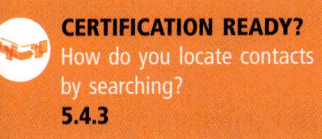

CERTIFICATION READY?
How do you locate contacts by searching?
5.4.3

4. Click the **Clear Search** button and collapse the Query Builder. The search criteria are cleared and all contacts are displayed.

   PAUSE. LEAVE Outlook open to use in the next exercise.

In the previous exercise, you used the new Instant Search feature. Results are immediately displayed when items matching the search criteria are located. Your Contacts folder currently contains very few contacts. As you add contacts, you might need to narrow the search results by using the expanded Query Builder. In the Query Builder, you can key *Pittsburgh* into the Mailing Address field so that results containing the letters in other fields are not displayed in the search results.

Searching for Items Related to a Contact

Occasionally, you will want to find all Outlook items related to a contact. For example, you might want to view messages about a specific meeting and the Calendar item scheduling the meeting. Using Instant Search in the Folder List enables you to search all Outlook folders at the same time to find items related to your search criteria.

SEARCH FOR ITEMS RELATED TO A CONTACT

GET READY. Before you begin these steps, be sure to launch Microsoft Outlook. Instant Search must be enabled. The contacts used in this exercise were entered in Lesson 5. Messages were created in previous lessons.

1. If necessary, click the **Folder List** button in the Navigation pane to display the Folder List and select **All Outlook Items** in the Instant Search dropdown list.
2. In the Instant Search box, key **Gabe**. As you key the search text, Outlook displays the matching Outlook items. The Gabe Mares contact record and the related messages are displayed, as shown in Figure 6-11.

Figure 6-11

Outlook items related to Gabe

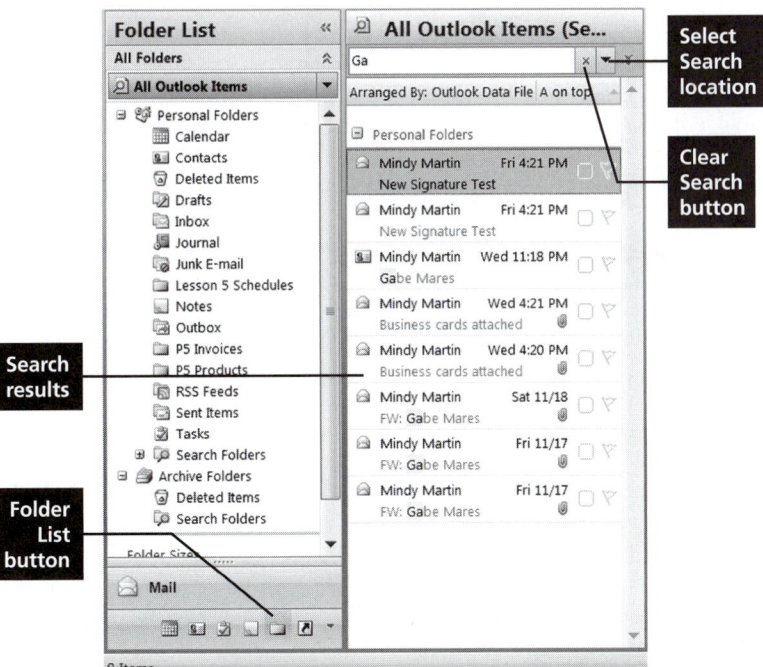

TROUBLESHOOTING Your search results might vary if you deleted any messages sent or received in previous lessons.

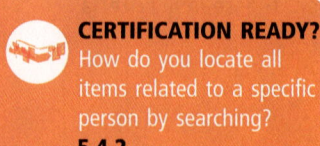

CERTIFICATION READY?
How do you locate all items related to a specific person by searching?
5.4.2

3. Click the **Clear Search** button to clear the search criteria.

PAUSE. LEAVE Outlook open to use in the next exercise.

In the previous exercise, you searched all Outlook items for the items related to Gabe Mares. As you keyed Gabe's name in the Instant Search box, items related to Gabe were found and displayed. In each item, the search text is highlighted in the result.

Creating a Custom Search Folder

Instant Search quickly finds Outlook items. However, you have to key the search text every time you perform a search. A *Search Folder* is a virtual folder that searches your email folders to locate items that meet the saved search criteria. A *virtual folder* is a folder that does not contain the actual items it displays. The items are actually located in other folders.

➔ **CREATE A CUSTOM SEARCH FOLDER**

GET READY. Before you begin these steps, be sure to launch Microsoft Outlook. The contacts used in this exercise were entered in Lesson 5. Messages were created in previous lessons.

1. If necessary, click the **Mail** button in the Navigation pane to display the Mail folder.
2. On the Standard toolbar, click the **New** arrow to display the dropdown list. Click the **Search Folder** option. The New Search Folder window is displayed. Scroll to the bottom of the list of options and click **Create a custom Search Folder**, as shown in Figure 6-12.

Figure 6-12

New Search Folder window

3. Click the **Choose** button to display the Custom Search Folder window shown in Figure 6-13.

Figure 6-13

Custom Search Folder window

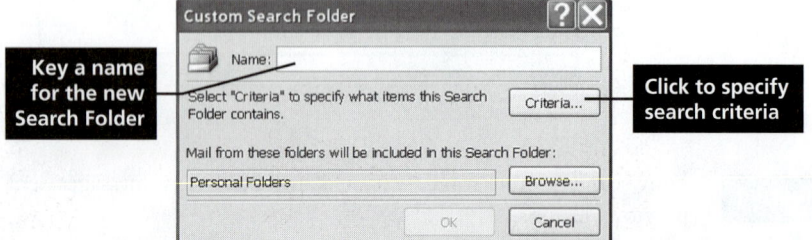

Advanced Contact Management | 1039

4. In the Name field, key **Messages about Jamie**. When naming a Search Folder, create a name that reflects the search criteria.

5. Click the **Criteria** button to display the Search Folder Criteria window shown in Figure 6-14.

Figure 6-14

Search Folder Criteria window

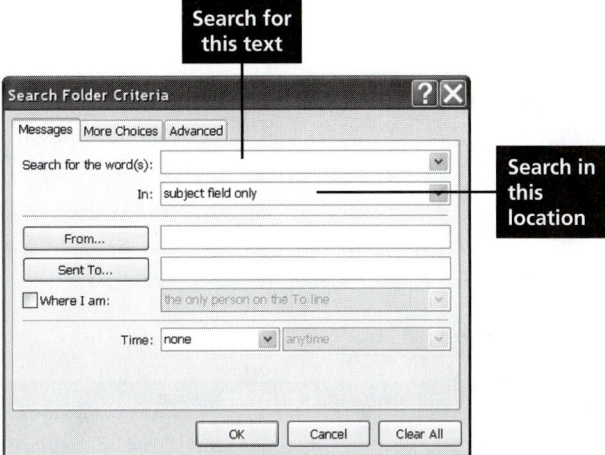

6. In the *Search for the word(s)* field, key **Jamie**. In the *In* field, select **subject field and message body** from the dropdown list. Click **OK** in each window to return to the Mail folder. The new Search Folder and the search results are automatically displayed, as shown in Figure 6-15.

Figure 6-15

Search Folder created

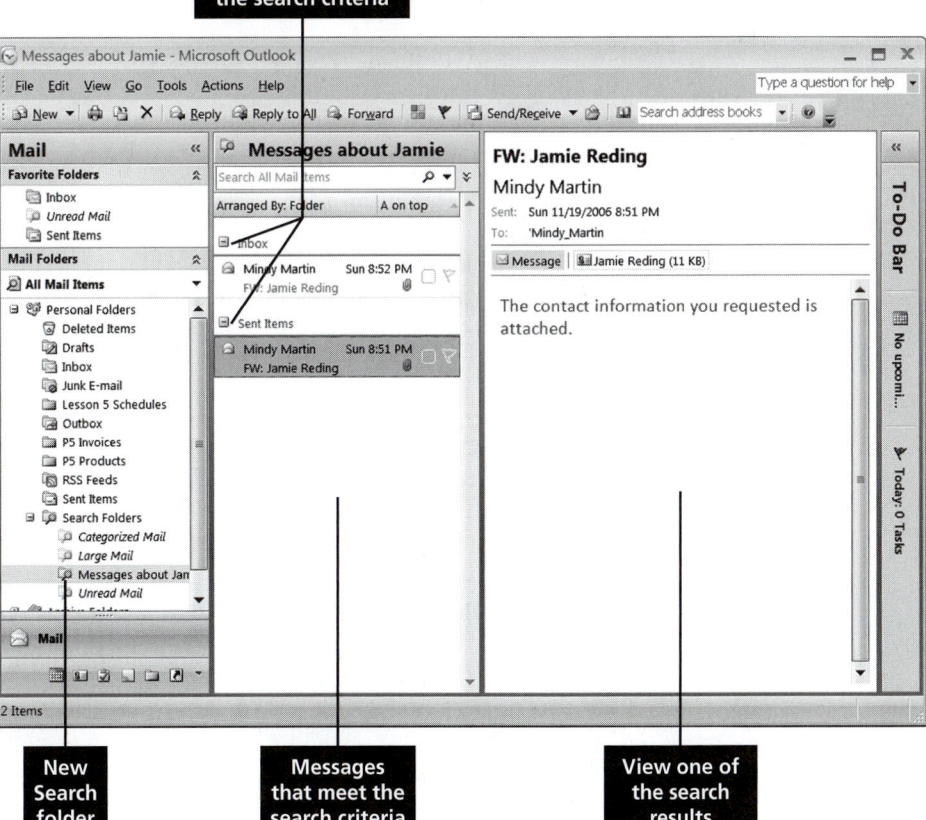

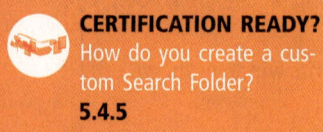

CERTIFICATION READY?
How do you create a custom Search Folder?
5.4.5

PAUSE. LEAVE Outlook open to use in the next exercise.

In the previous exercise, you created a custom Search Folder to identify any messages about Jamie Reding, one of your contacts. You can easily create Search Folders that identify messages exchanged with a specific contact or messages about a project or meeting.

TAKE NOTE* Search Folders are virtual folders. You can delete a Search Folder without deleting the displayed messages because the messages are actually located in other folders. However, if you click a message in the Search Folder and then delete the message, the message is deleted.

Outlook has several standard Search Folders as well. They are Categorized Mail, Large Mail, and Unread Mail. The folders are described in Table 6-2.

Table 6-2

Standard Search Folders

Search Folder	Content
Categorized Mail	Messages that have an assigned color category are displayed in this folder.
Large Mail	Messages larger than 100 kilobytes are displayed in this folder.
Unread Mail	Messages that are marked as Unread are displayed in this folder.

Creating a Secondary Address Book

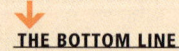

THE BOTTOM LINE

Previous versions of Outlook allowed you to create a private address book by creating an Outlook file with the .pab extension. Because the Contacts folder has more functionality and features than the private address book, Outlook 2007 does not allow you to create or use a personal address book. Instead, you can create a secondary address book.

Every Contacts folder has its own Outlook address book. Therefore, to keep your personal contacts separate from your business contacts, create an additional Contacts folder that has its own address book. The address book for an additional Contacts folder is a *secondary address book*. This provides all the functionality of the familiar Contacts folder and separates your personal information from your business information.

Creating a Secondary Address Book for Personal Contacts

Each Outlook Contacts folder has an associated Outlook address book. To create a secondary address book for personal contacts, create a secondary Contacts folder that contains the personal contact records.

→ CREATE A SECONDARY ADDRESS BOOK FOR PERSONAL CONTACTS

GET READY. Before you begin these steps, be sure to launch Microsoft Outlook.

1. If necessary, click the **Folder List** button in the Navigation pane to display the Folder List.
2. Click the **Contacts** folder in the Folder List.
3. Click the **New** arrow to display the dropdown menu and click **Folder**. The Create New Folder window is displayed.

4. In the Name field, key **My Contacts**. Because you selected the Contacts folder before creating a new folder, Contact Items is already displayed in the *Folder contains* field and the Contacts folder is selected in the *Select where to place the folder* list. Click **OK**. The My Contacts folder is created in the Contacts folder. It is slightly indented in the Folder List to indicate that it is in the Contacts folder, as shown in Figure 6-16.

Figure 6-16
My Contacts folder created

5. Click the **My Contacts** folder in the Folder List. Contacts are not displayed in the main pane because this folder does not contain any contacts yet.

PAUSE. LEAVE Outlook open to use in the next exercise.

> **CERTIFICATION READY?**
> How do you create a secondary address book for personal contacts?
> 4.4.1

An ***address book*** stores names and email addresses. When you key an address in the To, Cc, or Bcc field in a new message, the address book displays potential matches. If the name is a match, you can click the displayed name to fill the address field.

Importing a Secondary Address Book from a File

Manually keying a large number of contacts can be tedious. It's much easier to import the contact information. When you ***import*** a file, you bring information into a file from an external source. In this case, you import contact information from a Microsoft Excel file.

➔ **IMPORT A SECONDARY ADDRESS BOOK FROM A FILE**

USE the My Contacts folder you created in the previous exercise.

1. Click the **My Contacts** folder in the Folder List, if necessary.
2. Click the **File** menu and then click the **Import and Export** option. The Import and Export Wizard is displayed.
3. Click **Import from another program or file**, if necessary, in the list of available actions. Click the **Next** button.
4. Click **Microsoft Excel 97-2003** in the list of available import file types. Click the **Next** button.
5. Click the **Browse** button. Navigate to the data files for this lesson and click the **Source Personal Contacts** file. Click **OK** to close the Browse window and return to the Import a File window. Click the **Next** button.
6. Verify that **My Contacts** is selected as the destination folder. Click the **Next** button.

The ***Source Personal Contacts*** file is available on the companion CD-ROM.

7. Click the **Finish** button. The contacts are imported and displayed in the My Contacts folder, as shown in Figure 6-17.

Figure 6-17

My Contacts folder

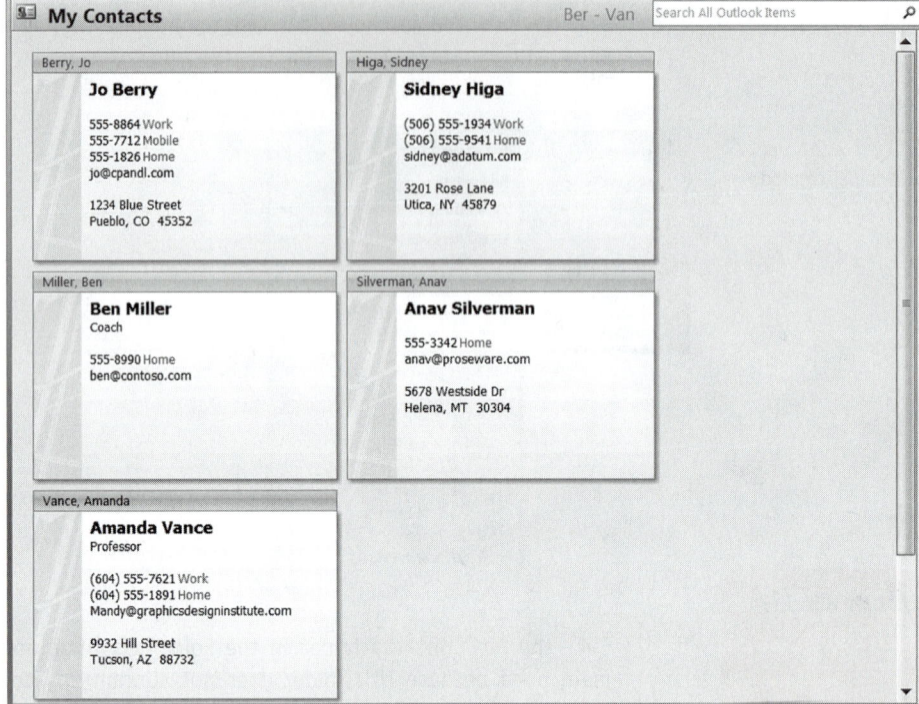

CERTIFICATION READY?
How do you import a secondary address book from a file?
4.4.2

CLOSE Outlook.

TAKE NOTE* If you are switching to Outlook 2007 from another program, Outlook's Import feature could save you time and effort.

Importing contact information is obviously much easier than keying the data into the fields. It also prevents errors from keying incorrect letters or numbers. One typographical error could result in calling a complete stranger instead of Great-Grandma Mabel on her birthday.

Advanced Contact Management | 1043

SUMMARY SKILL MATRIX

IN THIS LESSON YOU LEARNED HOW TO:

Edit an Electronic Business Card

Send an Electronic Business Card

Create a Contact from an Electronic Business Card

Use an Electronic Business Card in a Signature

Search for Contacts

Search for Items Related to a Contact

Create a Custom Search Folder

Create a Secondary Address Book for Personal Contacts

Import a Secondary Address Book from a File

■ Knowledge Assessment

Fill in the Blank

Complete the following sentences by writing the correct word or words in the blanks provided.

1. You can _____ contact information from an external source.
2. Outlook items are not stored in a(n) _____.
3. _____ can contain an image to set them apart from other contact records.
4. The _____ stores names and addresses.
5. The _____ can be used to contain information about personal contacts.
6. A(n) _____ identifies items in other folders that meet specific criteria.
7. A(n) _____ containing an electronic business card can be added automatically in every message you send.
8. _____ displays search results as they are identified.
9. The _____ displays all the Outlook folders.
10. The _____ folder contains contact records.

Multiple Choice

Circle the correct choice.

1. What is the default view in the Contacts folder?
   A. Address Cards
   B. Detailed Address Cards
   C. Business Cards
   D. Phone List

2. What can you do with an electronic business card?
   A. Send it as an attachment
   B. Include it in your signature
   C. Create a contact record from it
   D. All of the above

3. When is an electronic business card created?
   A. When the contact record is created
   B. When the electronic business card is viewed
   C. When the electronic business card is modified
   D. When the electronic business card is sent with a message

4. How many areas are in the Edit Business Card window?
   A. One
   B. Three
   C. Four
   D. Eight

5. Why is a .vcf file automatically attached to a message containing an electronic business card?
   A. Outlook 2007 requires the .vcf file to create a new contact.
   B. Users of other email applications can use the .vcf file.
   C. The .vcf file contains the graphic used in the electronic business card.
   D. The .vcf file contains your signature.

6. Which Outlook search feature displays results immediately?
   A. Immediate Search
   B. Fast Find
   C. Search Folder
   D. Instant Search

7. Which folder is a virtual folder?
   A. Search Folder
   B. Contacts folder
   C. Secondary Contacts folder
   D. Sent Items folder

8. Which folder is *not* a standard Search Folder?
   A. Categorized Mail
   B. Unread Mail
   C. Mail with Attachments
   D. Large Mail

9. Where can you store personal contacts in Outlook 2007?
   A. Private address book
   B. Personal address book
   C. Search Folder
   D. Secondary address book

10. Which of the following is an easy way to enter contact information stored in another application?
    A. Import
    B. Key the data
    C. Send the data in an email message
    D. All of the above

Advanced Contact Management | 1045

■ Competency Assessment

Project 6-1: Edit an Electronic Business Card

Diane Tibbott was recently hired by Tailspin Toys. She decided to use the teddy bear image to brighten up her electronic business card.

GET READY. Launch Outlook if it is not already running.

1. If necessary, click the **Contacts** button in the Navigation pane to display the Contacts folder. Click the **Contacts** folder if necessary.
2. Double-click the **Diane Tibbott** contact. The Diane Tibbott – Contact window is displayed.
3. In the Options group on the Ribbon, click the **Business Card** button to display the Edit Business Card window.
4. In the Card Design area in the upper-right of the window, select **Background Image** in the Layout field.
5. Click the **Change** button. The Add Card Picture dialog box is displayed. Navigate to the data files for this lesson. Click the *bear background* file and click **OK**. The bear image is added to the card preview.
6. In the Card Design area, click the **Image Align** field. Change the value to **Fit to Edge**. In the card preview, the image fills the card.
7. Click **OK** to close the Edit Business Card window. Click the **Save & Close** button to return to the Contacts folder.

    LEAVE Outlook open for the next project.

The *bear background* image is available on the companion CD-ROM.

Project 6-2: Send an Electronic Business Card

Diane Tibbott wants to stay in touch with her friends at Wingtip Toys. She decided to send her new electronic business card to her former supervisor.

1. If necessary, click the **Mail** button in the Navigation pane to display the Mail folder.
2. Click the **New** button in the Standard toolbar. The Message window is displayed. By default, the Message tab is selected.
3. Click the **To** field. Key *Molly@wingtiptoys.com*.
4. Click the **Subject** field. Key *Let's keep in touch!*
5. Click in the message area. Key *I attached my new electronic business card. Write when you have time.* Press Enter.
6. In the Include group on the Ribbon, click the **Insert Business Card** button. A dropdown list is displayed.
7. Click **Diane Tibbott**. The electronic business card is inserted and the .vcf file is attached.
8. Click the **Send** button.

    LEAVE Outlook open for the next project.

Proficiency Assessment

Project 6-3: Use an Electronic Business Card in a Signature

Management has decided that every message sent to clients must include an electronic business card. Rather than manually inserting the electronic business card into every message, Diane decided to create a signature containing her electronic business card.

1. If necessary, click the **Mail** button in the Navigation pane to display the Mail folder.
2. Click the **New** button in the Standard toolbar to open a new Message window.
3. Click the **Signature** button in the Include group on the Ribbon. In the dropdown list, click **Signatures** to display the Signatures and Stationery window.
4. Click the **New** button to display the New Signature dialog box.
5. To name the new signature, key **Diane** into the *Type a name for this signature* field. Click **OK**.
6. Click the empty **Edit signature** box. Key **Diane Tibbott** and press [Enter]. Key **Software Development Team Lead** and press [Enter]. Key **Tailspin Toys** and press [Enter]. Key **Diane@tailspintoys.com** and press [Enter].
7. Click the **Insert Business Card** button above the Edit Signature box to display the Insert Business Card window.
8. Click the **Diane Tibbott** contact record and click **OK** to insert the electronic business card into the signature.
9. Click **OK** to close the Signatures and Stationery window and return to the Message window.
10. In the Include group on the Ribbon, click the **Signature** button and then click **Diane**. The signature is inserted in the message.
11. **CLOSE** the message without saving or sending it.

    LEAVE Outlook open for the next project.

Project 6-4: Create a Custom Search Folder

Diane wants to monitor messages about the team's new software development project. The project has been nicknamed 007 for the fictional character James Bond. All messages about the project must contain "007" in the Subject field. Diane decided to create a Search Folder to collect messages about the project.

1. If necessary, click the **Mail** button in the Navigation pane to display the Mail folder.
2. On the Standard toolbar, click the **New** arrow to display the dropdown list. Click the **Search Folder** option to display the New Search Folder window. Scroll to the bottom of the list of options and click **Create a custom Search Folder**.
3. Click the **Choose** button to display the Custom Search Folder window.
4. In the Name field, key **Project 007**.
5. Click the **Criteria** button to display the Search Folder Criteria window.
6. In the *Search for the word(s)* field, key **007**. In the *In* field, select **in subject field only** from the dropdown list if necessary. Click **OK** in each window to return to the Mail folder.
7. Create a new message. In the To field, key your email address. In the Subject field, key **007**. In the message body, key **Testing Search Folder**. Click the **Send** button.
8. Click the **Send/Receive** button if the 007 message has not arrived. After the message arrives, click the **Project 007** folder to view its content. It should contain the 007 message in the Sent Items folder and the 007 message in the Inbox.

    LEAVE Outlook open for the next project.

Mastery Assessment

Project 6-5: Create a Secondary Address Book

Diane works for a new company, but she wants to stay in touch with friends she made at Wingtip Toys. Diane decided to create a secondary address book before she imports personal contacts for her friends.

1. If necessary, click the **Folder List** button in the Navigation pane to display the Folder List.
2. Click the **Contacts** folder in the Folder List.
3. Click the **New** arrow to display the dropdown menu and click **Folder**. The Create New Folder window is displayed.
4. In the Name field, key **Diane's Contacts**. Because you selected the Contacts folder before creating a new folder, Contact Items is already displayed in the *Folder contains* field and the Contacts folder is selected in the *Select where to place the folder* list. Click **OK**. The Diane's Contacts folder is created in the Contacts folder.
   LEAVE Outlook open for the next project.

Project 6-6: Import a Secondary Address Book from a File

After creating the Diane's Contacts folder, Diane can import contact records for her friends at Wingtip Toys.

1. Click the **Diane's Contacts** folder in the Folder List, if necessary.
2. Click the **File** menu and then click the **Import and Export** option to display the Import and Export Wizard.
3. Click **Import from another program or file** in the list of available actions. Click the **Next** button.
4. Click **Microsoft Excel 97-2003** in the list of available import file types. Click **Next** button.
5. Click the **Browse** button. Navigate to the data files for this lesson and click the **Source Diane's Contacts** file. Click **OK** to close the Browse window and return to the Import a File window. Click the **Next** button.
6. Verify that **Diane's Contacts** is selected as the destination folder. Click the **Next** button.
7. Click the **Finish** button. The contacts are imported and displayed in the Diane's Contacts folder.
   CLOSE Outlook.

> **CD**
> The *Source Diane's Contacts* file is available on the companion CD-ROM.

INTERNET READY

Microsoft provides templates for a wide variety of electronic business cards. Sophisticated, casual, fun, and serious designs are available. Go to www.Microsoft.com. Search for electronic business cards. Download a style that appeals to you. Modify the card and use it as your electronic business card.

Workplace Ready

Organizing Outlook Items

Nicole Holliday is an instructor at the School of Fine Arts. Every session, a batch of fresh students registers for Nicole's classes. Nicole teaches several classes that require students to submit electronic files. The school doesn't set up mailboxes for each class, so Nicole uses Outlook to organize her messages.

Every session, Nicole sets up a new email folder for each class. She creates rules that sort messages from each student into the correct folder. A few weeks after classes end, Nicole archives the class folders that are no longer needed.

Because Nicole also teaches at a second school, she created a secondary address book to separate the contact information between the two schools. Incorrectly addressing a message to a staff member at the wrong school would be embarrassing.

Calendar Basics

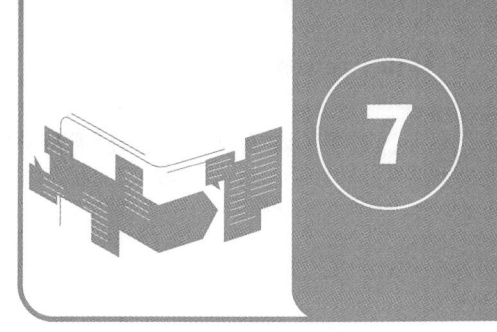

LESSON SKILL MATRIX

Creating a One-Time Appointment — 1050	Students will learn how to create a one-time appointment.
Scheduling a Recurring Appointment — 1051	Students will learn how to schedule a recurring appointment.
Creating an Appointment from a Message — 1053	Students will learn how to create an appointment from a message.
Creating an Appointment from a Task — 1055	Students will learn how to create an appointment from a task.
Marking an Appointment as Private — 1056	Students will learn how to mark an appointment as private.
Managing Events — 1057	Students will learn how to manage events.

As a marketing assistant, Terry Eminhizer knows the value of time. Terry manages her schedule and the schedules of two marketing representatives who are constantly on the road. Setting up travel arrangements, confirming appointments with clients, and generally smoothing out the bumps for the marketing representatives gives them more time to make bigger sales. Time is money.

KEY TERMS
appointment
banner
busy
event
free
out of office
private
recurring appointment
tentative

Software Orientation

Microsoft Outlook's Appointment Window

The Appointment window displayed in Figure 7-1 enables you to schedule an appointment or event. Scheduled appointments and events are displayed on your calendar.

Figure 7-1

Outlook's Appointment window

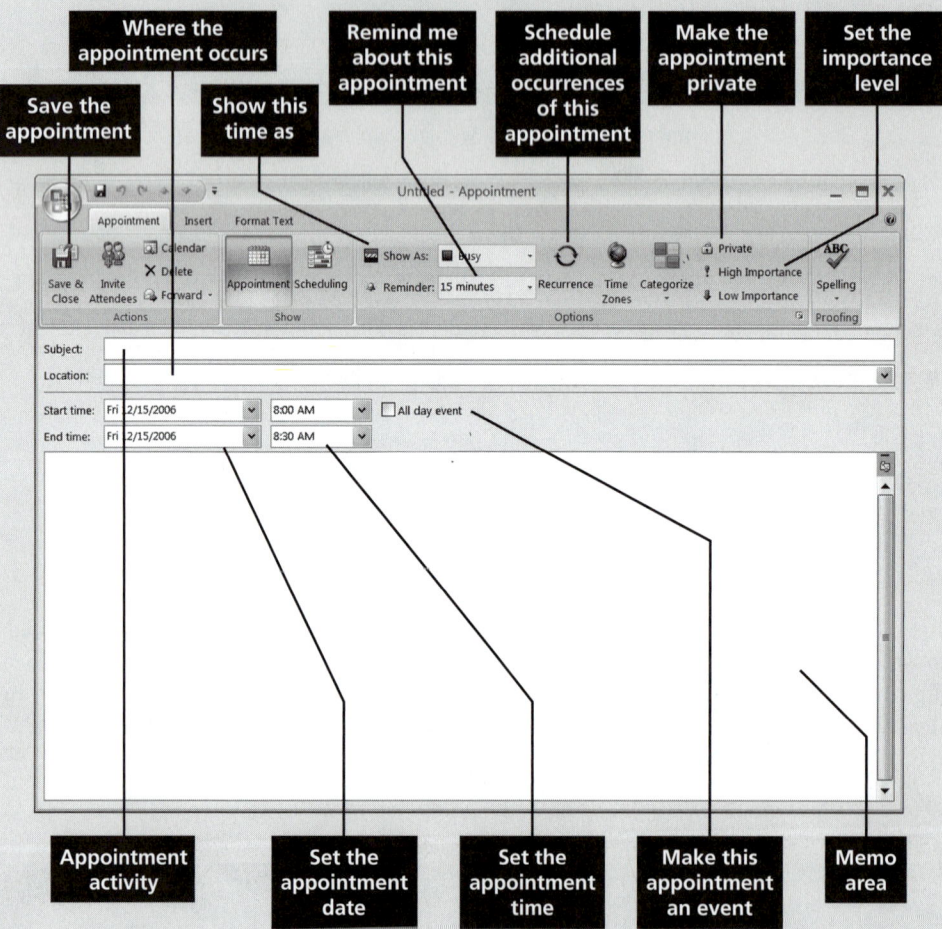

Use the Appointment window to create an appointment or event. Refer to Figure 7-1 as you complete the following exercises.

Managing Appointments

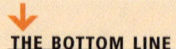

THE BOTTOM LINE

An *appointment* is a scheduled activity that does not require sending invitations to other people or resources. An appointment can occur once or occur at regular intervals.

Creating a One-Time Appointment

Appointments can involve other people, but they do not require invitations sent through Outlook. Appointments can include activities such as doctor appointments and picking up your daughter after soccer practice.

Calendar Basics | 1051

 CREATE A ONE-TIME APPOINTMENT

GET READY. Before you begin these steps, be sure to launch Microsoft Outlook.

1. Click the **Calendar** button in the Navigation pane to display the Calendar folder. Click the **Month** button to display the Month view, if necessary.
2. Click next Friday's date on the monthly calendar.

 You can also select the date in the Appointment window. If the date is displayed in the monthly calendar, it is easier to select the date there. For appointments that occur several months in the future, it is easier to select the date in the Appointment window.

3. On the Standard toolbar, click the **New** button. The Appointment window in Figure 7-1 is displayed. The date selected in the monthly calendar is already displayed in the *Start time* and *End time* fields.
4. In the Subject field, key **Blood Drive**.
5. In the Location field, key **Van in the South parking lot**.
6. In the *Start time* fields, select or key **2:00 PM**. By default, each appointment is 30 minutes long. Because you need to fill out forms before donating and eat a few cookies after donating, select an End time of **3:00 PM**.
7. Click the **Save & Close** button in the Actions group on the Ribbon. The appointment is displayed on the calendar.

   PAUSE. LEAVE Outlook open to use in the next exercise.

CERTIFICATION READY?
How do you create a one-time appointment, meeting or event?
2.1.1

In the previous exercise, you created a one-time appointment to donate blood at the company blood drive. By default, when you select a future date in the calendar, the displayed time of the appointment in the Appointment window will be the start of the work day.

The *Show as* field in the Appointment window determines how the time is displayed on your calendar. When others look at your calendar, this tells them if you are available and how definite your schedule is for a specific activity. You can choose from four options displayed in Table 7-1.

Table 7-1

Show time as options

Show As	Description
Free	No activities are scheduled for this time period. You are available.
Busy	An activity is scheduled for this time period. You are not available for other activities.
Tentative	An activity is scheduled for this time period, but the activity might not occur. You might be available for other activities.
Out of Office	You are out of the office.

Scheduling a Recurring Appointment

A ***recurring appointment*** is an appointment that occurs at regular intervals. Recurrences can be scheduled based on daily, weekly, monthly, and yearly intervals.

 SCHEDULE A RECURRING APPOINTMENT

GET READY. Before you begin these steps, be sure to launch Microsoft Outlook.

1. Click the **Calendar** button in the Navigation pane to display the Calendar folder. Click the **Month** button to display the Month view, if necessary.

2. Click the third Monday of the month on the monthly calendar. If the third Monday of this month has passed, click the third Monday of next month.

> **TAKE NOTE*** In the Month view, click the lower part of the square to select the day. Clicking the top part of the square displays the Day view for that date.

3. On the Standard toolbar, click the **New** button. The Appointment window in Figure 7-1 is displayed. The date selected in the monthly calendar is already displayed in the *Start time* and *End time* fields.
4. In the Subject field, key **Engineering Lunch**.
5. In the Location field, key **Conference Room B**.
6. In the *Start time* fields, key **12:15 PM**. Key or select an End time of **1:15 PM**.
7. Click the Memo area. Key **New techniques and troubleshooting**.
8. Click the **Recurrence** button in the Options group on the Ribbon. The Appointment Recurrence window is displayed, as shown in Figure 7-2.

Figure 7-2

Appointment Recurrence window

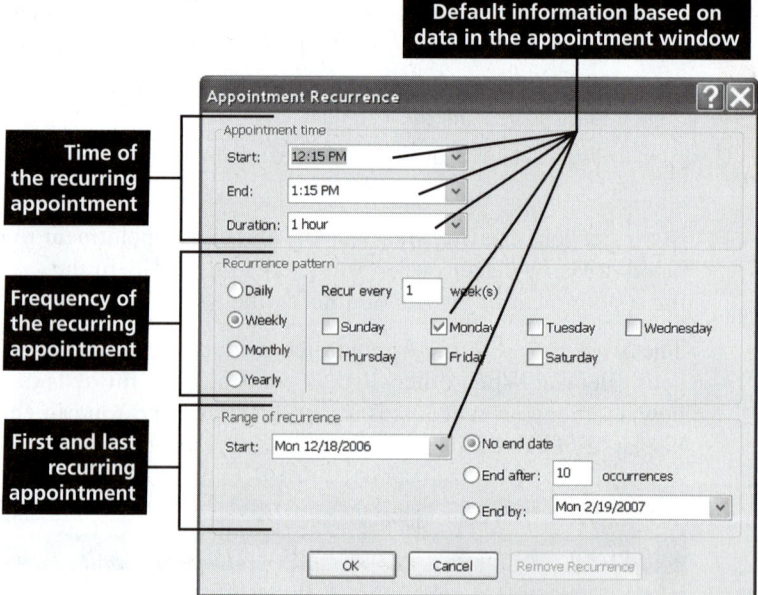

9. In the Appointment Recurrence window, click **Monthly** in the Recurrence pattern area. Selecting a different frequency changes the patterns available for selection on the right side in the Recurrence pattern area.
10. On the right side in the Recurrence pattern area, click the radio button to select **The third Monday of every 1 month(s)**. Because the date of the first recurring appointment was the third Monday of the month, the third Monday of every month is offered as a likely pattern.
11. Click **OK** to set the recurrence pattern and return to the Appointment window. The recurrence pattern is displayed in the Appointment window, as shown in Figure 7-3.

Figure 7-3

Recurring appointment

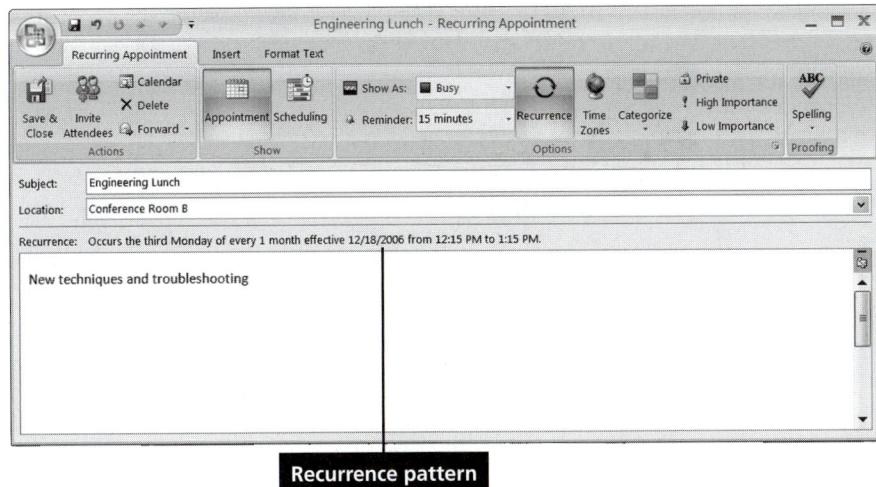

Recurrence pattern

CERTIFICATION READY?
How do you create a recurring appointment, meeting, or event?
2.1.2

12. Click the **Save & Close** button in the Actions group on the Ribbon. The appointment is displayed on the monthly calendar. Click the **Forward** button at the top of the monthly calendar to verify that the recurring appointment is displayed in next month's calendar. Click the **Back** button at the top of the monthly calendar to return to the current month.

    PAUSE. LEAVE Outlook open to use in the next exercise.

In the previous exercise, you created a recurring appointment. Recurring appointments are common in many calendars. Weekly soccer games, monthly lunch dates with an old friend, and semi-annual company dinners are examples of recurring appointments.

Creating an Appointment from a Message

Sometimes, a message can lead to an appointment. For example, your son's cross-country running coach sends you a message about the awards banquet or you receive a message that a farewell lunch will be held Thursday for a coworker in your department. Simply use the email message to create an appointment.

➔ CREATE AN APPOINTMENT FROM A MESSAGE

GET READY. Before you begin these steps, be sure to launch Microsoft Outlook.

1. If necessary, click the **Mail** button in the Navigation pane to display the Mail folder.
2. Click the **New** button in the Standard toolbar to display the Message window.
3. In the To field, key your email address. In the Subject field, key **Vice President Duerr visiting Thursday afternoon**. In the message area, key **Vice President Bernard Duerr is visiting this division on Thursday. An employee meeting will be held in the company cafeteria from 2:00 PM to 4:00 PM. Attendance is mandatory.** Click the **Send** button.
4. Return to your Inbox, if necessary. Click the **Send/Receive** button if the message has not arrived yet.
5. Double-click the **Vice President Duerr visiting Thursday afternoon** message to open it.
6. Click the **Move to Folder** button in the Actions group on the Ribbon. In the dropdown list, click **Other Folder**. The *Move Item to* window is displayed, as shown in Figure 7-4.

Figure 7-4

Move Item to window

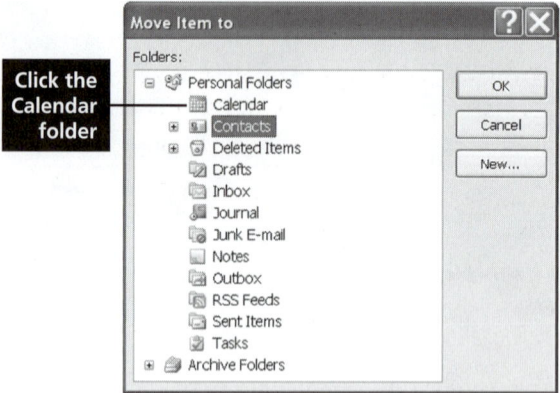

7. In the *Move Item to* window, click **Calendar** and then click **OK**. An Appointment window is opened. The message text is displayed in the Memo area of the Appointment window. The message subject is displayed in the Subject field in the Appointment window.
8. In the Appointment window, key **Company cafeteria** into the Location field.
9. Key **Thursday** into the *Start time* field instead of a date. Key or select a Start time of **2:00 PM**.

> **TAKE NOTE** You can key text in the *Start time* and *End time* fields rather than a date. Outlook translates the text into a date.

10. In the *End time* field, key an End time of **4:00 PM**. The Appointment window should be similar to Figure 7-5.

Figure 7-5

Creating an appointment from a message

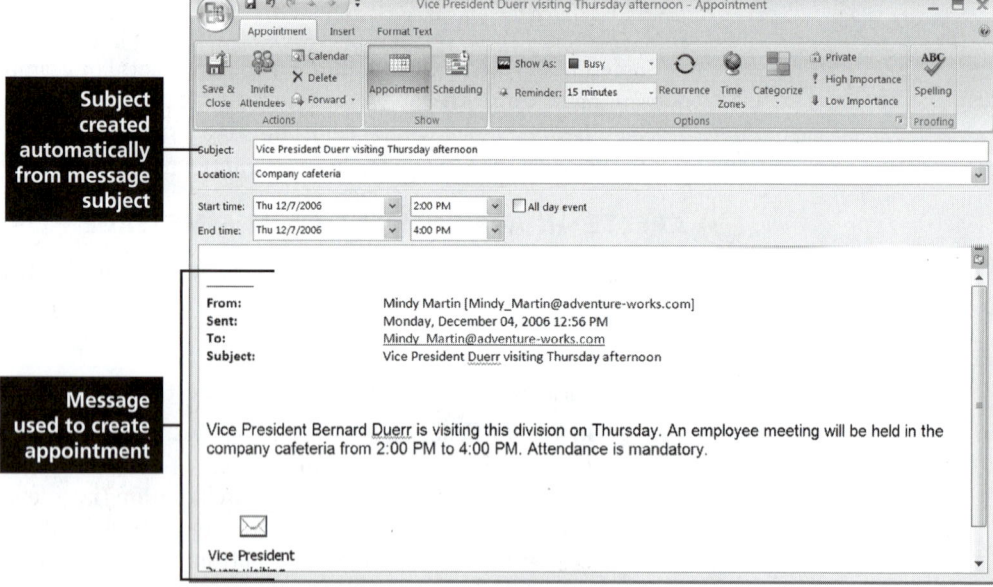

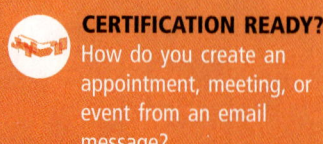

CERTIFICATION READY?
How do you create an appointment, meeting, or event from an email message?
2.1.3

11. Click the **Save & Close** button in the Actions group on the Ribbon.
12. Click the **Calendar** button in the Navigation pane to display the Calendar folder. The appointment created from the message is displayed.

PAUSE. LEAVE Outlook open to use in the next exercise.

In the previous exercise, you created an appointment from a message you received. The message text is saved automatically in the Appointment window's memo area. This stores the related message with the appointment.

Creating an Appointment from a Task

Tasks describe activities you have to do. Appointments tell you when activities are performed. Tasks frequently become appointments when the time to perform a task is scheduled.

➔ CREATE AN APPOINTMENT FROM A TASK

GET READY. Before you begin these steps, be sure to launch Microsoft Outlook.

1. Click the **Calendar** button in the Navigation pane to display the Calendar folder. Click the **Month** button to display the Month view, if necessary.
2. Click the **View** menu. Point to **To-Do Bar** and then click **Normal**. The To-Do Bar is displayed to the right of the monthly calendar. Your scheduled appointments are listed in the To-Do Bar. No tasks are displayed as shown in Figure 7-6.

Figure 7-6
To-Do Bar displayed

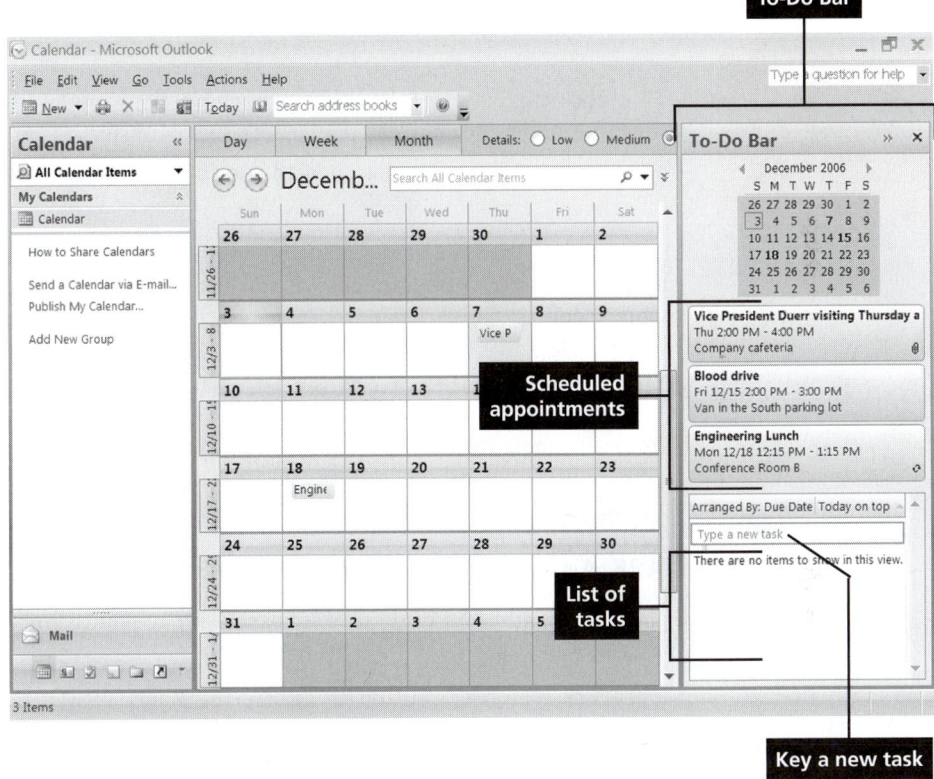

3. Click the **Type a new task** field, and key **Lunch with Vice President Duerr**. Press **Enter**. The task is created.
4. Click the **Lunch with Vice President Duerr** task. Drag it to Thursday's date on the calendar. You already have an appointment for the employee meeting from 2:00 PM to 4:00 PM for that date.
5. Double-click the **Lunch with Vice President Duerr** item in the calendar. An Appointment window containing the task information is displayed.
6. Click the **All day event** checkbox to clear the checkbox. The time fields become available.
7. Key a Start time of **12:30 PM** and an End time of **1:45 PM**. The Appointment window should be similar to Figure 7-7.

Figure 7-7

Creating an appointment from a task

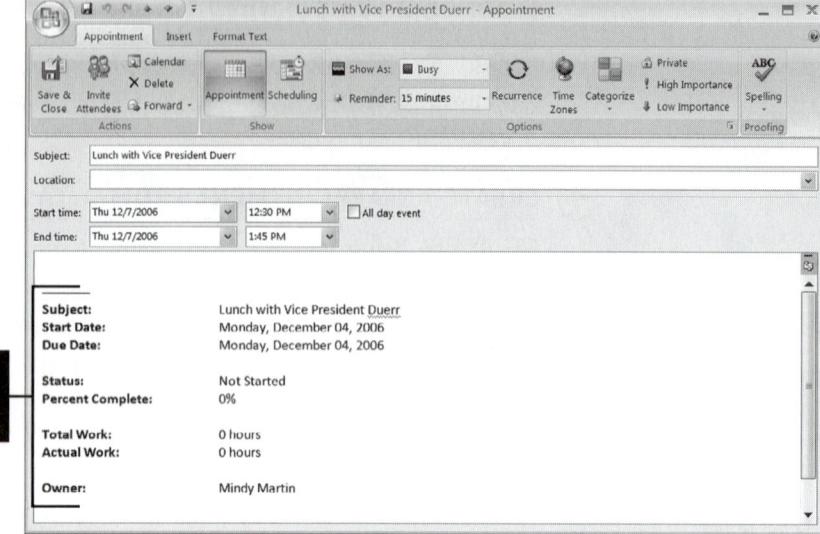

8. Click the **Save & Close** button in the Actions group on the Ribbon. The appointment created from the task is displayed on the calendar.

   PAUSE. LEAVE Outlook open to use in the next exercise.

CERTIFICATION READY?

How do you create an appointment, meeting, or event from a task?

In the previous exercise, you created an appointment from a task. The task text is saved automatically in the Appointment window's memo area, storing the information with the appointment.

Marking an Appointment as Private

You can choose to mark an appointment as *private*. This feature protects the details of an activity from a casual observer, but it does not ensure privacy. Any person who has Read privileges to your calendar could access the information through a variety of methods.

➔ **MARK AN APPOINTMENT AS PRIVATE**

GET READY. Before you begin these steps, be sure to launch Microsoft Outlook.

1. Click the **Calendar** button in the Navigation pane to display the Calendar folder. Click the **Month** button to display the Month view if necessary.
2. Click next Friday's date on the monthly calendar. The Blood drive is already scheduled for 2:00 PM on that date.

TROUBLESHOOTING To ensure privacy for the details of your appointments, meetings, or events, create a separate Calendar folder that is not shared with other users.

3. On the Standard toolbar, click the **New** button. The Appointment window in Figure 7-1 is displayed. The date selected in the monthly calendar is already displayed in the *Start time* and *End time* fields.
4. In the Subject field, key **Interview Rebecca Laszlo for receptionist**.
5. In the Location field, key **My office**.
6. In the *Start time* fields, key or select a time of **4:30 PM**. Key or select an End time of **5:00 PM**, if necessary.
7. Click the **Private** button in the Options group on the Ribbon.
8. Click the **Save & Close** button in the Actions group on the Ribbon. The appointment is displayed on your monthly calendar.

   PAUSE. LEAVE Outlook open to use in the next exercise.

CERTIFICATION READY?

How do you mark an appointment, meeting or event as private?

Calendar Basics | 1057

In the previous exercise, you created a one-time appointment to interview an applicant for the department receptionist. You clicked the Private button before saving the appointment. You can also open an existing appointment and click the Private button to turn on or turn off the Private feature for that appointment. Be sure to save the modified appointment after changing the Private status.

In the Day view, a lock is displayed next to a private appointment. Without permission, other users cannot open the appointment to view the details.

■ Managing Events

THE BOTTOM LINE

An *event* is an activity that lasts one or more days. In your calendar, an event is displayed as a banner at the top of the day. A *banner* is text displayed at the top of a day to indicate an event. For scheduling purposes, an event is displayed as free time. You are still available for appointments or meetings.

MANAGE EVENTS

GET READY. Before you begin these steps, be sure to launch Microsoft Outlook.

1. Click the **Calendar** button in the Navigation pane to display the Calendar folder. Click the **Month** button to display the Month view, if necessary.
2. On the Standard toolbar, click the **New** button. The Appointment window in Figure 7-1 is displayed.
3. In the Subject field, key **Anniversary**.
4. In the *Start time* field, key the date of your anniversary or a family member's anniversary.
5. Click the **All day event** checkbox to select the option. The time fields are dimmed.
6. Click the **Private** button in the Options group on the Ribbon.
7. Click the **Recurrence** button in the Options group on the Ribbon. The Appointment Recurrence window is displayed.
8. In the Appointment Recurrence window, click **Yearly** in the Recurrence pattern area. Selecting a different frequency changes the patterns available for selection on the right side in the Recurrence pattern area.
9. On the right side in the Recurrence pattern area, click the radio button to select **Every [month] [date]**.
10. Click **OK** to set the recurrence pattern and return to the Appointment window. The recurrence pattern is displayed in the Appointment window.
11. In the Options group on the Ribbon, click the **Reminder** dropdown list. Click the **1 week** option.
12. Click the **Save & Close** button in the Actions group on the Ribbon. The appointment is added to your calendar.
13. Click the **Forward** button at the top of the monthly calendar to verify that the recurring event is displayed on the correct date. Click the **Back** button at the top of the monthly calendar to return to the current month.
    CLOSE Outlook.

CERTIFICATION READY?
How do you create a recurring appointment, meeting, or event and mark the recurring appointment, meeting, or event as private?
2.1.2 and 2.1.5

In the previous exercise, you created a private recurring event for the date of your wedding anniversary. The Appointment window is used to create an event. The methods of creating new appointments from messages or tasks that you performed in the earlier exercises in this lesson can also be used to create events.

SUMMARY SKILL MATRIX

IN THIS LESSON YOU LEARNED HOW TO:
Create a One-Time Appointment
Schedule a Recurring Appointment
Create an Appointment from a Message
Create an Appointment from a Task
Mark an Appointment as Private
Manage Events

Knowledge Assessment

Matching

Match the term with its definition.

a. appointment
b. banner
c. busy
d. calendar
e. event
f. free
g. private
h. recurring appointment
i. task
j. tentative

_____h_____ 1. An appointment that occurs at regular intervals

_____e_____ 2. An activity that lasts one or more days

_____a_____ 3. A scheduled activity that does not require sending invitations to other people or resources

_____i_____ 4. An activity that has to be performed

_____j_____ 5. An activity is scheduled for this time period, but the activity might not occur

_____b_____ 6. Text displayed at the top of a day to indicate an event

_____g_____ 7. Feature that protects the details of an activity from a casual observer

_____c_____ 8. An activity is scheduled for this time period

_____d_____ 9. Enables you to create a schedule

_____f_____ 10. No activities are scheduled for this time period

True/False

Circle T if the statement is true or F if the statement is false.

T F 1. Use the Appointment window to schedule an event.

T **F** 2. Appointments require invitations sent through Outlook.

T **F** 3. By default, each appointment is one hour long.

T F 4. You are not available for other activities when your time is displayed as busy.

T F 5. Recurrences can be scheduled based on daily, weekly, monthly, and yearly intervals.

T F 6. You can key text in the *Start time* and *End time* fields rather than a date.
T F 7. A message is deleted automatically when it is used to create an appointment.
T F 8. A task cannot be used to create an appointment unless the task is private.
T F 9. Marking an appointment as private does not ensure that users who can view your calendar cannot view the details of the private appointment.
T F 10. An event is displayed as a banner in your calendar.

Competency Assessment

Project 7-1: Schedule Vacation

First things first. Before you create appointments, schedule your vacation.

GET READY. Launch Outlook if it is not already running.

1. Click the **Calendar** button in the Navigation pane to display the Calendar folder.
2. On the Standard toolbar, click the **New** button. The Appointment window is displayed.
3. In the Subject field, key **Vacation**.
4. In the *Start time* field, key the date of the first day of your vacation.
5. In the *End time* field, key the date of the last day of your vacation.
6. Click the **All day event** checkbox to select the option. The time fields are dimmed.
7. Click the **Save & Close** button in the Actions group on the Ribbon. The appointment is added to your calendar.

   LEAVE Outlook open for the next project.

Project 7-2: Create a One-Time Appointment

You have been selected to create a presentation about a new product your company will sell in the coming year. You will deliver the presentation at a company dinner on Wednesday. Schedule the time to prepare the presentation.

1. Click the **Calendar** button in the Navigation pane to display the Calendar folder.
2. Click next Monday's date on the monthly calendar.
3. On the Standard toolbar, click the **New** button. The Appointment window is displayed.
4. In the Subject field, key **Prepare new product presentation**.
5. In the *Start time* fields, key or select the time of **9:30 AM**. Key or select the End time of **2:00 PM**.
6. Click the **Save & Close** button in the Actions group on the Ribbon. The appointment is added to the calendar.

   LEAVE Outlook open for the next project.

Proficiency Assessment

Project 7-3: Schedule a Recurring Appointment

Every week, you collect sales information to track the difference between sales goals and actual sales. Create a recurring appointment every Monday to gather the information and post the sales information for the managers to review.

1. Click the **Calendar** button in the Navigation pane to display the Calendar folder.
2. Click next Monday's date on the monthly calendar.

3. On the Standard toolbar, click the **New** button. The Appointment window is displayed.
4. In the Subject field, key **Prepare Sales Report**.
5. In the *Start time* fields, key or select **8:30 AM**. Key or select an End time of **9:30 AM**.
6. Click the **Recurrence** button in the Options group on the Ribbon. The Appointment Recurrence window is displayed.
7. Click **OK** to accept the recurrence pattern and return to the Appointment window.
8. Click the **Save & Close** button in the Actions group on the Ribbon. The appointment is added to the calendar.

LEAVE Outlook open for the next project.

Project 7-4: Create an Appointment from a Message

A friend sent you a message about a concert in August. Create an appointment from the message.

1. If necessary, click the **Mail** button in the Navigation pane to display the Mail folder.
2. Click the **New** button in the Standard toolbar to display the Message window.
3. In the To field, key your email address. In the Subject field, key **Concert!** In the message area, key **[Insert name of favorite musical performer] is coming to [Insert name of local concert hall]! Mark August 10 on your calendar! I already bought our tickets!** Click the **Send** button.
4. Return to your Inbox, if necessary. Click the **Send/Receive** button if the message has not arrived yet.
5. Double-click the **Concert** message to open it.
6. Click the **Move to Folder** button in the Actions group on the Ribbon. In the dropdown list, click **Other Folder**. The *Move Item to* window is displayed.
7. In the *Move Item to* window, click **Calendar**, and then click **OK**. An Appointment window is opened.
8. Key **August 10** in the *Start time* field. Key or select a Start time of **7:00 PM**.
9. Key or select an End time of **11:00 PM**.
10. Click the **Save & Close** button in the Actions group on the Ribbon.

LEAVE Outlook open for the next project.

■ Mastery Assessment

Project 7-5: Create an Appointment from a Task

Last week, a coworker asked you to review a new marketing presentation. He finished the presentation yesterday. Turn the task into an appointment to review the presentation tomorrow after lunch.

1. Click the **Calendar** button in the Navigation pane to display the Calendar folder.
2. Display the To-Do Bar, if necessary.
3. Click the **Type a new task** field, and key **Review presentation for Gary Schare**. Press **Enter**. The task is created.
4. Click the **Review presentation for Gary Schare** task. Drag it to tomorrow's date on the calendar.
5. Double-click the **Review presentation for Gary Schare** item in the calendar. An Appointment window is displayed.
6. Click the **All day event** checkbox to clear the checkbox. The time fields become available.

7. Key or select a Start time of **3:30 PM** and an End time of **5:00 PM**.
8. Click the **Save & Close** button in the Actions group on the Ribbon. The appointment is added to the calendar.

   LEAVE Outlook open for the next project.

Project 7-6: Mark an Appointment as Private

In Project 7-4, you created an appointment for the concert. Your taste in music might not be appreciated by everyone who views your calendar. Make the appointment private.

1. Click the **Calendar** button in the Navigation pane to display the Calendar folder.
2. Display August in the calendar.
3. Double-click the **Concert** appointment to open it.
4. Click the **Private** button in the Options group on the Ribbon.
5. Click the **Save & Close** button in the Actions group on the Ribbon. The private appointment is added to the calendar.

   CLOSE Outlook.

INTERNET READY

Use the Internet to find some local events that you would like to attend. A local sports game or a concert performed by your favorite artist could be fun. Schedule the activities in your calendar.

8 Managing Meetings

LESSON SKILL MATRIX

Creating a One-Time Meeting	Students will learn how to create a one-time meeting.
Inviting Mandatory and Optional Attendees	Students will learn how to invite mandatory and optional attendees.
Determining When Attendees Can Meet	Students will learn how to determine when attendees can meet.
Responding to a Meeting Request	Students will learn how to respond to a meeting request.
Tracking Responses to a Meeting Request	Students will learn how to track responses to a meeting request.
Changing a Meeting Time	Students will learn how to change a meeting time.
Proposing a New Meeting Time	Students will learn how to propose a new meeting time.
Accepting a Proposed New Meeting Time	Students will learn how to accept a proposed new meeting time.
Adding and Updating a New Attendee	Students will learn how to add and update a new attendee.
Creating a Recurring Meeting	Students will learn how to create a recurring meeting.
Changing One Occurrence of a Recurring Meeting	Students will learn how to change one occurrence of a recurring meeting.
Scheduling a Meeting Resource	Students will learn how to schedule a meeting resource.
Canceling a Meeting	Students will learn how to cancel a meeting.

Gabe Mares reviewed the list of bug reports for Project Snow. The list was much longer than it should be at this stage in the software development cycle. It was obviously time to call a meeting to identify the reason for the long list of problems and determine how the problems could be resolved to meet the project deadlines.

KEY TERMS
cancel
group schedule
mandatory attendee
meeting
meeting organizer
meeting request
occurrence
optional attendee
recurring meeting
resource

Managing Meetings | 1063

■ SOFTWARE ORIENTATION

Microsoft Outlook's Meeting Window

The Meeting window displayed in Figure 8-1 enables you to create a meeting involving other people or resources. Scheduled meetings are displayed on your calendar.

Figure 8-1

Outlook's Meeting window

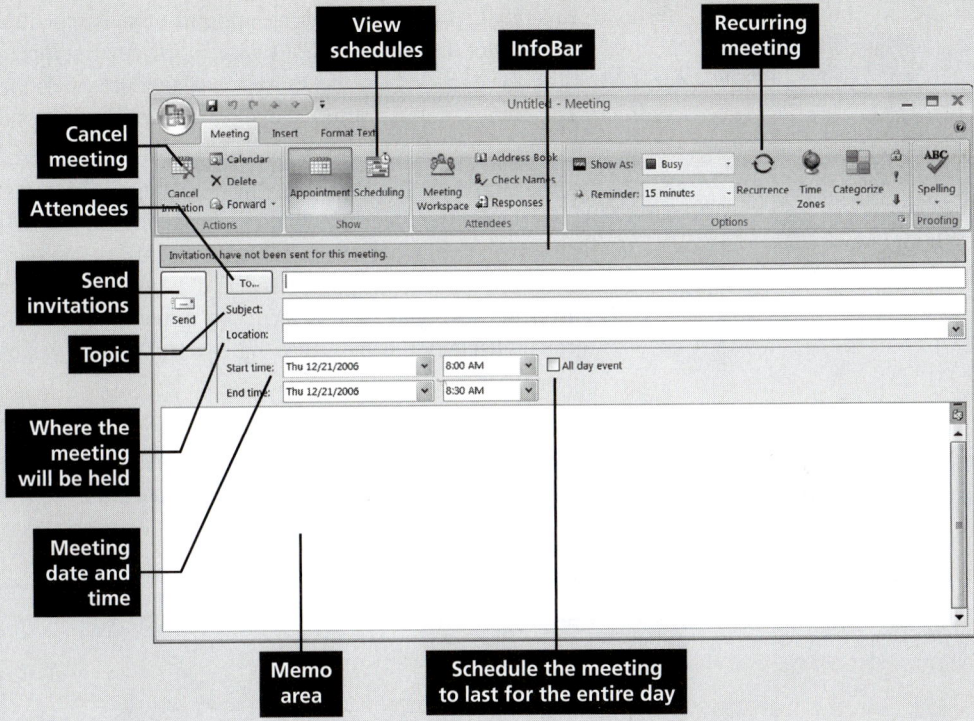

Use the Meeting window to create a meeting. Refer to Figure 8-1 as you complete the following exercises.

■ **Creating a Meeting**

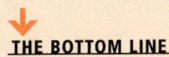
THE BOTTOM LINE

A *meeting* is a scheduled activity that requires sending invitations to other people or resources. Basically, a meeting is an appointment that requires other attendees. Therefore, Outlook's Meeting window, shown in Figure 8-1, is very similar to the Appointment window. However, the Meeting window also includes the To field to invite attendees and the Send button to send the invitations. A meeting can occur once or at regular intervals.

➢ Creating a One-Time Meeting

You can find more information on appointments in Lesson 7.

Meeting a goal often requires more than one person. Working with others to accomplish a goal usually requires meetings. Use Outlook to start planning a good meeting by selecting the right time, the right place, and the right people to accomplish the goal. A *meeting request* is an Outlook item that creates a meeting and invites attendees.

CREATE A ONE-TIME MEETING

GET READY. Before you begin these steps, be sure to launch Microsoft Outlook.

1. Click the **Calendar** button in the Navigation pane to display the Calendar folder. Click the **Month** button to display the Month view, if necessary.
2. Click the third Monday of the month on the monthly calendar. If you have already passed the third Monday of this month, select the third Monday of next month.

> **TROUBLESHOOTING**
>
> If you completed Lesson 7, a recurring appointment is scheduled for 8:30 AM to 9:30 AM every Monday to prepare a sales report. An Engineering Lunch is scheduled for 12:15 PM to 1:15 PM on the third Monday of every month. If you did not complete Lesson 7, the busy times shown on your schedule will differ.

3. On the Standard toolbar, click the **New** arrow. Click **Meeting Request** on the drop-down menu. The Meeting window shown in Figure 8-1 is displayed. By default, the beginning of your workday, 8:00 AM in this example, is in the *Start time* field for the meeting and the time in the *End time* field is 30 minutes after the meeting starts. Because you have a recurring appointment scheduled for 8:30 AM, the InfoBar displays the message *Adjacent to another appointment on your Calendar*.
4. Click the **Subject** field and key **Discuss Annual Convention**. In the Location field, key **Conference Room A**.
5. Click the **Scheduling** button in the Show group on the Ribbon. Scheduling information is displayed, as shown in Figure 8-2.

Figure 8-2

Viewing schedules

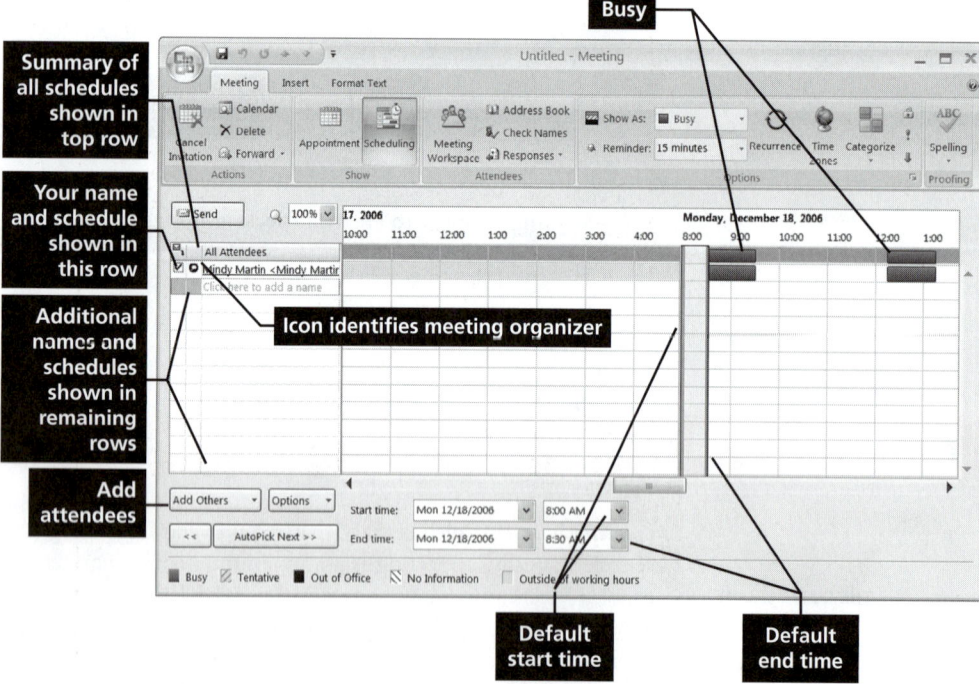

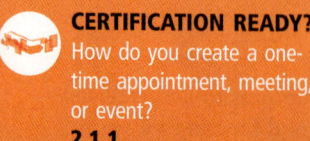

CERTIFICATION READY?
How do you create a one-time appointment, meeting, or event?
2.1.1

PAUSE. LEAVE the Meeting window open to use in the next exercise.

In the previous exercise, you started the process of creating a one-time meeting. In the next exercise, you will select the right people to make this meeting a success.

Inviting Mandatory and Optional Attendees

A ***mandatory attendee*** is a person who must attend the meeting. An ***optional attendee*** is a person who should attend the meeting, but whose presence is not required. When you select a meeting time, choose a time slot when all mandatory attendees are available.

INVITE MANDATORY AND OPTIONAL ATTENDEES

GET READY. Before you begin these steps, complete the previous exercise. The mandatory attendee used in this exercise must have an active email account and be able to respond to your meeting invitation.

ANOTHER WAY

If the person who will respond to your invitation is not in the address book, click the *Click here to add a name* text in the Meeting window. Key the desired email address. Verify that the icon next to the keyed name is *Required Attendee*.

1. In the Meeting window, click the **Add Others** button and click **Add from Address Book**. The Select Attendees and Resources: Contacts window is displayed, as shown in Figure 8-3.

Figure 8-3

Select Attendees and Resources: Contacts window

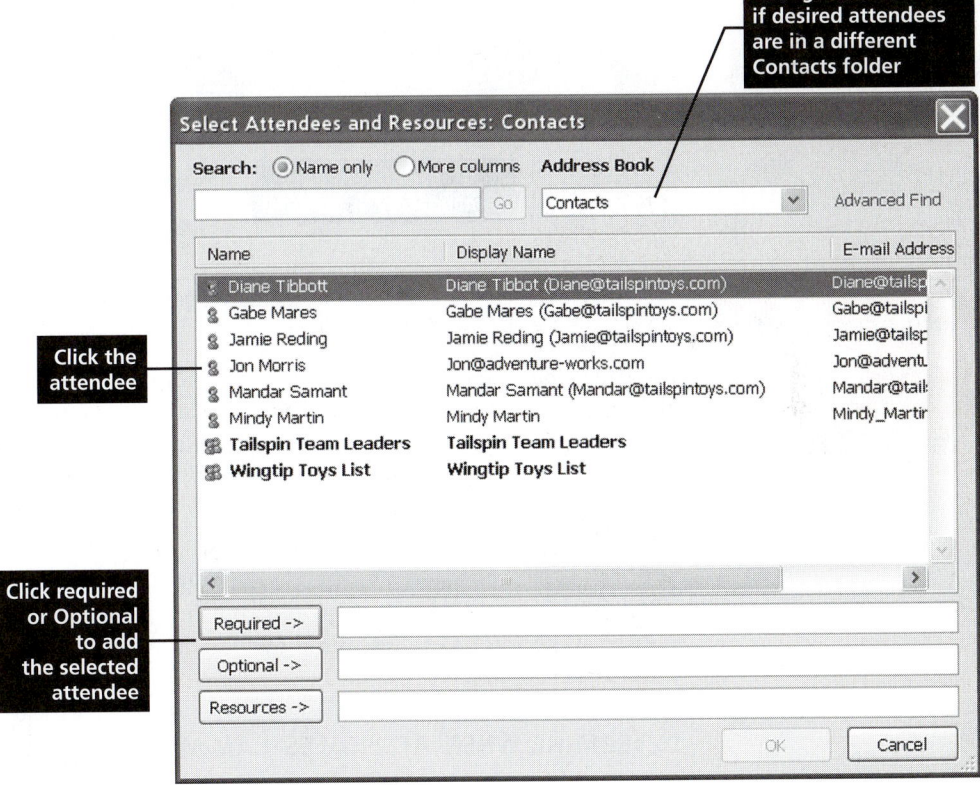

2. Click the contact information for the person who can respond to your invitation. In this example, Mindy clicks **Jon Morris'** contact record. Click the **Required** button. Jon is a mandatory attendee. Your mandatory attendee will be the real email account that can respond to your invitation.

> **TROUBLESHOOTING** If you invite a different Outlook user as your mandatory attendee, create a contact record for the new user before completing this exercise or key the new user's email address directly into the *To* field.

3. Click **Gabe Mares'** contact information. Click the **Optional** button. Gabe is an optional attendee. Click **OK** to return to the Meeting window. Your mandatory attendee and Gabe have been added to the list of attendees, as shown in Figure 8-4.

Figure 8-4

Attendees displayed

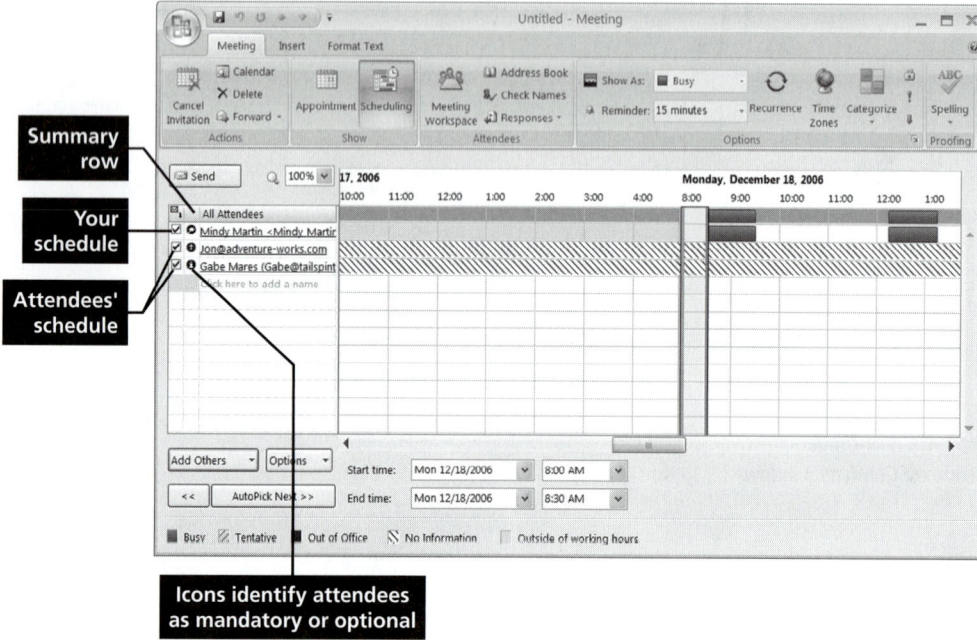

PAUSE. LEAVE the Meeting window open to use in the next exercise.

In the previous exercise, you selected a mandatory attendee and an optional attendee. When planning a meeting, you should always invite at least one mandatory attendee. If a mandatory attendee is not needed to accomplish a goal at the meeting, you might not need a meeting at all. In the next exercise, you will select a time for the meeting.

Determining When Attendees Can Meet

> Viewing schedules for others in your company or group can make scheduling much easier. With schedules displayed for all attendees, it is clear when all attendees are free to participate in your meeting.

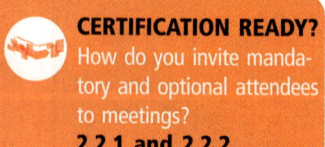

CERTIFICATION READY?
How do you invite mandatory and optional attendees to meetings?
2.2.1 and 2.2.2

➡ DETERMINE WHEN ATTENDEES CAN MEET

GET READY. Before you begin these steps, complete the previous exercises.

1. In the *Start time* field, key or select **10:00 AM**. Notice that the green and red vertical bars indicating the start and end time for the meeting moved to enclose the 10:00 AM to 10:30 AM time slot.

2. Click the **red vertical line** and drag it to the right so that the bars enclose the 10:00 AM to 11:00 AM time slot. Notice that the *End time* field changed to 11:00 AM.

3. Change the *Start time* field to **8:00 AM** and change the *End time* field to **9:00 AM**, if necessary. The green and red vertical lines move. The meeting time overlaps your scheduled appointment.

4. Click the **AutoPick Next** button. Outlook examines the available calendar information and selects the first open hour. The meeting times are changed to the 9:30 AM to 10:30 AM time slot.

5. You don't want to rush your previous appointment, so click the **AutoPick Next** button again. The meeting times are changed to starting at 10:00 AM and ending at 11:00 AM, as shown in Figure 8-5.

Figure 8-5

Meeting time selected

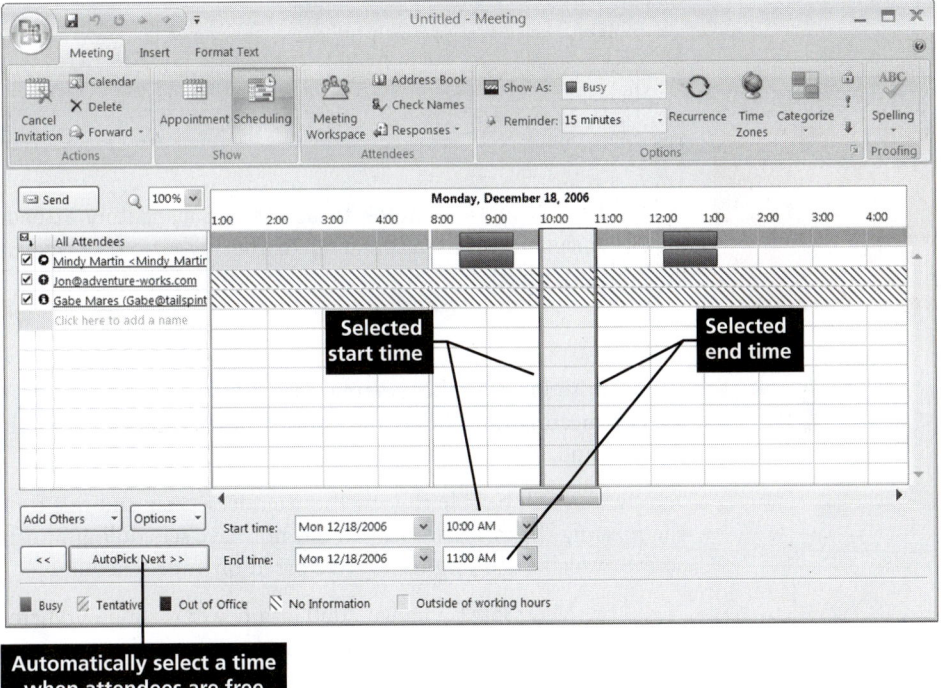

6. Click the **Appointment** button in the Show group on the Ribbon. The To field is automatically filled with the attendees' email addresses, and the *Start time* and *End time* fields are filled.

7. Click the message area. Key the following message. **Jon, please let me know if this time is convenient for you. Gabe, I hope you can attend. Coffee and pastries will be available.** Press Enter. **Mindy**

> **TROUBLESHOOTING** The email addresses provided in these exercises belong to unused domains owned by Microsoft. When you send a message to these addresses, you will receive an error message stating that the message could not be delivered. Delete the error messages when they arrive.

8. Compare your Meeting window to Figure 8-6. Click the **Send** button. Your calendar is updated, and the 10:00 AM to 11:00 AM time slot is displayed as busy.

Figure 8-6

Meeting invitation

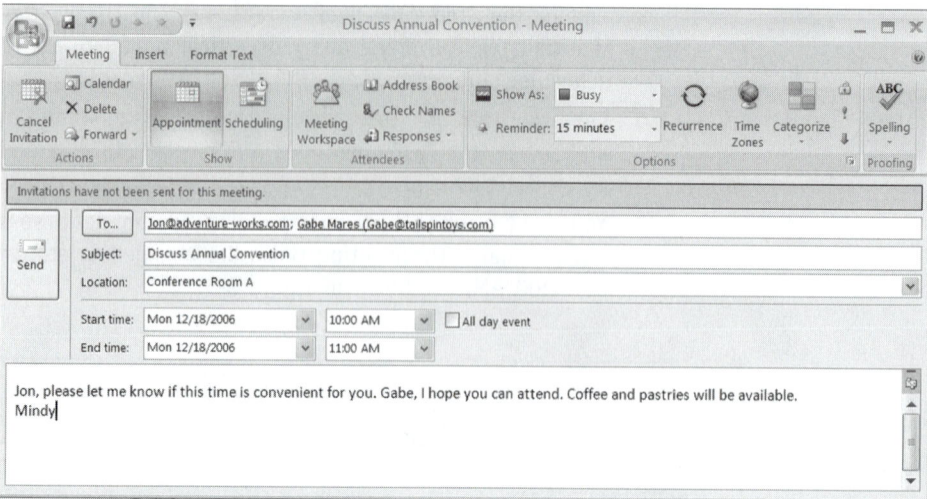

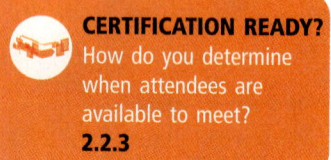

CERTIFICATION READY?
How do you determine when attendees are available to meet?
2.2.3

PAUSE. CLOSE Outlook to access the mandatory attendee's account, if necessary. If someone else is responding to the invitation, leave Outlook open to use in the next exercise.

In the previous exercise, you examined the available scheduling information for the people you want to invite to the meeting, manually selected a meeting time, and then let Outlook select a meeting time. You wrote a brief message and sent the meeting invitations. Your calendar was updated.

Ideally, you will be able to view the attendees' busy and free times before selecting a time for the meeting. In this exercise, you did not have scheduling information for the other attendees, so the available meeting times were based on your schedule.

If you use Microsoft Exchange 2000 or a newer version of Microsoft Exchange, you can view a group schedule. A *group schedule* displays scheduling information for several people. For example, you could view scheduling information for all the people in a public Contacts folder.

You used the message area to write a brief note to the attendees. However, this space can also be used to key an agenda for the meeting. You can also attach documents to the invitation before sending it. To attach documents, click the Insert tab and click the Attach File button in the Include group on the Ribbon.

Responding to a Meeting Request

By default, a meeting request arrives in your Inbox. It offers five options at the top of the message. You can accept the invitation, accept tentatively, decline, propose a new time, or view your calendar.

RESPOND TO A MEETING REQUEST

GET READY. Before you begin these steps, launch Microsoft Outlook, if necessary. Complete the previous exercises. To complete this exercise, you must have access to the email account that received the invitation for the mandatory attendee. If you do not have access to the email account, the account owner should respond to the invitation.

1. In the mandatory attendee's account, click the **Mail** button in the Navigation pane to display the Mail folder, if necessary.
2. If the Discuss Annual Convention message has not arrived, click the **Send/Receive** button.
3. Click the **Discuss Annual Convention** message in the message list. The message is displayed in the Preview pane, as shown in Figure 8-7.

Figure 8-7

Meeting invitation received

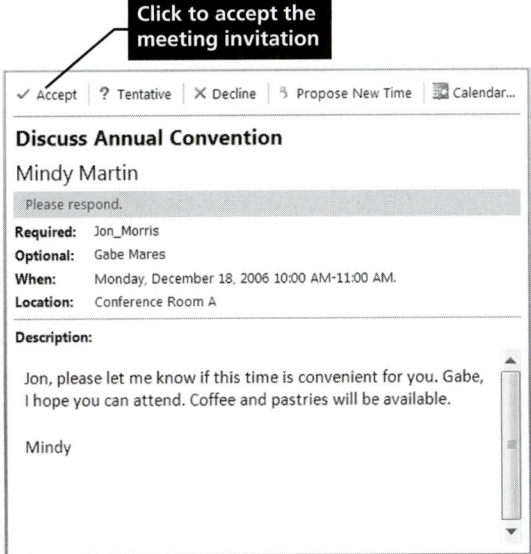

4. Click the **Accept** button. A dialog box is displayed that enables you to send your response now, add a comment before sending the response, or choose to not send a response.

5. Click the **Send the response now** option, if necessary. Click **OK**. The meeting request is removed from your Inbox, and the meeting is added to your calendar.

   PAUSE. CLOSE Outlook to return to your account, if necessary. If someone else responded to the invitation, leave Outlook open to use in the next exercise.

Accepting a meeting request automatically adds the meeting to your calendar, displaying the meeting time as busy. If you tentatively accept the invitation, the time is displayed as tentative in your calendar.

Tracking Responses to a Meeting Request

> When an attendee responds to your meeting invitation, you receive a message. If the attendee included comments in the response, the comments are contained in the message. The meeting information stored in your calendar keeps track of the responses. Opening the Meeting window to view a summary of the responses is much more efficient than manually tracking every email you receive.

➔ TRACK RESPONSES TO A MEETING REQUEST

GET READY. Before you begin these steps, complete the previous exercises. The mandatory attendee used in this exercise must have an active email account that received and responded to your meeting invitation.

1. In your account, click the **Mail** button in the Navigation pane to display the Mail folder, if necessary.

2. If the Accepted: Discuss Annual Convention message has not arrived, click the **Send/Receive** button.

3. Click the **Accepted: Discuss Annual Convention** message in the message list. The message is displayed in the Preview pane, as shown in Figure 8-8.

Figure 8-8

Message accepting the meeting invitation

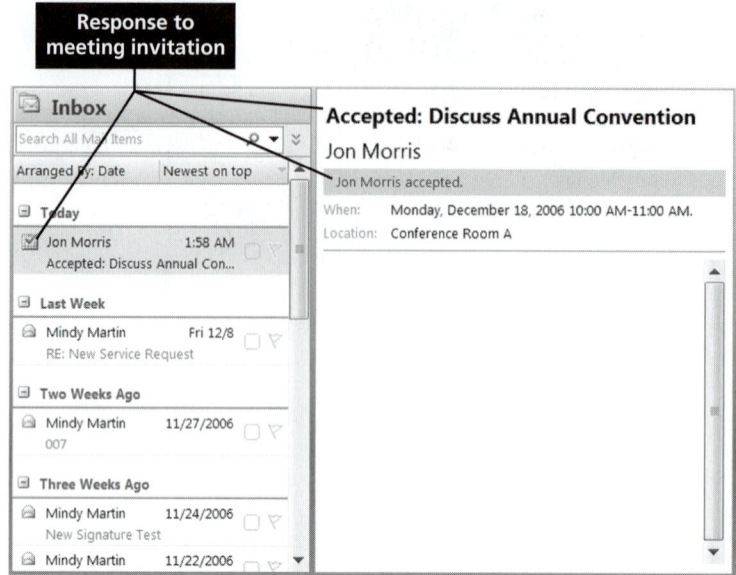

4. Click the **Calendar** button in the Navigation pane to display the Calendar folder. Click the **Month** button to display the Month view, if necessary.

5. Navigate to and double-click the **Discuss Annual Convention** meeting item on the calendar. The Discuss Annual Conference – Meeting window is displayed, as shown in Figure 8-9. The InfoBar contains a summary of the responses received.

Figure 8-9

Summary of responses received

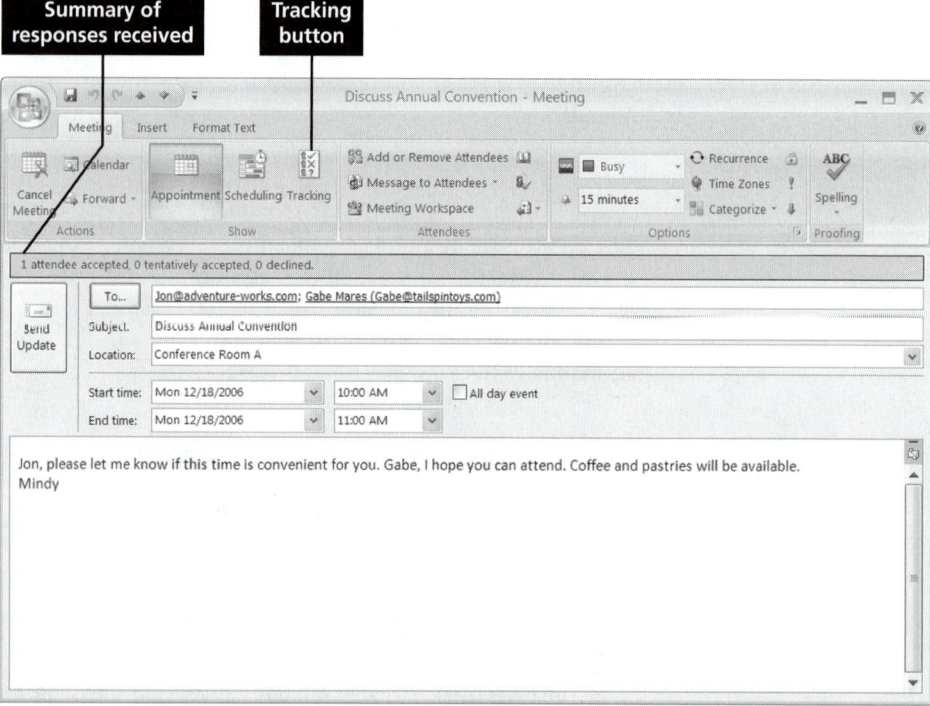

6. Click the **Tracking** button. Detailed tracking information is displayed, as shown in Figure 8-10. You can see at a glance which attendees have responded.

Figure 8-10

Details about responses received

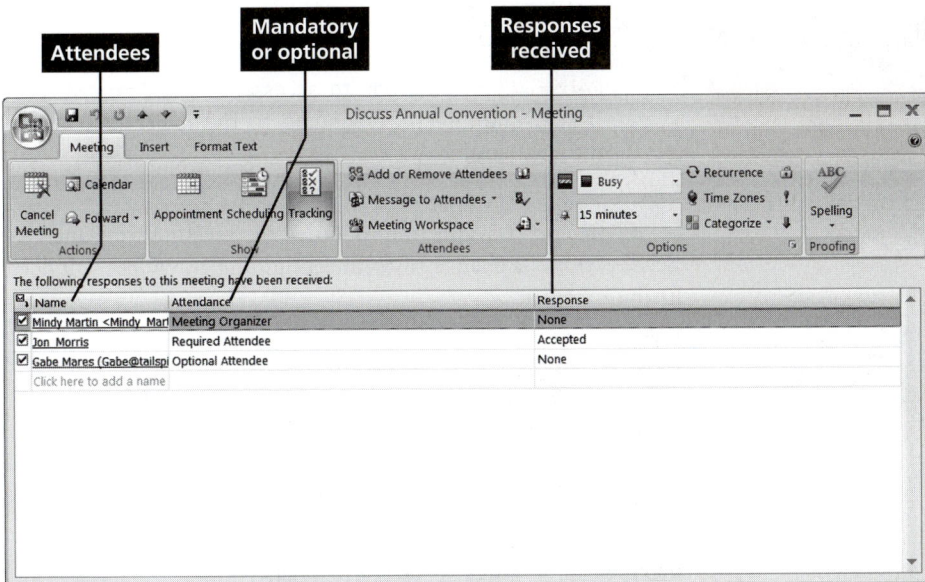

CERTIFICATION READY?
How do you track responses to meeting requests?
2.2.4

7. Close the Meeting window without saving changes.

   PAUSE. LEAVE Outlook open to use in the next exercise.

In the previous exercise, you received a response to the meeting invitations you sent earlier. Tracking responses is a simple task, regardless of the number of attendees invited.

Modifying a Meeting

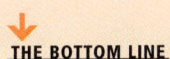

THE BOTTOM LINE

When you are trying to get a group of people to sit at the same table at the same time, problems can emerge. One person will go out of town on an emergency business trip. Another person has to attend a meeting with a higher priority. Necessary audio-visual equipment is shipped to a trade show. The list of potential problems is endless. Modifying a meeting and updating the attendees is a simple task in Outlook.

Changing a Meeting Time

The most common modifications to a meeting are changing the time and the location of a meeting. In Outlook, you can modify the meeting information and then send an update to all attendees.

➔ CHANGE A MEETING TIME

GET READY. Before you begin these steps, complete the previous exercises. The mandatory attendee used in this exercise must have an active email account and be able to respond to your message.

1. In your account, click the **Calendar** button in the Navigation pane to display the Calendar folder. Click the **Month** button to display the Month view, if necessary.
2. Double-click the **Discuss Annual Convention** meeting item on the calendar. The Discuss Annual Conference – Meeting window is displayed, as shown in Figure 8-9.
3. Click the **Start time** field. Key or select **10:30 AM**. Press **Enter**. The *End time* field automatically changes to 11:30 AM.

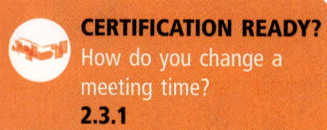

CERTIFICATION READY?
How do you change a meeting time?
2.3.1

4. Click the **Send Update** button below the InfoBar to send the modified information to the attendees.

   PAUSE. CLOSE Outlook to access the mandatory attendee's account, if necessary. If someone else is responding to the invitation, leave Outlook open to use in the next exercise.

In the previous exercise, you modified the meeting time and sent an update to the attendees. Because this is a change to the meeting time, attendees will need to respond to the meeting invitation again.

Proposing a New Meeting Time

Meeting times are set by the *meeting organizer*, the person who creates the meeting and sends meeting invitations. When a meeting invitation is received, the attendee can suggest a different time for the meeting that better fits the attendees' schedule.

→ PROPOSE A NEW MEETING TIME

GET READY. Before you begin these steps, launch Microsoft Outlook, if necessary. Complete the previous exercises. To complete this exercise, you must have access to the email account that received the invitation for the mandatory attendee. If you do not have access to the email account, the account owner should propose a new time when responding to the updated meeting invitation.

1. In the mandatory attendee's account, click the **Mail** button in the Navigation pane to display the Mail folder, if necessary.
2. If the Discuss Annual Convention message has not arrived, click the **Send/Receive** button.
3. Click the **Discuss Annual Convention** message in the message list. The message is displayed in the Preview pane, as shown in Figure 8-11.

Figure 8-11

Updated meeting invitation received

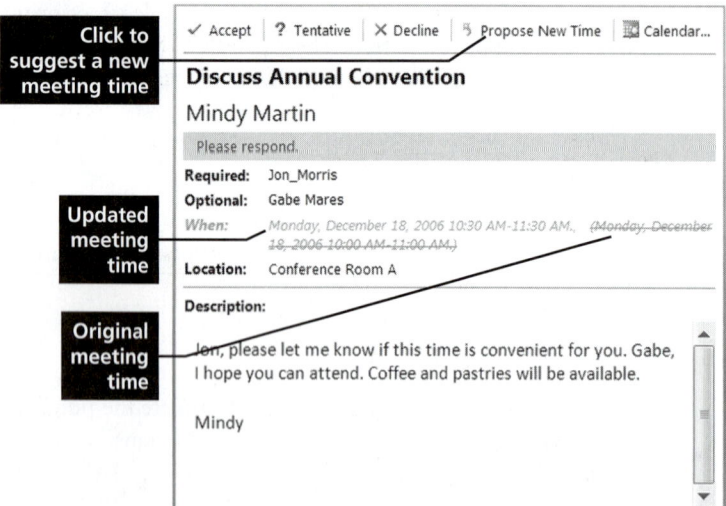

4. Click the **Propose New Time** button at the top of the message. The Propose New Time window is displayed, as shown in Figure 8-12.

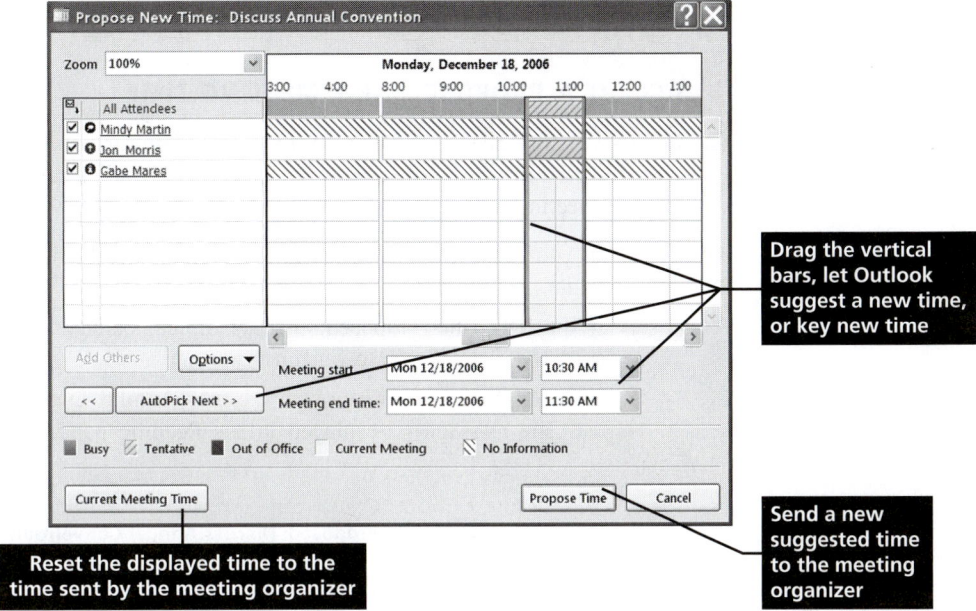

Figure 8-12

Propose New Time window

5. Verify that 10:30 is in the *Start time* field. Click the **End time** field. Key **12:00 PM**. Click the **Propose Time** button. A Message window is displayed.

6. In the message area, key the following message. **Let's add 30 minutes and conclude the meeting by offering a sampling of foods available for the convention luncheon.** Press **Enter**. **Jon**

7. Compare your message to Figure 8-13 and click the **Send** button.

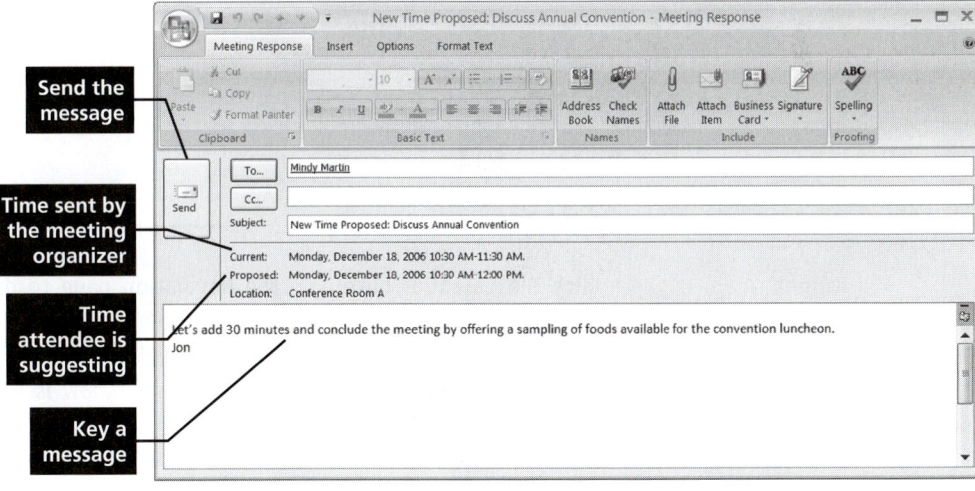

Figure 8-13

New Time Proposed message

CERTIFICATION READY?
How do you change a meeting time?
2.3.1

PAUSE. CLOSE Outlook to return to your account, if necessary. If someone else responded to the invitation, leave Outlook open to use in the next exercise.

The meeting organizer and the attendees might evaluate several different meeting times. If you share your calendar, you can prevent some message exchanges regarding meeting times by keeping your free and busy times up-to-date in your calendar. In the previous exercise, offering food samples is a good reason to extend the meeting time.

Accepting a Proposed New Meeting Time

The meeting organizer has the final word on setting the meeting time. When an attendee proposes a new meeting time, the meeting organizer must evaluate the proposed time and accept or decline the proposal.

➔ ACCEPT A PROPOSED NEW MEETING TIME

GET READY. Before you begin these steps, complete the previous exercises. The mandatory attendee used in this exercise must have an active email account that received and responded to your meeting invitation.

1. In your account, click the **Mail** button in the Navigation pane to display the Mail folder, if necessary.
2. If the New Time Proposed: Discuss Annual Convention message has not arrived, click the **Send/Receive** button.
3. Click the **New Time Proposed: Discuss Annual Convention** message in the message list. The message is displayed in the Reading pane, as shown in Figure 8-14.

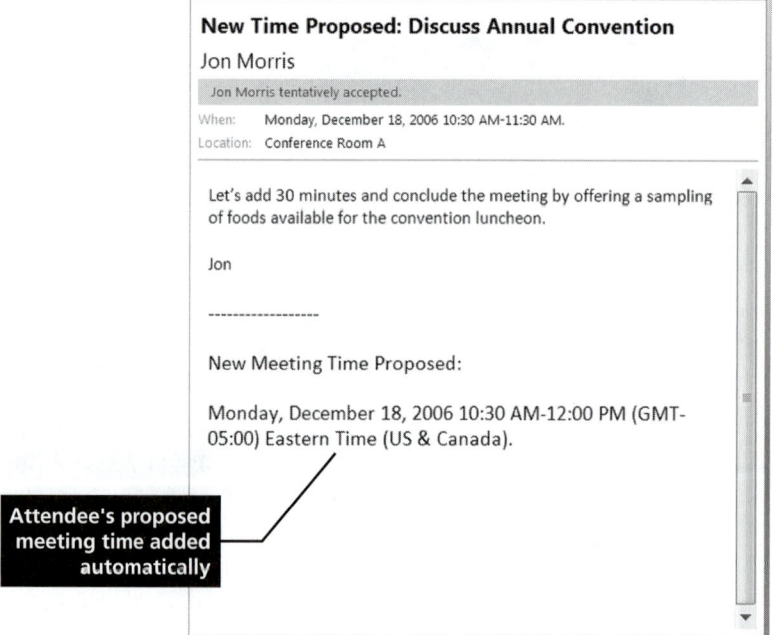

Figure 8-14

Message from attendee proposing the new time

4. Click the **Calendar** button in the Navigation pane to display the Calendar folder. Click the **Month** button to display the Month view, if necessary.
5. Double-click the **Discuss Annual Convention** meeting item on the calendar. The Discuss Annual Conference – Meeting window is displayed, as shown in Figure 8-9. The InfoBar contains a summary of the responses received. Jon's previous acceptance has been changed to a tentative acceptance because he proposed a new time for the meeting.
6. Click the **Scheduling** button. Click **Accept Proposal**. Click **Send Update**.

PAUSE. LEAVE Outlook open to use in the next exercise.

Managing Meetings | 1075

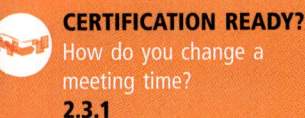

TROUBLESHOOTING If the proposed time or the Accept Proposal button is not displayed, you can manually change the start and end time of the meeting and click Send to send the update to the attendees.

In the previous exercise, you accepted a new meeting time proposed by an attendee. Anyone invited to the meeting can suggest a new date and time for the meeting. Only the meeting organizer can accept or decline the suggested time and change the meeting time.

CERTIFICATION READY?
How do you change a meeting time?
2.3.1

When the meeting time is changed and you click the Send Update or Send button, attendees are notified of the new time. They must accept or decline the meeting again, as they did for the initial invitation.

Adding and Updating a New Attendee

When you create a meeting, you select the attendees needed to meet the meeting's objective. When the selected attendees learn about the meeting, they can suggest other individuals who should be invited to the meeting. For example, say that you created a meeting about software issues experienced by a client. You invited the project manager, the lead software developer on the team, and the service representative working with the client. The project manager suggests that you invite the trainer who has been working on-site with the client's equipment. You quickly add an attendee to invite the trainer.

 ADD AND UPDATE A NEW ATTENDEE

GET READY. Before you begin these steps, launch Microsoft Outlook, if necessary. Complete the previous exercises.

1. In your account, click the **Calendar** button in the Navigation pane to display the Calendar folder.
2. Double-click the **Discuss Annual Convention** meeting item on the calendar. The Discuss Annual Conference – Meeting window is displayed, as shown in Figure 8-9.
3. Click the **Add or Remove Attendees** button in the Attendees group on the Ribbon. The Select Attendees and Resources: Contacts window is displayed, as shown in Figure 8-3. The mandatory attendee and Gabe Mares are already displayed in the fields.
4. Click the **Diane Tibbott** contact record and click the **Optional** button. Click **OK** to return to the Meeting window.
5. Click the **Send Update** button. Outlook recognizes that the list of attendees has changed and displays the Send Update to Attendees dialog box shown in Figure 8-15.

Figure 8-15

Send Update to Attendees dialog box

6. Click **OK** to only send the message to the added attendee. The updated meeting information is sent to Diane Tibbott.

PAUSE. LEAVE Outlook open to use in the next exercise.

CERTIFICATION READY?
How do you add a meeting attendee and send meeting updates only to new attendees?
2.3.2 and 2.3.4

In the previous exercise, you added a new attendee to the meeting and sent the updated meeting information only to Diane, the new attendee. This eliminates sending meeting information to the original attendees. In this example, the amount of information sent is minimal. However, if you had attached documents or other files, the time saved and storage space conserved for every attendee would be more obvious.

1076 | Lesson 8

Managing a Recurring Meeting

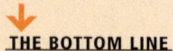
THE BOTTOM LINE

A *recurring meeting* is a meeting that occurs at regular intervals. The meeting always has the same attendees, location, and purpose. The interval could be a number of days, weeks, or months. For example, status meetings commonly occur at weekly or monthly intervals.

Creating a Recurring Meeting

The process of creating a recurring meeting is very similar to creating a one-time meeting. The only difference is setting the recurrence pattern.

 CREATE A RECURRING MEETING

GET READY. Before you begin these steps, be sure to launch Microsoft Outlook.

1. In your account, click the **Calendar** button in the Navigation pane to display the Calendar folder. Click the **Month** button to display the Month view, if necessary.
2. Click next Friday on the monthly calendar.
3. On the Standard toolbar, click the **New** arrow. Click **Meeting Request** on the drop-down menu. The Meeting window shown in Figure 8-1 is displayed. By default, the beginning of your workday, 8:00 AM in this example, is in the *Start time* field for the meeting and the time in the *End time* field is 30 minutes after the meeting starts.
4. Click the **Subject** field and key **Project Status**. In the Location field, key **Dept Room 62**.
5. Click the **Scheduling** button in the Show group on the Ribbon. Scheduling information is displayed.
6. Click the **Add Others** button and click **Add from Address Book**. The Select Attendees and Resources: Contacts window is displayed.
7. Press **Ctrl** while clicking the four Tailspin Toys employees. Click **Required**. Click **OK** to return to the Meeting window.
8. Change the *Start time* field to **9:00 AM** and change the *End time* field to **10:00 AM**, if necessary. The green and red vertical lines move.
9. Click the **Recurrence** button in the Options group on the Ribbon. The Appointment Recurrence window is displayed, as shown in Figure 8-16.

Figure 8-16

Appointment Recurrence window

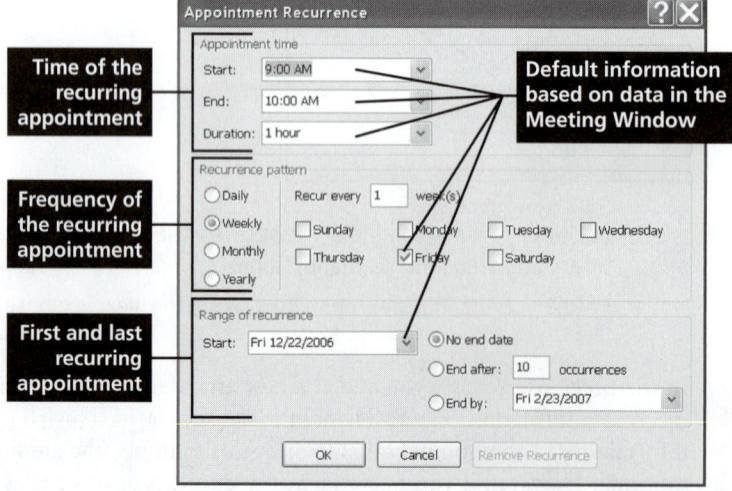

10. Outlook presents the most likely recurrence pattern when the Appointment Recurrence window is displayed. In this case, the pattern is correct. The Project Status meeting will be held every Friday. Click **OK** to accept the recurrence pattern and return to the meeting window.
11. Click the **Appointment** button in the Show group on the Ribbon. The To field is automatically filled with the attendees' email addresses, and the recurrence pattern is displayed.
12. Compare your Meeting window to Figure 8-17. Click the **Send** button. Your calendar is updated, and the 9:00 AM to 10:00 AM time slot is displayed as busy for every Friday.

Figure 8-17

Meeting request for a recurring meeting

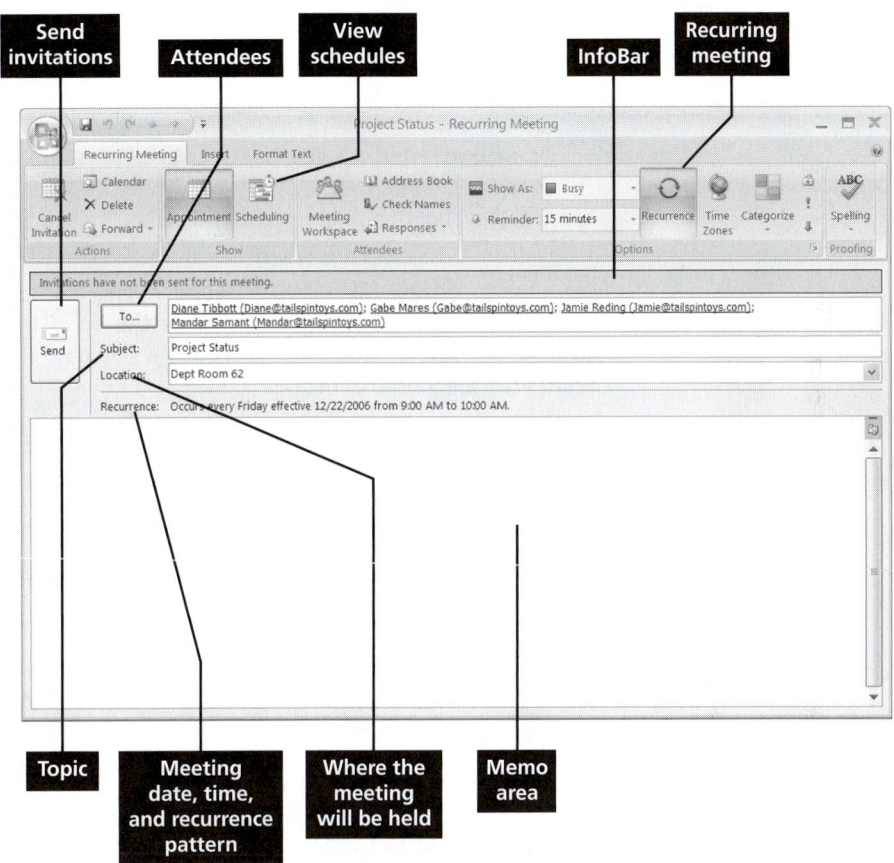

PAUSE. LEAVE Outlook open to use in the next exercise.

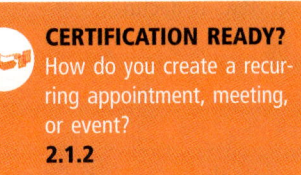

CERTIFICATION READY?
How do you create a recurring appointment, meeting, or event?
2.1.2

In the previous exercise, you created a recurring meeting. The attendees will meet every Friday morning to review the status of their active projects.

TROUBLESHOOTING If the location of a meeting is scheduled as a resource and the room is not available for any of the recurrent meetings, you will not be able to schedule the recurrent meeting. You will learn more about scheduling resources later in this lesson.

Changing One Occurrence of a Recurring Meeting

A single meeting in a series of recurring meetings is an ***occurrence***. When a recurring meeting is held regularly for a long period of time, an occurrence will eventually conflict with some other event. You will need to change the time of a single occurrence of the meeting.

CHANGE ONE OCCURRENCE OF A RECURRING MEETING

GET READY. Before you begin these steps, complete the previous exercise to create the recurring meeting.

1. In your account, click the **Calendar** button in the Navigation pane to display the Calendar folder. Click the **Month** button to display the Month view, if necessary.
2. Double-click the second occurrence of the **Project Status** meeting item on the calendar. The Open Recurring Item dialog box is displayed, as shown in Figure 8-18.

Figure 8-18

Open Recurring Item dialog box

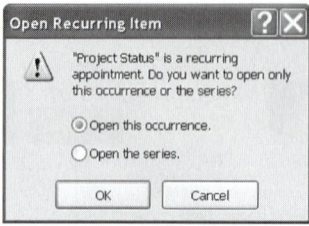

3. Click **OK** to open the single occurrence. The Project Status – Meeting window is displayed. The meeting information applies to the single occurrence.
4. Click the **Start time** field. Key or select **10:00 AM** and press [Enter]. The *End time* automatically changes to 11:00 AM. Click the **Send Update** button. In your calendar, the single occurrence is modified to show the new time. The other occurrences are not changed.

   PAUSE. LEAVE Outlook open to use in the next exercise.

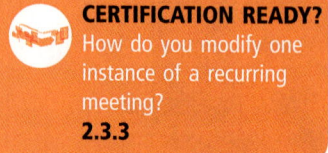

CERTIFICATION READY?
How do you modify one instance of a recurring meeting?
2.3.3

In the previous exercise, you changed the time of one meeting in a series of recurring meetings. When you changed one occurrence, your calendar was updated and updates were sent to the attendees. You can change the date, time, and location of a single occurrence.

■ Scheduling a Meeting Resource

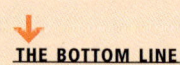

THE BOTTOM LINE

In Outlook, a *resource* is an item or a location that can be invited to a meeting. Resources can include cars, presentation equipment, and conference rooms. You can invite a resource to a meeting just like you invite attendees. A resource has its own mailbox and maintains its own schedule. It accepts invitations for free times and updates its calendar. It declines invitations if the requested time is already scheduled.

SCHEDULE A MEETING RESOURCE

GET READY. Before you begin these steps, be sure to launch Microsoft Outlook.

TROUBLESHOOTING Scheduling a resource requires Microsoft Exchange and a resource with a separate mailbox.

1. Click the **Calendar** button in the Navigation pane to display the Calendar folder. Click the **Month** button to display the Month view, if necessary. Click next Thursday's date.
2. On the Standard toolbar, click the **New** arrow. Click **Meeting Request** on the dropdown menu. The Meeting window shown in Figure 8-1 is displayed.
3. Click the **Subject** field and key **Project Presentation Review**. In the Location field, key **Dept Room 62**.

Managing Meetings | 1079

ANOTHER WAY

You can create contact records for the resources you use. This enables you to select the resource in the address book rather than keying the resource's address in the Meeting window.

4. Click the **Scheduling** button in the Show group on the Ribbon. Scheduling information is displayed.
5. Change the *Start time* field to **9:00 AM** and change the *End time* field to **10:00 AM**. The green and red vertical lines move.
6. Click the **Add Others** button and click **Add from Address Book**. The Select Attendees and Resources: Contacts window is displayed.
7. Click **Diane Tibbott** and click **Required**. Click **OK** to return to the Meeting window.
8. Click the **Click here to add a name** text in the Meeting window. Key **AV01@tailspintoys.com**. Press [Enter]. You are inviting a slide projector to your meeting with Diane.
9. Click the icon next to the keyed address and select **Resource (Room or Equipment.)** A dialog box will be displayed asking if you want to change the location to AV01. Click **No**.
10. Click the **Appointment** button in the Show group on the Ribbon.
11. Compare your Meeting window to Figure 8-19. Click the **Send** button. Your calendar is updated to display the meeting.

Figure 8-19

Inviting a resource to a meeting

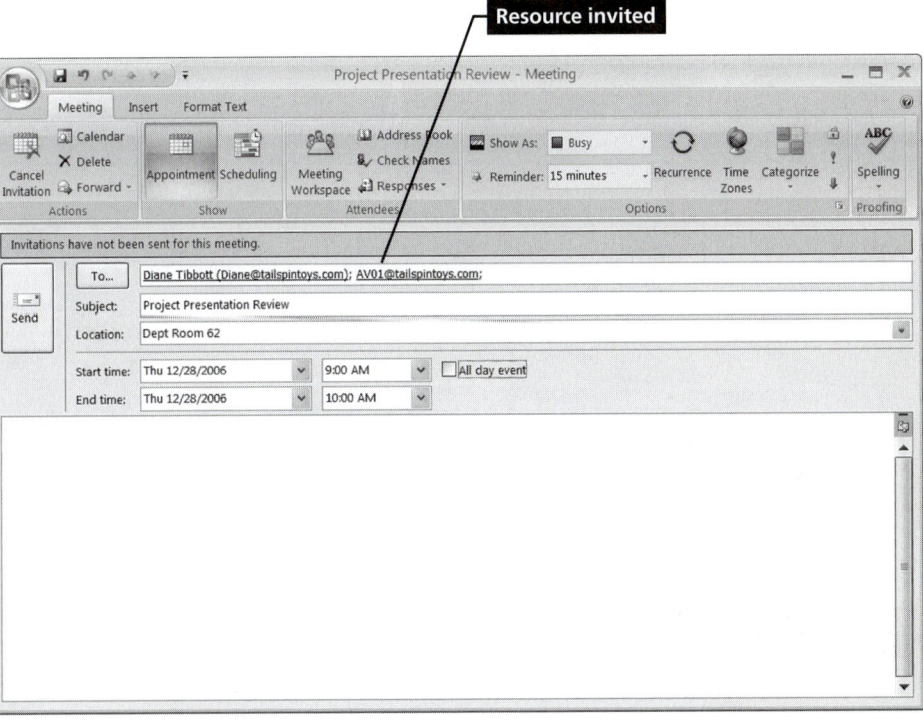

PAUSE. LEAVE Outlook open to use in the next exercise.

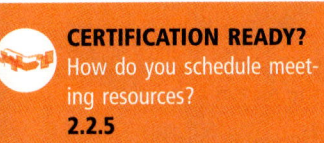

CERTIFICATION READY?
How do you schedule meeting resources?
2.2.5

In the previous exercise, you invited AV01, a slide projector, to your meeting with Diane. In the meeting, you plan to review a presentation Diane created, so the equipment is essential to the meeting.

■ Cancelling a Meeting

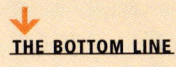

THE BOTTOM LINE

Regardless of how much planning went into creating a meeting, some meetings are cancelled. When you *cancel* a meeting, it is deleted from your calendar and the attendees are notified. Reasons for cancelling a meeting are varied. For example, mandatory attendees could become unavailable or issues are resolved before the scheduled meeting occurs.

CANCEL A MEETING

GET READY. Before you begin these steps, complete the exercises to create the Discuss Annual Convention meeting.

TAKE NOTE* Only the meeting organizer can cancel a meeting.

1. Click the **Calendar** button in the Navigation pane to display the Calendar folder. Click the **Month** button to display the Month view, if necessary.
2. Double-click the **Discuss Annual Convention** meeting item on the calendar. The Discuss Annual Convention – Meeting window is displayed.
3. Click the **Cancel Meeting** button in the Actions group on the Ribbon.
4. Click the **Memo area**. Delete any existing text and key the following message. **This meeting was cancelled because Jon had an emergency appendectomy earlier today. He is recovering at Mountain View Hospital and we expect him to return to the office next week. We'll reschedule the meeting after he returns.** Press Enter. **Mindy**
5. Compare your Meeting window to Figure 8-20 and click the **Send Cancellation** button. The message is sent and the meeting is removed from your calendar.

Figure 8-20

Cancelling a meeting

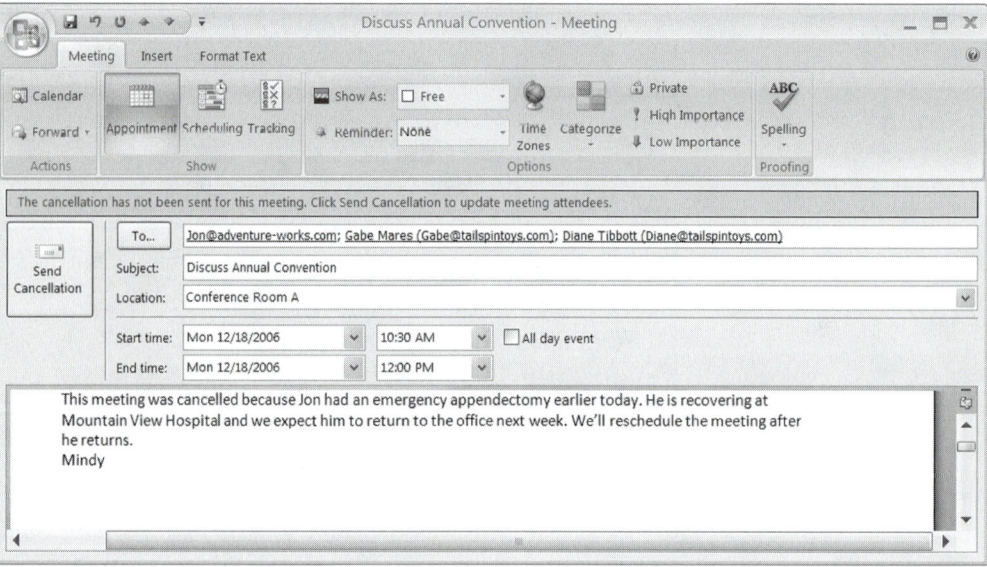

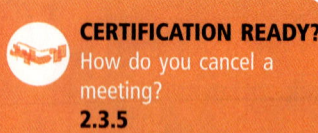

CERTIFICATION READY?
How do you cancel a meeting?
2.3.5

CLOSE Outlook.

In the previous exercise, you cancelled a meeting. A cancellation notice was sent to the attendees. If you need to track cancelled meetings or keep a record of the reason a meeting was cancelled, the cancellation notice is saved in your Sent Items folder.

In the attendee's mailbox, the cancellation notice is automatically assigned a High Importance. The attendee opens the message and clicks the Remove from Calendar button in the Respond group on the Ribbon. The attendee's calendar is updated.

SUMMARY SKILL MATRIX

IN THIS LESSON YOU LEARNED HOW TO:
Create a One-Time Meeting
Invite Mandatory and Optional Attendees
Determine When Attendees Can Meet
Respond to a Meeting Request
Track Responses to a Meeting Request
Change a Meeting Time
Propose a New Meeting Time
Accept a Proposed New Meeting Time
Add and Update a New Attendee
Create a Recurring Meeting
Change One Occurrence of a Recurring Meeting
Schedule a Meeting Resource
Cancel a Meeting

■ Knowledge Assessment

Matching

Match the term with its definition.

- a. cancel
- b. group schedule
- c. mandatory attendee
- d. meeting
- e. meeting organizer
- f. meeting request
- g. occurrence
- h. optional attendee
- i. recurring meeting
- j. resource

_____ 1. A single meeting in a series of recurring meetings

_____ 2. An item or a location that can be invited to a meeting

_____ 3. Displays scheduling information for several people

_____ 4. A meeting that occurs at regular intervals

_____ 5. Delete a meeting

_____ 6. A scheduled activity that requires sending invitations to other people or resources

_____ 7. The person who creates the meeting and sends meeting invitations

_____ 8. A person who should attend the meeting, but whose presence is not required

_____ 9. Outlook item that creates the meeting and invites attendees

_____ 10. A person who must attend the meeting

True/False

Circle T if the statement is true or F if the statement is false.

T | F 1. Outlook's Meeting window is exactly like the Appointment window.
T | F 2. Only people or resources in your address book can be invited to a meeting.
T | F 3. Every meeting should have at least one mandatory attendee.
T | F 4. Your calendar is updated when you send a meeting request.
T | F 5. When an attendee accepts a meeting request, the attendee's schedule displays the meeting time as tentative.
T | F 6. Any attendee can propose a new meeting time.
T | F 7. When you add an attendee, you can send updated information to only the new attendee.
T | F 8. A recurring meeting can occur only 10 times.
T | F 9. To be scheduled, a resource must have its own mailbox.
T | F 10. Any attendee can cancel a meeting.

■ Competency Assessment

Project 8-1: Create a One-Time Meeting

It's time to launch a new project at Tailspin Toys. Gather the team leaders in a meeting to divide the duties.

GET READY. Launch Outlook if it is not already running.

1. Click the **Calendar** button in the Navigation pane to display the Calendar folder.
2. Click next Thursday's date.
3. On the Standard toolbar, click the **New** arrow. Click **Meeting Request** on the dropdown menu. The Meeting window is displayed.
4. Click the **Subject** field and key **Decoder: Project Launch**. In the Location field, key **Dept Room 62**.
5. Click the **Scheduling** button in the Show group on the Ribbon. Scheduling information is displayed.
6. Click the **Add Others** button and click **Add from Address Book**. The Select Attendees and Resources: Contacts window is displayed.
7. Click **Jamie Reding's** contact information and click the **Required** button. Click **Mandar Samant's** contact information and click the **Required** button. Click **OK** to return to the Meeting window.
8. Change the current *End time* value so the meeting is one hour long. Click the **AutoPick Next** button. If necessary, click the **AutoPick Next** button again or key **10:00 AM** in the *Start time* field.
9. Click the **Appointment** button in the Show group on the Ribbon. The To field is automatically filled with the attendees' email addresses and the *Start time* and *End time* fields are filled.
10. Click the **Send** button. Your calendar is updated, and the slot is displayed as busy.
LEAVE Outlook open for the next project.

Project 8-2: Create a Recurring Meeting

After the Decoder project is launched, set up a recurring meeting to monitor the project's status.

1. Click the **Calendar** button in the Navigation pane to display the Calendar folder.
2. Click the Thursday following the Decoder project launch.
3. On the Standard toolbar, click the **New** arrow. Click **Meeting Request** on the dropdown menu. The Meeting window is displayed.
4. Click the **Subject** field and key **Decoder: Project Status**. In the Location field, key **Dept Room 62**.
5. Click the **Scheduling** button in the Show group on the Ribbon. Scheduling information is displayed.
6. Click the **Add Others** button and click **Add from Address Book**. The Select Attendees and Resources: Contacts window is displayed.
7. Click **Jamie Reding's** contact information and click the **Required** button. Click **Mandar Samant's** contact information and click the **Required** button. Click **OK** to return to the Meeting window.
8. Change the *Start time* field to **10:00 AM** and change the *End time* field to **11:00 AM**, if necessary. The green and red vertical lines move to enclose the specified time slot.
9. Click the **Recurrence** button in the Options group on the Ribbon. The Appointment Recurrence window is displayed.
10. Click **OK** to accept the weekly recurrence pattern and return to the meeting window.
11. Click the **Appointment** button in the Show group on the Ribbon. The To field is automatically filled with the attendees' email addresses, and the recurrence pattern is displayed.
12. Click the **Send** button. Your calendar is updated and the 10:00 AM to 11:00 AM time slot is displayed as busy for every Thursday.

    LEAVE Outlook open for the next project.

■ Proficiency Assessment

Project 8-3: Add an Attendee to a Recurring Meeting

Diane Tibbott has been assigned to the Decoder project. Add her as an attendee to the recurring Decoder project status meeting.

1. Click the **Calendar** button in the Navigation pane to display the Calendar folder.
2. Double-click the first **Decoder: Project Status** meeting. The Open Recurring Item dialog box is displayed.
3. Click the **Open the Series** option and click **OK**.
4. Click the **Scheduling** button in the Show group on the Ribbon. Scheduling information is displayed.
5. Click the **Add Others** button and click **Add from Address Book**. The Select Attendees and Resources: Contacts window is displayed.
6. Click **Diane Tibbott's** contact information and click the **Required** button. Click **OK** to return to the Meeting window.
7. Click the **Appointment** button in the Show group on the Ribbon. Diane Tibbott has been added in the To field.

8. Click the **Send Update** button. The Send Update to Attendees dialog box is displayed.
9. Click **OK**. The updated meeting information is sent to Diane Tibbott.

LEAVE Outlook open for the next project.

Project 8-4: Change the Meeting Time of a Recurring Meeting

Diane is currently assigned to the TopHat project that is coming to a close, and it takes priority over the Decoder project. To be able to participate in both meetings, Diane asked you to hold the Decoder: Project Status meeting later in the day. Change the start time of the recurring status meetings to 1:00 PM.

1. Click the **Calendar** button in the Navigation pane to display the Calendar folder.
2. Double-click the first **Decoder: Project Status** meeting. The Open Recurring Item dialog box is displayed.
3. Click the **Open the Series** option and click **OK**.
4. Click the **Scheduling** button in the Show group on the Ribbon. Scheduling information is displayed.
5. Click the **Recurrence** button in the Options group on the Ribbon. The Appointment Recurrence window is displayed.
6. Key **1:00 PM** in the Start field. Verify that 2:00 PM is the time in the End field and click **OK**.
7. Click the **Appointment** button in the Show group on the Ribbon. The Recurrence pattern below the location field has been modified.
8. Click the **Send Update** button.

LEAVE Outlook open for the next project.

■ Mastery Assessment

Project 8-5: Change an Occurrence of a Recurring Meeting

The TopHat project plans to camp in your meeting room for a week of intensive testing. Change the location of the first Decoder: Project Status meeting.

1. Click the **Calendar** button in the Navigation pane to display the Calendar folder.
2. Double-click the first **Decoder: Project Status** meeting. The Open Recurring Item dialog box is displayed.
3. Click **OK** to open this occurrence of the meeting.
4. Click the **Location** field. Change the location to **Dept Room 50**. The room is smaller and less popular as a meeting room due to a peculiar odor that has persisted since the building was purchased.
5. Click the **Send Update** button.

LEAVE Outlook open for the next project.

Project 8-6: Cancel a Meeting

The upper management at Tailspin Toys has changed. New leadership brings new priorities. The Decoder project has been cancelled. Cancel the Decoder project launch meeting and the recurring project status meeting.

1. Click the **Calendar** button in the Navigation pane to display the Calendar folder.
2. Double-click the **Decoder: Project Launch** meeting. The Meeting window is displayed.

3. Click the **Cancel Meeting** button in the Actions group on the Ribbon.
4. Click the **Send Cancellation** button.
5. Double-click the first **Decoder: Project Status** meeting. The Open Recurring Item dialog box is displayed.
6. Click the **Open the Series** option and click **OK**.
7. Click the **Cancel Meeting** button in the Actions group on the Ribbon.
8. Click the **Send Cancellation** button. If a dialog box is displayed stating that the meeting request contains embedded attachments, click **Yes** to send the cancellation notice.

    CLOSE Outlook.

INTERNET READY

Your coworkers might not work in your office. Between telecommuting and traveling to client locations, you might find that several attendees do not attend meetings in person. Use the Internet to investigate meeting methods that can be used when all of the attendees are not in the same location.

9 Managing Tasks

LESSON SKILL MATRIX

Creating a One-Time Task — 1088	Students will learn how to create a one-time task.
Creating a Recurring Task — 1089	Students will learn how to create a recurring task.
Creating a Task from a Message — 1091	Students will learn how to create a task from a message.
Modifying a Task — 1092	Students will learn how to modify a task.
Making a Task Private — 1093	Students will learn how to make a task private.
Completing a Task — 1094	Students will learn how to complete a task.
Assigning a Task to Someone Else — 1095	Students will learn how to assign a task to someone else.
Responding to an Assigned Task — 1097	Students will learn how to respond to an assigned task.
Reporting the Status of an Assigned Task — 1098	Students will learn how to report the status of an assigned task.
Searching for Tasks — 1099	Students will learn how to search for tasks.

Developing and releasing a new product are complicated processes that can take months or years to complete. Ruth Ann Ellerbrock knows this from firsthand experience. She has managed the product development team at Trey Research for five years. In five years, her team has released only three new products. Ruth Ann and her team use the Tasks folder to track the multitude of tasks required to accomplish the goal of releasing solid, marketable new products.

KEY TERMS
assign
complete
Deferred
In Progress
owner
recurring task
task
task request
Tasks folder
to-do item

Managing Tasks | 1087

SOFTWARE ORIENTATION

Microsoft Outlook's Task Window

Create and modify your tasks in the Task window shown in Figure 9-1.

Figure 9-1
Outlook's Task window

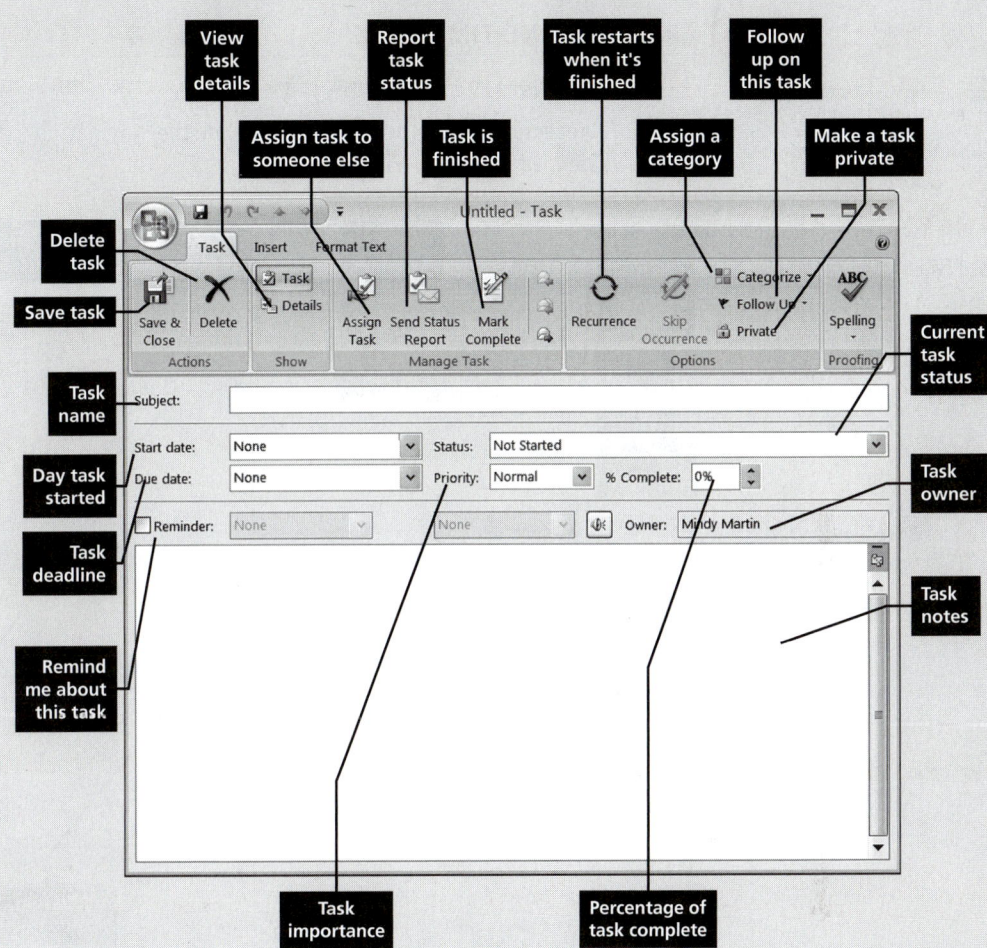

Use the Task window to create and track tasks that you are managing or performing. Keep your task information readily available in one location.

■ Creating New Tasks

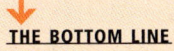
THE BOTTOM LINE

Some days, it seems like everyone is telling you what to do. Keep track of everything you have to accomplish by creating tasks. A ***task*** is an Outlook item that can be tracked from creation to completion. Tasks are stored in the ***Tasks folder***.

Creating a One-Time Task

Create a one-time task to track your progress on a task that only needs to be completed once. For example, create a task to register for a specific trade show. When you have registered for the trade show, the task is complete. You won't need to register for the trade show every week or every month.

➡️ **CREATE A ONE-TIME TASK**

GET READY. Before you begin these steps, be sure to launch Microsoft Outlook.

1. If necessary, click the **Tasks** button in the Navigation pane to display the Tasks folder, as shown in Figure 9-2.

Figure 9-2

Tasks folder

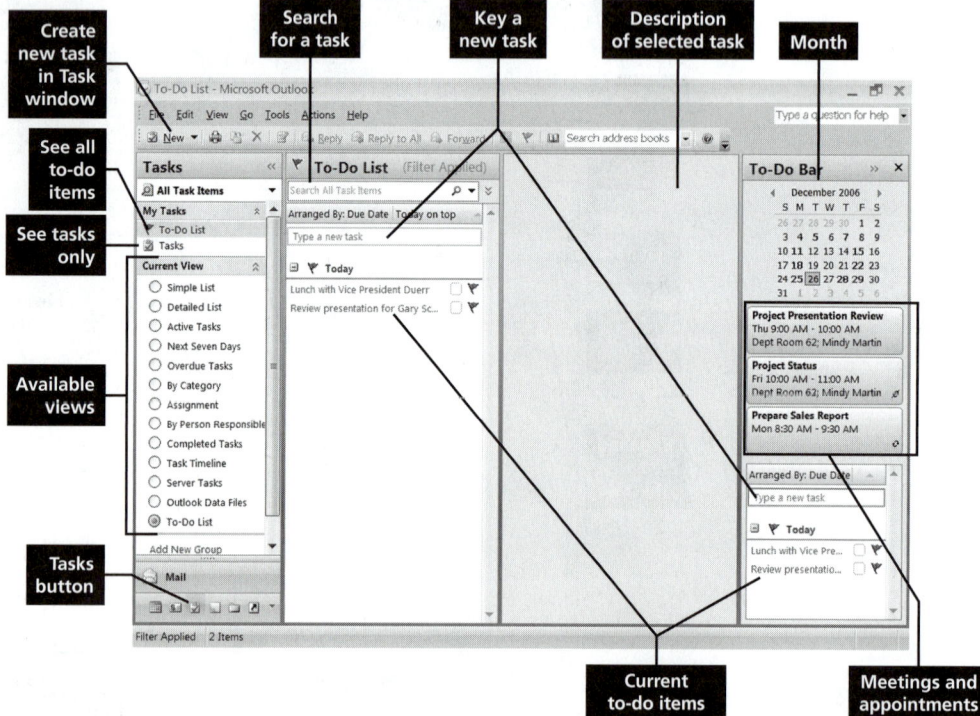

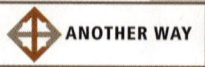 Depending on the exercises you completed in previous lessons, you might have items displayed in the To-Do List.

2. Click the **New** button on the Standard toolbar. A Task window is displayed, as shown in Figure 9-1.

ANOTHER WAY In every Outlook folder, you can create a new task by selecting Task in the New dropdown menu or by pressing **Ctrl+Shift+K**.

3. In the Subject field, key **Create marketing brochure**.
4. In the *Due date* field, key or select the date five weeks from today.
5. In the Priority field, select **Low**.
6. In the task note area, key **Photographer is Ann Beebe**.
7. Compare your Task window to Figure 9-3. Click the **Save & Close** button in the Actions group on the Ribbon.

Figure 9-3

Creating a new task

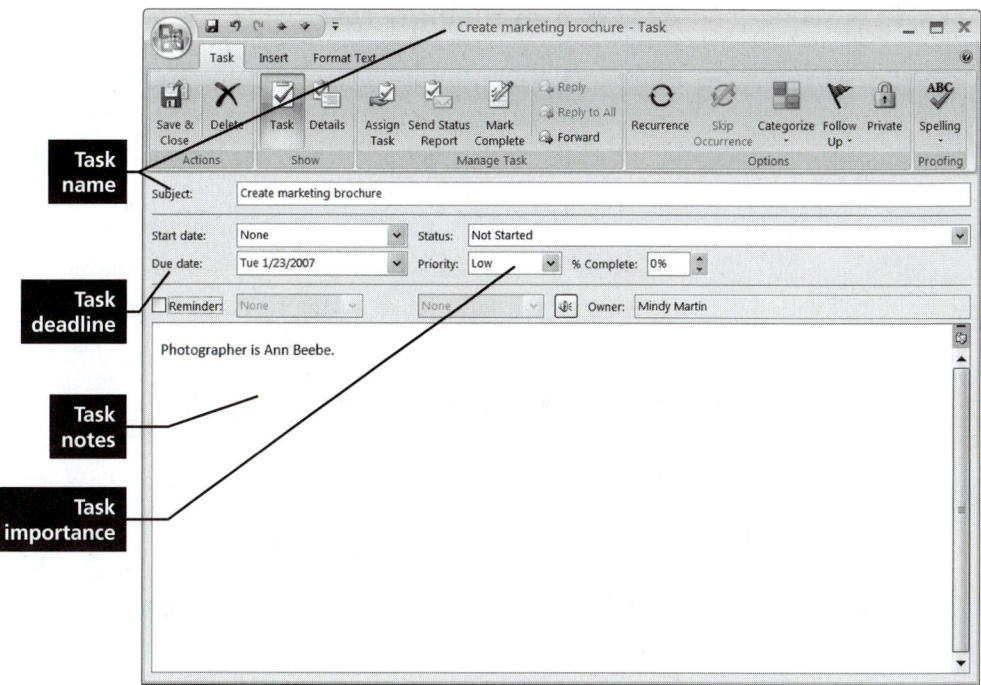

8. Compare your To-Do List to Figure 9-4. The new task is displayed below the Next Month heading because the deadline occurs next month.

Figure 9-4

New task created

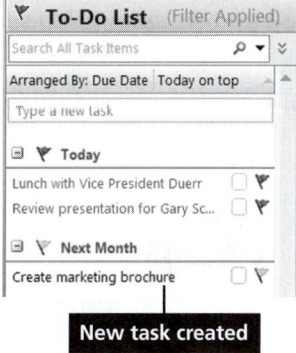

PAUSE. LEAVE Outlook open to use in the next exercise.

In the previous exercise, you created a one-time task. When any task is created, it is automatically flagged for follow-up. Any Outlook item flagged for follow-up is a *to-do item*. Thus, creating a task creates a to-do item.

To-do items can include messages and contacts with a follow-up flag. To-do items are displayed on the To-Do Bar. Because to-do items are not all tasks, you can have more to-do items than tasks on your To-Do Bar.

Creating a Recurring Task

X REF

You can find more information on completing a task later in this lesson.

A *recurring task* is a task that must be completed at regular intervals. Common recurring tasks include creating a status report every week or turning in your travel receipt to the accounting department every month. When you mark a recurring task as complete, the task is automatically re-created with the next due date displayed.

CREATE A RECURRING TASK

GET READY. Before you begin these steps, be sure to launch Microsoft Outlook.

1. If necessary, click the **Tasks** button in the Navigation pane to display the Tasks folder.
2. Click the **New** button on the Standard toolbar. A Task window is displayed as shown in Figure 9-1.
3. In the Subject field, key **Summarize team's progress on Vault project**.
4. In the *Start date* field, select the second Monday in January of next year.
5. Click the **Recurrence** button in the Options group on the Ribbon. The Task Recurrence window is displayed, as shown in Figure 9-5.

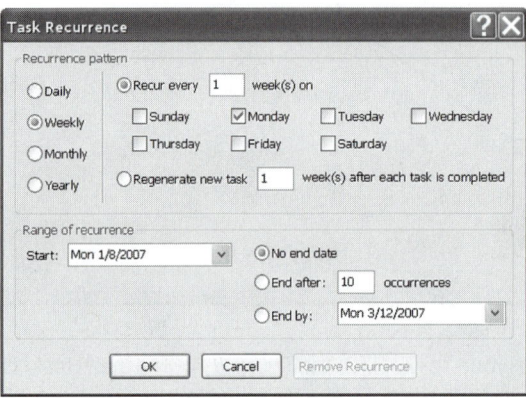

Figure 9-5

Task Recurrence window

6. Click the **End by** radio button. In the *End by* field, key or select the second Monday in July. This ends the recurring task in six months.
7. Click **OK** to return to the Task window.
8. Compare your Task window to Figure 9-6. Depending on the current date, the number of days before the first deadline will differ. Click the **Save & Close** button in the Actions group on the Ribbon.

Figure 9-6

Creating a new recurring task

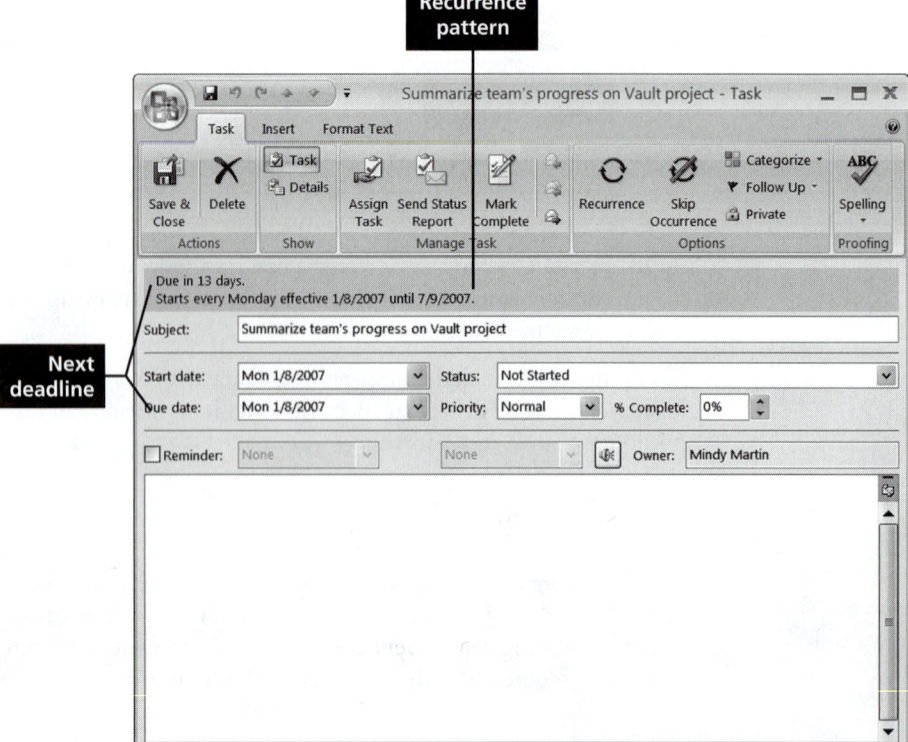

TAKE NOTE * The "Due in" date message is only displayed if the deadline is 14 days or fewer in the future.

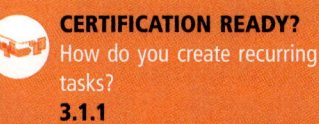

CERTIFICATION READY?
How do you create recurring tasks?
3.1.1

9. Examine your To-Do List. The new task is displayed below a heading. The heading title depends on the amount of time between today's date and the first deadline.

PAUSE. LEAVE Outlook open to use in the next exercise.

In the previous exercise, you created a recurring task that starts in January and ends after six months. Frequently, start and end dates coincide with project deadlines.

Creating a Task from a Message

Email messages are used to convey a variety of information. Sometimes, a message contains information about tasks that must be performed. To prevent additional data entry, use the message to create a tracked task.

⊙ **CREATE A TASK FROM A MESSAGE**

GET READY. Before you begin these steps, be sure to launch Microsoft Outlook. This exercise requires exchanging messages with another Outlook user with an active email account who can respond to a message or who has the ability to access and use another user's Outlook profile.

1. If necessary, click the **Mail** button in the Navigation pane to display the Mail folder in your account.
2. Click the **New** button in the Standard toolbar to display a Message window.
3. Click the **To** field and key the recipient's email address. The recipient is the Outlook user who will create a task from this message.
4. Click the **Subject** field and key **Travel Itinerary**.
5. In the message area, key the following message.

   Hi, Press ⎣Enter⎦. **Please give a copy of your itinerary to Arlene Huff before you leave next Friday.** Press ⎣Enter⎦. **Thanks,** Press ⎣Enter⎦. **Mindy**

6. Click the **Send** button to send the message.
7. In the recipient's account, click the **Send/Receive** button if the Travel itinerary message has not arrived.
8. Click the **Travel itinerary** message in the message list. Drag it to the Tasks button on the Navigation pane and drop the message on the Tasks button. A Task window containing information from the message is automatically opened, as shown in Figure 9-7.

Figure 9-7

Creating a task from a message

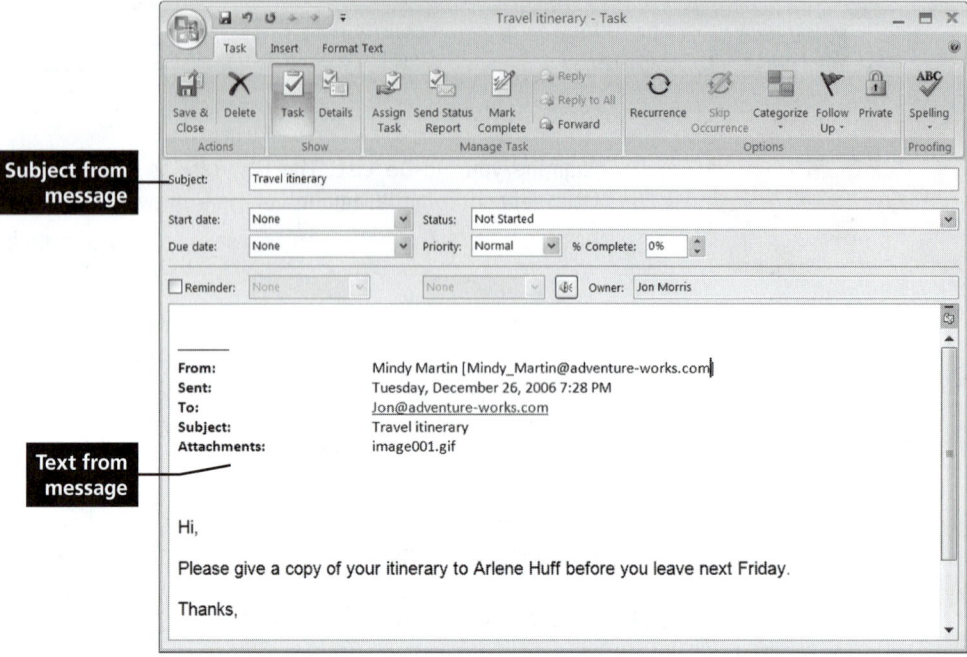

9. In the Task window, click the **Due date** field. Key or select next Friday's date.
10. Click the **Save & Close** button in the Actions group on the Ribbon.
11. Click the **Tasks** button in the Navigation pane to display the Tasks folder. Examine your To-Do List. The new task is displayed below the Next Week heading.

    PAUSE. CLOSE Outlook to return to your account if necessary. If you exchanged tasks with another user so that you received the task in your mailbox, leave Outlook open to use in the next exercise.

CERTIFICATION READY?
How do you create a task from a message?
3.1.2

In the previous exercise, you created a task from a message. Using this method to create a task keeps the related message with the task.

Modifying and Completing a Task

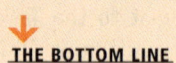

THE BOTTOM LINE

After a task is created, you will modify the task to change its status and update the amount of the task that has been completed. You can also mark a task as private, keeping the details hidden from other users. When you finish a task, mark it as complete.

Modifying a Task

Tracking the status of a task includes modifying the task's status and percentage complete. You can also modify a task's characteristics, such as its importance.

➔ MODIFY A TASK

GET READY. Before you begin these steps, be sure to launch Microsoft Outlook and complete the first exercise in this lesson.

1. If necessary, click the **Tasks** button in the Navigation pane to display the Tasks folder.

2. Double-click the **Create marketing brochure** task. The task is opened in a Task window.
3. Click the **Status** field. Select **In Progress**. The *In Progress* status indicates that work on the task has started.
4. Click the **% Complete** field. Click the field's arrows to select **50%** or key **50%** in the field.
5. In the Priority field, select **High**.
6. Compare your Task window to Figure 9-8. Click the **Save & Close** button in the Actions group on the Ribbon.

Figure 9-8

Modifying a task

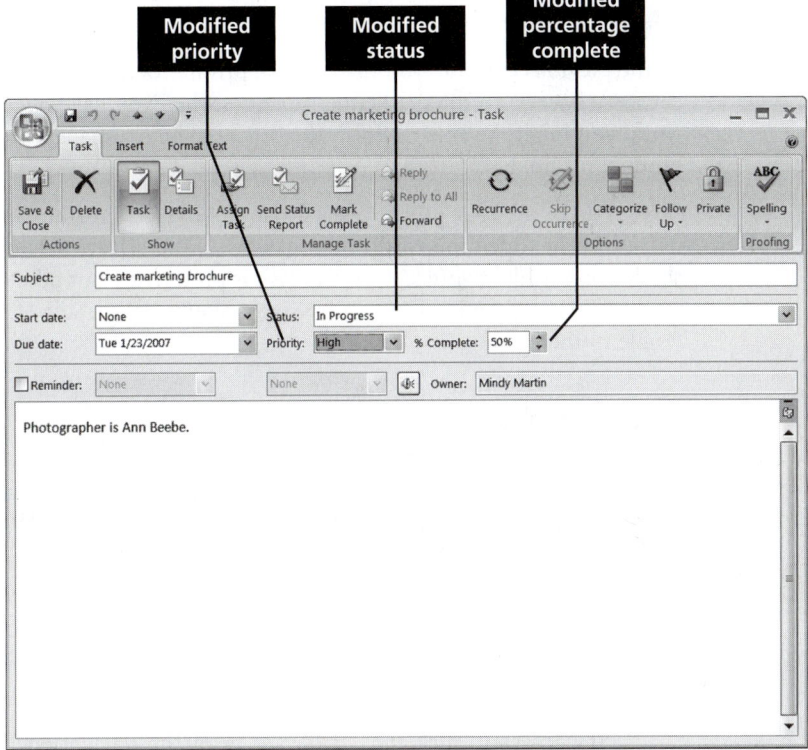

7. Double-click the **Create marketing brochure** task. The task is opened in a Task window.
8. Click the **Status** field. Select **Deferred**. The *Deferred* status indicates that the task has been postponed without changing the deadline or the percentage complete.
9. Click the **Save & Close** button in the Actions group on the Ribbon.

   PAUSE. LEAVE Outlook open to use in the next exercise.

CERTIFICATION READY?
How do you set the status, priority, and percent complete of a task?
3.1.3

In the previous exercise, you modified an existing task. Shortly after changing the task's importance to High, the release date for the product described in your marketing brochure was delayed. You changed the status of the task to Deferred. You are not currently working on the task, but the task characteristics remain unchanged. The priority is still high, and it is still halfway complete.

Making a Task Private

Like appointments and meetings, you can mark a task as private. This protects the details of the task from casual observers on your network.

MAKE A TASK PRIVATE

GET READY. Before you begin these steps, be sure to launch Microsoft Outlook. Complete the previous exercise.

1. If necessary, click the **Tasks** button in the Navigation pane to display the Tasks folder.
2. Double-click the **Create marketing brochure** task. The task is opened in a Task window.
3. Click the **Private** button in the Options group on the Ribbon.
4. Click the **Save & Close** button in the Actions group on the Ribbon.

   PAUSE. LEAVE Outlook open to use in the next exercise.

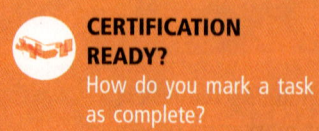

CERTIFICATION READY?
How do you mark a task as private?

In the previous exercise, you made a task private. Because the task was deferred, you have decided to work on the marketing brochure when you have free time. With a bit of hard work, you might be able to finish the brochure before management decides to take the product off hold.

In your account, your private tasks do not look different from any other task. To see that your task is private, open the task. In a private task, the Private button in the Options group on the Ribbon is highlighted. A private task is protected from other casual observers on your network. Without permission to access your account, the details of any private task will not be visible to them.

Completing a Task

When you finish a task, mark the task as ***complete***. A completed task is removed from your To-Do List. To see information about your tasks that have been marked as complete, click the Completed Tasks view in the Navigation pane.

 COMPLETE A TASK

GET READY. Before you begin these steps, be sure to launch Microsoft Outlook and complete the first exercise in this lesson.

1. If necessary, click the **Tasks** button in the Navigation pane to display the Tasks folder.
2. Double-click the **Create marketing brochure** task. The task is opened in a Task window.
3. Click the **Mark Complete** button in the Manage Task group on the Ribbon. The Task window closes and the task is moved to the Completed Tasks list so it is no longer displayed on your To-Do List.
4. Click the **Completed Tasks** button in the Navigation pane to see your completed task. Click the **To-Do List** button in the Navigation pane to return to your normal view.

   PAUSE. LEAVE Outlook open to use in the next exercise.

CERTIFICATION READY?
How do you mark a task as complete?

In the previous exercise, you marked a task as complete. Completed tasks are not displayed on your To-Do List. As your list of completed tasks grows over time, the Completed Tasks view becomes a record of the tasks you have accomplished.

Managing Tasks | 1095

Working with Assigned Tasks

THE BOTTOM LINE In the previous section, you created, modified, and completed tasks. In this section, you will assign tasks to other Outlook users and respond to tasks assigned to you.

Assigning a Task to Someone Else

The task *owner* is the only Outlook user who can modify a task. The creator of a task is automatically the task owner. To transfer ownership of a task, you can *assign* the task to another Outlook user.

→ **ASSIGN A TASK TO SOMEONE ELSE**

GET READY. Before you begin these steps, be sure to launch Microsoft Outlook.

TROUBLESHOOTING You cannot assign a task to yourself; therefore, this series of exercises requires exchanging messages with a partner using Outlook 2007. If you do not have a partner, you can use a different Outlook profile tied to a separate email account. If you need to create a profile, see Outlook's Help topics for more information.

TAKE NOTE* This exercise is performed in your account.

1. If necessary, click the **Tasks** button in the Navigation pane to display the Tasks folder.
2. Click the **New** arrow and click the **Task Request** option. A *task request* assigns a task to another user. The Task request window is displayed, as shown in Figure 9-9. It contains components from a Task window and a Message window.

Figure 9-9

Task request window

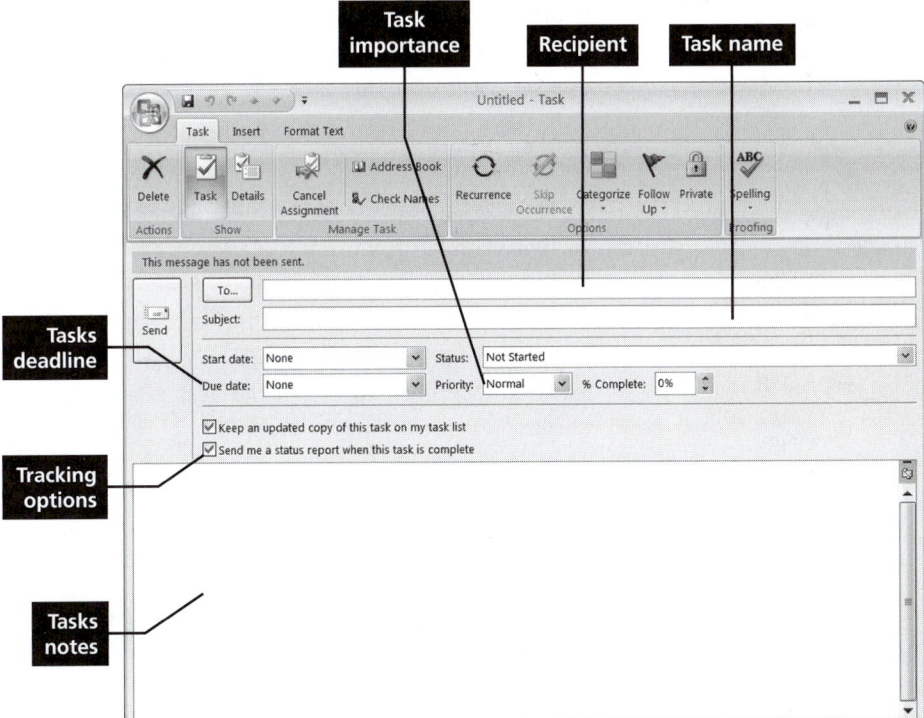

3. Click the **To** field and key your partner's email address. Your partner is the Outlook user who will own this task.
4. Click the **Subject** field and key **Prepare training materials for new employees**.
5. Click the **Due date** field. Key or select next Friday's date.
6. In the Priority field, select **High**.
7. In the message area, key the following message.

   Hi, Press Enter. **Please prepare training materials and a schedule for the one-day training seminar next week.** Press Enter. **Thanks,** Press Enter. Key your name.

8. Click the **Send** button to send the task request. Based on the tracking options you selected, the task is displayed on your To-Do List. If necessary, click the **Prepare training materials for new employees** task on your To-Do List. Note that your partner is identified as the task owner, as shown in Figure 9-10.

Figure 9-10

Assigned task displayed after task request sent

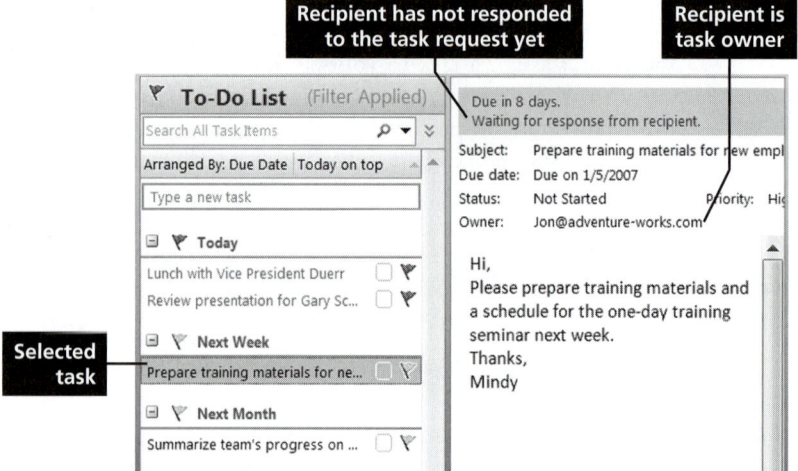

9. Click the **New** arrow and click the **Task Request** option. The Task request window is displayed.
10. Click the **To** field and key your partner's email address. Your partner is the Outlook user who will own this task.
11. Click the **Subject** field and key **Greet new employees**.
12. Click the **Due date** field. Key or select next Friday's date.
13. In the message area, key the following message.

    Hi, Press Enter. **It's a good idea to introduce ourselves to the new employees before the training session starts next Friday.** Press Enter. Key your name.

14. Click the **Send** button to send the task request.

    PAUSE. CLOSE Outlook to access your partner's account, if necessary. Otherwise, leave Outlook open to use in the next exercise.

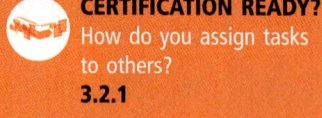

CERTIFICATION READY?
How do you assign tasks to others?
3.2.1

In the previous exercise, you sent two task requests to your partner. When you send a task request, the recipient becomes the task owner when you click the Send button. You can only recover ownership of the task if the recipient declines the task *and* you return the task to your task list.

The *Keep an updated copy of this task on my task list* option is selected by default. When the owner updates the task, it will also be updated on your task list if a connection is available.

Managing Tasks | 1097

Responding to an Assigned Task

A task request is received in your mailbox like any other message. When you receive a task request, you can accept the task, decline the task, or assign the task to another Outlook user.

RESPOND TO AN ASSIGNED TASK

GET READY. Before you begin these steps, be sure to launch Microsoft Outlook. Complete the previous exercise.

TAKE NOTE*

This exercise is performed in your partner's account.

1. In your partner's account, click the **Mail** button in the Navigation pane to display the Mail folder, if necessary. If the task requests sent in the previous exercise have not arrived, click the **Send/Receive** button on the Standard toolbar.
2. In the Inbox, double-click the **Task Request: Prepare training materials for new employees** message to open it, as shown in Figure 9-11.

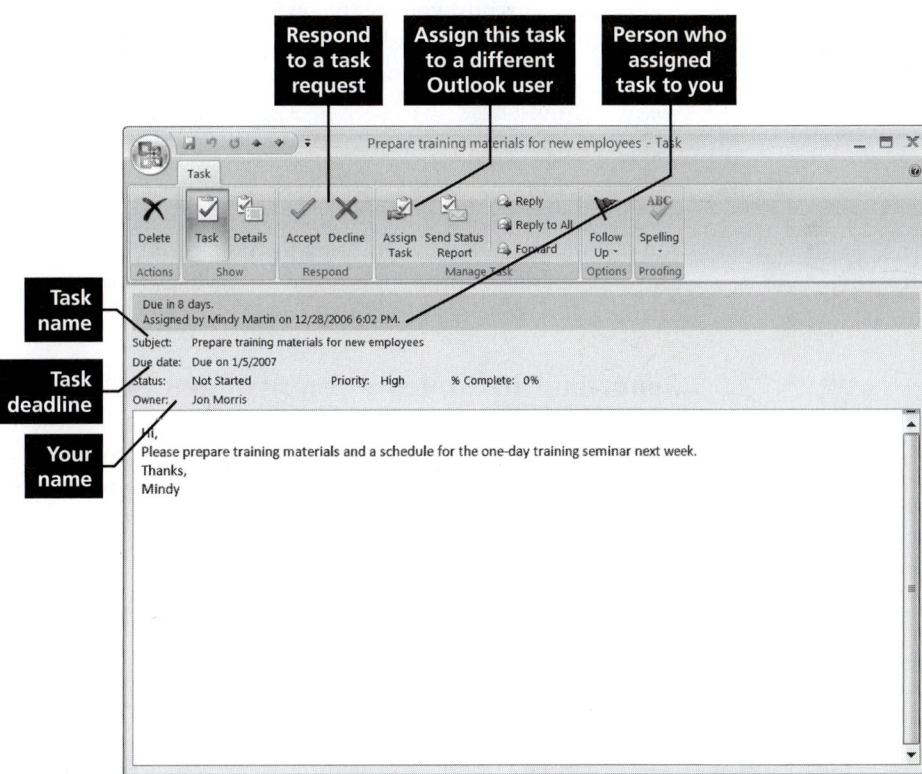

Figure 9-11
Task request received

3. In the Task window, click the **Accept** button in the Respond group on the Ribbon. As shown in Figure 9-12, a small dialog box is displayed asking if you want to edit the message sent with the response.

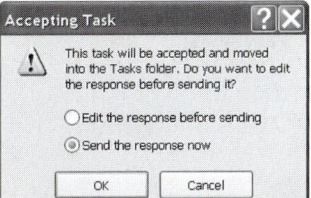

Figure 9-12
Accepting Task dialog box

4. Click **OK** to send the response now. The task acceptance is sent and the task is added to your task list.
5. In the Inbox, double-click the **Task Request: Greet new employees** message to open it.
6. In the Task window, click the **Decline** button in the Respond group on the Ribbon. The small Declining Task dialog box is displayed, asking if you want to edit the message sent with the response.
7. In the Declining Task dialog box, click the **Edit the response before sending** option and click **OK**.
8. In the Task window, key **I will be out of town next Friday.** Click the **Send** button. You have declined this task, so it is not added to your task list.

   PAUSE. LEAVE Outlook open to use in the next exercise.

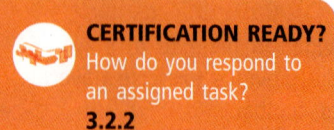

CERTIFICATION READY?
How do you respond to an assigned task?
3.2.2

In the previous exercise, you received two task requests. You accepted one task and declined the second. Currently, you are the owner of both tasks. When you decline a task request, you are still the owner of the task until the person who sent the original task request returns the declined task to his or her task list.

When a task you assigned to another user is declined, you will receive a Task Declined: Task Name message. Double-click the message to open it. Click the Return to Task List button in the Manage Task group on the Ribbon. Until you return the task to your task list, you are not the task owner. Even though the other user declined the task, he or she is the task owner until you reclaim ownership by returning the task to your task list. Therefore, the *Greet new employees* task in the previous exercise still belongs to your partner, even though he or she declined the task.

Reporting the Status of an Assigned Task

> When you update a task assigned to you, the task copy kept on any previous owner's task list is automatically updated if the previous owner chose the tracking options when assigning the task. You can also choose to send a status report to previous task owners or interested individuals.

REPORT THE STATUS OF AN ASSIGNED TASK

GET READY. Before you begin these steps, be sure to launch Microsoft Outlook. Complete the previous exercises.

TAKE NOTE This exercise is performed in your partner's account.

1. In your partner's account, click the **Tasks** button in the Navigation pane to display the Tasks folder if necessary.
2. Double-click the **Prepare training materials for new employees** task. The Task window is displayed.
3. Click the **% Complete** field. Key or select **50%**.

Managing Tasks | 1099

4. Click the **Send Status Report** button in the Manage Task group on the Ribbon. A Message window is displayed. The person who assigned the task to you is displayed in the To field. The message content details the task's current status, as shown in Figure 9-13.

Figure 9-13

Task Status report

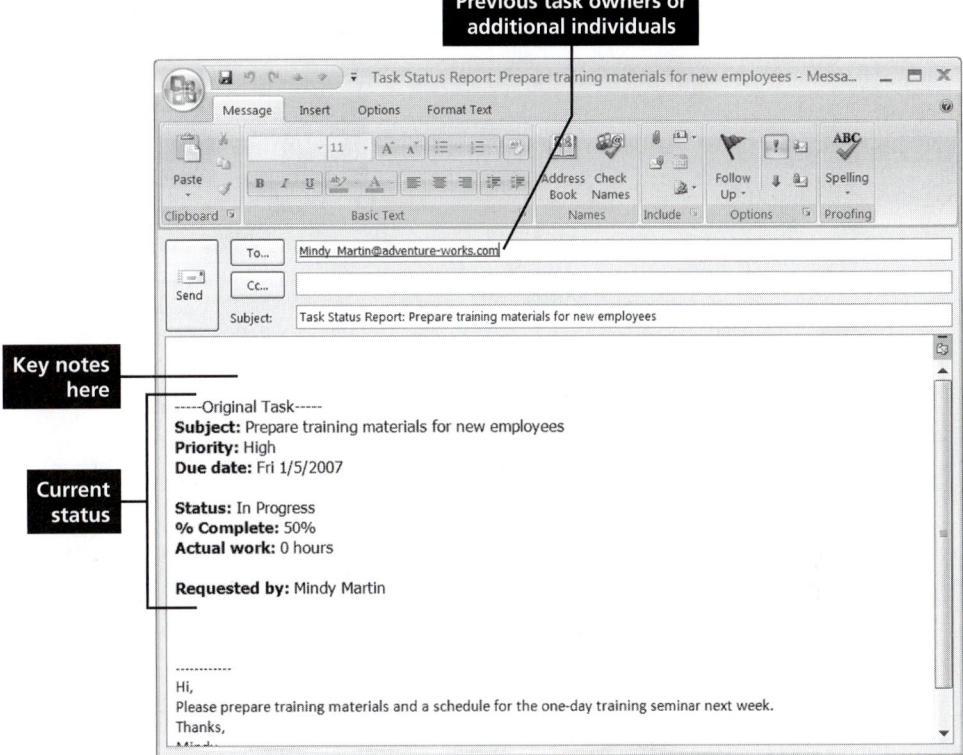

CERTIFICATION READY?
How do you send a status report on an assigned task?
3.2.3

5. Click the **Send** button. Close the Task window.

   PAUSE. CLOSE Outlook to access your account, if necessary. Otherwise, leave Outlook open to use in the next exercise.

In the previous exercise, you sent a status report to the person who assigned the task to you. The name was filled in automatically. To see any individuals who will be automatically updated, open the task to display the Task window and click the Details button in the Show group on the Ribbon. The *Update list* field identifies individuals who are automatically updated. When you send a status report, these names will be placed automatically in the To field.

■ Searching for Tasks

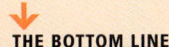

Outlook's new Instant Search feature makes it simple to quickly find a task. Use Instant Search to find any text in the task item. Use text in the subject or task notes area to find a task.

 SEARCH FOR TASKS

GET READY. Before you begin these steps, be sure to launch Microsoft Outlook. Instant Search must be enabled. Complete the previous exercises in this lesson.

1. In your account, click the **Tasks** button in the Navigation pane to display the Tasks folder if necessary. Click the **To-Do List** button in the Current View area on the Navigation pane, if necessary.

2. In the Instant Search box, verify that **Search All Task Items** is selected.

3. In the Instant Search box, key **greet**. As you key the search text, Outlook displays the matching task items, as shown in Figure 9-14. Note that the Task Request message in the Sent Items folder is also displayed.

Figure 9-14

Instant Search results

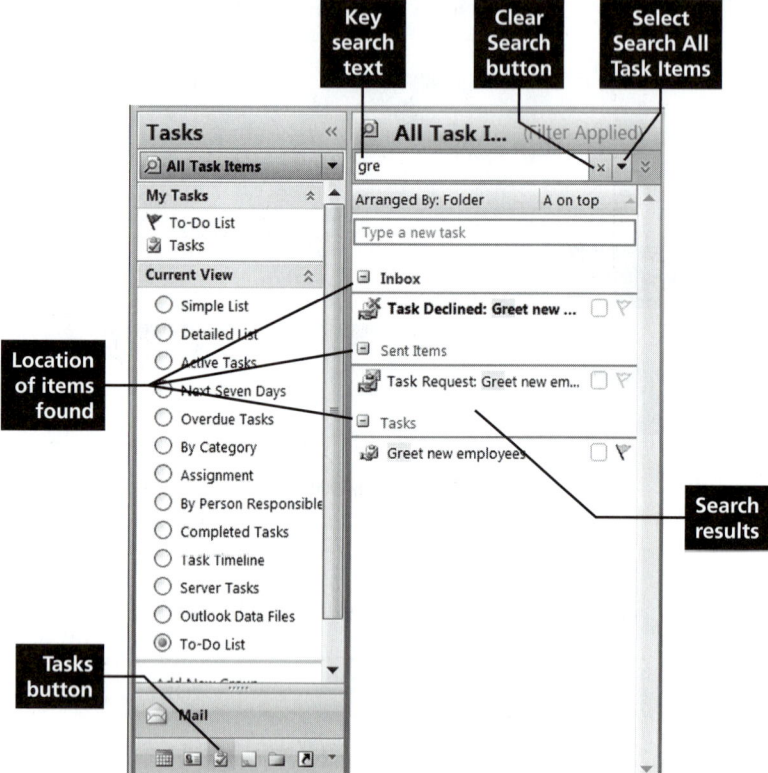

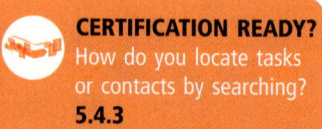

CERTIFICATION READY?
How do you locate tasks or contacts by searching?
5.4.3

4. Click the **Clear Search** button to clear the search criteria.
   CLOSE Outlook.

In the previous exercise, you used Outlook's new Instant Search feature to locate specific tasks. Task requests located in the Mail folders are also included in the search results.

Managing Tasks | 1101

SUMMARY SKILL MATRIX

IN THIS LESSON YOU LEARNED HOW TO:
Create a One-Time Task
Create a Recurring Task
Create a Task from a Message
Modify a Task
Make a Task Private
Complete a Task
Assign a Task to Someone Else
Respond to an Assigned Task
Report the Status of an Assigned Task
Search for Tasks

■ Knowledge Assessment

Fill in the Blank

Complete the following sentences by writing the correct word or words in the blanks provided.

1. A(n) __recurring__ task occurs at regular intervals.
2. Click the Tasks button to view the __Task Folder__.
3. After you start a task, the task's status is __In progress__.
4. The To-Do List displays tasks and __To Do Items__.
5. The task owner can __Assign__ the task to another Outlook user.
6. A(n) __Complete__ task is not displayed on your To-Do List.
7. You can track a(n) __Task__ from creation to completion.
8. A(n) __Deffered__ task is postponed.
9. Only the task __Owner__ can modify a task.
10. Use a(n) __Task Request__ to assign a task to another user.

Multiple Choice

Circle the correct choice.

1. Which of the following can be a to-do item?
    A. Task
    B. Message
    C. Flagged contact
    D. All of the above

2. What is the difference between a task and a to-do item?
   A. A task takes longer to complete.
   B. To-do items are displayed on the To-Do List.
   C. Tasks can be tracked.
   D. There is no difference between a task and a to-do item.

3. What folder must be active to create a task?
   A. Tasks folder
   B. Mail folder
   C. Contacts folder
   D. Any Outlook folder

4. What is automatically created when you create a task?
   A. To-do item
   B. Deadline
   C. Task request
   D. Message

5. What happens when you complete a recurring task?
   A. The task is deleted.
   B. The task is assigned to another Outlook user.
   C. An entry is made in your calendar.
   D. The task is automatically re-created with the next due date displayed.

6. How do you protect the details of a task from casual observers on your network?
   A. Complete the task.
   B. Make the task private.
   C. Assign the task to another Outlook user.
   D. Hide the task.

7. Who owns a task you assign to another Outlook user?
   A. You
   B. You and the other Outlook user
   C. The other Outlook user
   D. No one owns the task

8. Who owns a task when you assign the task to another user and the task is declined?
   A. You
   B. You and the other Outlook user
   C. The other Outlook user
   D. No one owns the task

9. Where does a task request arrive?
   A. Tasks folder
   B. Mail folder
   C. To-Do List
   D. Task Requests folder

10. What new feature finds tasks quickly?
    A. Instant Search
    B. Search folder
    C. Sort tasks
    D. All of the above

Competency Assessment

Project 9-1: Create a One-Time Task

Eugene Kogan is setting up a small business to bake and sell cupcakes. He believes that "personal cakes" will be popular at children's parties, open houses, and office events. Before he can get started, Eugene needs to create a list of tasks. He is a procrastinator, so he knows that deadlines are needed to keep him focused on the business.

GET READY. Launch Outlook if it is not already running.

1. If necessary, click the **Tasks** button in the Navigation pane to display the Tasks folder.
2. Click the **New** button on the Standard toolbar. A Task window is displayed.
3. In the Subject field, key **Cupcakes - Identify potential clients.** In the *Due date* field, key or select the date two weeks from today. Click the **Save & Close** button in the Actions group on the Ribbon.
4. Click the **New** button on the Standard toolbar. A Task window is displayed.
5. In the Subject field, key **Cupcakes - Identify competitors.** In the *Due date* field, key or select the date two weeks from today. Click the **Save & Close** button in the Actions group on the Ribbon.
6. Click the **New** button on the Standard toolbar. A Task window is displayed.
7. In the Subject field, key **Cupcakes - Research prices and recurring expenses.** In the *Due date* field, key or select the date two weeks from today. Click the **Save & Close** button in the Actions group on the Ribbon.
8. Click the **New** button on the Standard toolbar. A Task window is displayed.
9. In the Subject field, key **Cupcakes - Identify initial equipment and financial investment needed.** In the *Due date* field, key or select the date four weeks from today. Click the **Save & Close** button in the Actions group on the Ribbon.
10. Click the **New** button on the Standard toolbar. A Task window is displayed.
11. In the Subject field, key **Cupcakes - Identify time investment required.** In the *Due date* field, key or select the date four weeks from today. Click the **Save & Close** button in the Actions group on the Ribbon.
12. Click the **New** button on the Standard toolbar. A Task window is displayed.
13. In the Subject field, key **Cupcakes - Research and select marketing methods.** In the *Due date* field, key or select the date four weeks from today. Click the **Save & Close** button in the Actions group on the Ribbon.
14. Click the **New** button on the Standard toolbar. A Task window is displayed.
15. In the Subject field, key **Cupcakes - Write a business plan.** In the *Due date* field, key or select the date six weeks from today. Click the **Save & Close** button in the Actions group on the Ribbon.

    LEAVE Outlook open for the next project.

Project 9-2: Modify Tasks

Eugene has made progress on making his cupcake dream come true. Update his progress on each of the tasks.

1. If necessary, click the **Tasks** button in the Navigation pane to display the Tasks folder.
2. Double-click the **Cupcakes - Identify potential clients** task. The task is opened in a Task window.
3. Click the **Status** field. Select **In Progress**.

4. Click the **% Complete** field. Click the field's arrows to select **50%** or key **50%** in the field.
5. Click the **Save & Close** button in the Actions group on the Ribbon.
6. Double-click the **Cupcakes - Identify competitors** task. The task is opened in a Task window.
7. Click the **Status** field. Select **In Progress**.
8. Click the **% Complete** field. Click the field's arrows to select **25%** or key **25%** in the field.
9. Click the **Save & Close** button in the Actions group on the Ribbon.
10. Double-click the **Cupcakes — Research prices and recurring expenses** task. The task is opened in a Task window.
11. Click the **Status** field. Select **In Progress**.
12. Click the **% Complete** field. Click the field's arrows to select **75%** or key **75%** in the field.
13. Click the **Save & Close** button in the Actions group on the Ribbon.

    LEAVE Outlook open for the next project.

■ Proficiency Assessment

Project 9-3: Assign a Task to Another Outlook User

Eugene has been researching his business prospects for several weeks now. He is ready to pull the information together in a business plan. However, Eugene knows that a business plan is a critical document. For example, the business plan is necessary for obtaining funds from a bank. Although Eugene has many important business skills, he decided to ask his cousin, a technical writer at Litware, Inc., to write the business plan.

> **TROUBLESHOOTING**
>
> You cannot assign a task to yourself; therefore, Projects 9-3 and 9-4 require exchanging messages with a partner using Outlook 2007. If you do not have a partner, you can use a different Outlook profile tied to a separate email account. If you need to create a profile, see Outlook's Help topics for more information.

TAKE NOTE*

This exercise is performed in your account.

1. If necessary, click the **Tasks** button in the Navigation pane to display the Tasks folder.
2. Double-click the **Cupcakes — Write a business plan** task. The task is opened in a Task window.
3. Click the **Assign Task** button in the Manage Task group on the Ribbon.
4. Click the **To** field and key the recipient's email address.
5. In the Priority field, select **High**.
6. In the message area, key the following message.

    Hi, Press Enter. **Please let me know if you need any additional information.** Press Enter. **Thanks!**
7. Click the **Send** button to send the task request.

    PAUSE. CLOSE Outlook to access your partner's account if necessary. Otherwise, leave Outlook open to use in the next exercise.

Managing Tasks | 1105

Project 9-4: Accept an Assigned Task

Eugene's cousin is helping Eugene by sorting through all of the information to create a business plan. His cousin understands the importance of creating a professional document that will give Eugene the best chance of obtaining financing from the bank.

> **TAKE NOTE**
> This exercise is performed in your partner's account.

1. In your partner's account, click the **Mail** button in the Navigation pane to display the Mail folder if necessary. If the task request sent in the previous project has not arrived, click the **Send/Receive** button on the Standard toolbar.
2. In the Inbox, double-click the **Task Request: Cupcakes — Write a business plan** message to open it.
3. In the Task window, click the **Accept** button in the Respond group on the Ribbon. A small dialog box is displayed asking if you want to edit the message sent with the response.
4. Click **OK**. The task acceptance is sent and the task is added to the task list.

   PAUSE. CLOSE Outlook to access your account if necessary. Otherwise, leave Outlook open to use in the next project.

■ Mastery Assessment

Project 9-5: Complete Tasks

At the end of two weeks, Eugene has completed several tasks on time. He marks these tasks as complete.

1. If necessary, click the **Tasks** button in the Navigation pane to display the Tasks folder.
2. Double-click the **Cupcakes - Identify potential clients** task. The task is opened in a Task window.
3. Click the **Mark Complete** button in the Manage Task group on the Ribbon. The Task window closes and the task is moved to the Completed Tasks list so it is no longer displayed on your To-Do List.
4. Double-click the **Cupcakes - Identify competitors** task. The task is opened in a Task window.
5. Click the **Mark Complete** button in the Manage Task group on the Ribbon. The Task window closes and the task is moved to the Completed Tasks list so it is no longer displayed on your To-Do List.
6. Double-click the **Cupcakes — Research prices and recurring expenses** task. The task is opened in a Task window.
7. Click the **Mark Complete** button in the Manage Task group on the Ribbon. The Task window closes and the task is moved to the Completed Tasks list so it is no longer displayed on your To-Do List.

   LEAVE Outlook open for the next project.

Project 9-6: Find and Delete Tasks

Eugene has been operating his cupcake business on the side for the last six months. He has decided that it's time to evaluate the possibility of quitting his day job and making cupcakes full time. Find and delete any current tasks related to the cupcake business. (This project will clean up your folders after completing all of these projects.)

1. In your account, click the **Tasks** button in the Navigation pane to display the Tasks folder, if necessary.

2. In the Instant Search box, verify that **Search All Task Items** is selected.
3. In the Instant Search box, key **Cupcake**. As you key the search text, Outlook displays the matching task items.
4. Select each item in the search results and click the **Delete** button on the Standard toolbar.
5. Click the **Clear Search** button to clear the search criteria.
   CLOSE Outlook.

INTERNET READY

Have you thought of starting a business? Create a task list to research your business idea. Use the Internet to research your business idea and the tasks involved.

Workplace Ready

Break It Down

Earning a degree, managing a project, and training new workers seem like unrelated activities. What do they have in common? All three activities are complicated processes that seem daunting when you look at the whole. However, each activity is made up of smaller steps. Enroll in a series of specific classes to earn a degree. Perform specific actions when you manage a project. Teach workers to follow specific steps.

Break down a large goal into smaller tasks that you can perform yourself or assign to others for completion. Start with the ultimate goal. Break it down into a list of steps to be completed. Convert the steps into tasks. Match the tasks with the people available to perform the tasks.

When you assign tasks to other people, make sure that the task owner has all the tools needed to complete the task. The task owner needs the ability and authority to perform the task. Ability includes skill and equipment. Authority ensures that the task owner can obtain any necessary information or assistance from other workers.

When you create tasks, remember these important tips.

- Break down large jobs into manageable tasks.
- Match tasks to people.
- Ensure that the task owner has the ability and authority to succeed.

10 Categories and Outlook Data Files

LESSON SKILL MATRIX

Assigning Outlook Items to Color Categories	Students will learn how to assign Outlook items to color categories.
Modifying and Creating Color Categories	Students will learn how to modify and create color categories.
Sorting Items by Color Categories	Students will learn how to sort items by color categories.
Searching for Items by Category	Students will learn how to search for items by category.
Creating a Data File	Students will learn how to create a data file.
Selecting a Data File for a Mail Account	Students will learn how to select a data file for a mail account.
Changing Data File Settings	Students will learn how to change data file settings.

Bart Duncan is a sales representative for Contoso, Ltd. He sells insurance policies to businesses. He works with large corporations, small businesses, and new businesses that are struggling to grow. He categorizes his clients based on the client's number of employees. To make the client's status easily visible, Bart uses five color categories based on size. His two most important clients have separate color categories to indicate their importance in his sales activities.

KEY TERMS
color category
compact
Outlook Personal Folders file
sort

Categories and Outlook Data Files | 1109

■ SOFTWARE ORIENTATION

Microsoft Outlook's Color Categories Window

The Color Categories window displayed in Figure 10-1 enables you to create, modify, and delete color categories.

Figure 10-1

Outlook's Color Categories window

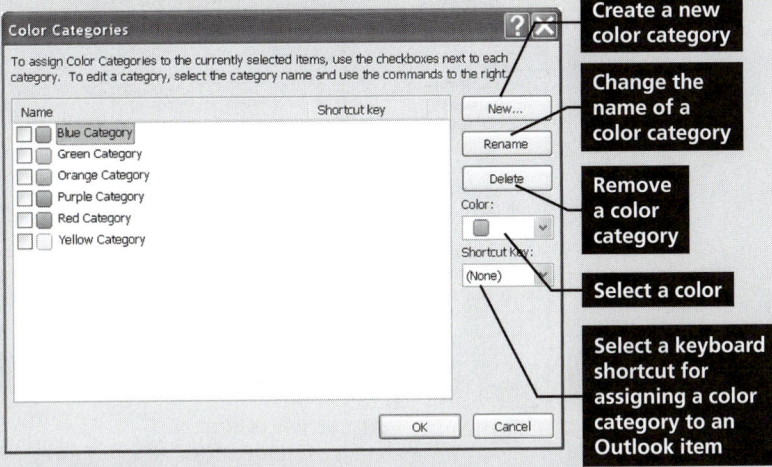

Use the Color Categories window to customize the new color categories for your use. Refer to Figure 10-1 as you complete the following exercises.

■ Working with Categories

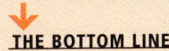
THE BOTTOM LINE

A *color category* assigns a color to an Outlook item, providing a new way to visually indicate relationships among Outlook items. For example, assign a color to all Outlook items related to a specific project or a specific person. Create new color categories to increase the number of categories available for your use. Use color categories to sort or find Outlook items.

Assigning Outlook Items to Color Categories

Color categories provide a quick visual method of identifying related Outlook items. A quick glace at any Outlook window reveals the relationship between the items. For example, assign the red category to all Outlook items related to your supervisor. Your supervisor's contact record, messages exchanged with your supervisor, and meetings scheduled with your supervisor can be assigned to the same color category.

➔ ASSIGN OUTLOOK ITEMS TO COLOR CATEGORIES

GET READY. Before you begin these steps, be sure to launch Microsoft Outlook.

1. Click the **Folder List** button in the Navigation pane to display the Folder List.
2. In the Instant Search box, select **Search All Outlook Items,** if necessary.
3. In the Instant Search box, key **Tibbott**. All Outlook items related to Diane Tibbott are displayed, as shown in Figure 10-2.

Figure 10-2

Search results

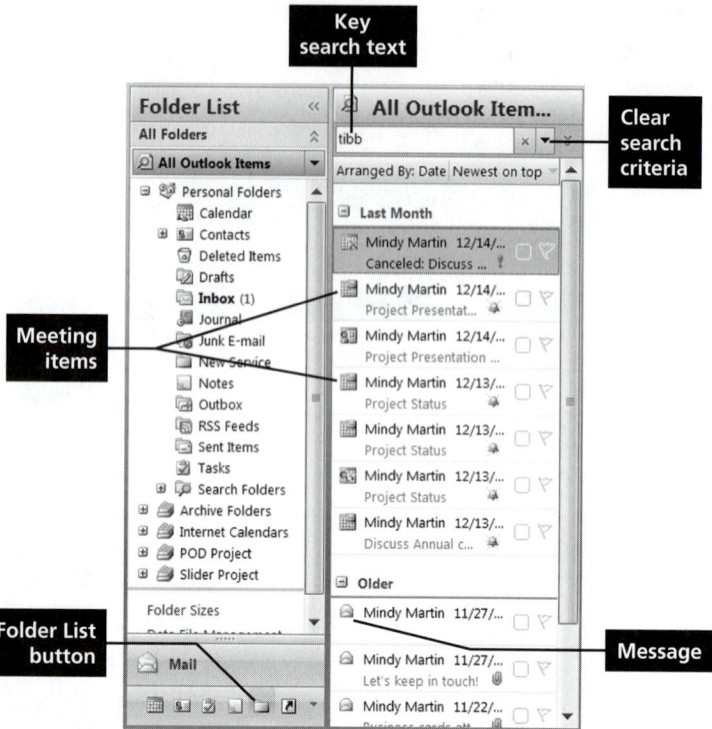

TROUBLESHOOTING The Outlook items in the search results depend on the exercises and projects you completed in previous lessons. They could differ from the results shown here.

4. Click the first item on the list. Scroll to the end of the list. Press **Shift** and click the last item on the list. All the search results are selected.
5. Right-click one of the selected items. On the shortcut menu, point to **Categorize** and click the **Red Category** option. All the items are assigned to the Red Category. If you have not used Red Category before, a dialog box allowing you to rename the category is displayed, as shown in Figure 10-3.

Figure 10-3

Rename Category dialog box

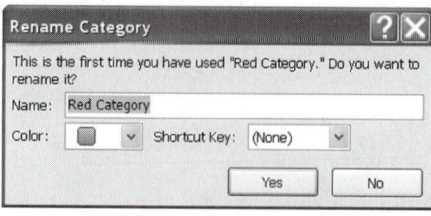

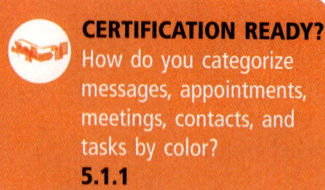

CERTIFICATION READY?
How do you categorize messages, appointments, meetings, contacts, and tasks by color?
5.1.1

6. Click **No** in the Rename Category dialog box. You will rename the category in the next exercise.
7. Click the **Clear Search** button to clear the search criteria.

   PAUSE. LEAVE Outlook open to use in the next exercise.

 REF

You can find more information on creating rules in Lesson 4.

In the previous exercise, you found all the Outlook items related to a specific contact and assigned them to a category. Every Outlook item can be assigned to one or more color categories. You can also create rules to assign a color category automatically to messages you send and receive.

Categories and Outlook Data Files | 1111

Modifying and Creating Color Categories

Color categories can be created and renamed to meet your needs. Use names that identify the Outlook items assigned to the color category. Project names or an individual's name clearly identify a color category.

➡ MODIFY AND CREATE COLOR CATEGORIES

GET READY. Before you begin these steps, complete the previous exercise.

1. Click the **Mail** button in the Navigation pane to display the Mail folder. Click the **Inbox**, if necessary. Click any message in the message list. An Outlook item must be selected to activate the Categorize button on the Standard toolbar.
2. Click the **Categorize** button and click the **All Categories** option. The Color Categories window in Figure 10-1 is displayed.
3. Click **Red Category** in the list of categories. Click the **Rename** button. The Red Category text becomes active.
4. Key **Diane Tibbott** and press ⟨Enter⟩.
5. Click **OK** to rename the category and close the Color Categories window.
6. Click the **Categorize** button and click the All **Categories** option. The Color Categories window in Figure 10-1 is displayed.
7. Click the **New** button. The Add New Category window shown in Figure 10-4 is displayed.

Figure 10-4

Add New Category window

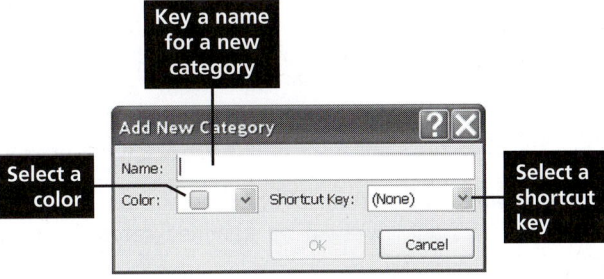

8. In the Name field, key **Slider Project**. In the Color field, select **Dark Olive**. Click **OK**. The new category is displayed in the Color Categories window.
9. Click **OK** to close the Color Categories window.
10. In the main Outlook window, click the **Categorize** button on the Standard toolbar to view the modified list of categories, as shown in Figure 10-5.

Figure 10-5

Modified list of available categories

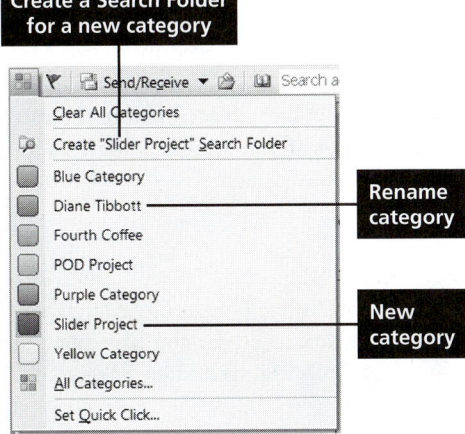

1112 | Lesson 10

CERTIFICATION READY?
How do you categorize messages, appointments, meetings, contacts, and tasks by color?
5.1.1

11. Because a message was selected when you created the new color category, the message is assigned to the category. Right-click the selected message. Point to **Categorize** and select the **Clear All Categories** option. The category is removed from the message.

    PAUSE. LEAVE Outlook open to use in the next exercise.

In the previous exercise, you renamed an existing category and created a new category. The colors offered in the Color field differ enough from each other to make the color categories distinct and easily recognizable.

You can also create categories that don't use a color. To create a colorless category, select None in the Color field in the Add New Category window.

Sorting Items by Color Category

To *sort* items, you arrange the items in a sequence based on specific criteria. After assigning Outlook items to a color category, you can use the color category as a sort criterion.

 SORT ITEMS BY COLOR CATEGORY

GET READY. Before you begin these steps, be sure to launch Microsoft Outlook.

1. If necessary, click the **Mail** button in the Navigation pane to display the Mail folder.
2. Click the **View** menu. Point to **Arrange by**, and click **Categories**. The messages in the message list are rearranged.

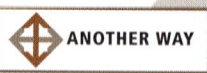 To sort items, you can click the *Arranged By: Date* text below the Instant Search box. Click *Categories* in the dropdown menu.

CERTIFICATION READY?
How do you sort Outlook items by color category?

3. Scroll down to the bottom of the message list to view the categorized message if necessary. Messages without an assigned category appear at the top of the list.
4. Click the **View** menu. Point to **Arrange by**, and click **Date** to sort the messages by date. The messages are arranged by the default date sort.

    PAUSE. LEAVE Outlook open to use in the next exercise.

In the previous exercise, you sorted messages by color category. In the Contacts folder, you can click the By Category radio button in the Navigation pane to sort contacts by category. The Tasks and Notes folders have the same By Category viewing option in the Navigation pane.

In the Calendar folder, click the View menu, point to Current View, and click By Category. Calendar items without a category are displayed first. Calendar items assigned to a color category are displayed next. The items are placed in groups based on the color categories. The order of the groups is determined alphabetically by the names of the color categories. For example, the category "Apple" will be placed before the category "Banana," regardless of the color assigned to the categories. If you added holidays to your calendar in Lesson 10, the holidays are displayed in the Holiday category.

Searching for Items by Category

Outlook's new Instant Search feature allows you to search for Outlook items that meet a variety of search criteria. In previous lessons, you keyed text used as the search criterion. You can modify the Instant Search Query Builder fields to allow you to search by category.

 You can find more information on using text as a search criterion in the Instant Search box in Lesson 6.

Categories and Outlook Data Files | 1113

→ SEARCH FOR ITEMS BY CATEGORY

GET READY. Before you begin these steps, complete the previous exercises in this lesson.

1. Click the **Mail** button in the Navigation pane to display the Calendar folder. Click the **Folder List** button to display the complete list of Outlook folders.
2. Click the **Expand the Query Builder** button next to the Instant Search box. The Query Builder is expanded, as shown in Figure 10-6.

Figure 10-6

Expanded Query Builder

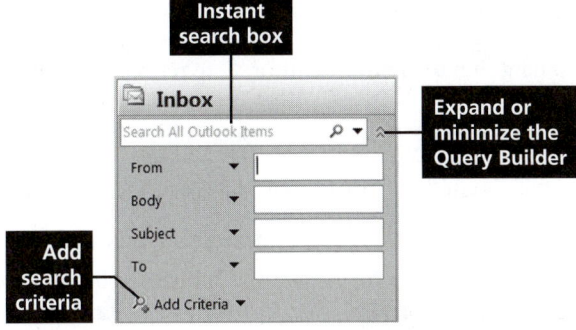

3. Click the **Add Criteria** arrow to display the dropdown menu. Click **Categories** on the dropdown menu. The Categories field is added to the Query Builder.
4. Click the **Categories** arrow to display the dropdown list of categories. Click the **Diane Tibbott** category. The search criterion is displayed in the Instant Search box, the Categories search criterion field is deleted from the Query builder, and the search results are displayed as they are located. See Figure 10-7.

Figure 10-7

Search criterion selected

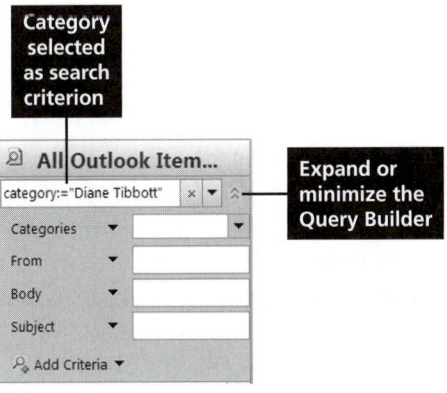

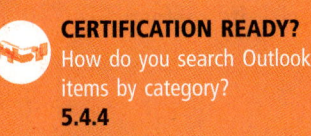

CERTIFICATION READY?
How do you search Outlook items by category?
5.4.4

5. Click the **Clear Search** button. The search criterion is cleared. Click the **Minimize the Query Builder** button to minimize the Query Builder, if necessary.

PAUSE. LEAVE Outlook open to use in the next exercise.

 REF

You can find more information on Search Folders in Lesson 6.

In the previous exercise, you added a selection criterion to the Instant Search Query Builder. Other characteristics, such as the Importance flag and sensitivity, can be used to locate Outlook items.

When searching for categorized messages, use the Categorized Mail Search Folder. It provides quick access to categorized messages without specifying search criteria.

Working with Data Files

THE BOTTOM LINE

Your Outlook data is saved in an *Outlook Personal Folders file*, identified by the .pst extension. An Outlook .pst file is also known as a data file. When you backup your Outlook data or create archive files, you are creating or using Outlook Personal Folders files.

Creating a Data File

Outlook automatically creates .pst files the first time it is launched. You can create additional data files to archive items or store related information in a separate .pst file.

➔ **CREATE A DATA FILE**

X REF

You can find more information on archiving Outlook items in Lesson 3.

GET READY. Before you begin these steps, be sure to launch Microsoft Outlook.

1. Click the **Folder List** button in the Navigation pane to display the Folder List.
2. Click the **New** arrow to display the dropdown list of new items you can create. Click **Outlook Data File**. The New Outlook Data File window is displayed, as shown in Figure 10-8.

Figure 10-8

New Outlook Data File window

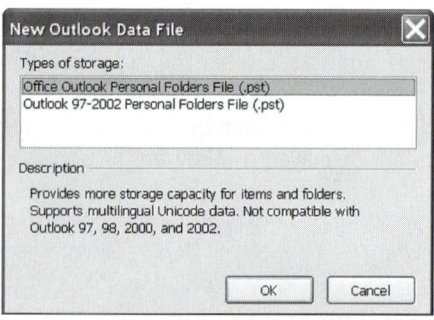

3. In the New Outlook Data File window, click **OK**. The Create or Open Outlook Data File window is displayed.
4. In the *File name* field, key **Slider** to identify the name of the .pst file. Click **OK**. The Create Microsoft Personal Folders window is displayed.
5. In the Create Microsoft Personal Folders window, key **Slider Project** in the Name field to identify the name of the folder that will be displayed in Outlook's folder list in the Navigation pane. Click **OK**. The Slider Project folder is displayed in the Navigation pane.
6. Click the plus sign (**+**) next to the Slider Project folder to display its contents, as shown in Figure 10-9.

Categories and Outlook Data Files | 1115

Figure 10-9

New Outlook data file created

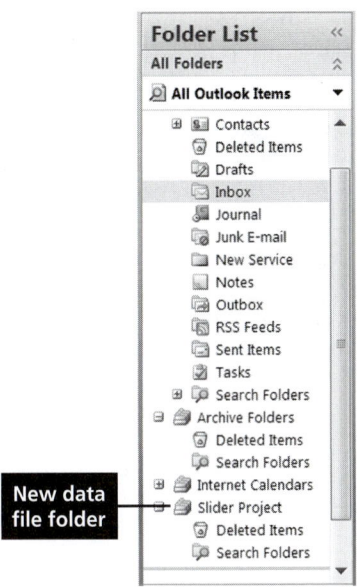

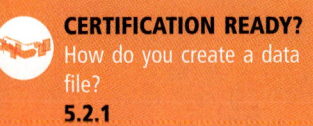

Depending on the exercises and projects you completed in previous lessons, the Outlook folders displayed in your Folder List could differ from the folders in Figure 10-9.

CERTIFICATION READY?
How do you create a data file?
5.2.1

PAUSE. LEAVE Outlook open to use in the next exercise.

In the previous exercise, you created a new Outlook Personal Folders file. Folders and Outlook items created or placed in the Slider Project folder are saved to the new .pst file. Optionally, when you create a new Outlook Personal Folders file, you can protect the folder with a password. This provides a convenient way to transfer Outlook data from your old computer to your new computer.

Selecting a Data File for a Mail Account

When messages are received, they are delivered to the Inbox, which is part of your default Outlook data file. If you create a new data file, you can choose to direct messages into the new data file. Normally, users will use this feature only if they send and receive messages in two or more email accounts.

TAKE NOTE*

Refer to the Outlook Help to find more information about configuring Outlook to send and receive messages through a second email account.

➔ SELECT A DATA FILE FOR A MAIL ACCOUNT

GET READY. Before you begin these steps, complete the previous exercise.

1. Click the **Mail** button in the Navigation pane to display the Mail folder. Click the **Folder List** button in the Navigation pane to display the Folder List.
2. Click the **Tools** menu, and click the **Account Settings** option. The Account Settings window is displayed. Your email account is listed. If you receive messages from more than one email account, the additional accounts will also be displayed.
3. Click your email account.

4. Click the **Change Folder** button near the bottom of the window. The New E-mail Delivery Location window is displayed, as shown in Figure 10-10.

Figure 10-10

New E-mail Delivery Location window

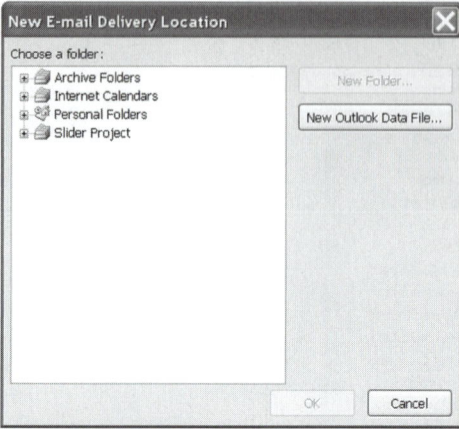

5. In the New E-mail Delivery Location window, click the **Slider Project** folder. Click the **New Folder** button. The Create Folder dialog box is displayed.

6. In the Create folder dialog box, key **Inbox** in the Name field and click **OK**.

7. In the New E-mail Delivery Location window, click the **Inbox** folder you just created in the Slider Project folder. Click **OK**. In the Account Settings window, you can see that mail will be delivered to Slider.pst.

8. Click the **Change Folder** button near the bottom of the window. The New E-mail Delivery Location window is displayed.

9. In the New E-mail Delivery Location window, click the plus sign (**+**) next to the Personal Folders folder and then click the **Inbox** folder in the Personal Folders folder. Click **OK**. This returns Outlook to your original data file settings. In the Account Settings window, you can see that mail will be delivered to the original location.

10. Click the **Close** button to close the Account Settings window.

PAUSE. LEAVE Outlook open to use in the next exercise.

CERTIFICATION READY?
How do you add an Outlook data file to, or remove it from, a mail profile?
5.2.2

In the previous exercise, you selected a new data file for an email account. All arriving messages will be delivered to the new data file.

Changing Data File Settings

After creating a data file, you can modify some of its characteristics. Characteristics include the data file's name, size, and password protection.

⊕ **CHANGE DATA FILE SETTINGS**

GET READY. Before you begin these steps, complete the previous exercise.

1. If necessary, click the **Mail** button in the Navigation pane to display the Mail folder.

 ANOTHER WAY

You can also access a data file's characteristics through the menu. Click the File menu and click the Data File Management option to display the Account Settings window. In the Account Settings window, click the data file's name and click the Settings button.

Categories and Outlook Data Files | 1117

2. Right-click the **Personal Folders** folder in the Navigation pane. Click **Properties for "Personal Folders"** on the shortcut menu. The Outlook Today — [Personal Folders] Properties window is displayed, as shown in Figure 10-11.

Figure 10-11

Outlook Today — [Personal Folders] Properties window

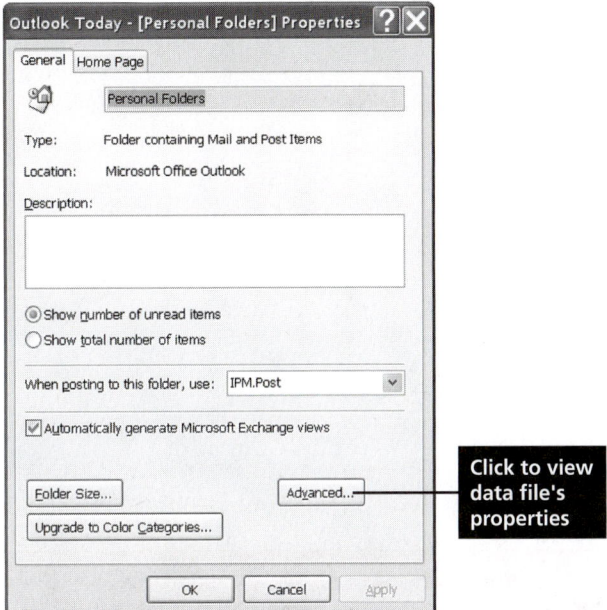

3. Click the **Advanced** button. The Personal Folders window is displayed. The name of the data file is already selected in the Name field. If you changed the name of your data file or selected a different data file, the name of this window will reflect the name of the data file.
4. Key **Original Data File**, replacing the existing data file name.
5. Click the **Change Password** button to display the Change Password window. To change the password, you would key the old password and key the new password twice. Instead, click the **Cancel** button to close the Change Password window.
6. Click the **Compact Now** button. A small alert window informs you that the data file is compacting.
7. Click the **Cancel** button to close the Personal Folders window. Click the **Cancel** button to close the Outlook Today — [Personal Folders] Properties window.

   CLOSE Outlook.

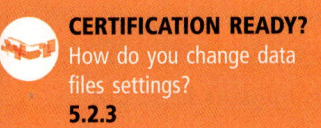

CERTIFICATION READY?
How do you change data files settings?
5.2.3

In the previous exercise, you accessed the data file settings. To *compact* your data file, a process that reduces the size of the data file, you clicked the Compact Now button. Compacting your data file is always a good idea to save space. Renaming the data file is not necessary unless you use more than one data file.

A password can be used to protect the information stored in the data file. However, you are solely responsible for remembering your password. Microsoft and your network administrator will not be able to help you access the data file if your password is lost or forgotten.

Summary Skill Matrix

In This Lesson You Learned how to:
Assign Outlook Items to Color Categories
Modify and Create Color Categories
Sort Items by Color Categories
Search for Items by Category
Create a Data File
Select a Data File for a Mail Account
Change Data File Settings

Knowledge Assessment

Matching

Match the term with its definition.

a. archive
b. color category
c. compact
d. criteria
e. Instant Search
f. Outlook Personal Folders file
g. rule
h. search
i. search folder
j. sort

_____ 1. Color assigned to an Outlook item, providing a way to visually indicate relationships among Outlook items

_____ 2. Defines an action that happens automatically when messages are received or sent

_____ 3. A virtual folder that searches your email folders to locate items that meet the saved search criteria

_____ 4. Try to find items that meet specific criteria

_____ 5. Characteristics used to select items

_____ 6. Search function that displays items as they are found

_____ 7. Process that reduces the size of a data file

_____ 8. Arrange items in a sequence based on specific criteria

_____ 9. Store messages in a separate folder to reduce the number of messages in the folders you use most often

_____ 10. File containing stored Outlook data

True/False

Circle T if the statement is true or F if the statement is false.

T | F   1. You can create new color categories.
T | F   2. A color category indicates a relationship among Outlook items.
T | F   3. Rules can't be used to assign color categories.
T | F   4. A color category must use a color.
T | F   5. You can use color categories to sort Outlook items.
T | F   6. When sorted, items without a color category are displayed below items with a color category.
T | F   7. Use Outlook's Instant Search feature to create a Search Folder.
T | F   8. Outlook automatically creates data files the first time it is launched.
T | F   9. Archived Outlook items are stored in data files.
T | F 10. Outlook data files can be protected by a password.

■ Competency Assessment

Project 10-1: Assign an Outlook Item to a Color Category

Terry Crayton at Trey Research is starting a new project. She will be working closely with Charles Fitzgerald. She decides to assign a color category to their correspondence.

GET READY. Launch Outlook if it is not already running.

TROUBLESHOOTING The email addresses provided in these exercises belong to unused domains owned by Microsoft. When you send a message to these addresses, you will receive an error message stating that the message could not be delivered. Delete the error messages when they arrive.

1. Click the Mail button in the Navigation pane to display the Mail folder, if necessary.
2. On the Standard toolbar, click the New button. The Message window is displayed.
3. In the To field, key Charles@treyresearch.net.
4. In the Subject field, key Project Team.
5. In the message area, key the following message.
   Hi Charles, Press [Enter] twice. I look forward to working with you on the new project. The product sounds like an interesting challenge. Press [Enter] twice. Terry
6. Click the Send button.
7. Click the Sent Items folder in the Navigation pane.
8. Click the Project Team message in the message list.
9. Click the Categorize button on the Standard toolbar. Click Green Category in the dropdown list. If you have not used Green Category before, a dialog box allowing you to rename the category is displayed.
10. Click No in the Rename Category dialog box.

    LEAVE Outlook open for the next project.

Project 10-2: Modify a Color Category

The new project that Terry Crayton and Charles Fitzgerald are leading has been named. Change the name of Green Category to POD Project.

1. Click the **Mail** button in the Navigation pane to display the Mail folder, if necessary.
2. Click the **Sent Items** folder in the Navigation pane.
3. Click the **Project Team** message in the message list.
4. Click the **Categorize** button on the Standard toolbar. Click **All Categories** in the dropdown list. The Color Categories window is displayed.
5. Click **Green Category** in the list of categories. Click the **Rename** button. The Green Category text becomes active.
6. Key **POD Project** and press **Enter**.
7. Click **OK** to rename the category and close the Color Categories window.
   LEAVE Outlook open for the next project.

■ Proficiency Assessment

Project 10-3: Sort Items by Color Category

A week later, Terry Crayton needs to find the message she sent to Charles. Because only one message has been sent, sorting the sent messages is the simplest way to find the message.

1. Click the **Mail** button in the Navigation pane to display the Mail folder if necessary.
2. Click the **Sent Items** folder in the Navigation pane.
3. Click the **View** menu. Point to **Arrange by**, and click **Categories**. The messages in the message list are rearranged.
4. Scroll down the list of messages to view the message in the POD Project category.
5. Click the **View** menu. Point to **Arrange by**, and click **Date** to sort the messages by date.
   LEAVE Outlook open for the next project.

Project 10-4: Search Items by Category

Several weeks later, the POD project is in full swing. Terry has added new contacts, and dozens of messages have been exchanged with POD Project team members. Searching is the easiest way to view all Outlook items associated with the project.

1. Click the **Mail** button in the Navigation pane to display the Calendar folder. Click the **Folder List** button to display the complete list of Outlook folders.
2. Click the **Expand the Query Builder** button next to the Instant Search box. The Query Builder is expanded.
3. If the Categories field is not displayed on the expanded Query Builder, click the **Add Criteria** arrow to display the dropdown menu. Click **Categories** on the dropdown menu. The Categories field is added to the Query Builder.
4. Click the **Categories** arrow to display the dropdown list of categories. Click the **POD Project** category. The search criterion is displayed in the Instant Search box, and the search results are displayed as they are located.
5. Click the **Clear Search** button. The search criterion is cleared. Click the **Minimize the Query Builder** button to minimize the Query Builder, if necessary.
   LEAVE Outlook open for the next project.

Categories and Outlook Data Files | 1121

■ Mastery Assessment

Project 10-5: Create a Data File

Terry has been assigned to the POD project exclusively. She creates a new data file that she will use until the project is complete.

1. Click the **Folder List** button in the Navigation pane to display the Folder List, if necessary.
2. Click the **New** arrow to display the dropdown list of new items you can create. Click **Outlook Data File**. The New Outlook Data File window is displayed.
3. In the New Outlook Data File window, click **OK**. The Create or Open Outlook Data File window is displayed.
4. In the *File name* field, key **POD** to identify the name of the .pst file. Click **OK**. The Create Microsoft Personal Folders window is displayed.
5. In the Create Microsoft Personal Folders window, key **POD Project** in the Name field to identify the name of the folder that will be displayed in Outlook's folder list in the Navigation pane. Click **OK**. The POD Project folder is displayed in the Navigation pane.

   LEAVE Outlook open for the next project.

Project 10-6: Select a Data File for a Mail Account

After creating the new data file, Terry has to add the data file to her mail account.

1. Click the **Mail** button in the Navigation pane to display the Mail folder. Click the **Folder List** button in the Navigation pane to display the Folder List.
2. Click the **Tools** menu and click the **Account Settings** option. The Account Settings window is displayed. Your email account is listed.
3. Click your email account.
4. Click the **Change Folder** button near the bottom of the window. The New E-mail Delivery Location window is displayed.
5. In the New E-mail Delivery Location window click the **POD Project** folder. Click the **New Folder** button. The Create Folder dialog box is displayed.
6. In the Create folder dialog box, key **Inbox** in the Folder Name field and click **OK**.
7. In the New E-mail Delivery Location window click the **Inbox** folder you just created in the Slider Project folder. Click **OK**. In the Account Settings window, you can see that mail will be delivered to POD.pst.
8. Before finishing these projects, you will change the data file to your default data file. Click the **Change Folder** button near the bottom of the window. The New E-mail Delivery Location window is displayed.
9. In the New E-mail Delivery Location window, expand the Personal Folders folder and click the **Inbox** folder. Click **OK**. This returns your original data file settings. In the Account Settings window, you can see that mail will be delivered to the original location.
10. Click the **Close** button to close the Account Settings window.

    CLOSE Outlook.

INTERNET READY

If you subscribe to an email provider such as Earthlink or Roadrunner, your account comes with several mailboxes. Many people use one mailbox for business correspondence, one mailbox for personal correspondence, and one mailbox for shopping or other activities. Access your account on the Internet to configure a mailbox, add a data file in Outlook, and associate the mailbox with the data file in Outlook.

Circling Back

The Baldwin Museum of Science is planning a major event this summer. Ajay Manchepalli, the Director of Special Exhibits, has worked tirelessly to arrange an exhibit of Egyptian antiquities. In a small town like Sun Ridge, Wisconsin, this is a major coup. As the plan for the event develops, Ajay must schedule a whirlwind of appointments and meetings leading up to the big event, as well as help coordinate the travel arrangements of several attendees.

Project 1: Modify Your Calendar

Ajay makes several calls to antiquities experts and officials in Egypt every day. He has modified his work schedule so that he is available during the day in Egypt. Change the work week to match Ajay's schedule and display Egypt's time zone so that Ajay calls during Egypt's day.

GET READY. Launch Outlook if it is not already running.

1. If necessary, click the **Calendar** button in the Navigation pane to display the Calendar folder.
2. Click the **Tools** menu, and click **Options**. The Options window is displayed.
3. Click the **Calendar Options** button to display the Calendar Options window.
4. Click the **Time Zone** button. The Time Zone window is displayed.
5. In the Current Windows time zone area, click the **Time zone** field and select **(GMT-06:00) Central Time (US & Canada)**. Click the **Label** field and key **Ajay**.
6. Click the **Show an additional time zone** checkbox.
7. Click the **Label** field in the Additional time zone area. Key **Egypt**, and press **Tab**.
8. In the Time zone field, select **(GMT + 02:00) Cairo**.
9. Click **OK** in the Time Zone window.
10. In the Calendar Options window, click the **Start time** field. Key or select **2:00 AM**. Click the **End time** field. Key or select **10:00 AM**.
11. Click **OK** in the Calendar Options window and the Options window to return to the Calendar folder.
12. Click the **Day** button to display the Day view. Note that both time zones are displayed.

    LEAVE Outlook open for the next project.

Project 2: Schedule Appointments and Events

The Egypt: Sands of Mysteries exhibit is scheduled for the month of August next year. Ajay has several appointments scheduled for next week. He meets with an insurance agent on Monday, and a telephone call is already scheduled with an antiquities expert in Egypt. Add the appointments and the Sands of Mysteries exhibit to Ajay's calendar.

GET READY. Launch Outlook if it is not already running. Complete the previous project.

1. Click the **Calendar** button in the Navigation pane to display the Calendar folder. Click the **Month** button to display the Month view, if necessary.
2. Click the **Forward** button at the top of the monthly calendar as many times as necessary to display August of next year.
3. Click the empty area of the August 1 box.
4. On the Standard toolbar, click the **New** button. The Appointment window is displayed. Because you clicked August 1 in the Month view, August 1 is the date in the *Start time* and *End time* fields.
5. Click the **All day event** checkbox to select the option. The time fields are dimmed.

6. In the *End time* field, select **August 31** of next year.
7. In the Subject field, key **Egypt: Sands of Mysteries exhibit**.
8. Click the **Save & Close** button on the Ribbon.
9. Click the **Back** button at the top of the monthly calendar as many times as necessary to return to the current month.
10. Click next Monday's date on the monthly calendar.
11. On the Standard toolbar, click the **New** button. The Appointment window is displayed.
12. In the Subject field, key **Susan Metters - Insurance**.
13. In the Location field, key **Here**. Susan will come to Ajay's office.
14. In the *Start time* field, select or key **9:00 AM**. Select an *End time* of **10:00 AM**.
15. Click the **Save & Close** button on the Ribbon.
16. Click next Wednesday's date on the monthly calendar.
17. On the Standard toolbar, click the **New** button. The Appointment window is displayed.
18. In the Subject field, key **Professor Lorraine Nay**.
19. In the Location field, key **Phone**. Lorraine is in Cairo, so Ajay will call her before lunch in Cairo.
20. In the *Start time* field, select or key **3:00 AM**. Select an *End time* of **3:30 AM**.
21. Click the **Save & Close** button on the Ribbon.
    LEAVE Outlook open for the next project.

Project 3: Create Tasks

To make the project more manageable, Ajay creates tasks. He bases the tasks on the participants' home city. All participants will be booked on Blue Yonder Airlines.

GET READY. Launch Outlook if it is not already running.

1. If necessary, click the **Tasks** button in the Navigation pane to display the Tasks folder.
2. Click the **New** button on the Standard toolbar. A Task window is displayed.
3. In the Subject field, key **Sands of Mysteries Exhibit - Make five reservations to Sun Ridge from Chicago**.
4. In the *Due date* field, key or select the date for next Friday.
5. In the Priority field, select **High**.
6. In the task note area, key the following list of names. These executives are travelling from Chicago to Sun Ridge.
   Michael Allen
   Stephanie Conroy
   Bob Gage
   Roger Lengel
   Deborah Poe
7. Click the **Save & Close** button in the Actions group on the Ribbon.
8. Click the **New** button on the Standard toolbar. A Task window is displayed.
9. In the Subject field, key **Sands of Mysteries Exhibit - Make five reservations to Sun Ridge from Las Vegas**.
10. In the *Due date* field, key or select the date for next Friday.
11. In the Priority field, select **High**.

12. In the task note area, key the following list of names. These executives are travelling from Las Vegas to Sun Ridge.

    Grant Culbertson

    Brian Groth

    Jenny Lysaker

    Laura Norman

    Kevin Verboort

13. Click the **Save & Close** button in the Actions group on the Ribbon.

    LEAVE Outlook open for the next project.

Project 4: Assign a Task

Rachel Valdez has offered to help make the arrangements. Assign Rachel the task of making reservations from Seattle to Sun Ridge.

GET READY. Launch Outlook if it is not already running.

> **TROUBLESHOOTING**
>
> The email addresses provided in these exercises belong to unused domains owned by Microsoft. When you send a message to these addresses, you will receive an error message stating that the message could not be delivered. Delete the error messages when they arrive.

1. If necessary, click the **Tasks** button in the Navigation pane to display the Tasks folder.
2. Click the **New** arrow and click the **Task Request** option.
3. Click the **To** field and key **Rachel@margiestravel.com**.
4. In the Subject field, key **Sands of Mysteries Exhibit - Make five reservations to Sun Ridge from Seattle**.
5. In the *Due date* field, key or select the date for next Friday.
6. In the Priority field, select **High**.
7. In the task note area, key the following list of names. These executives are travelling from Seattle to Sun Ridge.

    Terry Adams

    Kari Hension

    Tamara Johnston

    Paula Nartker

    Benjamin C. Willett

8. Click the **Send** button to send the task request.

    CLOSE Outlook.

Appendix A
MCAS for Windows Vista and Office 2007

The Microsoft Certified Application Specialist (MCAS) program is part of the new and enhanced Microsoft Business Certifications. This program is designed to validate skills using the 2007 Microsoft Office system.

In order to prepare for the certification exams, students need to study each application in depth. The information contained in this book covers only a portion of the skills needed to complete the exams successfully. The tables below outline the skills covered in this Office survey text. For skills not covered in this survey text, a reference appears in the table to the specific lesson in the complete MOAC application text covering that application. Students would need to review the material in the books referenced in this manner before attempting the certification exam.

INTRODUCTION TO WINDOWS VISTA

This unit on Vista is intended as a brief overview of the new operating system and is not meant to prepare students for the Windows Vista certification exam, 77-600. The certification skills that are covered are listed in the table below.

LESSON SKILL MATRIX FOR 77-600: WINDOWS VISTA FOR THE INFORMATION WORKER

Matrix Skill	Skill Number	Lesson Number
Word—Change research options	1.4.2	1
Windows—Create a folder, rename a folder	4.2.1, 4.2.2	1
Windows—Search by using keywords	4.4.4	1
PowerPoint—Save presentations as appropriate file types	4.3.6	1
Windows—Create, delete, rename, and move files	4.6.3	1
Windows—Copy data files to a CD or DVD	4.6.4	1
Excel—Save workbooks for use in previous versions of Excel	5.4.1	1
Excel—Add keywords and other information to workbook properties	5.3.3	1
Access—Open databases	6.1.1	1
Word—Save to appropriate format	6.1.1	1
Windows—Customize the Start menu	6.1.1	1
Windows—Locate information in Windows Help and Support	7.2.1	1

ACCESS

For coverage of required certification skills not contained within this Access unit, please see *Microsoft Official Academic Course: Microsoft Office Access 2007* (referred to as *Access* in the table below). The specific lessons where skills are covered are noted.

LESSON SKILL MATRIX FOR EXAM 77-605: USING MICROSOFT OFFICE ACCESS 2007

Matrix Skill	Skill Number	Lesson Number
Define data needs and types	1.1	1
Define table fields	1.1.1	1
Define appropriate table field data types for fields in each table	1.1.2	1
Define tables in databases	1.1.3	1
Define and print table relationships	1.2	3
Create relationships	1.2.1	3
Modify relationships	1.2.2	3
Print table relationships	1.2.3	3
Add, set, change, or remove primary keys	1.3	3
Define and modify primary keys	1.3.1	3
Define and modify multi-field primary keys	1.3.2	3
Split databases	1.4	8
Create databases	2.1	2
Creating databases using templates	2.1.1	2
Create blank databases	2.1.2	2
Create tables	2.2	2
Create custom tables in Design view	2.2.1	See *Access* Lesson 9
Create tables by copying the structure of other tables	2.2.2	2
Create tables from templates	2.2.3	2
Modify tables	2.3	4
Modify table properties	2.3.1	4
Rename tables	2.3.3	4
Delete tables	2.3.4	4
Summarize table data by adding a Total row	2.3.5	See *Access* Lesson 9
Create fields and modify field properties	2.4	4
Create commonly used fields	2.4.1	4
Modify field properties	2.4.2	4
Create and modify multi-valued fields	2.4.3	4
Create and modify attachment fields	2.4.4	4
Create forms	2.5	5, also see *Access* Lesson 10
Create forms using Design View	2.5.1	5
Create datasheet forms	2.5.2	5
Create multiple item forms	2.5.3	See *Access* Lesson 10
Create split forms	2.5.4	See *Access* Lesson 10
Create subforms	2.5.5	See *Access* Lesson 10
Create PivotTable forms	2.5.6	See *Access* Lesson 10

continued

Matrix Skill	Skill Number	Lesson Number
Create forms using Layout view	2.5.7	5
Create simple forms	2.5.8	5
Create reports as a simple report	2.6.1	6
Create reports by using the Report Wizard	2.6.2	6
Create reports by using Design view	2.6.3	6
Define group headers	2.6.4	See *Access* Lesson 11
Create aggregate fields	2.6.5	See *Access* Lesson 11
Set the print layout	2.6.6	See *Access* Lesson 11
Create labels by using the Label Wizard	2.6.7	See *Access* Lesson 11
Add controls	2.7.1	See *Access* Lesson 7
Add controls, Bind controls to fields	2.7.1, 2.7.2	See *Access* Lesson 7
Define the tab order of controls	2.7.3	See *Access* Lesson 7
Format controls	2.7.4	See *Access* Lesson 7
Arrange control	2.7.5	See *Access* Lesson 7
Arrange controls	2.7.5	See *Access* Lesson 7
Apply and change conditional formatting on controls	2.7.6	See *Access* Lesson 7
Apply AutoFormats to forms and reports	2.7.7	5
Apply AutoFormats to forms and reports	2.7.7	6
Enter, edit, and delete records	3.1	3
Navigate among records	3.2	3
Find and replace data	3.3	3
Attach documents to and detach from records	3.4	3
Import data	3.5	See *Access* Lesson 14
Import data from a specific source	3.5.1	See *Access* Lesson 14
Link to an external data source	3.5.2	See *Access* Lesson 14
Save and run import specifications	3.5.3	See *Access* Lesson 14
Create queries	4.1	7
Create queries based on a single table	4.1.1	7
Create queries based on more than one table	4.1.2	7
Create action queries	4.1.3	See *Access* Lesson 12
Create crosstab queries	4.1.4	See *Access* Lesson 12
Create subqueries	4.1.5	See *Access* Lesson 12
Save filters as queries	4.1.6	See *Access* Lesson 12
Modify queries	4.2	7
Add tables to and remove tables from queries	4.2.1	7
Add criteria to queries	4.2.2	7
Create joins	4.2.3	See *Access* Lesson 12
Create calculated fields in queries	4.2.4	See *Access* Lesson 12
Add aliases to query fields	4.2.5	See *Access* Lesson 12
Create sum, average, min/max, and count queries	4.2.6	See *Access* Lesson 12
Sort data within tables	5.1.1	3
Sort data within queries	5.1.2	7
Sort data within reports	5.1.3	6
Sort data within forms	5.1.4	5

continued

Matrix Skill	Skill Number	Lesson Number
Filter data within tables	5.2.1	3
Filter data within queries	5.2.2	7
Filter data within reports	5.2.3	6
Filter data within forms	5.2.4	5
Remove a filter	5.2.5	3
Create and modify charts	5.3	See *Access* Lesson 13
Create charts	5.3.1	See *Access* Lesson 13
Format charts	5.3.2	See *Access* Lesson 13
Change chart types	5.3.3	See *Access* Lesson 13
Export data	5.4	See *Access* Lesson 14
Export from tables	5.4.1	See *Access* Lesson 14
Export from queries	5.4.2	See *Access* Lesson 14
Save and run export specifications	5.4.3	See *Access* Lesson 14
Save database objects as other file types	5.5	See *Access* Lesson 13
Print database objects	5.6	See *Access* Lesson 13
Back up databases	6.1.2	8
Compact and repair databases	6.1.3	8
Save databases as a previous version	6.1.4	See *Access* Lesson 15
Encrypt databases by using passwords	6.2.1	8
Configure database options	6.2.2	8
Set database properties	6.2.3	See *Access* Lesson 15
Identify object dependencies	6.2.4	8
Print database information	6.2.5	8
Reset or refresh table links	6.2.6	8

EXCEL

For coverage of required certification skills not contained within this Excel unit, please see *Microsoft Official Academic Course: Microsoft Office Excel 2007* (referred to as *Excel* in the table below). The specific lessons where skills are covered are noted.

LESSON SKILL MATRIX FOR 77-602: USING MICROSOFT OFFICE EXCEL 2007

Matrix Skill	Skill Number	Lesson Number
Fill a series	1.1.1	2
Copy a series	1.1.2	2
Restrict data using data validation	1.2.1	6
Remove duplicate rows from spreadsheets	1.2.2	6
Cut, copy, and paste data and cell contents	1.3.1	2
Change views within a single window	1.4.1	1
Split windows	1.4.2	1

continued

Matrix Skill	Skill Number	Lesson Number
Open and arrange new windows	1.4.3	1
Copy worksheets	1.5.1	5
Reposition worksheets within workbooks	1.5.2	5
Rename worksheets	1.5.3	5
Hide and unhide worksheets	1.5.4	5
Insert and delete worksheets	1.5.5	5
Use themes to format worksheets	2.1.1	4
Show and hide gridlines and headers	2.1.2	4
Add color to worksheet tabs	2.1.3	4
Format worksheet backgrounds	2.1.4	4
Insert and delete cells, rows, and columns	2.2.1	3, 4
Format rows and columns	2.2.2	4
Hide and unhide rows and columns	2.2.3	4
Modify row height and column width	2.2.4	4
Apply number formats	2.3.1	3
Create custom cell formats	2.3.2	3
Apply and modify cell styles	2.3.3	3
Format text in cells	2.3.4	3
Convert text to columns	2.3.5	See *Excel* Lesson 8
Merge and split cells	2.3.6	3
Add and remove cell borders	2.3.7	3
Insert, modify, and remove hyperlinks	2.3.8	3
Apply Quick Styles to tables	2.4.1	6
Add rows to tables	2.4.2	6
Insert and delete rows and columns in tables	2.4.3	6
Create formulas that use absolute and relative cell references	3.1.1	7
Create formulas that reference data from other worksheets or workbooks	3.1.2	7
Manage named ranges	3.1.3	7
Use named ranges in formulas	3.1.4	7
Use SUM, COUNT, COUNTA, AVERAGE, MIN, and MAX	3.2.1	7
Create and modify list ranges	3.3.1	7
Use SUMIF, SUMIFS, COUNTIF, COUNTIFS, AVERAGEIF, and AVERAGEIFS	3.4.1	See *Excel* Lesson 8
Use VLOOKUP and HLOOKUP	3.5.1	See *Excel* Lesson 8
Use IF, AND, OR, NOT, and IFERROR	3.6.1	See *Excel* Lesson 8
Use PROPER, UPPER, LOWER, SUBSTITUTE	3.7.1	See *Excel* Lesson 8
Convert text to columns	3.7.2	See *Excel* Lesson 8
Display and print formulas	3.8	7
Select appropriate data sources for charts	4.1.1	8
Select appropriate chart types to represent data sources	4.1.2	8
Format charts using Quick Styles	4.1.3	8
Add and remove chart elements	4.2.1	8
Move and size charts	4.2.2	8
Change chart types	4.2.3	8

continued

Matrix Skill	Skill Number	Lesson Number
Manage conditional formats using the rule manager	4.3.1	3
Allow more than one rule to be true	4.3.2	3
Apply conditional formats	4.3.3	3
Insert and modify pictures from files	4.4.1	See *Excel* Lesson 10
Insert and modify SmartArt graphics	4.4.2	See *Excel* Lesson 10
Insert and modify shapes	4.4.3	See *Excel* Lesson 10
Group and ungroup data	4.5.1	6
Subtotal data	4.5.2	6
Sort data using single or multiple criteria	4.6.1	6
Filter data using AutoFilter	4.6.2	6
Filter and sort data using conditional formatting	4.6.3	6
Filter and sort data using cell attributes	4.6.4	6
Insert, display, modify, and resolve tracked changes	5.1.1	See *Excel* Lesson 11
Insert, display, modify, and delete comments	5.1.2	See *Excel* Lesson 11
Protect workbooks and worksheets	5.2.1	See *Excel* Lesson 11
Enable workbooks to be changed by multiple users	5.2.2	See *Excel* Lesson 11
Remove private and other inappropriate data from workbooks	5.3.1	See *Excel* Lesson 11
Restrict permissions to a workbook	5.3.2	See *Excel* Lesson 11
Add digital signatures	5.3.4	See *Excel* Lesson 11
Mark workbooks as final	5.3.5	See *Excel* Lesson 11
Using the correct format, save a workbook as a template, a Web page, a macro-enabled document, or another format	5.4.2	2
Define the area of a worksheet to be printed	5.5.1	2
Insert and move a page break	5.5.2	4
Set margins	5.5.3	4
Add and modify headers and footers	5.5.4	4
Change the orientation of a worksheet	5.5.5	4
Scale worksheet content to fit a printed page	5.5.6	4

OUTLOOK

For coverage of required certification skills not contained within this Outlook unit, please see *Microsoft Official Academic Course: Microsoft Office Outlook 2007* (referred to as *Outlook* in the table below). The specific lessons where skills are covered are noted.

LESSON SKILL MATRIX FOR 77-604: USING MICROSOFT OFFICE OUTLOOK 2007

Matrix Skill	Skill Number	Lesson Number
Send messages to multiple recipients	1.1.1	2
Reply to a message	1.1.2	2
Resend a message	1.1.3	2

continued

Matrix Skill	Skill Number	Lesson Number
Forward a message	1.1.4	2
Create and modify a personal signature	1.2.1	2
Create internal and external Out of Office Messages	1.2.2	2
Attach files and items to a message	1.3.1	2
Preview a message attachment in Outlook	1.3.2	2
Save attachments to a specific location	1.3.3	2
Open a message attachment	1.3.4	2
Show, hide, or move the reading pane	1.7.1	1
Set message sensitivity level	1.4.1	See *Outlook* Lesson 3
Set mail importance level	1.4.2	See *Outlook* Lesson 3
Digitally sign a message	1.5.1	See *Outlook* Lesson 3
Restrict permissions to a message	1.5.2	See *Outlook* Lesson 3
Encrypt a message	1.5.3	See *Outlook* Lesson 3
Add or remove a flag for follow up	1.6.1	See *Outlook* Lesson 3
Delay delivery of a message	1.6.2	See *Outlook* Lesson 3
Request read or delivery receipts	1.6.3	See *Outlook* Lesson 3
Create email polls using standard or custom voting buttons	1.6.4	See *Outlook* Lesson 3
Request that replies be sent to a specific email address	1.6.5	See *Outlook* Lesson 3
Automatically preview messages	1.7.2	2
Create a one-time appointment, meeting, or event	2.1.1	7, 8
Create a recurring appointment, meeting, or event	2.1.2	7, 8
Create an appointment, meeting, or event from an email message	2.1.3	7, 8
Create an appointment, meeting, or event from a task	2.1.4	7
Mark an appointment, meeting, or event as private	2.1.5	7
Invite mandatory attendees to meetings	2.2.1	8
Invite optional attendees to meetings	2.2.2	8
Determine when attendees are available to meet	2.2.3	8
Track responses to meeting requests	2.2.4	8
Schedule meeting resources	2.2.5	8
Change a meeting time	2.3.1	8
Add a meeting attendee	2.3.2	8
Modify one instance of a recurring meeting	2.3.3	8
Send meeting updates only to new attendees	2.3.4	8
Cancel a meeting	2.3.5	8
Define your work week	2.4.1	See *Outlook* Lesson 10
Display multiple time zones	2.4.2	See *Outlook* Lesson 10
Change time zones	2.4.3	See *Outlook* Lesson 10
Add predefined holidays to the calendar	2.4.4	See *Outlook* Lesson 10
Configure free/busy privacy settings	2.5.1	See *Outlook* Lesson 10
Share your calendar with other Outlook users on your network	2.5.2	See *Outlook* Lesson 10
Send calendar information in an email message	2.5.3	See *Outlook* Lesson 10
Publish calendar information to Office Online	2.5.4	See *Outlook* Lesson 10
View a calendar shared by another Outlook user on your network	2.6.1	See *Outlook* Lesson 10

continued

Matrix Skill	Skill Number	Lesson Number
Subscribe to an Internet Calendar	2.6.2	See *Outlook* Lesson 10
View multiple calendars in overlay mode	2.6.3	See *Outlook* Lesson 10
Create recurring tasks	3.1.1	9
Create a task from a message	3.1.2	9
Set the status, priority, and percent complete of a task	3.1.3	9
Mark a task as complete	3.1.4	9
Mark a task as private	3.1.5	9
Assign tasks to others	3.2.1	9
Respond to an assigned task	3.2.2	9
Send a status report on an assigned task	3.2.3	9
Create a contact from a blank contact	4.1.1	5
Create a contact from a message header	4.1.2	5
Create a contact from an electronic business card	4.1.3	6
Save a contact received as a contact record	4.1.4	5
Modify contact information	4.1.5	5
Edit an electronic business card	4.2.1	6
Send an electronic business card to others	4.2.2	6
Use an electronic business card as an automatic signature in messages	4.2.3	6
Create and modify distribution lists	4.3	5
Create a secondary address book for personal contacts	4.4.1	6
Import a secondary address book from a file	4.4.2	6
Categorize messages, appointments, meetings, contacts, and tasks by color	5.1.1	4, 10
Sort Outlook items by color category	5.1.2	10
Create a data file	5.2.1	10
Add an Outlook data file to, or remove it from, a mail profile	5.2.2	10
Change data file settings	5.2.3	10
Create and move mail folders	5.3.1	3
Move mail between folders	5.3.2	3
Specify where a copy of a sent message is saved	5.3.3	2
Empty the Deleted Mail and Sent items folders	5.3.4	3
Manage junk email messages	5.3.5	See *Outlook* Lesson 3
Search all email folders in a single search	5.4.1	See *Outlook* Lesson 3
Locate all items related to a specific person by searching	5.4.2	6
Locate tasks or contacts by searching	5.4.3	6, 9
Search Outlook items by category	5.4.4	10
Create a custom Search Folder	5.4.5	6
Create a rule to move email messages	5.5.1	5
Create a rule to categorize email	5.5.2	5
Create a rule to forward email	5.5.3	5
Create a rule to delete email	5.5.4	5
Show, hide, or minimize the To Do Bar	5.6.1	1
Customize the To Do Bar	5.6.2	1
Select the default format for messages	5.6.3	See *Outlook* Lesson 3
Configure Outlook to be accessible through the Web	5.6.4	See *Outlook* Lesson 10

POWERPOINT

For coverage of required certification skills not contained within this PowerPoint unit, please see *Microsoft Official Academic Course: Microsoft Office PowerPoint 2007* (referred to as *PowerPoint* in the table below). The specific lessons where skills are covered are noted.

LESSON SKILL MATRIX FOR EXAM 77-603: USING MICROSOFT OFFICE POWERPOINT 2007

Matrix Skill	Skill Number	Lesson Number
Create presentations from blank presentations	1.1.1	2
Create presentations from templates	1.1.2	2
Create presentations from existing presentations	1.1.3	2
Create presentations from Microsoft Office Word outlines	1.1.4	2
Apply themes to slide masters	1.2.1	4
Format slide master backgrounds	1.2.2	4
Add elements to slide masters	1.3	4
Change presentation orientation	1.4.1	7
Add, change and remove transitions between slides	1.4.2	4
Set slide size	1.4.3	7
Arrange slides	1.5	2
Insert and remove text boxes	2.1.1	3
Size text boxes	2.1.2	3
Format text boxes	2.1.3	3
Select text orientation and alignment	2.1.4	3
Set margins	2.1.5	3
Create columns in text boxes	2.1.6	3
Cut, copy and paste text	2.2.1	1
Apply Quick Styles from the Style Gallery	2.2.2	3
Format font attributes	2.2.3	3
Use the Format Painter to format text	2.2.4	3
Create and format bulleted and numbered lists	2.2.5	3
Format paragraphs	2.2.6	3
Insert and modify WordArt	2.2.7	3
Reuse slides from an existing presentation	2.3.1	2
Copy elements from one slide to another	2.3.2	1
Insert hyperlinks	2.3.3	4
Insert media clips	2.3.4	6
Apply built-in animations	2.4.1	4
Modify animations	2.4.2	4
Create custom animations	2.4.3	4
Create a SmartArt diagram	3.1.1	5
Create SmartArt diagrams from bullet points	3.1.2	5
Add text to SmartArt diagrams	3.2.1	5
Change theme colors	3.2.2	See *PowerPoint* Lesson 7

continued

Appendix A

Matrix Skill	Skill Number	Lesson Number
Add effects by using Quick Styles	3.2.3	5
Change the layout of diagrams	3.2.4	See *PowerPoint* Lesson 7
Change the orientation of charts	3.2.5	See *PowerPoint* Lesson 7
Add or remove shapes within SmartArt	3.2.6	See *PowerPoint* Lesson 7
Change diagram types	3.2.7	See *PowerPoint* Lesson 7
Insert pictures from file	3.3.1	6
Insert shapes	3.3.2	6
Insert clip art	3.3.3	6
Add text to shapes	3.3.4	6
Apply Quick Styles to shapes and pictures	3.4.1	6
Add, change and remove illustration effects	3.4.2	6
Size, scale, and rotate illustrations and other content	3.5.1	6
Order illustrations and other content	3.5.2	6
Group and align illustrations and other content	3.5.3	6
Use gridlines and guides to arrange illustrations and other content	3.5.4	6
Insert charts	3.6.1	5
Change chart types	3.6.2	5
Format fill and other effects	3.6.3	5
Add chart elements	3.6.4	See *PowerPoint* Lesson 6
Insert tables in a slide	3.7.1	5
Apply Quick Styles to tables	3.7.2	See *PowerPoint* Lesson 5
Change alignment and orientation of table text	3.7.3	See *PowerPoint* Lesson 5
Add images to tables	3.7.4	See *PowerPoint* Lesson 5
Insert, delete and modify comments	4.1.1	See *PowerPoint* Lesson 9
Show and hide markup	4.1.2	See *PowerPoint* Lesson 9
Add digital signatures to presentations	4.2.1	See *PowerPoint* Lesson 9
Identify presentation features not supported by previous versions	4.3.1	See *PowerPoint* Lesson 9
Remove inappropriate information using Document Inspector	4.3.2	See *PowerPoint* Lesson 9
Restrict permissions to a document using Information Rights Management (IRM)	4.3.3	See *PowerPoint* Lesson 9
Mark presentations as final	4.3.4	See *PowerPoint* Lesson 9
Compress images	4.3.5	6
Customize handout masters	4.4.1	7
Print a presentation in various formats	4.4.2	2
Show only specific slides in presentations	4.5.1	7
Rehearse and time the delivery of a presentation	4.5.2	7
Use presentation tools	4.5.3	7
Package presentations for a CD	4.5.4	7
Set slide show options	4.5.5	7

WORD

For coverage of required certification skills not contained within this Word unit, please see *Microsoft Official Academic Course: Microsoft Office Word 2007* (referred to as *Word* in the table below). The specific lessons where skills are covered are noted.

LESSON SKILL MATRIX FOR EXAM 77-601: USING MICROSOFT OFFICE WORD 2007

Matrix Skill	Skill Number	Lesson Number
Work with templates	1.1.1	See *Word* Lesson 6
Apply Quick Styles to a document	1.1.2	2
Format documents by using Themes	1.1.3	2
Customize Themes	1.1.4	2
Format document backgrounds	1.1.5	5
Insert blank pages and cover pages	1.1.6	6
Format pages	1.2.1	5
Create and modify headers and footers	1.2.2	5
Create and format columns	1.2.3	6
Create, modify, and update tables of contents	1.3.1	See *Word* Lesson 13
Create, modify, and update indexes	1.3.2	See *Word* Lesson 13
Insert document and navigation tools	1.3.4	See *Word* Lesson 12
Customize Office Word 2007 options	1.4.1	10
Change research options	1.4.2	10
Apply styles	2.1.1	3
Create and modify styles	2.1.2	3
Format characters	2.1.3	3
Format paragraphs	2.1.4	4
Set and clear tabs	2.1.5	4
Cut, copy, and paste text	2.2.1	7
Find and replace text	2.2.2	7
Control pagination	2.3	6
Create and modify sections	2.3.2	6
Insert sections	2.5	6
Insert SmartArt graphics	3.1.1	9
Insert pictures from files and clip art	3.1.2	9
Insert shapes	3.1.3	9
Format text wrapping	3.2.1	9
Format by size, scaling, and rotation	3.2.2	9
Apply Quick Styles	3.2.3	9
Set contrast, brightness, and coloration	3.2.4	9
Add text to SmartArt graphics and shapes	3.2.5	9
Compress pictures	3.2.6	9
Insert and modify WordArt	3.3.1	See *Word* Lesson 11
Insert pull quotes	3.3.2	See *Word* Lesson 11

continued

Matrix Skill	Skill Number	Lesson Number
Insert and modify drop caps	3.3.3	See *Word* Lesson 11
Insert text boxes	3.4.1	See *Word* Lesson 11
Format text boxes	3.4.2	See *Word* Lesson 11
Link text boxes	3.4.3	See *Word* Lesson 11
Insert building blocks in documents	4.1.1	7
Save frequently used data as building blocks	4.1.2	7
Insert formatted headers and footers from Quick Parts	4.1.3	5
Insert fields from Quick Parts	4.1.4	7
Create tables and lists	4.2.1	4
Sort content	4.2.2	8
Modify list formats	4.2.3	8
Apply Quick Styles to tables	4.3.1	8
Modify table properties	4.3.2	8
Merge and split table cells	4.3.3	8
Perform calculations in tables	4.3.4	8
Change the position and direction of cell contents	4.3.5	8
Create and modify sources	4.4.1	See *Word* Lesson 15
Insert citations and captions	4.4.2	See *Word* Lesson 14
Insert and modify bibliographies	4.4.3	See *Word* Lesson 15
Select reference styles	4.4.4	See *Word* Lesson 15
Create, modify, and update tables of figures and tables of authorities	4.4.5	See *Word* Lesson 14 and Lesson 15
Create merged documents	4.5.1	See *Word* Lesson 16
Merge data into form letters	4.5.2	See *Word* Lesson 16
Create envelopes and labels	4.5.3	2, also see *Word* Lesson 16
Move through a document quickly by using the Find and Go To commands	5.1.1	7
Change windows view	5.1.2	1
Compare document versions	5.2.1	See *Word* Lesson 17
Merge document versions	5.2.2	See *Word* Lesson 17
Combine revisions from multiple authors	5.2.3	See *Word* Lesson 17
Manage track changes	5.3	See *Word* Lesson 17
Display markup	5.3.1	See *Word* Lesson 17
Enable, disable, accept, and reject tracked changes	5.3.2	See *Word* Lesson 17
Change tracking options	5.3.3	See *Word* Lesson 17
Insert, modify, and delete comments	5.4	See *Word* Lesson 17
Identify document features that are not supported by previous versions	6.1.2	See *Word* Lesson 17
Remove inappropriate or private information by using Document Inspector	6.1.3	See *Word* Lesson 17
Restrict permissions to documents	6.2.1	See *Word* Lesson 17
Mark documents as final	6.2.2	See *Word* Lesson 17
Set passwords	6.2.3	See *Word* Lesson 17
Protect documents	6.2.4	See *Word* Lesson 17
Authenticate documents by using digital signatures	6.3.1	See *Word* Lesson 17
Insert a line for a digital signature	6.3.2	See *Word* Lesson 17

Appendix B
Microsoft Office Professional 2007

TO USE MICROSOFT OFFICE PROFESSIONAL 2007, YOU WILL NEED:

COMPONENT	REQUIREMENT
Computer and processor	500 megahertz (MHz) processor or higher[1]
Memory	256 megabyte (MB) RAM or higher[1,2]
Hard disk	2 gigabyte (GB); a portion of this disk space will be freed after installation if the original download package is removed from the hard drive.
Drive	CD-ROM or DVD drive
Display	1024x768 or higher resolution monitor
Operating system	Microsoft Windows XP with Service Pack (SP) 2, Windows Server 2003 with SP1, or later operating system[3]
Other	Certain inking features require running Microsoft Windows XP Tablet PC Edition or later. Speech recognition functionality requires a close-talk microphone and audio output device. Information Rights Management features require access to a Windows 2003 Server with SP1 or later running Windows Rights Management Services.
	Connectivity to Microsoft Exchange Server 2000 or later is required for certain advanced functionality in Outlook 2007. Instant Search requires Microsoft Windows Desktop Search 3.0. Dynamic Calendars require server connectivity.
	Connectivity to Microsoft Windows Server 2003 with SP1 or later running Microsoft Windows SharePoint Services is required for certain advanced collaboration functionality. Microsoft Office SharePoint Server 2007 is required for certain advanced functionality. PowerPoint Slide Library requires Office SharePoint Server 2007. To share data among multiple computers, the host computer must be running Windows Server 2003 with SP1, Windows XP Professional with SP2, or later.
	Internet Explorer 6.0 or later, 32 bit browser only. Internet functionality requires Internet access (fees may apply).
Additional	Actual requirements and product functionality may vary based on your system configuration and operating system.

[1] 1 gigahertz (GHz) processor or higher and 512 MB RAM or higher recommended for **Business Contact Manager**. Business Contact Manager not available in all languages.
[2] 512 MB RAM or higher recommended for **Outlook Instant Search**. Grammar and contextual spelling in **Word** is not turned on unless the machine has 1 GB memory.
[3] Office Clean-up wizard not available on 64 bit OS.

Appendix C

Standard Forms for Business Documents

Reference manuals, such as *The Gregg Reference Manual,* provide a variety of letter and memorandum styles, as well as styles for reports and other documents. Many businesses also have their own styles for documents. This Appendix includes two basic styles-for a business letter and a memorandum. It also shows the most common format for a continuation page (used for either letters or memos).

Table C-1

Parts of a Letter

PARTS OF LETTER	LOCATION / DESCRIPTION
Heading	
Letterhead or return address	Often appears on preprinted stationery; can also be created in Word. Includes the company name, address, and other contact information.
Date line	Two inches from the top of the page on letterhead stationery or on the third line below a Word letterhead. Use date format shown in Figure C-1.
Opening	
Inside address	Starts on the fourth line below the date; consists of name and address (and possibly company name and job title) of person to whom you are writing.
Salutation	On the second line below the inside address; typically includes a courtesy title (Mr., Mrs., Ms., Miss) and ends with a colon.
Body	
Message	Content of the letter, single spaced with one blank line between paragraphs.
Closing	
Complimentary closing	On the second line below the last line of the body of the letter. Common closings are "Sincerely" or "Sincerely yours" followed by a comma.
Writer's identification	On the fourth line below the closing, to leave space for a signature; includes the writer's name and job title (and sometimes the department).
Reference initials	On the second line below the writer's name and title; consists of the typist's initials in small letters.
Enclosure notation	On new line below the reference initials if letter has an enclosure. Specify the number of enclosures. Can also use "Attachment" if enclosure if attached.
Optional features	Filename notation indicates document name for reference purposes; delivery notation indicates method of delivery (other than regular mail); copy notation indicates people who will receive copies of the letter (usually begins with "c:" or "cc:").

Figure C-1

Business letter style

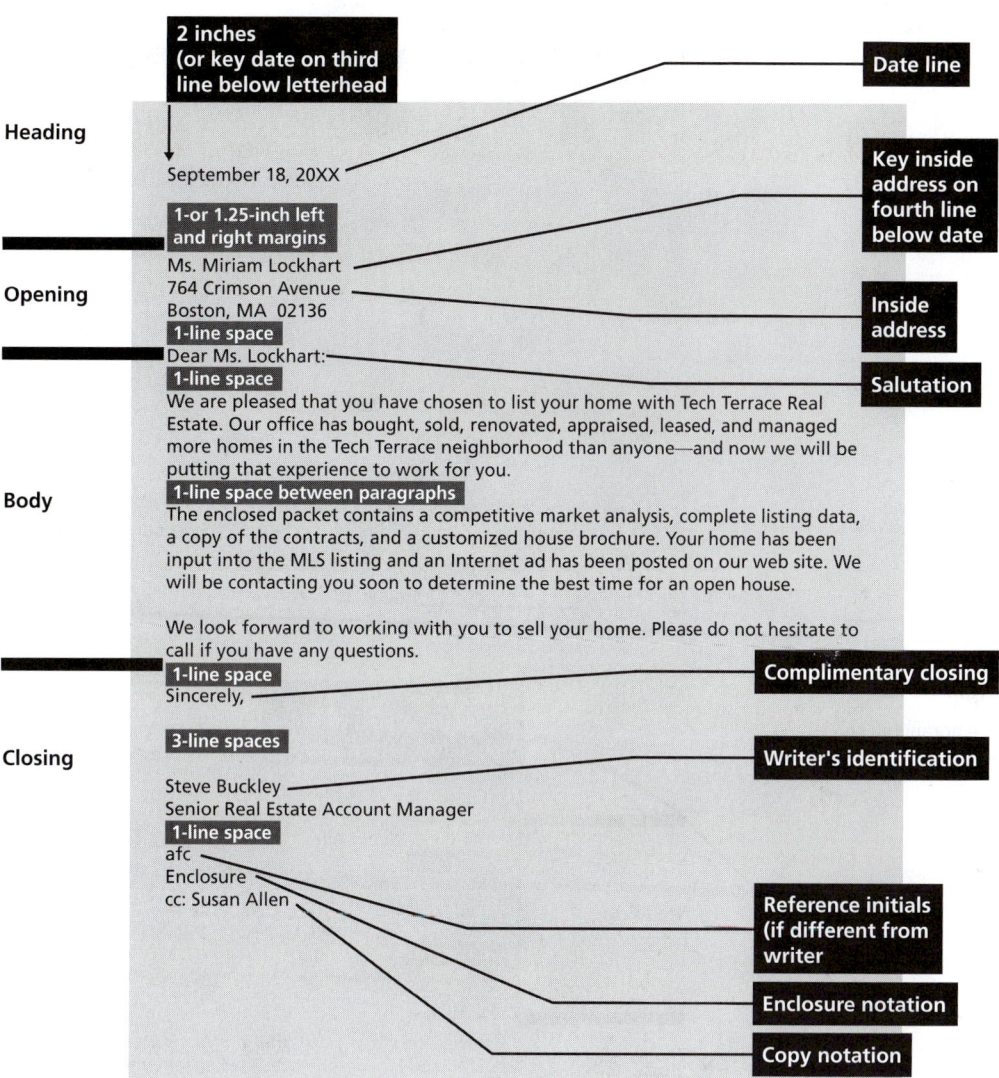

Figure C-2

Continuation page header for two-page (or longer) letter or memo

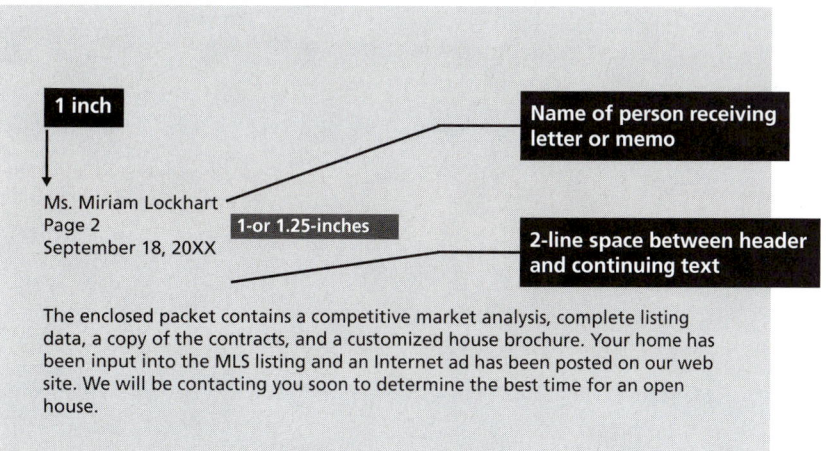

Table C-2

Parts of a Memo

PARTS OF MEMO	LOCATION / DESCRIPTION
Heading	Starts 2 inches from top of page using plain paper or letterhead stationery or on third line below Word letterhead. Consists of guide words ("MEMO TO," "FROM," "DATE," and "SUBJECT") in capital letters followed by a colon. Entries after guide words align at a 1-inch left tab setting. Use date format shown in Figure C-3.
Body	Starts on the third line below the memo heading; contains message, single spaced, with one blank line between paragraphs.
Closing	On the second line below the last paragraph; includes reference initials (the typist's initials in small letters). Might also include an enclosure notation, a file name notation, and a copy notation or distribution list.

Figure C-3

Memorandum style

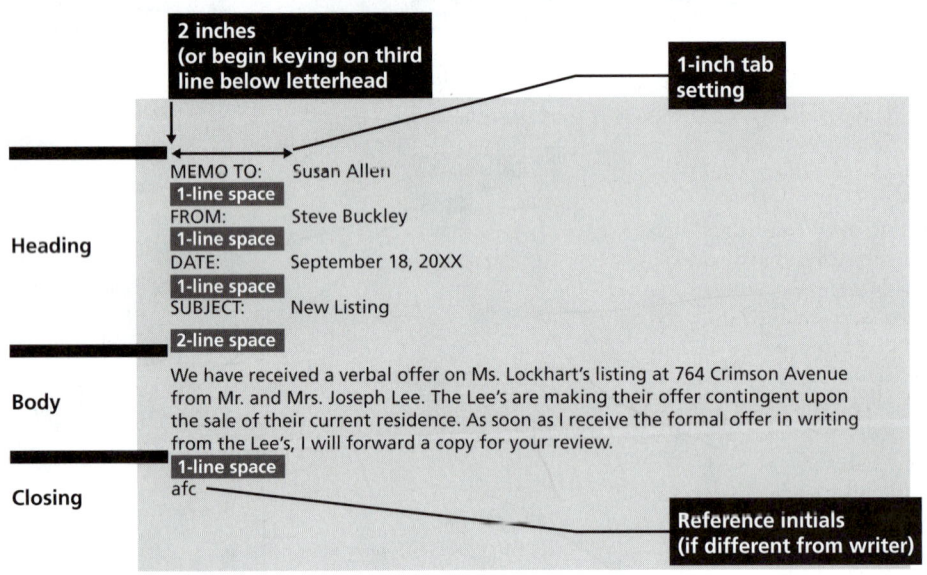

Glossary

A

absolute cell reference in a formula, a reference to a specific cell. Absolute references point to the same cell even when the formula that contains the reference is copied or moved to a different cell

action determines what happens when a message meets the conditions defined in the rule; a button or text block programmed to perform a specific action, such as jumping to a slide or starting a program

active cell the cell in which you can enter data. A thick black border surrounds the active cell

add-in supplemental program that can be installed to extend the capabilities of Word by adding custom commands and specialized features

address book stores names and email addresses

animation an effect you apply to placeholders or other content to move the content in unique ways on the slide

annotate to write or draw on a slide during a presentation

appointment a scheduled activity that does not require sending invitations to other people or resources

archive store messages in a separate folder to reduce the number of messages in the folders you use most often

ascending sorting text from beginning to end, such as from A to Z, 1 to 10, and January to December

ascending order sort order in which alphabetic data appears A to Z, numeric data appears from lowest to highest or smallest to largest, and dates appear from oldest to most recent

aspect ratio the relationship of width to height in a picture or shape

assign transfer ownership of a task to another Outlook user

assistant in an organization chart, a person who reports directly to a superior

attachment file sent as part of an email message

Attribute a formatting characteristic of text or a cell

auto fill an Excel feature that automatically fills cells with data from another cell or range of cells or completes a data series

AutoArchive automatic function that archives messages

AutoComplete a feature in Microsoft Office Excel that completes text entries that you start to key in a column of data if the first few letters that you key match an existing entry in that column; automatically completes the names of the months and days of the week

AutoFilter a built-in set of filtering capabilities that you can apply to worksheet data

AutoFormat command that applies a predefined format that you select to a form or report

AutoPreview displays the first three lines of every message in the message list

axis a line bordering the chart plot area used as a frame of reference for measurement

B

back up to create a copy of data for safekeeping; a copy of a database file

back-end file in a split database, the database that contains the tables

background the empty area of the desktop where windows open and display content

badges small square labels that contain key tips

banner text displayed at the top of a day to indicate an event

Blank Form tool tool that creates a new blank form in Layout view

boundary the line that divides columns or rows on an Excel worksheet

Building Blocks reusable pieces of content or other document parts that are stored in galleries and can be inserted into a document whenever needed

bulleted list groups of items or phrases that present related ideas

busy an activity is scheduled for this time period. You are not available for other activities

button an element you can click in order to select a command or action

C

cancel delete a meeting

cascades arrange windows to overlap one another in an orderly fashion, starting in the upper left corner of the desktop. The active window, which is on top, displays in its entirety, while only the top and left of the other windows are visible

Categorized Mail standard Search folder that displays messages that have an assigned color category

cell the intersection of a column and a row in a worksheet

character any single letter, number, symbol, or punctuation mark

character a letter, number, punctuation, mark, or symbol

character styles styles that are applied to individual characters or words that you have selected within a paragraph rather than affecting the entire paragraph

chart a graphical representation of numeric data in a worksheet

chart area the entire chart and all its elements

chart sheet a sheet in a workbook that contains only a chart

clip art pre-drawn artwork in a wide variety of styles. Office clip art files can include drawn graphics, photographs, sounds, and animated graphics

Clip Organizer a series of folders in which installed or downloaded clip art files are stored on your system

Clipboard a temporary storage area that can hold one item at a time. Use to copy and move files, folders, and selected data

collapsed hide the contents of a folder in a list or menu

color category color assigned to an Outlook item, providing a way to visually indicate relationships among Outlook items

column (Excel) a vertical line of cells. Columns are identified by a letter or letters

columns (Word) vertical blocks of text in which text flows from the bottom of one column to the top of the next

column heading the letter that appears at the top of the columns on a worksheet

column width the number of characters that will fit in a column. Default column width is 8.43 characters

command a button you click or a box where you enter information that tells Word what you want it to do

common filters popular filters available as context menu commands, depending on the type and values of the field

compact process that reduces the size of a data file

comparison operator a sign used in comparison criteria to compare two values

complete a task is 100 percent finished

composite key Two or more primary keys used in a table

compress decrease the size of a picture file by reducing the resolution

condition identifies the characteristics used to determine the messages affected by a rule

conditional formatting formatting that is applied based on established criteria

Connection Status menu a menu that lets you choose between searching help topics online and help topics offline

constant numbers or text values entered directly into a formula. Constant values are not calculated

constrain to force a drawing object into a particular shape or alignment

contact collection of information about a person or company

Contacts folder electronic organizer that enables you to create, view, and edit contact information

Content controls tiny programs that include a label for instructing you on the type of text to include and a placeholder that reserves a place for your new text

context menu a shortcut menu that displays when you right-click an item

copy place a duplicate of a selection on the Office Clipboard

copy pointer a plus (+) symbol that allows you to use the mouse to copy data from a selected range to a new location

criteria conditions you specify to limit which records are included in the result of a sort, query, or filter

crop trim the vertical or horizontal edges of an object, or to remove a portion of a picture or shape that is not needed. The cropped portion is hidden until you compress the picture

current slide the slide that is currently being edited

custom show a group of slides in a presentation that can be shown separately from the entire presentation

cut remove a selection from a worksheet and place it on the Office Clipboard

D

data information keyed into an Excel workbook cell

data labels text that provides additional information about a data marker, which represents a single data point or value that originates from a worksheet cell

data marker a bar, area, dot, slice, or other symbol in a chart that represents a single data point or value that originates from a worksheet cell. Related data markers in a chart constitute a data series

data series all the data points for a particular category of plotted information

data type kind of information a field contains—whether it is text, number, date/time, or some other type

database tool for collecting and organizing information

Database Documenter creates a report that shows details, or definitions, about a selected object and opens it in Print Preview

database management system (DBMS) a system for managing data that allows the user to store, retrieve, and analyze information

Database Splitter a wizard that splits a database into two files

Datasheet visual representation of the data contained in a table or of the results returned by a query

decrypting removing the password from a file that has been encrypted

default a predefined setting. You can accept Excel's default option settings or you can change them

Deferred status indicating that a task has been postponed without changing the deadline or the percentage complete

Deleted Items folder deleted items are held in this folder until the folder is emptied. Emptying the folder removes the items from your computer

descending order sort order in which alphabetic data appears Z to A, numeric data appears from highest to lowest or largest to smallest, and dates appear from most recent to oldest

desktop the main screen that appears once the computer is started

destination location A new storage location for a moved or copied file. Also, target

dialog box a box that displays options or information you can specify to execute a command

dialog box launcher a small arrow in the lower right corner of a group that you click to launch a dialog box

distribution list group of individual contacts saved together as a single contact

document properties details about a file that describe or identify it

document theme a set of predefined formatting options that include sets of theme colors, fonts, and effects

Drafts folder Outlook messages you write but haven't sent are stored in this folder

duplicate contact contact records containing the same information

duplicate value values in the row are an exact match of all the values in another row

E

electronic business card digital version of paper business cards. They can be sent as attachments, used as signatures, and used to create a contact record

embedded data that has been placed in a destination application so that it can be edited with the tools of its original source applications

embedded chart a chart that is placed on a worksheet rather than on a separate chart sheet

embedded object an inserted picture that becomes part of the document

encrypting to scramble data in a way that can only be reconverted by an authorized user who has the password

event an activity that lasts one or more days

exception identifies the characteristics used to exclude messages from being affected by the rule

expanded to open, or increase in size to display content that would otherwise be hidden

external reference a reference to a cell or range on a worksheet in another Excel workbook, or a reference to a defined name in another workbook. External references are sometimes called links

F

field (Excel) column in a database table

field (Word) a placeholder that tells Word where to insert changeable data into a document

field list a window that lists all the fields in the underlying record source or database object

files a set of information stored with a single name

fill handle a small black square in the lower-right corner of selected cells. You can click the handle to drag the contents of one cell to adjacent cells or to create a series such as a series of dates

filter to find items that meet certain criteria while excluding items that do not meet the criteria; a set of rules for determining which records will be displayed

filter a rule that Excel uses to determine which worksheet rows to display

filter by form tool that creates a blank form similar to the original—useful for filtering on several fields in a form or to find a specific record

first-line indent in a paragraph, the first line indents more than the following lines

floating object a picture or drawing object that can be positioned precisely on the page, including behind or in front of text

folder common name for Outlook components

folders a place where you can items such as files and other folders

font a set of characters that have the same design and are designed to appear a certain way

footer (Excel) a line of text that appears at the bottom of each page of a printed worksheet

footer (PowerPoint) information such as a date, slide number, or text phrase that appears at the bottom of each slide in a presentation

footer (Word) text that is printed at the bottom of a page or worksheet

foreign key a primary key from one table that is used in another table

form database object that simplifies the process of entering, editing, and displaying data

Form Design tool that creates a new blank form in Design view

Form tool creates a simple form that includes all the fields from the underlying data source

Form Wizard form-building tool that allows you to choose the form fields, style, and layout

Format Painter a tool to copy character, paragraph, or cell formatting from one selection to another

formatting layout and presentation of document, including size and style of font

formula a set of mathematical instructions used to perform calculations in a table or worksheet cell

formula bar a bar at the top of the Excel window where you can enter or edit cell entries or formulas

free no activities are scheduled for this time period. You are available

freeze make certain rows or columns visible on your screen even when you scroll your worksheet

front-end file database that contains the queries, forms, reports, and other objects created from the tables

function a predefined formula that performs a calculation

G

gadgets a program or tool usually displayed on the Sidebar, designed to provide information at a glance

gridlines (Excel) the lines that display around the worksheet cells

gridlines (PowerPoint) horizontal and vertical lines that can be used as guides when positioning objects on a slide

gridlines (Word) vertical and horizontal lines that help you align graphics and other objects in your documents

group schedule displays scheduling information for several people. Requires Microsoft Exchange 2000 or a more recent version of Microsoft Exchange

group worksheets selecting multiple worksheets to enter and edit data on them or format them at the same time

grouping organizing data so that it can be viewed as a collapsible and expandable outline

groups related commands within the tabs on the Ribbon

guides nonprinting vertical and horizontal lines that you can move or copy to align objects on a slide

H

handout a printed copy of a presentation

hanging indent in a paragraph, the first full line of text is not indented, but the following lines are

header (Excel) a line of text that appears at the top of each page of a printed worksheet

header (PowerPoint) information such as a date, slide number, or text phrase that appears at the top of each page of a presentation's handouts or notes

header (Word) text that is printed at the top of a page

header row in a table, the first row; it is formatted differently and usually contains headings for the entire table

hide to make a row, column, worksheet, or workbook invisible

horizontal alignment how text is positioned between the left and right margins, including left-aligned, centered, right-aligned, and justified

hyperlink a shortcut or jump that opens a document stored on a network server, an intranet, or the Internet

I

I-beam shape of the mouse pointer when it is moved over the text area of a document

icon a small picture that represents an item or command

import bring information into a file from an external source

In Progress status indicating that work on the task has started

Inbox folder by default, new messages are placed in this folder when they arrive

Indent the space between a paragraph and the document's left and/or right margin

indent level the distance of a paragraph of text from the placeholder's left border

index a collection of information about items stored on a computer, used to increase the speed and accuracy of a search

indexed location a location that is included in the Windows Vista index

inline object a picture or drawing object that moves along with the text around it

innermost field secondary sort field in a multi-field sort

Input mask a set of placeholder characters that force you to enter data in a specific format

insertion point a blinking vertical line that signals you can begin keying text

item a record stored in Outlook

J

Junk E-Mail folder messages identified as spam are placed in this folder when they arrive

K

key tips small letters and numbers that appear on the Ribbon when you press Alt; used for executing commands with the keyboard

keyword a word or phrase that describes a subject or category on which you can search

L

label entries that identify the numeric data in a worksheet

landscape orientation page setup in which a page is wider than it is tall

Large Mail a standard Search folder that displays messages larger than 100 kilobytes

layout a predefined arrangement of placeholders for text or objects (such as charts or pictures)

leaders dotted, dashed, or solid lines that fill the space before a tab

legend a box that identifies the patterns or colors that are assigned to a data series or categories in a chart

line spacing the amount of space between lines of text in a paragraph

linked data that has been placed in a destination application so that it maintains a link with its source file; changes to the source file are also made in the linked object

linked object an inserted object that includes a connection to the object's source

Linked Table Manager Lists the paths to all currently linked tables

M

mandatory attendee a person who must attend the meeting

margins the blank areas at the top, bottom, and sides of a document

mathematical operator the formula component that specifies what calculations are to be performed. The most common operators are = (equal), + (addition), – (subtraction), * (multiplication), and / (division)

maximize to expand a window to fill the desktop

meeting a scheduled activity that requires sending invitations to other people or resources

meeting organizer the person who creates the meeting and sends meeting invitations

meeting request Outlook item that creates a meeting and invites attendees

menu a list of additional options from which you can choose

merged cell a single cell that is created by combining two or more selected cells

message header text automatically added at the top of a message; The message header contains the sender's email address, the names of the servers used to send and transfer the message, the subject, the date, and other basic information about the message

microphone sound recording device attached to your computer

Microsoft Office Button displays a menu of basic commands for opening, saving, and printing files as well as more advanced options

Mini toolbar a small toolbar with popular commands that appears when you point to selected text

minimize to reduce a window to a button on the taskbar

mixed reference in formulas, a cell reference in which the column is absolute and the row is relative or vice versa

mouse an input device commonly used to select features and command

mouse pointer the icon that moves on the screen in response to the movement of the mouse on your desk

move pointer a four-point symbol that allows you to use the mouse to move data from one worksheet location to another

multi selection a feature that enables you to select multiple pieces of text that are not next to each other

Multi-valued field a field that allows you to select more than one value from a list

N

name a meaningful shorthand that makes it easier to understand the purpose of a cell reference, constant, formula, or table

Navigation pane provides access to Outlook components such as Contacts and the Calendar folder

negative indent a paragraph that extends into the left margin

nonprinting characters symbols that Word inserts into a document when you use certain formatting commands, such as paragraph and indents

normal forms standards and guidelines of database design that can be used to determine if a database is structured correctly

Normal view PowerPoint's default view, suited for editing individual slides; includes the Slide pane, Notes pane, and Slides/Outline pane

normalization process of applying rules to a database design to ensure that information is divided into the appropriate tables

note additional information associated with a slide

Notes Page view a view that displays a single slide and its associated notes

numbered list a group of steps, procedures, or actions that are listed in numeric order

O

Object Dependencies describes how objects in a database are dependent on or rely on other components to function properly

objects elements in a database such as tables, queries, forms, and reports

occurrence a single meeting in a series of recurring meetings

Office Clipboard an area in memory for storing up to 24 copied or cut items so they can be selectively pasted in other locations

offline files Copies of network files that are stored locally

operand the components of a formula that identify the values to be used in the calculation; these can be a constant value, a cell reference, a range of cells, or another formula

optional attendee a person who should attend the meeting but whose presence is not required

order the way in which objects stack up on a slide as you create them

organization chart a diagram that shows the relationships among personnel or departments in an organization

orientation (Excel) a setting that specifies the direction a worksheet appears on a printed page, either vertically (portrait orientation) or horizontally (landscape orientation)

orientation (Word) the direction that material appears on a page when printed

orphan a line of text that is left alone at the bottom of a page

out of office you are not in the office during this time period

Outbox outgoing messages are held in this folder until you are connected to the Internet. When an Internet connection is detected, the message is sent

outermost field primary sort field in a multi-field sort

outline symbols symbols that you use to change the view of an outlined worksheet. You can show or hide detailed data by pressing the plus sign, minus sign, and the numbers 1, 2, 3 indicating the outline level

Outlook Personal Folders file file containing stored Outlook data. It is identified by the .pst extension

owner only Outlook user who can modify a task

P

page break (Excel) divider that breaks a worksheet into separate pages for printing

page break (Word) the location in a document where one page ends and a new page begins

Page Break Preview: a view that allows you to see the dividers that break a worksheet into separate pages for printing

panes a section of an area on the screen, such as a section of a window

paragraph spacing the amount of space above or below a paragraph

paragraph styles formats that are applied to all the text in the paragraph where your insertion point is located, whether or not you have it all selected

parameter query query in which the user interactively specifies one or more criteria values

paste a command used to insert a cut or copied selection stored on the Office Clipboard to a cell or range in a worksheet

path the route Windows takes from a storage device through folders and subfolders to a specific destination.

placeholder on a slide, a box that holds a specific type of content, such as text

plot area the area bounded by the axes

point a measurement of the height of characters in a cell or the height of a row. One point is equal to 1/72 inch

point size refers to the height of characters, with one point equaling approximately 1/72 [comp: note fraction] of an inch

portrait orientation page setup in which the page is taller than it is wide

Presenter view a viewing mode that allows the presenter to see notes on one screen while the audience views slides on another screen

primary key column in a database that uniquely identifies each row

Print Preview (Word) command that enables you to view your document as it will look when it is printed, and also provides the ability to make changes

Print Preview (Excel) the Excel window that allows you to view a full-page preview of what your worksheet will look like when it is printed

private feature that protects the details of an activity from a casual observer, but it does not ensure privacy

program a set of instructions that a computer uses to perform a task, such as word processing or photo editing

Q

query database object that enables stored data to be searched and retrieved

query criterion a rule that identifies the records that you want to include in the query result

Quick Access Toolbar a toolbar at the top left of the screen that contains the commands that you use most often, such as Save, Undo, and Redo

Quick Styles (Excel) predefined formats that you can apply to your worksheet to instantly change its look and feel

Quick Tables (PowerPoint) built-in preformatted tables, such as calendars and tabular lists, you can insert and use in your documents

Quick Style (Word) built-in formatting for text, graphics, SmartArt diagrams,

charts, WordArt, pictures, tables, and shapes

R

range a group of adjacent cells that you select to perform operations on all of the selected cells

Reading pane displays the text of a selected email message

record row in a database table

record source tables or queries from which a query gets its data

recurring appointment an appointment that occurs at regular intervals

recurring meeting a meeting that occurs at regular intervals

recurring task a task that must be completed at regular intervals

Recycle Bin a place where deleted items are stored until they are removed permanently or restored to their original location

redo repeat your last action

redundant data duplicate information in a database

reference identifies a cell or a range of cells on a worksheet and tells Excel where to look for the values you want to use in a formula

referential integrity prevents orphaned records

relational database group of database tables that are connected or linked by a defined relationship that ties the information together

relative cell reference in formulas, a cell reference that changes "relative" to the location to which they are copied or moved

report database object that presents information in a format that is easy to read and print

reset discard all the formatting changes that you made to a picture

resource an item or a location that can be invited to a meeting

restore make an item available for use. For example, moving an item out of the Deleted Items folder restores it for use

restore down to return a window to its previous size and position on the desktop

retention rules guidelines that determine the length of time correspondence must be kept

Ribbon located across the top of the screen, it contains tabs and groups of commands

row a horizontal line of cells

row heading the row number that appears to the left of a worksheet

row height the top-to-bottom height of a row, given in points or in pixels. You

can change row height by using the Format command in the Home tab Editing group or by dragging the bottom of the row selector

rule defines an action that happens automatically when messages are received or sent

rulers (Excel) horizontal and vertical measures that help you position objects on a slide

ruler (Word) a measuring tool that helps you align text and displays indents, tabs, and margins

S

Save store a document for future use

Save As save a document with a new name or in a different location

scaling specifying a percentage of the original dimensions to enlarge or reduce a picture or shape

scaling (Excel) expanding or shrinking how a worksheet appears on a printed page

scope location within which the name is recognized without qualification

ScreenTip brief description of an item's purpose displayed when the mouse hovers on the item

Scroll box a box you can click and drag to move more quickly horizontally or vertically through the document

Scroll buttons buttons you can click to move up or down through the document one line at a time

Scrollbars appear on the right and/or bottom of the document window; contain buttons and boxes you can use to move through the document

Search Folder a virtual folder that searches your email folders to locate items that meet the saved search criteria

search results The items that match the specified criteria

secondary address book the address book for an additional Contacts folder

section break used to enable layout or formatting changes in a portion of a document

select identify the cell or range of cells in which you want to enter data or apply formatting

select query most basic type of Access query that creates subsets of data, displayed in Datasheet view, that can be used to answer specific questions or to supply data to other database objects

Sent Items folder items are automatically moved to this folder after they have been sent

shortcut menu a list of commands or options relevant to the current task that displays when you right-click an item p. 55

shortcuts a link to a program, feature, or command

sidebar a vertical bar usually located along the right side of the desktop where gadgets can be displayed

signature text or images that are automatically placed at the end of outgoing messages

slide master a slide that stores information about the formats applied in a presentation, such as theme, fonts, layouts, and colors

Slide sorter view PowerPoint view that allows slides to be easily sorted

Slide show view PowerPoint view that displays each slide in sequential order

SmartArt graphics a visual representation of your information; can help communicate your message and ideas

sort to arrange data alphabetically, numerically, or chronologically

source location The location where an item is originally stored

speech recognition process of converting a speech signal to a sequence of words

speech recognition rate measures the amount of successful and unsuccessful speech recognition results returned from the recognizer

speech user interface appears on screen to indicate current mode when speech recognition is running on your computer

split cells to divide one cell into two or more cells

spoofing providing false information in a message header

stacks Tile windows horizontally so they display one above the other without overlapping

Start button a round button with the Microsoft Windows logo on it that you click to open the Start menu

Start menu a menu that provides access to all the programs, files, and folders stored on your computer

string any sequence of letters or numbers that you key

style a set of formatting attributes you can apply as a group to a cell or range of cells

subject topic of a message

submenu a secondary list of choices that falls under a main menu

subordinates in an organization chart, persons or departments who are subordinate to another person or department

syntax The way words are arranged

T

tab area of activity on the Ribbon

table (Access) most basic database object; stores data in categories

table an arrangement of columns and rows used to organize information

tabs areas of activity in the Ribbon

target the page, slide, or file that appears when a link is clicked

task an Outlook item that can be tracked from creation to completion

task request assigns a task to another user

taskbar a row, usually across the bottom of the desktop, that displays icons that let you access frequently-used features, programs, and commands

Tasks folder store tasks in this folder

template (Excel) Worksheets that are already set up to track certain kinds of data, such as sales reports, invoices, and purchase orders

template (Outlook) an existing rule provided by Outlook that contains specific pieces that can be customized to create new rules

template (PowerPoint) a predesigned presentation

template (Word) a predesigned document

tentative an activity is scheduled for this time period, but the activity might not occur; You might be available for other activities

text box a container that holds text on a slide

Text pane the fly-out pane that allows you to key information for a SmartArt diagram

theme a scheme of complementing colors

thumbnail a small picture of a page or slide

tiles Arrange windows so that they display without overlapping Tile horizontally to stack windows one above the other; Tile vertically to arrange windows side by side

title descriptive text that is automatically aligned to an axis or centered at the top of a chart

To Do Bar new feature that summarizes information about appointments and tasks

to-do item any Outlook item flagged for follow-up

top-level shape in an organization chart, the person or department at the head of the organization

U

undo cancel or undo your last command

unhide to make a hidden workbook, worksheet, row, or column visible

Unread Mail standard Search folder that displays unread messages

V

validation rule expression that limits the values that can be entered in the field

validation text specifies the text in the error message that appears when users violate a validation rule

vertical alignment how text is positioned between the top and bottom margins of the page

virtual folder a folder that does not contain the actual items it displays

W

warning icon icon that appears in speech user interface when speech recognition is busy

watermark text or graphic that is printed lightly behind text on a page

widow a line of text that is left alone at the top of a page

wildcard symbol that represents a character or multiple characters in a search string

Wizard consists of steps that walk you through completing a process in Microsoft Office applications

WordArt a feature used to turn text into a formatted graphic

workbook an Excel file that can contain multiple worksheets

worksheet an Excel document used to organize numerical data that can then be analyzed or otherwise manipulated

Z

zero-length string contains no characters and is used to indicate that no value exists for a field

zoom make a worksheet appear bigger (zoom in) or smaller (zoom out) on your screen

Index

A

Absolute cell reference, 460
Accent color, 390
Accepting Task dialog box, 1097
Accept Proposal button, 1075
Access
　change views in, 737–739
　create and modify queries, 871–893
　create database tables, 749–763
　create forms, 832–847
　create reports, 854–866
　database basics, 731–732
　database tools, 743–744
　defining data needs and types, 739–744
　modify tables and fields, 794–819
　navigate in, 730–739
　opening screen, 730
　work with tables/database records, 768–789
Access Help, 16–18, 40–42, 730, 902
Access Options dialog box, 902, 904
Accessories folder, 30–31
Accounting format, 386
Action, 606–608, 984
Action Settings dialog box, 607–608
Active cell, 322, 337, 339–341, 349
Active item, 29
Active window, 63, 65
Add Entrance Effect dialog box, 614–615
Add Existing Fields button, 834, 859, 861
Add-ins, 306–307, 322
Addition, create formula to perform, 455–456
Add New Category window, 1111–1112
Add New Field column, 808–809
Add Printer Wizard, 14
Address book, 1041
Address Cards view, 1012
Add Space After Paragraph, 178
Add Space Before Paragraph, 178
Add word to dictionary dialog box, 98
Adjust group, 286, 288–289, 673, 675, 677
Advanced Filter/Sort, 866, 889, 891
Advanced Layout dialog box, 288
Advanced options, in Word, 302–304
Advanced sort criteria, 890
AIFE file format, 691
Align Button, 688
Align Center, 688
Align Left, 688

Alignment
　in PowerPoint
　　automatic, 669
　　justify, 564, 581
　　of paragraphs, 562–564
　　text, 579–580
　in Word, 174–176
Alignment commands, 176, 359–360
Alignment group, 261, 366
Align Middle, 688
Align Right, 688
Align Text Left, 564
Align Text Right, 564
Align Top, 688
Allow Multiple Values property, 814, 816
Allow Text to Be Dragged and Dropped checkbox, 235
Allow Value List Edits property, 816
Allow Zero Length field property, 802, 804
All Programs menu, 30–31, 34
Alt+Enter property sheet for object, 795
Animation
　add built-in, 612–613
　create customized, 614–617
　defined, 613
　modify, 613–614
Annotate slides, with pen pointer, 716–717
Append Only field property, 802, 805
Apply Names dialog box, 466
Apply to selected pictures only check box, 289, 678
Appointment Recurrence window, 1052, 1076–1077
Appointment(s), 934
　create, from message, 1053–1054
　create, from task, 1055–1056
　defined, 1050
　managing, 1050–1057
　mark, as private, 1056
　one-time, 1051
　recurring, 1051–1053
Appointment window, 1050–1052, 1054
Archive, 969
Archive Outlook items, 969–971
Archive Package, 719
Area chart, 485, 645
Arrange All, 119–121, 326
Arrange group, 687
Arrange tools, 684
Arrange Windows dialog box, 417
Arrow. *See* Dialog Box Launcher
Arrow pointer, 716
Ascending order
　in Access, 780, 843–845, 864
　in Excel, 431, 435, 438–439
　in Word, 259
ASF file format, 693

Aspect ratio, 673, 702
Aspect theme colors, 597
Assets template database, 753
Assigned task
　assign, 1095–1096
　report status of, 1098–1099
　respond to, 1097–1098
Assistant, 649
Attachment
　defined, 951
　open, 953–954
　preview, 950–951
　save, 951–953
　send, 949–950
　send contact as, 1009
Attachment data type, 742, 778
Attachment dialog box, 817
Attachment field, 778, 817–819
Attachments dialog box, 778
Attendees
　add and update new, 1075
　determine when to meet, 1066–1068
　invite, 1065–1066
Attributes, 362
AU file format, 691
Author property, 15
AutoArchive, 969–970
AutoComplete, 338–339
AutoCorrect: English (U.S) dialog box, 298–299
AutoCorrect dialog box, 300
Auto fill, 342–343
AutoFilter, 439–441
AutoFit button and menu, 255
AutoFit Column Width, 384–385
AutoFit Contents, 256
AutoFit Window, 256
AutoFormat, apply, 840–842, 861–862
AutoFormat Attributes to Apply, 841
AutoFormat dialog box, 841, 862
AutoFormat group, 840–842
AutoFormat menu, 862
AutoFormat options, 840
AutoFormat Wizard, 842, 862
Automated replies, 959–960
Automatically align, 669
Automatic page break, 397
AutoNumber data type, 740, 774, 802
AutoPreview, 947–948
AutoRecover feature, in Word, 301–302
AutoSum function, 467–468
AVERAGE function, 260, 469, 471–473
AVI file format, 693
Axis. *See* Chart axis

B

Back button, 49–50
Back-end file, 912

Background, 25–26, 196–197. *See also* Theme background
Background Color section, 363
Background Styles gallery, 599
Back up, 68
Backup, 900–901
Badges, 10
Ball Point Pen, 717
Banded row style, 444
Banner, 277–279, 702, 1057
Bar chart, 485–486, 645
Basic shapes, insert, 680–681
Black Screen, 717
Blank cells, 439
Blank database, create, 754–756
Blank Database pane, 755–756
Blank document, 114
Blank Form tool, 837
Blank presentation, open, 526–527
Blank slide, 506, 528–529
Block arrow shape, 278
Block Cycle layout, 652
Blue text link, 41
BMP file format, 666
Bold, 155, 159. *See also* Formatting
Border, 674
　around cells, 367–368
　around paragraphs, 182–183
　formatting, 578–580
　insert page, 198
Border line, change, 489–490
Borders and Shading dialog box, 182–183, 198
Boundary, 383–387
Bound Column property, 816
Brightness, adjust picture, 284–174, 673
Bring Forward, 687
Bring to Front, 687
Browsed at a kiosk (full screen), 713
Browsed by an individual (window), 713, 715
Browse Office Help list, 18
Browse Office 2007 Help list, 18
Bubble chart, 485
Building blocks
　create, 231–232
　defined, 230
　use built-in, 229–230
Building Blocks Organizer, 229–230
Built-in animation, 612–613
Built-in building blocks, 229–230
Built-in formula, 447–448
Built-in margin, 396–398
Built-in theme, 388–389
Bulleted list, 540
　convert, to diagram, 652–653
　create in Word, 179–180
　defined, 568
　gallery of styles, 567
Bulleted text, 272, 574, 620, 650–651

1147

1148 | Index

Bullets and Numbering dialog box, 566–567, 619
Bullets menu, 263
Business card. *See* Electronic business card
Business letter, start, 133–134
Business template, 751
Busy option, 1051
Button, defined, 25–26

C

Calculator, 31
Calculator—View menu, 89
Calendar, 1050–1057
Calendar button, 927, 929
Calendar folder, 929, 933, 1051, 1054–1057, 1064, 1070–1071, 1074–1076, 1078, 1080, 1112–1113
Cancel, meeting, 1075–1076
Can't rename table message, 797
Caption property field, 807
Cascade, 62–64
Case, change in Word, 159–160
Case-sensitive criteria, 437
Categorized Mail Search Folder, 1113
Category property, 15
Cc, 941–942
CD drive, 39
CD format, store presentation on, 719
Cell attributes, 438, 442
Cell reference, 460–461
Cell(s), 322
  add new, to worksheet, 357–358
  align contents, 361
  change direction of text in table, 259
  change position of text in, 259–260
  clear formatting, 375
  defined, 248
  delete, from worksheet, 358–359
  enter data in, 328
  manually format contents, 359–368
  merge and split, 260–261, 366–367
  perform calculations in, 259–260
  place hyperlink in, 371–372
  placing borders around, 367–368
  remove duplicate, from worksheet, 434–435
  restrict entries to certain data types, 431–433
  select, 359–360
  select, edit, delete contents of, 329–331
  and specific values, 433
  unmerge, 366
  use ranges in formulas, 463–466
  wrap text in, 365–366
Cells group, 359–361, 385
Cell Size group, 258
Cell Size options, 386
Cell style, 369–371
Centered alignment, 175–176
Change case, 155, 159–160

Change lookup column message, 815
Character, 362
  defined, 157
  display non-printing, 187–188
  formatting, in Word, 155–161
  wildcard, 237, 776–778
Character formats, 561–562
Character spacing, 559–560
Character style, 163
Chart
  building, 639–645
  defined, 641
  formatting, with Quick Styles, 645–646
  insert, from content placeholder, 639–642
Chart area, 488
Chart axis, 488, 492
Chart diagram, 648
Chart elements
  add, 491–492
  delete, 492–494
  list of, 488
  move, 493
  use mouse to select, 489
Chart Elements box, 489
Chart layout, apply different, 643–644
Chart Layout gallery, 646
Chart Quick Styles gallery, 647–648
Chart(s)
  add elements to, 489–490
  build, 480–484
  change border line, 487–488
  choose, for data, 482–483
  create, 480
  defined, 480
  delete, 482
  delete elements from, 490–491
  format, with Quick Style, 485
  format data series, 488
  manually format parts of, 486–489
  modify, 489–492
  modify legend, 488–489
  move, 491
  resize, 491–492
  select data to include in, 480–481
  See also entries for individual charts
Charts Dialog Box Launcher, 482, 486
Charts group, 486
Chart Sheet, 483, 493
Chart subtype, 485–486
Chart title, 488, 639, 644
Chart Tools, 642
Chart type
  change from two-dimensional, to three-dimensional, 643
  choose, 642–643
  choose different, 643
  list of, 485
  See also entries for individual chart types
Choose a SmartArt Graphic dialog box, 271, 647–649, 652
Choose File dialog box, 817
Choose Location dialog box, 719
Classic Photo Album template, 532

Clear, 337
Clear All Filters, 784, 845, 866
Clear All Sorts button, 779–781, 843, 863, 889, 891
Clear command, 375
Clear filter from field name command, 866
Clear Formatting command, 155, 161–162, 188–189
Clear Highlighting, 236
Click, defined, 25
Clip art
  add, to slide, 662–665
  defined, 275, 664
  insert, from file, 666–667
  insert and resize, 274–275
Clip art on Office Online, 665
Clip Art pane, 274–275
Clip Art task pane, 273, 659–663, 691
Clipboard, 66–68, 231–232
Clipboard Dialog Box Launcher, 335, 343–345
Clipboard group, 160, 335, 343–344, 366–367. *See also entries for individual commands*
Clipboard task pane, 231–232, 344–345
Clipboard tools, 515
Clip Organizer, 663
Close, 4–6, 112, 119, 504
Clustered bar chart, 484
Collapse arrow, 61
Collapsed, 60–61
Collect Without Showing Office Clipboard, 343, 345
Color
  adjust picture, 284–285
  change chart's fill color, 486–487
  changing, of worksheet tab, 390–391
  customize theme by selecting, 387–388
  insert page, 194
  See also Document theme; Font
Color Categories dialog box, 985
Color category
  assign Outlook items to, 1105–1106
  defined, 1105
  modify and create, 1107–1108
  search for item by category, 1109
  sort items by, 1108
Colored background, 194–195
Color/grayscale drop-down list, 546
Color scale, 372–373
Colors dialog box, 179–180, 361, 569
Column break, 216
Column chart, 482–483, 643
Column Count property, 814
Column heading, 383, 391
Column Heads property, 814
Column labels, 320
Column(s), 320
  add and remove, in table, 443–444
  change widths of, 219–220
  create, 218
  defined, 218
  format, 219

format entire, 383–384
headings for, 49–50
hide and unhide, 384–385
insert or delete, 380–381
move, 254–255
remove duplicate, from worksheet, 432–433
resize, 252–254
set, in text box, 582–584
width of, 380–383
Columns dialog box, 219–220, 584
Column shortcut menu, 806
COM Add-ins dialog box, 304–305
Command, defined, 8
Commas, selecting, in speech recognition, 96–97
Comments property, 15
Common filters, 842–844
Communicate group, 1012
Compact, 1113
Compact and Repair command, 899–890
Company name, contacts grouped by, 1008
Composite key, 773
Compress, defined, 287
Compression Settings dialog box, 287, 675
Compress Pictures dialog box, 286–287, 675–676
Computer, protect, 305–306
Computer folder, 51
Computer monitor, displaying slides on, 704
Condition, of message rule, 982
Conditional formatting
  allow multiple rules to be true, 372
  apply specific, 372–373
  defined, 370–371
  filter data using, 439–440
  sort data by using, 435–436
  use Rule Manage to apply, 371–372
Conditional Formatting Rules Manager, 371–372
Conditional Rule Manager, 371
Connection Status menu, 17–18
Constant, 453
Constrain, 678
Contact(s)
  in Address Cards view, 1012
  create, from blank contact, 1004–1006
  create, from electronic business card, 1032–1033
  create, from existing contact, 1006
  create, from message header, 1011–1012
  defined, 1003
  grouped by company name, 1012
  modify information, 1007–1008
  in Phone List view, 1012
  save, received in Outlook format, 1009–1010
  save information, 1009–1010
  search for, 1035–1036
  search for items related to, 1037–1038
  send, as attachment, 1012–1013
  view and delete, 1012–1013

Index | 1149

Contacts button, 927
Contacts folder, 930, 932, 1003
Contacts window, 1003, 1005–1007, 1014–1015
Content controls, 202
Content placeholder, 639–642, 664–665. *See also* Text placeholder
Contents of computer folder, 61
Context menu, 34
Continuous section break, 219
Contrast, adjust picture, 286–288, 675
Convert Text to Table command, 250
Convert to Range, 446
Convert to SmartArt gallery, 652–653
Copies group, 548
Copy, 251, 337, 518
   cell formatting with Format Painter, 368–369
   data, 344–347
   files and folders, 67–69
   text, in Word, 233–235
   worksheet, 411–412
Copy and Paste commands, 67–68, 70
Copy pointer, 344
Copy to Folder dialog box, 718–719
COUNTA function, 468–469
COUNT function, 468
Create Back-end Database dialog box, 912
Create Building Block dialog box, 231–232
Create from Selection dialog box, 464–465
Create Graphic group, 651
Create New Folder button, 13
Create New Folder dialog box, 965, 978–979
Create New Theme Colors dialog box, 390, 597–598
Create Rule dialog box, 988
Criteria
   and AutoFilter, 439
   defined, 431
   sort data in single criterion, 435–436
   sort data on multiple, 436–437
   See also Query criterion
Crop, 670–671
Ctrl+; (enter current date), 340
Ctrl+: (enter current time), 340
Ctrl+Arrow (move to start and end of data ranges), 327
Ctrl+C (copy), 345, 347
Ctrl+C copy command, 233
Ctrl+C copy database object, 760
Ctrl+D (fill cell), 342
Ctrl+End shortcut key, 124
Ctrl+Enter manual page break, 218
Ctrl+F (Find and Replace dialog box), 420
Ctrl+G (Go To dialog box), 424
Ctrl+Home shortcut key, 124
Ctrl+K (insert hyperlink), 371
Ctrl+L (align left), 361
Ctrl+Page Up shortcut key, 124
Ctrl+P paste command, 234

Ctrl+R (align right), 342, 361
Ctrl+(switch between formulas and values), 474
Ctrl+V (paste), 345–346
Ctrl+V paste database, 761
Ctrl+X cut command, 233
Ctrl+Y (insert row or column), 383
Ctrl+Y (redo), 348
Ctrl+Z (undo), 348, 362
Currency data type, 742
Currency format category, 365
Currency value ($) character, 341
Current item, 29
Current slide, defined, 509
Custom Animation task pane, 613–614, 616, 653
Custom filter box, 781
Custom Filter dialog box, 844–845, 892
Customize AutoFormat dialog box, 842
Customize Classic Start Menu dialog box, 32
Customized animation, 614–617
Customized Start menu, 34
Customize Keyboard dialog box, 305
Customize options screen, in Word, 305–306
Customize Quick Access Toolbar button, 306
Customize Start Menu dialog box, 32, 34
Custom Margin, 203, 398
Custom Search Folder window, 1038
Custom show
   create, 590–591
   defined, 708–710
Custom Shows dialog box, 708–709
Cut, 337, 344–348, 359
Cut and Paste command, 66–68
Cut command, 251, 257, 517–518
Cut text, 233–234
Cycle category of SmartArt graphics, 273
Cycle diagram, 652

D

Data
   choose chart for, 482–483
   copy and paste, 343–345
   cut and paste, 345–346
   filter, 437–440, 777, 779–781
   filter, with common filters, 842–844
   filter, within query, 889–891
   filter, within report, 862–864
   find and replace, 773–775
   locate, with Find command, 418–419
   populate worksheet with, 336–340
   refer to, in another worksheet or workbook, 459–460
   replace, with Replace command, 420
   restrict cell entries to certain data type, 429–431

   select, to include in chart, 480–481
   sort, 433–437
   sort, within form, 840–842
   sort, within query, 886–889
   sort, within report, 860–862
   summarize, with functions, 464–468
Data bar, 374–375
Database
   backup, 900–901
   compact and repair, 901–902
   configure options for, 902–904
   create, 749–756
   create blank, 754–756
   defined, 731
   encrypt and decrypt, 905–907
   split, 911–912
   use template to create, 749–754
   See also Record(s); Table, database; *and entries for specific databases*
Database documenter, 908–909
Database management system (DBMS), 731, 813
Database object, 735, 760, 762–763
Database splitter, 912
Database Splitter Wizard, 904, 911
Database Tools tab, 904. *See also entries for individual commands*
Data file
   change settings, 1116–1117
   create, 1114–1115
   select, for mail account, 1115–1116
Data File Management option, 1116
Data labels, 488, 491–493
Data marker, 484–485, 639, 646
Data series, 639, 646
   chart for, 484–485
   copy, with mouse, 344
   defined, 484
   format, 490
   move, with mouse, 344–345
Datasheet form, 837–840
Datasheet view
   Access table in, 738–739
   blank record in, 771
   enter data in, 756
   set field properties in, 800–801
Data tab
   ensure data integrity, 431–435
   filter data, 439–442
   set up data in table format, 444–446
   sort, 435–439
   subtotal data, 442–444
   See also entries for individual commands and groups
Data type, 806
   define, for fields, 740–742
   defined, 741–742
   See also entries for individual types
Data Type & Formatting group, 818
Data validation, 432–434
Data validation rules, 805–806. *See also* Validation rule field property

Date
   in Excel, 339–340, 439, 474
   in PowerPoint
     insert, 603–605
     placeholder for, 705
Date and Time dialog box, 89–90
Date format, 340, 365
Date Navigator, 934
Date/Time data type, 740–741
DBMS. *See* Database management system (DBMS)
Decimal (.) character, 341
Decimal Places field property, 802
Decrease Font Size, 361
Decrease List Level, 539
Decrypting, 905–906
Default, defined, 361
Default column width, 382, 384–385
Default General format, 457
Default mail folders, 966
Default Office theme, 389
Default row height, 384
Default Start menu, 33
Default value field property, 800
Default view table property, 796
Default Width, 385
Define Custom Show dialog box, 708–709
Define Name, 464–465
Delete
   cells, 359
   chart, 484
   chart elements, 492–493
   column or row, 382–383
   worksheet from workbook, 416
   See also Recycle Bin
Delete button, 13
Delete Column command, 810
Delete confirmation dialog box, 55
Delete dialog box, 359
Deleted items folder, empty, 969
Deleted Items mail folder, 966
Delete field confirmation message, 811
Delete field message, 811
Delete menu, 772–773
Delete Record, 771–773
Delete slide, 509
Delete table confirmation message, 798
Delivery, package presentation for, 719
Descending order
   in Access, 780, 843–845, 864
   in Excel, 431, 435
   in Word, 259
Description table property, 796
Design tab, 252, 394, 444, 882. *See also entries for individual commands*
Design view
   create form in, 834–836
   create report in, 859–861
   query in, 883
   table in, 738–739
Desktop, 5, 25–36
Destination location, 67
Detail, 861
Details pane, 49–50

Developer, 322
Diagram. *See* SmartArt diagram
Dialog box, defined, 8
Dialog Box Launcher, 8, 155, 158–159, 363, 494
Digital camera, 39
Digital video camcorder, 39
Disk drives, 39
Display Control property, 816
Display delete confirmation dialog check box, 55
Display Form menu, 902
Display Navigation Pane checkbox, 902, 904
Display Views on SharePoint table property, 796
Distribution list
  create, 1013–1015
  defined, 1013
  modify, 1015–1016
  selected members window, 1014
  untitled window, 1014
Division, formula to perform, 457–458
Document
  in Access, 777–778
  in Word
    change appearance of, 135–140
    change views, 115–116
    choose different file format, 134–135
    create, 133–137
    editing, 228–246, 316–317
    find text in, 235–237
    format, using document theme, 137–139
    formatting add content to header or footer, 201–202
    add page numbers, 199
    add watermark, 196–197
    choose paper size, 204
    insert header or footer, 199–201
    insert page border, 198
    insert page color, 196
    select page orientation, 202–204
    set margins, 202–203
    format using Quick Styles, 135–137
    insert blank page into, 222
    navigate, 122–124, 238–241
    print, 140–142
    replace text in, 237–238
    title for, 114
    use Quick Parts to add content to, 229–232
    work with existing, 114–127
Documenter dialog box, 908–909
Document file, on opening screen, 4
Document Information Panel, 14
Document map, 238–243
Document properties, 15–16
Documents folder, 51
Document theme
  in Excel
    built-in, 388–389
    choose, for worksheet, 388–389
    customize, by selecting colors, 389–390
    customize, by selecting font and font effects, 390–391
  defined, 385
  in Word
    format document using, 137–140
    Theme Colors, 138–139
    Theme Effects, 138, 140
    Theme Fonts, 138–139
Document Views group, 115
Donut chart, 485
Double-headed arrow, 255–256
Double left arrow button, 858
Double right arrow button, 858
Down Arrow shortcut key, 124
Downloading Template dialog box, 753
Drafts mail folder, 968
Draft view, 116–117
Drag-and-drop, 66–68
  in Excel, 344
  in Word, 233, 254
Drawing tools, 275
Drawing Tools Format, 570, 573, 678–683, 687–689
Draw lines, 678–680
Draw Table command, 250
Duplicate Contact Detected window, 1009–1010, 1032
Duplicates dialog box, 434–435
Duplicate value, 432–433
DVD, store presentation on, 719
DVD drive, 39

E

Edit Business Card window, 1025, 1027
Edit/Delete menu, 786
Edit Hyperlink dialog box, 606
Editing
  in Outlook, 1027–1030
  in Word, 223–246, 316–317
  copy and move text, 233–235
  drag-and-drop, 235
  find text, 235–237
  navigate in long document, 238–241
  Quick Parts to add content to document, 229–232
  replace text, 237–238
Editing group, 126, 337, 375, 436, 468
Edit Name dialog box, 465
Edit Relationship dialog box, 785, 787
Edit Signature box, 957, 1033
Education template, 750–751
Effect Options dialog box, 614, 616
Effects, 614–616
Electronic business card
  create contact from, 1032–1033
  editing, 1027–1030
  send, 1030–1031
  use, in signature, 1033–1035
Electronic postage software, 145
Embedded chart, 483, 493–494
Embedded object, 277
Embedded worksheet, 637
Embedding TrueType fonts, 719
Emphasis effects, 616
Enable AutoComplete, 338
Encrypting, 905–907
End shortcut key, 124
Enforce Referential Integrity, 787
Entrance effects, 616
Envelope, 143–147, 210
Envelopes and Labels dialog box, 144–145, 147
E-postage Properties button, 145, 147
Equal sign (=), 260, 455
Erase All Ink on Slide command, 717
Error Alert, 432–433
Error checking, 902, 904
Esc key
  to cancel search, 236
  to restore arrow pointer, 716
  specify show loop continuously, 713
Even Page break, 219
Event, 1057
Excel
  basic formulas and functions, 454–494
  creating and editing workbook, 337–375
  Home tab, 337
  insert chart in PowerPoint, 640–641
  managing worksheets, 410–424
  opening screen, 322
  views in, 322–324, 326, 393, 462
  working with data, 431–446
  worksheet formatting, 382–400
Excel dialog box, 366
Excel Ribbon, 635. *See also* Ribbon
Excel Spreadsheet command, 637
Excel worksheet, 635–637
Exception, of message rule, 981, 984
Exclamation point, in formula, 462
Exit command, 6
Exit effects, 616
Expand arrow, 61
Expanded, 60–61
Expanded Query Builder, 1036–1037, 1113
Expression Builder, 805
Extensible markup language (XML) format, 531
External out of office message, 960

F

Featured Online Templates, 749, 754
Felt Tip Pen, 717
Field
  in Access
    create, 807–810
    create multi-valued field, 811–813
    define data types for, 740–742
    define input masks for, 803–804
    delete, 810–811
    modify multi-valued, 814
    size of, 806
  in Word
    defined, 231
    insert, from Quick Parts, 230–231
Field code, 231
Field dialog box, in Word, 230
Field List, 810, 816, 834–837, 860–861, 884
Field properties, 799–807
  define text length, 801
  fig., 799
  modify, 800–801
  set, in datasheet view, 800–801
Fields & Columns group, 777, 807–819. *See also* entries for individual commands
Field size field property, 802
Fields List pane, 859, 861
Fields Templates menu, 777
Field template, 807, 809
File
  defined, 29
  delete, 55–56
  move, 66
File as field, 1006
File format
  choose different, 530–531
  choose different, in Word, 134–135
  save workbook in different, 350–351
File list, 49–50, 61
Filename, 326
Filename extension, 326
File New Database dialog box, 752
Files of Type menu, 12
Fill, 337
Fill color, 363
Fill command, 342–343
Fill effects, 387. *See also* Document theme
Fill Effects dialog box, 196
Fill formatting, 342–343
Fill handle, 342–343
Fill options, 337, 342–343, 571
Filter by form, 846–847
Filter data, 431, 439–442, 779, 781–783
Filtered query, 892
Filtered/Unfiltered button, 783
Filter Indicator, 771
Filter menu, 781–783, 892
Filter On Load table property, 796
FilterOnLoan property, 866
Filter(s), 37, 436
  data within query, 891–893
  data within report, 864–866
  filter data with common, 844–846
  remove, 783–784
Filter table property, 796
Find All, 421
Find and Replace dialog box, 236–238, 420–422, 776–777
Find dialog box, 236
Find Duplicates Query Wizard, 874–876
Find Next, 421–422
Find Printer button, 547
Find & Select feature, 424
Find Unmatched Query Wizard, 879–881
Find What box, 776
First-line indent, 173–174
First Name box, 752
First normal form (1NF), 742

Index | 1151

Fit slide to current window button, 511
Fixed Column Width, 256
Flash drive, 39
Floating object, 288
Flowchart, in Word, 280–281
Folder
    copy to different, 67–68
    create and move mail folder, 964–966
    create and rename, 53–55
    defined, 29, 930
    delete, 55–56
    delete and restore, 966–967
    move, 66
    move messages to different, 967–968
    select items in, 52–53
    See also Window; *and entries for specific folders*
Folders button, 49–50
Folders list, 60–61, 925, 930–931
Folder window, 37–39, 49–51
Font
    change, 155–157
    choose, 361
    color of, 155, 159, 362, 560–561
    customize document theme by selecting, 390–391
    defined, 361
    size of, 155, 361, 556–558, 651
    See also Document theme; Theme fonts
Font command, 359
Font dialog box, 7, 159, 363, 560
Font effects, 390–391, 558.
    See also Document theme
Font group, 155, 363, 367, 556.
    See also entries for individual commands and tabs
Font group's dialog box launcher, 560
Font menu, 156–157
Font Size menu, 156
Font Size tool, 557
Font styles, apply, 558
Font tool, 557
Footer, 603–605, 705, 861
    add content to, 201–202, 395–396
    defined, 201, 394
    insert, 199–201
    insert predefined, 395
    margins for, 398
    visible in Page Layout View, 393
Foreign key, 774
Form
    create, in Design view, 834–836
    create, in Layout view, 836–837
    create datasheet form, 837–840
    create simple, 832–833
    sort data within, 842–844
    Format, 188–189, 439
Format Background dialog box, 600–601
Format Cells dialog box, 7, 323–324, 363–364, 367, 371, 459
Format commands, 383
Format Data Series dialog box, 488
Format dialog box, 489
Format field property, 802

Format Page Numbers command, 199
Format Painter, 161–162, 368–369, 385, 561–562
Format Picture dialog box, 675
Format Shape dialog box, 290
Format Shapes, 682–684
Format tab, to format chart elements, 489
Format Text Effects dialog box, 570
Formatting
    apply fill and border, to text box, 578–580
    charts with Quick Styles, 645–646
    clear, 375
    copy character formats with Format Painter, 561–562
    data series, 490
    defined, 558
    manually, cell contents, 359–368
    manually, parts of chart, 488–491
    with Quick Style, 487
    set options for text box, 577–580
    shapes, 682–684
    of WordArt graphic, 570–573
    worksheet, 381–400
    See also Conditional formatting
Formatting characters, 155–161
Formatting paragraphs, in Word, 171–194
Form Design button, 836
Form filter, 846
Forms group, 832. *See also entries for individual commands*
Forms objects, 735
Form tool, 833
Formula bar, 322
    defined, 339
    for editing, 455
    formula always displayed in, 459–460
    numeric values in, 340
Formula dialog box, in Word, 259–260
Formula(s), 454
    addition, 455–456
    basic, 455–458
    built-in, 447–448
    cell ranges in, 463–466
    cell references in, 458–463
    control appearance of, 473–474
    controlling appearance of, 473–474
    create, operating on named range, 466–470
    create subtotals, 471–473
    defined, 259–260, 455
    display, on screen, 473–474
    division, 457–458
    exclamation point in, 462
    in Formula bar, 459–460
    multiplication, 456
    print, 474
    structure of, 457
    subtraction, 456
    summarize data with functions, 466–470
    using cell ranges in, 463–466
    using cell references in, 458–463

    using relative cell reference in, 458–460
    using templates with built-in, 447–448
    See also entries for individual commands and groups
Form view, 835
Form Wizard, 838–840
Forward a message button, 940, 948
Forward button, 49–50
Fraction (/) character, 341
Frame slides, 548
Free option, 1051
Freeze, 419–420
Front-end file, 912
Full Screen Reading view, 115–116
Function, 260
Function Arguments dialog box, 467–470
Function Library group, 468
Function(s), 466–470. *See also entries for individual functions*

G

Gadgets, 25
Gallery. *See individual galleries*
General and Compatibility options, in Word, 304
General format, 364–365, 457
Getting Started help topic, 41
Getting Started with Microsoft Office Access, 730–732, 755, 754. *See also entries for individual options*
GIF file format, 666
Glow color, 677
Google Desktop Search Office Add-in, 307
Go To command, 238–239
Go To feature, 387, 422–424
Go To Special dialog box, 422–423
Grammar, checking in Word, 127
Grammar Settings dialog box, 300–301
Grayscale mode, 548
Greater than operator, 441
Greater than or equal to operator, 441
Green text link, 41
Gridline, 117–118, 256, 391, 393, 667–669, 681
Gridlines and Guides dialog box, 668–669
Group, defined, 506. *See also entries for individual groups*
Group, Sort, and Total pane, 863–864
Group data, 431, 442–443
Group Footer, 861
Group Header, 861
Groups, 7, 730
Group schedule, 1068
Group worksheets, 416–418
Grow, 155
Guides, 667–669

H

Handout, 546, 703–705
Handout Master tab, 705
Handout Master view, 703
Hanging indent, 173–174

Hard disk, 39
Hard disk drive, 39
Header, 605, 705, 861
    add content to, 201–202, 395–396
    defined, 201, 394
    insert, 199–201
    insert predefined, 395
    margins for, 398
    message, 1011–1012
Header & Footer group, 199, 201, 393–395
Header & Footer Tools, 200–202
Header row, create, 257–258
Help and Support, 40–41, 80
Help button, on opening screen, 4
Help command, 506
Hidden slide, display, 714–715
Hide command, 386–387, 414–415, 418–419
Hide Slide button, 706–707
Hierarchy category of SmartArt graphics, 273
Hierarchy layout, 647–649
Highlighter, 717
Highlight text, 160–161
High quality, 548
Home shortcut key, 124
Home tab, 126, 556
    AutoSum function, 467–468
    Cells group on, 383
    format cells and ranges, 356
    placement on Ribbon, 337
    See also entries for individual commands and groups
Horizontal alignment, 175–176, 257
Horizontal axis, 492, 639
Horizontal gridline, 639
Http://, 371
Hyperlink
    add to slide, 605–606
    color for built-in document theme, 389
    defined, 371
    edit, 372
    place, in cell, 371–372
    remove, 372
Hyperlink data type, 742

I

I-beam, 127, 516–517
Icons, 28. *See also entries for specific icons*
Icon set, 374–375
Illustrations group, 271. *See also entries for individual commands*
Illustrator, 687
IME Mode field property, 802
Import, 1041–1042
Inbox mail folder, 966
Increase Font Size, 361
Increase List Level, 539–539
Indent, 172–174, 538–539
Index, 35
Indexed field property, 802
Indexed location, 35
Inline object, 288
Innermost field, 781
Input Mask field property, 802–804, 806
Input Mask Wizard message, 803–804

Input Method Editor, 802
Insert
  column or row, 382–383
  new worksheet into workbook, 415–416
  predefined header or footer, 395
  See also Paste
Insert Address button, 144, 146–147
Insert Business Card window, 1031, 1033
Insert Chart dialog box, 486, 642
Insert dialog box, 357–358, 415–416
Insert Function dialog box, 467, 469–470
Insert group, 201
Insert Hyperlink dialog box, 605
Insertion point, 55, 114, 127
Insert Item dialog box, 950
Insert Object dialog box, 637
Insert Outline dialog box, 537
Insert Picture dialog box, 276–277
Insert SmartArt Graphic icon, 647
Insert subtotal, 431
Insert tab, 271
  build charts, 482–486
  format chart with Quick Style, 487
  manually format parts of chart, 488–491
  modify chart, 491–494
  See also entries for individual commands and groups
Insert Table dialog box, 249, 633
Insert Worksheet tab, 415
Instant Search feature, 1037
Instant Search Query Builder field, 1128–1129
Instant Search results, 1096
Interactive whiteboard, 706
Internal out of office message, 957–958
Invalid Entry, 432, 446
Issues database template, 747
Italic, 155, 159. *See also* Formatting
Item, in Outlook, 924, 926

J

JPEG file format, 666
Junk E-mail mail folder, 966
Justify alignment, 175–176, 564, 581

K

Keep Lines Together command, 215–216
Keep On Top, 18
Keep with Next command, 216
Keyboard
  navigate presentation from, 513
  navigate records using, 769–770
Keyboard commands, for navigating records, 770
Keyboard shortcut document, 10, 124
Keystroke, use, to navigate Word document, 123–124
KeyTips, 9–10
  apply italic formatting, 558
  center-align text, 564
  Copy command, 517
  Cut command, 518
  exit from Slide Show view, 549
  left-align text, 564

open new, blank presentation, 526
open Print dialog box, 547
Paste command, 517
remove all annotations on slide, 717
repeat last issued command, 559
show or hide guides, 668
switch to Slide Show view, 509
undo delete text box, 586
Keyword
  assign, 15–16
  defined, 16, 664
Keywords property, 15

L

Label
  create, in Word, 153
  data, 488, 491–492
  defined, 338
  entering, 338–339
  print, in Word, 146–148
  Short/Over, 466
  See also AutoComplete
Labels Options dialog box, 147–148
Landscape orientation, 204, 398–399, 700–701
Large Mail search folder, 1040
Layers palette, 687
Layout, 527–528. *See also entries for individual layouts*
Layout gallery, 528
Layout tab, 254. *See also entries for individual commands*
Layout tab command, 491–492
Layout view, create form in, 836–837
Leaders, 187
Left-aligned, 175–176
Left Arrow shortcut key, 124
Left indent marker, 173–174
Legend, 488, 490–491, 639
Legend keys, 488–489
Less than operator, 441
Less than or equal to operator, 441
Letter, create, 209
Limit To List property, 816
Line. *See* Document theme
Line chart, 484–485, 645
Lines, 678–680
Line spacing
  defined, 177
  set paragraph, 564–565
  set within paragraph, 176–178
Line spacing menu, 176
Line Spacing option, 564–565
Link Child Fields table property, 796
Linked, 637
Linked files, 719
Linked object, 277
Linked Table Manager, 910–911
Link Master Fields table property, 796
List
  change formatting, 263–264
  change indent levels in, 538–539
  create numbered, 565–566
  create outline-style, 262–263
  multilevel, 262–263
  sort contents of, 263
  subtotal data in, 443–444
  See also Bulleted list
List category of SmartArt graphics, 273

List formatting, 263–264
List Items Edit Form property, 816
List layout, 649
List Rows property, 816
List value, 439
Live preview, 596
Lock *aspect ratio* check box, 673
Lock Aspect Ration box, 284
Logical values, 439
Look for tab, 847
Look In list, 950
Lookup column, 813, 815
Lookup field properties, 814–816
Lookup Wizard, 811–814

M

Magnification. *See* Zoom
Magnifying glass, 141
Mail account, select data file for, 1131–1134
Mail button, 940
Mail folder, 926–927, 930–931, 964–966
Mailing labels, create, 153
Manage Attachments, 778
Manage Task group, 1095
Mandatory meeting invitees, 1065–1066
Manual page break, 217–218, 397
Margins, 202–203, 397–398, 583–584
Match case, 421, 776
Mathematical operator, 455
Matrix category of SmartArt graphics, 273
Matrix layout, 649
MAX function, 470, 472
Maximize, 39
Maximize/Restore Down window, 121–122
Media clips, 690–693. *See also* Movie; Sound
Media field text filters, 844
Meeting organizer, 1072–1073
Meeting request, defined, 1063
Meeting resource, scheduling, 1078–1079
Meeting(s)
  accept proposed new time, 1074–1071
  cancel, 1079–1080
  change time, 1071–1072
  create one-time, 1063–1064
  determine when attendees can meet, 1066–1068
  invite mandatory and optional attendees to, 1065–1066
  propose new time, 1072–1073
  recurring, 1071–1078
  responses to requests for, 1069–1070
  track responses to requests for, 1069–1071
Memo data type, 742
Memo field, 802, 805
Menu, 8, 25
Menu bar, in Outlook, 924, 926
Merge and Center command, 366
Merge cells, 260, 366–367
Merge group, 260
Message area, 941–942
Message bar, 730

Message header, create contact from, 1011–1012
Message list
  open attachment from, 953
  save attachment from, 951–952
Message list button, 940
Message(s)
  add signature to, 956–957
  attach file to, 949–950
  automatically previewing, 945–946
  composing, 939–941
  create appointment from, 1053–1054
  create internal out of office message, 957–958
  create rule to categorize messages from selected, 985–988
  create rule to delete message from scratch, 991
  create rule to forward, by copying existing, 988–990
  create task from, 1087–1088
  forward, 948
  resend, 942–944
  save copy sent message in different location, 944–945
  send, 941–942
  send report to, 946–947
  See also Attachment
Message window, 939
Metro theme, 486
Microphone, 76–79
Microsoft Clip Organizer, 275
Microsoft Exchange Server, 957–958
Microsoft Office
  open and close office applications, 4–6
  opening screen, 4
  Windows basics, 24–42
  Windows Vista Speech Recognition, 76–101
  working in Office window, 6–10
  working with files and folders, 49–70
  working with Microsoft Office Button, 10–16
  working with Microsoft Office Help, 16–18
Microsoft Office Access dialog box, 772, 903
Microsoft Office Access Message box, 905
Microsoft Office application, 5–6
Microsoft Office Button, 10–16
  in Access, 732, 856
  assign keywords, 15–16
  choose printer, 14
  defined, 10–11
  in Excel, 322, 326, 447
  Open Dialog box, 11–13
  open existing document, 11–13
  on opening screen, 4–6
  save document, 13
  set standard properties, 14–15
  in Word, 114, 235
Microsoft Office Help button, 16–18
Microsoft Office Online, 447, 532, 693

Index | 1153

Microsoft Office window
    KeyTips, 9–10
    Mini toolbar, 8
    onscreen tools, 6
    Quick Access toolbar, 8–9
    Ribbon, 6–8
    work in, 6–10
Microsoft Windows Serer 2003, 754
Microsoft Windows Vista, 754
Microsoft Windows XP, 14, 754
MIDI file format, 691
MIN function, 470, 472
Minimize, 4, 39, 114, 121–122
Minimize button, 506
Mini toolbar, 8, 362, 369
Mixed reference, 461
Modify command, 370
Modify Style dialog box, 164–165
More Colors command, 196
More Columns command, 221
More Forms menu, 838
More Shading Colors, 181
More Watermarks command, 197
Motion Path effects, 616
Mouse, 344–345
    defined, 26
    to identify desktop items, 27–28
    navigate document using, 122–123
Mouse pointer, 26, 582
Move Cells dialog box, 345
Move Chart dialog box, 493
Move Items dialog box, 967–968
Move *Item* to window, 1053–1054
Move or Copy dialog box, 411–412
Move pointer, 344
Movie, add, to slide, 692–693
Movie from Clip Organizer, 693
Movie from File, 693
Movie Tools Options tab, 693
MPEG file format, 693
MPS file format, 691
Multi-field primary key, 774–775
Multilevel list, 262–263
Multiple-criteria sort, 436–439
Multiple monitors area, 713
Multiple windows, open and arrange, 62–64
Multiplication, formula to perform, 456
Multi-selection, 126
Multi-valued field, 811–814
Music folder, 51
My Contacts folder, 1041–1042

N

Name box, 322, 328
Name Manager, 464–466
Name ranged, 463–466
Navigate presentation, 511–513
Navigation button, 770–771
Navigation group, 201
Navigation options, in Slide Show view, 715
Navigation pane
    in Access, 730, 733–737, 856
    in Microsoft Office window, 49–50, 59–61
    in Outlook, 924–926
Negative indent, 173–174
Negative numbers, 341
Negative value, 341, 456

Network drive, 39
New button, 940
New E-mail Delivery Location window, 1134
New from Existing Presentation dialog box, 536
New Name, 463–465
New Outlook Data File window, 1130
New Presentation dialog box, 525
New Query dialog box, 872–873
New Search Folder window, 1038
New Signature dialog box, 955, 1033
New Slide button, 533
New Slide gallery, 533
New Time Proposed window, 1073
New Values field property, 802
New window button, 119, 121
New Workbook window, 447
Next Page break, 114, 122–123, 219
Non-printing characters, display, 187–188
Non-text content, tools for adding, 529
Normal cell style, 370
Normal form, 744
Normalization, 743
Normal margin, 398
Normal view, 324, 509–509, 513
Not equal to operator, 441
Notes, 542–543, 925
Notes folder, 929–931
Notes Master button, 705
Notes Page master, 705
Notes Pages, in Print Preview, 546
Notes Page view, 507–509, 512, 543
Notes pane, 507, 509–510, 512, 542–543
Notification area, 25–26
Number commands, 359
Number data type, 742, 802
Numbered list, 178, 565–566
Number format, 178, 363–365, 457
Number group, 364–365
Numbers
    add page numbers to worksheet, 394–395
    entering values, 340–341
    serial, 340
    serial number date system, 474
    See also Date
Numbers value, 439

O

Object Definition report, 909
Object dependencies, identify, 907–908
Object Designers options, 904
Object(s)
    align, 687–688
    crop, 670–671
    group, 688–690
    rotate, 669–670
    set order of, 684–687
    size or scale, 671–674
    See also Picture
Occurrence, 1075–1078
Odd Page break, 219
Office button, 506
Office Clipboard, 345–347
Office Diagnostics program, 902

Office theme, 389
Office window, view of screen, 4
Offline file, 37
OLE object data type, 742
Omit checkbox, 147
1NF. *See* First normal form (1NF)
One-time appointment, 1051
One-time task, create, 1084–1085
One-to-many relationship, 785–786
On-screen tools, 6, 925–926
Onscreen view, use Zoom and Scroll to change, 419–420
On Top button, 18
Open and Repair, 13
Open dialog box, 11–13
Open document, 4, 114
Open in Browser, 13
Opening Mail Attachment dialog box, 953
Opening screen
    in Access, 730
    in Microsoft Word, 114
    in Outlook, 924, 940
    in PowerPoint, 506
Open or Save dialog box, 16
Open Recurring item dialog box, 1078
Open with Transform, 13
Operand, 455
Operators, 441. *See also* Mathematical operator
Optional meeting attendees, 1065–1066
Options dialog box, 719
Options group, 201
Order, 687
Order By On Load property, 796, 844
Order By property, 796
Organization chart
    defined, 647
    figure, 650
    insert, 647–649
Orientation, 204
    adjust slide, 700–702
    defined, 701
    set, 398–399
    See also Page orientation
Orientation table property, 796
Orphan control, 214–215
Orphan record, 787
Or tab, 847
Other Actions button, 943
Other group, 872. *See also entries for individual commands*
Outbox mail folder, 966
Outdenting, 539
Outermost field, 781
Outgoing message, 957. *See also* Message
Outline group, 443
Outline-style list, 262–263
Outline symbol, 443
Outline tab, add text on, 515
Outline view, 117, 546
Outlook
    advanced contact management, 1027–1042
    Appointment window, 1046
    Calendar basics, 1046–1057
    categories and data files, 1125–1135

Color Categories window, 1069
Contact basics, 1001–1016
Edit Business Card window, 1027
email basics, 938–958
Folders List, 964
managing mail with folders, 964–971
managing meetings, 1063–1080
managing tasks, 1083–1096
Meeting window, 1063
message window, 939
opening screen, 940
personalize, 931–935
processing messages with rules, 978–993
rules and alerts windows, 978
save contact received in Outlook format, 1009–1010
Task window, 1083
working in Outlook window, 924–931
Outlook items
    archive, 969–971
    assign color categories to, 1125
Outlook Personal Folders file, 1130
Outlook Today—(Personal Folders) Properties window, 1135
Out of Office Assistant, 957–958
Out of office message, 957–958
Out of Office option, 1051

P

.pab extension, 1040
Package for CD dialog box, 718–719
Page Background group, 196–198
Page border, insert, 198
Page break
    defined, 218, 396–397
    insert and delete manual, 217–218
    See also entries for individual break types
Page Break Preview, 396–397
Page color, insert, 196
Page Color menu, 196
Page Down shortcut key, 124
Page Footer, 861
Page Header, 861
Page layout, in Word, 202–204
Page Layout command, 348–349, 381–400. *See also entries for individual commands and tabs*
Page Layout view, 323–324, 393–396
Page Number placeholder, 705
Page numbers, add, 199
Page orientation, select, 203–204
Page Setup dialog box
    in Excel, 397–398
    in PowerPoint, 701
    in Word, 175–176, 203–204
Page Setup group, 203–204, 220
Page Up shortcut key, 124
Page Width button, 119
Panes, 29
Paper size, in Word, 204
Paragraph dialog box, 172, 176–178, 214–216
Paragraph group, 556, 567

Paragraph line spacing, set, 564–565
Paragraph mark, 232
Paragraphs
    in PowerPoint, 538, 562–564
    in Word
        change alignment, 174–176
        clear formats from paragraph, 188–189
        clear tabs, 188
        controlling behavior of, 214–216
        create bulleted list, 179–180
        create numbered list, 178–179
        display non-printing characters, 187–188
        forcing, to top of page, 216
        Indents and Spacing tab, 172
        line spacing, 176–178
        manually, 172–183
        place border around paragraph, 182–184
        set indents, 172–174
        set tabs on ruler, 184–186
        shade paragraph, 180–182
        spacing around paragraph, 177–178
        spacing of, 177–178
        style of, 163
        Tab dialog box, 184, 186–188
Parameter query, 886, 888
Parental Controls dialog box, 310
Parentheses, to change order of calculation, 456–458
Password, 25, 906, 1135
Paste, 67–68, 70, 251, 337, 344–348, 517–518.
    See also Insert
Paste Columns, 257
Paste List, 466
Paste Names, 466
Paste Rows, 257
Paste Special drop-down arrow, 637
Paste Table As dialog box, 761
Path, 50
Pattern, change chart's, 488–489
Pattern Style, 363
Pen pointer, 716–717
Percentage (%) character, 341
Personal contacts, create secondary address book for, 1040–1041
Personal folder, 51
Personalize Word, 297–298
Personalizing Outlook, 931–935
Personal signature, create, 954–956
Personal template, 750
Phone List view, 1012
Photoshop, 687
Picture
    add special effects to, 676–677
    adjust brightness, contrast, and color, 286
    adjust brightness and contrast of, 675
    apply Quick Style to, 284–286, 674–675
    arrange text around, 287–288
    compress, 288–289
    cropping, resizing, scaling, and rotating, 282–284
    format, 667–678
    insert, 271–277
    insert, from file, 275–277
    reset, 289–290
    rotate, 669–670
    use ruler, gridlines, and guides, 667–669
    See also Clip art; SmartArt graphic
Picture Border menu, 285
Picture Effects, 285–286, 677
Picture file format, 666
Picture Quick Style gallery, 285
Pictures folder, 51
Picture Styles gallery, 674
Picture Styles group, 290
Picture Tools, 282. *See also entries for individual commands*
Picture Tools Format tab, 684, 687
Pie chart, 484–485, 645
Placeholder(s)
    add text to, 513–515
    content, 639–641, 664–665
    defined, 515
    handout, 704
    Header, Date, Footer, and Page Number, 705
    subtitle, 538
    title, 514
Play CD Audio Track, 691
Plot area, 488
PNG file format, 666
Pointer Options, 717
Points, 361. *See also* Font
Point size, 157
Portrait orientation
    in Excel, 398–399
    in PowerPoint, 700–702
    in Word, 204
Position group, 201
Positive value (+) character, 341
Postal abbreviation, 1006
Postcard, create, 211–212
PowerPoint
    add graphics and media clips to presentation, 661–693
    add tables, charts, and SmartArt graphics to slides, 632–654
    change views in, 506–511
    delivering presentation, 700–719
    designing presentation, 594–622
    navigating presentation, 511–513
    opening screen, 506
    presentation basics, 525–549
    working with text, 513–518, 556–586
PowerPoint Viewer, 719
Precision field property, 802
Predefined layout or style, 487
Presentation, PowerPoint
    add media clips to, 690–693
    apply theme to, 595–596
    blank, 526–527
    compress images in, 677–678
    create, from template, 531–533
    create new, from existing one, 536
    insert chart in, 639–642
    navigate, 511–513
    package, for delivery, 718–719
    preview, 549
    print, 544–548
    print, in Grayscale mode, 548
    rearrange slides in, 540–541
    rehearse timing of, 709–711
    reuse slide from different, 534–536
    start, from Microsoft Office Outline, 537–540
    view, in Slide Sorter view, 540–541
Presentation title, 506
Presentation tools, 714–715
Presentation views, 506–511, 703
Presented by a speaker (full screen), 713
Presenter view, 543
Preview
    of attachment, 950–951
    of presentation, 548–549
    See also Print Preview
Previous page, 114, 122–123
Price field number filters, 845
Price field shortcut menu, 842
Primary key, 740
    define and modify, 773–774
    define and modify multi-field, 774–775
Print comments and ink markup, 548
Print dialog box, 14, 142–143, 348–350, 547–548
Printed Watermark dialog box, 197
Printer, 348–349
    add, in Microsoft Windows Vista, 1436
    add, in Microsoft Windows XP, 14
    choose, with Microsoft Office Button, 14
    set, as default, 14
Print hidden slides, 548
Printing
    in Excel
        formulas, 474
        prepare document for, 396–400
        set print area, 348–349
        worksheet, 348–350
        worksheet's gridline, 393
    in Word
        document, 140–143
        envelope, 143–146
        label, 146–148
Print Layout view, 116, 118, 217–218, 258
Print options, 547–548
Print presentation, 544–548
Print Preview
    in Access, 787–788
    in Excel, 349, 396–397
    in PowerPoint, 544–546
    in Word, 140–141
Print range group, 547
Print Table Definition dialog box, 909
Private, 1056, 1089–1090
Process category of SmartArt graphics, 273
Process layout, 649
PRODUCT function, 472
Program, 55
Program Files folder, 58–59
Projection options, 706
Proofing options, configure, 299–301
Properties, set standard, 14–15
Properties dialog box, 15
Property Sheet pane, 795–796
Propose New Time window, 1073
Pyramid category of SmartArt graphics, 273
Pyramid layout, 649

Q

Queries objects, 735
Query
    add criteria to, 884–887
    add table to, 882–884
    create, 872–874
    create, from multiple tables, 876–879
    defined, 872
    filter data within, 891–893
    modify, 882–888
    remove table from, 884
    sort data within, 888–891
Query Builder, 1036
Query criterion, 884–887
Query setup group, 884
Query Wizard, 872
Quick Access Toolbar, 4, 8–9
    in Access, 856
    to delete information from database field, 773
    in Excel, 304–306, 322
    in PowerPoint, 506
    in Word, 143
    See also entries for individual commands
Quick Launch toolbar, 25–26, 65
Quick Parts, 201, 229–232
Quick Print command, 9
Quick Style
    in Excel
        format chart with, 487
        format table with, 444–445
    in PowerPoint
        apply SmartArt diagram to, 653–207
        apply to picture, 674–675
        apply to table, 638
        apply to text box, 577–578
        formatting charts with, 645–646
    in Word
        apply to picture in Word, 284–286
        apply to table, 252–253
        defined, 137
        format document using, 135–137
        formatting text with, 162–165
        options of, 279
Quick Style gallery, 136, 253, 638
Quick Style picture borders, 674
Quick Style thumbnail, 577
Quick Table, insert, 251

R

Radar chart, 485
Random transition, 610
Range(s)
    change size of, 465
    create, for subtotaling, 471–473
    create formula operating on named, 466
    defined, 342
    keep track of, 465–466
    modify, in subtotal, 472
    naming, 463–465

Index | 1155

Reading Highlight, 236
Reading pane
  containing message with attachment, 950–951
  description, 926
  open attachment from, 953
  on Outlook's opening screen, 924, 940
  personalizing outlook, 931–932
  save attachment from, 952
Really Simple Syndication (RSS), 966
Realtors®, 336
Recent Pages menu, 59
Recolor gallery, 675
Recolor menu, 287
Record Narration button, 713
Record navigation buttons, 770–771
Record(s)
  defined, 740
  enter data into, 771
  find unmatched, 879–881
  input mask, 772
  navigate among, using keyboard, 769–770
  navigate among, using navigation buttons, 770–771
Record Sound, 691
Record source, 856, 874
Recurrence pattern, 1086
Recurring appointment, 1051–1053
Recurring meeting
  change one occurrence of, 1075–1078
  create, 1072–1075
Recurring task
  create, 1085–1087
  defined, 1085
Recycle Bin, 51, 56–57
Recycle Bin icon, 25–28, 50
Redo, 9, 348, 357
Redundant data, 743
Reference, cell, 458
Referential integrity, 787
Reflection effect, 677
Rehearsal toolbar, 710–711
Rehearse timing, of presentation, 709–711
Relational database, 743. *See also* Table relationships
Relationship category of SmartArt graphics, 273
Relationship layout, 649
Relationship Report command, 788
Relationships, table, 784–788
Relative cell reference, 458–461
Relative to Original Picture Size box, 284
Remove duplicate rows, 431
Remove Page Numbers command, 199
Remove Space After Paragraph, 178
Remove Space Before Paragraph, 178
Remove Watermark command
Rename Category dialog box, 1126
Rename Column, 809
Rename command, 797–798
Rename dialog box, 991
Rename worksheet, 412–413
Repeat, last issued command, 559
Repeat. *See* Redo
Replace All, 422
Replace command, 422, 775

Replace text, 237–238
Replace With box, 776–777
Reply to All button, 946
Reply to a message button, 940
Report
  create, 854–856
  in Design view, 859–861
  using Report Wizard, 856–859
  defined, 856
  filter data within, 864–866
  with resized columns, 855
  sort data within, 862–864
Report Footer, 861
Report Header, 861
Reports group, 854. *See also* entries for individual commands
Reports objects, 735
Report Wizard, 854, 856–859
Report Wizard Fields screen, 856
Report Wizard Grouping screen, 857
Report Wizard Layout screen, 857
Report Wizard Sort screen, 857
Report Wizard Style screen, 857
Report Wizard title screen, 858
Required Attendee, 1065
Required field property, 802
Research options, change, 308–310
Research Options dialog box, 308–309
Research Task Pane, 308–310. *See also* entries for individual commands
Reset Window Position, 121
Resize text box, 575–577
Resize window, 121
Resource, meeting, 1078–1079
Restore all items, 57. *See also* Recycle Bin
Restore down, 39
Restore Down button, 38–39
Restore Down/Maximize, 4, 114, 506
Results should be list, 693
Retention rules, 969
Reuse Slides task pane, 534–535
Ribbon
  in Access, 730
  defined, 7–8
  in Excel, 322, 482
  on opening screen, 4, 6–8
  in PowerPoint, 506, 556, 635
  in Word, 114
  See also entries for individual commands and tabs
Ribbon's View tab, 322
Right-aligned, 175–176
Right Arrow object, 686
Right Arrow shortcut key, 124
Rooms Wizard report, 858
Rotate pictures, 669–670
Rotation handle, 582
Row height, modify, 383–385
Row labels, 322
Row(s), 322
  add and remove, in table, 445–446
  create header for, 257–258
  format entire, 385–386
  hide and unhide, 386–387
  insert or delete, 382–383
  insert total row in table, 445
  move, 256–257
  remove duplicate, from worksheet, 434–435

resize, 254–256
view and print headings, 393
Row Source property, 816
RSS. *See* Really Simple Syndication (RSS)
RSS Feeds mail folder, 966
Rule Address dialog box, 989
Rule Manager, 373–374
Ruler
  in Excel, 396
  in PowerPoint, 667–669, 681
  in Word, 117–118, 173–174, 184–186
Rule(s)
  copy, 988–990
  create, to categorize message from selected, 985–988
  create, to delete messages from scratch, 991
  create, to move message from template, 978–984
  create rule to forward message by copying existing, 988–990
  defined, 978
  delete, 993
  managing, 992
  parts of, 984
  rename, 988
  run, 984–985
  sequencing, 992–993
  turn off, 993
Rules Wizard
  with available actions based on selected message, 986
  with default selection, 979
  with destination folder identified, 981
  and exceptions, 981
  to forward messages, 990
  with new rule displayed, 983
  with rule displayed for approval, 983
  with search phrase identified, 980
  with template to move messages selected, 979
Rule templates, 978–985
Run Rules Now dialog box, 984

S

San serif font, 157
Save As dialog box, 13
  in Access, 762–763, 797, 833, 900–901
  in Excel, 350
Save As options, 531
Save button, 9
Save design changes message, 796
Save options, in Word, 301–302
Save Sent item button, 944
Save workbook, 350–351
Scale, 399–400
Scale field property, 802
Scale to fit paper, 548
Scaling, 671–674
Scanner, 39
Scatter chart, 485
Schedules, viewing, 1064
Scope, 464
ScreenTip, 59, 66, 512
  chart element in, 489
  defined, 27–28
  displays chart type name, 486

hyperlink address, 372
  scrolling, 344
Screen tip, on scroll bar, 123
Scroll, 419–420
Scrollbar, 123, 326–327
Scroll box and button, 114, 122–123
Scroll lock, 328
Scroll tools, 511–512
Search, from Start menu, 35–37
Search box, 49–50
Search Fields As Formatted checkbox, 776
Search Folder, 1038
Search Folder Criteria window, 1039
Search for a function box, 469
Search results, 37
Search Text window, 980, 991
Secondary address book, 1040–1042
Second normal form (2NF), 744
Section break, 218–219
Select, 28
Select Browse Object menu, 123
Select button, 126
Select cells and ranges, 359–360
Select command, 420, 484
Select Data Source dialog box, 642
Select Folder dialog box, 945
Select how presentations will play in the viewer drop-down list, 719
Selection and Visibility pane, 685–687
Selection menu, 783
Select Object, 114, 122–123
Select query, 874
Self-running or individual presentation, 706
Send and receive messages button, 940
Send Backward, 687
Send button, 942
Send to Back, 687
Send To menu, 69
Send Update to Attendees dialog box, 1071
Sent Items folder, 942
Sent Items mail folder, 966
Separate digits of entry (,) character, 341
Serial number date system, 474
Serial numbers, 340
Serif font, 157
Service Properties dialog box, 309
Set as Default Printer, 14
Set Database Password dialog box, 906
Settings dialog box, 304
Settings tab, 433
Set Up Show dialog box, 707, 711–713
Set up Speech Recognition dialog box, 76–77
Shading, paragraph, 180–182
Shadow styles, 560
Shape Effects, 682
Shape Fill, 488–489, 682
Shape Outline, 489–490, 682
Shape(s)
  add, 278–282
  add text to, 281–282, 681–682
  create flowchart, 280–281
  format, 682–684
  insert, 278–279, 680–681
  See also Picture; SmartArt diagram;

Index

SmartArt graphic
Shapes button, 606–604
Shapes gallery, 678–679
Shapes menu, 277
Shape Styles gallery, 279
Shape text, 651
Sheet background, format, 391–392
Shift+F2 display Zoom box, 796
Shortcut keys, 10, 25–26, 925.
    See also KeyTips
Shortcut menu, 8, 53–55, 762,
    779–780, 782, 797,
    863, 865
Short/Over label, 466
Show all windows in the Taskbar, 462
Show as field, 1051
Show Document Text command, 201
Show/Hide, in Word, 117–118,
    187–188, 218, 222, 232
Show/Hide group, 796
Show/Hide tools, 507
Show Numbers, 90
Show Office Clipboard
    Automatically, 347
Show Only Row Source Values
    property, 816
Show Table dialog box, 785, 883
Shrink Font, 155
Shutter Bar Open/Close button, 735
Sidebar, 25–26
Side-by-side bar chart, 486
Side ruler, 396
Signature
    add, to all outgoing messages, 957
    add, to single message, 956–957
    personal, 954–956
    use electronic business card in,
        1033–1035
Signatures and Stationary dialog
    box, 954–956
Signatures and Stationary window,
    1033
Simple form, 832–833
Simple query, create, 872–874
Simple Query Wizard, 873–874,
    878–879. *See also* Query
Simple report, create, 854–856
Single left arrow button, 858
Size and Position dialog box, 672–674
Size dialog box, 283–284
Size Dialog Box Launcher, 284
Size group, 494
Sizing, 671–674
Sleeping, speech recognition, 87
Slide advance, 611–612
Slide layout, 527–528, 601–603
Slide Master
    add new element to, 620–622
    apply theme to, 618–619
    change background, 619–620
Slide Master view, 617
Slide number, 603–605
Slide orientation, select, 700–701
Slide pane, 507, 510, 512
Slide(s)
    add action to, 606–608
    add hyperlink to, 605–606
    add movie to, 692–693
    add new, to template, 533–534
    add note to, 542–543
    add picture to, 662–667
    add shapes to, 678–684

add sound to, 690–692
add text box to, 574–575
add text to blank, 528–529
adjust orientation, 700–701
annotate, with pen pointer,
    716–717
blank, 528–529
current, 509
delete, 541–542
highlight text on, 717
move, in Slide Sorter view, 541
omitting selected, from
    presentation, 706–709
organize objects on, 684–690
rearrange, in presentation,
    540–541
reuse, from different
    presentation, 534–536
set size, 701–702
ways to present, 706
Slide show
    create custom, 590–591
    display hidden slide during,
        714–715
    guidelines for presenting, 544
    Set Up Show dialog box,
        711–713
    text links in, 608–609
    See also Presentation
Slide show button, 507
Slide Show tab, 713
Slide Show view, 509, 531
    exit from, 549
    navigation options in, 715
    preview presentation in, 549
    Rehearsal toolbar in, 710
Slides option, in Print Preview, 546
Slide Sorter view
    defined, 507–509
    move slide in, 541
    scroll tools, 512
    transition and timing symbols
        in, 611
    view presentation in, 540–541
    visible in hidden slide in, 707
Slides/Outline pane, 507, 509–512
Slides Per Page button, 703–705
Slides sized for drop-down list, 702
Slide timing, 709–711
Slide transition, 609–610
SmartArt diagram
    add text to, 649–651
    apply Quick Style to, 653
    convert bulleted list to, 652–653
    defined, 649
SmartArt graphic, 271–274
    add, to slide, 647–653
    categories, 273
    choose, 647
    defined, 273
    modify, 653–220
    replace text, 272
    See also entries for individual types
        of graphics
SmartArt layouts, 647
SmartArt Quick Style gallery, 653
SmartArt shapes, 683
SmartArt Tools, 273
SmartArt Tools Design tab, 651
SmartArt Tools Format tab, 687
SmartArt types, 647
SmartTags field property, 802

Snap objects to grid check box, 669
Soft edges effect, 676
Sort
    contents of list, 263
    data within query, 888–891
    defined, 780
    within view, 862–864
Sort ascending order, 431, 435,
    438–439
Sort command, 436, 780
Sort data
    multiple-criteria, 436–437
    in single criterion, 435–436
    by using cell attributes, 438–439
    by using conditional formatting,
        437–438
Sort descending order, 431, 435
Sort dialog box, 258–259, 431,
    435–436, 438
Sorted query, 889, 891
Sort & Filter group, 779–784,
    843–845, 847, 864–866,
    893, 901. *See also entries*
    for individual commands
Sort Largest to Smallest, 864
Sort Newest to Oldest, 864
Sort Options dialog box, 437
Sort Order to Newest, 864
Sort Smallest to Largest, 864
Sort Text dialog box, 263
Sort Warning message, 435
Sound
    add, to slide, 690–692
    choose, 690
    from Clip Organizer, 691
    from File, 691
Sound effects, 610
Sound icon, 691
Sound Tools Options tab, 691, 693
Source box, 433
Source location, 67
Spacing, 172–174, 176–178
Special character, 158–159, 341, 362
Special effects
    add, to picture, 676–677
    apply, to WordArt, 572–573
Speech Dictionary dialog box, 91
Speech Properties dialog box, 94
Speech recognition
    common commands in, 81
    defined, 79
    dictating text in, 95–96
    edit text, 96–99
    format text, 100–101
    languages available in, 86
    navigate, 90–94
    setting up, 76–86
    set up microphone, 76–79
    sleeping, 87
    speech user interface, 85
    tabs added to list, 101
    talk to computer, 79–84
    text in, 95–101
    train computer to understand
    turn on and off, 87–88
    user, 85–86
    voice commands, 89–90
    warning icon, 85
    WordPad dialog box, 101
Speech Recognition Control Panel, 94
Speech recognition rate, 79
Speech Recognition Tutorial, 82–83

Speech Recognition Voice Training
    Wizard, 85–86
Speech user interface, 85
Spelling checker
    in PowerPoint, 537
    in Word, 127
Spelling panel, in speech
    recognition, 98
Split, merged cells, 366
Split cells, 258–259
Split Cells dialog box, 258–259
Split command, 324–325
Split database, 911–912
Split window, 120–121, 324–325
Spreadsheet. *See* Worksheet(s)
Spreadsheet Solutions, 415–416
Stacked bar chart, 486
Stacks, 63–64, 687
Standard color, 363, 489
Standard properties, set, 14–15
Standard toolbar, in Outlook,
    924, 926, 940
Standard Width dialog box, 385
Start Button, 25–26, 28
Start menu, 25, 114
    identify items on, 29–31
    open and close, 28–29
    on opening screen, 4–5
    search from, 35–37
    select settings for, 32–34
Start menu settings, select, 32–34
Status bar, 4
    in Outlook, 924, 926
    in PowerPoint, 506
    in Word, 114
Status property, 15
STDEV function, 472
STDEVP function, 472
Stock chart, 485
Storage device, 39, 69
Strikethrough, 155, 560
String, 421
Style, 369–371
    apply, 162–163
    formatting text with, 162–165
    modify, 164–165
Style box, 433
Style dialog box, 370–371
Style Set menu options, 137
Subdatabasheet Name table
    property, 796
Subdatasheet expanded table
    property, 796
Subfolder, 55
Subject property, 15
Subordinate, 649
Subscript, 155
Subtitle placeholder, 538
Subtle Emphasis dropdown
    menu, 164
SUBTOTAL function, 471–473
Subtotal group, 443–444
Subtotaling
    build formulas to subtotal and
        total, 472–473
    group and ungroup data for,
        442–443
    modify range in, 472
    select ranges for, 471–473
    subtotal data in list, 443–444
Subtraction, formula to perform, 456
SUM function, 260, 466–468, 472

Summary function, 471
Superscript, 155
Surface chart, 485
Switch Windows, 119, 121, 325, 462
Synchronous Scrolling command, 121
Syntax, 37
Syntax rule, for creating names, 463

T

Tab, to enter data in several cells, 338
Tab dialog box, 184, 186–188.
    See also entries for individual commands
Table, database
  create one from another, 760–761
  create template from, 757–759
  define, 742–744
  delete, 798–799
  modify properties, 795–796
  rename, 797–798
  save, 762–763
  sort data within, 779–781
  See also Table
Table fields, define, 739–740
Table format, 444–446
Table properties, 795–796, 806
Table Properties dialog box, 255–257
Table Quick Styles gallery, 638
Table relationships, 784
  defined, 785–786
  modify, 786–787
  print, 787–788
Table Row command, 445
Table(s)
  in Access
    add, to query, 882–884
    create query from multiple, 876–879
    relationship between, 743
    View menu for, 737
  in Excel
    add and remove rows or columns in, 445–446
    insert total row in, 445
  in PowerPoint
    apply Quick Style to, 638
    defined, 634
    insert, 632–635
  in Word
    apply Quick Style to, 252–253
    change direction of text in cell, 259
    change position of text in cell, 261–262
    create, 248–251
    create header row, 257–258
    defined, 248
    draw, 249–250
    formatting, 252–254
    insert, by dragging, 248–249
    managing, 254–261
    merge and split cells, 260–261
    move row or column, 256–257
    perform calculations in table cell, 259–260
    resize row or column, 254–256
    set horizontal alignment, 257
    sort contents of, 258–259
    turn table style options on or off, 253–254
    use Insert Table dialog box, 249
  See also entries for individual table types
Tables Group commands, 756.
    See also entries for individual commands
Tables object, 735
Table style options, turn, on or off, 253–254
Table Styles Group, 444–445
Table Templates menu, 757–759
Table Tools, 444
  Design tab on, 252–254
  Layout tab on, 254–261
Tabs, 7, 184–186, 188, 730. *See also entries for individual tabs*
Target, defined, 606
Task
  assigned, 1091–1095
  complete, 1090
  create, from message, 1087–1088
  create appointment form, 1055–1056
  create one-time, 1084–1085
  create recurring, 1085–1087
  defined, 1083
  make private, 1089–1090
  modify, 1088–1089
  search for, 1095–1096
Taskbar, 114
  defined, 25–26
  on opening screen, 4
Taskbar and Start Menu Properties dialog box, 32
Task Declined, 1094
Task Input Panel, 934
Task list, 934
Task Recurrence window, 1086
Task request, 1091–1092
Tasks button, 925
Tasks folder, 929, 931, 1083–1084
Task Status report, 1095
Task window, 1083. *See also entries for individual commands*
Template
  access, from Microsoft Office Online, 532
  add new slide, 533–534
  Classic Photo Album, 532
  create Access database, 755–754
  create database table from, 757–759
  create new rules, 978–985
  create presentation from, 531–533
  defined, 532
  functions of, 754
  use to create new workbook, 337
  use with built-in formulas, 447–448
  See also entries for individual templates
Template database, 755–754
Tentative option, 1051
Text
  colors of, for help, 41
  in Excel, wrap, 367–368
  in PowerPoint
    add, on Outline tab, 515
    add, to placeholder, 513–515
    add, to SmartArt diagram, 649–651
    copy and move, from one slide to another, 517–518
    edit and delete, in Notes pane, 542
    highlight, on slide, 717
    orient, in text box, 581–583
    select, replace, delete, 516–517
    set up columns in, 584–586
    working with, in text box, 580–586
  in speech recognition, 95–101
  in Word
    add, to shape, 281–282
    arrange, around picture, 287–288
    change position of, in cell, 261–262
    delete, 125, 127
    enter, 124–125
    find, 235–237
    replace, 125, 127
    replace text in, 237–238
    select, 125–126
    use Clipboard to copy and move text, 233–234
    use mouse to copy or move, 234–235
    wrap, 127
    wrapping, 218
Text Align field property, 802
Text box
  add, to handout placeholder, 704
  add, to slide, 574–575
  align text in, 580–581
  apply fill and border formatting to, 578–580
  apply quick style to, 577–578
  defined, 575
  delete, 586
  orient text in, 581–583
  resize, 575–577
  set formatting options for, 577–580
  set margins in, 583–584
Text Box Tools, 282
Text cells, 468
Text data type, 742, 802
Text Filter option, 441
Text Format field property, 802
Text formatting tools, 556
Text group, 394
Text Highlight Color, 155, 160–161
Text length, define, 801
Text links, in slide show, 608–609
Text Outline Theme Colors palette, 572
Text pane, 651
Text placeholder, 513–515, 581
Textured background, 600–601
Texture gallery, 600
Text Wrapping options, 287–288
Theme, 532, 595–596. *See also* Document theme
Theme background, 599
Theme color,
  in Word, 138–139
  in Excel, 363, 489
  in PowerPoint, 571, 594, 596–598
  See also Document theme
Theme Effects, 138, 140, 594
Theme fonts, 138–139, 390–391, 594, 596, 598. *See also* Document theme
Themes gallery, 594

Third normal form (3NF), 744
3-D chart, in Excel, 485–486
3-D effects, in Word, 279
Three-dimensional chart type, in PowerPoint, 643
3NF. *See* Third normal form (3NF)
Thumbnail, 117–118, 136, 528, 577
TIFF file format, 666
Tiles, 64
Time, 474
Timing, rehearse, 709–711
Timing symbols, 611
Title, 322, 337
Title and Content layout, 528
Title bar, 924, 926, 943
Title placeholder, 514
Title property, 15
Title slide, 515
To, 941–942
To-Do bar
  customize, 934
  defined, 926
  fig., 1055
  in opening screen, 924
  to-do items and tasks, 1085
  view, hide, and minimize, 933
To-Do Bar Options dialog box, 934
To-do item, 1085
Toggle Field button, 847
Toggle Filter button, 782–784, 866
Toolbar, 49–50
Tools group, 446
Top-level shape, 649
Top ruler, 396
Total, build formulas to, 472–473
Total row, insert, in table, 445
Transition, modify, 610–611
Transition gallery, 610
Transition symbols, 611
TrueType fonts, embedding, 719
Trust Center options screen, 307–308
2-D chart, 485
Two-dimensional chart type, 643
2NF. *See* Second normal form (2NF)
Typeface, 558. *See also* Font

U

Underline, 155, 158. *See also* Formatting
Undo, 9
  in Excel, 330, 348, 362
  in PowerPoint, 542, 680
  in Word, 250
Ungroup, 442–443
Unhide, 387, 414–415, 418–419
Unicode Compression field property, 802
Unmatched records, find, 879–881
Unmerge cells, 366
Unread Mail search folder, 1040
Unset Database Password dialog box
Up Arrow shortcut key, 124
Up One Level button, 12
Use hardware graphics acceleration, 713
Use Return Address box, 147
Using timings, if present option, 713

V

Validation rule, defined, 806
Validation rule field property, 802, 805–806

Validation Rule table property, 796
Validation text, 806
Validation text field property, 802
Validation Text table property, 796
Value fields, 468
Values, entering, 340–341
VAR function, 472
VARP function, 472
Vertical alignment, 176
Vertical axis, 488, 492
Vertical axis label, 639
Vertical gridline, 639
Vertical axis title, 639
View1157
   in Access, 737–739
   in Excel, 323–324, 326, 393, 462
   in Outlook, 927–931
   in Word, 119–122
   See also entries for individual views
Viewer Package, 719
View Options menu, 116
View Reference Sheet, 80
View Ruler, 114
View Slide by Slide button, 121
View tab, 115
View toolbar, 506, 508
Violet text, 41
Virtual folder, 1038
Voice commands, 89–90. *See also* Speech recognition

W

Walls, chart, 488
Warning icon, 85
Watermark, 196–198
WAV file format, 691
Web Layout view, 116
Web page, 371. *See also* Hyperlink
Welcome screen, of Windows Vista, 24–26
Whiteboard, interactive, 706
White Screen, 717
Widow/orphan control, 214–215
Wildcard character, 237, 776–777

Window control button, 49–50
Windows
   active, 63, 65
   browse through recently opened, 58–59
   change active, 65
   changing Excel's view, 322–324
   navigating through, 58–61
   open and arrange multiple, 62–64
   open new, 325–326
   split, 324–325
Windows group, 462
Windows Help and Support, 40–41, 80
Windows Photo Gallery folder icon, 59
Windows SharePoint Services, 814
Windows Vista
   add printer in, 14
   desktop elements of, 25–26
   folder windows, 37–39
   log on to, 24–26
   mouse to identify desktop items, 27–28
   shut down, 42
   Start menu for, 28–29
Windows Vista Speech Recognition, 75–101
Wipe dialog box, 615–616
WMA file format, 691
WMF file format, 666, 693
WMV file format, 693
Word
   add pictures and shapes to document, 271–290
   character formatting, 155–165
   creating tables and lists, 248–264
   customizing, 297–310
   document basics, 133–148
   document formatting, 196–204
   editing basics, 229–241
   managing text flow, 214–222
   opening screen, 114
   paragraph formatting, 172–189
   personalize, 297–298

   start presentation from, 537–540
   work with existing document, 114–127
WordArt, 568–574
WordArt fill color, change, 570–571
WordArt graphic, 568–573
WordArt Outline color, 571–572
WordArt special effects, apply, 572–573
WordArt styles, format text with, 573–574
Word options, 297–308
Word Options dialog box, 142–143, 298–307. *See also entries for individual options*
WordPad
   Date and Time dialog box, 89–90
   potential client list, 95–96
   Show Numbers, 90
WordPad dialog box, 101
WordPad file menu, 90
Workbook(s)
   defined, 322
   delete worksheet from, 416
   existing, 326–331
   hide and unhide worksheets in, 418–419
   insert new worksheet into, 415–416
   multiple worksheets in, 416–418
   open existing, 326
   refer to data in another, 461–462
   reposition workbook in, 413
   save, 350–351
   save editing, 14
   select, edit, delete contents of cell in, 329–331
   start, from scratch, 337–338
Workbook title, 325
Workbook View group, 322
Worksheet(s), 635–637
   add new cell to, 357–358
   add page numbers to, 394–395
   choose theme for, 388–389

   copy, 411–412
   defined, 322
   delete, from workbook, 416
   delete cell from, 358–359
   enter data in cell of, 328
   formatting, 381–400
   hide and unhide, 414–415
   hide and unhide, in workbook, 418–419
   insert new, into workbook, 415–416
   multiple, 416–418
   navigate, 326–328, 423–424
   organize, 410–420
   print, 348–350
   refer to data in another, 461–462
   remove duplicate cells, rows, or columns from, 434–435
   rename, 412–413
   reposition, in workbook, 413
   scale, to fit on printed page, 399–400
   select, edit, delete contents of, 329–331
   set orientation on page, 398–399
   use absolute cell reference in, 460–461
   view and print gridlines, 393
Worksheet tab, 322, 391–392
Wrap text, 365–366

X

XY (scatter) chart, 485

Y

Year. *See* Date
Yes/No data type, 741–742
YMCA, 154

Z

Zero length property menu, 804
Zero-length string, 804
Zoom, 118–119, 419–420, 510–511, 543, 796
Zoom slider, 114, 118
Zoom tool, 506–507

Photo Credits

Unit 1
Lesson 1
Courtesy Microsoft
Lesson 2
Alaska Stock Images
Lesson 3
Purestock
Lesson 4
"PhotoDisc, Inc."

Unit 2
Lesson 1
Digital Vision
Lesson 2
Corbis Digital Stock
Lesson 3
Purestock/Superstock
Lesson 4
Corbis Digital Stock
Lesson 5
"PhotoDisc, Inc."
Lesson 6
Corbis Digital Stock
Lesson 7
Purestock/Superstock
Lesson 9
Digital Vision
Lesson 10
Corbis Digital Stock

Unit 3
Lesson 1
Corbis Digital Stock
Lesson 2
PhotoDisc/Getty Images
Lesson 3
"Ryan McVay/PhotoDisc, Inc./Getty Images"
Lesson 4
Corbis Digital Stock
Lesson 5
Corbis Digital Stock
Lesson 6
Digital Vision
Lesson 7
PhotoDisc/Getty Images
Lesson 8
"PhotoDisc, Inc."

Unit 4
Lesson 1
Corbis Digital Stock
Lesson 2
Corbis Digital Stock
Lesson 3
"PhotoDisc, Inc."
Lesson 4

Purestock Lesson 5
"PhotoDisc, Inc."
Lesson 6
PhotoDisc/Getty Images
Lesson 7
"PhotoDisc, Inc."

Unit 5
Lesson 1
PhotoDisc/Getty Images
Lesson 2
Digital Vision
Lesson 3
"PhotoDisc, Inc."
Lesson 4
"PhotoDisc, Inc./Getty Images"
Lesson 5
ImageState
Lesson 6
Corbis Digital Stock
Lesson 7
Corbis Digital Stock

Unit 6
Lesson 1
Corbis Digital Stock
Lesson 2
Corbis Images
Lesson 3
Corbis Digital Stock
Lesson 4
"PhotoDisc, Inc."
Lesson 5
Digital Vision
Lesson 6
Purestock
Lesson 7
Corbis Digital Stock
Lesson 8
ImageState
Lesson 9
Corbis Digital Stock
Lesson 10
ImageState

sweetg@live.com